Foundations of Behavioral Research

Foundations of Behavioral Research

SECOND EDITION

Fred N. Kerlinger

New York University

Holt, Rinehart and Winston, Inc.
New York Chicago San Francisco Atlanta
Dallas Montreal Toronto London Sydney

Library of Congress Catalog Card Number 72–91751
ISBN: 03-085462-8
Printed in the United States of America
3 4 5 6 7 8 9 0 032 9 8 7 6 5 4 3 2

To Betty, Paul, and Stephen

Preface

Some activities command more interest, devotion, and enthusiasm from man than others. So it seems to be with science and art. Why this is so is an interesting and significant psychological question to which there is no unequivocal answer. All that seems to be clear is that once men become immersed in scientific research or artistic expression they devote very large portions of their thoughts, energies, and emotions to these activities. It seems a far cry from science to art. But in one respect at least they are similar: men make passionate commitments to them.[1]

This is a book on scientific behavioral research. Above everything else, it aims to convey the exciting quality of research in general, and in the behavioral sciences and education in particular. A large portion of the book is focused on abstract conceptual and technical matters, but behind the discussion is the conviction that research is a deeply absorbing and vitally interesting business.

It may seem strange in a book on research that I talk about interest, enthusiasm, and passionate commitment. Shouldn't we be objective? Shouldn't we develop a hardheaded attitude toward psychological, sociological, and educational phenomena? Yes, of course. But more important is somehow to catch the essential quality of the excitement of discovery that comes from research well done. Then the difficulties and frustrations of the research enterprise, while they never vanish, are much less significant. What I am trying to say is that strong subjective involvement is a powerful motivator for acquiring an objective approach to the study of phenomena. It is doubtful that any significant work is ever done without great personal involvement. It is doubtful that

[1]The term "passionate commitment" is Polanyi's. M. Polanyi, *Personal Knowledge.* Chicago: University of Chicago Press, 1958.

students can learn much about science, research design, and research methods without considerable personal involvement. Thus I would encourage students to discuss, argue, debate, and even fight about research. Take a stand. Be opinionated. Later try to soften the opinionation into intelligent conviction and controlled emotional commitment.

The writing of this book has been strongly influenced by the book's major purpose: to help students understand the fundamental nature of the scientific approach to problem solution. Technical and methodological problems have been considered at length. One cannot understand any complex human activity, especially scientific research activity, without some technical and methodological competence. But technical competence is empty without an understanding of the basic intent and nature of scientific research: the controlled and objective study of the relations among phenomena. All else is subordinate to this. Thus the book, as its name indicates, strongly emphasizes the *fundamentals* or *foundations* of behavioral research.

To accomplish the major purpose indicated above, the book has four distinctive general features. First, it is a treatise on scientific research; it is limited to what is generally accepted as the scientific approach. It does not discuss historical research, legal research, library research, philosophical inquiry, and so on.[2] It emphasizes, in short, understanding scientific research problem solution.

Second, the student is led to grasp the intimate and often difficult relations between a research problem and the design and methodology of its solution. While methodological problems are treated at length, the book is not a "methods" book. Stress is always on the research problem, the design of research, and the relation between the two. The student is encouraged to think relationally and structurally.

Third, the content of much of the book is tied together with the notions of set, relation, and variance. These ideas, together with those of probability theory, statistics, and measurement, are used to integrate the diverse content of research activity into a unified and coherent whole.

Fourth, a good bit of the book's discussion is slanted toward psychological and educational research problems. It seemed to me that a foundational research book was needed in education. But there is little scientific research in education that is uniquely educational; for the most part it is behavioral research, research basically psychological and sociological in nature. In sum, while this is a book on the intellectual and technical foundations of scientific behavioral research in general, it emphasizes psychological and educational problems and examples, while not ignoring other behavioral disciplines.

The book's content is organized into ten parts. In Part 1, the language and approach of science are studied. Its three chapters discuss the nature of science, scientific problems and hypotheses, and the notions of variables, constructs, and definitions. Part 2 presents the conceptual and mathematical foundations.

[2]Historical and methodological research are briefly discussed in Appendix B.

Much of the presentation of conceptual and technical matters, as indicated above, is based on the ideas of set, relation, and variance. These terms are defined using modern mathematical theory. Fortunately the theory is simple, though the reader may feel a bit strange at first. After becoming accustomed to the language and thinking, however, he will find that he possesses powerful instruments for understanding later subjects.

It is impossible to do competent research or to read and understand research reports without understanding the probabilistic and statistical thinking of scientists. Parts 3, 4, and 5 are thus devoted mainly to probabilistic thinking, sampling, randomness, and the nature and purpose of statistics and statistical inference, including a generous exposure to that great invention, analysis of variance. The first chapter of this part, however, discusses the highly important subject of the principles of analysis and interpretation. This chapter and the following chapter on crossbreaks or cross-partitions—the analysis of frequencies and percentages—were inserted at this point hopefully to make clear the purpose of quantitative analysis and statistics. Indeed, this is what Parts 3, 4, and 5 are about: drawing inferences from data with quantitative methods. Interpretation is in essence drawing inferences, and the ultimate purpose of quantitative analysis and statistics is interpretation.

Parts 1 through 5, then, provide an important part of the conceptual and mathematical foundations of behavioral research. The remainder of the book uses these foundations to attack problems of design, measurement, and observation and data collection.

Part 6, "Designs of Research," is the structural heart of the book. Here the major designs of experimental and nonexperimental research are outlined and explained. Part 7, on types of research, follows naturally from Part 6: so-called ex post facto research and the distinctions among laboratory experiments, field experiments, field studies, and survey research are explored.

Part 8 addresses itself mainly to theoretical measurement problems, while Part 9 addresses itself to practical and technical problems of gathering the data necessary for scientific problem solution. Standard methods of observation and data collection—interviews, objective tests and scales, direct observation of behavior, projective methods, content analysis, and the use and analysis of available materials—are extensively discussed and illustrated. Sociometry, *Q* methodology, and the semantic differential might have been subsumed under other methods. Because of their importance, distinctive nature, and frequent use by behavioral scientists, and because elementary yet detailed discussions of *Q* and the semantic differential seem not to exist, each has been assigned a separate chapter.

The book ends with fairly extended but elementary discussions of multiple regression analysis, multivariate analysis, and factor analysis. The very nature of behavioral research is multivariate: many variables act in complex ways to influence other variables. While some of the complexity can be handled with analysis of variance, it is only with multivariate methods that the complexity of many psychological, sociological, and educational problems can be adequately attacked. We are in the midst of a revolution in research thinking and practice. Behavioral research is right now changing from a predominantly univariate emphasis to a multivariate emphasis. The change is extensive and profound. Even the nature of theory and problems is changing. Before finishing the book, I hope the reader will become convinced of the necessity of considering at some length such relatively difficult subjects as multiple regression and factor analysis.

Some word on the book's level and audience is in order. The book is a behavioral science text intended for graduate students who have elementary backgrounds in psychology, statistics, and measurement. While many terms and ideas used in educational and psychological problems are defined, some familiarity with terms like intelligence, aptitude, socioeconomic status, authoritarianism, and the like is assumed. All technical terms are defined, though many students will probably need instructor help with some of them.

As usual, statistical terms and ideas may hinder the student's progress. While it is possible to study the book and master its contents without statistical background, the student who has had an elementary statistics course will probably find the going easier. Suggestions are given in Part 4 to help the student conquer certain statistical difficulties.

Foundations of Behavioral Research can be used in courses of either one or two semesters. When used in one-semester courses, it should be selectively studied. Although individual instructors will of course make their own selection decisions, the following parts and chapters are suggested for a single semester course: Parts 1 and 2 and Chapters 8–12, 17, 19, 23, and 25–29. (Chapters 25, 26, and 27 can also be omitted.) For a two-semester course, all or most of the chapters may well be studied. Whatever selection is made, it should be borne in mind that later discussions often presuppose understanding of earlier discussions.

To aid student study and understanding, and to help surmount some of the inherent difficulties of the subject, several devices have been used. One, many topics have been discussed at length. If a choice had to be made between repetition and possible lack of student understanding, material was repeated, though in different words with different examples. Two, many examples from actual research as well as many hypothetical examples have been used. The student who reads the book through will have been exposed to a large number and a wide variety of problems, hypotheses, designs, and data and to many actual research studies in the social sciences and education.

Three, an important feature of the book is the frequent use of simple numerical examples in which the numbers are only those between 0 and 9. The fundamental ideas of statistics, measurement, and design can be conveyed as well with small numbers as with large numbers, without the additional burden of tedious arithmetic computations. It is suggested that the reader work through each example at least once. Intelligent handling of data is indispensable to intelligent understanding of research design and methodology.

Four, most chapters have study suggestions that include suggested readings as well as problems designed to help integrate and consolidate the material presented in the chapters. Many of them arose from practical use with graduate students. Answers to most of the computational problems have been given immediately after the problems. An answer, if checked against a supplied answer and found to be correct, reassures the student about computational details. He should not have to waste time wondering about right answers. Understanding the procedures is what is important and not the calculations as such.

How does this edition of *Foundations* differ from the first edition? First, most of the errors and gaucheries in the first edition have been detected and corrected. Second, the book is longer because research itself has become more complex and diverse. For example, Monte Carlo methods, almost unknown some years ago, are becoming more and more important in modern research and thus require explanation and illustration. The addition of study suggestions to almost all chapters—at the suggestion of a number of users of the book—has also contributed to the book's greater length. Third, two new chapters on multiple regression and related methods, ignored in the first edition, have been added. Multivariate analysis can be ignored or treated superficially only at the cost of the book being obsolescent, even obsolete.

Fourth, more than half the research examples used in the first edition have been replaced, usually by more recent examples from more diverse sources. Fifth, there is considerably more material on the computer in this edition. A contemporary book on research that does not discuss the computer would indeed be an anomaly.

Although much of the text and some of the organization of the book have been changed, its basic approach and purpose remain the same: understanding of principles of research through relatively lengthy explanation and many examples. No one can be completely satisfied with the organization and content of a book. One of the goals of both the first and second editions has been to supply enough materials for instructors and students of diverse background and taste to select what they need. Even so, the content of the book is still highly selective when one considers the very great diversity and depth of modern behavioral research and methods. I hope my selection will serve the teaching and learning needs of most instructors and students.

All books are cooperative enterprises. Though one person may undertake the actual writing, he is dependent on many others for ideas, criticism, and support. Among the many persons who contributed to both editions of this book, I am most indebted to those mentioned below. I here express my sincere thanks to them.

Three individuals read the entire original manuscript of the first edition and made many valuable and constructive suggestions for improvement: Professors Theodore Newcomb, Dale Harris, and Jum Nunnally. Professor Newcomb also furnished the early prodding and encouragement needed to get the book going. Professor Harris contributed from his wide research experience insights whose worth cannot be weighed. Professor Nunnally's trenchant and penetrating analysis was invaluable, especially with a number of difficult technical matters.

Professors Newcomb and Harris also read the manuscript of this edition and again made valuable suggestions. Professors Ellis Page and William Asher and two unknown critics provided detailed criticisms of the published first edition with suggestions for change. Professor Page also read and criticized the manuscript of this edition. Many of the suggestions of these men have been followed. Professor Ernest Nagel helped me greatly with certain logical scientific problems. His thinking helped me improve and hopefully clarify several sections of the book in both editions.

I am grateful to the many teachers and students who have corresponded with me about aspects of the book (especially the errors). Published reviews of the book have also been helpful. All suggested corrections and changes have been given careful consideration. In some cases I have made changes. In other cases I have not—for instance, I have stubbornly refused to remove or change the strong emphasis I have given to set theory. If anything, I have given it greater emphasis! I owe a large debt in the writing of the revision to my colleague and friend, Professor Elazar Pedhazur. He has ferreted out weaknesses and made many suggestions for improvement.

I also want to express my gratitude to my colleagues and students of the Psychology Laboratory, University of Amsterdam. They pointed out errors and ambiguities in the text, some of which I have been able to correct.

It is doubtful that either edition of this book could have been written without the sabbatical leaves given me in 1961–1962 and 1970–1971 by New York University. I am indeed grateful to the University for its generous sabbatical policy.

The price a family pays for an author's book is high. Its members put up with his obsession and his unpredictable writing ups and downs. I express my gratitude and indebtedness to my wife and sons by dedicating the book to them.

Fred N. Kerlinger

Amsterdam, The Netherlands
January 1973

Contents

PART 2. SETS, RELATIONS, AND VARIANCE

PART 3. PROBABILITY, RANDOMNESS, AND SAMPLING

PART 4. ANALYSIS, INTERPRETATION, STATISTICS, AND INFERENCE

PART 7. TYPES OF RESEARCH

PART 8. MEASUREMENT

Foundations of Behavioral Research

PART 1

The Language and Approach of Science

CHAPTER 1

Science and the Scientific Approach

To understand any complex human activity we must grasp the language and approach of the individuals who pursue it. So it is with understanding science and scientific research. One must know and understand, at least in part, scientific language and the scientific approach to problem-solving.

One of the most confusing things to the student of science is the special way the scientist uses ordinary words. To make matters worse, he invents new words. There are good reasons for this specialized use of language, which will become evident later. Suffice it to say now that we must understand and learn the language of psychological and educational scientists. When a psychological investigator tells us about his independent and dependent variables we must know what he means. When he tells us that he has randomized his experimental procedures, we must not only know what he means—we must understand why he does what he does.

Similarly, the scientist's approach to his problems must be clearly understood. It is not so much that this approach is different from the layman's. It *is* different, of course, but it is not strange and esoteric. Quite the contrary. When understood, it will seem natural and almost inevitable that the scientist does what he does. Indeed, we will probably wonder why much more human thinking and problem-solving are not consciously structured along such lines.

The purpose of Part 1 of this book, then, is to help the student learn and understand the language and approach of science and research. In the chapters of this part many of the basic constructs of the social and educational scientist will be studied. In some cases it will not be possible to give complete and satisfactory definitions because of lack of background at this early point in our development. In such cases we shall attempt to formulate and use reasonably accurate first approximations to later, more satisfactory definitions. Let us begin our study by considering how the scientist approaches his problems and how this approach differs from what might be called a commonsense approach.

Science and Common Sense

Whitehead has pointed out that in creative thought common sense is a bad master. "Its sole criterion for judgment is that the new ideas shall look like the old ones."[1] This is well said. Common sense may often be a bad master for the evaluation of knowledge. But how are science and common sense alike and how are they different? From one viewpoint, science and common sense are alike. This view would say that science is a systematic and controlled extension of common sense, since common sense, as Conant points out, is a series of concepts and conceptual schemes satisfactory for the practical uses of mankind.[2] But these concepts and conceptual schemes may be seriously misleading in modern science—and particularly in psychology and education. It was self-evident to many educators of the last century—it was only common sense—to use punishment as a basic tool of pedagogy. Now we have evidence that this older commonsense view of motivation may be quite erroneous. Reward seems more effective than punishment in aiding learning.

Science and common sense differ sharply in five ways. These disagreements revolve around the words "systematic" and "controlled." First, the uses of conceptual schemes and theoretical structures are strikingly different. While the man in the street uses "theories" and concepts, he ordinarily does so in a loose fashion. He often blandly accepts fanciful explanations of natural and human phenomena. An illness, for instance, may be thought to be a punishment for sinfulness. An economic depression may be attributed to Jews. The scientist, on the other hand, systematically builds his theoretical structures, tests them for internal consistency, and subjects aspects of them to empirical test. Furthermore, he realizes that the concepts he is using are man-made terms that may or may not exhibit a close relation to reality.

Second, the scientist systematically and empirically tests his theories and hypotheses. The man in the street tests his "hypotheses," too, but he tests them in what might be called a selective fashion. He often "selects" evidence simply because it is consistent with his hypothesis. Take the stereotype: Blacks are

[1] A. Whitehead, *An Introduction to Mathematics*. New York: Holt, Rinehart and Winston, 1911, p. 157.

[2] J. Conant, *Science and Common Sense*. New Haven: Yale University Press, 1951, pp. 32–33. A *concept* is a word that expresses an abstraction formed by generalization from particulars. "Aggression" is a concept, an abstraction that expresses a number of particular actions having the similar characteristic of hurting people or objects. A *conceptual scheme* is a set of concepts interrelated by hypothetical and theoretical propositions. (See *ibid.*, pp. 25, 47–48.) A *construct* is a concept with the additional meaning of having been created or appropriated for special scientific purposes. "Mass," "energy," "hostility," "introversion," and "achievement" are constructs. They might more accurately be called "constructed types" or "constructed classes," classes or sets of objects or events bound together by the possession of common characteristics defined by the scientist. The term "variable" will be defined in a later chapter. For now let it mean a symbol or name of a characteristic that takes on different numerical values.

musical. If a person believes this, he can easily "verify" his belief by noting that many blacks are musicians. Exceptions to the stereotype, the unmusical or tone-deaf black, for example, are not perceived. The sophisticated social scientist, knowing this "selection tendency" to be a common psychological phenomenon, carefully guards his research against his own preconceptions and predilections and against selective support of his hypotheses. For one thing, he is not content with armchair exploration of a relation; he must test the relation in the laboratory or in the field. He is not content, for example, with the presumed relations between methods of teaching and achievement, between intelligence and creativity, between values and administrative decisions. He insists upon systematic, controlled, and empirical testing of these relations.

A third difference lies in the notion of control. In scientific research, control means several things. For the present let it mean that the scientist tries systematically to rule out variables that are possible "causes" of the effects he is studying other than the variables that he has hypothesized to be the "causes." The layman seldom bothers to control his explanations of observed phenomena in a systematic manner. He ordinarily makes little effort to control extraneous sources of influence. He tends to accept those explanations that are in accord with his preconceptions and biases. If he believes that slum conditions produce delinquency, he will tend to disregard delinquency in nonslum neighborhoods. The scientist, on the other hand, seeks out and "controls" delinquency incidence in different kinds of neighborhoods. The difference, of course, is profound.

Another difference between science and common sense is perhaps not so sharp. It was said earlier that the scientist is constantly preoccupied with relations among phenomena. So is the layman who invokes common sense for his explanations of phenomena. But the scientist consciously and systematically pursues relations. The layman's preoccupation with relations is loose, unsystematic, uncontrolled. He often seizes, for example, on the fortuitous occurrence of two phenomena and immediately links them indissolubly as cause and effect.

Take the relation tested in a study by Hurlock.[3] In more recent terminology, this relation might be expressed: Positive reinforcement (reward) produces greater increments of learning than does negative reinforcement (punishment) or no reinforcement. The relation is between reinforcement (or reward and punishment) and learning. Educators and parents of the nineteenth century often assumed that negative reinforcement (punishment) was the more effective agent in learning. Educators and parents of the present often assume that positive reinforcement (reward) is more effective. Both may say that their viewpoints are "only common sense." It is obvious, they may say, that if you reward (or punish) a child he will learn better. The scientist, on the other hand, while he may personally espouse one or the other or neither of these viewpoints, would probably insist on systematic and controlled testing of both (and other) relations, as Hurlock did.

A final difference between common sense and science lies in different ex-

[3]E. Hurlock, "An Evaluation of Certain Incentives Used in Schoolwork," *Journal of Educational Psychology*, XVI (1925), 145–159.

planations of observed phenomena. The scientist, when attempting to explain the relations among observed phenomena, carefully rules out what have been called "metaphysical explanations." A metaphysical explanation is simply a proposition that cannot be tested. To say, for example, that people are poor and starving because God wills it, that studying hard subjects improves the child's moral character, or that it is wrong to be authoritarian in the classroom is to talk metaphysically.

None of these propositions can be tested; thus they are metaphysical. As such, science is not concerned with them. This does not mean that a scientist would necessarily spurn such statements, rule them out of life, say they are not true, or claim they are meaningless. It simply means that *as a scientist* he is not concerned with them. In short, science is concerned with things that can be publicly observed and tested. If propositions or questions do not contain implications for such public observation and testing, they are not scientific questions.

Four Methods of Knowing

Charles Peirce, the great American philosopher, said that there are four general ways of knowing or, as he put it, of fixing belief.[4] The first is the *method of tenacity*. Here men hold firmly to the truth, the truth that they know to be true because they hold firmly to it, because they have always known it to be true. Frequent repetition of such "truths" seems to enhance their validity. Recent psychological evidence has shown us that men will often cling to their beliefs in the face of clearly conflicting facts. And they will also infer "new" knowledge from propositions that may be false.

A second method of knowing or fixing belief is the *method of authority*. This is the method of established belief. If the Bible says it, it is so. If a noted physicist says there is a God, it is so. If an idea has the weight of tradition and public sanction behind it, it is so. As Peirce points out, this method is superior to the method of tenacity, because human progress, although slow, can be achieved using the method. Actually, life could not go on without the method of authority. We must take a large body of facts and information on the basis of authority. Thus, it should not be concluded that the method of authority is unsound; it is only unsound under certain circumstances.

The *a priori method* is the third way of knowing or fixing belief. (Cohen and Nagel call it the *method of intuition*.) It rests its case for superiority on the assumption that the propositions accepted by the "a priorist" are self-evident. Note that a priori propositions "agree with reason" and not necessarily with experience. The idea seems to be that men, by free communication and intercourse, can reach the truth because their natural inclinations tend toward truth. The difficulty with

[4]J. Buchler, ed., *Philosophical Writings of Peirce*. New York: Dover, 1955, chap. 2. In the ensuing discussion, I am taking some liberties with Peirce's original formulation in an attempt to clarify the ideas and to make them more germane to the present work. For a good discussion of the four methods, see M. Cohen and E. Nagel, *An Introduction to Logic and Scientific Method*. New York: Harcourt, 1934, pp. 193–196.

this rationalistic position lies in the expression "agree with reason." Whose reason? Suppose two good men, using rational processes, reach different conclusions, as they often do. Which one is right? Is it a matter of taste, as Peirce puts it? If something is self-evident to many men—for instance, that learning hard subjects trains the mind and builds moral character, that American education is inferior to Russian and European education, that women are poor drivers—does this mean it is so? According to the a priori method, it does—it just "stands to reason."

The fourth method is the *method of science*. Peirce says:

> To satisfy our doubts, . . . therefore, it is necessary that a method should be found by which our beliefs may be determined by nothing human, but by some external permanency—by something upon which our thinking has no effect. . . . The method must be such that the ultimate conclusion of every man shall be the same. Such is the method of science. Its fundamental hypothesis . . . is this: There are real things, whose characters are entirely independent of our opinions about them . . .[5]

The scientific approach[6] has one characteristic that no other method of attaining knowledge has: self-correction. There are built-in checks all along the way to scientific knowledge. These checks are so conceived and used that they control and verify the scientist's activities and conclusions to the end of attaining dependable knowledge outside himself. Even if a hypothesis seems to be supported in an experiment, the scientist will test alternative hypotheses that, if also supported, may cast doubt on the first hypothesis. A scientist does not accept a statement as true, even though the evidence at first looks promising. He insists upon testing it. He also insists that any testing procedure be open to public inspection.

As Peirce says, the checks used in scientific research are anchored as much as possible in reality lying outside the scientist and his personal beliefs, perceptions, biases, values, attitudes, and emotions. Perhaps the best single word to express this is *objectivity*. But, as we shall see later, the scientific approach involves more than this. The point is that more dependable knowledge is attained through science because science ultimately appeals to evidence: propositions are subjected to empirical test. An objection may be raised: Theory, which the scientist uses and exalts, is part of man himself. But, as Polanyi points out, "A theory is something other than myself";[7] thus a theory helps the scientist to attain greater objectivity. In short, scientists systematically and consciously use the self-corrective aspect of the scientific approach.

Science and Its Functions

What is science? This question is not easy to answer. Indeed, no definition of science will be directly attempted. We shall, instead, talk about notions and views of science and then try to explain the functions of science.

[5]Buchler, *op cit.*, p. 18.

[6]This book's position is that there is no one scientific method as such. Rather, there are a number of methods that scientists can and do use, but it can probably be validly said that there is one scientific approach.

[7]M. Polanyi, *Personal Knowledge*. Chicago: University of Chicago Press, 1958, p. 4.

Science is a badly misunderstood word. There seem to be three popular stereotypes that impede understanding of scientific activity. One is the white coat-stethoscope-laboratory stereotype. The scientist is perceived as a peculiar person who works with facts in laboratories. He uses complicated equipment, does innumerable experiments, and piles up facts for the ultimate purpose of improving the lot of mankind. Thus, while he is somewhat of an unimaginative grubber after facts, he is redeemed by his noble motives. And you can believe him when, for example, he tells you that such-and-such a toothpaste is good for you or that you should not smoke cigarettes.

The second stereotype of the scientist is that he is a brilliant individual who thinks, spins complex theories, and generally spends his time in the ivory tower aloof from the world and its problems. This scientist is a rather impractical theorist, even though his thinking and theory occasionally lead to results of practical significance like atomic bombs.

The third stereotype equates science with engineering and technology. The building of bridges, the improvement of automobiles and missiles, the automation of industry, the invention of teaching machines, and the like are thought to be science. The scientist's job, in this conception, is to work at the improvement of man's inventions and artifacts. The scientist himself is conceived to be a sort of highly skilled engineer working to make life smooth and efficient.

These notions impede student understanding of science, the activities and thinking of the scientist, and scientific research in general. In short, they make the student's task harder than it would otherwise be. Thus they should be cleared away to make room for more adequate notions.

In the scientific world itself there are two broad views of science: the static and the dynamic.[8] The *static view*, the view that seems to influence most laymen and students, is that science is an activity that contributes systematized information to the world. The scientist's job is to discover new facts and to add them to the already existing body of information. In short, science is even conceived to be a body of facts. Science, in this view, is also a way of explaining observed phenomena. The emphasis, then, is on the *present state of knowledge and adding to it*, on the extent of knowledge, and on the present set of laws, theories, hypotheses, and principles.

The *dynamic view*, on the other hand, regards science more as an *activity*, what scientists *do*. The present state of knowledge is important, of course. But it is important mainly because it is a base for further scientific theory and research. This has been called a *heuristic view*. The word "heuristic," meaning serving to discover or reveal, now has the notion of self-discovery connected with it. A heuristic method of teaching, for instance, emphasizes students' discovering things for themselves. The heuristic view in science emphasizes theory and interconnected conceptual schemata that are fruitful for further research. A heuristic emphasis is a discovery emphasis.

It is the heuristic aspect of science that distinguishes it in good part from engineering and technology. On the basis of a heuristic hunch, the scientist takes

[8]Conant, *op. cit.*, pp. 23–27.

a risky leap. As Polanyi says, "It is the plunge by which we gain a foothold at another shore of reality. On such plunges the scientist has to stake bit by bit his entire professional life."[9] Heuristic may also be called problem-solving, but the emphasis is on imaginative and not routine problem-solving. The heuristic view in science stresses problem-solving rather than facts and bodies of information. Alleged established facts and bodies of information are important to the heuristic scientist because they help lead to further theory, further discovery, and further investigation.

Still avoiding a direct definition of science—but certainly implying one—we now look at the function of science. Here we find two distinct views. The practical man, the nonscientist generally, thinks of science as a discipline or activity aimed at improving things, at making progress. Some scientists, too, take this position. The function of science, in this view, is to make discoveries, to learn facts, to advance knowledge in order to improve things. Branches of science that are clearly of this character receive wide and strong support. Witness the strong support in the last forty to fifty years of medical research and military research. This function of science, to improve man's lot, seems to be supported by most laymen and many scientists. The criterion of practicality is preeminent here. It can be argued that most educational research has been and is now dominated by this view.[10]

A very different view of the function of science is well expressed by Braithwaite: "The function of science . . . is to establish general laws covering the behaviors of the empirical events or objects with which the science in question is concerned, and thereby to enable us to connect together our knowledge of the separately known events, and to make reliable predictions of events as yet unknown."[11] The connection between this view of the function of science and the dynamic-heuristic view discussed earlier is obvious, except that an important element is added: the establishment of general laws—or theory, if you will. If we are to understand modern behavioral research and its strengths and weaknesses, we must explore the elements of Braithwaite's statement. We do so by considering the aims of science, scientific explanation, and the role and importance of theory.

The Aims of Science, Scientific Explanation, and Theory

The basic aim of science is theory. Perhaps less cryptic, the basic aim of science is to explain natural phenomena. Such explanations are called theories. Instead of trying to explain each and every separate behavior of children, the scientific psychologist seeks general explanations that encompass and link together many different behaviors. Rather than try to explain children's methods of solving

[9]Polanyi, *op cit.*, p. 123.

[10]See F. Kerlinger, "Practicality and Educational Research," *School Review*, LXVII (1959), 281–291; "Research in Education," in R. Ebel, V. Noll, and R. Bauer, eds., *Encyclopedia of Educational Research*, 4th ed. New York: Macmillan, 1969, pp. 1127–1144.

[11]R. Braithwaite, *Scientific Explanation*. Cambridge: Cambridge University Press, 1955, p. 1.

arithmetic problems, for example, he seeks general explanations of all kinds of problem-solving. He might call such a general explanation a theory of problem-solving.

This discussion of the basic aim of science as theory may seem strange to the student, who has probably been inculcated with the notion that human activities have to pay off in practical ways. If we said that the aim of science is the betterment of mankind, most readers would quickly read the words and accept them. But the *basic* aim of science is not the betterment of mankind. It is theory. Unfortunately, this sweeping and really complex statement is not too easy to understand. Still, we must try because it is important.

Other aims of science that have been stated are: explanation, understanding, prediction, and control. If we accept theory as the ultimate aim of science, however, explanation and understanding become simply subaims of the ultimate aim. This is because of the definition and nature of theory:

A theory is a set of interrelated constructs (concepts), definitions, and propositions that present a systematic view of phenomena by specifying relations among variables, with the purpose of explaining and predicting the phenomena.

This definitions says three things. One, a theory is a set of propositions consisting of defined and interrelated constructs. Two, a theory sets out the interrelations among a set of variables (constructs), and in so doing, presents a systematic view of the phenomena described by the variables. Finally, a theory explains phenomena. It does so by specifying what variables are related to what variables and how they are related, thus enabling the researcher to predict from certain variables to certain other variables.

One might, for example, have a theory of school failure. One's variables might be intelligence, verbal and numerical aptitudes, anxiety, social class membership, and motivation. The phenomenon to be explained, of course, is school failure—or, perhaps, more accurately, school achievement. School failure is explained by specified relations between each of the six variables and school failure, or by combinations of the six variables and school failure. The scientist, successfully using this set of constructs, then, "understands" school failure. He is able to "explain" and, to some extent at least, "predict" it.

It is obvious that explanation and prediction can be subsumed under theory. The very nature of a theory lies in its explanation of observed phenomena. Take reinforcement theory. A simple proposition flowing from this theory is: If a response is rewarded (reinforced) when it occurs, it will tend to be repeated. The psychological scientist who first formulated some such proposition did so as an expanation of the observed repetitious occurrences of responses. *Why* did they occur and reoccur with dependable regularity? Because they were rewarded. This is an explanation, although it may not be a satisfactory explanation to many people. Someone else may ask *why* reward increases the likelihood of a response's occurrence. A full-blown theory would have the explanation. Today, however, there is no really satisfactory answer. All we can say is that, with a high degree of probability, the reinforcement of a response makes the response occur and reoccur. In other words, the propositions of a theory, the statements of relations, constitute the explanation, as far as that theory is concerned, of observed natual phenomena.

Now, about prediction and control. It can be said that scientists do not really have to be concerned with explanation and understanding. Only prediction and control are necessary. Proponents of this point of view may say that the adequacy of a theory is its predictive power. If by using the theory we are able to predict successfully, then the theory is confirmed and this is enough. We need not necessarily look for further underlying explanations. Since we can predict reliably, we can control because control is deducible from prediction.

The prediction view of science has validity. But as far as this book is concerned, prediction is considered to be an aspect of theory. By its very nature, a theory predicts. That is, when from the primitive propositions of a theory we deduce more complex ones, we are in essence "predicting." When we explain observed phenomena, we are always stating a relation between, say, the class A and the class B. Scientific explanation boils down to specifying the relations between one class of empirical events and another, under certain conditions. We say: If A, then B, A and B referring to classes of objects or events.[12] But this *is* prediction, prediction from A to B. Thus a theoretical explanation implies prediction. And we come back to the idea that theory is the ultimate aim of science. All else flows from theory. This is perhaps what is meant by the expression "There is nothing more practical than a good theory."

There is no intention here to discredit or denigrate research that is not specifically and consciously theory-oriented. Much valuable social scientific and educational research is preoccupied with the shorter-range goal of finding specific relations; that is, merely to discover a relation is part of science. The ultimately most usable and satisfying relations, however, are those that are the most generalized, those that are tied to other relations in a theory.

The notion of generality is important. Theories, because they are general, apply to many phenomena and to many people in many places. A specific relation, of course, is less widely applicable. If, for example, one finds that test anxiety is related to test performance, this finding, though interesting and important, is less widely applicable and less understood than if one first found the relation in a network of interrelated variables that are parts of a theory. Modest, limited, and specific research aims, then, are good. Theoretical research aims are better because, among other reasons, they are more widely applicable and more general.

Scientific Research – a Definition

Fortunately, it is easier to define scientific research than it is to define science and theory. It would not be easy, however, to get scientists and researchers to agree

[12]Statements of the form "If p, then q," called conditional statements in logic, are part of the core of scientific inquiry. They and the concepts or variables that go into them are the central ingredients of theories. The logical foundation of scientific inquiry that underlies much of the reasoning in this book has been outlined in Kerlinger, "Research in Education," *op. cit.*, 1132–1134.

on such a definition. Even so, we attempt one here:

Scientific research is systematic, controlled, empirical, and critical investigation of hypothetical propositions about the presumed relations among natural phenomena.

This definition requires little explanation since it is mostly a condensed and formalized statement of much that was said earlier or that will be said soon. Two points need emphasis, however. First, when we say that scientific research is systematic and controlled, we mean, in effect, that scientific investigation is so ordered that investigators can have critical confidence in research outcomes. As we shall see later, this means that the research observations are tightly disciplined. Among the many alternative explanations of a phenomenon, all but one are systematically ruled out. One can thus have greater confidence that a tested relation is as it is than if one had not controlled the observations and ruled out alternative possibilities.

Second, scientific investigation is empirical. If the scientist believes something is so, he must somehow or other put his belief to a test outside himself. Subjective belief, in other words, must be checked against objective reality. The scientist must always subject his notions to the court of empirical inquiry and test. He is hypercritical of the results of his own and others' research results. Every scientist writing a research report has other scientists reading what he writes while he writes it. Though it is easy to err, to exaggerate, to overgeneralize when writing up one's own work, it is not easy to escape the feeling of scientific eyes constantly peering over one's shoulder.

The Scientific Approach

The scientific approach is a special systematized form of all reflective thinking and inquiry. Dewey, in his famous analysis of reflective thinking, *How We Think*, has given a general paradigm of problematical inquiry.[13] The present discussion of the scientific approach is based on Dewey's analysis. Dewey's treatment, however, is altered somewhat to suit the scientific framework in which we are working.

Problem-Obstacle-Idea

The scientist will usually experience an obstacle to understanding, a vague unrest about observed and unobserved phenomena, a curiosity as to why something is as it is. His first and most important step is to get the idea out in the open, to express the problem in some reasonably manageable form. Rarely or never will the problem spring full-blown at this stage. He must struggle with it, try it out, live with it. Dewey says, "There is a troubled, perplexed, trying situation, where the difficulty is, as it were, spread throughout the entire situation, infecting it as a whole."[14]

[13] J. Dewey, *How We Think*. Boston: Heath, 1933, pp. 106–118.
[14] *Ibid.*, p. 108.

Sooner or later, explicitly or implicitly, he states the problem, even if his expression of it is inchoate and tentative. Here he intellectualizes, as Dewey puts it, "what at first is merely an *emotional* quality of the whole situation,"[15] In some respects, this is the most difficult and most important part of the whole process. Without some sort of statement of the problem, the scientist can rarely go further and expect his work to be fruitful.

Hypothesis

After intellectualizing the problem, after turning back on experience for possible solutions, after observing relevant phenomena, the scientist may formulate a hypothesis. A hypothesis is a conjectural statement, a tentative proposition, about the relation between two or more phenomena or variables. Our scientist will say, "If such-and-such occurs, then so-and-so results."

Reasoning-Deduction

This step or activity is frequently overlooked or underemphasized. In some respects it is perhaps the most important part of Dewey's contribution to the analysis of reflective thinking. The scientist now deduces the consequences of the hypothesis he has formulated. Conant, in talking about the rise of modern science, says that the new element added in the seventeenth century was the use of deductive reasoning.[16] Here is where experience, knowledge, and perspicuity are important. Often the scientist, when deducing the consequences of a hypothesis he has formulated, will arrive at a problem quite different from the one he started with. On the other hand, he may find that his deductions lead him to believe that the problem cannot be solved with present technical tools. For example, before modern statistics was developed, certain behavioral research problems were insoluble. It was difficult, if not impossible, to test two or three interdependent hypotheses at one time. It was next to impossible to test the interactive effect of variables. And we now have reason to believe that certain problems are insoluble unless they are tackled in a multivariate manner. An example of this is teaching methods and their relation to achievement and other variables. It is likely that teaching methods, *per se*, do not differ much if we study only their simple effects. Teaching methods probably work differently under different conditions, with different teachers, and with different pupils.

An example may help us understand this reasoning-deduction step. Suppose an investigator becomes intrigued with aggressive behavior. He wonders why people are often aggressive in situations where aggressiveness may not be too appropriate. He has noted that aggressive behavior seems to occur when people have experienced difficulties of one kind or another. (Note the vagueness of the problem here.) After thinking for some time, reading the literature for clues, and making further observations, he formulates a hypothesis: Frustration leads to aggression. He defines "frustration" as prevention from reaching a goal and "ag-

[15]*Ibid.*, p. 109.
[16]Conant, *op. cit.*, p. 46.

gression" as behavior characterized by physical or verbal attack on other persons or objects.

He may now reason somewhat as follows. If frustration leads to aggression, then we should find a great deal of aggression among children who are in schools that are restrictive, schools that do not permit children much freedom and self-expression. Similarly, in difficult social situations, assuming such situations are frustrating, we should expect more aggression than is "usual." Reasoning further, if we give experimental subjects interesting problems to solve and then prevent them from solving them, we can predict some kind of aggressive behavior.

Reasoning may, as indicated above, change the problem. We may realize that the initial problem was only a special case of a broader, more fundamental and important problem. We may, for example, start with a narrower hypothesis: Restrictive school situations lead to negativism in children. Then we can generalize the problem to the form: Frustration leads to aggression. While this is a different form of thinking from that discussed earlier, it is important because of what can almost be called its heuristic quality. Reasoning can help lead to wider, more basic, and thus more significant problems, as well as provide operational (testable) implications of the original hypothesis.

Observation-Test-Experiment

It should be clear by now that the observation-test-experiment phase is only part of the scientific enterprise. If the problem has been well stated, the hypothesis or hypotheses adequately formulated, and the implications of the hypotheses carefully deduced, this step is almost automatic—assuming that the investigator is technically competent.

The essence of testing a hypothesis is to test the *relation* expressed by the hypothesis. We do not test the variables, as such; we test the relation between the variables. All observation, all testing, all experimentation is for one large purpose: putting the problem relation to empirical test. To test without knowing at least fairly well what and why one is testing is usually to blunder. Simply to have a vague and poorly stated problem (such as "What effect does the core curriculum have on students?") and then to test students for their achievement in, say, social studies is an inadequate procedure that can lead only to ignorance and, worse, to misguided information. Similarly, to say one is going to study grouping practices (grouping children by intellectual level, reading level, and the like) of teachers without knowing, really, why one is doing it or without stating a relation between grouping practices and some other variable or variables is research nonsense.

Another point about testing hypotheses is that we do not test a hypothesis directly. As indicated in the previous step on reasoning, we test the deduced implications of the hypothesis. Our hypothesis might be, "Writing remarks on student papers will improve future papers," which was deduced, say, from a broader hypothesis, "Reinforcement of responses leads to an increment in the response rate and strength." We are not testing "writing remarks on student papers" nor "the improvement of future papers." We are testing the relation between them.

Dewey emphasized that the temporal sequence of reflective thinking or inquiry is not fixed. We can repeat and reemphasize what he says in our own framework. The steps of the scientific approach are not neatly fixed. The first step is not neatly completed before the second step begins. Further, we may test before adequately deducing the implications of the hypothesis. The hypothesis itself may seem to need elaboration or refinement as a result of deducing implications from it.[17]

Feedback to the problem, the hypotheses, and, finally, the theory of the results of research is highly important. Learning theorists and researchers, for example, have frequently altered their theories and research as a result of experimental findings.[18] Theorists and researchers have been working on the effects of early environment and training on later development. Their research has yielded varied evidence converging on this extremely important theoretical and practical problem.[19] Part of the essential core of scientific research is the constant effort to replicate and check findings, to correct theory on the basis of empirical evidence, and to find better explanations of natural phenomena. One can even go so far as to say that science has a cyclic aspect. A researcher finds, say, that *A* is related to *B* in such-and-such a way. He then does more research to determine under what other conditions *A* is similarly related to *B*. Other researchers challenge his theory and his research, offering explanations and evidence of their own. The original researcher, hopefully, alters his work in the light of his own and others' evidence. The process never ends.

Let us summarize the so-called scientific approach to inquiry. First there is doubt, a barrier, an indeterminate situation crying out to be made determinate. The scientist experiences vague doubts, emotional disturbance, inchoate ideas. He struggles to formulate the problem, even if inadequately. He studies the literature, scans his own experience and the experience of others. Often he simply has to wait for an inventive leap of the mind. Maybe it will occur; maybe not. With the problem formulated, with the basic question or questions properly asked, the rest is much easier. Then the hypothesis is constructed, after which its empirical implications are deduced. In this process the original problem, and of course the original hypothesis, may be changed. It may be broadened or narrowed. It may even be abandoned. Last, but not finally, the relation expressed by the hypothesis is tested by observation and experimentation. On the basis of the research evidence, the hypothesis is accepted or rejected. This information is then fed back to the original problem, and the problem is kept or altered as dictated by the evi-

[17]Hypotheses and their expression will often be found inadequate when implications are deduced from them. A frequent difficulty occurs when a hypothesis is so vague that one deduction is as good as another – that is, the hypothesis may not yield to precise test.

[18]E. Hilgard and G. Bower, *Theories of Learning*, 3d ed. New York: Appleton, 1966.

[19]For example, E. Bennett et al., "Chemical and Anatomical Plasticity of Brain," *Science*, CXLVI (1964), 610–619; J. Hunt, *Intelligence and Experience*. New York: Ronald, 1961; M. Whiteman and M. Deutsch, "Social Disadvantage as Related to Intellective and Language Development." In M. Deutsch, I. Katz, and A. Jensen, eds., *Social Class, Race, and Psychological Development*. New York: Holt, Rinehart and Winston, 1968, pp. 86–114.

dence. Dewey pointed out that one phase of the process may be expanded and be of great importance, another may be skimped, and there may be fewer or more steps involved. Research is rarely an orderly business anyway. Indeed, it is much more disorderly than the above discussion may imply. Order and disorder, however, are not of primary importance. What is much more important is the controlled rationality of scientific research as a process of reflective inquiry, the interdependent nature of the parts of the process, and the paramount importance of the problem and its statement.

CHAPTER 2

Problems and Hypotheses

Many people think that science is basically a fact-gathering activity. It is not. As Cohen says:

> There is . . . no genuine progress in scientific insight through the Baconian method of accumulating empirical facts without hypotheses or anticipation of nature. Without some guiding idea we do not know what facts to gather . . . we cannot determine what is relevant and what is irrelevant.[1]

The scientifically uninformed person often has the idea that the scientist is a highly objective individual who gathers data without preconceived ideas. Poincaré long ago pointed out how wrong this idea is. He said:

> It is often said that experiments should be made without preconceived ideas. That is impossible. Not only would it make every experiment fruitless, but even if we wished to do so, it could not be done.[2]

Problems

It is not always possible for a researcher to formulate his problem simply, clearly, and completely. He may often have only a rather general, diffuse, even confused notion of the problem. This is in the nature of the complexity of scientific research. It may even take an investigator years of exploration, thought, and research before he can clearly say what questions he has been seeking answers to. Nevertheless, adequate statement of the research problem is one of the most important

[1]M. Cohen, *A Preface to Logic.* New York: Meridian, 1956, p. 148.
[2]H. Poincaré, *Science and Hypothesis.* New York: Dover, 1952, p. 143.

parts of research. That it may be difficult or impossible to state a research problem satisfactorily at a given time should not allow us to lose sight of the ultimate desirability and necessity of doing so. Nor should the difficulty be used as a rationalization to avoid stating the problem.

Bearing this difficulty in mind, a fundamental principle can be stated: If one wants to solve a problem, one must generally know what the problem is. It can be said that a large part of the solution lies in knowing what it is one is trying to do. Another part lies in knowing what a problem is and especially what a scientific problem is.

What is a good problem statement? Although research problems differ greatly, and although there is no one "right" way to state one, certain characteristics of problems and problem statements can be learned and used to good advantage. To start, let us take two or three examples of published research problems and study their characteristics. First, take the problem of the study by Hurlock mentioned in Chapter 1: What are the effects on pupil performance of different types of incentives?[3] Note that the problem is stated in question form. The simplest way is here the best way. Also note that the problem states a relation between variables, in this case between the variables incentives and pupil performance (achievement).

A *problem*, then, is an interrogative sentence or statement that asks: What relation exists between two or more variables? The answer is what is being sought in the research. If the problem is a scientific one, it will almost always contain two or more variables. In the Hurlock example, the problem statement relates incentive to pupil performance. Another problem, by Page, is: Do teacher comments cause improvement in student performance?[4] One variable is teacher comments (or reinforcement), and the other variable is student performance. The relational part of the question is expressed by the word "cause." Still another problem, by Harlow, is more complex: Under what conditions does learning how to learn transfer to new situations?[5] One variable is "learning how to learn" (or set); the other variable is transfer (of learning).[6]

Criteria of Problems and Problem Statements

There are three criteria of good problems and problem statements. One, the problem should express a relation between two or more variables. It asks, in effect, questions like: Is A related to B? How are A and B related to C? How is A related to B under conditions C and D? The rare exceptions to this dictum occur mostly in taxonomic or methodological research. (See Appendix B.)

[3]E. Hurlock, "An Evaluation of Certain Incentives Used in Schoolwork," *Journal of Educational Psychology*, XVI (1925), 145–159. When citing problems and hypotheses from the literature, I have not always used the words of the authors. In fact, the statements of some of the problems are mine and not those of the cited authors. Some authors use only problem statements; some use only hypotheses; others use both.

[4]E. Page, "Teacher Comments and Student Performance: A Seventy-Four Classroom Experiment in School Motivation," *Journal of Educational Psychology*, XLIX (1958), 173–181.

[5]H. Harlow, "The Formation of Learning Sets," *Psychological Review*, LVI (1949), 51–65.

[6]Problems have the same form in different behavioral sciences. Here is a sociological problem suggested by Etzioni (there are others below): Does conflict enhance or impede the efficiency of organizations? A. Etzioni, *Modern Organizations.* Englewood Cliffs, N.J.: Prentice-Hall, 1964, p. 27.

Two, the problem should be stated clearly and unambiguously in question form. Instead of saying, for instance, "The problem is . . . ," or "The purpose of this study is . . . ," ask a question. Questions have the virtue of posing problems directly. The purpose of a study is not necessarily the same as the problem of a study. The purpose of the Hurlock study, for instance, was to throw light on the use of incentives in school situations. The problem was the question about the relation between incentives and performance. Again, the simplest way is the best way: ask a question.

The third criterion is often difficult to satisfy. It demands that the problem and the problem statement should be such as to *imply* possibilities of empirical testing. A problem that does not contain implications for testing its stated relation or relations is not a scientific problem. This means not only that an actual relation is stated, but also that the variables of the relation can somehow be measured. Many interesting and important questions are not scientific questions simply because they are not amenable to testing. Certain philosophic and theological questions, while perhaps important to the individuals who consider them, cannot be tested empirically and are thus of no interest to the scientist as a scientist. The epistemological question, "How do we know?," is such a question. A medieval theological classic is "How many angels can dance on the head of a pin?" Education has many interesting but nonscientific questions, such as, "Does democratic education improve the learning of youngsters?" "Are group processes good for children?" These questions can be called metaphysical in the sense that they are, at least as stated, beyond empirical testing possibilities. The key difficulties are that some of them are not relations, and most of their constructs are very difficult or impossible to so define that they can be measured.[7]

Hypotheses

A *hypothesis* is a conjectural statement of the relation between two or more variables. Hypotheses are always in declarative sentence form, and they relate, either generally or specifically, variables to variables. There are two criteria for "good" hypotheses and hypothesis statements. They are the same as two of those for problems and problem statements. One, hypotheses are statements about the relations between variables. Two, hypotheses carry clear implications for testing the stated relations. These criteria mean, then, that hypothesis statements contain two or more variables that are measurable or potentially measurable and that they specify how the variables are related. A statement that lacks either or both these characteristics is no hypothesis in the scientific sense of the word.[8]

[7]Webb, working from a different point of view, has proposed the following criteria of research problems: knowledge (of the researcher); dissatisfaction (skepticism, going against the tide, etc.); generality (wideness of applicability). Webb's article is doubly valuable because he effectively disposes of irrelevant criteria, such as confirmability, cupidity ("payola"), conformity ("Everybody's doing it"). W. Webb, "The Choice of Problem," *American Psychologist*, XVI (1961), 223–227.

[8]There are legitimate hypotheses that, at least on the surface, lack the relation criterion. For instance, in factor-analytic investigations, to be discussed later, we might have some such problem statement as: What are the factors underlying social attitudes? A hypothesis such as this might be used: There are two underlying factors behind social attitudes: (I) liberalism and (II) conservatism. In this book, however, relational statements will be emphasized.

Let us take three hypotheses from the literature and apply the two criteria to them. First, consider a very simple hypothesis: Group study contributes to higher grade achievement.[9] We have here a relation stated between one variable, group study, and another variable, grade achievement. Since measurement of the variables is readily conceivable, implications for testing the hypothesis, too, are readily conceivable. The criteria are satisfied. A second hypothesis is different because it states the relation in the so-called null form: Practice in a mental function has no effect on the future learning of that mental function.[10] Note that the relation is stated directly and clearly: one variable, practice in a mental function, is related to another variable, future learning, by the words "has no effect on." On the criterion of potential testability, however, we meet with difficulty. We are faced with the problem of so defining "mental function" and "future learning" that they are measurable. If we can solve this problem satisfactorily, then we definitely have a hypothesis. Indeed, we have a famous one—but one that has usually not been stated as a hypothesis but as a fact by many educators of the past and the present.

The third hypothesis represents a very numerous and important class. Here the relation is indirect, concealed, as it were. It customarily comes in the form of a statement that Groups *A* and *B* will differ on some characteristic. For example: Middle-class children more often than lower-class children will avoid finger-painting tasks.[11] Note that this statement is one step removed from the actual hypothesis, which might be stated: Finger-painting behavior is in part a function of social class. If the latter statement were the hypothesis stated, then the first might be called a subhypothesis, or a specific prediction based on the original hypothesis.

Let us consider another hypothesis of this type but removed one step further: Individuals having the same or similar occupational role will hold similar attitudes toward a cognitive object significantly related to the occupational role.[12] ("Cognitive objects" are any concrete or abstract things perceived and "known" by individuals. People, groups, the government, and education are examples of cognitive objects.) The relation in this case, of course, is between occupational role and attitudes (toward a cognitive object related to the role, for example, role of educator and attitudes toward education). In order to test this hypothesis, it would be necessary to have at least two groups, each representing a different occupational role, and then to compare the attitudes of the groups. For instance, we might take a group of teachers and compare their attitudes toward education to those of, say, a group of businessmen. Thus the hypothesis, as stated, is really a "difference" hypothesis. Still, it, too, can be reduced to the general relational

[9]J. Blue, "The Effects of Group Study on Grade Achievement," *Journal of Educational Psychology*, XLIX (1958), 118–123.

[10]A. Gates and G. Taylor, "An Experimental Study of the Nature of Improvement Resulting from Practice in a Mental Function," *Journal of Educational Psychology*, XVI (1925), 583–592.

[11]T. Alper, H. Blane, and B. Adams, "Reactions of Middle and Lower Class Children to Finger Paints as a Function of Class Differences in Child-Training Practices," *Journal of Abnormal and Social Psychology*, LI (1955), 439–448.

[12]F. Kerlinger, "The Attitude Structure of the Individual: A Q-Study of the Educational Attitudes of Professors and Laymen," *Genetic Psychology Monographs*, LIII (1956), 283–329.

form with which we started: Attitudes toward cognitive objects significantly related to occupational roles are in part a function of the behavior and expectations associated with the roles.

The Importance of Problems and Hypotheses

There is little doubt that hypotheses are important and indispensable tools of scientific research. There are three main reasons for this belief. One, they are, so to speak, the working instruments of theory. Hypotheses can be deduced from theory and from other hypotheses. If, for instance, we are working on a theory of aggression, we are presumably looking for causes and effects of aggressive behavior. We might have observed cases of aggressive behavior occurring after frustrating circumstances. The theory, then, might include the proposition: Frustration produces aggression.[13] From this broad hypothesis we may deduce more specific hypotheses, such as: To prevent children from reaching goals they find desirable (frustration) will result in their fighting with each other (aggression); if children are deprived of parental love (frustration), they will react in part with aggressive behavior.

The second reason is that hypotheses can be tested and shown to be probably true or probably false. Isolated facts are not tested, as we said before; only relations are tested. Since hypotheses are relational propositions, this is probably the main reason they are used in scientific inquiry. They are, in essence, predictions of the form, "If A, then B," which we set up to test the relation between A and B. We let the facts have a chance to establish the probable truth or falsity of the hypothesis.

Three, hypotheses are powerful tools for the advancement of knowledge because they enable man to get outside himself. Though constructed by man, hypotheses exist, can be tested, and can be shown to be probably correct or incorrect apart from man's values and opinions. This is so important that we venture to say that there would be no science in any complete sense without hypotheses.

Just as important as hypotheses are the problems behind the hypotheses. As Dewey has well pointed out, research usually starts with a problem, with a problematic situation. Dewey says that there is first an indeterminate situation in which ideas are vague, doubts are raised, and the thinker is perplexed.[14] He further points out that the problem is not enunciated, indeed cannot be enunciated, until one has experienced such an indeterminate situation.

The indeterminacy, however, must ultimately be removed. Though it is true, as stated earlier, that a researcher may often have only a general and diffuse notion of his problem, sooner or later he has to have a fairly clear idea of what the problem is. Though this statement seems self-evident, one of the most difficult things to do, apparently, is to state one's research problem clearly and completely.

[13] J. Dollard et al., *Frustration and Aggression*. New Haven: Yale University Press, 1939.
[14] J. Dewey, *Logic: The Theory of Inquiry*. New York: Holt, Rinehart and Winston, 1938, pp. 105–107.

In other words, you must know what you are trying to find out. When you finally do know, the problem is a long way toward solution.

Virtues of Problems and Hypotheses

Problems and hypotheses, then, have important virtues. One, they direct investigation. The relations expressed in the hypotheses tell the investigator, in effect, what to do. Two, problems and hypotheses, because they are ordinarily generalized relational statements, enable the researcher to deduce specific empirical manifestations implied by the problems and hypotheses. We may say, following Allport and Ross: If it is indeed true that people of extrinsic religious orientation (they *use* religion) are prejudiced, whereas people of intrinsic religious orientation (they *live* religion) are not, then it follows that churchgoers should be more prejudiced than nonchurchgoers. They should perhaps also have a "jungle" philosophy: general suspicion and distrust of the world.[15]

There are important differences between problems and hypotheses. Hypotheses, if properly stated, can be tested. While a given hypothesis may be too broad to be directly tested, if it is a "good" hypothesis, then other testable hypotheses can be deduced from it. The point is that facts or variables are not tested as such. The relations stated by the hypotheses are tested. And a problem really cannot be scientifically solved unless it is reduced to hypothesis form, because a problem is a question, usually of a broad nature, and is not directly testable. One does not test the questions: Does anxiety affect achievement? Do ghetto conditions produce delinquency? One tests one or more hypotheses implied by these questions. For example: Test anxiety reduces achievement test scores, and delinquency rates are higher in ghetto than in nonghetto areas of cities.

Problems and hypotheses advance scientific knowledge by helping the investigator confirm or disconfirm theory. Suppose a psychological investigator gives a number of subjects three or four tests, among which is a test of anxiety and an arithmetic test. Routinely computing the intercorrelations between the three or four tests, he finds that the correlation between anxiety and arithmetic is negative. He concludes, therefore, that the greater the anxiety the lower the arithmetic score. But it is quite conceivable that the relation is fortuitous or even spurious. If, however, he had hypothesized the relation on the basis of theory, the investigator could have greater confidence in the results. The investigator who does not hypothesize a relation in advance, in short, does not give the facts a chance to prove or disprove anything.[16]

[15]G. Allport and J. Ross, "Personal Religious Orientation and Prejudice," *Journal of Personality and Social Psychology*, V (1967), 432–443.

[16]The words "prove" and "disprove" are not to be taken here in their usual literal sense. It should be remembered that a hypothesis is never really proved or disproved. To be more accurate we should probably say something like: The weight of evidence is on the side of the hypothesis, or the weight of the evidence casts doubt on the hypothesis. Braithwaite says: "Thus the empirical evidence of its instance never proves the hypothesis: in suitable cases we may say that it *establishes* the hypothesis, meaning by this that the evidence makes it reasonable to accept the hypothesis; but it never *proves* the hypothesis in the sense that the hypothesis is a logical consequence of the evidence." (R. Braithwaite, *Scientific Explanation*. Cambridge: Cambridge University Press, 1955, p. 14.)

This use of the hypothesis is similar to playing a game of chance. The rules of the game are set up in advance, and bets are made in advance. One cannot change the rules after an outcome, nor can one change one's bets after making them. That would not be "fair." One cannot throw the dice first and then bet. Similarly, if one gathers data first and then selects a datum and comes to a conclusion on the basis of the datum, one has violated the rules of the scientific game.

The game is not "fair" because the investigator can easily capitalize on, say, two significant relations out of five tested. What happens to the other three? They are usually forgotten. But in a fair game every throw of the dice is counted, in the sense that one either wins or does not win on the basis of the outcome of each throw. The main point, perhaps, is that the purpose of hypotheses is to direct inquiry. As Darwin pointed out long ago, all observations have to be for or against some view if they are to be of any use.

A final point about hypotheses has already been made, but it needs formal statement, even repetition. Hypotheses incorporate the theory, or part of it, in testable or near-testable form. Earlier, an example of reinforcement theory was given in which testable hypotheses were deduced from the general problem. The importance of recognizing this function of hypotheses may be shown by going through the back door and using a theory that is very difficult, or perhaps impossible, to test. Freud's theory of anxiety includes the construct of repression. Now, by repression Freud meant the forcing of unacceptable ideas deep into the unconscious. In order to test the Freudian theory of anxiety it is necessary to deduce relations suggested by the theory. These deductions will, of course, have to include the repression notion, which includes the construct of the unconscious. Hypotheses can be formulated using these constructs; in order to test the theory, they have to be so formulated. But testing them is another, more difficult matter because of the extreme difficulty of so defining terms such as "repression" and "unconscious" that they can be measured. To the present, no one has succeeded in defining these two constructs without seriously departing from the original Freudian meaning and usage. Hypotheses, then, are important bridges between theory and empirical inquiry.

Problems, Values, and Definitions

To clarify further the nature of problems and hypotheses, two or three common errors will now be discussed. First, scientific problems are not moral and ethical questions. Are punitive disciplinary measures bad for children? Should an organization's leadership be democratic? What is the best way to teach college students? To ask these questions is to ask value and judgmental questions that science cannot answer. Many so-called hypotheses are not hypotheses at all. For instance: The small-group method of teaching is better than the lecture method. This is a value statement; it is an article of faith and not a hypothesis. If it were possible to state a relation between the variables, and if it were possible to define the variables so as to permit testing the relation, then we might have a hypothesis. But there is no way to test value questions scientifically.

A quick and relatively easy way to detect value questions and statements is to look for words such as "should," "ought," "better than" (instead of "greater than"), and similar words that indicate cultural or personal judgments or preferences. Value statements, however, are tricky. While a "should" statement is obviously a value statement, certain other kinds of statements are not so obvious. Take the statement: Authoritarian methods of teaching lead to poor learning. Here there is a relation. But the statement fails as a scientific hypothesis because it uses two value expressions or words, "authoritarian methods of teaching" and "poor learning," neither of which can be defined for measurement purposes without deleting the words "authoritarian" and "poor." The word "poor" is obviously a value word: it expresses a value judgment. To attain scientific respectability, the expression "poor learning" has to be deleted and some expression substituted such as "decreased problem-solving behavior," which implies measurement possibilities but no value judgment. The expression "authoritarian methods of teaching" is perhaps almost hopeless at present, although its definition is conceivable. The trouble is that the mere use of the word "authoritarian" expresses a value judgment, at least in this case. As used today, it says, in effect, that such methods are "bad." Another difficulty is that at present we do not know what "authoritarian methods of teaching" means. Most often it seems to refer to the personal teaching biases of the person using this method.[17]

Other kinds of statements that are not hypotheses or are poor ones are frequently formulated, especially in education. Consider, for instance: The core curriculum is an enriching experience. Another type, too frequent, is the vague generalization: Reading skills can be identified in the second grade; The goal of the unique individual is self-realization; Prejudice is related to certain personality traits.

Another common defect of problem statements often occurs in doctoral theses: the listing of methodological points or "problems" as subproblems. These methodological points have two characteristics that make them easy to detect: (1) they are not substantive problems that spring from the basic problem; and (2) they relate to techniques or methods of sampling, measuring, or analyzing. They are usually not in question form, but rather contain the words "test," "determine," "measure," and the like. "To determine the reliability of the instruments used in this research," "To test the significance of the differences between the means," and "To assign pupils at random to the experimental groups" are symptomatic of this mistaken notion of problems and subproblems.

Generality and Specificity of Problems and Hypotheses

One difficulty that the research worker usually encounters and that almost all students working on a thesis find bothersome is the generality and specificity of

[17]An almost classic case of the use of the word "authoritarian" is the statement sometimes heard among educators: The lecture method is authoritarian. This seems to mean that the speaker does not like the lecture method and he is telling us that it is bad. Similarly, one of the most effective ways to criticize a teacher is to say that he is authoritarian.

problems and hypotheses. If the problem is too general, it is usually too vague and cannot be tested. Thus, it is scientifically useless, though it may be interesting to read. Problems and hypotheses that are too general or too vague are common. For example: Creativity is a function of the self-actualization of the individual; Democratic education enhances social learning and citizenship; Authoritarianism in the college classroom inhibits the creative imagination of students. These are interesting problems. But, in their present form, they are worse than useless scientifically, because they cannot be tested and because they give one the spurious assurance that they are hypotheses that can "some day" be tested.

Terms such as "creativity," "self-actualization," "democracy," "authoritarianism," and the like have, at the present time at least, no adequate empirical referents.[18] Now, it is quite true that we can define "creativity," say, in a limited way by specifying one or two creativity tests. This may be a legitimate procedure. Still, in so doing, we run the risk of getting far away from the original term and its meaning. This is particularly true when we speak of artistic creativity. We are often willing to accept the risk in order to be able to investigate important problems, of course. Yet terms like "democracy" are almost hopeless to define. Even when we do define it, we often find we have destroyed the original meaning of the term.

The other extreme is too great specificity. Every student has heard that it is necessary to narrow problems down to workable size. This is true. But, unfortunately, we can also narrow the problem out of existence. In general, the more specific the problem or hypothesis the clearer are its testing implications. But triviality may be the price we pay. While the researcher cannot handle problems that are too broad because they tend to be too vague for adequate research operations, in his zeal to cut the problems down to workable size or to find a workable problem, he may cut the life out of it. He may make it trivial or inconsequential. A thesis, for instance, on the simple relation between the speed of reading and size of type, while important and maybe even interesting, is too thin for doctoral study. Too great specificity is perhaps a worse danger than too great generality. At any rate, some kind of compromise must be made between generality and specificity. The ability effectively to make such compromises is a function partly of experience and partly of much critical study of research problems.

The Multivariate Nature of Behavioral Research and Problems

Until now the discussion of problems and hypotheses has been pretty much limited to two variables, x and y. We must hasten to correct any impression that such problems and hypotheses are the norm in behavioral research. Researchers in psychology, sociology, education, and other behavioral sciences have become keenly aware of the multivariate nature of behavioral research. Instead of saying:

[18]Although many studies of authoritarianism have been done with considerable success, it is doubtful that we know what authoritarianism in the classroom means. For instance, an action of a teacher that is authoritarian in one classroom may not be authoritarian in another classroom. The alleged democratic behavior exhibited by one teacher may even be called authoritarian if exhibited by another teacher. Such elasticity is not the stuff of science.

If p, then q, it is often more appropriate to say: If $p_1, p_2, \ldots, p_k$, then q; or: If p_1, then q, under conditions r, s, and t.

An example may clarify the point. Instead of simply stating the hypothesis: If frustration, then aggression, it is more realistic to recognize the multivariate nature of the determinants and influences of aggression by saying, for example: If high intelligence, middle class, male, and frustrated, then aggression. Or: If frustration, then aggression, under the conditions of high intelligence, middle class, and male. Instead of one x, we now have four x's. Although one phenomenon may be the most important in determining or influencing another phenomenon, it is unlikely that most of the phenomena of interest to behavioral scientists are determined simply. It is much more likely that they are determined multiply. It is much more likely that aggression is the result of several influences working in complex ways. Moreover, aggression itself has multiple aspects. After all, there are different kinds of aggression.

Problems and hypotheses thus have to reflect the multivariate complexity of psychological, sociological, and educational reality. Although we will talk of one x and one y, especially in the early part of the book, it must be understood that contemporary behavioral research, which used to be almost exclusively univariate in its approach, is rapidly becoming multivariate. (For now, "univariate" means one x and one y. "Univariate," strictly speaking, applies to y. If there is more than one x or more than one y, the word "multivariate" is used, at least in this book.) We will soon encounter multivariate conceptions and problems. And later parts of the book will be especially concerned with a multivariate approach and emphasis.

Concluding Remarks – The Special Power of Hypotheses

One will sometimes hear that hypotheses are unnecessary in research, that they unnecessarily restrict the investigative imagination, that the job of science and scientific investigation is to find out things and not to labor the obvious, that hypotheses are obsolete, and the like. Such statements are quite misleading. They misconstrue the purpose of hypotheses.

It can almost be said that the hypothesis is the most powerful tool man has invented to achieve dependable knowledge. Man observes a phenomenon. He speculates on possible causes. Naturally, his culture has a stock of answers to account for most phenomena, many correct, many incorrect, many a mixture of fact and superstition, many pure superstition and mythology. It is the scientist's business to doubt most explanations of the phenomena of his field. His doubts are systematic. He insists upon subjecting explanations of phenomena to controlled empirical test. In order to do this, he must so formulate explanations that they are amenable to controlled empirical test. He formulates the explanations in the form of theories and hypotheses. In fact, the explanations *are* hypotheses. The scientist simply disciplines the business by writing systematic and testable hypotheses. If an explanation cannot be formulated in the form of a testable hypothesis, then it can be considered to be a metaphysical explanation and thus not amenable to scientific investigation. As such, it is dismissed by the scientist as being of no interest.

The power of hypotheses goes further than this, however. A hypothesis is a prediction. It says that if *x* occurs, *y* will also occur. That is, *y* is predicted from *x*. If, then, *x* is made to occur (vary), and it is observed that *y* also occurs (varies concomitantly), then the hypothesis is confirmed. This is more powerful evidence than simply observing, without prediction, the covarying of *x* and *y*. It is more powerful in the betting-game sense discussed earlier. The scientist makes a bet that *x* leads to *y*. If, in an experiment, *x* does lead to *y*, then he collects his money. He has won the bet. He cannot just enter the game at any point and pick a perhaps fortuitous common occurrence of *x* and *y*. Games are not played this way (at least in our culture). He must play according to the rules, and the rules in science are made to minimize error and man's fallibility. Hypotheses are part of the rules of the game.

Even when hypotheses are not confirmed, they have power. Even when *y* does not covary with *x*, knowledge is advanced. Negative findings are sometimes as important as positive ones, since they cut down the total universe of ignorance and sometimes point up fruitful further hypotheses and lines of investigation. *But the scientist cannot tell positive from negative evidence unless he uses hypotheses.* It is possible to conduct research without hypotheses, of course, particularly in exploratory investigations. But it is hard to conceive modern science in all its rigorous and disciplined fertility without the guiding power of hypotheses.

Study Suggestions

1. Use the following constructs to write research problems and hypotheses: level of aspiration, frustration, academic achievement, race, intelligence, verbal aptitude, social class, sex, reinforcement, teaching methods, reading readiness, introversion, incentives, anti-Semitism, occupational choice, permissiveness, ego involvement, education, income, classroom climate, need for achievement, social prestige, ethnic beliefs.
2. Seven problems from the research literature are given below. Study them carefully and construct one or two hypotheses based on them.
   (a) Do teacher comments cause improvement in student performance?[19]
   (b) Does learning how to learn transfer to new situations?[20]
   (c) Is similarity in belief more influential than race in accepting others?[21]
   (d) Does practice in a mental function improve future learning of the mental function?[22]
   (e) How does organizational climate affect administrative performance?[23]
   (f) Does forced compliance induce change in belief?[24]

[19]Page, *op. cit.*

[20]Harlow, *op. cit.*

[21]M. Rokeach and L. Mezei. "Race and Shared Belief as Factors in Social Choice." *Science*, CLI (1966), 167–172.

[22]Gates and Taylor, *op. cit.*

[23]N. Frederiksen, O. Jensen, and A. Beaton, *Organizational Climates and Administrative Performance.* Princeton, N.J.: Educational Testing Service, 1968.

[24]L. Festinger and J. Carlsmith, "Cognitive Consequences of Forced Compliance," *Journal of Abnormal and Social Psychology*, LVIII (1959), 203–211; E. Schein, "The Chinese Indoctrination Program for Prisoners of War: A Study of Attempted 'Brainwashing.'" In E. Maccoby, T. Newcomb, and E. Hartley, eds., *Readings in Social Psychology*, 3d ed. New York: Holt, Rinehart and Winston, 1958, pp. 311–334.

   (g) How does the socioeconomic status of blacks affect the social distance they accord whites?[25]
3. Seven hypotheses are given below. Discuss possibilities of testing them. Then read one or two of the original studies to see how the author(s) tested them.
   (a) The greater the cohesiveness of a group the greater its influence on its members.[26]
   (b) Prejudiced people identify minority-group members by their faces more readily than do unprejudiced people.[27]
   (c) The extent of role conflict is a function of the number and magnitude of incompatible expectations placed on or held by the individual.[28]
   (d) Deductive and associative types of concept learning depend on age of children and their instructional sets.[29]
   (e) The learning and retention of unfamiliar but meaningful verbal material is facilitated by the advance introduction of relevant subsuming concepts (organizers).[30]
   (f) Pseudoprogressives will assess teachers exhibiting seemingly progressive (but not really progressive) behavior more positively than will genuine progressives.[31]
   (g) The probability of the occurrence of responses is increased if the responses are followed by statements consonant with the attitude of the respondents.[32]
4. To give the student a preliminary feeling for multivariate problems, three of them are given below.
   (a) How do academic aptitude, high school achievement, and level of aspiration influence academic achievement?[33]
   (b) What are the relative contributions to the verbal achievement of white and black elementary school pupils of home background, school facilities, and pupil attitudes?[34]
   (c) How are early experiences in the home and parental dominance, on the one hand, related to curiosity about people and desire for close personal relations, on the other hand?[35]

[25]F. Westie and D. Howard, "Social Status Differentials and the Race Attitudes of Negroes," *American Sociological Review*, XIX (1954), 584–591.

[26]S. Schachter et al., "An Experimental Study of Cohesiveness and Productivity," *Human Relations*, IV (1951), 229–238.

[27]G. Allport and B. Kramer, "Some Roots of Prejudice," *Journal of Psychology*, XXII (1946), 9–39.

[28]J. Getzels and E. Guba, "Role, Role Conflict, and Effectiveness: An Empirical Study," *American Sociological Review*, XIX (1954), 164–175.

[29]H. Amster, "Effect of Instructional Set and Variety of Instances of Children's Learning," *Journal of Educational Psychology*, LVII (1960), 74–85.

[30]D. Ausubel, "The Use of Advance Organizers in the Learning and Retention of Meaningful Verbal Material," *Journal of Educational Psychology*, LI (1960), 267–272.

[31]E. Pedhazur, "Pseudoprogressivism and Assessment of Teacher Behavior," *Educational and Psychological Measurement*, XXIX (1969), 377–386.

[32]C. Golightly and D. Byrne, "Attitude Statements as Positive and Negative Reinforcements," *Science*, CXLVI (1964), 798–799.

[33]L. Worrell, "Level of Aspiration and Academic Success," *Journal of Educational Psychology*, L (1959), 47–54.

[34]J. Coleman et al., *Equality of Educational Opportunity*. Washington, D.C.: U.S. Government Printing Office, 1966.

[35]A. Roe and M. Siegelman, *The Origin of Interests*. Washington, D.C.: American Personnel and Guidance Association, 1964.

CHAPTER 3

Constructs, Variables, and Definitions

Scientists operate on two levels: theory-hypothesis-construct and observation. More accurately, they shuttle back and forth between these levels. A psychological scientist may say, "Early deprivation produces learning deficiency." This statement is a hypothesis consisting of two concepts, "early deprivation" and "learning deficiency," joined by a relation word, "produces." It is on the theory-hypothesis-construct level. Whenever the scientist utters relational statements and whenever he uses concepts, or constructs, as we shall call them, he is operating, so to speak, at this level.

The scientist must also operate at the level of observation. He must gather data that test his hypotheses. In order to do this, he must somehow get from the construct level to the observation level. He cannot simply make observations of "early deprivation" and "learning deficiency." He must so define these constructs that observations are possible. The problem of this chapter is to examine and clarify the nature of scientific concepts or constructs and the way in which behavioral scientists get from the construct level to the observation level, how they shuttle from one to the other.

Concepts and Constructs

The terms "concept" and "construct" have similar meanings. Yet there is an important distinction. A *concept* expresses an abstraction formed by generalization from particulars. "Weight" is a concept: it expresses numerous observations of things that are more or less "heavy" or "light." "Mass," "energy," and "force" are concepts used by physical scientists. They are, of course, much more abstract than concepts such as "weight," "height," and "length."

A concept of more interest to readers of this book is "achievement." It is an abstraction formed from the observation of certain behaviors of children. These behaviors are associated with the mastery or "learning" of school tasks—reading words, doing arithmetic problems, drawing pictures, and so on. The various observed behaviors are put together and expressed in a word—"achievement." "Intelligence," "aggressiveness," "conformity," and "honesty" are all concepts used to express varieties of human behavior of interest to behavioral scientists.

A *construct* is a concept. It has the added meaning, however, of having been deliberately and consciously invented or adopted for a special scientific purpose. "Intelligence" is a concept, an abstraction from the observation of presumably intelligent and nonintelligent behaviors. But as a scientific construct, "intelligence" means both more and less than it may mean as a concept. It means that scientists consciously and systematically use it in two ways. One, it enters into theoretical schemes and is related in various ways to other constructs. We may say, for example, that school achievement is in part a function of intelligence and motivation. Two, "intelligence" is so defined and specified that it can be observed and measured. We can make observations of the intelligence of children by administering X intelligence test to them, or we can ask teachers to tell us the relative degrees of intelligence of their pupils.

Variables

Scientists somewhat loosely call the constructs or properties they study "variables." Examples of important variables in sociology, psychology, and education are: sex, income, education, social class, organizational productivity, occupational mobility, level of aspiration, verbal aptitude, anxiety, religious affiliation, political preference, ego strength, task orientation, authoritarianism, conformity, intelligence, achievement. It can be said that a variable is a property that takes on different values. Putting it redundantly, a variable is something that varies. While this way of speaking gives us an intuitive notion of what variables are, we need a more general and yet more precise definition.

A *variable* is a symbol to which numerals or values are assigned. For instance, x is a variable: it is a *symbol* to which we assign numerical values. The variable x may take on any justifiable set of values—for example, scores on an intelligence test or an attitude scale. In the case of intelligence we assign to x a set of numerical values yielded by the procedure designated in a specified test of intelligence. This set of values, often called IQ's, ranges from low to high, from, say, 50 to 150.

A variable, x, however, may have only two values. If sex is the construct under study, then x can be assigned 1 and 0, 1 standing for one of the sexes and 0 standing for the other. It is still a variable. Other examples of two-valued variables are: alive-dead, citizen-noncitizen, middle class-working class, teacher-nonteacher, Republican-Democrat, and so on. Such variables are often called dichotomies or dichotomous variables.

Some of the variables used in behavioral research are true dichotomies—that is, they are characterized by the presence or absence of a property: male-female, alive-dead, employed-unemployed. Some variables are polytomies. A good example is religious preference: Protestant, Catholic, Jew, Other.[1] Most variables, however, are theoretically capable of taking on continuous values. It has been common practice in behavioral research to convert continuous variables to dichotomies or polytomies. For example, intelligence, a continuous variable, has been broken down into high and low intelligence, or into high, medium, and low intelligence. Variables such as anxiety, introversion, and authoritarianism have been treated similarly. Note that while it is not possible to convert a truly dichotomous variable such as sex to a continuous variable, it is always possible to convert a continuous variable to a dichotomy or a polytomy. As we will see later, such conversion can serve a useful conceptual purpose. But it is poor practice in the analysis of data because it throws information away.

Constitutive and Operational Definitions of Constructs and Variables

The distinction made earlier between "concept" and "construct" leads naturally to another important distinction: that between kinds of definitions of constructs and variables. Words or constructs can be defined in two general ways. First, we can define a word by using other words, which is what a dictionary usually does. We can define "intelligence" by saying it is "operating intellect," "mental acuity," or "the ability to think abstractly." Note that such definitions use other concepts or conceptual expressions in lieu of the expression being defined.

Second, we can define a word by telling what actions or behaviors it expresses or implies. Defining "intelligence" this way requires that we specify what behaviors of children are "intelligent" and what behaviors are "not intelligent." We may say that a child of seven who successfully reads a story we give him to read is "intelligent." If the child cannot read the story, we may say he is "not intelligent." In other words, this kind of definition can be called a behavioral or observational definition. Both "other word" and "observational" definitions are used constantly in everyday living.

There is a looseness about this discussion that would disturb a scientist. Though he uses the types of definition just described, he does so in a more precise and articulated manner. We express this usage by defining and explaining Margenau's distinction between constitutive and operational definitions.[2]

A *constitutive definition* defines a construct with other constructs. For instance, we can define "weight" by saying that it is the "heaviness" of objects. Or we can define "anxiety" as "subjectified fear." In both cases we have substituted one concept for another. Some of the constructs of a scientific theory may be defined constitutively. Torgerson, borrowing from Margenau, says that

[1]Such dichotomies and polytomies have been called "qualitative variables." The questionable nature of this designation will be discussed later.

[2]H. Margenau, *The Nature of Physical Reality*. New York: McGraw-Hill, 1950, chaps. 4, 5, and 12. The present discussion leans heavily on Margenau and on Torgerson's excellent presentation of the same distinction: W. Torgerson, *Theory and Methods of Scaling*. New York: Wiley, 1958, pp. 2–5.

all constructs, in order to be scientifically useful, must possess constitutive meaning.[3] This means that they must be capable of being used in theories.

An *operational definition* assigns meaning to a construct or a variable by specifying the activities or "operations" necessary to measure it. Alternatively, an operational definition is a specification of the activities of the researcher in measuring a variable or in manipulating it. An operational definition is a sort of manual of instructions to the investigator. It says, in effect, "Do such-and-such in so-and-so a manner." In short, it defines or gives meaning to a variable by spelling out what the investigator must do to measure it.

A well-known, if extreme, example of an operational definition is: Intelligence (anxiety, achievement, and so forth) is scores on X intelligence test, or intelligence is what X intelligence test measures. Notice that this definition tells us what to do to measure intelligence. It says nothing about how well intelligence is measured by the specified instrument. (Presumably the adequacy of the test was ascertained prior to the investigator's use of it.) In this usage, an operational definition is an equation where we say, "Let intelligence equal the scores on X test of intelligence." We also seem to be saying, "The meaning of intelligence (in this research) is expressed by the scores on X intelligence test."

There are, in general, two kinds of operational definitions: (1) *measured* and (2) *experimental*. The definition given above is more closely tied to measured than to experimental definitions. A *measured* operational definition describes how a variable will be measured. For example, achievement may be defined by a standardized achievement test, by a teacher-made achievement test, or by grades. Hare defined the consensus of a group as follows: "The amount of consensus in the group is measured by having each individual rate the ten pieces of camping equipment before discussion, the group rate the equipment during the discussion, and the individuals again rate them after discussion."[4] A study may include the variable *consideration*. It can be defined operationally by listing behaviors of children that are presumably considerate behaviors and then requiring teachers to rate the children on a five-point scale. Such behaviors might be when the children say to each other, "I'm sorry," or "Excuse me," when one child yields a toy to another on request (but not on threat of aggression), or when one child helps another with a school task.

An *experimental* operational definition spells out the details (operations) of the investigator's manipulations of a variable. Reinforcement can be operationally defined by giving the details of how subjects are to be reinforced (rewarded) and not reinforced (not rewarded) for specified behaviors. In the Hurlock study discussed earlier, for example, some children were praised, some blamed, and some ignored. Dollard et al. define frustration as prevention from reaching a goal, or ". . . interference with the occurrence of an instigated goal response at its proper time in the behavior sequence . . ."[5] This definition contains clear implications for experimental manipulations. Barker, Dembo, and Lewin, apparently

[3]*Ibid.*, p. 5.

[4]A. Hare, "A Study of Interaction and Consensus in Different Sized Groups," *American Sociological Review*, XVII (1952), 261–267.

[5]J. Dollard et al., *Frustration and Aggression*. New Haven: Yale University Press, 1939, p. 7.

influenced by the definition of Dollard et al., operationally defined frustration by describing children put into a playroom with "a number of highly attractive, *but inaccessible*, toys."[6] (The toys were put behind a wire-net partition; the children could see them but not touch them.) Other examples of both kinds of operational definitions will be given later.

Scientific investigators must sooner or later face the necessity of measuring the variables of the relations they are studying. Sometimes measurement is easy, sometimes difficult. To measure sex or social class is easy; to measure creativity, anxiety, or organizational effectiveness is difficult. The importance of operational definitions cannot be overemphasized. They are indispensable ingredients of scientific research because they enable researchers to measure variables and because they are bridges between the theory-hypothesis-construct level and the level of observation. There can be no scientific research without observations, and observations are impossible without clear and specific instructions on what and how to observe. Operational definitions are such instructions.

Though indispensable, operational definitions yield only limited meanings of constructs. No operational definition can ever express all of a variable. No operational definition of intelligence can ever express the rich and diverse meaning of human intelligence. This means that the variables measured by scientists are always limited and specific in meaning. The "creativity" studied by psychologists is not the "creativity" referred to by artists, though there will of course be common elements.

Some scientists say that such limited operational meanings are the only meanings that "mean" anything, that all other definitions are metaphysical nonsense. They say that discussions of anxiety are metaphysical nonsense, unless adequate operational definitions of anxiety are available and are used. This view is extreme, though it has healthy aspects. To insist that every term we use in scientific discourse be operationally defined would be too narrowing, too restrictive, and, as we shall see, scientifically unsound.[7]

Despite the dangers of extreme operationism, it can be safely said that operationism has been and still is a healthy influence because, as Skinner puts it, "The operational attitude, in spite of its shortcomings, is a good thing in any science but especially in psychology because of the presence there of a vast vocabulary of ancient and nonscientific origin."[8] When the terms used in education are considered, it is clear that education, too, has a vast vocabulary of ancient and nonscientific terms. Consider these: the whole child, horizontal and vertical enrichment, meeting the needs of the learner, core curriculum, emotional adjustment, and curricular enrichment.

[6]R. Barker, T. Dembo, and K. Lewin, "Frustration and Regression." In R. Barker, J. Kounin, and H. Wright, *Child Behavior and Development*. New York: McGraw-Hill, 1943, p. 443.

[7]For a good discussion of this point, see F. Northrop, *The Logic of the Sciences and the Humanities*. New York: Macmillan, 1947, chaps VI and VII. Northrop says, for example, "The importance of operational definitions is that they make verification possible and enrich meaning. They do not, however, exhaust scientific meaning" (p. 130). Margenau makes the same point in his extended discussion of scientific constructs. (See Margenau, *op. cit.*, pp. 232ff.)

[8]B. Skinner, "The Operational Analysis of Psychological Terms." In H. Feigl and M. Brodbeck, eds., *Readings in the Philosophy of Science*. New York: Appleton, 1953, p. 586.

To clarify constitutive and operational definitions—and theory, too—look at Fig. 3.1, which has been adapted after Margenau and Torgerson. The diagram is supposed to illustrate a well-developed theory. The single lines represent theoretical connections or relations between constructs. These constructs, labeled with lower-case letters, are defined constitutively; that is, c_4 is defined somehow by c_3, or vice versa. The double lines represent operational definitions. The C constructs are directly linked to observable data; they are indispensable links to empirical reality. But it is important to note that not all constructs in a scientific theory are defined operationally. Indeed, it is a rather thin theory that has all its constructs so defined.

Let us build a "small theory" of underachievement to illustrate these notions. Suppose an investigator believes that underachievement is, in part, a function of pupils' self-concepts. He believes that pupils who perceive themselves "inadequately," who have negative self-percepts, also tend to achieve less than their potential capacity and aptitude indicate they should achieve. He further believes that ego-needs (which we will not define here) and motivation for achievement (call this *n*-ach, or need for achievement) are tied to underachievement. Naturally, he is also aware of the relation between aptitude and intelligence and achievement in general. A diagram to illustrate this "theory" might look like Fig. 3.2.

The investigator has no *direct* measure of self-concept, but he assumes that he can draw inferences about an individual's self-concept from a figure-drawing test. He operationally defines self-concept, then, as certain responses to the figure-drawing test. This is probably the most common method of measuring psychological (and educational) constructs. The heavy single line between c_1 and C_1 indicates the relatively direct nature of the presumed relation between self-concept and the test. (The double line between C_1 and the level of observation indicates an

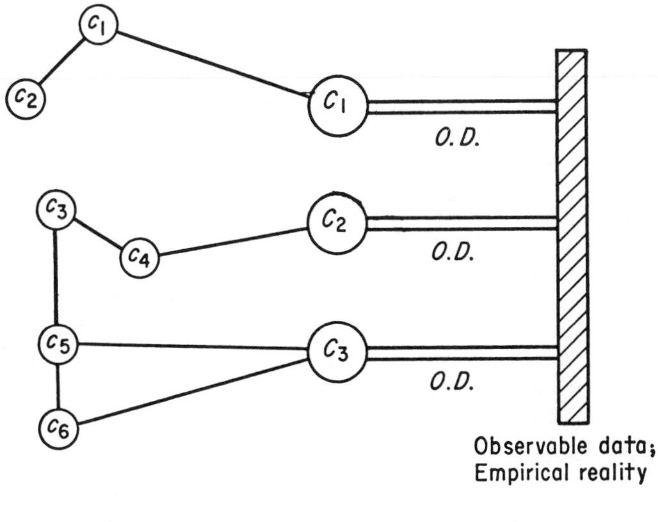

FIG. 3.1 Constructs defined operationally—that is, connected to observable data by operational definitions (*O. D.*'s): C_1, C_2, C_3. Constructs defined constitutively: $c_1, c_2, \ldots, c_6$

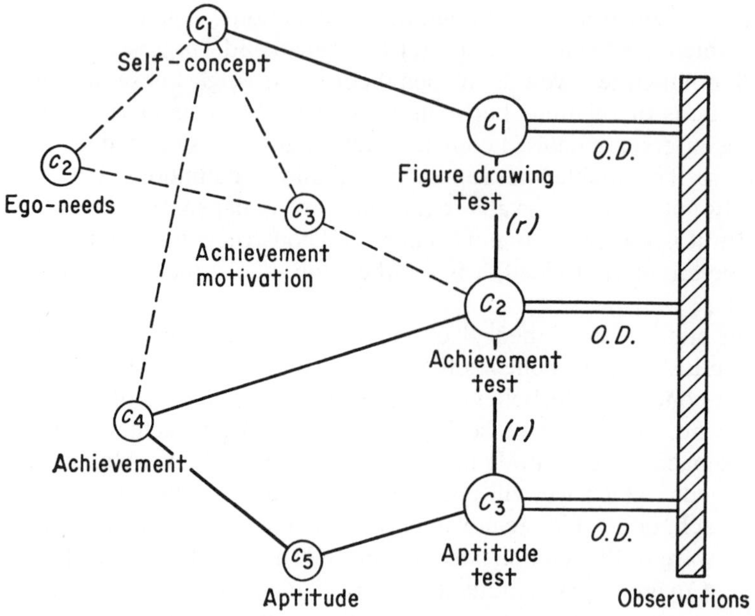

FIG. 3.2

operational definition, as it did in Fig. 3.1.) Similarly, the construct achievement (c_4) is operationally defined as the discrepancy between measured achievement (C_2) and measured aptitude (c_5). In this model the investigator has no direct measure of achievement motivation, no operational definition of it. In another study, naturally, he may specifically hypothesize a relation between achievement and achievement motivation, in which case he will try to define achievement motivation operationally.

A single solid line between concepts—for example, the one between the construct achievement (c_4) and achievement test (C_2)—indicates a relatively well-established relation between postulated achievement and what standard achievement tests measure. The single solid lines between C_1 and C_2 and between C_2 and C_3 indicate obtained relations between the test scores of these measures. (The lines between C_1 and C_2 and between C_2 and C_3 are labeled r for "relation," or "coefficient of correlation.")

The broken single lines indicate postulated relations between constructs that are not relatively well established, are more tenuous. A good example of this is the postulated relation between self-concept and achievement motivation. One of the aims of science is to make these broken lines solid lines by bridging the operational definition-measurement gap. In this case, it is quite conceivable that both self-concept and achievement motivation can be operationally defined and directly measured.

In essence, this is the way the behavioral scientist operates. He shuttles back and forth between the level of theory-constructs and the level of observation. He does this by operationally defining the variables of his theory that are amenable to such definition and then by estimating the relations between the operationally defined and measured variables. From these estimated relations he makes inferences as to the relations between the constructs. In the above example, he calculates the relation between C_1 (Figure-drawing test) and C_2 (Achievement test) and, if the relation is established on this observational level, he infers that a relation exists between c_1 (Self-concept) and c_4 (Achievement).

Types of Variables

Independent and Dependent Variables

With definitional background behind us, we return to variables. Variables can be classified in several ways. In this book three kinds of variables are very important and will be emphasized: (1) independent and dependent variables, (2) active and attribute variables, and (3) continuous and categorical variables.

The most important and useful way to categorize variables is as independent and dependent. This categorization is highly useful because of its general applicability, simplicity, and special importance in conceptualizing and designing research and in communicating the results of research. An *independent variable* is the *presumed* cause of the *dependent variable*, the *presumed* effect. The independent variable is the antecedent; the dependent is the consequent. When we say: If A, then B, we have the conditional conjunction of an independent variable (A) and a dependent variable (B).

The terms "independent variable" and "dependent variable" come from mathematics, where X is the independent and Y the dependent variable. This is probably the best way to think of independent and dependent variables, because there is no need to use the touchy word "cause" and related words, and because such use of symbols applies to most research situations. Indeed, it can even be said that in scientific research the relations between X's and Y's are constantly pursued. And there is no theoretical restriction on numbers of X's and Y's. When, later, we consider multivariate thinking and analysis, we will deal with several independent and several dependent variables.

In experiments the independent variable is the variable manipulated by the experimenter. When, for example, an educational investigator studies the effect of different teaching methods, he may manipulate method, the independent variable, by using different methods. In nonexperimental research, where there is no possibility of manipulation, the independent variable is the variable that has presumably been "manipulated" before he got it. He may, for instance, study the presumed effects on achievement of a ready-made teaching situation in which different methods have already been used. Methods, here, is also the independent variable. Or he may study the effect on school achievement of parental attitudes. Here parental attitudes is the independent variable.

The dependent variable, of course, is the variable predicted *to*, whereas the independent variable is predicted *from*. The dependent variable, Y, is the presumed effect, which varies concomitantly with changes or variation in the independent variable, X. It is the variable that is not manipulated. Rather, it is observed for variation as a presumed result of variation in the independent variable. In predicting from X to Y, we can take any value of X we wish, whereas the value of Y we predict to is "dependent on" the value of X we have selected. The dependent variable is ordinarily the condition we are trying to explain. The most common dependent variable in education, for instance, is achievement or "learning." We want to account for or explain achievement. In doing so we have a large number of possible X's or independent variables to choose from.

When the relation between intelligence and school achievement is studied, intelligence is the independent and achievement the dependent variable. (Is it conceivable that it might be the other way around?) Other independent variables that can be studied in relation to the dependent variable, achievement, are social class, methods of teaching, personality types, types of motivation (reward and punishment), attitudes toward school, class atmosphere, and so on. When the presumed determinants of delinquency are studied, such determinants as slum conditions, broken homes, lack of parental love, and the like, are independent variables and, naturally, delinquency (more accurately, delinquent behavior) is the dependent variable. In the frustration-aggression hypothesis mentioned earlier, frustration is the independent variable and aggression the dependent variable. Sometimes a phenomenon is studied by itself, and either an independent or a dependent variable is implied. This is the case when teacher behaviors and characteristics are studied. The usual implied dependent variable is achievement or child behavior in general. Teacher behavior can, of course, be a dependent variable.

The relation between an independent variable and a dependent variable can perhaps be more clearly understood if we lay out two axes at right angles to each other, one axis representing the independent variable and the other axis the dependent variable. (When two axes are at right angles to each other, they are called *orthogonal* axes.) Following mathematical custom, X, the independent variable, is the horizontal axis and Y, the dependent variable, the vertical axis. (X is called the *abscissa* and Y the *ordinate*.) X values are laid out on the X axis and Y values on the Y axis. A very common and useful way to "see" and interpret a relation is to plot the pairs of XY values, using the X and Y axes as a frame of reference. Let us suppose, in a study of child development, that we have two sets of measures: the X measures chronological age, the Y measures reading age:[9]

X: Chronological Age (in Months)	Y: Reading Age (in Months)
72	48
84	62
96	69
108	71
120	100
132	112

These measures are plotted in Fig. 3.3.

[9] *Reading age* is so-called growth age. Seriatim measurements of individuals' growths—in height, weight, intelligence, and so forth—are expressed as the average chronological age at which they appear in the standard population. The data reported above are from one of the author's studies: F. Kerlinger, "The Statistics of the Individual Child: The Use of Analysis of Variance with Child Development Data," *Child Development*, XXV (1954), 265–275. This article refers to the original sources of the growth data.

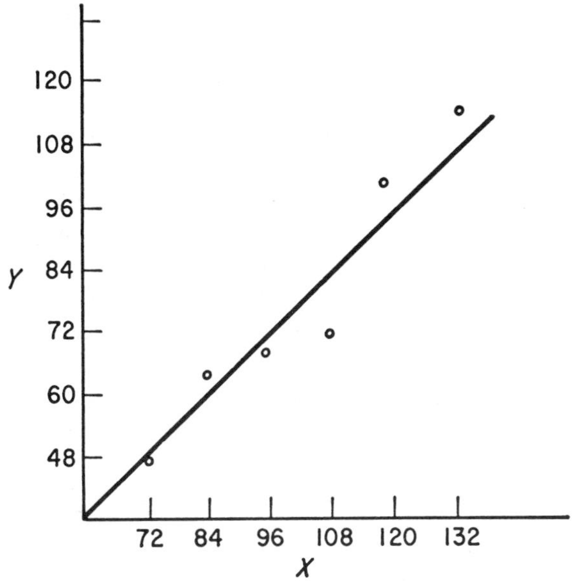

FIG. 3.3 *Y*: reading age (in months); *X*: chronological age (in months)

The relation between chronological age (*CA*) and reading age (*RA*) can now be "seen" and roughly approximated. Note that there is a pronounced tendency, as might be expected, for more advanced *CA* to be associated with higher *RA*, medium *CA* with medium *RA*, and less advanced *CA* with lower *RA*. In other words, the relation between the independent and dependent variables, in this case between *CA* and *RA*, can be seen from a graph such as this. A straight line has been drawn in to "show" the relation. It is a rough average of all the points of the plot. Note that if one has knowledge of independent variable measures and a relation such as that shown in Fig. 3.3 one can predict with considerable accuracy the dependent variable measures. Plots like this can, of course, be used with any independent and dependent variable measures.

The student should be alert to the possibility of a variable being an independent variable in one study and a dependent variable in another. A good example is the variable "group cohesiveness." It is possible to study the determinants of cohesiveness and equally possible to study the presumed results of cohesiveness. In the former case cohesiveness is the dependent variable; in the latter it is the independent variable.

It is quite possible to consider school achievement as an independent variable, even though it is usually treated as a dependent variable. In studies of success in college, for instance, achievement in high school is often used as a predictor, or an independent variable. Here we have the interesting case of achievement being now the independent and now the dependent variable—achievement in different educational situations, naturally. Anxiety has been studied as an independent variable affecting the dependent variable achievement.[10] But anxiety

[10]See S. Sarason et al., *Anxiety in Elementary School Children*. New York: Wiley, 1960.

can readily be conceived and used as a dependent variable—for example, if we wished to study the effectiveness of types of teaching or types of teacher supportive behavior, or types of tests, in reducing anxiety.[11] It is also possible—but too rarely done—to treat a variable as independent in one study and dependent in another study. We can even give a variable this dual role in the same study. In other words, the independent and dependent variable classification is really a classification of *uses* of variables rather than a distinction between different *kinds* of variables.

Active and Attribute Variables

A classification that will be useful in our later study of research design is based on the distinction between experimental and measured variables. It is important when planning and executing research to distinguish between these two types of variables. Manipulated variables will be called *active* variables; measured variables will be called *attribute* variables.

Any variable that is manipulated, then, is an active variable. Any variable that cannot be manipulated is an attribute variable. When one uses different methods of teaching, rewarding the children of one group and punishing those of another, creating anxiety through worrisome instructions, one is *actively* manipulating the variables methods, reinforcement, and anxiety.

On the other hand, it is impossible, or at least difficult, to manipulate many variables. All variables that are human characteristics—intelligence, aptitude, sex, socioeconomic status, field dependence, education, need for achievement, and attitudes, for example—are attribute variables. Subjects come to our studies with these variables (attributes) ready-made. They are, so to speak, already manipulated. Early environment, heredity, and other circumstances have made individuals what they are.[12] The word "attribute," moreover, is accurate enough when used with inanimate objects or referents. Organizations, institutions, groups, populations, homes, and geographical areas have attributes. Organizations are variably productive; institutions become outmoded; groups differ in cohesiveness; geographical areas vary widely in resources.

This active-attribute distinction is general, flexible, and useful. We will see that some variables are by their very nature always attributes, but other variables that are attributes can also be active. This latter characteristic makes it possible to investigate the "same" relations in different ways. A good example is the variable anxiety. We can measure the anxiety of subjects. Anxiety is in this case

[11] *Ibid.*, p. 280.

[12] Such variables are also called *organismic* variables. Any property of an individual, any characteristic or attribute, is an organismic variable. It is part of the organism, so to speak. In other words, organismic variables are those characteristics that individuals have in varying degrees when they come to the research situation. The term individual differences implies organismic variables.

Another related classification, used mainly by psychologists, is *stimulus* and *response* variables. A *stimulus variable* is any condition or manipulation by the experimenter of the environment that evokes a response in an organism. A *response variable* is any kind of behavior of the organism. The assumption is made that for any kind of behavior there is always a stimulus. Thus the organism's behavior is a response. This classification is reflected in the well-known equation: $R = f(O, S)$, which is read: "Responses are a function of the organism and stimuli," or "Response variables are a function of organismic variables and stimulus variables."

obviously an attribute variable. But we can manipulate anxiety, too. We can induce different degrees of anxiety, for example, by telling the subjects of one experimental group that the task they are about to do is difficult, that their intelligence is being measured, and that their futures depend on the scores they get. The subjects of another experimental group are told to do their best but to relax, the outcome is not too important and will have no influence on their futures. Actually, we cannot assume that the measured (attribute) and the manipulated (active) "anxieties" are the same. We may assume that both are "anxiety" in a broad sense, but they are certainly not the same.

Continuous and Categorical Variables

A distinction especially useful in the planning of research and the analysis of data—that between continuous and categorical variables—has already been introduced. Its later importance, however, justifies more extended consideration.

A *continuous* variable is capable of taking on an ordered set of values within a certain range. This definition means, first, that the values of a continuous variable reflect at least a rank order, a larger value of the variable meaning more of the property in question than a smaller value. The values yielded by a scale to measure dogmatism, for instance, express differing amounts of dogmatism from high through medium to low. Second, continuous measures in actual use are contained in a range, and each individual obtains a "score" within the range. A scale to measure dogmatism may have the range 1 through 7. Most scales in use in the behavioral sciences also have a third characteristic: there are a theoretically infinite set of values within the range. (Rank-order scales are somewhat different; they will be discussed later in the book.) That is, a particular individual's score may be 4.72 rather than simply 4 or 5.

Categorical variables, as I will call them, belong to a kind of measurement called nominal. (It will be explained in Chapter 25.) In nominal measurement, there are two or more subsets of the set of objects being measured. Individuals are categorized by their possession of the characteristic that defines any subset. "To categorize" means to assign an object to a subclass or subset of a class or set on the basis of the object's having or not having the characteristic that defines the subset. The individual being categorized either has the defining property or does not have it; it is an all-or-none kind of thing. The simplest examples are dichotomous categorical variables: sex, Republican-Democrat, white-black. Polytomies, variables with more than two subsets or partitions, are fairly common, especially in sociology and economics: religious preference, education (usually), nationality, occupational choice, and so on.

Categorical variables—and nominal measurement—have simple requirements: all the members of a subset are considered the same and all are assigned the same name (nominal) and the same numeral. If the variable is religious preference, for instance, all Protestants are the same, all Catholics are the same, and all "others" are the same. If an individual is a Catholic—operationally defined in a suitable way—he is assigned to the category "Catholic" and also assigned a "1" in that category. In brief, he is counted as a "Catholic." Categorical variables are "democratic": there is no rank order or greater-than-and-less-than among the categories, and all members of a category have the same value: 1.

The expression "qualitative variables" has sometimes been applied to categorical variables, especially to dichotomies, probably in contrast to "quantitative variables" (our continuous variables). Such usage reflects a somewhat distorted notion of what variables are. They are always quantifiable, or they are not variables. If x has only two subsets and can take on only two values, 1 and 0, these are still values, and the variable varies. If x is a polytomy, like religious preference, we quantify again by assigning 1's and 0's to individuals. If an individual, say, is a Catholic, then put him in the Catholic subset and assign him a 1. It is extremely important to understand this because, for one thing, it is the basis of quantifying many variables—even experimental treatments—for complex analysis. In multiple regression analysis, as we will see later in the book, all variables, continuous and categorical, are entered as variables into the analysis. Earlier, the example of sex was given, 1 being assigned to one sex and 0 to the other. We can set up a column of 1's and 0's just as we would set up a column of IQ's or dogmatism scores. The column of 1's and 0's is the quantification of the variable sex. There is no mystery here. The method is easily extended to polytomies.[13]

Constructs, Observables, and Intervening Variables

In much of the previous discussion of this chapter it has been implied, though not explicitly stated, that there is a sharp difference between constructs and observed or observable variables. In fact, we can say that constructs, as constructs, are nonobservables, and variables, when operationally defined, are observables. The distinction is important, because if we are not always keenly aware of the level of discourse we are on when talking about variables, we can hardly be clear about what we are doing.

Constructs have been called intervening variables.[14] *Intervening variable* is a term invented to account for internal and directly unobservable psychological processes that in turn account for behavior. Tolman, using William James' picturesque expression, says, ". . . the sole 'cash-value' of mental processes lies . . . in this their character as a set of intermediate functional processes which interconnect between the initiating causes of behavior, on the one hand, and the final resulting behavior itself, on the other."[15] An intervening variable is an "in-the-head" variable. It cannot be seen, heard, or felt. It is inferred from behavior.

[13]Such variables have been called "dummy variables." Since they are highly useful and powerful, even indispensable, in modern research data analysis, they should be clearly understood. See F. Kerlinger and E. Pedhazur, *Multiple Regression Analysis in Behavioral Research.* New York: Holt, Rinehart and Winston, 1973, chaps. 6 and 7, and Chapter 36 of this volume. A *polytomy* is a division of the members of a group into three or more subdivisions. The method of "coding" variables described above—and other methods—are explained in Chapter 36. See also Chapters 5 and 25.

[14]E. Tolman, *Behavior and Psychological Man.* Berkeley, Calif.: University of California Press, 1958, pp. 115–129.

[15]*Ibid.*, p. 116.

"Hostility" is inferred from presumably hostile or aggressive acts. "Learning" is inferred from, among other things, increases in test scores. "Anxiety" is inferred from test scores, from skin responses, from heart beat, and so on.

The scientist, using such terms, is always aware that he is talking about invented constructs the "reality" of which he has inferred from behavior. If he wants to study the effects of different kinds of motivation, he must know that "motivation" is an intervening variable, a construct invented by man to account for presumably "motivated" behavior. He must know that its "reality" is only a postulated reality. He can only judge that a youngster is motivated or not motivated by observing the youngster's behavior. Still, in order to study motivation, he must measure it. But he cannot measure it directly because it is an in-the-head variable, an intervening variable, an unobservable entity. Other men have invented the construct to stand for "something" *presumed to be* inside the individual, "something" prompting him to behave in such-and-such manner. This means that he must always measure presumed indicants of motivation and not motivation itself. He must, in other words, always measure some kind of behavior, be it marks on paper, spoken words, or meaningful gestures, and then make inferences about presumed characteristics.

Examples of Constructs and Operational Definitions

A number of constructs and operational definitions have already been given. To illustrate and perhaps clarify the preceding discussion, especially that in which the distinction was made between experimental and measured variables and between constructs and operationally defined variables, several and varied examples of constructs and operational definitions are given below. If a definition is experimental, it is labeled (E). If it is measured, it is labeled (M).

The student should note that operational definitions differ in degree of specificity. Some are quite closely tied to observations. "Test" definitions like "Intelligence is defined as score on X intelligence test" are very specific. A definition like "Frustration is prevention from reaching a goal" is more general and requires further specification, such as that of the Barker, Kounin, and Wright definition, in order to be directly measurable.

Social Class "... two or more orders of people who are believed to be, and are accordingly ranked by the members of a community, in socially superior and inferior positions."[16] (M) (To be operational this definition has to be specified by questions aimed at people's beliefs about other people's positions.)

This is a subjective definition of social class. Social class, or social status, is also defined more objectively by using such indices as occupation, income, and education, or by combinations of such indices. For example, "To get an index of SES (socioeconomic status), we combined a measure of occupational level with one of income."[17] (Then details of the definition follow.) (M)

[16]W. Warner and P. Lunt, *The Social Life of a Modern Community*. New Haven: Yale University Press, 1941, p. 82.

[17]R. Sears, E. Maccoby, and H. Levin, *Patterns of Child Rearing*. New York: Harper & Row, 1957, pp. 423–424.

Anxiety (Test Anxiety) "Our measure of test anxiety was a revised and shortened version of the Test Anxiety (TA) questionnaire which is described elsewhere."[18] (M) (The authors refer to a research study that describes the construction and development of the TA Scale. It is always good practice to refer to the original sources of tests and scales.)

Achievement (School, Arithmetic, Spelling) Achievement is customarily defined operationally by citing a standardized test of achievement (for example, Iowa Every-Pupil Tests of Basic Skills, Elementary); by grade-point averages; or by teacher judgments.

"The criterion of school achievement, grade-point average . . . was generally obtained by assigning weights of 4, 3, 2, 1, and 0 to grades of A, B, C, D, and F, respectively. Only courses in the so-called 'solids,' that is, mathematics, science, social studies, foreign language, and English, were used in computing grade-point averages."[19] (M)

Social Organization (of Classes) ". . . has to do with the amount of social grouping and pupil autonomy in a class. A class scoring high was one in which it was relatively common to find the class broken up into two or more groups working independently, and in which the teachers talked relatively little."[20] (M) (Note the relative looseness of this definition, a looseness introduced by such words as "relatively common" and "relatively little." But it is not too difficult to tighten it.

Popularity Popularity is often defined operationally by the number of sociometric choices an individual receives from other individuals (in his class, play group, and so on). Individuals are asked: "With whom would you like to work?", "With whom would you like to play?", and the like. Each individual is required to choose one, two, or more individuals from his group on the basis of such criterion questions.

"The sociometric popularity score (choices received) based on a criterion of enjoyment of participation, and the expansiveness (choices made), confidence (choices expected) . . ."[21] (M)

Reinforcement Reinforcement definitions come in a number of forms. Most of them involve, one way or another, the principle of reward. But note that both positive and negative reinforcement may be used.

". . . statements of *agreement* or *paraphrase*."[22] (E) Then the author gives specific experimental definitions of "reinforcement." For example, "In the second 10 minutes, every opinion statement *S* made was recorded by *E* and reinforced. For two groups, *E* agreed with every opinion statement by saying: 'Yes, you're

[18]I. Sarnoff et al., "A Cross-Cultural Study of Anxiety among American and English School Children," *Journal of Educational Psychology*, XLIX (1958), 129–136.

[19]W. Holtzman and W. Brown, "Evaluating the Study Habits and Attitudes of High School Students," *Journal of Educational Psychology*, LIX (1968), 404–409.

[20]D. Medley and H. Mitzel, "Some Behavioral Correlates of Teacher Effectiveness," *Journal of Educational Psychology*, L (1959), 239–246.

[21]E. Borgatta, "Analysis of Social Interaction: Actual, Role-Playing, and Projective," *Journal of Abnormal and Social Psychology*, LI (1955), 394–405.

[22]W. Verplanck, "The Control of the Content of Conversation: Reinforcement of Statements of Opinion," *Journal of Abnormal and Social Psychology*, LI (1955), 668–676.

right,' 'That's so,' or the like, or by nodding and smiling affirmation if he could not interrupt."[23] (E)

"... the model and the child were administered alternately 12 different sets of story items ... To each of the 12 items, the model consistently expressed judgmental responses in opposition to the child's moral orientation ... and the experimenter reinforced the model's behavior with verbal approval responses such as 'Very good,' 'That's fine,' and 'That's good.' The child was similarly reinforced whenever he adopted the model's class of moral judgments in response to his own set of items."[24] (E) (This is called "social reinforcement.")

"Specified Comment students, regardless of teacher or student differences, all received comments designated in advance for each letter grade, as follows:

A. Excellent! Keep it up.
B. Good work. Keep it up.
C. Perhaps try to do still better?
D. Let's bring this up.
F. Let's raise this grade!

Teachers were instructed to administer the comments 'rapidly and automatically, trying not even to notice who the students are.'"[25] (E) Two other experimental conditions, Free Comment and No Comment, were also operationally (experimentally) defined by the author.

Acquisition (of Learning or Conditioning) "... probability of occurrence, expressed as the number of trials on which a given subject produces a CR, or the percentage of subjects giving a CR on a given trial."[26] (E-M) (CR means conditioned response.)

Extinction (of Learning or Conditioning) "... the decrease of response strength of nonreinforcement."[27] (E-M)

Response Set "... a general 'tendency to agree or disagree with questionnaire items, regardless of their content.'" (M) The authors later operationalize this definition in different ways. One of these is: "An Overall Agreement Score (OAS) was computed for each *S* by taking the mean of their responses to the 360 items."[28]

Community Reputation This is a variable of Newcomb's study of the attitudes of Bennington College girls. It was operationally defined by having knowledgeable students choose other students sociometrically. Twenty-eight criteria were used. For each of these the student judges nominated three individuals.

[23] *Ibid.*

[24] A. Bandura and F. McDonald, "Influence of Social Reinforcement and the Behavior of Models in Shaping Children's Moral Judgments," *Journal of Abnormal and Social Psychology*, LXVII (1963), 274–281.

[25] E. Page, "Teacher Comments and Student Performance: A Seventy-Four Classroom Experiment in School Motivation," *Journal of Educational Psychology*, XLIX (1958), 173–181.

[26] G. Kimble, *Hilgard and Marquis' Conditioning and Learning*, 2d ed. New York: Appleton, 1961, p. 82.

[27] *Ibid.*

[28] A. Couch and K. Keniston, "Yeasayers and Naysayers: Agreeing Response Set as a Personality Variable," *Jounal of Abnormal and Social Psychology*, LX (1960), 151–174.

Examples of the criteria are:

1. *Most absorbed* in social life, weekends, etc.
2. *Most influenced* by faculty authority.
3. *Least likely* to engage actively in pursuits related to college interest.[29]

Values "'Rank the ten goals in the order of *their importance to you.*' (1) financial success; (2) being liked; (3) success in family life; (4) being intellectually capable; (5) living by religious principles; (6) helping others; (7) being normal, well adjusted; (8) cooperating with others; (9) doing a thorough job; (10) occupational success."[30] (M)

Approval-Disapproval (of Pupils by Teachers) ". . . time samples of classroom behavior were spread over an entire school year . . . interactions between teachers and pupils were classified into two categories: (a) praise contacts (teacher initiated interactions with a child in which she verbally expressed approval of some behavior which the child had displayed), and (b) blame contacts (teacher initiated interactions with a child in which she verbally expressed disapproval for some bit of behavior which the child had displayed)."[31] (M)

Honesty "A child was considered 'dishonest' on the *Clapp-Young Arithmetic Test* in the correction of his paper if the inside of the test booklet showed: (a) that he had changed his answer by drawing a circle around his wrong response and had made an X for the correct response; (b) that he had erased the wrong response and marked the correct one; (c) that he marked the correct response when checking his paper but his work on the outside of the test booklet did not agree with his answer."[32] (M)

Leadership "We have chosen to measure two specific dimensions of leader behavior, 'Initiating Structure' and 'Consideration.' Initiating Structure refers to the leader's behavior in delineating the relationship between himself and the members of the work-group, and in endeavoring to establish well-defined patterns of organization, channels of communication, and methods of procedure. Consideration refers to behavior indicative of friendship, mutual trust, respect, and warmth in the relationship between the leader and the members of his staff."[33] (M) (Later, the author defines the two dimensions more precisely and operationally.)

Cohesiveness ". . . group cohesiveness refers to the degree to which the members of a group desire to remain in the group."[34] (M) (The author goes on to elaborate and operationalize the definition.)

[29]T. Newcomb, *Personality and Social Change.* New York: Holt, Rinehart and Winston, 1943, pp. 66–67, 184–185.

[30]T. Newcomb, *The Acquaintance Process.* New York: Holt, Rinehart and Winston, 1961, pp. 40 and 83.

[31]W. Meyer and G. Thompson, "Sex Differences in the Distribution of Teacher Approval and Disapproval among Sixth-Grade Children," *Journal of Educational Psychology*, XLVII (1956), 385–396.

[32]Sister M. Gross, "The Effect of Certain Types of Motivation on the 'Honesty' of Children," *Journal of Educational Research*, XL (1946), 133–140.

[33]A. Halpin, *The Leadership Behavior of School Superintendents.* Chicago: Midwest Administration Center, University of Chicago, 1956, p. 4.

[34]D. Cartwright, "The Nature of Group Cohesiveness." In D. Cartwright and A. Zander, eds., *Group Dynamics*, 3d ed. New York: Harper & Row, 1968, 91–109.

Institutional Quality (Excellence) "... the average academic ability of the entering student body and the per-student expenditures for 'educational and general' purposes (meaning, primarily, salaries for faculty and staff)."[35] (M)

Before leaving operational definitions, we should discuss something that may puzzle the student. In reading the literature, as often as not the student will not encounter operational definitions as such. Investigators may or may not *explicitly* define their terms operationally. A good research report, of course, should be so written that another investigator, if he chooses, can repeat the research. This implies that he will be able to measure the variables or manipulate the experimental conditions in the same way the original investigator did. To do this, naturally, he must know clearly and explicitly how to measure the variables or how to manipulate the experimental conditions. Therefore report writers must include operational definitions directly or indirectly. The commonest practice seems to be to mention the variables of the study early in the report and later to discuss the instruments used to measure the variables, or to discuss the experimental procedures used to manipulate the independent variables. Obviously the variables are thus operationally defined. An investigator will state a hypothesis, for example, that contains his variables: Underachievement is a function of inadequate self-concept. He will then probably discuss the hypothesis and in so doing say something about the concepts "underachievement" and "self-concept." But he may not define them operationally at this point. Later, in his section on method or procedure he will explain how he intends to measure underachievement and self-concept.

The benefits of operational thinking can be great. Although operationism can be carried to extremes, and although extreme operationism is dangerous because it tends to shut out the recognition of the importance of constructs and constitutive definitions in scientific theory and research and also tends to narrow research to perhaps trivial problems, there can be little doubt that it is a healthy scientific influence. As Underwood has said, in one of his fine chapters on operational definitions:

> ... I would say that operational thinking makes better scientists. The operationist is forced to remove the fuzz from his empirical concepts ...
>
> ... operationism facilitates communication among scientists because the meaning of concepts so defined is not easily subject to misinterpretation.[36]

Study Suggestions

1. Make up operational definitions for the following constructs. When possible, write two such definitions: an experimental one and a measured one.

permissiveness	underachievement
reinforcement	leadership

[35]A. Astin, "Undergraduate Achievement and Institutional 'Excellence,'" *Science*, CLXI (1968), 661–668.

[36]B. Underwood, *Psychological Research*. New York: Appleton, 1957, p. 53.

reading ability	class atmosphere
achievement	delinquency
interests	organizational conflict
needs	self-other attitudes
transfer of training	conformity

Notice that some of these concepts or variables—for example, needs and transfer of training—are difficult to define operationally. Why?

2. It is instructive and broadening for specialists to read outside their fields. This is particularly true for students of behavioral research. It is suggested that the student of a particular field read two or three research studies in one of the best journals of another field. If you are in psychology, read a sociology journal, say the *American Sociological Review*. If you are in education or sociology, read a psychology journal, say the *Journal of Personality and Social Psychology*. Students not in education can sample the *Journal of Educational Psychology* or the *American Educational Research Journal*. When you read, jot down the names of the variables and compare them to the variables in your own field. Are they primarily active or attribute variables? Note, for instance, that psychology's variables are more "active" than sociology's. What implications does the nature of the variables of a field have for research in the field?

PART 2

Sets, Relations, and Variance

CHAPTER 4

Sets

Science works basically with group, class, or set concepts. When a scientist discusses individual events or objects, he does so by considering such objects as members of sets of objects. But this is true of human discourse in general. We say "goose," but the word "goose" is meaningless without the concept of a goose-like group called "geese." We say "She's a beauty," but really mean she is a member of a class of beautiful women called "beauties." When we talk about a child and his problems, we inevitably must talk of the groups, classes, or sets of objects to which he belongs: A seven-year old (first set), second-grade (second set), bright (third set), and healthy (fourth set) boy (fifth set).

A *set* is a well-defined collection of objects or elements.[1] A set is well defined when it is possible to tell whether a given object does or does not belong to the set. Terms like aggregate, class, school, family, flock, and group indicate sets. There are two ways to define a set: (1) by listing all the members of the set, and (2) by giving a rule for determining whether objects do or do not belong to the set. Call (1) a "list" definition and (2) a "rule" definition. In research the rule definition is usually used, although there are cases where all members of a set are actually or imaginatively listed. For example, suppose we study the relation between voting behavior and political preference. Political preference can be defined as being a registered Republican or Democrat. We then have a large set of all people with political preferences with two smaller *subsets*: the subset of Republicans and the subset of Democrats. This is a rule definition of sets. Of course, we might list all registered Democrats and all registered Republicans to define our two subsets, but this is often difficult if not impossible. Besides, it is unnecessary;

[1]J. Kemeny, J. Snell, and G. Thompson, *Introduction to Finite Mathematics*, 2d ed., Englewood Cliffs, N.J.: Prentice-Hall, 1966, p. 58.

the rule is usually sufficient. Such a rule might be: A Republican is any person who is registered in the Republican party. Another such rule might be: A Republican is any person who says he is a Republican.

Subsets

A *subset* of a set is a set that results from selecting sets from an original set. Each subset of a set is part of the original set. More succinctly and accurately, "A set B is a subset of a set A whenever all the elements of B are elements of A."[2] We designate sets by capital letters: A, B, K, L, X, Y, and so forth. If B is a subset of A, we write $B \subset A$, which means "B is a subset of A," "B is contained in A," or "All members of B are also members of A."

Whenever a population is sampled, the samples are subsets of the population. Suppose an investigator samples four eleventh-grade classes out of all the eleventh-grade classes in a large high school. The four classes form a subset of the population of all the eleventh-grade classes. Each of the four classes of the sample, too, can be considered a subset of the four classes—and also the total population of classes. All the children of the four classes can be broken down into two subsets of boys and girls. Whenever a researcher breaks down or partitions a population or a sample into two or more groups he is "creating" subsets using a "rule" or criterion to do so. Examples are numerous: religious preferences into Protestant, Catholic, Jew; intelligence into high and low; and so on. Even experimental conditions can be so viewed. The classic experimental-control group idea is a set-subset idea. Individuals are put into the experimental group; this is a subset of the whole sample. All other individuals used in the experiment (the control-group individuals) form a subset, too.

Set Operations

There are two basic set operations: *intersection* and *union*. An operation is simply "a doing-something to." In arithmetic we add, subtract, multiply, and divide. We "intersect" and "union" sets. We also "negate" them.

Intersection is the overlapping of two or more sets; it is the elements of two or more sets shared in common by the two or more sets. The symbol for intersection is $\cap$ (read "intersection" or "cap"). The intersection of the sets A and B is written $A \cap B$, and $A \cap B$ is itself a set. More precisely, it is the set that contains those elements of A and B that belong to *both* A and B. Intersection is also written $A \cdot B$, or simply AB.

Let $A = \{0, 1, 2, 3\}$; let $B = \{2, 3, 4, 5\}$. (Note that we use braces, "{ }," to symbolize sets.) Then $A \cap B = \{2, 3\}$. This is shown in Fig. 4.1. $A \cap B$, or $\{2, 3\}$, is a new set composed of the members *common* to both sets. Note that $A \cap B$ might indicate the *relation* between the sets, the elements shared in common by A and B.

[2] R. Kershner and L. Wilcox, *The Anatomy of Mathematics*. New York: Ronald, 1950, p. 35.

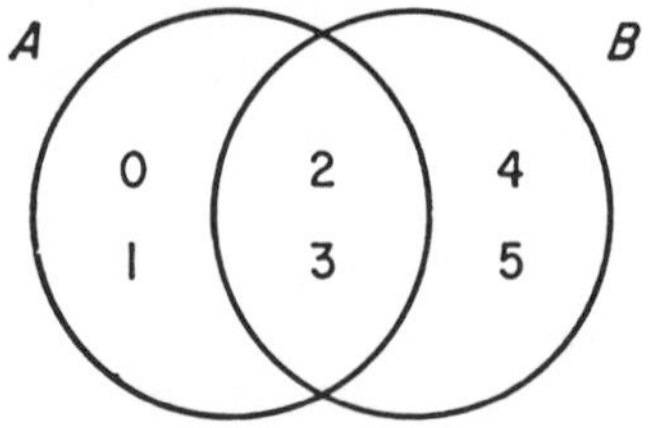

FIG. 4.1

The *union* of two sets is written $A \cup B$. $A \cup B$ is a set that contains all the members of A and all the members of B. Mathematicians define $A \cup B$ as a set that contains those elements that belong either to A or to B or to both. In other words, we "add" the elements of A to those of B to form a new set $A \cup B$. Take the example of Fig. 4.1. A included 0, 1, 2, and 3; B included 2, 3, 4, and 5. $A \cup B = \{0, 1, 2, 3, 4, 5\}$. Note that the union of A and B in Fig. 4.1 is indicated by the whole area of the two circles. Note also that we do not count the members of $A \cap B$, $\{2, 3\}$, twice.

Examples of union in research would be putting males and females together, $M \cup F$, or Republican and Democrats together, $R \cup D$. Let A be all the children of the elementary schools and B all the children of the secondary schools of X school district. Then $A \cup B$ is the set of all the school children in the district.

The Universal and Empty Sets; Set Negation

The *universal set*, labeled U, is the set of all elements under discussion. It can be called the *universe of discourse* or *level of discourse*. (It is much like the terms *population* and *universe* in sampling theory.) This means that we limit our discussion to the fixed set of elements—all of them—from this fixed class, U. If we were to study determinants of achievement in the elementary school, for example, we might define U as all pupils in grades one through six. We can also define U, alternatively, as the scores on an achievement test of these same pupils. Subsets of U, perhaps to be studied separately, might be the scores of Grade 1 pupils, the scores of Grade 2 pupils, and so on.

U can be large or small. Returning to the example of Fig. 4.1, $A = \{0, 1, 2, 3\}$ and $B = \{2, 3, 4, 5\}$. If $A \cup B = U$, then $U = \{0, 1, 2, 3, 4, 5\}$. Here U is quite small. Let A = {Jane, Mary, Phyllis, Betty}, and B = {Tom, John, Paul}. Then, if these individuals are all we are talking about U = {Jane, Mary, Phyllis, Betty, Tom, John, Paul}. And, of course, $U = A \cup B$. This is another example of a small U. In research U's are more often large. If we sample the schools of a large county, then U is all the schools in the county, a rather large U. U might also be all the children or all the teachers in these schools, still larger U's.

In research it is important to know the U we are studying. Any ambiguity in the definition of U can lead to erroneous conclusions. Such ambiguities are common. If the characteristics of teachers are studied, it is imperative to define as precisely as possible what teachers we mean. Elementary and secondary teachers may differ considerably in some characteristics. In his study of teacher characteristics, for instance, Ryans separated elementary and secondary teachers. In effect, he defined two U's.[3] (It is possible, of course, to say that U was all elementary and secondary teachers and that U was broken down into two subsets.) Or the characteristics themselves might form a U, though it would be no mean job to define U in this case.

Like all sets, U is defined by a list or by a rule. In the case of teachers in the example just given, we would most likely use a rule definition. In the beginning of his study, Ryans limited the U of elementary teachers to those of Grades 3 and 4. He later defined U to include teachers from Grades 1 through 6.[4] With large U's rule definitions are ordinarily used because a list would be unwieldy and because it is often impossible to obtain or compile a list.

The *empty set* is the set with no members in it. We label it E. It can also be called the *null set*. Though it may seem peculiar to the student that we bother with sets with no members, the notion is quite useful, even indispensable. With it we can convey certain ideas economically and unambiguously. To indicate that there is no relation between two sets of data, for example, we can write the set equation $A \cap B = E$, which simply says that the intersection of the sets A and B is empty, meaning that no member of A is a member of B, and vice versa.

Let $A = \{1, 2, 3\}$; Let $B = \{4, 5, 6\}$. Then $A \cap B = E$. Clearly there are no members common to A and B. The set of possibilities of the Democratic and Republican presidential candidates both winning the national election is empty. The set of occurrences of rain without clouds is empty. The empty set, then, is another way of expressing the falsity of propositions. In this case we can say that the statement "Rain without clouds" is false. In set language this can be expressed $P \cap \sim Q = E$, where P = the set of all occurrences of rain, Q = the set of all occurrences of clouds, and $\sim Q$ = the set of all occurrences of no clouds.

The *negation* or *complement* of the set A is written $\sim A$. It means all members of U not in A. If we let A = all men, when U = all human beings, then $\sim A$ = all women (not-men). Simple dichotomization seems to be a fundamental basis of human thinking. In order to think, categorization is necessary: one must, at the most elementary level, separate objects into those belonging to a certain set and those not belonging to the set. We must distinguish men and not-men, me and not-me, early and not-early, good and not-good.

If $U = \{0, 1, 2, 3, 4\}$, and $A = \{0, 1\}$, then $\sim A = \{2, 3, 4\}$. A and $\sim A$ are of course subsets of U. An important property of sets and their negation is expressed in the set equation: $A \cup \sim A = U$. Note, too, that $A \cap \sim A = E$.

Set Diagrams

We now pull together and illustrate the basic set ideas already presented by diagramming them. Sets can be depicted with various kinds of figures, but rectangles

[3] D. Ryans, *Characteristics of Teachers*. Washington, D.C.: American Council on Education, 1960.
[4] *Ibid.*, p. 63.

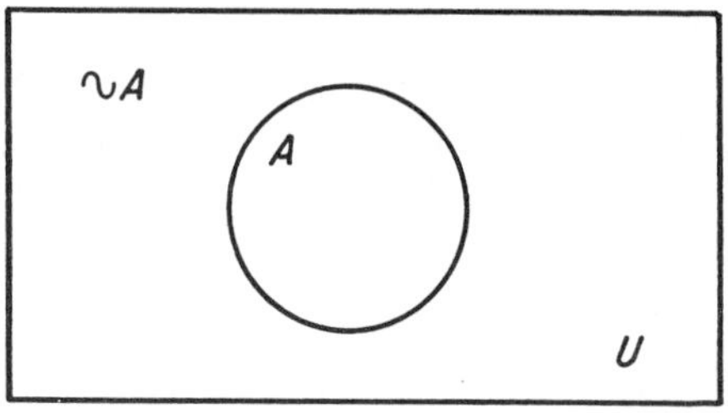

FIG. 4.2

and circles are ordinarily used. They have been adapted from a system invented by John Venn. In this book rectangles, circles, and ovals will be used. Look at Fig. 4.2. U is represented by the rectangle. All members of the universe under discussion are in U. A set A has been drawn inside U. The members of the set A are a subset of U. All members of U not in A form another subset of U: $\sim A$. Note, again, that $A \cup \sim A = U$. Note, too, that $A \cap \sim A = E$, that is, there are no members common to both A and $\sim A$.

Next, we depict, in Fig. 4.3, two sets, A and B, both subsets of U. From the diagram it can be seen that $A \cap B = E$. We adopt a convention: when we wish to indicate a set or a subset, we shade it either horizontally, vertically, or diagonally. The set $A \cup B$ has been shaded in Fig. 4.3.

Intersection, probably the most important set notion from the point of view of this book, is indicated by the shaded portion of Fig. 4.4. The situation can be expressed by the equation $A \cap B \neq E$; the intersection of the sets A and B is *not* empty.

When two sets, A and B, are equal, they have the same set elements or members. The Venn diagram would show two congruent circles in U. In effect, only one circle would show. When $A = B$, then $A \cap B = A \cup B = A = B$.

We diagram $A \subset B$; A is a subset of B, in Fig. 4.5. B has been shaded horizontally, A vertically. Note that $A \cup B = B$ (whole shaded area) and $A \cap B = A$ (area shaded both horizontally and vertically). All members of A are also in B, or all a's are also b's, if we let $a =$ any member of A and $b =$ any member of B.

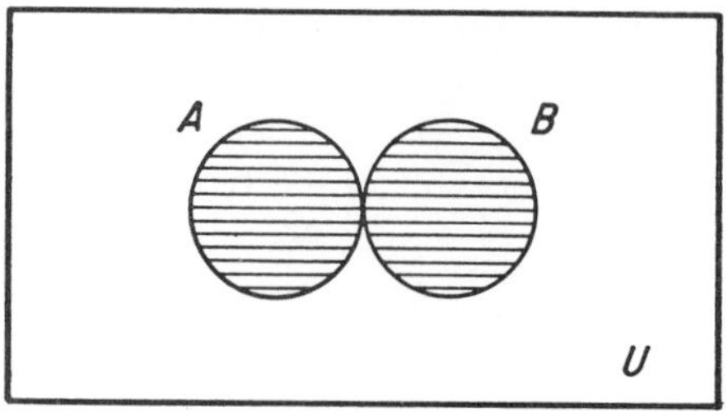

$A \cup B$

FIG. 4.3

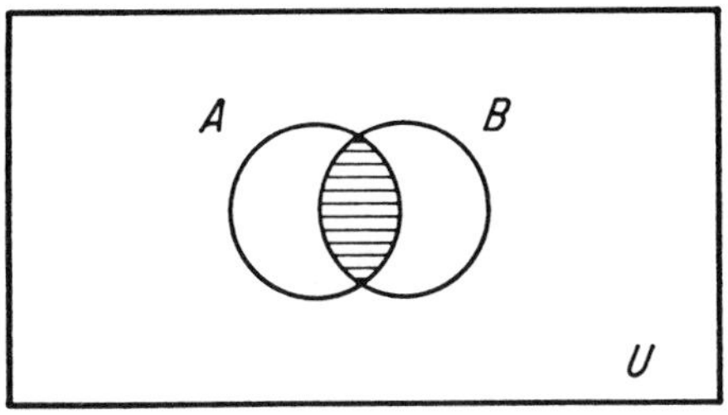

$A \cap B$

FIG. 4.4

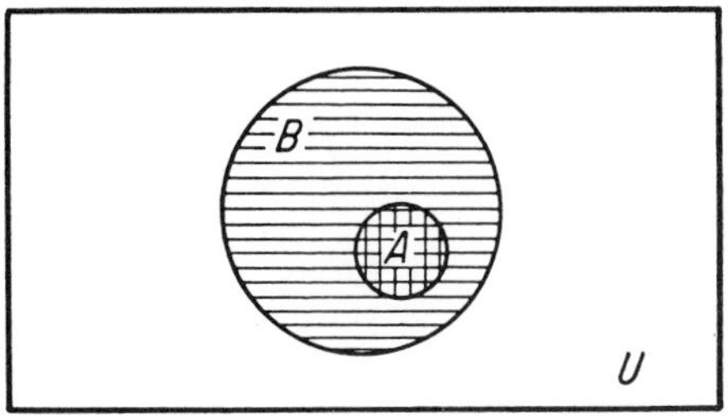

$A \subset B$

FIG. 4.5

Set Operations with More than Two Sets

Set operations are not limited to two subsets of U. Let A, B, and C be three subsets of U. Suppose the intersection of these three subsets of U is not empty, as shown in Fig. 4.6. The triply hatched area shows $A \cap B \cap C$. Note that there are four intersections, each hatched differently: $A \cap B$, $A \cap C$, $B \cap C$, and $A \cap B \cap C$.

Although four or more sets can be diagrammed, such diagrams become cumbersome and not easy to draw and inspect. There is no reason, however, why the intersection and union operations cannot be applied symbolically to four or more sets.

Partitions and Cross Partitions

It is obvious that U can be broken down into subsets that intersect. U can also be broken into subsets that do not exhaust all of U (unless we use set negation). On the other hand, U can be broken down into subsets that do not intersect and that exhaust all of U. When this is done the process is called *partitioning*.

Partitioning breaks a universal set down into subsets that are *disjoint* and *exhaustive* of the universal set. In set language, let U be a universe, and let A and

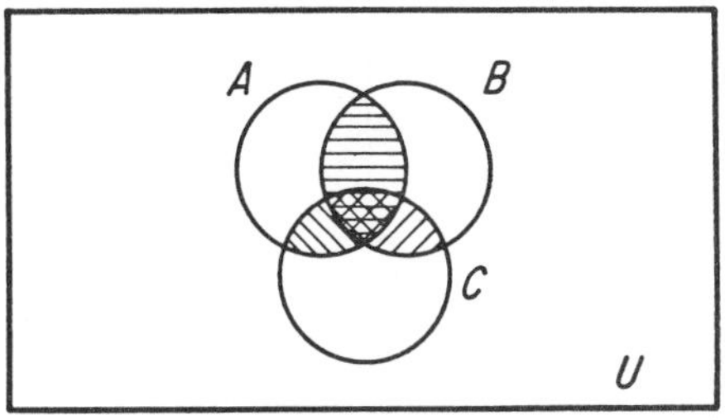

$A \cap B \cap C$

FIG. 4.6

B be subsets of U that are partitions. We label subjects of A: $A_1, A_2, \ldots, A_k$ and of B: $B_1, B_2, \ldots, B_k$. Now, $[A_1, A_2]$ and $[B_1\ B_2]$,[5] for example, are partitions if:

$$A_1 \cup A_2 = U \quad \text{and} \quad A_1 \cap A_2 = E$$
$$B_1 \cup B_2 = U \quad \text{and} \quad B_1 \cap B_2 = E$$

Diagrams make this clearer. The partitioning of U, represented by a rectangle, separately into the subsets A_1 and A_2 and into B_1 and B_2, is shown in Fig. 4.7. Note that both partitionings have been performed on the same U. We have met many examples of such partitions: middle class-working class, high income-low income, introvert-extrovert, Democrat-Republican, field dependence-field independence pass-fail, approve-disapprove, and so on. Some of these are true dichotomies; others are continuous variables.

It is possible to put the two partitions together into a *cross partition*. A *cross partition* is a new partitioning that arises from successively partitioning the same set U by forming all subsets of the form $A \cap B$. In other words, perform the A partitioning, then the B partitioning on the same U, or the same square. This is shown in Fig. 4.8. Each cell of the partitioning is an intersection of the subsets of A and B. We shall find in a later chapter that such cross-partitioning is very important in research design and in the analysis of data.

Anticipating later developments, we give a research example of a cross partition. Such examples are called *crossbreaks*. Crossbreaks provide the most elementary way to show a relation between two variables. The example is from Miller and Swanson's study of child-rearing practices. One of the tables they report is a crossbreak in which the variables are social class (middle class and working class) and weaning (early and late). The data, converted to percentages by the writer, are given in Table 4.1.[6] The frequencies reported by Miller and Swanson are given in the lower right corner of each cell. Evidently there is a relation between social class and weaning. Middle-class mothers show a tendency to wean their children earlier than lower-class mothers do. The two conditions of disjointness and exhaustiveness are satisfied. The intersection of any two cells

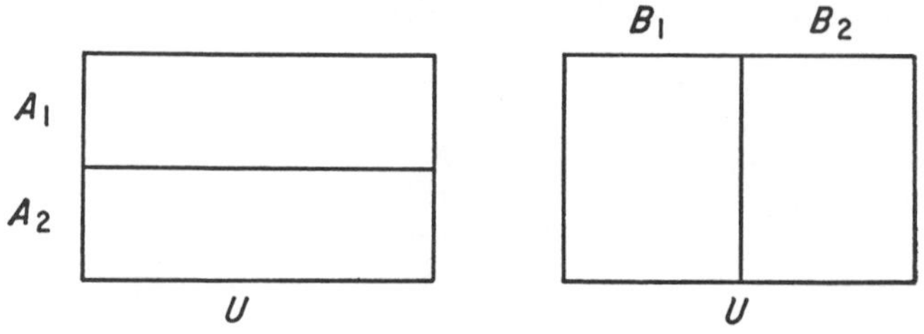

FIG. 4.7

[5]Partitions are usually set off by square brackets, [ ], while sets and subsets are set off by curled brackets or braces, { }.

[6]D. Miller and G. Swanson, *Inner Conflict and Defense*. New York: Holt, Rinehart and Winston, 1960, p. 426.

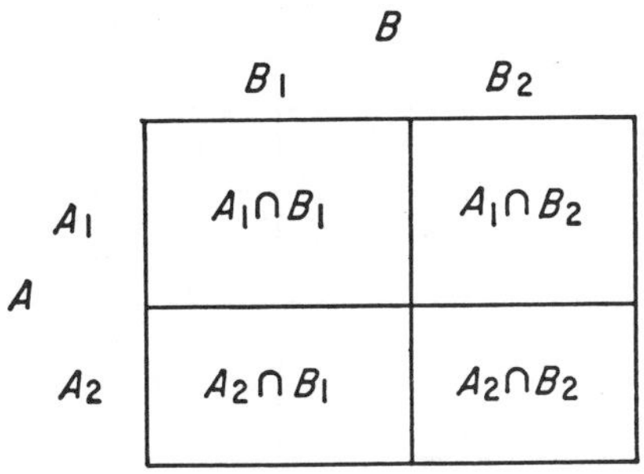

FIG. 4.8

is empty, for example, $(A_1 \cap B_1) \cap (A_2 \cap B_2) = E$. And the cells exhaust all the cases: $(A_1 \cap B_1) \cup \cdots \cup (A_2 \cap B_2) = U$.

Partitioning extends beyond two partitions, of course. Instead of dichotomies, we can have polytomies; instead of success-failure, for instance, we can have success-partial success-failure. A variable can theoretically be partitioned into any number of subsets, though there are usually practical limitations. There is no theoretical limitation, either, on the number of variables in a cross partition, but practical considerations usually limit the number to three or four.

TABLE **4.1** CROSSBREAK TABLE: RELATION BETWEEN SOCIAL CLASS AND WEANING. MILLER AND SWANSON STUDY

		Weaning	
		Early (B_1)	Late (B_2)
Social Class	Middle Class (A_1)	60% (33)	40% (22)
	Working Class (A_2)	35% (17)	65% (31)

Here is an example of a larger and more complex cross partition. We assign variable names to the set letters of a $2 \times 3 \times 2$ cross partition. It has been laid out in Fig. 4.9. Let U be all fourth-grade children in X school system. Let U be partitioned and cross-partitioned according to three variables, A, B, and C, A being sex, B intelligence, and C motivation. Let U be partitioned first into A_1 and A_2, male and female. Let U be partitioned next into B_1, B_2, B_3, or high, medium, and low intelligence.[7] Finally, let U be partitioned into C_1 and C_2, high and low motivation (to do school work).

Next, we cross-partition or crossbreak A_1 and A_2 and B_1, B_2, and B_3 by forming subsets from the intersections of A and B, such as $A_1 \cap B_1$, $A_1 \cap B_2, \ldots,$ $A_2 \cap B_3$. We do the same, theoretically, for A and C and B and C. Actually, we

[7]Naturally there has to be a clear-cut system for setting up the categories. Such systems will be discussed when we study research design.

	B_1		B_2		B_3	
	C_1	C_2	C_1	C_2	C_1	C_2
A_1	$A_1B_1C_1$	$A_1B_1C_2$	$A_1B_2C_1$	$A_1B_2C_2$	$A_1B_3C_1$	$A_1B_3C_2$
A_2	$A_2B_1C_1$	$A_2B_1C_2$	$A_2B_2C_1$	$A_2B_2C_2$	$A_2B_3C_1$	$A_2B_3C_2$

U

FIG. 4.9

do not have to do all this. What we do do, after we have $A_1 \cap B_1, \ldots, A_2 \cap B_3$ is to cross-partition these intersection subsets with C_1 and C_2, arriving at the triple subsets, $A_1 \cap B_1 \cap C_1$, $A_1 \cap B_1 \cap C_2, \ldots, A_2 \cap B_3 \cap C_2$. (For simplicity we write these subsets in the diagram: $A_1B_1C_1$, $A_1B_1C_2$, and so forth.) This gives us $2 \times 3 \times 2 = 12$ cells, each of which represents the intersection of three sets.

To classify any single individual, we learn whether "he" is a male or a female, whether he has high, medium, or low intelligence, and whether his motivation is high or low. We do this for each individual until all individuals or members of U are appropriately classified and assigned to their appropriate cells. Since our initial rules said that (1) the cells must be disjoint $[(A_1 \cap B_1 \cap C_2) \cap (A_2 \cap B_1 \cap C_3) = E$, for example], and (2) the union of all the cells must equal the universe $[(A_1 \cap B_1 \cap C_1) \cup (A_1 \cap B_1 \cap C_2) \cup \cdots \cup (A_2 \cap B_3 \cap C_2) = U]$, no individual can be in more than one cell and every individual must be assigned to a cell. An example or two may clarify all this. If one of the children is female, has high intelligence, and low motivation, she is in cell $A_2B_1C_2$, whereas a boy of medium intelligence and high motivation is in cell $A_1B_2C_1$.

Defining Sets

There are certain symbolic ways to define or specify sets. List definitions have already been mentioned: one merely lists all the members of a set, for example: $A = \{$Opus 101, Opus 106, Opus 109, Opus 110, Opus 111$\}$, which is the set of Beethoven's last five piano sonatas. Rule definitions are more interesting and more practical because most sets, especially in research, are too large and too difficult to list. A rule definition is:

$$A = \{a \mid a \text{ is one of the last five Beethoven piano sonatas}\}$$

(The sign "|" is read "such that." Another rule definition is:

$$B = \{b \mid b \text{ is a fourth-grade female pupil in the Berkeley, California, school system}\}$$

Many rule definitions, especially in mathematics, are more succinct—for example:

$$C = \{x | x \text{ is a rank, and } 1 \leqslant x \leqslant 10\}$$

which says that C is a set of ranks, x_i, where $i = 1, 2, \ldots, 10$.

Levels of Discourse

When we talk about anything we talk about it in a context or frame of reference. The expressions context and frame of reference are closely related to U, the universe of discourse. The universe of discourse must be able to include any objects we talk about. If we go to another U, another level of discourse, the new level will not include all the objects. Indeed, it may not include any of the objects. If we are talking about people, for instance, we do not—or perhaps I should say "should not"—start talking about birds and their habits unless we somehow relate birds and their habits to people and make it clear that this is what we are doing. There are two levels of discourse or universes (U's) of discourse here: people and birds. When discussing the democratic implications of segregation, we should not abruptly shift to religious problems—unless, of course, we somehow relate the latter to the former. Otherwise we lose our original universe of discourse, or we cannot assign the objects of the level, religion, perhaps, to the old level, the education of black children.

In research, similarly, we should not mix or shift our universes of discourse. Set-thinking helps us avoid such mixing and shifting. As an extreme example, suppose an investigator decided to study the toilet training, authoritarianism, musical aptitude, creativity, intelligence, reading achievement, and general scholastic achievement of ninth-grade youngsters. While it is conceivable that some sort of relation or relations could be teased out of this array of variables, it is more conceivable that it is an intellectual mess. At any rate, remember sets. Ask yourself: "Do the objects I am discussing or am about to discuss belong to the set or sets of my present discussion?" If so, then you are on one level of discourse. If not, then another level of discourse, another set, or set of sets, is entering the discussion. If this happens without your knowing it, the result is confusion. In short, ask: "What is my U and the subsets of my U?"

In addition, define your universal set precisely. "Precisely" means: give a clear rule that tells you when an object is or is not a member of U. Similarly, define subsets of U and the subsets of the subsets of U. If the objects of U are people, then you cannot have a subset with objects that are not people. (Though you might have the set A of people and set $\sim A$ of "not-people," this logically amounts to U being people. "Not-people" is a class on the dimension of "people," by definition or convention.)

The set idea is fundamental in human thinking. This is because all human thinking probably depends on putting things into categories and labeling the categories, as indicated earlier. What we do is to group together classes of objects —things, people, events, phenomena in general—and name these classes. Such names are then concepts, labels that we no longer need to learn anew and that we can use for efficient thinking.

Set theory is also a general and widely applicable tool of conceptual and analytic thinking. Its most important applications pertinent to research methodology are probably to the study of relations, logic, sampling, probability, measurement, and data analysis. But sets can be applied to other areas and problems that are not considered technical in the sense, say, that probability and measurement are. Piaget, for example, has used set algebra to help explain the thinking of children.[8] Hunt has applied sets to his study of concept learning.[9] Coombs presented his important theory of data largely in set terms.[10] Warr and Smith, with remarkable ingenuity and insight, used set theory to test different models of inference about personal traits—with rather surprising results.[11] Later in this book, measurement will be defined using a single set-theoretic equation. In addition, basic principles of sampling, analysis, and of research design will hopefully be clarified with sets and set theory. Unfortunately, most social scientists and educators are still not aware of the generality, power, and flexibility of set thinking. It can be safely predicted, however, that researchers in the social sciences and education will find set thinking and theory increasingly useful in the conceptualization of theoretical and research problems.

Study Suggestions

1. Draw two overlapping circles, enclosed in a rectangle. Label the following parts: the universal set U, the subsets A and B, the intersection of A and B, and the union of A and B.
   (a) If you were working on a research problem involving fifth-grade children, what part of the diagram would indicate the children from which you might draw samples?
   (b) What might the sets A and B represent?
   (c) What meaning might the intersection of A and B have?
   (d) How would you have to change the diagram to represent the empty set? Under what conditions would such a diagram have research meaning?
2. Consider the following cross partition:

	Republican (B_1)	Democrat (B_2)
Male (A_1)		
Female (A_2)		

What is the meaning of the following sets—that is, what would we call any object in the sets?

[8] J. Piaget, *Logic and Psychology*. New York: Basic Books, 1957. Also, B. Inhelder and J. Piaget, *The Growth of Logical Thinking from Childhood to Adolescence*. New York: Basic Books, 1958.

[9] E. Hunt, *Concept Learning*. New York: Wiley, 1962.

[10] C. Coombs, "A Theory of Data," *Psychological Review*, LXVII (1960), 143–159.

[11] P. Warr and J. Smith, "Combining Information about People: Comparisons Between Six Models," *Journal of Personality and Social Psychology*, XVI (1970), 55–65.

(a) $(A_1 \cap B_1)$; $(A_2 \cap B_2)$
(b) A_1; B_1
(c) $(A_1 \cap B_1) \cup (A_1 \cap B_2) \cup (A_2 \cap B_1) \cup (A_2 \cap B_2)$
(d) $(A_1 \cap B_1) \cup (A_2 \cap B_1)$

3. Using the following sets, make a cross partition: intelligence test scores of third-grade children; socioeconomic backgrounds of the children; the children's sex.
4. Under what conditions will the following set equation be true?

$$n(A \cup B) = n(A) + n(B)$$

[*Note:* $n(A)$ means the number of objects in the set A.]
5. Suppose a researcher in sociology wants to do a study of the influence of sex and race on occupational status. How can he conceptualize the problem in set terms? [*Hint:* Let A = sex, B = social class, and C = occupational status, and study Fig. 4.9.]
6. How are sets related to variables? Can we talk about the partitioning of variables? Is it meaningful to talk about subsets and variables? Explain.

CHAPTER 5

Relations

Relations are the essence of science. Cohen says, ". . . science is not a knowledge of mere particulars, but rather a knowledge of the way in which classes are related."[1] We know that large things are large only by comparing them to other smaller things. We thus establish the relations "greater than" and "less than." An educational scientist can "know" about achievement only as he studies achievement in relation to nonachievement and in relation to other variables. There is no "fact" of achievement in and of itself. Scientific "facts" are relations. The relations between intelligence and achievement, between group pressure and conformity, between aptitude and motivation, are, when established, "facts."

The relational nature of human knowledge is clearly seen even when seemingly obvious "facts" are analyzed. Is it a fact that a stone is hard? To speak of the truth or falsity of this statement we must first examine sets and subsets of different kinds of stones. Then, after operationally defining "hard," we compare the "hardness" of stones to other "hardnesses." The "simplest" facts turn out, on analysis, to be not so simple. Northrop, discussing concepts and facts, says, "The only way to get pure facts, independent of all concepts and theory, is merely to look at them and forthwith to remain perpetually dumb . . ."[2]

The dictionary tells us that a relation is a bond, a connection, a kinship. For most people this definition is good enough. But what do "bond," "connection," and "kinship" mean? Again, the dictionary says that a bond is a tie, a binding force, and that a connection is, among other things, a union, a relationship, an

[1]M. Cohen, *A Preface to Logic*. New York: Meridian, 1957, p. 170.

[2]F. Northrop, *The Logic of the Sciences and the Humanities*. New York: Macmillan, 1947, p. 317. See also, M. Cohen and E. Nagel, *An Introduction to Logic and Scientific Method*. New York: Harcourt, 1934, pp. 217–219.

alliance. But a union, a tie, between what? And what do "union," "tie," and "binding force" mean? Such definitions, while intuitively helpful, are too ambiguous for scientific use.

Relations as Sets of Ordered Pairs

Relations in science are always between classes or sets of objects. One cannot "know" the relation between social class and school achievement by studying one child. "Knowing" the relation is achieved only by abstracting the relation from sets of children, or more accurately, from sets of characteristics of children. Let us take examples of relations and intuitively develop a notion of what a relation is.

Let A be the set of all fathers and B the set of all sons. If we pair each father with his son (or sons), we have the relation "father-son." We might also call this relation "fatherhood," even though daughters have not been considered. Similarly we might pair parents (elements of A, each pair of parents being considered as an element) with their children. This would be the relation of "parenthood," or maybe "family."

Let A be the set of all husbands and B the set of all wives. The set of pairs then defines the relation "marriage." In other words, a new set is formed, a set of pairs with husbands always listed first and wives second and each husband paired only with his own wife.

Suppose the set A consists of the scores of a specified group of children on an intelligence test and the set B scores on an achievement test. If we pair each child's IQ with his achievement score, we define a relation between intelligence and achievement. Notice that we cannot so easily assign a name like "parenthood" or "marriage" to this relation. Suppose the sets of scores are as follows:

IQ	Achievement
136	55
125	57
118	42
110	48
100	42
97	35
90	32

Consider the two sets as one set of pairs. Then this set is a relation.

If we graph the two sets of scores on X and Y axes, as we did in Chapter 3 (Fig. 3.3), the relation becomes easier to "see." This has been done in Fig. 5.1. Each point is defined by two scores. For example, the point farthest to the right is defined by (136, 55), and the point farthest to the left is (90, 32). Graphs like Fig. 5.1 are convenient ways to express relations.

We are now prepared to define "relation" formally: *A relation is a set of ordered pairs.* Any relation *is* a set, a certain kind of set: a set of ordered pairs. An *ordered pair* is two objects, or a set of two elements, in which there is a fixed order

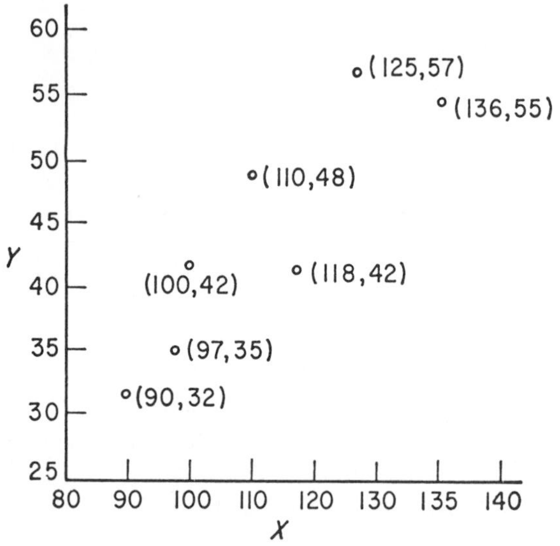

FIG. 5.1 *Y*: achievement; *X*: IQ

for the objects to appear. Actually, we speak of ordered pairs which means, as indicated earlier, that the members *of each pair* always appear in a certain order. If the members of the sets *A* and *B* are paired, then we must specify whether the members of *A* or the members of *B* come first in each pair. If we define the relation of marriage, for example, we specify the set of ordered pairs with, say, husbands always placed first in each pair. In other words, the pair (a, b) is not the same as the pair (b, a). (Ordered pairs are enclosed thus: ( ). A set of ordered pairs is indicated in this manner: $\{(a, k), (b, l), (c, m)\}$.

We have fortunately left the previous ambiguity of the dictionary definition behind. The definition of relations as sets of ordered pairs, though it may seem a bit strange and even curious to the student, is unambiguous and general. Moreover, the scientist, like the mathematician, can work with it.

Determining Relations in Research

Though we have avoided ambiguity with our definition of relations, we have not cleared up the definitional and especially the practical problem of "determining" relations. There is another way to define a relation that may help us. Let *A* and *B* be sets. If we pair each individual member of *A* with every member of *B*, we obtain *all the possible pairs* between the two sets. This is called the *Cartesian product* of the two sets and is labeled $A \times B$. A relation is then defined as a subset of $A \times B$, that is, *any* subset of ordered pairs drawn from $A \times B$ is a relation.[3]

To illustrate this idea very simply, let the set $A = \{a_1, a_2, a_3\}$ and the set $B =$

[3]See R. Kershner and L. Wilcox, *The Anatomy of Mathematics*. New York: Ronald, 1950, chap. 5, for an excellent discussion of relations.

$\{b_1, b_2, b_3\}$.[4] Then the Cartesian product, $A \times B$, can be diagrammed as in Fig. 5.2. That is, we generate nine ordered pairs: (a_1, b_1), (a_1, b_2), . . . , (a_3, b_3). With large sets, of course, there would be many pairs, in fact mn pairs, where m and n are the numbers of elements in A and B, respectively.

This is not very interesting—at least in the present context. What do we do to determine or "discover" a relation? We determine empirically which elements of A "go with" which elements of B according to some criterion. Obviously there are many subsets of pairs of $A \times B$, most of which do not "make sense" or which do not interest us. Kershner and Wilcox say that a relation is "a method for distinguishing some ordered pairs from others; it is a scheme for singling out certain pairs from all of them."[5] According to this way of viewing relations, the relation of "marriage" is a method or procedure for distinguishing married couples from all possible pairings of men and women. In this way we can even think of religion as a relation. Let $A = \{a_1, a_2, \ldots, a_n\}$ be the set of all people in the United States, and let $B = \{$Catholic, Protestant, Jew, and so forth$\}$ be the set of religions. If we order pairs, in this case each person with his religion, then we have the "relation" of religion, or perhaps more accurately, "religious affiliation."

Lest the student be too disturbed by the perhaps jarring sensation of defining a relation as a subset of $A \times B$, we may hastily add, again, that many of the possible subsets of ordered pairs of $A \times B$, naturally, will make no sense. Then, too, some of them may make very good sense. Perhaps the main point to be made is that our definition of relation is unambiguous and completely general. No matter what sets of ordered pairs we pick, it *is* a relation. It is up to *us* to decide whether or not the sets we pick make scientific sense according to the dictates of the problems to which we are seeking answers and the hypotheses we are testing. But we should not automatically rule out relations just because they seem at the moment not to make sense.

The student may wonder why so much trouble has been taken to define relations. First, the ordered pair definition, as already indicated, is unambiguous. Second, it applies to research situations generally and thus is a useful intellectual tool that helps us to unify varied kinds of relations in varied kinds of research situations. Third, it tells us, in effect, what we must do to study relations empirically: we must somehow study ordered pairs and find ways to distinguish meaningful

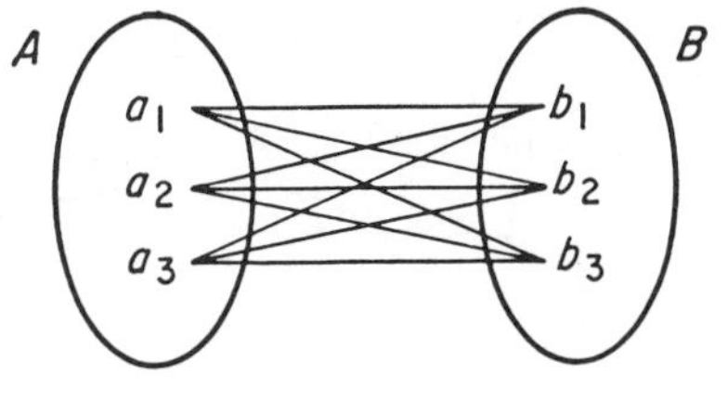

FIG. 5.2

[4]The subscript integers merely label and distinguish individual members of sets. They do not imply order. Note, too, that there do not have to be equal numbers of members in the two sets.

[5]Kershner and Wilcox, *op. cit.*, p. 46.

ordered pairs from those that are not meaningful to a particular research problem.

Rules of Correspondence and Mapping

Any objects—people, coffee beans, numbers, railroad cars, gambling outcomes, points in space, symbols, and so on and on—can be members of sets and can be related in the ordered-pair sense. It is said that the members of one set are *mapped* on to the members of another set by means of a rule of correspondence. A *rule of correspondence* is a prescription or a formula that tells us how to map the objects of one set on to the objects of another set. It tells us, in brief, how the correspondences between set members are achieved.

To illustrate the mapping and correspondence notions, study Fig. 5.3, which shows a simplified ordinary map on the left and the names of map objects on the right. We have here literally a mapping, a mapping of actual geographical objects on to the names of the objects (or vice versa). This is of course a relation, a set of ordered pairs, each geographical object being paired with its name.

In a relation the two sets whose objects are being related are named the *domain* and the *range*, or D and R. D is always the set of first elements, and R the set of second elements. Suppose we have a group of boys and girls and want to study the relation between sex and some other variable. We assign 1 to male and 0 to female. An illustration of the mapping is given in Fig. 5.4, where to each member of the domain is appropriately assigned a member of the range. $D = \{\text{Jane, Arthur, Michael, Alberta, Ruth}\}$, and $R = \{0, 1\}$. The rule of correspondence says: If the object of D is female assign a 0, if male assign a 1.

In other words, objects, especially numbers, are assigned to other objects—persons, places, numbers, and so on—according to rules. The process is highly varied in its applications but simple in its conception. This is why sets are stressed in this book: they are generally applicable and simple in conception. Instead of

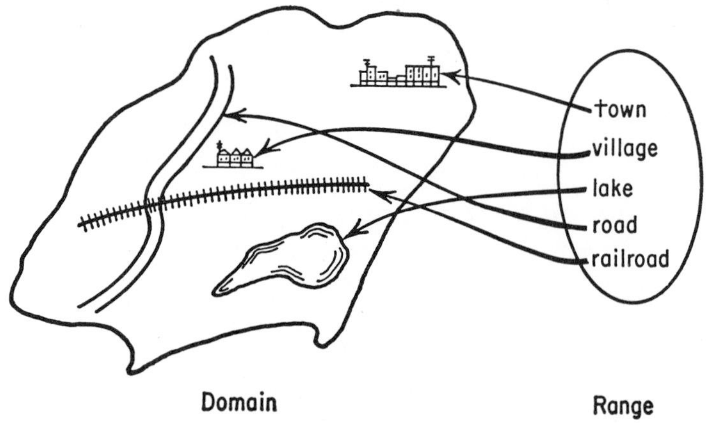

FIG. 5.3

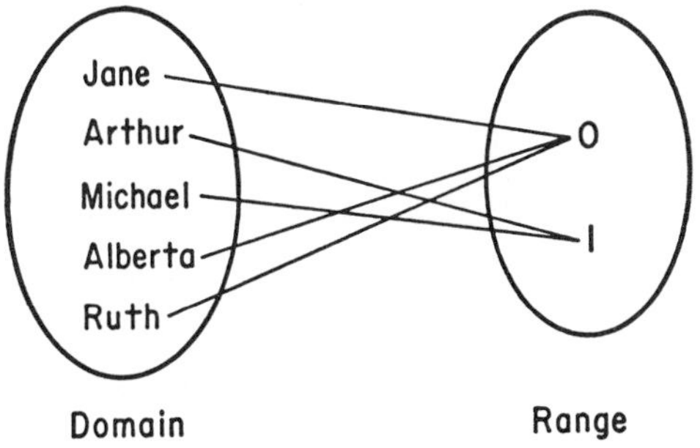

FIG. 5.4

thinking of all the different ways of expressing relations separately, we realize that they are all sets of ordered pairs and that the objects of one set are simply mapped on to the objects of another set. All the varied ways of expressing relations—as mappings, correspondences, equations, sets of points, tables, or statistical indices—can be reduced to sets of ordered pairs.

Functions

A *function* is a rule, a rule of correspondence. It is a rule, often designated by the letters f, g, F, and so on, that assigns to each member of a domain *some one* member of a range. All functions are relations, sets of ordered pairs. Figure 5.4 depicts a function: to each member of the domain {Jane, Arthur, Michael, Alberta, Ruth} one and only one member of the range {0, 1} is assigned.

Functions are written in various ways. One frequent way is $y = f(x)$. Here x stands for the objects of the domain; $f(x)$ denotes the objects assigned to the x's of the domain. That is, $f(x)$ stands for the objects of the range. These objects are called the *values* of f at x; $y = f(x)$ is ordinarily read, "y is a function of x." Unfortunately, this tends to be confused with commonsense usages of the word function: school achievement is a function of intelligence. This usage seems to mean that one thing depends on or is caused by another. This is not the meaning intended here; $y = f(x)$ is better read "y equals the object (a set member) that corresponds to x."

Another way to write functions, one that is close to the purposes of this chapter, is exemplified in this equation: $f = \{(x, y);\ x \text{ is a number and } y = x + 2\}$. Translated into words, this says: "The function, f, or the rule of correspondence, is equal to the set of ordered pairs (x, y) such that x is a number and each corresponding y, also a number, is equal to $x+2$." In brief, given a value of x, say 4, we add 2 to it to obtain y, in this case 6. The rule is f which, spelled out, is the expression on the right side of the equation.

It was said above that all functions are relations. It should be understood, however, that not all relations are functions. A function can have assigned to any member of its domain only one member of its range. If we pair sons and fathers, with sons always coming first, we have a function—and, of course, a relation. Each

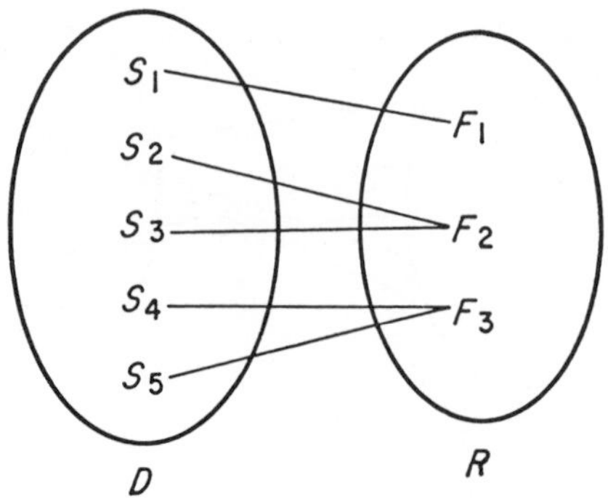

FIG. 5.5

son can have assigned to him only one father. This is shown in Fig. 5.5 where five sons are "related" to three fathers. Note that each object of the domain has only one object of the range associated with it: each son can have only one father.

Figure 5.6 turns the situation around. Fathers come first and sons second. Notice that F_2 and F_3 have two lines connecting them to objects of R. Thus Fig. 5.6 illustrates a relation but not a function.

It is important for the student of research at least to know what a function is. Functions, functional expressions, and functional laws occur frequently in research literature. More important, one of the principal goals of science is to discover and state functional laws, laws of the kind, "If p, then q," which can be stated $q=f(p)$. In addition to discovering relations, the scientist would like to state precise mathematical functional laws which he can use for prediction from independent variables to dependent variables. For example, learning theorists have long used functional equations. The famous so-called learning curves and the equations that underlie them are functions—and, of course, relations. The relation in this case is between time or practice, the independent variables (or domains), and correct or incorrect responses, the dependent variables (the ranges). The student, reading the learning theory literature, is in difficulty if he knows nothing about relations and functions.

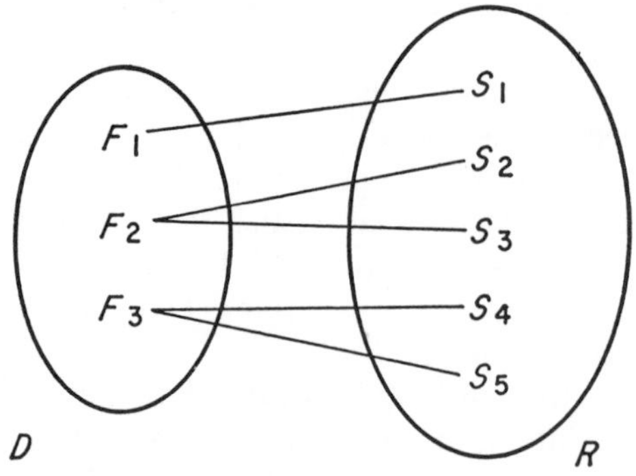

FIG. 5.6

More and more, in fact, social scientists are using sets, relations, and functions in their work. Though the mathematical statements look complex and abstruse to the uninitiated, they are fortunately based on the relatively simple and unambiguous ideas outlined in these chapters. More to the scientific point, they are powerful tools for conceptualizing the foundations of scientific thinking and research and for aiding the discovering and testing of relations.

Some Ways To Show Relations

It was said earlier that relations can be expressed in various ways. In the previous discussion, some of these ways were illustrated. One way was simply to list and pair the members of sets. Figs. 5.2, 5.3, 5.4, 5.5, and 5.6 illustrate the method. Another way to illustrate a relation is with graphs. Fig. 5.1 is an example. Still another way is with equations.

Tables are often convenient ways to show relations. The situation indicated in Fig. 5.4 might be expressed in a table. Here is one table that shows the ordered pairs clearly:

x	Jane	Arthur	Michael	Alberta	Ruth
y	0	1	1	0	0

Here is a simple example from actual research. Newcomb, in studying the acquaintance process, reports a table that epitomizes the relation between need for affiliation and attitude change.[6] The substantive details need not concern us here since we are interested only in tables as convenient devices to show relations. Part of Newcomb's table is given in Table 5.1.

TABLE **5.1** RELATION BETWEEN NEED FOR AFFILIATION AND ATTITUDE CHANGE, NEWCOMB STUDY[a]

	Change of Attitude	No Change of Attitude
High Need for Affiliation	6	0
Low Need for Affiliation	2	6

[a]The numbers are the numbers of individuals who exhibited the joint characteristics indicated by the variables on the top and side of the table. For example, 2 individuals with low need for affiliation showed change of attitude.

The table is of course a cross partition or crossbreak. Actually, it condenses a set of 14 ordered pairs, the first members being individuals and the second members 1's and 0's. The mapping, or functional rule, is contained in the intersection of the subsets (the four cells) and their joint names. For example, the lower left cell is $A_2 \cap B_1$, using the convention adopted in Chapter 4, A_2 is Low Need for Affiliation, and B_1 is Change of Attitude. The two individuals who satisfy both

[6]T. Newcomb, *The Acquaintance Process*. New York: Holt, Rinehart and Winston, 1961, p. 140.

these conditions (part of the rule) are mapped from their domain (containing 14 individuals) on to $A_2 \cap B_1$, which is part of the range of the four intersections (cells). The other 12 individuals are similarly mapped. We have here a relation that is also a function. In a later chapter we will examine similar crossbreaks, as well as other kinds of tables that express relations and functions.

It is instructive to examine statistical measures of relation together with graphs. Suppose we have two sets, X and Y, consisting of scores of the same individuals on two tests. The scores are:

X	Y
1	1
2	1
2	2
3	3

The two sets form a set of ordered pairs. This set is of course a relation. (Is it a function?) It can also be written, letting R stand for relation $R = \{(1, 1), (2, 1), (2, 2), (3, 3)\}$.

Though we can often get a rough idea of the direction and degree of a relation by inspection of lists of ordered pairs, such a method is imprecise. Graphs, such as those of Figs. 5.1 and 5.7, tell us more. It can more easily be "seen" that X values "go along" with Y values: higher values of Y accompany higher values of X, and lower values of Y accompany lower values of X. In this case the relation, or correlation, as it is commonly called, is positive. If we had the equation: $R = \{(1, 3), (2, 1), (2, 2), (3, 1)\}$, the relation would be negative. (The student should plot these values. Note that this relation is not a function because the X value of 2 has two different Y values paired with it. This is easily seen in the graph. A function can never have more than one Y value with each X value.)

If the equation were $R = \{(1, 2), (2, 1), (2, 2), (3, 2)\}$, the relation would be null or zero. This is plotted in Fig. 5.8. It can be seen that Y values do not "go along" with X values in any systematic way. This does not mean that there is "no" relation. There is always a relation—by definition—since there is a set of ordered pairs. It is commonly said, however, that there is "no" relation. It is more accurate to say that the relation is null or zero.

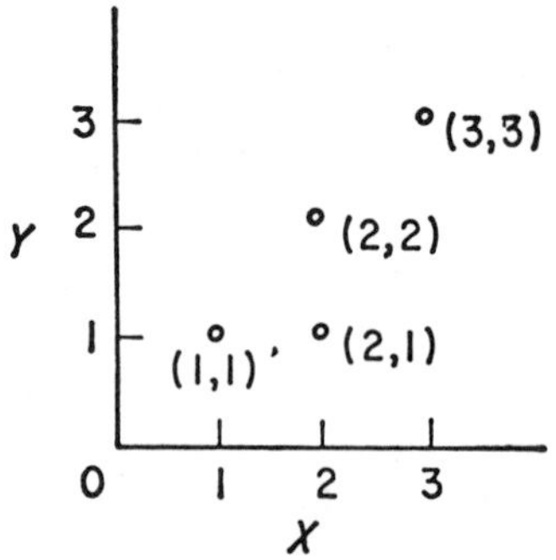

FIG. 5.7

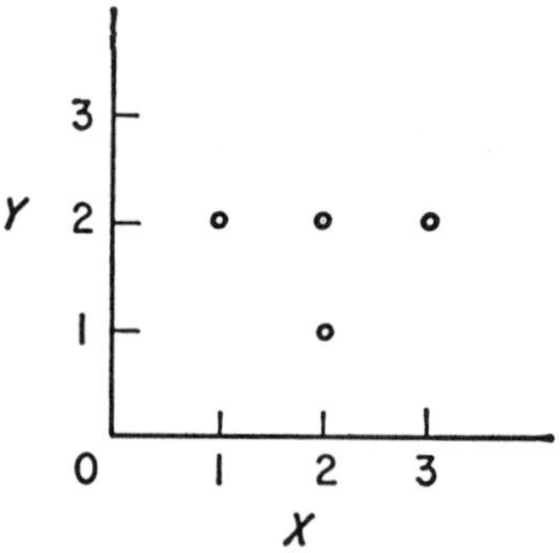

FIG. 5.8

Social scientists commonly calculate indices of relation, usually called coefficients of correlation, between sets of ordered pairs in order to obtain more precise estimates of the direction and degree of relations. If one such index, the product-moment coefficient of correlation, or r, is calculated for the ordered pairs of Fig. 5.7, $r = .85$ is obtained. For the pairs of $R = \{(1, 3), (2, 1), (2, 2), (3, 1)\}$, the relation we said was negative, $r = -.85$. For the pairs of Fig. 5.8, the set of pairs that showed a null or zero relation, $r = 0$.[7]

Product-moment and related coefficients of correlation, then, are based on the concomitant variation of the members of sets of ordered pairs. If they *covary*, vary together—high values with high values, medium values with medium values, and low values with low values, or high values with low values, and so on—it is said that there is a positive or negative relation as the case may be. If they do not covary, it is said there is "no" relation. The most useful such indices range from $+1.00$ through 0 to -1.00, $+1.00$ indicating a perfect positive relation, -1.00 a perfect negative relation, and 0 no discernible relation, or zero relation. Some indices range only from 0 to $+1.00$. Other indices may take on other values.

Most coefficients of relation tell us how similar the rank orders of two sets of measures are. Table 5.2 presents three examples to illustrate this going together of rank orders. The coefficients of correlation are given with each of the sets of ordered pairs. I and II are fairly obvious: the rank orders of the X and Y scores of I go together perfectly. So do the X and Y scores of II, but in the opposite direction. In III, no relation between the rank orders can be discerned. In I and II, one can predict perfectly from X to Y, but in III one cannot predict values of Y from knowledge of X. Coefficients of correlation are rarely 1.00 or 0. They ordinarily take on intermediate values.

TABLE **5.2** THREE SETS OF ORDERED PAIRS SHOWING DIFFERENT DIRECTIONS AND DEGREES OF CORRELATION

(I) $r = 1.00$		(II) $r = -1.00$		(III) $r = 0$	
X	Y	X	Y	X	Y
1	1	1	5	1	2
2	2	2	4	2	5
3	3	3	3	3	3
4	4	4	2	4	1
5	5	5	1	5	4

Study Suggestions

1. The following selected references contain excellent discussions of sets, relations, and functions. Students should try to study the pertinent sections of at least two of these books.

[7]Methods of calculating these r's and other coefficients of correlation are discussed in statistics texts. These texts also discuss at greater length than is possible in this book the interpretation of correlation coefficients.

Kershner, R., and Wilcox, L., *The Anatomy of Mathematics*. New York: Ronald, 1950, pp. 41–60. The most abstract and in some ways the most satisfactory of all the references. Its rigorous treatment of sets, relations, and functions is especially good. The text is difficult, however, and is recommended for more advanced students.

Report of the Commission on Mathematics. *Appendices*. New York: College Entrance Examination Board, 1959. This is an excellent reference, with clear, simple exposition. Chap. 2 is highly recommended; chap. 9 is good.

2. Five examples of relations and/or functions are given below. Assume that the first-named set is the domain and the second the range. Why are all of these relations? Which are functions?
   (a) Book pages and page numbers
   (b) Chapter numbers and pages of a book
   (c) Population table headings or categories and population figures in a census report
   (d) A class of third-grade children and their arithmetic scores on a standardized test
   (e) $y = 2x$
   (f) $y > 5 - x$ [*Hint:* Substitute values for x and y and plot some points.]

An educational investigator has studied the relation between anxiety and school achievement. Express the relation in set language.

4. In this book, the expressions "cause" and "causal relations" will be used sparingly. Indeed, they will be avoided, whenever possible—not because they are "bad" or "wrong" but because they lead to technical and philosophical difficulties that are better bypassed. Besides, there is no real necessity to think causally in science.[8] All that is really necessary is to use so-called conditional statements of the kind encountered earlier: If p, then q. Nevertheless, if a scientist wishes to use the word "cause"—which many do—what basic condition must his relations satisfy? That is, what kind of relation is necessary even to consider using the word "cause"? Why? [*Hint:* Set up one or two figures like those of Figs. 5.5 and 5.6 but use numbers to represent values of the variables X and Y.]

[8] See the end of Chapter 22 for a brief discussion of causal ideas in scientific research and the position taken in this book.

CHAPTER 6

Variance

To study scientific problems and to answer scientific questions, we must study differences among phenomena. Without differences, without variation, there is no way to determine the relations among variables. If we want to study the relation between race and achievement, for instance, we are helpless if we have only achievement measures of white children. We must have achievement measures of children of more than one race. In short, race must vary; it must have variance. It is necessary to explore the variance notion analytically and in some depth. To do so adequately, it is also necessary to skim some of the cream off the milk of statistics.

Studying sets of numbers as they are is unwieldy. It is usually necessary to reduce the sets in two ways: (1) by calculating averages or measures of central tendency, and (2) by calculating measures of variability. The measure of central tendency used in this book is the *mean*. The measure of variability most used is the *variance*. Both kinds of measures epitomize sets of scores, but in different ways. They are both "summaries" of whole sets of scores, "summaries" that express two important facets of the sets of scores: their central or average tendency and their variability. Solving research problems without these measures is next to impossible. We start our study of variance, then, with some simple computation.

Calculation of Means and Variances

Take the set of numbers $X = \{1, 2, 3, 4, 5\}$. The mean is defined:

$$M = \frac{\Sigma X}{n} \tag{6.1}$$

n = the number of cases in the set of scores; Σ means "the sum of" or "add them up." X stands for any one of the scores, that is, each score is an X. The formula, then, says, "Add the scores and divide by the number of cases in the set." Thus:

$$M = \frac{1+2+3+4+5}{5} = \frac{15}{5} = 3$$

The mean of the set X is 3.

Calculating the variance, while not as simple as calculating the mean, is still simple. The formula is:[1]

$$V = \frac{\Sigma x^2}{n} \tag{6.2}$$

V means variance; n and Σ are the same as in Eq. 6.1. Σx^2 is called the *sum of squares*; it needs some explanation. The scores are listed in a column:

	X	x	x^2
	1	−2	4
	2	−1	1
	3	0	0
	4	1	1
	5	2	4
ΣX:	15		
M:	3		
Σx^2:			10

In this calculation x is a deviation from the mean. It is defined:

$$x = X - M \tag{6.3}$$

Thus, to obtain x, simply subtract from X the mean of all the scores. For example, when $X = 1$, $x = 1-3 = -2$; when $X = 4$, $x = 4-3 = 1$; and so on. This has been done above. Equation 6.2, however, says to square each x. This has also been done above. (Remember, that the square of a negative number is always positive.) In other words, Σx^2 tells us to subtract the mean from each score to get x, square each x to get x^2, and then add up the x^2's. Finally, the average of the x^2's is taken by dividing Σx^2 by n, the number of cases. Σx^2, the *sum of squares*, is a very important statistic which we will use often.

The variance, in the present case, is

$$V = \frac{(-2)^2 + (-1)^2 + (0)^2 + (1)^2 + (2)^2}{5} = \frac{4+1+0+1+4}{5} = \frac{10}{5} = 2$$

[1] "V" will be used for "variance" in this book. Other symbols commonly used are σ^2 and s^2. It is not necessary to go into their usage here. In this text, N is used for the number of cases in U, whereas n is used for the number of cases in a subset or sample of U. Appropriate subscripts will be added and explained as necessary. For example, if we wish to indicate the number of elements in the set A, a subset of U, we can write n_A or n_a. Similarly we attach subscripts to x, V, and so on. When double subscripts are used, such as r_{xy}, the meaning will usually be obvious.

The variance is also called the *mean square* (when it is calculated in a slightly different way which we take up in a future chapter). It is called this because, obviously, it is the mean of the x^2's. Clearly it is not difficult to calculate the mean and the variance.[2]

The question is: Why calculate the mean and the variance? The rationale for calculating the mean is easily disposed of. In research, means of different experimental groups are compared to study relations. We may be testing the relation between organizational climates and productivity, for instance. We may have used three kinds of climates and may be interested in the question of which climate has the greatest effect on productivity. In such cases means are customarily compared. For instance, of three groups, each operating under one of three climates, A_1, A_2, and A_3, which has the greatest mean on, say, a measure of productivity?

The rationale for computing and using the variance in research is more difficult to explain. In the usual case of ordinary scores the variance is a measure of the dispersion of the set of scores. It tells us how much the scores are spread out. If a group of pupils is very heterogeneous in reading achievement, then the variance of their reading scores will be large compared to the variance of a group that is homogeneous in reading achievement. The variance, then, is a measure of the spread of the scores; it describes the extent to which the scores differ from each other.[3] The remainder of this chapter and later parts of the book will explore other aspects of the use of the variance statistic.

Kinds of Variance

Variances come in a number of forms. When you read the research and technical literature, you will frequently come across the term sometimes with a qualifying adjective, sometimes not. To understand the literature, it is necessary to have a good idea of the characteristics and purposes of these different variances. And to design and do research, one must have a rather thorough understanding of the variance concept as well as considerable mastery of statistical variance notions and manipulations.

A goodly part of statistics consists in comparing variances. To obtain answers to research questions, to test research hypotheses, different kinds of variance are compared. Take a simple example. A teacher has two classes that he knows are approximately equal in arithmetic ability, that is, the means of the classes are approximately equal. The teacher thinks, however, that the classes differ

[2]The method of calculating the variance used in this chapter differs from the methods ordinarily used. In fact, the method given above is impracticable in most situations. Our purpose is not to learn statistics, as such. Rather, we are pursuing basic ideas. Methods of computation, examples, and demonstrations have been constructed to aid this pursuit of basic ideas. The student should therefore *not* learn the computational methods of this chapter.

[3]For descriptive purposes, the square root of the variance is ordinarily used. It is called the *standard deviation*. Because of certain mathematical properties, however, the variance is more useful in research. It is suggested that the student supplement his study with study of appropriate sections of an elementary statistics text, since it will not be possible in this book to discuss all the facets of meaning and interpretation of means, variances, and standard deviations. A good elementary text for this purpose is: A. Edwards, *Statistical Analysis*, 3d ed. New York: Holt, Rinehart and Winston, 1969.

considerably in variability. He can easily check his belief by calculating the variances of both classes and then dividing the smaller variance into the larger variance. If the resu t of this operation is large—"large" means considerably greater than 1—then his belief is substantiated. If the ratio is small, then his belief is not substantiated. From this simple beginning the comparison of variances gets very elaborate indeed, as we will see.

Population and Sample Variances

The *population variance* is the variance of U, a universe or population of measures. If all the measures of a defined universal set, U, are known, then the variance is known. More likely, however, all the measures of U are not available. In such cases the variance is estimated by calculating the variance of one or more samples of U. A good deal of statistical energy goes into this important problem. A question may arise: How variable is the intelligence of the citizens of the United States? This is a U or population question. If there were a complete list of all the millions of people in the United States—and there were also a complete list of intelligence test scores of these people—the variance could be simply if wearily computed. No such list exists. So samples—hopefully representative samples—of Americans are tested and means and variances computed. The samples are used to estimate the mean and variance of the whole population.

Sampling variance is the variance of statistics computed from samples. The means of four random samples drawn from a population will differ. If the sampling is random and the samples are large enough, the means should not vary too much. That is, the *variance of the means* should be relatively small.[4]

Systematic Variance

Perhaps the most general way to classify variances is as *systematic variance* and *error variance*. *Systematic variance* is the variation in measures due to some known or unknown influences that "cause" the scores to lean in one direction more than another. Any natural or man-made influences that cause events to happen in a certain predictable way are systematic influences. The achievement test scores of the children in a wealthy suburban school will tend to be *systematically* higher than the achievement test scores of the children in a city slum area

[4]Unfortunately, in much actual research only one sample is usually available—and this one sample is frequently small. We can, however, estimate the sampling variance of the means by using what is called the *standard variance of the mean(s)*. (The term "standard error of the mean" is usually used. The standard error of the mean is the square root of the standard variance of the mean.) The formula is

$$V_M = \frac{V_s}{n_s}$$

where V_M is the standard variance of the mean, V_s the variance of the sample, and n_s the size of the sample.

Notice an important conclusion that can be reached from this equation. If the size of the sample is increased, V_M is decreased. In other words, to be more confident that the sample is close to the population mean, make n large. Conversely, the smaller the sample, the riskier the estimate.

school. Expert teaching may systematically influence the achievement of children —as compared to the achievement of children taught inexpertly.

"Fair" dice will turn up all the numbers 1 through 6 about equally often. Loaded dice, on the other hand, lean in one direction systematically: certain numbers will turn up more often than other numbers. Similarly, marked cards and crooked roulette wheels show systematic variance.

There are many, many causes of systematic variance. The scientist seeks to separate those in which he is interested from those in which he is not interested. And he must also separate from his systematic variances variance that is random. Indeed, research may narrowly and technically be defined as controlled study of variances.

Between-Groups (Experimental) Variance

One important type of systematic variance in research is between-groups or experimental variance. *Between-groups* or *experimental variance*, as the name indicates, is the variance that reflects systematic differences between *groups* of measures. The variance discussed previously as score variance reflects the differences between individuals in a group. We can say, for instance, that, on the basis of present evidence and current tests, the variance in intelligence of a random sample of eleven-year-old children is about 225 IQ points.[5] This figure is a statistic that tells us how much the individuals differ from each other. Experimental variance, on the other hand, is the variance due to the differences between *groups* of individuals. It is often called "between-groups" variance. If the achievement of northern and southern children in comparable schools is measured, there would be differences between the northern and southern groups. Groups as well as individuals differ or vary, and it is possible and appropriate to calculate the variance between these groups.

Between-groups variance and experimental variance are fundamentally the same. Both arise from differences between groups. Between-groups variance is a term that covers all cases of systematic differences between groups, experimental and nonexperimental. Experimental variance is usually associated with the variance engendered by active manipulation of independent variables by experimenters. In this book the term "between groups" will most often be used. It will be clear from the context of future discussions whether experimental manipulation is or is not involved.

Here is a simple example of between-groups—in this case experimental—variance. Suppose an investigator tests the relative efficacies of three different methods of teaching a physical education skill. After teaching three groups of children, each group being taught by a different method, he calculates the means

[5] This is obtained simply by squaring the standard deviation reported in a test manual. The standard deviation of the California Test of Mental Maturity for eleven-year-old children is about 15, and $15^2 = 225$.

of the groups. Suppose that they are 30, 23, and 19. The mean of the three means is 24, and we calculate the variance *between the means* or *between the groups*:

		x	x^2
	30	6	36
	23	−1	1
	19	−5	25
ΣX:	72		
M:	24		
Σx^2:			62

$$V_b = \frac{62}{3} = 20.67$$

In other words, the three means are treated as three scores, and their variance is calculated as before. This variance between groups (V_b) is an index of the variability of the three group means, or the variability of the three groups taken as wholes. Later we will see how V_b is used.

In the methods experiment just described, presumably the methods tend to "bias" the skill scores one way or another. This is, of course, the experimenter's purpose: he wants Method A, say, to increase all the skill scores of an experimental group. He may believe that Method B will have no effect on skill, and that Method C will have a depressing effect. If he is correct, the scores under Method A should all tend to go up, whereas under Method C they should all tend to go down. Thus the scores of the groups, as wholes—and, of course, their means—differ systematically. Methods is an *active* variable, a variable deliberately manipulated by the experimenter with the conscious intent to "bias" the scores differentially. Thus any experimenter-manipulated variables are intimately associated with systematic variance. When Bennett et al. gave their experimental groups of rats different degrees of early experience—environmental complexity and training (enriched experiences), control condition (the usual rat colony condition), and reduced experience (isolation)—they were deliberately attempting to build systematic variance into their outcome measures (weight, thickness, and chemical activity of the brain).[6]

The basic idea behind the famous "classical design" of scientific research, in which experimental and control groups are used, is that, through careful control and manipulation, the experimental group's outcome measures (also called "criterion measures") are made to vary systematically, to all go up or down together, while the control group's measures are ordinarily held at the same level. The variance, of course, is between the two groups, that is, the two groups are made to differ. For example, in an interesting experiment on arithmetic readiness in the kindergarten child, Koenker manipulated experimental groups by giving them an enriched-numbers and arithmetic-concepts program.[7] He held his control groups constant or at the same level by not giving them a readiness program, by letting

[6]E. Bennett et al., "Chemical and Anatomical Plasticity of Brain," *Science*, CXLVI (1964), 610–619.

them have the regular kindergarten program "without enrichment." Statistically speaking, he was trying to increase the between-groups variance. (He succeeded.)

This is clear and easy to see in experiments. In research that is not experimental, in research where already existing differences between groups are studied, it is not always so clear and easy to see that one is studying between-groups variance. But the idea is the same. The principle may be stated in a somewhat different way: The greater the differences between groups, the more an independent variable or variables can be presumed to have operated. If there is little difference between groups, on the other hand, then the presumption must be that an independent variable or variables have not operated, that their effects are too weak to be noticed, or that their influences have canceled each other out. We judge the effects of independent variables that have been manipulated or that have worked in the past, then, by between-groups variance. It makes no difference whether the independent variables have or have not been manipulated. The principle is the same.

To illustrate the principle, we can go back to the example of anxiety and school achievement discussed earlier. It is possible to manipulate anxiety by having two experimental groups and inducing anxiety in one and not in the other. This can be done by giving each group the same test with different instructions. We tell the members of one group that their grades depend wholly on the test. We tell the members of the other group that the test does not matter particularly, that its outcome will not affect grades. On the other hand, the relation between anxiety and achievement may also be studied by comparing groups of individuals on whom it can be assumed that different environmental and psychological circumstances have acted to produce anxiety. (Of course, the experimentally induced anxiety and the already existing anxiety—the stimulus variable and the organismic variable—are not assumed to be the same.) A study to test the hypothesis that different environmental and psychological circumstances act to produce different levels of anxiety has been done by Sarnoff et al.[8] The investigators predicted that, as a result of the English 11-plus examinations, English school children would exhibit greater test anxiety than would American school children. In the language of this chapter, the investigators hypothesized a between-groups variance larger than could be expected by chance because of the differences between English and American environmental, educational, and psychological conditions. (The hypothesis was supported.)

Error Variance

It is probably safe to say that the most ubiquitous kind of variance in research is error variance. *Error variance* is the fluctuation or varying of measures due to chance. Error variance is random variance. It is the variation in measures due to

[7]R. Koenker, "Arithmetic Readiness at the Kindergarten Level," *Journal of Educational Psychology*, XLII (1948), 218–223.

[8]I. Sarnoff et al., "A Cross-Cultural Study of Anxiety among American and English School Children," *Journal of Educational Psychology*, XLIX (1958), 129–136. Also reported in S. Sarason et al., *Anxiety in Elementary School Children*. New York: Wiley, 1960, pp. 151–157.

the usually small and self-compensating fluctuations of measures—now here, now there; now up, now down. The sampling variance discussed earlier in the chapter, for example, is random or error variance.[9]

It can be said that error variance is the variance in measures due to ignorance. Imagine a great dictionary in which everything in the world—every occurrence, every event, every little thing, every great thing—is given in complete detail. To understand any event that has occurred, that is now occurring, or that will occur, all one needs to do is look it up in the dictionary. With this dictionary there are obviously no random or chance occurrences. Everything is accounted for. In brief, there is no error variance; all is systematic variance. Unfortunately—or more likely, fortunately—we do not have such a dictionary. Many, many events and occurrences cannot be explained. Much variance eludes identification and control. This is error variance—at least as long as identification and control elude us.

While seemingly strange and even a bit bizarre, this mode of reasoning is useful, provided we remember that some of the error variance of today may not be the error variance of tomorrow. Suppose that we do an experiment on teaching problem-solving in which we assign pupils to three groups at random. After we finish the experiment, we study the differences between the three groups to see if the teaching has had an effect. We know that the scores will always show minor fluctuations, now plus a point or two or three, now minus a point or two or three, which we can probably never control. Something or other makes these scores fluctuate in this fashion. According to the view under discussion, they do not just fluctuate for no reason; there is probably no "absolute randomness." Assuming determinism, there must be some cause or causes for the fluctuations. True, we can learn some of them and possibly control them. When we do this, however, we have systematic variance.

We find out, for instance, that sex "causes" the scores to fluctuate, since boys and girls are mixed in the experimental groups. (We are, of course, talking figuratively here. Obviously sex does not make scores fluctuate.) So we do the experiment and control sex by using, say, only boys. The scores still fluctuate, though to a somewhat lesser extent. We remove another presumed cause of the perturbations: intelligence. The scores still fluctuate, though to a still lesser extent. We go on removing such sources of variance. We are controlling systematic variance. We are also gradually identifying and controlling more and more unknown variance.

Now note that before we controlled or removed these systematic variances, before we "knew" about them, we would have to label all such variance error variance—partly through ignorance, partly through inability to do anything about such variance. We could go on and on doing this and still there would be variance left over. Finally we give in; we "know" no more; we have done all we can. There will still be variance. A practical definition of error variance, then, would be: *Error variance* is the variance left over in a set of measures after all known sources

[9]It will be necessary in this chapter and the next to use the notion of "random" or "randomness." Ideas of randomness and randomization will be discussed in considerable detail in Chapter 8. For the present, however, randomness means that there is no known way that can be expressed in language of correctly describing or explaining events and their outcomes. Random events cannot be predicted, in other words. A random sample is a subset of a universe, its members so drawn that each member of the universe has an equal chance of being selected.

of systematic variance have been removed from the measures. This is so important it deserves a numerical example.

An Example of Systematic and Error Variance

Suppose a teacher is interested in knowing whether writing critical comments on student essays, in addition to assigning grades, is more effective in improving subsequent student writing than merely assigning grades.[10] Call "critical comments" and "no critical comments" the variable A, partitioned into A_1 and A_2. The teacher assigns ten students at random to two groups and assigns treatments A_1 and A_2 at random. She gives a written assignment and follows the procedure indicated. A week later she gives a similar assignment and grades the papers. The scores are as follows:

	A_1	A_2
	6	3
	5	5
	7	1
	8	4
	4	2
M:	6	3

A_1 is the critical comments-plus-grades group, A_2 the grades-only group. The means are different; they vary. Thus there is between-groups variance. Calculating it just as we did with an earlier example, we get:

		x	x^2
	6	1.5	2.25
	3	−1.5	2.25
M:	4.5		
Σx^2:			4.50

$$V_b = \frac{4.50}{2} = 2.25$$

In other words, we calculate the between-groups variance just as we earlier calculated the variance of the five scores 1, 2, 3, 4, and 5. We simply treat the two means as though they were individual scores, and go ahead with an ordinary variance calculation. The between-groups variance, V_b, is, then, 2.25. An appropriate statistical test would show that the difference between the means of the two groups is what is called a "statistically significant" difference. (The meaning of this will be taken up in another chapter.)[11]

[10]This little example is a miniature experiment modeled after Page's much larger experiment: E. Page, "Teacher Comments and Student Performance: A Seventy-Four Classroom Experiment in School Motivation," *Journal of Educational Psychology*, XLIX (1958), 173–181.

[11]The method of computation used here is *not* what would be used to test statistical significance. It is used here purely as a pedagogical device. Note, too, that the small numbers of cases in the examples given and the small size of the numbers are used only for simplicity of demonstration. Actual research data, of course, are usually more complex, and many more cases are needed. In actual analysis of variance the correct expression for the between sum of squares is: $ss_b = n\Sigma x_b^2$. (See Footnote 12, Chapter 13.) For pedagogical simplicity, however, we retain Σx_b^2, later replacing it with ss_b.

If we put the 10 scores in a column and calculate the variance, we obtain:

	X	x	x^2
	6	1.5	2.25
	5	.5	.25
	7	2.5	6.25
	8	3.5	12.25
	4	−.5	.25
	3	−1.5	2.25
	5	.5	.25
	1	−3.5	12.25
	4	−.5	.25
	2	−2.5	6.25
M:	4.5		
Σx^2:			42.50

$$V_t = \frac{42.50}{10} = 4.25$$

This is the total variance, V_t. $V_t = 4.25$ contains all sources of variation in the scores. We already know that one of these is the between-groups variance, $V_b = 2.25$. Let us calculate still another variance. We do this by calculating the variance of A_1 alone and the variance of A_2 alone and then averaging the two:

	A_1	x	x^2	A_2	x	x^2
	6	0	0	3	0	0
	5	−1	1	5	2	4
	7	1	1	1	2	4
	8	2	4	4	1	1
	4	−2	4	2	−1	1
ΣX:	30			15		
M:	6			3		
Σx^2:			10			10

$$V_{A_1} = \frac{10}{5} = 2 \qquad V_{A_2} = \frac{10}{5} = 2$$

The variance of A_1 is 2, and the variance of A_2 is 2. The average is 2. Since each of these variances was calculated *separately* and then *averaged*, we call the average variance calculated from them the "within-groups variance." We label this variance V_w, meaning within variance, or within-groups variance. Thus $V_w = 2$. It is important to note here that this variance is unaffected by the difference between the two means.[12]

Now write an equation: $V_t = V_b + V_w$. This equation says that the total variance is made up of the variance between the groups and the variance within the

[12]This is easily shown by subtracting a constant of 3 from the scores of A_1. This makes the mean of A_1 equal to 3. Then, if the variance of A_1 is calculated, it will be the same as before: 2. Obviously the within-groups variance will be the same: 2.

groups. Is it? Substitute the numerical values: $4.25 = 2.25 + 2.00$. Our method works—it shows us, too, that these variances are additive (as calculated).

The variance ideas under discussion can perhaps be clarified with a diagram. In Fig. 6.1, a circle broken up into two parts has been drawn. Let the area of the total circle represent the total variance of the 10 scores, or V_t. The larger shaded portion represents the between-groups variance, or V_b. The smaller unshaded portion represents the error variance, or V_w or V_e. From the diagram one can see that $V_t = V_b + V_e$. (Note the similarity to set thinking and the operation of union.)

A measure of all sources of variance is represented by V_t and a measure of the between-groups variance (or a measure of the effect of the experimental treatment) by V_b. Evidently, adding critical comments to the papers of the A_1 group "caused" the scores on subsequent A_1 individuals' papers to rise. But what is V_w, the within-groups variance? Since, of the total variance, we have accounted for a known source of variance, via the between-groups variance, we assume that the variance remaining is due to chance or random factors. We call it error variance. But, you may say, surely there must be other sources of variance? How about individual differences in intelligence, sex, and so on? Since the teacher assigned the students to the experimental groups at random, we assume that these sources of variance are equally, or approximately equally, distributed between A_1 and A_2. And because of the random assignment we cannot isolate and identify any other sources of variance. So we call the variance remaining error variance, knowing full well that there are probably other sources of variance but assuming, and hoping our assumption is correct, that they have been equally distributed between the two groups.

A Subtractive Demonstration: Removing Between-Groups Variance from Total Variance

Let us demonstrate all this another way by removing from the original set of scores the between-groups variance, using a simple subtractive procedure. First, we let

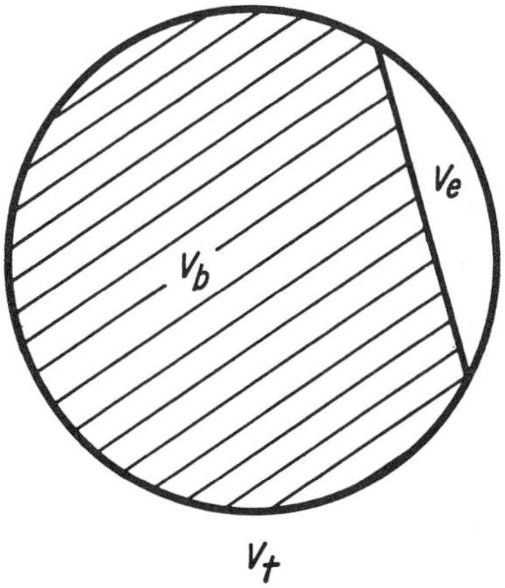

FIG. 6.1

each of the means of A_1 and A_2 be equal to the total mean. The total mean is 4.5. (See above where the mean of all 10 scores was calculated.) Second, we adjust each individual score of A_1 and A_2 by subtracting or adding, as the case may be, an appropriate constant. Since the mean of A_1 is 6, $6-4.5=1.5$ is the constant to be *subtracted* from each A_1 score. The mean of A_2 is 3. Therefore we add $4.5-3=1.5$ to each of the A_2 scores.

Study the "corrected" scores. Compare them with the original scores. Note that they vary less than they did before. Naturally. We removed the between-groups variance, a sizeable portion of the total variance. The variance that remains is that portion of the total variance due, presumably, to chance. We calculate the variance of the "corrected" scores of A_1, A_2, and the total, and note these surprising results:

Correction:	-1.5	$+1.5$
	A_1	A_2
	$6-1.5=4.5$	$3+1.5=4.5$
	$5-1.5=3.5$	$5+1.5=6.5$
	$7-1.5=5.5$	$1+1.5=2.5$
	$8-1.5=6.5$	$4+1.5=5.5$
	$4-1.5=2.5$	$2+1.5=3.5$
ΣX:	22.5	22.5
M:	4.5	4.5

	A_1	x	x^2	A_2	x	x^2
	4.5	0	0	4.5	0	0
	3.5	-1	1	6.5	2	4
	5.5	1	1	2.5	-2	4
	6.5	2	4	5.5	1	1
	2.5	-2	4	3.5	-1	1
ΣX:	22.5			22.5		
M:	4.5			4.5		
Σx^2:			10			10

$$V_{A_1}=\frac{10}{5}=2 \qquad V_{A_2}=\frac{10}{5}=2$$

The within-groups variance is the same as before. It is unaffected by the correction operation. Obviously the between-groups variance is now zero. What about the total variance, V_t? Calculating it, we obtain $\Sigma x_t^2=20$, and $V_t=20/10=2$. Thus the within-groups variance is now equal to the total variance. The reader should study this example carefully until he has firmly grasped what has happened and *why*.

Although the previous example is perhaps sufficient to make the essential points, it may solidify the student's understanding of these basic variance ideas if we extend the example by putting in and pulling out another source of variance. The reader may recall that we knew that the within-groups variance contained variation due to individual differences. Now assume that, instead of randomly assigning all the students to the two groups, the teacher had matched the students on intelligence—and intelligence was related to the criterion measure. That is, she put into the two groups members of pairs with IQ's approximately equal. The outcome of the experiment might be:

	A_1	A_2
	6	3
	5	1
	7	4
	4	2
	8	5
M:	6	3

Note carefully that the *only* difference between this setup and the previous one is that the matching has caused the scores to covary: the A_1 and A_2 measures now have nearly the same rank order. In fact, the coefficient of correlation between the two sets of scores is 0.90. We have here another source of variance: that due to individual differences in intelligence which is reflected in the rank order of the pairs of criterion measures. (The precise relation between the rank order and matching ideas and their effects on variance will be taken up in another chapter. The student should take it on faith for the present that matching produces systematic variance.)

This variance can be calculated and extracted as before, except that there is an additional operation. First equalize the A_1 and A_2 means and "correct" the scores as before. This yields:

Correction:	-1.5	$+1.5$
	A_1	A_2
	4.5	4.5
	3.5	2.5
	5.5	5.5
	2.5	3.5
	6.5	6.5
M:	4.5	4.5

Second, by equalizing the rows (making each *row* mean equal to 4.5 and "correcting" the row scores accordingly) we find the following data:

Correction:	A_1	A_2	Original Means	Corrected Means
0	$4.5 + 0 = 4.5$	$4.5 + 0 = 4.5$	4.5	4.5
$+1.5$	$3.5 + 1.5 = 5.0$	$2.5 + 1.5 = 4.0$	3.0	4.5
-1.0	$5.5 - 1.0 = 4.5$	$5.5 - 1.0 = 4.5$	5.5	4.5
$+1.5$	$2.5 + 1.5 = 4.0$	$3.5 + 1.5 = 5.0$	3.0	4.5
-2.0	$6.5 - 2.0 = 4.5$	$6.5 - 2.0 = 4.5$	6.5	4.5
M:	4.5	4.5	$M_t = 4.5$	

The doubly corrected measures now show very little variance. The variance of the ten doubly corrected scores is 0.10, very small indeed. There is no between-groups (columns) or between-individuals (rows) variance left in the measures, of course. After double correction, all of the total variance is error variance. (As we will see later, when the variances of both columns and rows are extracted like this—although with a quicker and more efficient method—there is no within-groups variance.)

This has been a long operation. A brief recapitulation of the main points may be useful. Any set of measures has a total variance. If the measures from which this variance is calculated have been derived from the responses of human beings, then there will always be at least two sources of variance. One will be due to systematic sources of variation like individual differences of the subjects whose characteristics or accomplishments have been measured and differences between the groups or subgroups involved in research. The other will be due to chance or random error, fluctuations of measures that cannot be accounted for. Sources of systematic variance tend to make scores lean in one direction or another. This is reflected in differences in means, of course. If sex is a systematic source of variance in a study of school achievement, for instance, then the sex variable will tend to act in such a manner that the achievement scores of girls will tend to be higher than those of boys. Sources of random error, on the other hand, tend to make measures fluctuate now this way now that way. Random errors, in other words, are self-compensating; they tend to balance each other out.

In any experiment or study, the independent variable (or variables) is a source of systematic variance—at least it should be. The researcher "wants" the experimental groups to differ systematically. He usually seeks to maximize such variance while controlling or minimizing other sources of variance, both systematic and error. The experimental example given above illustrates the additional idea that these variances are additive, and that because of this additive property, it is possible to analyze a set of scores into systematic and error variance.

Components of Variance

The discussion so far may have convinced the student that any total variance has what will be called "components of variance." The case just considered, however, included one experimental component, A_1 and A_2, one component due to individual differences, and a third component due to random error. We now study the case of two components of systematic experimental variance. To do this, we synthesize the experimental measures, creating them from *known* variance components. We go backwards, in other words. Because we start from "known" sources of variance, from "known" scores, there will be no error in the synthesized scores.

We have a variable X which has three values. Let $X = \{0, 1, 2\}$. We also have another variable Y, which has three values. Let $Y = \{0, 2, 4\}$. X and Y, then, are *known* sources of variance. We assume an ideal experimental situation where there are two independent variables acting *in concert* to produce effects on a dependent variable, Z. That is, each score of X operates with each score of Y to produce a dependent variable score Z. For example, the X score, 0, has no influence. The X score, 1, operates with Y as follows: $\{(1+0), (1+2), (1+4)\}$. Similarly, the X score, 2, operates with Y: $\{(2+0), (2+2), (2+4)\}$. All this is easier to see if we generate Z in clear view:

			Y					Z	
		0	2	4			0	2	4
	0	0+0	0+2	0+4		0	0	2	4
X	1	1+0	1+2	1+4	=	1	1	3	5
	2	2+0	2+2	2+4		2	2	4	6

The set of scores in the 3×3 matrix (a matrix is any rectangular set or array of numbers) is the set of Z scores. The purpose of this example will be lost unless the reader remembers that in practice we do *not* know the X and Y scores; we only know the Z scores. In actual experimental situations we manipulate or set up X and Y. But we only hope they are effective. They may not be. In other words, the sets $X = \{0, 1, 2\}$ and $Y = \{0, 2, 4\}$ can never be known like this. The best we can do is to estimate their influences by estimating the amount of variance in Z due to X and to Y.

The sets X and Y have the following variances:

	X	x	x^2	Y	y	y^2
	0	−1	1	0	−2	4
	1	0	0	2	0	0
	2	1	1	4	2	4
ΣX:	3			6		
M:	1			2		
Σx^2:			2			8

$$V_x = \frac{2}{3} = .67 \qquad V_y = \frac{8}{3} = 2.67$$

The set Z has variance as follows:

	Z	z	z^2
	0	−3	9
	2	−1	1
	4	1	1
	1	−2	4
	3	0	0
	5	2	4
	2	−1	1
	4	1	1
	6	3	9
ΣX:	27		
M:	3		
Σx^2:			30

$$V_z = \frac{30}{9} = 3.33$$

Now $.67 + 2.67 = 3.34$, or $V_z = V_x + V_y$, within errors of rounding.

This example illustrates that, under certain conditions, variances operate additively to produce the experimental measures we analyze. While the example is "pure" and therefore unrealistic, it is not unreasonable. It is possible to think of X and Y as independent variables. They might be level of aspiration and pupil attitudes. And Z might be verbal achievement, a dependent variable. That real scores do not behave exactly this way does not alter the idea. They behave approximately this way. We plan research to make this principle as true as possible, and we analyze data as though it were true. And it works!

Covariance

Covariance is really nothing new. Recall, in an earlier discussion of sets and correlation, that we talked about the relation between two or more variables being analogous to the intersection of sets. Let X be $\{0, 1, 2, 3\}$, a set of attitude measures for four children. Let Y be $\{1, 2, 3, 4\}$, a set of achievement measures of the same children, but not in the same order. Let R be a set of ordered pairs of the elements of X and Y, the rule of pairing being: each individual's attitude and achievement measures are paired, with the attitude measure placed first. Assume that this yields $R = \{(0, 2), (1, 1), (2, 3), (3, 4)\}$. By our previous definition of relation, this set of ordered pairs is a relation, in this case the relation between X and Y. The results of the calculations of the variance of X and the variance of Y are:

	X	x	x^2	Y	y	y^2
	0	−1.5	2.25	2	− .5	.25
	1	− .5	.25	1	−1.5	2.25
	2	.5	.25	3	.5	.25
	3	1.5	2.25	4	1.5	2.25
ΣX:	6			10		
M:	1.5			2.5		
Σx^2:			5.00			5.00

$$V_x = \frac{5}{4} = 1.25 \qquad V_y = \frac{5}{4} = 1.25$$

We now set ourselves a problem. (Note carefully in what follows that we are going to work with deviations from the mean, x's and y's, and not with the original raw scores.) We have calculated the variances of X and Y above by using the x's and y's, that is, the deviations from the respective means of X and Y. If we can calculate the variance of any set of scores, is it not possible to calculate the relation *between* any two sets of scores in a similar way? Is it conceivable that we can calculate the variance of the two sets simultaneously? And if we do so, will this be a measure of the variance of the two sets together? Will this variance also be a measure of the relation between the two sets?

What we want do do is to use some statistical operation analogous to the set operation of intersection, $X \cap Y$. To calculate the variance of X or of Y, we squared the deviations from the mean, the x's or the y's, and then added and averaged them. A natural answer to our problem is to perform an analogous operation on the x's and y's *together*. To calculate the variance of X, we did this first: $(x_1 \cdot x_1), \ldots, (x_4 \cdot x_4) = x_1^2, \ldots, x_4^2$. Why, then, not follow this through with *both* x's and y's, multiplying the ordered pairs like this: $(x_1 \cdot y_1), \ldots, (x_4 \cdot y_4)$? Then, instead of writing Σx^2 or Σy^2, we write Σxy, as follows:

x	$\cdot$	y	$=$	xy
-1.5	$\cdot$	$-.5$	$=$	.75
$-.5$	$\cdot$	-1.5	$=$	.75
.5	$\cdot$	.5	$=$	.25
1.5	$\cdot$	1.5	$=$	2.25
				$\Sigma xy = 4.00$

$$V_{xy} = CoV_{xy} = \frac{4}{4} = 1.00$$

If we calculate the variance of these products—symbolized as V_{xy} or CoV_{xy}—we obtain 1.00, as indicated above. This 1.00, then, can be taken as an index of the relation between the two sets. But it is an unsatisfactory index because its size fluctuates with the ranges and scales of different X's and Y's. That is, it might be 1.00 in this case and 8.75 in another case, making comparisons from case to case difficult and unwieldy.

Before going further, let us give names to Σxy and V_{xy}. Σxy is called the *cross product*, or the sum of the cross products. V_{xy} is called the *covariance*. We will write it CoV with suitable subscripts. Returning to the problem, we need a measure that is comparable from problem to problem. Such a measure—an excellent one, too—is obtained simply by writing a fraction or ratio: the covariance, CoV_{xy}, divided by an average of the variances of X and Y. The average usually taken is the square root of the product of V_x and V_y. The whole formula for our index of relation, then, is

$$R = \frac{CoV_{xy}}{\sqrt{V_x \cdot V_y}}$$

This is one form of the well-known product-moment coefficient of correlation. Using it with our little problem, we obtain:

$$R = \frac{1.00}{\sqrt{(1.25)(1.25)}} = \frac{1.00}{1.25} = .80$$

This index, usually written r, can range from $+1.00$ through 0 to -1.00, as we learned in Chapter 5.

So we have another important source of variation in sets of scores, provided the set elements, the X's and Y's, have been ordered into pairs after conversion into deviation scores. The variation is aptly called *covariance* and is a measure of the relation between the sets of scores.

It can be seen that the definition of relation as a set of ordered pairs leads to several ways to define the relation of the above example:

$$R = \{(x, y); x \text{ and } y \text{ are numbers, } x \text{ always coming first}\}$$

$$xRy = \text{the same as above or ``}x \text{ is related to } y\text{''}$$

$$R = \{(0, 2), (1, 1), (2, 3), (3, 4)\}$$

$$R = \{(-1.5, -.5), (-.5 - 1.5), (.5, .5), (1.5, 1.5)\}$$

$$R_{xy} = \frac{CoV_{xy}}{\sqrt{V_x \cdot V_y}} = \frac{1.00}{1.25} = .80$$

Common Factor Variance

The previous discussion of covariance and correlation leads naturally to another expression used a great deal in statistics and research: *common factor variance*. Common factor variance is the variance shared by two or more variables. The term *factor* is a construct used to indicate a common entity or influence present in different variables. In brief, a factor is a source of variance common to two or more variables. Common factor variance will be symbolized: V_{co}. If only two variables, A and B, are under study, and if certain operations are performed, then the common factor variance is the covariance. The operations alluded to involve too much statistics so we will tackle the problem another way. If a coefficient of correlation has been calculated, then the common factor variance is the coefficient of correlation squared. Squaring the coefficient calculated in the previous section, for example, yields $.80^2 = .64$. This number now has a direct meaning. It means that 64 percent of the variance of B is shared in common with A, or vice versa.[13]

Assume that $r = 1.00$. (We change R to r, the usual symbol for the coefficient of correlation.) Then $r^2 = 1.00$, and all the variance of the sets A and B is common factor variance. The same is true if $r = -1.00$, since $(-1.0)^2 = 1$. Now assume that $r = .00$. Then, obviously, there is no variance common to the two variables. If we let $V(A)$ equal the variance of the set A, and $V(B)$ equal the variance of the set B, then $V(A \cap B)$ equals the variance common to the two sets or variables. In this case $V(A \cap B) = 0$, or $A \cap B = E$, the empty set.

Diagrams to illustrate $r = .00$ and $r = 1.00$ would show the extreme possibilities of set intersection. With $r = .00$, the two sets do not intersect; there would be no overlapping or common area. No variance is shared by A and B. With $r = 1.00$ (or $r = -1.00$), the two sets intersect completely, that is, there is complete overlapping or common area—virtual identity. The variances of A and B are one and the same.

Now take the case above where $r_{xy} = .80$ and $r^2_{xy} = .64$, or 64 percent. We attempt to show the percentage of variance shared in common by the two vari-

[13]The squared coefficient of correlation is called the *coefficient of determination*. If the two correlated variables are A and B, it indicates the percentage of variance in B associated with or "determined by" the variance in A.

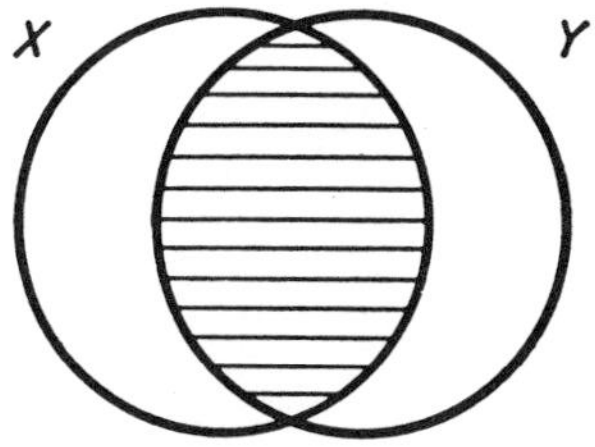

FIG. 6.2

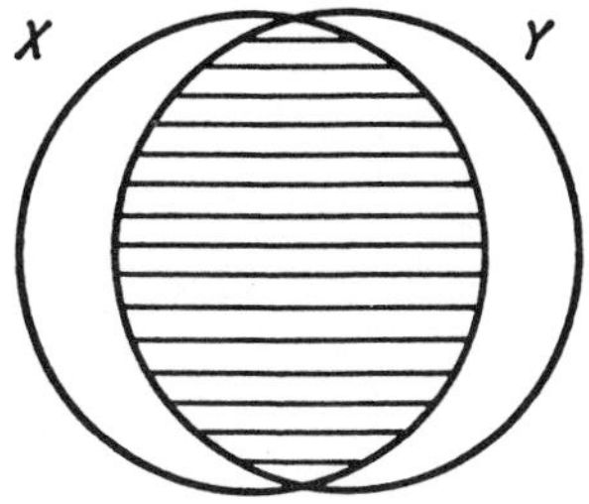

FIG. 6.3

ables (Fig. 6.2).[14] If $r = .90$, then $r^2 = .81$, or 81 percent (Fig. 6.3). On the other hand, take a contrasting case of little shared variance, $r = .30$ and $r^2 = .09$, or 9 percent (Fig. 6.4).

This reasoning can be applied to more than two variables. Assume that we have three variables A, B, and C. Let these variables be represented by the sets A, B, and C. Further, $r_{ab} = .70$, $r_{ac} = .60$, and $r_{bc} = .60$. Then $r^2_{ab} = .49$, $r^2_{ac} = .36$, and $r^2_{bc} = .36$. This is approximately depicted in Fig. 6.5.

Consider the sets A and B and $A \cap B$, just as we did before. Note that about half the areas of the A and B circles are shared ($r^2_{ab} = .49$). Now consider A and C and $A \cap C$ separately. Here the shared area is 36 percent. Sets B, C, and $B \cap C$ are interpreted in the same manner. If we had only the sets (variables) A and B, then the common factor variance would be $A \cap B$, and similarly for A and C considered apart from B, and B and C considered apart from A. But now we have an area of the three circles common to all three variables (triply hatched area of Fig. 6.5). This represents the common factor variance, or, in set terms: $V(A \cap B \cap C)$. In other words, $V(A \cap B \cap C)$, or V_{co}, represents whatever the three variables or measures share in common. In later chapters of the book these ideas will serve us well.

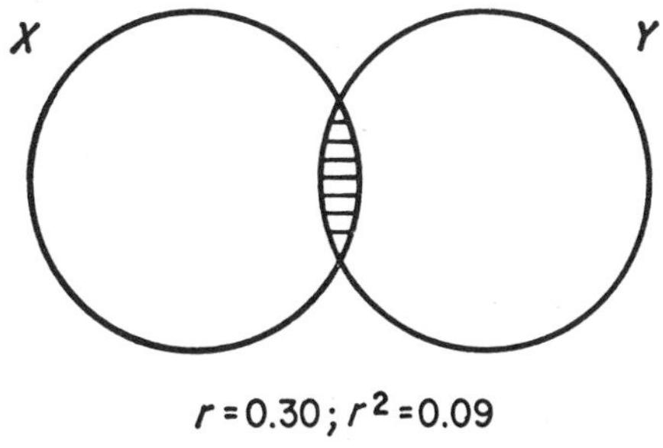

FIG. 6.4

[14]It should be noted that circles usually do not represent actual areas: they are diagrammatic representations of abstractions and are usually not to be literally perceived and interpreted. In what ensues, however, the circles are used to represent areas (roughly). This is a special case, where we consider each variable represented by a circle to be equal to 1. Strictly speaking, the above use of set theoretical ideas is not congruent with precise use of set theory. As in other places in the book, however, I hope that pedagogical necessity justifies the somewhat loose usage of mathematical and other ideas.

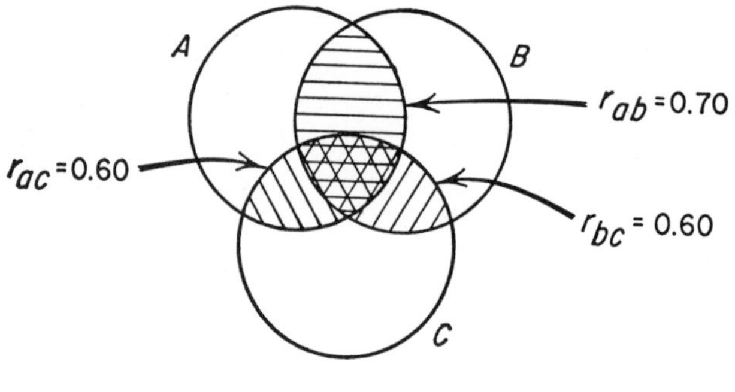

FIG. 6.5

Study Suggestions

1. A social psychologist has done an experiment in which one group, A_1, was given a task to do in the presence of an audience, and another group, A_2, was given the same task to do without an audience. The scores of the two groups on the task, a measure of digital skill, were:

A_1	A_2
5	3
5	4
9	7
8	4
3	2

   (a) Calculate the means and variances of A_1 and A_2, using the method described in the text.
   (b) Calculate the between-groups variance, V_b, and the within-groups variance, V_w.
   (c) Arrange all ten scores in a column, and calculate the total variance, V_t.
   (d) Substitute the calculated values obtained in (b) and (c), above, in the equation: $V_t = V_b + V_w$. Interpret the results.
   [*Answers:* (a) $V_{a_1} = 4.8$; $V_{a_2} = 2.8$; (b) $V_b = 1.0$; $V_w = 3.8$; (c) $V_t = 4.8$.]
2. Add 2 to each of the scores of A_1 in 1, above, and calculate V_t, V_b, and V_w. Which of these variances changed? Which stayed the same? Why?
   [*Answers:* $V_t = 7.8$; $V_b = 4.0$; $V_w = 3.8$.]
3. Equalize the means of A_1 and A_2, in 1, above, by adding a constant of 2 to each of the scores of A_2. Calculate V_t, V_b, and V_w. What is the main difference between these results and those of 1, above? Why?
4. Suppose a sociological researcher obtained measures of conservatism (A), attitude toward religion (B), and anti-Semitism (C) from 100 individuals. The correlations between the variables were: $r_{ab} = .70$; $r_{ac} = .40$; $r_{bc} = .30$. What do these correlations mean? [*Hint:* Square the r's before trying to interpret the relations. Also, think of ordered pairs.]

*5. *Special note:* As early as possible in their study, students of research should start to understand and use the computer. Therefore, from this point on in the book, its use will be encouraged. At the ends of chapters, study suggestions using the computer will be marked with asterisks; these suggestions can be omitted without loss of continuity. To start, the student should read Appendix

C. Then he should learn how to do simple statistical operations using available computer programs and existing facilities at his institution. All installations, for example, have programs for calculating means and standard deviations and for generating random numbers. The present study suggestion will be a useful beginning.

The purpose of this study suggestion is to give the student an intuitive feeling for the variability of simple statistics, the relation between population and sample variances, and between-groups and error variances. Choices are given for students who know how to program and for those who do not, and for those who have a computer available and for those who do not. Generate 20 sets of 100 random numbers between 0 and 99, or 0 and 100. Have the computer calculate sums, means, and variances of each of the 20 sets of numbers, as well as the sum, mean, and variance of all 2000 numbers. (Either write a program to do this, or use a local program. For those with no computer available, Appendix D contains 40 sets of 100 random numbers each of the numbers 0 through 100, with calculated statistics. Simply take any 20 of these 40 sets, preferably at random.

(a) Arrange the 20 means and variances in rank order from highest to lowest. (If you have a friend who is a programmer, he can easily write a short routine in the basic program to do this. Or you can find such a routine in the McCracken reference given at the end of Appendix C, pp. 70–71.) Do the highest and lowest means and variances differ much from the mean and variance of the total group of 2000 numbers? In general, do the means and variances differ much from the general mean and variance?

(b) Calculate the variance of the 20 means. This is, of course, the between-groups variance, V_b. Calculate the error variance, using the formula: $V_e = V_t - V_b$. Now, substitute the obtained variances in the equation: $V_t = V_b + V_e$.

(c) Discuss the meaning of the results after reviewing the discussion in the text.

PART 3

Probability, Randomness, and Sampling

CHAPTER 7

Probability

Probability is an obvious and simple subject. It is a baffling and complex subject. It is a subject we know a great deal about, and a subject we know nothing about. Kindergartners can study probability, and philosophers do. It is dull; it is interesting. Such contradictions are the stuff of probability.

Take the expression "laws of chance." The expression itself is contradictory. Chance or randomness, by definition, is the absence of law. If events can be explained lawfully, they are not random. Then why say "laws of chance"? The answer, too, is contradictory—seemingly. It is possible to gain knowledge from ignorance if we view randomness as ignorance. This is because random events, *in the aggregate*, occur in lawful ways with monotonous regularity. From the disorder of randomness the scientist welds the order of scientific prediction and control.

It is not easy to explain these disconcerting statements. Indeed, philosophers disagree on the answers. Fortunately there is no disagreement on the empirical probabilistic events—or at least very little. Almost all scientists and philosophers will agree that if two dice are thrown a number of times, there will probably be more sevens than twos or twelves. They will also agree that certain events like finding a hundred-dollar bill or winning a sweepstakes are extremely unlikely.

Definition of Probability

What is probability? We ask this question and immediately strike a perplexing problem. Philosophers cannot seem to agree on the answer.[1] This seems to be be-

[1]For discussions of the disagreement, see J. Kemeny, *A Philosopher Looks at Science*. New York: Van Nostrand Reinhold, 1959, chap. 4, 11. Margenau, *The Nature of Physical Reality*, New York: McGraw-Hill, 1950, chap. 13.

cause there are two broad definitions, among others, which seem irreconcilable: the a priori and the a posteriori. The *a priori definition* we owe to a controversial, interesting, and very human genius, Simon Laplace.[2] The probability of an event is the number of favorable cases divided by the total number of (equally possible) cases, or $p = f/(f+u)$, where p is probability, f the number of favorable cases, and u the number of unfavorable cases. The method of calculating probability implied by the definition is a priori in the sense that probability is given, that we can determine the probabilities of events before empirical investigation. This definition is the basis of theoretical mathematical probability.

The *a posteriori*, or *frequency, definition* is empirical in nature. It says that, in an actual series of tests, probability is the ratio of the number of times an event occurs to the total number of trials. With this definition, one approaches probability empirically by performing a series of tests, counting the number of times a certain kind of event happens, and then calculating the ratio. The result of the calculation is the probability of the certain kind of event.

A brief and simple example will make the distinction clear. The a priori probability of throwing a 6 with a die is 1/6, since there are 6 sides to the die, and any side is equally likely to turn up as any other. (Note that the latter part of this statement uses the important assumption of equiprobability—which is not always justified.) That is, out of six possible outcomes, there is one only that is "favorable." Thus $p = 1/6$. Similarly, if one throws two dice, the a priori probability of a 12 is 1/36 since there are 36 possibilities $(6+6, 6+5, \ldots, 6+1, \ldots, 5+5, 5+4, \ldots, 1+1)$ and among these possibilities only one $(6+6)$ yields a 12.

The same samples with an a posteriori or frequency definition, on the other hand, would lead to throwing a die a large number of times and counting the number of 6's to obtain the probability that a 6 will turn up on any one throw. If we throw a die 60 times, the a priori definition tells us that a 6 should appear 10 times, or close to 10 times. (Actually, this is not accurate. There should be many throws. How many is many? An infinite number!) At this point, I took a die and threw it 60 times, shaking it thoroughly before each throw. Six turned up 8 times. The frequency interpretation of probability would say, then, that the probability that 6 will turn up is 8/60. This is called a *relative frequency*. With a small number of throws, obviously, this is not a very good definition of probability.

Practically speaking and for our purposes, the distinction between the a priori and a posteriori definition is not too vital. Following Margenau, we put the two together by saying that the a priori approach supplies a constitutive definition of probability, whereas the a posteriori approach supplies an operational definition of probability.[3] We need to use both approaches; we need to supplement one with the other.

[2]For a good brief discussion of Laplace and his work, see J. Newman, *The World of Mathematics*, vol. 2. New York: Simon and Schuster, 1956, pp. 1316–1324. For Laplace's own definition of probability, see *ibid.*, pp. 1325–1333. Discussions of the two kinds of definitions are given by Margenau, *op. cit.*, chap. 13. (Laplace was famous for using that exasperating expression of mathematicians and statisticians, "It is easy to see that . . . .")

[3]Margenau, *op. cit.*, p. 264.

Sample Space, Sample Points, and Events

To calculate the probability of any outcome, first determine the total number of possible outcomes. With a die the outcomes are 1, 2, 3, 4, 5, 6. Call this the set U. U is the *sample space*, or universe of possible outcomes. The sample space includes all possible outcomes of an "experiment" that are of interest to the experimenter. The primary elements of U are called *elements* or *sample points*. Then let us write $U = \{1, 2, 3, 4, 5, 6\}$, and bring this chapter in line with the set reasoning and method of Part II. Letting x_i = any sample point or element in U, we write $U = \{x_1, x_2, \ldots, x_n\}$. Examples of different U's are: (1) all possible outcomes of tossing two dice (see below), (2) all kindergarten children in such-and-such a school system, and (3) all eligible voters in X County.

Sometimes the determination of the sample space is easy; sometimes it is difficult. The problem is directly analogous to the definition of sets of Chapter 4: sets can be defined by listing all the members of the set, and by giving a rule for the inclusion of elements in a set. In probability theory, both kinds of definition are used. What is U in tossing two coins? We list all the possibilities: $U = \{(H, H), (H, T), (T, H), (T, T)\}$. This is a list definition of U. A rule definition—although we would not use it—might be: $U = \{x; x \text{ is all combinations of } H \text{ and } T\}$. In this case U is the Cartesian product. Let $A_1 = \{H_1, T_1\}$, the first coin; let $A_2 = \{H_2, T_2\}$, the second coin. Recalling that a Cartesian product of two sets is the set of *all* ordered pairs whose first entry is an element of one set and whose second entry is an element of another set, we can diagram the generation of the Cartesian product of this case, $A_1 \times A_2$, as in Fig. 7.1. Notice that there are four lines connecting A_1 and A_2. Thus there are four possibilities: $\{(H_1, H_2), (H_1, T_2), (T_1, H_2), (T_1, T_2)\}$. This thinking and procedure can be used in defining many sample spaces of U's, although the actual procedure can be tedious.

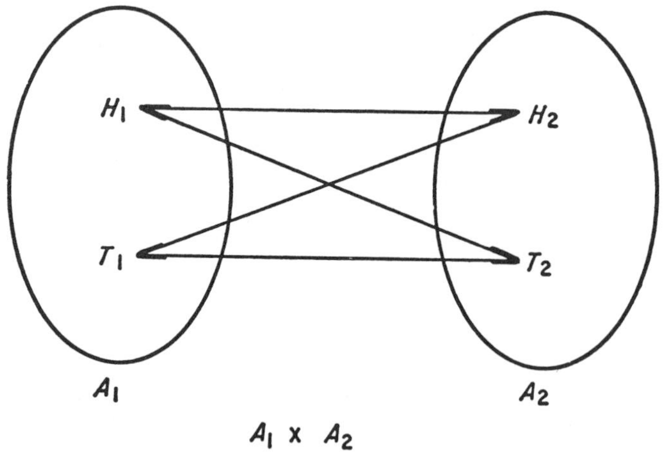

FIG. 7.1

With two dice, what is U? Think of the Cartesian product of two sets and you will probably have little trouble. Let A_1 be the outcomes or points of the first die: $\{1, 2, 3, 4, 5, 6\}$. Let A_2 be the outcomes or points of the second die. Then $U = A_1 \times A_2 = \{(1, 1), (1, 2), \ldots, (5, 6), (6, 6)\}$. We can diagram this as we diagrammed the coin example, but counting the lines would be more difficult. There are too many of them. We can know the number of possible outcomes simply by $6 \times 6 = 36$, or in a formula: mn, where m is the number of possible outcomes of the first set, and n is the number of possible outcomes of the second set.

It is often possible to solve difficult probability problems by using trees. Trees define sample spaces, logical possibilities, with clarity and precision. A *tree* is a diagram that gives all possible alternatives or outcomes for combinations of sets by providing paths and set points. This definition is a bit unwieldy. Illustration is better. Take the coin example (we turn the tree on its side). Its tree is shown in Fig. 7.2.

To determine the number of possible alternatives, just count the number of alternatives or points at the "top" of the tree. In this case, there are four alternatives. To name the alternatives, read off, for each end point, the points that led to it, for example, the first alternative is (H_1, H_2). Obviously, three, four, or more coins can be used. The only trouble is that the procedure is tedious because of the large number of alternatives. The tree for three coins is illustrated in Fig. 7.3. There are eight possible alternatives, outcomes, or sample points: $U = \{(H_1, H_2, H_3), (H_1, H_2, T_3), \ldots, (T_1, T_2, T_3)\}$. (The elements of this set are called ordered triples.)

Sample points of a sample space may seem a bit confusing to the reader, because two kinds of points have been discussed without differentiation. Another term and its use may help clear up this possible confusion. An *event* is a subset of U. Any element of a set is also a subset of the set. Recall that with set $A = \{a_1, a_2\}$, for example, both $\{a_1\}$ and $\{a_2\}$ are subsets of A, as well as $\{a_1, a_2\}$, and $\{\ \}$, the empty set. Identically, all the outcomes of Figs. 7.2 and 7.3, for example,

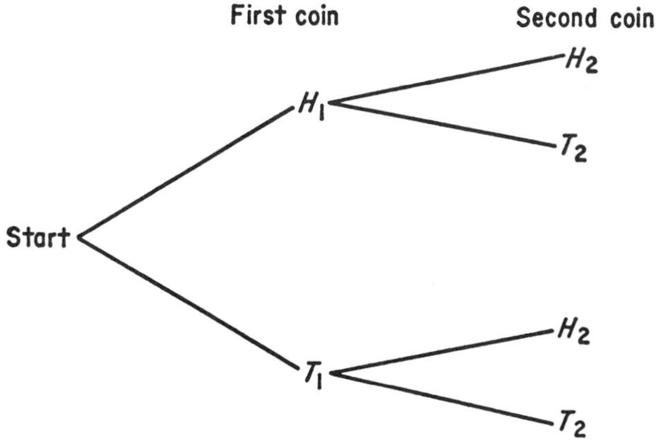

FIG. 7.2

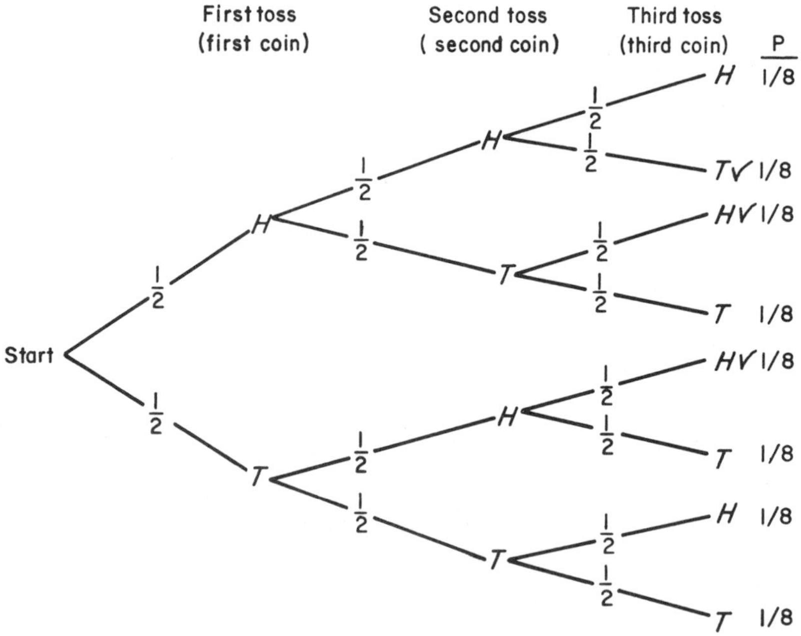

FIG. 7.3

(H_1, T_2), (T_1, H_2), and (T_1, H_2, T_3), are subsets of their respective U's. Therefore they are events, too—by definition. But in the usual usage, events are more encompassing than points. All points are events (subsets), but not all events are points. Or, a point or outcome is a special kind of event, the simplest kind. Any time we state a proposition, we describe an event. We ask, for instance, "If two coins are thrown, what is the probability of getting two heads?" The "two heads" is an event. It so happens, in this case, that it is also a sample point. But suppose we asked, "What is the probability of getting at least one head?" "At least one head" is an event, but not a sample point, because it includes, in this case, three sample points: (H_1, H_2), (H_1, T_2), and (T_1, H_2). (See Fig. 7.2).

Determining Probabilities with Coins

Suppose we toss a new coin three times. We write $p(\text{H}) = 1/2$ and $p(\text{T}) = 1/2$, meaning the probability of heads is 1/2, and similarly for tails. We assume, then, equiprobability. The sample space for three tosses of a coin (or one toss of three coins) is: $U = \{(H, H, H), (H, H, T), (H, T, H), (H, T, T), (T, H, H), (T, H, T), (T, T, H), (T, T, T)\}$. Note that if we pay no attention to the order of heads and tails, we obtain one case of 3 heads, one case of 3 tails, three cases of 2 heads and 1 tail, and three cases of 2 tails and 1 head. The probability of each of the eight outcomes is obviously 1/8. Thus the probability of 3 heads is 1/8, and the probability of 3 tails is 1/8. The probability of 2 heads and 1 tail, on the other hand, is 3/8, and similarly for the probability of 2 tails and 1 head.

The probabilities of all the points in the sample space must add up to 1.00. It also follows that *probabilities are always positive*. If we write a probability tree for the three-toss experiment, it looks like Fig. 7.3. Each complete path of the tree (from the start to the third toss) is a sample point. All the paths comprise the sample space. The single path sections are labeled with the probabilities, in this case all of them are labeled with "1/8." This leads naturally to the statement of a basic principle: If the outcomes at the different points in the tree, that is, at the first, second, and third tosses, are independent of each other (that is, if one outcome does not influence another in any way), then the probability of any sample point (*HHH* perhaps) is the product of the probabilities of the separate outcomes. For example, the probability of 3 heads is $1/2 \times 1/2 \times 1/2 = 1/8$.

Another principle is: *To obtain the probability of any event, add the probabilities of the sample points that comprise that event.* For example, what is the probability of tossing 2 heads and 1 tail? We look at the paths in the tree that have 2 heads and 1 tail. We find that there are 3 of them. (They are checked in Fig. 7.3.) Thus, $1/8 + 1/8 + 1/8 = 3/8$. In set language, we find the subsets (events) of U and note their probabilities. The subset of U of the type "2 heads and 1 tail" are, from the tree or the previous definition of U, $\{(H, H, T), (H, T, H), (T, H, H)\}$. Call this the set A_1. Then $p(A_1) = 3/8$.

This procedure can be followed with the experiment of 100 tosses, but it is much too laborious. Instead, to get the theoretical expectations, we merely multiply the number of tosses by the probability of any one of them, $100 \times 1/2 = 50$, to get the *expected* number of heads (or tails). This can be done because all the probabilites are the same. A big and important question is: In actual experiments in which we throw 100 coins, will we get *exactly* 50 heads? No, not often: about 8 times in 100 such experiments. This can be written: $p = 8/100$ or .08. (Probabilities can be written in fractional or decimal forms, more usually in decimal form.)

An Experiment with Dice

I threw two new dice 72 times under carefully controlled conditions. If I add the number of spots on the two dice on all 72 throws, I will obtain a set of sums from 2 to 12. Some of these outcomes (sums) will turn up more frequently than others simply because there are more ways for them to do so. For example, there is only one way for 2 or for 12 to turn up: $1+1$ and $6+6$, but there are three ways for a 4 to turn up: $1+3$, $3+1$, and $2+2$. If this be so, then the probabilities for getting different sums must be different. The game of craps is based on these differences in frequency expectations.

To solve the a priori probability problem, we must first define the sample space: $U = \{(1, 1), (1, 2), (1, 3), \ldots, (6, 4), (6, 5), (6, 6)\}$. That is, we pair each number of the first die with each number of the second die in turn (the Cartesian product again). This can easily be seen if we set up this procedure in a matrix (see Table 7.1). Suppose we want to know the probability of the event—a very important event, too—"a 7 turns up." Simply count the number of 7's in the table. There are six of them nicely arrayed along the center diagonal. There are 36 sample points in U, obtained by some method of enumerating them, as above, or

TABLE **7.1** MATRIX OF POSSIBLE OUTCOMES WITH TWO DICE

		Second Die					
		1	2	3	4	5	6
	1	2	3	4	5	6	7
	2	3	4	5	6	7	8
First	3	4	5	6	7	8	9
Die	4	5	6	7	8	9	10
	5	6	7	8	9	10	11
	6	7	8	9	10	11	12

simply by using the formula mn, which says: Multiply the number of possibilities of the first thing by the number of possibilities of the second thing. This method can be defined: When there are m ways of doing something, A, and n ways of doing something else, B, then, if the n ways of doing B are independent of the m ways of doing A, there are $m \cdot n$ ways of doing both A and B.[4]

Applied to the dice problem, $mn = 6 \times 6 = 36$. Assuming equipossibility again, the probability of any *single* outcome is 1/36. The probability of a 12, for instance, is 1/36. The probability of a 4, however, is different. Since 4 occurs three times in the table above, we must add the probabilities for each of these elements of the sample space: $1/36 + 1/36 + 1/36 = 3/36$. Thus $p(4) = 3/36 = 1/12$. As we have seen, the probability of a 7 is $p(7) = 6/36 = 1/6$. The probability of an 8 is $p(8) = 5/36$. Note, too, that we can calculate the probabilities of combinations of events. Gamblers often bet on such combinations. For example, what is the probability of a 4 *or* a 10? In set language, this is a *union* question: $p(4 \cup 10)$. Count the number of 4's and 10's in the table. There are three 4's and three 10's. Thus $p(4 \cup 10) = 6/36$.

Counting, in Table 7.1, the probabilities of each kind of outcome, we lay out a table of expected frequencies (f_e) for 36 throws. Then simply double these frequencies to get the expected (a priori) frequencies for 72 throws. We juxtapose against these expected frequencies the frequencies obtained when two dice were actually thrown 72 times. The absolute differences between expected and obtained frequencies are then apparent. The results are laid out in Table 7.2.

The discrepancies are not great. In fact, by actual statistical test, they do not differ significantly from chance expectation. The a priori method seems to have virtue.

Compound Events

It is possible to do compound experiments and calculate the probabilities of compound events. For example, if a die is thrown *and* a coin is tossed, what is the probability of the event 4 *and* tails? Any particular combination of die face and

[4]This principle can be extended to more than two things. If, for example, there are three things, A, B, and C, then the formula is mnr.

TABLE 7.2 EXPECTED AND OBTAINED FREQUENCIES OF SUMS OF TWO DICE THROWN 72 TIMES

Sum of Dice	2	3	4	5	6	7	8	9	10	11	12
$f_e(36)$	1	2	3	4	5	6	5	4	3	2	1
$f_e(72)$	2	4	6	8	10	12	10	8	6	4	2
$f_o(72)$	4	2	6	6	10	15	7	11	6	4	1
Difference	2	2	0	2	0	3	3	3	0	0	1

coin face has a probability of 1/12, since, say, $p(T) = 1/2$ and $p(4) = 1/6$, and $1/2 \times 1/6 = 1/12$. One can ask: What is the probability of getting an even-numbered die face *and* heads? (The probability is 1/4. Why?) One draws a tree similar to that of Figure 7.3, except that both kinds of events, die outcomes and coin outcomes, must appear in the tree.

Compound events are more interesting than single events—and more useful in research. Relations can be studied with them. Take the following hypothetical example. Suppose that 100 people respond to two questions, one on liberalizing abortion and the other on the protection of private property. If we assume that there is no relation whatever between the two questions—probably a questionable assumption—and 60 percent of the people respond Yes to the first question and 70 percent Yes to the second question, the probability of the joint event, Yes to both questions, is $.60 \times .70 = .42$. What use might this be in actual research? If we wanted to know whether there was a relation between the attitudes expressed by the two questions, then the joint percentage obtained from actual data could be compared to the 42 percent, since the latter is the percentage that would occur when there was a zero relation between the two questions. Suppose, for instance, we actually obtained a joint percentage of 55. Then it would appear that the answer to the first question is somehow related to the answer to the second question. Actual research constantly assesses the probabilities of compound events to ascertain the existence of relations between sets of events. More on this shortly.

We have based most of the discussion until now on the assumption of equiprobability. But in many situations the assumption is not justified. Notice how absurd it would be to reason like this: The probability of one's dying tomorrow is one-half. Why? Because one will either die tomorrow or not die tomorrow. Since there are two possibilities, they each have probability of occurrence of one-half. Any insurance company that operated this way would go out of business. Suppose that a political scientist were studying, among other things, the relation between political preferences and religious preferences. If he assumed that the probabilities that a Catholic would be a Democrat or a Republican were equal, he would err seriously. Obviously, researchers have to know something about the phenomena they are studying. Some attempt must be made, before using probability theory, to check the assumptions being used. This is not always easy.

Some Formal Theory

We have the *sample space* U, with subsets $A, B, \ldots$. The elements of U—and *of* $A, B, \ldots$—*are* $a_i, b_i, \ldots$, that is, $a_1, a_2, \ldots, a_n$ and $b_1, b_2, \ldots, b_n$, and so forth. A, B, and so forth, are *events*. Actually, although we have often talked about the probability of a single occurrence, we really mean the probability of a type of occurrence. When we talk about the probability of any single event of U, for instance, we can only do so because any particular member of U is conceived as representative of all of U. And similarly for the probabilities of subsets $A, B, \ldots, K$ of U. The probability of U is 1; the probability of E, the empty set, is 0. Or $p(U) = 1.00$; $p(E) = 0$. To determine the probability of any subset of U, a *measure* of the set must be assigned. In order to assign such a measure, we must assign a *weight* to each element of U and thus to each element of the subsets of U. A weight is defined:[5]

> A *weight* is a positive number assigned to each element, x, in U, and written $w(x)$, such that the sum of all these weights, $\Sigma w(x)$, is equal to 1.

This is a function notion; w is called a *weight function*. It is a rule that assigns weights to elements of a set, U, in such a way that the sum of the weights is equal to 1, that is, $w_1 + w_2 + w_3 + \cdots + w_n = 1.00$, and $w_i = 1/n$. The weights are equal, assuming equiprobability; each weight is a fraction with 1 in the numerator and the number of cases, n, is the denominator. In the previous experiment of the tosses of a coin (Fig. 7.3), the weights assigned to each element of U, U being all the outcomes, are all 1/8. The sum of all the weight functions, $w(x)$, is $1/8 + 1/8 + \cdots + 1/8 = 1$. In probability theory, the sum of the elements of the sample space must always equal 1.

To get from weights to the measure of a set is easy. We define the measure of a set thus: The *measure* of a set is the sum of the weights of the elements of the set:[6]

$$\sum_{x \text{ in } U} w(x) \quad \text{or} \quad \sum_{x \text{ in } A} w(x)$$

We write $m(A)$, meaning "The measure of the set A." This simply means the sum of the weights of the elements in the set A.

By way of example, suppose that we randomly sample children from the 400 children of the fourth grade of a school system. Then U is all 400 children. Each child is a sample point of U. Each child is an x in U. The probability of selecting any one child at random is 1/400. Let A = the boys in U, and B = the girls in U. There are 100 boys and 300 girls. Each boy is assigned the weight 1/400, and each girl is assigned the weight 1/400. Suppose we wish to sample, all together, 100

[5]The approach used here follows to some extent that found in J. Kemeny, J. Snell, and G. Thompson, *Introduction to Finite Mathematics*, 2d ed. Englewood Cliffs, N.J.: Prentice-Hall, 1966, chap. IV, and J. Kemeny, H. Mirkil, J. Snell, and G. Thompson, *Finite Mathematical Structures*. Englewood Cliffs, N.J.: Prentice-Hall, 1959, chap. 30.

[6]Note that the sum of the weights in a subset A of U does not have to equal 1. In fact, it is usually less than 1.

children. Our expectation is, then, 25 boys and 75 girls in the sample. The measure of the set A, $m(A)$, is the sum of the weights of all the elements in A. Since there are 100 boys in U, we sum the 100 weights: $1/400 + 1/400 + \cdots + 1/400 = 100/400 = 1/4$, or

$$m(A) = \sum_{x \text{ in } A} w(x) = \frac{1}{4}$$

Similarly,

$$m(B) = \sum_{x \text{ in } B} w(x) = \frac{3}{4}$$

For the set B, the girls, we sum 300 weights, each of them being 1/400. In short, the sums of the weights are the probabilities. That is, the measure of a set is the probability of a member of the set being chosen. Thus we can say that the probability that a member of the sample of 400 children will be a boy is 1/4, and the probability that the selected member will be a girl is 3/4. To determine the expected frequencies, simply multiply the sample size by these probabilities: $1/4 \times 100 = 25$ and $3/4 \times 100 = 75$.

Probability has three fundamental properties:

1. The measure of any set, as defined above, is greater than or equal to 0 and less than or equal to 1. In brief, probabilities (measures of sets) are either 0, 1, or in between.
2. The measure of a set, $m(A)$, equals 0 if and only if there are no members in A, that is, A is empty.
3. Let A and B be sets. If A and B are disjoint, that is, $A \cap B = E$, then:

$$m(A \cup B) = m(A) + m(B)$$

This equation simply says that when no members of A and B are shared in common, then the probability of either A or B or both is equal to the combined probabilities of A and B.

There is no need to give an example to illustrate (1). We have had several earlier. To illustrate (2), assume, in the boys-girls example, that we asked the probability of drawing a teacher in the sample. But U did not include teachers. Let C be the set of fourth-grade teachers. In this case, the set C is empty, and $m(C) = 0$. Use the same boys-girls example to illustrate (3). Let A be the set of boys, B the set of girls. Then $m(A \cup B) = m(A) + m(B)$. But $m(A \cup B) = 1.00$, because they were the only subsets of U. And we learned that $m(A) = 1/4$ and $m(B) = 3/4$. It is obvious that the equation holds.

Compound Events and Their Probabilities

It is now necessary to examine compound events and their probabilities. First, we examine certain counting problems and the ways in which counting is related to set theory and probability theory. It will be found that if the basic theory is understood, the application of probability theory to research problems is considerably facilitated. In addition, the interpretation of data becomes less subject to error.

Assume that a group of sixth-grade children has been studied, that there are 100 children altogether in the group, 60 boys and 40 girls. A useful function is the *numerical function*, which assigns to any set the number of members in the set. The number of members in A is $n(A)$. In this case $n(U)=100$, $n(A)=60$, and $n(B)=40$, where A is the set of boys and B the set of girls, both subsets of U, the 100 sixth-grade children. If there is no overlap between two sets, $A \cap B = E$, then the following equation holds:

$$n(A \cup B) = n(A) + n(B) \tag{7.1}$$

Recall that earlier the frequency definition of probability was given as:

$$p = \frac{f}{f+u} \tag{7.2}$$

where f is the number of favorable cases, and u the number of unfavorable cases. The numerator is $n(F)$ and the denominator $n(U)$, the total number of possible cases. Similarly, we can divide through the terms of Eq. 7.1 by $n(U)$:

$$\frac{n(A \cup B)}{n(U)} = \frac{n(A)}{n(U)} + \frac{n(B)}{n(U)} \tag{7.3}$$

This reduces to probabilities, analogously to Eq. 7.2:

$$p(A \cup B) = p(A) + p(B) \tag{7.4}$$

Using the example of the 100 children, and substituting values in Eq. 7.3, we get

$$\frac{100}{100} = \frac{60}{100} + \frac{40}{100}$$

which yields for Eq. 7.4:

$$1.00 = .60 + .40$$

In many cases, two (or more) sets in which we are interested are not disjoint. Rather, they overlap. When this is so, then $A \cap B \neq E$, and it is not true that $n(A \cup B) = n(A) + n(B)$. Look at Fig. 7.4.

Here A and B are subsets of U; sample points are indicated by dots. The number of sample points in A is 8; the number in B is 6. There are two sample points in $A \cap B$. Thus the equation above does not hold. If we calculate all the points in $A \cup B$ with Eq. 7.1, we get $8+6=14$ points. But there are only 12 points. The equation has to be altered to a more general equation that fits all cases:

$$n(A \cup B) = n(A) + n(B) - n(A \cap B) \tag{7.5}$$

It should be clear that the error when Eq. 7.1 is used results from counting the two points of $A \cap B$ twice. Therefore we subtract $n(A \cap B)$ once, which

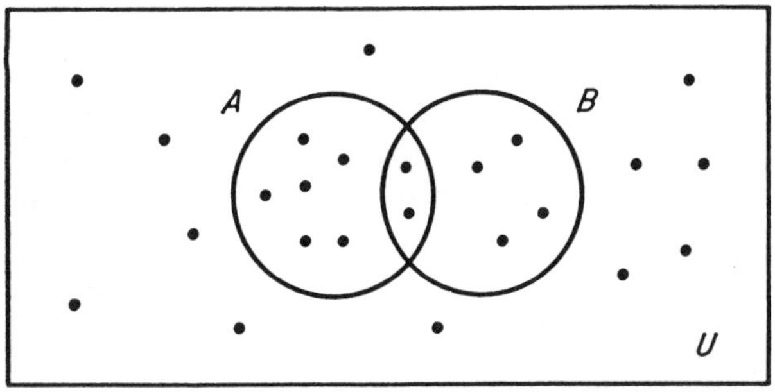

FIG. 7.4

corrects the equation. It now fits any possibility. If, for example, $n(A \cap B) = E$, the empty set, Eq. 7.5 reduces to (7.1). Eq. 7.1 is a special case of (7.5). Calculating the number of sample points in $A \cup B$ of Fig. 7.4, then, we get: $n(A \cup B) = 8+6-2 = 12$. If we divide Eq. 7.5 through by $n(U)$, as in (7.3):

$$p(A \cup B) = p(A) + p(B) - p(A \cap B) \tag{7.6}$$

Substituting our number of dots or sample points, we find that

$$\frac{12}{24} = \frac{8}{24} + \frac{6}{24} - \frac{2}{24}$$
$$.50 = .33 + .25 - .08$$

In a random sample of U, then, the probabilities of an element being a member of $A, B, A \cap B$, and $A \cup B$, respectively, are .33, .25, .08, and .50.

Independence, Mutual Exclusiveness, and Exhaustiveness

Think of the following equations, variants of which must be asked by any researcher. Does the occurrence of this event, A, preclude the possibility of the occurrence of this other event, B? Does the occurrence of event A have an influence on the occurrence of event B? Are the events A, B, and C related? When A has occurred, does this influence the outcomes of B—and, perhaps, C? Do the events A, B, C, and D exhaust the possibilities? Or are there, perhaps, other possibilities E, F, and so on? Suppose, for instance, that a researcher is studying board of education decisions and their relation to, say, political preference, religious preference, education, and other variables. In order to relate these variables to board decisions, he has to have some method of classifying the decisions. One of the first questions he must ask is, "Have I exhausted all possibilities in my classification system?" He should also ask, "If a board makes one kind of decision, does this preclude the possibility of making another kind of decision?" "If the board members vote Yes on this issue, does this make it logically impossible for them to vote Yes on the next issue?" Perhaps the most important question the researcher can ask, however, is, "If a board makes a particular decision, does this decision influence its action on any other decision?"

We have been talking about exhaustiveness, mutual exclusiveness, and independence. We now define them in a more detailed manner and use them in probability examples.

Let A and B be subsets of U. We ask the questions: Are there any other subsets of U (other than the empty set)? Do A and B exhaust the sample space? Are all the sample points of the sample space U included in A or in B? A simple example is: Let $A = \{H, T\}$; let $B = \{1, 2, 3, 4, 5, 6\}$. If we toss a coin and throw a die together, what are the possibilities? Unless *all* the possibilities are exhausted, we cannot solve the probability problem. There are 12 possibilities (2×6). The sets A and B exhaust the sample space. (This is of course obvious, since A and B generated the sample space.) Now take a more realistic example. Suppose a researcher is studying religious preferences. He sets up the following system to categorize individuals: {Protestants, Catholics, Jews}. What he has done, implicitly, is to set up U = all people (with or without religious preferences) and subsets of U, A = Protestants, B = Catholics, C = Jews. The set question is: Does $A \cup B \cup C = U$? Has he exhausted all religious preferences? How about Buddhists? How about atheists? And so on.

Exhaustiveness, then, simply means that the subsets of U use up all the sample space, or $A \cup B \cup \cdots \cup K = U$, where $A, B, \ldots, K$ are subsets of U, the sample space. In probability language, this means: $p(A \cup B \cup \cdots \cup K) = 1.00$. Unless the sample space, U, is used up, so to speak, probabilities cannot be adequately calculated. For example, in the religious-preference example, suppose we thought that $A \cup B \cup C = U$, but in fact there were a large number of individuals with no particular religious preference. So, really, $A \cup B \cup C \cup D = U$, where D is the subset of individuals with no religious preference. The probabilities calculated on the assumption of this equation would be quite different than those based on the assumption of the earlier equation.

Mutual exclusiveness is easier to understand. Succinctly, two events, A and B, are *mutually exclusive* when they are disjoint, or when $A \cap B = E$. That is, when the intersection of two (or more) sets is the empty set—or when two sets have no elements in common—the sets are said to be mutually exclusive. This is the same as saying, again in probability language, $p(A \cap B) = 0$. It is more convenient for the researcher when events are mutually exclusive, because he can then add the probabilities of events. We state a principle in set and probability terms: If the events (sets) A, B, and C are *mutually exclusive*, then $p(A \cup B \cup C) = p(A) + p(B) + p(C)$. This is the special case of the more general principle we discussed in the previous section. (See Eqs. 7.1, 7.4, 7.5, and 7.6 and the accompanying discussion, above.)

One of the chief purposes of research design is to set up conditions of independence of events so that conditions of dependence of events can be adequately studied. Two events, A and B, are *statistically independent* if the following equation holds:

$$p(A \cap B) = p(A) \cdot p(B) \tag{7.7}$$

which says that the probability of A and B both occurring is equal to the probability of A times the probability of B. Easy and clear examples of independent events are dice throws and coin tosses. If A is the event of a die throw and B is the event of a coin toss, and $p(A) = 1/6$ and $p(B) = 1/2$, then, if $p(A) \cdot p(B) = 1/6 \cdot 1/2 = 1/12$, A and B are independent. If we toss a coin ten times, one toss has no influence on any other toss. The tosses are independent. So are the throws of dice. Similarly, when we simultaneously throw a die and toss a coin, the events of throwing a die, A, and tossing a coin, B, are independent. The outcome of a die throw has no influence on the toss of a coin—and vice versa. Unfortunately, this neat model does not always apply in research situations.

The commonsense notion of the so-called law of averages is utterly erroneous, but it nicely illustrates lack of understanding of independence. It says something to the effect that if there is a large number of occurrences of an event, then the chance of that event occurring on the next trial is smaller. Suppose a coin is being tossed. Heads has come up five times in a row. The commonsense notion of the "law of averages" would lead one to believe that there is a greater chance of getting tails on the next toss. Not so. The probability is still 1/2. Each toss is an independent event. Let's look at an example.

Suppose students in a college class are taking an examination. They are working under the usual conditions of no communication, no looking at each other's papers, and so forth. The responses of any student can be considered independent of the responses of any other student. Can the responses to the items within the test be considered independent? Suppose that the answer to one item later in the test is embedded in an item earlier in the test. The probability of getting the later item correct by chance, say, is 1/4. But the fact that the answer was given earlier can change this probability. With some students it might even become 1.00. What is important for the researcher to know is that independence is often difficult to achieve and that lack of independence when research operations assume independence can seriously affect the interpretation of data.

Suppose we rank order examination papers and then assign grades on the basis of the ranks. This is a perfectly legitimate and useful procedure. But it must be realized that the grades given by the rank-order method are not independent (if they ever could be). Take five such papers. After reading them one is ranked as the first (the best), the second next, and so on through the five papers. We assign the number "1" to the first, "2" to the second, "3" to the third, "4" to the fourth, and "5" to the fifth. After using up 1, we have only 2, 3, 4, and 5 left. After using up 2, only 3, 4, and 5 remain. When we assign 4, obviously we must assign 5 to the remaining examination. In short, the assignment of 5 was influenced by the assignment of 4—and also 1, 2, and 3. The assignment events are not independent. One may ask, "Does this matter?" Suppose we take the ranks, treat them as scores, and make inferences about mean differences between groups, say between two classes. The statistical test used to do this is probably based on the coin-dice paradigm with its pristine independence. But we have not followed this model—one of its most important assumptions, independence has been ignored.

When research events lack independence, statistical tests lack a certain validity. A χ^2 test, for example, assumes that the events—responses of individuals to an interview question, say—recorded in the cells of a crossbreak table, are independent of each other. If the recorded events are not independent of each other, then the basis of the statistical test and the inferences drawn from it are corrupted.

It will be instructive to illustrate this discussion of independence with research examples, actual and hypothetical. In a fascinating account of research on the aggressive behavior of apes, Hebb and Thompson present the data of Table 7.3.[7] The problem was the relation between sex and aggression. Samples of the behavior of 30 adult chimpanzees were taken in an effort to study individual differences in ape temperament. Without going into details, it can be said that one analysis of the observations showed that males and females displayed friendly behavior about equally often, but that males were more aggressive. Hebb and Thompson's data on this observation seem to say: "Watch out for males!" But, the authors point out, this is quite out of line with the experience of the apes' caretakers. Nineteen out of 20 cuts and scratches were inflicted by females! Then Hebb and Thompson pursued the interesting, if disconcerting, idea of tabulating incidence of aggressive acts in two ways: (1) when such were preceded by quasi-aggression, that is, by warning of attack, and (2) when aggressive acts were preceded by friendly behavior. The resulting incidences of behavior are given in Table 7.3. The table seems to indicate: "Watch out for females when they are friendly!"

TABLE **7.3** EXAMPLE OF DATA EXHIBITING POSSIBLE LACK OF INDEPENDENCE, HEBB DATA[a]

	Males ($n = 8$)	Females ($n = 22$)
Quasi-Aggression, then Aggression	37	0
Friendly Behavior, then Aggression	0	15

[a]Table entries are numbers of acts of male and female chimpanzees of the kinds indicated by the margin labels on the left.

The data in the table cannot be validly analyzed statistically, since the numbers indicate the frequency of kinds of acts. But all 37 acts by males may have been committed by only one or two of them. If one ape had committed all 37 acts, then it should be clear that the acts were not independent of each other. The ape might simply have had a bad temper. And bad tempers notoriously create lack of independence in animal and human acts.

The second example is hypothetical. Suppose a researcher decides to sample 100 board of education decisions. He has a variety of ways to do this. He can sample many decisions from a few boards, or he can sample many decisions from

[7]D. Hebb and W. Thompson, "The Social Significance of Animal Studies." In G. Lindzey, ed., *Handbook of Social Psychology*, vol. I. Reading, Mass.: Addison-Wesley, 1954, pp. 532–562. The table is on p. 546.

many boards. Or he may do both. If he wants to be assured of the independence of the decisions, then he should sample many decisions from many boards of education. Theoretically, he should take only one decision from each board. Then he is assured of independence—at least as much as such assurance is possible. True, his sample of education boards might include two in adjoining districts, one of which watches the other's decisions before making its own. But this is not too likely. As soon as he takes more than one decision from the same board, however, he must entertain the notion that decisions of the kind A may influence decisions of the kind B. Decision A may influence decision B, for example, because the board members may wish to appear consistent. Both decisions may involve expenditures for instructional equipment, and since the board adopted a liberal policy on A it must adopt a liberal policy on B.

Suppose an investigator calculated the probability that an obtained result—for example, the difference between two means—was due to chance. This probability was 5/100, or .05. This means that there were approximately five chances in 100 that his result was due to chance. That is, if he repeated the experimental conditions 100 times *without* the experimental manipulation, approximately five of those times he could obtain a mean difference as large as the one he obtained *with* the experimental manipulation. Feeling shaky about the result—after all, there *are* five chances in 100 that the result could have been due to chance—he carefully repeated the whole experiment. He obtained substantially the same result (luck!). Having controlled everything carefully to be sure the two experiments were independent, he calculated the probability that the two results were due to chance. This probability was approximately .02. Thus we see both one of the values of independence in experimentation and the importance of replication of results.[8]

Note, finally, that the formula for independence works two ways. One, it tells us, if events are independent and we know the probabilities of the separate events, the probability of both events occurring *by chance*. If it is found that dice repeatedly show 12's, say, then there is probably something wrong with the dice. If a gambler notes that another gambler seems always to win, he will of course get suspicious. The chances of continually winning a fair game or a relatively fair game are small. It can happen, of course, but it is unlikely to happen. In research, it is unlikely that one would get two or three significant results by chance. *Something* beyond chance must probably be operating—hopefully the independent variable.

Two, the formula can be turned around, so to speak. It can tell the researcher what he must do to allow himself the advantage of the multiplicative probabilities.

[8]The method of calculating these combined probabilities was proposed by Fisher and is described in F. Mosteller and R. Bush, "Selected Quantitative Techniques." In G. Lindzey, ed., *Handbook of Social Psychology*, vol. I. Reading, Mass.: Addison-Wesley, 1954, pp. 328–331. The astute student may wonder why the set principle applied to probability, $p(A \cap B) = p(A) \cdot p(B)$, is not applicable. That is, why not calculate $.05 \times .05 = .0025$? Mosteller and Bush explain this point. Since it is a rather difficult and moot point, we do not consider it in this book. All the reader need do is to remember that the probability of getting, say, a substantial difference between means in the same direction on repeated experiments is considerably smaller than getting such a difference once. Thus one can be surer of one's data and conclusions, other things equal.

He must, if it is at all possible, plan his research so that events are independent. That this is easier said than done will become quite evident before this book is finished.

Conditional Probability

In all research and perhaps especially in social scientific and educational research, events are often not independent. Look at independence in another way. When two variables are related they are not independent. Our previous discussion of sets makes it clear; if $A \cap B = E$, then there is no relation (more accurately, a zero relation), or A and B are independent; if $A \cap B \neq E$, then there is a relation, or A and B are not independent. When events are not independent, scientists can sharpen their probabilistic inferences. The meaning of this statement can be explicated to some extent by studying conditional probability. In addition, its study may give the student more insight into both probability and scientific problems of sampling and prediction.

When events are not independent, the probability approach must be altered. Here is a simple example. What is the probability that, of any married couple picked at random, both mates are Republicans? First, assuming equiprobability and that everything else is equal, the sample space U (all the possibilities) is $\{RR, RD, DR, DD\}$, where the husband comes first in each possibility or sample point. Thus the probability that both husband and wife are Republicans is $p(RR) = 1/4$. But suppose we know that one of them is a Republican. What is the probability of both's being Republicans now? U is reduced to $\{RR, RD, DR\}$. The knowledge that one is a Republican deletes the possibility DD, thus reducing the sample space. Therefore, $p(RR) = 1/3$. Suppose we have the further information that the wife is a Republican. Now, what is the probability that both mates are Republicans? Now $U = \{RR, DR\}$. Thus $p(RR) = 1/2$. The new probabilities are, in this case, "conditional" on prior knowledge or facts.

Definition of Conditional Probability

Let A and B be events in the sample space, U, as usual. The conditional probability is denoted: $P(A \mid B)$, which is read, "The probability of A, given B." For example, we might say, "The probability that a husband and wife are both Republicans, given that the husband is a Republican," or, much more difficult to answer, though more interesting, "The probability of high effectiveness in college teaching, given the Ph.D. degree." Of course, we can write $p(B \mid A)$, too. The formula for the conditional probability involving two events is:[9]

$$p(A \mid B) = \frac{p(A \cap B)}{p(B)} \tag{7.8}$$

The formula simply takes an earlier notion of probability and alters it for the conditional probability situation. Remember that in probability problems the

[9]The theory extends to more than two events, but will not be discussed in this book.

TABLE **7.4** PROBABILITY MATRIX SHOWING JOINT PROBABILITIES OF TWO INDEPENDENT EVENTS

		Second Toss		
		H_2	T_2	
First Toss	H_1	¼	¼	½
	T_1	¼	¼	½
		½	½	

denominator has to be the sample space. The formula above changes the denominator of the ratio and thus *changes the sample space. The sample space has, through knowledge, been cut down from U to B.* To demonstrate this point take two examples, one of independence of simple probability and one of dependence or conditional probability.

Toss a coin twice. The events are independent. What is the probability of getting heads on the second toss if heads appeared on the first toss? We already know: 1/2. Let us calculate the probability using Eq. 7.8. First we write a probability matrix (see Table 7.4). For the probabilities of heads (H) and tails (T) on the first toss, read the marginal entries on the right side of the matrix. Similarly for the probabilities of the second toss: they are on the bottom of the matrix. Thus $p(H_1) = 1/2, p(H_2) = 1/2$, and $p(H_2 \cap H_1) = 1/4$. Therefore,

$$p(H_2 \mid H_1) = \frac{p(H_2 \cap H_1)}{p(H_1)} = \frac{1/4}{1/2} = \frac{1}{2}$$

The result agrees with our previous simpler reasoning. If we make the problem a bit more complex, however, maybe the formula will be of more use. Suppose, somehow, that the probability of getting heads on the second toss were increased to .60 instead of .50—the events are still independent. Does this change the situation? The new situation is set up in Table 7.5. (The .30 in the cell $H_1 \cap H_2$ is calculated with the probabilities on the margins: $.50 \times .60 = .30$. This is permissible since we know that the events are independent. If they are not independent, conditional probability problems cannot be solved without knowledge

TABLE **7.5** MATRIX OF JOINT PROBABILITIES OF TWO INDEPENDENT EVENTS, UNEQUAL PROBABILITIES OF EVENTS

		Second Toss		
		H_2	T_2	
First Toss	H_1	.30	.20	.50
	T_1	.30	.20	.50
		.60	.40	1.00

of at least one of the values.) The formula gives us:

$$p(H_2 \mid H_1) = \frac{p(H_2 \cap H_1)}{p(H_1)} = \frac{.30}{.50} = .60$$

But this .60 is the same as the simple probability of H_2. When events are independent, we get the same results. That is, in this case:

$$p(H_2 \mid H_1) = p(H_2)$$

and in the general case:

$$p(A \mid B) = p(A) \tag{7.9}$$

We have another definition or condition of independence. If Eq. 7.9 holds, the events are independent.

An Academic Example

There are more interesting examples of conditional probability than coins and other such chance devices. Take the interesting, if baffling and frustrating, problem of predicting the success of doctoral students in the graduate school. Can the coin-dice models be used in such a complex situation? Yes—under certain conditions. Unfortunately, these conditions are difficult to arrange. There is some limited success, however. Provided that we have certain empirical information, the model can be quite useful. Assume that the administrators of a graduate school are interested in predicting the success of their doctoral students. They are distressed by the poor performance of many of their graduates and want to set up a selection system. The school continues to admit all doctoral applicants as in the past, but for three years all incoming students take the Miller Analogies Test (MAT), a test that has been found to be fairly successful in predicting doctoral success. An arbitrary cutoff point of a raw score of 65 is selected.

The school administration finds that 30 percent of all the candidates of the three-year period score 65 or above. Each is categorized as a success (s) or failure (f). The criterion is simple: Does he or she get the degree? If so, this is defined as success. It is found that 40 percent of the total number succeed. To determine the relation between MAT score and success or failure, the administration, again using a cutoff point of 65, determines the proportions shown in Table 7.6.

The MAT divides the successful group in half (.20 and .20), but sharply differentiates in the failure group (.10 and .50). Now, the questions are asked: What is the probability of getting the doctor's degree if a candidate gets an MAT score of 65 or higher? What is the probability of a candidate's getting the degree if

TABLE **7.6** JOINT PROBABILITIES, GRADUATE-SCHOOL PROBLEM

	Success (s)	Failure (f)	
$\geqq 65$	.20	.10	.30
< 65	.20	.50	.70
	.40	.60	1.00

he gets an MAT score lower than 65? The computations are:

$$p(S \mid \geqslant 65) = \frac{p(S \cap \geqslant 65)}{p(\geqslant 65)} = \frac{.20}{.30} = .67$$

$$p(S \mid < 65) = \frac{p(S \cap < 65)}{p(< 65)} = \frac{.20}{.70} = .29$$

Clearly, it would seem that the MAT is a good predictor of success in the program.

Note carefully what happens in all these cases. When we write $p(A \mid B)$ instead of simply $p(A)$, in effect we cut down the sample space from U to B. Take the example just given. The probability of success without any other knowledge is a probability problem on the whole sample space U. This probability is .40. But given knowledge of MAT score, the sample space is cut down from U to a subset of U, $\geqslant 65$. The actual number of occurrences of the success event, of course, does not change; the same number of persons succeed. But the probability fraction gets a new denominator. Put differently, the probability estimate is refined by knowledge of "pertinent" subsets of U. In this case, $\geqslant 65$ and < 65 are "pertinent" subsets of U. By "pertinent" subsets we mean that the variable implied is related to the criterion variable, success and failure.

Maybe the following mode of looking at the problem will help. An area interpretation of the graduate-student problem is diagrammed in Fig. 7.5. The idea of a *measure of a set* is used here. Recall that a measure of a set or subset is the sum of the weights of the set or subset. The weights are assigned to the elements of the set or subset. Figure 7.5 is a square with ten equal parts on each side. Each part is equal to 1/10 or .10. The area of the whole square is the sample space U, and the

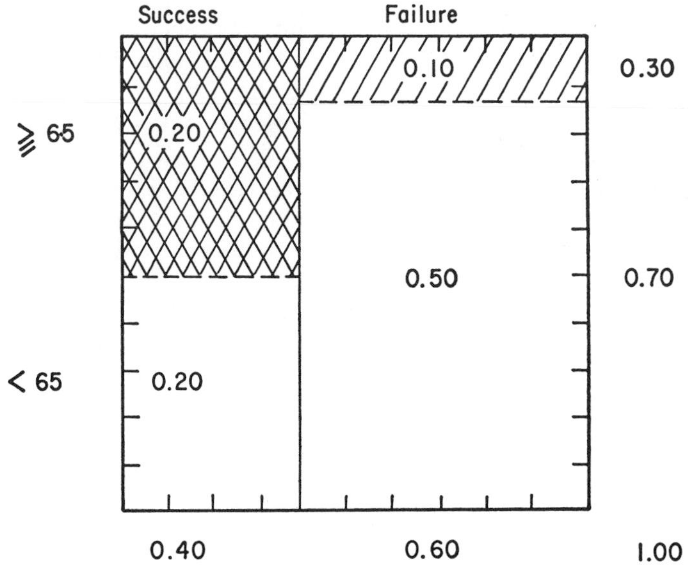

FIG. 7.5

measure of U, $m(U)$, equals 1.00. This simply means that all the weights assigned to all the elements of the square add up to 1.00. The measures of the subsets have been inserted: $m(F) = .60$, $m(<65) = .70$, $m(S \cap \geqslant 65) = .20$. The measures of these subsets can be calculated by multiplying the lengths of their sides. For example, the area of the upper left (doubly hatched) box is $.5 \times .4 = .20$. Recall that the probability of any set (or subset) is the measure of the set (or subset). So the probability of any of the boxes in Fig. 7.5 is as indicated. We can find the probability of any two boxes by adding the measures of sets; for example, the probability of success is $.20 + .20 = .40$.

These measures (or probabilities) are defined on the whole area, or $U = 1.00$. The probability of success is equal to .40/1.00. We have knowledge of the students' performances on the MAT. The areas indicating the probabilities associated with $\geqslant 65$ and < 65 are marked off by horizontal dashed lines. The simple probability of $\geqslant 65$ is equal to $.20 + .10 = .30$, or .30/1.00. The whole shaded area on the top indicates this probability. The areas of the "success" and "failure" measures are indicated by the heavy lines separating them on the square.

Our conditional probability problem is: What is the probability of success, given knowledge of MAT scores, or given $\geqslant 65$ (it could also be < 65, of course)? We have a new small sample space, indicated by the whole shaded area at the top of the square. In effect U has been cut down to this smaller space because we know the "truth" of the smaller space. Instead of letting this smaller space be equal to .30, we now let it be equal to 1.00. (You might say it becomes a new U.) Consequently the measures of the boxes that constitute the new sample space must be recalculated. For instance, instead of calculating the probability of $p(\geqslant 65 \cap S) = .20$ because it is 2/10 of the area of the whole square, we must calculate, since we now know that the elements in the set $\geqslant 65$ do have MAT scores greater than or equal to 65, the probability on the basis of the area of $\geqslant 65$ (the whole shaded area at the top of the square). Having done this, we get $.20/.30 = .67$, which is exactly what we got when we used Eq. 7.8.

What happens is that the additional knowledge makes U no longer relevant as the sample space. *All probability statements are relative to a sample space.* The basic question, then, is that of adequately defining the sample space. In the earlier problem of husbands and wives, we asked the question: What is the probability of both mates being Republican? The sample space was $U = \{RR, RD, DR, DD\}$. But when we add the knowledge that one of them is certainly a Republican and ask the same question, in effect we make the original U irrelevant to the problem. A new sample space, call it U', is required. Consequently the probability that both are Republicans is different when we have more knowledge.

We can calculate other probabilities similarly. Suppose we wanted to know the probability of failure, given an MAT score less than 65. Look at Fig. 7.5. The probability we want is the box on the lower right, labeled .50. Since we know that the score is < 65, we use this knowledge to set up a new sample space. The two lower boxes whose area equals $.20 + .50 = .70$ represent this sample space. Thus we calculate the new probability: $.50/.70 = .71$. The probability of failure to get the degree if one has an MAT score less than 65 is .71.

Study Suggestions

1. Suppose that you are sampling ninth-grade youngsters for research purposes. There are 250 ninth graders in the school system, 130 boys and 120 girls.
   (a) What is the probability of selecting any youngster?
   (b) What is the probability of selecting a girl? A boy?
   (c) What is the probability of selecting either a boy or a girl? How would you write this problem in set symbols? [*Hint:* Is it equivalent to set intersection or union?]
   (d) Suppose you drew a sample of 100 boys and girls. You got 90 boys and 10 girls. What conclusions might you reach?
   [*Answers:* (a) 1/250; (b) 120/250, 130/250; (c) 1.]
2. Toss a coin and throw a die once. What is the probability of getting heads on the coin *and* a six on the die? Draw a tree to show all the possibilities. Label the branches of the tree with the appropriate weights or probabilities. Now answer some questions. What is the probability of getting:
   (a) tails and either a 1, a 3, or a 6?
   (b) heads and either a 2 or a 4?
   (c) heads or tails and a 5?
   (d) heads or tails and a 5 or a 6?
   [*Answers:* (a) 1/4; (b) 1/6; (c) 1/6; (d) 1/3.]
3. Toss a coin and roll a die 72 times. Write the results side-by-side on a ruled sheet as they occur. Check the obtained frequencies against the theoretical expected frequencies. Now check your answer to each of the questions in question 2. Do the obtained results come close to the expected results? (For example, suppose you calculated a certain probability for 2(a), above. Now count the number of times tails is paired with a 1, a 3, or a 6. Does the obtained fraction equal the expected fraction?)
4. Note Fig. 7.6. There are 20 elements in U, of which 4 are in A, 6 in B, and 2 in $A \cap B$. If you randomly select one element, what is the probability
   (a) that it will be in A?
   (b) that it will be in B?
   (c) that it will be in $A \cap B$?
   (d) that it will be either in A or B? [*Hint:* Remember the equation: $p(A \cup B) = p(A) + p(B) - p(A \cap B)$.]
   (e) that it will be neither in A nor in B.
   (f) that it will be in B but not in A.
5. Consider Fig. 7.7. There are 20 elements in U, 4 in B, and 8 in A. If an element of U is selected at random, what are the probabilities that the element will be in
   (a) A?
   (b) B?
   (c) $A \cap B$?
   (d) $A \cup B$?
   (e) U?
   [*Answers:* (a) 2/5; (b) 1/5; (c) 1/5; (d) 2/5; (e) 1.]

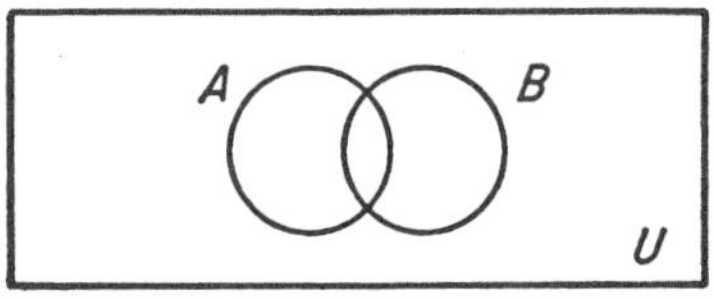

FIG. 7.6

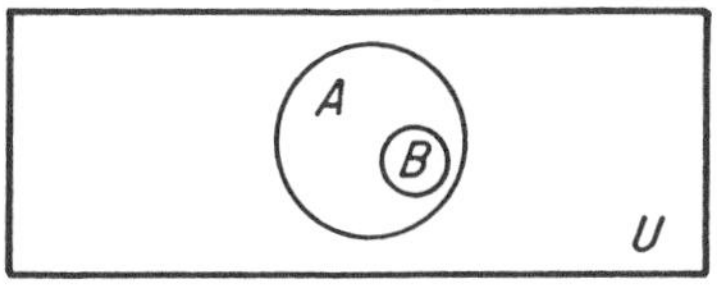

FIG. 7.7

6. Using Fig. 7.7, answer the following questions:
   (a) Given *A* (knowing that a sampled element came from *A*), what is the probability of *B*?
   (b) Given *B*, what is the probability of *A*?
   [*Answers:* (a) 1/2; (b) 1.]
7. Using Fig. 7.6, answer the following questions:
   (a) Given *B*, what is the probability of *A*?
   (b) Given *A*, what is the probability of *B*?
   [*Answers:* (a) 1/3; (b) 1/2.]
8. Suppose one had a two-item four-choice multiple-choice test, with the four choices of each item labeled *a*, *b*, *c*, and *d*. The correct answers to the two items are *c* and *a*.
   (a) Write out the sample space. (Draw a tree; see Fig. 7.3.)
   (b) What is the probability of any testee getting both items correct by guessing?
   (c) What is the probability of getting at least one of the items correct by guessing?
   (d) What is the probability of getting both items wrong by guessing?
   (e) Given that a testee gets the first item correct, what is the probability of him getting the second item correct by guessing?
   [*Answers:* (b) 1/16; (c) 7/16; (d) 9/16; (e) 1/4.]

CHAPTER 8

Sampling and Randomness

Imagine the many situations in which we want to know something about people, about events, about things. To learn something about people, for instance, we take some few people whom we know—or do not know—and study them. After our "study," we come to certain conclusions about people, often people in general. Some such method is behind much folk wisdom. Commonsensical observations about people, their motives, and their behaviors derive, for the most part, from observations and experiences with relatively few people. We make such statements as: "Adolescents are delinquent"; "People nowadays have no sense of moral values"; "Politicians are corrupt"; and "Public school pupils are not learning the three R's."

The basis for making such statements is simple. People, mostly through their limited experiences, come to certain conclusions about other people and about their environment. In order to come to such conclusions, they must *sample* their "experiences" of other people. Actually, they take relatively small samples of all possible experiences. The term "experiences" here has to be taken in a broad sense. It can mean direct experience with other people—for example, first-hand interaction with, say, Germans or Jews. Or it can mean indirect experience: hearing about Germans or Jews from friends, acquaintances, parents, and others. Whether experience is direct or indirect, however, does not concern us too much at this point. Let us assume that all such experience is direct. An individual believes he "knows" something about Jews and says he "knows" they are clannish, because he has had direct experience with a number of Jews. He may even say, "Some of my best friends are Jews, and I know that . . ." The point is that his conclusions are based on a sample of Jews, or a sample of the behaviors of Jews, or both. He can never "know" all Jews; he must depend, in the last analysis, on samples. Indeed, most of the world's knowledge is based on samples, most often on inadequate samples.

Sampling, Random Sampling, and Representativeness

Sampling is taking any portion of a population or universe as representative of that population or universe. This definition does not say that the sample taken—or drawn, as researchers say—*is* representative. It says, rather, taking a portion of the population and *considering* it to be representative. When a school administrator visits certain classrooms in his system "to get the feel of the system," he is sampling classes from all the classes in the system. He is probably assuming that if he visits, say, eight to ten classes out of forty "at random," as he may say, he will get a fair notion of the quality of teaching going on in the system. Or he may visit one teacher's class two or three times to sample her teaching. He is now sampling behaviors, in this case teaching behaviors, from the universe of all possible behaviors of the teacher. Such sampling is necessary and legitimate.

Random sampling is that method of drawing a portion (or sample) of a population or universe so that each member of the population or universe has an equal chance of being selected. This definition has the virtue of being easily understood. Unfortunately, it is not entirely satisfactory because it is limited. A better definition is: *Random sampling* is that method of drawing a portion (sample) of a population or universe so that all possible samples of fixed size n have the same probability of being selected.[1] This definition is general and thus more satisfactory than the earlier definition.

Define a universe to be studied as all fourth-grade children in X school system. Suppose there are 200 such children. They comprise the population (or universe). We select one child at random from the population. His (or her) chance of being selected is 1/200, if the sampling procedure is random. Likewise, a number of other children are similarly selected. Let us assume that after selecting a child we return him (or the symbol assigned to him) to the population. Then the chance of selecting any second child is also 1/200. (If we do not return him to the population, then the chance each of the remaining children has, of course, is 1/199. This is called *sampling without replacement*. When the sample elements are returned to the population after being drawn, the procedure is called *sampling with replacement*.)

Suppose from the population of the 200 fourth-grade children in X school system we decide to draw a random sample of 50 children. This means, if the sample is random, that all possible samples of 50 have the same probability of being selected—a very large number of possible samples. To make the ideas involved comprehensible, suppose a population consists of four children, a, b, c, and d, and we draw a random sample of two children. Then the list of all the possibilities, or the *sample space*, is: (a, b), (a, c), (a, d), (b, c), (b, d), (c, d). There are six

[1] W. Feller, *An Introduction to Probability Theory and Its Applications*, 2nd ed. New York: Wiley, 1957, p. 29.

possibilities. If the sample of two is drawn at random, then its probability is 1/6. Each of the pairs has the same probability of being drawn. This sort of reasoning is needed to solve many research problems, but we will usually confine ourselves to the simpler idea of sampling connected with the first definition. The first definition, then, is a special case of the second general definition—the special case in which $n = 1$.

Unfortunately, we can never be sure that a random sample is representative of the population from which it is drawn. Remember that any particular sample of size n has the same probability of being selected as any other sample of the same size. Thus, a particular sample may not be representative at all. We should know what "representative" means. Ordinarily, "representative" means to be typical of a population, that is, to exemplify the characteristics of the population. From a research point of view, "representative" must be more precisely defined, though it is often difficult to be precise. We must ask: What characteristics are we talking about? So, in research, a "representative sample" means that the sample has approximately the characteristics of the population relevant to the research in question. If sex and socioeconomic class are variables (characteristics) relevant to the research, a representative sample will have approximately the same proportions of men and women and middle-class and working-class individuals as the population. When we draw a random sample, we *hope* that it will be representative, that the relevant characteristics of the population will be present in the sample in approximately the same way they are present in the population. But we can never be sure; there is no guarantee.

What we rely on is the fact, as Stilson points out, that the characteristics typical ("characteristic") of a population are those that are the most frequent and therefore most likely to be present in any particular random sample.[2] When sampling is random, the sampling variability is predictable. We learned in Chapter 7, for example, that if we throw two dice a number of times, the probability of a 7 turning up is greater than that of a 12 turning up. (See Table 7.1.)

A sample drawn at random is unbiased in the sense that no member of the population has any more chance of being selected than any other member. We have here a democracy in which all members are equal before the bar of selection. Rather than using coins or dice, let's use a research example. Suppose we have a population of 100 children. The children differ in intelligence, a variable relevant to our research. We want to know the mean IQ of the population, but for some reason we can only sample 30 of the 100 children. If we sample randomly, there are a large number of possible samples of 30 each. The samples have equal probabilities of being selected. The means of most of the samples will be relatively close to the mean of the population. A few will not be close. The probability of selecting a sample with a mean close to the population mean, then, is greater than the probability of selecting a sample with a mean not close to the population mean—if the sampling has been random.

If we do not draw our sample at random, however, some factor or factors

[2]D. Stilson, *Probability and Statistics in Psychological Research and Theory*. San Francisco: Holden-Day, 1966, p. 35.

unknown to us may predispose us to select a biased sample, in this case perhaps one of the samples with a mean not close to the population mean. The mean IQ of this sample will then be a biased estimate of the population mean. If the 100 children were known to us, we might unconsciously tend to select the more intelligent children. It is not so much that we *would* do so; it is that our method *allows* us to do so. Random methods of selection do not allow our own biases or any other systematic selection factors to operate. The procedure is objective, divorced from our own predilections and biases.

Random sampling has another virtue that we cannot yet adequately discuss and understand because we need to know more about statistics. Nevertheless, it has to be mentioned, if only briefly. Modern statistical theory is based on random sampling and its definition. In a random sample, remember, every element of the population has an equal chance of being selected. In order to estimate population values from sample values, or statistics (sample values, like means, are called statistics), one needs estimates of the variability of the sample values. Strictly speaking, the application of statistical theory, which largely involves estimating variability of sample values, is possible only when the probability of the selection of population elements is known. We will understand better what is meant at a later point in our development.

The reader may be experiencing a vague and disquieting sense of uneasiness, even dissatisfaction. If we can't be sure that random samples are representative, how can we have confidence in our research results and their applicability to the populations from which we draw our samples? Why not select samples systematically so that they *are* representative? The answer is complex. First—and again—we cannot ever be sure. Second, random samples are more likely to include the characteristics typical of the population if the characteristics are frequent in the population. In actual research, we draw random samples whenever we can and hope and assume that the samples are representative. We learn to live with uncertainty, but try to cut it down whenever we can—just as we do in ordinary day-to-day living, but more systematically and with considerable knowledge of and experience with random sampling and random outcomes. Fortunately, our lack of certainty does not impair our research functioning.

Randomness

The notion of randomness is at the core of modern probabilistic methods in the natural and behavioral sciences. But it is difficult to define "random." The dictionary notion of haphazard, accidental, without aim or direction, does not help us much. In fact, scientists are quite systematic about randomness; they carefully select random samples and plan random procedures.

The position can be taken that nothing happens at random, that for any event there is a cause. The only reason, this position might say, that one uses the word random is that human beings do not know enough. To omniscience nothing is random. Suppose an omniscient being has an omniscient newspaper. It is a gigantic newspaper in which every event down to the last detail—for tomorrow, the next day, and the next day, and on and on into indefinite time—is carefully inscribed.[3] There is nothing unknown. And, of course, there is no randomness. Randomness is, as it were, ignorance, in this view.

Taking a cue from this argument, we define randomness in a backhand way. We say events are random if we cannot predict their outcomes. For instance, there is no known way to win a penny-tossing game. Whenever there is no system for playing a game that ensures our winning (or losing), then the event-outcomes of the game are random. More formally put, *randomness* means that there is no known law, capable of being expressed in language, that correctly describes or explains events and their outcomes.[4] In a word, when events are random we cannot predict them individually. Strange to say, however, we can predict them quite successfully in the aggregate. That is, we can predict the outcomes of large numbers of events. We cannot predict whether a coin tossed will be heads or tails. But, if we toss the coin 1000 times, we can predict, with considerable accuracy, the total numbers of heads and tails.

An Example of Random Sampling

To give the reader a feeling for randomness and random samples, we now do an experiment using a table of random numbers. A table of random numbers contains numbers generated mechanically so that there is no discernible order or system in them. It was said above that if events are random they cannot be predicted. But now we are going to predict the *general nature* of the outcomes of our experiment. We select, from a table of random digits, ten samples of ten digits each. Since the numbers are random, each sample should be representative of the universe of digits. The universe can be variously defined. We simply define it as the complete set of digits in the Rand Corporation table of random digits.[5] These digits are 0, 1, 2, 3, 4, 5, 6, 7, 8, 9. We now draw samples from the table. The means of the ten samples will, of course, be different, but they should fluctuate within a relatively narrow range, with most of them fairly close to the mean of all 100 numbers and to the theoretical mean of the whole population of random numbers. And the number of even numbers in each sample of 10 should be approximately equal to the number of odd numbers—though, again, there will be fluctuations, some of them perhaps extreme but most of them comparatively modest. The samples are given in Table 8.1.

The means of the samples are given below each sample. The mean of U, the theoretical mean of the whole population of Rand random numbers, $\{0, 1, 2, 3, 4, 5, 6, 7, 8, 9\}$, is 4.5. The mean of all 100 numbers, which can be considered a

[3]See J. Kemeny, *A Philosopher Looks at Science*. New York: Van Nostrand Reinhold, 1959, p. 39.

[4]*Ibid.*, pp. 68–75.

[5]The source of random numbers used was: Rand Corporation, *A Million Random Digits With 100,000 Normal Deviates*. New York: Free Press, 1955. This is a large and carefully constructed table of random numbers. There are many other such tables, however, that are good enough for most practical purposes. Modern statistics texts have such tables. Useful tables of nonrepeating random numbers can be found in: A. Rosander, *Elementary Principles of Statistics*. New York: Van Nostrand Reinhold, 1951, pp. 681–683. Appendix D at the end of this book contains 4000 computer-generated random numbers.

TABLE 8.1 TEN SAMPLES OF RANDOM NUMBERS

	1	2	3	4	5	6	7	8	9	10	
	9	0	8	0	4	6	0	7	7	8	
	7	2	7	4	9	4	7	8	7	7	
	6	2	8	1	9	3	6	0	3	9	
	7	9	9	1	6	4	9	4	7	7	
	3	3	1	1	4	1	0	3	9	4	
	8	9	2	1	3	9	6	7	7	3	
	4	8	3	0	9	2	7	2	3	2	
	1	4	3	0	0	2	6	9	7	5	
	3	1	8	8	4	5	2	1	0	3	
	2	1	4	8	9	2	9	3	0	1	
Mean:	5.0	3.9	5.3	2.4	5.7	3.8	5.2	4.4	5.0	4.9	Total mean = 4.56

sample of U, is 4.56. This is, of course, very close the mean of U. It can be seen that the means of the ten samples vary around 4.5, the lowest being 2.4 and the highest 5.7. Only two of these means differ from 4.5 by more than 1. A statistical test—later we will learn the rationale of such tests—shows that the ten means do not differ from each other significantly. (The expression "do not differ from each other significantly" means that the differences are not greater than the differences that would occur by chance.) And by another statistical test nine of them are "good" estimates of the population mean of 4.5 and one (2.4) is not.

Changing the sampling problem, we can define the universe to consist of odd and even numbers. Let's assume that in the entire universe there is an equal number of both. In our sample of 100 numbers there should be approximately 50 odd and 50 even numbers. There are actually 54 odd and 46 even numbers. A statistical test shows that the deviation of 4 for odd and 4 for even does not depart significantly from chance expectation.[6]

Similarly, if we sample human beings, then the numbers of men and women in the samples should be approximately in proportion to the numbers of men and women in the population—if the sampling is random and the samples are large enough. If we measure the intelligence of a sample, and the mean intelligence quotient of the population is 100, then the mean of the sample should be close to 100. Of course, we must always bear in mind the possibility of selection of the deviant sample, the sample with a mean, say, of 80 or less or 120 or more. Deviant samples *do* occur, but they are less likely to occur. The reasoning is similar to that for coin-tossing demonstrations. If we toss a coin three times, it is less likely that 3 heads or 3 tails will turn up than it is that 2 heads and 1 tail or 2 tails and 1 head will turn up, because $U = \{HHH, HHT, HTH, HTT, THH\ THT, TTH, TTT\}$. There is only one HHH point and one TTT point, while there are three points with two H's and three with two T's.

[6]The nature of such statistical tests, as well as the reasoning behind them, will be explained in detail in Part IV. The student should not be too concerned if he does not completely grasp the statistical ideas expressed here. Indeed, one of the purposes of this chapter is to introduce some of the basic elements of such ideas.

Randomization

Suppose an investigator wishes to test the hypothesis that counseling helps underachievers. He wants to set up two groups of underachievers, one to be counseled, one not to be counseled. Naturally, he also wishes to have the two groups equal in other independent variables that may have a possible effect on achievement. One way he can do this is to assign the children to both groups at random by, say, tossing a coin for each child in turn and assigning the child to one group if the toss is heads and to the other group if the toss is tails. (Note that if he had three experimental groups he would probably not use coin-tossing. He might use a die.) Or he can use a table of random numbers and assign the children as follows: if an odd number turns up, assign a child to one group, and if an even number turns up, assign the child to the other group. He can now assume that the groups are approximately equal in all possible independent variables. The larger the groups, the safer the assumption. Just as there is no guarantee, however, of not drawing a deviant sample, as discussed earlier, there is no guarantee that the groups *are* equal or even approximately equal in all possible independent variables. Nevertheless, it can be said that the investigator has used randomization to equalize his groups, or, as it is said, to control influences on the dependent variable other than that of the manipulated independent variable.

An "ideal" experiment is one in which *all* the factors or variables likely to affect the experimental outcome are controlled. If we *knew* all these factors, in the first place, and *could* control them, in the second place, then we might have an ideal experiment. But the sad case is that we can never know all the pertinent variables nor could we control them even if we did know them. Randomization, however, comes to our aid.

Randomization is the assignment of objects (subjects, treatments, groups) of a universe to subsets of the universe in such a way that, for any given assignment to a subset, every member of the universe has an equal probability of being chosen for that assignment. The idea of randomization seems to have been discovered or invented by Sir Ronald Fisher, who illustrated the idea with his famous lady and her cup of tea.[7] The lady says that she can tell whether the milk or the tea was first added to the cup. Fisher showed how to test her claim, using probability theory and chance notions. In any case, randomization and what can be called the principle of randomization is one of the great intellectual achievements of our time. It is not possible to overrate the importance of the idea and the practical measures that come from it to improve experimentation and inference from obtained results.

Randomization can perhaps be clarified in two or three ways: by stating the principle of randomization, by describing how one uses it in practice, and by demonstrating how it works with objects and numbers. The importance of the idea deserves all three.

The *principle of randomization* may be stated thus: Since, in random procedures, every member of a population has an equal chance of being selected, members with certain distinguishing characteristics—male or female, high or low

[7]R. Fisher, *The Design of Experiments*, 6th ed. New York: Hafner, 1951, pp. 11 ff.

intelligence, Republican or Democrat, dogmatic or not dogmatic, and so on and on—will, if selected, probably be counterbalanced in the long run by the selection of other members of the population with the "opposite" quantity or quality of the characteristic. We can say that this is a practical principle of what usually happens; we cannot say that it is a law of nature. It is simply a statement of what most often happens when random procedures are used.

We say that subjects are assigned at random to experimental groups, and that experimental treatments are assigned at random to groups. For example, in the example cited above of an experiment to test the effectiveness of counseling on achievement, subjects can be assigned to two groups at random by using random numbers or by tossing a coin. When the subjects have been so assigned, the groups can be randomly designated as experimental and control groups using a similar procedure. We will encounter a number of examples of randomization as we go along.

A Randomization Demonstration

To show how, if not why, the principle of randomization works, we now set up a sampling and design experiment. The voting records of 100 senators of the Eighty-Sixth Congress on 12 important issues were reported in the *New York Times* on September 20, 1959. Omitting the two senators from Hawaii (they only voted on two of the issues), we have a population of 98 senators from which we can sample. In this population there are 64 Democrats and 34 Republicans, 65 northerners and 33 southerners. Each senator voted on each issue either Yea or Nay, except when he "paired for" or "paired against" an issue, or was absent. Thus we have a population of senators that can be broken down into subpopulations of Republicans and Democrats, northerners and southerners, "Yeaers" and "Nayers."

Let us pretend we are going to do an experiment using three groups, with 20 senators in each group. The nature of the experiment is not too relevant here, but let us say we want to test the efficacy of a film depicting the horrors of nuclear warfare in changing the attitudes of the senators toward nuclear test bans. We want the three groups of senators to be approximately equal in all possible characteristics. To accomplish this, we assign numbers from 1 through 98 to the senators in the *Times* table (omitting the senators from Hawaii), and then we select the 60 senators for the experiment in blocks of 20 using three separate pages of a large table of random numbers, the pages themselves being selected at random by entering the entire table anywhere and choosing three numbers at random.

We choose 20 two-digit numbers from the first page chosen, limiting our choices to numbers 1 through 98. Then we go to the second and third pages chosen and follow a similar procedure. The three groups of 20 numbers are given in Table 8.2, together with political party affiliation and regional origin (North-South) of each senator. In addition, for a purpose to be mentioned later, we enter the senatorial votes on Issues 1 and 5, assigning a 1 if a senator voted Yea and a 0 if he voted Nay.

How "equal" are the groups? In the total population of 98 senators, 64 are

TABLE **8.2** THREE GROUPS OF RANDOMLY SELECTED EIGHTY-SIXTH CONGRESS SENATORS, THEIR POLITICAL PARTY AND REGION, AND THEIR VOTES ON TWO ISSUES[a]

I	*PP*	*R*	1	5	II	*PP*	*R*	1	5	III	*PP*	*R*	1	5
34	*D*	*S*	0	1	60	*D*	*S*	0	0	4	*D*	*N*	0	0
35	*R*	*S*	0	1	42	*D*	*S*	1	0	38	*D*	*N*	0	0
50	*D*	*S*	0	0	66	*D*	*N*	0	0	75	*D*	*N*	1	0
15	*R*	*N*	0	1	98	*D*	*N*	0	0	37	*D*	*N*	1	1
86	*D*	*S*	0	1	41	*D*	*S*	0	0	30	*D*	*S*	0	0
29	*D*	*S*	0	1	51	*D*	*S*	0	0	31	*D*	*N*	1	0
79	*D*	*N*	1	0	9	*R*	*N*	0	1	65	*D*	*S*	0	1
16	*D*	*N*	1	0	1	*R*	*N*	1	1	13	*D*	*N*	0	0
21	*D*	*N*	1	0	46	*R*	*N*	0	1	7	*D*	*N*	0	0
17	*R*	*N*	1	1	40	*D*	*N*	0	0	67	*D*	*N*	1	0
76	*D*	*N*	0	0	53	*R*	*N*	1	1	2	*R*	*N*	0	1
87	*R*	*N*	0	1	32	*D*	*S*	0	1	85	*R*	*N*	1	1
8	*R*	*N*	1	1	93	*R*	*N*	1	1	78	*R*	*N*	0	1
92	*D*	*S*	0	1	89	*D*	*S*	0	1	12	*D*	*S*	0	0
57	*R*	*N*	1	1	90	*D*	*S*	1	0	84	*R*	*N*	0	1
52	*D*	*S*	0	1	64	*D*	*N*	1	0	20	*D*	*N*	0	0
26	*D*	*N*	1	1	63	*R*	*N*	0	1	44	*D*	*S*	0	0
11	*D*	*S*	0	1	43	*R*	*N*	0	1	23	*R*	*N*	0	1
36	*D*	*S*	0	0	80	*D*	*S*	0	0	73	*D*	*N*	0	0
96	*D*	*S*	0	0	3	*D*	*N*	0	0	72	*R*	*N*	0	1

[a]*PP* = Political Party; *R* = Region; *D* = Democrat; *R* = Republican (in body of table); 1 and 5 = Issues 1 and 5. See text for other explanations.

Democrats and 34 are Republicans, or 65 percent and 35 percent. In the total sample of 60, there are 41 Democrats and 19 Republicans, or 68 percent and 32 percent, a difference of only 3 percent. There are 65 northerners and 33 southerners in the population, or 66 percent and 34 percent. In the sample of 60, there are 38 northerners and 22 southerners, or 63 percent and 37 percent, again a difference of 3 percent. We calculate the frequencies for the three groups of 20 senators each. The data on political party and region are summarized in Table 8.3. It can be seen that the obtained frequencies in each sample on both variables are close to the expected frequencies.[8] In the total sample of 60, we would expect 39 Democrats and 39 northerners. Our sample gave us 41 Democrats and 38 northerners. These differences are only chance fluctuations. We have evidently succeeded in "equalizing" the groups on political party and region. In addition, the total sample of 60 and the three samples of 20 each seem to be representative of the total population of 98—at least in these two variables.

Now we check on the voting of the senators. To do this, we use Issues 1 and 5. We simply count the 1's (Yeas) in each column and compare the totals to the

[8]The expected frequencies are calculated as follows: Take the proportions of Democrats, Republicans, northerners, and southerners in the total population of 98 and, using these proportions (or percentages), calculate the frequencies to be expected in the samples of 20. For example, 64 senators are Democrats, and 64/98 = .65. Thus 20 × .65 = 13, which is the number of Democrats to be expected in each of the samples of 20.

TABLE **8.3** OBTAINED AND EXPECTED FREQUENCIES OF POLITICAL PARTY (DEMOCRAT) AND REGION (NORTH) IN SAMPLES OF 20 SENATORS[a]

	Groups I		II		III		Total	
	PP	*R*	*PP*	*R*	*PP*	*R*	*PP*	*R*
Obtained	14	10	13	12	14	16	41 (68%)	38 (63%)
Expected	13	13	13	13	13	13	39 (65%)	39 (66%)
Deviation	1	3	0	1	1	3	2	1

[a]Only the larger of the two totals of the Democrat-Republican split, the Democrat, is reported, and similarly, North is reported. *PP* = Political Party; *R* = Region. Expected frequencies have been rounded.

expected number of 1's obtained by counting the Yeas on each issue, calculating the proportion of Yeas on the issues in each sample of 20 and in the total sample of 60. For instance, in the total group of 98 senators there were 29 Yeas cast for Issue 1 and 50 Yeas for Issue 5, or proportions of 29/98 = .30 and 50/98 = .51. Multiplying 20 by .30 and by .51 gives us 6 and 10, respectively, as the numbers of Yeas expected on Issues 1 and 5. Similarly, multiplying 60 by .30 and by .51 yields expected frequencies of 18 and 31. Table 8.4 reports the results of this analysis. All deviations obtained from expected frequencies are small (with one possible exception: Group I, Issue 5). They do not deviate much from chance expectations.

Random Assignment

Instead of viewing this demonstration as a sampling problem, we can view it as an experimental *assignment* problem. Suppose we have the 60 senators available for our experiment. We are not interested, say, in the 60 senators as a random sample of the whole Senate; we are only interested in testing the efficacy of the film mentioned earlier in changing attitudes toward a nuclear test ban. In other words, the 60 senators are handed to us; they are available; they are not a random sample of the 98 senators. This is like many research situations where we must work with groups as they are, intact. We must take as they are intact classes of

TABLE **8.4** OBTAINED AND EXPECTED FREQUENCIES OF SENATORIAL YEA AND NAY VOTES ON ISSUES 1 AND 5[a]

	Groups I		II		III		Total	
	1	5	1	5	1	5	1	5
Obtained	7	13	6	9	5	8	18	30
Expected	6	10	6	10	6	10	18	31
Deviation	1	3	0	1	1	2	0	1

[a]If a senator voted Yea, this was counted as a frequency. The table is read, for example (first column): In the first sample of 20 senators (I), 7 voted Yea where 6 were expected to vote Yea, yielding a difference of 1.

fifth and sixth graders, a class or two of sophomores, a willing PTA. In such cases we can, hopefully, use random assignment to groups.

To assign the 60 senators to three groups, we number them from 1 to 60 and draw the numbers 1 through 60 from a table of random numbers in some specified way. The first 20 numbers that are drawn—and the senators associated with the numbers—constitute one group, the second 20 numbers constitute another group, and similarly for the third 20 numbers and a third group. (We would then assign the experimental treatments at random to the three groups.) This is called "random assignment"; it is a close relative of random sampling. Both operate on the principle of randomization. In fact, we can regard the random assignment as random sampling. In this case, it would be random sampling of the 60 senators viewed as a population. That is, each of the groups of 20 senators *is* a random sample of the total group of 60 senators. (It is *not* a random sample of the 98 senators.) In short, we randomly assign subjects in order to have experimental groups that we can *assume* to be equal, within chance limits, in all possible characteristics.

We can now do our experiment believing that the three groups are "equal." They may not be, of course. Like deviant samples from populations, we can have deviant assignment. The probabilities are in our favor, however. As we have already seen, the procedure usually works well. Our checking of the characteristics of the senators in the three groups showed that the groups were fairly "equal" in political preference, region, and Yea and Nay votes. Thus we can have greater confidence that if the groups become unequal in attitudes toward a nuclear test ban, the differences are probably due to our experimental manipulation and not to differences among the groups before we started.

Sample Size

A rough and ready rule taught to beginning students of research is: Use as large samples as possible. Whenever a mean, a percentage, or other statistic is calculated from a sample, a population value is being estimated. A question that must be asked is: How much error is there likely to be in statistics calculated from samples of different sizes? The curve of Fig. 8.1 roughly expresses the relations between sample size and error, error meaning deviation from population values. The curve says that the smaller the sample the larger the error, and the larger the sample the smaller the error.

Take the following rather extreme example of ten sets of two numbers each selected at random (using a table of random numbers) from a population of 293 IQ's given by Tate. These IQ's were themselves a sample from a much larger population of IQ's. We consider them to be a population from which we draw our small samples. Study Table 8.5. Note that the means of the samples diverge rather widely: The range is from 84.5 to 108.5, or 24.0 IQ points. The mean of all 20 scores is 93.55. With very small samples like these we cannot depend too much on any one mean as an estimate of the population value, but apparently we can depend much more on the total mean (calculated from 20 IQ's) as such an estimate. (The mean of the population of 293 IQ's is 95.0.)

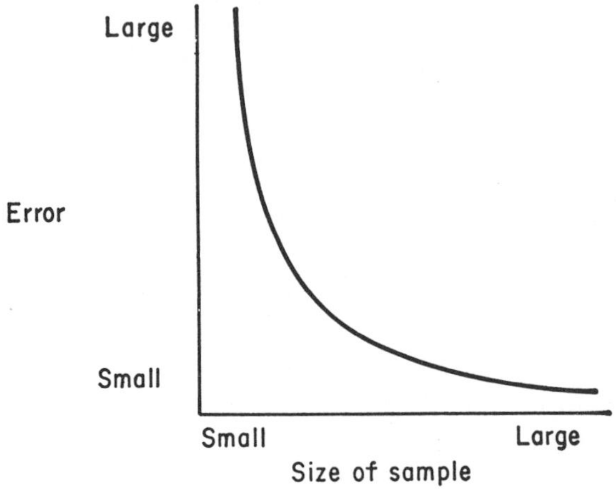

FIG. 8.1

Four more samples of 20 IQ's were drawn at random from the Tate data. The five means (including the mean of the sample of 20 IQ's in Table 8.5) were: 93.55; 90.20; 97.50; 94.80; and 90.50. The mean of all 100 IQ's was 93.31.

TABLE **8.5** SAMPLES ($n = 2$) OF IQ'S FROM A POPULATION OF 293 IQ'S OF FOURTH-GRADE CHILDREN[a]

	Samples									
	117	85	84	92	83	82	83	96	93	101
	75	84	107	103	87	96	100	121	103	79
Mean:	96.0	84.5	95.5	97.5	85.0	89.0	91.5	108.5	98.0	90.0
										Total mean = 93.55

[a]From M. Tate, *Statistics in Education*. New York: Macmillan, 1955, pp. 537–545.

We are now in a position to answer some questions. First, statistics calculated from large samples are more accurate, other things equal, than those calculated from small samples. The range of the means of samples of 20 was 90.20 to 97.50, or 7.30 IQ points, a relatively small range when the variability of the IQ's is considered (the range is from 54 to 125). The range of the means of the 10 samples of two IQ's each, on the other hand, was from 84.5 to 108.5, or 24.0 IQ points. Also attesting to the greater accuracy of larger samples are the means of our samples of 20. They were generally closer to the population mean of 95.0 than the means of the samples of two.

It should now be fairly clear why the research and sampling principle is: Use large samples.[9] Large samples are not advocated because large numbers are good in and of themselves. They are advocated in order to give the principle of randomization, or simply randomness, a chance to "work," to speak somewhat anthropomorphically. For a rather dramatic example of what is meant, look back at the data of Table 8.2. Look at the political party of the first ten cases of Group

[9]The situation is more complex than this simple statement indicates. Samples that are too large can be dangerous; the reasons will be explained in a later chapter.

III. They are all Democrats. Suppose, now, that we had chosen to work experimentally only with two groups of 10 each and one of our groups was the one with these 10 Democrats and the other had the remaining 10 cases of Group III in it. If our experiment had anything to do with political preference, the results might be biased. With groups of 20, however, there is less danger.[10]

Kinds of Samples

The discussion of sampling has until now been confined to simple random sampling. The purpose is to help the student understand fundamental principles; thus the idea of simple random sampling, which is behind much of the thinking and procedures of modern research, is emphasized. The student should realize, however, that simple random sampling is not the only kind of sampling used in behavioral research. Indeed, it is relatively uncommon, at least for describing characteristics of populations and the relations between such characteristics. It is, nevertheless, the model on which all scientific sampling is based.

Other kinds of samples can be broadly classified into probability and nonprobability samples (and certain mixed forms). *Probability samples* use some form of random sampling in one or more of their stages. *Nonprobability samples* do not use random sampling; they thus lack the virtues being discussed. Still, they are often necessary and unavoidable. Their weakness can to some extent be mitigated by using knowledge, expertise, and care in selecting samples and by replicating studies with different samples.[11]

One form of nonprobability sampling is *quota sampling*, in which knowledge of strata of the population – sex, race, region, and so on – is used to select sample members that are representative, "typical," and suitable for certain research purposes. Quota sampling derives its name from the practice of assigning quotas, or proportions of kinds of people, to interviewers. Such sampling has been used a good deal in public opinion polls. Another form of nonprobability sampling is *purposive sampling*, which is characterized by the use of judgment and a deliberate effort to obtain representative samples by including presumably typical areas or groups in the sample. So-called *"accidental" sampling*, the weakest form of sampling, is probably also the most frequent. In effect, one takes available samples at hand: classes of seniors in high school, sophomores in college, a convenient PTA, and the like. This practice is hard to defend. Yet, used with reasonable knowledge and care, it is probably not as bad as it has been said to be. The most sensible advice seems to be: Avoid accidental samples unless you can get no other samples – random samples are usually expensive and, in general, hard to come by – and, if you do use them, use extreme circumspection in analysis and interpretation of data.

[10]This run of 10 Democrats is unusual. It has happened very seldom in all the random sampling the author has done. *But it can and does happen.*

[11]See I. Chein, "An Introduction to Sampling." In C. Selltiz et al., *Research Methods in Social Relations*, rev. ed. New York: Holt, Rinehart and Winston, 1959, pp. 509–545. This is a good introduction to sampling methods. A clear exposition of different kinds of sampling can also be found in F. Stephan and P. McCarthy, *Sampling Opinions*. New York: Wiley, 1963 (1958), chap. 3.

Probability sampling includes a variety of forms. The most general of these are stratified sampling and cluster sampling. In *stratified sampling*, the population is divided into strata, such as men and women, black and white, and the like, from which random samples are drawn. *Cluster sampling*, the most used method in surveys, is the successive random sampling of units, or sets and subsets. In educational research, for example, school districts of a state or county can be randomly sampled, then schools, then classes, and finally pupils. Another kind of probability sampling—if, indeed, it can be called probability sampling—is *systematic sampling*. Here the first sample element is randomly chosen from numbers 1 through k and subsequent elements are chosen at every kth interval. For example, if the element randomly selected from the elements 1 through 10 is 6, then the subsequent elements are 16, 26, 36, and so on. The student who will pursue research further should, of course, know much more about these methods and should consult one or more of the excellent references on the subject.[12]

Randomness, randomization, and random sampling are among the great ideas of science, as indicated earlier. While research can, of course, be done without using ideas of randomness, it is difficult to conceive how it can have viability and validity, at least in most aspects of behavioral scientific research. Modern notions of research design, sampling, and inference, for example, are literally inconceivable without the idea of randomness. One of the most remarkable of paradoxes is that through randomness, or "disorder," we are able to achieve control over the often obstreperous complexities of psychological, sociological, and educational phenomena. We impose order, in short, by exploiting the known behavior of sets of random events. One is perpetually awed by what can be called the structural beauty of probability, sampling, and design theory and by its great usefulness in solving difficult problems of research design and planning and the analysis and interpretation of data.

Before leaving the subject, let's return to a view of randomness mentioned earlier. To an omniscient being, there is no randomness. By definition such a being would "know" the occurrence of any event with complete certainty.[13] As Poincaré points out, to gamble with such a being would be a losing venture. Indeed, it would not *be* gambling. When a coin was tossed ten times, he (or she) would predict heads and tails with complete certainty and accuracy. When dice were thrown, he would know infallibly what the outcomes will be. He would even be able to predict every number in a table of random numbers! And certainly he would have no need for research and science. What I seem to be saying is that randomness is a term for ignorance. If we, like the omniscient being, knew all the contributing causes of events, then there would be no randomness. The beauty of it, as indicated above, is that man uses this "ignorance" and turns it to knowledge.

[12]See footnote 11. One of the best references, especially for survey sampling, is: L. Kish, "Selection of the Sample." In L. Festinger and D. Katz, eds., *Research Methods in the Behavioral Sciences.* New York: Holt, Rinehart and Winston, 1953, pp. 175–239.

[13]For an eloquent discussion of this point, see Poincaré's essay on chance. H. Poincaré, *Science and Method.* New York: Dover, 1952, pp. 64–90.

How he does this should become more and more apparent as we go on with our study.

Study Suggestions

A variety of experiments with chance phenomena is recommended: games using coins, dice, cards, roulette wheels, and tables of random numbers. Such games, properly approached, can help one learn a great deal about fundamental notions of modern scientific research, statistics, probability, and, of course, randomness. Try the problems given in the suggestions below. Do not become discouraged by the seeming laboriousness of such exercises here and later on in the book. It is evidently necessary and, indeed, helpful occasionally to go through the routine involved in certain problems. After working the problems given, devise some of your own. If you can devise intelligent problems, you are probably well on your way to understanding.

1. From a table of random numbers draw 50 numbers, 0 through 9. (Use the random numbers of Appendix D, if you wish.) List them in columns of 10 each.
   (a) Count the total number of odd numbers; count the total number of even numbers. What would you expect to get by chance? Compare the obtained totals with the expected totals.
   (b) Count the total number of numbers 0, 1, 2, 3, 4. Similarly count 5, 6, 7, 8, 9. How many of the first group should you get? The second group? Compare what you do get with these chance expectations. Are you far off?
   (c) Count the odd and even numbers in each group of 10. Count the two groups of numbers 0, 1, 2, 3, 4 and 5, 6, 7, 8, 9 in each group of 10. Do the totals differ greatly from chance expectations?
   (d) Add the columns of the five groups of 10 numbers each. Divide each sum by 10. (Simply move the decimal point one place to the left.) What would you expect to get as the mean of each group if only chance were "operating"? What did you get? Add the five sums and divide by 50. Is this mean close to the chance expectation? [*Hint:* To obtain the chance expectation, remember the population limits.]
2. This is a class exercise and demonstration. Assign numbers arbitrarily to all the members of the class from 1 through N, N being the total number of members of the class. Take a table of random numbers and start with any page. Have a student wave a pencil in the air and blindly stab at the page of the table. Starting with the number the pencil indicates, choose n two-digit numbers between 1 and N (ignoring numbers greater than N and repeated numbers) by, say, going down columns (or any other specified way). n is the numerator of the fraction n/N, which is decided by the size of the class. If $N = 30$, for instance, let $n = 10$. Repeat the process twice on different pages of the random numbers table. You now have three equal groups (if N is not divisible by 3, drop one or two persons at random. Write the random numbers on the blackboard in the three groups. Have each class member call out his height in inches. Write these values on the blackboard separate from the numbers, but in the same three groups. Add the three sets of numbers in each of the sets on the blackboard, the random numbers and the heights. Calculate the means of the six sets of numbers. Also calculate the means of the total sets.
   (a) How close are the means in each of the sets of numbers? How close are the means of the groups to the mean of the total group?
   (b) Count the number of men and women in each of the groups. Are the sexes spread fairly evenly among the three groups?

(c) Discuss this demonstration. What do you think is its meaning for research?

3. In Chapter 6, it was suggested that the student generate 20 sets of 100 random numbers between 0 and 100 and calculate means and variances. If you did this, use the numbers and statistics in this exercise. If you did not, use the numbers and statistics of Appendix D at the end of the book.
   (a) How close to the population mean are the means of the 20 samples? Are any of the means "deviant"? (You might judge this by calculating the standard deviation of the means and adding and subtracting two standard deviations to the total mean.)
   (b) On the basis of (a), above, and your judgment, are the samples "representative"? What does "representative" mean?
   (c) Pick out the third, fifth, and ninth group means. Suppose that 300 subjects had been assigned at random to the three groups and that these were scores on some measure of importance to a study you wanted to do. What can you conclude from the three means, do you think?

PART 4

Analysis, Interpretation, Statistics, and Inference

CHAPTER

Principles of Analysis and Interpretation

The research analyst breaks down data into constituent parts to obtain answers to research questions and to test research hypotheses. The analysis of research data, however, does not in and of itself provide the answers to research questions. Interpretation of the data is necessary. To interpret is to explain, to find meaning. It is difficult or impossible to explain raw data; one must first analyze the data and then interpret the results of the analysis.

Analysis means the categorizing, ordering, manipulating, and summarizing of data to obtain answers to research questions. The purpose of analysis is to reduce data to intelligible and interpretable form so that the relations of research problems can be studied and tested. A primary purpose of statistics, for example, is to manipulate and summarize numerical data and to compare the obtained results with chance expectations. A researcher hypothesizes that styles of leadership affect group-member participation in certain ways. He plans an experiment, executes the plan, and gathers data from his subjects. Then he must so order, break down, and manipulate the data that he can answer the question: How do styles of leadership affect group-member participation? It should be apparent that this view of analysis means that the categorizing, ordering, and summarizing of data should be planned early in the research. The researcher should lay out analysis paradigms or models even when working on the problem and hypotheses. Only in this way can he see, even if only dimly, whether his data and its analysis can and will answer the research questions.

Interpretation takes the results of analysis, makes inferences pertinent to the research relations studied, and draws conclusions about these relations. The researcher who interprets research results searches them for their meaning and implications. This is done in two ways. One, the relations *within* the research study and its data are interpreted. This is the narrower and more frequent use of the term interpretation. Here interpretation and analysis are closely intertwined. One almost automatically interprets as one analyzes. That is, when one calculates, say, a coefficient of correlation, one almost immediately infers the existence of a relation and draws out its significance for the research problem as one orders, breaks down, and manipulates the data.

Two, the broader meaning of the research data is sought. This is done by comparing the results and the inferences drawn within the data to theory and to other research results. One seeks the meaning and implications *between* one's research results and conclusions either of one's own or of other researchers.[1] More important, one compares one's results with the demands and expectations of theory.

An example that may illustrate these ideas is research on the perception of teacher characteristics.[2] On the basis of so-called directive-state and social perception theory,[3] it was predicted that perceptions or judgments of desirable characteristics of effective teachers will in part be determined by the attitudes toward education of the individuals making the judgments. Suppose, now, that we have measures of attitudes toward education and measures of the perceptions or judgments of the characteristics of effective teachers. We correlate the two sets of measures: the correlation is substantial. This is the analysis. The data have been broken down into the two sets of measures, which are then compared by means of a statistical procedure.

The result of the analysis, a correlation coefficient, now has to be interpreted. What is its meaning? Specifically, what is its meaning within the study? What is its broader meaning in the light of previous related research findings and interpretations? And what is its meaning as confirmation or lack of confirmation of theoretical prediction? If the "internal" prediction holds up, one then relates the finding to other research findings which may or may not be consistent with one's present finding.

The correlation was substantial. Within the study, then, the correlation datum is consistent with theoretical expectation. Directive-state theory says that central states influence perceptions. Attitude is a central state; it should therefore influence perception. The specific deduction is that attitudes toward education influence perceptions of the effective teacher. We measure both variables and correlate the measures. From the correlation coefficient we make an inferential leap to the hypothesis: since it is substantial, as predicted, the hypothesis is

[1]This distinction is due to M. Jahoda, M. Deutsch, and S. Cook. *Research Methods in Social Relations*. New York: Holt, Rinehart and Winston, 1951, Vol. I, pp. 252 ff.

[2]F. Kerlinger and E. Pedhazur, "Educational Attitudes and Perceptions of Desirable Traits of Teachers," *American Educational Research Journal*, V (1968), 543–560.

[3]*Directive-state theory* is a broad theory of perception that says in effect that our perceptions of cognitive objects are colored by our emotions, needs, wants, motives, attitudes, and values. These latter are, so to speak, directive states within the individual influencing his perceptions and judgments. See J. Bruner, "Social Psychology and Perception." In E. Maccoby, T. Newcomb, and E. Hartley, eds., *Readings in Social Psychology*, rev. ed. New York: Holt, Rinehart and Winston, 1958, pp. 85–94. A more complete discussion can be found in: F. Allport, *Theories of Perception and the Concept of Structure*. New York: Wiley, 1955, chaps. 13, 14, and 15.

supported. We then attempt to relate the finding to other research and other theory. In this case the finding is consistent with much of the research on directive-state and social perception theory, though it may be a far cry from laboratory experiments on perceptions of sizes of coins and perceptions of food objects to measurement of educational attitudes and perceptions of desirable teacher characteristics.

Frequencies and Continuous Measures

In Chapter 3, a distinction was made between categorical variables and continuous variables. A continuous variable is one that is capable of taking on an ordered set of values within a certain range, whereas a categorical variable is one that has two or more subsets of the set of objects being measured and the subsets are separate and distinct, they are not ordered, and any member of a subset is conceived to have the same value on the variable as any other member of the subset. A similar distinction can be made with quantitative data. They come in two general forms: frequencies and continuous measures. Obviously, continuous measures are associated with continuous variables and frequencies with categorical variables. Although both kinds of variables and measures can be subsumed under the same measurement frame of reference, in practice it is useful, even necessary, to distinguish them.

Frequencies are simply the numbers of objects in sets and subsets. Let U be the universal set with N objects. Then N is the *number* of objects in U. Let U be partitioned into $A_1, A_2, \ldots, A_k$. Let $n_1, n_2, \ldots, n_k$ be the numbers of objects in $A_1, A_2, \ldots, A_k$. Then $n_1, n_2, \ldots, n_k$ are called frequencies.

It is helpful to look at this as a function. Let X be any set of objects with members $\{x_1, x_2, \ldots, x_n\}$. We wish to measure an attribute of the members of the set; call it M. Let $Y = \{0, 1\}$. Let the measurement be described as a function:

$$f = \{(x, y); x \text{ is a member of the set } X, \text{ and } y \text{ is either } 1 \text{ or } 0 \text{ depending on } x\text{'s possessing or not possessing } M\}$$

This is read: f, a function, or rule of correspondence, equals the set of ordered pairs (x, y) such that x is a member of X, y is 1 or 0, and so on. If x possesses M (determined in some empirical fashion), then assign a 1. If x does not possess M, assign a 0. Obviously this works very well with variables like sex, religious preference, social class membership, and so on. It can also be adapted to continuous measures by definition and convention. To find the frequency of objects with characteristic M, count the number of objects that have been assigned 1.

With continuous measures, the basic idea is the same. Only the rule of correspondence, f, and the numerals assigned to objects change. The rule of correspondence is more elaborate and the numerals are generally 0, 1, 2, . . . and fractions of these numerals. In other words, we write a measurement equation:

$$f = \{(x, y); x \text{ is an object, and } y = \text{any numeral}\}$$

which is the generalized form of the function.[4] This digression is important, be-

[4]This equation and the ideas behind it will be explained in detail in Chapter 25.

cause it helps us to see the basic similarity of frequency analysis and continuous measure analysis.

Rules of Categorization

The first step in any analysis is categorization. It was said earlier (Chapter 4) that partitioning is the foundation of analysis. We will now see why. Categorization is merely another word for partitioning—that is, a *category* is a partition or a subpartition. If a set of objects is categorized in some way, it is simply partitioned according to some rule. The rule tells us, in effect, how to assign set objects to partitions and subpartitions. If this is so, then the rules of partitioning we studied earlier apply to problems of categorization. We need only explain the rules, relate them to the basic purposes of analysis, and put them to work in practical analytic situations.

Five rules of categorization are given below. Two of them, (2) and (3), are the exhaustiveness and disjointness rules discussed in Chapter 4. Two others, (4) and (5), can actually be deduced from the fundamental rules, (2) and (3). Nevertheless, we list them as separate rules for practical reasons.

1. Categories are set up according to the research problem and purpose.
2. The categories are exhaustive.
3. The categories are mutually exclusive and independent.
4. Each category (variable) is derived from one classification principle.
5. Any categorization scheme must be on one level of discourse.

Rule 1 is the most important. If categorizations are not set up according to the demands of the research problem, then there can be no adequate answers to the research questions. We constantly ask: Does my analysis paradigm conform to the research problem? Does the analysis scheme enable me to test my hypotheses adequately? Suppose the hypothesis were: Religious education enhances the moral characteristics of children. Religious education has been defined as "parochial school education," moral characteristics as "honesty." The hypothesis is, therefore: Parochial children are more honest than public school children. (We ignore the difficulty in designing an adequate test of this and related hypotheses.) Whatever data are gathered, whatever analysis is used, both data and analysis must bear on this hypothesis.

The simplest type of analysis is a frequency analysis. We randomly sample parochial and public schools, randomly sample n children from each school, and measure their honesty. Let us suppose that the best we can do is to label each child as *honest* or *not honest*. The paradigm for the frequency analysis would look like this:

	Honest	Not Honest
Parochial		
	FREQUENCIES	
Public		

If we had continuous measures for the *honesty* variable, then the paradigm would be different:

Parochial (1)		Public (2)
.		.
.	*Y* Measures	.
.		.
.		.

It is obvious that both paradigms bear directly on the hypothesis: both enable the researcher to test the hypothesis, albeit in quite different ways. The point is that an analytical paradigm is, in effect, another way to state a problem, a hypothesis, a relation. That one paradigm uses frequencies while the other uses continuous measures in no way alters the relation tested. In other words, both modes of analysis are logically similar: they both test the proposition that the type of education affects honesty. They differ in the data they use, in statistical tests, and in sensitivity and power.

There are several things a researcher might do that would be irrelevant to the problem. If he included one, two, or three variables in the study with no theoretical or practical reason for doing so, then the analytic paradigm would be at least partly irrelevant to the problem. To take an extreme example, suppose a researcher collected achievement test data from both types of schools and tested the achievement differences. This would probably have no bearing on the problem, since the researcher is interested in the moral differences and not the achievement differences between the two types of schools and, of course, between religious instruction and no religious instruction. He might bring other variables into the picture that have little or no bearing on the problem, for example, differences in teacher experience and training or teacher-pupil ratios. If, on the other hand, he thought that certain variables, like sex, family religious background, and perhaps personality variables, might interact with religious instruction to produce differences, then he might be justified in building such variables into the research problem and consequently into the analytic paradigm.[5]

Rule 2, on exhaustiveness, means that all subjects, all objects of U, must be used up. All individuals in the universe must be capable of being assigned to the cells of the analytic paradigm. With the example just considered, each child either goes to parochial school or to public school. If, somehow, the sampling had included children who attend private schools, then the rule would be violated because there would be a number of children who could not be fitted into the 2×2 paradigm. If the research problem called for private school pupils, then the 2×2

[5]In the next chapter, elementary consideration will be given to frequency analysis with more than one independent variable. In later chapters there will be much more detailed consideration of both frequency and continuous measure analysis with several independent variables. The reader should not now be concerned with complete understanding of examples like those given above and in Figs. 9.1 and 9.2. They will be clarified later.

paradigm would have to be changed to a 3×2 paradigm, the rubric Private being added to Parochial and Public.

The exhaustiveness criterion is not always easy to satisfy. With some categorical variables, there is no problem. If sex is one of the variables, any individual has to be male or female. Suppose, however, that a variable under study were religous preference and we set up, in a paradigm, Protestant-Catholic-Jew. Now suppose some subjects were atheists or Buddhists. Clearly the categorization scheme violates the exhaustiveness rule: some subjects would have no cells to which to be assigned. Depending on numbers of cases and the research problem, we might add another rubric, Others, to which we assign any subjects who are not Protestants, Catholics, or Jews. Another solution, especially when the number of Others is small, is to drop these subjects from the study. Still another solution is to put these other subjects, if it is possible to do so, under an already existing rubric. Other variables where this problem is encountered are political preference, social class, types of education, types of teacher training, and so on.

Rule 3 is one that often causes research workers concern. To demand that the categories be mutually exclusive means, as we learned earlier, that each object of U, each research subject (actually the measure assigned to each subject), must be assigned to one cell and one cell only of an analytic paradigm. This is a function of operational definition. Definitions of variables must be clear and unambiguous so that it is unlikely that any subject can be assigned to more than one cell. If religious preference is the variable being defined, then the definition of membership in the subsets Protestant, Catholic, and Jew must be clear and unambiguous. It may be "registered membership in a church." It may be "born in the church." It may simply be the subject's identification of himself as a Protestant, a Catholic, or a Jew. Whatever the definition, it must enable the investigator to assign any subject to one and only one of the three cells.

The independence part of Rule 3 is often difficult to satisfy, especially with continuous measures—and sometimes with frequencies. *Independence* means that the assignment of one object to a cell in no way affects the assignment of any other object to that cell or to any other cell. Random assignment from an infinite or very large universe, of course, satisfies the rule. Without random assignment, however, we run into problems. When assigning objects to cells on the basis of the object's possession of certain characteristics, the assignment of an object now may affect the assignment of another object later.

Rule 4, that each category (variable) be derived from one classificatory principle, is sometimes violated by the neophyte. If one has a firm grasp of partitioning, this error is easily avoided. The rule means that, in setting up an analytic design, each variable has to be treated separately, because each variable is a separate dimension. One does not put two or more variables in one category or one dimension. If one were studying, for instance, the relations between social class, sex, and drug addiction, one would not put social class and sex on one dimension. If one were studying the relations between methods of teaching, types of motivation, and school achievement, one would not lump together methods of teaching and types of motivation on one dimension. Such an error might look like the following design:

Method 1	Method 2	Type *a*	Type *b*
	ACHIEVEMENT SCORES		

It is clear that the paradigm violates the rule: it has one category derived from two classificatory principles. Correct paradigms might look like those of Fig. 9.1 (frequency analysis) or Fig. 9.2 (continuous measure analysis). If the student will use different letters for each variable, A, B, C, . . . , with breakdowns $A_1, A_2, \ldots,$ $B_1, B_2, \ldots,$ he is not as likely to make this error.

		Methods			
		A_1		A_2	
	Types	B_1	B_2	B_1	B_2
Achieve-ment	C_1		FREQUENCIES		
	C_2				

FIG. 9.1

		Methods	
		A_1	A_2
Types	B_1	ACHIEVEMENT	
	B_2	SCORES	

FIG. 9.2

Rule 5 is the hardest to explain because the term "level of discourse" is hard to define. It was defined in an earlier chapter as a set that contains all the objects that enter into a discussion. If we use the expression "universe of discourse," we tie the idea to set ideas. When talking about U_1, do not bring in U_2 without good reason and without making it clear that you are doing so.[6]

In research analysis, it is usually the measures of the dependent variable that are analyzed. Take the problem of the relations among methods, intelligence, and achievement. Methods and intelligence are the independent variables; achievement is the dependent variable. The objects of analysis are the achievement

[6]For a discussion of levels of discourse and relevance, see F. Kerlinger, "Research in Education." In R. Ebel, V. Noll, and R. Bauer, eds., *Encyclopedia of Educational Research*, 4th ed. New York: Macmillan, 1969, pp. 1127–1144, especially p. 1131.

measures. The independent variables and their categories are actually used to structure the dependent variable analysis. The universe of discourse, U, is the set of dependent variable measures. The independent variables can be conceived as the partitioning principles that are used to break down or partition the dependent variable measures. If, suddenly, we switch to another kind of dependent variable measure, then we may have switched levels or universes of discourse.

Kinds of Statistical Analysis

There are many kinds of statistical analysis and presentation that cannot be discussed in detail in this book. Later discussions of certain more advanced forms of statistical analysis have as their purpose basic understanding of statistics and statistical inference and the relation of statistics and statistical inference to research. In this section, the major forms of statistical analysis are discussed briefly to give the reader an overview of the subject; they are discussed, however, only in relation to research. It is assumed that the reader has already studied the simpler descriptive statistics. Those who have not can find good discussions in elementary textbooks.[7]

Frequency Distributions

Although frequency distributions are used primarily for descriptive purposes, they can be used for other purposes in research. For example, one can test whether two or more distributions are sufficiently similar to warrant merging them. Suppose one were studying the verbal learning of boys and girls in the sixth grade. After obtaining large numbers of verbal learning scores, one can compare and test the differences between the boy and girl distributions.[8] If the test shows the distributions to be the same—and other criteria are satisfied—they can perhaps be combined for other analysis.

Observed distributions can also be compared to theoretical distributions. The best-known such comparison is with the so-called normal distribution. It may be important to know that obtained distributions are normal in form, or, if not normal, depart from normality in certain specifiable ways. Such analysis can be useful in both theoretical and applied work and research. In theoretical study of abilities it is important to know whether such abilities are in fact distributed normally. Since a number of human characteristics have been found to be normally distributed,[9] researchers can ask significant questions about "new" characteristics being investigated.

A more interesting use of distributions in research might be in the study of

[7]For example, A. Edwards, *Statistical Analysis*, 3d ed. New York: Holt, Rinehart and Winston, 1969; P. Lohnes and W. Cooley, *Introduction to Statistical Procedure: With Computer Exercises*. New York: Wiley, 1968. The latter book is especially useful because it integrates computer thinking and programming into the discussions.

[8]See W. Hays, *Statistics*. New York: Holt, Rinehart and Winston, 1963, pp. 580 ff.

[9]A. Anastasi, *Individual Differences*, 3d ed. New York: Macmillan, 1958, pp. 26 ff. The student of research in education, psychology, and sociology should study Anastasi's outstanding contribution to our understanding of individual differences. Her book also contains many examples of distributions of empirical data.

prejudice in different regions and with different groups. In addition to asking whether scores on a measure of anti-Semitism, for instance, are normally distributed—which would be an important theoretical and practical finding—we might ask how distributions of such scores differ. If we find a relatively normal distribution in the Northeast and a skewed or rather flat one in the Midwest, this would be important information of possible theoretical import. We might then want to inquire into the presumed causes of such different distributions.

Applied educational research of the evaluative kind can profit from careful study of distributions of intelligence, aptitude, and achievement scores. Is it conceivable that an innovative learning program can change the distributions of the achievement scores, say, of third and fourth graders? Can it be that massive early education programs can change the shape of distributions, as well as the general levels of scores?

Allport's study of social conformity many years ago showed that even a complex behavioral phenomenon like conformity can be profitably studied using distribution analysis.[10] Allport was able to show that a number of social behaviors—stopping for red lights, parking violations, religious observances, and so on—were distributed in the form of a J curve, with most people conforming, but with predictable smaller numbers not conforming in different degrees.

Hook and Kim tested the notion that large size of boys contributes to delinquent behavior in XYY individuals.[11] ("XYY" refers to a genetic pattern; X and Y are chromosomes. XYY boys tend to be taller than most; they are also believed to be more delinquent. The research question is whether the delinquency is influenced by height itself or by other factors.) To test the notion, they compared the distributions of the heights of white and black boys in two institutions for antisocial behavior with the published height distributions of healthy white and black children. If boys with the XYY pattern became large and developed antisocial behavior because of their height, then there should be more very tall boys than expected in institutions for antisocial boys. If, on the other hand, the boys became antisocial because of the XYY pattern (and not the height), then there should be no overrepresentation of very tall boys in a sample of XYY boys. That is, height itself is ruled out by using known distributions against which to compare the subject distributions. (They found that large height itself was not exclusively responsible for the frequency of delinquency among XYY individuals.)

Distributions, like graphs (to be considered in the next section) have probably been too little used in the behavioral sciences and education. The study of relations and the testing of hypotheses are almost automatically associated with correlations and comparisons of averages. The use of distributions is considered less often. Some research problems, however, can be solved better by using distribution analysis. Studies of pathology and other unusual conditions are perhaps best approached through a combination of distribution analysis and probabilistic

[10]F. Allport, "The J-Curve Hypothesis of Conforming Behavior." In T. Newcomb and E. Hartley, eds., *Readings in Social Psychology*. New York: Holt, Rinehart and Winston, 1947, pp. 55–67.

[11]E. Hook and D. Kim, "Height and Anti-Social Behavior in XY and XYY Boys," *Science*, CLXXII (1971), 284–286.

notions. What is the probability in the Hook and Kim study, for example, that so many very tall boys will occur by chance in this distribution? Moreover, distribution analysis may give a more complete picture of a phenomenon than other methods do.

Graphs and Graphing

One of the most powerful tools of analysis is the graph. A *graph* is a two-dimensional representation of a relation or relations. It exhibits pictorially sets of ordered pairs in a way no other method can. If a relation exists in a set of data, a graph will not only clearly show it; it will show its nature: positive, negative, linear, quadratic, and so on. While graphs have been used a good deal in the behavioral sciences, they, like distributions, probably have not been used enough. To be sure, there are objective ways of epitomizing and testing relations, such as correlation coefficients, comparison of means, and other statistical methods, but none of these so vividly and uniquely describes a relation as a graph.

Look back at the graphs in Chapter 5 (Figs. 5.1 and 5.7). Note how they convey the nature of the relations. Later we will use graphs in a more interesting way to show the nature of rather complex relations among variables. To give the student just a taste of the richness and interest of such analysis, we anticipate later discussion; in fact, we will try to teach a complex idea through graphs.

The three graphs of Fig. 9.3 show three hypothetical relations between age, as an independent variable, and verbal achievement (VA), as dependent variable, of middle-class children (A), and working-class children (B). One can call these growth graphs. The horizontal axis is the abscissa; it is used to indicate the independent variable, or X. The vertical axis is the ordinate; it is used to indicate the dependent variable, or Y. Graph (a) shows the same positive relation between age and VA with both A and B samples. It also shows that the A children exceed the B children. Graph (b), however, shows that both relations are positive, but that as time goes on the A children's achievement increases more than the B children's achievement. This seems to be the sort of phenomenon that Coleman et al. found

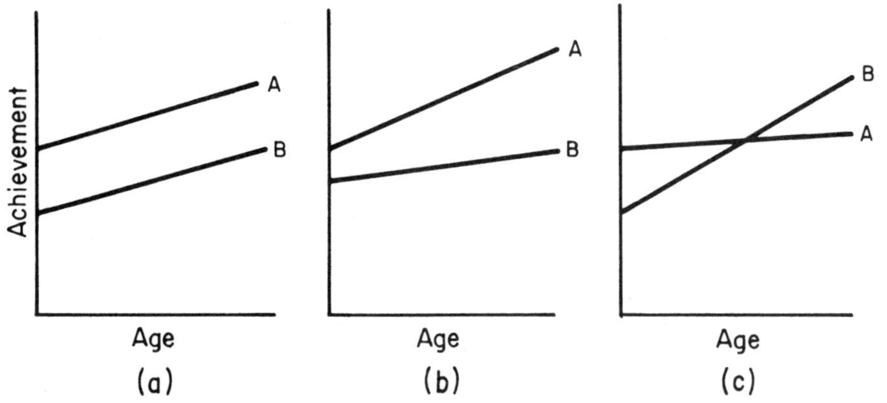

FIG. 9.3

when comparing the verbal achievement of majority- and minority-group children in grades 3, 6, 9, and 12.[12] Graph (c) is more complex. It shows that the A children were superior to the B children at an early age and remained the same to a later age, but the B children, who started lower, advanced and continued to advance over time until they exceeded the A children. This sort of relation is unlikely with verbal achievement, but it can occur with other variables.

The phenomenon shown in graphs (b) and (c) is known as *interaction.* Briefly, it means that two (or more) variables interact in their "effect" on a dependent variable. In this case, age and group status interact in their relation to verbal achievement. Expressed differently, interaction means that the relation of an independent variable to a dependent variable is different in different groups, as in this case, or at different levels of another independent variable. It will be explained in detail when we study analysis of variance and multiple regression analysis.

While means are one of the best ways to report complex data, complete reliance on them can be unfortunate. Most cases of significant mean differences between groups are also accompanied by considerable overlap of the distributions. Clear examples are given by Anastasi, who points out the necessity of paying attention to overlapping and gives examples and graphs of sex distribution differences, among others.[13] In short, students of research are advised to get into the habit, from the beginning of their study, of paying attention to and understanding distributions of variables and to graphing relations of variables.

Measures of Central Tendency and Variability

There is little doubt that measures of central tendency and variability are the most important tools of behavioral data analysis. Since much of this book will be preoccupied with such measures—indeed, a whole section is called "The Analysis of Variance"—we need only characterize averages and variances. The three main averages, or measures of central tendency, used in research, the mean, median, and mode, are epitomes of the sets of measures from which they are calculated. Sets of measures are too many and too complex to grasp and understand readily. They are "represented" or epitomized by measures of central tendency. They tell what sets of measures "are like" on the average. But they are also compared to test relations. Moreover, individual scores can be usefully compared to them to assess the status of the individual. We say, for instance, that individual A's score is such-and-such a distance above the mean.

While the mean is the most used average in research, and while it has desirable properties that justify its preeminent position, the median, the midmost measure of a set of measures, and the mode, the most frequent measure, can some-

[12]J. Coleman et al., *Equality of Educational Opportunity*. Washington, D.C.: U.S. Govt. Printing Office, 1966. See, especially, pp. 20 ff. and 220 ff.

[13]Anastasi, *op. cit.*, pp. 453 ff.

[14]Consult: S. Siegel, *Nonparametric Statistics for the Behavioral Sciences*. New York: McGraw-Hill, 1956, pp. 111–116 and pp. 179–184. Types of means and other measures of central tendency are exceptionally well discussed in: M. Tate, *Statistics in Education*. New York: Macmillan, 1955, chap. II. Tate also gives a number of good examples of distributions and graphs of various kinds. Though old, this is a valuable book.

times be useful in research. For instance, the median, in addition to being an important descriptive measure, can be used in tests of statistical significance where the mean is inappropriate.[14] The mode is used mostly for descriptive purposes, but it can be useful in research for studying characteristics of populations and relations. Suppose that a mathematical aptitude test was given to all incoming freshmen in a college that has just initiated open admissions, and that the distribution of scores was bimodal. Suppose, further, that only a mean was calculated, compared to means of previous years, and found to be considerably lower. The simple conclusion that the average mathematical aptitude of incoming freshmen was considerably lower than in previous years conceals the fact that because of the open admissions policy many freshmen were admitted who had deficient backgrounds in mathematics. While this is an obvious example, deliberately chosen because it *is* obvious, it should be noted that obscuring important sources of differences can be more subtle. It often pays off in research, in other words, to calculate medians and modes as well as means. Multimodal distributions are signals of the possible operation of variables not taken into account.[15]

The principal measures of variability are the variance and the standard deviation. They have already been discussed and will be discussed further in later chapters. We therefore forego discussion of them here, except to say that research reports should always include variability measures. Means should almost never be reported without standard deviations (and N's, the sizes of samples), because adequate interpretation of research by readers is virtually impossible without variability indices. Another measure of variability that has in recent years become more important is the *range*, the difference between the highest and lowest measures of a set of measures. It has become possible, especially with small samples (with N about 20 or 15 or less), to use the range in tests of statistical significance.

Measures of Relations

There are many useful measures of relations: the product-moment coefficient of correlation (r), the rank-order coefficient of correlation (*rho*), the distance measure (D), the coefficient of contingency (C), the coefficient of multiple correlation (R), and so on. Almost all coefficients of relation, no matter how different in derivation, appearance, calculation, and use, do essentially the same thing: express the extent to which the pairs of sets of ordered pairs vary concomitantly. In effect, they tell the researcher the magnitude and (usually) the direction of the relation. Some of them vary in value from -1.00 through 0 to $+1.00$, -1.00 and 1.00 indicating perfect negative and positive association, respectively, and 0 indicating no discernible relation.

Measures of relations are comparatively direct indices of relations in the sense that from them one has some direct idea of the degree of the covarying of the variables. The square of the product-moment coefficient of correlation, for example, is a direct estimate of the amount of the variance shared by the variables. One can say, at least roughly, how high or low the relation is. This is in contrast to

[15]See *ibid.*, pp. 79 ff.

measures of statistical significance which say, in effect, that a relation is or is not "significant" at some specified level of significance. Ideally, any analysis of research data should include both kinds of indices, measures of the significance of a relation and measures of the magnitude of the relation.

Measures of relations, but especially product-moment coefficients of correlation, are unusual in that they themselves are subject to extensive and elaborate forms of analysis, mainly multiple regression analysis and factor analysis (see below). They are thus extremely useful and powerful tools of the researcher.

Analysis of Differences

The analysis of differences, particularly the analysis of differences between means, occupies a rather large part of statistical analysis and inference. It is important to note two things about differences analysis. One, it is by no means confined to the differences between measures of central tendency. Almost any kind of difference—between frequencies, proportions, percentages, ranges, correlations, and variances—can be so analyzed. Take variances. Suppose an educational psychologist wants to know if a certain form of instruction has the effect of making pupils more heterogeneous in concept learning. The difference between the variances of groups taught by different methods can be easily tested. Or one might want to know whether groups set up to be homogeneous are homogeneous on variables other than those used to form the groups.

The second point is more important. All analysis of differences is really for the purpose of studying relations. Suppose one believes that changing art preferences toward greater complexity will transfer to music preferences and sets up three experimental groups, one of which is given the greater complexity manipulation.[16] One finds the predicted differences between the means of the three groups on music preferences, with the one given the complexity manipulation the highest. It is not really these differences that interest us, however. It is the relation of the study: that between the complexity modification on art preference and the modification toward greater music complexity preference. Differences between means, then, really reflect the relation between the independent variable and the dependent variable. If there are no significant differences among means, the correlation between independent variable and dependent variable is zero. And, conversely, the greater the differences the higher the correlation, other things equal.

Suppose an experiment to study the effect of random reinforcement of opinion utterance on rate of opinion utterance has been done and the experimental group, which received random reinforcement, had a mean of 6 utterances in a specified period of time, and the control group, which received a regular rate of reinforcement, had a mean of 4 utterances.[17] The difference is statistically significant, and we conclude from the significant difference that there is a relation between reinforcement and opinion utterance rate. In earlier chapters, relations be-

[16] V. Renner, "Effects of Modification of Cognitive Style on Creative Behavior," *Journal of Personality and Social Psychology*, XIV (1970), 257–262.

[17] The idea for this problem comes from: W. Verplanck, "The Control of the Content of Conversation: Reinforcement of Statements of Opinion," *Journal of Abnormal and Social Psychology*, LI (1955), 668–676.

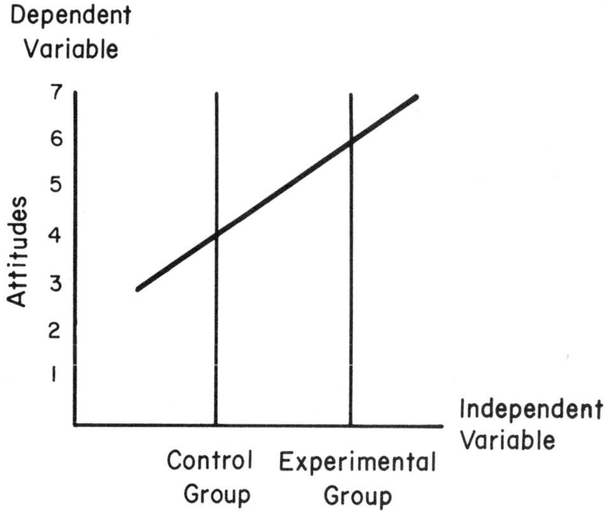

FIG. 9.4

tween measured variables were plotted to show the nature of the relations. It is possible, too, to graph the present relation between the experimental (manipulated) independent variable and the measured dependent variable. This has been done in Fig. 9.4, where the means have been plotted as indicated. While the plotting is more or less arbitrary—for instance, there are no real baseline units for the independent variable—the similarity to the earlier graphs is apparent and the basic idea of a relation is clear.

If the reader will always keep in mind that relations are sets of ordered pairs, the conceptual similarity of Fig. 9.4 to earlier graphs will be evident. In the earlier graphs, each member of each pair was a score. In Fig. 9.4, an ordered pair consists of an experimental treatment and a score. If we assign 1 to the experimental group and 0 to the control group, two ordered pairs might be: (1, 8), (0, 3).

Analysis of Variance and Related Methods

A sizable part of this book will be devoted to analysis of variance and related methods. So there is little need to say much here. The reader need only put this important method of analysis in perspective. Analysis of variance is what its name implies—and more: a method of identifying, breaking down, and testing for statistical significance variances that come from different sources of variation. That is, a dependent variable has a total amount of variance, some of which is due to the experimental treatment, some to error, and some to other causes. Analysis of variance's job is to work with these different variances and sources of variance. Strictly speaking, analysis of variance is more appropriate for experimental than for nonexperimental data, even though its inventor, Fisher, used it with both kinds.[18] We will consider it, then, a method for the analysis of data yielded by

[18]R. Fisher, *Statistical Methods for Research Workers*, 11th ed. New York: Hafner, 1950, pp. 227 ff.

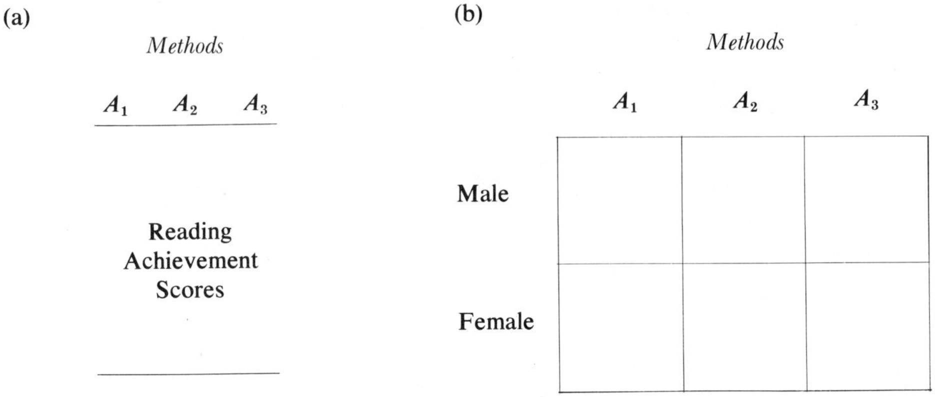

FIG. 9.5

experiments in which randomization and manipulation of at least one independent variable have been used.

For the purposes of this book, analysis of variance is more important for its basic ideas and paradigms than for its flexibility or power. We emphatically state that there is no better way to study research design than through an analysis of variance approach. Those proficient with the approach almost automatically think of alternative analysis of variance models when confronted with new research problems. Suppose an experienced investigator is asked to test three methods of teaching reading. He will immediately think of a simple one-way analysis of variance, which will look like the paradigm on the left [marked (a)] of Fig. 9.5. If he thinks that sex is an important variable to include, then the paradigm will look like that on the right (b). Other variables, too, can be added, but there are practical limitations. Clearly, analysis of variance is an important method of studying differences.

Profile Analysis

Profile analysis is basically the assessment of the similarities of the profiles of individuals or groups. A *profile* is a set of different measures of an individual or group, each of which is expressed in the same unit of measure. An individual's scores on a set of different tests constitute a profile, if all scores have been converted to a common measure system, like percentiles, ranks, and standard scores. Profiles have been used mostly for diagnostic purposes—for instance, the profiles of the Differential Aptitude Test are used to assess and advise junior high school pupils. But they are becoming increasingly important in psychological and educational research, as we will see later when we study, among other things, the semantic differential and *Q* methodology.

Profile analysis has special problems that require researchers' careful consideration. As Cronbach and Gleser have pointed out, similarity is not a general characteristic of persons; it is similarity only with respect to specified characteristics or complexes of characteristics.[19] Another difficulty—or, rather, set of diffi-

[19]L. Cronbach and G. Gleser, "Assessing Similarity Between Profiles," *Psychological Bulletin*, L (1953), 456–473 (p. 457).

culties—lies in what information one is willing to sacrifice in calculating indices of profile similarity. Such decisions, of course, depend on the research problem. When one uses the product-moment coefficient of correlation—which is a profile measure—one loses level; that is, differences between means are sacrificed. This is loss of *elevation*. Product-moment *r*'s take only *shape* into account. Further, *scatter*—differences in variability of profiles—is lost in the calculation of certain other kinds of profile measures. In short, information can be and is lost.[20] The student will find excellent help and guidance with profile analysis in Nunnally's book on psychometrics, though the treatment is not elementary.[21]

Multivariate Analysis

Perhaps the most important forms of statistical analysis, especially at the present stage of development of the behavioral sciences and education, are multivariate analysis and factor analysis. *Multivariate analysis* is a general term used to categorize a family of analytic methods whose chief characteristic is the simultaneous analysis of k independent variables and m dependent variables.[22] If an analysis includes, for instance, four independent variables and two dependent variables, handled simultaneously, it is a multivariate analysis.

It can be argued that, of all methods of analysis, multivariate methods are the most powerful and appropriate for behavioral scientific and educational research. The argument to support this statement is long and involved and would sidetrack us from our subject. Basically, it rests on the idea that behavioral problems are almost all multivariate in nature and cannot be solved with a bivariate (two-variable) approach—that is, an approach that considers only one independent and one dependent variable at a time. This has become strikingly clear in much educational research where, for instance, the determinants of learning and achievement are complex: intelligence, motivation, social class, instruction, school and class atmosphere and organization, and so on. Evidently variables like these work with each other, sometimes against each other, mostly in unknown ways, to affect learning and achievement.[23] In other words, to account for the complex psychological and sociological phenomena of education requires design and analytic tools that are capable of handling the complexity, which manifests itself above all in multiplicity of independent and dependent variables. A similar argument can be given for psychological and sociological research.

This argument and the reality behind it impose a heavy burden on those teaching and learning research approaches and methods. It is unrealistic, even wrong, to approach research by teaching and learning an approach that is basically bivariate in conception. But multivariate methods are, like the behavioral reality they try to mirror, complex. The pedagogical necessity, as far as this book is con-

[20]*Ibid.*, pp. 460–461. See, also, J. Nunnally, "Analysis of Profile Data," *Psychological Bulletin*, LIX (1962), 311–319.

[21]J. Nunnally, *Psychometric Theory*. New York: McGraw-Hill, 1967, chap. 11.

[22]In this book we will not be excessively concerned about the terminology used with multivariate analysis. To some, multivariate analysis includes factor analysis and other forms of analysis, like multiple regression analysis. "Multivariate" to these individuals means more than one independent variable *or* more than one dependent variable, *or* both. Others in the field use "multivariate analysis" only for the case of *both* multiple independent and multiple dependent variables.

[23]Coleman, *op. cit.*

cerned, is to try to convey the fundamentals of research thinking, design, methods, and analysis mainly through a modified bivariate approach, to extend this approach as much as possible to multivariate conceptions and methods, and to hope that the student will pursue matters further after having gotten an adequate foundation. We have already encountered multivariate thinking, if not analysis itself. This approach will be continued and extended as we move along.

Multivariate techniques are largely logical extensions of univariate techniques. *Multiple regression analysis* is a method of analyzing the contributions of two or more independent variables to one dependent variable. Educational researchers can study the combined and separate effects on school achievement, say, of intelligence, aptitude, social class, race, home background, school atmosphere, teacher characteristics, and so on.[24] Of the multivariate methods, with the possible exception of factor analysis, it is perhaps the most useful and flexible. It can handle any number and kind of independent variables, continuous and categorical, though practical considerations usually restrict the number of variables.

Canonical correlation is a logical extension of multiple regression. Indeed, it *is* a multiple regression method. It adds more than one dependent variable to the multiple regression model. In other words, it handles the relations between sets of independent variables and sets of dependent variables. As such, it is a theoretically powerful method of analysis. It has limitations, however, that can restrict its usefulness, mainly in the interpretation of the results it yields.

Discriminant analysis is also closely related to multiple regression. Its name indicates its purpose: to discriminate groups from one another on the basis of sets of measures. It is also useful in assigning individuals to groups on the basis of their scores on tests. While this explanation is not adequate, it is sufficient for now.

It is difficult at this stage to characterize, even at a superficial level, the technique known as multivariate analysis of variance, because we have not yet studied analysis of variance. We therefore postpone its discussion until Chapter 36.

Factor analysis is essentially different in kind and purpose from the other multivariate methods. Its fundamental purpose is to help the researcher discover and identify the unities or dimensions, called *factors*, behind many measures. We now know, for example, that behind many measures of ability and intelligence lie fewer general dimensions or factors. Verbal aptitude and mathematical aptitude are two of the best known such factors. In measuring social attitudes, religious, economic, and educational factors have been found.

Before concluding this discussion of multivariate methods, we must take note of an important and rather startling fact so that later work can be put into better perspective and certain analytic difficulties clarified. The rather startling fact, little understood at this time, is that multiple regression can do all the analysis of variance does—and more. In Part 5, we go into analysis of variance in considerable detail. Why? If multiple regression analysis can do all analysis of variance can do, and more, why bother with analysis of variance? The answer is complex and

[24]This statement has limitations, especially about the separate contributions of independent variables, that will be discussed in Chapter 35.

cannot be fully given here. One reason is that multiple regression, while a powerful tool, is not as easy to understand. Analysis of variance, on the other hand, is well suited to teaching statistics, statistical inference, and research design. So we will first study analysis of variance almost as though multiple regression analysis did not exist. Later in the book we will bring the two approaches together into an extremely useful, flexible, and powerful team.

Indices

Index can be defined in two related ways. One, an index is an observable phenomenon that is substituted for a less observable phenomenon. A thermometer, for example, gives readings of numbers that stand for degrees of temperature. The numerals on a speedometer dial indicate the speed of a vehicle. Test scores indicate achievement levels, verbal aptitudes, degrees of anxiety, and so on.

A definition perhaps more useful to the researcher is: An index is a number that is a composite of two or more other numbers. An investigator makes a series of observations, for example, and derives some single number from the measures of the observations to summarize the observations, to express them succinctly. By this definition, all sums and averages are indices: they include in a single measure more than one measure. But the definition also includes the idea of indices as composites of different measures. Coefficients of correlation are such indices. They combine different measures in a single measure or index.

IQ is an index: mental age divided by chronological age. (Mental age is itself an index since it is a composite of more than one measure.) There are indices of social-class status. For example, one can combine income, occupation, and place of residence to obtain a rather good index of social class. An index of cohesiveness can be obtained by asking members of a group whether they would like to stay in the group. Their responses can be combined in a single number.

Indices are most important in scientific analysis. They simplify comparisons. Indeed, they enable research workers to make comparisons that otherwise could not be made or that could be made only with considerable difficulty. Raw data are usually much too complex to be grasped and used in mathematical and statistical manipulations. They must be reduced to manageable form. The percentage is a good example. Percentages transform raw numbers into comparable form.

Indices generally take the form of quotients: one number is divided by another number. The most useful such indices range between 0 and 1.00 or between -1.00 through 0 to $+1.00$. This makes them independent of numbers of cases and aids comparison from sample to sample and study to study. (They are generally expressed in decimal form.) There are two forms of quotients: ratios and proportions. A third form, the percentage, is a variation of the proportion.

A *ratio* is a composite of two numbers that relates one number to the other in fractional or decimal form. Any fraction, any quotient, is a ratio. Either or both the numerator and denominator of a ratio can themselves be ratios. The chief purpose and utility of a ratio is relational: it permits the comparison of otherwise noncomparable numbers. In order to do this, it is perhaps best to put the larger of the two numbers of the quotient in the denominator. This of course satisfies the condition mentioned above of having the ratio values range between 0 and 1.00, or between -1.00 through 0 to $+1.00$. This is not absolutely necessary, however. If, for example, we wished to compare the ratio of male to female high school graduates to the ratio of male and female graduates of junior high school graduates over several years, the ratio could sometimes be less than 1.00 and sometimes greater than 1.00, since it is possible that the preponderance of one sex over the other in one year might change in another year.

Sometimes ratios give more accurate information (in a sense) than the parts of which they are composed. If one were studying the relation between educational variables and tax rate, for instance, and if one were to use actual tax rates, an erroneous notion of the relation may be obtained. This is because tax rates on property are often misleading. Some communities with high *rates* actually have relatively low levels of taxation. The assessed valuation of property may be low. To avoid the discrepancies between one community and another, one can calculate, for each community, the ratio of assessed valuation to true valuation. Then an adjusted tax rate, a "true" tax rate, can be calculated by multiplying the tax rate in use by this fraction. This will yield a more accurate figure to use in calculations of relations between the tax rate and other variables.

Newcomb, in his study of the acquaintance process, invented an interesting ratio index.[25] As an index of agreement, Newcomb counted the issues among a large number of issues on which pairs of individuals agreed and disagreed. For each pair of subjects, the following ratio was computed:

$$\frac{\text{Number of agreeing responses to items of importance to both members}}{\text{Number of disagreeing responses to items of importance to both members}}$$

It is a fraction with the numerator one of two or more observed frequencies and the denominator the sum of the observed frequencies. The probability definition given earlier, $p = s/(s+f)$, where s = number of successes and f = number of failures, is a proportion. Take any two numbers, say 20 and 60. The ratio of the two numbers is $20/60 = .33$. (It could also be $60/20 = 3$.) If these two numbers were the observed frequencies of the presence and lack of presence of an attribute in a total sample, where $N = 60 + 20 = 80$, then a proportion would be: $20/(60+20) = .25$. Another proportion, of course, is $60/80 = .75$.

A *percentage* is simply a proportion multiplied by 100. With the above example, $20/80 \times 100 = 25$ percent. The main purpose of proportions and percentages is to reduce different sets of numbers to comparable sets of numbers with a common base. Any set of frequencies can be transformed to proportions or percentages in order to facilitate statistical manipulation and interpretation.[26]

A word of caution is in order. Because they are often a mixture of two

[25]T. Newcomb, *The Acquaintance Process*. New York: Holt, Rinehart and Winston, 1961, pp. 281–282.

[26]Percentages should not be used with small numbers, though proportions may always be used. The reason for the percentage computation restriction is that the relatively larger percentages give a sense of accuracy not really present in the data. For example, suppose 6 and 4 are two observed frequencies. To transform these frequencies to 60 percent and 40 percent is a bit absurd.

fallible measures, indices can be dangerous. The IQ is a good example. The numerator of the fraction is itself an index since MA, mental age, is a composite of a number of measures. A better example is the so-called Achievement Quotient: $AQ = 100 \times EA/MA$, where EA = Educational Age, and MA = Mental Age. Here, both the numerator and the denominator of the fraction are complex indices. Both are mixtures of measures of varying reliability. What is the meaning of the resulting index? How can we interpret it sensibly? It is hard to say. In short, while indices are indispensable aids to scientific analysis, they must be used with circumspection and care.

The Interpretation of Research Data

Scientists, in evaluating research, can disagree on two broad fronts: data and the interpretation of data. Disagreements on data focus on such problems as the validity and reliability of measurement instruments, and the adequacy and inadequacy of research design, methods of observation, and analysis. Assuming competence, however, major disagreements ordinarily focus upon the interpretation of data. Most psychologists, for example, will agree on the data of reinforcement experiments. Yet they disagree vigorously on the interpretation of the data of the experiments. Such disagreements are in part a function of theory. In a book like this we cannot labor interpretation from theoretical standpoints. We must be content with a more limited objective: the clarification of some common precepts of the interpretation of data *within* a particular research study or series of studies.

Adequacy of Research Design, Methodology, Measurement, and Analysis

One of the major themes of this book is the appropriateness of methodology to the problem under investigation. The researcher usually has a choice of research designs, methods of observation, methods of measurement, and types of analysis. All of these must be congruent; they must fit together. One does not use, for example, an analysis appropriate to frequencies with, say, the continuous measures yielded by an attitude scale. Most important, the design, methods of observation, measurement, and statistical analysis must all be appropriate to the research problem.

An investigator must carefully scrutinize the technical adequacy of the methods, the measurements, and the statistics. The adequacy of data interpretation crucially depends upon such scrutiny. A frequent source of interpretative inadequacy, for example, is neglect of measurement problems. It is urgently necessary to pay particular attention to the reliability and validity of the measures of the variables. (See Chapters 26 and 27.) Simply to accept without question their reliability and validity is a gross error. The researcher must be especially careful to question the validity of his measures, since the whole interpretative framework can collapse on this one point alone. If an educational investigator's problem includes the variable anxiety, and the statistical analysis shows a positive relation between anxiety and, say, achievement, the investigator must ask himself and the data whether the anxiety measured is the type of anxiety germane to the problem.

He may, for example, have measured test anxiety when the problem variable is really general anxiety. Similarly, he must ask himself whether his measure of achievement is valid for the research purpose. If the research problem demands application of principles but the measure of achievement is a standardized test that emphasizes factual knowledge, the interpretation of the data can be erroneous.

In other words, we face here the obvious, but too easily overlooked, fact that adequacy of interpretation is dependent on each link in the methodological chain, as well as on the appropriateness of each link to the research problem and the congruence of the links to each other. This is clearly seen when we are faced with negative or inconclusive results.

Negative and Inconclusive Results

Negative or inconclusive results are much harder to interpret than positive results. When results are positive, when the data support the hypotheses, one interprets the data along the lines of the theory and the reasoning behind the hypotheses. Although one carefully asks critical questions, upheld predictions are evidence for the validity of the reasoning behind the problem statement.

This is one of the great virtues of scientific prediction. When we predict something and plan and execute a scheme for testing the prediction, and things turn out as we say they will, then the adequacy of our reasoning and our execution seems supported. We are never sure, of course. The outcome, though predicted, may be as it is for reasons quite other than those we fondly espouse. Still, that the whole complex chain of theory, deduction from theory, design, methodology, measurement, and analysis has led to a predicted outcome is cogent evidence for the adequacy of the whole structure. We make a complex bet with the odds against us, so to speak. We then throw the research dice or spin the research wheel. If our predicted number comes up, the reasoning and the execution leading to the successful prediction would seem to be adequate. If we can repeat the feat, then the evidence of adequacy is even more convincing.

But now take the negative case. Why were the results negative? Why did the results not come out as predicted? Note that any weak link in the research chain can cause negative results. They can be due to any one, or several, or all of the following: incorrect theory and hypotheses, inappropriate or incorrect methodology, inadequate or poor measurement, and faulty analysis. All these must be carefully examined. All must be scrutinized and the negative results laid at the door of one, several, or all of them. If we can be fairly sure that the methodology, the measurement, and the analysis are adequate, then negative results can be definite contributions to scientific advance, since only then can we have some confidence that our hypotheses are not correct.

Unhypothesized Relations and Unanticipated Findings

The testing of hypothesized relations is strongly emphasized in this book. This does not mean, however, that other relations in the data are not sought and tested. Quite the contrary. The practicing researcher is always keen to seek out and study relations in his data. The unpredicted relation may be an important key to deeper understanding of theory. It may throw light on aspects of the problem not anticipated when the problem was formulated. Therefore researchers, while emphasizing hypothesized relations, should always be alert to unanticipated relations in their data.

Suppose we have hypothesized that the homogeneous grouping of pupils will be beneficial to bright pupils but not beneficial to pupils of lesser ability. The hypothesis is upheld, say. But we notice an apparent difference between suburban and rural areas: the relation seems stronger in the suburban areas; it is reversed in some rural areas! We analyze the data using the suburban-rural variable. We find that homogeneous grouping seems to have a marked influence on bright children in the suburbs, but that it has little or no influence in rural areas. This would be an important finding indeed.

One of the best examples of an unexpected finding occurred in the well-known Hawthorne studies.[27] Elaborate procedures were set up to study the effects of different working conditions on the output of a group of women workers. Various changes were successively made in the women's working conditions—for example, change in payment, increased rest periods, shorter working day. The output curve rose. The researchers became suspicious, however. Was something else at work? They did away with the changes and restored the women to their original working conditions. The output rose even more! This unexpected finding led them to recast their thinking. As Homans says, ". . . the increase in the output rate . . . could . . . be related to . . . the development of an organized social group in a peculiar and effective relation with its supervisors."[28]

Unpredicted findings must be treated with more suspicion than predicted findings. Before being accepted, they should be substantiated in independent research in which they are specifically predicted and tested. Only when a relation is deliberately and systematically tested with the necessary controls built into the design can we have much faith in it. The unanticipated finding may be fortuitous or spurious.

Proof, Probability, and Interpretation

The interpretation of research data culminates in conditional probabilistic statements of the "If p, then q" kind. We enrich such statements by qualifying them in some such way as: If p, then q, under conditions r, s, and t. Ordinarily we eschew causal statements, because we are aware that they cannot be made without grave risk of error.

Perhaps of greater practical importance to the researcher interpreting data is the problem of proof. Let us flatly assert that nothing can be "proved" scientifically. All one can do is to bring evidence to bear that such-and-such a proposition is true.[29] Proof is a deductive matter, and experimental methods of inquiry are not methods of proof. They are controlled methods of bringing evidence to bear on

[27]G. Homans, "Group Factors in Worker Productivity," In H. Proshansky and B. Seidenberg, eds., *Basic Studies in Social Psychology*. New York: Holt, Rinehart and Winston, 1965, pp. 592–604.

[28]*Ibid.*, p. 596.

[29]Kerlinger, *op. cit.*, p. 1134.

the probable truth or falsity of relational propositions. In short, no scientific investigation ever proves anything. Thus the interpretation of the analysis of research data can never use the term proof in the logical sense of the word. Interpretation, rather, must concern itself with the evidence for or against the validity of tested hypotheses.

Fortunately, for practical research purposes it is not necessary to worry excessively about causality and proof. Evidence at satisfactory levels of probability is sufficient for scientific progress. Causality and proof were discussed in this chapter to sensitize the reader to the danger of loose usage of the terms. The understanding of scientific reasoning, and practice and reasonable care in the interpretation of research data, while no guarantees of the validity of one's interpretations, are helpful guards against inadequate inference from data to conclusions.

Study Suggestions

1. Suppose you wish to study the relation between social class and test anxiety. What are the two main possibilities for analyzing the data (omitting the possibility of calculating a coefficient of correlation)? Set up two analytic structures.
2. Assume that you want to add sex as a variable to the problem above. Set up the two kinds of analytic paradigms.
3. Suppose an investigator has tested the effects of three methods of teaching reading on reading achievement. He had 30 subjects in each group and a reading achievement score for each subject. He also included sex as an independent variable: half the subjects were male and half female. What does his analytic paradigm look like? What goes into the cells?
4. Study Fig. 9.5. Do these analysis of variance designs or paradigms represent partitioning of variables? Why? Why is partitioning important in setting up research designs and in analyzing data? Do the rules of categorization (and partitioning) have any effect on the interpretation of data? If so, what effects might they have? (Consider the effects of violations of the two basic partitioning rules.)

CHAPTER 10

The Analysis of Crossbreaks

So far, we have talked mostly *about* analysis. Now we must learn how to do analysis. The simplest way to analyze data to study relations is by cross-partitioning frequencies. A cross partition, as we learned in Chapter 4, is the juxtaposition of subsets of U. We form subsets of the form $A \cap B$ from the subsets A and B of U. Examples were given in Chapter 4; more will be given shortly. The expression "cross partition" refers to an abstract process of set theory. In this text, when the cross partition idea is applied to the analysis of frequencies to study relations between variables, we call the cross partitions "crossbreaks." The kind of analysis to be shown is also called *contingency analysis*.

We can no longer get along without some statistics. So we here introduce a form of statistical analysis usually associated with frequencies, the χ^2 (chi square) test, and the idea of statistical "significance." This study of crossbreaks and χ^2 should help ease us into statistics.

In a Gallup poll study, Catholic priests were asked, "Should priests be allowed to marry?"[1] The investigators evidently thought there was a relation between answers to this question and age. They therefore tabulated the results, in percentages, as in Table 10.1. There appears to be a relation between age and priests' opinions on marriage of the Catholic clergy: most young priests evidently believe in marriage for priests, whereas most older priests do not.

Teacher mortality has plagued the education profession. Why do teachers leave teaching and go into other occupations? Some indirect light was thrown on the subject by Rosenberg who, in a study of students' values, asked students, in

[1] *New York Times*, April 11, 1971.

TABLE **10.1** RELATION BETWEEN AGE OF PRIESTS AND OPINIONS ON CLERGY MARRIAGE, PERCENTAGES

Age	Yes	No	No Opinion
Under 40	77	17	6
Over 40	36	56	8

1950 and again in 1952, whether they would like to become teachers.[2] He also determined whether the students held values that were "people-oriented" (work with people rather than things; be helpful to others) or "non-people-oriented." One of the relations he reported is given in Table 10.2.[3] The data in the table seem to say that, among students who choose teaching as a profession, those who are not oriented toward people are more likely to leave teaching than those who are.

Tables 10.1 and 10.2 are both crossbreaks or cross partitions, and they both use percentages, a common and useful practice.

TABLE **10.2** PEOPLE-ORIENTED VALUES AND CHANGE OF OCCUPATIONAL CHOICE, ROSENBERG STUDY. (IN PERCENT)

	Remained Teachers, 1952	Left Teaching, 1952
People-Oriented	57	43
Non-People-Oriented	19	81

Data and Variable Terminology

In Chapter 3 a distinction was made between active and attribute variables, the former meaning an experimental or manipulated variable and the latter a measured variable. The term "attribute" was used because it is general and can cover the properties of any objects, animate or inanimate. Unfortunately, however, "attribute" has sometimes been used to mean what have been called categorical variables in this book. In this usage, for example, sex, race, religion, and similar categorical variables have been called attributes. They have also been called "qualitative variables." Both usages seem ill-advised. An attribute is any property of any object, whether the object is measured in an all-or-none way or with a set of continuous measures. We so use it in this book not to upset any conventional usage, if that were possible, but rather to clarify the distinction between experimental and measured variables.

The use of the expression "qualitative variable" has been criticized before (Chapter 3). In short, there is no such thing as a variable that is qualitative. Since we can always assign 1's and 0's to categorical variables, they are thus capable of

[2] M. Rosenberg, "Factors Influencing Change in Occupational Choice." In P. Lazarsfeld and M. Rosenberg, eds., *The Language of Social Research.* New York: Free Press, 1955, pp. 250–259.

[3] *Ibid.*, p. 251. Rosenberg's table has been changed slightly by reversing the variables.

quantification. That this is not mere word quibbling will become evident later in the book.

What we have called categorical variables are also called, perhaps more accurately, "nominal variables." This is because they belong to what we will later learn is the level of measurement called "nominal." Since in this and later chapters we have to be quite clear about the difference between continuous and categorical variables, let us briefly anticipate a later discussion and define measurement. When the numbers or symbols assigned to objects have no number meaning beyond presence or absence of the property or attribute being measured, the measurement is called "nominal." A variable that is nominal is, of course, what we have been calling "categorical." To name something ("nominal") is to put it into a category ("categorical").

All this is perhaps clarified by the following set equation, which is a general definition of measurement:[4]

$$f = \{(x, y): x = \text{any object, and } y = \text{any numeral}\}$$

which is read: f is a rule of correspondence that is defined as a set of ordered pairs, (x, y), such that x is some object and y is some numeral assigned to x. This is a general definition that covers all cases of measurement. Obviously, y can be a set of continuous measures or simply the set $\{0, 1\}$. Categorical or nominal variables are those variables where $y = \{0, 1\}$, 0 and 1 being assigned on the basis of the object x either possessing or not possessing some defined property or attribute. Continuous variables are those variables where $y = \{0, 1, 2, \ldots, k\}$, or some numerical system where the numbers mean more or less of the attribute in question. (It is mathematically difficult to define "continuous measures," and the definition just given is not satisfactory. Nevertheless, the reader will know what is meant.)

The level of measurement of this chapter is mostly nominal. Even when continuous variables are used, they are converted to categorical variables. In general, this should not be done, because it throws information (variance) away. Nevertheless, there are times when, in the judgment of the researcher, it is necessary or desirable to treat a continuous variable as a categorical variable. For example, it may be possible to measure a potentially continuous variable only in a crude way by, say, having an observer judge whether or not objects possess or do not possess an attribute. While there are degrees of aggressive behavior, it may only be possible to say that an individual did or did not exhibit aggressive behavior, or it may be sufficient for the purposes of the research. Ideally, it is desirable to assign continuous values to individuals; this is usually better measurement. But the property may be so gross or so elusive that only nominal measurement is possible.

Crossbreaks: Definitions and Purpose

A *crossbreak* is a numerical tabular presentation of data, usually in frequency or percentage form, in which variables are cross-partitioned in order to study the

[4]F. Kerlinger, "Research in Education." In R. Ebel, V. Noll, and R. Bauer, eds., *Encyclopedia of Educational Research*, 4th ed. New York: Macmillan, 1969, pp. 1127–1144 (p. 1137).

relations between them.[5] It is a common form of analysis that can be used with almost any kind of data. Its principal use, however, is with categorical or nominal data. Apart from its actual research use, the crossbreak is a valuable pedagogical device. Its clarity and simplicity make it an effective tool for learning how to structure research problems and how to analyze data. Crossbreaks are cross partitions, as indicated earlier. Therefore the partitioning rules and the set notions already learned can be easily applied to their analysis.

Crossbreaks enable the researcher to determine the nature of the relations between variables. But they have other side purposes. They can be used to organize data in convenient form for statistical analysis. A statistical test is then applied to the data. Indices of association, too, are readily calculated.

Another purpose of crossbreaks is to control variables. As we will see later, crossbreaks enable us to study and test a relation between two variables while controlling a third variable. In this way "spurious" relations can be unmasked and the relations between variables can be "specified"—that is, differences in degree of relation at different levels of a control variable can be determined.

Still another purpose of crossbreaks was alluded to above: their study and use sensitize the student and practicing researcher to the design and structure of research problems. There is something salutary about reducing a research problem to a crossbreak. In fact, if you cannot write a diagrammatic paradigm of your research problem in either analysis of variance or crossbreak form, then the problem is not clear in your mind, or you do not really have a research problem.

Simple Crossbreaks and Rules for Crossbreak Construction

The simplest form a crossbreak can take is a 2×2 table. Examples of 2×2 crossbreaks in percentage form have already been given. A third example, this time in frequency form, is given in Table 10.3. The data for the table were taken from a tabulation of twelve roll calls of the House of Representatives of the Eighty-Eighth Congress, 1963–1964, by Wirt, Morey, and Brakeman.[6] (The figures in parentheses are percentages.) They represent the vote of the House on a resolution to enlarge the House Rules Committee from 12 to 15 members, a political and procedural issue of considerable importance. More important for our purpose, they represent the relation between political affiliation and voting on the resolution. Before discussing the interpretation of the tabled data, however, we need to know how it was set up.

There seem to be no generally accepted rules on the setup of crossbreaks. We know, however, that they are cross partitions and thus must follow the rules of

[5]Crossbreaks are also used in descriptive ways. The investigator may not be interested in relations, as such: he may want only to describe a situation that exists. For instance, take the case where a table breaks social-class membership against possession of TV sets, refrigerators, and so on. This is a descriptive comparison rather than a variable crossbreak, even though we might conceivably call possession of a TV set, for instance, by some variable name. Our concern is exclusively with the analysis of data gathered to test or explore relations.

[6]F. Wirt, R. Morey, and L. Brakeman, *Introductory Problems in Political Research*. Englewood Cliffs, N.J.: Prentice-Hall, 1970, p. 73 (Table 6.3). I set up the crossbreak.

TABLE **10.3** CROSSBREAK OF POLITICAL AFFILIATION AND ROLL CALL VOTE ON HOUSE RULES COMMITTEE ENLARGEMENT, HOUSE OF REPRESENTATIVES, EIGHTY-EIGHTH CONGRESS[a]

	Yea	Nay	
Democrat	207 (.81)	48 (.19)	255
Republican	28 (.16)	148 (.84)	176
	235	196	(431)

[a]The figures in the body of the table and at the bottom and the right side are frequencies. The decimal figure in parentheses are proportions or percentages calculated across the rows, e.g., 207/255 = .81 and 48/255 = .19.

partitioning or categorization discussed earlier: the categories are set up according to the research hypotheses; they are independent and mutually exclusive; they are exhaustive; each category is derived from one and only one classification principle; all categories are on one level of discourse.

A 2×2 crossbreak, in variable symbols, is given in Fig. 10.1. A_1 and A_2 are the partitions of the variable A; B_1 and B_2 are the partitions of the variable B. The cells $A_1B_1, \ldots, A_2B_2$ are simply the intersections of the subsets of A and B: $A_1 \cap B_1, \ldots, A_2 \cap B_2$. Any object in U, the universe of objects, can be categorized as A_1B_1, A_1B_2, A_2B_1, or A_2B_2. If U is a sample of children, and A is sex and B is delinquency, then an A_1B_1 member is a delinquent boy, whereas an A_2B_2 child is a nondelinquent girl. Larger tables—2×3, 2×4, 3×2, and so on—are merely extensions of the idea.

In the three-variable case, strictly speaking, a cube is necessary. Let there be three variables A, B, C, each dichotomized (for simplicity). The actual situation would look like Fig. 10.2. Each cell is a cube with a triple label. All visible cubes have been properly labeled. If the variables A, B, and C were sex, social class, and delinquency, then, for example, an $A_2B_2C_1$ cell member would be a working-class girl who is delinquent. Since handling cubes is cumbersome, we use a simpler

	B_1	B_2
A_1	A_1B_1	A_1B_2
A_2	A_2B_1	A_2B_2

FIG. 10.1

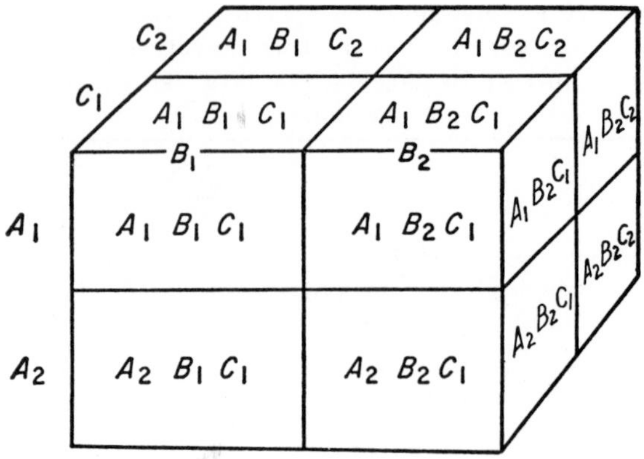

FIG. 10.2

system. The three-variable crossbreak table can look like that of Fig. 10.3. We return to three-variable crossbreaks later.

	B_1		B_2	
	C_1	C_2	C_1	C_2
A_1	$A_1B_1C_1$	$A_1B_1C_2$	$A_1B_2C_1$	$A_1B_2C_2$
A_2	$A_2B_1C_1$	$A_2B_1C_2$	$A_2B_2C_1$	$A_2B_2C_2$

FIG. 10.3

Calculation of Percentages

Calculate percentages from the independent variable to the dependent variable. In studies where it is not possible to label the variables as independent and dependent, the rule, of course, does not apply. But in most cases it does apply.[7] In Table 10.3, for example, the percentages are calculated from Democrat and Republican to Yea and Nay. They are in parentheses in the table.

Return to Table 10.2, the data from the Rosenberg study. Does the table indicate a relation greater than chance between people orientation of teachers and teachers' remaining in teaching (or occupational choice)? Do the proportions in the four cells of the table depart significantly from the proportions to be expected by chance? If they do, we say that there is a relation between the variables. Suppose a statistical test has been done and its result indicates greater than chance departure of the proportions. (We will see how to do such a test shortly.) We say,

[7]Zeisel states the rule differently: "... *percentages should be computed in the direction of the causal factor.*" H. Zeisel, *Say It With Figures*, 4th ed. New York: Harper & Row, 1957, p. 24.

then, that there is a statistically significant relation between people orientation and remaining in or leaving teaching.

But what is the nature of the relation? This can be determined by inspecting the table. It can be seen that lack of people orientation appears to be a factor in leaving teaching. Most of those teachers in this sample who were not people-oriented left teaching: 81 percent of non-people-oriented teachers left teaching versus 19 percent who stayed in teaching. Note that among the teachers with orientation toward people the difference was not nearly as great: 57 percent versus 43 percent.

Crossbreaks with frequencies can sometimes be interpreted the way they are, but it is usually better to convert the frequencies to percentages following the rule given above: calculate from the independent variable to the dependent variable one row (or column) at a time. To do this, first add the frequencies in the rows and in the columns and enter these sums at the bottom and side of the table. In Table 10.3, these sums have been entered. They are called "marginal frequencies," or "marginals." (Actually, to calculate the percentages, only the row sums of Table 10.3 need be calculated. Both row and column sums will be needed later.) In the relation of Table 10.3, the independent variable is clearly political affiliation, and the dependent variable is vote on the issue, or Yea and Nay. Sometimes, however, determining which variable is which is not so simple. At any rate, we calculate the percentages across the rows, or from the independent variable (rows) to the dependent variable (columns).[8]

Now, calculate the percentages (or proportions). Take each row separately. Take the Democrat row of Table 10.3: $207/255 = .81$, and $48/255 = .19$. The percentages are obtained simply by multiplying these proportions by 100, which amounts to moving the decimal two places to the right. Now do the Republican row: $28/176 = .16$, and $148/176 = .84$. (Notice that each row must total to 1.00, or 100 percent.) The relation is now clear: of the Democrats 81 percent voted Yea and 19 percent voted Nay, and of the Republicans 16 percent voted Yea and 84 percent Nay. Notice how the percentage crossbreak highlights the relation. The relation is obscured in the frequency table, owing to an unequal number of Democrats (255) and Republicans (176). The percentage calculation transforms both rows to a common base and enhances the comparison—and the relation.

The reader may wonder about two things: Why not calculate the percentages the other way: from the dependent variable to the independent variable? Why not calculate the percentages over the whole table? There is nothing inherently wrong with either of these calculations. In the first case, however, we would be asking the data a different question. In the second case, we merely transform the frequency data to percentage or proportion data without changing the pattern of the frequencies.

[8]Researchers often construct their tables the other way, i.e., the independent variable is at the top and the dependent variable at the side. It doesn't really matter, of course, provided one does the calculation correctly. With more than one independent variable, constructing the table is more complex. Wherever possible, we follow the system used in Tables 10.1, 10.2, and 10.3.

In the Rosenberg problem, the problem is really pointed toward accounting for teachers leaving teaching. The question, then, is: Do teachers who are not people-oriented leave teaching? The hypothesis implied by this question is: Teachers who are not people-oriented leave teaching. We have a statement of the kind If p, then q: If non-people-oriented, then leave teaching. There can be no doubt of the independent and dependent variables. Therefore, the calculation of the percentages is determined, since we must ask: Given non-people orientation, what proportion of teachers leave teaching? This question is answered in the second row of Table 10.2: 81 percent. (Of course, the first row is also important in the overall relation.) If the percentages are calculated down the columns, this is tantamount to the question: Given teachers who have left teaching, what proportion is non-people-oriented? The answer happens to be 37 percent (see later), which hardly gives the correct impression of the relation.

Percentage Calculation and Conditional Probability

Fortunately, it is possible to clarify the percentage calculation rule by giving its theoretical rationale. This is necessary because percentages are often calculated the "wrong" way, and it is hard to detect such "errors." (See Study Suggestion 5 at the end of the chapter.) We can also throw light on the meaning of calculating proportions over the whole table. To do so, we return to the idea of conditional probability discussed in Chapter 7. We will also see something of the power of set theory and probability in their applications to research and analysis.

Note, first, that Fig. 10.1 represents the Cartesian product (see Chapter 5) of the sets A and B, or $A \times B$. Note, too, that A_1B_1, A_1B_2, etc. are abbreviated symbolism for $A_1 \cap B_1$, $A_1 \cap B_2$, and so on. Recall the conditional probability equation:

$$p(A \mid B) = \frac{p(A \cap B)}{p(B)}$$

Let A = leave teaching (LT), and B = non-people orientation (NPO). Then the equation becomes:

$$p(LT \mid NPO) = \frac{p(LT \cap NPO)}{p(NPO)}$$

It is easier to obtain the needed probability from the original frequencies. They are given in Table 10.4. (They were calculated from Rosenberg's percentage table and the total N of 108.) $LT \cap NPO$, the intersection of LT and NPO, or the joint event of leaving teaching and being non-people-oriented, is of course the lower right cell: 21 teachers who were non-people-oriented left teaching. Thus, $p(LT \cap NPO)$ is obtained by calculating: $21/108 = .1944$. $p(NPO)$ is calculated by using the marginal sum corresponding to NPO: $26/108 = .2407$. Substituting in the above equation gives: $.1944/.2407 = .81$. But this is the percentage calculated across the rows in Table 10.2! The percentages of the other three cells are similarly calculated.

In other words, *the percentages calculated from the independent variable to the dependent variable are the conditional probabilities* whose correct statements are derived from the original research problem. Calculation down the columns of Table 10.4 gives quite a different—and erroneous—picture. It is tantamount to writing: $p(NPO \mid LT)$, or the probability of non-people orientation, given left teaching. The conditional probability statement, $p(A \mid B)$, expresses a relation between an independent variable and a dependent variable, A being the *dependent* and B the *independent* variable. When we say "conditional," we mean A is "dependent" on B. More accurately—and as explained in Chapter 7—the specification of B changes the sample space. Using the symbols of Fig. 10.1, we calculate the joint probability of A_1B_1:

$$p(A_1 \cap B_1) = \frac{n(A_1 \cap B_1)}{n(U)}$$

where $n(A_1 \cap B_1)$ is the number of cases in A_1B_1, and $n(U) = N =$ all the cases. This is: $47/108 = .44$, the probability of any case in the whole sample falling into the A_1B_1 cell. Now, suppose we know a teacher is people-oriented. This means the sample space has been cut down to the top row of the table. Thus we calculate the probability with the new sample space:

$$p(B_1 \mid A_1) = \frac{p(A_1 \cap B_1)}{p(A_1)}$$

Translating this into the symbols of the example, we have:

$$p(RT \mid PO) = \frac{p(PO \cap RT)}{p(PO)} = \frac{47/108}{82/108} = .57$$

which is the proportion obtained for the cell by calculating across the row, or from the independent variable to the dependent variable. To calculate the cell on the lower right of Table 10.4, we write and calculate:

$$p(LT \mid NPO) = \frac{p(NPO \cap LT)}{p(NPO)} = \frac{21/108}{26/108} = .81$$

TABLE **10.4** FREQUENCIES OF TABLE 10.2: PEOPLE-ORIENTED VALUES AND CHANGE OF OCCUPATIONAL CHOICE[a]

	Remained Teachers, 1952	Left Teaching, 1952	
People-Oriented	47	35	82
Non-People-Oriented	5	21	26
	52	56	108

[a]Frequencies calculated from percentages given in Table 10.2 and the total N of 108.

Let's now calculate the proportions two other ways and compare them to the calculations from the independent variable to the dependent variable. First, calculate down the columns and we obtain the proportions in the upper left corner of Table 10.5. For example, the entry in the upper right cell is calculated (from Table 10.4): 35/56 = .63. Second, calculate the proportions over the whole table, and obtain the entries in the lower right of each cell. For the lower right cell (from Table 10.4): 21/108 = .19. Both sets of proportions, if interpreted, lead to conclusions rather different from those yielded by the proportions calculated from independent variable to dependent variable (in parentheses in Table 10.5). Study of the differences is left to the reader.

TABLE **10.5** PROPORTIONS OBTAINED BY CALCULATING (a) DOWN THE COLUMNS, (b) OVER THE WHOLE TABLE, AND (c) FROM INDEPENDENT VARIABLE TO DEPENDENT VARIABLE, FREQUENCIES OF TABLE 10.4[a]

	Remained Teachers, 1952	Left Teaching, 1952	
People-Oriented	.90 (.57) .44	.63 (.43) .32	(1.00)
Non-People-Oriented	.10 (.19) .05	.37 (.81) .19	(1.00)
	1.00	1.00	

[a]Calculations down columns: upper left in each cell. Calculations over whole table: lower right in each cell. Calculations from independent variable to dependent variable: in parentheses.

Statistical Significance and the χ^2 Test

We must now interrupt our study of crossbreaks to learn a little statistics and thus anticipate the work and study of the next chapter. While it is possible to talk about crossbreaks and how they are constructed without statistics, it is not really possible to go into the analysis and interpretation of frequency data without at least some statistics. So we examine one of the simplest and yet most useful of statistical tests, the χ^2 (chi square) test.

Look at the frequencies of Table 10.4. Do they really express a relation between people orientation and change of occupational choice? Or could they have happened by chance? Are they one pattern among many patterns of frequencies that one would get picking numbers from a table of random numbers, such selection being limited only by the given marginal frequencies? Such questions have to be asked of every set of frequency results obtained from samples. Until they *are* answered, there is little or no point in going further with data interpretation. If our results could have happened by chance, of what use is our effort to interpret them?

What does it mean to say that an obtained result is "statistically significant"—that it departs "significantly" from chance expectation? Suppose that we were to do an actual experiment 100 times just as we toss a coin 100 times. Each experiment is like a coin toss or a throw of the dice. The outcome of each experiment can be considered a sample point. The sample space, properly conceived, is an infinite number of such experiments or sample points. For convenience, we conceive of the 100 replications of the experiment as the sample space U. This is nothing new. It is what we did with the coins and the dice.

Take a simple example. A university administration is considering the wisdom of changing the marking system, but it wants to know faculty attitudes toward the proposed change, since it has found from experience that if most of the faculty does not approve a change the new system can run into serious trouble. By means of a suitable procedure 100 faculty members, selected at random, are asked their attitudes toward the proposed change. Sixty faculty members approve the change, and 40 disapprove. The administration now has to ask: Is this a "significant" majority? The administration reasons this way. If the faculty members were completely indifferent, their responses would be like chance: now this way, now that way. The expected frequency on an indifference hypothesis would of course be 50/50, the result to be expected by chance.

To answer the question whether 60/40 differs significantly from indifference or chance a statistical test known as χ^2 is performed. A table (Table 10.6) is set

TABLE **10.6** CALCULATION OF χ^2: FACULTY APPROVAL AND DISAPPROVAL OF PROPOSED CHANGE IN MARKING SYSTEM

	Approve	Disapprove
f_o	60	40
f_e	50	50
$f_o - f_e$	10	-10
$(f_o - f_e)^2$	100	100
$\frac{(f_o - f_e)^2}{f_e}$	$\frac{100}{50} = 2$	$\frac{100}{50} = 2$

up to obtain the necessary terms for the calculation of χ^2. The term f_o means "frequency obtained" and f_e means "frequency expected." The function of statistical tests is to compare obtained results with those to be expected on the basis of chance. Here, then, we compare f_o with f_e. On the indifference or chance assumption, we write 50 and 50. But 60 and 40 were obtained. The difference is 10. Could a difference as large as 10 have happened by chance? Another way to put the question is: If we performed the same experiment 100 times and only chance were operating—that is, the faculty members answered the questions indifferently or, in effect, randomly—how many times in the 100 could we expect to get a deviation as large as 60/40? If we tossed a coin 100 times, we know that sometimes we would get 60 heads and 40 tails and 40 heads and 60 tails. How many times would such a large discrepancy, if it *is* a large discrepancy, happen by chance? The χ^2 test is a convenient way to get an answer.

We now write a χ^2 formula:

$$\chi^2 = \sum \left[\frac{(f_o - f_e)^2}{f_e} \right] \tag{10.1}$$

which simply says: "Subtract each expected frequency, f_e, from the comparable obtained frequency, f_o, square this difference, divide the difference squared by the expected frequency, f_e, and then add up these quotients." This was done in Table 10.6. To make sure the reader knows what is happening, we write it out:

$$\chi^2 = \frac{(60-50)^2}{50} + \frac{(40-50)^2}{50} = \frac{100}{50} + \frac{100}{50} = 4$$

But what does $\chi^2 = 4$ mean? χ^2 is a measure of the departure of obtained frequencies from the frequencies expected by chance. Provided we have some way of knowing what the chance expectations are, and provided the observations are independent, we can always calculate χ^2. The larger χ^2 is the greater the obtained frequencies deviate from the expected chance frequencies. The value of χ^2 ranges from 0, which indicates no departure of obtained from expected frequencies, through a large number of increasing values.

In addition to the formula, above, it is necessary to know the so-called *degrees of freedom* of the problem and to have a χ^2 table. Chi-square tables are found in almost any statistics book, together with instructions on how to use them. So are explanations of degrees of freedom. We may say here that "degrees of freedom" means the latitude of variation a statistical problem has. In the problem above, there is one degree of freedom because the total number of cases is fixed, 100, and as soon as one of the frequencies is given the other is immediately determined. That is, there are no degrees of freedom when two numbers must sum to 100 and one of them, say 40, is given. Once 40, or 45, or any other number is given, there are no more places to go. The remaining number has no freedom to vary.[9]

To understand more about what is going on here, suppose we calculate all the χ^2's for all possibilities: 40/60, 41/59, 42/58, . . . , 50/50, . . . , 60/40. Doing so, we get the set of values given in Table 10.7. (In reading the table, it is helpful to conceive of the first frequency of each pair as "Heads," or "Agrees with," or "Male," or any other variable.) Only two of these χ^2's, the values of 4.00 associated with 40/60 and 60/40, are statistically significant. They are statistically significant because by checking the χ^2 table for one degree of freedom we find an entry of 3.841 at what is called the .05 level of significance. All the other χ^2's in Table 10.7 are less than 3.841. Take the χ^2 for 42/58, which is 2.56. If we consult the table, 2.56 falls between the values of χ^2 with probabilities of .10 and .25, or 2.706 and 1.323, respectively. This is actually a probability of about .14. In most

[9]Similarly, if one calculates a mean of 100 scores, one uses up one degree of freedom, by imposing one restriction on the data. Probably the best explanation of degrees of freedom is Walker's. See H. Walker, "Degrees of Freedom," *Journal of Educational Psychology*, XXXI (1940), 253–269, and H. Walker, *Mathematics Essential for Elementary Statistics*, rev. ed. New York: Holt, Rinehart and Winston, 1951, chap. 22.

TABLE **10.7** FREQUENCIES AND CORRESPONDING χ^2's[a]

Frequencies	χ^2
40/60	4.00
41/59	3.24
42/58	2.56
43/57	1.96
44/56	1.44
45/55	1.00
46/54	.64
47/53	.36
48/52	.16
49/51	.04
50/50	0

[a]*The values of* χ^2 for 51/49. . . . , 60/40 are, of course, the same as those in the table but in reverse order.

cases, we do not need to bother finding out where it falls. All we need to do is to note that it does not make the .05 grade of 3.841. If it does not, we say that it is not statistically significant—*at the .05 level.* The reader may now ask: "What is the .05 level?" and "Why the .05 level?" "Why not .10 or even .15?" To answer these questions, we must digress a little.

Levels of Statistical Significance

The .05 level means that an obtained result that is significant at the .05 level could occur *by chance* only 5 times in 100 trials. With our responses to the administrations's question of 60 Agrees and 40 Disagrees, we can say that a discrepancy as large as this *will happen by chance* only about 5 times in 100 trials. It *can* happen more often or less often, but it probably will happen about 5 times in 100.

A level of statistical significance is to some extent chosen arbitrarily.[10] But it is certainly not completely arbitrary. Another level of significance frequently used is the .01 level. The .05 and .01 levels correspond fairly well to two and three standard deviations from the mean of a normal probability distribution. (A normal probability distribution is the symmetric bell-shaped curve which the student has probably often seen. We take it up later.)

Think back to the coin-tossing experiment, when a penny was tossed 100 times. Heads turned up 52 times and tails 48 times. Consult Table 10.7. $\chi^2 = .16$, a result clearly not significant. But suppose the coin had been tossed not one set of 100 tosses but 100 sets of 100 tosses, which would be tantamount to 100 experiments. From these 100 experiments we would get a variety of results: 58/42, 46/54, 51/49, and so on. About 95 or 96 of these experiments would yield heads within the bounds of 40 and 60. That is, only 4 or 5 of the experiments would yield less than 40 or greater than 60 heads. Similarly, if we perform an experiment

[10]The .05 level was apparently first chosen by Fisher. See R. Fisher, *Statistical Methods for Research Workers*, 11th ed. New York: Hafner, 1950, pp. 80 ff.

and find a difference between two means which, after an appropriate statistical test, is at the .05 level of significance, then we have reason to believe that the obtained mean difference is not merely a chance difference. It *could* be a chance difference, however. If the experiment were done 100 times and there really were no difference between the means, 5 of these 100 replications might show differences as large as the actual obtained differences.

While this discussion may help to clarify the meaning of statistical significance, it does not yet answer all the questions asked before. The .05 level was originally chosen—and has persisted with researchers—because it is considered a reasonably good gamble. It is neither too high nor too low for most social scientific research. Many researchers prefer the .01 level of significance. This is quite a high level of certainty. Indeed, it is "practical certainty." Some researchers say that the .10 level might sometimes be used. Others say that 10 chances in 100 are too many, so that they are not willing to risk a decision with such odds. Others say that the .01 level, or 1 chance in 100, is too stringent, that "really" significant results may be discarded in this manner.

Should a certain level of significance be chosen and adhered to? This is a difficult question. The .05 and .01 levels have been widely advocated. There is a newer trend of thinking that advocates reporting the significance levels of all results. That is, if a result is significant at the .12 level, say, it should be reported accordingly. Some practitioners object to this practice. They say that one should make a bet and stick to it. Another school of thought advocates working with what are called "confidence intervals."[11] In this book, the statistical "levels" approach will be used because it is simpler. For the student who does not plan to do any research, the matter is not serious. But it is emphasized that those who will engage in research should study other procedures, such as statistical estimation methods, confidence intervals, and exact probability methods.

To illustrate the calculation and use of the χ^2 test with crossbreaks, we now apply it to the frequency data of Table 10.4. Formula 10.1 is used, but with crossbreak tables its application is more complicated than its use in Table 10.6. The main difference is the calculation of the expected frequencies. The necessary calculations are given in Table 10.8. The expected frequencies, f_e, are in the upper

[11]Most investigators simply say that the results are not significant if they do not make the .05 or .01 grade. For a penetrating discussion of this obviously difficult issue, which cannot be adequately discussed here, see W. Rozeboom, "The Fallacy of the Null-Hypothesis Significance Test." *Psychological Bulletin*, LVII (1960), 416–428. Rozeboom advocates the use of confidence intervals and the reporting of precise probability values of experimental outcomes. See also J. Nunnally, "The Place of Statistics in Psychology," *Educational and Psychological Measurement*, XX (1960), 641–650; H. Walker and J. Lev, *Statistical Inference*. New York: Holt, Rinehart and Winston, 1953, pp. 52 ff. The basic idea is that, instead of categorically rejecting hypotheses if the .05 grade is not made, we say the probability is .95 that the unknown value falls between .30 and .50. Now, if the obtained empirical proportion is, say, .60, then this is evidence for the correctness of the investigator's substantive hypothesis, or in null hypothesis language, the null hypothesis is rejected. A well-balanced discussion of these and other statistical problems can be found in C. Harris, "Statistical Methods," in R. Ebel et al., *op. cit.*, pp. 1307–1318. A discussion of the difference between the terms "significance" and "confidence" can be found in R. Chandler, "The Statistical Concepts of Confidence and Significance," *Psychological Bulletin*, LIV (1957), 429–430. See, also, W. Hays, *Statistics*. New York: Holt, Rinehart and Winston, 1963, chap. 9.

TABLE **10.8** CALCULATION OF χ^2, DATA OF TABLE 10.4

39.4815[a] 47 7.5185[b]	42.5185 35 −7.5185	82
12.5185 5 −7.5185	13.4815 21 7.5185	26
52	56	108

[a](82 × 52)/108 = 39.4815; (82 × 56)/108 = 42.5185; etc.
[b]47 − 39.4815 = 7.5185; etc.

left corner of each cell; they are calculated as shown in footnote *a* of the table. The obtained frequencies, f_o, are given in the right center of each cell. The $f_o - f_e$ terms, required by the formula, are given in the lower left corner of the cells. They are the same in all cells, except for sign. This will be true in 2 × 2 tables. The χ^2 formula simply requires squaring these differences, dividing the squares by the expected frequencies, and summing the results. These calculations are indicated at the bottom of the table. $\chi^2 = 11.4698$, at one degree of freedom. (Why one degree of freedom?) Looking up the tabled χ^2 value, one degree of freedom at the .01 level, we read 6.635. Since our value exceeds this substantially, it can be said that χ^2 is statistically significant, the obtained results are probably not chance results, and the relation expressed in the table is a "real" one in the sense that it is probably not due to chance.[12]

$$\chi^2 = \Sigma\left[\frac{(f_o - f_e)^2}{f_e}\right]$$

$$= \frac{(47.0 - 39.4815)^2}{39.4815} + \frac{(35.0 - 42.5185)^2}{42.5185} + \frac{(5.0 - 12.5185)^2}{12.5185} + \frac{(21.0 - 13.4815)^2}{13.4815}$$

$$= 11.4698$$

χ^2, like other statistics that indicate statistical significance, tells us nothing about the magnitude of the relation. It is a test of the independence of the variables in the sense of independence discussed in Chapter 9. It is not, strictly speaking, a measure of association. One of the oldest problems of statistics is indexing the strength or magnitude of association or relation between categorical variables. Its complexity forbids discussion here. But we give one statistic, even though it is not the best one, because it is easily applicable and can be used with any size contingency or crossbreak table. It is C, the *coefficient of contingency*:

$$C = \sqrt{\frac{\chi^2}{\chi^2 + N}} \qquad (10.2)$$

[12]Note that χ^2 needs a correction if N is small. The approximate rule is that the so-called correction for continuity is used—it consists merely of subtracting .5 from the absolute difference between f_0 and f_e in the χ^2 formula *before squaring*—when *expected* frequencies are less than 5 in 2 × 2 tables.

If we substitute the value of χ^2 calculated above and insert it and N in the equation, we obtain:

$$C = \sqrt{\frac{11.4698}{11.4698 + 108}} = \sqrt{.0960} = .3098 = .31$$

which is a rough and conservative index of the strength of the relation.

C is inadequate partly because it cannot reach 1.00, has no sign, and is not readily interpretable in various terms, as is r, for instance. Nevertheless, it yields a measure of association that is useful if used with circumspection.[13] Generally speaking, the best advice for handling categorical data is to calculate χ^2 to determine statistical significance, calculate C (or other measures: see footnote 13), calculate the percentages as outlined earlier, and then interpret the data using all the information.

Types of Crossbreaks and Tables

In general there are three types of tables: (1) one-dimensional, (2) two-dimensional, and (3) k-dimensional. The number of dimensions of a table is determined by the number of variables: a one-dimensional table has one variable, a two-dimensional table has two variables, and so on. It makes no difference how many categories any single variable has; the dimensions of a table are always fixed by the number of variables. We have already considered the two-dimensional table where two variables, one independent and one dependent, are set against each other. It is often fruitful and necessary to consider more than two variables simultaneously. Theoretically, there is no limit to the number of variables that can be considered at one time. The only limitations are practical ones: insufficient sample size and difficulty of comprehension of the relations contained in a multidimensional table.

One-Dimensional Tables

There are two kinds of one-dimensional table. One is a "true" one-dimensional table; it is of little interest to us since it does not express a relation. Such tables occur commonly in newspapers, government publications, magazines, and so forth. In reporting the number or proportion of males and females in San Francisco, the number of cars of different makes produced in 1972, the number of children in each of the grades of X school system, we have "true" one-dimensional tables. One variable only is used in the table.

Social scientists sometimes choose to report their data in tables that look one-dimensional but are really two-dimensional. Consider a table reported by Child, Potter, and Levine.[14] In this study the values expressed in third-grade children's textbooks were content-analyzed. Table 10.9 shows the percentages of

[13]The reader is urged to study the subject further. See Hays, *op. cit.*, pp. 603–614. The more advanced student may wish to study a newer and quite different approach, predictive association. The original source is: L. Goodman and H. Kruskal, "Measures of Association for Cross Classification," *Journal of the American Statistical Association*, XLIX (1954), 732–764. While Goodman and Kruskal's method seems not be have been used much in the behavioral sciences, it probably should be because it is congruent with a conditional probability approach.

[14]I. Child, E. Potter, and E. Levine, "Children's Textbooks and Personality Development: An Exploration in the Social Psychology of Education," *Psychological Monographs*, LX (1946), No. 3.

instances in which rewards were given for various modes of acquisition. (In the original table, only the column of percentages on the left was given.) The table looks one-dimensional, but it really expresses a relation between two variables, mode of acquisition and reward.

The key point is that tables of this kind are not really one-dimensional. In Table 10.9, one of the variables, reward, is incompletely expressed. To make this clear, simply add another column of percentages beside those in the original table. (This has been done in the table.) This column can be labeled "Not Rewarded." Now we have a complete two-dimensional table, and the relation becomes obvious. (Sometimes this cannot be done because data for "completing" the table are lacking.)

TABLE **10.9** CHILD, POTTER, AND LEVINE DATA

Mode of Acquisition	% in which rewarded	(% in which not rewarded)
Effort	93	(7)
Buying, Selling, Trading	80	(20)
Asking, Wishing, Taking What is Offered	68	(32)
Dominance, Aggression, Stealing, Trickery	41	(59)

Two-Dimensional Tables

Two-dimensional tables or crossbreaks have two variables, each with two or more subclasses. The simplest form of a two-dimensional table, as we have seen, is called two-by-two, or simply 2×2. Two-dimensional tables are by no means limited to the 2×2 form. In fact, there is no logical limitation on the number of subclasses that each variable can have. Let us look at a few examples of $m \times n$ tables.

Miller and Swanson have reported tests of a number of interesting hypotheses.[15] One hypothesis predicted a relation between the social-class membership of parents and the type of discipline they use, as shown in Table 10.10.[16] χ^2 is

TABLE **10.10** RELATION BETWEEN SOCIAL CLASS AND TYPE OF DISCIPLINE, MILLER AND SWANSON STUDY

	Discipline		
	Psychological	Mixed	Corporal
Middle Class	29 .76	5 .13	4 .11
Working Class	9 .12	28 .36	40 .52

[15]D. Miller and G. Swanson, *Inner Conflict and Defense*. New York: Holt, Rinehart and Winston, 1960. Appendix D of this book contains a large number of crossbreaks.

[16]*Ibid.*, p. 426. The textual discussion is on pp. 73 ff. It would be profitable for the student to study the author's theoretical reasoning and predictions in connection with the tables given in Appendix D. This book is a sophisticated theoretical-empirical study which, aside from its intrinsic interest, well repays study.

TABLE **10.11** RELATION BETWEEN SOCIAL CLASS AND TYPE OF REWARD, MILLER AND SWANSON STUDY

	Type of Reward		
	Psychic	Neither	Concrete
Middle Class	25 .66	6 .16	7 .18
Working Class	12 .16	37 .48	28 .36

49.45, highly significant. This is, of course, a 2 × 3 table which the reader can easily interpret for himself. (The percentages, or proportions, have been inserted in the cells to aid interpretation.)

A similar table from the same book is given in Table 10.11.[17] Again, χ^2 is highly significant (29.52), and the interpretation is fairly simple. (The student should be sure he is able to interpret Tables 10.10 and 10.11, as well as earlier tables, before reading further.)

Another example of a two-dimensional table that can help us make two or three important points, as well as give us interesting data to study, is from Stouffer's conformity-tolerance study.[18] Stouffer studied the relation between tolerance, on the one hand, and several other sociological variables, on the other hand. One of the latter was education. Stouffer sought an answer to the question: What is the relation between the amount of education and degree of tolerance? The crossbreak given in Table 10.12 is instructive because (1) it is a 5 × 3 type and thus more complex than previous types; (2) it juxtaposes an ordinal variable, education, against a classification of a presumably continuous variable, tolerance; and (3) it

TABLE **10.12** RELATION BETWEEN EDUCATION AND TOLERANCE, STOUFFER STUDY

	Percentage of Distribution of Scores on Scale of Tolerance			
Education	Less Tolerant	In-Between	More Tolerant	*N*
College Graduates	5	29	66	308
Some College	9	38	53	319
High School Graduates	12	46	42	768
Some High School	17	54	29	576
Grade School	22	62	16	792

[17] *Ibid.*

[18] S. Stouffer, *Communish, Conformity, and Civil Liberties.* New York: Doubleday, 1955. Copyright © 1955 by Samuel A. Stouffer. Reprinted by Permission of Doubleday & Company, Inc. This book contains exhaustive crossbreak analyses. It can almost be considered a text and model of how to analyze relations via crossbreaks. Stouffer's untiring specifications of his data are especially valuable. For example, see chap. 4 where he juxtaposes age, education, tolerance, and other variables.

illustrates a point that seems to confuse students, namely that the m and n numbers of an $m \times n$ crossbreak tell the number of subclasses or subcategories, and not the number of variables. Study of the table shows that a relation between the two variables exists: evidently the more education the more tolerance.

Two-Dimensional Tables, "True" Dichotomies, and Continuous Measures

Many two-dimensional tables report "true" nominal data, data of variables that are truly dichotomous: sex, alive-dead, and the like. Yet many such tables have one or both variables presumably continuous and artificially dichotomized or trichotomized. An interesting example of a 2×2 table with one variable, oral explanation, a "natural" or "true" dichotomy, and the other variable, oral anxiety, a continuous variable artificially dichotomized at the median was used by Whiting and Child in their book, *Child Training and Personality.*[19] In studying their larger problem, the authors hypothesized that societies fostering oral anxiety in their socialization process explain illness orally. Part of their evidence is given in Table 10.13. The data are statistically significant. The hypothesis is upheld.[20]

TABLE **10.13** RELATION BETWEEN ORAL ANXIETY AND ORAL EXPLANATIONS OF ILLNESS, WHITING AND CHILD STUDY

	Societies with Oral Explanation	Societies without Oral Explanation
Societies above Median on Oral Anxiety	17	3
Societies below Median on Oral Anxiety	6	13

Three- and k-Dimensional Tables

It is theoretically possible to crossbreak any number of variables, but in practice the limit is three or four, more often three. The reasons for such limitation are obvious: very large N's are required and, more important, the interpretation of data becomes considerably more difficult. Another point to bear in mind is: Never

[19]J. Whiting and I. Child, *Child Training and Personality.* New Haven: Yale University Press, 1953, p. 156. The frequencies in the table are numbers of societies and not individuals. The total N was 75 (75 societies). This book, like others previously cited (Miller and Swanson; Gross), is an excellent example of sophisticated theoretical reasoning and careful empirical testing of hypotheses. It is particularly instructive because of the ingenuity and flexibility shown in quantifying complex variables.

[20]Whiting and Child used a somewhat unusual method of testing statistical significance. See *ibid.*, pp. 163–166. Percentages are not given in Table 10.14 because the use of percentages with so few cases is questionable. Percentages with small numbers of cases are misleading. It is difficult, however, to define "small numbers of cases." A rule of thumb might be: do not calculate percentages if a marginal frequency is less than 30.

use a complex analysis when a simpler one will accomplish the analytic job. Still, three- and even four-dimensional tables can be useful and can supply indispensable information.

The analysis of three or more variables simultaneously has two main purposes. One is to study the relations among three or more variables. Take a three-dimensional example, and call the variables *A*, *B*, and *C*. We can study the following relations: between *A* and *B*, between *A* and *C*, between *B* and *C*, and between *A*, *B*, and *C*. The second purpose is to control one variable while studying the relation between the other two variables. For instance, we can study the relation between *B* and *C* while controlling *A*. An important use of this notion is to help detect spurious relations. Another use is to "specify" a relation, to tell us when or under what conditions a relation is more or less pronounced.

Specification

". . . is the process of describing the conditions under which a particular relationship may exist or not exist, or may exist to a greater or lesser degree."[21] Specifying relations through crossbreaks is an important part of analysis, because one can possibly detect spurious relations and spell out conditions under which a relation exists or does not exist.

Suppose an investigator was interested in the hypothesis that level of aspiration is positively related to success in college: the higher the level of aspiration, the greater the probability of graduating. Suppose further that he had a relatively crude dichotomous measure of level of aspiration.[22] He also had, of course, a measure of success in college: Did a student graduate, or didn't he? The variables and categories, then, are Hi *LA* (high level of aspiration), Lo *LA*, *SC* (success in college), and *NSC* (not successful in college). He drew a random sample of 400 sophomores from a college and obtained level of aspiration measures from them. He divided the 400 students into halves on the basis of the level-of-aspiration measures. At the end of three years he further categorized the students on the basis of having graduated or not. Suppose the results were those shown in Table 10.14.[23] There is evidently a relation between the variables: $\chi^2 = 64$, significant at the .001 level, and $C = .37$.

The investigator shows the results to a colleague, a rather sour individual, who says they are questionable, that if social class were brought into the picture the relation might be quite different. He reasons that social class and level of aspiration are strongly related, and that the original relation might hold for middle-class students but not for working-class students. Disconcerted, the investigator goes back to his data, and, since he luckily has indices of social class

[21]W. Goode and P. Hatt, *Methods in Social Research*. New York: McGraw-Hill, 1952, p. 356.

[22]There is no logical reason why the investigator could not have used three, four, or more categories for the level-of-aspiration measure. In fact, with adequate continuous measures there are more powerful methods of analysis.

[23]The *LA* marginal totals of the table have been made equal to simplify the analysis. The *SC* and *NSC* totals have also been made equal. Similarly, the marginal totals of Table 10.16 have been made equal. It is highly unlikely that such equal marginal totals would be obtained. Thus the example is not realistic. Nevertheless, it is useful for demonstrating the points to be made.

TABLE **10.14** RELATION BETWEEN LEVEL OF ASPIRATION AND SCHOOL ACHIEVEMENT, HYPOTHETICAL DATA

	SC	*NSC*	
Hi *LA*	140	60	200
Lo *LA*	60	140	200
	200	200	(400)

for all the subjects, he finds, when he works out the three-variable crossbreak, the results shown in Table 10.15.

The overall χ^2 is 144, significant at the .001 level. $C = .51$. The table frequencies depart very significantly from chance expectation. But what contributes to this result? Inspection of the data shows that the investigator's colleague was right: the relation between level of aspiration and success in college is considerably more pronounced with middle-class students than with working-class students.

The investigator can study the relations in more depth by calculating percentages separately for the middle-class and working-class sides of Table 10.15.

TABLE **10.15** RELATIONS AMONG LEVEL OF ASPIRATION, SOCIAL CLASS, AND SCHOOL ACHIEVEMENT, HYPOTHETICAL DATA

	MC		*WC*		
	Hi *LA*	Lo *LA*	Hi *LA*	Lo *LA*	
SC	80	20	60	40	200
NSC	20	80	40	60	200
	100	100	100	100	(400)
	(200)		(200)		

In this case, since the frequencies in each row of the halves of the table total to 100, the frequencies are, in effect, percentages. It can be seen that the relation between level of aspiration and college success is stronger with middle-class students than it is with working-class students.[24]

In the analysis above, the data were specified: it was shown, by introducing the social-class variable, that the relation was stronger with one group than with another. But this is the same phenomenon as that discussed in Chapter 9: interaction. (See Fig. 9.1 and accompanying discussion.) We said earlier that interaction means an independent variable affects a dependent variable differently at different levels or facets of another independent variable. This is virtually what

[24]It is possible and desirable to break down a table of this kind into its components and to calculate the χ^2's that contribute to the components. Such procedures are beyond the scope of this chapter, though they are closely related to similar analysis of variance procedures, to be discussed in Part 5.

we have in Table 10.15: the relation between level of aspiration and college success is different in the two social classes.

Crossbreaks, Relations, Ordered Pairs, Graphing

The relations among crossbreaks, relations, and correlations are interesting and instructive. A relation is a set of ordered pairs. Two of the ways in which we can express a set of ordered pairs are by listing the pairs and by graphing the pairs. A coefficient of correlation is an index expressing degree of relation. A crossbreak expresses the ordered pairs in a table.

To show how these ideas are related, take the fictitious data of Table 10.16, where $U = 23$ pupils. The relation being studied is between sex and level of aspiration. We partition U into male (M) and female (F). We also partition U into high level of aspiration (Hi LA) and low level of aspiration (Lo LA). We thus have a two-variable partition or crossbreak.

Suppose that of the 23 members of U we count 12 M's and 11 F's. We also count 13 Hi LA's and 10 Lo LA's. This gives us the marginal totals of a crossbreak. It does not tell us how many members there are in each cell. We must now count the number of M pupils who are also Hi LA, the number of M pupils who are also Lo LA, the number of F pupils who are also Hi LA, and the number of F pupils who are also Lo LA. We find the numbers to be those of Table 10.16. These frequencies depart significantly from chance.[25] There is a significant relation between sex and level of aspiration.

TABLE **10.16** RELATION BETWEEN SOCIAL CLASS AND SCHOOL ACHIEVEMENT, FICTITIOUS DATA

		B_1 Hi LA	B_2 Lo LA	
A_1	M	10	2	12
A_2	F	3	8	11
		13	10	

Look at this another way. Let $A_1 = M, A_2 = F, B_1 =$ Hi LA, and $B_2 =$ Lo LA. How do we set up the ordered pairs of the crossbreak? We do so by assigning each of the 23 subjects one of the combinations (1, 1), (0, 1), (1, 0), (0, 0). Assign 1's to A_1 and B_1 and 0's to A_2 and B_2. If a subject is male (A_1) *and* has a high level of aspiration (B_1), then he is an A_1B_1; consequently the ordered pair assigned to him is (1, 1). The first 10 subjects in Table 10.17 belong to the A_1B_1 category and are thus assigned (1, 1). Similarly, the remaining subjects are assigned ordered pairs of numbers according to their subset membership. The full list of 23 ordered pairs

[25]As judged by Finney's tables. See S. Siegel, *Nonparametric Statistics*. New York: McGraw-Hill, 1956, pp. 256–270. When the frequencies are relatively small, the Finney tables give a more accurate test of significance than the χ^2 test. The Finney tables can also be found in: E. Pearson and H. Hartley, eds. *Biometrika Tables for Statisticians*, Vol. I. Cambridge: Cambridge University Press, 1954, pp. 188 ff.

is given in Table 10.17. The categories or crossbreak (set) intersections have been indicated.

The relation is the set of ordered pairs of 1's and 0's. Table 10.17 is simply a different way of expressing the same relation shown in Table 10.16. We can calculate a coefficient of correlation for both tables. If, for example, we calculate a coefficient of correlation, a product-moment *r*, of the Table 10.17 data, we obtain .56. (The product-moment *r* calculated with 1's and 0's is called a *phi* (ϕ) coefficient.[26])

Graph the relation. Let there be two axes, *A* and *B*, at right angles to each other, and let *A* and *B* represent the two variables of Tables 10.17 (and 10.16). We are interested in studying the relation between *A* and *B*. Figure 10.4 shows the graphed ordered pairs. It also shows a "relation" line run through the larger clusters of pairs. Where is the relation? We ask: Is there a set of ordered pairs that defines a significant relation between *A* and *B*? We have *paired* each individual's score on *A* with his "score" on *B* and plotted the pairs on the *A* and *B* axes. Going

TABLE **10.17** ORDERED-PAIR ARRANGEMENT OF THE DATA OF TABLE 10.16

Ss	*A*	*B*	
1	1	1	
2	1	1	
3	1	1	
4	1	1	
5	1	1	
6	1	1	A_1B_1
7	1	1	
8	1	1	
9	1	1	
10	1	1	
11	0	1	
12	0	1	A_2B_1
13	0	1	
14	1	0	
15	1	0	A_1B_2
16	0	0	
17	0	0	
18	0	0	
19	0	0	A_2B_2
20	0	0	
21	0	0	
22	0	0	
23	0	0	

[26]This is not a recommended procedure. It is used here to help clarify analytic procedures and not to illustrate how ϕ is calculated. When both variables are true dichotomies, ϕ is used. This is not the case here.

back to the substance of the relation, we pair each individual's "score" on sex with his level-of-aspiration "score." In this manner we obtain a set of ordered pairs, and this subset *is* a relation. Our real question, then, is not: Is there a relation between A and B? But rather: *What* is the relation between A and B?

We can see from Fig. 10.4 that the relation between A and B is fairly strong. This is determined by the ordered pairs: the pairs are mostly (a_1, b_1) and (a_2, b_2). There are comparatively few (a_1, b_2) and (a_2, b_1). In words, male "scores" pair with high level-of-aspiration scores (1, 1), and female scores pair with low level-of-aspiration scores (0, 0) with comparatively few exceptions (5 cases out of 23). We cannot name this relation succinctly, as we can relations such as "marriage," "brotherhood," and the like. We might, however, call it "sex-level of aspiration," meaning that there is a relation in the ordered pair sense.

It should be clear that there are several ways to analyze the same data. The importance of understanding the different methods, their relations to the problems under investigation, and their relations to each other cannot be overemphasized. It is not so much technical competence as depth and flexibility of comprehension that one gets from using and understanding different methods. Too much analysis is done routinely and uncomprehendingly. While it is pointless to think when one does not need to—as Whitehead long ago pointed out—it is dangerous not to think and not to know what one is doing, both when planning research and the analysis of the data to be obtained in the research and when actually doing the analysis.

No method of analysis is perfect. For a benefit obtained by one method, we often lose a benefit obtained by another method. Pick the method that seems best suited to the research problem and the research data. Study it, use it, and interpret results obtained by it with care. Understand the methods you use as best you can, and, as with statistics, do not allow yourself to worry excessively about assumptions and restrictions. They are important, of course, but significant research is

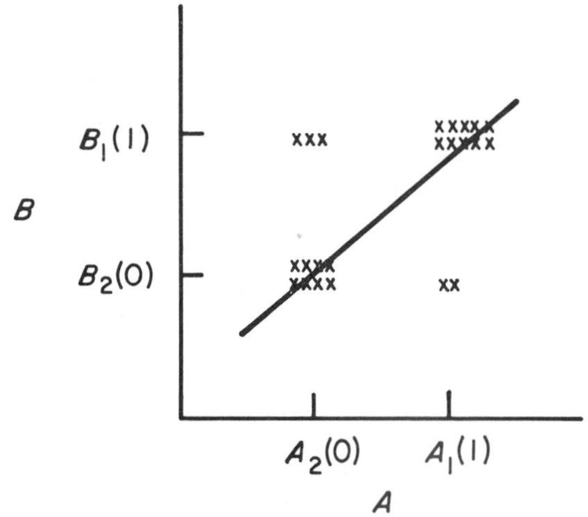

FIG. 10.4.

more important. Few investigators can hope to understand thoroughly all statistics, all methods of observation, and all methods of analysis, especially in the early stages of study. Understanding in depth comes only with study and experience. Try the methods described above. You will probably find that as you do so you will begin to enjoy yourself. When this happens, real learning has begun. Later, we will study even more interesting—and certainly more powerful—methods.

Addendum: Other Kinds of Crossbreaks

There are other kinds of crossbreaks than those described in the chapter. They have not been described because the purpose here was to emphasize basic understanding of the use of frequency (and percentage) analysis in scientific behavioral research, and to tie such analysis to previous ideas of sets and relations.

Unfortunately, sociologists and psychologists have used widely divergent methods and have had too little appreciation of the common nature of their research. Psychologists for the most part use continuous measures and the techniques suitable to such measures: means, standard deviations, *t* tests, *F* tests, correlations, and so on. They report crossbreaks and frequency analysis much less often. Sociologists, on the other hand, often make primary use of frequency and crossbreak analysis. Our purpose is to acquaint the student with the practices so that he can read the literature intelligently and, more important, choose the forms of analysis suited to his problems.

One precept should be borne in mind: Do not use crossbreak analysis if your data warrant a more powerful mode of analysis. If your dependent variable has continuous measures, it is ordinarily wasteful to use crossbreak analysis. We never consciously and deliberately throw variance away. It is the working stuff of analysis. And crossbreaking continuous measures throws variance away. If you have an attitude scale and you dichotomize or trichotomize it into high and low, or high, middle, and low, you are throwing away variance and information.

The forms of analysis that a discipline tends to use are naturally influenced by the variables of the field. Sociologists use crossbreak and related analyses a good deal because many sociological variables either are categorical or are treated as categorical: income, education, religion, occupation, sex, and so on. Psychological variables, on the other hand, tend to be continuous, as said earlier: anxiety, intelligence, attitude, aggressiveness, achievement, and so on. But psychological and sociological research problems and methods have been drawing closer and closer together in recent years, thus in effect demanding that psychologists and sociologists master and use the tools that in the past have customarily been associated with one or the other. This is good. It will enable behavioral scientists to be just that by centering attention on problems and their study rather than on methods and techniques. Indeed, the day has long gone when it was possible to identify research problems clearly as sociological or psychological. I pick up the *American Sociological Review* and find that a surprising number of the variables are psychological. I pick up the *Journal of Personality and Social Psychology* and find many sociological variables.

Study Suggestions

1. What does specification have to do with spuriousness? Make up one or two examples to show what you mean.
2. In the important Kerner Commission Report on civil disorders (riots) in the United States, a large number of relations are presented in table form. Here is

one of the tables, from a Newark survey, which gives the percentages of responses to the question, "Sometimes I hate white people," given by rioters (R) and people not involved (NI).[27]

	R ($N = 105$)	NI ($N = 126$)
Agree	72.4%	50.0%
Disagree	27.6	50.0

(a) Interpret the table. Examine the data carefully before interpreting.
(b) Calculate the frequencies (e.g., $.724 \times 105 = 76$). Are the percentages calculated the "right" way? Calculate them across the rows, e.g., $76/139 = .55$. Does the interpretation change? How?
(c) If you think the percentages are calculated incorrectly in the data above, why are they incorrect?

3. Shortly after the late President Kennedy took office, there was a battle in the Rules Committee of the House of Representatives. Representative Rayburn wanted to increase the number of members of the committee so that it would no longer be dominated by a conservative coalition. When the vote was taken in the House, the Rayburn forces won 217 to 212. One can ask: Is there a relation between political affiliation and voting on the issue? The data are:[28]

	For	Against
Democrats	195	64
Republicans	22	148

Calculate χ^2 and C. Also calculate the appropriate percentage table. Interpret. Is there another possible interpretation? That is, might there be an independent variable other than political affiliation operating?
[*Answers:* $\chi^2 = 159.61$ (.001); $C = .52$.]

4. In their study of defense mechanisms and social class, Miller and Swanson[29] published a large number of interesting tables, among which are the following. Interpret each of these tables, first calculating percentages, χ^2's, and C's. (The variables are self-explanatory.)

(a)

	Obedience Requests	
	Arbitrary	Explained
Middle Class	16	27
Working Class	28	10

(b)

	Weaning	
	Early	Late
MC	33	22
WC	17	31

(c)

	Type of Reward		
	Psychic	Mixed	Concrete
MC	25	6	7
WC	12	37	28

(d)

	Discipline		
	Psychological	Mixed	Corporal
MC	29	5	4
WC	9	28	40

[27] *Report of the National Advisory Commission on Civil Disorders*. New York: Bantam, 1968, p. 176.
[28] Organized from figures published in the *New York Times*, February 15, 1961, sec. 4, p. 1.
[29] Miller and Swanson, *op. cit.*, pp. 426 ff.

Notice, particularly, in these four examples, that studying frequencies and χ^2's alone does not tell us very much about the relations. Interpret the tables. [*Answers:* χ^2's: (a) 9.40; (b) 5.26; (c) 29.52; (d) 49.45. C's: (a) .32; (b) .22; (c) .45; (d) .55. Note that these χ^2's were calculated using the correction for continuity. Simply subtract .5 from $f_0 - f_e$ before squaring.]

CHAPTER 11

Statistics: Purpose, Approach, and Method

The Basic Approach

The basic principle behind the use of statistical tests of significance can be summed up in one sentence: *Compare obtained results with chance expectation.* When a research study is done and statistical results obtained, they are checked against the results expected by chance. In Chapter 7 we met examples of checking empirical results of coin-tossing and dice-throwing against theoretical expectations. For example, if a die is thrown a large number of times, the expected proportion of occurrences of a 4, say, is one-sixth of the total number of throws. In Chapter 10 we learned that the rationale of the χ^2 test was the comparison of numbers of observed frequencies of events with the numbers of frequencies expected by chance. Indeed, the statistical ideas of Chapter 10 were presented before those of this chapter in part to give the student preliminary experience with obtained and expected results.

Two dice were thrown 72 times in a demonstration described in Chapter 7. Theoretically, 7 should turn up $1/6 \times 72 = 12$. But Table 7.2 showed that 7 turned up 15 times in 72 throws rather than 12 times. We ask an important question: Does this obtained result differ from the theoretically expected result *significantly*? Or: Does this obtained result differ from chance expectation enough to warrant a belief that something other than chance is at work?

Such questions are the essence of the statistical approach. The statistician is a skeptic. He does not believe in the "reality" of empirical results until he has applied statistical tests to them. He assumes that all results are chance results until shown to be otherwise. He is what might be called an inveterate probabilist. The core of his approach to empirical data is to set up chance expectation as his hypothesis and to try to fit the empirical data to the chance model. If the empirical data "fit" the chance model, then it is said that they are "not significant." If they do not fit the chance model, if they depart "sufficiently" from the chance model, it is said that they are "significant."

This and several succeeding chapters are devoted to the statistical approach to research problems. In this chapter we extend the discussion of Chapter 7 on probability to basic conceptions of the mean, variance, and standard deviation. The so-called law of large numbers and the normal probability curve are also explained and interpreted, and some idea is given of their potent use in statistics. In the next chapter we tackle the idea of statistical testing itself. These two chapters are the foundation.

Definition and Purpose of Statistics

Statistics is the theory and method of analyzing quantitative data obtained from samples of observations in order to study and compare sources of variance of phenomena, to help make decisions to accept or reject hypothesized relations between the phenomena, and to aid in making reliable inferences from empirical observations.

Four purposes of statistics are suggested in this definition. The first is the commonest and most traditional: to reduce large quantities of data to manageable and understandable form. It is impossible to digest 100 scores, for instance, but if a mean and a standard deviation are calculated, the scores can be readily interpreted by a trained person. The definition of "statistic" stems from this traditional usage and purpose of statistics. A *statistic* is a measure calculated from a sample. A statistic contrasts with a *parameter*, which is a population value. If, in U, a population or universe, we calculate the mean, this is a parameter. Now take a subset (sample) A of U. The mean of A is a statistic. For our purpose, parameters are of theoretical interest only. They are not usually known. They are *estimated* with statistics. Thus we deal mostly with sample or subset statistics. These samples or subsets are usually conceived to be representative of U. Statistics are, then, epitomes or summaries of the samples—and often, presumably, of the populations—from which they are calculated. Means, medians, variances, standard deviations, percentiles, percentages, and so on, calculated from samples, are statistics.

A second purpose of statistics is to aid in the study of populations and samples. This use of statistics is so well known that it will not be discussed. Besides, we studied something of populations and samples in earlier chapters.

A third purpose of statistics is to aid in decision making. If an educational psychologist needs to know which of three methods of programmed instruction promotes the most learning with the least cost, he can use statistics to help him gain this knowledge. This use of statistics is comparatively recent. Some of the basic ideas of statistical decision theory, without the technical ramifications, will be used in this book. In fact, this purpose is subsumed under the inference purpose to be discussed below.

Although most decision situations are more complex, we use an example that is quite familiar by now. A decision-maker dice gambler would first lay out the outcomes for dice throws. These are, of course, 2 through 12. He notes the differing frequencies of the numbers. For example, 2 and 12 will probably occur much less often than 7 or 6. He calculates the probabilities for the various outcomes. Finally, on the basis of how much money he can expect to make, he devises a betting system. He decides, for instance, that, since 7 has a probability of 1/6, he will require that his opponent give him, say, odds of 5 to 1 instead of even money on the first throw. (We here take liberties with craps.) To make this whole thing a bit more dramatic, suppose that two players operate with different decision-makers.[1] One player, *A*, proposes the following game: *A* will win if 2, 3, or 4 turns up; his opponent, *B*, will win if 5, 6, or 7 turns up (outcomes 8 through 12 are to be disregarded). It is obvious that *A*'s decision-maker is faulty. It is based on the assumption that 2, 3, 4, 5, 6, and 7 are equiprobable. *B* should have a good time with this game.

The fourth and last purpose of statistics, to aid in making reliable inferences from observational data, is closely allied to, indeed, is part of, the purpose of helping to make decisions among hypotheses. An *inference* is a proposition or generalization derived by reasoning from other propositions, or from evidence. Generally speaking, an inference is a conclusion arrived at through reasoning. In statistics, a number of inferences may be drawn from tests of statistical hypotheses. We "conclude" that methods A and B really differ. We conclude from evidence, say $r = .67$, that two variables are really related.

Statistical inferences have two characteristics. One, the inferences are usually made *from samples to populations*. When we say that the variables *A* and *B* are related because the statistical evidence is $r = .67$, we are inferring that because $r = .67$ in *this* sample it is $r = .67$, or near .67, in the population from which the sample was drawn. The second kind of inference is used when investigators are not interested in the populations, or only interested secondarily in them. An educational investigator is studying the presumed effect of the relationships between board of education members and chief educational administrators, on the one hand, and teacher morale, on the other hand. His hypothesis is that, when relationships between boards and chief administrators are strained, teacher morale is lower than otherwise. He is interested only in testing this hypothesis in Y County. He makes the study and obtains statistical results that support the hypothesis, for example, morale is lower in system A than in systems B and C. He *infers*, from the statistical evidence of a difference between system A, on the one hand, and systems B and C, on the other hand, that his hypothetical proposition is correct—in Y County. And it is possible for his interest to be strictly limited to Y County.

To summarize much of the above discussion, the purposes of statistics can be reduced to one major purpose: *to aid in inference-making*. This is one of the basic purposes of research design, methodology, and statistics. Scientists want to draw inferences from data. Statistics, via its power to reduce data to manageable

[1]This example is suggested by I. Bross, *Design for Decision*. New York: Macmillan, 1953, p. 28.

forms (statistics) and its power to study and analyze variances, enables scientists to attach probability estimates to the inferences they draw from data. Statistics says, in effect, "The inference you have drawn is correct at such-and-such a level of significance. You may act as though your hypothesis were true, remembering that there is such-and-such a probability that it is untrue." It should be reasonably clear why some contemporary statisticians call statistics the discipline of decision making under uncertainty. It should also be reasonably clear that, whether you know it or not, you are always making inferences, attaching probabilities to various outcomes or hypotheses, and making decisions on the basis of statistical reasoning. Statistics, using probability theory and mathematics, simply makes the process more exact.

Binomial Statistics

When things are counted, the number system used is simple and useful. Whenever objects are counted, they are counted on the basis of some criterion, some variable or attribute, in research language. Many examples have already been given: heads, tails, numbers on dice, sex, aggressive acts, political preference, and so on. If a person or a thing possesses the attribute, the person or thing is "counted in," we say. When something is "counted in" because it possesses the attribute in question, it is assigned a 1. If it does not possess the attribute, it is assigned a 0. This is a binomial system.

Earlier, the mean was defined as $M = \Sigma X/n$. The variance is $V = \Sigma x^2/n$, where $x = X - M$ (each x is a deviation from the mean). The standard deviation is $SD = \sqrt{V}$. Of course, these formulas work with any scores. Here we use them only with 1's and 0's. And it is useful to alter the formula for the mean. The formula $\Sigma X/n$ is not general enough. It assumes that all scores are equiprobable. A more general formula, which can be used when equiprobability is not assumed, is

$$M = \Sigma\,[X \cdot w(X)] \qquad (11.1)$$

where $w(X)$ is the weight assigned to an X. $w(X)$ simply means the probability each X has of occurring. The formula says: Multiply each X, each score, by its weight (probability), and then add them all up. Notice that if all X's are equally probable, this formula is the same as $\Sigma\, X/n$.

The mean of the set $\{1, 2, 3, 4, 5\}$ is

$$M = \frac{1+2+3+4+5}{5} = \frac{15}{5} = 3$$

By formula 11.1 it is, of course, the same, but its computation looks different:

$$M = 1 \cdot 1/5 + 2 \cdot 1/5 + 3 \cdot 1/5 + 4 \cdot 1/5 + 5 \cdot 1/5 = 3$$

Why the hair-splitting? Let a coin be tossed. $U = \{H, T\}$. The *mean number of heads* is, by Eq. 11.1,

$$M = 1 \cdot 1/2 + 0 \cdot 1/2 = 1/2$$

Let two coins be tossed. $U = \{HH, HT, TH, TT\}$. The mean number of heads, or the *expectation* of heads, is

$$M = 2 \cdot 1/4 + 1 \cdot 1/4 + 1 \cdot 1/4 + 0 \cdot 1/4 = 4/4 = 1$$

This means that if two coins are tossed many times, the average number of heads per toss is 1. If we sample one person from 30 men and 70 women, the mean of men is: $M = 3/10 \cdot 1 + 7/10 \cdot 0 = .3$. The mean for women is: $M = 3/10 \cdot 0 + 7/10 \cdot 1 = .7$. These are the means for one outcome. (This is a little like saying "an average of 2.5 children per family.")

What has been said in these examples is that the mean of any single experiment (a single coin toss, a sample of one person) is the probability of the occurrence of one of two possible outcomes (heads, a man) which, if the outcome occurs, is assigned a 1 and, if it does not occur, is assigned a 0. This is tantamount to saying: $p(1) = p$ and $p(0) = 1 - p$. In the one-toss experiment, let 1 be assigned if heads turns up and 0 if tails turns up. Then $p(1) = 1/2$ and $p(0) = 1 - 1/2 = 1/2$. In tossing a coin twice, let 1 be assigned to each head that occurs and 0 to each tail. We are interested in the outcome "heads." $U = \{HH, HT, TH, TT\}$. The mean is

$$M = 1/4 \cdot 2 + 1/4 \cdot 1 + 1/4 \cdot 1 + 1/4 \cdot 0 = 1$$

Can we arrive at the same result in an easier manner? Yes. Just add the means for each outcome. The mean of the outcome of one coin toss is 1/2. For two coin tosses it is simply $1/2 + 1/2 = 1$. To assign probabilities with one coin toss, we weight 1 (heads) with its probability and 0 (tails) with its probability. This gives $M = p \cdot 1 + (1-p) \cdot 0 = p$. Take the men-women sampling problem. Let $p =$ the probability of a man's being sampled on a single outcome and $1 - p = q =$ the probability of a woman's being sampled on a single outcome. Then $p = 3/10$ and $q = 7/10$. We are interested in the mean of a man being sampled. Since $M = p \cdot 1 + q \cdot 0 = p$, $M = 3/10 \cdot 1 + 7/10 \cdot 0 = 3/10 = p$. The mean is 3/10 and the probability is 3/10. Evidently $M = p$, or the mean is equal to the probability.

How about a series of outcomes? We write S_n for the sum of n outcomes. One example, the tossing of two coins, was given above. Let us take the men-women sampling problem. The mean of a man's occurring is 3/10 and of a woman's occurring 7/10. We sample 10 persons. What is the mean number of men? Put differently, what is the *expectation* of men? If we sum the 10 means of the individual outcomes, we get the answer:

$$\begin{aligned} M(S_{10}) &= M_1 + M_2 + \cdots + M_{10} \\ &= 3/10 + 3/10 + \cdots + 3/10 = 30/10 = 3 \end{aligned} \tag{11.2}$$

In a sample of 10, we expect to get the answer: 3 men. The same result could have been obtained by $3/10 \cdot 10 = 3$. But $3/10 \cdot 10$ is pn, or

$$M(S_n) = pn \tag{11.3}$$

In n trials the mean number of occurrences of the outcome associated with p is pn.

The Variance

Recall that in Chapter 6 the variance was defined as $V = \Sigma\, x^2/n$. Of course, it will be the same in this chapter, with a change in symbols (for the same reason given with the formula for the mean):

$$V = \Sigma\,[w(X)\,(X-M)^2] \tag{11.4}$$

To make clear what a variance—and a standard deviation—is in probability theory, we work two examples. Recall that, binomially, only two outcomes are possible: 1 and 0. Therefore X is equal to 1 or 0. We set up a table to help us calculate the variance of the heads outcome of a coin throw:

Outcome	X	$w(X) = p$	$(X-M)^2$
H	1	1/2	$(1-1/2)^2 = 1/4$
T	0	1/2	$(0-1/2)^2 = 1/4$

The variance is, then,

$$V = 1/2(1-1/2)^2 + 1/2(0-1/2)^2 = 1/2 \cdot 1/4 + 1/2 \cdot 1/4 = 1/8 + 1/8 = 2/8 = 1/4$$

The mean is 1/2 and the variance is 1/4. The standard deviation is simply the square root of the variance, or $\sqrt{1/4} = 1/2$.

The variance of an individual outcome, however, does not have too much meaning. We really want the variance of the sum of a number of outcomes. If the outcomes are independent, the variance of the sum of the outcomes is the sum of the variances of the outcomes:

$$V(S_n) = V_1 + V_2 + \cdots + V_n \tag{11.5}$$

Or, analogously to Eqs. 11.2 and 11.3, if all the outcomes have the same mean:

$$V(S_n) = nV_i \qquad (i = 1, 2, \ldots, n) \tag{11.6}$$

For 10 coin tosses, the variance of heads, then, is $V(H_{10}) = 10 \cdot 1/4 = 10/4 = 2.5$.

Earlier we showed that $M(S_n) = np$. We now want a formula for the variance. That is, instead of Eq. 11.5 we want a direct, simple formula. With a little algebraic manipulation we can arrive at such a formula:

$$V = p(1-p) = pq \tag{11.7}$$

This is the variance of one outcome. The variance of the number of times that an outcome occurs is, analogously to Eqs. 11.2, 11.3, and 11.6, the sum of the individual outcome variances, or

$$V(S_n) = npq \tag{11.8}$$

The standard deviation is

$$SD(S_n) = \sqrt{npq} \tag{11.9}$$

Equations 11.3, 11.8, and 11.9 are important and useful. They can be applied in many statistical situations. Take two or three applications of the formula: first, the Agree-Disagree problem of the last chapter. Since a sample of 100 was taken, $n = 100$. On the assumption of equiprobability, $p = 1/2$ and $q = 1/2$. Therefore, $M(S_{100}) = np = 100 \cdot 1/2 = 50$, $V(S_{100}) = npq = 100 \cdot 1/2 \cdot 1/2 = 25$, and $SD(S_{100}) = \sqrt{25} = 5$. It was found that there were 60 Agrees. So, this is a deviation of two standard deviations from the mean of 50, $60 - 50 = 10$, and $10/5 = 2$. Second, take the coin-tossing experiment of the chapter on probability. In one experiment, 52 heads turned up in 100 tosses. The calculations are the same as those just given. Since there were 52 heads, the deviation from the mean, or expected frequency, is $52 - 50 = 2$. In standard deviation terms or units, this is $2/5 = .4$ standard deviation units from the mean. We now get back to one of the original questions we asked: Are these differences "statistically significant"? We found, via χ^2, that the result of 60 Agrees was statistically significant and that the result of 52 heads was not statistically significant. Can we do the same thing with the present formula? Yes, we can. Further, the beauty of the present method is that it is applicable to all kinds of numbers, not just to binomial numbers. Before demonstrating this, however, we must study, if only briefly, the so-called law of large numbers and the properties of the standard deviation and the normal probability curve.

The Law of Large Numbers

The law of large numbers took Jacob Bernoulli twenty years to work out. In essence it is so simple that one wonders why he took so long to develop it.[2] Roughly, the law says that as you increase the size of samples, you also decrease the probability that the observed value of an event, A, will deviate from the "true" value of A by no more than a fixed amount, k. Provided the members of the samples are drawn independently, the larger the sample the closer the "true" value of the population is approached. The law is also a gateway to the testing of statistical hypotheses, as we shall see.

Toss a coin 1, 10, 50, 100, 400, and 1000 times. Let heads be the outcome in which we are interested. We calculate means, variances, standard deviations, and two new measures. The first of these new measures is the proportion of favorable outcomes, heads in this case, in the total sample. We call this measure H_n and define it as $H_n = S_n/n$. (Recall that S_n is the total number of times the favorable outcome occurs in n trials.) Then, the fraction of the time that the favorable outcome occurs is H_n. The mean of H_n is p, or $M(H_n) = p$. [This follows from Eq. 11.3, where $M(S_n) = pn$, and since $H_n = S_n/n$, $M(H_n) = M(S_n)/n = np/n = p$.] In short, $M(H_n)$ equals the expected probability. The second measure is the variance of H_n. It is defined: $V(H_n) = pq/n$. The variance, $V(H_n)$, is a measure of the variability of the mean, $M(H_n)$. Later more will be said about the square root of $V(H_n)$, called the *standard error of the mean*. The results of the calculation are given in Table 11.1.

[2]A brief statement of the law by Bernoulli himself can be found in J. Newman, *The World of Mathematics*, vol. 3. New York: Simon and Schuster, 1956, pp. 1452–1455. For more exact statements than are possible in this text, see *ibid.*, pp. 1448–1449. A rigorous mathematical treatment is given in J. Kemeny et al., *Finite Mathematical Structures*. Englewood Cliffs, N.J.: Prentice-Hall, 1959, pp. 165–178.

TABLE **11.1** MEANS, VARIANCES, STANDARD DEVIATIONS, AND EXPECTED PROBABILITIES OF THE OUTCOME HEADS WITH DIFFERENT SIZE SAMPLES[a]

n	$M(S_n) = np$	$V(S_n) = npq$	$SD(S_n)$	$M(H_n) = p$	$V(H_n) = pq/n$
1	½	.25	.50	½	¼
10	5	2.50	1.58	½	1/40
50	25	12.50	3.54	½	1/200
100	50	25.00	5.00	½	1/400
400	200	100.00	10.00	½	1/1600
1000	500	250.00	15.81	½	1/4000

[a]See text for explanation of symbols in this table.

Notice that, although the means, variances, and standard deviations of the sums increase with the sizes of the samples, the $M(H_n)$'s or p's remain the same. That is, the average number of heads, or $M(H_n)$, is always 1/2. But the variance of the average number of heads, $V(H_n)$, gets smaller and smaller as the sizes of the samples increase. Again, $V(H_n)$ is a measure of the variability of the averages. As Table 11.1 clearly indicates, the average number of outcomes should come closer and closer to the "true" value, in this case 1/2. (The student should ponder this example carefully before going further.)

The Normal Probability Curve and the Standard Deviation

The normal probability curve is the lovely bell-shaped curve encountered so often in statistics and psychology textbooks. Its importance stems from the fact that chance events in large numbers tend to distribute themselves in the form of the curve. The so-called theory of errors uses the curve. Many natural phenomena, physical and psychological, distribute themselves in approximately normal form. Height, intelligence, and achievement are three familiar examples. The means of samples distribute themselves normally.[3] It is hard to conceive of modern statistics without this curve. Every statistics text has a table called the "table of the normal deviate," or "table of the normal curve."

The most important statistical reason for using the normal curve is to be able easily to interpret the probabilities of the statistics one calculates. If the data are, as is said, "normal" or approximately normal, one has a clear interpretation for what one does.

[3]The reader should avoid the untested belief that all or even most phenomena are normally distributed. Whenever possible, data should be checked by appropriate methods, especially by plotting or graphing. Data are often subtle. Take height, for example. In the whole population, height is probably normally distributed. But suppose we are studying men of high talent. Is height normally distributed? (Some people may think short people are more talented; others that tall people are more talented.) Havelock Ellis, in his study of British genius, lists 270 men of high talent according to their heights: 103 tall, 57 medium, and 100 short. Although we can well question the sampling and the source data, the example is instructive. (See H. Ellis, *A Study of British Genius*. Boston: Houghton Mifflin, 1926, pp. 278–281.) Margenau gives a powerful *rational* argument for normality: H. Margenau, *The Nature of Physical Reality*. New York: McGraw-Hill, 1950, pp. 114–115. For an enlightening discussion of the normality concept, see M. Tate, *Statistics in Education*. New York: Macmillan, 1955, pp. 203–209.

There are two types of graphs ordinarily used in research in the social sciences and education. In one of these, as we have seen, the values of a dependent variable are plotted against the values of an independent variable. The second major type of graph has a different purpose: to show the distribution of a single variable. On the horizontal axis, values are laid out similarly to the first type of graph. But, on the vertical axis, *frequencies* or frequency intervals or probabilities are laid out.

We draw a normal curve and lay out two sets of values on the horizontal axis. In one set of values, we use IQ's with a mean of 100 and a standard deviation of 16. Say we have a sample of 400 and the data (the IQ's) are in approximately normal form. (It is said that the data are "normally distributed.") The curve looks like that of Fig. 11.1. Imagine a Y (vertical) axis with frequencies (or proportions) marked off on the axis. The major characteristics of normal curves are unimodality (one curve), symmetry (one side the same as the other), and certain mathematical properties. It is the mathematical properties that interest us, because they allow us to make statistical inferences of considerable power.

A standard deviation can be conceived as a length along the base line of the curve from the mean or middle of the base line out to the right or left to the point where the curve inflects. It can also be visualized as a point on the base line a certain distance from the mean. One standard deviation from the mean of this particular distribution is $100 + 16 = 116$. The distance from 100 to 116 has been indicated by a heavy line in Fig. 11.1. Similarly, one standard deviation below the mean is $100 - 16 = 84$. Two standard deviations are represented by $100 + (2)(16) = 132$ and $100 - (2)(16) = 68$. If one can be reasonably confident that one's data are normally distributed, then one can draw a curve like the one above, mark the mean, and lay out the standard deviations. This has also been done in Fig. 11.1 The base line has also been labeled in *standard deviation units* (labeled z in the figure). That is, instead of IQ's of 100, 116, and 68, for instance, standard deviation scores can be used. They are 0, +1, −2, and so on; points between these marked points can be indicated. For example, one half of a standard deviation above the mean, in raw scores, is $100 + (1/2)(16) = 108$. In standard deviation scores, it is $0 + .5 = .5$. These standard deviation scores are called *standard*

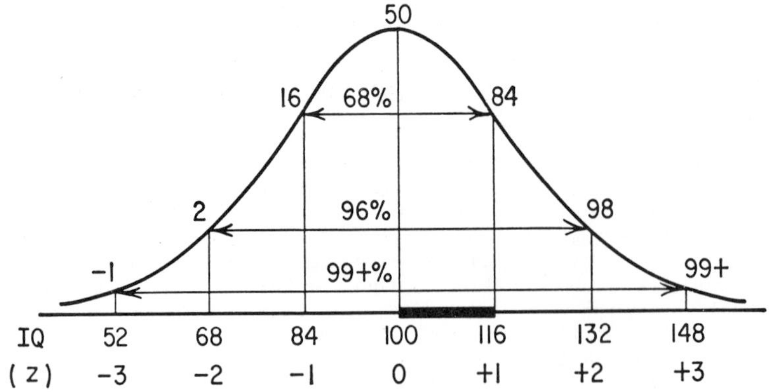

FIG. 11.1

scores or z scores. z scores range, in practical usage, from about -3 through 0 to about $+3$.[4]

If z scores are used, and the total area under the curve is set equal to 1.00, the curve is said to be in *standard form*. This immediately suggests probability. Portions of the area of the curve are conceived as probabilities and interpreted as such. If the total area under the whole curve is equal to 1.00, then if a vertical line is drawn upward from the base line at the mean ($z = 0$) to the top of the bell, then the areas to the left and to the right of the vertical line are each equal to 1/2 or 50 percent. But vertical lines might be drawn elsewhere on the base line, at one standard deviation above the mean ($z = 1$) or two standard deviations below the mean ($z = -2$). To interpret such points in area terms—and in probability terms—we must know the area properties of the curve.

The *approximate* percentages of the areas one, two, and three standard deviations above and below the mean have been indicated in Fig. 11.1. For our purposes, it is not necessary to use the exact percentages. The area between $z = -1$ and $z = +1$ is approximately 68 percent. The area between $z = -2$ and $z = +2$ is approximately 98 percent. (The exact figure is .9544. We use .96 because it makes interpretation easier.) The area between $z = -3$ and $z = +3$ is 99+ percent. Similarly all other possible baseline distances and their associated areas can be translated into percentages of the whole curve. An important point to remember is that, since the area of the whole curve is equal to 1.00, or 100 percent, and thus is equivalent to U in probability theory, the percentages of area can be interpreted as probabilities. In fact, the normal probability table entries are given in percentages of areas corresponding to z scores.

Interpretation of Data Using the Normal Probability Curve–Frequency Data

We now inquire about the probabilities of events. To do this, we first go back to tossing coins. Strictly speaking, the frequencies of heads and tails are discontinuous events, whereas the normal probability curve is continuous. But this need not worry us, since the approximations are close. It is possible to specify with great accuracy and considerable ease the probabilities that chance events will occur. Instead of calculating exact probabilities, as we did before, we can estimate probabilities from knowledge of the properties of the normal curve.

Suppose we again, somewhat wearily, perhaps, toss 100 coins. We found that the mean number of times heads will probably turn up is $M(S_{100}) = np = 100 \cdot 1/2 = 50$, and the standard deviation was $SD(S_{100}) = \sqrt{V(S_{100})} = \sqrt{npq} = \sqrt{100 \cdot 1/2 \cdot 1/2} = \sqrt{25} = 5$. Using the percentages of the curve (probabilities), we can make proba-

[4]To transform any raw score to a z score, use the formula $z = x/s$, where $x = X - M$ and s is the sample standard deviation. The x's are called deviation scores. Now we can divide the standard deviation into any x to convert the X (raw score) to a z score. As an example, take $X = 120$. Then $z = (120 - 100)/16 = 20/16 = 1.25$. That is, a raw score of 120 is equivalent to a z score of 1.25. Or, it is one and a quarter standard deviations above the mean.

bility statements. We can say, for example, that in 100 tosses the probability that heads will turn up between one standard deviation below the mean ($z = -1$) and one standard deviation above the mean ($z = +1$) is approximately .68. Roughly, then, there are two out of three chances that the number of heads will be between 45 and 55 (50 ± 5). There *is* one chance in three, approximately, that the number of heads will be less than 45 or greater than 55. That is, $q = 1 - p = 1 - .68 = .32$, approximately.

Take two standard deviations above and below the mean. These points would be $50 - (2)(5) = 40$ and $50 + (2)(5) = 60$. Since we know that about 95 or 96 percent of the cases will probably fall into this band, that is, between $z = -2$ and $z = +2$, or between 40 and 60, we can say that the probability that the number of heads will be no less than 40 or no greater than 60 is about .95 or .96. That is, there are only about 4 or 5 chances in 100 that less than 40, or more than 60, heads will occur. It can happen. But it is unlikely to happen. (Recall that earlier it was said that by the exact probability method of calculation the probability was about .96.)

If we want or need to be practically certain (as in certain kinds of medical or engineering research), then we can go out to three standard deviations, $z = -3$ and $z = +3$, or perhaps somewhat less than three standard deviations. (The .01 level is about two and a half standard deviations.) Three standard deviations means the numbers of heads between 35 and 65. Since three standard deviations above and below the mean in Fig. 11.1 take up more than 99 percent of the area of the curve, we can say that we are practically certain that the number of heads in 100 tosses of a fair coin will not be less than 35 nor more than 65. The probability is greater than .99. If you tossed a coin 100 times and got, say, 68 heads, you might conclude that there was probably something wrong with the coin. Of course, 68 heads can occur, but it is very, very unlikely that they will.

The earlier Agree-Disagree problem is treated exactly the same as the coin problem above. The result of 60 Agrees and 40 Disagrees is unlikely to happen. There are only about 4 chances in 100 that 60 Agrees and 40 Disagrees will happen by chance. We knew this before from the χ^2 test and from the exact probability test. Now we have a third way that is generally applicable to all kinds of data—provided the data are distributed normally or approximately so.

Interpretation of Data Using the Normal Probability Curve–Continuous Data

Suppose we have the social studies test scores of a sample of 100 fifth-grade children. The mean of the scores is 70; the standard deviation is 10. From previous knowledge we know that the distribution of test scores on this test is approximately normal. Obviously we can interpret the data using the normal curve. Our interest is in the reliability of the mean. How much can we depend on this mean? With future samples of similar fifth-grade children, will we get the same mean? If the mean is undependable, that is, if it fluctuates widely from sample to sample, obviously any interpretation of the test scores of individual children is in jeopardy. A score of 75 might be average this time, but if the mean is unreliable this 75 might be, on a future testing, a superior score. In other words, we must have a dependable or reliable mean.

Imagine giving this same test to the same group of children again and again and again. Go further. Imagine giving the test under exactly the same conditions 100,000 times. Assume that all other things are equal: the children learn nothing new in all these repetitions; they do not get fatigued; environmental conditions remain the same; and so on.

If we calculate a mean and a standard deviation for each of the many times, we obtain a gigantic distribution of means (and standard deviations). What will this distribution be like? First, it will form a beautiful bell-shaped normal curve. Means do. They have the property of falling nicely into the normal distribution, even when the original distributions from which they are calculated are not normal. This is because we assumed "other things equal" and thus have no source of mean fluctuations other than chance. The means will fluctuate, but the fluctuations will all be chance fluctuations. Most of these fluctuations will cluster around what we will call the "true" mean, the "true" value of the gigantic population of means. A few will be extreme values. If we repeated the 100 coin-tosses experiment many many times, we would find that heads would cluster around what we know is the "true" value: 50. Some would be a little higher, some a little lower, a few considerably higher, a few considerably lower. In brief, the heads and the means will obey the same "law." Since we assumed that nothing else is operating, we must come to the conclusion that these fluctuations are due to chance. And chance errors, given enough of them, distribute themselves into a normal distribution. This is the theory. It is called the *theory of errors*.

Continuing our story of the mean, if we had the data from the very many administrations of the social studies test to the same group, we could calculate a mean and a standard deviation. The mean so calculated would be very close to the "true" mean. If we had an infinite number of means from an infinite number of test administrations and calculated the mean of the means, we would then obtain the "true" mean. Similarly for the standard deviation of the means. Naturally, we cannot do this, for we do not have an infinite or even a very large number of test administrations. There is fortunately a simple way to solve the problem. It consists in accepting the mean calculated from the sample as the "true" mean and then estimating how accurate this acceptance (or assumption) is. To do this, a statistic known as the *standard error of the mean* is calculated. It is defined:

$$SE_M = \frac{\sigma_{\text{pop}}}{\sqrt{n}} \tag{11.10}$$

where the standard error of the mean is SE_M; the standard deviation of the population (σ is read "sigma"), σ_{pop}, and the number of cases in the sample, n.

There is a little snag here. We do not know, nor can we know, the standard deviation of the population. Recall that we also did not know the mean of the population, but that we estimated it with the mean of the sample. Similarly, we estimate the standard deviation of the population with the standard deviation of the sample. Thus the formula to use is

$$SE_M = \frac{SD}{\sqrt{n}} \tag{11.11}$$

The social studies test mean can now be studied for its reliability. We calculate:

$$SE_M = \frac{10}{\sqrt{100}} = \frac{10}{10} = 1$$

Again imagine a large population of means of this test. If they are put into a distribution and the curve of the distribution plotted, the curve would look something like the curve of Fig. 11.2. Keep firmly in mind: this is an imaginary distribution of means of samples. It is *not* a distribution of scores. It is easy to see that the means of this distribution are not very variable. If we double the standard error of the mean we get 2. Subtract and add this to the mean of 70: 68 to 72. The probability is approximately .95 that the population ("true") mean lies within the interval 68 to 72, that is, approximately 5 percent of the time the means of random samples of this size will lie outside this interval.

If we do the same calculation for the intelligence test data of Fig. 11.1, we obtain

$$SE_M = \frac{16}{\sqrt{400}} = \frac{16}{20} = .80$$

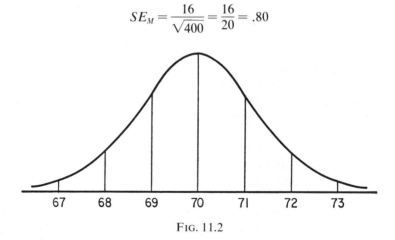

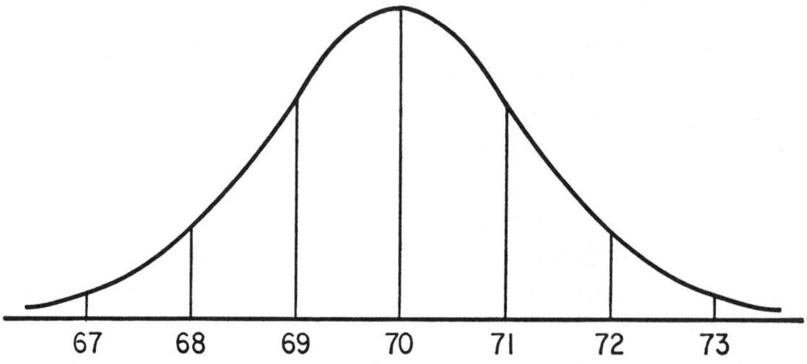

FIG. 11.2

[5]Even with relatively small samples, the mean is quite stable. (See the IQ data in Chapter 8.) Five samples of 20 IQ's each were drawn from a population of IQ's with a mean of 95. The means of the five samples were calculated. Standard errors of the mean were calculated for the first two samples, and interpretations were made. Then comparisons were made to the "true" value of 95. The mean of the first sample was 93.55 with a standard deviation of 12.22. $SE_M = 2.73$. The .05 level range of means was: 88.09 to 99.01. Obviously 95 falls within this range. The mean of the second sample was more deviant: 90.20. The standard deviation was 9.44. $SE_M = 2.11$. The .05 level range was 85.98 to 94.42. Our 95 does not fall in this range. The .01 level range is: 83.87 to 96.53. Now 95 is encompassed. This is not bad at all for samples of only 20. For samples of 50 or 100 it would be even better. The mean of the five means was 93.31; the standard deviation of these means was 2.73. Compare this to the standard errors calculated from the two samples: 2.73 and 2.11. In the next chapter a more convincing demonstration of the stability of means will be given.

Three standard errors above and below the mean of 100 give the range 97.60 to 102.40, or we can say that the "true" mean very probably (less than 1 percent chance of being wrong) lies within the interval 98 to 102. Means *are* reliable—with fair-size samples.[5]

The standard error of the mean, then, is a standard deviation. It is a standard deviation of an infinite number of means. Only chance error makes the means fluctuate. Thus the standard error of the mean—or the standard deviation of the means, if you like—is a measure of chance or error in its effect on one measure of central tendency.

A caution is in order. All of the theory discussed is based on the assumptions of random sampling and independence of observations. If these assumptions are violated, the reasoning, while not entirely invalidated, practically speaking, is open to question. Estimates of error may be biased to a greater or lesser extent. The trouble is we cannot tell how much a standard error is biased. Years ago Guilford gave interesting examples of the biases encountered when the assumptions are violated.[6] With large numbers of Air Force pilots, he found that estimates of standard errors were sometimes considerably off. No one can give hard and fast rules. The best maxim probably is: Use random sampling and keep observations independent, if at all possible.

If random sampling cannot be used, and if there is doubt about the independence of observations, calculate the statistics and interpret them. But be circumspect about interpretations and conclusions; they may be in error. Because of such possibilities of error, it has been said that statistics are misleading, and even useless. Like any other method—consulting authority, using intuition, and the like—statistics *can* be misleading. But even when statistical measures are biased, they are usually less biased than authoritative and intuitive judgments. It is not that numbers lie. The numbers do not know what they are doing. It is that the human beings using the numbers may be informed or misinformed, biased or unbiased, knowledgeable or ignorant, intelligent or stupid. Treat numbers and statistics neither with too great respect nor too great contempt. Calculate statistics and act as though they were "true," but always maintain a certain reserve toward them, a willingness to disbelieve them if the evidence indicates such disbelief.[7]

[6]J. Guilford, *Fundamental Studies in Psychology and Education*, 3d ed. New York: McGraw-Hill, 1956, pp. 169–173.

[7]Study suggestions for this chapter are given at the end of the next chapter.

CHAPTER 12

Testing Hypotheses and the Standard Error

The standard error, as an estimate of chance fluctuation, is the measure against which the outcomes of experiments are checked. Is there a difference between the means of two experimental groups? If so, is the difference a "real" difference or merely a consequence of the many relatively small differences that could have arisen by chance? To answer this question, the standard error of the differences between means is calculated and the obtained difference is compared to this standard error. If it is sufficiently greater than the standard error, it is said to be a "significant" difference. Similar reasoning can be applied to any statistic. Thus, there are many standard errors: of correlation coefficients, of differences between means, of means, of medians, of proportions, and so on. The purpose of this chapter is to examine the general notion of the standard error and to see how hypotheses are tested using the standard error.

Examples: Differences between Means

Gross, Mason, and McEachern, in their study of board of education members and superintendents, administered a questionnaire on division of labor between board and superintendent to a sampling of board members and superintendents.[1] The hypothesis tested was that incumbents of subordinate (superintendent) and superordinate (board of education) positions will assign more responsibility to their own position than incumbents of the other position will assign to it. The means of the two groups on the instrument, which indicated relative amount of judged responsibility, were 1.41 and 2.54 for board members and superintendents, respectively.

[1]N. Gross, W. Mason, and A. McEachern, *Explorations in Role Analysis*. New York: Wiley, 1958, pp. 123–126.

(The higher the mean the greater the responsibility assigned to the superintendent role.) The direction of the difference was as predicted. Is the size of the difference, 1.13, sufficient to warrant the authors' claim that their hypothesis was supported? A test of the statistical significance of this difference showed that it was highly significant.

The point of this example in the present context is that the mean difference was tested for statistical significance with a standard error. The standard error in this case was the standard error of the differences between two means. The difference was found to be significant. This means that superintendents judged the responsibility of their role significantly higher than did board of education members. Now let us look at an example in which the difference between means was not significant.

Gates and Taylor, in a well-known early study of transfer of training, set up two matched groups of 16 pupils each.[2] The experimental group was given practice in digit memory; the control group was not. The mean gain of the experimental group right after the practice period was 2.00; the mean gain of the control group was .67, a mean difference of 1.33. Four to five months later, the children of both groups were tested again. The mean score of the experimental group was 4.71; the mean score of the control group was surprising—4.77. The mean gains over the initial tests were .35 and .36. Statistical tests are hardly necessary with data like these.

Absolute and Relative Differences

Since differences between statistics, especially between means, are tested and reported a great deal in the literature, we must try to get some perspective on the absolute and relative sizes of such statistics. Although the discussion uses differences between means as examples, the same points apply to differences between proportions, correlation coefficients, and so on. In a study by Ojemann and Wilkinson, a difference of .24 in grade-point averages, which was statistically significant, was obtained between the means of an experimental group and a control group.[3] Now, contrast this seemingly small difference to one of the mean differences between experimental and control groups obtained by Mann and Janis in their study of the long-term effects of role playing on smoking: 13.50 and 5.20.[4] (These are mean decreases in number of cigarettes smoked each day; the difference is statistically significant.)

The problem here is actually two problems: one of absolute and relative size of differences and one of practical or "real" significance versus statistical significance. What appears to be a very small difference may, upon close examination, not be so small. In the Ojemann and Wilkinson experiment, the means of the

[2]A. Gates and G. Taylor, "An Experimental Study of the Nature of Improvement Resulting from Practice in a Mental Function," *Journal of Educational Psychology*, XVI (1925), 583–592.

[3]R. Ojemann and F. Wilkinson, "The Effect on Pupil Growth of an Increase in Teachers' Understanding of Pupil Behavior," *Journal of Experimental Education*, VIII (1939), 143–147.

[4]L. Mann and I. Janis, "A Follow-Up on the Long-Term Effects of Emotional Role Playing," *Journal of Personality and Social Psychology*, VIII (1968), 339–342.

experimental and control groups were 3.21 and 2.97. But they were working with grade-point averages, which had a range of only 1 through 4. A difference of .24 can, of course, be trivial, even though statistically significant. The Mann and Janis difference of $13.50 - 5.20 = 8.30$ seems to be practically as well as statistically significant. Just think: this is a difference of eight cigarettes a day! The researcher has to use experienced and informed judgment as well as a careful examination of the size of the scale, the size of the sample—the larger the N, the greater the probability of statistical significance—the nature of the variable, and the circumstances of the study.

One should ordinarily not be enthusiastic about mean differences like .20, .15, .08, and so on, but one has to be intelligent about it. Suppose that a very small difference is reported as statistically significant, and you think this ridiculous. But also suppose that it was the mean difference between the cerebral cortex weights of groups of rats under enriched and deprived experiences in the early days of their lives.[5] To obtain *any* difference in brain weight due to experience is an outstanding achievement and, of course, an important scientific discovery. Nevertheless, in most cases very small differences, even though statistically significant, must be treated with skepticism.

Correlation Coefficients

Correlation coefficients are reported in large quantities in research journals. Questions as to the significance of the coefficients—and the "reality" of the relations they express—must be asked. For example, to be statistically significant a coefficient of correlation calculated between 30 pairs of measures has to be approximately .31 at the .05 level and .42 at the .01 level. With 100 pairs of measures the problem is less acute (the law of large numbers again). To carry the .05 day, an r of .16 is sufficient; to carry the .01 day, an r of about .23 does it. If r's are less than these values, they are considered to be not significant.

If one draws, say, 30 pairs of numbers from a table of random numbers and correlates them, theoretically the r should be near zero. Clearly, there should be near-zero relations between sets of random numbers, but occasionally sets of pairs can yield statistically significant and reasonably high r's *by chance*.[6] At any rate, coefficients of correlation, as well as means and differences, have to be weighed in the balance for statistical significance by stacking them up against their standard errors. Fortunately, this is easy to do, since r's for different levels of significance and for different sizes of samples are given in tables in most statistics texts. Thus, with r's it is not necessary to calculate and use the standard error of an r. The reasoning behind the tables has to be understood, however.[7]

[5] E. Bennett et al., "Chemical and Anatomical Plasticity of Brain," *Science*, CXLVI (1964), 610–619. (See, especially, remarks on p. 618.)

[6] As indicated earlier, 4000 random numbers in 40 sets of 100 each are given in Appendix D, which also describes a test of the significance of the correlations.

[7] There has been a good deal of misunderstanding about the assumptions that have to be satisfied to calculate coefficients of correlation. No assumptions have to be satisfied simply to calculate r's. The assumptions come in only when we wish to infer from the sample to the population. See W. Hays, *Statistics*. New York: Holt, Rinehart and Winston, 1963, pp. 509–510 and 528.

In presenting data on the validity of their Test Anxiety Scale (TASC), Sarason et al. present a number of coefficients of correlation between the TASC and mean school achievement of children and between teacher ratings (TR) of test anxiety and mean achievement.[8] Most of the *r*'s between the TASC and achievement were low. In Greenwich, Conn., only one *r* out of eight was significant. It was $-.234$ ($n = 120$). In Milford, Conn., however, all the *r*'s were significant. The samples were considerably larger. Curiously, the *r*'s between TR and achievement were considerably higher but with a larger range: $-.127$ to $-.533$. All were significant. Here is a case of a type that occurs frequently in the literature where *r*'s are low and borderline. It has been said that it is inappropriate to bother with *r*'s of .10, .20, and .30. With *r*'s of about .10 or less, this point is well taken, but with *r*'s of about .30, it is not. If an *r* of .30 is statistically significant, it may help the investigator later to find an important relation—if he can clear up, say, his measurement problems. That is, he may, by dropping a statistically significant *r* of .30, be losing a valuable lead for theory and subsequent research. The point is that *r*'s, like other statistics, must be tested for statistical significance.

Hypothesis Testing: Substantive and Null Hypotheses

The main research purpose of inferential statistics is to test research hypotheses by testing statistical hypotheses. Another way to put it is that inferential statistics helps the researcher make decisions between alternative hypotheses.

Broadly speaking, the scientist uses two types of hypothesis, substantive and statistical. A *substantive hypothesis* is the usual type of hypothesis discussed in Chapter 2 in which a conjectural statement of the relation between two or more variables is expressed, for example, "The greater the cohesiveness of a group the greater its influence on its members"[9] is a substantive hypothesis. An investigator's theory dictates that this variable is related to that variable. The statement of the relation is a substantive hypothesis.

A substantive hypothesis itself, strictly speaking, is not testable. It has first to be translated into operational and experimental terms. One very useful way to test substantive hypotheses is through statistical hypotheses. A *statistical hypothesis* is a conjectural statement, in statistical terms, of statistical relations deduced from the relations of the substantive hypothesis. This rather clumsy statement needs translation. A statistical hypothesis expresses an aspect of the original substantive hypothesis in quantitative and statistical terms. $M_A > M_B$, Mean *A* is greater than Mean *B*; $r > +.20$, the coefficient of correlation is greater than $+.20$; $M_A > M_B > M_C$, at the .01 level; the interaction *F* ratio is significant at the .05 level; and so on. A statistical hypothesis is a prediction of how the statistics used in analyzing the quantitative data of a research problem will turn out.

Statistical hypotheses must be tested against something, however. It is not

[8] S. Sarason et al., *Anxiety in Elementary School Children*. New York: Wiley, 1960, p. 129.

[9] S. Schachter et al., "An Experimental Study of Cohesiveness and Productivity," *Human Relations*, IV (1951), 229–238.

possible simply to test a statistical hypothesis as it stands. That is, we do not directly test the statistical proposition $M_A > M_B$ in and of itself. We test it against an alternative proposition. Naturally, there can be several alternatives to $M_A > M_B$. The alternative usually selected is the null hypothesis, which was invented by Sir Ronald Fisher. The *null hypothesis* is a statistical proposition which states, essentially, that there is no relation between the variables (of the problem). The null hypothesis says, "You're wrong, there is no relation; disprove me if you can." It says this in statistical terms such as $M_A = M_B$, or $M_A - M_B = 0$; $r_{xy} = 0$; F is not significant; t is not significant; and so on.[10]

Fisher says, "Every experiment may be said to exist only in order to give the facts a chance of disproving the null hypothesis."[11] Aptly said. What does it mean? Suppose you entertain a hypothesis to the effect that teaching method A is superior to teaching method B. If you satisfactorily solve the problems of defining what you mean by "superior," of setting up an experiment, and the like, you now must specify a statistical hypothesis. In this case, you might say $M_A > M_B$ (the mean of method A is, or will be, greater than the mean of method B on such-and-such a criterion measure). Assume that after the experiment the two means are 68 and 61, respectively. It would seem that your substantive hypothesis is upheld since $68 > 61$, or M_A is greater than M_B. As we have already learned, however, this is not enough since this difference may be one of the many possible similar differences due to chance and its fluctuations.

In effect, we set up what can be called the chance hypothesis: $M_A = M_B$, or $M_A - M_B = 0$, or $M_B - M_A = 0$. These are all null hypotheses. What we do, then, is write hypotheses. First we write the statistical hypothesis which reflects the operational-experimental meaning of the substantive hypothesis. Then we write the null hypothesis against which we test the first type of hypothesis. Here are the two kinds of hypothesis suitably labeled:

$$H_1: M_A > M_B$$
$$H_o: M_A = M_B$$

H_1 simply means "Hypothesis 1." There is often more than one such hypothesis. They are labeled H_1, H_2, H_3, and so on. H_o means "null hypothesis." Note that the null hypothesis could in this case have been written:

$$H_o: M_A - M_B = 0$$

This form shows where the null hypothesis got its name; the difference between M_A and M_B is zero. But it is a little unwieldy in this form, especially when there are three or more means or other statistics being tested. $M_A = M_B$ is general, and

[10]Many graduate students use the null form of hypothesis in writing their theses. Instead of saying that method A is more conducive to learning arithmetic than method B, to take a simple example, they may say that there is no difference between methods A and B. In the author's opinion, this is poor practice because it begs the scientific question. Assume that an investigator believes $M_A > M_B$, but hypothesizes $M_A = M_B$. Then, either $M_A > M_B$ *or* $M_A < M_B$, which is a wide range. The power of the substantive hypothesis, that the investigator can make a more or less specific *nonchance* prediction, is lost.

[11]R. Fisher, *The Design of Experiments*, 6th ed. New York: Hafner, 1951, p. 16.

of course means the same as $M_A - M_B = 0$ and $M_B - M_A = 0$. Notice that we can write quite easily $M_A = M_B = M_C = \cdots = M_N$.

The null hypothesis is a succinct way to express the testing of obtained data against chance expectation. It expresses the chance expectation. The standard error is a tool used in testing the null hypothesis. We can express these ideas in variance terms. How much does the obtained result vary? Does it vary significantly? Vary from what?—from chance. The null hypothesis and the statistical tests that use it give us the answers to these questions.

The General Nature of a Standard Error

If this were the best of all possible research worlds, there would be no random error. And if there were no random error, there would be no need for statistical tests of significance. The word "significance" would be meaningless, in fact. Any difference at all would be a "real" difference. But such is never the case, alas. There are *always* chance errors (and biased errors, too), and in educational, sociological, and psychological research they often contribute substantially to the total variance. Standard errors are measures of this error, and are used, as has repeatedly been said, as a sort of yardstick against which experimental or "variable" variance is checked.

The *standard error* is the standard deviation of the sampling distribution of any given measure—the mean or the correlation coefficient, for instance. In most cases, population or universe values (parameters) cannot be known; they must be estimated from sample measures, usually from single samples.

Suppose we draw a random sample of 100 children from eighth-grade classes in such-and-such a school system. It is difficult or impossible, say, to measure the whole universe of eighth-grade children for reasons we need not go into here. We calculate the mean and the standard deviation from a test we give the children and find these statistics to be $M = 110$; $SD = 10$. An important question we must ask ourselves is "How accurate is this mean?" Or, if we were to draw a large number of random samples of 100 eighth-grade pupils from this same population, will the means of these samples be 110 or near 110? And, if they are near 110, how near? What we do, in effect, is to set up a *hypothetical distribution of sample means*, all calculated from samples of 100 pupils each drawn from the parent population of eighth-grade pupils. If we could calculate the means of this population *of means*, or if we knew what it was, everything would be simple. But we do not know this value, and we are not able to know it since the possibilities of drawing different samples are so numerous. The best we can do is to *estimate it with our sample value, or sample mean*. We simply say, in this case, let the sample mean equal the mean of the population mean—and hope we are right. Then we must test our equation. This we do with the standard error.

A similar argument applies to the standard deviation of the whole population (of the original scores). We do not know and probably can never know it. But we can estimate it with the standard deviation calculated from our sample. Again, we say, in effect, let the standard deviation of the sample equal the standard deviation of the population. We know they are probably not the same value, but we also know, if the sampling has been random, that they are probably close.

In Chapter 11 the sample standard deviation was used as a substitute for the standard deviation of the population in the formula for the *standard error of the mean:*

$$SE_M = \frac{SD}{\sqrt{n}} \tag{12.1}$$

This is also called the *sampling error*. Just as the standard deviation is a measure of the dispersion of the original scores, the standard error of the mean is a measure of the dispersion of the distribution of sample means. It is *not* the standard deviation of the population of individual scores if, for example, we could test every member of the population and calculate the mean and standard deviation of this population.

A Monte Carlo Demonstration

To give us material to work with, we now resort to the computer and what are called Monte Carlo methods. A Monte Carlo procedure is an empirical study of statistics using random numbers. In the behavioral sciences, the term Monte Carlo is usually applied to an empirical study of some method or model that a scientist wishes to explore. This is just what we do now: use an elementary form of Monte Carlo to test a most important theorem of statistics and to explore the variability of means and the use of the standard error of the mean. We also want to lay a foundation for understanding the use of the computer in studying random processes.

The Procedure

A computer program was written to generate 4000 random numbers evenly distributed between 0 and 100 (so that each number has an equal chance of being "drawn") in 40 sets of 100 numbers each, and to calculate various statistics with the numbers.[12] Consider this set of 4000 numbers a population, or U. The mean of U is 50.33 (by actual computer calculation) and the standard deviation 29.17. We wish to estimate this mean from samples that we draw randomly from U. Of course, in a real situation we would usually not know the mean of the population. One of the virtues of Monte Carlo procedures is that we can know what we ordinarily do not know. In fact, this is partly why we are using Monte Carlo.

Five of the 40 sets of 100 numbers were drawn at random. (The sets drawn were 5, 7, 8, 16, and 36. See Appendix D.) The means and standard deviations of the five sets were calculated. So were the five standard errors of the mean. These statistics are reported in Table 12.1. We want to give an intuitive notion of what the standard error of the mean is and then we want to show how it is used.

First, calculate the *standard deviation of this sample of means*. If we simply

[12]See footnote 6.

TABLE **12.1** MEANS, STANDARD DEVIATIONS, AND STANDARD ERRORS OF THE MEAN, FIVE SAMPLES OF 100 RANDOM NUMBERS (0 THROUGH 100)[a]

	Samples 1	2	3	4	5
M:	53.21	49.64	51.37	49.02	55.51
SD:	29.62	27.91	29.83	26.72	29.23
SE_M:	2.96	2.79	2.98	2.67	2.92

[a]Population statistics: $M = 50.33$; $SD = 29.17$; $N = 4000$.

treat the five means as ordinary scores and calculate the mean and standard deviation, we obtain: $M_1 = 51.75$; $SD = 2.38$. The mean of all 4000 scores is 50.33. Each of the five means is a sample estimate of this population mean. Notice that three of them, 49.64, 51.37, and 49.02, are rather close to the population mean, and two of them, 53.21 and 55.51, are farther away from it. So it seems that three of the samples provide good estimates of the population mean and two do not—or do they?

The standard deviation of 2.38 is *akin to* the standard error of the mean. (It is, of course, not the standard error of the mean, because it has been calculated from only five means.) Suppose only one sample, the first with $M = 53.21$ and $SD = 29.62$, had been drawn—and this is the usual situation in research—and the standard error of the mean calculated:

$$SE_M = \frac{SD}{\sqrt{N}} = \frac{29.62}{\sqrt{100}} = 2.96$$

This value is an estimate of the standard deviation of the population *means* of many, many samples of 100 cases, each randomly drawn from the population. Our population has 40 groups and thus 40 means. (Of course, this is not many, many means. This is done for pedagogical reasons.) The standard deviation of these means is actually 3.10. The SE_M calculated with the first sample, then, is close to this population value: 2.96 as an estimate of 3.10.

The five standard errors of the mean are given in the third data line of Table 12.1. They fluctuate very little—from 2.67 to 2.98—even though the means of the sets of 100 scores vary considerably. The standard deviation of 2.38 calculated from the five means is only a fair estimate of the standard deviation of the population of means. Yet it *is* an estimate. The interesting and important point is that the standard error of the mean, which is a "theoretical" estimate, calculated from the data of any one of the five groups, is an accurate estimate of the variability of the means of samples of the population.

To reinforce these ideas, let's now look at another Monte Carlo demonstration of much greater magnitude. The computer program used to produce the 4000 random numbers for the example discussed above was used to produce 15 more sets of 4000 random numbers each, evenly distributed between 0 and 100. That is, a total of 80,000 random numbers, in 20 sets of 4000 each, were generated. The theoretical mean, again, of numbers between 0 and 100 is 50. Consider each of the

20 sets as a sample of 4000 numbers. The means of the 20 sets are given in Table 12.2.

The 20 means cluster closely around 50: the lowest is 49.3175, the highest is 51.1450, and most of them are near 50. The mean of the 20 means is 50.0401, very close indeed to the theoretical expectation of 50. The standard deviation of the 20

TABLE **12.2** MEANS FROM 20 SETS OF 4000 COMPUTER-GENERATED RANDOM NUMBERS (0 THROUGH 100)[a]

50.3322	49.9447	50.1615	50.0995
50.1170	49.5960	51.0585	51.1450
49.8200	49.3175	49.5822	50.6440
49.8227	49.9022	49.7505	49.8437
49.5875	50.6180	50.0990	49.3605

[a]Mean of means = 50.0401; standard deviation of the means = .4956; standard error of the mean, first sample = .4611.

means is .4956. The standard deviation of the first sample of 4000 cases (see Footnote *a*, Table 12.1) is 29.1653. If we use this standard deviation to calculate the standard error of the mean, we obtain: $SE_M = 29.1653/\sqrt{4000} = .4611$. Note that this estimate of the standard error of the mean is close to the calculated standard deviation of the 20 means. We would not go wrong using it to assess the variability of the means of samples of 4000 random numbers. Clearly, means of large samples are highly stable statistics, and standard errors are good estimates of their variability.

Generalizations

Three or four generalizations of great usefulness in research can now be made. One, means of samples are stable in the sense that they are much less variable than the measures from which they are calculated. This is, of course, true by definition. Variances, standard deviations, and standard errors of the mean are even more stable; they fluctuate within relatively narrow ranges. Even when the sample means of our example varied by as much as four or five points, the standard errors fluctuated by no more than a point and a half. This means that we can have considerable faith that estimates of sample means will be rather close to the mean of a population of such means. And the law of large numbers tells us that the larger the sample size, the closer to the population values the statistics will probably be.

A difficult question for researchers is: Do these generalizations always hold, especially with nonrandom samples? The validity of the generalizations depends on random sampling and the principle of randomization. If the sampling is not random, we cannot really know whether or not the generalizations hold. Nevertheless, we often have to act as though they do hold, even with nonrandom samples. Fortunately, if we are careful about studying our data to detect substantial sample idiosyncrasy, we can use the theory profitably. For example, samples can be checked for easily checked expectations. If one expects about equal numbers of males and females in a sample, or known proportions of young and old or Republican and Democrat, it is simple to count these numbers. (Even random samples are checked in this way. See Study Suggestion 5.) There are experts who insist on random sampling as a condition of the validity of the theory—and they are correct. But if the theory is forbidden to us with nonrandom samples, much use of statistics and the inferences that accompany statistics would have to be abandoned. The reality is that the statistics seem to work very well even with nonrandom samples—provided the researcher knows the limitations of such samples, is even more careful than he would be with random samples, and replicates his studies. But this is not the last word on this subject; we return to it later in the book.

The Central Limit Theorem

Before studying the actual use of the standard error of the mean, we should look, if briefly, at an extremely important generalization about means: *If samples are drawn from a population at random, the means of the samples will tend to be normally distributed.* The larger the n's, the more this is so. And the shape and kind of distribution of the original population makes no difference. That is, the population distribution does not have to be normally distributed.[13]

For example, the distribution of the 4000 random numbers in Appendix D is rectangular, since the numbers are evenly distributed. If the central limit theorem is empirically valid, then the means of the 40 sets of 100 scores each should be approximately normally distributed. If so, this is a remarkable thing. And it is so, though one sample of 40 means is hardly sufficient to show the trend too well. Therefore, three more populations of 4000 different evenly distributed random numbers, partitioned into 40 subsets of 100 numbers each, were generated on the computer. The means calculated for the $4 \times 40 = 160$ subsets of 100 numbers each were calculated and put into one distribution. A frequency polygon of the means is given in Fig. 12.1. It can be seen that the 160 means look almost like the bell-shaped normal curve. Apparently the central limit theorem "works." And bear in mind that this distribution of means was obtained from rectangular distributions of numbers.

Why go to all this bother? Why is it important to show that distributions of means approximate normality? We work with means a great deal in data analysis, and if they are normally distributed then one can use the known properties of the normal curve to interpret obtained research data. Knowing that approximately 96 percent of the means will lie between two standard deviations (standard errors) above and below the mean is valuable information, because an obtained result can be assessed against the known properties of the normal curve. In the last chapter we saw the use of the normal curve in interpreting means. We now turn to what is perhaps a more interesting use of the curve in assessing the differences between means.

[13]See Hays, *op. cit.*, pp. 238–242. Hays gives a neat example to show how the theorem works (pp. 240–241). Another good discussion with examples is given by G. Snedecor and W. Cochran, *Statistical Methods*, 6th ed. Ames, Iowa: Iowa State University Press, 1967, pp. 51–56.

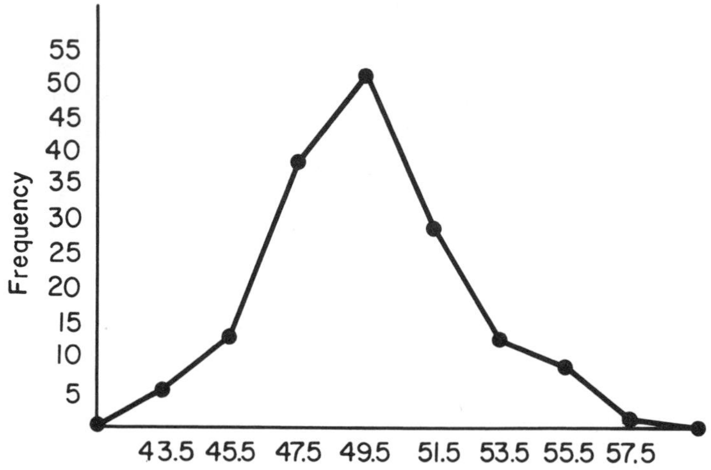

FIG. 12.1

The Standard Error of the Differences between Means

One of the most frequent and useful strategies in research is to compare means of samples. From differences in means we infer effects of independent variables. Any linear combination of means is also governed by the central limit theorem. That is, differences in means will be normally distributed, given large enough samples. (A linear combination is any equation of the first degree, e.g., $Y = M_1 - M_2$. $Y = M_1^2 - M_1$ is not linear.) Therefore we can use the same theory with differences between means that we use with means.

Suppose we have two randomly selected groups of 100 eighth-grade pupils each. We show a movie on intergroup relations to one group, for example, and none to the other group. Next, we give both groups an attitude measure. The mean score of Group A (saw the movie) is 110 and the mean score of Group B (did not see the movie) is 100. Our problem is: Is the difference of 10 units a "real" difference, a statistically significant difference? Or is it a difference that could have arisen by chance—more than 5 times in 100, say, or some other amount—when no difference actually exists?

If we similarly draw double samples of 100 and calculate the differences between the means of these samples, and go through the same experimental procedure, will we consistently get this difference of 10? Again, we use the standard error to evaluate our differences, but this time we have a *sampling distribution of differences between means*. It is as if we took each $M_i - M_j$ and considered it as an X. Then the several differences between the means of the samples are considered as the X's of a new distribution. At any rate, the standard deviation of this sampling distribution of differences is *akin* to the standard error. But this procedure is only for illustration; actually we do not do this. Here, again, we estimate the standard error from our first two groups, A and B, by using the formula:

$$SE_{M_A - M_B} = \sqrt{SE_{M_A}{}^2 + SE_{M_B}{}^2} \tag{12.2}$$

where $SE_{M_A}{}^2$ and $SE_{M_B}{}^2$ are the standard errors squared, respectively, of Groups A and B, as previously stated.[14]

Suppose we did the experiment with five double groups, that is, ten groups, two at a time. The five differences between the means were 10, 11, 12, 8, 9. The mean of these differences is 10; the standard deviation is 1.414. This 1.414 is again *akin to* the standard error of the sampling distribution of the differences between the means, in the same sense as the standard error of the mean in the previous discussion. Now, if we calculate the standard error of the mean for each group (by making up standard deviations for the two groups, $SD_A = 8$ and $SD_B = 9$), we obtain:

$$SE_{M_A} = \frac{SD_A}{\sqrt{n_A}} = \frac{8}{\sqrt{100}} = .8, \qquad SE_{M_B} = \frac{SD_B}{\sqrt{n_B}} = \frac{9}{\sqrt{100}} = .9$$

By Eq. 12.2 we calculate the standard error of the differences between the means:

$$SE_{M_A - M_B} = \sqrt{SE_{M_A}{}^2 + SE_{M_B}{}^2} = \sqrt{(.8)^2 + (.9)^2} = \sqrt{.64 + .81}$$
$$= \sqrt{1.45} = 1.20$$

What do we do with the 1.20 now that we have it? If the scores of the two groups had been chosen from a table of random numbers and there were no experimental conditions, we would expect no difference between the means. But we have learned that there are always relatively small differences due to chance factors. These differences are random. *The standard error of the differences between the means is an estimate of the dispersion of these differences.* But it is a measure of these differences that is an estimate for the whole population of such differences. For instance, the standard error of the differences between the means is 1.20. This means that, by chance alone, around the difference of 10 between M_A and M_B there will be random fluctuations—now 10, now 10.2, now 9.8, and so on. Only rarely will the differences exceed, say, 13 or 7 (about three times the SE). Another way of putting it is to say that the standard error of 1.20 indicates the limits (if we multiply the 1.20 by the appropriate factor) beyond which sample differences between the means probably will not go.

What has all this to do with our experiment? It is precisely here that we evaluate the experimental results. The standard error of 1.20 estimates random fluctuations. Now, $M_A - M_B = 10$. Could this have arisen by chance, as a result of random fluctuations as just described? It should by now be halfway clear that this cannot be, except under very unusual circumstances. We evaluate this difference of 10 by comparing it to our estimate of random or chance fluctuations. *Is it one of them?* We make the comparison by means of the t ratio, or t test (formerly called the critical ratio):[15]

$$t = \frac{M_A - M_B}{SE_{M_A - M_B}} = \frac{110 - 100}{1.20} = \frac{10}{1.20} = 8.33$$

[14]Other formulas are applicable under other circumstances, for example, if we start off with matched pairs of subjects.

[15]The term "critical ratio" (*CR*) is a fraction in which a statistic is divided by its standard error. With samples larger than 30, the t ratio and the *CR* are almost the same. The *CR*'s can be referred to any table of the normal deviate. The t ratios must be referred to a t table, especially with n's less than 30. We use the t ratio in this text because it is more general (includes the *CR*) and because it is a more accurate test. In addition, it is intimately related to the more general F ratio of analysis of variance, to be studied in Part 5.

This means that our measured difference between M_A and M_B would be 8.33 standard deviations away from a hypothesized mean of zero (zero difference, no difference between the two means).

We would not have any difference, theoretically, if our subjects were well randomized and there had been no experimental manipulation. We would have, in effect, two distributions of random numbers from which we could expect only chance fluctuations. But here we have, comparatively, a huge difference of 10, compared to an insignificant 1.20 (our estimate of random deviations). Decidedly, something is happening here besides chance. And this something is just what we are looking for. It is, presumably, the effect of the movie, or the effect of the experimental condition, other conditions having been sufficiently controlled, of course.

Look at Fig. 12.2. It represents *a population of differences between means* with a mean of zero and a standard deviation of 1.20. (The mean is set at zero, because we assume that the mean of all the mean differences is zero.) Where would the difference of 10 be placed on the base line of the diagram? In order to answer this question, the 10 must first be converted into standard deviation (or standard error) units. (Recall standard scores from the last chapter.) This is done by dividing by the standard deviation (standard error), which is 1.20: $10/1.2 = 8.33$. But this is what we got when we calculated the t ratio. It is, then, simply the difference between M_A and M_B, 10, expressed in standard deviation (standard error) units. Now we can put it on the base line of the diagram. Look far to the right for the little dot. Clearly the difference of 10 is a deviate. It is so far out, in fact, that it probably does not belong to the population in question. In short, the difference between M_A and M_B is statistically significant, so significant that it amounts to what Bernoulli called "moral certainty." Such a large difference, or deviation from chance expectation, can hardly be attributed to chance. The odds are actually greater than a billion to one. It *can* happen. But it is hardly likely to happen.[16]

Such is the standard error and its use. The standard errors of other statistics are used in the same way. A very important, useful, and neat tool. It is a basic instrument in contemporary research. Indeed, it would be hard to imagine modern research methodology, and impossible to imagine modern statistics, without the standard error. As a key to statistical inference its importance cannot be overestimated. Much of statistical inference boils down to a family of fractions epitomized by the fraction,

$$\frac{\text{Statistic}}{\text{Standard error of the statistic}}$$

[16]An important question is: How large a difference, or in the language of statistics, how far away from the hypothetical mean of zero must a deviation be to be significant? This question cannot be answered definitively in this book. The .05 level is 1.96 standard deviations from the mean, and the .01 level is 2.58 standard deviations from the mean. But there are complications, especially with small samples. The student must, as usual, study a good statistics text. A simple rule is: 2 standard deviations (*SE*'s) are significant (about the .05 level); 2.5 standard deviations are very significant (about the .01 level); and 3 standard deviations are highly significant (a little less than the .001 level).

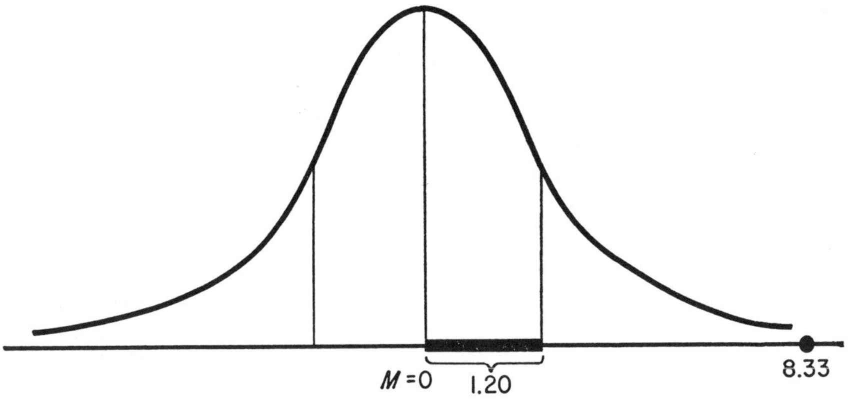

FIG. 12.2

Statistical Inference

To *infer* is to derive a conclusion from premises or from evidence. To *infer statistically* is to derive probabilistic conclusions from probabilistic premises. We conclude probabilistically, that is, at a specified level of significance. We infer, probabilistically, if an experimental result deviates from chance expectation, if the null hypothesis is not "true," that a "real" influence is at work. If, in the teaching methods experiment, $M_A > M_B$ and $M_A \neq M_B$, or H_1 is "true" and H_o is not "true," we infer that method A is "superior" to method B, "superior" being accepted in the sense defined in the experiment.

Another form of inference, discussed at length in the chapter on sampling, is that from a sample to a population. Since, for instance, 55 percent of a random sample of 2000 people in the United States say they will vote for a certain presidential candidate, it is inferred that the whole population of the United States, if asked, will respond similarly. This is rather a big inference. One of the gravest dangers of research—or perhaps I should say, of any human reasoning—is the inferential leap from sample data to population fact. In education, inferential leaps of no mean size are constantly being made. Witness the recommendations for teaching elementary school youngsters foreign languages on the basis of little research. Aided by large inferential leaps, teaching machines by the thousands are being made and sold. But scientists, too, make inferential leaps, often very large ones—with one important difference. The scientist is (or should be) aware that he is making such leaps and that they are always risky.

It can be said, in sum, that statistics enables the scientist to test substantive hypotheses indirectly by enabling him to test statistical hypotheses directly (if it is at all possible to test anything directly). In this process, he uses the null hypothesis, which he considers to be a hypothesis written by chance. He tests the "truth" of substantive hypotheses by subjecting null hypotheses to statistical tests on the basis of probabilistic reasoning. He then makes appropriate inferences. Indeed, the objective of all statistical tests is to test the justifiability of inferences.

Study Suggestions

1. Good references on statistics, fortunately, are plentiful. Those given below are only a small sample. The student should select one or two of them to supplement his study. The references marked with an asterisk are especially recommended to the beginning student. In reading a statistics book, you should not be too discouraged if you do not completely understand everything you read the first or second times. Some of the references below will contain passages that may be difficult at first. Most of the difficulties will disappear as you acquire an understanding of the language and methods of the statistician.

   *Diamond, S., *Information and Error*. New York: Basic Books, 1959, chaps. 5, 6, and 7. Witty and original, this different kind of statistics book has excellent presentation. It is well worth one or two months of study. *Highly recommended.*

   *Edwards, A., *Statistical Analysis*, 3d ed. New York: Holt, Rinehart and Winston, 1969. A good book for the beginning student. The text is clear and readable, though one sometimes wishes for more detailed explanation. See, especially, chaps. 3, 4, 10, and 11.

   Hays, W. *Statistics*. New York: Holt, Rinehart and Winston, 1963. This book is superb. It is thorough, clear, well balanced, and research-oriented—but it is not elementary. Its careful study (or of the new 1973 edition of it) should be a goal of serious students and researchers. *Very highly recommended.*

   Lohnes, P., and Cooley, W., *Introduction to Statistical Procedures: with Computer Exercises*. New York: Wiley, 1968. This book is the precursor of a new kind of statistics text. The authors have thoroughly integrated computer thinking, programming, and use with elementary statistics, a most valuable and commendable effort. Monte Carlo is a major feature of the book.

   Snedecor, G., and Cochran, W., *Statistical Methods*, 6th ed. Ames, Iowa: Iowa State University Press, 1967. A solid, authoritative, and very helpful work, but not elementary.

2. The proportions of men and women voters in a certain county are .70 and .30, respectively. In one election district of 400 people, there are 300 men and 100 women. Can it be said that the district's proportions of men and women voters differ significantly from those of the county?
   [*Answer:* No. $\chi^2 = 2.66$.]
3. An investigator in the field of prejudice experimented with various methods of answering the prejudiced person's remarks about minority group members. He randomly assigned 32 subjects to two groups, 16 in each group. With the first group he used method A; with the second group he used method B. The means of the two groups on an attitude test, administered after the methods were used, were A: 27; B: 25. Each group had a standard deviation of 4. Do the two group means differ significantly?
   [*Answer:* No. $(27-25)/1.4 = 2/1.4 = 1.3$.]
4. In Stouffer's fine study of tolerance and civil liberties, two independent samples totaling approximately 5900 were drawn.[17] It is customary in survey research to check the accuracy of the sampling by comparing proportions of sociological variables—rural-urban, sex, education, and so on—with the proportions reported in the national census. One such comparison, drawn from many made by Stouffer, is urban-rural. The percentage figures are: Survey:

[17]S. Stouffer, *Communism, Conformity, and Civil Liberties*. Garden City, N.Y.: Doubleday, 1955.

64 percent; Census: 66 percent.[18] Does the survey figure differ significantly from the census figure? ($n = 4900$.) [*Hint:* What proportion are you testing? Against what expectation?]
[*Answer:* The difference is significant: $t = 3$, approximately.]

*5. The evenly distributed 4000 random numbers discussed in the text, and the statistics calculated from the random numbers are given in Appendix D at the end of the book. Use a table of random numbers—the 4000 random numbers will do—and wave a pencil in the air with eyes closed and let it come to rest at any point in the table. Going down the columns from the place the table was entered, copy out 10 numbers in the range from 1 through 40. Let these be the numbers of ten of the 40 groups. The means, variances, and standard deviations are given right after the table of 4000 random numbers. Copy out the means of the groups randomly selected. Round the means; i.e., 54.33 becomes 54, 47.87 becomes 48, and so on.
   (a) Calculate the mean of the means, and compare it to the population mean of 50 (really 50.33). Did you come close?
   (b) Calculate the standard deviation of the 10 means.
   (c) Take the first group selected and calculate the standard error of the mean, using $N = 100$ and the reported standard deviation. Do the same for the fourth and ninth groups. Are the SE_M's alike? Interpret the first SE_M. Compare the results of (b) and (c).
   (d) Calculate the differences between the first and sixth means and the fourth and tenth means. Test the two differences for statistical significance. Should they be statistically significant? Give the reason for your answer. Make up an experimental situation and imagine that the fourth and tenth means are your results. Interpret.
   (e) Discuss the central limit theorem in relation to (d), above.

6. To now, the variance and the standard deviation have been calculated with N in the denominator. In statistics books, the student will encounter the variance formula as: $V = \Sigma x^2/N$, or $V = \Sigma x^2/(N-1)$. The first formula is used when only describing a sample or population. The second is used when estimating the variance of a population variation with the sample variance (or standard deviation). With N large, there is little practical difference. In Part 5, we will see that the denominators of variance estimates always have $N-1$, $k-1$, and so on. These are really degrees of freedom. Most computer programs use $N-1$ to calculate standard deviations. Perhaps the best advice is to use $N-1$ always. Even when it is not appropriate, it will not make that much difference.
   The student should read a good discussion in a statistics text of the reason for using $N-1$ in the variance formula. Hays' discussion (see reference in Study Suggestion 1, above, pp. 206–208) is very good. In addition, study of the idea of degrees of freedom will help future work in statistics. See Hays, pp. 310–311. A particularly good mathematical discussion is: H. Walker, *Mathematics Essential for Elementary Statistics*, rev. ed. New York: Holt, Rinehart and Winston, 1951, chap. 22.

[18]*Ibid.*, p. 238.

PART 5

Analysis of Variance

CHAPTER 13

Analysis of Variance: Foundations

The analysis of variance is not just a statistical method. It is an approach and a way of thinking. From one point of view at least, modern statistical methods culminate in analysis of variance, multiple regression analysis, and factor analysis. These methods are general. They have aims of scientific data analysis hardly conceived fifty years ago. They attain their results in fundamentally the same way, although the methods and outcomes are different: the total variance of any statistical situation is broken down into component sources of variance.

In this chapter and in Chapters 14 and 15 we explore the analysis of variance. The emphasis will be on the few fundamental and general notions that underlie the method. The chapters are not meant merely to teach analysis of variance and related methods as statistics. Their intent is to convey the basic ideas of the methods in relation to research and research problems. To accomplish the pedagogical purpose, simple examples will be used. It makes little difference whether 5 scores or 500 scores are used, or if 2 or 20 variables are used. The fundamental ideas, the theoretical conceptions, are the same. In this chapter, *simple one-way analysis of variance* is discussed. The next two chapters consider so-called factorial analysis of variance and the analysis of variance of correlated groups or subjects. By then the student should have a good basis for the study of research design.[1]

Variance Breakdown: A Simple Example

In Chapter 6, two sets of scores were analyzed in a variance fashion. The *total variance* of all the scores was broken down into a *between-groups variance* and a

[1]At this point the student should review Chapter 6. The basic ideas presented in that chapter will be applied in this one.

within-groups variance. We now pick up the theme of Chapter 6 by using, in altered form, the two-group example given there, and by correcting the method of calculation. Then we extend analysis of variance ideas considerably.

Suppose an educational investigator is interested in the relative efficacies of two methods of teaching, A_1 and A_2. Selecting ten students as a sample, he divides them into two groups at random and assigns the experimental treatments to the two groups at random. After a suitable length of time, he measures the learning of the students of both groups on a measure of achievement. The results, together with certain computations, are given in Table 13.1.

TABLE **13.1** TWO SETS OF HYPOTHETICAL EXPERIMENTAL DATA WITH SUMS, MEANS, AND SUMS OF SQUARES

	A_1	x	x^2	A_2	x	x^2	
	4	0	0	3	0	0	
	5	1	1	1	−2	4	
	3	−1	1	5	2	4	
	2	−2	4	2	−1	1	
	6	2	4	4	1	1	
ΣX:	20			15			$\Sigma X_t = 35$
M:	4			3			$M_t = 3.5$
Σx^2:			10			10	

Our job with the data given, is to locate and calculate the different variances that make up the total variance. The total variance and the other variances are calculated as before, with an important difference. Instead of using N or n in the denominator of variance fractions, we use so-called degrees of freedom. Degrees of freedom are ordinarily defined as one case less than N or n, that is, $N-1$ and $n-1$. In the case of groups, instead of k (the number of groups), we use $k-1$. While this method has a great advantage from a statistical point of view, from a mathematical-conceptual point of view it makes our job a bit more difficult. First, we do the computations, and then return to the difficulty.

To calculate the total variance, we use the formula:

$$V_t = \frac{\Sigma x^2}{N-1} \tag{13.1}$$

where Σx^2 = the sum of squares, as before, $x = X - M$, or deviation from the mean of any score, and N = number of cases in the total sample. To calculate V_t, simply take all the scores, regardless of their grouping, and calculate the necessary terms of Eq. 13.1, as in Table 13.2. Since $N-1 = 10-1 = 9$, $V_t = 22.50/9 = 2.5$. Thus, if we arrange the data of Table 13.1 without regard to the two groups, $V_t = 2.5$.

There is variance between the groups and this variance is due, presumably, to the experimental manipulation. That is, the experimenter did something to one group and something different to the other group. These different treatments should make the groups and their means different. They will have *between-groups variance*. Take the two means, treat them like any other scores (X's), and calculate their variance (see Table 13.3).

TABLE **13.2** CALCULATION OF V_t OF DATA OF TABLE 13.1

	X	x	x^2
	4	.5	.25
	5	1.5	2.25
	3	−.5	.25
	2	−1.5	2.25
	6	2.5	6.25
	3	−.5	.25
	1	−2.5	6.25
	5	1.5	2.25
	2	−1.5	2.25
	4	.5	.25
ΣX:	35		
M:	3.5		
Σx^2:			22.50

TABLE **13.3** CALCULATION OF V_b OF DATA OF TABLE 13.1

	X	x	x^2
	4	.5	.25
	3	.5	.25
ΣX:	7		
M:	3.5		
Σx^2:			.50

$$V_b = \frac{\Sigma x_b^2}{k-1} = \frac{.50}{2-1} = .50$$

There is a remaining source of variance left over: the ubiquitous random error. We saw in Chapter 6 that this could be obtained by calculating the variance *within* each group separately and then averaging these separate variances. We do this using the figures given in Table 13.1. Each group has $\Sigma x^2 = 10$. Dividing each of these sums of squares by its degrees of freedom, we get:

$$\frac{\Sigma x_{A_1}^2}{n_{A_1}-1} = \frac{10}{4} = 2.5$$

and

$$\frac{\Sigma x_{A_2}^2}{n_{A_2}-1} = \frac{10}{4} = 2.5$$

The averaging yields, of course, 2.5. Therefore the *within-groups variance*, V_w, is 2.5.

Three variances have been calculated: $V_t = 2.5$, $V_b = .50$, $V_w = 2.5$. The theoretical equation given in Chapter 6 says that the total variance is made up of separate sources of variance: the between-groups and the within-groups variances.

Logically, they should add up to the total variance. The theoretical equation is

$$V_t = V_b + V_w \tag{13.2}$$

Since 2.5 is not equal to .50 and 2.5, something must be wrong. The trouble is easily located. Degrees of freedom were used in the denominators of the variance formula instead of N, n, and k. Had N, n, and k been used, the relation of Eq. 13.2 would have held (see Chapter 6).

The student may ask: Why not follow the N, n, and k procedure? And if you cannot follow it, why bother with all this? The answer is that the calculation of the variances with N, n, and k is mathematically correct but statistically "unsatisfactory." Another important aspect of the analysis of variance is the estimation of population values. It can be shown that using degrees of freedom in the denominators of the variance formula yields unbiased estimates of the population values, a matter of great statistical concern. The reason we bother going through the present procedure is to show the reader clearly the mathematical basis of the reasoning. One should remember, though, that variances, as used in the analysis of variance, are not necessarily additive.

Sums of squares, on the other hand, are always additive. (They are calculated from the scores and not *divided* by anything.) The sum of squares, of course, is also a measure of variability. Except at the final stage of analysis of variance, sums of squares are calculated, studied, and analyzed. To convince ourselves of the additive property of sums of squares, note that the between-groups and the within-groups sums of squares add to the total sum of squares. If we multiply the between-groups sum of squares by n, the number of cases in each group:

$$\Sigma x_t^2 = n\Sigma x_b^2 + \Sigma x_w^2$$

or numerically, $22.50 = (5)(.50) + 20$. (Why Σx_b^2 is multiplied by 5 will be taken up later.)

The *t*-Ratio Approach

Using the data of Table 13.1, we calculate several statistics for the A_1 and A_2 data separately: the variances, standard deviations, standard errors of the means, and standard variances of the means.[2] These calculations are shown in Table 13.4. (Note that V is now calculated with $n-1$ instead of n.)

Now we consider the central statistical idea behind the analysis of variance. The question the investigator has to ask himself is: Do the means differ significantly? It is obvious that 4 does not equal 3, but the question has to be asked statistically. We know that if sets of random numbers are drawn, the means of the

[2]The methods of analysis used in the first part of this chapter are not used in actual calculation. They are too cumbersome. They are used here purely for pedagogical reasons. Unfortunately, the usual method of calculation tends to obscure the important relations and operations underlying the analysis of variance.

TABLE **13.4** VARIOUS STATISTICS CALCULATED FROM TABLE 13.1 DATA

	A_1	A_2
V:	$\frac{\Sigma x^2}{n-1} = \frac{10}{4} = 2.5$	$\frac{10}{4} = 2.5$
SD:	$\sqrt{2.5} = 1.58$	$\sqrt{2.5} = 1.58$
SE_M:	$\frac{SD}{\sqrt{n}} = \frac{1.58}{\sqrt{5}} = .705$	$\frac{1.58}{\sqrt{5}} = .705$
SV_M:	$\frac{V}{n} = \frac{2.5}{5} = .50$	$\frac{2.5}{5} = .50$

sets will not be equal. They should, however, not be too different, that is, they should differ only within the bounds of chance fluctuations. Thus the question becomes: Does 4 differ from 3 *significantly*? Again the null hypothesis is set up: H_0: $M_{A_1} - M_{A_2} = 0$, or $M_{A_1} = M_{A_2}$. The substantive hypothesis was: H_1: $M_{A_1} > M_{A_2}$. Which hypothesis does the evidence support? In other words, it is not simply a question of 4 being absolutely greater than 3. It is, rather, a question of whether 4 differs from 3 beyond the differences to be expected by chance.

This question can be quickly answered using the method of the last chapter. First, calculate the standard error of the differences between the means:

$$SE_{M_{A_1}-M_{A_2}} = \sqrt{SE_{M_{A_1}}{}^2 + SE_{M_{A_2}}{}^2} = \sqrt{(.705)^2 + (.705)^2}$$
$$= \sqrt{.994} = .997 = 1.00 \text{ (rounded)}$$

Now, the t ratio:

$$t = \frac{M_{A_1} - M_{A_2}}{SE_{M_{A_1}-M_{A_2}}} = \frac{4-3}{1.00} = \frac{1}{1} = 1$$

Since the difference being evaluated is no greater than the measure of error, it is obvious that it is not significant. The numerator and the denominator of the t ratio are equal. The difference, $4-3=1$, is clearly one of the differences that could have occurred with random numbers. Remember that a "real" difference would be reflected in the t ratio by a considerably larger numerator than denominator.

The Analysis of Variance Approach

In the analysis of variance, the approach is conceptually similar, although the method differs. The method is general: differences of more than two groups can be tested for statistical significance, whereas the t test applies only to two groups. (With two groups, as we shall see shortly, the results of the two methods are really identical.) The method of analysis of variance uses variances entirely, instead of using actual differences and standard errors, even though the actual difference-standard error reasoning is behind the method. Two variances are always pitted against each other. One variance, that presumably due to the experimental (independent) variable or variables is pitted against another variance, that presumably due to error or randomness. This is a case, again, of information versus error, as Diamond would put it,[3] or, as information theorists say, information versus noise. To get a grip on this idea, go back to the problem.

We found that the between-groups variance was .50. Now we must find a variance that is a reflection of error. This is the within-groups variance. After all, since we calculate the within-groups variance, essentially, by calculating the variance of each group separately and then averaging the two (or more) variances, this estimate of error is unaffected by the differences between the means. Thus, *if nothing else is causing the scores to vary*, it is reasonable to consider the within-groups variance a measure of chance fluctuation. If this is so, then we can *stack up the variance due to the experimental effect, the between-groups variance, against this measure of chance error, the within-groups variance*. The only question is: How is the within-groups variance calculated?

Remember that the variance of a population of means can be estimated with the standard variance of the mean (the standard error squared). One way to obtain the within-groups variance is to calculate the standard variance of each of the groups and then average them for all of the groups. This should yield an estimate of error that can be used to evaluate the variance of the means of the groups. The reasoning here is basic. To evaluate the differences between the means, it is necessary to refer to a theoretical population of means that would be gotten from the random sampling of groups of scores like the groups of scores we have. In the present case, we have two means from samples with five scores in each group. (It is well to remember that we might have three, four, or more means from three, four, or more groups. The reasoning is the same.) If the sampling has been random and nothing else has operated—that is, there have been no experimental manipulations and no other systematic influences at work—then it is possible to estimate the variance of the means of the population of means with the standard variance of the means (SE_M^2, or simply SV_M). Each group provides such an estimate. These estimates will vary to some extent among themselves. We can pool them by averaging to form an overall estimate of the variance of the population means.

Recall that the standard error of the mean formula was: $SE_M = SD/\sqrt{n}$. Simply square this expression to get the standard variance of the mean: $SE_M^2 = (SD)^2/n = SV_M = V/n$. The variances of each of the groups was 2.5. Calculating the standard variances, we obtain for each group: $SV_M = V/n = 2.50/5 = .50$. Averaging them obviously yields .50. Note carefully that each standard variance was calculated from each group *separately and then averaged*. Therefore this average standard variance is uninfluenced by differences between the means, as noted earlier. The average standard variance, then, is a *within-groups variance*. It is an estimate of random errors.

But if random numbers had been used, the same reasoning applies to the between-groups variance, the variance calculated from the actual means. We cal-

[3]S. Diamond, *Information and Error*. New York: Basic Books, 1959.

culated a variance from the means of 4 and 3: it was .50. If the numbers were random, estimating the variance of the population of means should be possible by calculating the variance of the obtained means.

Note carefully, however, that if any extraneous influence has been at work, if anything like experimental effects have operated, then no longer will the variance calculated from the obtained means be a good estimate of the population variance of means. If an experimental influence—or some influence other than chance—has been operative, the effect may be to increase the variance of the obtained means. In a sense, this is the purpose of experimental manipulation: to increase the variance between means, to make the means different from each other. This is the crux of the analysis of variance matter. *If* an experimental manipulation has been influential, then it should show up in differences between means above and beyond the differences that arise by chance alone. And the between-groups variance should show the influence by becoming greater than expected by chance. Clearly we can use V_b, then, as a measure of experimental influence. Equally clearly, as we showed above, we can use V_w as a measure of chance variation. Therefore, we have almost reached the end of a rather long but profitable journey: we can evaluate the between-groups variance, V_b, with the within-groups variance, V_w. Or information, experimental information, can be weighed against error or chance.

It would conceivably be possible to evaluate V_b by subtracting V_w from it. In the analysis of variance, however, V_b is divided by V_w. The ratio so formed is called the F ratio. (The F ratio was named by Snedecor in honor of Ronald Fisher, the inventor of the analysis of variance. It was Snedecor who worked out the F tables used to evaluate F ratios.) One calculates the F ratio from observed data and checks the result against an F table. (The F table with direction for its use can be found in any recent statistics text.) If the obtained F ratio is as great or greater than the appropriate tabled entry, the differences that V_b reflects are statistically significant. In such a case the null hypothesis of no differences between the means is rejected at the chosen level of significance. In the present case:

$$F = \frac{V_b}{V_w} = \frac{.50}{.50} = 1$$

One obviously does not need the F table to see that the F ratio is not significant. Evidently the two means of 4 and 3 do not differ from each other significantly. In other words, of the many possible random samples of pairs of groups of five cases each, this particular case could easily be one of them. Or it is possible to say that 4 and 3 could readily belong to the same population of means. Had the difference been considerably greater, great enough to tip the F-ratio balance scale, then the conclusion would have been quite different, as we shall see.[4]

[4]Note that the t test and analysis of variance yielded the same result. With only two groups, or one degree of freedom $(k-1)$, $F = t^2$, or $t = \sqrt{F}$. This equality shows that it does not matter, in the case of two groups, whether t or F is calculated. (But the analysis of variance is a bit easier to calculate than t, in most cases.) With three or more groups, however, the equality breaks down; F must always be calculated. Thus F is the general test of which t is a special case.

An Example of a Statistically Significant Difference

Suppose that the investigator had obtained quite different results. Say the means had been 6 and 3, rather than 4 and 3. We now take the above example and *add a constant of 2 to each A_1 score.* This operation of course merely restores the scores used in Chapter 6. It was said earlier that adding a constant to a set of scores (or subtracting a constant) changes the mean by the constant *but has no effect whatever on the variance.* The figures are given in Table 13.5.

TABLE **13.5** HYPOTHETICAL EXPERIMENTAL DATA FOR TWO GROUPS: TABLE 13.1 DATA ALTERED

	A_1	x	x^2	A_2	x	x^2
	$4+2=6$	0	0	3	0	0
	$5+2=7$	1	1	1	-2	4
	$3+2=5$	-1	1	5	2	4
	$2+2=4$	-2	4	2	-1	1
	$6+2=8$	2	4	4	1	1
ΣX:	30			15		
M:	6			3		
Σx^2:			10			10
V:	$\frac{10}{4}=2.5$			$\frac{10}{4}=2.5$		
SV:	$\frac{V}{n}=\frac{2.5}{5}=.50$			$\frac{2.5}{5}=.50$		

It is important to note carefully that the Σx^2 amounts are the same as they were before, 10. Note, too, that the variances, V, are the same, 2.5. So are the standard variances, each being .50. As far as these statistics are concerned, then, there is no difference between this example and the previous example. But now we calculate the between-groups variance (Table 13.6). V_b is nine times greater than

TABLE **13.6** CALCULATION OF BETWEEN-GROUPS VARIANCE OF TABLE 13.5 DATA

	X	x	x^2
	6	1.5	2.25
	3	-1.5	2.25
ΣX:	9		
M:	4.5		
Σx^2:			4.50

$$V_b = \frac{\Sigma x_b^2}{k-1} = \frac{4.50}{2-1}$$

$$= 4.50$$

it was before: 4.50 versus .50. But V_w *is exactly the same as it was before*. This is the important point. To repeat: adding a constant to one set of scores—which is tantamount to an experimental manipulation, since one of the purposes of an experiment of this kind is to augment or diminish one set of measures (the experimental group measures) while the other set does not change (the control group measures)—has no effect on the within-groups variance while the between-groups variance changes drastically. Another way to put this is to say that *the estimates of* V_b *and* V_w *are independent of each other*. (If they are not, by the way, the F test is vitiated.)

The F ratio is $F = V_b/V_w = 4.50/.50 = 9$. Evidently information is much greater than error. Does this mean that the difference $6-3=3$ is a statistically significant difference? If we check an F table, we find that, in this case, an F ratio of 5.32 or greater is significant at the .05 level. (The details of how to read an F table are omitted here. They are not essential to the argument.) To be significant at the .01 level, the F ratio in this case would have to be 11.26 or greater. Our F ratio is 9. It is greater than 5.32 but less than 11.26. It seems that the difference of 3 is a statistically significant difference at the .05 level. Therefore, $6 \neq 3$, and the null hypothesis is rejected.

Calculation of One-way Analysis of Variance

Simple one-way analysis of variance is easier to do than the above procedure and discussion have indicated. To show the method, the example just considered will be used. By now the reader should be able to follow the procedure without difficulty. Note that deviation scores (x's) are not used at all. One can calculate entirely with raw scores. There will be certain differences in the variances. In the preceding examples, standard variances were used in order to show the underlying rationale of the analysis of variance. In the following method, however, although the same method is used, certain steps are omitted because it is possible to arrive at the ultimate goal, the F ratio and the conclusions thereto, in a much easier way.

The calculations of Table 13.7 speak for themselves and can easily be followed. First, in the body of the table, note that the raw scores, the X's, are each squared.[5] Then they are added to yield the ΣX^2's at the bottom of the table (190 and 55). The purpose of doing this is to obtain $\Sigma X_t^2 = 245$ $(190+55)$, at the right and bottom. Read ΣX_t^2: "The total sum of all the squared X's." The ΣX's and M's are calculated as usual (even though we do not really need the M's, except for later interpretation). Next, each group sum is squared and written $(\Sigma X)^2$. They are $(30)^2 = 900$ and $(15)^2 = 225$. (Be careful here. A frequent mistake is to confuse ΣX^2 and $(\Sigma X)^2$.) At the bottom right of the table proper, ΣX_t, $(\Sigma X_t)^2$, M_t, and

[5]The calculations of Table 13.7 are not difficult to do by hand. With most realistic problems, however, a desk calculator is needed. Whether or not one uses a computer, desk calculator skill is essential for the researcher. There are always auxiliary calculations that have to be done.

TABLE **13.7** CALCULATION OF ANALYSIS OF VARIANCE: FICTITIOUS DATA

	X_{A_1}	$X_{A_1}^2$	X_{A_2}	$X_{A_2}^2$	
	6	36	3	9	$N = 10$
	7	49	1	1	$n = 5$
	5	25	5	25	$k = 2$
	4	16	2	4	
	8	64	4	16	
ΣX:	30		15		$\Sigma X_t = 45$
$(\Sigma X)^2$:	900		225		$(\Sigma X_t)^2 = 2025$
M:	6		3		$M_t = 4.5$
ΣX^2:		190		55	$\Sigma X_t^2 = 245$

$$C = \frac{(\Sigma X_t)^2}{N} = \frac{(45)^2}{10} = \frac{2025}{10} = 202.50$$

$$\text{Total} = \Sigma X_t^2 - C = 245 - 202.50 = \mathit{42.50}$$

$$\text{Between} = \left[\frac{(\Sigma X_{A_1})^2}{n_{A_1}} + \frac{(\Sigma X_{A_2})^2}{n_{A_2}} \right] - C$$

$$= \left[\frac{(30)^2}{5} + \frac{(15)^2}{5} \right] - 202.50 = (180 + 45) - 202.50 = \mathit{22.50}$$

Source	*df*	*s.s.*	*m.s.*	*F*
Between Groups	$k - 1 = 1$	22.50	22.50	9. (.05)
Within Groups	$N - k = 8$	20.00	2.50	
Total	$N - 1 = 9$	42.50		

ΣX_t^2 are entered. They are simply the total statistics and are calculated in the same way as the individual group statistics.

Next, the calculations of the sums of squares (hereafter, *ss*). In the analysis of variance, mostly sums of squares are calculated and used. The variances are reserved for the final analysis of variance table (at the bottom of Table 13.7). What we are after in this procedure are the total, the between and the within *sums of squares*, or ss_t, ss_b, and ss_w. First, the calculation of C, the correction term. Since we are using raw scores, and since we are aiming at sums of squares, which are the *sums of the deviations* squared, we must reduce the raw scores to deviation scores. To accomplish this, we subtract C from every calculation. This accomplishes the reduction: it changes, in effect, X's to x's. The actual calculation of C is obvious. Here it is 202.50.

The total sum of squares, ss_t, is now calculated: 42.50. The between, or between-groups, or between-means, sum of squares is not as obvious. The sum of each group's scores is squared and then divided by the number of scores in the group. These averages are then added. From this sum C is subtracted. The result is the between-groups sum of squares, or ss_b. And this is all there is to the simple one-way analysis of variance. The within sum of squares, ss_w is calculated by subtraction. The following equation is important and should be remembered:

$$ss_t = ss_b + ss_w \tag{13.3}$$

Recall Eq. 13.2: $V_t = V_b + V_w$. Equation 13.3 is the same equation in the sum of squares form. Equation 13.2 cannot be used since, as was pointed out earlier, it is a theoretical formulation that only works exactly under the conditions specified. Equation 13.3 always works precisely; that is, sums of squares in the analysis of variance are always additive. So, with a little algebraic manipulation we see that $ss_w = ss_t - ss_b$. To obtain the within sum of squares, in other words, simply subtract the between from the total sum of squares. In the table, $42.50 - 22.50 = 20$. (It is, of course, possible to calculate the within sum of squares directly.)

After completing the above calculation, we enter the degrees of freedom (*df*) in the final table. Although formulas have been entered, they are not necessary to the operation. For the total degrees of freedom, simply take one less than the total number of subjects used. If, for example, there were three experimental groups with 30 *S*s in each group, the total degrees of freedom are $N - 1 = 90 - 1 = 89$. The between-groups degrees of freedom are one less than the number of experimental groups. With three experimental groups, $k - 1 = 3 - 1 = 2$. With the example of Table 13.7, $k - 1 = 2 - 1 = 1$. The within-groups degrees of freedom, like the within-groups sum of squares, are obtained by subtraction. In this case, $9 - 1 = 8$. Next, divide the degrees of freedom into the sums of squares (*s.s./df*) to obtain the between and within mean squares, labeled "*m.s.*" in the table. In the analysis of variance, the variances are called "mean squares." Finally, obtain the *F* ratio by dividing the within or error variance or mean square into the between variance or mean square: $F = m.s._b / m.s._w = 22.50/2.50 = 9$. This final *F* ratio, also called the variance ratio, is checked against appropriate entries in an *F* table to determine its significance, as discussed previously.

A Research Example

To illustrate the research use of one-way analysis of variance, data from an early experimental study by Hurlock, described earlier in this book are given in Table 13.8.[6] The data were not analyzed in this manner by Hurlock, the analysis of variance not being available at the time of the study. Hurlock divided 106 fourth- and sixth-grade pupils into four groups, E_1, E_2, E_3, and *C*. Five forms of an addition test, *A*, *B*, *C*, *D*, and *E*, were used. Form *A* was administered to all the *S*s on the first day. For the next four days the experimental groups, E_1, E_2, and E_3, were given a different form of the test. The control group, *C*, was separated from the other groups and given different forms of the test on four separate days. The *S*s of

[6] E. Hurlock, "An Evaluation of Certain Incentives Used in Schoolwork," *Journal of Educational Psychology*, XVI (1925), 145–159. The first three lines of figures in Table 13.8 are reported by Hurlock. All the other figures were calculated by the author from these figures. The analysis of variance was done by recreating necessary figures from Hurlock's reported figures. A simple way to do one-way analysis of variance from reported means, standard deviations, and *n*'s is given in Diamond, *op. cit.*, pp. 129–130.

TABLE **13.8** SUMMARY DATA AND ANALYSIS OF VARIANCE OF DATA FROM HURLOCK STUDY

	E_1 Praised	E_2 Reproved	E_3 Ignored	E_4 Control
n:	27	27	26	26
M:	20.22	14.19	12.38	11.35
SD:	7.68	6.78	6.06	4.21
Source	*df*	*s.s.*	*m.s.*	*F*
Between Groups	3	1260.06	420.02	10.08 (.001)
Within Groups	102	4249.29	41.66	
Total	105	5509.35		

Group C were told to work as usual. But each day before the tests were given, the E_1 group was brought to the front of the room and *praised* for its good work. Then the E_2 group was brought forward and *reproved* for its poor work. The members of the E_3 group were *ignored.* On the fifth day of the experiment, Form E was administered to all groups. Scores were the number of correct answers on this form of the test. Summary data are given in Table 13.8, together with the table of the final analysis of variance.

Since $F = 10.08$, which is significant at the .001 level, the null hypothesis of no differences between the means has to be rejected. Evidently the experimental manipulations were effective. There is not much difference between the Ignored and Control groups, a very interesting finding. The Praised group has the largest mean, with the Reproved group mean in between the Praised group and the other two groups. The student can complete the interpretation of the data.[7]

Strength of Relations: Correlation and the Analysis of Variance

Tests of statistical significance like t and F unfortunately do not reveal to the research scientist the magnitude or strength of the relations he is studying. A t test of the difference between two means, if significant, simply tells the investigator that there *is* a relation. That there is a relation between two variables is inferred from the significant difference between the means. An F test, similarly, if significant, simply says that a relation exists. The relational fact is inferred from the significant differences between two, three, or more means. A statistical test like F says in a relatively indirect way that there is or is not a relation between the independent variable (or variables) and the dependent variable.

In contrast to tests of statistical significance like t and F, coefficients of correlation are relatively direct measures of relations. They have an easily "seen"

[7]After an analysis of variance of this kind, some investigators test pairs of means with t tests. Unless specific differences between means, or groups of means, have been predicted, this procedure is questionable. We take up this problem later in the chapter.

and direct intuitive message since the joining of two sets of scores more obviously seems like a relation, plus the fact that this follows our earlier definition of a relation as a set of ordered pairs. If, for example, $r = .90$, it is easy to see that the rank orders of the measures of two variables are very similar. But t and F ratios are one or two steps removed from the actual relation. An important research technical question, then, is how t and F, on the one hand, and measures like r, on the other hand, are related.

We first calculate a simple measure of relation between an independent variable and a dependent variable. In an analysis of variance, the variable on the margins of the data table—methods of incentive as in the Hurlock example—is the independent variable. The measures in the body of the table reflect the dependent variable: arithmetic achievement in the Hurlock example. The analysis of variance works with the relation between these two kinds of variables. If the independent variable has had an effect on the dependent variable, then the "equality" of the means of the experimental groups that would be expected if the numbers being analyzed were simply random numbers is upset. The effect of a really influential independent variable is to make means unequal. We can say, then, that any relation that exists between the independent and dependent variables is reflected in the inequality of the means. The more unequal the means, the wider apart they are, the higher the relation, other things equal.

If no relation exists between the independent variable and the dependent variable, then it is as though we had sets of random numbers, and consequently, random means. The differences between the means would only be chance fluctuations. An F test would show them not to be significantly different. If a relation does exist, if there is a tie or bond between the independent and dependent variables, the imposition of *different* aspects of the independent variable, like different methods of instruction, should make the measures of the dependent variable vary accordingly. Method A_1 might make achievement scores go up, whereas method A_2 might make them go down or stay about the same. Note that we have the same phenomenon of concomitant variation that we did with the correlation coefficient. Take two extreme cases: a strong relation and a zero relation. We lay out a hypothetically strong relation between methods and achievement in Table 13.9.

Note that the dependent variable scores vary directly with the independent variable methods: Method A_1 has high scores, method A_2 medium scores, and method A_3 low scores. The relation is also shown by comparing methods and the means of the dependent variable.

Compare the example of Table 13.9 with chance expectation. If there were no relation between methods and achievement, then the achievement means would not covary with methods. That is, the means would be nearly equal. In order to show this, I wrote the 12 achievement scores of Table 13.9 on separate slips of paper, mixed them up thoroughly in a hat, threw them all on the floor, and picked them up 4 at a time, assigning the first four to A_1, the second four to A_2, and the third four to A_3. The results are shown in Table 13.10.

Now it is difficult, or impossible, to "see" a relation. The means differ, but not much. Certainly the relation between methods and achievement scores (and

TABLE **13.9** HYPOTHETICALLY STRONG RELATION BETWEEN METHODS OF INSTRUCTION AND ACHIEVEMENT

Independent Variable (Methods of Instruction)	Dependent Variable (Achievement)	Means
Method A_1	10 9 9 8	9
Method A_2	7 7 7 7	7
Method A_3	5 4 4 3	4

means) is not nearly as clear as it was before. Still, we have to be sure. Analyses of variance of both sets of data were performed. The F ratio of the data of Table 13.9 (strong relation) was 57.59, highly significant, whereas the F ratio of the data of Table 13.10 (low or zero relation) was 1.29, not significant. The statistical tests confirm our visual impressions. We now know that there is a relation between methods and achievement in Table 13.9 but not in Table 13.10.

TABLE **13.10** HYPOTHETICALLY ZERO RELATION BETWEEN METHODS OF INSTRUCTION AND ACHIEVEMENT

Independent Variable (Methods of Instruction)	Dependent Variable (Achievement)	Means
Method A_1	4 8 10 7	7.25
Method A_2	3 5 4 9	5.25
Method A_3	7 7 7 9	7.50

The problem, however, is to show the relation between significance tests like the F test and the correlation method. This can be done in several ways. We illustrate with two such ways, one graphical and one statistical. In Fig. 13.1 the data

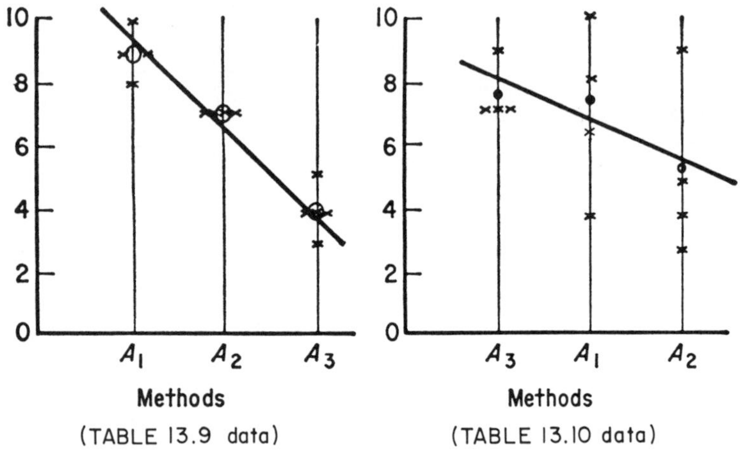

FIG. 13.1

of Tables 13.9 and 13.10 have been plotted much as continuous X and Y measures in the usual correlation problem are plotted, with the independent variable—Methods—on the horizontal axis, and the dependent variable—Achievement—on the vertical axis, as usual. To indicate the relation, lines have been drawn as near to the means as possible. A diagonal line making a 45-degree angle with the horizontal axis would indicate a strong relation. A horizontal line across the graph would indicate a zero relation. Note that the plotted scores of the data of Table 13.9 clearly indicate a strong relation: the height of the plotted scores (crosses) and the means (circles) varies with the method. The plot of the data of Table 13.10, even with a rearrangement of the methods for purposes of comparison, shows a weak relation or no relation.

Let us now look at the problem statistically. It is possible to calculate correlation coefficients with data of this kind. If one has done an analysis of variance, a simple (but not entirely satisfactory) coefficient is yielded by the following formula:

$$E = \sqrt{\frac{ss_b}{ss_t}} \tag{13.4}$$

Of course, ss_b and ss_t are the between-groups sum of squares and the total sum of squares, respectively. One simply takes these sums of squares from the analysis-of-variance table to calculate the coefficient. The symbol E is the letter associated with the Greek symbol η (Greek *eta*) that is usually used with this coefficient. E, usually called the *correlation ratio*, is a general coefficient or index of relation often used with data that are not linear. (*Linear*, roughly speaking, means that, if two variables are plotted one against another, the plot tends to follow a straight line. This is another way of saying what was said in Chapter 12 about linear combinations.) Its values vary from 0 to 1.00. We are interested here only in its use with analysis of variance and in its power to tell us the *degree* of relation between independent and dependent variables.

Recall that the means of the data of Table 13.1 were 3 and 4. They were not significantly different. Therefore there is no relation between the independent variable (methods) and the dependent variable (achievement). If an analysis of variance of the data of Table 13.1 is done, using the method outlined in Table 13.7, $ss_b = 2.50$ and $ss_t = 22.50$. $E = \sqrt{2.50/22.50} = \sqrt{.111} = .33$ yields the correlation between methods and achievement. Since we know that the data are not significant ($F = 1$), E is not significant. In other words, $E = .33$ is here tantamount to a zero relation. Had there been no difference at all between the means, then, of course, $E = 0$. If $ss_b = ss_t$, then $E = 1.00$. This can happen only if all the scores of one group are the same, and all the scores of the other group are the same as, and yet different from, those of the first group, which is highly unlikely. For example, if the A_1 scores were 4, 4, 4, 4, 4, and the A_2 scores were 3, 3, 3, 3, 3, then $ss_b = ss_t = 2.5$, and $E = \sqrt{2.5/2.5} = 1$. It is obvious that there is no within-groups variance—again, extremely unlikely.

Take the data of Table 13.7. The means are 6 and 3. They are significantly different, since $F = 9$. Calculate E:

$$E = \sqrt{\frac{ss_b}{ss_t}} = \sqrt{\frac{22.50}{42.50}} = \sqrt{.529} = .727 = .73$$

Note the substantial increase in E. And since F is significant, $E = .73$ is significant. There is a substantial relation between methods and achievement.

The Hurlock study E is more interesting: $E = \sqrt{1260.06/5509.35} = \sqrt{.229} = .48$, which is of course significant. In the Hurlock study, other things equal, incentive is substantially related to arithmetic achievement, as defined.

By now the student has sufficient background to interpret E in variance terms. In Chapter 6, this was done for r, where it was explained that r^2 indicated the variance shared by two variables. This variance was called *common-factor variance*. E can be given a similar interpretation. If E is squared, E^2 indicates, in essence, the variance shared by the independent and dependent variables. Perhaps more to the point, E indicates the proportion of the variance of the dependent variable, say achievement, determined by the variance of the independent variable, methods, or incentives. For example, in the Hurlock example, $E^2 = (.48)^2 = .23$, which indicates that 23 percent of the variance of the arithmetic addition scores is accounted for by the different modes of incentives used by Hurlock.

Other measures of association or correlation that can be used with the analysis of variance are readily available. Fortunately, they are based on the same basic idea: the relations between different variances. One of these is the *intraclass coefficient of correlation, RI*. Like the correlation ratio E, RI is a general measure of association readily used with the analysis of variance.[8]

Although it would take us too far afield to discuss RI in detail, it is worthwhile to indicate one of the RI formulas to show how it is calculated with one-way

[8]E. Haggard, *Intraclass Correlation and the Analysis of Variance*. New York: Holt, Rinehart and Winston, 1958. Intraclass correlation is an important idea, as Haggard competently shows in his book. Fisher, of course, discussed RI many years earlier. In fact, in his *Statistical Methods*, one chapter is entitled "Intraclass Correlation and the Analysis of Variance." See R. Fisher, *Statistical Methods for Research Workers*, 11th ed. New York: Hafner, 1950, chap. VII.

analysis of variance. The formula is:

$$RI = \frac{ms_b - ms_w}{ms_b + (n-1)ms_w} \tag{13.5}$$

All the symbols are familiar: they are the between-groups variance (ms_b), or between-groups mean square, the within-groups variance (ms_w), and the number of cases in each group (n). Now, calculate RI for the Hurlock example, using the statistics of Table 13.8:[9]

$$RI = \frac{420.02 - 41.66}{420.02 + (26.50 - 1)(41.66)} = \frac{378.36}{1482.35} = .255 = .26$$

Compare this value of .26 to the value of E^2, .23. RI is comparable to E^2 rather than to E. Both RI and E^2 indicate the proportion of variance in a dependent variable due to the presumed influence of an independent variable.

The purpose of this exposition of E and RI is not to discuss the relative merits of these and other indices.[10] It is, rather to point up the similarity of the principle and structure of the analysis of variance and correlational methods. RI, like E, depends on the relative magnitudes of the different variances. The larger the variance due to the independent variable, indicated by ss_b or ms_b, relative to the total variance or to the variance due to error, the larger the correlation. Under certain conditions, RI can be defined as the proportion of between-groups variance to the total variance, or ms_b/ms_t.[11] It is thus seen that the conceptualization of E and that of RI are similar.

The total variance, of course, is the variance of the dependent variable, Y. What E^2 and RI tell us is the proportion of the variance of Y attributable to X (the independent variable). The achievement means in the Hurlock example varied significantly. This variance can be attributed to X, the experimental manipulation. The total variance is the total variance of Y, arithmetic achievement. (Remember that in an experimental situation—or we might also call it an analysis of variance situation—it is the variances of the Y scores that are analyzed.)

[9]In the calculation n is slightly altered, because the n's were unequal. (See Haggard, *op. cit.*, p. 14.) Ordinarily this is no problem, since n's are usually equal.

[10]Different indices, the relations between them, and their relative merits are not easy problems. Hays (*Statistics*. New York: Holt, Rinehart and Winston, 1963, pp. 381–384, 406–407) argues cogently for a measure called omega-squared (ω^2), which is a conservative estimate of the magnitude of the relation between the independent and dependent variables. E^2 is an upward-biased estimate; that is, it is too large. If calculated with the following formula, however, the bias is corrected (Diamond, *op. cit.*, p. 131):

$$_cE^2 = 1 - \frac{ms_w}{ss_t/(N-1)}$$

Applied to the Hurlock data, $_cE^2 = .21$ (.2136) compared to $E^2 = .23$ (.2287). Hays' omega-squared is .21 (.2045). $RI = .26$ (.2552). It is obvious that E^2 corrected for bias is close to omega-squared. In this book, we use E^2 and RI because E^2 is equivalent to an important index used in multiple regression analysis, R^2, the multiple coefficient of correlation, to be discussed in detail near the end of the book, and because of a special use and interpretation of RI to be discussed in this chapter. In any case, the magnitudes of the various indices are usually similar. If the student will scale E^2 and RI down a little, the resulting estimates will usually be good ones.

[11]See Haggard, *op. cit.*, pp. 12 and 54.

Components of Variance

The analysis of variance is usually used to test statistical hypotheses about the significance of the differences between means. But it has another important use that needs emphasis. This is the problem of estimating *component variances*. Each statistical problem has a total amount of variance. As in probability theory, we let this amount of variance equal 100 percent. Then each variance source contributes so much percent of the variance. It is certainly important and useful to know what proportion of the variance of a dependent variable an experimental independent variable contributes. It is often also important to know what proportion of the total variance the error variance is. (This notion is used in measurement theory, for example.)

It is possible to derive expressions for the average values of the variances of large numbers of samples from a large population. It can be shown that ms_w, the within-groups variance, is an unbiased or best estimate of the variance of this population. Thus, if we let σ^2 be the symbol for the population variance, then ms_w is an unbiased estimate of σ^2. The between-groups variance ms_b is defined as $ms_b = n \Sigma x_b^2/(k-1)$, where Σx_b^2 is the sum of squares calculated from the means (as previously shown), and k is the number of groups.[12] This between-groups variance is also an estimate of the variance of the population. If the samples have been random samples from the same population, then these two estimates, ms_w and ms_b, should be pretty nearly the same.

Now let us assume that ms_w and ms_b are not equal, that ms_b is significantly greater than ms_w. In this case, we must reason that there is something in ms_b over and above chance. Thus we must conclude that *ms_b includes both error variance and some systematic variance*. That is, ms_b includes ms_w, plus some other variance. If we had a way to estimate these components of variance of ms_b, we would have valuable information as to the relative contributions of systematic and error variance, or the contribution of the independent variable and the contribution of error to the total variance. Luckily, this is easily determined. Subtract the within-groups variance from the between-groups variance and divide the remainder by the number of cases in each group, n. This gives the component of variance due to the independent variable. Now add to this the component due to error. Dividing each of these components by the sum of the two, we obtain the relative contributions (percentages) of each to the total variance. Examples will clarify the procedure.

Take the fictitious data of Table 13.7, where the means of 6 and 3 were found to be significantly different. The computations of the components of variance are laid out in Table 13.11. The independent variable, the experimental manipulation, contributes 62 percent of the total variance. Contrast this to the data of Table 13.1, the problem in which the difference between the means of 4 and 3 was not significant. The between-groups and within-groups variances were both 2.50.

[12]The reasoning behind this equation is as follows. The definition of an unbiased estimate of the variance of the population of means is $V_M = \Sigma x^2/(n-1)$. But from our reasoning on the standard error and the standard variance, we know that $V_M = SV_M = V/n$. Substituting in the first equation, we get $V/n = \Sigma x^2/(k-1)$, and thus $V = n \Sigma x^2/(k-1)$. It should be noted here that the expression, $n \Sigma x_b^2$, indicated in Footnote 11, Chapter 6, is really the *between sum of squares*—and not Σx_b^2, as indicated in Chapter 6 and subsequent chapters. That is, instead of writing Σx_b^2, statisticians write ss_b, which is really $n \Sigma x_b^2$.

TABLE **13.11** COMPUTATION OF COMPONENTS OF VARIANCE FOR DATA OF TABLE 13.7

n	$m.s.$	Components of Variance	Percent
5	22.50	$\frac{20}{5} = 4.00$	62
	−2.50	2.50	38
	20.00	6.50	

Therefore $2.5 - 2.5 = 0$, and the between-groups component of variance is 0, contributing nothing to the total variance. (If this sounds confusing, remember that it is a theoretical estimation of population variances. Actually, in the obtained data, some variance was contributed by the difference between the means, but did not exceed chance expectation.)

Actual research examples are more interesting. The Hurlock example (Table 13.8) components of variance are calculated in Table 13.12. The independent variable, the incentives, contributed approximately 26 percent of the total variance.

TABLE **13.12** CALCULATION OF COMPONENTS OF VARIANCE OF HURLOCK EXAMPLE[a]

n	$m.s.$	Components of Variance	Percent
26.50	420.02	$\frac{378.36}{26.50} = 14.28$	26
	−41.66	41.66	74
	378.36	55.94	

[a] $n = 26.50$ is an average of the four group n's.

Insight into the nature of *RI*, the intraclass coefficient of correlation, is achieved when we compare the *RI*'s for these examples with the percentages of the between-groups components of variance. In each case they are the same. In fact, the procedure outlined for calculating components of variance is algebraically identical to the formula previously given for *RI*. Therefore *RI* tells us not only about the relative homogeneity and heterogeneity of the scores in the groups and the group means, and thus about the relation between the independent and dependent variables; it also tells us the approximate proportion of the total variance of the dependent variable accounted for by the independent variable. Probably most important, however, for the purposes of this book and its central theme, *RI* is an excellent illustration of the logical identity of different research approaches and different statistical approaches.

Broadening the Structure: Planned Comparisons and Post Hoc Tests

The approach used in this chapter and the next two chapters, while pedagogically useful, is too rigid. That is, the emphasis is on neat paradigms that have as their culmination the F test and some measure of relation. Actual research, however, frequently does not fit into such nice shapes and thinking. Nevertheless, the basic analysis of variance notions can be used in a broader and freer way, with an expansion of the design and statistical possibilities. We examine such possibilities within the general framework of this chapter.

Post Hoc Tests

Suppose an experiment like Hurlock's has been done and the experimenter has the data of Table 13.8. He knows that the overall differences among the means are statistically significant. But he does not know which differences contribute to the significance. Can he simply test the differences between all pairs of means to tell which are significant? Yes and No, but generally No. Such tests are not independent and, with sufficient numbers of tests, one of them can be significant by chance. In short, such a "shotgun" procedure capitalizes on chance. Moreover, they are blind and what has been called "no-headed."

There are several ways to do post hoc tests, but we mention only one of them briefly.[13] The Scheffé test, if used with discretion, is a general method that can be applied to all comparisons of means after an analysis of variance.[14] If and only if the F test is significant, one can test all the differences between means; one can test the combined mean of two or more groups against the mean of one other group; or one can select any combination of means against any other combination. Such a test with the ability to do so much is very useful. But we pay for the generality and usefulness: the test is quite conservative. To attain significance, differences have to be rather substantial. The main point is that post hoc comparisons and tests of means can be done, mainly for exploratory and interpretative purposes. One examines one's data in detail; one rummages for insights and clues.

Since it would take us too far afield, the mechanics of the Scheffé test are not given here. (But see Study Suggestion 7 at the end of the chapter.) Suffice it to say that, when applied to the Hurlock data of Table 13.8, it shows that the Praised mean is significantly greater than the other three means and that none of the other differences is significant. This is important information, because it points directly to the main source of the significance of the overall F ratio: praise versus reproof, ignoring, and control. (However, the difference between an average of means 1 and 2 versus an average of means 3 and 4 is also statistically significant.) Although one can see this from the relative sizes of the means, the Scheffé test makes things precise—in a conservative way. Moreover, research data are not always as clear as Hurlock's.

[13]For an excellent description of such tests, see T. Ryan, "Multiple Comparisons in Psychological Research," *Psychological Bulletin*, LVI (1959), 26–47. See, also, T. Ryan, "Significance Tests for Multiple Comparisons of Proportions, Variances, and Other Statistics," *Psychological Bulletin*, LVII (1960), 318–328. Perhaps the best reference is R. Kirk, *Experimental Design: Procedures for the Behavioral Sciences*. Belmont, Calif.: Brooks/Cole, 1968, chap. 3.

[14]H. Scheffé, "A Method for Judging All Contrasts in the Analysis of Variance." *Biometrika*, XL (1953), 87–104. See, also, Hays, *op. cit.*, pp. 483 ff. Hays' discussion of the problems of this section is particularly good.

Planned Comparisons

While post hoc tests are important in actual research, especially for exploring one's data and for getting leads for future research, the method of planned comparisons is perhaps more important scientifically. Whenever hypotheses are formulated and systematically tested and empirical results support them, this is much more powerful evidence on the empirical validity of the hypotheses than when "interesting" (sometimes translate: "support my predilections") results are found *after* the data are obtained. This point was made in Chapter 2 where the power of hypotheses was explained.

In the analysis of variance, an overall F test, if significant, simply indicates that there are significant differences somewhere in the data. Inspection of the means can tell one, though imprecisely, which differences are important. To test hypotheses, however, more or less controlled and precise statistical tests are needed. There is a large variety of possible comparisons in any set of data that one can test. But which ones? As usual, the research problem and the theory behind the problem should dictate the statistical tests. One designs research, at least whenever one can, in part to test substantive hypotheses.

Suppose the reinforcement theory behind the Hurlock study said, in effect, that any kind of reinforcement, positive or negative, will improve performance, and that positive reinforcement will improve it more than negative reinforcement. This would mean that E_1 and E_2 of Table 13.8, taken together or separately, will be significantly greater than E_3 and E_4 taken together or separately. That is, both Praised (positive reinforcement) and Reproved (negative reinforcement) will be significantly greater than Ignored (no reinforcement) and Control (no reinforcement). In addition, the theory says that the effect of positive reinforcement is greater than the effect of negative reinforcement. Thus Praised will be significantly greater than Reproved. These implied tests can be written symbolically:

$$H_1\text{:}\quad C_1 = \frac{M_1 + M_2}{2} > \frac{M_3 + M_4}{2}$$

$$H_2\text{:}\quad C_2 = M_1 > M_2$$

where C_1 indicates the first comparison and C_2 the second. We have here the ingredients of one-way analysis of variance, but the simple overall test and its democracy of means have been radically changed. That is, the plan and design of the research have changed under the impact of the theory and the research problem.

When the Scheffé test is used, the overall F ratio must be significant because none of the Scheffé tests can be significant if the overall F is not significant. When planned comparisons are used, however, no overall F test need be made. The focus is on the planned comparisons and the hypotheses. The number of comparisons and tests made are limited by the degrees of freedom. In the Hurlock example, there are three degrees of freedom $(k-1)$; therefore, three tests can be made. These tests have to be *orthogonal* to each other—that is, they must be independent. We keep the comparisons orthogonal by using what are called *orthogonal coefficients*, which are weights to be attached to the means in the comparisons.

The coefficients, in other words, specify the comparisons. The coefficients or weights for H_1 and H_2, above, are:

$$H_1: \quad 1/2 \quad 1/2 \quad -1/2 \quad -1/2$$
$$H_2: \quad 1 \quad -1 \quad 0 \quad 0$$

For comparisons to be orthogonal, there are two conditions to be met: the sum of each set of weights must equal 0, and the sum of the products of any two sets of weights must also be zero. It is obvious that both of the above sets sum to zero. Test the sum of the products: $(1/2)(1)+(1/2)(-1)+(-1/2)(0)+(-1/2)(0)=0$. Thus the two sets of weights are orthogonal.

It is important to understand orthogonal weights thoroughly, as well as the two conditions just given. The first set of weights simply stands for: $(M_1+M_2)/2-(M_3+M_4)/2$. The second set stands for: M_1-M_2. Now, suppose we also wanted to test the notion that the Ignored mean is greater than the Control mean. This is tested by: M_3-M_4, and is cooled: H_3: 0 0 1 -1. Henceforth, we will call these *weight vectors*. The values of the vector sum to zero. What about its sum of products with the other two vectors?

$$H_1 \times H_3: \quad (1/2)(0)+(1/2)(0)+(-1/2)(1)+(-1/2)(-1)=0$$
$$H_2 \times H_3: \quad (1)(0)+(-1)(0)+(0)(1)+(0)(-1)=0$$

The third vector is orthogonal to, or independent of, the other two vectors. The third comparison can be made. If these three comparisons are made, no other is possible because the available $k-1=4-1=3$ degrees of freedom are used up.

Suppose, now, that instead of the H_3 above, we wanted to test the difference between the average of the first three means against the fourth mean. The coding is: 1/3 1/3 $1/3-1$. This is tantamount to: $(M_1+M_2+M_3)/3-M_4$. Is the vector orthogonal to the first two? Calculate:

$$(1/2)(1/3)+(1/2)(1/3)+(-1/2)(1/3)+(-1/2)(-1)=1/6+1/6-1/6+1/2=4/6=2/3$$

Since the sum of the products does not equal zero, it is not orthogonal to the first vector, and the comparison should not be made. The comparison implied by the vector would yield redundant information. In this case, the comparison using the third vector supplies information already given in part by the first vector.

The method of calculating the significance of the differences of planned comparisons need not be detailed. Besides, at this point we do not need the actual calculations. Our purpose is hopefully a larger one: to show the flexibility and power of analysis of variance when properly conceived and understood. F tests are used with each comparison, or, in this case, with each degree of freedom. The details of calculations can be found in Hays' and other texts.[15] The basic idea of planned comparisons is quite general, and we use it again when we study research design. We will even find that coding (the weights) is invaluable in multiple regres-

[15]Hays, *op. cit.*, pp. 473 ff. In the Hurlock example, H_1 and H_2, above, were both statistically significant at the .01 level, but H_3 was not significant.

sion analysis: by using appropriate coding of experimental variables, we can do analysis of variance with multiple regression analysis.

We have come a long, perhaps hard, way on the analysis of variance road. One may wonder why so much space has been devoted to the subject. There are several reasons. One, the analysis of variance has wide practical applicability. It is hard to conceive of contemporary educational, psychological, and sociological research without it. Analysis of variance takes many forms that are applicable in psychology, sociology, economics, political science, agriculture, biology, education, and other fields. It frees us from working with only one independent variable at a time and gives us a powerful lever for solving measurement problems. It increases the possibilities of making our experiments exact and precise. The analysis of variance also permits us to test several hypotheses at one time, as well as to test hypotheses that cannot be tested in any other way, at least with precision. Thus its generality of application is great.

More germane to the purposes of this book, the analysis of variance gives us an insight into modern research approaches and methods. No other method of statistical analysis gives quite so much. It does this by focusing sharply and constantly on variance thinking, by making clear the close relation between research problems and statistical methods and inference, and by clarifying the structure, the architecture, of research design.

Study Suggestions

1. There are a number of good references on analysis of variance, varying in difficulty and clarity of explanation (for the beginning student). Three of these were given in the study suggestions of Chapter 12. Diamond's (chap. 8) presentation, which stresses understanding of principles, is refreshing and clear. Hays' (chaps. 12, 14) discussion is as usual excellent, but more advanced. It is *highly recommended* for careful study. The first part of Snedecor and Cochran's chap. 10 is useful for the beginning student. Snedecor and Cochran also give a number of fairly easy examples, some with calculations and all with answers. The following references, though of varying degrees of difficulty and clarity, are very good to excellent. The Winer book is a staple for practising researchers, partly because of its detailed computational guidance. It should not be used as a beginning book, however. Edwards' book has long guided psychology students through the ramifications of analysis of variance. It and the Winer book are better suited to the material of Chapters 14 and 15 than to this chapter. The Lindquist book is older but very good; it is also rather difficult. Like the Hays book, it is only for the student with some statistical background. If one had to choose a single reference, it should probably be Kirk's fine book.

   Edwards, A. *Experimental Design in Psychological Research*, 3d ed. New York: Holt, Rinehart and Winston, 1968.

   Kirk, R. *Experimental Design: Procedures for the Behavioral Sciences.* Belmont, Calif.: Brooks/Cole, 1968.

   Lindquist, E. *Design and Analysis of Experiments.* Boston: Houghton Mifflin, 1953.

   Winer, B. *Statistical Principles in Experimental Design*, 2d ed. New York: McGraw-Hill, 1971.

2. A university professor has conducted an experiment to test the relative efficacies of three methods of instruction: A_1, Lecture; A_2, Large-Group Discussion; and A_3, Small-Group Discussion. From a universe of sophomores, 30 were selected at random and randomly assigned to three groups. The three methods were randomly assigned to the three groups. The students were tested for their achievement at the end of four months of the experiment. The scores for the three groups are given below.

   Test the null hypothesis, using simple one-way analysis of variance and the .01 level of significance. Calculate E and RI. Interpret the results. Draw a graph of the data similar to those in the text.

	Methods	
A_1 (Lecture)	A_2 (Large-Group Discussion)	A_3 (Small-Group Discussion)
4	5	3
7	6	5
9	3	1
6	8	4
9	3	4
6	2	5
5	5	7
7	6	3
7	7	5
10	5	3

[*Answers:* $F = 7.16$ (.01); $E = .59$; $RI = .38$.][16]

3. From a table of random numbers—you can use those in Appendix D—draw three samples of 10 each of numbers 0 through 9.
   (a) Make up a research study, with problem and hypotheses, and imagine that the three sets of numbers are your results.
   (b) Do an analysis of variance of the three sets of numbers. Calculate E, E^2, and RI. Draw a graph of the results like those of Fig. 13.1. Interpret the results both statistically and substantively.
   (c) Add a constant of 2 to each of the scores of the group with the highest mean. Do the calculations and graph of (b), above, again. Interpret. What changes take place in the statistics? [Examine the sums of squares especially, taking careful note of the within-groups variances (mean squares) of both examples.]
   (d) Calculate the components of variance and then interpret them.
4. Take the scores of the highest and lowest groups in Study Suggestion 2, above (Groups A_1 and A_3).
   (a) Do an analysis of variance, and calculate the square root of F, $\sqrt{F}$. Now do a t test as described in Chapter 12. Compare the t obtained with $\sqrt{F}$.
   (b) Is it legitimate, after doing the analysis of variance of the three groups, to calculate the t ratio as instructed and then to draw conclusions about the

[16]From now on, errors of rounding will occur. The student should carry one or two more decimal places than he will need. If the answers obtained do not agree exactly with those given—say a discrepancy between the second decimal places, e.g., $F = 7.16$ and 7.12, or 7.21—do not be concerned. As calculations become more complex, errors of rounding play a more and more important part. For a discussion of rounding, see P. Dwyer, *Linear Computations*. New York: Wiley, 1951, pp. 13–14.

difference between the two methods? (Consult your instructor, if necessary. This point is difficult.)

(c) Calculate E, E^2, and RI. Compare them to E, E^2, and RI of Study Suggestion 2, above. Discuss.

[*Answers:* (a) $F = 14.46$; $\sqrt{F} = 3.80$; $t = 3.80$; (c) $E = .67$; $RI = .57$.]

5. Aronson and Mills tested the interesting and perhaps humanly perverse hypothesis that individuals who undergo an unpleasant initiation to become members of a group have more liking for the group than do members who do not undergo such an initiation.[17] Three groups of 21 young women each were subjected to three experimental conditions: (1) *severe condition*, in which the Ss were asked to read obscene words and vivid descriptions of sexual activity in order to become members of a group; (2) *mild condition*, in which Ss read words related to sex but not obscene; and (3) *control condition*, in which Ss were not required to do anything to become members of the group. After a rather elaborate procedure, the Ss were asked to rate the discussion and the group members of the group to which they then ostensibly belonged. The means and standard deviations of the total ratings are *severe*: $M = 195.3$, $SD = 31.9$; *mild*: $M = 171.1$, $SD = 34.0$; *control*: $M = 166.7$, $SD = 21.6$. Each n was 21.

(a) Do an analysis of variance of these data. Interpret the data. Is the hypothesis supported?

(b) Calculate RI. Is the relation strong? Would you expect the relation to be strong in an experiment of this kind?

[*Answers:* (a) $F = 5.39$ (.01); (b) $RI = .17$.]

6. Suppose that the 40 groups of 100 random numbers (total $N = 4000$) and the means and standard deviations in Appendix D were the result of a gigantic experiment. Can you do an analysis of the 40 groups of numbers? If so, what results would you expect? Would the F ratio probably be significant or not significant? Why? What should the magnitude of E and RI be, low or high? Why? What would the total, between groups, and within groups degrees of freedom be?

7. Use the Scheffé test to calculate the significance of all the differences between the three means of Study Suggestion 2, above. Here is one way to do the Scheffé test. Calculate the standard error of the differences between two means with the following formula:

$$SE_{M_i - M_j} = \sqrt{ms_w\left(\frac{1}{n_i} + \frac{1}{n_j}\right)} \tag{13.6}$$

where ms_w = within-groups mean square, and n_i and n_j are the numbers of cases in groups i and j. For the example, this is:

$$SE_{M_{A1} - M_{A2}} = \sqrt{(3.26)\left(\frac{1}{10} + \frac{1}{10}\right)} = .81$$

Then calculate the statistic S (for Scheffé):

$$S = \sqrt{(k-1)F_{.05(k-1,m)}} \tag{13.7}$$

where k = number of groups in the analysis of variance, and the F term is the .05 level F ratio obtained from an F table at $k - 1$ $(3 - 1 = 2)$ and $m = N - k =$

[17] E. Aronson and J. Mills, "The Effect of Severity of Initiation on Liking for a Group," *Journal of Abnormal and Social Psychology*, LIX (1959), 177–181.

$30-3=27$ degrees of freedom. This is 3.35. Thus,

$$S=\sqrt{(3-1)(3.35)}=\sqrt{6.70}=2.59$$

The final step is to multiply the results of formulas 13.6 and 13.7:

$$S \times SE_{M_i-M_j}=(2.59)(.81)=2.10$$

Any difference, to be statistically significant at the .05 level, must be as large or larger than 2.10. Now use this statistic in the example.

8. In analysis of variance, there are three kinds of models: I, Fixed Effects; II, Random Effects; and III, Mixed. The discussion in this book is directed to Model I, Fixed Effects, since most use of analysis of variance is based on this model and since the objective is basic understanding of the rationale of analysis of variance. The more advanced student, especially in psychology where Models II and III can be meaningfully used, will want to understand and perhaps use Models II and III. See Hays, *op. cit.*, pp. 357–358; 413 ff.
9. Here are three studies in various aspects of education. They all used one-way analysis of variance but in different ways. Select two of them for study. They also used post hoc tests of the significance of the differences between means. Pay particular attention to how this was done.

   Allen, D. "Some Effects of Advance Organizers and Level of Question on the Learning and Retention of Written Social Studies Materials." *Journal of Educational Psychology*, LXI (1970), 333–339.

   DiVesta, F., and Walls, R. "Transfer of Solution Rules in Problem Solving." *Journal of Educational Psychology*, LVIII (1967), 319–326.

   Wittrock, M. "Replacement and Nonreplacement Strategies in Children's Problem Solving." *Journal of Educational Psychology*, LVIII (1967), 69–74.

CHAPTER 14

Factorial Analysis of Variance

Two Research Examples

Educators have long believed that praise and blame, reward and punishment, have different effects on learning. In previous centuries, great emphasis was put upon the efficacy of punishing pupils for poor work. Good work was only to be expected, because it was only right and proper that children should do good work. If the children did poor work, they were considered to be bad, and their teachers were admonished to correct this defect, even by ruthless and cruel methods if necessary.

In the twentieth century educational thought has changed radically. Influenced by more enlightened thinking, by increased knowledge of the growth of the child, and by more valid knowledge of the learning process in general, we now believe that learning is encouraged more by reward than by punishment. But is it possible that reward and punishment have varying effects on different kinds of children in different kinds of educational institutions with different kinds of teachers?

Thompson and Hunnicutt attempted to answer part of this question in an experimental manner.[1] Five groups of fifth-grade children were used—four experimental and one control. The children were divided into the four experimental groups as follows. On the basis of an extroversion-introversion test, the children were split into two groups, those above the median and those below the median (a common method of dividing experimental groups), and called "extroverts" and "introverts." Six alternate forms of a cancellation test were given in six test periods of 30 seconds each. Two of the four classes were designated as "praise" groups and two as "blame" groups. The fifth group, the control group, was neither

[1]G. Thompson and C. Hunnicutt, "The Effect of Praise and Blame on the Work Achievement of 'Introverts' and 'Extroverts,'" *Journal of Educational Psychology*, XXXV (1944), 257–266.

praised nor blamed. (In subsequent discussion, this control group will be omitted from consideration, since it is not pertinent to our purpose.) In effect, then, the authors had two independent variables, praise-blame and extroversion-introversion, and one dependent variable, achievement (via cancellation score gains).

The results showed that both praise and blame increased cancellation scores. More important, it was found that extroverts who were blamed and introverts who were praised achieved higher scores. Apparently an interaction existed between the two independent variables.

We concentrate here on the basic design and omit other details. What Thompson and Hunnicutt did, in effect, was to assign the total number of students to four groups by dichotomizing the entire group on extroversion-introversion, and by administering the experimental treatments of praise-blame to half of each of these two groups. The design looks like Fig. 14.1. Although Thompson and Hunnicutt did not clearly conceptualize or analyze the study in this way, it is a good example of a factorial design.

		Incentive	
		Praise	Blame
	Extrovert	CANCELLATION	
Type		TEST	
	Introvert	SCORES	

FIG. 14.1

Factorial designs look like the crossbreaks we studied earlier (Chap. 10). There is an important difference, however. Crossbreaks have frequencies or percentages in the cells, whereas factorial designs have measures of the dependent variable in the cells. In Fig. 14.1, cancellation test scores are in the cells. Compare this to Fig. 10.2 or 10.3 in Chapter 10. After a little exposure to factorial designs and problems, the student should have no difficulty distinguishing them from crossbreaks.

Note that three statistical hypotheses can be tested: the significance of the differences between praise-blame, between extrovert-introvert, and the significance of the interaction or mutual interplay of these two variables. An important characteristic of factorial analysis of variance is that several hypotheses can be tested simultaneously. Thompson and Hunnicutt were naturally interested in the effects of praise and blame, but they were *more* interested in whether praise and blame worked differently with different kinds of children, in this case with extroverts and introverts. In other words, they wanted to know whether or not praise-blame *interacted* with extroversion-introversion. They asked these questions of the data, the theoretical and practical implications of which are important: Does praise work better with introverts than with extroverts? Does blame work better with extroverts? (The answer to both questions was Yes.)

If someone injures us or treats us badly, we will probably dislike him. Or we may dislike a person for other reasons. What will our feeling be toward still another person who treats the disliked person badly? Will we like him? Suppose a second person rewards or otherwise treats a friend of ours nicely. Will we like him for being nice to our friend? In an unusual experiment designed to test these propositions, Aronson and Cope randomly assigned 80 subjects (*S*s) to four experimental conditions which reflected two independent variables to be explained shortly.[2] The *S*s were asked by the experimenter to write stories about pictures supplied them. They were told that creativity was being studied. The experimenter gave highly adverse judgments of the stories to half the subjects (*harsh* condition) and adverse judgments to the other half but in a gentle way (*pleasant* condition). This treatment constituted one independent variable. Presumably the harsh treatment would engender antipathy and dislike of the experimenter, whereas the pleasant treatment would not.

A second independent variable was manipulated as follows. Just before the experimenter finished his evaluation of a subject's story, as described above, a "supervisor" entered the scene, took the experimenter outside, and either praised his work (*pleasant* condition) or castigated him for poor work (*harsh* condition)—within the hearing of the experimental *S*s. The dependent variable was ingenious: a secretary told the *S*s that Dr. Cope, the "supervisor," needed help getting subjects. Would they help Dr. Cope by making phone calls? The number of phone calls offered by the subject was the measure of the dependent variable. The paradigm of the experimental design and the results are given in Table 14.1.

TABLE **14.1** DESIGN AND DATA OF ARONSON AND COPE EXPERIMENT: MEAN NUMBERS OF PHONE CALLS VOLUNTEERED ON BEHALF OF "SUPERVISOR" BY SUBJECTS[a]

		Supervisor		
		Harsh	Pleasant	
Experimenter	Harsh	12.1	6.2	9.15
	Pleasant	6.3	13.5	9.90
		9.20	9.85	

[a]The marginal sums were inserted by the author to show the similarity of the main effects.

In a factorial experiment, the independent variables are called the *main effects*. Note that the main effects are expressed by the means in the margins of the table: at the right side, 9.15 and 9.90, and at the bottom, 9.20 and 9.85. These main effects means do not differ too much. Bur Aronson and Cope did not expect them to differ. Their main interest was in the *interaction* of the two independent variables in their effect on the dependent variable. That is, they expected that the subjects would volunteer more phone calls for the supervisor who had been harsh to the experimenter who had been harsh to them, and fewer calls for the supervisor who had been pleasant to the harsh experimenter. Conversely, they expected the *S*s to volunteer more phone calls for the supervisor who had been pleasant to

[2]E. Aronson and V. Cope, "My Enemy's Enemy Is My Friend," *Journal of Personality and Social Psychology*, VIII (1968), 8–12.

the experimenter who had been pleasant to them than for the supervisor who had been harsh to the experimenter who had been pleasant to them. This is an *interaction hypothesis*. We explain it more later. In any case, the hypothesis was supported: the interaction was statistically significant.

The Nature of Factorial Analysis of Variance

In factorial analysis of variance two or more independent variables vary independently or interact with each other to produce variation in a dependent variable. *Factorial analysis of variance is the statistical method that analyzes the independent and interactive effects of two or more independent variables on a dependent variable.*

One of the most significant and revolutionary developments in modern research design and statistics is the planning and analysis of the simultaneous operation and interaction of two or more variables. Scientists have long known that variables do not act independently. Rather, they often act in concert. The virtue of one method of teaching contrasted with another method of teaching depends on the teachers using the methods. The educational effect of a certain kind of teacher depends, to a large extent, on the kind of pupil being taught. An anxious teacher may be quite effective with anxious pupils but less effective with nonanxious pupils. Different methods of teaching in colleges and universities may depend on the intelligence and personality of both professors and students. In the Thompson and Hunnicutt study, the effect of praise or blame on pupil performance depended on the extroversion or introversion of the students. In the Aronson and Cope experiment, the effect on phone-call volunteering of the treatment by the supervisor of the experimenter depended on the treatment of the subject by the experimenter.

The traditional conduct of experimental research has been to study the effect of one independent variable on one dependent variable. Educational scientists knew that the study of the effects of different pedagogical methods and techniques on educational outcomes was in part a function of other variables, such as the intelligence of the students, the personality of the teachers, the social background of both the teachers and the students, and the general atmosphere of the class and the school. But in the past researchers believed that the most effective research method was to vary one independent variable while controlling, as best one could, other independent variables that might contribute to the variance of the dependent variable. (Indeed, it is true of many researchers today.)

It is by no means implied that scientists did not arrive at important and valid generalizations before the advent of modern research design and statistics. They did. Factorial analysis of variance and other multivariate notions, however, as well as the research designs they imply, make it possible to expand greatly our conceptions and our methods of research and analysis.

In the studies summarized above, the conclusions go beyond the simple differences between effects or groups. It was possible to qualify the conclusions in important ways because the authors studied the simultaneous working of the two independent variables. They were consequently able to talk about the *differential effect* of their variables. They could say, for example, that treatment A_1 is effective when coupled with level B_1, but not effective when alone or when coupled with level B_2, and that, perhaps, A_2 is effective only when coupled with B_1. The balance of this chapter will be devoted to clarifying these statements, as well as explaining the logic and machinery of factorial analysis of variance.

A Simple Fictitious Example

As usual we take a simple, if unrealistic, example that highlights the basic problems and characteristics of factorial analysis of variance. Assume that an educational investigator is interested in the relative efficacy of two methods of teaching, A_1 and A_2. Call this variable methods. He believes that methods of teaching, in and of themselves, do not differ very much. They differ only when used with certain kinds of students, by certain kinds of teachers, in certain kinds of educational situations, and with certain kinds of motives. Studying all of these variables at one time is too large an order for him, though not necessarily impossible. So he decides to study methods and motivations, which gives him two independent variables and one dependent variable. Call the dependent variable achievement. (Some type of achievement measure will be used, perhaps scores on a standardized test.)

The investigator conducts an experiment with eight sixth-grade children. (Obviously in a real experiment he would work with many more than eight children.) He randomly assigns the eight children to four groups, two per group. He also randomly assigns methods A_1 and A_2 and motivations B_1 and B_2 to the four groups. Refer back to the earlier discussion on partitions of sets. Recall that we can partition and cross-partition sets of objects. The objects can be assigned to a partition or subpartition on the basis of the possession of certain characteristics. But they can also be assigned at random—and then presumably be "given" certain characteristics by the experimenter. In either case the partitioning logic is the same. The experimenter will end up with four subpartitions: A_1B_1, A_1B_2, A_2B_1, and A_2B_2. The experimental paradigm is shown in Fig. 14.2.

Each cell in the design is the intersection of two subsets. For instance, method A_1 combined with motivation B_2 is conceptually $A_1 \cap B_2$. Method A_2 combined with motivation B_2 is the intersection $A_2 \cap B_2$. In this design, we write simply A_1B_2 and A_2B_2 for simplicity. Now two children have been assigned at random to each of these four cells. This means that each child will get a combina-

		Methods	
		A_1	A_2
Motivations	B_1	A_1B_1	A_2B_1
	B_2	A_1B_2	A_2B_2

FIG. 14.2

tion of two experimental manipulations, but each pair of children will get a different combination.

Call A_1 "recitation," and A_2 "no recitation." Call B_1 "praise," and B_2 "blame." The children in cell A_1B_1, then, will be taught with recitation and will be praised for their work. The children in cell A_1B_2 will be taught with recitation but will be "blamed" for their work. And similarly for the other two cells. If the experimental procedures have been adequately handled, it is possible to conceive of the variables as being independent, that is, two separate experiments are actually being run with the same subjects. One experiment manipulates methods; the other, types of motivations. The design of the experiment, in other words, makes it possible for the investigator to test *independently* the effects on a dependent variable, in this case, achievement, of (1) methods and (2) types of motivation. To show this and other important facets of factorial designs, let us jump to the hypothetical data of the experiment. These "data" are reported in Table 14.2, together with the necessary computations for a factorial analysis of variance.

TABLE **14.2** DATA OF HYPOTHETICAL FACTORIAL EXPERIMENT WITH ANALYSIS OF VARIANCE CALCULATIONS

Types of Motivation	*Methods* A_1	A_2	
B_1	8 6	4 2	
ΣX $(\Sigma X)^2$ M	14 196 (7)	6 36 (3)	$\Sigma X_{B_1} = 20$ $(\Sigma X_{B_1})^2 = 400$ $M_{B_1} =$ (5)
B_2	8 6	4 2	
ΣX $(\Sigma X)^2$ M	14 196 (7)	6 36 (3)	$\Sigma X_{B_2} = 20$ $(\Sigma X_{B_2})^2 = 400$ $M_{B_2} =$ (5)
ΣX_A $(\Sigma X_A)^2$ M_A	28 784 (7)	12 144 (3)	$\Sigma X_t = 40$ $(\Sigma X_t)^2 = 1600$ $M_t =$ (5) $\Sigma X_t^2 = 240$

First, we calculate the sums of squares that we would for a simple one-way analysis of variance. There is of course a *total sum of squares*, calculated from all the scores, using C, the correction term:

$$C = \frac{(40)^2}{8} = \frac{1600}{8} = 200$$

$$\text{Total} = 240 - 200 = \mathit{40}$$

Since there are four groups, there is a sum of squares associated with the means of the four groups. Simply conceive of the four groups placed side by side as in simple analysis of variance, and calculate the sum of squares as in the last chapter. Now, however, we call this the "*between all groups*" *sum of squares* to distinguish it from sums of squares to be calculated later.

$$\text{Between all groups} = \left(\frac{196}{2}+\frac{36}{2}+\frac{196}{2}+\frac{36}{2}\right)-200 = \mathit{32}$$

This sum of squares is a measure of the variability of all four group means. Therefore, if we subtract this quantity from the total sum of squares, we should obtain the sum of squares due to error, the random fluctuations of the scores within the cells (groups). This is familiar: it is the *within-groups sum of squares*:

$$\text{Within groups} = 40-32 = \mathit{8}$$

Since the experiment is concerned with methods and types of motivation, we need not bother with the final analysis of variance table. Instead, we go on to calculate the sum of squares of experimental concern.

To calculate the *sum of squares for methods*, proceed exactly as with the simple analysis of variance: treat the scores (X's) and sums of scores (ΣX's) of the columns (methods) as though these two groups were not subdivided:

	A_1	A_2
	8	4
	6	2
	8	4
	6	2
ΣX:	28	12

The calculation is:

$$\begin{matrix}\text{Between methods}\\ (A_1, A_2)\end{matrix} = \left(\frac{(28)^2}{4}+\frac{(12)^2}{4}\right)-200 = \left(\frac{784}{4}+\frac{144}{4}\right)-200 = \mathit{32}$$

Similarly, treat types of motivation (B_1 and B_2) as though there were no methods (A_1 and A_2):

	B_1	B_2
	8	8
	6	6
	4	4
	2	2
ΣX:	20	20

The calculation of the between-types sum of squares is really not necessary. Since the sums (and the means) are the same, the between types sum of squares is zero:

$$\begin{matrix}\text{Between types} \\ (B_1, B_2)\end{matrix} = \left(\frac{(20)^2}{4} + \frac{(20)^2}{4}\right) - 200 = 0$$

There is another possible source of variance, the variance due presumably to the *interaction* of the two independent variables. The between-all-groups sum of squares comprises the variability due to the means of the four groups: 7, 3, 7, 3. This sum of squares was 32. If this were not a contrived example, part of this sum of squares would be due to methods, part to types of motivation, and a remaining part left over, *which is due to the joint action, or interaction, of* methods and Types. In many cases it would be relatively small, no greater than chance expectation. In other cases, it would be large enough to be statistically significant; it would exceed chance expectation. In the present problem it is clearly zero since the between-methods sum of squares was 32, and this is equal to the between-all-groups sum of squares. To complete the computational cycle we calculate:[3]

$$\text{Interaction: methods} \times \text{types} = \text{between all groups} - (\text{between methods} + \text{between types}) = 32 - (32 + 0) = 0$$

We are now in a position to set up the final analysis of variance table. We postpone this, however, until we perform a minor operation on these scores.

We use exactly the same scores, but rearrange them slightly: we reverse the scores of A_1B_2 and A_2B_2. Since all the individual scores (X's) are exactly the same, the total sum of squares must also be exactly the same. Further, the sums and sums of squares of B_1 and B_2 (Types) must also be exactly the same. Table 14.3 shows just what was done and its effect on the means of the four groups.

TABLE **14.3** DATA OF HYPOTHETICAL FACTORIAL EXPERIMENT OF TABLE 14.2 WITH B_2 FIGURES REARRANGED

Types of Motivation	*Methods* A_1	A_2	
B_1	8	4	
	6	2	
ΣX	14	6	$\Sigma X_{B_1} = 20$
M	(7)	(3)	$M_{B_1} = (5)$
B_2	4	8	
	2	6	
ΣX	6	14	$\Sigma X_{B_2} = 20$
M	(3)	(7)	$M_{B_2} = (5)$
ΣX	20	20	$\Sigma X_t = 40$
M	(5)	(5)	$M_t = (5)$
			$\Sigma X_t^2 = 240$

[3]In a more complex factorial analysis of variance it is not possible to calculate the interactions so easily. Since the purpose of these chapters is not basically computational, we do not take up the calculation of more complex forms of analysis of variance. See A. Edwards, *Experimental Design in Psychological Research*, 3d ed. New York: Holt, Rinehart and Winston, 1968, chaps. 10–12.

Study the figures of Tables 14.2 and 14.3 and note the differences. To emphasize the differences, the means have been circled in both tables. To make the differences still clearer, the means of both tables have been laid out in Table 14.4. The little table on the left shows two variabilities: between all four means and between A_1 and A_2 means. In the little table on the right, there is only one variability, that between the four means. In both tables, the variability of the four means is the same since they both have the same four means: 7, 3, 7, 3. Obviously, there is no

TABLE **14.4** MEANS OF THE DATA OF TABLES 14.2 AND 14.3

Table 14.2 Means				Table 14.3 Means			
	A_1	A_2			A_1	A_2	
B_1	7	3	5	B_1	7 ↘	↗ 3	5
B_2	7	3	5	B_2	3 ↗	↘ 7	5
	7	3			5	5	

variability of the B means in both tables. There are two differences between the tables, then: the A means and the arrangement of the four means inside the squares. If we analyze the sum of squares of the four means, the between-all-groups sums of squares, we find that B_1 and B_2 contribute nothing to it in both tables, since there is no variability with 5, 5, the means of B_1 and B_2. In the table on the right, the A_1 and A_2 means of 5 and 5 contribute no variability. In the table on the left, however, the A_1-A_2 means differ considerably, 7 and 3, and thus they contribute variance.

Assuming for the moment that the means of 7 and 3 differ significantly, we can say that methods of the data of Table 14.2 had an effect irrespective of types of motivation. That is, $M_{A_1} \neq M_{A_2}$, or $M_{A_1} > M_{A_2}$. As far as this experiment is concerned, methods differ significantly *no matter what the type of motivation.* And, obviously, types of motivation had no effect, since $M_{B_1} = M_{B_2}$. In Table 14.3, on the other hand, the situation is quite different. Neither methods nor types of motivation had an effect *by themselves.* Yet there *is* variance. The problem is: What is the source of the variance? It is in the *interaction of the two variables*, the interaction of methods and types of motivation.

If we had performed an experiment and obtained data like those of Table 14.3, then we could come to the likely conclusion that there was an interaction between the two variables in their effect on the dependent variable. In this case, we would interpret the results as follows. Methods A_1 and A_2, operating in and of themselves, do not differ in their effect. Types of motivation B_1 and B_2, in and of themselves, do not differ in their effect. When methods and types of motivation are allowed to "work together," when they are permitted to interact, they are significantly effective. Specifically, method A_1 is superior to method A_2 when combined with type of motivation B_1. When combined with type of motivation B_2, it is inferior to A_2. This interaction effect is indicated on the right-hand side of Table 14.4 by the crisscrossed arrows. Qualitatively interpreting the original methods, we find that "recitation" seems to be superior to "no recitation" under the condition of "praise," but that it is inferior to "no recitation" under conditions of "blame" (reproof).

It is instructive to note, before going further, that interaction can be studied and calculated by a subtractive procedure. In a 2×2 design, this procedure is simple. Subtract one mean from another in each row, and then calculate the variance of these differences. Take the fictitious means of Table 14.4. If we subtract the Table 14.2 means, we get $7-3=4$; $7-3=4$. Clearly the mean square is zero. Thus, the interaction is zero. Follow the same procedure for the Table 14.3 means (right-hand side of the table): $7-3=4$; $3-7=-4$. If we now treat these two differences as we did means in the last chapter and calculate the sum of squares and the mean square, we will arrive at the interaction sum of squares and the mean square, 32 in each case. The reasoning behind this procedure is simple. If there were no interaction, we would expect the differences between row means to be approximately equal to each other and to the difference between the means at the bottom of the table, the methods means, in this case. Note that this is so for the Table 14.2 means: the bottom-row difference is 4, and so are the differences of each of the rows. The row differences of Table 14.3, however, deviate from the difference between the bottom-row (methods) means. They are 4 and −4, whereas the bottom-row difference is $5-5=0$.

From this discussion and a little reflection, it can be seen that a significant interaction can be caused by one deviant row. For example, the means of the above example might be:

7	3	5
5	5	5
6	4	

Subtract the rows. $7-3=4$; $5-5=0$; and $6-4=2$. There is obviously some variance in these remainders.[4]

It will be profitable to write the final analysis of variance tables in which the different variances and F ratios are calculated. Táble 14.5 gives the final analysis of variance tables for both examples.[5] The sum of squares and mean square and the resulting F ratio of 16 on the left-hand side of the table indicate what we already know from the preceding discussion: Methods are significantly different (at the .05 level), and types of motivation and interaction are not significant. The parallel figures of the right-hand side of the table indicate that only the interaction is significant.

[4]For a more complete discussion, see E. Lindquist, *Design and Analysis of Experiments in Psychology and Education.* Boston: Houghton Mifflin, 1953, pp. 119, 125. Lindquist also discusses more complex examples.

[5]The between-all-groups sums of squares have not been included in the table. They are only useful for calculating the within-groups sums of squares. The degrees of freedom for the main effects (methods and types) and for between all groups and within groups are calculated in the same way as in the simple analysis of variance. This should become apparent upon studying the table. The interaction degrees of freedom is the product of the degrees of freedom of the main effects, that is, $1 \times 1 = 1$. If methods had had four groups and types three groups, the interaction degrees of freedom would have been $3 \times 2 = 6$.

TABLE **14.5** FINAL ANALYSIS OF VARIANCE TABLES: DATA OF TABLES 14.2 AND 14.3

		Data of Table 14.2			*Data of Table 14.3*		
Source	*df*	*s.s.*	*m.s.*	*F*	*s.s.*	*m.s.*	*F*
Between Methods (A_1, A_2)	1	32	32	16(.05)	0	0	....
Between Types (B_1, B_2)	1	0	0	....	0	0	....
Interaction: A × B	1	0	0	....	32	32	16(.05)
Within Groups	4	8	2		8	2	
Total	7	40			40		

Interaction: An Example

In the last chapter, it was said that if sampling was random the means of the k groups would be approximately equal. If, for example, there were four groups and the general mean, M_t, was 4.5, then it would be expected that each of the means would be approximately 4.5. Similarly, in factorial analysis of variance, if random samples of numbers are drawn for each of the cells, then the means of the cells should be approximately equal. If the general mean, M_t, were 10, then the best expectation for any cell means in the factorial design would be 10. These means, of course, would very rarely be exactly 10. Indeed, some of them might be considerably far from 10. The fundamental statistical question is: Do they differ from 10 significantly? The means of combinations of means, too, should hover around 10. For example, in a design like that of the previous example the A_1 and A_2 means should be approximately 10, and the B_1 and B_2 means should be approximately 10. In addition, the means of each of the cells, A_1B_1, A_1B_2, A_2B_1, and A_2B_2, should hover around 10.

Using a table of random numbers, I drew 60 digits, 0 through 9, to fill the six cells of a factorial design. The resulting design has two levels or independent variables, A and B. A is subdivided into A_1, A_2, and A_3, B into B_1 and B_2. This is called a 3 × 2 factorial design. (The examples of Tables 14.2 and 14.3 are 2 × 2 designs.)

Conceive of A as types of appeal. In a social psychological experiment designed to test hypotheses of the best ways to appeal to prejudiced people to change their attitudes, the question is asked: What kinds of appeal work best to change prejudiced attitudes?[6] Assume that three types of appeal, "Religious," "Fair-Play," "Democratic," have been tried with unclear results. The investigator suspects that the situation is more complex, that types of appeal interact with the

[6]The idea for this fictitious experiment was taken from an actual experiment: A. Citron, I. Chein, and J. Harding, "Anti-Minority Remarks: A Problem for Action Research," *Journal of Abnormal and Social Psychology*, XLV (1950), 99–126.

manner of appeal in which appeals are made. So he sets up a 3×2 factorial design, in which the second variable, B, is divided into B_1 and B_2, impassioned and calm manner of appeal. That is, the religious appeal is given in an impassioned manner to some subjects and in a calm manner to others, and similarly for the other two types of appeal. We will not explore this research problem further, but simply use it to color the abstract and perhaps skeleton quality of our discussion. Imagine the experiment to have been done with the results given in Table 14.6, which gives the design paradigm and the means of each cell, as well as the means of the two variables, A and B, and the general mean, M_t. These means were calculated from the 60 random numbers drawn in lots of 10 each and inserted in the cells.

TABLE **14.6** TWO-WAY FACTORIAL DESIGN: MEANS OF GROUPS OF OF RANDOM NUMBERS 0 THROUGH 9

	Type of Appeal			
Manner of Appeal	A_1 Religious	A_2 Fair-Play	A_3 Democratic	Manner Means
B_1 Impassioned	4.1	5.0	3.9	4.33
B_2 Calm	5.6	3.9	4.2	4.57
Type means	4.85	4.45	4.05	$M_t = 4.45$

We hardly need a test of statistical significance to know that these means do not differ significantly. Their total range is 3.9 to 5.6. The mean expectation, of course, is the mean of the numbers 0 through 9, or 4.5. The closeness of the means to $M_t = 4.45$ or to 4.5 is remarkable, even for random sampling. At any rate, if these were the results of an actual experiment, the experimenter would probably be most chagrined. Types of appeal, manner of appeal, and the interaction between them are all insignificant.

Remark how many different outcome possibilities other than chance there would be if one or both variables had been effective. The three means of appeal, M_{A_1}, M_{A_2}, and M_{A_3}, might have been significantly different, with the means of manner, M_{B_1}, and M_{B_2}, not significantly different. Or the manner means might be significantly different, with the appeal means not significantly different; or both sets of means could be different; or both could turn out not to be different, with their interaction significant. The possibilities of *kinds* of differences and interactions are considerable, too, although it would take too many words and numbers to illustrate even a small number of them. If the student will juggle the numbers a bit, he can get considerable insight into both statistics and design possibilities. Since our present preoccupation is with interaction, let us alter the means to create a significant interaction. We increase the A_1B_1 mean by 2, decrease the A_1B_2 mean by 2, increase the A_3B_2 mean by 1, and decrease the A_3B_1 mean by 1. We let the A_2

means stand as they are, and alter the main effect means accordingly. The changes are shown in Table 14.7.

The table should be studied carefully. Compare it to Table 14.6. Interaction has been produced by the arbitrary alterations. The cell means have been unbalanced, so to speak, while the marginal means (A_1, A_2, A_3, B_1, B_2) are almost undisturbed. The total mean remains unchanged at 4.45. The three A means are the same. (Why?) The two B means are changed very little. A factorial analysis of

TABLE **14.7** MEANS OF TABLE 14.6 ALTERED SYSTEMATICALLY BY ADDING AND SUBTRACTING CONSTANTS

Manner of Appeal	*Type of Appeal*			
	A_1	A_2	A_3	Manner Means
B_1	(4.1 + 2) 6.1	5.0	(3.9 − 1) 2.9	4.67
B_2	(5.6 − 2) 3.6	3.9	(4.2 + 1) 5.2	4.23
Type Means	4.85	4.45	4.05	4.45

variance of the appropriately altered random numbers—which, of course, are no longer random—yields the final analysis of variance table given in Table 14.8.

Neither of the main effects (appeal and manner) is significant. That is, the means of A_1, A_2, and A_3 do not differ significantly from chance. Neither do the means of B_1 and B_2. The only significant F ratio is that of interaction, which is significant at the .05 level.[7] Evidently the alteration of the scores has had an effect. If we were interpreting the results, as given in Tables 14.7 and 14.8, we

TABLE **14.8** FINAL ANALYSIS OF VARIANCE TABLE OF ALTERED RANDOM-NUMBER DATA

Source	*df*	*s.s.*	*m.s.*	*F*
Between All Groups	5	70.15		
Within Groups	54	476.70	8.83	
Between Appeals (A_1, A_2, A_3)	2	6.40	3.20	< 1.0 (*n.s.*)
Between Manners (B_1, B_2)	1	2.82	2.82	< 1.0 (*n.s.*)
Interaction: $A \times B$	2	60.93	30.47	3.45 (.05)
Total	59	546.85		

[7]The random numbers that generated Table 14.6 were also subjected to an analysis of variance. The F ratios were not significant.

would say that, in and of themselves, neither type of appeal to the bigot nor the manner of appeal differ. But a religious appeal delivered in an impassioned manner and a democratic appeal in a calm manner seem to be most effective. Perhaps a bit more clearly, the democratic appeal in an impassioned manner is relatively ineffectual, as is the religious appeal in a calm manner. (It is not possible to say much about the fair play appeal.)

Factorial Analysis of Variance with Three or More Variables

Factorial analysis of variance works with more than two independent variables. Three, four, and more variables are possible and do appear in the literature. Designs with more than four variables, however, are uncommon and not too fruitful. It is not so much because the statistics become complex and unwieldy. Rather, it is a matter of practicality. It is very difficult just to get enough subjects to fill the cells of complex designs. And it is even more difficult to manipulate four, five, or six independent variables at one time. For instance, take an experiment with four independent variables. The smallest arrangement possible is $2 \times 2 \times 2 \times 2$, which yields 16 cells into each of which some minimum number of subjects must be put. If 10 *S*s are placed in each cell, it will be necessary to handle the total of 160 *S*s in four different ways. Yet one should not be dogmatic about the number of variables. Perhaps in the next ten years factorial designs with more than four variables will become common with the increased support of behavioral research and the use of high speed computers. Indeed, when we later study multiple regression analysis we will find that factorial analysis of variance can be done with multiple regression analysis and that four and five factors are easily accommodated *analytically*. That is, the complexities of analysis of variance calculations with four or five independent variables are considerably simplified. Such analytic facilitation of calculations, however, in no way changes the *experimental* difficulties of managing several manipulated independent variables.

The simplest form of a three-variable factorial analysis of variance is a $2 \times 2 \times 2$ design. Consider the immediately preceding sample. Suppose the investigator decided to use, in a new experiment, a third independent variable. He drops the fair play appeal and keeps the religious and democratic appeals. He has noticed that there seems to be a greater effect on the prejudiced person if he personalizes the appeal. So he adds another variable, C, which he calls personalization. This variable he defines as the degree of appeal to the person as an individual rather than as a member of any group. In the design this variable has two *modes* which he calls "personalized" and "objectified," C_1 and C_2. The design now looks like that in Fig. 14.3.

The researcher can now test seven hypotheses: the differences between A_1 and A_2 (appeal), between B_1 and B_2 (manner), and between C_1 and C_2 (mode). These are the *main effects*. Four interactions can also be tested: $A \times B$, $A \times C$, $B \times C$, and $A \times B \times C$. A final analysis of variance table would look like Table 14.9. It is evident that a great deal of information can be obtained from this one

		Appeals			
		A_1 (Religious)		A_2 (Democratic)	
	Mode	C_1 Personalized	C_2 Objectified	C_1 Personalized	C_2 Objectified
Manner	B_1 (Impassioned)	$A_1B_1C_1$	$A_1B_1C_2$	$A_2B_1C_1$	$A_2B_1C_2$
	B_2 (Calm)	$A_1B_2C_1$	$A_1B_2C_2$	$A_2B_2C_1$	$A_2B_2C_2$

FIG. 14.3

experiment. Contrast it with the one variable experiment in which only *one* hypothesis can be tested. The difference is not only great—it indicates a fundamentally different way of conceptualizing research problems.

TABLE **14.9** FINAL ANALYSIS OF VARIANCE TABLE FOR THE $2 \times 2 \times 2$ DESIGN OF FIG. 14.3

Source	*df*	*s.s.*	*m.s.*	*F*
Between Appeals (A_1, A_2)	1			
Between Manners (B_1, B_2)	1			
Between Modes (C_1, C_2)	1			
Interaction: $A \times B$	1			
Interaction: $A \times C$	1			
Interaction: $B \times C$	1			
Interaction: $A \times B \times C$	1			
Within Groups	$N-7$			
Total	$N-1$			

In most studies using factorial designs, the main effects are probably of most interest. Interactions, particularly triple and higher-order interactions, seem for the most part not to be significant.[8] Even so, this information is important. To know, say, that a variable, A, is effective in and of itself and across conditions or levels of other variables is important information, and it cannot be known unless the interaction is specifically tested.

Interactions are called first-order, second-order, third-order, and so on. A two-variable interaction, $A \times B$, is a first-order interaction; a three-variable inter-

[8]Nevertheless, higher-order interactions *can* be significant, though relatively rare. Here are two interesting researches that have reported significant *triple* interactions: I. Katz et al., "Effects of Race of Tester, Approval-Disapproval, and Need on Negro Children's Learning," *Journal of Personality and Social Psychology*, VIII (1968), 38–42; J. Rapier, "Learning Abilities of Normal and Retarded Children as a Function of Social Class," *Journal of Educational Psychology*, LIX (1968), 102–110. Triple interactions are difficult to grasp. The best way to handle them, probably, is to make up sets of two-dimensional tables so that the relations are clarified.

action, $A \times B \times C$, is a second-order interaction. Though infrequent compared to significant main effects, significant first-order interactions occur frequently enough to warrant serious attention. Students of research must be able to handle them. In the opinion of some behavioral researchers, especially in education, the study of interactions is become increasingly important and should become a central concern of researchers.[9]

By now the reader no doubt realizes that in principle the breakdowns of the independent variables are not restricted to just two or three subpartitions. It is quite possible to have 2×4, 2×5, 4×6, $2 \times 3 \times 3$, $2 \times 5 \times 4$, $4 \times 2 \times 3 \times 5, \ldots.$ Laughlin et al., in their study of concept attainment, used a $2 \times 2 \times 2 \times 8 \times 3$ design![10] As always, the problem under investigation and the judgment of the researcher are the criteria that determine what a design and its concomitant analysis shall be.

Advantages of Factorial Analysis of Variance

Factorial analysis of variance, as we have seen, accomplishes several things, all of which are important advantages of the approach and method. One, it enables the researcher to manipulate and control two or more variables simultaneously. In educational research, not only is it possible to study the effects of teaching methods on achievement; we can also study the effects of both methods *and*, say, kinds of reinforcement. In psychological research, we can study the separate and combined effects of many kinds of independent variables, such as anxiety, guilt, reinforcement, types of persuasion, status, race, and group atmosphere, on many kinds of dependent variables, such as compliance, conformity, learning, transfer, discrimination, perception, and attitude change. In addition, we can control variables such as sex, social class, and home enivornment.

A second advantage of the factorial approach has just been touched upon: variables that are not manipulated can be controlled. We may be interested, for example, only in the differential effects of certain methods. Certain variables that are known or suspected to influence achievement, such as sex or social class, may at the time be merely distracting complications. But they must be controlled. We can "control" them by building them into the research design. Not only can they be controlled; they can yield information of possible value and significance. One easy way to control the sex variable is to confine an experiment to one of the sexes only. But why not introduce sex as a variable in a factorial design? We may find

[9]See G. Bracht, "Experimental Factors Related to Aptitude-Treatment Interaction," *Review of Educational Research*, XL (1970), 627–645; L. Cronbach and R. Snow, "Individual Differences in Learning Ability as a Function of Instructional Variables." Report to Office of Education, U.S. Dept. of HEW. Stanford, Calif.: School of Education, Stanford University, 1969. The Cronbach and Snow report is definitive—and discouraging. They found the research of ability-trait interaction (ATI) to be frustrating and inconclusive. There are enough first-order interactions now appearing in both psychological and educational research, however, to be encouraging. See D. Berliner and L. Cahen, "Trait-Treatment Interaction and Learning," in F. Kerlinger, ed., *Review of Research in Education*, Vol. I. Itasca, Ill.: Peacock, 1973 (in press).

an interaction between an independent variable and sex, which would probably be important information.

A third advantage is that factorial analysis is more precise than one-way analysis. Here we see one of the virtues of combining research design and statistical considerations. It can be said that, other things equal, factorial designs are "better" than one-way designs. This value judgment has been implicit in most of the preceding discussion. The precision argument adds weight to it and will be elaborated shortly.

The final advantage—and, from a large scientific viewpoint, perhaps the most important one—is the study of the interactive effects of independent variables on dependent variables. This has been discussed. But a highly important point must be added. Factorial analysis enables the research *to hypothesize interactions* because the interactive effects can be directly tested. If we go back to conditional statements and their qualification, we see the core of the importance of this statement. In a one-way analysis, we simply say: If p, then q; If such-and-such methods, then so-and-so outcomes. In factorial analysis, however, we utter richer conditional statements. We can say: If p, then q *and* If r, then q, which is tantamount to talking about the main effects in a factorial analysis. In the problem of Table 14.3, for instance, p is methods (A) and r is types of motivation (B). We can also say, however: If p *and* r, then q, which is equivalent to the interaction of methods and types of motivation. Interaction can also be expressed by: If p, then q, under condition r.

On the basis of theory, previous research, or hunch, researchers can hypothesize interactions. One hypothesizes that an independent variable will have a certain effect only in the presence of another independent variable. Berkowitz, for example, in studying the relation between anti-Semitism and displacement of aggression, asked whether prejudiced persons were more likely to respond to frustration with displaced aggression than less prejudiced individuals.[11] This is an interaction hypothesis, as we will see. Berkowitz split 48 female subjects into two groups on the basis of their scores on a measure of anti-Semitism.[12] Each of these two groups was then split into two groups based on high and low aggressive drive.

[10]P. Laughlin et al., "Concept Attainment by Individuals versus Cooperative Pairs as a Function of Memory, Sex, and Concept Rule," *Journal of Personality and Social Psychology*, VIII (1968), 410–417.

[11]L. Berkowitz, "Anti-Semitism and the Displacement of Aggression," *Journal of Abnormal and Social Psychology*, LIX (1959), 182–187.

[12]It has become common practice to partition a continuous variable into dichotomies or other polytomies. In the Berkowitz study, for instance, a continuous measure, anti-Semitism, was dichotomized. In the Thompson and Hunnicutt study, introversion-extroversion, a continuous variable, was dichotomized. It was pointed out earlier that creating a categorical variable out of a continuous variable throws variance away and thus should be avoided. We will learn in a later chapter that factorial analysis of variance can be done with multiple regression analysis and that, with such analysis, it is not necessary to sacrifice any variance by conversion of variables. Nevertheless, there are countervailing arguments. One, if a difference is statistically significant and the relation is substantial, the variable conversion does not matter. The danger is in concealing a relation that in fact exists. Two, there are times when conversion of a variable may be wise—for example, for exploration of a new field or problem and when measurement of a variable is at best rough and crude. In other words, while the rule is a good one, it is best not to be inflexible about it. Much good, even excellent, research has been done with continuous variables that have been partitioned for one reason or another.

(This variable was a control variable and is dropped from further consideration.) The third variable was hostility arousal. In one experimental group the experimenter aroused hostility by using sarcasm, deprecating performances, and questioning the student's ability to do well in college. The nonhostility *S*s were treated in a neutral manner. Each *S* was paired with a confederate of the experimenter with whom the *S* was to work to solve a problem. *S*s were asked whether they liked their partners by means of two questions that could be scored 0 ("definitely yes") to 23 ("definitely no"). This measure of liking was the dependent variable. It was predicted that the more anti-Semitic *S*s would exhibit more displaced aggression, induced by the hostility arousal, than the less anti-Semitic *S*s. This should be manifested in less liking for the work partners by the highly anti-Semitic *S*s. We have here, then, an interaction hypothesis.

The mean liking-for-partner scores as a function of anti-Semitism and hostility arousal are given in Table 14.10. (This table was constructed from part of Berkowitz's larger table.) None of the main effects—anti-Semitism, aggressive drive, or

TABLE **14.10** MEAN LIKING-FOR-PARTNER SCORES AS RELATED TO HOSTILITY AND ANTI-SEMITISM, BERKOWITZ STUDY[a]

	Hostility Arousal	No Hostility Arousal
High Anti-Semitism	18.4	14.2
Low Anti-Semitism	12.2	16.3

[a]The higher the score the less the liking for partner.

hostility—was, in and of itself significant. But the interaction of the data of Table 14.10 was significant. It seems clear that when hostility is aroused, high anti-Semitic individuals responded with more displaced aggression than low anti-Semitic individuals. The interaction hypothesis was supported—a finding of both theoretical and practical significance.

Factorial Analysis of Variance and Precision

In a simple one-way analysis of variance, there are two *identifiable* sources of variance: that presumed to be due to the experimental effects and that presumably due to error or chance variation. We now look at the latter more closely. When subjects have been assigned to the experimental groups at random, the only possible estimate of chance variation is the within-groups variance. But—and this is important—it is clear that the within-groups variance contains not only variance due to error; it also contains variance due to individual differences among the subjects. Two simple examples are intelligence and sex. There are, of course, many others. If both girls and boys are used in an experiment, randomization can be used in order to balance the individual differences that are concomitant to sex.

Then the number of girls and boys in each experimental group will be approximately equal. We can also arbitrarily assign girls and boys in equal numbers to the groups. This method, however, does not accomplish the overall purpose of randomization, which is to equalize the groups on *all* possible variables. It *does* equalize the groups as far as the sex variable is concerned, but we can have no assurance that other variables are equally distributed among the groups. Similarly for intelligence. Randomization, if successful, will equalize the groups such that the intelligence test means and standard deviations of the groups will be approximately equal. Here, again, it is possible arbitrarily to assign youngsters to the groups in a way to make the groups approximately equal, but then there is no assurance that other possible variables are similarly controlled, since randomization has been interfered with.

Now, let us assume that randomization has been "successful". Then theoretically there will be no differences between the groups in intelligence and all other variables. *But there will still be individual differences in intelligence—and other variables—within each group.* With two groups, for instance, Group 1 might have IQ's ranging from, say, 88 to 145, and Group 2 might have IQ's ranging from 90 to 142. This range of IQ's, in and of itself, shows, just as the presence of boys and girls within the groups shows, that there are individual differences in intelligence *within* the groups. If this be so, then how can we say that the within-groups variance can be an estimate of error, of chance variation?

The answer is that it is the best we can do under the design circumstances. If the design is of the simple one-way kind, there is no other measure of error obtainable. So we calculate the within-groups variance and treat it as though it were a "true" measure of error variance. It should be clear that the within-groups variance will be larger than the "true" error variance, since it contains variance due to individual differences as well as error variance. Therefore, an F ratio may not be significant when in fact there is "really" a difference between the groups. Obviously if the F ratio is significant, there is not so much to worry about, since the between-groups variance is sufficiently large to overcome the spuriously high estimate of error variance.

To summarize what has been said, let us rewrite an earlier theoretical equation. The earlier equation was

$$V_t = V_b + V_w \tag{14.1}$$

Since the within-groups variance contains more variance than error variance, the variance due to individual differences, in fact, we can write

$$V_w = V_i + V_e \tag{14.2}$$

where V_i = variance due to individual differences and V_e = "true" error variance. If this be so, then we can substitute the right-hand side of Eq. 14.2 for the V_w in Eq. 14.1:

$$V_t = V_b + V_i + V_e \tag{14.3}$$

In other words, Eq. 14.3 is a shorthand way to say what we have been saying above.

The practical research significance of Eq. 14.3 is considerable. If we can find a way to control or measure V_i, to separate it from V_w, then it follows that a more accurate measure of the "true" error variance is possible. Put differently, our ignorance of the variable situation is decreased because we identify and isolate more systematic variance. A portion of the variance that was attributed to error is identified. Consequently the within-groups variance is reduced.

Many of the principles and much of the practice of research design is occupied with this problem, which is essentially a problem of control—the control of variance. When it was said earlier that factorial analysis of variance was more precise than simple one-way analysis of variance, we meant that, by setting up levels of an independent variable, say sex or social class, we decrease the estimate of error, the within-groups variance, and thus get closer to the "true" error variance. Instead of writing Eq. 14.3, let us now write a more specific equation, substituting for V_i, the variance of individual differences, V_{sc}, the variance for social class—and reintroducing V_w:

$$V_t = V_b + V_{sc} + V_w \tag{14.4}$$

Compare this equation to Eq. 14.1. More of the total variance, other than the between-groups variance, has been identified and labeled. This variance, V_{sc} has in effect been taken out of the V_w of Eq. 14.1.

Some Research Examples

A large number of interesting uses of factorial analysis of variance have been reported in recent years in the psychological and educational literature. Indeed, one is confronted with an embarrassment of riches, especially compared to the paucity of one-way analysis. A number of examples of different kinds have been selected to illustrate further the usefulness and strength of the method. We include more examples than usual because of the complexity of factorial analysis, its frequency of use, and its manifest importance.

Attitudes toward the Negro

Young, Benson, and Holtzman, in a nonexperimental and important study of students attitudes toward the Negro in a southern university, used a 2 × 2 factorial analysis to study the possible interaction of two variables, sex and year.[13] This study is also distinctive because the sampling procedure was random. Two surveys of student attitudes, measured with a 26-item attitude scale (embedded in a larger scale), were made in 1955 and 1958. No appreciable change from 1955 to 1958 was found in the student body as a whole, but a factorial analysis of variance using the variables year of survey, sex, and fraternity (or sorority) membership yielded interesting results. The authors state that they were specifically looking for significant interactions, despite the overall lack of a significant difference between the 1955 and 1958 means. They found fraternity affiliation to be related

[13] R. Young, W. Benson, and W. Holtzman, "Changes in Attitudes toward the Negro in a Southern University," *Journal of Abnormal and Social Psychology*, LX (1960), 131–133.

to attitudes: the F ratio for fraternity membership and no fraternity membership was significant at the .05 level. Unaffiliated students were more tolerant of the Negro. The only other significant F ratio (.05 level) was that for the interaction between sex and year. The data (means) reported are given in Table 14.11.

TABLE **14.11** MEANS OF CROSS-CLASSIFICATION OF SEX AND YEAR: YOUNG, BROWN, AND HOLTZMAN STUDY

	Year of Survey	
	1955	1958
Men	44.8	47.9
Women	45.1	42.3

This is a good example of interaction. Study of the table shows that both male and female students changed from 1955 to 1958, but that they changed in opposite directions. In 1958 the men were *less* tolerant than they had been in 1955, whereas the women were *more* tolerant in 1958 than they had been in 1955.

Comments on Test Papers

In a study already mentioned, Page analyzed his data in several ways.[14] One of these analyses, a factorial analysis of variance, should be of interest to educators. Recall that Page used three types of reinforcements on tests: no comment, free comment, and specified comment. Objective tests were returned to students with (1) no comment at all on them; (2) free comment, that is, the teachers made any comments they thought desirable; (3) specified comment(s), which were short remarks provided by Page to be used by the teachers. The criterion measures were scores on the next test given. Page found significant differences between the three treatments. But he also explored the interaction between the types of comment and the pupils' letter grades (A, B, and so forth). The interaction was significant and surprising. He found that the F (failing) pupils' performance mostly caused the interaction. Contrary to the expectation of common sense, the failing students profited most from the free comments on the tests. The mean score (rank) of the free comment students was considerably higher than that of any of the other mean scores. Had Page not used factorial analysis and the idea behind the method, he would not have made this rather startling discovery.

The Effects of Teacher Expectancy

Ever since the publication of Rosenthal and Jacobson's study of the alleged effects on children's IQ's of teachers "knowing" the children's presumed intelligence, controversy has been intense and several studies have been done to test the

[14]E. Page, "Teacher Comments and Student Performance: A Seventy-Four Classroom Experiment in School Motivation," *Journal of Educational Psychology*, XLIX (1958), 173–181.

experimental ideas in a manner believed to be more satisfactory than Rosenthal and Jacobson's.[15] Let's look briefly at two recent studies.[16]

Fleming and Antonnen tested large numbers of second-grade students with the Kuhlman-Anderson Intelligence Test. Although there were four independent variables in a $4 \times 2 \times 3 \times 2$ design, we are concerned only with the treatments variable, which consisted of four different kinds of test information given to the teachers: IQ's, no IQ information, the percentiles of the children on another intelligence test, and, most important, IQ's inflated by 16 points. At the end of the term, the Kuhlman-Anderson Test was administered again. Although the mean differences for the other three variables of the factorial design were statistically significant, the treatment differences were not significant, casting doubt on the Rosenthal hypothesis. Note that the authors were able to test a large number of hypotheses, as well as their central hypothesis.

José and Cody studied the effects of three independent variables: treatments, sex of pupils, and grade level. Four pupils in each class, the experimental-group pupils, were randomly selected to be "academic bloomers," and the teachers were told that these pupils had scored high on a test of "academic blooming." They were told nothing about the control-group children. At the end of 16 weeks, the children's intelligence and reading and arithmetic achievement were tested. There were, then, three dependent variables that could have been influenced by the expectancies of the teachers. The three factorial analyses of variance ($2 \times 2 \times 2$) showed that only the mean differences in grade level were statistically significant. None of the treatment differences ("academic bloomer" versus control children) was significant.

The use of the grade-level variable acts as a salutary control: one expects the differences between the grade levels to be statistically significant. Had they not been, one would suspect some sort of deficiency in the research. These two studies show the use of experimentation in regular school settings and the neat applicability of factorial design and analysis to the problem investigated. Studies like these have cast severe doubt on the Rosenthal hypothesis.[17]

Pseudoprogressivism

Pedhazur used factorial analysis of variance to help study the relation between progressivism in educational attitudes, or rather, "pseudoprogressivism," and assessment of teacher behavior.[18] He focused on the teacher who professes to be

[15]R. Rosenthal and L. Jacobson, *Pygmalion in the Classroom.* New York: Holt, Rinehart and Winston, 1968. For published criticisms, see: R. Snow, "Unfinished Pygmalion," (review) *Contemporary Psychology,* XIV (1969), 197–199; R. Thorndike, "Review of R. Rosenthal and L. Jacobson, *Pygmalion in the Classroom.*" *American Educational Research Journal,* V (1968), 708–711. Both reviews are devastating.

[16]E. Fleming and R. Antonnen, "Teacher Expectancy or My Fair Lady," *American Educational Research Journal,* VIII (1971), 241–252; J. José and J. Cody, "Teacher-Pupil Interaction as It Relates to Attempted Changes in Teacher Expectancy of Academic Ability and Achievement," *American Educational Research Journal,* VIII (1971), 39–49.

[17]For a review of studies, see T. Barber and M. Silver, "Fact, Fiction, and the Experimenter Bias Effect," *Psychological Bulletin Monograph,* LXX (1970), 1–29.

[18]E. Pedhazur, "Pseudoprogressivism and Assessment of Teacher Behavior," *Educational and Psychological Measurement,* XXIX (1969), 377–386.

progressive but who, in word and in deed, betrays attitudes antithetical to the principles of progressivism. He categorized teachers and students of education as "pseudo" or "genuine" by their responses to an educational attitudes scale and a scale to measure dogmatism (D Scale). This was the principal independent variable. The second independent variable was teaching experience, which was measured simply by whether *S*s were teachers or students of education. The dependent variable, assessment of teacher behavior, was measured by an instrument called Teachers at Work (TAW), which consisted of classroom episodes that apparently were characterized by democracy and progressive ideas but in fact were the antithesis of both.

Pedhazur's results, obtained from 159 teachers and 174 students of education, supported his notion that pseudoprogressive teachers and students would endorse the TAW statements and "genuine" progressives would not. The means of the former and the latter, respectively, on the TAW were 17.08 and 13.67 for teachers and 17.99 and 15.10 for students of education. Both were statistically significant at the .01 level. In words, pseudoprogressives endorse descriptions of phoney "democratic" teacher behaviors more than do genuine progressives.

Learning by Discovery

One of the oldest debates in education—it probably springs from basic philosophical differences—is that on learning by discovery. Should we let students "discover" the solutions to problems or should we "direct" them to solutions? Wittrock taught 292 college students by one of four methods to decipher transposition codes.[19] The four methods amounted to a 2×2 factorial design, though a third independent variable (not considered here) was used. Instead of a detailed description of the methods, the paradigm of the design with one set of results is given in Table 14.12.

TABLE **14.12** MEAN LEARNING SCORES, RULE AND ANSWER TREATMENTS, WITTROCK STUDY

	Rule Given	Rule Not Given	
Answer Given	9.52	7.59	8.56[a]
Answer Not Given	9.73	2.76	6.25
	9.63	5.18	

[a]Marginal means calculated from table means. *F* ratios: Rule = 490.74 (.001); Answer = 131.77 (.001); Interaction: Rule by Answer = 157.47 (.001).

The *S*s designated Rule were given rules for the solutions of problems. The *S*s designated Answer were given answers to some problems. Then there were

[19]M. Wittrock, "Verbal Stimuli in Concept Formation: Learning by Discovery," *Journal of Educational Psychology*, LIV (1963), 183–190. Only one of several sets of results reported by Wittrock is given above.

*S*s who were not given either rules or answers. The two main effects and the interaction were statistically significant, indicating that learning (of this kind) is enhanced by giving rules and by giving answers. When rules were not given, giving answers enhanced learning. When rules were given, giving the answer did not enhance learning. (Study the table carefully.)

A Further Word on Interaction

To now, we have said nothing about kinds of interaction of independent variables in their joint influence on a dependent variable. To leap to the core of the matter of interactions, let us lay out several sets of means to show the main possibilities. There are, of course, many possibilities, especially when one includes higher-order interactions. The six examples in Table 14.13 indicate the main possibilities with two independent variables. The first three setups show the three possibilities of significant main effects. They are so obvious that they need not be discussed. (There is, naturally, another possibility: neither *A* nor *B* is significant.)

TABLE **14.13** VARIOUS SETS OF MEANS SHOWING DIFFERENT KINDS OF MAIN EFFECTS AND INTERACTION

	A_1	A_2	
B_1	30	20	25
B_2	30	20	25
	30	20	

(a) *A* significant; *B* not significant; Interaction not significant

	A_1	A_2	
B_1	30	30	30
B_2	20	20	20
	25	25	

(b) *A* not significant; *B* significant; Interaction not significant

	A_1	A_2	
B_1	30	20	25
B_2	40	30	35
	35	25	

(c) *A* significant; *B* significant; Interaction not significant

	A_1	A_2	
B_1	30	20	25
B_2	20	30	25
	25	25	

(d) Interaction significant (symmetrical)

	A_1	A_2	
B_1	30	20	25
B_2	20	20	20
	25	20	

(e) Interaction significant (not symmetrical)

	A_1	A_2	
B_1	20	20	20
B_2	30	20	25
	25	20	

(f) Interaction significant (not symmetrical)

When there is a significant interaction, on the other hand, the situation is not so obvious. The setups (*d*), (*e*), and (*f*) show three common possibilities. In (*d*), what might be called a "classical" pattern is shown. The means crisscross, as indicated by the arrows in the table. Here the interpretation is symmetrical: opposite at the two levels of *B*. It can be said, for example, that *A* is effective in one direction at B_1, but is effective in the other direction at B_2. Or, $A_1 > A_2$ at B_1, but $A_1 < A_2$ at B_2. In this chapter, the simple fictitious example of Table 14.3 was of this kind. (See also Table 14.4.) The fictitious example of Table 14.7, where interaction was deliberately induced by adding and subtracting constants, is another symmetric case. An example from actual research was given in Table 14.11. An almost classic example occurs in the Berkowitz study, reported in Table 14.10. Interactions in which the means cross over like these are called *disordinal* interactions.

The setups in (*e*) and (*f*), however, are different. Here one independent variable is effective at one level only of the other independent variable. In (*e*), $A_1 > A_2$ at B_1, but $A_1 = A_2$ at B_2. In (*f*), $A_1 = A_2$ at B_1, but $A_1 > A_2$ at B_2. The interpretation changes accordingly. In the case of (*e*), we would say that A is effective at B_1 level, but makes no difference at B_2 level. The case of (*f*) would take a similar interpretation. Such interactions are called *ordinal* interactions.

A simple way to study the interaction with a 2×2 setup (it is more complex with more complex models) is to subtract one entry from another in each row, as we did earlier. If this be done for (*a*), we get, for rows B_1 and B_2, 10 and 10. For (*b*), we get 0 and 0, and for (*c*), 10 and 10 again. When these two differences are equal, as in these cases, there is no interaction. But now try it with (*d*), (*e*), and (*f*). We get 10 and -10 for (*d*), 10 and 0 for (*e*), and 0 and 10 for (*f*). When these differences are significantly unequal, interaction is present. The student can interpret these differences as an exercise.

It is also possible—and often very profitable—to graph interactions. Set up one independent variable by placing the experimental groups (A_1, A_2, and so on) at equal intervals on the horizontal axis and appropriate values of the dependent variable on the vertical axis. Then plot, against the horizontal axis group positions ($A_1 A_2$, and so on), the mean values in the table at the levels of the other independent variable (B_1, B_2, and so on). This method can quite easily be used with 2×3, 3×3, and other such designs. The plots of (*a*), (*c*), (*d*), and (*e*) are given in Fig. 14.4.

We can discuss these graphs briefly since both graphs and graphing relations have been discussed before.[22] In effect, we ask first if there is a relation between the main effects (independent variables) and the measures of the dependent variables. Each of these relations is plotted as in the preceding chapter, except that the relation between one independent variable and the dependent variable is plotted at both levels of the other independent variables; for instance, A is plotted against the dependent variable (vertical axis) at B_1 and B_2. The slope of the lines roughly indicates the extent of the relation. In each case, we have chosen to plot the relations using A_1 and A_2 on the horizontal axis. If the plotted line is horizontal, obviously there is no relation. There is no relation between A and the dependent variable at level B_2 in (*e*) of Fig. 14.4, but there is a relation at level B_1. In (*a*), there is a relation between A and the dependent variable at both levels, B_1 and B_2. The same is true of (*c*). The nearer the line comes to being diagonal, the higher the relation. If the two lines make approximately the same angle in the same direction (that is, they are parallel), as in (*a*) and (*c*), the relation is approximately the same

[20]Extended discussions of interactions can be found in: Edwards, *op. cit.*, pp. 210–215, 220–225, 235–244; W. Hays, *Statistics*. New York: Holt, Rinehart and Winston, 1963, pp. 386–392. More thorough discussion—but without graphs—can be found in: E. Lindquist, *op. cit.*, pp. 20–23, 118–120, 123–127. A valuable and clear discussion of ordinal and disordinal interactions and the virtue of graphing significant interactions is given in: A. Lubin, "The Interpretation of Significant Interaction" *Educational and Psychological Measurement*, XXI (1961), 807–817.

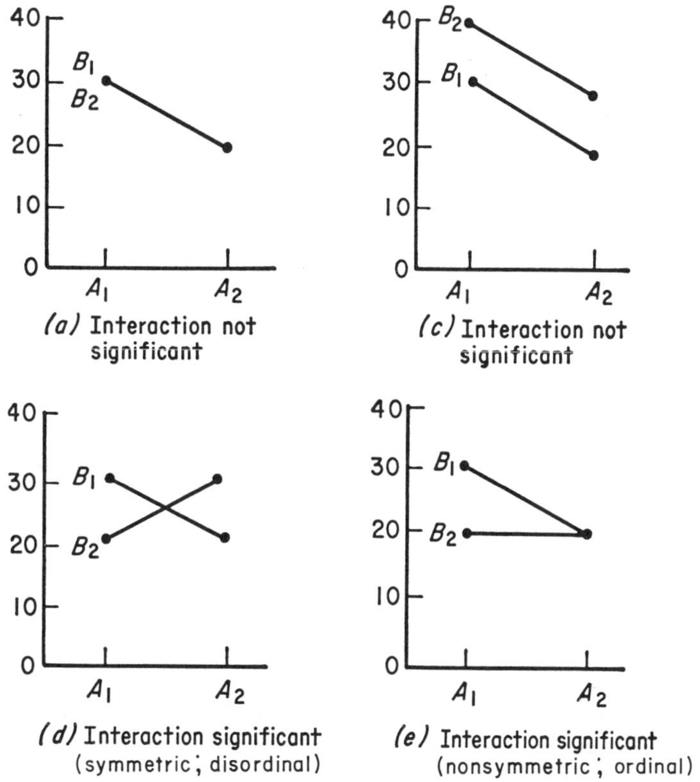

FIG. 14.4

magnitude at each level. To the extent that the lines make different angles with the horizontal axis (are not parallel), to this extent there is interaction present.

If the graphs of Fig. 14.4 were plotted from actual research data, we could interpret them as follows. Call the measures of the dependent variable (on the vertical axis) Y. In (*a*), A is related to Y *regardless of* B. It makes no difference what B is; A_1 and A_2 differ significantly. The interpretation of (*c*) is similar: A is related to Y at both levels of B. There is no interaction in either (*a*) or (*c*). In (*d*) and (*e*), however, the case is very different. The graph of (*d*) shows interaction. A is related to Y, but the kind of relation depends on B. Under the B_1 condition, A_1 is greater than A_2. But under the B_2 condition A_2 is greater than A_1. The graph of (*e*) says that A is related to Y at level B_1 but not at level B_2, or A_1 is greater than A_2 at B_1 but at B_2 they are equal. (Note that it is possible to plot B on the horizontal axis. The interpretations would differ accordingly.)

Notes of Caution

As Lindquist has pointed out, interaction is not always a result of the "true" interaction of experimental treatments.[23] There are, rather, three possible causes

[21]Lindquist, *op. cit.*, p. 124.

of a significant interaction. One is "true" interaction, the variance contributed by the interaction that "really" exists between two variables in their mutual effect on a third variable. Another is error. A significant interaction *can* happen by chance, just as the means of experimental groups can differ significantly by chance. A third possible cause of interaction is some extraneous, unwanted, uncontrolled effect operating at one level of an experiment but not at another. Such a cause of interaction is particularly to be watched for in nonexperimental uses of the analysis of variance, that is, in the analysis of variance of data gathered after independent variables have already operated. Suppose, for example, that the levels in an experiment on methods was schools. Extraneous factors in such a case can cause a significant interaction. Assume that the principal of one school, although he had consented to having the experiment run in his school, was negative in his attitude toward the research. This attitude could easily be conveyed to teachers and pupils, thus contaminating the experimental treatment, methods. In short, significant interactions must be handled with the same care as any other research results. They are interesting, even dramatic, as we have seen. Thus they can perhaps cause us momentarily to lose our customary caution.

Two related difficulties of factorial analysis are unequal *n*'s in the cells of a design and the experimental and nonexperimental use of the method. If the *n*'s in the cells of a factorial design are not equal (and are disproportionate, i.e., not in proportion from row to row or column to column), the orthogonality or independence of the independent variables is impaired. While adjustments can be made, they are a bit awkward and not too satisfactory. When doing experiments, the problem is not severe because subjects can be assigned to the cells at random—except, of course, for attribute variables—and the *n*'s kept equal or nearly equal. But in the nonexperimental use of factorial analysis, the *n*'s in the cells get pretty much beyond the control of the researcher. Indeed, even in experiments, when more than one categorical variable is included (like race and sex), *n*'s almost necessarily become unequal.

To understand this, take a simple example. Suppose we split a group in two by sex and have, say, 50 males and 50 females. A second variable is political preference and we want to come up with two equal groups of Republicans and Democrats. But suppose that sex is correlated with political preference. Then there may be, for example, more males who are Republican compared to females who are Republican, creating a disproportion. This is shown in Table 14.14. Now add another independent variable and the difficulties magnify greatly.

What can we do, then, in nonexperimental research? Can't we use factorial analysis of variance? The answer is complex and is evidently not clearly understood. Factorial analysis of variance paradigms can and should be used because they guide and clarify research. There are devices for surmounting the unequal *n* difficulty. One can make adjustments of the data, or one can equalize the groups by elimination of subjects at random. These are unwieldy devices, however. The best analytic solution seems to be to use multiple regression analysis. While the problems do not all disappear, many of them cease to be problems in the multiple regression framework. In general, factorial analysis of variance is best suited to experimental research in which the subjects can be randomly assigned to cells, the

TABLE **14.14** EXAMPLE OF DISPROPORTION AND UNEQUAL CELL n'S ARISING FROM NONEXPERIMENTAL VARIABLES

	Republican	Democrat	
Males	30	20	50
Females	20	30	50
	50	50	

[a]The cell entries are frequencies.

n's thus kept equal and the assumptions behind the method more or less satisfied. Nonexperimental research or experimental research that uses a number of nonexperimental (attribute) variables is better served with multiple regression analysis. With equal n's and experimental variables, multiple regression analysis *yields exactly the same sums of squares, mean squares, and F ratios, including interaction F ratios as the standard factorial analysis.* Nonexperimental variables, which are a grave problem for factorial analysis, are routine in multiple regression analysis. We return to all this in Chapter 36.

Study Suggestions

1. Here are some varied and interesting psychological or educational studies that have used factorial analysis of variance in one way or another. Read and study two of them and ask yourself: Was factorial analysis the appropriate analysis? That is, might the researchers have used, say, a simpler form of analysis?

   Carlsmith, J., and Gross, A. "Some Effects of Guilt on Compliance." *Journal of Personality and Social Psychology*, XI (1969), 232–239.

   Coop, R., and Brown, L. "Effects of Cognitive Style and Teaching Method on Categories of Achievement." *Journal of Educational Psychology*, LXI (1970), 400–405.

   Scandura, J. "Learning Verbal and Symbolic Statements of Mathematical Rules." *Journal of Educational Psychology*, LVIII (1967), 356–364.

   Staats, A., and Staats, C. "Attitudes Established by Classical Conditioning." *Journal of Abnormal and Social Psychology*, LVII (1958), 37–40.

   Tallmadge, G., and Shearer, J. "Interactive Relationships Among Learner Characteristics, Types of Learning, Instructional Methods, and Subject Matter Variables." *Journal of Educational Psychology*, LXII (1971), 31–38.

2. Suppose a research worker has done an experiment in which he tested two methods of instruction, A_1 and A_2. A second independent variable was social class: middle class and working class, B_1 and B_2. The dependent variable was achievement. The results are summarized as follows (the tabled entries are means):

		Methods A_1	A_2	
Social	B_1	78	70	74
Class	B_2	72	60	66
		75	65	($M_t = 70$)

The A effect was significant at the .01 level. So was the B effect. The interaction was not significant.

(a) Interpret the results specifically and discuss the differences between the means and the relations they presumably reflect.

(b) Draw a graph of the results, and interpret the graph.

3. Use Study Suggestion 2 again, but now assume that the tabled entries are a bit different:

	A_1	A_2	
B_1	70	78	74
B_2	72	60	66
	71	69	$(M_t = 70)$

The only change is that the A_1B_1 and A_2B_1 means have been interchanged. (Of course, the marginal means at the bottom of the table, too, are changed.) A factorial analysis of variance shows that this time the A means are not significantly different, and the B means, as before, are significantly different. The interaction is also significant.

(a) Interpret the results. Compare the interpretation to that of problem 2.

(b) Draw a graph, and then interpret it. Compare this graph to the one drawn in problem 2.

(c) What value does factorial analysis of variance have in research situations like this? Could you reach the same conclusions by two separate experiments? For example, suppose the investigator conducted two experiments, one with middle-class subjects and another with working-class subjects. What might the results have been like? Why?

4. We are interested in testing the relative efficacies of different methods of teaching foreign languages (or any other subject). We believe that foreign language aptitude is a possibly influential variable. How might an experiment be set up to test the efficacies of the methods? Now add a third variable, sex, and lay out the paradigms of both researches. Discuss the logic of each design from the point of view of statistics. What statistical tests of significance would you use? What part do they play in interpreting the results?

5. Write two problems and the hypotheses to go with them, using any three (or four) variables you wish. Scan the problems and hypotheses in Study Suggestions 2 and 3, Chapter 2, and the variables given in Chapter 3. Or use any of the variables of this chapter. Write at least one hypothesis that is an interaction hypothesis.

6. From the random numbers of Appendix D draw 40 numbers, 0 through 9, in groups of 10. Consider the four groups as $A_1B_1, A_2B_1, A_1B_2, A_2B_2$.

(a) Do a factorial analysis of variance as outlined in the chapter. What should the A, B and $A \times B$ (interaction) F ratios be like?

(b) Add 3 to each of the scores in the group with the highest mean. Which F ratio or ratios should be affected? Why? Do the factorial analysis of variance. Are your expectations fulfilled?

(c) Take one of the problem and hypothesis sets you wrote in 5, above. Assume that the results of (b) apply to the problem and the hypothesis. Interpret the "results."

CHAPTER 15

Analysis of Variance: Correlated Groups

Suppose an investigator wants to test the effects of marijuana and alcohol on driving.[1] He can, of course, set up a one-way or factorial analysis design, assign subjects at random to experimental groups, and conduct the experiment. Instead, he decides to use subjects as their own controls. That is, each subject undergoes three experimental treatments or conditions: marijuana (A_1), alcohol (A_2), and control (A_3), and after each one he operates a driving simulator. The number of driving errors is the dependent variable measure. A paradigm of the design of the experiment with fictitious scores is given in Table 15.1. Note that the sums of both

TABLE **15.1** DESIGN OF MARIJUANA, ALCOHOL, AND SIMULATOR DRIVING EXPERIMENT: REPEATED MEASURES (FICTITIOUS SCORES)

Subjects	Marijuana (A_1)	Alcohol (A_2)	Control (A_3)	Sums, Rows
1	18	27	16	61
2	24	29	21	74
.	.	.	.	.
.	.	.	.	.
.	.	.	.	.
36	21	25	20	66
Sums	710	820	680	$\Sigma X_t = 2210$

[1]The idea and some of the data of this example came from an actual research study: A. Crancer et al., "Comparison of the Effects of Marihuana and Alcohol on Simulated Driving Performance," *Science*, CLXIV (1969), 851–854.

columns *and* rows are given in the table. Note, too, that the design looks like that of one-way analysis of variance, with one exception: the sums of the rows, which are the sums of each subject's scores across the three treatments, are included.

This is a radically different situation from the earlier models in which subjects were assigned at random to experimental groups. Here all subjects undergo all treatments. Therefore, each subject is his own control, so to speak. More generally, instead of independence we now have dependence or correlation between groups. What does correlation between groups mean? It is not easy to answer with a simple statement.

Definition of the Problem

In one-way and factorial analysis of variance, the independence of groups, subjects, and observations is a sine qua non of the designs. In both approaches subjects are assigned to experimental groups at random. There is no question of correlation between groups—by definition. Except for variables specifically put into the design—like adding sex to treatments—variance due to individual differences is randomly distributed among the experimental groups, and the groups are thus "equalized." Variance due to individual differences is known to be substantial. If it can be isolated and extracted from the total variance, then there should be a substantial increase in precision, because this source of variation in the scores can be subtracted from the total variance. Thus a smaller error variance to use to evaluate the effects of the treatments is created.

In Chapter 14, we subtracted the sum of squares due to social class in a factorial design (see Eqs. 14.1 through 14.4), thus reducing the within-groups variance, the error term. The reasoning in this chapter is the same: isolate and extract variance in the dependent variable due to individual differences. To make this abstract discussion concrete, we use an easy example in which the idea of matching is introduced. Using the same subjects in the different experimental groups and matching subjects on one, two, or more variables involves the same basic idea of correlation between groups.[2]

A Fictitious Example

A principal of a school and the members of his staff decided to introduce a program of education in intergroup relations as an addition to the school's curriculum. One of the problems that arose was in the use of motion pictures. Films were shown in the initial phases of the program, but the results were not too encouraging. The staff hypothesized that the failure of the films to have impact might have resulted from their not making any particular effort to bring out the possible applications of the film to intergroup relations. They decided to test the hypothesis

[2]In the example that follows, matching is used in order to show the applicability of correlated-groups analysis to a common research situation, because matching is probably a little easier to understand, and because certain points about correlation and its effect can be made better. The student should bear in mind, however, that the basic ideas are the same in both kinds of design and analysis. This point will be clarified later. Another point to bear in mind is that when we say correlation between groups, we mean positive correlation.

that seeing the films and then discussing them would improve the viewers' attitudes toward minority group members more than would just seeing the films.

For a preliminary study the staff randomly selected a group of students from the total student body and paired the students on intelligence and socioeconomic background until ten pairs were obtained, each pair being approximately equal in intelligence and socioeconomic background. The reasoning behind the experiment was that intelligence and socioeconomic background are related to attitudes toward minority groups. Each member of each pair was randomly assigned to either an experimental or a control group, and then both groups were shown a new film on intergroup relations. The A_1 (experimental) group had a discussion session after the picture was shown; the A_2 (control) group had no such discussion after the film. Both groups were tested with a scale designed to measure attitudes toward minority groups. The attitude scores and the necessary calculations for an analysis of variance procedure to be described are given in Table 15.2.

TABLE **15.2** ATTITUDE SCORES AND CALCULATIONS FOR ANALYSIS OF VARIANCE—FICTITIOUS EXAMPLE

	Groups					
Pairs	A_1 (Experimental)		A_2 (Control)		Σ	Σ^2
1	8	64	6	36	14	196
2	9	81	8	64	17	289
3	5	25	3	9	8	64
4	4	16	2	4	6	36
5	2	4	1	1	3	9
6	10	100	7	49	17	289
7	3	9	1	1	4	16
8	12	144	7	49	19	361
9	6	36	6	36	12	144
10	11	121	9	81	20	400
ΣX:	70		50		$\Sigma X_t = 120$	
$(\Sigma X)^2$:	4900		2500		$(\Sigma X_t)^2 = 14{,}400$	
M:	7		5		$\Sigma X_t^2 = 930$	
					$\Sigma(\Sigma)^2 = 1804$	

First we do a one-way analysis of variance as though the investigators had not matched the subjects. We disregard the matching procedure and analyze the scores as though all the subjects had been randomly assigned to the two groups without regard to intelligence and socioeconomic background. The necessary calculations are:

$$C = \frac{14{,}400}{20} = 720$$

$$\text{Total} = 930 - 720 = \mathit{210}$$

$$\begin{array}{c}\text{Between columns}\\(A_1, A_2)\end{array} = \left(\frac{4900}{10} + \frac{2500}{10}\right) - 720 = \mathit{20}$$

The final analysis of variance table of this analysis is given in Table 15.3. Since the F ratio of 1.89 is not significant, the two group means of 7 and 5 do not differ significantly. The interpretation of these data would lead the experimenters to believe that the film plus discussion had no effect. This conclusion would be erroneous. The difference in this case is really significant at the .01 level. Let us assume that this statement is true; if it *is* true, then there must be something wrong with the analysis.

TABLE **15.3** FINAL ANALYSIS OF VARIANCE TABLE, ONE-WAY ANALYSIS OF FICTITIOUS DATA OF TABLE 15.2

Source	*df*	*s.s.*	*m.s.*	F
Between Groups (A_1, A_2)	1	20.00	20.0	1.89 (n.s.)
Within Groups	18	190.00	10.56	
Total	19	210.00		

An Explanatory Digression

When subjects are matched on variables *significantly related to the dependent variable*, correlation is introduced into the statistical picture. In Chapter 14 we saw that it was often possible to identify and control more of the total variance of an experimental situation by setting up levels of one or more variables presumably related to the dependent variable. The setting up of two or three levels of social class, for example, makes it possible to identify the variance in the dependent-variable scores due to social class. Now, simply shift gears a bit. The matching of the present experiment has actually set up ten levels, one for each pair. The members of the first pair had IQ's of 130 and 132, say, the members of the second pair 124 and 125, and so on to the tenth pair, the members of which had IQ's of 89 and 92. Each pair (level) has a different mean. Now, if intelligence is substantially correlated positively with the dependent variable, then the dependent variable pairs of scores should reflect the matching on intelligence. That is, the dependent variable pairs of scores should also be more like each other than they are like other dependent-variable scores. So the matching on intelligence has "introduced" variance between pairs on the dependent variable, or *between-rows variance*.

Consider another hypothetical example to dramatize what happens when there is correlation between sets of scores. Suppose that an investigator has matched three groups of subjects on intelligence, and that intelligence was perfectly correlated with the dependent variable, achievement of some kind. This is highly unlikely, but let's go along with it to get the idea. The first trio of subjects had IQ's of 141, 142, and 140; the second trio 130, 126, and 128; and so on through the fifth trio of 82, 85, and 82. If we check the rank orders in columns of the three sets of scores, they are exactly the same: 141, 130, . . . , 82; 142, 126, . . . , 85; 140, 128, . . . , 82. Since we assume that $r = 1.00$ between intelligence and achievement, then the rank orders of the achievement scores must be the same in the three groups. The assumed achievement test scores are given on the left-hand side of Table 15.4. The rank orders of these fictitious scores, from high to low, are given in parentheses beside each achievement score. Note that the rank orders are the same in the three groups.

TABLE **15.4** CORRELATED AND UNCORRELATED SCORES, FICTITIOUS EXAMPLE

I. Correlated Groups				II. Uncorrelated Groups			
A_1	A_2	A_3	M	A_1	A_2	A_3	M
73 (1)	74 (1)	72 (1)	73	63 (2)	74 (1)	46 (5)	61.00
63 (2)	65 (2)	61 (2)	63	45 (5)	55 (3)	61 (2)	53.67
57 (3)	55 (3)	59 (3)	57	50 (4)	50 (4)	59 (3)	53.00
50 (4)	50 (4)	53 (4)	51	57 (3)	65 (2)	53 (4)	58.33
45 (5)	44 (5)	46 (5)	45	73 (1)	44 (5)	72 (1)	63.00
			$M_t = 57.80$				$M_t = 57.80$

Now suppose that the correlation between intelligence and achievement were approximately zero. In such a case, no prediction could be made of the rank orders of the achievement scores, or, to put it another way, the achievement scores would not be matched. To simulate such a condition of zero correlation, I broke up the rank orders of the scores on the left-hand side of Table 15.4 with the help of a table of random numbers. After drawing three sets of numbers 1 through 5, I rearranged the scores in columns according to the random numbers. (Before doing this, all the column rank orders were 1, 2, 3, 4, 5.) The first set of random numbers was 2, 5, 4, 3, 1. The second number of column A_1 was put first. I next took the fifth number of A_1 and put it second. This process was continued until the former first number became the fifth number. The same procedure was used with the other two groups of numbers, with, of course, different sets of random numbers. The final results are given on the right-hand side of Table 15.4. The means of the rows are also given, as are the ranks of the column scores (in parentheses).

First, study the ranks of the two sets of scores. In the left-hand portion of the table, labeled I, are the correlated scores. Since the ranks are the same in each column, the average correlation between columns is 1.00. The numbers of the set labeled II, which are essentially random, present quite a different picture. The 15 numbers of both sets are exactly the same. So are the numbers in each column (and their means). Only the row numbers—and, of course, the row means—are different. Look at the rank orders of II. No systematic relations can be found between them. The average correlation should be approximately zero, since the numbers were randomly shuffled. Actually it is .11.

Now study the variability of the row means. Note that the variability of the means of I is considerably greater than that of II. If the numbers are random, the expectation for the mean of any row is the general mean. The means of the rows of II hover rather closely around the general mean of 57.80. The range is $63-53=10$. But the means of the rows of I do not hover closely around 57.80; their variability is much greater, as indicated by a range of $73-45=28$. Calculating the variances of these two sets of means (called *between-rows variance*), we obtain 351.60 for I and 58.27 for II. The variance of I is six times greater than the variance of II. This large difference is a direct effect of the correlation that is present in the scores of I but not in II. It may be said that the between-rows variance is a direct index of individual differences. The reader should pause here and go over this example, especially the examples of Table 15.4, until the effect of correlation on variance is clear to him.

What is the effect of the estimate of the error variance of correlated scores? Clearly the variance due to the correlation is *systematic* variance, which must be removed from the total variance if a more accurate estimate of error variance is desired. Otherwise the error variance estimate will include the variance due to individual differences and the result will thus be too large. In the example of Table 15.4, we know that the shuffling procedure has concealed the systematic variance due to the correlation. By rearranging the scores the possibility of identifying this variance is removed. This variance is still in the scores of II, but it cannot be extracted. To show this, we calculate the variances of the error terms of I and II; that of I is 3.13; that of II, 149.79. By removing from the total variance the variance due to the correlation, it is possible to reduce the error term greatly, with the result that the error variance of I is 48 times smaller than the error variance of II. If there is substantial systematic variance in the sets of measures, then, and it is possible to isolate and identify this variance, it is clearly worthwhile to do so.

Actual research data will not be as dramatic as the above example. Correlations are almost never 1. But they are often greater than .50 or .60. *The higher the correlation, the larger the systematic variance that can be extracted from the total variance and the more the error term can be reduced.* This principle becomes very important not only in designing research, but also in measurement theory and practice. Sometimes it is possible to build correlation into the scores and then extract the variance due to the resulting correlated scores. For example, we can obtain a "pure" measure of individual differences by using the same subjects on different trials. Obviously a subject's own scores will be more alike than they will be like the scores of others.

Re-examination of Table 15.2 Data

We return to the fictitious research data of Table 15.2 on the effects of films on attitudes toward minority groups. Earlier we calculated a between-columns sum of squares and variance exactly as in one-way analysis of variance. We found that the difference between the means was not significant when this method was used. From the above discussion, we can surmise that if there is correlation between the two sets of scores, then the variance due to the correlation should be removed from the total variance and, of course, from the estimate of the error variance. If the correlation is substantial, this procedure should make quite a difference: the error term should get considerably smaller. The correlation between the sets of scores of A_1 and A_2 of Table 15.2 is .93. Since this is a high degree of correlation, the error term when properly calculated should be much lower that it was before.

The additional operation required is simple. Just add the scores in each row of

Table 15.2 and calculate the *between-rows* sum of squares and the variance. Square the sum of each row and divide the result by the number of scores in the row; for example, in the first row: $8+6=14$; $(14)^2/2=196/2=98$. Repeat this procedure for each row, add the quotients, and then subtract the correction term C. This yields the *between-rows* sum of squares. (Since the number of scores in each row is always 2, it is easier, especially with a desk calculator, to add all the squared sums and then divide by 2.)

$$\begin{matrix}\text{Between rows}\\ (1,2,\ldots,10)\end{matrix}=\left[\frac{(14)^2+(17)^2+\cdots+(20)^2}{2}\right]-720=902-720=\mathit{182}$$

This between-rows sum of squares is a measure of the variability due to individual differences, as indicated earlier.

We have extracted from the total sum of squares the between-columns and the between-rows sums of squares. Now, set up a familiar equation:

$$ss_t=ss_b+ss_w \tag{15.1}$$

This is the equation used in one-way analysis of variance. The analysis of Table 15.3 is an example. We must alter this equation to suit the present circumstances. The former between-groups sum of squares, ss_b, is relabeled ss_c, which means the sum of squares of the columns. The sum of squares of the rows, ss_r, is added, and ss_w must be relabeled since we now no longer have a within-groups variance. (Why?) We label it ss_{res}, meaning the sum of squares of the *residuals*. As the name indicates, the *residual* sum of squares means the sum of squares left over after the sums of squares of columns and rows have been extracted from the total sum of squares. The equation then becomes

$$ss_t=ss_c+ss_r+ss_{\text{res}} \tag{15.2}$$

Briefly, the total variance has been broken down into two identifiable or systematic variances and one error variance. And this error variance is a more accurate estimate of error or chance variation of the scores than that of Table 15.3.

Rather than substitute in the equation, we set up the correct final analysis of variance table (Table 15.5). The F ratio of the columns is now $20.00/.89=22.47$, which is significant at the .001 level. In Table 15.3 the F ratio was not significant.

TABLE **15.5** FINAL COMPLETE ANALYSIS OF VARIANCE TABLE: DATA OF TABLE 15.2

Source	*df*	*s.s.*	*m.s.*	*F*
Between Columns (A_1, A_2)	1	20.	20.00	22.47 (.001)
Between Rows (1, 2, · · · , 10)	9	182.	20.22	22.72 (.001)
Residual	9	8.	.89	
Total	19	210.		

This is quite a difference. Since the between-columns variance is exactly the same, the difference is due to the greatly decreased error term, now .89 when it was 10.56 before. By calculating the rows sum of squares and the variance, it has been possible to reduce the error term to about 1/12 of its former magnitude. In this situation, obviously, the former error variance of 10.56 was greatly over-inflated. Returning to the original problem, it is now possible to say that adding discussion after the motion picture seems to have had a significant effect on attitudes toward minority groups.

Further Considerations

Before we leave this example, three or four additional points need to be made. The first involves the error term and the within-groups and residual variances. When the variances of the columns and the rows are calculated, it is not possible to calculate a within-groups variance, since there is in effect only one score per cell. Also bear in mind that both error variances, as calculated, *are only estimates of the error variance*. In the one-way situation the only estimate possible is the within-groups variance. In the present situation a better estimate is possible, "better" in the sense that it contains less systematic variance. When it is possible to extract systematic variance we do so. It was possible to do so with the data of Table 15.2.

A second point is: Why not use the t test? The answer is simple: Do so if you wish. If there is only one degree of freedom, that is, two groups, then $t = \sqrt{F}$, or $F = t^2$. The t ratio of the data of Table 15.5 is simply: $\sqrt{22.47} = 4.74$. But if there is more than one degree of freedom, the t test must give way to the F test. Moreover, the analysis of variance yields more information. The analysis of Table 15.5 tells us that the difference between the mean attitude scores of the experimental and control groups is significantly different. The t test would have yielded the same information. But Table 15.5 also tells us, simply and clearly, that the matching was effective, or that the correlation between the dependent variable scores of the two groups is significant. Had the between-rows F ratio not been significant, we would know that the matching had not been successful—important information indeed. Finally, the calculations of the analysis of variance, once understood, are easily remembered, whereas the equations used for estimating the standard error of the differences between the means seem to confuse the beginning student. (The simple formula given earlier has to be altered because of the correlation.)

Three, post hoc tests of the significance of the differences between individual means can be made—of course with more than two groups. The Scheffé and other tests are applicable.[3]

Finally, and most important, the principles discussed above are applicable to a variety of research situations. Their application to matching is perhaps the least important, though maybe the easiest to understand. Whenever the same subjects and repeated measures are used, the principles apply. When different classes or different schools are used in educational research, the principles apply: vari-

[3]See B. Winer, *Statistical Principles in Experimental Design*. New York: McGraw-Hill, 1962, pp. 80 ff. and pp. 113 ff., and R. Kirk, *Experimental Design: Procedures for the Behavioral Sciences*. Belmont, Calif.: Brooks/Cole, 1968, chap. 3.

ance due to class and school differences can be extracted from the data. Indeed, the principles can be invoked for any research in which different experimental treatments are used in different units of a larger organization, institution, or even geographical area—provided these units differ in variables of significance to the research.

To see what is meant, imagine that the rows of the left side of Table 15.4 are different schools or classes in a school system, that the schools or classes differ significantly in achievement, as indicated by the row means, and that A_1, A_2, and A_3 are experimental treatments of an experiment done in each of the schools or classes. (See Study Suggestion 2.)

Two-way analysis of variance is useful in the solution of certain measurement problems, particularly in psychology and education, as we will see later in Part 8. Individual differences are a constant source of variance that needs to be identified and analyzed. A good example is its use in the study of raters and ratings. One can separate the variance of raters from the variance of the objects being rated. The reliability of measuring instruments can be studied because the variance of the items can be separated from the variance of the persons responding to the items. We return again and again to these important points and the principles behind them.

Extracting Variances by Subtraction

To make sure that the reader understands the points being made, previous examples are repeated here. In Table 15.6, two sets of numbers, labeled I and II, are given. The numbers in these sets are exactly the same; only their arrangements differ. In I, there is no correlation between the two columns of numbers; the coefficient of correlation is exactly zero. This is analogous to the assignment of subjects to the two groups at random. One-way analysis of variance is applicable. In II, on the other hand, the A_2 numbers have been rearranged so that there is correlation between the A_1 and A_2 numbers. (Check the rank orders.) In fact, $r = .90$. One-way analysis of variance is not applicable here. If it is used with the numbers of II, the result would be exactly the same as it would be with the numbers of I, but then we would be disregarding the variance due to the correlation.

The calculations in Table 15.6 yield all the sums of squares except the residual sums of squares, which are obtained by subtraction. Since the calculations are so straightforward, we proceed directly to the final analysis of variance tables which are given in Table 15.7. The sums of squares for totals, columns, and rows are entered as indicated, with the appropriate degrees of freedom. The between-rows degrees of freedom are the number of rows minus one $(5-1=4)$. The residual degrees of freedom, like the interaction degrees of freedom in factorial analysis of variance, are obtained by multiplying the between-columns and between-rows degrees of freedom: $1\times4=4$. Or simply subtract the between-columns and between-rows degrees of freedom from the total degrees of freedom: $9-1-4=4$. The residual sums of squares, similarly, are obtained by subtracting the between-columns and between-rows sums of squares from the total sums of squares. For I, $22.5-2.5-10.0=10$; for II, $22.5-2.5-19.0=1$.

TABLE **15.6** ANALYSES OF VARIANCE OF RANDOMIZED AND CORRELATED FICTITIOUS DATA

	I $r = .00$				II $r = .90$			
	A_1	A_2	Σ	Σ^2	A_1	A_2	Σ	Σ^2
	1	5	6	36	1	2	3	9
	2	2	4	16	2	4	6	36
	3	4	7	49	3	3	6	36
	4	6	10	100	4	5	9	81
	5	3	8	64	5	6	11	121
ΣX:	15	20	$\Sigma X_t = 35$		15	20	$\Sigma X_t = 35$	
$(\Sigma X)^2$:	225	400	$(\Sigma X_t)^2 = 1225$				$(\Sigma X_t)^2 = 1225$	
M:	3	4	$\Sigma X_t^2 = 145$				$\Sigma X_t^2 = 145$	
			$\Sigma(\Sigma)^2 = 265$				$\Sigma(\Sigma)^2 = 283$	

I:

$$C = \frac{1225}{10} = 122.50$$

$$\text{Total} = 145 - 122.50 = \mathit{22.50}$$

$$\text{Between } C = \frac{225 + 400}{5} - 122.50 = \mathit{2.50}$$

$$\text{Between } R = \frac{6^2 + 4^2 + \cdots + 8^2}{2} - 122.50 = 132.50 - 122.50 = \mathit{10}$$

II:

$$C = \frac{1225}{10} = 122.50$$

$$\text{Total} = 145 - 122.50 = \mathit{22.50}$$

$$\text{Between } C = \frac{225 + 400}{5} - 122.50 = \mathit{2.50}$$

$$\text{Between } R = \frac{3^2 + 6^2 + \cdots + 9^2}{2} - 122.50 = 141.50 - 122.50 = \mathit{19}$$

These analyses need little elaboration. Note particularly that where there is correlation, the between-columns F ratio is significant, but where the correlation is zero it is not significant. Note, too, the error terms. For I ($r = .00$), it is 2.5. For II ($r = .90$), it is .25, which is *ten* times smaller.

TABLE **15.7** FINAL ANALYSIS OF VARIANCE TABLES

		I ($r = .00$)			II ($r = .90$)		
Source	*df*	*s.s.*	*m.s.*	*F*	*s.s.*	*m.s.*	*F*
Between C	1	2.5	2.5	1. (*n.s.*)	2.5	2.50	10. (.05)
Between R	4	10.0	2.5		19.0	4.75	
Residual $C \times R$	4	10.0	2.5		1.0	.25	
Total	9	22.5			22.5		

Removal of Systematic Sources of Variance

We now use the subtractive procedure of Chapter 6 to remove the two systematic sources of variance in the two sets of scores. First, remove the between-columns variance by correcting each mean so that it equals the general mean of 3.5. Then correct each score in each column similarly (as done for I and II in Table 15.8).

TABLE **15.8** REMOVAL OF BETWEEN-COLUMNS VARIANCE BY EQUALIZING COLUMN MEANS AND SCORES

	I ($r = .00$)			II ($r = .90$)		
Correction	.5	−.5		.5	−.5	
	A_1	A_2	M	A_1	A_2	M
	1.5	4.5	3.0	1.5	1.5	1.5
	2.5	1.5	2.0	2.5	3.5	3.0
	3.5	3.5	3.5	3.5	2.5	3.0
	4.5	5.5	5.0	4.5	4.5	4.5
	5.5	2.5	4.0	5.5	5.5	5.5
M:	3.5	3.5	$M_t = 3.5$	3.5	3.5	$M_t = 3.5$

If we now calculate the total sums of squares of I and II, in both cases we obtain 20. Compare this result to the former figure of 22.5. The correction procedure has reduced the total sums of squares by 2.5. These are of course the sums of squares between columns. Note, again, that the correction procedure has had no effect whatever on the variance within each of the four groups of scores. Nor has it had any effect on the means of the rows.

Now remove the rows variance by letting each row mean equal 3.5, the general mean, and by correcting the row scores accordingly. This has been done in Table 15.9, which should be carefully studied. Note that the variability of both sets of scores has been reduced, but that the variability of the correlated set (II) has been sharply reduced. In fact, the scores of II have a range of only $4 - 3 = 1$, whereas the range of the I scores is $5 - 2 = 3$. The matching of the scores in II and its concomitant correlation enables us, via the corrective procedure, to reduce the error term sharply by "correcting out" the variance due to the correlation. The only variance now in the twice-corrected scores is the residual variance. "Residual variance" is an apt term. It is the variance left over after the two systematic variances have been removed. If we calculate the *total* sums of squares of I and

TABLE **15.9** REMOVAL OF BETWEEN-ROWS VARIANCE BY EQUALIZING ROW MEANS AND SCORES

I ($r = .00$)				II ($r = .90$)			
Correction	A_1	A_2	M	Correction	A_1	A_2	M
+ .5	2.0	5.0	3.5	+ 2.0	3.5	3.5	3.5
+ 1.5	4.0	3.0	3.5	+ .5	3.0	4.0	3.5
0	3.5	3.5	3.5	+ .5	4.0	3.0	3.5
− 1.5	3.0	4.0	3.5	− 1.0	3.5	3.5	3.5
− .5	5.0	2.0	3.5	− 2.0	3.5	3.5	3.5
M:	3.5	3.5	(3.5)		3.5	3.5	(3.5)

II, we find them to be 10 and 1, respectively. If we calculate the sums of squares *within* the groups as with one-way analysis of variance, we find them also to be 10 and 1. Evidently there is no more systematic variance left in the scores—only error variation remains. The most important point to note is that the residual sum of squares of the uncorrelated scores is ten times greater than the residual sum of squares of the correlated scores. Exactly the same operation was performed on both sets of scores. With the uncorrelated scores, however, it is not possible to extract as much variance as with the correlated scores.

Research Examples

Transfer of Individually Derived Principles

In a study that compared *rules given* for problem solution (*G* problems) with no directions for solution, or *derived solutions* (*D* problems), Haslerud and Meyers used subjects as their own controls.[4] They had the *S*s solve problems in the two ways (the problem was coding) after having been trained in both ways. They were tested on a later test which included *G* and *D* problems, with the result that they did better on the *G* (rule-given) problems than on the *D* (rule-derived) problems. But on a second test a week later, the results were reversed: the scores on those problems that had been rule-derived (*D*) by the *S*s *increased*, whereas the scores on the problems that had been rule-given (*G*) *decreased*. Each *S* was used as his own control, so to speak, since the scores analyzed (with *t* tests) were $D_2 - D_1$ and $G_2 - G_1$, or difference scores, where D_2 and D_1 were the numbers of correct codings on the second and first tests, respectively, of rule-derived problems—and similarly for G_2 and G_1 rule-given problem scores.[5]

Learning Sets of Isopods

In an interesting and effective demonstration of the use of subjects as their own controls, in which two-way analysis of variance and the testing of learning theory with lower organisms was used, Morrow and Smithson showed that isopods (small crustaceans) can learn to learn.[6] Many students, humanists, sociologists, educators, and even psychologists have criticized learning theorists and other psychological investigators for using animals in their research. While there can be legitimate criticism of psychological and other behavioral research, criticizing it because animals are used is part of the frustrating but apparently unavoidable irrationality that plagues all human effort. Yet, it does have a certain charm and

[4]G. Haslerud and S. Meyers, "The Transfer Value of Given and Individually Derived Principles," *Journal of Educational Psychology*, XLIX (1958), 293–298.

[5]Giving examples of published research analyses does not necessarily mean endorsement or recommendation of methods of analysis used. In the above case, for example, the use of difference scores, a common practice, is questionable, since they are systematically less reliable than the scores from which they are calculated. See R. Thorndike and E. Hagen, *Measurement and Evaluation in Psychology and Education*, 3d ed. New York: Wiley, 1969, pp. 195–198, for a clear explanation of the difficulties involved.

[6]J. Morrow and B. Smithson, "Learning Sets in an Invertebrate," *Science*, CLXIV (1969), 850–851. Copyright 1969 by the American Association for the Advancement of Science.

can itself be the object of scientific investigation![7] In any case, one of the reasons for testing similar hypotheses with different species is the same reason we replicate research in different parts of the United States and in other countries: generality. How much more powerful a theory is if it holds up with southerners, northerners, easterners, and westerners, with Germans, Japanese, Israelis, and Americans—and with rats, pigeons, horses, and dogs. Morrow and Smithson's study attempted to extend learning theory to little creatures whose learning one might think to be governed by different laws than the learning of men and rats. They succeeded—to some extent at least.

They trained eight isopods, through water deprivation and subsequent reinforcement for successful performance (wet blotting paper), to make reversals of their "preferences" for one or the other arm of a T maze. When the *S*s had reached a specified criterion of correct turns in the maze, the training was reversed—that is, turning in the direction of the other arm of the T maze was reinforced until the criterion was reached. This was done with each isopod for nine reversals. The question is: Did the animals learn to make the reversals sooner as the trials progressed? Such learning should be exhibited by fewer and fewer errors.

Morrow and Smithson analyzed the data with two-way analysis of variance. The mean number of errors of the initial trial and the nine reversal trials consistently got smaller: 27.5, 23.6, 18.6, 14.3, 16.8, 13.9, 11.1, 8.5, 8.6, 8.6. The two-way analysis of variance table is given in Table 15.10.[8] The ten means differ significantly, since the *F* ratio for columns (reversal trials), 4.78, is significant at the .01 level. That there is correlation between the columns, and thus individual differences among the isopods, is shown by the *F* ratio for rows, 3.15, also significant at the .01 level. It is a piquant note that even little crustaceans are individuals!

TABLE **15.10** ANALYSIS OF VARIANCE OF MORROW AND SMITHSON DATA

Source	*df*	*s.s.*	*m.s.*	*F*
Between Columns	9	3095.95	343.994	4.78 (.01)
Between Rows	7	1587.40	226.771	3.15 (.01)
Residual	63	4532.85	71.950	
Total	79	9216.20		

Study Suggestions

1. Do two-way analysis of variance of the two sets of fictitious data of Table 15.6. Use the text as an aid. Interpret the results. Now do two-way analysis of

[7]Bugelski has written an excellent defense of the use of rats in learning research that students of behavioral research should read: B. Bugelski, *The Psychology of Learning*. New York: Holt, Rinehart and Winston, 1956, pp. 33–44. Another equally excellent essay on a somewhat broader base is: D. Hebb and W. Thompson, "The Social Significance of Animal Studies." In G. Lindzey and E. Abelson, eds., *The Handbook of Social Psychology*, 2d ed. Reading, Mass: Addison-Wesley, 1968, vol. II, pp. 729–774.

[8]I did the analysis of variance from the original data given by Morrow and Smithson in their Table 1.

variance of the two sets of Table 15.8; do the same for Table 15.9. Lay out the final analysis of variance tables and compare. Think through carefully how the adjustive corrections have affected the original data.

2. Three sociologists were asked to judge the general effectiveness of the administrative offices of ten elementary schools in a school district. One of their measures was administrative flexibility. (The higher the score the greater the flexibility.) The ten ratings on this measure of the three sociologists are given below:

	S_1	S_2	S_3
1	9	7	5
2	9	9	6
3	7	5	4
4	6	5	3
5	3	4	2
6	5	6	4
7	5	3	1
8	4	2	1
9	5	4	4
10	7	5	5

(a) Do a two-way analysis of variance as described in the chapter.
(b) Do the three sociologists agree in their mean ratings? Does one of the sociologists appear to be severe in his ratings?
(c) Are there substantial differences among the schools? Which school appears to have the greatest administrative flexibility? Which school has the least flexibility?

[*Answers:* (a) F (columns) = 24.44 (.001); F (rows) = 14.89 (.001); (b) no; yes; (c) yes: no. 2; no. 8.]

3. Draw 30 digits, 0 through 9, from a table of random numbers. (Use Appendix D, if you wish.) Divide them arbitrarily into three groups of 10 digits each.
(a) Do a two-way analysis of variance. Assume that the numbers in each row are data from one individual.
(b) Now add constants to the three numbers of each row as follows: 20 to the first two rows, 15 to the second two rows, 10 to the third two rows, 5 to the fourth two rows, and 0 to the last two rows. Do a two-way analysis of variance of these "data."
(c) In effect, what have you done by "biasing" the row numbers in this fashion?
(d) Compare the sum of squares and the mean squares of (a) and (b). Why are the *total* sums of squares and mean squares different? Why are the *between-columns* and the *residual* sums of squares and mean squares the same? Why are the *between-rows* sums of squares and mean squares different?
(e) Create a research problem out of all this and interpret the "results." Is the example realistic?

CHAPTER 16

Nonparametric Analysis of Variance and Related Statistics

It is, of course, possible to analyze data and to draw inferences about relations among variables without statistics. Sometimes, for example, data are so obvious that a statistical test is not really necessary. If all the scores of an experimental group are greater than (or less than) those of a control group, then a statistical test is superfluous. It is also possible to have statistics of a quite different nature than those we have been studying, statistics that use properties of the data other than the strictly quantitative. We might infer an effect of X on Y, in several experimental groups, if there are long runs of similar scores in one of the groups, since, on the basis of chance, long runs are unlikely. For instance, if the experimental group has all, or nearly all, the scores or labels of a certain kind, one infers that something other than chance is operating.

Indeed, there are many ways to approach and analyze data other than comparing means and variances. But the basic principle is always the same if we continue to work in a probabilistic world: compare obtained results to chance or theoretical expectations. If, for example, we administer four treatments to subjects and expect that one of the four will excel the others, we can compare the mean of the favored group with the average of the other three groups in an analysis of variance and planned comparisons manner. But suppose our data are highly irregular in one or more ways and we fear for the validity of the usual tests of significance. What can we do? We can rank order all the observations, for one thing. If none of the four treatments has any more influence than any other, we expect the ranks to disperse themselves among the four groups more or less evenly. If treatment A_2, however, has a preponderance of high (or low) ranks, then we conclude that the usual expectation is upset. Such reasoning is a good part of the basis of so-called nonparametric statistics.

In this chapter we examine in some detail three forms of nonparametric analysis of variance. Other forms of nonparametric statistics will be briefly mentioned. The chapter has two main purposes: to introduce the reader to the ideas behind nonparametric statistics, but especially nonparametric analysis of variance, and to bring out the essential similarity of most inference-aiding methods.

The student should be aware that careful study of nonparametric statistics gives depth of insight into statistics and statistical inference. The insight gained is probably due to the considerable loosening of thinking that seems to occur when working tangential to the usual statistical structure. One sees, so to speak, a broader perspective; one can even invent statistical tests, once the basic ideas are well understood. In short, statistical and inferential ideas are generalized on the basis of relatively simple fundamental ideas.

Parametric and Nonparametric Statistics

A *parameter*, as we learned in an earlier chapter, is a population value. If all the scores of a defined population are available and a mean is calculated, this mean is a parameter. Similarly, the variance and the standard deviation of a population are parameters. It may not be possible to calculate population measures. They are still referred to as parameters. A *statistic*, on the other hand, is a measure calculated from a sample. In Chapter 8 we drew random samples from a population of intelligence test scores and calculated statistics from the samples, our purpose being to estimate the parameter known as the mean.

Whenever statistical tests, parametric or nonparametric, are used, certain assumptions are made. Nonparametric statistical tests are hemmed in by fewer and less stringent assumptions than parametric tests. They are particularly free of assumptions about the characteristics or the form of the distributions of the populations of research samples. Thus they are also called distribution-free tests. As Siegel puts it, "A nonparametric statistical test is a test whose model does not specify conditions about the parameters of the population from which the sample was drawn."[1]

Assumption of Normality

The most famous assumption behind the use of many parametric statistics is the *assumption of normality*. It is assumed in using the t and F tests (and thus the analysis of variance), for example, that the samples with which we work have been drawn from populations that are normally distributed. It is said that, if the populations from which samples are drawn are not normal, then statistical tests that depend on the normality assumption are vitiated. As a result, the conclusions drawn from sampled observations and their statistics will be in question. When in doubt about the normality of a population, or when one knows that the population is not normal, one should use a nonparametric test that does not make the nor-

[1]S. Siegel, *Nonparametric Statistics for the Behavioral Sciences*. New York: McGraw-Hill, 1956, p. 31.

mality assumption, it is said. Some teachers urge students of education and psychology to use *only* nonparametric tests on the questionable ground that most educational and psychological populations are not normal. The issue is not this simple.

Homogeneity of Variance

The next most important assumption is known as the *homogeneity of variance* assumption. It is assumed, in analysis of variance, that the variances within the groups are statistically the same. That is, variances are assumed to be homogeneous from group to group, within the bounds of random variation. If this is not true, the F test is vitiated. There is good reason for this statement. We saw earlier that the within-groups variance was an average of the variances within the two, three, or more groups of measures. If the variances differ widely, then such averaging is questionable. The effect of widely differing variances is to inflate the within-groups variance. Consequently an F test may be not significant when in reality there are significant differences between the means.

These two assumptions have both been examined rather thoroughly by empirical methods. Artificial populations have been set up, samples drawn from them, and t and F tests performed. The evidence to date is that the importance of normality and homogeneity is overrated,[2] a view that is shared by the author. Unless there is good evidence to believe that populations are rather seriously nonnormal and that variances are heterogeneous, it is usually unwise to use a nonparametric statistical test in place of a parametric one. The reason for this is that parametric tests are almost always more powerful than nonparametric tests. (The power of a statistical test is the probability that the null hypothesis will be rejected when it is actually false.) Relative simplicity and number of calculations are hardly good scientific arguments for using statistical tests. Current fashion may be one argument, but it lacks scientific cogency.

To return to the evidence on normality and homogeneity, Lindquist says, "... the F distribution is amazingly insensitive to the form of the distribution of criterion measures in the parent population ..."[3] Lindquist also says, on the basis of Norton's data, that unless variances are so heterogeneous as to be readily apparent, that is, relatively large differences exist, the effect on the F test will

[2]Two important large-scale studies were done by Norton and by Boneau. Lindquist gives an admirable summary of the Norton study: E. Lindquist, *Design and Analysis of Experiments*. Boston: Houghton Mifflin, 1953, pp. 78–86. Boneau discusses the whole problem of assumptions and reports his own definitive study in a brilliant article: C. Boneau, "The Effects of Violations of Assumptions Underlying the t Test," *Psychological Bulletin*, LVII (1960), 49–64. Another useful article by Boneau is C. Boneau, "A Note on Measurement Scales and Statistical Tests," *American Psychologist*, XVI (1961), 260–261. An excellent but more general article is N. Anderson, "Scales and Statistics: Parametric and Nonparametric," *Psychological Bulletin*, LVIII (1961), 305–316. Two recent empirical demonstrations of the robustness of analysis of variance and the t test are: P. Games and P. Lucas, "Power of the Analysis of Variance of Independent Groups on Non-Normal and Normally Transformed Data," *Educational and Psychological Measurement*, XXVI (1966), 311–327; B. Baker, C. Hardyck, and L. Petrinovich, "Weak Measurements vs. Strong Statistics: An Empirical Critique of S. S. Stevens' Proscriptions on Statistics," *Educational and Psychological Measurement*, XXVI (1966), 291–309.

[3]Lindquist, *op. cit.*, p. 81.

probably be negligible. Boneau confirms this. He says that in a large number of research situations the probability statements resulting from the use of t and F tests, even when these two assumptions are violated, will be highly accurate.[4] In brief, in most cases in education and psychology, it is probably safer—and usually more effective—to use parametric tests rather than nonparametric tests. Anderson, in an excellent and definitive article on the whole subject, says, "It was concluded that parametric procedures are the standard tools of psychological statistics, although nonparametric procedures are useful minor techniques."[5]

Continuity and Equal Intervals of Measures

A third assumption is that the measures to be analyzed are continuous measures with equal intervals. As we shall see in a later chapter, this assumption is behind the arithmetic operations of adding, subtracting, multiplying, and dividing. Parametric tests like the F and t tests of course depend on this assumption, but many nonparametric tests do not. A rank-order method, for example, may take no account of the continuity and equal intervals of measures.

Despite the conclusions of Lindquist, Boneau, Anderson, and others, it is well to bear these assumptions in mind. It is not wise to use statistical procedures—or, for that matter, any kind of research procedures—without due respect for the assumptions behind the procedures. If they are too seriously violated, the conclusions drawn from research data may be in error. To the reader who has been alarmed by some statistics books the best advice probably is: Use parametric statistics, as well as the analysis of variance, routinely, but keep a sharp eye on data for gross departures from normality, homogeneity of variance, and equality of intervals. Be aware of measurement problems and their relation to statistical tests, and be familiar with the basic nonparametric statistics so that they can be used when necessary. Also bear in mind that nonparametric tests are often quick and easy to use and are excellent for preliminary, if not always definitive, tests.

Nonparametric Analysis of Variance

The nonparametric analysis of variance methods studied here, like so many other nonparametric methods, depend on ranking. We study two basic forms: one-way analysis and two-way analysis.

One-Way Analysis of Variance: The Kruskal-Wallis Test

An investigator interested in the differences in conservatism of three boards of education is unable to administer a measure of conservatism to the board members. He therefore has an expert judge rank order all the members of the three boards on the basis of private discussions with them. The three boards have six, six, and five members, respectively. The ranks of the board members are given in Table 16.1.

[4]Boneau, "The Effects of Violations of Assumptions Underlying the *t* Test," *op. cit.*, p. 62. There is one case that is particularly difficult to resolve, however: when variances are heterogeneous and the sample sizes of experimental groups differ.

[5]Anderson, *op. cit.*, p. 315.

TABLE **16.1** RANKS OF 17 MEMBERS OF THREE BOARDS OF EDUCATION ON JUDGED CONSERVATISM

	Boards		
	I	II	III
	12	11	4
	14	16	3
	10	5	8
	17	7	1
	15	6	9
	13	2	
Σ Ranks:	81	47	25
M:	13.50	7.83	5.00

If there were no differences in conservatism between the three boards, then the ranks should be randomly distributed in the three columns. If they are randomly distributed in the three columns, then the sums of the ranks (or their means) in the three columns should be approximately equal.[6] On the other hand, if there are differences in conservatism between the three groups, then the ranks in one column should be higher than the ranks in another column—with a consequent higher sum or mean of ranks.

Kruskal and Wallis give a simple formula for assessing the significance of these differences.[7] The formula is:

$$H = \frac{12}{N(N+1)} \Sigma \frac{R^2}{n} - 3(N+1) \tag{16.1}$$

where N is the total number of ranks, n the number of ranks in one group, and R the sum of the ranks in any one column. Applying Eq. 16.1 to the ranks of Table 16.1, we first calculate $\Sigma(R^2/n)$:

$$\Sigma \frac{R^2}{n} = \frac{(81)^2}{6} + \frac{(47)^2}{6} + \frac{(25)^2}{5} = 1093.50 + 368.17 + 125.0 = 1586.67$$

Substituting in Eq. 16.1, we find:

$$H = \frac{12}{17(17+1)} \cdot 1586.67 - 54 = 62.22 - 54 = \mathit{8.22}$$

H is approximately distributed as χ^2. The degrees of freedom are $k-1$, where k is the number of columns or groups, or $3-1=2$. Checking the χ^2 table, we find this to be significant at the .02 level. Thus the ranks are not random.

The Kruskal and Wallis method is analogous to one-way analysis of variance. It can be used for experimental and nonexperimental data and is simple and

[6]Kendall has ingeniously shown how it is appropriate to add ranks: M. Kendall, *Rank Correlation Methods*. London:Griffin, 1948, p. 1.

[7]W. Kruskal and W. Wallis, "Use of Ranks in One-Criterion Variance Analysis," *Journal of the American Statistical Association*, XLVII (1952), 583–621. The test is also described in statistics texts, for example: Siegel, *op. cit.*, pp. 184–193, and W. Hays, *Statistics*. New York: Holt, Rinehart and Winston, 1963, pp. 637–639.

effective. Cases arise in psychological, sociological, and educational research where the measurement is such that it is doubtful whether parametric analysis is legitimate. Of course, doubtful measures can also be transformed.[8] But in many cases it is easily possible to rank order the scores and do the analysis on the ranks. There are also research situations in which the only form of measurement possible is rank order, or ordinal, measurement. The Kruskal and Wallis test is most useful in such situations. But it is also useful when data are quite irregular but amenable to ranking. In situations in which subjects are matched or the same subjects are observed more than once (see Chapter 15), other similar forms of analysis are available. Three of these are described below.

As indicated in an earlier chapter, it is desirable to know the degree of association between independent and dependent variables. In the usual analysis of variance, E^2, RI, and omega-squared (ω^2) can be calculated. With ranks a useful measure that is directly comparable to E^2 can be calculated: Kendall's W, the coefficient of concordance. One can also calculate the intraclass coefficient of correlation of ranks. We take up these matters using the same set of simple numbers to illustrate the techniques. The research examples to go with the numbers, however, will be varied.

Two-Way Analysis of Variance: The Friedman Test

In situations in which subjects are matched or the same subjects are observed more than once, a form of rank-order analysis of variance, first devised by Friedman, can be used.[9] An ordinary two-way analysis of variance of the ranks can also be used.

An educational researcher, concerned with the relation between role and perception of teaching competence, asked groups of professors to rate each other on an instructor evaluation rating instrument. He also asked administrators and students to rate the same professors. Since the numbers of professors ("peers"), administrators, and students differed, he lumped the ratings of the members of each rating group together by averaging. In effect the hypothesis stated that the three groups of raters would differ significantly in their ratings. The researcher also wanted to know whether there were significant differences among the professors. The data of one part of the study are given in Table 16.2.

There are a number of ways these data can be analyzed. First, of course, ordinary two-way analysis of variance can be used. If the numbers being analyzed seem to conform reasonably well with the assumptions discussed earlier, this

[8]The problem of transformation of scores exceeds the bounds of this book. An enlightened discussion for behavioral science students is: F. Mosteller and R. Bush, "Selected Quantitative Techniques," In G. Lindzey, ed., *Handbook of Social Psychology*. Reading, Mass.: Addison-Wesley, 1954, vol. I, pp. 324–328. Perhaps the most complete discussion—but a difficult one—is: M. Bartlett, "The Use of Transformations." *Biometrics*, III (1947), 39–52. The essence of the idea of transformations is that measures that are not respectable, owing to lack of normality and other reasons, are transformed to respectability via a linear function of the sort $y=f(x)$, where y is a transformed score, x the original score, and f is some operation ("the square root of") on x.

[9]M. Friedman, "The Use of Ranks to Avoid the Assumption of Normality Implicit in the Analysis of Variance," *Journal of the American Statistical Association*, XXXII (1937), 675–701. The Friedman test is also described in the references mentioned earlier.

TABLE **16.2** HYPOTHETICAL DATA (MEANS) OF RATINGS, WITH RANKS, OF PROFESSORS BY PEERS, ADMINISTRATORS, AND STUDENTS[a]

Professors		Peers			Administrators			Students		ΣR
A	(3)	28	(3)	(1)	19	(1)	(2)	22	(1)	5
B	(1)	22	(1)	(2)	23	(2)	(3)	36	(3)	6
C	(2)	26	(2)	(1)	24	(3)	(3)	29	(2)	7
D	(2)	44	(6)	(1)	34	(4)	(3)	48	(6)	16
E	(1)	35	(4)	(2)	39	(6)	(3)	40	(4)	14
F	(2)	40	(5)	(1)	38	(5)	(3)	45	(5)	15
ΣR:	11			8			17			

[a]The numbers in the table are composite ratings. The numbers in parentheses to the right and left of the compositve ratings are ranks. Those to the right are the ranks in columns; those to the left are the ranks in rows. The higher the number, the greater the perceived competence.

would be the best analysis. In the analysis of variance, the F ratio for columns (between raters) is 4.71, significant at the .05 level, and the F ratio for rows is 12.73, significant at the .01 level. From this analysis, the hypothesis of the investigator is supported. This is indicated by the significant differences between the means of the three groups. The professors, too, differ significantly.

Now assume that the investigator is disturbed by the type of data he has and decides to use nonparametric analysis of variance. Clearly he should not use the Kruskal-Wallis method; he decides to use the Friedman method, rank ordering the data *by rows*. In so doing he tests the differences between the columns. Obviously if two or more raters are given the same ranking system, say 1, 2, 3, 4, 5, it is apparent that the sums and means of the ranks of the different raters will always be the same. In this analysis, then, he concentrates on the differences between the raters and ignores the differences between the professors (as rated). In what follows, then, we concentrate on the ranks in the parentheses to the *left* of each composite rating. Also concentrate on the sums of the ranks in the *columns* at the bottom of the table and ignore the sums in the last column of the table.

The formula given by Friedman is:

$$\chi_r^2 = \frac{12}{kn(n+1)} \Sigma R^2 - 3k(n+1) \tag{16.2}$$

where $\chi_r^2 = \chi^2$, ranks; k is the number of rankings; n the number of objects being ranked; R the sum of the ranks in each column; and ΣR^2 is the sum of these squared sums. First calculate ΣR^2:

$$\Sigma R^2 = (11)^2 + (8)^2 + (17)^2 = 474$$

Now determine k and n. The number of rankings is k, or the number of times that the rank-order system, whatever it is, is used. Here $k = 6$. The number of objects being ranked, n, or the number of ranks, is 3. (Actually, the raters are not being ranked: 3 is the number of ranks in the rank-order system being used.) Now calculate χ_r^2:

$$\chi_r^2 = \frac{12}{(6)(3)(4)} \cdot 474 - (3)(6)(4) = 79 - 72 = 7$$

This value is checked against a χ^2 table, at $df = n - 1 = 3 - 1 = 2$. The value is significant at the .05 level.[10]

The investigator was also interested in the significance of the differences between the professors as rated. Clearly if these differences are not significant, there may be something wrong with the raters and/or the rating system. Note that the reasoning is the same here—with minor modifications—as it was with one-way analysis of variance of ranks. If the rating composites in Table 16.2 are random, then the totals of the ranks (ΣR's) will be roughly the same. What is tested, in effect, is whether they *are* random. Returning to the example, the investigator then assigns ranks to the rating composites in *columns* (in parentheses to the *right* of each rating composite). These are the ranks that the rater groups assigned to the six professors. The professor who is rated high should get the higher ranks, which can be determined by adding his ranks across the rows. The data for all six professors appear in Table 16.2. (See ΣR column on the right-hand side of the table.) This time $k = 3$ and $n = 6$. We calculate χ_r^2 using Eq. 16.2 again:

$$\chi_r^2 = \frac{12}{(3)(6)(7)} \cdot 787 - (3)(3)(7) = \mathit{11.95}$$

Checking this value in a x^2 table, at $df = n - 1 = 6 - 1 = 5$, we find it to be significant at the .05 level. The instructors, as rated, seem to be different.

Compare these results to the ordinary analysis of variance results. In the latter, the three groups were found to be significantly different at the .05 level. In the case of the significance of the differences between the professors, the analysis also showed significance. In general, the methods should agree fairly well.[11]

The Coefficient of Concordance, W

Perhaps a more direct test of the investigator's hypothesis is provided by using a measure of the association of the ranks. Such a measure, called the *coefficient of*

[10]With n and k relatively small, the significance level is in doubt. For details, see Siegel, *op. cit.*, pp. 166–169.

[11]Using another method of analysis of variance based on ranges rather than variances, the results of the Friedman test are confirmed. This method, called the *studentized range test*, is useful. For details, see E. Pearson and H. Hartley, eds., *Biometrika Tables for Statisticians*. Cambridge: Cambridge University Press, 1954, vol. I, pp. 51–54 and 176–179. Ranges are good measures of variation for small samples but not for large samples. The principle of the studentized range test is similar to that of the F test in that a "within-groups range" is used to evaluate the range of the means of the groups. Another useful method, that of Link and Wallace, is described in detail in Mosteller and Bush, *op. cit.*, pp. 304–307. Both methods have the advantage that they can be used with one-way and two-way analyses. Still another method, which has the unique virtue of testing an ordered hypothesis of the ranks, is the L test: E. Page, "Ordered Hypotheses for Multiple Treatments: A Significance Test for Linear Ranks," *Journal of the American Statistical Association*, LVIII (1963), 216–230. While this test seems to be excellent, it is tied to tables of L, which are evidently found only in Page's article.

concordance, W, has been worked out by Kendall.[12] We are now interested in the degree of agreement or association in the ranks of the columns of Table 16.2. Each rater group has virtually assigned a rank to each professor. If there were no association whatever between two of the rater groups, and a rank-order coefficient of correlation were computed between the ranks, it should be near zero. On the other hand, if there is agreement, the coefficient should be significantly different from zero.

The coefficient of concordance, W, expresses the average agreement, on a scale from .00 to 1.00, between the ranks. There are two ways to define W. The Kendall method will be presented first. According to this method W can be expressed as the ratio between the *between-groups* (or ranks) sum of squares and the *total* sum of squares of a complete analysis of variance of the ranks. This ratio, then, is the correlation ratio squared, E^2, of ranked data.

Where there are k rankings of n individual objects, Kendall's coefficient of concordance is defined by

$$W = \frac{12S}{k^2(n^3 - n)} \qquad (16.3)$$

S is the sum of the deviations squared of the totals of the n ranks from their mean. S is a between-groups sum of squares for ranks. It is like ss_b. (In fact, if we divide S by k, S/k, we obtain the between sum of squares we would obtain in a complete analysis of variance of the ranks.)

Consider the data of Table 16.3, which simply reproduces the ranks on the right of the columns of Table 16.2, plus certain calculations to be used later. We are interested in the six ranks of the three-column measures and their overall relation. Add them across the rows. The sums of the six rows are 5, 6, 7, 16, 14, and 15. Then S can be calculated in two ways. In the first method, square each total, add them up, and subtract the total of all the ranks squared divided by n. In a formula, $S = \Sigma X^2 - (\Sigma X_t)^2/n$, where ΣX is the sum of the ranks in any row (or column), $\Sigma X_t =$ the sum of all the ranks. Using this formula, we find that

$$S = (5^2 + 6^2 + \cdots + 15^2) - (63)^2/6 = 787 - 661.5 = \mathit{125.5}$$

Kendall uses another method that gives the same results: subtract each individual sum of ranks from the mean of the sums, square the resulting figures, and then add them. The mean of the six totals is $63/6 = 10.5$. Therefore,

$$S = (5 - 10.5)^2 + (6 - 10.5)^2 + \cdots + (15 - 10.5)^2$$

$$= (-5.5)^2 + (-4.5)^2 + \cdots + (4.5)^2 = \mathit{125.5}$$

Since $k = 3$ and $n = 6$,

$$W = \frac{12 \times 125.50}{3^2(6^3 - 6)} = \frac{1506}{9(216 - 6)} = \frac{1506}{1890} = .797 = \mathit{.80}$$

The relation between the three sets of ranks is substantial.

[12]Kendall, *op. cit.*, chap. 6.

To evaluate the significance of W, the following formula for the F ratio can be used:

$$F = \frac{(k-1)W}{1-W} \tag{16.4}$$

By substitution we find that

$$F = \frac{(3-1)(.797)}{1-.797} = \frac{1.594}{.203} = 7.85$$

TABLE **16.3** RANKS OF HYPOTHETICAL DATA OF TABLE 16.2 WITH CALCULATIONS FOR ANALYSIS OF VARIANCE

Professors	Peers	Administrators	Students	Σ	Σ^2
A	3	1	1	5	25
B	1	2	3	6	36
C	2	3	2	7	49
D	6	4	6	16	256
E	4	6	4	14	196
F	5	5	5	15	225
ΣX	21	21	21		$\Sigma X_t = 63$
					$(\Sigma X_t)^2 = 3969$
					$\Sigma X_t^2 = 273$
					$\Sigma(\Sigma)^2 = 787$

$$C = \frac{3969}{18} = 220.50$$

$$\text{Total} = 273 - 220.50 = \mathit{52.50}$$

$$\text{Between raters} = 0$$

$$\text{Between professors} = \frac{787}{3} - 220.50 = \mathit{41.83}$$

Source	*df*	*s.s.*	*m.s.*	*F*
Between raters	2	0	0	
Between professors	5	41.83	8.366	7.84 (0.01)
Residual	10	10.67	1.067	
Total	17	52.50		

The significance of the F ratio (which is significant at the .01 level) will not be discussed here. The reader can check such methods in the Kendall or Siegel books. We now note that we could have used Friedman's χ_r^2 to obtain the F ratio, as follows:

$$F = \frac{(k-1)\chi_r^2}{k(n-1) - \chi_r^2} \tag{16.5}$$

Previously we found that $\chi_r^2 = 11.95$. Thus,

$$F = \frac{(3-1)(11.95)}{3(6-1) - 11.95} = \frac{23.90}{3.05} = 7.84$$

Now, let us do a two-way analysis of variance of the ranks, treating the ranks as though they were scores. The calculations are given in Table 16.3. Note that the F ratio calculated by Eqs. 16.4 and 16.5 and by the analysis of variance are the same (within errors of rounding). Now, we perform one more calculation, E^2:

$$E^2 = \frac{ss_b}{ss_t} = \frac{41.83}{52.50} = .797 = .80$$

This is the same as W. (Note that if we multiply the between-sum of squares by k, we obtain S: $41.83 \times 3 = 125.5$.) Since the above methods produce results similar to those of earlier analyses of the relations among variances, further discussion is unnecessary. (The possibilities have still not been exhausted, though. For example, RI, the intraclass coefficient of correlation can be calculated with ranks.) The reader will find it profitable to go through the calculations of these various methods carefully.

Properties of Nonparametric Methods[13]

A rather large number of good nonparametric methods are now readily available, most of them in Siegel's excellent book. They are usually based on some property of data that can be tested against chance expectation. For example, the odds and evens of coin-tossing are a dichotomous property that is conveniently tested with binomial statistics (see Chapter 7). Another data property is range. With small samples, the range is a good index of variability. A "quick and dirty" method of calculating the standard error of the mean (MB, pp. 323–324), for instance, is:

$$SE_{M(e)} = \frac{\text{Largest observation} - \text{Smallest observation}}{N}$$

A t test of the difference between two means can be made with the following formula:

$$t_e = \frac{\bar{X}_1 - \bar{X}_2}{1/2(R_1 + R_2)}$$

where t_e = estimated t; R_1 = range of group 1, and R_2 = range of group 2 (see MB, p. 324).

Another property of data is what can be called periodicity. If there are different kinds of events (heads and tails, male and female, religious preference, etc.), and numerical data from different groups are combined and ranked, then by chance there should not be long runs of any particular event, like a long run of females in one experimental group. The runs test is based on this idea.

[13]To expedite referencing, the following abbreviations will be used: MB: Mosteller and Bush, *op. cit.*; S: Siegel, *op. cit.*

Still another property of data was discussed in Chapter 11: distribution. The distributions of different samples can be compared with each other or with a "criterion" group (like the normal distribution) for deviations. The Kolmogorov–Smirnov test (S, pp. 47–52, 127–136) tests goodness of fit of the distributions. It is a useful and powerful test, especially for small samples.

The most ubiquitous property of data, perhaps, is rank order. Whenever data can be ranked, they can be checked against each other and against chance expectation. Many, perhaps most, nonparametric tests are rank order tests. The Kruskal-Wallace and the Friedman tests are, of course, both based on rank order. Rank-order coefficients of correlation are extremely useful. W is one of these. So are the Spearman rank-order coefficient of correlation (S, pp. 202–213) and Kendall's *tau* (S, pp. 213–223).

There are several points to all this. One, nonparametric methods are virtually inexhaustible. There seems to be no end to what can be done, given the simple principles involved and the various properties of data that can be exploited. Two, different properties of data can be used to help inference-making. While means and variances have nice properties and powerful advantages, we are by no means restricted to them. Range, periodicity, distribution, rank order, and other properties can be used. Three—and familiar to the point of tedium—most nonparametric methods use the same principle that underlies so much of statistics and statistical inference: assess obtained results against chance or other theoretical expectation. There is no magic to nonparametric statistics. The same principles apply.

Study Suggestions

1. A teacher interested in studying the effect of workbooks, decides to conduct a small experiment with her class. She randomly divides the class into 3 groups of 7 pupils each, calling these groups A_1, A_2, and A_3. A_1 was taught without any workbooks, A_2 was taught with the occasional use of workbooks at the teacher's direction, and A_3 was taught with heavy dependence on workbooks. At the end of four months, the teacher tested the children in the subject matter. The scores she obtained were in percentage form, and she knew that it might be questionable to use parametric analysis of variance.[14] So she used the Kruskal-Wallis method. The data are as follows:

A_1	A_2	A_3
.55	.82	.09
.32	.24	.35
.74	.91	.25
.09	.36	.36
.48	.86	.20
.61	.80	.07
.12	.65	.36

[14]When scores are in percentage form, they can easily be transformed to scores amenable to parametric analysis. The appropriate transformation is called the *arc-sine transformation*, a table for which can be found in R. Fisher and F. Yates, *Statistical Tables for Biological, Agricultural, and Medical Research*, 5th ed. New York: Hafner, 1957, Table X, p. 70.

Convert the percentages into ranks (from 1 through 21) and calculate H. Interpret. (To be significant, H must be 5.99 or greater for the .05 level, and 9.21 for the .01 level. This is at $k-1=2$ degrees of freedom, the χ^2 table.)

Note: Two cases of tied percentages and consequently tied ranks occur in these data. When ties occur, simply take the median (or mean) of the ties. For example, there are three .36's in the above table, occurring at the tenth, eleventh, and twelfth ranks. The median (or mean) is 11. All three .36's, then, will be assigned the rank of 11. The next higher rank must then be 13, since 10, 11, and 12 have been "used up." Similarly there are two .09's, which occur at the second and third ranks. The median of 2 and 3 is 2.5. Both .09's are assigned 2.5 and the next higher rank, of course, is 4. [*Answer* $H=7.79$ (.05).]

2. An educational sociologist, studying the relation between racial membership and overall school achievement, used the usual analysis of variance procedure to test the significance of the differences between his racial groups. He obtained $F=7.34$, which is significant at the .01 level. A statistician, criticizing his work, used a nonparametric test on the data and obtained $H=8.50$, which is also significant at the .01 level.
   (a) Is there any difference in the interpretation of these two results?
   (b) From a purely statistical point of view, *is* there any difference?
3. The relation between the discussion behavior of members of boards of education and their decisions was studied by a social psychological researcher. In this research, a particularly complex facet of discussion behavior, say antagonistic behavior, was to be measured. He wondered if this behavior could be reliably measured. The researcher trained three observers and had them rank order the antagonistic behavior of the members of one board of education during a two-hour session. The ranks of the three observers are given below (high ranks show high antagonism):
   (a) What is the degree of agreement or concordance between the three observers? (Use W.)

		Observers	
Board Members	0_1	0_2	0_3
1	3	2	2
2	2	4	1
3	6	6	7
4	1	1	3
5	7	7	6
6	4	3	5
7	5	5	4

   (b) Is W statistically significant? (If $F \geqslant 5.32$, W is significant at the .01 level. If $F \geqslant 9.58$, W is significant at the .001 level.)
   (c) Can the social psychologist say that he is reliably measuring "antagonism" or "antagonistic behavior"?
   (d) Use another method to calculate the W of (a).
   [*Answers:* (a) $W=.86$; (b) $F=12.00$ (.001); (c) yes.]
4. Use the numerical example of Problem 3 and calculate a two-way analysis of variance, using Friedman's method.
   (a) What is $\chi_r{}^2$? Is it statistically significant? (At $df=6$, if $\chi_r{}^2 \geqslant 12.59$, it is significant at the .05 level.)

(b) Do the board of education members differ in antagonistic behavior? Could you have known this from the results of Problem 3?
(c) Compare these results with those of Problem 3.
(d) Calculate F, using Eq. 16.5. Compare this F to that calculated in Problem 3.
[*Answers:* (a) $\chi_r^2 = 15.43$ (.05); (b) yes.]

PART

Designs of Research

CHAPTER 17

Research Design: Meaning, Purpose, and Principles

Research design is the plan, structure, and strategy of investigation conceived so as to obtain answers to research questions and to control variance. The *plan* is the overall scheme or program of the research. It includes an outline of what the investigator will do from writing the hypotheses and their operational implications to the final analysis of data. The *structure* of the research is more specific. It is the outline, the scheme, the paradigm of the operation of the variables.[1] When we draw diagrams that outline the variables and their relation and juxtaposition, we build structural schemes for accomplishing operational research purposes. *Strategy*, as used here, is also more specific than plan. It includes the methods to be used to gather and analyze the data. In other words, strategy implies *how* the research objectives will be reached and *how* the problems encountered in the research will be tackled.

Purposes of Research Design

Research design has two basic purposes: (1) *to provide answers to research questions* and (2) *to control variance*. Naturally, research design does not *do* these things; only the investigator does. Design helps the investigator obtain answers to the questions of research and also helps him to control the experimental, extraneous, and error variances of the particular research problem under study. Since all research activity can be said to have the purpose of providing answers to research

[1]A "paradigm" is a model, or an example. The word "model" is a synonym for a paradigm, but "paradigm" evades the value connotation of "model." Diagrams, graphs, and verbal outlines are paradigms. The word will be used here, however, in the sense of a structure and a guiding model, particularly in connection with research design.

questions, it is possible to omit this purpose from the discussion and to say that research design has one grand purpose: to control variance. Such a delimitation of the purpose of design, however, is dangerous. Without strong stress on the research questions and on the use of design to help provide answers to these questions, the study of design can degenerate into an interesting, but sterile, technical exercise.

Research designs are invented to enable the researcher to answer research questions as validly, objectively, accurately, and economically as possible. Any research plan is deliberately and specifically conceived and executed to bring empirical evidence to bear on the research problem. Research problems can be and are stated in the form of hypotheses. At some point in the research they are stated so that they can be empirically tested. There is a wide range of possibilities of testing; theoretically, at least, as many designs of research exist as there are possibilities. Designs are carefully worked out to yield dependable and valid answers to the research questions epitomized by the hypotheses. We can make one observation and infer that the hypothesized relation exists on the basis of this one observation, but it is obvious that we cannot accept the inference so made. On the other hand, it is also possible to make hundreds of observations and to infer that the hypothesized relation exists on the basis of these many observations. In this case we may or may not accept the inference as valid. The result depends on how the observations and the inference were made. Adequately planned and executed design helps greatly in permitting us to rely on both our observations and our inferences.

How does design accomplish this? Research design sets up the framework for "adequate" tests of the relations among variables. Design tells us, in a sense, what observations to make, how to make them, and how to analyze the quantitative representations of the observations. Strictly speaking, design does not "tell" us precisely what to do, but rather "suggests" the directions of observation-making and analysis. An adequate design "suggests," for example, how many observations should be made, and which variables are active and which are attribute. We can then act to manipulate the active variables and to categorize the attribute variables. A design tells us what type of statistical analysis to use. Finally, an adequate design outlines possible conclusions to be drawn from the statistical analysis.

An Example

It has been said that colleges and universities discriminate against women in hiring and in admissions.[2] Suppose we wish to test discrimination in admissions. We set up an experiment as follows. To a random sample of 200 colleges we send applications for admission basing the applications on several model cases selected over a range of tested ability with all details the same except for sex. Half the applications will be those of men and half women. Other things equal, we expect approximately equal numbers of acceptances and rejections. Acceptance, then, is

[2]The idea for the example to be used came from an unusual and ingenious experiment: E. Walster, T. Cleary, and M. Clifford, "The Effect of Race and Sex on College Admission," *Sociology of Education*, XLIV (1971), 237–244.

the dependent variable. It is measured on a three-point scale: full acceptance, qualified acceptance, rejection. Call male A_1 and female A_2. The paradigm of the design is given in Fig. 17.1.

The design is the simplest possible, given minimum requirements of control. The two treatments will be assigned to the colleges at random. Each college, then, will receive one application, which will be either male or female. The difference between the means, M_{A_1} and M_{A_2}, will be tested for statistical significance with a t or F test. The substantive hypothesis is: $M_{A_1} > M_{A_2}$, or more males than females will be accepted for admission. If there is no discrimination in admissions, then $M_{A_1} = M_{A_2}$, statistically. Suppose that an F test indicates that the means are not significantly different. Can we then be sure that there is no discrimination practiced (on the average)? While the design of Fig. 17.1 is satisfactory as far as it goes, perhaps it does not go far enough.

A Stronger Design

Walster and her colleagues (see footnote 2), in their study of discrimination in admissions, used two other independent variables, race and ability, in a factorial design. We drop race—it was not statistically significant, nor did it interact significantly with the other variables—and concentrate on sex and ability. If a college bases its selection of incoming students strictly on ability, there is no discrimination (unless, of course, ability selection is called discrimination). Add ability to the design of Fig. 17.1; use three levels. That is, in addition to the applications being designated male and female, they are also designated as high, medium, and low ability. For example, three of the applications may be: male, medium ability; female, high ability; female, low ability. Now, if there is no significant difference between sexes *and* the interaction between sex and ability is not significant, this would be considerably stronger evidence for no discrimination than that yielded by the design and statistical test of Fig. 17.1. We now use the expanded design to explain this statement and to discuss a number of points about research design. The expanded design is given in Fig. 17.2.

The design is a 2 × 3 factorial. One independent variable, A, is sex, the same as in Fig. 17.1. The second independent variable, B, is ability, which is manipu-

Treatments

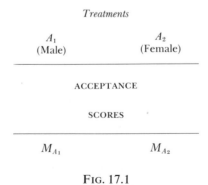

A_1 (Male)	A_2 (Female)
ACCEPTANCE	
SCORES	
M_{A_1}	M_{A_2}

FIG. 17.1

lated by indicating in several ways what the ability levels of the students are.[3] Let's assume that we believe discrimination against women takes a more subtle form than simply across-the-board exclusion: that it is the women of lower ability who are discriminated against (compared to men). This is an interaction hypothesis. At any rate, we use this problem and the paradigm of Fig. 17.2 as a basis for discussing some elements of research design.

Research problems suggest research designs. Since the hypothesis just discussed is one of interaction, a factorial design is evidently appropriate. A is *sex*; B is *ability*. A is partitioned into A_1 and A_2, and B into B_1, B_2, and B_3.

The paradigm of Fig. 17.2 suggests a number of things. First and most obvious, a fairly large number of subjects is needed. Specifically, $6n$ subjects are necessary ($n =$ number of Ss in each cell). If we decide that n should be 10, then we must have 60 Ss for the experiment. Note the "wisdom" of the design here. If we were only testing the treatments and ignoring ability, only $2n$ Ss would be needed.

Second, the design indicates that the "subjects" (colleges, in this case) can be randomly assigned to both A and B because both are experimental variables. If ability were a nonexperimental attribute variable, however, then the subjects could be randomly assigned to A_1 and A_2, but not to B_1, B_2, and B_3. Third, according to the design the observations made on the "subjects" must be made independently. The score of one college must not affect the score of another college. This is a statistical requirement of factorial design. The mere act of reducing a design to an outline like that of Fig. 17.2 in effect prescribes the operations necessary for obtaining the measures that are appropriate for the statistical analysis. An F test depends on the assumption of the independence of the measures of the dependent variable. If ability here is an attribute variable and individuals are measured for intelligence, say, then the independence requirement is in greater jeopardy because of the possibility of one subject seeing another subject's paper, because

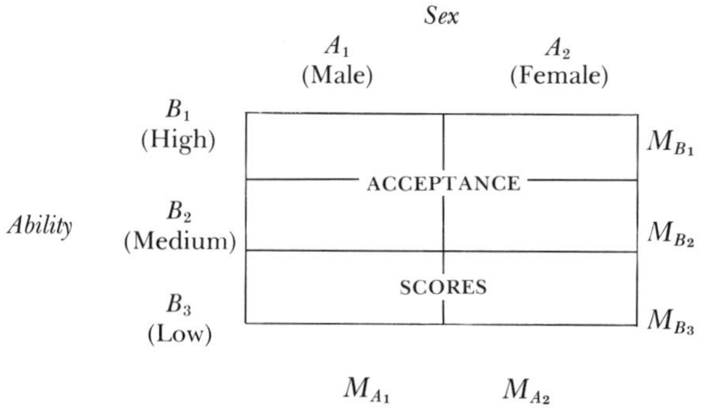

FIG. 17.2

[3] It is important not to be confused by the names of the variables. Sex and ability are ordinarily attribute variables and thus nonexperimental. In this case, however, they are manipulated. The student records sent to the colleges were systematically adjusted to fit the six cells of Fig. 17.2. A case in the A_1B_2 cell, for instance, would be the record of a male of medium ability. It is this record that the college judges for admission.

teachers may unknowingly (or knowingly) "help" children with answers, and for other reasons. Researchers try to prevent such things—not on moral grounds but to satisfy the requirements of sound design and sound statistics.

A fourth point is quite obvious to us by now: Fig. 17.2 suggests factorial analysis of variance, F tests, measures of association, and, perhaps, post hoc tests. If the research is well designed before the data are gathered—as it certainly was by Walster et al.—most statistical problems can be solved. In addition, certain troublesome problems can be avoided before they arise or can even be prevented from arising at all. With an inadequate design, however, problems of appropriate statistical tests may be very troublesome. One reason for the strong emphasis in this book on treating design and statistical problems concomitantly is to point out ways to avoid these problems. If design and statistical analysis are planned simultaneously, the analytical work is usually straightforward and uncluttered.

The last function of design discussed here is this: it outlines clearly the possible conclusions the investigator can reach, by specifically outlining or suggesting the statistical tests that can be made. A simple one-variable randomized design with two partitions, for example, two treatments, A_1 and A_2, permits only a statistical test of the difference between the two statistics yielded by the data. These statistics might be two means, two medians, two ranges, two variances, two percentages, and so forth. Only one statistical test is ordinarily possible. With the design of Fig. 17.2, however, three statistical tests are possible: (1) between A_1 and A_2; (2) among B_1, B_2, and B_3; and (3) the interaction of A and B. In most investigations, all the statistical tests are not of equal importance. The important ones, naturally, are those directly related to the research problems and hypotheses.

In the present case the interaction hypothesis [or (3), above] is the important one, since the discrimination is supposed to depend on ability level. Colleges may practice discrimination at different levels of ability. As suggested above, females (A_2) may be accepted more than males (A_1) at the higher ability level (B_1), whereas they may be accepted less at the lower ability level (B_3). This can be expressed symbolically:

$$\begin{aligned} H_3\colon\ A_2 &> A_1 \mid B_1 \qquad \text{(or: } A_1 = A_2 \mid B_1\text{)} \\ A_1 &= A_2 \mid B_2 \qquad (?) \\ A_1 &> A_2 \mid B_3 \end{aligned}$$

which simply says what we said above, except that the second line is unsure. The "|" in the symbolism indicates "under the condition," so that the first line is read "A_2 is greater than A_1, under condition B_1."

It should be evident that research design is not static. A knowledge of design can help us to plan and do better research and can also suggest the testing of hypotheses. Probably more important, we may be led to realize that the design of a study is not in itself adequate to the demands we are making of it. What is meant by this somewhat peculiar statement?

Assume that we formulate the interaction hypothesis as outlined above without knowing anything about factorial design. We set up a design consisting, actually, of two experiments. In one of these experiments we test A_1 against A_2 under con-

B_1 Condition Treatments		*B_3 Condition Treatments*	
A_1	A_2	A_1	A_2
M_{A_1}	M_{A_2}	M_{A_1}	M_{A_2}

FIG. 17.3

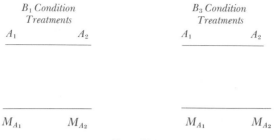

dition B_1. In the second experiment we test A_1 against A_2 under condition B_3. The paradigm would look like that of Fig. 17.3. (To make matters simpler, we are only using two levels of B, B_1 and B_3, thus reducing the design to 2×2.)

The important point to note is that no *adequate* test of the hypothesis is possible with this design. A_1 can be tested against A_2 under both B_1 and B_3 conditions, to be sure. But it is not possible to know, clearly and unambiguously, whether there is a significant interaction between A and B. Even if $M_{A_1} > M_{A_2}|B_3$, as hypothesized, the design does not offer a clear confirmation of the fact of interaction, since we cannot obtain any information about the difference between B_1 and B_3. This information is necessary to test the interaction hypothesis. If the statistical conditions were as indicated in the expression above, then there is good *presumptive* evidence that the interaction hypothesis is true. But presumptive evidence is not good enough, especially when we know that it is possible to obtain better evidence.

In Fig. 17.3, suppose the means of the cells were, from left to right: 30, 30; 40, 30. This result would seem to support the interaction hypothesis, since there is a significant difference between A_1 and A_2 at level B_3, but not at level B_1. But we could not know this to be certainly so, even though the difference between A_1 and A_2 is statistically significant. Figure 17.4 shows how this would look if a factorial design had been used.

	A_1	A_2	
B_1	30	30	30
B_3	40	30	35
	35	30	

FIG. 17.4

(The figures in the cells and on the margins are means.) Assuming that the main effects, A_1 and A_2; B_1 and B_3, were significant, it is still possible that the interaction is not significant. Unless the interaction hypothesis is specifically tested, the evidence for interaction is merely presumptive, because the authentic ring of a planned statistical interaction test that a factorial design provides is lacking. It should be clear that a knowledge of design could have improved this experiment.

Research Design as Variance Control

The main technical function of research design is *to control variance*. A research design is, in a manner of speaking, a set of instructions to the investigator to gather and analyze his data in certain ways. It is therefore a control mechanism. The statistical principle behind this mechanism, as stated earlier is: *Maximize systematic variance, control extraneous systematic variance, and minimize error variance*. In other words, we must *control variance*.

According to this principle, by constructing an efficient research design the investigator attempts (1) to maximize the variance of the variable or variables of his substantive research hypothesis, (2) to control the variance of extraneous or "unwanted" variables that may have an effect on his experimental outcomes, but in which he is not interested, and (3) to minimize the error or random variance, including so-called errors of measurement. Let us look at an example.

An Example

An educational investigator decides to test the hypothesis that the teaching of reading is facilitated more by an opportunistic method than by a systematic method.[4] The *systematic method*, call it A_1, uses a course of study that is definitely outlined and organized and oriented basically to the subject matter. The *opportunistic method*, call it A_2, explores the inclinations and interest of children. The teacher waits for opportunities to introduce reading skills, on the supposition that this study will be better motivated by the children's interests. The investigator knows very well that other possible independent variables influence reading outcomes: intelligence, sex, social class background, previous experience with verbal materials, and so on. He has reason to believe that the methods may work differently with different kinds of children. They may work one way with children of different intelligence levels and another way with children of varying home backgrounds. Children from relatively strict homes may respond better to one method than to the other method, and the same is true for children from relatively permissive homes.

What kind of design should the investigator set up? To answer this question, it is important to assemble and label the variables and to know clearly what questions the investigator wants to answer. The variables are:

Methods	*Type of Home*
systematic, A_1	restrictive, B_1
opportunistic, A_2	permissive, B_2

He might also include *intelligence* as an independent variable, but he decides not to do so. Instead, he decides that random assignment will take care of intelligence and other possible influential independent variables. His dependent variable

[4]The idea for this example was taken from A. Gates, M. Batchelder, and J. Betzner, "A Modern Systematic versus an Opportunistic Method of Teaching," *Teachers College Record*, XXVII (1926), 679–700. The design notions used in the example are not those of the original authors, who used a matching method.

measure is provided by a standardized reading test to be administered after four months of the experiment.

The investigator's problem seems to call for a factorial design. There are two reasons for this choice. One, there are two independent variables. Two, the investigator has quite clearly an interaction hypothesis in mind, though he may not have stated it in so many words, since he has the belief that the methods will work differently with different kinds of children. We set up the design structure in Fig. 17.5.

Note that all the marginal and cell means have been appropriately labeled. Note, too, that there is one *active variable*, methods, and one *attribute variable*, type of home.[5] The experimenter obviously cannot use randomization with the attribute variable. All he can do is to categorize his subjects as coming from restrictive and permissive homes and assign them accordingly to B_1 and B_2. He can, however, and *does* randomly assign the children to A_1 and A_2, the methods groups. This he does in two stages: (1) he randomly assigns the B_1, restrictive home, children to A_1 and A_2, and (2) he assigns the B_2, permissive home, children to A_1 and A_2. By so randomizing the subjects the investigator can assume that before the experiment begins, the children in A_1 are approximately equal to the children in A_2 in all possible characteristics.

Our present concern is with the different roles of variance in research design and the variance principle. Before going further, we name the variance principle for easy reference—the "maxmincon" principle. The origin of this name is obvious: *max*imize the systematic variance under study; *con*trol extraneous systematic variance; and *min*imize error variance—with two of the syllables reversed for euphony.

Before tackling the application of the maxmincon principle in the present example, an important point should be discussed. Whenever we talk about variance, we must be sure to know *what* variance we are talking about. We speak of

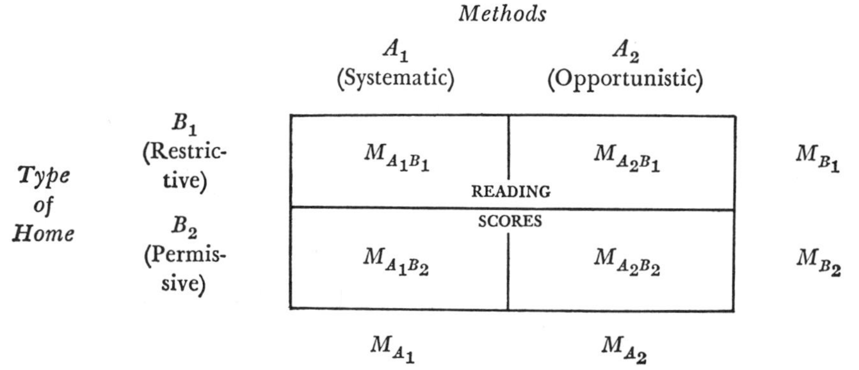

FIG. 17.5

[5]It will be remembered from Chapter 3 that an *active variable* is an experimental or manipulated variable, and an *attribute variable* is a measured variable, or a variable that is a characteristic, e.g., intelligence, social class, and occupation (people), and cohesiveness, productivity, and restrictive–permissive atmosphere (organizations, groups, and the like).

the variance of the methods, of intelligence, of sex, of type of home, and so on. This sounds as though we were talking about the independent variable variance. This is true and not true. We always mean *the variance of the dependent variable, the variance of the dependent variable measures*, after the experiment has been done.[6] Our way of saying "independent variable variance" stems from the fact that, by manipulation and control of independent variables, we *influence*, presumably, the variance of the dependent variable. Somewhat inaccurately put, we "make" the measures of the dependent variable behave or vary as a presumed result of our manipulation and control of the independent variables. In an experiment, it is the dependent variable measures that are analyzed. Then, from the analysis we *infer* that the variances present in the total variance of the dependent variable measures are due to the manipulation and control of the independent variables and to error. Now, back to our principle.

Maximization of Experimental Variance

The experimenter's most obvious, but not necessarily most important, concern is to maximize what we will call the *experimental variance*. This term is introduced to facilitate subsequent discussions and, in general, simply refers to the variance of the dependent variable influenced by the independent variable or variables of the substantive hypothesis. In this particular case, the experimental variance is the variance in the dependent variable presumably due to methods, A_1 and A_2, and types of home, B_1 and B_2. Although experimental variance can be taken to mean only the variance due to a manipulated or *active* variable, like methods, we shall also consider *attribute* variables, like intelligence, sex, and, in this case, type of home, experimental variables. One of the main tasks of an experimenter is to maximize this variance. He must "pull" the methods apart as much as possible to make A_1 and A_2 (and A_3, A_4, and so on, if they are in the design) as unlike as possible.

If the independent variable does not vary substantially, there is little chance of separating its effect from the total variance of the dependent variable, so much of which is often due to chance. It is necessary to give the variance of a relation a chance to show itself, to separate itself, so to speak, from the total variance, which is a composite of variances due to numerous sources and chance. Remembering this subprinciple of the maxmincon principle, we can write a research precept: *Design, plan, and conduct research so that the experimental conditions are as different as possible*.[7]

In the present research example, this subprinciple means that the investigator

[6] This is not true in so-called correlational studies where, when we say "the variance of the independent variable," we mean just that. When correlating two variables, we study the variances of the independent and dependent variables "directly."

[7] There are, of course, exceptions to this subprinciple, but they are probably rare. An investigator might want to study the effects of small gradations of, say, motivational incentives on the learning of some subject matter. Here he would not make his experimental conditions as different as possible. Still, he would have to make them vary somewhat or there would be no discernible resulting variance in the dependent variable.

must take pains to make A_1 and A_2, the systematic and opportunistic methods, as different as possible. Next, he must so categorize his types of homes into restrictive and permissive, B_1 and B_2, that they are as different as possible on the restrictive-permissive dimension. This latter problem is essentially one of measurement. In an experiment, the investigator is like a puppeteer making the independent variable puppets do what he wants. He holds the strings of the A_1 and A_2 puppets in his right hand and the strings of the B_1 and B_2 puppets in his left hand. (We assume there is no influence of one hand on the other, that is, the hands must be independent.) He makes the A_1 and A_2 puppets dance apart, and he makes the B_1 and B_2 puppets dance apart. He then watches his audience (the dependent variable) to see and measure the effect of his manipulations. If he is successful in making A_1 and A_2 dance apart, and if there is a relation between A and the dependent variable, the audience reaction—if separating A_1 and A_2 is funny, for instance—then he should get a reaction from the audience, laughter. He may even observe that he only gets laughter when A_1 and A_2 dance apart and, at the same time, B_1 or B_2 dance apart (interaction again).

Control of Extraneous Variables

The control of extraneous variables means that the influences of independent variables extraneous to the purposes of the study are minimized, nullified, or isolated. In other words, the variance of such variables is in effect reduced to zero or near zero, or, what amounts to fundamentally the same thing, it is separated from the variance of other independent variables.

There are three ways to control extraneous variables. The first is the easist, if it is possible: to eliminate the variable as a variable. If we are worried about intelligence as a possible contributing factor in studies of achievement, its effect on the dependent variable can be virtually eliminated by using subjects of only one intelligence level, say IQ's within the range of 90 to 110. If we are studying achievement, and racial membership is a possible contributing factor to the variance of achievement, it can be eliminated by using only members of one race. The subprinciple here is: *To eliminate the effect of a possible influential independent variable on a dependent variable, one can choose subjects so that they are as homogeneous as possible on that independent variable.*

This method of controlling unwanted or extraneous variance is very effective. If we select only one sex for an experiment, then we can be sure that sex cannot be a contributing independent variable. But then we lose the power of generalization; for instance we can say nothing about the relation under study with girls if we use only boys in the experiment. If the range of intelligence is restricted, then we can discuss only this restricted range. Is it possible that the relation, if discovered, is nonexistent or quite different with children of high intelligence or children of low intelligence? We simply do not know; we can only surmise or guess.

The second way to control extraneous variance is through randomization. This is the best way, in the sense that you can have your cake and eat some of it, too. Theoretically, randomization is the only method of controlling *all* possible extraneous variables. Another way to phrase it is: if randomization has been thoroughly accomplished, then the experimental groups can be considered statistically equal in all possible ways. This does not mean, of course, that the groups *are* equal in all the possible variables. We already know that by chance the groups can be unequal, but the probability of their being equal is greater, with proper randomization, than the probability of their not being equal. For this reason control of the extraneous variance by randomization is a powerful method of control. All other methods leave many possibilities of inequality. If we match for intelligence, we may successfully achieve statistical equality in intelligence (at least in those aspects of intelligence measured), but we may suffer from inequality in other significantly influential independent variables like aptitude, motivation, and social class. A subprinciple that springs from this equalizing power of randomization, then, is: *Whenever it is possible to do so, randomly assign subjects to experimental groups and conditions, and randomly assign conditions and other factors to experimental groups.*

The third means of controlling an extraneous variable is to build it right into the design as an independent variable. For example, assume that sex was to be controlled in the experiment discussed earlier and it was considered inexpedient or unwise to eliminate it. One could add a third independent variable, sex, to the design. Unless one were interested in the actual difference between the sexes on the dependent variable or wanted to study the interaction between one or two of the other variables and sex, however, it is unlikely that this form of control would be resorted to. One might want information of the kind just mentioned and also want to control sex, too. In such a case, adding it to the design as a variable might be desirable. The point is that building a variable into an experimental design "controls" the variable, since it then becomes possible to extract from the total variance of the dependent variable the variance due to the variable. (In the above case, this would be the "between-sexes" variance.)

These considerations lead to another subprinciple: *An extraneous variable can be controlled by building it into the research design as an attribute variable, thus achieving control and yielding additional research information about the effect of the variable on the dependent variable and about its possible interaction with other independent variables.*

The fourth way to control extraneous variance is to match subjects. The control principle behind matching is the same as that for any other kind of control, the control of variance. Matching is similar—in fact, it might be called a corollary—to the principle of controlling the variance of an extraneous variable by building it into the design. The basic principle is to split a variable into two or more parts, say into high and low intelligence in a factorial design, and then randomize within each level as described above. Matching is a special case of this principle. Instead of splitting the subjects into two, three, or four parts, however, they are split into $N/2$ parts, N being the number of subjects used; thus the control of variance is identified and built into the design.

In using the matching method several problems may be encountered. To begin with, the variable on which the subjects are matched must be fairly substantially related to the dependent variable or the matching is a waste of time. Even worse, it can be misleading. In addition, matching has severe limitations. If we try to match, say, on more than two variables, or even more than one, we lose subjects. It is difficult to find matched subjects on more than two variables. For instance, if one decides to match intelligence, sex, and social class, one may be fairly successful in matching the first two variables but not in finding pairs that are fairly equal on all three variables. Add a fourth variable and the problem becomes very difficult, often impossible to solve.

Let us not throw the baby out with the bath, however. When there is a substantial correlation between the matching variable or variables and the dependent variable (> .50 or .60), then matching reduces the error term and thus increases the precision of an experiment, a desirable outcome. If the same subjects are used with different experimental treatments—called repeated measures or randomized blocks design—we have powerful control of variance. How match better on all possible variables than by matching a subject with himself? Unfortunately, other negative considerations usually rule out this possibility. It should be forcefully emphasized that matching of any kind is no substitute for randomization. If subjects are matched, *they should then be assigned to experimental groups at random.* Through a random procedure, like tossing a coin or using odd and even random numbers, the members of the matched pairs are assigned to experimental and control groups. If the same subjects undergo all treatments, then the order of the treatments should be assigned randomly. This adds randomization control to the matching, or repeated measures, control.[8]

A subprinciple suggested by this discussion is: *When a matching variable is substantially correlated with the dependent variable, matching as a form of variance control can be profitable and desirable. Before using matching, however, carefully weigh its advantages and disadvantages in the particular research situation. Complete randomization or the analysis of covariance may be better methods of variance control.*

Still another form of control, statistical control, was discussed at length in Part 5, but one or two further remarks are in order here. Statistical methods are, so to speak, forms of control in the sense that they isolate and quantify variances. But statistical control is inseparable from other forms of design control. If matching is used, for example, an appropriate statistical test must be used, or the matching effect, and thus the control, will be lost.

Minimization of Error Variance

Error variance is the variability of measures due to random fluctuations whose basic characteristic is that they are self-compensating, varying now this way, now that way, now positive, now negative, now up, now down. Random errors tend to balance each other so that their mean is zero, but systematic variance is in essence predictable. Error variance is unpredictable.

[8]See D. Campbell and J. Stanley, *Experimental and Quasi-Experimental Designs for Research.* Skokie, Ill.: Rand McNally, 1963, pp. 15, 49.

There are a number of determinants of error variance, for instance, factors associated with individual differences among subjects. Ordinarily we call this variance due to individual differences "systematic variance." But when such variance cannot be, or is not identified and controlled, we have to lump it with the error variance. Because many determinants interact and tend to cancel each other out (or at least we assume that they do), the error variance has this random characteristic.

Another source of error variance is that associated with what are called errors of measurement: variation of responses from trial to trial, guessing, momentary inattention, slight temporary fatigue and lapses of memory, transient emotional states of subjects, and so on.

Minimizing error variance has two principal aspects: (1) the reduction of errors of measurement through controlled conditions, and (2) an increase in the reliability of measures. The more uncontrolled the conditions of an experiment, the more the many determinants of error variance can operate. This is one of the reasons for carefully setting up controlled experimental situations and conditions. In studies under field conditions, of course, such control is difficult; still, constant efforts must be made to lessen the effects of the many determinants of error variance. This can be effected, in part, by specific and clear instructions to subjects and by excluding from the experimental situation problems that are extraneous to the research purpose.

To increase the reliability of measures is to reduce the error variance. Pending fuller discussion later in the book, reliability can be taken to be the *accuracy* of a set of scores. To the extent that scores do not fluctuate randomly, to this extent they are reliable. Imagine a completely unreliable measurement instrument, one that could not allow us to predict the future performance of individuals at all, one that would give one rank ordering of a sample of subjects and a completely different rank ordering on another administration. With such an instrument, it would not be possible to identify and extract systematic variances, since the scores yielded by the instrument would be like the numbers in a table of random numbers. This is the extreme case. Now imagine differing amounts of reliability and unreliability in the measures of the dependent variable. The more reliable the measures, the better we can identify and extract systematic variances and the smaller the error variance in relation to the total variance.

Another reason for reducing error variance as much as possible is to give systematic variances a chance to show their significance—if they *are* significant. We cannot do this if the error variance, and thus the error term, is too large. If a relation exists, we seek to discover it. One way of discovering this relation or of letting it appear, is by finding significant differences between means. But if the error variance is relatively large due to uncontrolled errors of measurement (and thus unreliable), the systematic variances—called earlier "between" variances—will not have a chance to be significant. Thus the relation, although it exists, will probably not be, or perhaps cannot be, discovered.

The problem of error variance can be put into a neat mathematical nutshell: remember the equation,

$$V_t = V_b + V_e$$

where V_t is the total variance in a set of measures; V_b is the between-groups variance, the variance presumably due to the influence of the experimental variables; and V_e is the error variance (in analysis of variance, the within-groups variance and the residual variance). Obviously, the larger V_e is, the smaller V_b must be, with a given amount of V_t.

Better yet, consider the following equations:

$$t = \frac{\text{statistic}}{\text{standard error of the statistic}}$$

and

$$F = \frac{V_b}{V_e}$$

Both equations say the same thing: in order for the numerators of the fractions on the right to be accurately evaluated for significant departures from chance expectations, the denominators should be accurate measures of random error.

A familiar example should make this clear. Recall that in the discussions of factorial analysis of variance and the analysis of variance of correlated groups we talked about variance due to individual differences being present in experimental measures. We said that, while adequate randomization would effectively equalize experimental groups, there would be variance in the scores due to individual differences, for instance, differences due to intelligence, aptitude, and so forth. Now, in some situations, these individual differences can be quite large. If they are, then the error variance and, consequently, the denominators of the t and F equations, above, will be "too large" relative to the numerators; that is, the individual differences will have been randomly scattered among, say, two, three, or four experimental groups. Still, they are sources of variance and, as such, will inflate the within-groups or residual variance or the standard variance (standard error squared), the denominators of the above equations.

Study Suggestion

We have noted, that research design has the purposes of obtaining answers to research questions and controlling variance. Explain in detail what this statement means. How does a research design control variance? Why should a factorial design control more variance than a one-way design? How does a design that uses matched subjects or repeated measures of the same subjects control variance? What is the relation between the research questions and hypotheses and a research design? In answering these questions, make up a research problem to illustrate what you mean (or use an example from the text).

CHAPTER 18

Inadequate Designs and Design Criteria

All man's disciplined creations have form. Architecture, poetry, music, painting, mathematics, scientific research—all have form. Man puts great stress on the content of his creations, often not realizing that without strong structure, no matter how rich and how significant the content, the creations may be weak and sterile.

So it is with scientific research. The scientist needs viable and plastic form with which to express his scientific aims. Without content—without good theory, good hypotheses, good problems—the design of research is empty. But without form, without structure adequately conceived and created for the research purpose, little of value can be accomplished. Indeed, it is no exaggeration to say that many of the failures of behavioral research have been failures of disciplined and imaginative form.

The principal focus of this chapter is on inadequate research designs. Such designs have been so common, especially in education, that they must be discussed. More important, the student should be able to recognize them and understand *why* they are inadequate. This negative approach has a virtue: the study of deficiencies forces one to ask why something is deficient, which in turn centers attention on the criteria used to judge both adequacies and inadequacies. So the study of inadequate designs leads us to the study of the criteria of research design. We take the opportunity, too, to describe the symbolic system to be used and to identify an important distinction between experimental and so-called ex post facto research.

Experimental and Ex Post Facto Approaches

Discussion of design must be prefaced by an important distinction: that between the experimental and so-called ex post facto approaches to research. Indeed, this distinction is so important that a separate chapter will be devoted to it later. The literal meaning of ex post facto is "from what is done afterward." It means something done or occurring *after* an event with a retroactive effect on the event. It is used in contradistinction to "experimental" in this text, and has been assigned a specific and, hopefully, unambiguous meaning.

An experiment is taken to mean a scientific investigation in which an investigator manipulates and controls one or more independent variables and observes the dependent variable or variables for variation concomitant to the manipulation of the independent variables. An *experimental design*, then, is one in which the investigator *manipulates* at least one independent variable. Hurlock manipulated incentives to produce different amounts of retention. Fleming and Antonnen manipulated IQ information given to teachers in their study of the effects of teacher expectancy: some of the teachers were told that certain pupils had IQ's much higher than they actually did have.

In a *true* experiment, the investigator has the power to assign subjects to experimental groups. Ideally, he should have the power to *select* his subjects, at random if possible, but unfortunately, this ideal situation is frequently denied him. If the experimenter does not have the *power* either to assign subjects to experimental groups or to assign experimental treatments to the groups, then his study may be an experiment, but not a *true* experiment.

In ex post facto research one cannot manipulate or assign subjects or treatments, because the independent variable or variables have already occurred, so to speak. The investigator starts with observation of the dependent variable and retrospectively studies independent variables for their possible effects on the dependent variable. When Getzels and Jackson compared the characteristics of highly intelligent "noncreative" children and less intelligent "creative" children, their "creative" and "noncreative" and highly intelligent and less intelligent groups had already been formed for them.[1] These independent variables had already "occurred," so to speak. Getzels and Jackson could not manipulate creativity or intelligence, nor could they assign, randomly or otherwise, subjects to groups or treatments to subjects (unless, of course, they had chosen another independent variable to manipulate, say methods of teaching). While experimental and ex post facto research differ sharply, then, on these and other counts, they share structural and design features, which we will attempt to point out in this and the following chapters on design.

The ideal of science is the controlled experiment. Except, perhaps, in taxonomic research, research with the purpose of discovering, classifying, and measuring natural phenomena and the factors behind such phenomena, the controlled experiment is the desired model of science. It may be difficult for many students to accept this rather categorical statement since its logic is not readily apparent. Earlier it was said that the main goal of science was to discover relations among phenomena. Why, then, assign a priority to the controlled experiment? Do not other methods of discovering relations exist? Yes, of course they do. The main

[1] J. Getzels and P. Jackson, "Occupational Choice and Cognitive Functioning: Career Aspirations of Highly Intelligent and of Highly Creative Adolescents," *Journal of Abnormal and Social Psychology*, LXI (1960), 119–123.

reason for the preeminence of the controlled experiment, however, is that the researcher can have more confidence that the relations he discovers *are* the relations he thinks they are, since he discovers them under the most carefully *controlled* conditions of inquiry known to man. The unique virtue of experimental inquiry, then, is control.

In short, a perfectly conducted experimental research, which yields information that A is related to B, is more trustworthy than a perfectly conducted ex post facto research. Why this is so should become more apparent as we advance in our study of research design.

Symbolism and Definitions

Before discussing inadequate designs, explanation of the symbolism to be used in these chapters is necessary. X means an *experimentally manipulated* independent variable (or variables). X_1, X_2, X_3, etc. mean independent variables 1, 2, 3, and so on, though we usually use X alone, even when it can mean more than one independent variable. (We also use X_1, X_2, etc. to mean partitions of an independent variable, but the difference will always be clear.) The symbol (X) indicates that the independent variable is *not manipulated*—is not under the direct control of the investigator, but is *measured* or *imagined*. The dependent variable is Y, or perhaps more accurately, the measure of the dependent variable. Y_b is the dependent variable *before* the manipulation of X, and Y_a the dependent variable *after* the manipulation of X. With $\sim X$, we borrow the negation sign of set theory; $\sim X$ "not-X") means that the experimental variable, the independent variable X, *is not* manipulated. (Note: (X) is a nonmanipulable variable and $\sim X$ is a manipulable variable that is *not* manipulated.) The symbol [R] will be used for the random assignment of subjects to experimental groups and the random assignment of experimental treatments to experimental groups.

The explanation of $\sim X$, just given, is not quite accurate, because in some cases $\sim X$ can mean a different aspect of the treatment X rather than merely the absence of X. In an older language, *the* experimental group was the group that was given the so-called experimental treatment, X, while the control group did not receive it, $\sim X$. For our purposes, however, $\sim X$ will do well enough, especially if we understand the generalized meaning of "control" discussed below. An *experimental group*, then, is a group of subjects receiving some aspect, some manipulation, of X. In testing the frustration-aggression hypothesis, the experimental group is the group whose subjects are systematically frustrated. In contrast, the control group is one that is given "no" treatment.

In modern multivariate research, it is necessary to expand these notions. They are not changed basically; they are only expanded. It is quite possible to have more than one experimental group, as we have seen. Different degrees of manipulation of the independent variable are not only possible; they are often also desirable or even imperative. Furthermore, it is possible to have more than one control group, a statement that at first seems like nonsense. How can one have different degrees of "no" experimental treatment?—because the notion of *control* is generalized. When there are more than two groups, and when any two of them are treated differently, one or more groups serve as "controls" on the others. Recall that control is always control of variance. With two or more groups treated differently, variance is engendered by the experimental manipulation. So the traditional notion of X and $\sim X$, treatment and no treatment, is generalized to $X_1, X_2, \ldots, X_k$, different forms or degrees of treatment.

If X is circled, $\textcircled{X}$, this means that the investigator "imagines" the manipulation of X, or he assumes that X occurred and that it is *the* X of his hypothesis. It may also mean that X is measured and not manipulated. Actually, we are saying the same thing here in different ways. The context of the discussion should make the distinction clear. Suppose an educational sociologist is studying delinquency and the frustration-aggression hypothesis. He observes delinquency, Y, and imagines that his delinquent subjects were frustrated in their earlier years, or $\textcircled{X}$. All ex post facto designs will have $\textcircled{X}$. Generally, then, $\textcircled{X}$ means an independent variable not under the experimental control of the investigator.

One more point—each design in this chapter will ordinarily have an *a* and a *b* form. The *a* form will be the experimental form, or that in which X is manipulated. The *b* form will be the ex post facto form, that in which X is not under the control of the investigator, or $\textcircled{X}$. Obviously, $\textcircled{\sim X}$ is also possible.

Faulty Designs

There are three or four inadequate designs of research that have been used, and unfortunately are still used, in behavioral research. It is doubtful that the investigators who use these designs are aware of their inadequacies. These inadequacies are basically structural weaknesses that lead to no control or poor control of independent variables. The faulty designs to be discussed furnish us with examples that, although poor, are instructive. Dangers cannot be avoided if they are not recognized.

Design 18.1: One Group

(a)	X	Y	(Experimental)
(b)	$\textcircled{X}$	Y	(Ex post facto)

[2]D. Campbell, "Factors Relevant to the Validity of Experiments in Social Settings," *Psychological Bulletin*, LIV (1957), 297–312. This is an excellent article. The author has been influenced by Campbell's thinking and the thinking of Solomon, Stouffer, and Underwood, but has altered their formulations to fit the design discussion of this book. See S. Stouffer, "Some Observations on Study Design," *American Journal of Sociology*, LV (1950), 355–361; R. Solomon, "An Extension of Control Group Design," *Psychological Bulletin*, XLVI (1949), 137–150; B. Underwood, *Psychological Research*. New York: Appleton, 1957, chaps. 4 and 5; and D. Campbell and J. Stanley, *Experimental and Quasi-Experimental Designs for Research*. Skokie: Ill.: Rand McNally, 1963. Recently, Solomon's four-group design (see Chapter 19, Design 19.6) idea has been applied to deprivation and enrichment research: R. Solomon and M. Lessac, "A Control Group Design for Experimental Studies of Developmental Processes," *Psychological Bulletin*, LXX (1968), 145–150.

This design has also been called the "One-Shot Case Study," an apropos expression.[2] Case studies fall under this rubric, but so do certain types of research. Design 18.1(a) is an "experimental" type. For example, a school faculty decides to institute a new curriculum, and also decides to "study" or "evaluate" the effects of the new curriculum, represented by X, a manipulated independent variable. After one year, Y, student achievement, and perhaps student attitudes—but more likely, faculty opinion—are studied. Student achievement is found to be "the same" or "better," say. The value of the new curriculum is established.[3]

Design 18.1(b) is the ex post facto form of the one-group design. Here the dependent variable Y, the outcome, is studied or examined, and the independent variable X is assumed or imagined. A case in point would be to study delinquency by taking a group of juvenile delinquents and looking into the past for causative factors that might have led to their antisocial behavior.

Scientifically speaking, Design 18.1 is worthless; worse, it can be badly misleading. As Campbell points out, the minimum of useful scientific information requires at least one formal comparison.[4] The new-curriculum example requires, *at the least,* comparison of a group that experienced the curriculum with a group that did not experience it. The design is worthless scientifically because Y, the presumed effect, might have occurred as it did without X, the presumed cause. The presumed effect of the new curriculum, say such-and-such achievement, might well have been about the same under any kind of curriculum. The point is not that the new curriculum did or did not have an effect, but that, in the absence of any formal, controlled comparison of the performance of the members of the "experimental" group with the performance of the members of some other group not experiencing the new curriculum, nothing can be said about its effect. Unfortunately, much *has* been said about the presumed results of such "experiments," and faith has even been placed in these utterances.

An important dictinction must be emphasized. We are not saying that the method is *universally* worthless and misleading, but that it is *scientifically* worthless and misleading. In studying life we depend on such "experimental" evidence. We act, we say, on the basis of our experience, and this is the only way we *can* act. We hope that we use our experience rationally and critically. Thus, the paradigm of thinking in practical affairs, which is implied by Design 18.1, is not being criticized, although it might well be. It is only when such a paradigm is labeled as scientific, or believed to be scientific, that difficulties arise. Even in high intellectual pursuits, this paradigm must be used. Freud's brilliant observations and analyses of neurotic behavior seem to fall into this category. The only quarrel we have is not with Freud but rather with the assertions that his conclusions were "scientifically established."

[3]The implication here is not that *evaluation,* in the sense of informed and careful discussion and appraisal, is undesirable. It is often not feasible to use controlled experiments in such situations. To call such appraisal "research," or to set up an experiment of the one-group kind, however, is misleading.

[4]Campbell, *op. cit.*, p. 298.

Design 18.2: One-Group, before-after (Pretest-Posttest)

(a)	Y_b	X	Y_a	(Experimental)
(b)	Y_b	(X)	Y_a	(Ex post facto)

Design 18.2 is only a small improvement on Design 18.1. The essential characteristic of this mode of research is that a group is compared with itself. Theoretically, there is no better control since all possible independent variables associated with the subjects' characteristics are controlled. The procedure dictated by such a design is as follows. A group is measured on the dependent variable, Y, before any experimental manipulation. This is usually called a *pretest*. Two important dependent variables that are used quite frequently are school achievement and attitudes. Let us assume that the attitudes toward women of a group of subjects are to be measured. An experimental manipulation designed to change these attitudes is accomplished. An experimenter might expose the group to expert opinion on women's rights. After the interposition of this X, the attitudes of the subjects are again measured. The difference scores, or $Y_a - Y_b$, are examined for change in attitudes.

At face value, this would seem a good way to accomplish the experimental purpose. After all, if the difference scores are statistically significant, does this not indicate a change in attitudes? The situation, however, is not so simple—there are a number of other factors that may have contributed to the change in scores. Campbell gives an excellent, detailed discussion of these factors,[5] only a brief discussion of which can be given here.

Measurement, History, Maturation First is the possible effect of the measurement procedure: measuring subjects changes them. Could it be that the post-X measures were influenced not by the manipulation of X but by increased sensitization due to the pretest? In some research situations, this factor may make no difference; in others, it may make a considerable difference. Controversial attitudes, for example, seem to be especially susceptible to such sensitization. Campbell calls the measures of such variables *reactive measures*, because they themselves cause the subject to react. Achievement measures, though probably less reactive, are still reactive. Measures involving memory are quite reactive. If you take a test now, you are more likely to remember later things that were included in the test. In short, observed changes may be due to reactive measures.

Two other important sources of extraneous variance are *history* and *maturation*. Between the Y_b and Y_a testings, many things can occur other than X. In other words, extraneous independent variables can operate in the interval. The longer the period of time, the greater the chance of extraneous variables affecting the subjects and thus the Y_a measures. This is what Campbell calls *history*. These variables or events are *specific* to the particular experimental situation. *Maturation*,

[5]*Ibid.*, pp. 298–300. The first point discussed, the possible interaction effect of the pretest, seems first to have been pointed out by Solomon in his excellent article, cited above, pp. 140–141. Campbell has elaborated Solomon's original point: Campbell, *op. cit.*, pp. 298–299. See, also, Campbell and Stanley, *op. cit.*, pp. 7–12. We ignore here the problems involved in using change, or difference, scores.

on the other hand, covers events that are not specific to any particular situation. They are, rather, *general*. They are connected with change or growth in the organism studied. The mental age of a child increases with time. This increase can easily affect achievement measures. Children learn during any given time interval, and the learning may affect the dependent variable measure. In fact, this is one of the exasperating features of educational research. Children refuse to stand still while studies are progressing. Again, the longer the time interval, the greater the possibility that such extraneous variables, such unwanted possible sources of systematic variance, will influence the dependent variable measures.

The Regression Effect A statistical phenomenon that has misled and baffled researchers is the so-called *regression effect*. Scores of tests change as a statistical fact of life: on retest, on the average, they *regress* toward the mean. The regression effect operates because of the imperfect correlation between the pretest and posttest scores. If $r_{ab} = 1.00$, then there is no regression effect; if $r_{ab} = .00$, the effect is at a maximum in the sense that the best prediction of any posttest score from pretest score is the mean. With the moderate and sizable, but imperfect, correlations found in practice, the net effect is that lower scores on the pretest tend to be higher and higher scores lower on the posttest—when, in fact, no real change has taken place in the dependent variable. Thus, if low-scoring subjects—the underprivileged, for example—are used in a study, their scores on the posttest will probably be higher than on the pretest due to the regression effect. This can deceive the researcher into believing that his experimental intervention has been effective when it really has not. Similarly, if one studies only high pretest scorers, one might erroneously conclude, say, that, a school program had had a depressing effect on them. Not necessarily so. The lower scores may be due to the regression effect.

How does this work? There are many chance factors at work in any set of scores.[6] On the pretest some high scores are higher than "they should be" due to chance, and similarly with some low scorers. On the posttest it is unlikely that the high scores will be maintained, because the factors that made them high were chance factors—which, after all, are uncorrelated on the pretest and posttest. Thus the high scorer will tend to drop on the posttest. A similar argument applies to the low scorer.

Any research design has to be constructed with the regression effect in mind. There is no way in Design 18.2 to control it. If there were a control group, then one could "control" the regression effect, since both experimental and control groups have pretest and posttest. If the experimental manipulation has had a "real" effect, then it should be apparent over and above the regression effect. That is, the scores of both groups, other things equal, are affected the same by regression

[6]Much of this explanation is due to Anastasi's clear and excellent discussion of the regression effect: A. Anastasi, *Individual Differences*, 3d ed. New York: Macmillan, 1958, pp. 203–205. For a more complete and equally excellent discussion, see R. Thorndike, *Concepts of Over- and Underachievement*. New York: Teachers College Press, 1963, pp. 11–15. This little book is an analytic tour de force that students of research should study carefully. Thorndike clearly and authoritatively describes a number of difficult research problems; he also recommends solutions to the problems.

and other effects. So, if the groups differ in the posttest, it should be due to the experimental manipulation.

Design 18.2 is inadequate not so much because extraneous variables and the regression effect can operate (the extraneous variables operate whenever there is a time interval between pretest and posttest), but *because we do not know whether or not they have operated, whether or not they have affected the dependent-variable measures*. The design affords no opportunity to control or to test such possible influences.

Design 18.3: Simulated before-after

$$\begin{array}{ccc} & X & Y_a \\ \hline Y_b & & \end{array}$$

The peculiar title of this design stems in part from its very nature. Like Design 18.2 it is a before-after design. Instead of using the before and after (or pretest-posttest) measures of one group, we use as pretest measures the measures of another group which are chosen to be as similar as possible to the experimental group and thus a control group of a sort. (The line between the two levels, above, indicates separate groups.) This design satisfies the condition of having a control group and is thus a gesture toward the comparison that is necessary to scientific investigation. Unfortunately, the controls are weak, a result of our inability to know that the two groups were equivalent before X, the experimental manipulation.

Design 18.4: Two Groups, No Control

$$\text{(a)} \quad \begin{array}{cc} X & Y \\ \hline \sim X & Y \end{array} \quad \text{(Experimental)}$$

$$\text{(b)} \quad \begin{array}{cc} \textcircled{X} & Y \\ \hline \textcircled{\sim X} & \sim Y \end{array} \quad \text{(Ex post facto)}$$

Design 18.4 is common. In (a) the experimental group is administered treatment X; the "control" group, taken to be, or assumed to be, similar to the experimental group, is not given X. The Y measures are compared to ascertain the effect of X. Groups or subjects are taken "as they are," or they may be matched. The ex post facto version of the same design is labeled (b). An effect, Y, is observed to occur in one group (top line) but not in another group, or to occur in the other group to a lesser extent (indicated by the $\sim Y$ in the bottom line). The first group is found to have experienced X, the second group not to have experienced X.

This design has a basic weakness. The two groups are *assumed* to be equal in independent variables other than X. It is sometimes possible to check the equality of the groups roughly by comparing them on different pertinent variables, for example, age, sex, income, intelligence, ability, and so on. This should be done if it is at all possible, but, as Stouffer says, ". . . there is all too often a wide-open gate through which other uncontrolled variables can march."[7] Because randomization is not used—that is, the subjects are not assigned to the groups at random—it is not possible to assume that the groups are equal. Design 18.4(b) is weaker than (a) because *X* is manipulated in (a) but not in (b). Both versions of the design, however, suffer seriously from lack of control of independent variables due to lack of randomization.

Criteria of Research Design

After examining some of the main weaknesses of inadequate research designs, we are in a good position to discuss what can be called criteria of research design. Along with the criteria, we will enunciate certain principles that should guide researchers. Finally, the criteria and principles will be related to Campbell's notions of internal and external validity, which, in a sense, express the criteria another way.

Answer Research Questions?

The main criterion or desideratum of a research design can be expressed in a question: *Does the design answer the research questions?* or *Does the design adequately test the hypotheses?* Perhaps the most serious weakness of designs often proposed by students is that they are not capable of adequately answering the research questions. A common example of this lack of congruence between the research questions and hypothesis, on the one hand, and the research design, on the other, is matching subjects for reasons irrelevant to the research and then using an experimental group-control group type of design. Students often assume, because they match pupils on intelligence and sex, for instance, that their experimental groups are equal. They have heard that one should match subjects for "control" and that one should have an experimental group and a control group. Frequently, however, the matching variables may be irrelevant to the research purposes. That is, if there is no relation between, say, sex and the dependent variable, then matching on sex is irrelevant.

Another example of this weakness is the case where three or four experimental groups are needed—for example, three experimental groups and one control group, or four groups with different amounts of *X*, the experimental treatment—and the investigator uses only two because he has heard that an experimental group and a control group are necessary and desirable.

The example discussed in Chapter 17 of testing and interaction hypothesis by performing, in effect, two separate experiments is another example. The hypothesis to be tested was that discrimination in college admissions is a function of both sex and ability level, that it is women of low ability who are excluded (in contrast to men of low ability). This is an interaction hypothesis and probably calls for a factorial-type design. To set up two experiments, one for college applicants of high ability and another for applicants of low ability, is poor practice because such a design, as shown earlier, cannot decisively test the stated hypothesis.

[7]Stouffer, *op. cit.*, p. 522.

Similarly, to match subjects on ability and then set up a two-group design would miss the research question entirely. These considerations lead to a general and seemingly obvious precept:

Design research to answer research questions.

Control of Extraneous Independent Variables

The second criterion is *control*, which means control of independent variables: the independent variables of the research study and extraneous independent variables. Extraneous independent variables, of course, are variables that may influence the dependent variable but that are not part of the study. In the admissions study of Chapter 17, for example, geographical location (of the colleges) may be a potentially influential extraneous variable that can cloud the results of the study. If colleges in the east, for example, exclude more women than colleges in the west, then geographical location is an extraneous source of variance in the admissions measures—which should somehow be controlled. The criterion also refers to control of the variables of the study. Since this problem has already been discussed and will continue to be discussed, no more need be said here. But the question must be asked: *Does this design adequately control independent variables?*

The best single way to answer this question satisfactorily is expressed in the following principle:

Randomize whenever possible: select subjects at random; assign subjects to groups at random; assign experimental treatments to groups at random.

While it may not be possible to *select* subjects at random, it may be possible to *assign* them to groups at random. This "equalizes" the groups in the statistical sense discussed in Parts 4 and 5. If such random assignment of subjects to groups is not possible, then every effort should be made to assign experimental treatments to experimental groups at random. And, if experimental treatments are administered at different times with different experimenters, times and experimenters should be assigned at random. To the extent that randomization is ignored or is not possible, to this extent research design is weak. The whole structure of probabilistic-statistical reasoning depends upon randomization. So, again, whenever possible, *randomize*.

The principle that makes randomization pertinent is complex and difficult to execute:

Control the independent variables so that extraneous and unwanted sources of systematic variance have minimal opportunity to operate.

As we have seen earlier, randomization theoretically satisfies this principle (see Chapter 8). When we test the empirical validity of an "If p, then q" proposition, we manipulate p and observe that q covaries with the manipulation of p. But how confident can we be that our If p, then q statement is really "true"? Our confidence is directly related to the completeness and adequacy of the controls. If we use a design similar to Designs 18.1 through 18.4, we cannot have too much confidence in the empirical validity of the If p, then q statement, since our control of extraneous independent variables is weak or nonexistent. Because such control is not always possible in much psychological, sociological, and educational research, should we then give up research entirely? By no means. Nevertheless, we must be aware of the weaknesses of intrinsically poor design. Frequently it is possible to construct and use a better design than is at first thought possible.

Generalizability

The third criterion, *generalizability*, is independent of other criteria because it is different in kind. This is an important point that will shortly become clear. It means simply: *Can we generalize the results of a study to other subjects, other groups, and other conditions*? Perhaps the question is better put: *How much* can we generalize the results of the study? or *To whom and what* can we generalize the results of the study? This is probably the most complex and difficult question that can be asked of research data because it touches not only upon technical matters like sampling and research design, but also to larger problems of basic and applied research. In basic research, for example, generalizability is not the first consideration, because the central interest is the relations among variables and *why* the variables are related as they are.[8] This puts an emphasis on the internal rather than the external aspects of the study. In applied research, on the other hand, the central interest forces more concern for generalizability because one certainly wishes to apply the results to other persons and to other situations. If the reader will ponder the following two examples of basic and applied research, he can get closer to this distinction.

In Chapter 14 we examined a study by Berkowitz on hostility arousal, anti-Semitism, and displaced aggression. This is clearly basic research: the central interest was in the relations among hostility, anti-Semitism, and displaced aggression. While no one would be foolish enough to say that Berkowitz was not concerned with hostility, anti-Semitism, and displaced aggression in general, the emphasis was on the relations among the variables *of the study*. Contrast this study with the effort of Walster et al. to determine whether colleges discriminate against women. Naturally, Walster and her colleagues were particular about the internal aspects of their study. But they perforce had to have another interest: Is discrimination practiced among colleges in general? Their study is clearly applied research, though one cannot say that basic research interest was absent. The considerations of the next section may help to clarify generalizability.

Internal and External Validity

Two general criteria of research design have been discussed at length by Campbell and by Campbell and Stanley.[9] These notions constitute one of the most sig-

[8]For a brief discussion of basic and applied research, see F. Kerlinger, "Research in Education." In R. Ebel, V. Noll, and R. Bauer, eds., *Encyclopedia of Educational Research*, 4th ed. New York: Macmillan, 1969, pp. 1127–1143, esp. p. 1128. This article also cites a number of references on basic and applied research.

[9]Campbell, *op. cit.*; Campbell and Stanley, *op. cit.* Readers are urged to study these sources, since the above discussion can only define and highlight internal and external validity.

nificant, important, and enlightening contributions to research methodology in the last two or three decades.

Internal validity asks the question: Did *X*, the experimental manipulation, really make a significant difference? The three criteria of the last chapter are actually aspects of internal validity. Indeed, anything affecting the *controls* of a design becomes a problem of internal validity. If a design is such that one can have little or no confidence in the relations, as shown by significant differences between experimental groups, say, this is a problem of internal validity. Henceforth, when the term internal validity is used, it will be a general way of denoting the control criterion discussed earlier.

A difficult criterion to satisfy, *external validity* means *representativeness* or *generalizability*. When an experiment has been completed and a relation found, to what populations can it be generalized? Can we say that *A* is related to *B* for *all* school children? All eighth-grade children? All eighth-grade children in this school system or the eighth-grade children of this school only? Or must the findings be limited to the eighth-grade children with whom we worked? This is a very important scientific question that should always be asked—*and answered.*

Not only must sample generalizability be questioned. It is necessary to ask questions about the ecological and variable representativeness of studies. If the social setting in which the experiment was conducted is changed, will the relation of *A* and *B* still hold? Will *A* be related to *B* if the study is replicated in a lower-class school? In a western school? In a southern school? These are questions of *ecological representativeness.*

Variable representativeness is more subtle. A question not often asked, but that should be asked, is: Are the variables of this research representative? When an investigator works with psychological and sociological variables, he assumes that his variables are "constant." If he finds a difference in achievement between boys and girls, he assumes that sex as a variable is "constant."

In the case of variables like achievement, aggression, aptitude, and anxiety, can the investigator assume that the "aggression" of his suburban subjects is the same "aggression" to be found in city slums? Is the variable the same in a European suburb? The representativeness of "anxiety" is more difficult to ascertain. When we talk of "anxiety," what kind of anxiety do we mean? Are all kinds of anxiety the same? If anxiety is manipulated in one situation by verbal instructions and in another situation by electric shock, are the two induced anxieties the same? If anxiety is manipulated by, say, experimental instruction, is this the same anxiety as that measured by an anxiety scale?[10] Variable representativeness, then, is another aspect of the larger problem of external validity, and thus of generalizability.

Unless special precautions are taken and special efforts made, the results of research are frequently not representative, and hence not generalizable. Campbell and Stanley say that internal validity is the sine qua non of research design, but that the ideal design should be strong in both internal validity and external validity,

[10]This is the problem of the equivalence of definitions. See A. Baldwin, "The Study of Child Behavior and Development." In P. Mussen, ed., *Handbook of Research Methods in Child Development.* New York: Wiley, 1960, pp. 12–13.

even though they are frequently contradictory.[11] This point is well taken. In these chapters, the main emphasis will be on internal validity, with a vigilant eye on external validity.

The negative approach of this chapter was taken in the belief that an exposure to poor but commonly used and *accepted* procedures, together with a discussion of their major weaknesses, would provide a good starting point for the study of research design. This method is especially justified because the student has already been exposed to good designs and design principles in previous chapters, though they may not have been so labeled. Other inadequate designs are possible, but all such designs are inadequate on design-structural principles alone. This point should be emphasized because in the next chapter we will find that a perfectly good design structure can be poorly used. Thus it is necessary to learn and understand the two sources of research weakness: intrinsically poor designs and intrinsically good designs poorly used.

Study Suggestions

1. A college faculty group is to study a core curriculum program instituted during the previous year. All incoming freshmen are to be required to take this program. Discuss the problems and difficulties the researchers face. How much faith can be put in their findings?
2. The faculty of a university school of education decides to begin a new curriculum for all undergraduates and to study its effectiveness. A faculty research group is asked to study the program for two years. The research group, wishing to have a group with which to compare the new curriculum group, requests that the regular program be continued for two years and that students be allowed to volunteer for the new program or the regular program. In this way, the group feels it will have an experimental group and a control group.

   Discuss the group's proposal critically. Would you have faith in its findings at the end of the two years? Give reasons for reacting positively or negatively to the proposal.
3. Imagine that you are a graduate school professor and that you are asked to judge the worth of a proposed doctoral thesis. The doctoral student is a school superintendent who is instituting a new type of administration into his school system. He plans to study the effects of the new administration for a three-year period and then write his thesis. To keep the study objective he will not study any other school situation.

   Discuss the candidate's proposal, keeping this question in mind: If the study is completed, should he be awarded the degree? Is such a study suitable for doctoral work?
4. In your opinion, should all research be held rather strictly to the criterion of generalizability? If so, why? If not, why not? Which field is likely to have more basic research: psychology or education? Why? What implication does your conclusion have for generalizability?
5. What relation does replication of research have to do with generalizability? Explain.

[11]Campbell and Stanley, *op. cit.*

CHAPTER 18

General Designs of Research

Design is data discipline. The implicit purpose of all research design is to impose controlled restrictions on observations of natural phenomena. The research design tells the investigator, in effect: Do this and this; don't do that or that; be careful with this; ignore that; and so on. It is the blueprint of the research architect and engineer. If the design is poorly conceived structurally, the ultimate product will be faulty. If it is at least well conceived structurally, the ultimate product has a greater chance of being worthy of serious scientific attention. In this chapter, our main preoccupation is seven or eight "good" basic designs of research. In addition, however, we take up certain conceptual foundations of research and two or three problems related to design—for instance, the rationale of control groups and the pro's and con's of matching.

Conceptual Foundations of Research Design

The conceptual foundation for understanding research design was laid in Chapters 4 and 5, where sets and relations were defined and discussed. Recall that a *relation* is a set of ordered pairs. (It can also be a set of ordered triples, quadruples, and so on.) Recall, too, that a *Cartesian product* is all the possible ordered pairs of two sets. A *partition* breaks down a universal set U into subsets that are *disjoint* and *exhaustive*. A *cross partition* is a new partitioning that arises from successively partitioning U by forming all subsets of the form $A \cap B$. These definitions were elaborated in Chapters 5 and 6. We now apply them to design and analysis ideas.

Take two sets, A and B, partitioned into A_1 and A_2, B_1 and B_2. The Cartesian product of the two sets is:

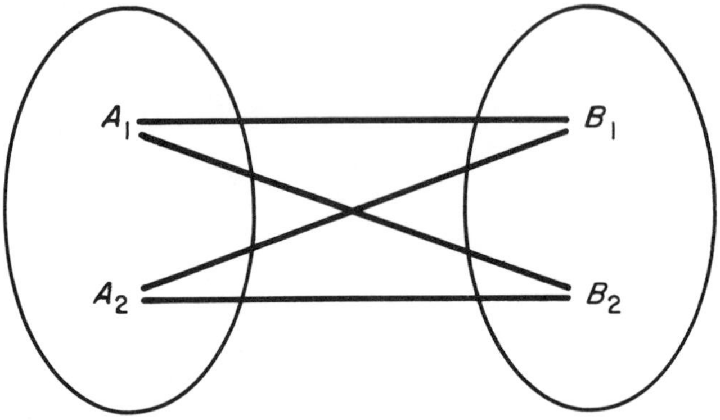

The ordered pairs, then, are: $A_1B_1, A_1B_2, A_2B_1, A_2B_2$. Since we have a set of ordered pairs, this is a relation. It is also a cross partition. The reader should look back at Figs. 4.7 and 4.8 of Chapter 4 to help clarify these ideas, and to see the application of the Cartesian product and relation ideas to research design. For instance, A_1 and A_2 can be two aspects of any independent variable: experimental-control, two methods of teaching, male and female, and so on.

A *design* is some subset of the Cartesian product of the independent variables and the dependent variable. It is possible to pair each dependent variable measure, which we call Y in this discussion, with some aspect or partition of an independent variable. The simplest possible cases occur with one independent variable and one dependent variable. In Chapter 10, an independent variable, A, and a dependent variable, B, were partitioned into $[A_1, A_2]$ and $[B_1, B_2]$ and then cross-partitioned to form the by-now familiar 2×2 crossbreak, with frequencies or percentages in the cells. We concentrate, however, on similar cross partitions of A and B, but with continuous measures in the cells.

Take A alone, using a one-way analysis of variance design. Suppose we have three experimental treatments, A_1, A_2, and A_3, and, for simplicity, two Y scores in each cell. This is shown on the left of Fig. 19.1, labeled (a). Say that six subjects have been assigned at random to the three treatments, and that the scores of the six individuals after the experimental treatment are those given in the figure.

The right side of Fig. 19.1, labeled (b), shows the same idea in ordered-pair or relation form. The ordered pairs are $A_1Y_1, A_1Y_2, A_2Y_3, \ldots, A_3Y_6$. This is, of course, not a Cartesian product, which would pair A_1 with all the Y's, A_2 with all the Y's, and A_3 with all the Y's, a total of $3 \times 6 = 18$ pairs. Rather, Fig. 19.1(b) is a subset of the Cartesian product, $A \times B$. Research designs are subsets of $A \times B$, and the design and the research problem define or specify how the subsets are set up. The subsets of the design of Fig. 19.1 are presumably dictated by the research problem.

When there is more than one independent variable, the situation is more complex. Take two independent variables, A and B, partitioned into $[A_1, A_2]$ and

(a)

A_1	A_2	A_3
7	7	3
9	5	3

(b)

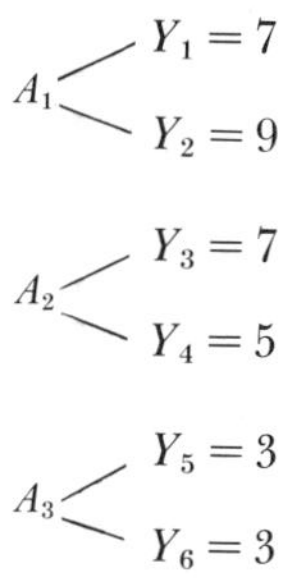

FIG. 19.1

$[B_1, B_2]$.[1] We must now have ordered triples (or two sets of ordered pairs): ABY. Study Fig. 19.2. On the left side of the figure, labeled (a), the 2×2 factorial analysis of variance design and example used in Chapter 14 (Table 14.3) is given, with the measures of the dependent variable, Y, inserted in the cells. That is, eight subjects were assigned at random to the four cells. Their scores, after the experiment, are $Y_1, Y_2, \ldots, Y_8$. The right side of the figure, labeled (b), shows the ordered triples, ABY, as a tree. Obviously these are subsets of $A \times B \times Y$ and are relations. The same reasoning can be extended to larger and more complex designs, like a $2 \times 2 \times 3$ factorial ($ABCY$) or a $4 \times 3 \times 2 \times 2$ ($ABCDY$). (In these designations, Y is usually omitted because it is implied.) Other kinds of designs can be similarly conceptualized, though their depiction in trees can be laborious. We simply want to emphasize the foundation ideas of design and need not give more examples.

In sum, a research design is some subset of the Cartesian product of the independent and the dependent variables. With only one independent variable, the single variable is partitioned; with more than one independent variable, the indedent variables are cross-partitioned. With three or more independent variables, the conceptualization is the same; only the dimensions differ, for example, $A \times B \times C$ and $A \times B \times C \times D$ and the cross partitions thereof. Whenever possible, it is desirable to have "complete" designs—a complete design is a cross partition of the independent variables[2]—and to observe the two basic conditions of disjointness and exhaustiveness. That is, the design must not have a case (a subject's score) in more than one cell of a partition or cross partition, and all the cases must be used up. Moreover, the basic minimum of any design is at least a partition of the independent variable into two subsets, for example, A into A_1 and A_2. (In this sense, then, Designs 18.1 and 18.2 are wanting.)

The term "general designs" means that the designs given in the chapter are symbolized or expressed in their most general and abstract form. Where a simple X, meaning independent variable, is given, it must be taken to mean more than

[1]The reader should not confuse this with the earlier AB frequency paradigm, in which A was the independent variable and B the dependent variable.

[2]There are also "incomplete" designs, but "complete" designs are emphasized more in this book. See R. Kirk, *Experimental Design: Procedures for the Behavioral Sciences.* Belmont, Calif.: Brooks/Cole, 1968, especially Table 1.4-1, p. 12.

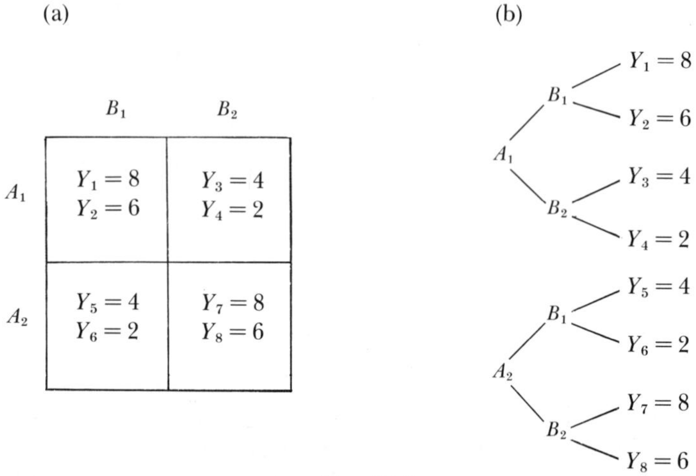

FIG. 19.2

one X—that is, X is partitioned into two or more experimental groups. For instance, Design 19.1, to be studied shortly, has X and $\sim X$, meaning experimental and control groups, and thus is a partition of X. But X can be partitioned into a number of X's, perhaps changing the design from a simple one-variable design to, say, a factorial design. The basic symbolism associated with Design 19.1, however, remains the same. These complexities will hopefully be clarified in this and succeeding chapters. Suffice it for now to remember that designs are relations, the subsets of ordered pairs being the symbols of the independent variables—A_1, A_2, B_1, B_2, X, $\sim X$, and so on—and the measures of the dependent variable, Y; complete designs are Cartesian products of the independent variables; and all designs are some form of partitions or cross partitions, subject to the rules of partitioning.

A final point needs to be made before we take up the designs. Research designs arose from experimental needs. They were invented to impose control on experimental variables. This point was made earlier when analysis of variance was discussed. Although some analysis of variance designs have been adapted for use in ex post facto research, their rationale is based on experimental ideas and conditions. So, along with the idea that the controlled experiment is the ideal of scientific research, we must say that research design is basically experimental in conception. The application of the designs to ex post facto research is at best somewhat questionable, even occasionally awkward and inappropriate. Nevertheless, the position is taken here that some well-conceived design is better than no design or badly conceived design, and we must do whatever we can to strengthen both experimental and ex post facto research.

The Designs

Unlike the designs of the last chapter, those of this section will have no ex post facto counterparts, because the ex post facto approach precludes the possibility of randomization. This problem will be discussed in detail in a later chapter.

Design 19.1: Experimental Group-Control Group: Randomized Subjects

$\boxed{R}$	X	Y	(Experimental)
	$\sim X$	Y	(Control)

Design 19.1, with two groups as above, and its variants with more than two groups, are probably the "best" designs for many experimental purposes in education and psychology. Its structural similarity to Design 18.4 is apparent. The R placed before the paradigm indicates that subjects have been *randomly assigned* to the experimental group (top line) and the control group (bottom line). This randomization removes the objections mentioned in Chapter 18. Theoretically, *all* possible independent variables are controlled. Practically, of course, this may not be so. If enough subjects are included in the experiment to give the principle of randomization a chance to "operate," then we have powerful control indeed. In other words, the claims of internal validity are rather well satisfied.

External validity is another matter. Too often subjects cannot be *selected* from a defined population at random. We must be satisfied with, or at least reconciled to, the nonrandom selection of subjects. Thus, while Design 19.1 gives us good answers to internal validity questions, unless subjects (and, theoretically, situations) have been selected at random, we cannot generalize beyond the samples at our disposal. This problem is not as difficult to resolve as it seems, however. By replicating experiments, with and without variants, it is possible to increase generalizability considerably. If, for instance, an experiment is repeated at different times and in different places with the hypothesized relations holding up in each experiment, then we can have much more confidence in the scientific validity of the relations.

If extended to more than two groups and if it is capable of answering the research questions asked, Design 19.1, then, has the following advantages: (1) it has the best built-in theoretical control system of any design, with one or two possible exceptions in special cases; (2) it is flexible, being theoretically capable of extension to any number of groups with any number of variables; (3) if extended to more than one variable, it can test several hypotheses at one time; and (4) it is statistically and probabilistically elegant.

We do not mean to say that Design 19.1 is the be-all and end-all of research design—it is not universal or perfect. Obviously, it cannot, as it stands, test experiments of change as well as do pretest-posttest designs, and if extended to more than one independent variable, practical considerations may limit its applicability in behavioral research situations. From most research viewpoints, however, it is very effective for two reasons:

1. The control group (or several experimental groups) gives the comparability required by science. Comparisons are essential in *all* scientific investigation. The classical experimental group-control group design using equated experimental and control groups (through randomization) provides such comparisons in an efficient manner, which makes it an intellectual achievement of the first order.

2. The second reason for its virtue is randomization. In order to make the experimental group-control group idea valid, it is necessary for the experimenter to have some assurance that his groups are approximately (statistically) equal on *any* variables possibly related to the dependent variable or variables. Matching cannot accomplish this, as we learned earlier, nor can intuitive or experienced judgments.

Many students find it hard to believe that a table of random numbers can be so effective. We hope our earlier Monte Carlo demonstrations have convinced them. We also hope that our rather generous citation of factorial studies has bolstered faith in the multivariable extensions of this design: 2×2, 3×2, $3 \times 2 \times 4$, and so on.

Before taking up other designs, we need to examine the notion of the control group, one of the creative inventions of the last hundred years, and certain extensions of Design 19.1. The two topics go nicely together.

The Notion of the Control Group and Extensions of Design 19.1 Evidently the word "control" and the expression "control group" did not appear in the scientific literature before the late nineteenth century.[3] The notion of controlled experimentation, however, is much older: Boring says that Pascal used it as early as 1648. Solomon searched the psychological literature and could not find a single case of the use of a control group before 1901.[4] He says that control-group design apparently had to await statistical developments and the development of statistical sophistication among psychologists.

Perhaps the first use of control groups in psychology occurred in 1901.[5] One of the two men who did this research, E. L. Thorndike, extended the basic and revolutionary ideas of this first research series to education.[6] Thorndike's controls, in this gigantic study of 8564 pupils in many schools in a number of cities, were independent educational groups. Among other comparisons, he contrasted the gains in intelligence test scores presumably engendered by the study of English, history, geometry, and *Latin* with the gains in intelligence test scores presumably engendered by the study of English, history, geometry, and *shopwork*. He tried, in effect, to compare the influence of Latin and shopwork. He also made other comparisons of a similar nature. Despite the weaknesses of design and control, Thorndike's experiments and those he stimulated others to perform were remarkable for their insight. Thorndike even berated colleges for not admitting students of stenography and typing who had not studied Latin, because he claimed to have shown that the influence of various subjects on intelligence was similar. It is

[3]E. Boring, "The Nature and History of Experimental Control," *American Journal of Psychology*, LXVII (1954), 573–589.

[4]R. Solomon, "An Extension of Control Group Design," *American Journal of Psychology*, LXVII (1954), 573–589. Perhaps the notion of the control group was used in other fields, though it is doubtful that the idea was well developed. Solomon (*ibid.*, p. 175) also says that the Peterson and Thurstone study of attitudes in 1933 was the first serious attempt to use control groups in the evaluation of the effects of educational procedures. One cannot find the expression "control group" in the famous eleventh edition (1911) of the *Encyclopaedia Britannica*, even though experimental method is discussed.

[5]E. Thorndike and R. Woodworth, "The Influence of Improvement in One Mental Function upon the Efficiency of Other Functions," *Psychological Review*, VIII (1901), 247–261, 384–395, 553–564.

[6]E. Thorndike, "Mental Discipline in High School Subjects," *Journal of Educational Psychology*, XV (1924), 1–22, 83–98.

interesting to note that he thought huge numbers of subjects were necessary—he called for 18,000 more cases. He was also quite aware, in 1924, of the need for random samples.[7]

The notion of the control group needs generalization. Assume that in an educational experiment we have four experimental groups as follows. A_1 is reinforcement of every response, A_2 reinforcement at regular time intervals, A_3 reinforcement at random intervals, and A_4 no reinforcement. Technically, there are three experimental groups and one control group, in the traditional sense of the control group. However, A_4 might be another "experimental treatment"; it might be some kind of minimal reinforcement. Then, in the traditional sense, there would be *no* control group. The traditional sense of the term "control group" lacks generality. If the notion of control is generalized, the difficulty disappears. Whenever there is more than one experimental group and any two groups are given different treatments, control is present in the sense of comparison previously mentioned. As long as there is an attempt to make two groups systematically different on a dependent variable, a comparison is possible. Thus the traditional notion that an experimental group should receive the treatment not given to a control group is a special case of the more general rule that comparison groups are necessary for the internal validity of any scientific research.

If we assume this reasoning to be correct, we can set up designs such as the following:

	X_1	Y
[R]	X_2	Y
	X_3	Y

or

	X_{1a}	Y
	X_{1b}	Y
[R]	X_{2a}	Y
	X_{2b}	Y

These designs will be more easily recognizable if they are set up in a different notation in the form used in Part 5, as in Fig. 19.3. The design on the left is a

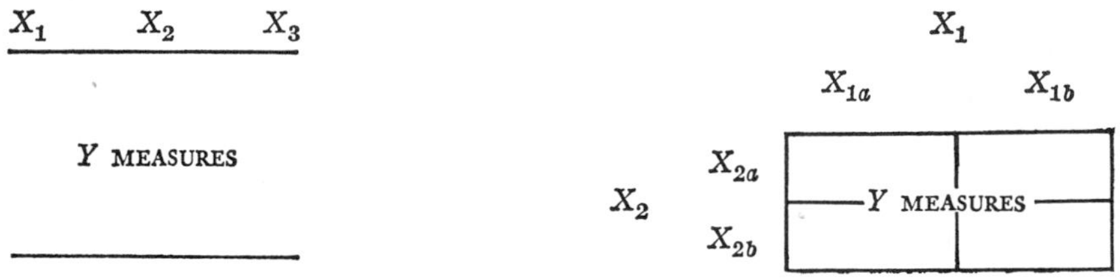

FIG. 19.3

[7]See *Ibid.*, pp. 93, 97, and 85, for the three points mentioned.

simple one-way analysis of variance design and the one on the right a 2×2 factorial design. In the right-hand design, X_{1a} might be experimental and X_{1b} control, with X_{2a} and X_{2b} either a manipulated variable or a dichotomous attribute variable. It is, of course, the same design as that shown in Fig. 19.2(a).

Design 19.2: Experimental Group-Control Group: Matched Subjects

	X	Y	(Experimental)
$\boxed{M_r}$			
	$\sim X$	Y	(Control)

The structure of Design 19.2 is the same as that of Design 19.1. The only difference is that, instead of all subjects being assigned at random to groups, they are matched on one or more attributes. For the design to take its place as an "adequate" design, however, randomization must enter the picture, as noted by the small r attached to the M (for "matched"). It is not enough that matched subjects are used; the members of each pair must be assigned to the two groups at random. Ideally, too, whether a group is to be an experimental or a control group is also decided at random. In either case, each decision can be made by flipping a coin or by using a table of random numbers, letting odd numbers mean one group and even numbers the other group. If there are more than two groups, naturally, a random number system must be used.

As in Design 19.1, it is possible, though not often easy, to use more than two groups. (The difficulty of matching more than two groups was discussed earlier.) There are times, however, when a matching design is an inherent element of the research situation. When the same subjects are used for two or more experimental treatments, or when subjects are given more than one trial, matching is inherent in the situation. In educational research, when schools or classes are in effect variables—when, say, two or more schools or classes are used and the experimental treatments are administered in each school or class—then Design 19.2 is the basis of the design logic. Study the paradigm of a schools design in Fig. 19.4. It is seen that variance due to the differences between schools, and such variance can be substantial, can be readily estimated.

Schools	X_{e_1} Experimental 1	X_{e_2} Experimental 2	X_c Control
1			
2			
3		Y MEASURES	
4			
5			

FIG. 19.4

Matching—Pro and Con

Matching is not limited to the matching of subjects. If we think of matching in variance terms, we can readily apprehend this point. When certain subsets of the total set of sampled units are more alike than other subsets, the variance due to the differences between the subsets is probably present. The extreme case is when the same subjects are used on more than one trial, because a subject is naturally more like himself than he is like other persons. The three experimental groups of Fig. 19.4 can be the same subjects on different trials, which introduces systematic variance, individual differences variance. When pretests and posttests are used, matching is of course present, too. Schools are known to differ in important characteristics: classes differ, school districts differ, neighborhoods differ, teachers differ. These differences can be used in the study and the variances arising from their use can be isolated by building their sources into the design. In fact, failure to build such variables into designs can lead to the confounding of the experimental variables.[8] And to have correlation between groups, due to matching or repeated measures of individuals or units like classes and schools, and not to take advantage of the correlation is a statistical and design blunder.[9]

Design 19.3: Before and after Control Group (Pretest-Posttest)

(*a*)	$\boxed{R}$	Y_b	X	Y_a	(Experimental)
		Y_b	$\sim X$	Y_a	(Control)
(*b*)	$\boxed{M_r}$	Y_b	X	Y_a	(Experimental)
		Y_b	$\sim X$	Y_a	(Control)

Design 19.3 has many advantages and is frequently used. Its structure is similar to that of Design 18.2, with two important differences: Design 18.2 lacks a control group and randomization. Design 19.3 is similar to Designs 19.1 and 19.2, except

[8]The term "confounding," often used in treatises of statistical and research design, means the "mixing" of the variance of one or more independent variables, usually extraneous to the research purpose, with the independent variable or variables of the research problem. As a result it cannot be clearly said that the relation found is between the independent variables and the dependent variable of the research, or between the extraneous independent variables and the dependent variable, or both. Underwood points out that there is only one basic principle of research design: ". . . design the experiment so that the effects of the independent variables can be evaluated unambiguously." [B. Underwood, *Psychological Research*. New York: Appleton, 1957, p. 86.] When this cannot be done—it is a difficult procedure—more likely than not the independent variables have been confounded. The term evidently came from statistics, where "confounding" is sometimes deliberately practiced.

[9]It must be emphasized that deliberate matching is in general not a desirable procedure. *And matching is never a substitute for randomization.* Remember, too, that the correlation between the matching variable or variables and the dependent variable must be substantial (greater than .50, say) to be productive, and that only the variable or variables matched on—and, perhaps, variables substantially correlated with these variables—are controlled. A better procedure, in general, is analysis of covariance or other regression procedure, a subject we will examine in Chapter 21 and in our final chapters.

that the "before" or pretest feature has been added. It is used frequently to study change. Like Designs 19.1 and 19.2, it can be expanded to more than two groups.

In Design 19.3(a), subjects are assigned to the experimental group (top line) and the control group (bottom line) at random and are pretested on a measure of Y, the dependent variable. The investigator can then check the equality of the two groups on Y. The experimental manipulation X is performed, after which the groups are again measured on Y. The difference between the two groups is tested statistically. An interesting and difficult characteristic of this design is the nature of the scores usually analyzed: difference, or change, scores, $Y_a - Y_b = D$. Unless the effect of the experimental manipulation is strong, the analysis of difference scores is not advisable. If they *are* analyzed, however, a t or F test is used. Because of this and other difficulties, it would easily be possible to devote a whole chapter to this one design. For an extended discussion, the student is referred to the Campbell and Stanley monograph (see footnote 14, pp. 13–24). Only the main strengths and weaknesses of the design will be discussed here. At the end of the discussion the analytic difficulties just mentioned will be taken up.

Probably most important, Design 19.3 overcomes the great weakness of Design 18.2, because it supplies a comparison control group against which the difference, $Y_a - Y_b$, can be checked. With only one group, we can never know whether history, maturation (or both), or the experimental manipulation X produced the change in Y. When a control group is added, the situation becomes radically altered. After all, if the groups are equated (through randomization), the effects of history and maturation, if present, should be present in both groups. If the mental ages of the children of the experimental group increase, so should the mental ages of the children of the control group. Then, if there is still a difference between the Y measures of the two groups, it should not be due to history or maturation. That is, if something happens to affect the experimental subjects between the pretest and the posttest, this something should also affect the subjects of the control group. Similarly, the effect of testing—Campbell's *reactive* measures—should be controlled. For if the testing affects the members of the experimental group it should similarly affect the members of the control group. (There is, however, a concealed weakness here, which will be discussed later.) This is the main strength of the well-planned and well-executed before-after, experimental-control group design.

On the other hand, before-after designs have a troublesome aspect, which decreases the external validity of the experiment, although the internal validity is not affected. This source of difficulty is the pretest. A pretest can have a *sensitizing effect* on subjects. For example, the subjects may possibly be altered to certain events in their environment that they might not ordinarily notice. If the pretest is an attitude scale, it can sensitize subjects to the issues or problems mentioned in the scale. Then, when the X treatment is administered to the experimental group, the subjects of this group may be responding not so much to the attempted influence, the communication, or whatever method is used to change attitudes, as to a combination of their increased sensitivity to the issues *and* the experimental manipulation.

Since such interaction effects are not immediately obvious, and since they contain a threat to the external validity of experiments, it is worthwhile to consider them a bit further. One would think that, since both the experimental and the control groups are pretested, the effect of pretesting, if any, would ensure the validity of the experiment. Let us assume that no pretesting was done, that is, that Design 19.2 was used. Other things equal, a difference between the experimental and the control groups after experimental manipulation of X can be assumed to be due to X. There is no reason to suppose that one group is more sensitive or more alert than the other, since they both face the testing situation *after* X. But when a pretest is used, the results differ. While the pretest sensitizes both groups, it can make the experimental subjects respond to X, wholly or partially, because of the sensitivity. What we have, then, is a lack of generalizability: it may be possible to generalize to pretested groups but not to unpretested ones. Clearly such a situation is disturbing to the researcher, since who wants to generalize to pretested groups?

If this weakness is important, why do we say that this is a good design? While the possible interaction effect described above may be serious in some research, it is doubtful that it is very serious in educational research, provided that adequate precautions are taken. Testing is an accepted and normal part of most school and college situations, and as such, should have no great sensitizing effect. Still, there may be times when it does. The rule Campbell and Stanley give is a good one: when highly unusual testing procedures are to be used, it is best to use designs that do not involve pretests.

Difference Scores Look at Design 19.3 again, particularly at changes between Y_b and Y_a. One of the most difficult problems that has plagued—and intrigued—researchers, measurement specialists, and statisticians is how to study and analyze such difference, or change, scores. In a book of the scope of this one, it is impossible to go into the problems in detail. General precepts and cautions, however, can be outlined. One would think that the application of analysis of variance to difference scores yielded by Design 19.3 and similar designs would be effective. Such analysis *can* be done if the experimental effects are substantial. But difference scores, as we pointed out in Chapter 15, are usually less reliable than the scores from which they are calculated. Differences between the experimental and control groups can be not significant when in fact an effect is substantial. Cronbach and Furby even say that change scores should not be used, that the essential question is whether the experimental and control groups differ.[10] So what should be done?

The generally recommended procedure is to use so-called residualized or regressed gain scores, which are scores calculated by predicting the posttest scores from the pretest scores on the basis of the correlation between pretest and posttest, and then subtracting these predicted scores from the posttest scores to obtain the residual gain scores. (The reader should not be concerned if this pro-

[10]L. Cronbach and L. Furby, "How Should We Measure 'Change'—or Should We?" *Psychological Bulletin*, LXXIV (1970), 68–80. For a definitive analysis and study of growth measures, see R. Thorndike, "Intellectual Status and Intellectual Growth," *Journal of Educational Psychology*, LVII (1966), 121–127.

cedure is not too clear at this stage. Later, after we study regression and analysis of covariance, it should become clearer.) The effect of the pretest scores is removed from the posttest scores; that is, the residual scores are posttest scores purged of the pretest influence. Then the significance of the difference between the means of these scores is tested. All this can be accomplished by using either the procedure just described and a regression equation or by analysis of covariance, which will be explained in Chapter 21.

Even the use of residual gain scores and analysis of covariance is not perfect, however. If subjects have not been assigned at random to the experimental and control groups, the procedure will not save the situation. When groups differ systematically before experimental treatment in other characteristics pertinent to the dependent variable, statistical manipulation does not correct such differences.[11] If, however, a pretest is used, use random assignment and analysis of covariance, remembering that the results must always be treated with special care. Finally, multiple regression analysis may provide the best solution of the problem, as we will see later.[12]

Design 19.4: Simulated before-after, Randomized

$$\boxed{R} \qquad \begin{array}{lll} & X & Y_a \\ \hline Y_b & & \end{array}$$

The value of this design is doubtful, even though it is included among the adequate designs. The scientific demand for a comparison is satisfied: there is a comparison group (lower line). A major weakness of Design 18.3 (a pallid version of Design 19.4) is remedied by the randomization. Recall that with Design 18.3 we were unable to assume beforehand that the experimental and control groups were equivalent. Design 19.4 calls for subjects to be assigned to the two groups at random. Thus, it can be assumed that they are statistically equal. Such a design might be used when one is worried about the reactive effect of pretesting, or when, due to the exigencies of practical situations, one has no other choice. Such a situation occurs when one has the opportunity to try a method or some innovation only once. To test the method's efficacy, one provides a base line for judging the effect of X on Y by pretesting a group similar to the experimental group. Then Y_a is tested against Y_b.

[11]Cronbach and Furby, *op. cit.*, p. 78.

[12]It is unfortunate that the complexities of design and statistical analysis may discourage the student, sometimes even to the point of feeling hopeless. But that is the nature of behavioral research: it merely reflects the exceedingly complex character of psychological, sociological, and educational reality. This is at one and the same time frustrating and exciting. Like marriage, behavioral research is difficult and often unsuccessful—but not impossible. Moreover, it is the only way to acquire reliable understanding of our behavioral world. The point of view of this book is that we should learn and understand as much as we can about what we are doing, use reasonable care with design and analysis, and then *do* the research without fussing too much about analytic matters. The main thing is always the research problem and our interest in it. This does not mean a cavalier disregard of analysis. Educational research, particularly, has suffered enough from this. It simply means reasonable understanding and care and healthy measures of both optimism and skepticism.

This design's validity breaks down if the two groups are not both randomly selected from the same population or if the subjects are not assigned to the two groups at random. Even then, it has the weaknesses mentioned in connection with other similar designs, namely, other possible variables may be influential in the interval between Y_b and Y_a. In other words, Design 19.4 is superior to Design 18.3, but it should not be used if a better design is available.

Design 19.5: Three-Group, before-after

	Y_b	X	Y_a	(Experimental)
$\boxed{R}$	Y_b	$\sim X$	Y_a	(Control 1)
		X	Y_a	(Control 2)

This design is better. In addition to the assets of Design 19.3 it provides a way to avoid possible interactive effects due to the pretest. This is achieved by the second control group (third line). (It seems a bit strange to have a control group with an X, but the group of the third line is really a control group.) With the Y_a measures of this group available, it is possible to check the interaction effect. Suppose the mean of the experimental group is significantly greater than the mean of the first control group (second line). We may doubt whether this difference was really due to X. It might have been produced by increased sensitization of the subjects after the pretest and the interaction of their sensitization and X. We now look at the mean of Y_a of the second control group (third line). It, too, should be significantly greater than the mean of the first control group. If it is, we can assume that the pretest has not unduly sensitized the subjects, or that X is sufficiently strong to override any sensitization-X interaction effect.

Design 19.6: Four-Group, before-after (Solomon)

	Y_b	X	Y_a	(Experimental)
$\boxed{R}$	Y_b	$\sim X$	Y_a	(Control 1)
		X	Y_a	(Control 2)
		$\sim X$	Y_a	(Control 3)

This design, proposed by Solomon,[13] is strong and aesthetically satisfying. It has potent controls. Actually, if we change the designation of Control 2 to Experimental 2, we have a combination of Designs 19.3 and 19.1, our two best designs, where the former design forms the first two lines and the latter the second two lines. The virtues of both are combined in one design. Campbell says that this design has become the new ideal for social scientists.[14] While this is a strong state-

[13]Solomon, *op. cit.*, pp. 137–150. Although this design can have a matching form, it is not discussed here nor is it recommended. The symbolism used above is not Solomon's.

[14]D. Campbell, "Factors Relevant to the Validity of Experiments in Social Settings," *Psychological Bulletin*, LIV (1957), 297–312. See, also, D. Campbell and J. Stanley, *Experimental Designs and Quasi-Experimental Designs for Research*. Skokie, Ill.: Rand McNally, 1963.

ment, probably a bit too strong, it indicates the high esteem in which the design is held.

Among the reasons why it is a strong design is that the demand for comparison is well satisfied with the first two lines *and* the second two lines, the randomization assures statistical equivalence of the groups, and history and maturation are controlled with the first two lines of the design. The possible interaction effect due to possible pretest subject sensitization is controlled by the first three lines. By adding the fourth line possible temporary contemporaneous effects that may have occurred between Y_b and Y_a can be controlled. Because Designs 19.1 and 19.3 are combined, we have the power of each test separately and the power of replication because, in effect, there are two experiments. If Y_a of Experimental is significantly greater than Control 1, and Control 2 is significantly greater than Control 3, together with a consistency of results between the two experiments, this is strong evidence, indeed, of the validity of our research hypothesis.

What is wrong with this paragon of designs? It certainly looks fine on paper. There seem to be only two sources of weakness. One is practicability—it is harder to run two simultaneous experiments than one and the researcher encounters the difficulty of locating more subjects of the same kind.

The other difficulty is statistical. Note that there is a lack of balance of groups. There are four actual groups, but not four complete sets of measures. Using the first two lines, that is, with Design 19.3, one can subtract Y_b from Y_a and do an analysis of covariance. With the second two lines, one can test the Y_a's against each other with a t test or F test, but the problem is how to obtain one overall statistical approach. One solution is to test the Y_a's of Controls 2 and 3 against the average of the two Y_b's (the first two lines), as well as to test the significance of the difference of the Y_a's of the first two lines. In addition, Solomon originally suggested a 2×2 factorial analysis of variance, using the four Y_a sets of measures.[15] Solomon's suggestion is outlined in Fig. 19.5. A careful study will reveal that this is a fine example of research thinking, a nice blending of design and analysis. With this analysis we can study the main effects, X and $\sim X$, and Pretested and Not Pretested. What is more interesting, we can test the interaction of pretesting and X and get a clear answer to the previous problem.

While this and other complex designs have decided strengths, it is doubtful that they can be used routinely. In fact, they should probably be saved for very important experiments in which, perhaps, hypotheses already tested with simpler designs are again tested with greater rigor and control. Indeed, it is recommended

	X	$\sim X$
Pretested	Y_a, Experimental	Y_a, Control 1
Not Pretested	Y_a, Control 2	Y_a, Control 3

FIG. 19.5

[15]Solomon, *op. cit.*, p. 146; Campbell, *op. cit.*, p. 303.

that designs like 19.5 and 19.6 and certain variants of Design 19.6, to be discussed later, be reserved for definitive tests of research hypotheses after a certain amount of preliminary experimentation has been done.

Variants of Basic Designs

Designs 19.1 through 19.6 are the *basic* experimental designs. Some variants of these designs have already been indicated. Additional experimental and control groups can be added as needed, but the core ideas remain the same. It is always wise to consider the possibility of adding experimental and control groups. Within reason, the addition of such groups provides more evidence of the validity of the study hypotheses as we saw clearly with Design 19.6. We saw that this design was a combination of two other basic designs, combining the strengths of both and adding replication power, as well as further controls. Such advantages lead to the principle that, whenever we consider a research design, we should consider the possibility of adding experimental groups as *replications* or *variants* of experimental and control groups.

Important variants of the basic design are *time designs*. The form of Design 19.6 can be altered to include a span of time:

Y_b	X	Y_a	
Y_b	$\sim X$	Y_a	
	X		Y_a
	$\sim X$		Y_a

The Y_a's of the third and fourth lines are observations of the dependent variable at any specified later date. Such an alteration, of course, changes the purpose of the design and may cause some of the virtues of Design 19.6 to be lost. We might, if we had the time, the patience, and the resources, retain all the former benefits and still extend in time by adding two more groups to Design 19.6 itself.

Compromise Designs

It is possible, indeed necessary, to use designs that are compromises with true experimentation. Recall that true experimentation requires at least two groups, one receiving an experimental treatment and one not receiving the treatment or receiving it in different form. The true experiment requires the manipulation of at least one independent variable, the random assignment of subjects to groups, and the random assignment of treatments to groups. When one or more of these prerequisites is missing for one reason or another, we have a *compromise design*. Although there are many possibilities, only one will be discussed at length below.

Compromise Experimental Group-Control Group Design Perhaps the most commonly used design is the experimental group-control pattern in which one has no clear assurance that the experimental and control groups are equivalent.

The structure of this design has already been considered in Design 19.3. The compromise form is as follows:

Design 19.7: Compromise Experimental Group-Control Group

Y_b	X	Y_a	(Experimental)
Y_b	$\sim X$	Y_a	(Control)

The difference between Designs 19.3 and 19.7 is sharp. In Design 19.7, there is no randomized assignment of subjects to groups, as in 19.3(a), nor is there matching of subjects and then random assignment, as in 19.3(b). Design 19.7, therefore, is subject to the weaknesses due to the possible lack of equivalence between the groups in variables other than X. Researchers commonly take pains to establish equivalence by other means, and to the extent they are successful in doing so, to this extent the design is valid. This is done in ways discussed below.

The fact must be faced that frequently in research it is extremely difficult or impossible to equate groups by random selection or random assignment, or by matching. Should one then give up doing the research? By no means. Every effort should be made, first, to select and to assign at random. If both of these are not possible, perhaps matching and random assignment can be accomplished. If they are not, an effort should be made at least to use samples from the same population or to use samples as alike as possible. The experimental treatments should be assigned at random. Then the similarity of the groups should be checked using any information available—sex, age, social class, and so on. The equivalence of the groups should be checked using the means and standard deviations of the pretests: t tests and F tests will do. The distributions should also be checked. Although one cannot have the assurance that randomization gives, if these items all check one can go ahead with the study knowing at least that there is no evidence against the equivalence assumption.

These precautions increase the possibilities of attaining internal validity. There are still difficulties, all of which are subordinate to one main difficulty, called *selection.* (These other difficulties will not be discussed here. For detailed discussion, see the Campbell and Stanley chapter previously cited. Another valuable reference is Underwood's book, *Psychological Research.*[16])

Selection is one of the difficult and troublesome problems of research. Since its aspects will be discussed in detail in Chapter 22 on ex post facto research, only a brief description will be given here. One of the most important reasons for the emphasis on random selection, and especially random assignment, is to avoid the difficulties of selection. When subjects are selected into groups on bases extraneous to the research purposes, we call this "selection," or more accurately, "self-selection." To take an example, let us assume that volunteers are used in the experimental group and other subjects are used as controls. If the volunteers differ in a characteristic related to Y, the dependent variable, the ultimate difference

[16]Underwood, *op. cit.*, chaps. 4 and 5.

between the experimental and control groups may be due to this characteristic rather than to X. Volunteers, for instance, may be more intelligent (or less intelligent) than nonvolunteers. If we were doing an experiment with some kind of learning as the dependent variable, obviously the volunteers might perform better on Y because of superior intelligence, despite the initial likeness of the two groups on the pretest. (Note that, if we had used only volunteers and had assigned them to experimental and control groups at random, the selection difficulty disappears. External validity or representativeness, however, is decreased.)

Another more frequent example in educational research is to take some school classes for the experimental group and others for the control group. If a fairly large number of classes are selected and assigned at random to experimental and control groups, there is no great problem. But if they are not assigned at random, certain ones may select themselves into the experimental groups, and these classes may have characteristics that predispose them to have higher mean Y scores than the other classes. For example, their teachers may be more alert, more intelligent, more aggressive. These characteristics interact with the selection to produce, irrespective of X, higher experimental group than control group Y scores. In other words, something that influences the selection process, as do the volunteer subjects, also influences the dependent variable measures. This happens even though the pretest may show the groups to be the same on the dependent variable. The X manipulation is "effective," but it is not effective in and of itself. It is effective because of selection, or *self-selection.*

Time Designs

A common research problem, especially in studies of the development and growth of children, involves the study of individuals and groups using time as a variable. Such studies are longitudinal studies of subjects, often children, at different points in time. One such design among many might be:

Design 19.8: A Longitudinal Time Design

$$Y_1 \qquad Y_2 \qquad X \qquad Y_3 \qquad Y_4$$

Note the similarity to Design 18.2, where a group is compared to itself. The use of Design 19.8 allows us to avoid one of the difficulties of Design 18.2. Its use makes it possible to separate reactive measurement effects from the effect of X. It also enables us to see, if the measurements have a reactive effect, whether X has an effect over and above that effect. The reactive effect should show itself at Y_2; this can be contrasted with Y_3. If there is an increase at Y_3 over and above the increase at Y_2, it can be attributed to X. A similar argument applies for maturation and history.

One difficulty with longitudinal or time studies, especially with children, is the growth or learning that occurs over time. Children do not stop growing and learning for research convenience. The longer the time period, the greater the problem. In other words, time itself is a variable in a sense. With a design like Design 18.2, $Y_b \;\; X \;\; Y_a$, the time variable can confound X, the experimental independent variable. If there is a significant difference between Y_a and Y_b, one cannot tell whether X or a time variable caused the change. But with Design 19.8, one has other measures of Y and thus a base line against which to compare the change in Y presumably due to X.

Campbell and Stanley believe that history is the most serious problem with this design. The idea here is that it was not X that produced a change in Y but some other event or combination of events occurring during the experimental period. History *is* a problem, but if other X's are operative, they should show up between, say, Y_1 and Y_2, as well as between Y_2 and Y_3. If there are constantly recurring extraneous events or variables other than the experimental X, naturally history will decrease the internal validity of a time study. Researchers must be particularly alert to such other possibilities to prevent their occurrence, and should either take them into account in the interpretation of results or demonstrate that the experimental manipulation X is greater than such extraneous influences.

Take an educational example to illustrate time research and possible extraneous influences. Suppose a board of education, concerned about the morale of its teaching staff, institutes a new policy calculated to improve morale. The administrative staff has two measures of staff morale gathered at three-month intervals, Y_1 and Y_2. The new policy, X, is instituted. The staff's morale is measured again on two subsequent occasions, Y_3 and Y_4. Assume that the results, when graphed (time data should probably always be graphed), are as shown in Fig. 19.6. It can be seen that X seems to have had an effect over and above the effect of time. While morale seems to have been increasing before X, a relatively sharp rise occurred after X. Then the previous rate of rise continued. The only trouble is: Did something else occur between Y_2 and Y_3 to cause the rise in morale? It is probably unlikely, but one must examine the situation carefully. Maybe the superintendent took some other action at the same time the board of education changed the policy in question.

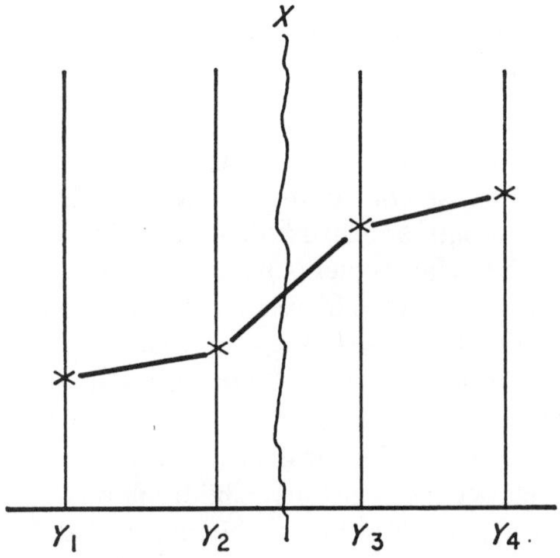

FIG. 19.6

It is easy to transfer the above examples to studies of child growth and learning data. The *Y*'s might be measurements of reading proficiency; *X* might be a new method of teaching reading. Results like those of Fig. 19.6 would look encouraging to the teacher. Here we have to be even more cautious. If a learning study is being done, one or more control groups are essential for reasons already considered and also because of the Hawthorne effect.[17] Almost any change, any extra attention, any experimental manipulation, or even the absence of manipulation but the knowledge that a study is being done, is enough to cause subjects to change. In short, if we pay attention to people, they respond. In the example, above, perhaps any method, as long as it was different from the usual classroom routine, would cause reading scores to rise—thus the need for a control group to which another placebo method could be given. (It is difficult to conceive of a control group in the board of education-staff morale situation.)

The statistical analysis of time measures is a special and troublesome problem: the usual tests of significance applied to time measures can yield spurious results. One reason is that such data tend to be highly variable, and it is easy to interpret changes not due to *X* as due to *X*. That is, in time data, individual and mean scores tend to move around a good bit. It is easy to fall into the trap of seeing one of these shifts as "significant," especially if it accords with our hypothesis. If we can legitimately assume that influences other than *X*, both random and systematic, are uniform over the whole series of *Y*'s, the statistical problem can be solved.[18] But such an assumption may be, and probably often is, unwarranted.

The researcher who does time studies should make a special study of the statistical problems and should consult a statistician. For the practitioner, this statistical complexity is unfortunate in that it may discourage needed practical studies. Since longitudinal single-group designs are particularly well-suited to individual class research, it is recommended that in longitudinal studies of methods or studies of children in educational situations analysis be confined to drawing graphs of results and interpreting them qualitatively. Crucial tests, especially those for published studies, however, must be buttressed with statistical tests.

Naturally, there are possible variations of Design 19.8. One important variation is to add one or more control groups; another is to add more time observations. Still another is to add more *X*'s, more experimental interventions.

Concluding Remarks

It is important to remember that the designs of this chapter are general: they are stripped down to bare essentials to show underlying structure. Having the underlying structures well in mind, the student is in a position to use the more specific designs of analysis of variance and related paradigms. One can of course study

[17]This effect is named after the Hawthorne plant of the Western Electric Corporation where it was first noted. A good, brief, and readily available account of some of this research may be found in G. Homans, "Group Factors in Worker Productivity," in H. Proshansky and B. Seidenberg, eds., *Basic Studies in Social Psychology*. New York: Holt, Rinehart and Winston, 1965, pp. 592–604.

[18]For a statistical discussion, see A. Edwards, *Experimental Design in Psychological Research*, 3d ed. New York: Holt, Rinehart and Winston, 1968, chap. 14.

just the more specific designs, but knowing the general designs enhances flexibility in the sense that they can be more readily adapted to research needs. This point was brought out in Chapter 13, where planned comparisons and post hoc tests were discussed. In any case, links between general and specific paradigms of designs will be taken up in Chapters 20 and 21.

A second point to be made is that basic design ideas and paradigms have stemmed from experimental considerations. Again, the ideal of scientific investigation is the controlled experiment. But as we have pointed out repeatedly, much behavioral research is nonexperimental and its data must be analyzed. The closer the approximation to controlled experimental design the better. Therefore, design created for experimental research is the ideal, the criterion. To the extent that the criteria of experimental design have to be compromised, to that extent research results and conclusions are weakened. So we constantly look toward the ideal even though we are quite aware that we cannot attain it. The point is that we should depart from our principles and criteria only with great reluctance, whether the research is experimental or nonexperimental.

Third, the important thing in studying and using research designs is to understand their rationale, their purposes, and their strengths and weaknesses. Knowing details of many designs and possibilities is not nearly as important as understanding the general nature of the designs and what they are for. Research problems and studies differ greatly and the researcher has to be able to adapt general principles and paradigms to the demands of specific problems. A 2×2 factorial design, for example, can be conceived as a four-group one-way analysis of variance with planned comparisons. How it is conceived and handled depends, as usual, on the research questions asked.

Finally, we need to know that two strong tendencies seem to exist among behavioral researchers: one toward experimental research and one toward nonexperimental research. We have the individual who says that most behavioral research should be experimental and then the individual who says experiments are absurd. Perhaps half the research in psychology and education, and most of the research in sociology and anthropology, is nonexperimental. Some psychological, sociological, and educational researchers even say that the most important and interesting research problems do not lend themselves to an experimental approach.

Ideally, we should, whenever possible, approach research problems and test research hypotheses both experimentally and nonexperimentally. Whenever an independent variable can be manipulated, an experimental approach can and should be used. Many important variables, however, cannot be studied experimentally, because they are not manipulable—at least not in our society. Think of intelligence, child training, religious values, honesty, characteristics of teachers, home environment, and many others. Some of these variables can conceivably be manipulated, but by their very nature most of them cannot be. Many other variables are inherently manipulable: reinforcement, drill, teaching methods, school and class environments, and certain teacher behaviors. There are other variables that are both measurable and manipulable. Anxiety and frustration are examples.

In short, the very multiplicity and complexity of variables tell us that it is misleading to insist upon a preponderance of experimental or nonexperimental research in education, psychology, and sociology.

Study Suggestions

1. The first sentence of this chapter is: "Design is data discipline." What does this sentence mean? Justify it.
2. Suppose you are an educational psychologist and plan to test the hypothesis that feeding back psychological information to teachers effectively enhances the children's learning by increasing the teachers' understanding of the children. Outline an *ideal* research design to test this hypothesis, assuming that you have complete command of the situation and plenty of money and help. (*These are important conditions*, which are included to free the reader from the practical limitations that so often compromise good research designs.) Set up two designs, each with complete randomization, both following the paradigm of Design 19.1. In one of these use only one independent variable and one-way analysis of variance. In the second, use two independent variables and a simple factorial design.

   How do these two designs compare in their control powers and in the information they yield? Which one tests the hypothesis better? Why?
3. Design research to test the hypothesis of Study Suggestion 2, above, but this time compromise the design by not having randomization. Compare the relative efficacies of the two approaches. In which of them would you put greater faith? Why? Explain in detail.
4. In a study of the relation between the attitudes of children toward school and counseling in the junior high school, an investigator took 30 eighth-grade children who, because of disciplinary problems, had been referred for counseling during the previous year, and matched each child with another eighth-grade child, not referred for counseling, on sex and intelligence. He compared the attitudes of the two groups toward school at the beginning and at the end of the year and found a significant difference at the beginning of the year but no significant difference at the end. He concluded that counseling had a salutary effect on children's attitudes toward school.

   Criticize this research: Is it good? Is it bad? How good? How bad? Bear the following in mind: sampling, group comparability, and control.

CHAPTER 21

Research Design and Applications: Randomized Groups

It is difficult to tell anyone how to do research. About all one can do is to try to make sure that the beginner has a grasp of the possibilities. The selection among the possibilities then becomes *his* problem. In tackling a research problem, the investigator should let his mind roam, speculate about possibilities, even guess. Once the possible alternatives are known, the intuitive stage of thinking can enrich the research conception by leading more effectively to the analytical stage of organizing and structuring the problem. The investigator is then ready to plan his approach to the problem and to decide what research and analytical methods he will use to execute his ideas. Good research design is not pure analysis. Intuitive thinking, too, is essential because it helps the investigator to arrive at solutions that are not routine. Perhaps most important, it should be remembered that intuitive thinking and analytical thinking depend upon knowledge, understanding, and experience.

The main purposes of this chapter and the next are to enrich previous design and statistical discussions with actual research examples and to suggest basic possibilities for structuring research, so that the student can ultimately solve research problems.

Simple Randomized Subjects Design

In Chapters 13 and 14 the statistics of simple one-way and factorial analysis of variance were discussed and illustrated. The design behind the earlier discussion is here called *randomized subjects design*. The general design paradigm is Design 19.1:[1]

$$\boxed{R} \quad \frac{X \qquad Y}{\sim X \qquad Y}$$

Research Examples

Examples of Design 19.1 in behavioral research, strange to say, are not numerous. Three examples are given below. Two used random assignment; one probably did not. Unfortunately, some investigators do not report *how* subjects are assigned to groups. The need for reporting on method of subject selection and subject assignment to experimental groups should by now be obvious.

Clark and Walberg: Massive Rewards and Reading While there is a great deal of research with animals on the effects of reinforcement on learning, little controlled experimentation seems to have been done in the classroom. Clark and Walberg, working with black children one to four years behind in their school work, used massive reinforcement to determine its effect on reading achievement.[2] An unusual feature of the study was the random assignment of pupils to classes and of classes to experimental and control groups. At the beginning of the experiment *all* pupils were given praise for their work. After the reward rates per child and per teacher stabilized (six sessions), the teachers of the experimental groups were instructed to double or triple the rewards, while the teachers of the control groups were told "to keep up the good work." At the end of a three-week period, all the children took a reading test.

The means of the experimental and control groups were 31.62 and 26.86, significantly different at the .01 level ($F = 9.52$, at 1 and 108 degrees of freedom).[3] Judging from this study, deprived children who are massively reinforced score significantly higher in reading than children who are given moderate reinforcement. This study is a good example of simple means competently and effectively applied.

Wickens: Stimulus and Response Generalization Study An interesting, ingenious, and important study with significant implications for education is Wickens' study of stimulus and response generalization using conditioning.[4] This

[1]Henceforth, when the term "general design" is used, we refer to the type of paradigm given above and discussed in Chapters 18 and 19. "Analysis of variance design" will refer to the type of paradigm used in the earlier statistical chapters, in this chapter, and in Chapter 21.

[2]C. Clark and H. Walberg, "The Influence of Massive Rewards on Reading Achievement in Potential Urban Dropouts," *American Educational Research Journal*, V (1968), 305–310.

[3]I calculated the intraclass coefficient of correlation; it was .13, which is the proportion of the total variance contributed by the independent variable, or massive reinforcement. This is substantial, especially when we realize the difficulty of the task and the deprivation Clark and Walberg faced. Note that they also controlled intelligence; we will examine how they did this in Chapter 21. An important and interesting sidelight of this study is that to the administrators and teachers the reinforcement idea was revolutionary!

[4]D. Wickens, "Studies of Response Generalization in Conditioning. I. Stimulus Generalization during Response Generalization," *Journal of Experimental Psychology*, XXXIII (1943), 221–227.

study is noteworthy on two related counts: (1) evidently no randomization was used, and (2) randomization was probably deemed unnecessary. The second point needs elaboration. With any type of human response, especially physiological response, that is universal to *homo sapiens* and that *does not exhibit a wide range of individual differences*, it is sometimes fairly safe not to randomize. If all people are pretty much alike in a characteristic under study, it obviously makes no difference whether or not randomization is used. In this respect, any single individual is representative of the whole human race. The possession of blood, a heart beat, and lungs are examples. Of course, the type of blood and the rate of the heart beat and lung action, when used as variables, radically change the picture. At any rate, in Wickens' study, it was probably assumed that all subjects are conditionable. Still, it would have been better to assign subjects to groups at random, because we know that there are individual differences in conditioning or conditionability. It is conceivable that such differences might affect the experimental outcomes.

Returning to Wickens' experiment, the responses of subjects to shock were conditioned to a tone. After being conditioned, the subjects' hands were turned over and their conditioned responses to the first tone and to other tones were tested. Three experimental groups and one control group were used. Groups I, II, and III, the experimental groups, were conditioned and then tested differently. Although the details do not concern us, in general, the *S*s were conditioned to one tone and either tested with that tone or with tones one or two octaves above or below the original conditioned tone. The results, in mean number of responses (flexion in a new hand position), indicated that stimulus generalization and response generalization had occurred. The means for the four groups were: I, 5.87; II, 3.69; III, 4.19; and control, .16.

Wickens did a one-way analysis of variance of the data of Groups I, II, and III to show that they did not differ in mean response. The *F* ratio was not significant. This demonstrated stimulus generalization (since the *S*s responded similarly to the original tone *and* to the tones one and two octaves away from the original tone). He then tested each of the experimental groups against the control group. Each comparison was significant, which demonstrated response generalization (because the control group was shocked but not conditioned, and the responses were given with the hand turned over).

Golightly and Byrne: Attitude as Reinforcement Can people be helped to learn discriminations by reinforcing correct responses *with attitude statements* that are in agreement with their attitudes? The traditional kind of reinforcement is "Yes-No," "Right-Wrong," and the like. Instead of saying "Right" and "Wrong," suppose we say, when a subject makes a correct response, "The Democratic Party is good"—and the subject is a Democrat. Will attitude statements of this sort act as reinforcers just as grain to pigeons and "Right-Wrong" to children do? Golightly and Byrne tested the idea using three groups of 20 *S*s each (assigned randomly) in a Design 19.1 and one-way analysis of variance framework.[5] The first of these, *traditional reward-punishment*, was reinforced with "Right" and "Wrong" when correct and incorrect responses were made. (The discrimination was between

[5]C. Golightly and D. Byrne, "Attitude Statements as Positive and Negative Reinforcements," *Science*, CXLVI (1964), 798–799.

large and *small*, and *large* was correct for half the *S*s and *small* for the other half.) The second group, *attitude similarity-dissimilarity*, was reinforced with attitude statements: if a discrimination was correct, an attitude statement with which the *S* agreed was presented to him; if incorrect, an attitude statement with which he disagreed was presented. The third group was a *control*: its members received statements that were attitude-neutral. Evidently planned comparisons were used, both experimental groups being tested against the control group separately.

First, the traditional reinforcement group was superior to both the other two groups, an expected result. More important, the attitude similarity group was superior to the control group: $F = 26.78$, $df = 1, 54$, significant at the .001 level. Evidently attitude statements can be effective reinforcers of discrimination learning. This is probably no great surprise to many people. After all, they may say, if you want someone to learn to like you, agree with his opinions. But the matter is more complex than this. In fact, this study is theoretically important because it brought learning and social psychological theory together and demonstrated, experimentally in an unusual way, the reinforcement power of opinion statements. It is also a good example of Design 19.1.

Factorial Designs

The basic general design is still Design 19.1, though the variation of the basic experimental group-control group pattern is drastically altered by the addition of other experimental factors or independent variables. Following an earlier definition of factorial analysis of variance, *factorial design is the structure of research in which two or more independent variables are juxtaposed in order to study their independent and interactive effects on a dependent variable.*

The reader may at first find it a bit difficult to fit the factorial framework into the general experimental group-control group paradigm of Design 19.1. The discussion of the generalization of the control-group idea in Chapter 19, however, should have clarified the relations between Design 19.1 and factorial designs. The discussion is now continued. We have the independent variables A and B and the dependent variable Y. The simplest factorial design, the 2×2, has three possibilities: both A and B active; A active, B attribute (or vice versa); and both A and B attribute. The last possibility, both independent variables attributes, is the ex post facto case. Returning to the experimental group-control group notion, A can be divided into A_1 and A_2, experimental and control, as usual, with the additional independent variable B partitioned into B_1 and B_2. Since this structure is familiar to us by now, we need only discuss one or two procedural details.

The ideal subject assignment procedure is to assign subjects to the four cells at random. If both A and B are active variables, this is possible and easy. Simply give the subjects numbers arbitrarily from 1 through N, N being the total number of subjects. Then, using a table of random numbers, write down numbers 1 through N as they turn up in the table. Place the numbers into four groups as they turn up and then assign the four groups of subjects to the four cells. To be safe, assign the groups of subjects to the experimental treatments (the four cells) at random, too. Label the groups 1, 2, 3, and 4. Then draw these numbers from a table of random numbers. Assume that the table yielded the numbers in this order: 3, 4, 1, 2. Assign Group 3 subjects to the upper left cell, Group 4 subjects to the upper right cell, and so on.

Often B will be an attribute variable, like sex, intelligence, achievement, anxiety, self-perception, race, and so on. The subject assignment must be altered. First, since B is an attribute variable, there is no possibility of assigning subjects to B_1 and B_2 at random. If B were the variable sex, the best we can do is to assign males first at random to the cells A_1B_1 and A_2B_1, and then females to the cells A_1B_2 and A_2B_2. With the ex post facto case where both variables are assigned, random assignment is, of course, not possible. Strictly speaking, however, it is doubtful that factorial analysis of variance should be used with much ex post facto data. There is a more suitable alternative, multiple regression analysis, which we study in Chapters 35 and 36.

Factorial Designs with More than Two Variables

We can often improve the design and sharpen up the information obtained from a piece of research by adding groups. Instead of A_1 and A_2, and B_1 and B_2, an experiment may profit from A_1, A_2, A_3, and A_4, and B_1, B_2, and B_3. Practical and statistical problems increase and sometimes become quite difficult as variables are added. Suppose we have a $3 \times 2 \times 2$ design that has $3 \times 2 \times 2 = 12$ cells, each of which has to have at least two subjects, and preferably many more. (It is possible, but not very sensible, to have only one subject per cell if one can have more than one. There are, of course, designs that have only one subject per cell.) If we decide that 10 subjects per cell are necessary, $12 \times 10 = 120$ subjects will have to be obtained and assigned at random. The problem is more acute with one more variable and the practical manipulation of the research situation is also more difficult. But the successful handling of such an experiment allows us to test a number of hypotheses and yields a great deal of information. The combinations of three-, four-, and five-variable designs give a wide variety of possible designs: $2 \times 5 \times 3$, $4 \times 4 \times 2$, $3 \times 2 \times 4 \times 2$, $4 \times 3 \times 2 \times 2$, and so on.

Research Examples of Factorial Designs

Examples of two- and three-dimensional factorial designs were described in Chapter 14. (The restudy of these examples is recommended, because the reasoning behind the essential design can now be more easily grasped.) Since a number of examples of factorial designs were given in Chapter 14, we confine the examples given here to three studies with unusual features.

Frederiksen, Jensen, and Beaton: Organizational Climate and Administrative Performance The first example is a 2×2 factorial-type design conceived to test highly interesting ideas about relations between organizational climates and administrative performance.[6] In that part of the study we outline—the whole study is a large one—one independent variable was innovation and originality vs.

[6]N. Frederiksen, O. Jensen, and A. Beaton, *Organizational Climates and Administrative Performance.* Princeton, N.J.: Educational Testing Service, 1968.

rules and standard procedures, and the second independent variable was global supervision vs. detailed supervision. Both variables were manipulated. There were a number of dependent variables derived from an unusual instrument called the In-Basket Test, among them overall quality of administrative performance, productivity, plans and discusses, and so on. The design is shown in Fig. 20.1.

Although the results were disappointing—very few statistical tests were significant—the design is theoretically and practically important. Note the unusual nature of the independent variables, which, incidentally, were manipulated by varied written instructions to administrators taking the In-Basket Test. Studies using variables that reflect different administrative and organizational ideas and practices are rare. And the dependent variables, too, are of theoretical and practical interest: they reflect many facets of executive behavior and style.

Lana: Pretest Interaction Effects[7] This is a methodological study using the Solomon design discussed in Chapter 19 as Design 19.6. It may be recalled that this design is a four-group design, with one experimental group and three control groups, the experimental group and one control group being administered pretests. Lana put Solomon's and Campbell's notions to empirical test. Do pretests have a sensitizing effect on attitudes? Recall one of the major purposes of the Solomon design: to control for possible pretest effects on Y, the dependent variable. Recall also that Solomon suggested, among other statistical analyses, a 2×2 factorial analysis of the four sets of posttest measures to separate the pretest-posttest variance from the variance of the other independent variables. Lana adopted these ideas and put them to good use.

Group I, the experimental group, and Group II, the first control group, were administered an attitudinal pretest. Groups III and IV were not given the pretest. One experimental variable, then, was Pretest-No Pretest. Another experimental variable was Communication-No Communication. Unlike most such attitudinal studies, this latter variable was less important than the pretest variable. The design and part of Lana's data are given in Table 20.1.[8] The difference between the communication and no communication means was significant at the .05 level. The pretest–no-pretest means difference was not significant, but most important, the interaction was not significant. The pretest apparently had no sensitizing effect.

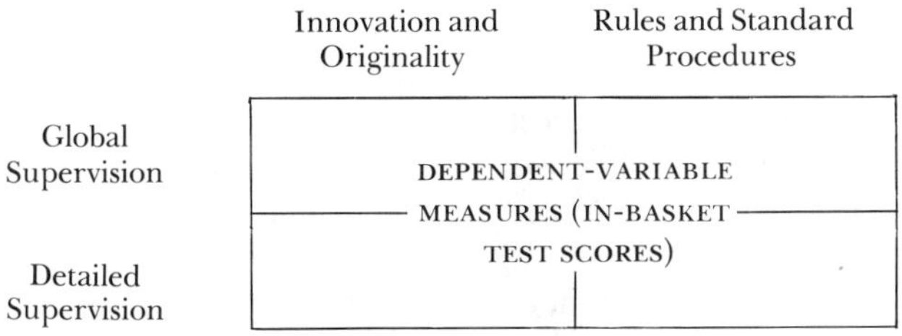

FIG. 20.1

[7]R. Lana, "Pretest-Treatment Interaction Effects in Longitudinal Studies," *Psychological Bulletin*, LVI (1959), 293–300.

[8]Lana actually used five groups. His design and analysis were more elaborate than indicated above. Still, the basic design is shown. Additional tests were control tests.

TABLE **20.1** DESIGN AND DATA OF LANA STUDY OF PRETEST INTERACTION EFFECT

	Pretest	No-Pretest
Communication	42.96	42.90
No communication	40.28	40.77

To understand this clever study and its findings, we must know clearly what Lana was trying to do: he was testing the hypothesis that the pretest and the treatment would interact. Listening to Campbell's warning about the danger of pretesting, we might expect that pretested groups, because they were pretested, would be sensitized to receive the communication whereas unpretested groups would not be so sensitized. This sensitization, if present, would be demonstrated by a difference between the means of the pretested communication-no communication groups with no such difference present between the means of the unpretested communication-no communication groups. That is, in Table 20.1, the means of the two cells on the top of the table would differ significantly, but the means of the bottom cells would not differ significantly.

Hoyt: Teacher Knowledge and Pupil Achievement[9] This study was planned to answer an important theoretical and practical educational question: What are the effects on the achievement and attitudes of pupils if the teachers are given knowledge of the characteristics of their pupils? An earlier study by Ojemann and Wilkinson had purported to show that such knowledge feedback enhances pupil achievement and personality.[10] Hoyt's study explored several related aspects of the basic question and used recent design and statistical developments to enhance the internal validity of the investigation. He used three factorial designs: $2 \times 2 \times 3$; $2 \times 3 \times 3 \times 3$; and 3×3. The first design was used three times for each of three school subjects, and the second and third were used twice, once in each of two school systems.

We sketch the design for the first of these designs. The independent variables were treatments, ability level, sex, and schools. The three treatments were: no information (N), test scores (T), and test scores plus other information (TO). These are self-explanatory. They were assigned at random to experimental groups. Ability levels were high, medium, and low IQ. The remaining two variables, sex and schools, are obvious. Eighth-grade students were assigned at random *within sex and scholastic aptitude populations*.[11] The design is shown in Fig. 20.2. Since this design is complex, it will be well to examine what a final analysis of variance table of such a design would look like and to know the hypotheses that can be tested. Before doing so, however, it should be noted that the achievement results were mostly indeterminate (or negative). With one interaction exception, the F

[9]K. Hoyt, "A Study of the Effects of Teacher Knowledge of Pupil Characteristics on Pupil Achievement and Attitudes towards Classwork," *Journal of Educational Psychology*, XLVI (1955), 302–310.

[10]R. Ojemann and F. Wilkinson, "The Effect on Pupil Growth of an Increase in Teachers' Understanding of Pupil Behavior," *Journal of Experimental Education*, VIII (1939), 143–147.

[11]Though not often done, this is desirable. The procedure is to select and assign within each sex separately and within each ability level separately.

		Treatments					
		N		*T*		*TO*	
	Sex	M	F	M	F	M	F
School A	High IQ						
	Medium IQ			DEPENDENT			
	Low IQ			VARIABLE			
School B	High IQ			MEASURES			
	Medium IQ						
	Low IQ						

FIG. 20.2

ratios were not significant. A notable positive result was that pupil attitudes toward teachers seemed to improve when there were increases in teacher knowledge, an interesting and important finding.

The sources of variance and degrees of freedom of the analysis of variance table are given in Table 20.2. One experiment yields 14 tests! Naturally, a number

TABLE **20.2** SOURCES OF VARIANCE AND DEGREES OF FREEDOM FOR A $3 \times 3 \times 2 \times 2$ FACTORIAL DESIGN WITH VARIABLES TREATMENTS, ABILITY, SEX, AND SCHOOL (TOTAL AND WITHIN DEGREES OF FREEDOM ARE OMITTED)

Source	*df*
Main Effects:	
*Between Treatments	2
Between Ability Levels	2
Between Sexes	1
Between Schools	1
First-Order Interactions:	
*Interaction: Treatments × Ability	4
*Interaction: Treatments × Sex	2
*Interaction: Treatments × School	2
Interaction: Ability × Sex	2
Interaction: Ability × School	2
Interaction: Sex × School	1
Second-Order Interactions:	
*Interaction: Treatments × Ability × Sex	4
*Interaction: Treatment × Ability × School	4
Interaction: Ability × Sex × School	2
Third-Order Interaction:	
Interaction: Treatment × Ability × Sex × School	4
Within	
Total	

of these tests are not important and can be ignored. The tests of greatest importance (marked with asterisks in the table) are those involving the treatment variable. The most important test is between treatments, the first of the main effects. Next in importance, perhaps equally important, are the interactions involving treatments. Take the interaction treatments × sex. If this were significant, it would mean that the amount of information a teacher possesses about students has an influence on student achievement, but boys are influenced differently than girls. Boys with teachers who possess information about their pupils may do better than boys whose teachers do not have such information, whereas it may be the opposite with girls, or it may make no difference one way or the other.[12]

Second-order or triple interactions are harder to interpret. It is probably true that they are rarely significant. If they *are* significant, however, they require special study; one of the best ways to study them is by graphic representation (discussed in an earlier chapter). Crossbreak tables of means are also helpful. The student will find guidance in Edwards' book.[13]

Evaluation of Randomized Subjects Designs

Randomized subjects designs are all variants or extensions of Design 19.1, the basic experimental group-control group design in which subjects are assigned to the experimental and control groups at random. As such they have the strengths of the basic design, the most important of which is the randomization feature and the consequent ability to assume the preexperimental approximate equality of the experimental groups in all possible independent variables. History and maturation are controlled because very little time elapses between the manipulation of X and the observation and measurement of Y. There is no possible contamination due to pretesting.

Two other strengths of these designs, springing from the many variations possible, are flexibility and applicability. They can be used to help solve many behavioral research problems, since they seem to be peculiarly well-suited to the types of design problems that arise from social scientific and educational problems and hypotheses. The one-way designs, for example, can incorporate any number of methods, and the testing of methods is a major educational need. The variables that constantly need control in behavioral research—sex, intelligence, aptitude, social class, schools, and many others—can be incorporated into factorial designs and thus controlled. With factorial designs, too, it is easily possible to have mixtures of active and attribute variables, another important need.

[12]The student will find it helpful to lay out and study the tables for these interactions. For example, the one under discussion would be:

	N	*T*	*TO*
Female			
Male			

Fill in the means and interpret the results for the various combinations.

[13]A. Edwards, *Experimental Design in Psychological Research*, 3d ed. New York: Holt, Rinehart and Winston, 1968, chaps. 11, 12.

There are weaknesses, too. One criticism has been that randomized subjects designs do not permit tests of the equality of groups as do before-after designs. Actually, this is not a valid criticism for two reasons: with enough subjects and randomization, it can be assumed that the groups are equal, as we have seen; and it *is* possible to check the groups for equality on variables other than Y, the dependent variable. Data on such variables as intelligence, aptitude, and achievement usually exist in readily available school records. It is an easy matter to run an analysis of variance on, say, intelligence.

Another difficulty is statistical. One should have equal numbers of cases in the cells of factorial designs. (It is possible to work with unequal n's, but it is both clumsy and a threat to interpretation. Small discrepancies can be cured by dropping out cases at random.) This imposes a limitation on the use of such designs, because it is often not possible to have equal numbers in each cell. One-way randomized designs are not so delicate: unequal numbers are not a difficult problem.[14]

Compared to matched groups designs, randomized subjects designs are usually less precise, that is, the error term is ordinarily larger, other things equal. It is doubtful, however, whether this is a matter for great concern. In some cases it certainly is—for example, where a very sensitive test of a hypothesis is needed. In much behavioral research, though, it is probably desirable to consider as nonsignificant any effect that is insufficiently powerful to make itself felt over and above the random noise of a randomized subjects design.

All in all, then, these are powerful, flexible, useful, and widely applicable designs. In the opinion of the writer, they are the best all-round designs, perhaps the first to be considered when planning the design of a research study.

Study Suggestions

1. In studying research design, it is useful to do analyses of variance—as many as possible: simple one-way analyses and two-variable factorial analyses. Try even a three-variable analysis. By means of this statistical work you can get a better understanding of the designs. You may well attach variable names to your "data," rather than work with numbers alone. Some useful suggestions for projects with random numbers follow.
   (a) Draw three groups of random numbers, 0 through 9. Name the independent and dependent variables. Express a hypothesis and translate it into design-statistical language. Do a one-way analysis of variance. Interpret.
   (b) Repeat 1(a) with five groups of numbers.
   (c) Now increase the numbers of one of your groups by 2, and decrease those of another group by 2. Repeat the statistical analysis.
   (d) Draw four groups of random numbers, 10 in each group. Set them up, at random, in a 2×2 factorial design. Do a factorial analysis of variance.
   (e) Bias the numbers of the two right-hand cells by adding 3 to each number. Repeat the analysis. Compare with the results of 1(d).

[14]The advanced student will find a discussion of unequal n's, the problem of disproportionality, and how to adjust for inequalities in G. Snedecor and W. Cochran, *Statistical Methods*, 6th ed. Ames, Iowa: Iowa State University Press, 1967, chap. 16. A generally better way to handle the problem is with multiple regression analysis (see Chapter 36). Complex studies like the Hoyt study, above, are also probably better handled with multiple regression analysis.

(f) Bias the numbers of the data of 1(d), as follows: add 2 to each of the numbers in the upper left and lower right cells. Repeat the analysis. Interpret.

2. Look up Study Suggestion 2, Chapter 13. Three groups are used. What general design does this example fall under? Why? Is there a "control group"?
3. Look up Study Suggestions 2 and 3, Chapter 14. Work through both examples again. (Are they easier for you now?) Pay particular attention to 3(c).
4. Suppose that you are the principal of an elementary school. Some of the fourth- and fifth-grade teachers want to dispense with workbooks. The superintendent does not like the idea, but he is willing for you to test the notion that workbooks do not make much difference. (One of the teachers even suggests that workbooks may have bad effects on both teachers and pupils.) Set up two research plans and designs to test the efficacy of the workbooks: a one-way design and a factorial design. Consider the variables achievement, intelligence, and sex. You might also consider the possibility of teacher attitude toward workbooks as an independent variable.
5. Here is a difficult research design problem. Imagine that you are the chairman of a committee appointed to evaluate the effects of a core curriculum soon to be established in your school's undergraduate division. The proponents of the program say that the core program is superior to the conventional program on all counts: achievement, student attitude, and so on. Draw up a research plan and design to test the efficacy of the new program. What are the limitations of the design? What would be the limitations of *any* design with a problem of this kind?
6. Suppose an investigation using methods and sex as the independent variables and achievement as the dependent variable has been done with the results shown in Table 20.3. The numbers in the cells are fictitious means. The F ratios of Methods and Sex are not significant. The interaction F ratio is significant at the .01 level. Interpret these results statistically and substantively. To do the latter, name the three methods.

TABLE **20.3** HYPOTHETICAL DATA (MEANS) OF A FICTITIOUS FACTORIAL EXPERIMENT

	Methods			
Sex	A_1	A_2	A_3	
Male	45	45	36	42
Female	35	39	40	38
	40	42	38	

7. Read the following two studies, one in education and one in social psychology. They are important and interesting researches, well designed and well executed.

Davis, J., and Klausmeier, H. "Cognitive Style and Concept Identification," *Journal of Educational Psychology*, LXI (1970), 423–430.
Jones, E. "Conformity as a Tactic of Ingratiation," *Science*, CXLIX (1965), 144–150.

(a) In your opinion, did the authors test their hypotheses adequately?
(b) One of the independent variables of the Davis and Klausmeier study is field dependence (cognitive style), which is known to be correlated with

intelligence. The authors did not include intelligence as a variable of the study. Does this create problems in the interpretation of the results? If so, why?

(c) Rearrange Tables 1 and 2 of the Jones report into 2×2 tables of means. Interpret.

8. Suppose a researcher has done a $3 \times 2 \times 2$ factorial study. Lay out the final analysis of variance table, labeling the three effects A, B, and C. Include the degrees of freedom in the table. Now name three independent variables and a dependent variable to fit the model. Have A be significant, B not significant, C significant, and the $A \times B$ interaction significant. Interpret the results. (*Note:* There are seven possible statistical tests. See Table 14.9, Chapter 14—but be careful: there is a difference.)

CHAPTER 21

Research Design and Applications: Correlated Groups

One basic principle is behind all correlated-groups[1] designs: there is systematic variance in the dependent variable measures due to the correlation between the groups *in some variable related to the dependent variable*. This correlation and its concomitant variance can be introduced into the measures—and the design—in three ways: (1) use the same units, for example, subjects, in each of the experimental groups, (2) match units on one or more independent variables that are related to the dependent variable, and (3) use more than one group of units, like classes or schools, in the design. Despite the seeming differences among these three ways of introducing correlation into the dependent variable measures, they are basically the same. We now examine the design implications of this basic principle and discuss the three ways of implementing the principle.

The General Paradigm

With the exception of correlated factorial designs and so-called nested designs, all analysis of variance paradigms of correlated groups designs can be easily outlined. The general paradigm is given in Fig. 21.1. To emphasize the sources of variance, means of columns and rows have been indicated. The individual dependent variable measures (Y's) have also been inserted.[2] It can be seen that there are two

[1]The word "group" should be taken to mean set of scores. Then there is no confusion when a repeated trials experiment is classified as a multigroup design.

[2]It is useful to know the system of subscripts to symbols used in mathematics and statistics. A rectangular table of numbers is called a *matrix*. The entries of a matrix are letters and/or numbers. When letters are used, it is common to identify any particular matrix entry with two (sometimes more) subscripts. The first of these indicates the number of the *row*, the second the number of the *column*. Y_{32}, for instance, indicates the Y measure in the third row and the second column. Y_{57} indicates the Y

	Treatments					
Units	X_1	X_2	X_3	. . .	X_k	
1	Y_{11}	Y_{12}	Y_{13}	. . .	Y_{1k}	M_1
2	Y_{21}	Y_{22}	Y_{23}	. . .	Y_{2k}	M_2
3	Y_{31}	Y_{32}	Y_{33}	. . .	Y_{3k}	M_3
.	.	.	.	. . .	.	.
.	.	.	.	. . .	.	.
.	.	.	.	. . .	.	.
n	Y_{n1}	Y_{n2}	Y_{n3}		Y_{nk}	M_n
	M_{X_1}	M_{X_2}	M_{X_3}	. . .	M_{X_k}	(M_t)

FIG. 21.1

sources of systematic variance: that due to columns, or treatments, and that due to rows—individual or unit differences. Analysis of variance must be the two-way variety.

The student who has studied the correlation-variance argument of Chapter 15, where the statistics and some of the problems of correlated-groups designs were presented, will have no difficulty with the variance reasoning of Fig. 21.1. The intent of the design is to maximize the between-treatments variance, identify the between-units variance, and minimize the error (residual) variance. The *max-mincon* principle applies here as elsewhere. The only difference, really, between designs of correlated groups and randomized subjects is the rows or units variance.

Units

The units used do not alter the variance principles in the slightest. It is necessary to understand this point clearly. The usual conception of the correlated-groups design seems to be fixed rather rigidly in the matching of subjects. The word "units" was deliberately used in Fig. 21.1 to overcome this conception and to substitute a generalized conception. In principle it does not matter what is substituted for "units." "Subjects," "pairs," "classes," "schools," "school districts," "cities," and "counties" are all appropriate substitutions for "units." The important consideration is whether the units, whatever they are, differ from each other. If they do, *variance between units* is introduced. In this sense, talking about correlated groups or subjects is the same as talking about variance between groups or subjects. The notion of individual differences is extended to *unit differences.*

The real value of correlated-groups designs would seem to be that not only do they enable the investigator to isolate and estimate the variance due to correlation; they also guide him to design research to capitalize on the differences that frequently exist between units. If a research study involves different classes in the

measure of the fifth row and the seventh column. It is also customary to generalize this system by adding letter subscripts. In this book, i symbolizes *any row number* and j *any column number. Any* number of the matrix is represented by Y_{ij}; *any* number of the third row, Y_{3j}; and *any* number of the second column, Y_{i2}.

same school, these classes are a possible source of variance. Thus it may be wise to use "classes" as units in the design. The well-known differences between schools are very important sources of variance in educational research. They may be handled factorially, or they may be handled in the manner of the designs in this chapter. Indeed, if one looks carefully at a factorial design with two independent variables, one of them *schools*, and at a correlated groups design with units *schools*, one finds, in essence, the same design. Study Fig. 21.2. On the left is a factorial design and on the right a correlated-groups design. But they look the same! They are the same, in variance principle. (The only differences might be numbers of scores in the cells and statistical treatment.)

		Treatments A_1	A_2
Schools	B_1		
	B_2		
	B_3		

Factorial Design

Schools	*Treatments* A_1	A_2
1		
2		
3		

Correlated-Groups Design

FIG. 21.2

One-group Repeated Trials Design

In the one-group repeated trials design, as the name indicates, one group is given different treatments at different times or is measured at different times. In a learning experiment, the same group of subjects may be given several tasks of different complexity, or the experimental manipulation may be to present learning principles in different orders, say from simple to complex, from complex to simple, from whole to part, from part to whole. Many longitudinal studies fall into this category. Studies of the physical and mental growth of children using this design have been successful, despite its inherent weaknesses. This success is probably due to the resistance of growth processes to other than massive external influences.

It was said earlier that the best possible matching of subjects is to match a subject with himself, so to speak. The difficulties in using this solution of the control problem have also been mentioned. One of these difficulties resembles pretest sensitization, which may produce an interaction between the pretest and the experimentally manipulated variable. Another is simply that subjects mature and learn over time. A subject who has experienced one or two trials of an experimental manipulation and is facing a third trial is a different person from the one who faced trial one. Experimental situations differ a great deal, of course. In some situations, repeated trials may not unduly affect the performances of subjects on later trials; in other situations, they may. The problem of how individuals learn or become unduly sensitized during an experiment is a difficult one to solve. In short, *history*, *maturation*, and *sensitization* are possible weaknesses of repeated trials. The regression effect can also be a weakness because, as we saw in an earlier chapter, low scorers tend to get higher scores and high scorers lower scores on retesting simply due to the imperfect correlation between the groups. A control group is, of course, needed.

Despite the basic time difficulties, there may be occasions when a one-group repeated trials design is useful. Certainly in ex post facto analyses of "time" data this is the implicit design. If we have a series of growth measurements of children, for instance, the different times at which the measurements were made correspond to treatments. The paradigm of the design is the same as that of Fig. 21.1. Simply substitute "subjects" for "units" and label $X_1, X_2, \ldots$ "trials."

From this general paradigm special cases can be derived. The simplest case is the one-group, before-after design, Design 18.2(a), where one group of subjects was given an experimental treatment preceded by a pretest and followed by a posttest. Since the weaknesses of this design have already been mentioned, further discussion is not necessary. It should be noted, though, that this design, especially in its ex post facto form, closely approximates much commonsense observation and thinking. A person may observe educational practices today and decide that they are not too good. In order to make this judgment, he implicitly or explicitly compares today's educational practices with educational practices of the past. From a number of possible causes, depending on his particular bias, he will select one or more reasons for what he believes to be the sorry state of educational affairs: "progressive education," "educationists," "moral degeneration," "lack of firm religious principles," and so on.

Two-group, Experimental Group–Control Group Designs

This design has two forms, the better of which (repeated here) was described in Chapter 19 as Design 19.2:

$\boxed{M_r}$	X	Y	(Experimental)
	$\sim X$	Y	(Control)

In this design, subjects are first matched and then assigned to experimental and control groups at random. In the other form, subjects are matched but not assigned to experimental and control groups at random. The latter design can be indicated by simply dropping the subscript *r* from $\boxed{M_r}$ (described in Chapter 18 as Design 18.4, one of the inadequate designs).

The design-statistical paradigm of this warhorse of designs is shown in Fig. 21.3. The insertion of the symbols for the means shows the two sources of system-

	Treatments		
Pairs	X_e	X_c	
1	Y_{1e}	Y_{1c}	M_1
2	Y_{2e}	Y_{2c}	M_2
3	Y_{3e}	Y_{3c}	M_3
.	.	.	.
.	.	.	.
.	.	.	.
n	Y_{ne}	Y_{nc}	M_n
	M_e	M_c	

FIG. 21.3

atic variance: *treatments* and *pairs*, *columns* and *rows*. This is in clear contrast to the randomized designs of Chapter 20, where the only systematic variance was *treatments* or *columns*.

The most common variant of the two-group, experimental group–control group design is the before-after, two-group design. [See Design 19.3(b).] The design-statistical paradigm and its rationale are discussed later (see Table 21.2).

Research Examples of Two-group Designs

Hundreds of studies of the two-group, matched-subjects type have been published. In many, probably most, studies using matched subjects, the subjects have not been assigned to experimental and control groups at random. It is often impossible to tell whether investigators have or have not used randomization, since research reports frequently fail to report how subjects are assigned to groups. The studies described below have been chosen not only because they illustrate correlated groups design, matching, and control problems, but also because they are historically, educationally, and psychologically important. Two of them are studies of rare scope.

Thorndike's Transfer of Training Study

In 1924, E. L. Thorndike published a remarkable study of the presumed effect on intelligence of certain school subjects.[3] Students were matched according to scores on Form A of the measure of the dependent variable, intelligence. This test also served as a pretest. The independent variable was One Year's Study of Subjects, such as history, mathematics, and Latin. A posttest, Form B of the intelligence test, was given at the end of the year. Thorndike used an ingenious device to separate the differential effect of each school subject by matching on Form A of the intelligence test those pupils who studied, for instance, English, history, geometry, and *Latin* with those pupils who studied English, history, geometry, and *shopwork*. Thus, for these two groups, he was comparing the differential effects of *Latin* and *shopwork*. Gains in final intelligence scores were considered a joint effect of growth plus the academic subjects studied.

Despite its weaknesses, this was a colossal study. Thorndike was aware of the lack of adequate controls, as revealed in the following passage on the effects of selection:

> The chief reason why good thinkers seem superficially to have been made such by having taken certain school studies, is that good thinkers have taken such studies . . . When the good thinkers studied Greek and Latin, these studies seemed to make good thinkers. Now that the good thinkers study Physics and Trigonometry, these seem to make good thinkers. If the abler pupils should all study Physical Education and Dramatic Art, these subjects would seem to make good thinkers.[4]

[3]E. Thorndike, "Mental Discipline in High School Studies," *Journal of Educational Psychology*, XV (1924), 1–22, 83–98.

[4]*Ibid.*, p. 98.

Thorndike pointed the way to controlled educational research, which has led to the decrease of metaphysical and dogmatic explanations in education. His work struck a blow against the razor-strop theory of mental training, the theory that likened the mind to a razor that could be sharpened by stropping it on "hard" subjects.

It is not easy to evaluate a study such as this, the scope and ingenuity of which is impressive. One wonders, however, about the adequacy of the dependent variable, "intelligence" or "intellectual ability." Can school subjects studied for one year have much effect on intelligence? We now also believe that such large numbers of subjects are not necessary. Most important, though, Thorndike's experiment was not a "true" one. Strictly speaking, it was an ex post facto study. No randomization, of course, was possible. Thorndike measured the intelligence of students and let the independent variables, school subjects, operate. As mentioned above, he was aware of this control weakness in his experiment. The study is still a classic that deserves respect and careful study despite its weaknesses in history and selection (maturation was controlled).

The Eight-Year Study

Another ambitious attempt to answer an important educational question empirically was the Eight-Year Study,[5] which was designed to answer the question: How do "progressive" methods of education in high school compare with "traditional" methods in preparing youngsters for college? Thirty "progressive" high schools in different parts of the country were included in the study. Students in these schools studied under a core curriculum plan. After the students were in college, they were matched with students from "traditional" schools on sex, intelligence, and other variables. The college performances of the two groups were compared. In general, the results indicated that the students of the progressive schools performed somewhat better than the students from traditional schools.

This large-scale study, like the Thorndike study, is ex post facto in nature with serious control weaknesses, probably the most important of which is self-selection. Despite the matching, there may have been other crucial variables that distinguished the progressive school students from the traditional school students *when the study started.* Do children, for example, who go to progressive high schools differ significantly in motivation from children who go to traditional high schools? Do the parents of the progressive school children engender better attitudes toward learning than do the parents of traditional school children? (Some of the schools were university laboratory schools.) Even though this study can be criticized, it remains an important attempt to get objective evidence on complex and difficult educational questions.[6]

[5]W. Aikin, *The Story of the Eight-Year Study.* New York: Harper & Row, 1942.

[6]The study also broke new ground in measurement. Realizing that progressive educators stress qualities not measured by the usual tests of intelligence and achievement, the investigators devised measurement instruments. The most important of these were tests to measure the ability to think. See E. Smith et al., *Appraising and Recording Student Progress.* New York: Harper & Row, 1942.

Bandura and Menlove's Modeling and Extinction Study

We skip through the years to a recent use of pre- and post-measures. It has become difficult to find studies in psychology that use matching. But more and more psychological researchers, perhaps because of the nature of many problems that involve change, are using relatively complex designs with pre- and post-measures and tests. We choose one such study not only for pretests and posttests but also because it is one of a fine series of researches along similar theoretical and practical lines on the problems of social learning and modeling.[7]

The researchers first measured the animal-avoidance behavior of 48 nursery school children (the pretest). They then randomly assigned the children to three experimental groups: *single-model*, *multiple-model*, and *control*. *S*s in the single-model condition observed a movie in which a five-year old progressively approached a cocker spaniel. *S*s in the multiple-model condition observed boys and girls interacting positively with different dogs. Children in the control condition were shown other unrelated movies. The avoidance behavior was tested after the treatment (posttest), and again in a later follow-up.

Analyses used in the study were unusual: because of nonnormality of the score distributions, nonparametric tests were used. First, to test the *trend* effect—that is, the differences among the scores of the pretest, posttest, and follow-up—a Friedman nonparametric analysis was used. χ_r^2 was 15.79, significant at the .001 level. Recall that the Friedman test takes account of the correlation. Here, the differences among the experimental treatments of the same children were tested. Thus, there was significant change. Other tests showed that the two modeling conditions changed, but the control condition did not change. The significance of the differences among the three experimental treatments was tested using the Kruskal-Wallis one-way nonparametric analysis of variance. Change or difference scores obtained between pretest and follow-up were analyzed. H was 5.01, significant at the .05 level. Other analyses showed that the modeling treatments were effective.

The authors then added an ingenious twist to the study: they used the multiple-modeling procedure with the control group *S*s at the end of the experiment proper. These *S*s already had three approach scores: pretest, posttest, follow-up. Call the new fourth set of scores posttherapy. The significance of the differences among the four sets of scores—note carefully that each *S* had four scores and thus we have correlated groups—was tested with the Friedman test. χ_r^2 was 13.42, significant at the .01 level. Thus the modeling procedure was also effective with the controls.

To be quite clear on what was done, the three principal analyses used by Bandura and Menlove are summarized in Table 21.1, using symbolism already familiar to us or self-evident. Recall that the Kruskal-Wallis test is a one-way analysis and uses ranks of *all* the scores, while the Friedman test is a two-way analysis and uses ranks of each row separately. Bandura and Menlove, then, used

[7]A. Bandura and F. Menlove, "Factors Determining Vicarious Extinction of Avoidance Behavior through Symbolic Modeling," *Journal of Personality and Social Psychology*, VIII (1968), 99–108.

TABLE **21.1** PARADIGMATIC OUTLINE OF ANALYSES OF BANDURA AND MENLOVE MODELING STUDY

I.

Trends

Ss	Pretest	Posttest	Follow-Up
1	Y_{1pr}	Y_{1po}	Y_{1fu}
2	Y_{2pr}	Y_{2po}	Y_{2fu}
.	.	.	.
.	.	.	.
N	Y_{Npr}	Y_{Npo}	Y_{Nfu}

Friedman Test

II.

Experimental Conditions[a]

SM	MM	C
	CHANGE SCORES (FOLLOW-UP — PRETEST)	

Kruskal-Wallis Test

III.

Control Trends

Ss	Pretest	Posttest	Follow-Up	Posttherapy
1	Y_{1pr}	Y_{1po}	Y_{1fu}	Y_{1pt}
2	Y_{2pr}	Y_{2po}	Y_{2fu}	Y_{2pt}
.	.	.	.	.
.	.	.	.	.
12	Y_{12pr}	Y_{12po}	Y_{12fu}	Y_{12pt}

Friedman Test

[a]SM = single-modeling; MM = multiple-modeling; C = control.

Designs 19.1 and 19.3, and they chose statistical tests to match the demands of their designs. The reader is urged to read the original study for its theoretical and technical sophistication and its considerable practical psychological and educational interest and significance. When reading it, keep Table 21.1 before you. (The original report is neither easy nor complete.)

Multigroup Correlated-groups Designs

Units Variance

While it is difficult to match three and four sets of subjects, and while it is ordinarily not feasible or desirable in behavioral research to use the same subjects in each of the groups, there are natural situations in which correlated groups exist. These situations are particularly important in educational research. Until recently, the variances due to differences between classes, schools, school systems, and other "natural" units have not been well controlled or often used in the analysis of data. Perhaps the first indication of the importance of this kind of variance was given in Lindquist's fine book on statistical analysis in educational research.[8] In

[8]E. Lindquist, *Statistical Analysis in Educational Research.* Boston: Houghton Mifflin, 1940.

this book, Lindquist placed considerable emphasis on *schools variance*. Schools, classes, and other educational units tend to differ significantly in achievement, intelligence, aptitudes, and other variables. The educational investigator has to be alert to these *unit differences*, as well as to individual difference.

Consider an obvious example. Suppose an investigator chooses a sample of five schools for their variety and heterogeneity. He is of course seeking external validity: representativeness. He conducts an investigation using pupils from all five schools and combines the measures from the five schools to test the mean differences in some dependent variable. In so doing, he is ignoring the variance due to the differences among schools. It is understandable that the means do not differ significantly; the schools variance is mixed in with the error variance.

Gross errors can follow from ignoring schools variance. One such error is to select a number of schools and to designate certain schools as experimental schools and others as control schools. Here the between-schools variance gets entangled with the variance of the experimental variable. Similarly, classes, school districts, and other educational units differ and thus engender variance. The variances must be identified and controlled, whether it be by experimental or statistical control, or both.[9]

A Hypothetical Example of Schools Variance

In running an experiment in several schools, the best procedure is to seek to reproduce the experiment in *each* of the schools. The procedure is somewhat as follows. First, randomly select m schools from the N schools of some well-defined schools population (district or county elementary schools). Run the experiment in *each* of the schools. Avoid setting up an experimental school here and a control school there, because the between-schools variance is confounded by doing this. Analyze the between-schools variance. A design-statistical paradigm would resemble Fig. 21.1, except that one might have means instead of individual scores in the cells. (One might also have several class means or the individual scores in the cells.)

Since school situations vary, it may not be possible to perform all the experimental treatments in each school. It is possible in such cases, though much less desirable, to sample schools at random and to assign them to experimental treatments at random.[10] Even if the schools cannot be selected at random, a useful experiment can be performed.

[9]To be prepared to do research in school situations, the student needs more study of the design and statistical problems involved than the scope of this text permits. For example, the differences between the situations where students can be assigned to experimental treatments at random and where intact classes must be used should be understood. Three references for such study are: E. Lindquist, *op. cit.*, chaps. IV and V, especially pp. 104–132, 145–163; E. Lindquist, *Design and Analysis of Experiments in Psychology and Education*, Boston: Houghton Mifflin, 1953, chaps. 7 and 8; A. Edwards, *Experimental Design in Psychological Research*, 3d ed., New York: Holt, Rinehart and Winston, 1968, chap. 9. The type of design considered above is also called *randomized blocks design or random replications design*.

[10]See Lindquist, *Design and Analysis of Experiments in Psychology and Education*, chap. 7. On pp. 187–188 Lindquist gives a good research example.

		Units	*Methods (Treatments)* A_1	A_2	A_3
		1			
		2			
	B_1	3			
		4			
Levels (Devices, Types, etc.)		5		Y MEANS	
				OR	
		1		MEASURES	
		2			
	B_2	3			
		4			
		5			

FIG. 21.4

Factorial Correlated-groups Designs

There is little doubt that factorial models will be combined with the units notion to yield a valuable design: *factorial correlated-groups design.* The more complex designs become, of course, the more difficult the statistical and interpretative problems. These problems should not block the use of such designs, however. To show how useful they can be, simply add sex or intelligence levels, or any other pertinent variable, to the design of Fig. 21.1. Conceptually there is nothing difficult about this – Fig. 21.4 shows what such a design might look like.

The strengths and weaknesses of the factorial correlated-groups design are similar to those of the more complex factorial designs. The main strengths are the ability to isolate and measure variances and to test interactions. Note that the two main sources of variance, *treatments* (A) and *levels* (B), and the *units* variance can be evaluated; that is, the differences between the A, B, and *units* means can be tested for significance. In addition, three interactions can be tested: *treatments* by *levels*, *treatments* by *units*, and *levels* by *units*. If individual scores are used in the cells instead of means, the triple interaction, too, can be tested. Note how important such interaction can be, both theoretically and practically. For example, questions like the following can be answered: Do treatments work differently in different units? Do certain methods work differently at different intelligence levels or with different sexes or with children of different socioeconomic levels?[11]

[11]The advanced student in psychology and education will want to know how to handle units (schools, classes, etc.) variance in more complex factorial designs. Detailed guidance is given in Edwards, *op. cit.*, chap. 13.

Analysis of Covariance

The invention of the analysis of covariance by Ronald Fisher has extraordinary potential importance in educational and psychological research. It is frequently necessary to study groups as they are; subjects cannot be matched or assigned at random. Analysis of covariance comes to the investigator's assistance. Here is an example of the creative use of the variance principles common to correlation theory and to analysis of variance to solve a long-standing analytical problem. In essence, Fisher extended his basic notion of analyzing the total variance of a set of measures into systematic and error variances to the analysis of covariance.

Analysis of covariance is a form of analysis of variance that tests the significance of the differences between means of final experimental data by taking into account the correlation between the dependent variable and one or more covariates, and by adjusting initial mean differences in the experimental groups. That is, the analysis of covariance analyzes the differences between experimental groups on Y after taking into account initial differences in the Y measures (i.e., pretest measures) or differences in some pertinent independent variable. The measure used for the control (pretest measures or measures on a pertinent variable) is called the *covariate*.

Consider the case of a team of sociologists, psychologists, and educators who wish to assess the effects on deprived children's reading of a massive remedial program. Knowing that intelligence is an important pertinent variable in any study of reading, they wish to control it. They have an experimental group of deprived children and a control group of the same kind of children; the children are randomly assigned.[12] They also have the intelligence test scores of each child. They use these scores in an analysis of covariance. The analysis of covariance will correct initial differences *in intelligence* between the two groups, taking the correlation between the intelligence measures and the reading measures into account. In other words, the procedure virtually controls intelligence, somewhat as matching does. It actually removes the variance due to intelligence (as measured) from the dependent variable measures before the test of significance is applied. Sums of squares and mean squares "adjusted" for the covariance are used in the final analysis of variance table. In addition, the analysis of covariance easily yields three estimates of the correlation between the intelligence and reading measures, one of which is the best estimate of the "true" correlation between the measures.

Even if the researchers had no intelligence measures, they could use reading

[12]The practical difficulty of random assignment in a situation like this, though considerable, has perhaps been overemphasized. At the very least, an attempt should be made to have experimental and control groups with children randomly assigned. By now the reader will appreciate the difficulty of adequately assessing the effects of any program without the comparison afforded by such groups and by random assignment. Unfortunately, too many investigators *assume*, often without sufficient foundation, that setting up adequate research conditions is not possible. One should always try to set up conditions that will permit valid inferences from the data, compromising the conditions only after trying to set them up. It is likely that many educational assessments are compromised by misguided assumptions *before they start*. In the present case, administrators, teachers, and parents can be assured that the control-group children will be given the remedial treatment after the experiment. Indeed, as the Bandura and Menlove study showed, such postexperimental treatment can be made an integral part of the whole study. What can be called "compromise by misguided assumption" has probably ruined as many assessments of educational programs as ignorance.

pretest measures in the same way. The analysis of covariance would be used to analyze the final measures for significance, but the analysis would be adjusted for pretest differences between the groups. If the assumptions behind the analysis of covariance are not violated (too severely), the method can be used in much social scientific and educational research, particularly the latter, because measures of important variables that can be used as covariates are often available in school, college, university, and other files.

A Procedural Description of Analysis of Covariance

Covariance[13] was defined in Chapter 6 as the average of the cross products of the deviation scores of two variables, X and Y. (A deviation score is defined by $x = X - M_x$, or $y = Y - M_y$.) If a number of individuals have X scores and Y scores, intelligence test scores and reading scores, we then have a set of ordered pairs, with X scores first in all pairs. Reducing these scores to deviation scores, x and y, we have another set of ordered pairs, (x, y). If the x's and y's are multiplied, and these cross products are summed, we have a measure analogous to the sum of squares of the analysis of variance. It is called the *sum of cross products*, or Σxy. Just as the analysis of variance works with sums of squares and variances, the analysis of covariance works with the sums of cross products and covariances, as well as with the sums of squares.

The net outcome of the procedure is an analysis of covariance table that tests the significance of the differences of the Y means of the experimental groups after adjustment of the Y sums of squares. This adjustment in effect removes from the Y sums of squares that part due to the relation between X and Y. The higher the correlation between X and Y, the more effective the analysis of covariance. (If the correlation is zero or quite low, analysis of covariance is a waste of time.) What emerges for a final analysis of covariance table are the adjusted total, between-groups, and within-groups sums of squares.[14] Variances (mean squares) and the F ratio are calculated from these adjusted measures.

[13]A complete statistical description of the analysis of covariance is not apropos in this text. The objective is to acquaint the student with the general method and to show its relation to other forms of design and statistical analysis. A good brief discussion of the rationale of analysis of covariance can be found in M. Tate, *Statistics in Education.* New York: Macmillan, 1955, pp. 515–522. For computational purposes, Edwards' older book is good: A. Edwards, *Experimental Design in Psychological Research.* New York: Holt, Rinehart and Winston, 1950, chap. 17.

[14]It is well to note the three r's that were mentioned earlier. Since one formula for r is $r = \Sigma xy / \sqrt{\Sigma x^2 \Sigma y^2}$, and since analysis of covariance yields all these terms for total, between groups, and within groups, obviously three r's can be calculated. The r for total is the usual r between two sets of measures, and r for between groups is the correlation between the pairs of means. The key contribution of analysis of covariance is to yield the *within-groups r.* Since the sums of squares and cross products are calculated *within* each group separately, the differences between the groups do not influence the calculated r. Thus, the within r is the "best" estimate of the "true" r between X and Y. It is not often realized that many r's may be spuriously inflated or deflated by between-groups variance. Assume that an r is calculated between intelligence and school achievement, and the scores of girls and boys are included in the calculations. If there is a significant difference in achievement between girls and boys, and if most of the girls are in one group and most of the boys in another group, this between-groups difference may inflate the calculated r. An analysis of covariance of the same data would yield a within-groups r that would probably be lower than the original total r.

The paradigm of an analysis of covariance is like that of the before and after, or pretest and posttest, design (see Design 19.3). A paradigm of the research outlined above is given in Table 21.2, where $X =$ intelligence test scores and $Y =$ reading scores. (X might also be the pretest and Y the posttest.) The table is also a paradigm of the Clark and Walberg study briefly described in Chapter 20. We now reexamine it.[15]

Recall that massive reinforcement was used with the experimental group *S*s and moderate reinforcement with the control group *S*s and that a one-way analysis of variance yielded $F = 9.52$, significant at the .01 level. It is conceivable that the difference between the experimental and control groups was due to intelligence rather than to reinforcement. That is, even though the *S*s were assigned at random to the experimental groups, an initial difference in intelligence in favor of the experimental group may have been enough to make the experimental group reading mean significantly greater than the control group reading mean, since intelligence is substantially correlated with reading. With random assignment, it is unlikely to happen, but it can happen. To control this possibility, Clark and Walberg used analysis of covariance.

Study Table 21.2, which shows in outline the design and analysis. The means of the X and Y scores, as reported by Clark and Walberg, are given at the bottom of the table. The Y means are the main concern. They were significantly different. Although it is doubtful that the analysis of covariance will change this result, it is possible that the difference between the X means, 92.05 and 90.73, may have tipped the statistical scales, in the test of the difference between the Y means, in favor of the experimental group. The analysis of covariance F test, which uses Y sums of squares and mean squares purged of the influence of X, was significant at the .01 level: $F = 7.90$. Thus the mean reading scores of the experimental and control groups differed significantly, after being adjusted or controlled for intelligence.

TABLE **21.2** ANALYSIS OF COVARIANCE PARADIGM, CLARK AND WALBERG STUDY

	Experimental (Massive Reinforcement)		*Control* (Moderate Reinforcement)	
	X (Intelligence)	Y (Reading)	X (Intelligence)	Y (Reading)
Means:	92.05	31.62	90.73	26.86

[15]C. Clark and H. Walberg, "The Influence of Massive Rewards on Reading Achievement in Potential Urban School Dropouts," *American Educational Research Journal*, V (1968), 305–310.

We now outline a questionable procedure, which experts have condemned: the use of analysis of covariance with intact groups. We do this because in many situations, especially in educational research, nothing else is possible. The student should carefully keep in mind, however, that the procedure is a poor alternative to random assignment.

One of the major difficulties of educational and sociological research is our inability to set up experimental groups at will. Administrators and teachers, for example, are understandably reluctant to break up classes. The investigator often must use classes and other groups intact. Through the analysis of covariance it is often possible to control class or other group differences statistically. For example, three methods of teaching spelling, A_1, A_2, and A_3, are to be tested. The random assignment of subjects is not possible, but it *is* possible to use intact classes. It is known that intelligence is significantly related to spelling and that the classes will probably differ significantly in intelligence. The methods can be assigned to the intact classes at random, and intelligence test scores can be used as X measures in an analysis of covariance. The paradigm would look like that in Fig. 21.5, where $X =$ intelligence test scores and $Y =$ spelling scores. (The X measures can also be spelling pretest scores.)

While questionable, if the results of this type of experiment are treated with circumspection, they can be useful. The procedure has advantages. One, measures of intelligence and achievement usually exist before the experiment starts. Thus they can be used without the sensitization danger of pretests; an experiment can also be run without students knowing they are being tested. Closely allied to this is the advantage of experiments done in natural settings, a matter we take up in Part 7. Still another advantage is the precision of the analysis and the information it can yield.

Methods					
A_1		A_2		A_3	
X	Y	X	Y	X	Y

FIG. 21.5

Research Design and Analysis: Concluding Remarks

Four major objectives have dominated the organization and preparation of Part 6. The first was to acquaint the student with the principal designs of research. By so doing, it was hoped that narrowly circumscribed notions of doing research with, say, only one experimental group and one control group, or with matched subjects, or with one group, before and after, may be widened.

The second objective was to convey a sense of the balanced structure of good research designs. It is desirable to develop a sensitive feeling for the architecture of design, design that is formally as well as functionally fitted to the research problems we are seeking to solve.

The third objective was to help the reader understand the logic of experimental inquiry and the logic of the various designs. Research designs are alternative routes to the same destination: reliable and valid statements of the relations between variables. Some designs, if feasible, yield stronger relational statements than other designs.

In a certain sense, the fourth objective of Part 6 has been the most difficult to achieve: to help the student understand the relation between research design and statistics. Statistics is, in one sense, the technical discipline of handling variance. And, as we have seen, one of the basic purposes of design is to provide control of systematic and error variances. This is the reason for treating statistics in such detail in Parts 4 and 5 before considering design in Part 6. Fisher expresses this idea succinctly when he says, "Statistical procedure and experimental design are only two different aspects of the same whole, and that whole comprises all the logical requirements of the complete process of adding to natural knowledge by experimentation."[16]

A well-conceived design is no guarantee of the validity of research findings. Elegant designs nicely tailored to research problems can still result in wrong or distorted conclusions. Nevertheless, the chances of arriving at accurate and valid conclusions are better with sound designs than with unsound ones. This is relatively sure: if design is faulty, one can come to no clear conclusions. If, for instance, one uses a two-group, matched-subjects design when the research problem logically demands a factorial design, or if one uses a factorial design when the nature of the research situation calls for a correlated-groups design, no amount of interpretative or statistical manipulation can increase confidence in the conclusions of such research.

It is fitting that Fisher should have the last word on this subject. In the first chapter of his book, *The Design of Experiments*, he said:

> . . . If the design of an experiment is faulty, any method of interpretation which makes it out to be decisive must be faulty too. It is true that there are a great many experimental procedures which are well designed in that they *may* lead to decisive conclusions, but on other occasions may fail to do so; in such cases, if decisive conclusions are in fact drawn when they are unjustified, we may say that the fault is wholly in the interpretation, not in the design. But the fault of interpretation . . . lies in overlooking the characteristic features of the design which lead to the result being sometimes inconclusive, or conclusive on some questions but not on all. To understand correctly the one aspect of the problem is to understand the other.[17]

[16]R. Fisher, *The Design of Experiments*, 6th ed. New York: Hafner, 1951, p. 3.
[17]*Ibid.*, pp. 2–3.

Study Suggestions

1. Can memory be improved by training? William James, the great American psychologist and philosopher, did a memory experiment on himself.[18] He first learned 158 lines of a Victor Hugo poem, which took him $131\frac{5}{6}$ minutes. This was his baseline. Then he worked for 20-odd minutes daily, for 38 days, learning the entire first book of *Paradise Lost*. (Book I is 22 tightly printed pages of rather difficult verse!) This was training of his memory. He returned to the Hugo poem and learned 158 additional lines in $151\frac{1}{2}$ minutes. Thus he took longer after the training than before. Not satisfied, he had others do similar tasks – with similar results.

   On the basis of this work, what conclusions could James come to? Comment on his research design. What design among those in this book does his design approximate?
2. In a study of the response to peer and adult pressure of Soviet and American children, Bronfenbrenner asked 158 American sixth graders and 188 Soviet fifth graders (comparable ages to the American children) to respond to conflict situations under peer, adult, and neutral (anonymous) conditions.[19] He reported, among other things, two means that reflected adult orientation: Soviet = 14.82, American = 2.22 (the higher the value, the greater the adult orientation), the difference being significant at the .01 level.

   What problems do you think would be associated with interpreting these results? Concentrate your thinking on problems of comparability and control.
3. Kolb, basing his work on the outstanding work of McClelland on achievement motivation, did a fascinating experiment with underachieving high school boys of high intelligence.[20] Of 57 boys, he assigned 20 at random to a training program in which, through various means, the boys were "taught" achievement motivation (an attempt to build a need to achieve into the boys). The boys were given a pretest of achievement motivation in the summer, and given the test again six months later. The mean *change scores* were, for experimental and control groups, respectively, 6.72 and −.34, significant at the .005 level.
   (a) Comment on the use of change scores. Does their use lessen our faith in the statistical significance of the results?
   (b) Might factors other than the experimental training have induced the change?
4. The $2 \times 2 \times 2$ factorial design is used a good deal by social psychologists. Here are two unusual, excellent, even creative studies in which it was used:

   Carlsmith, J., and Gross, A. "Some Effects of Guilt on Compliance," *Journal of Personality and Social Psychology*, XI (1969), 232–239.

   Jones, E., et al. "Pattern of Performance and Ability Attribution: An Unexpected Primacy Effect," *Journal of Personality and Social Psychology*, X (1968), 317–340.

   Read one or both of these studies. (The Jones study is long, involved, and difficult, but well worth the effort. It has replication and systematic exploration of alternative hypotheses, as well as high theoretical and technical competence.) Note particularly the relations between the problem statements and the designs.

[18]W. James, *The Principles of Psychology*. New York: Holt, 1890, pp. 666–667.

[19]U. Bronfenbrenner, "Response to Pressure from Peers Versus Adults among Soviet and American School Children," *International Journal of Psychology*, II (1967), 199–207.

[20]D. Kolb, "Achievement Motivation Training for Underachieving High-School Boys," *Journal of Personality and Social Psychology*, II (1965), 783–792.

5. Lest the student believe that only continuous measures are analyzed and that analysis of variance alone is used in psychological and educational experiments, read the study by Freedman et al. on guilt and compliance.[21] There was an experimental group (*S*s induced to lie) and a control group, and the dependent variable was measured by whether a *S* did or did not comply with a request for help. The results were reported in crossbreak frequency tables.

   Read the study, and, after studying the authors' design and results, design one of the three experiments another way. Bring in another independent variable, for instance. Suppose that it was known that there were wide individual differences in compliance. How could this be controlled? Name and describe two kinds of design to do it.
6. One useful means of control by matching is to use pairs of identical twins. Why is this method a useful means of control? If you were setting up an experiment to test the effect of environment on measured intelligence and you had 20 pairs of identical twins and complete experimental freedom, how would you set up the experiment?
7. In what appears to be a classic study of teaching children to lose fears (of snakes), Bandura et al. used four experimental groups, pretests, matching, random assignment, and analysis of covariance.[22] It is suggested that advanced students read the study and lay out the main design of the research. (Note that, as in the Bandura and Menlove study cited earlier, the control group *S*s were given the experimental treatment when the experiment was over.)
8. In a study in which training on the complexities of art stimuli affected attitude toward music, among other things, Renner used analysis of covariance, with the covariate being measures from a scale to measure attitude toward music.[23] This was a pretest. There were three experimental groups. Sketch the design from this brief description. Why did Renner use the music attitude scale as a pretest? Why did she use analysis of covariance? (*Note:* The original report is well worth reading. The study, in part a study of creativity, is itself creative.)

[21]J. Freedman, S. Wallington, and E. Bless, "Compliance Without Pressure: The Effect of Guilt," *Journal of Personality and Social Psychology*, VII (1967), 117–124.

[22]A. Bandura, E. Blanshard, and B. Ritter, "Relative Efficacy of Desensitization and Modeling Approaches for Inducing Behavioral, Affective, and Attitudinal Changes," *Journal of Personality and Social Psychology*, XIII (1969), 173–199.

[23]V. Renner, "Effects of Modification of Cognitive Style on Creative Behavior," *Journal of Personality and Social Psychology*, XIV (1970), 257–262.

PART 2

Types of Research

CHAPTER 22

Ex Post Facto Research

Among the fallacies used by man, one of the most dangerous to science is that known as *post hoc, ergo propter hoc*: after this, therefore caused by this. We may joke, with a tinge of seriousness, "If I take an umbrella, it won't rain." We may even seriously say that delinquents are delinquent because of a lack of discipline in the schools or that religious education makes children more virtuous. It is very easy to assume that one thing causes another simply because it occurs before the other, and because one has such a wide choice of possible "causes." Then, too, many explanations often seem plausible. It is easy to believe, for instance, that the learning of children improves because we institute a new educational practice or teach in a certain way. We assume that the improvement in their learning was due to the new spelling method, to the institution of group processes into the classroom situation, to stern discipline and more homework (or little discipline and less homework). We rarely realize that children will usually learn something if they are given the opportunity to learn.

The social scientist and the educational scientist constantly face the problem of the post hoc fallacy. The sociologist who seeks the causes of delinquency knows that he must exercise extreme care in studying this problem. Slum conditions, broken homes, lack of love—each, or all, of these conditions are possible causes of delinquency. The psychologist seeking the roots of adult personality faces an even subtler problem: hereditary traits, child-rearing practices, educational influences, parental personality, and environmental circumstances are all plausible explanations. The educational scientist, with the goal of understanding the basis of successful school achievement, also faces a large number of reasonable possibilities: intelligence, aptitude, motivation, home environment, teacher personality, pupil personality, and teaching methods.

The danger of the post hoc assumption is that it can, and often does, lead to erroneous and misleading interpretations of research data, the effect being particularly serious when the scientist has little or no control over time and independent variables. When he is seeking to explain a phenomenon that has already occurred, he is confronted with the unpleasant fact that he does not have real control of the possible causes. Hence he must pursue a course of research action different in execution and interpretation from that of the scientist who experiments.

Definition

Ex post facto research[1] *is systematic empirical inquiry in which the scientist does not have direct control of independent variables because their manifestations have already occurred or because they are inherently not manipulable. Inferences about relations among variables are made, without direct intervention, from concomitant variation of independent and dependent variables.*

Assume that an investigator is interested in the relation between sex and creativity in children. He measures the creativity of a sample of boys and girls and tests the significance of the difference between the means of the two sexes. The mean of boys is significantly higher than the mean of girls. He concludes that boys are more creative than girls. This may or may not be a valid conclusion. The relation exists, true. With only this evidence, however, the conclusion is doubtful. The question is: Is the demonstrated relation really between sex and creativity? Since many other variables are correlated with sex, it might have been one or more of these variables that produced the difference between the creativity scores of the two sexes.

Basic Difference between Experimental Research and Ex Post Facto Research

The basis of the structure in which the experimental scientist operates is simple. He hypothesizes: If x, then y; if frustration, then aggression. Depending on circumstances and his personal predilections in research design, he uses some method to manipulate or measure x. He then observes y to see if concomitant variation, the variation expected or predicted from the variation in x, occurs. If it does, this is evidence for the validity of the proposition, $x \rightarrow y$, $x \rightarrow y$ meaning "If x, then y." Note that the scientist here predicts from a controlled x to y. To help him achieve control, he can use the principle of randomization and active manipulation of x and can assume, other things equal, that y is varying as a result of the manipulation of x.

In ex post facto research, on the other hand, y is observed, and an x, or several

[1]The complete definition of ex post facto research used in this book is somewhat different from that often accepted. The term was originally used by Chapin and Greenwood to mean a quasi-experiment in which an attempt is made to control independent variables by matching and symbolic means. Since this meaning is not broad enough for our purposes, "ex post facto" is here expanded to include all research that has the characteristics discussed in the text.

x's, are also observed, either before, after, or concomitant to the observation of y. There is no difference whatever in the basic logic: it can be shown that the argument structure and its *logical* validity are the same in experimental and ex post facto research.[2] And the basic purpose of both is also the same: to establish the *empirical* validity of so-called conditional statements of the form: If p, then q. The essential difference is direct control of p, the independent variable. In experimental research, p can be manipulated, which is rather direct "control." When Clark and Walberg had teachers give one group of subjects massive reinforcement and other teachers give another group moderate reinforcement, they were directly manipulating or controlling the variable reinforcement. Similarly, when Bandura and Menlove showed one group a movie with a single model, another group a movie with multiple models, and a third group a "neutral" movie, they were directly manipulating the variable modeling. In addition, subjects can be assigned at random to the experimental groups.

In ex post facto research, *direct* control is not possible: neither experimental manipulation nor random assignment can be used by the researcher. These are two essential differences between experimental and ex post facto approaches. Owing to lack of relative control of x and other possible x's, the "truth" of the hypothesized relation between x and y cannot be asserted with the confidence of the experimental situation. Basically, ex post facto research has, so to speak, an inherent weakness: lack of control of independent variables.

The most important difference between experimental research and ex post facto research, then, is *control*. In the experimental case, the investigator at least has manipulative control: he has at least one active variable. If an experiment is a "true" experiment, he can also exercise control by randomization. He can assign subjects to groups at random, or he can assign treatments to groups at random. In the ex post facto research situation, this kind of control of the independent variables is not possible. The investigator must take things as they are and try to disentangle them.

Take a well-known case. When an experimenter paints the skins of rats with carcinogenic substances (x), adequately controls other variables, and the rats ultimately develop carcinoma (y), the argument is compelling because x (and other possible x's, theoretically) is controlled and y is predicted. But when an investigator finds cases of lung cancer (y) and then goes back among the possible multiplicity of causes ($x_1, x_2, \ldots, x_n$) and picks cigarette-smoking (say x_3) as the culprit, he is in a more difficult and ambiguous situation. Neither situation is sure, of course; both are probabilistic. But in the experimental case the investigator can be *more* sure—considerably more sure if he has adequately made "other things equal"—that the statement If x, then y is empirically valid. In the ex post facto case, however, the investigator is always on shakier ground because he cannot say, with nearly as much assurance, "other things equal." He cannot control the independent variables by manipulation or by randomization. In short, the proba-

[2]The basic logic is set forth in: F. Kerlinger, "Research in Education." In R. Ebel, V. Noll, and R. Bauer, eds., *Encyclopedia of Educational Research*, 4th ed. New York: Macmillan, 1969, pp. 1127–1144 (pp. 1133–1134).

bility that x is "really" related to y is greater in the experimental situation than it is in the ex post facto situation, because the control of x is greater.

Self-Selection and Ex Post Facto Research

In an ideal social scientific research world, the drawing of random samples of subjects, and the random assignment of subjects to groups and treatments to groups, would always be possible. In the real world, however, one, two, or even all three of these possibilities do not exist. It is possible to draw subjects at random in both experimental and ex post facto research. But it is not possible, in ex post facto research, to assign subjects to groups at random or to assign treatments to groups at random. Thus subjects can "assign themselves" to groups, can "select themselves" into the groups on the basis of characteristics other than those in which the investigator may be interested. The subjects and the treatments come, as it were, already assigned to the groups.

Self-selection occurs when the members of the groups being studied are in the groups, in part, because they differentially possess traits or characteristics extraneous to the research problem, characteristics that possibly influence or are otherwise related to the variables of the research problem. Examples of self-selection may aid understanding.

In the well-known research on cigarette-smoking and cancer, the smoking habits of a large number of people were studied. This large group was divided into those who had lung cancer—or who had died of it—and those who did not have it. The dependent variable was thus the presence or absence of cancer. Investigators probed the subjects' backgrounds to determine whether they smoked cigarettes, and if so, how many. Cigarette-smoking was the independent variable. The investigators found that the incidence of lung cancer rose with the number of cigarettes smoked daily. They also found that the incidence was lower in the cases of light smokers and nonsmokers. They came to the conclusion that cigarette-smoking caused lung cancer.[3] This conclusion may or may not be true. But the investigators cannot come to this conclusion, although they *can* say that there is a statistically significant relation between the variables.

The reason they cannot state a causal connection is that there are a number of other variables, any one of which, or any combination of which, may have caused lung cancer. And they have not controlled other possible independent variables. They *cannot* control them, except by testing alternative hypotheses, a procedure to be explained later. Even when they also study "control groups" of people who have no cancer, self-selection may be operating. Maybe tense, anxious men are doomed to have lung cancer if they marry blonde women, for instance. It

[3]Careful scientific investigators will usually not say "cause." The word "cause" is used here to make the point more emphatic and because authoritative sources so use it: see *The New York Times*, Dec. 6, 1959, p. E-11, where the Surgeon General of the United States Public Health Service is directly quoted as saying: "the weight of evidence at present implicates smoking as the principal etiological (causative) factor in the increased incidence of lung cancer."

may just happen that this type of man also smokes cigarettes heavily. The cigarette-smoking is not what kills him—he kills himself by being born tense and anxious—and possibly by marrying a blonde. Such men are selected into the sample by investigators only because they smoke cigarettes. But such men select themselves into the sample because they commonly possess a temperament that happens to have cigarette-smoking as a concomitant.

Self-selection can be a subtle business. There are two kinds: self-selection into *samples* and into *comparison groups*. The latter occurs when subjects are selected because they are in one group or another: cancer and no cancer, college and no college, underachievement and no underachievement. That is, they are selected *because* they possess the dependent variable in greater or lesser degree. Self-selection into samples occurs when subjects are selected in a nonrandom fashion into a sample.

The crux of the matter is that when *assignment* is not random, there is always a loophole for other variables to crawl through. When we put subjects into groups, in the above case and in similar cases, or they "put themselves" into groups, on the basis of one variable, it is possible that another variable (or variables) correlated with this variable is the "real" basis of the relation. The usual ex post facto study uses groups that exhibit differences in the dependent variable. In some longitudinal-type studies the groups are differentiated first on the basis of the independent variable. But the two cases are basically the same, since group membership *on the basis of a variable* always brings selection into the picture.

For example, we may select college freshmen at random and then follow them to determine the relation between intelligence and success in college. The students selected themselves into college, so to speak. One or more of the characteristics they bring with them to college, other than intelligence—socioeconomic level, motivation, family background—may be the principal determinants of college success. That we start with the independent variable, in this case intelligence, does not change the self-selective nature of the research situation. In the sampling sense, the students selected themselves into college, which would be an important factor if we were studying college students and noncollege students. But if we are interested only in the success and nonsuccess *of college students*, self-selection into college is irrelevant, whereas self-selection into success and nonsuccess groups is crucial. That we measure the intelligence of the students when they enter college and follow them through to success and nonsuccess does not change either the selection problem or the ex post facto character of the research. In sum, the students selected themselves into college and selected themselves to succeed or not to succeed in college.

Large-Scale Ex Post Facto Research

Further study of research examples will help us evaluate ex post facto research in the behavioral sciences. Several examples have been given in the context of other problems. Now, we focus on the inherent nature of ex post facto research. In Parts 5 and 6, we necessarily concentrated on experimental research, because analysis of variance and research design have been developed in an experimental framework. This does not mean that experimental research is necessarily more important or even more frequent in the behavioral sciences. Indeed, it is probably no exaggeration to say that a large proportion of research in sociology, education, anthropology, and political science has been ex post facto. Though psychologists are much more inclined to be experimental in their approach—many more psychological than sociological variables, for example, are manipulable—it is probably safe to say that a substantial proportion of psychological studies, perhaps half or more than half, are ex post facto.

The Authoritarian Personality Study[4]

The Authoritarian Personality Study was actually a series of studies which together constitute an important and influential contribution to social scientific, particularly psychological, research. The general hypothesis of the study was that political, economic, and social beliefs are related to deep-seated personality characteristics. Another hypothesis was that adult personality is derived from early childhood experiences. In short, attitudes and beliefs were related to underlying personality trends. The investigators, among other things, studied anti-Semitism as part of a general characteristic called *ethnocentrism*. Later, the investigators extended their thought and work to a still larger construct, *authoritarianism*, which they conceived to be a broad personality syndrome that determines in part ethnocentrism, social attitudes, and certain other behaviors. The authoritarian personality was conceived to be conventional, cynical, destructive, aggressive, power-centered, and ethnocentric.

While this is an inadequate summary of the basic problems of a very complex study, it is sufficient for the present purpose. The study had to be ex post facto—although there have been later experimental studies in which authoritarianism has been manipulated and in which high authoritarianism and low authoritarianism, for instance, have been attribute variables—because authoritarianism, as defined, is a nonmanipulable variable. One of the major results of the study was information on the relation between authoritarianism and prejudice. It is obvious that when one studies such variables one is studying already existing sets of personality characteristics and attitudes. The subjects are ready-made authoritarians or nonauthoritarians (with gradations between) and come to the research with already well-formulated attitudes. One can conceive, somehow, of manipulating such variables, but the manipulation, as indicated previously, changes their nature. At any rate, whenever one studies the relations between variables that "al-

[4]T. Adorno et al., *The Authoritarian Personality.* New York: Harper & Row, 1950. An extensive critique of this book has been published: R. Christie and M. Jahoda, eds., *Studies in the Scope and Method of "The Authoritarian Personality."* New York: Free Press, 1954. Study of the latter volume is rewarding for the intermediate or advanced student of social scientific research. See, especially, the chapter by H. Hyman and P. Sheatsley, "The Authoritarian Personality—A Methodological Critique," pp. 50–122. More recent research reviews and critiques are: J. Kirscht and R. Dillehay, *Dimensions of Authoritarianism: A Review of Research and Theory.* Lexington: University of Kentucky Press, 1967; S. Messick and D. Jackson, "The Measurement of Authoritarian Attitudes," *Educational and Psychological Measurement,* XVIII (1958), 241–253; H. Titus and E. Hollander, "The California F Scale in Psychological Research: 1950–1955," *Psychological Bulletin,* LIV (1957), 47–64.

ready exist" in the individuals studied, or whenever one studies the determinants of such variables, one is deeply embedded in ex post facto research and its problems.

Social Class Influences on Learning Studies[5]

An extensive set of investigations into social-class influences on learning, the details of which do not concern us here, has greatly affected modern educators. These studies are ex post facto studies and, as such, are laden with interpretative difficulties. One of the principal aims of research in such studies is to attempt to explain differences in school achievement between middle-class and lower-class children. An investigator notes that there are striking differences in school achievement. Can these differences be attributed in part to social class membership? He examines the collective achievement scores of middle-class and lower-class children and consistently notes significant differences: middle-class children do better in school than lower-class children. He may then come to the conclusion that social class is a determinant of school achievement.

The ex post facto character of such research is clear. The investigator starts with the dependent variable, school achievement (or "learning"), and among the many possible influential independent variables, he selects social class. Naturally, he may pick other independent variables as well, variables such as intelligence and motivation, both of which are also related to school achievement and to social class. This makes no difference. It is not a matter of complexity; it is a matter of control. The social class researcher has no power to manipulate social class, nor has he the power of randomization. In this case, the relation between social class and school achievement seems well-established.

Even the relation between social class and measured intelligence seems to be well-established. Yet these "established" relations may be spurious, and they are more likely to be spurious in ex post facto than in experimental research, other things equal. The major determinants of the difference between the two groups in school achievement may be intelligence and motivation. Middle-class children may tend to have higher measured intelligence and higher motivation for school work than lower-class children. It may be these two variables that are the major determinants of school achievement—not social class. Social class membership "happens" to be a correlate of these two variables. It is, so to speak, part of the correlational baggage of intelligence, motivation, and school achievement rather than a determinant of school achievement in its own right.

[5]There are a large number of studies of social class and its relation to a number of variables, including such educational variables as curriculum choice, testing, grades, and educational motivation. Two pertinent references are A. Davis, *Social-Class Influences upon Learning*, Cambridge: Harvard University Press, 1948; and W. Warner, R. Havighurst, and M. Loeb, *Who Shall Be Educated?* New York: Harper & Row, 1944. More recent, extensive, and important studies are the Coleman and Wilson reports: J. Coleman et al., *Equality of Educational Opportunity*. Washington, D.C.: U.S. Government Printing Office, 1966; A. Wilson, "Educational Consequences of Segregation in a California Community." In U.S. Commission on Civil Rights, *Racial Isolation in the Public Schools*. Washington, D.C.: U.S. Government Printing Office, 1967, vol. 2, pp. 165–210. The Wilson report's central focus was social class, race, and school achievement.

Ideology, Consensus, and Operational Beliefs Studies

Political scientists have been interested in certain key questions, the answers to which have deep significance in a democracy. Two of these are: Does consensus exist among Americans on basic democratic beliefs? If such consensus exists, do Americans subscribe to specific operational beliefs and behaviors implied by the basic beliefs? Three important studies addressed to these and other related questions have been done in the last decade or so, and the answers to the questions are not simple.[6]

In one of the most recent of these studies, Free and Cantril obtained the responses of two probability samples of more than 3000 Americans to a variety of questions on political beliefs. They found distinct and sharp differences between what they called the *ideological spectrum* and the *operational spectrum* of beliefs. Americans, for instance, respond quite differently to abstract statements of beliefs than they do to more specific operational statements. Evidently they are ideologically conservative and operationally liberal.[7] A somewhat different conclusion, however, comes from two other large-scale studies.

Prothro and Grigg sampled (randomly), in a northern city and a southern city, the responses of registered voters to abstract and specific statements, like "Democracy is the best form of government" (abstract) and "A Negro should not be allowed to run for mayor of this city" (specific). They found high agreement among the voters with the abstract statements and much less agreement on the specific statements. Here people seem to be ideologically (abstractly) liberal and operationally conservative.

In the third, and perhaps most important and sophisticated study, McClosky administered to his respondents a wide variety of statements on personal background, personality traits, and political, economic, and social values, attitudes, and beliefs. His respondents were of two kinds: leaders or political influentials ($N =$ 3000+) and the general electorate in the United States ($N =$ 1500+) selected to be representative (in a Gallup poll). Like Prothro and Grigg, McClosky found greater support for general, abstract statements of democratic beliefs than for the specific application of the beliefs. For instance, 89 percent of the electorate sample agreed with the statement, "I believe in free speech for all no matter what their views might be," but 50 percent agreed with "A book that contains wrong political views cannot be a good book and does not deserve to be published." Moreover, McClosky found that the leaders were distinctly more democratic in their outlook and rejected antidemocratic sentiments more than the general electorate did.

We note two important points about these studies. One, they are clearly ex

[6]L. Free and H. Cantril, *The Political Beliefs of Americans*. New Brunswick, N.J.: Rutgers University Press, 1967; H. McClosky, "Consensus and Ideology in American Politics," *American Political Science Review*, LVIII (1964), 361–382; J. Prothro and C. Grigg, "Fundamental Principles of Democracy: Bases of Agreement and Disagreement," *Journal of Politics*, XXII (1960), 276–294.

[7]Although Free and Cantril's results can be questioned on the basis of the way they measured liberalism and conservatism, this is not our concern here. We are interested mainly in the general nature of the research.

post facto. There is no experimental manipulation whatever. While the sampling was random—except, perhaps, in the McClosky study—there was no possibility of random assignment. People were asked for their responses to questions and statements, and these responses were related to each other, mostly in percentage crossbreak form. That is, the relations between independent and dependent variables, as reflected in the responses *that people brought with them to the studies*, were analyzed. The beliefs of people, as expressed in their responses, were usually taken as dependent variables and related to other responses or sociological facts. There was literally no intervention by the researchers.

Small-Scale Ex Post Facto Research

Regional Differences in Prejudice[8]

In a well-executed study of a social problem that is difficult to probe experimentally, Pettigrew asked the question: Is anti-Negro prejudice more closely related to social factors and less so to personality factors in the South than in the North? In effect, this amounts to contrasting sociological and psychological explanations of prejudice. To test hypotheses derived from this question, Pettigrew administered authoritarianism, anti-Semitism, and anti-Negro scales to random samples of white adults in four northern and four southern towns.

One hypothesis predicted a simple difference between northern and southern anti-Negro prejudice, and the southern sample did have a significantly higher mean score than the northern sample. There was no significant mean difference on the authoritarianism measure, which was used as a control test. Pettigrew reasoned that, since the authoritarianism scale is presumed to measure "externalizing personality potential," and since the two regions did not differ on this scale but *did* differ on the anti-Negro scale, the hypothesis that externalizing personality factors are of equal importance in the North and the South, and that social-cultural factors are more important in the South than in the North, was supported.

Freedom and Equality Study[9]

A great deal of theoretical and empirical work has been done on prejudice. It can safely be said that because of this work we understand a good deal about the psychology and sociology of prejudice, its stereotypes, how it operates, and how it is supported. Much of the research has been ex post facto. For example, the many studies of sterotypes of minority-group members have been largely and perforce ex post facto. To understand phenomena like prejudice and stereotypes, after all, we have to know their incidence and their relations to other variables. Of course, further understanding of such phenomena is enhanced when we can change them. The former knowledge requires ex post facto research, while the latter requires an

[8]T. Pettigrew, "Regional Differences in Anti-Negro Prejudice," *Journal of Abnormal and Social Psychology*, LIX (1959), 28–36.

[9]M. Rokeach, *Beliefs, Attitudes, and Values*. San Francisco: Jossey-Bass, 1968, pp. 168–178.

experimental approach. The Pettigrew study just cited is an excellent example of the former demand. The research we are about to examine is an ex post facto part of theoretically based research that is both ex post facto and experimental. Without the knowledge yielded by the ex post facto work, it is doubtful that the later experimental work would have been possible.

Rokeach has had a number of groups, including a national sample, rank order two sets of what he calls terminal and instrumental values. Two of the terminal values, *freedom* and *equality*, have been particularly significant because they are evidently keys to fundamental differences in social and political value outlooks. Rokeach has found, for instance, that different groups reliably and significantly rank these two values (embedded among others) quite differently. In Table 22.1,

TABLE **22.1** COMPOSITE RANKS OF *Freedom* AND *Equality* OF DIFFERENT GROUPS (I), AND THEIR FREQUENCY OF MENTION AND COMPARABLE RANKS IN FOUR SAMPLES OF POLITICAL WRITINGS (II)

I.	Policemen (50)	Unemployed Whites (141)	Unemployed Negroes (28)	Calvinist Students (75)
Freedom	1[a]	3	10	8
Equality	12	9	1	9

II.	*Socialists*		*Hitler*		*Goldwater*		*Lenin*	
	Freq.[b]	Rank	Freq.	Rank	Freq.	Rank	Freq.	Rank
Freedom	+66	*1*	−48	*16*	+85	*1*	−47	*17*
Equality	+62	*2*	−71	*17*	−10	*16*	+88	*1*

[a]1 is the highest rank, 12 the lowest.
[b]Frequency is defined as number of favorable mentions minus number of unfavorable mentions.

the composite ranks of the two values given by different groups are given (I). The results are dramatic. Policemen and unemployed blacks are very, very different in their social value outlook. To the policemen, *freedom* is highly important, while *equality* is not, but to the blacks *equality* is all-important and *freedom* is not. Quite an upset of certain of our traditional ideas! In contrast, Calvinist students rank both values rather low.

Rokeach seems to have hit upon a fundamental difference in value outlook. His results are evidently not spurious. Study the bottom half of Table 22.1 (II). He and a colleague (James Morrison) counted the number of times that *freedom* and *equality* were mentioned favorably and unfavorably in the writings of socialists, Hitler, Goldwater, and Lenin. Again, there are striking contrasts, which need no elaboration. This is another excellent example of ex post facto research and its scientific usefulness in imaginative and competent hands.[10]

[10]Note that Rokeach, after the above research, did experiments in which he managed to change students' values: *ibid.*, pp. 173 ff.

A Study of Children's Reactions to Finger Painting[11]

A study that is particularly interesting, because it combines experimental and ex post facto approaches, is the Alper, Blane, and Adams study of the reactions of children of different social classes to finger-painting experience. Experimental manipulation was certainly involved, but the independent variable was not manipulated. Indeed, one might almost say that the dependent variable was manipulated! The general question the authors asked was: Do social-class differences in child-training practices result in class differences in personality? More specifically: Are there differences in approaches to finger painting between middle- and lower-class children?

Two groups of nursery school children, 18 middle-class children and 18 lower-class children, were introduced to two different finger-painting tasks. The children's behavior was measured on 16 variables: time began painting, acceptance of task, requests for help, washing, and so on. The two groups differed greatly in their reactions, and the differences were significant on most of the measures.

In a "control experiment," the same procedure was followed using crayons rather than finger paints. The only differences were procedural changes necessitated by the use of the two media (some of the subjects were different also). The two groups did not differ significantly in any of the 11 variables measured, a rather surprising contrast to the former results.

To call the Alper, Blane, and Adams study ex post facto may be questionable, because a control experiment was included. It is possible, however, to suppose that the two groups varied in the finger-painting tasks, not because of different child-rearing practices between the social classes, but because of some other variable. The study is classified as ex post facto research because it was not possible to manipulate the independent varible and because the subjects came to the study with their reactions ready-made, as it were.

Another noteworthy point is the ingenuity of the control experiment. The running of this second experiment is analogous to Pettigrew's testing of authoritarianism. Imagine the researchers' consternation if the differences between the two groups had been significant on the crayon tasks! Obviously their theoretical thinking would have had to be reviewed with a very critical eye.

Testing Alternative or "Control" Hypotheses

Most investigations begin with hypotheses; the empirical implications of these hypotheses are then tested. Although we "confirm" hypotheses in the manner described in earlier chapters, we can also "confirm" and "disconfirm" hypotheses under study by trying to show that alternative plausible hypotheses are or are not supported. Let us first consider alternative independent variables as antecedents of a dependent variable. The reasoning is the same. If we say "alternative inde-

[11]T. Alper, H. Blane, and B. Adams, "Reactions of Middle and Lower Class Children to Finger Paints as a Function of Class Differences in Child-Training Practices," *Journal of Abnormal and Social Psychology*, LI (1955), 439–448.

pendent variables," for example, we are in effect stating alternative hypotheses or explanations of a dependent variable.

In ex post facto studies, although one cannot have the confidence in the "truth" of an "If x, then y" statement that one can have in experiments, it *is* possible to set up and test alternative or "control" hypotheses. (Of course, alternative hypotheses can be and are tested in experimental studies, too.) This procedure has been formalized and explained by Platt who, influenced by Chamberlin, called it "strong inference."[12] Chamberlin aptly called the procedure the "method of working multiple hypotheses," and he outlined how the investigator's own "intellectual affections" can be guarded against. He said: "The effort is to bring up into view every rational explanation of new phenomena, and to develop every tenable hypothesis respecting their cause and history. The investigator thus becomes the parent of a family of hypotheses; and, by his parental relation to all, he is forbidden to fasten his affections unduly upon any one."[13]

Let x_1, x_2, and x_3 be three alternative independent variables, and let y be the dependent variable, the phenomenon to be "explained" with a statement of the form: If x, then y. Assume that x_1, x_2, and x_3 exhaust the possibilities. This assumption cannot actually be made—in scientific research it is practically impossible to exhaust all the causal possibilities. Still, it is assumed for pedagogical reasons.

An investigator has evidence that x_1 and y are substantially related. Having reason to believe that x_1 is the determinative factor, he holds x_2 and x_3 constant. He is assuming that one of the three factors is *the* factor, that either x_1 or x_2 or x_3 is *the* "true" independent variable. (Again, note the assumption. It may be none of them or some combination of all three.) Suppose that the investigator succeeds in eliminating x_2, that is, he shows that x_2 is not related to y. If he also succeeds in eliminating x_3, he can then conclude that x_1 is the influential independent variable. Since the alternative or "control" hypotheses have not been substantiated, the original hypothesis is strengthened.

Similarly, we can test alternative *dependent* variables, which imply alternative hypotheses, of course. We merely shift the alternatives to the dependent variable, as Alper, Blane, and Adams did when they set up the crayon experiment in juxtaposition to the finger-paint experiment. Pettigrew used the same method to test the relation between geographical region and authoritarianism and prejudices. In both of these studies alternative hypotheses were tested and found wanting.

Now consider a study by Sarnoff et al. in which it was predicted that English and American children would differ significantly in test anxiety but not in general anxiety.[14] The hypothesis was carefully delineated: If eleven-plus examinations are taken, then test anxiety results. (The eleven-plus examinations are given to

[12] J. Platt, "Strong Inference," *Science*, CXLVI (1964), 347–353; T. Chamberlin, "The Method of Multiple Working Hypotheses," *Science*, CXLVII (1965), 754–759. The Chamberlin article was originally published in *Science* in 1890 (vol. 15). A clear explanation of the logic behind testing alternative hypotheses is given in: M. Cohen and E. Nagel, *An Introduction to Logic and Scientific Method*. New York: Harcourt Brace Jovanovich, 1934, pp. 265–267.

[13] Chamberlin, *op. cit.*, p. 756.

[14] I. Sarnoff et al., "A Cross-Cultural Study of Anxiety among American and English School Children," *Journal of Educational Psychology*, XLIX (1958), 129–136.

English school children at eleven years of age to help determine their educational futures.) Since it was possible that there might be other independent variables causing the difference between the English and American children on test anxiety, the investigators evidently wished to rule out at least some of the major contenders. This they accomplished by carefully matching the samples: they probably reasoned that the difference in test anxiety might be due to a difference in general anxiety, since the measure of test anxiety obviously must reflect some general anxiety. If this were found to be so, the major hypothesis would not be supported. Therefore Sarnoff and his colleagues, in addition to testing the relation between examination and test anxiety, also tested the relation between examination and general anxiety.

In this kind of ex post facto control, instead of having alternative independent variables, say x_1 and x_2, we have alternative dependent variables, y_1 and y_2. We again assume that the alternatives exhaust the possibilities. If this is so, then x is either associated with y_1 (test anxiety), or with y_2 (general anxiety), or with both. To paraphrase the Sarnoff argument: Either the examination influences test anxiety or it influences general anxiety, or both; the examination influences test anxiety and it does not influence general anxiety. Therefore the examination influences test anxiety.

The method of testing alternative hypotheses, though important in all research, is particularly important in ex post facto studies, because it is one of the only ways to "control" the independent variables of such research. Lacking the possibility of randomization and manipulation, ex post facto researchers, perhaps more so than experimentalists, must be very sensitive to alternative hypothesis-testing possibilities.

Evaluation of Ex Post Facto Research

The reader may have concluded from the preceding discussion that ex post facto research is inferior to experimental research, but this conclusion would be unwarranted. It is easy to *say* that experimental research is "better" than ex post facto research, or that experimental research tends to be "trivial," or that ex post facto research is "merely correlational." Such statements, in and of themselves, are oversimplifications. What the student of research needs is a balanced understanding of the strengths and weaknesses of both kinds of research. To be committed unequivocally to experimentation or to ex post facto research may be poor policy.

The Limitations of Ex Post Facto Interpretation

Ex post facto research has three major weaknesses, two of which have already been discussed in detail: (1) the inability to manipulate independent variables, (2) the lack of power to randomize, and (3) the risk of improper interpretation. In other words, compared to experimental research, other things being equal, ex post facto research lacks control; this lack is the basis of the third weakness: the risk of improper interpretation.

The danger of improper and erroneous interpretations in ex post facto research stems in part from the plausibility of many explanations of complex events. It is easy for us to accept the first and most obvious interpretation of an established relation, especially if we work without hypotheses to guide the investigation, or proceed from the dependent variable to the independent variable. These two circumstances are closely related because research unguided by hypotheses, research "to find out things," is most often ex post facto research. Experimental research is more likely to be based on carefully defined hypotheses.

Hypotheses are if-then predictions. In a research experiment the prediction is from a well-controlled x to a y. If the prediction holds true, we are relatively safe in stating the conditional, If x, then y. In an ex post facto study under the same conditions, however, we are considerably less safe in stating the conditional, for reasons discussed earlier. Careful safeguards are more essential in the latter case, especially in the selection and testing of alternative hypotheses, such as the predicted lack of relation between the eleven-plus examination and general anxiety in the Sarnoff study. A predicted (or unpredicted) relation in ex post facto research may be quite spurious, but its plausibility and conformity to preconception may make it easy to accept. This is a danger in experimental research, but it is *less* of a danger than it is in ex post facto research because an experimental situation is so much easier to control.

Ex post facto research that is conducted without hypotheses, without predictions, research in which data are just collected and then interpreted, is even more dangerous in its power to mislead. Significant differences or correlations are located if possible and then interpreted. Assume that an educator decides to study the factors leading to underachievement. He selects a group of underachievers and a group of normal achievers and administers a battery of tests to both groups. He then calculates the means of the two groups on the tests and analyzes the differences with t tests. Among, say, twelve such differences, three are significant. The investigator concludes, then, that underachievers and normal achievers differ on the variables measured by these three tests. Upon analysis of the three tests, he thinks he understands what characterizes underachievers. Since all three of the tests seem to measure insecurity, therefore the cause of underachievement is insecurity.

Although the simplicity of this example is a bit exaggerated, studies very similar to this hypothetical one are often undertaken. When guided by hypotheses the results of such studies are more valid, but the results are still weak because they capitalize on chance relations, and above all, the explanation of the results seems so plausible—once a plausible explanation has been found. According to Merton, *post factum* explanations do not lend themselves to nullifiability, because they are so flexible. Whatever the observations, he says, new interpretations can be found to "fit the facts."[15]

The Value of Ex Post Facto Research

Despite its weaknesses, much ex post facto research must be done in psychology, sociology, and education simply because many research problems in the social

[15]R. Merton, *Social Theory and Social Structure*. New York: Free Press, 1949, pp. 90–91.

sciences and education do not lend themselves to experimental inquiry. A little reflection on some of the important variables in educational research—intelligence, aptitude, home background, parental upbringing, teacher personality, school atmosphere—will show that they are not manipulable. Controlled inquiry is possible, of course, but true experimentation is not. Sociological problems of education, such as extreme deviation in group behavior and its effect on educational achievement, and board of education decisions and their effects on teacher and administrator performance and morale, are mostly ex post facto in nature. Even if we would avoid ex post facto research, we cannot.

It can even be said that ex post facto research is more important than experimental research. This is, of course, not a methodological observation. It means, rather, that the most important social scientific and educational research problems do not lend themselves to experimentation, although many of them do lend themselves to controlled inquiry of the ex post facto kind. Consider Piaget's studies of children's thinking, Gross' study of boards of education and superintendents, the authoritarianism studies of Adorno et al., the enormously important study, *Equality of Educational Opportunity*. If a tally of sound and important studies in the behavioral sciences and education were made, it is possible that ex post facto studies would outnumber and outrank experimental studies.

Conclusions

Some students of research believe that much behavioral research, but particularly educational research, suffers from a serious lack of a rigorous experimental approach and that it will lag as long as this situation exists. The author believes that good experimental research is badly needed in all fields, and that large doses of poor ex post facto research should be avoided. Improvements in *educational* ex post facto research are badly needed. Perhaps a good rule to follow would be to ignore the results of any ex post facto study that does not test hypotheses. Exceptions to this stricture should be few and far between. Perhaps another good rule would be to be highly skeptical of any ex post facto study that tests only one hypothesis; that is, alternative "negative" hypotheses should be routinely tested. Researchers should predict significant relations *and* nonsignificant relations whenever possible.

A final piece of advice is this: always treat the results and interpretations of the data of ex post facto investigations with great care and caution. Where one must be careful with experimental results and interpretations, one must be doubly careful with ex post facto results and interpretations.

Addendum: Causality and Scientific Research

A great deal of work, especially in sociology, has been and is being done on the study and analysis of causal relations in ex post facto research. One of the principal approaches has been what is called path analysis, whose purpose appears to be to study and test alternative hypotheses or alternative independent variables and to help to establish causal connections and inferences. A good reference is a book by Blalock which examines this difficult subject in depth.[16] Without substantial knowledge of multiple regression analysis—beyond the treatment of the subject in this text—it is not possible to follow Blalock's and others' expositions. The advanced student, however, will certainly want to be aware of the developments.

The position taken in this book is that the study of cause and causation is an endless maze. One of the difficulties is that the word "cause" has surplus meaning and metaphysical overtones. Perhaps more important, it is not really needed. Scientific research can be done without invoking cause and causal explanations, even though the words and other words that imply cause are almost impossible to avoid and thus will occasionally be used. Blalock points out that causal laws cannot be demonstrated empirically, but that it is helpful to think causally.[17] We agree that causal laws cannot be demonstrated empirically, but we are equivocal about thinking causally. There is little doubt that scientists do think causally and that when they talk of a relation between p and q they *hope* or *believe* that p causes q. But no amount of evidence can demonstrate that p *does* cause q.

This position is not so much an objection to causal notions as it is an affirmation that they are not necessary to scientific work. Evidence *can* be brought to bear on the empirical validity of conditional statements of the "If p, then q" kind, alternative hypotheses can be tested, and probabilistic statements can be made about p and q—and other p's and q's and conditions r, s, and t. Invocation of the word "cause" and the expression "causal relation" does nothing really constructive. Indeed, it can be misleading.

In expert hands and used with circumspection, path analysis and related methods can help to clarify theoretical and empirical relations.[18] But when their espousal and use imply that causes are sought *and found*, such methods can also be misleading. In sum, the elements of deductive logic in relation to conditional statements, a probabilistic framework and method of work and inference, and the testing of alternative hypotheses are sufficient aids to scientific ex post facto work without the excess baggage of causal notions and methods presumably geared to strengthening causal inferences. We rest the case with some apt words of Bertrand Russell:

> . . . the word "cause" is so inextricably bound up with misleading associations as to make its complete extrusion from the philosophical vocabulary desirable . . . the reason physics has ceased to look for causes is that, in fact, there are no such things. The law of causality . . . is a relic of a bygone age, surviving, like the monarchy, only because it is erroneously supposed to do no harm.[19]

[16]H. Blalock, *Causal Inferences in Nonexperimental Research.* Chapel Hill, N.C.: University of North Carolina Press, 1961. Blalock cites the following two books as part of the basis of his own thinking: H. Wold and L. Jureen, *Demand Analysis.* New York: Wiley, 1953; H. Simon, *Models of Men.* New York: Wiley, 1957.

[17]Blalock, *op. cit.*, p. 6.

[18]For an extended discussion of the value and use of path analysis and so-called commonality analysis in studying relations, see F. Kerlinger and E. Pedhazur, *Multiple Regression in Behavioral Research.* New York: Holt, Rinehart and Winston, 1973 (in press), chap. 11.

[19]B. Russell, "On the Notion of Cause, with Applications to the Free-Will Problem." In H. Feigl and M. Brodbeck, eds., *Readings in the Philosophy of Science.* New York: Appleton, 1953, p. 387.

Study Suggestions

1. A social psychologist plans to investigate factors behind anti-Semitism. He believes that people who have had authoritarian parents and authoritarian upbringing tend to be anti-Semitic. Would a research project designed to test this hypothesis be experimental or ex post facto? Why?
2. An educational psychologist decides to test the hypothesis that intelligence and motivation are the principal determinants of success in school. Would his research most likely be experimental or ex post facto? Why?
3. An investigator is interested in the relation between role perception and social values.
   (a) Which is the independent variable? The dependent variable?
   (b) Whatever judgment you have made, can you justifiably reverse the variables?
   (c) Do you think a research project designed to investigate this problem would be basically experimental or ex post facto?
   (d) Can the investigator do two researches, one experimental and one ex post facto, both designed to test the same hypothesis?
   (e) If your answer to (d) was Yes, will the variables of the two problems be the same? Assuming that the relations in both researches were significant, will the conclusions be substantially the same?
4. A researcher is interested in teacher success. He selects two groups of teachers: one that has been highly successful and one that has not been too successful. He finds that successful teachers tend to be more outgoing, somewhat more dependent, and more interested in people than less successful teachers. Assuming that everything has been methodologically well-done, discuss the possible strengths and weaknesses of this research. Can the researcher plan an experiment to test these relations?
5. Suppose that you want to study the effects of the decisions of boards of education on various aspects of education, such as teacher morale, pupil achievement, relations between teachers and administrators, teacher clique formation. Would your research be experimental or ex post facto? Why?
6. In the study suggestions of Chapter 2, a number of problems and hypotheses were given. Take each of these problems and hypotheses and decide whether research designed to explore the problems and test the hypotheses would be basically experimental or ex post facto. Can any of the problems and hypotheses be tackled in both ways?

CHAPTER 23

Laboratory Experiments, Field Experiments, and Field Studies

Social scientific research can be divided into four major categories: laboratory experiments, field experiments, field studies, and survey research.[1] This breakdown stems from two sources, the distinction between experimental and nonexperimental research and that between laboratory and "field" research.

A Laboratory Experiment: Miller Studies of the Learning of Visceral Responses

A brilliant series of experiments by Neal Miller and his colleagues has upset another long-held and well-cherished belief: that learning occurs only with voluntary responses, and that the involuntary autonomic system is subject only to classical conditioning.[2] This means, in effect, that responses like moving the hand and talking can be brought under control and thus taught, but that involuntary responses, like heart rate, intestinal contractions, and blood pressure, cannot be brought under instrumental control and thus not "taught."[3] Miller and his colleagues' work has shown that, through instrumental conditioning, the heart rate can be changed, stomach contractions can be altered, and even urine formation

[1]This chapter owes much to L. Festinger and D. Katz, *Research Methods in the Behavioral Sciences*. New York: Holt, Rinehart and Winston, 1953, chaps. 2, 3, 4.

[2]N. Miller, "Learning of Visceral and Glandular Responses," *Science*, CLXIII (1969), 434–445.

[3]To understand Miller's studies, we must define certain psychological terms. In *classical conditioning* a neutral stimulus, inherently unable to produce a certain response, becomes able to by being associated repeatedly with a stimulus inherently capable of doing so. The most famous example is Pavlov's dog salivating at the clicking of a metronome, which had been repeatedly associated with meat powder. In *instrumental conditioning*, a reinforcement given to an organism immediately after it has made a response produces an increment in the response. Pigeons, for example, will peck their beaks bloody after having been subjected to certain forms of instrumental conditioning. In short, reward a response and it will be repeated. Voluntary responses or behavior are thought to be superior,

can be enhanced! This "discovery" is of enormous theoretical and practical importance. To show the nature of laboratory experiments, we take one of Miller's experiments. A rather "pure" example, it is also interesting and creative.

The idea of the experiment is simple: reward one group of rats when their heart rates go up, and reward another group when their heart rates go down. This is a straightforward example of the two-group design discussed earlier. Miller's big problem was control. There are a number of other causes of changed heart rate—for example, muscular exertion. To control such extraneous variables, Miller and a colleague (Trowill) paralyzed the rats with curare. But if the rats were paralyzed, what could be used as reward? They decided to use direct electrical stimulation of the brain. The dependent variable, heart rate, was continuously recorded with the electrocardiograph. When a small change in heart rate occurred (in the "right" way: up for one group, down for the other), an animal was given an electrical impulse to a reward center of its brain.[4] This was continued until the animals were "trained."

The increases and decreases of heart rate were statistically reliable but small: only five percent in each direction. So Miller and another colleague (DiCara) used the technique known as shaping, which, in this case, means rewarding first small changes and then requiring increasing changes in rate to obtain the rewards. This increased the heart rate changes to an average of 20 percent in either direction. Moreover, further research, using escape from mild shock as reinforcement, showed that the animals remembered what they had learned and "differentiated" the heart responses from other responses.

Miller has been successful in "training" a number of other involuntary responses: intestinal contraction, urine formation, and blood pressure, for example. In short, visceral responses *can* be learned and *can* be shaped. But can the method be used with people? Miller says that he thinks people are as smart as rats, but that it has not yet been completely proved. Although the use of curare might present difficulty, people can be hypnotized, says Miller. In any case, the results of his research furnish evidence for the idea that there is only one kind of learning.

A Field Experiment: Winter et al.'s Study of the Classic Personal Style

How much influence do educational institutions have on students? This old question has been attacked in ways that vary widely but rarely are so stimulating as in the studies to be described in this section and the next. Winter, Alpert, and

presumably because they are under the control of the individual, whereas involuntary responses are inferior because they are not. It has been believed that involuntary responses can be modified only by classical conditioning and not by instrumental conditioning. In other words, the possibility of "teaching" the heart, the stomach, and the blood is remote, since classical conditioning conditions are difficult to come by. If the organs are subject to instrumental conditioning, however, they can be brought under experimental control, they can be "taught," and they can "learn." For authoritative accounts of both kinds of conditioning and their relation to learning, see E. Hilgard and G. Bower, *Theories of Learning*, 3d ed. New York: Appleton, 1966, chaps. 3 and 5.

[4]Brain research has shown that mild electrical stimulation of a certain part of the brain acts as a reward for the organism. See J. and M. Olds, "Drives, Rewards, and the Brain." In *New Directions in Psychology II*. New York: Holt, Rinehart and Winston, pp. 329–410.

McClelland wanted to know if a New England boys' boarding school whose goals and purposes were utterly different from those of the usual American high school would significantly affect the values and attitudes of a group of high school boys.[5] A grant made it possible for a school of this kind to take for a summer 32 bright boys who were attending public high schools. The investigators used participant observation, and administered a number of tests to assess change. (*Participant observation* is a "method" of research used by anthropologists and sociologists in which the researcher lives and works within the group he is studying.) The 32 boys and a control group of 30 matched boys, who did not attend the school, were compared on the measures before and after the summer session. A second experimental group and a control group of boys were also compared the following summer. For comparison purposes, 23 regular students of the school were similarly tested.

There are five basic themes in schools like this, according to the researchers, and St. Grottlesex—the fictitious name of the school—was no exception: intellectualism; self-control; authority that is impersonal, strong and good; cynicism and sophistication; and antihumanitarianism. These themes reflect a traditionalism in education and socialization that is virtually absent in American high schools. They reflect the "classic personal style" of the English public school. Would the boys pick up this style, these themes?

The results were interesting, though equivocal. There were no differences between the experimental group and the control group on the tests of attitudes and values used. But on special tests of imagination or associative processes, there were significant differences on four variables. The boys expressed themselves negatively about shiftlessness, impulsiveness, and emotionality; showed a sophisticated and cynical approach; were positive toward authority; and were unconcerned about humanitarian goals. Evidently St. Grottlesex's themes got through to them.[6]

A Field Study: Newcomb's Bennington College Study

In one of the most important studies yet done of the influence on students of a college environment, Newcomb studied the entire student body of Bennington College, about 600 young women, from 1935 to 1939.[7] An unusual facet of the

[5]D. Winter, R. Alpert, and D. McClelland, "The Classic Personal Style," *Journal of Abnormal and Social Psychology*, LXVII (1963), 254–265.

[6]It is impossible in a brief summary to convey the flavor of this interesting report. Students, especially those in education, are urged to read the original. Despite its methodological looseness, this is important research.

[7]T. Newcomb, *Personality and Social Change*. New York: Holt, Rinehart and Winston, 1943. A shorter account, called "Some Patterned Consequences of Membership in a College Community," can be found in T. Newcomb and E. Hartley, eds., *Readings in Social Psychology*. New York: Holt, Rinehart and Winston, 1947, pp. 345–357. Recently a number of the Bennington students were restudied in follow-up research designed to test the permanence of the changes made by Bennington: T. Newcomb et al., *Persistence and Change: Bennington College and Its Students After Twenty-five Years*. New York: Wiley, 1967. In general, it was found that the changes had lasted: evidently Bennington's influence was persistent over the years. A definitive review of the research on the influence of college is: K. Feldman and T. Newcomb, *The Impact of College on Students*. San Francisco: Jossey-Bass, 1969. A brief account of the Bennington follow-up is given on pp. 317–320.

study was Newcomb's attempt to explain both social and personality factors in influencing attitude changes in the students. Although other hypotheses were tested, the principal hypothesis of the Bennington study was that new students would converge on the norms of the college group, and that the more the students assimilated to the college community, the greater would be the change in their social attitudes.

Newcomb used a number of paper-and-pencil attitude scales, written reports on students, and individual interviews. The study was longitudinal and ex post facto. The independent variable, while not easy to categorize, might be said to be the social norms of Bennington College. The dependent variables were social attitudes and certain behaviors of the students.

Newcomb found significant changes in attitudes between freshmen, on the one hand, and juniors and seniors, on the other. The changes were toward less conservatism on a variety of social issues. For example, the political preferences of juniors and seniors in the 1936 presidential election were much less conservative than those of freshmen and sophomores. Of 52 juniors and seniors, 15 percent preferred Landon (Republican), whereas of 52 freshmen, 62 percent preferred Landon. The percentages of preferences for Roosevelt (Democrat) were 54 percent and 29 percent. The mean scores of all students for four years on a scale designed to measure political and economic conservatism were: freshmen, 74.2; sophomores, 69.4; juniors, 65.9, and seniors, 62.4. Evidently the college had affected the students' attitudes.

Newcomb asked a further question: Would these attitudes have changed in other colleges? To answer this question, Newcomb administered his conservatism measures to students of Williams College and Skidmore College. The comparable mean scores of Skidmore students, freshmen through seniors, were: 79.9, 78.1, 77.0, and 74.1. Although Newcomb does not report a significance test, it seems that Skidmore (and Williams) students did not change as much and as consistently over time as did the Bennington students.

Characteristics and Criteria of Laboratory Experiments, Field Experiments, and Field Studies

A *laboratory experiment* is a research study in which the variance of all or nearly all of the possible influential independent variables not pertinent to the immediate problem of the investigation is kept at a minimum. This is done by isolating the research in a physical situation apart from the routine of ordinary living and by manipulating one or more independent variables under rigorously specified, operationalized, and controlled conditions.

Strengths and Weaknesses of Laboratory Experiments

The laboratory experiment has the inherent virtue of the possibility of relatively complete control. The laboratory experimenter can, and often does, isolate the research situation from the life around the laboratory by eliminating the many extraneous influences that may affect the dependent variable.

In addition to situation control, laboratory experimenters can ordinarily use random assignment and can manipulate one or more independent variables. There are other aspects to laboratory control: the experimenter in most cases can achieve a high degree of specificity in the operational definitions of his variables. The relatively crude operational definitions of field situations, such as many of those associated with the measurement of values, attitudes, aptitudes, and personality traits, do not plague the experimentalist, though the definitional problem is never simple. The Miller experiment is a good example. The operational definitions of reinforcement and heart rate change are precise and highly objective.

Closely allied to operational strength is the precision and replicability of laboratory experiments. *Precise* means accurate, definite, unambiguous. Precise measurements are made with precision instruments. In variance terms, the more precise an experimental procedure is, the less the error variance. The more accurate or precise a measuring instrument is, the more certain we can be that the measures obtained do not vary very much from their "true" values. This is the problem of reliability, which will be discussed in a later chapter.

Precise laboratory results are achieved mainly by controlled manipulation. By specifying exactly the conditions of the experiment, we reduce the risk that subjects may respond equivocally and thus introduce random variance into the experimental situation. Miller's experiment is a model of laboratory experimental precision.

The greatest weakness of the laboratory experiment is probably the lack of strength of independent variables. Since laboratory situations are, after all, situations that are created for special purposes, it can be said that the effects of experimental manipulations are usually weak. The production of increases and decreases in heart rate by electrical brain reinforcement, while striking, was a relatively small effect. Compare this to the relatively large effects of independent variables in realistic situations. In the Bennington study, for example, the college community apparently had a massive effect. In laboratory research on conformity, only small effects are usually produced by group pressure on individuals. Compare this to the relatively strong effect of a large group majority on an individual group member in a real-life situation. The board of education member, who knows that an action he wants carried goes against the wishes of the majority of his colleagues and perhaps the majority of the community, is under heavy and massive pressure to converge on the norm.

One reason for the preoccupation with laboratory precision and refined statistics is the weakness of laboratory effects. To detect a significant difference in the laboratory requires situations and measures with a minimum of random noise and accurate and sensitive statistical tests that will show relations and significant differences when they exist.

Another weakness is a product of the first: the artificiality of the experimental research situation. Actually, it is difficult to know if artificiality is a weakness or simply a neutral characteristic of laboratory experimental situations. When a research situation is deliberately contrived to exclude the many distractions of the environment, it is perhaps illogical to label the situation with a term that expresses in part the result being sought. The criticism of artificiality does not come from experimenters, who know that experimental situations are artificial; it comes from individuals lacking an understanding of the purposes of laboratory experiments.

The temptation to interpret the results of laboratory experiments incorrectly is great. While Miller's results are believed by social scientists to be highly significant, they can only tentatively be extrapolated beyond the laboratory. Similar results may be obtained in real-life situations, and there is evidence that they do in some cases. But this is not necessarily so. The relations must always be tested anew under nonlaboratory conditions. Miller's research, for instance, will have to be carefully and cautiously done with human beings in hospitals and even in schools.

Although laboratory experiments have relatively high internal validity, then, they lack external validity. Earlier we asked the question: Did X, the experimental manipulation, really make a significant difference? The stronger our confidence in the "truth" of the relations discovered in a research study, the greater the internal validity of the study. When a relation is discovered in a well-executed laboratory experiment, we generally can have considerable confidence in it, since we have exercised the maximum possible control of the independent variable and other possible extraneous independent variables. When Miller "discovered" that visceral responses could be learned and shaped, he could be relatively assured of the "truth" of the relation between reinforcement and visceral response—in the laboratory. He had achieved a high degree of control and of internal validity.

One can say: If I study this problem using field experiments, *maybe* I will find the same relation. This is an empirical, not a speculative, matter; we must put the relation to test in the situation to which we wish to generalize. If a researcher finds that individuals converge on group norms in the laboratory, as Sherif did,[8] does the same or similar phenomenon occur in community groups, faculties, legislative bodies? This lack of external validity is the basis of the objections of many educators to the animal studies of learning theory. Their objections are only valid if an experimenter generalizes from the behavior and learning of laboratory animals to the behavior and learning of children. Capable experimentalists, however, rarely blunder in this fashion—they know that the laboratory is a contrived environment.

Purposes of the Laboratory Experiment

Laboratory experiments have three related purposes. First, they attempt to discover relations under "pure" and uncontaminated conditions. The experimenter asks: Is x related to y? How is it related to y? How strong is the relation? He seeks to reduce a discovered relation to functional form. He would like to write an equation of the form $y = f(x)$, make predictions on the basis of the function, and perform further laboratory, and perhaps even field tests, to see if the empirical values of the dependent variable y agree with or depart from the predicted values.

A second purpose should be mentioned in conjunction with the first purpose:

[8]M. Sherif, "Formation of Social Norms: The Experimental Paradigm." In H. Proshansky and B. Seidenberg, eds., *Basic Studies in Social Psychology*. New York: Holt, Rinehart and Winston, 1965, pp. 461–471. This is a classic laboratory experiment with large implications for both theory and practice.

the testing of predictions derived from theory, primarily, and other research, secondarily. For instance, on the basis of Sherif's norm-convergence finding, one might predict to a number of other laboratory and field experimental situations, as Sherif did in his later studies of boys in camp situations. Asch, though, argued that Sherif's stimulus was ambiguous in the sense that different people would "interpret" it differently.[9] He wondered whether the convergence phenomenon would work with clear stimuli in a more realistic setting. A series of experiments showed that it did.

A third purpose of laboratory experiments is to refine theories and hypotheses, to formulate hypotheses related to other experimentally or nonexperimentally tested hypotheses, and, perhaps most important, to help build theoretical systems. This was one of Miller's and Sherif's major purposes. Although some laboratory experiments are conducted without this purpose, of course, most laboratory experiments are strongly theory-oriented.

The aim of laboratory experiments, then, is to test hypotheses derived from theory, to study the precise interrelations of variables and their operation, and to control variance under research conditions that are uncontaminated by the operation of extraneous variables. As such, the laboratory experiment is one of man's greatest achievements. Although weaknesses exist, they are weaknesses only in a sense that is really irrelevant. Conceding the lack of representativeness (external validity) the laboratory experiment still has the fundamental prerequisite of any research: internal validity.[10]

The Field Experiment

A field experiment is a research study in a realistic situation in which one or more independent variables are manipulated by the experimenter under as carefully controlled conditions as the situation will permit. The contrast between the laboratory experiment and the field experiment is not sharp: the differences are mostly matters of degree. Sometimes it is hard to label a particular study "laboratory experiment" or "field experiment." Where the laboratory experiment has a maximum of control, most field studies must operate with less control, a factor that is often a severe handicap to the experiment. The Miller and Winter et al. studies were deliberately chosen as examples because of their differences in control: compared to Miller's controls, Winter's were loose.

Strengths and Weaknesses of Field Experiments

Field experiments have values that especially recommend them to social psychologists, sociologists, and educators because they are admirably suited to many

[9]S. Asch, "Studies of Independence and Conformity: I. A. Minority of One against a Unanimous Majority," *Psychological Monographs*, LXX (1956), Whole No. 416; S. Asch, *Social Psychology*. Englewood Cliffs, N.J.: Prentice-Hall, 1952, chap. 16.

[10]In this discussion, guidance on the actual conduct of experiments has been omitted. The reader who wants to go much deeper and get practical guidance can profit from a fine and detailed chapter by two social psychologists: E. Aronson and J. Carlsmith, "Experimentation in Social Psychology." In G. Lindzey and E. Aronson, eds., *The Handbook of Social Psychology*, 2d ed. Reading, Mass.: Addison-Wesley, vol. II, pp. 1–79.

of the social and educational problems of interest to social psychology, sociology, and education. Indeed, one can even say that most educational experiments are field experiments, since they are done in actual schools and classrooms. Because independent variables can be manipulated and randomization can be used, the criterion of control can be satisfied—at least theoretically.

The control of the experimental field situation, however, is rarely as tight as that of the laboratory experimental situation. We have here both a strength and a weakness. The investigator in a field study, though he has the power of manipulation, is always faced with the unpleasant possibility that his independent variables are contaminated by uncontrolled environmental variables. We stress this point because the necessity of controlling extraneous independent variables is particularly urgent in field experiments. The laboratory experiment is conducted in a tightly controlled situation, whereas the field experiment takes place in a natural, often loose, situation. One of the main preoccupations of the field experimenter, then, is to try to make the research situation more closely approximate the conditions of the laboratory experiment. Of course this is often a difficult goal to reach, but if the research situation can be kept tight, the field experiment is powerful because stronger statements of the if-then type can be made.

As compensation for the blessing of control being mixed, the field experiment has two or three unique virtues. The variables in a field experiment usually have a stronger effect than those of laboratory experiments. The effects of field experiments are often strong enough to penetrate the distractions of experimental situations. The principle is: The more realistic the research situation, the stronger the variables. This is one advantage of doing research in educational settings. For the most part, research in school settings is similar to routine educational activities, and thus need not be necessarily viewed as something special and apart from school life. Despite the pleas of many educators for more realistic educational research, there is no special virtue in realism, as realism. Realism simply increases the strength of the variables. It also contributes to external validity, since the more realistic the situation, the more valid are generalizations to other situations likely to be.

Another virtue of field experiments is their appropriateness for studying complex social influences, processes, and changes in lifelike settings. The dynamics and interactions of small groups have been fruitfully studied in field experiments. Winter et al. studied the influence of a school's value system on high school students in a natural situation. In a field experiment in a factory, Coch and French manipulated participation in planning and studied its effect on various dependent variables—production, resignations, and aggression.[11] The broad hypothesis tested was that resistance to change can be overcome by increased participation in decisions or processes that may lead to change. Factory workers were divided into three groups. The members of the control group did not participate in any of the discussions or decisions about changes in the factory. Two experimental groups did participate in discussion and decision in different degrees: total participation and participation by representation. The results supported the hypothesis.

[11]L. Coch and J. French, "Overcoming Resistance to Change," *Human Relations*, I (1948), 512–532.

Field experiments are well suited both to the testing of theory and to the solution of practical problems. Methods experiments in education are usually practical in purpose and seek to determine which methods get the best results. Studies of college teaching, studies of homogeneous and heterogeneous grouping, experiments on underachievers, studies of systematic versus nonsystematic early instruction, and many others are oriented to practical outcomes. Although some educators strongly believe that most educational research should be applied research, in recent years other educators have urged increased theoretical research.[12]

Another characteristic of field experiments is that they are suited to testing broad hypotheses. A good example is the cohesiveness-attraction hypothesis of group dynamics: The greater the cohesiveness of a group, the greater its power to influence its members.[13] This is a broad generalization, but one that is not difficult to operationalize and test in field experiments. An important hypothesis adaptable to field experimentation is that principles learned through induction from concrete cases are transferred more to new situations than are principles taught as principles.[14]

Flexibility and applicability to a wide variety of problems are important characteristics of field experiments, the only two limitations being whether one or more independent variables can be manipulated and whether the practical exigencies of the research situation are such that a field experiment can be done on the particular problem under study. Surmounting these two limitations is not easy. When it *can* be done, a wide range of theoretical and practical problems is open to experimentation.

As indicated earlier, the main weakness of field experiments are practical. Manipulation of independent variables and randomization are perhaps the two most important problems. The manipulation of independent variables may be conceivable, but not possible or practicable in many field situations because, say, parents object when their children, who happen to have been randomly assigned to a control group, will not get a desirable experimental treatment. Or there may be objection to an experimental treatment because it deprives children of some gratification or puts them into conflict situations.

There is no theoretical reason why randomization cannot be used in field experiments. Nevertheless, difficulties are frequently met. Unwillingness to break up class groups or to allow children to be assigned to experimental groups at random are examples. Even if random assignment is possible and permitted, the independent variable may be seriously blurred, because the effects of the treatments cannot be isolated from other effects.

Teachers and children, for example, may discuss what is happening during the course of the experiment. To prevent such muddying of the variables, the experimenter should explain to administrators and teachers the necessity for random

[12]For a good discussion of the issues involved, see R. Travers, *An Introduction to Educational Research.* New York: Macmillan, 1958, chaps. 3 ff. See also F. Kerlinger, "The Mythology of Educational Research: The Methods Approach," *School and Society*, LXXXVIII (1960), 149–151.

[13]D. Cartwright, "The Nature of Group Cohesiveness." In D. Cartwright and A. Zander, eds., *Group Dynamics*, 3d ed. New York: Harper & Row, 1968, chap. 7.

[14]This is an altered form of the hypothesis of G. Haslerud and S. Meyers, "The Transfer Value of Given and Individually Derived Principles," *Journal of Educational Psychology*, XLIX (1958), 293–298.

assignment and careful control. Lacking the ability to randomize, the experimenter must abandon the research, modify it to suit the situation, or seek another situation where randomization is feasible and permissible.

An experimental field characteristic of a different nature is to some experimenters a weakness and to others a strength. A field investigator has to be, to some extent at least, a socially skilled operator. He should be able to work with people, talk to them, and convince them of the importance and necessity of his research. He should be prepared to spend many hours, even days and weeks, of patient discussion with people responsible for the institutional or community situation in which he is to work. For instance, if he is to work in a rural school system, he should have a knowledge of rural as well as general educational problems, and of the particular rural system he wishes to study. Some researchers become impatient with these preliminaries, because they are anxious to get the research job done. They find it difficult to spend the time and effort necessary in most practical situations. Others enjoy the inevitable socializing that accompanies field research.[15]

An important obstacle to good design, an obstacle that seems ordinarily to be overlooked, is the attitude of the researcher. For example, the planning of educational research often seems to be characterized by a negative attitude epitomized by such statements as, "That can't be done in schools," "The administrators and teachers won't allow that," and "Experiments can't be done on this problem in that situation." Starting with attitudes like this compromises any good research design before the research even begins. If a research design calls for the random assignment of teachers to classes, and if the lack of such assignment seriously jeopardizes the internal validity of the proposed study, every effort should be made to assign teachers at random. Educators planning research seem to assume that the administrators or the teachers will not permit random assignment. This assumption is not necessarily correct, however.

The consent and cooperation of teachers and administrators can often be obtained if a proper approach, with adequate and accurate orientation, is used, and if explanations of the reasons for the use of specific experimental methods are given. The points being emphasized are these: Design research to obtain valid answers to the research questions. Then, if it is necessary to make the experiment possible, and only then, modify the "ideal" design. With imagination, patience, and courtesy, many of the practical problems of implementation of research design can be satisfactorily solved.

One other weakness inherent in field experimental situations is lack of precision. In the laboratory experiment it is possible to achieve a high degree of precision or accuracy, so that laboratory measurement and control problems are usually simpler than those in field experiments. In realistic situations, there is always a great deal of systematic and random noise. In order to measure the effect of an independent variable on a dependent variable in the field experiment, it is not only necessary to maximize the variance of the manipulated variable and any

[15]Good advice on handling this aspect of field situations is given by J. French, "Experiments in Field Settings," in Festinger and Katz, *op. cit.*, pp. 118–129, and D. Katz, "Field Studies," *ibid.*, pp. 87–89.

assigned variables, but also to measure the dependent variable as precisely as possible. But in realistic situations, such as in schools and community groups, extraneous independent variables abound. And measures of dependent variables, unfortunately, are sometimes not sensitive enough to pick up the messages of our independent variables. In other words, the dependent variable measures are often so crude that they cannot pick up all the variance that has been engendered by the independent variables.

Field Studies

Field studies are ex post facto scientific inquiries aimed at discovering the relations and interactions among sociological, psychological, and educational variables in real social structures. In this book, *any* scientific studies, large or small, that systematically pursue relations and test hypotheses, that are ex post facto, and that are done in life situations like communities, schools, factories, organizations, and institutions will be considered field studies.

The investigator in a field study first looks at a social or institutional situation and then studies the relations among the attitudes, values, perceptions, and behaviors of individuals and groups in the situation. He ordinarily manipulates no independent variables. Before we discuss and appraise the various types of field studies, it will be helpful to consider examples. We have already examined field studies in Chapter 22 and in this chapter: the Rokeach *freedom-equality* study, the Pettigrew prejudice study, the *Authoritarian Personality* study, the Newcomb Bennington study. We now briefly examine two smaller field studies.

In a study of the relations between role conflict and role-taking effectiveness, Getzels and Guba studied Air Force officers who were also instructors at an Air Force school.[16] The amount of conflict between the role of an officer and his role as instructor was related to his rated effectiveness. It was found that the more acute this conflict became, the more ineffective the officer tended to be. Getzels and Guba thus used a ready-made educational situation to test hypotheses derived from role theory. This is a case where manipulation of the independent variables is unlikely.

Marquis, Guetzkow, and Heyns, in a unique and significant field study, studied 72 actual business and government decision-making conferences.[17] Through direct observation and questionnaires they determined the satisfaction of group members with the conferences and their outcomes, and the productivity of the conferences. It was found that group-member satisfaction increased with procedural structuring of the meetings, with cohesiveness of the groups, and with *opportunity* to talk (but not necessarily actual participation of group members). Cohesive groups were found to be no more productive than noncohesive groups. This is an especi-

[16]J. Getzels and E. Guba, "Role, Role Conflict, and Effectiveness," *American Sociological Review*, XIX (1954), 164–175.

[17]D. Marquis, H. Guetzkow, and R. Heyns, "A Social Psychological Study of the Decision-Making Conference." In H. Guetzkow, ed., *Groups, Leadership, and Men.* Pittsburgh: Carnegie Press, 1951, pp. 55–67.

ally good example of disciplined field observation, study, and analysis of important and practical decision-making and its correlates.

Types of Field Studies

Katz has divided field studies into two broad types: *exploratory* and *hypothesis-testing*.[18] The exploratory type, says Katz, *seeks what is* rather than *predicts relations* to be found. The Marquis, Guetzkow, and Heyns study more or less exemplifies this type, though so categorizing it might be criticized. Exploratory studies have three purposes: to discover significant variables in the field situation, to discover relations among variables,[19] and to lay the groundwork for later, more systematic and rigorous testing of hypotheses.

Throughout this book up to this point, the use and testing of hypotheses have been emphasized. It is well to recognize, though, that there are activities preliminary to hypothesis-testing in scientific research. In order to achieve the desirable aim of hypothesis-testing, preliminary methodological and measurement investigation must often be done. Some of the finest work of the twentieth century has been in this area. An example of this work is that done by the factor analyst, who is preoccupied with the discovery, isolation, specification, and measurement of underlying dimensions of achievement, intelligence, aptitudes, attitudes, situations, and personality traits.

The second subtype of exploratory field studies, research aimed at discovering or uncovering relations, is indispensable to scientific advance in the social sciences. It is necessary to know, for instance, the correlates of the variables of our science. Indeed, the scientific meaning of a construct springs from the relations it has with other constructs.

Assume that we have no scientific knowledge of the construct "intelligence": we know nothing of its causes or concomitants. For example, suppose that we know nothing whatsoever about the relation of intelligence to achievement. It is conceivable that we might do a field study in school situations. We might carefully observe a number of boys and girls who are said to be intelligent or nonintelligent by teachers (though right here we introduce contamination, because teachers must obviously judge intelligence, in part at least, by achievement). We may notice that a larger number of "more intelligent" children come from homes of higher socioeconomic levels; they solve problems in class more quickly than other children; they have a wider vocabulary, and so on. We now have some clues to the nature of intelligence, so that we can attempt to construct a simple measure of intelligence. Note that our "definition" of intelligence springs from what presumably intelligent and nonintelligent children *do*. A similar procedure could be followed with the variable "achievement."

Strengths and Weaknesses of Field Studies

Field studies are strong in realism, significance, strength of variables, theory orientation, and heuristic quality. The variance of many variables in actual field

[18]Katz, *op. cit.*, pp. 75–83.
[19]*Ibid.*, p. 75.

settings is large, especially when compared to the variance of the variables of laboratory experiments. Consider the contrast between the impact of social norms in a laboratory experiment like Sherif's and the impact of these norms in a community where, say, certain actions of teachers are frowned upon and others approved. Consider also the difference between studying cohesiveness in the laboratory where subjects are asked, for example, whether they would like to remain in a group (measure of cohesiveness) and studying the cohesiveness of a school faculty where staying in the group is an essential part of one's professional future. Compare the group atmosphere in the Bennington College Study and that in a field experiment where different atmospheres are planned by college instructors playing different roles. Variables such as social class, prejudice, conservatism, cohesiveness, and social climate can have a massive effect in these studies. The strength of variables is not an unalloyed blessing, however. In a field situation there is usually so much noise in the communication channel that even though the effects may be strong and the variance great, it is not easy for the experimenter to separate the variables.

The realism of field studies is obvious. Of all types of studies, they are closest to real life. There can be no complaint of artificiality here. (The remarks about realism in field experiments apply, a fortiori, to the realism of field studies.)

The application of scientific method to such human problems as delinquency, morale, prejudice, social and educational attitudes, value conflicts, child-rearing practices, educational deprivation and inequality, and authoritarianism was started in this century. Much has been learned by scientists seeking to understand the origin and the correlates of religious and other prejudice, or the relation between child-rearing practices and adult social behavior, or the relation between the values of society in general and the educational practices of schools. These are problems that are closer to practical men and women than are many other scientific problems.

Social significance, however, does not always mean scientific significance. Practical field studies designed only for the ultimate solution of practical problems will always be desirable. If they exclude theoretical scientific problems, however, they defeat the purpose of scientific research. The researcher can get so involved in the fascinating business of examining complex human attributes and activities that he may find it difficult to focus his mind on the theory he is trying to develop and to test. For instance, he may ask the question, Is there a relation between religious preference or political preference and authoritarian attitudes? But a more important scientific question lies behind this surface question: *Why* are religious and political preferences related to authoritarian attitudes? The answer to this theoretical problem would solve not just this one question but many other related, though perhaps not so obvious, questions. In other words, the social significance of field studies is definitely a strength, but without scientific vigilance social scientific and educational research can be weakened.

Field studies are highly heuristic. Any researcher knows that one of the research difficulties of a field study is to keep himself contained within the limits of his problem. Hypotheses frequently fling themselves at one. The field is rich in discovery potentiality. For example, an investigator may decide to test the hypothesis that the social attitudes of board of education members is a determinant of board of education policy decisions. After starting to gather data, however, he stumbles upon many interesting notions that can deflect the course of his investigation: the relation between the attitudes of board of education members and their election to the boards, the relation between the scope of men's business and professional interests and their seeking board of education membership, and the different conceptions of curriculum problems of board members, administrators, teachers, and parents.

Despite these strengths, the field study is a scientific weak cousin of laboratory and field experiments. Its most serious weakness, of course, is its ex post facto character. Thus statements of relations are weaker than they are in experimental research. To complicate matters further, the field situation almost always has a plethora of variables and variance. Think of the many possible independent variables that we might choose as determinants of school achievement. In an experimental study, these variables can be controlled to a large extent, but in a field study, they must be related somehow to achieve whatever degree of control we can get by more direct and less satisfactory means.

Another methodological weakness is the lack of precision in the measurement of field variables. In field *studies*, the problem of precision is more acute, naturally, than in field *experiments*. The problems encountered by Astin (and others) in measuring college environment[20] comprise one of many similar examples. Administrative environment, for example, was measured by students' perceptions of aspects of the environment. Much of the lack of precision is due to the greater complexity of field situations.

Other weaknesses of field studies are practical problems: feasibility, cost, sampling, and time. These difficulties are really *potential* weaknesses—none of them need be a real weakness. The most obvious questions that can be asked are: Can the study be done with the facilities at the investigator's disposal? Can the variables be measured? Will it cost too much? Will it take too much time and effort? Will the subjects be cooperative? Is random sampling possible? Anyone contemplating a field study has to ask and answer such questions. In designing research it is important not to underestimate the large amounts of time, energy, and skill necessary for the successful completion of most field studies. The field researcher needs to be a salesman, administrator, and entrepreneur, as well as investigator.[21]

Study Suggestions

1. Here are some studies and the chapters they appeared in. Go back to them and refresh your memory. Then identify each as a laboratory experiment, a field experiment, or a field study. Tell why you categorize each study as you do.

   Hurlock, 13
   Aronson and Cope, 14

[20] A. Astin, *The College Environment*. Washington, D.C.: American Council on Education, 1968.
[21] For details, see Katz, *op. cit.*, especially pp. 65 ff.

Berkowitz, 14
Young, Benson, and Holtzman, 14
Walster et al., 17
Thorndike, 19
Bandura and Menlove, 21

2. Is factorial analysis of variance more likely to be used in laboratory experiments, field experiments, or field studies? Why?
3. In Chapter 15, a study of the comparative effects of marijuana and alcohol was outlined. Suppose such a study is a laboratory experiment. Does that limit its usefulness and generalizability? Would such an experiment differ in generalizability from, say, a laboratory experiment of frustration and aggression?
4. Which kind of study is likely to be more generalizable: laboratory experiment, field experiment, or field study? Why?
5. It has been said that laboratory experiments are artificial, unrealistic, and not very useful to educators or education. Argue both sides of this question, bringing out the characteristics and strengths and weaknesses of laboratory and field research.
6. Outline plans for the design of a laboratory experiment, a field experiment, and a field study of the same basic problem: the relation between the cohesiveness of a group and its productivity. Keep the design simple. Check back to Chapter 3 for a definition of cohesiveness. Do the three designs study the same problem? That is, is the problem altered by the differences in the three kinds of study? How? Which design is "best," do you think?

CHAPTER 24

Survey Research

Survey research studies large and small populations (or universes) by selecting and studying samples chosen from the populations to discover the relative incidence, distribution, and interrelations of sociological and psychological variables.[1] Surveys covered by this definition are often called *sample surveys*, probably because survey research developed as a separate research activity, along with the development and improvement of sampling procedures. Surveys, as such, are not new. Social welfare studies were done in England as long ago as the eighteenth century.[2] Survey research in the social scientific sense, however, is quite new—it is a development of the twentieth century.

Survey research is considered to be a branch of social scientific research, which immediately distinguishes survey research from the status survey. The procedures and methods of survey research have been developed mostly by psychologists, sociologists, anthropologists, economists, political scientists, and statisticians.[3] These men have put a rigorous scientific stamp on survey research and, in the process, have profoundly influenced the social sciences.

[1]This chapter concentrates on the use of survey research in scientific research and neglects so-called status surveys, the aim of which is to learn the status quo rather than to study the relations among variables. There is no intention of derogating status surveys; they are useful, even indispensable. The intention is to emphasize the importance and usefulness of survey research in the scientific study of socially and educationally significant problems. The work of public opinion pollsters, such as Gallup and Roper, is also neglected. For a good account of polls and other surveys, see M. Parten, *Surveys, Polls, and Samples.* New York: Harper & Row, 1950, chap. 1. Though old, this book is still valuable.

[2]*Ibid.*, p. 5.

[3]A. Campbell and G. Katona, "The Sample Survey: A Technique for Social-Science Research." In L. Festinger and D. Katz, *Research Methods in the Behavioral Sciences.* New York: Holt, Rinehart and Winston, 1953, chap. 1.

The definition also links populations and samples. The survey researcher is interested in the accurate assessment of the characteristics of whole populations of people. He wants to know, for example, how many persons in the United States vote for a Republican candidate and the relation between such voting and variables like sex, race, religious preference, and the like. He wants to know the relation between the attitudes toward education and the public support of a school bond issue of the population of a school district. In short, the survey researcher wants to know something about U, the universe.

Only rarely, however, do survey researchers study whole populations: they study *samples* drawn from populations. From these samples they infer the characteristics of the defined population or universe. The study of samples from which inferences about populations can be drawn is needed because of the difficulties of attempting to study whole populations. Random samples can often furnish the same information as a census (an enumeration and study of an entire population) at much less cost, with greater efficiency, and sometimes greater accuracy.

Sample surveys attempt to determine the incidence, distribution, and interrelations among sociological and psychological variables. Although the approach and the techniques of survey research can be used on any set of objects that can be well-defined, survey research focuses on people, the vital facts of people, and their beliefs, opinions, attitudes, motivations, and behavior.

The social scientific nature of survey research is revealed by the nature of its variables, which can be classified as sociological *facts* and *opinions* and *attitudes*. *Sociological facts* are attributes of individuals that spring from their membership in social groups: sex, income, political and religious affiliation, socioeconomic status, education, age, living expenses, occupation, race, and so on.[4]

The second type of variable is psychological and includes opinions and attitudes, on the one hand, and behavior, on the other. The survey researcher is not interested primarily in the sociological variables, as such: he is primarily interested in what people think and what they do. The sociological variables are then related in some manner to the psychological variables. An example will show this quite well. Table 24.1 gives some of the data from Gross's study of the members of boards of education and superintendents of schools in Massachusetts.[5] The board members and superintendents were asked whether they thought there should be specific academic standards for promotion in the first six grades. The table shows

TABLE **24.1** RELATION BETWEEN ROLE AND BELIEFS ABOUT PROMOTION POLICIES—GROSS STUDY

	Belief about Academic Standards for Promotion			
	Desirable	No Opinion	Undesirable	N
School Board Members	84%	1%	15%	508
Superintendents	51%	0%	49%	105

[4]For a complete description of such social and personal facts, see Parten, *op. cit.*, pp. 169–174.
[5]N. Gross, *Who Runs Our Schools?* New York: Wiley, 1958, p. 115.

the pertinent percentages. Evidently there *is* a relation between role (the sociological and independent variable) and belief about promotion standards (the psychological and dependent variable). School board members seem to believe more in academic standards for promotion than do school superintendents.

Survey researchers, of course, also study the relations among psychological variables. For example, Gross also reports the relation between the educational progressivism of board members and the number of hours spent on board activities.[6]

Types of Surveys

Surveys can be conveniently classified by the following methods of obtaining information: personal interview, mail questionnaire, panel, telephone, and controlled observation. Of these, the personal interview far overshadows the others as perhaps the most powerful and useful tool of social scientific survey research. These survey types will be briefly described here; in later chapters, when studying methods of data collection, we shall return to two of them: the personal interview and controlled observation.

Interviews and Schedules

The best examples of survey research use the personal interview as the principal method of gathering information. This is accomplished in part by the careful and laborious construction of a schedule or questionnaire.[7] Schedule information includes factual information, opinions and attitudes, and reasons for behavior, opinions, and attitudes. Interview schedules are difficult to construct; they are time-consuming and relatively costly; but there is no other method that yields the information they do.

The *factual information* gathered in surveys includes the so-called sociological data mentioned previously: sex, marital status, education, income, political preference, religious preference, and the like. Such information is indispensable, since it is used in studying the relations among variables and in checking the adequacy of samples. These data, which are entered on a "face sheet," are called "face sheet information." Face sheet information, at least part of it, is ordinarily obtained at the beginning of the interview. Much of it is neutral in character and helps the interviewer establish rapport with the respondent. Questions of a more personal nature, such as those about income and personal habits, and questions that are more difficult to answer such as the extent of the knowledge or ability of the respondent, can be reserved for later questioning, perhaps at the end of the schedule.[8] The timing must necessarily be a matter of judgment and experience.

Other kinds of factual information include what respondents know about the subject under investigation, what respondents did in the past, what they are doing now, and what they intend to do in the future. After all, unless we observe be-

[6] *Ibid.*, p. 180.

[7] The term "schedule" will be used. It has a clear meaning: the instrument used to gather survey information through personal interview. "Questionnaire" has been used to label personal interview instruments and attitudinal or personality instruments. The latter are called "scales" in this book.

[8] Parten, *op. cit.*, p. 215.

havior directly, all data about respondents' behavior must come from them or from other people. In this special sense, past, present, and future behavior can all be classified under the "fact" of behavior, even if the behavior is only an intention. A major point of such factual questions is that the respondent presumably knows a good deal about his own actions and behavior. If he says he voted for a school bond issue, we can believe him—unless there is compelling evidence to the contrary. Similarly, we can believe him, perhaps with more reservation (since the event has not happened yet), if he says he is going to vote for a school bond issue.

Just as important, maybe even more important from a social scientific standpoint, are the beliefs, opinions, attitudes, and feelings that respondents have about cognitive objects.[9] Many of the cognitive objects of survey research may not be of interest to the researcher: investments, certain commercial products, political candidates, and the like. Other cognitive objects are more interesting: the United Nations, the Supreme Court, educational practices, integration, Federal aid to education, revenue sharing, college students, Jews, and the Women's Lib Movement.

The personal interview can be very helpful in learning a respondent's own estimate of his *reasons* for doing or believing something. When asked his reasons for his actions, intentions, or attitudes, a person may say he has done something, intends to do something, or feels a certain way about something. He may specify that a group affiliation or loyalty or an event may have influenced him. Or he may have heard about the issue under investigation via public media of communication. For example, a respondent may say that, while he was formerly opposed to Federal aid to education because he and his political party have always opposed government interference, he now supports Federal aid because he has read a great deal about the problem in newspapers and magazines and has come to the conclusion that Federal aid will benefit American education.

A respondent's desires, values, and needs may influence his attitudes and actions. When saying why he favors Federal aid to education the respondent may indicate that his own educational aspirations were thwarted and that he has always yearned for more education. Or he may indicate that his religious group has, as a part of its value structure, a deep commitment to the education of children. If the individual under study has accurately sounded his own desires, values, and needs—and can express them verbally—the personal interview can be very valuable.

Other Types of Survey Research

The next important type of survey research is the *panel* technique.[10] A sample of respondents is selected and interviewed, and then reinterviewed and studied at

[9]*Cognitive object* is an expression used to indicate the object of an attitude. Almost anything can be the object of an attitude, but the term is ordinarily reserved for important social "objects," for example, groups (religious, racial, educational) and institutions (education, marriage, political parties). A more general and probably better term, though one not in general use, is *referents*. See F. Kerlinger, "Social Attitudes and Their Criterial Referents: A Structural Theory," *Psychological Review*, LXXIV (1967), 110–122.

[10]See P. Lazarsfeld, "The Use of Panels in Social Research," in B. Berelson and M. Janowitz, *Supplement to Reader in Public Opinion and Communication*. New York: Free Press, 1953, pp. 511–519.

later times. The panel technique enables the researcher to study changes in behaviors and attitudes.

Telephone surveys have little to recommend them beyond speed and low cost. Especially when the interviewer is unknown to the respondent they are limited by possible nonresponse, uncooperativeness, and by reluctance to answer more than simple, superficial questions. Yet telephoning can sometimes be useful in obtaining information essential to a study. Its principal defect, obviously, is the inability to obtain detailed information.

The *mail questionnaire*, another type of survey, has been popular in education, although it has serious drawbacks unless it is used in conjunction with other techniques. Two of these defects are possible lack of response and the inability to check the responses given. These defects, especially the first, are serious enough to make the mail questionnaire worse than useless, except in highly sophisticated hands. Responses to mail questionnaires are generally poor. Returns of less than 40 or 50 percent are common. Higher percentages are rare. At best, the researcher must content himself with returns as low as 50 or 60 percent.

As a result of low returns in mail questionnaires, valid generalizations cannot be made.[11] Although there are means of securing larger returns and reducing deficiencies—follow-up questionnaires, enclosing money, interviewing a random sample of nonrespondents and analyzing nonrespondent data—these methods are costly, time-consuming, and often ineffective. As Parten says, "Most mail questionnaires bring so few returns, and these from such a highly selected population, that the findings of such surveys are almost invariably open to question."[12] The best advice would seem to be not to use mail questionnaires if a better method can possibly be used. If they are used, every effort should be made to obtain returns of at least 80 to 90 percent or more, and lacking such returns, to learn something of the characteristics of the nonrespondents.

The Methodology of Survey Research

Survey research has contributed much to the methodology of the social sciences. Its most important contributions, perhaps, have been to rigorous sampling procedures, the overall design and the implementation of the design of studies, the unambiguous definition and specification of the research problem, and the analysis of data.

In the limited space of a section of one chapter, it is obviously impossible to discuss adequately the methodology of survey research. Only those parts of the methodology germane to the purposes of this book, therefore, will be outlined: the survey or study design, the so-called flow plan or chart of survey researchers, and the check of the reliability and validity of the sample and the data-gathering methods. (Sampling was discussed in Part 3, analysis in Part 4.)

Survey researchers use a "flow plan" or chart to outline the design and sub-

[11]See Parten, *op. cit.*, pp. 391–402, for a discussion of the inadequacies of mail questionnaires and remedies for remediable deficiencies.

[12]Parten, *op. cit.*, p. 400.

sequent implementation of a survey.[13] The flow plan starts with the objectives of the survey, lists each step to be taken, and ends with the final report. First, the general and specific problems that are to be solved are as carefully and as completely stated as possible. Since, in principle, there is nothing very different here from the discussion of problems and hypotheses of Chapter 2, we can omit detailed discussion and give one simple hypothetical example. An educational investigator has been commissioned by a board of education to study the attitudes of community members toward the school system. On discussing the general problem with the board of education and the administrators of the school system, the investigator notes a number of more specific problems, such as: Is the attitude of the members of the community affected by their having children in school? Are their attitudes affected by their educational level?

One of the investigator's most important jobs is to specify and clarify the problem. To do this well, he should not expect just to ask people what they think of the schools, although this may be a good way to begin if one does not know much about the subject. He should also have specific questions to ask that are aimed at various facets of the problem. Each of these questions should be built into the interview schedule. Some survey researchers even design tables for the analysis of data at this point in order to clarify the research problem and to guide the construction of interview questions. Since this procedure is recommended, let us design a table to show how it can be used to specify survey objectives and questions.

Take the question: Is attitude related to educational level? The question requires that "attitude" and "educational level" be operationally defined. Positive and negative attitudes will be inferred from responses to schedule questions and items: If, in response to a broad question like, "In general, what do you think of the school system here?" a respondent says, "It is one of the best in this area," it can be inferred that he has a positive attitude toward the schools. Naturally, one question will not be enough. Related questions should be used, too. A definition of "educational level" is quite easy to obtain. It is decided to use three levels: (1) Some College, (2) High School Graduate, and (3) Non-High School Graduate. The analysis paradigm might look like Fig. 24.1.

	Positive Attitude	Negative Attitude
Some College		
High School Graduate		
Non-High School Graduate		

FIG. 24.1

[13]Campbell and Katona, *op. cit.*, pp. 39–41.

The virtue of paradigms like this is that the researcher can immediately tell whether he has stated a specific problem clearly and whether the specific problem is related to the general problem. It also gives him some notion as to how many respondents he will need to fill the table cells adequately, as well as provide him guidelines for coding and analysis. In addition, as Katz says, "By actually going through the mechanics of setting out such tables, the investigators are bound to discover complexities of a variable that need more detailed measurement and qualifications of hypotheses in relation to special conditions."[14]

The next step in the flow plan is the sample and the sampling plan. Because sampling is much too complex to be discussed here,[15] we outline only the main ideas. First, the universe to be sampled and studied must be defined. Are all citizens living in the community included: Community leaders? Those citizens paying school taxes? Those with children of school age? Those with children in school? Once the universe is defined, a decision is made as to how the sample is to be drawn and how many cases will be drawn. In the best survey research, random samples are used. Because of their high cost and greater difficulty of execution random samples are often bypassed for *quota samples*. In a quota (or quota control) sample, "representativeness" is presumably achieved by assigning quotas to interviewers—so many men and women, so many whites and Negroes, and so on. Quota sampling should be avoided in behavioral survey research: while it *may* achieve representativeness, it lacks the virtues of random sampling.

The next large step in a survey is the construction of the interview schedule and other measuring instruments to be used. This is a laborious and difficult business bearing virtually no resemblance to the questionnaires often hastily put together by neophytes. The main task is to translate the research question into an interview instrument and into any other instruments constructed for the survey. One of the problems of the study, for instance, may be: How are permissive and restrictive attitudes toward the discipline of children related to perceptions of the local school system? Among the questions to be written to assess permissive and restrictive attitudes, one might be: How do you feel children should be disciplined? After drafts of the interview schedule and other instruments are completed, they are pretested on a small representative sample of the universe. They are then revised and put in final form.

The steps outlined above constitute the first large part of any survey. Data collection is the second large part. Interviewers are oriented, trained, and sent out

[14]D. Katz, "Field Studies," in Festinger and Katz, *op. cit.*, pp. 80–81.

[15]See Chapter 8. An excellent but technical discussion is: L. Kish, "Selection of the Sample," in Festinger and Katz, *op. cit.*, chap. 5. Much more complete is Kish's book: L. Kish, *Survey Sampling*. New York: Wiley, 1965. Parten's chapters on the subject are detailed and useful: Parten, *op. cit.*, chaps. 4, 7, 8, and 9. A good brief reference on so-called area sampling is: M. Hansen and P. Hauser, "Area Sampling—Some Principles of Sample Design," in Berelson and Janowitz, *op. cit.*, pp. 546–554. Area sampling is the type most used in survey research. First, defined large areas are sampled at random. This amounts to partitioning of the universe and random sampling of the cells of the partition. The partition cells may be areas delineated by grids on maps or aerial photographs of counties, school districts, or city blocks. Then further subarea samples may be drawn at random from the large areas already drawn. Finally, all individuals or families or random samples of individuals and families may be drawn.

with complete instructions as to whom to interview and how the interview is to be handled. In the best surveys, interviewers are allowed no latitude as to whom to interview. They must interview those individuals and only those individuals designated, generally by random devices. Some latitude may be allowed in the actual interviewing and use of the schedule, but not much. The work of interviewers is also systematically checked in some manner. For example, every tenth interview may be checked by sending another interviewer to the same respondent. Interview schedules are also studied for signs of spurious answering and reporting.

The third large part of the flow plan is analytical. The responses to questions are coded and tabulated. *Coding* is the term used to describe the translation of question responses and respondent information to specific categories for purposes of analyses.[16] Take the example of Fig. 24.1. All respondents must be assigned to one of the three educational-level categories and a number (or other symbol) assigned to each level. Then each person must also be assigned to a "positive attitude" or "negative attitude" category. To aid in the coding, content analysis may be used. Content analysis is an objective and quantitative method for assigning types of verbal and other data to categories. Coding can mean the analysis of factual response data and then the assignment of individuals to classes or categories, or the assigning of categories to individuals, especially if one is preparing machine cards for machine analysis. Such cards consist of a large number of columns with a number of cells in each column. The fifth column may be assigned, say, to sex, and the first two cells of the column, or the numbers 0 and 1, used to designate female and male.

Tabulation is simply the recording of the numbers of types of responses in the appropriate categories, after which statistical analysis follows: percentages, averages, relational indices, and appropriate tests of significance.

The analyses of the data are studied, collated, assimilated, and interpreted. Finally, the results of this interpretative process are reported.

Checking Survey Data

Survey research has a unique advantage among social scientific methods: it is often possible to check the validity of survey data. Some of the respondents can be interviewed again, and the results of both interviews checked against each other. It has been found that the reliability of personal factual items, like age and income, is high.[17] The reliability of attitude responses is harder to determine because a changed response can mean a changed attitude. The reliability of average responses is, of course, higher than the reliability of individual responses. Fortunately, the researcher is usually more interested in averages, or group measures, than in individual responses.

[16]A discussion of simple coding can be found in: W. Goode and P. Hatt, *Methods in Social Research.* New York: McGraw-Hill, 1952, pp. 315–325. For detailed discussions of coding and coding problems, instructional materials are available at small cost from the Institute for Social Research, University of Michigan, Ann Arbor, Mich. 48104. The Institute also issues extensive bibliographies on survey research and related matters. One of its valuable publications on interviewing is its *Interviewer's Manual* (1969).

[17]Parten, *op. cit.*, pp. 496–498.

One way of checking the validity of a measuring instrument is to use an outside criterion. One compares one's results to some outside, presumably valid, criterion. For instance, a respondent tells us he voted in the last election of school board members. We can find out whether he did or not by checking the registration and voting records. Ordinarily, individual behavior is not checked, because information about individuals is hard to obtain, but group information is often available. This information can be used to test to some extent the validity of the survey sample and the responses of the respondents.

A good example of an outside check on survey data is the use of information from the last census. This is particularly useful in large-scale surveys, but it may also help in smaller ones. In studying the attitudes toward education of the people of a school district, for example, we draw a sample of citizens and wish to check its adequacy. We can check the proportions of men and women, races, educational level, ages, and so on. National sample information has been found to be remarkably close to census information. Stouffer made such comparisons in a national study of civil liberties. Table 24.2 reports some of the comparisons made by Stouffer in a large-scale study of civil liberties.[18]

TABLE **24.2** COMPARISON OF SAMPLE WITH CENSUS DATA, STOUFFER STUDY

Characteristic	Census	Survey
Urban	64.0%	66.0%
Male	47.7	46.6
Negro	9.2	8.9
College	15.4	17.1
High School	43.5	45.4
Grade School (or none)	41.1	37.5

With one exception, grade school education, no estimate is off by more than 2 percent, which is reassuring evidence of the adequacy of the sample. (It is also some evidence of the validity of the responses of individuals interviewed.) To be sure, Stouffer was dealing with a very large sample, but smaller samples have also been found to be quite accurate. In one of the Detroit-area studies of the University of Michigan, the sample was approximately 735. The check of the sample against the 1950 Census showed survey percentages on a number of items to be very close to census percentages. The percentages of religious affiliations of the Detroit people, as estimated by the sample and as reported by the Detroit Council of Churches were: Catholic: 37 percent (survey), 38 percent (Council); Protestant: 56 percent and 57 percent; Other: 5 percent and 2 percent; No preference: 2 percent and 3 percent.[19]

[18]From S. Stouffer, *Communism, Conformity, and Civil Liberties.* Garden City, N.Y.: Doubleday, 1955, pp. 237–238. Copyright © 1955 by Samuel A. Stouffer. Reprinted by permission of Doubleday & Company, Inc.

[19]Detroit Area Study, University of Michigan, *A Social Profile of Detroit.* Ann Arbor: University of Michigan, 1952, p. 36.

Similar methods can and should be used in all surveys. Certain routine factual questions can be used, and special methods devised. Methods of checking sample reliability and validity have been discussed by Parten and others.[20]

Two Studies

Many surveys have been done, both good and bad. Most of them would probably not interest the student because they are only refined attempts to obtain simple information—certain studies of presidential voting, of industrial plants, and so forth. There are, however, other surveys of considerable, even great, interest and significance to behavioral scientists. Two of these will be summarized and discussed below. One is the Stouffer study already mentioned. Its content and methodology are so unusual, even imaginative, and yet representative of the best of survey research, that its inclusion in this chapter is well justified. The other is a study of the role relationships of board of education members and superintendents. Its methodology, while following the lines of good survey research, goes beyond most surveys in certain respects. More important, it is strongly grounded in social scientific theory.

Stouffer's large and thorough study was anchored in the reactions of Americans to the danger of Communism inside and outside the United States and to danger from those individuals who, while trying to thwart the conspiracy, might sacrifice some of the liberties of Americans.[21] A number of questions were asked and answered: How do the attitudes of community leaders compare to the attitudes of the rank and file within the community? Do attitudes vary from one region of the country to another, with education, with religion?

The study is unique in one methodological respect: two large and independent area random samples of the people of the United States were interviewed by two separate and independent agencies using the same schedule. Each sample included more than 2400 cases, a total of almost 5000 cases! By using two separate samples, not only could external and internal checks of survey data be made; the results of one survey could be checked against the other. There has rarely been such a large-scale and thorough check on the adequacy of random sampling procedures. In addition, about 1500 community leaders were selected and interviewed independently of the larger samples. These leaders were not selected at random, but by role: mayors, chambers of commerce presidents, American Legion commanders, and so on.

Stouffer exhaustively analyzed the data. The reader who follows the analyses, the numerical data, and the evaluative discussions of the analyses will find them rewarding. To summarize the data and findings here would be impractical. Instead, one interesting example is reported in Table 24.3.[22] The question was asked of the leaders and the larger group in the sample: "If a person wanted to

[20]Parten, *op. cit.*, chap. 16; Campbell and Katona, *op. cit.*, pp. 41–48; H. Hyman, *Survey Design and Analysis*. New York: Free Press, 1955, pp. 151–172.

[21]Stouffer, *op. cit.*

[22]Figures taken from Stouffer, *op. cit.*, pp. 32–33.

TABLE **24.3** TABULATION OF RESPONSES TO QUESTION ON TOLERANCE OF RELIGIOUS NONCONFORMITY, STOUFFER STUDY[a] (IN PERCENT)

		Response		
		No	No Opinion	Yes
Community Leaders	AIPO	33	1	66
	NORC	35	2	63
National Cross Section	AIPO	60	3	37
	NORC	61	2	37

[a]"No Opinion" percentages filled in by subtraction. AIPO: American Institute of Public Opinion (one of the survey agencies); NORC: National Opinion Research Center (the other survey agency).

make a speech in your community against churches and religions, should he be allowed to speak or not?"

The data of Table 24.3 indicate: one, there is a relation between position in the community and tolerance: community leaders seem to be more tolerant than the average citizen. Two, the sampling (area random method) was quite effective. Note the closeness of the percentages of the national cross sections. This is a remarkable demonstration of the power of random sampling.

The gross, Mason, and McEachern study, using the role of the school superintendent as the main cognitive object, tested theoretically derived hypotheses about expectations and behaviors of superintendents and board of education members. One of these was that incumbents of a role position would assign more responsibility to the position than would incumbents of subordinate or superordinate positions.[23] Another was that the longer the members of a social system interact, the greater the consensus of their expectations of the behavior of incumbents of positions in that social system.[24]

Of the universe of 217 superintendents in Massachusetts, 105 were randomly selected and interviewed. The board of education members associated with these 105 superintendents were also studied. There were 517 such members of whom 508 were interviewed. The lengthy interview schedule was designed to test the hypotheses mentioned above, as well as to obtain other factual information. As in the Stouffer study, scales were also used, including scales to measure authoritarianism, ethnocentrism, political-economic conservatism, career satisfaction, level of aspiration, educational progressivism, and other variables.

In the course of the study, superintendents were asked about the civic motivation of board members. The investigators then related civic motivation to religion, among other variables. According to the results (given in Table 24.4),[25] Catholics seem to be less motivated by civic duty than non-Catholics. Another interesting finding was the relation between board of education members having children and "goodness" of motivation to become board members. Of the board

[23]N. Gross, W. Mason, and A. McEachern, *Explorations in Role Analysis: Studies of the School Superintendency Role.* New York: Wiley, p. 123.

[24]*Ibid.*, p. 177.

[25]*Ibid.*, p. 199.

TABLE **24.4** RELATION OF RELIGION TO CIVIC MOTIVATION, GROSS, MASON, AND MC EACHERN STUDY (IN PERCENT)

	Motivated by Civic Duty	
	Yes	No
Catholic	49.4	50.6
Non-Catholic	73.1	26.9

members with no children, 27 percent had "good" motivation (as reported by superintendents), whereas of those with children, 48 percent had "good" motivation.[26]

Applications of Survey Research to Education

Despite its evident potential value in helping to solve theoretical and applied educational problems, scientific survey research has not been used to any great extent by educators. Its distinctive educational usefulness, moreover, seems not to have been realized. Therefore this section is devoted to applications of survey research to education and educational problems.

Obviously, survey research is a useful tool for educational fact-finding. An administrator, a board of education, or a staff of teachers can learn a great deal about a school system or a community without contacting every child, every teacher, and every citizen. In short, the sampling methods developed in survey research can be very useful. It is unsatisfactory to depend upon relatively hit-or-miss, so-called representative samples based on "expert" judgments. Nor is it necessary to gather data on whole populations; samples are sufficient for many purposes.

Most research in education is done with relatively small nonrandom samples. If hypotheses are supported, they can later be tested with random samples of populations, and if again supported, the results can be generalized to populations of schools, children, and laymen. In other words, survey research can be used to test hypotheses already tested in more limited situations, with the result that external validity is increased.

School district reorganization is taking place all over the United States. Little reliable and valid information is available on the attitudes of citizens toward this reorganization. It might be profitable to draw random samples of citizens in communities that are entering reorganization discussions. Then, by using the panel method, changes in attitude can be studied as reorganization progresses and the information or misinformation of citizens accurately weighed. Practical information helpful to administrators and boards of education may thus be obtained, not to mention rich possibilities for testing theoretical hypotheses on the subject of change in attitude and information due to public information programs.

Survey research seems ideally suited to the study of integration and its impact on communities and their schools. Interviews of random samples of citizens and

[26]Gross, *Who Runs Our Schools?*, p. 165.

teachers of school districts just starting integration might provide valuable practical information on the fears and anxieties of the citizenry, so that appropriate measures to lessen these fears can be taken. The effect of these measures can also be studied similarly.

Survey research is probably best adapted to obtaining personal and social facts, beliefs, and attitudes. It is significant that, although hundreds of thousands of words are spoken and written about education and about what people presumably think about education, there is little dependable information on the subject. We simply do not know what people's attitudes toward education are. We have to depend on feature writers and so-called experts for this information. Boards of education frequently depend on administrators and local leaders to tell them what the people think. Will they support a bond issue? What would they think about a merger of two or three adjoining districts? How would they react to redistricting in neighborhood school areas to counteract segregation?

Advantages and Disadvantages of Survey Research

Survey research has the advantage of wide scope: a great deal of information can be obtained from a large population. A large population or a large school system can be studied with much less expense than that incurred by a census. While surveys tend to be more expensive than laboratory and field experiments and field studies, for the amount and quality of information they yield they are economical. Furthermore, existing educational facilities and personnel can be used to reduce the costs of the research.

Survey research information is accurate—within sampling error, of course. The accuracy of properly drawn samples is frequently surprising, even to experts in the field. A sample of 600 to 700 individuals or families can give a remarkably accurate portrait of a community—its values, attitudes, and beliefs.

With these advantages go inevitable disadvantages. First, survey information ordinarily does not penetrate very deeply below the surface. The scope of the information sought is usually emphasized at the expense of depth. This seems to be a weakness, however, that is not necessarily inherent in the method. The Gross, Mason, and McEachern and other studies show that it is possible to go considerably below surface opinions. Yet the survey seems best adapted to extensive rather than intensive research. Other types of research are perhaps better adapted to deeper exploration of relations.

A second weakness is a practical one. Survey research is demanding of time and money. In a large survey, it may be months before a single hypothesis can be tested. Sampling and the development of good schedules are major operations. Interviews require skill, time, and money. Surveys on a smaller scale can avoid these problems to some extent, even though it is generally true that survey research demands large investments of time, energy, and money. (When compared to the census, however, surveys are relatively inexpensive, as indicated earlier.)

Any research that uses sampling is naturally subject to sampling error. While it is true that survey information has been found to be relatively accurate, there is always the one chance in twenty or a hundred that an error more serious than might be caused by minor fluctuations of chance may occur. The probability of such an error can be diminished by building safety checks into a study—by comparing census data or other outside information and by sampling the same population independently.

A potential rather than an actual weakness of this method is that the survey interview can temporarily lift the respondent out of his own social context, which may make the results of the survey invalid. The interview is a special event in the ordinary life of the respondent. This apartness may affect the respondent so that he talks to, and interacts with, the interviewer in an unnatural manner. He is not himself, so to speak. For example, a mother, when queried about her child-rearing practices, may give answers that reveal methods she would like to use rather than those she *does* use. It is possible for interviewers to limit the effects of lifting respondents out of social context by skilled handling, especially by one's manner and by careful phrasing and asking of questions.[27]

Survey research also requires a good deal of research knowledge and sophistication. The competent survey investigator must know sampling, question and schedule construction, interviewing, the analysis of data, and other technical aspects of the survey. Such knowledge is hard to come by. Few investigators get this kind and amount of experience. As the value of survey research, both large- and small-scale, becomes appreciated, it can be anticipated that such knowledge and experience will be considered, at least in a minimal way, to be necessary for researchers.

Study Suggestion

Here are some good examples of survey research. Choose one of them and read the first chapter or chapters to get an idea of the problem of the study. Then go to the technical methodological appendix to see how the sampling and interviewing were done. (Most published survey research studies have such appendices.)

Gross and Stouffer studies. (See footnotes 18 and 23.)
Campbell, A., and Schuman, H. *Racial Attitudes in Fifteen American Cities*. Ann Arbor: Institute for Social Research, University of Michigan, 1968.
Free, L., and Cantril, H. *The Political Beliefs of Americans*. New Brunswick, N.J.: Rutgers University Press, 1967.
Glock, C., and Stark, R. *Christian Beliefs and Anti-Semitism*. New York: Harper & Row, 1966.
Hess, R., and Torney, J. *The Development of Political Attitudes in Children*. Chicago: Aldine, 1967.
Kahn, R., et al. *Organizational Stress: Studies in Role Conflict and Ambiguity*. New York: Wiley, 1964.
Sears, R., Maccoby, E., and Levin, H. *Patterns of Child Rearing*. New York: Harper & Row, 1957.
U.S. Commission on Civil Rights. *Racial Isolation in the Public Schools, Appendices*. Washington, D.C.: U.S. Govt. Printing Office, 1967, vol. 2, app. C 5.

[27]E. Maccoby and N. Maccoby, "The Interview: A Tool of Social Science," in G. Lindzey, ed., *Handbook of Social Psychology*, vol. I. Cambridge, Mass.: Addison-Wesley, 1954, pp. 449–481. See, especially, pp. 462–464.

PART 8

Measurement

CHAPTER 25

Foundations of Measurement

"In its broadest sense, measurement is the assignment of numerals to objects or events according to rules."[1] This definition of measurement succinctly expresses the basic nature of measurement. To understand the definition, however, requires the definition and explanation of each important term—a task to which much of this chapter will be devoted.

Suppose that we ask a male judge to stand seven feet away from an attractive young woman. The judge is asked to look at the young woman and then to estimate the degree to which she possesses five attributes: niceness, strength of character, personality, musical ability, and intelligence. The estimate is to be given numerically. In the number system a scale of numbers from 1 through 5 is used, 1 indicating a very small amount of the characteristic in question and 5 indicating a great deal of it. In other words, the judge, just by looking at the young woman, is to assess how "nice" she is, how "strong" her character is, and so on, using the numbers 1, 2, 3, 4, and 5 to indicate the amount of each characteristic she possesses.

This example may be a little ridiculous. Most of us, however, go through much the same procedure all our lives. We often judge how "nice," how "strong," how "intelligent" people are simply by looking at them and talking to them. It only seems silly when it is given as a serious example of measurement. Silly or serious, it *is* an example of measurement, since it satisfies the definition. The judge assigned numerals to objects according to rules. The objects, the numerals, and the rules

[1]S. Stevens, "Mathematics, Measurement, and Psychophysics," in S. Stevens, ed., *Handbook of Experimental Psychology*. New York: Wiley, 1951, p. 1. Campbell first proposed a definition of this nature. One of his definitions is "...the assignment of numbers to represent properties." N. Campbell, *What is Science?* New York: Dover, 1952 (1921), p. 110. Stevens' latest statement is: S. Stevens, "Measurement, Statistics, and the Schemapiric View," *Science*, CLXI (1968), 849–856.

for the assignment of the numerals to the objects were all specified. The numerals were 1, 2, 3, 4, and 5; the objects were the young women; the rules for the assignment of the numerals to the objects were contained in the instructions to the judge. Then the end-product of his work, the numerals, might be used to calculate measures of relation, analyses of variance, and the like.

The definition of measurement includes no statement about the quality of the measurement procedure. It simply says that, somehow, numerals are assigned to objects or to events. The "somehow," naturally, is important—but not to the definition. Measurement is a game we play with objects and numerals. Games have rules. It is, of course, important for other reasons that the rules be "good" rules, but whether the rules are "good" or "bad," the procedure is still measurement.

Why this emphasis on the definition of measurement and on its "rule" quality? There are three reasons. First, measurement, especially psychological and educational measurement, is misunderstood. It is not hard to understand certain measurements used in the natural sciences—length, weight, and volume, for example. Even measures more removed from common sense can be understood without wrenching elementary intuitive notions too much. But to understand that the measurement of such characteristics of individuals and groups as intelligence, aggressiveness, cohesiveness, and anxiety involves *basically and essentially* the same thinking and general procedure is much harder. Indeed, many say it cannot be done. Knowing and understanding that measurement is the assignment of numerals to objects or events by rule, then, helps to erase erroneous and misleading conceptions of psychological and educational measurement.

Second, the definition tells us that, if rules can be set up on some rational or empirical basis, measurement of anything is *theoretically* possible. This greatly widens the scientist's measurement horizons. He will not reject the possibility of measuring some property because the property is complex and elusive. He understands that measurement is a game that he may or may not be able to play with this or that property at this time. But he never rejects the possibility of playing the game, though he may realistically understand its difficulties.

Third, the definition alerts us to the essential neutral core of measurement and measurement procedures and to the necessity for setting up "good" rules, rules whose virtue can be empirically tested. No measurement procedure is any better than its rules. The rules given in the example above were poor. The procedure was a measurement procedure; the definition was satisfied. But it was a poor procedure for reasons that should become apparent later.

Definition of Measurement

To repeat our definition, "measurement is the assignment of numerals to objects or events according to rules." A *numeral* is a symbol of the form: 1, 2, 3, . . . , or I, II, III, ... It has no quantitative meaning unless we give it such a meaning; it is simply a symbol of a special kind. It can be used to label objects, such as baseball players, billiard balls, or individuals drawn in a sample from a universe. We could just as well use the word "symbol" in the definition. It is quite possible, even necessary, to assign symbols to objects or sets of objects according to rules. "Numeral" is used because measurement ordinarily uses numerals which, after being assigned quantitative meaning, become *numbers*. A *number*, then, is a numeral that has been assigned quantitative meaning.

The term "assigned" in the definition means *mapping*. Recall that earlier we talked about mapping the objects of one set onto the objects of another set. A function, *f*, is a rule, a *rule of correspondence*. It is a rule that assigns to each member of one set some one member of another set. The members of the two sets can be any objects at all. In mathematics, the members are generally numbers and algebraic symbols. In research, the members of one set can be individuals, or symbols standing for individuals, and the members of the other set can be numerals or numbers. In most psychological and educational measurement, numerals and numbers are mapped onto, or assigned to, individuals.[2]

The most interesting—and difficult—work of measurement is *the rule*. A *rule* is a guide, a method, a command that tells us what to do. A mathematical rule is *f*, a function; *f* is a rule for assigning the objects of one set to the objects of another set. In measurement a rule might say: "Assign the numerals 1 through 5 to individuals according to how nice they are. If an individual is very, very nice, let the number 5 be assigned to him. If an individual is not at all nice, let the number 1 be assigned. Assign to individuals between these limits numbers between the limits." Another rule is one we have already met a number of times: "If an individual is male, assign him a 1. If an individual is female, assign her a 0." Of course, we would have to have a prior rule or set of rules defining male and female.

Assume that we have a set, A, of five persons, three men and two women: a_1, a_3, and a_4 are men; a_2 and a_5 are women. We wish to "measure" sex. Assuming we have a prior rule that allows us unambiguously to determine sex, we use the rule given in the preceding paragraph: "If a person is male, assign 1; if female, assign 0." Let 0 and 1 be a set. Call it B. Then $B = \{0, 1\}$. The measurement diagram is shown in Fig. 25.1.

This procedure is the same as the one we used in Chapter 5 when discussing relations and functions. Evidently measurement is a relation. Since, to each member of A, the domain, one and only one object of B, the range, is assigned, the relation is a function. Are all measurement procedures functions, then? They are, provided the objects being measured are considered the domain and the numerals being assigned to, or mapped onto them, are considered the range.

Here is another way to bring set, relation-function, and measurement ideas together. Recall that a relation is a set of ordered pairs. So is a function. Any measurement procedure, then, sets up a set of ordered pairs, the first member of each pair being the object measured, and the second member the numeral assigned to the object according to the measurement rule, whatever it is. We can thus write a

[2]Usually, in a mapping, the members of the domain are said to be mapped onto members of the range. In order to preserve consistency with the definition of measurement given above and to be able always to conceive of the measurement procedure as a function, the mapping has been turned around. This conception of mapping, furthermore, is consistent with the earlier definition of a function as a rule that assigns to each member of the domain of a set some one member of the range. The rule tells *how* the pairs are to be ordered.

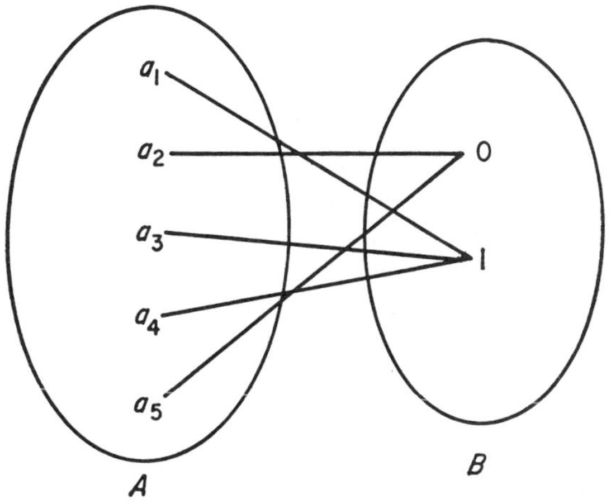

FIG. 25.1

general equation for any measurement procedure:

$$f = \{(x, y); x = \text{any object, and } y = \text{a numeral}\}$$

This is read: "The function, f, or the rule of correspondence, is equal to the set of ordered pairs (x, y) such that x is an object and each corresponding y is a numeral." This is a general rule and will fit any case of measurement.

Let us cite another example to make this discussion more concrete. The events to be measured, the x's, are five children. The numerals, the y's, are the ranks 1, 2, 3, 4, and 5. Assume that f is a rule that instructs a teacher as follows: "Give the rank 1 to the child who has the greatest motivation to do schoolwork. Give the rank 2 to the child who has the next greatest motivation to do schoolwork, and so on to the rank 5 which you should give to the child with the least motivation to do schoolwork." The measurement or the function is shown in Fig. 25.2.

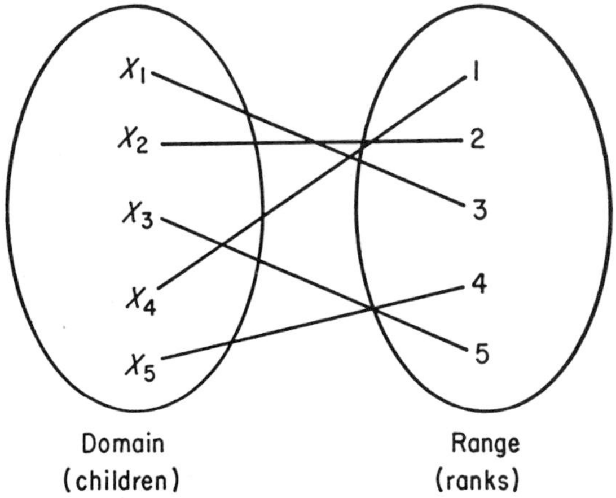

FIG. 25.2

Note that *f*, the rule of correspondence, might have been: "If a child has high motivation for schoolwork, give him a 1, but if a child has low motivation for schoolwork, give him a 0." Then the range becomes {0, 1}. This simply means that the set of five children has been partitioned into two subsets, to each of which will be assigned, by means of *f*, the numerals 0 and 1. A diagram of this would look like Fig. 25.1 with the set *A* being the domain and the set *B* the range.

To return to *rules*. Here is where evaluation comes into the picture. Rules may be "good" or "bad." With "good" rules we have "good," or sound, measurement, other things equal. With "bad" rules we have "bad," or poor, measurement. Many things are easy to measure, because the rules are easy to draw up and follow. To measure sex is easy, for example, since several simple and fairly clear criteria can be used to determine sex and to tell the investigator when to assign 1 and when to assign 0. It is also easy to measure certain other human characteristics: hair color, eye color, height, weight. Unfortunately, most human characteristics are much more difficult to measure, mainly because it is difficult to devise clear rules that are "good." Nonetheless, we must always have rules of some kind in order to measure anything.

Measurement and "Reality" Isomorphism

Measurement can be a meaningless business, as we have seen. How can this be avoided? The definition of sets of objects being measured, the definition of the numerical sets from which we assign numerals to the objects being measured, and the rules of assignment or correspondence have to be tied to "reality." When the hardness of objects is measured, there is little difficulty. If a substance *a* can scratch *b* (and not vice versa), then *a* is harder than *b*. Similarly, if *a* can scratch *b*, and *b* can scratch *c*, then (probably) *a* can scratch *c*. These are empirical matters that are easily tested, so that we can find a rank order of hardness. A set of objects can be measured for its hardness by a few scratch tests, and numerals can be assigned to indicate degrees of hardness. It is said that the measurement procedure and the number system are *isomorphic* to reality.

Isomorphism means identity or similarity of form. The question is asked: Is this set of objects isomorphic to that set of objects? Are the two sets the same or similar in some formal aspect? For example, the two sets of Fig. 25.3 are isomorphic as to cardinal number: they both have *three* members. They both have

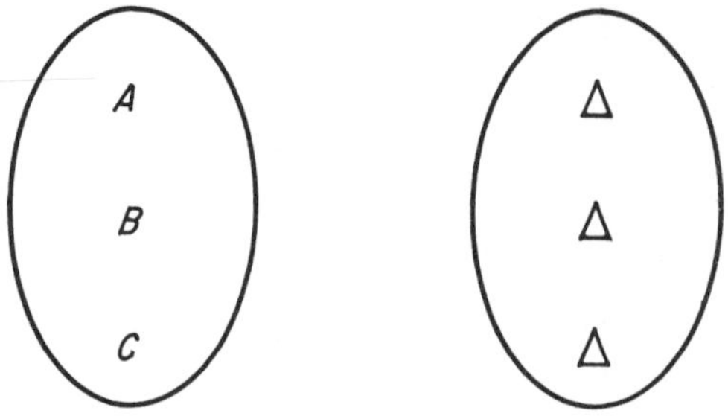

FIG. 25.3

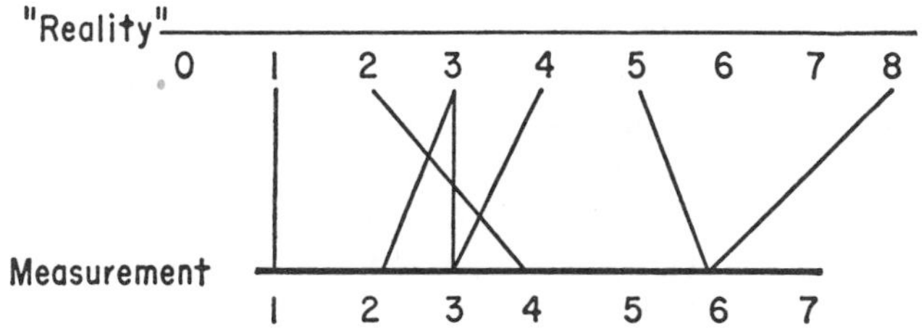

FIG. 25.4

"threeness." In measurement, the question must be asked: Is the measurement game we are playing tied to "reality"? Do the measurement procedures being used have some rational and empirical correspondence with "reality"?

To show the nature of this question of isomorphism, we can again use the idea of the correspondence of sets of objects. We may wish to measure the *persistence* of seven individuals. Suppose, also, that I am an omniscient being. I know the exact amount of persistence each individual possesses, that is, I know the "true" persistence values of each individual. (Assume that *persistence* has been adequately defined.) But *you*, the measurer, do not know these "true" values. It is necessary for you to assess the persistence of the individuals in some fallible way and you think you have found such a way. For instance, you might assess persistence by giving the individuals tasks to perform and noting the total time each individual requires to complete a task, or you might note the total number of times he tries to do a task before he turns to some other activity.[3] You use your method and measure the persistence of the individuals. You come out with, say, the seven values 6, 6, 4, 3, 3, 2, 1. Now I know the "true" values. They are: 8, 5, 2, 4, 3, 3, 1. This set of values is "reality." The correspondence of this set is shown in Fig. 25.4.

In two cases, you have assessed the "true" values exactly. You have "missed" all the others. Only one of these "misses," however, is serious, and there is a fair correspondence between the two rank orders of values. Note, too, that in my omniscience I knew that the "true" values of persistence run from 0 through 8, whereas your measurement system only encompasses 1 through 7.

While this example is a bit fanciful, it does show in a crude way the nature of the isomorphism problem. The ultimate question to be asked of any measurement procedure is: Is the measurement procedure isomorphic to reality? You were not too far off in measuring persistence. The only trouble is that we rarely discover as simply as this the degree of correspondence to "reality" of our measurements. In fact, we often do not even know whether we are measuring what we are trying to measure! Despite this difficulty, the scientist must *test*, in some manner, the isomorphism with "reality" of the measurement numbers game he is playing.

Properties, Constructs, and Indicants of Objects

We say we measure objects, but this is not quite true. We measure the properties, or the characteristics, of these objects. Even this qualification is not quite true,

[3]N. Feather, "The Study of Persistence," *Psychological Bulletin*, LIX (1962), 94.

however. We actually measure *indicants* of the properties of objects, so that when we say we measure objects we are really saying that we measure indicants of the properties of objects. This is generally true of all science, though the properties of some natural objects are much closer to direct observation than others. For instance, the property of sex associated with animal objects is closely tied to direct observation. As soon as relatively simple physical properties are left behind for more complex and elusive properties – which are of much greater interest to social scientists and educators – direct observation of properties is impossible. Hostility cannot be direct observed, nor can morale, anxiety, intelligence, creativeness, and talent. We must always *infer* these properties or characteristics from observation of presumed indicants of the properties.

Indicant is merely a convenient word used to mean something that points to something else. If a boy continually strikes other boys, we *may* say his behavior is an indicant of his underlying hostility. If someone's hands sweat excessively, we *may* say that he is anxious. A child plays a Schubert impromptu beautifully; we say she has "talent." If a child marks a certain number of objective-type items in an achievement test correctly, we say he has a certain level of achievement. In each of these cases, some identifiable behavior is an indicant of an underlying property. Obviously we are on much shakier ground when making such inferences from observed behavior than when directly observing properties like skin color, size, and sex. To measure a child's cooperativeness, dependency, and imaginativeness is very different from measuring his height, weight, or wrist-bone development. The fundamental process of measurement is the same, but the rules are much more difficult to prescribe. Moreover, the observations of the psychological properties are much further removed from the actual properties than are those of the physical properties. This is perhaps the single greatest difficulty of psychological and educational measurement.

The indicants from which properties are inferred are specified by operational definitions, definitions that specify the activities or "operations" necessary to measure variables or constructs. A *construct* is an invented name for a property. Many constructs have been used in previous chapters: authoritarianism, achievement, social class, intelligence, persistence, and so on. Constructs, commonly and somewhat inaccurately called variables, are defined in two general ways in science: by other constructs and by experimental and measurement procedures. These were earlier called constitutive and operational definitions. An operational definition is necessary in order to measure a property or a construct. This is done by specifying the observations of the behavioral indicants of the properties.

Numerals are assigned to the behavioral indicants of the properties. Then, after making observations of the indicants, the numbers (numerals) are substituted for the indicants and analyzed statistically. As an example, consider an investigator who is working on the relation between intelligence and honesty. He operationally defines *intelligence* as scores obtained on the Lorge-Thorndike Intelligence Test. *Honesty* is operationally defined as observations in a contrived situation permitting pupils to cheat or not to cheat. The intelligence numerals assigned to pupils can be the total number of items correct in the test, IQ's, or some other form of score. The honesty numerals assigned to pupils are the number of times they did not cheat when they could have cheated. The two sets of numbers may be correlated or otherwise analyzed. The coefficient of correlation, say, is .55, significant at the .01 level. All this is fairly straightforward and quite familiar. What is not so straightforward and familiar is this: if the investigator draws the conclusion that there is a significant positive relation between intelligence and honesty, he is making a very large inferential leap from behavior indicants in the form of marks on paper and observations of "cheating" behavior to psychological properties. That he may be mistaken should be quite obvious.

Levels of Measurement and Scaling

Classification and Enumeration

The first and most elementary step in any measurement procedure is to define the objects of the universe of discourse. Suppose U, the universal set, is defined as all tenth grade pupils in a certain high school. Next, the properties of the objects of U must be defined. All measurement requires that U be broken down into at least two subsets. The most elementary form of measurement would be to classify or categorize all the objects as possessing or not possessing some characteristic. Say this characteristic is maleness. We break U down into males and nonmales, or males and females. These are of course two *subsets* of U, or a *partitioning* of U. (Recall that partitioning a set consists of breaking it down into subsets that are *mutually exclusive* and *exhaustive*. That is, each set object must be assigned to one subset and one subset only, and all set objects in U must be so assigned.)

What we have done is to classify the objects of interest to us. We have put them into pigeonholes: we have partitioned them. The obvious simplicity of this procedure seems to cause difficulty for students. People spend much of their lives categorizing things, events, and people. Life could not go on without such categorizing, yet to associate the process with measurement seems difficult.

After a method of classification has been found, we have in effect a rule for telling which objects of U go into which classes or subsets or partitions. This rule is used and the set objects are put into the subsets. Here are the boys; here are the girls. Easy. Here are the middle-class children; here are the working-class children. Not as easy, but not too hard. Here are the delinquents; here are the nondelinquents. Harder. Here are the bright ones; here are the average ones; here are the dull ones. Much harder. Here are the creative ones; here are the noncreative ones. Very much harder.

After the objects of the universe have been classified into designated subsets, the members of the sets can be counted. In the dichotomous case, the rule for counting was given in Chapter 4: If a member of U has the characteristic in question, say *maleness*, then assign a 1. If the member does not have the characteristic, then assign a 0. (See Fig. 25.1.) When set members are counted in this fashion, all objects of a subset are considered to be equal to each other and unequal to the members of other subsets.

Measurement Postulates

There are four general levels of measurement: nominal, ordinal, interval, and ratio. These four levels lead to four kinds of scales. Some writers on the subject admit only ordinal, interval, and ratio measurement, while others say that all four belong to the measurement family. We need not be too fussy about this as long as we understand the characteristics of the different scales and levels.[4]

Before discussing the levels themselves, it will be wise to discuss three of the postulates basic to measurement. A *postulate* is an assumption that is an essential prerequisite to carrying out some operation or line of thinking. In this case, it is an assumption about the relations between the objects being measured. Although postulates are usually assumed to be true, in measurement it is necessary to test the postulates whenever possible. More than three postulates are really necessary in order to make it possible to equate objects, to rank order them, and to add them.[5]

The three postulates can be written:

1. Either $(a = b)$ or $(a \neq b)$, but not both
2. If $[(a = b)$ and $(b = c)]$, then $(a = c)$
3. If $[(a > b)$ and $(b > c)]$, then $(a > c)$

The first postulate says: "*a* is either equal to *b* or not equal to *b*, but not both." This postulate is necessary for classification. We must be able to assert either that one object is the same in a characteristic as another or that it is not the same. In measurement "the same" does not necessarily mean complete identify. It can mean "sufficiently the same to be classed as members of the same set." Two boys are the "same" in maleness, though it is conceivable that one boy may actually be more masculine than another. And the two boys certainly differ in many other characteristics. To be able to say "the two are the same," we must have a criterion or a set of criteria. If we wish to assign boys to social class categories, we might use the criterion of father's occupation and/or residence. The criterion must be sufficiently unambiguous to make classification possible, that is, to satisfy the condition the postulate states.

The second postulate says "If *a* equals *b*, and *b* equals *c*, then *a* equals *c*." If one member of a universe is the same as another member, and this second member

[4]The Stevens' position and definition of measurement cited earlier is a broad view that is followed in this text. A considerably more restrictive—yet defensible—position is that of Jones (and others) who requires that differences between measures be interpretable as *quantitative differences in the property measured.* "Quantitative," in the view of some experts, means that differences in magnitude between two attribute values must represent a corresponding quantitative difference in the attribute. L. Jones, "The Nature of Measurement." In R. Thorndike, ed., *Educational Measurement,* 2d ed. Washington, D.C.: American Council on Education, 1971, pp. 335–355. This view, strictly speaking, rules out, *as measurement,* nominal and ordinal scales. I believe that actual measurement experience in the behavioral sciences and education justifies the Stevens position. Again, it does not matter terribly, provided the student *understands* the general ideas being presented. I recommend that the more advanced student read Torgerson's and Nunnally's fine presentations: W. Torgerson, *Theory and Methods of Scaling.* New York: Wiley, 1958, chaps. 1 and 2; J. Nunnally, *Psychometric Theory.* New York: McGraw-Hill, 1967, chap. 1.

[5]See J. Guilford, *Psychometric Methods,* 2d ed. New York: McGraw-Hill, 1954, pp. 11–12. Some of the discussion that follows is based in part on Guilford and on the Stevens reference cited earlier.

is the same as a third member, then the first member is the same as the third member. This postulate enables a researcher to establish the equality of set members on a characteristic by comparing objects. More important, if the postulate is satisfied, objects not ordinarily amenable to observation may be assigned to subsets of a universe. For example, suppose we wish to assign individuals to two categories, "prejudiced" and "unprejudiced." Consider one such individual. We know that all or most members of the association he belongs to are prejudiced. We may therefore feel safe in assigning him and others like him to the category "prejudiced." Or we may be able to assign him to the category "prejudiced" on the basis of his response to another measuring instrument which is highly correlated with a prejudice measuring instrument.

The third postulate is of more immediate and practical importance for our purposes. It says, "If *a* is greater than *b*, and *b* is greater than *c*, then *a* is greater than *c*." This is the *transitivity* postulate. (So is 2 a transitivity postulate.) Other symbols or words can be substituted for "greater than" (">"), "less than" ("<"), "is at a greater distance than," "is stronger than," "precedes," "dominates," and so on. Most measurement in psychology and education depends on this postulate. It must be possible to assert ordinal- or rank-order statements like "*a* has more of a property than *b*; *b* has more of the property than *c*; therefore *a* has more of the property than *c*."

The preceding statements may seem obvious. It is easy and even justifiable to make many such statements, but not always. We cannot always take it for granted that the postulate is satisfied. In fact Coombs says that it is remarkably difficult to find examples of simple orders among social psychological variables.[6] In physical measurements the postulate is often satisfied: if stick *a* is longer than stick *b*, and stick *b* is longer than stick *c*, then stick *a* must be longer than stick *c*. If student *a* has more items right on a test than student *b*, and student *b* has more right than student *c*, student *a* must have more right than student *c*. But take the relation *dominance*: *a* may dominate *b* and *b* may dominate *c*, but it is possible that *a* does not dominate *c*. A wife may dominate her husband, and the husband may dominate the child, but the child may dominate his mother (the wife). If an investigator is studying dominance relations, he cannot simply assume that the postulate is correct. He must demonstrate that it is correct. To disabuse oneself of the notion that transitivity is obvious, think about the relations "loves," "likes," "is a friend of," or "accepts."

Nominal Measurement

The rules used to assign numerals to objects define the kind of scale and the level of measurement. The lowest level of measurement is *nominal* measurement (see earlier discussion of categorization). The numbers assigned to objects are numerical without having a number meaning; they cannot be ordered or added. They are *labels* much like the letters used to label sets. If individuals or groups are assigned 1, 2, 3, . . . , these numerals are merely names. For example, baseball and football

[6]C. Coombs, "Theory and Methods of Social Measurement," In L. Festinger and D. Katz, eds., *Research Methods in the Behavioral Sciences*. New York: Holt, Rinehart and Winston, 1953, p. 477.

players are assigned such numbers. Telephones are assigned such numbers. Groups may be given the labels I, II, and III or A_1, A_2, and A_3. We use nominal measurement in our everyday thinking and living. We identify others as "men," "women," "Protestants," "Australians," and so on. At any rate, the symbols assigned to objects, or rather, to the sets of objects, constitute nominal scales. Some experts think this is not measurement, as indicated previously. Such exclusion of nominal measurement would prevent much social scientific research procedure from being called measurement. Since the definition of measurement is satisfied, and since the members of labeled sets can be counted and compared, it would seem that nominal procedures *are* measurement.

The requirements of nominal measurement are simple. All the members of a set are assigned the same numeral and no two sets are assigned the same numeral. Postulates 1 and 2 have to be satisfied. We must know when objects are or are not equal. In psychological, sociological, and educational measurement, however, the "equal" should be enclosed in quotation marks. We mean "*approximately* equal," because of the complexity of human behavior, the fallibility of human judgment and response, and the usual errors of measurement.

Nominal measurement—at least in one simple form—was expressed in Fig. 25.1, where the objects of the range, $\{0, 1\}$, were mapped onto the a's, the objects of U, the five people, by the rule: If x is male, assign 1; if x is female, assign 0. This is how nominal measurement is quantified when only a dichotomy is involved. When the partition contains more than two categories, some other method must be used. Basically, nominal measurement quantification amounts to counting the objects in the cells of the subsets or partitions.

Ordinal Measurement

Ordinal measurement requires, as we saw earlier, that the objects of a set can be rank-ordered on an operationally defined characteristic or property. If the ordinal transitivity postulate is justified, then ordinal measurement is possible. That is, if we have three objects, a, b, and c, and a is greater than b, and b is greater than c; and if we can justifiably say, also, that a is greater than c, then the main condition for ordinal measurement is satisfied.

The procedure can be generalized in three ways. One, any number of objects of any kind can be measured ordinally simply by extension to $a, b, c, \ldots, n$. (Even though two objects may sometimes be equal, ordinal measurement is still possible.) We simply need to be able to say $a > b > c > \cdots > n$ on some property.

The second extension consists of using combined properties or combined criteria. Instead of using only one property, we can use two or more. For example, instead of ranking a group of college students on academic achievement by grade-point averages, we may wish to rank them on the combined criteria of grade-point average and test scores. (Grade-point averages, too, are composite scores.)

The third extension is accomplished by using criteria other than "greater than." "Less than" occurs to us immediately. "Precedes," "is above," and "is superior to" may be useful criteria. In fact, we might substitute a symbol other than "$>$" or "$<$." One such symbol is "$\circ$." It can be used to mean any operation, such as those just named, in which the transivity postulate is satisfied: $a \circ b$ might mean "a precedes b," or "a is subordinate to b," and $a \circ b \circ c$ might mean "a is superior to b, b is superior to c, and a is superior to c."

The numerals assigned to ranked objects are called *rank values*. Let R equal the set of *ranked objects:* $R = \{a > b > \cdots > n\}$. Let R^* equal the set of *rank values:* $R^* = \{1, 2, \ldots, n\}$. We assign the objects of R^* to the objects of R as follows: the largest object is assigned 1, the next in size 2, and so on to the smallest object which is assigned the last numeral in the particular series. If this procedure is used, the rank values assigned are in the reverse order. If, for instance, there are five objects, with a the largest, b the next, through e, the smallest, then:

Objects	R	R^*
a	1	5
b	2	4
c	3	3
d	4	2
e	5	1

Of course, one step can be skipped by assigning R^* directly: by assigning 5 to a, 4 to b, through 1 to e.

Ordinal numbers indicate rank order and nothing more. The numbers do not indicate absolute quantities, nor do they indicate that the intervals between the numbers are equal. For instance, it cannot be assumed that because the *numerals* are equally spaced the underlying properties they represent are equally spaced. If two subjects have the ranks 8 and 5 and two other subjects the ranks 6 and 3, we cannot say that the differences between the first and second pairs are equal. There is also no way to know that any individual has *none* of the property being measured. Rank-order scales are not equal-interval scales, nor do they have absolute zero points.

Interval Measurement (Scales)

Interval or *equal-interval* scales possess the characteristics of nominal and ordinal scales, especially the rank-order characteristic. In addition, numerically equal distances on interval scales represent equal distances in the property being measured. Thus, suppose that we had measured four objects on an interval scale and gotten the values 8, 6, 5, and 3. Then we can legitimately say that the difference between the first and third objects in the property measured, $8-5=3$, is equal to the difference between the second and fourth objects, $6-3=3$. Another way to express the equal-interval idea is to say that the *intervals* can be added and subtracted. An interval scale is assumed as follows:

a	b	c	d	e
1	2	3	4	5

The interval from a to c is $3-1=2$. The interval from c to d is $4-3=1$. We can add these two intervals $(3-1)+(4-3)=2+1=3$. Now note that the interval from a to d is $4-1=3$. Expressed in an equation: $(d-a)=(c-a)+(d-c)$. If these intervals were five pupils measured on an interval scale of achievement, then the differences in achievement between pupils a and c and between b and d would be equal. We could not say, however, that the achievement of d was twice as great as that of pupil b. (Such a statement would require one higher level of measurement.) Note that it is not *quantities* or *amounts* that are added and subtracted. It is *intervals* or *distances*.

Ratio Measurement (Scales)

The highest level of measurement is *ratio measurement*, and the measurement ideal of the scientist is the ratio scale. A ratio scale, in addition to possessing the characteristics of nominal, ordinal, and interval scales, has an absolute or natural zero that has empirical meaning. If a measurement is zero on a ratio scale, then there is a basis for saying that some object has none of the property being measured. Since there is an absolute or natural zero, all arithmetic operations are possible, including multiplication and division. Numbers on the scale indicate the actual amounts of the property being measured. If a ratio scale of achievement existed, then it would be possible to say that a pupil with a scale score of 8 has an achievement twice as great as a pupil with a scale score of 4.

Comparisons of Scales: Practical Considerations and Statistics

The basic characteristics of the four types of measurement and their accompanying scales have been discussed. What kinds of scales are used in behavioral and educational research? Mostly nominal and ordinal are used, though the probability is good that many scales and tests used in psychological and educational measurement approximate interval measurement well enough for practical purposes, as we shall see.

First, consider nominal measurement. When objects are partitioned into two, three, or more categories on the basis of group membership—sex, ethnic identification, married-single, Protestant-Catholic-Jew, and so forth—measurement is nominal. When continuous variables are converted to attributes, as when objects are divided into high-low and old-young, we have what can be called quasi-nominal measurement: although capable of at least rank order, the values are in effect collapsed to 1 and 0.

It is instructive to study the numerical operations and statistics that are, in a strict sense, legitimate and permissible with each type of measurement. With nominal measurement the counting of numbers of cases in each category and subcategory is, of course, permissible. Frequency statistics like χ^2, percentages, and certain coefficients of correlation (contingency coefficients) can be used. This sounds thin. Actually, it is a good deal. A good principle to remember is this: If one cannot use any other method, one can almost always partition or cross-partition subjects. If we are studying the relation between two variables and do not have any way to measure them adequately in an ordinal or interval fashion, some way can probably be found to divide the objects of study into at least two groups. For example, in studying the relation between the motivation of board of education members to become board members and their religion, as Gross and his colleagues did, we may be able to have knowledgeable judges divide the sample of board members into those with "good" motivation and those with "poor" motivation. Then we can cross-partition religion with the motivation dichotomy and thus study the relation.

Intelligence, aptitude, and personality test scores are, *basically and strictly speaking*, ordinal. They indicate with more or less accuracy not the *amounts* of intelligence, aptitude, and personality traits of individuals, but rather the *rank-order positions* of the individuals. To see this, we must realize that ordinal scales do not possess the desirable characteristics of equal intervals or absolute zeroes. Intelligence test scores are examples. It is not possible to say that an individual has zero intelligence. If he is alive, he must have some score above zero. But there is no absolute zero on an intelligence test scale. The zero is arbitrary, and without an absolute zero, addition of *amounts* of intelligence has little meaning, for arbitrary zero points can lead to different sums. On a scale with an arbitrary zero point the following addition is performed: $2+3=5$. Then the sum is 5 scale units above zero. But if the arbitrary zero point is inaccurate and the "real" zero point is at the scale position 4 scale points lower than the arbitrary zero position, then the former 2 and 3 should really be 6 and 7, and $6+7=13$!

The lack of a real zero in ordinal scales is not as serious as the lack of equal intervals. Even without a real zero, *distances* within a scale can be added, provided that these distances are equal (empirically). The situation might be somewhat as indicated in Fig. 25.5. The scale on the top ("true" scale) indicates the "true" values of a variable. The bottom scale (ordinal scale) indicates the rank-order scale used by an investigator. In other words, an investigator has rank-ordered seven persons quite well, but his ordinal numerals, which *look* equal in interval, are not "true," although they may be fairly accurate representations of the empirical facts.

Strictly speaking, the statistics that can be used with ordinal scales include rank-order measures such as the rank-order coefficient of correlation, ρ, Kendall's W, and rank-order analysis of variance, medians, and percentiles. If only these statistics (and others like them) are legitimate, how can statistics like r, t, and F be used with what are in effect ordinal measures? And they are so used, without a qualm by most researchers.

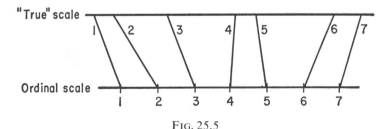

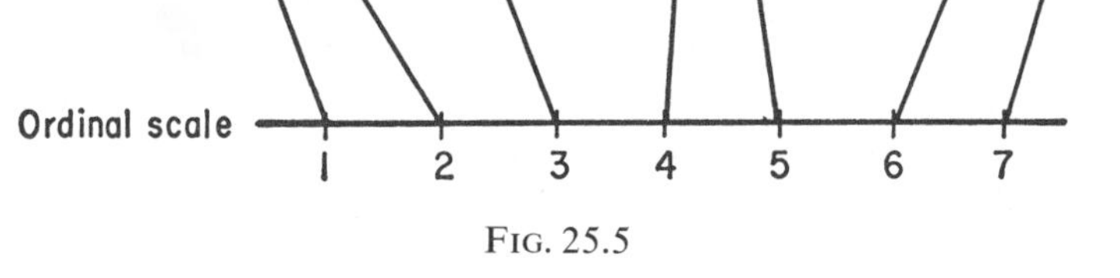

FIG. 25.5

Although this is a moot point, the situation is not as difficult as it seems. As Torgerson points out, some types of natural origin have been devised for certain types of measurement.[7] In measuring preferences and attitudes, for example, the neutral points (on either side of which are degrees of positive and negative favoring, approving, liking, and preferring) can be considered natural origins. Besides, ratio scales, while desirable, are not absolutely necessary because most of what we need to do in psychological measurement can be done with equal-interval scales.

The lack of equal intervals is more serious since distances *within* a scale theoretically cannot be added without interval equality. Yet, though most psychological scales are basically ordinal, we can with considerable assurance often assume equality of interval. The argument is evidential. If we have, say, two or three measures of the same variable, and these measures are all substantially and linearly related, then equal intervals can be assumed. This assumption is valid because the more nearly a relation approaches linearity, the more nearly equal are the intervals of the scales. This also applies, at least to some extent, to certain psychological measures like intelligence, achievement, and attitude tests and scales.

A related argument is that many of the methods of analysis we use work quite well with most psychological scales. That is, the results we get from using scales and assuming equal intervals are quite satisfactory.

The point of view adopted in this book is, then, a pragmatic one, that the assumption of interval equality works. Still, we are faced with a dilemma: if we use ordinal measures as though they were interval or ratio measures, we *can* err in interpreting data and the relations inferred from data, though the danger is probably not as grave as it has been made out to be. There is no trouble with the numbers, as numbers. *They* do not know the difference between ρ and r or between parametric and nonparametric statistics, nor do they know the assumptions behind their use. But *we* do, or should, know the differences and the consequences of ignoring the differences. On the other hand, if we abide strictly by the rules, we cut off powerful modes of measurement and analyses and are left with tools inadequate to cope with the problems we want to solve.

What is the answer, the resolution of the conflict? Part of the answer was given above: it is probable that most psychological and educational scales approximate interval equality fairly well. In those situations in which there is serious doubt as to interval equality, there are technical means for coping with some of the problems. The competent research worker should know something of scaling methods and certain transformations that change ordinal scales into interval scales.[8]

In the state of measurement at present, we cannot be sure that our measurement instruments have equal intervals. It is important to ask the question: How serious are the distortions and errors introduced by treating ordinal measurements as though they were interval measurements? With care in the construction of

[7]Torgerson, *op. cit.*, p. 30.

[8]M. Bartlett, "The Use of Transformations," *Biometrics*, III (1947), 39–52. (See, especially, pp. 49–50.) Guilford, *op. cit.*, chaps. 8 and 9.

measuring instruments, and especially with care in the interpretation of the results, the consequences are evidently not serious.

The best procedure would seem to be to treat ordinal measurements as though they were interval measurements, but to be constantly alert to the possibility of *gross* inequality of intervals. As much as possible about the characteristics of the measuring tools should be learned. Above all, we need to be particularly careful with the interpretation of ordinal data to which statistical analysis suitable for interval measurement has been applied. Much useful information has been obtained by this approach, with resulting scientific advances in psychology, sociology, and education. In short, it is unlikely that the educational researcher will be seriously led astray by heeding this advice, if he is knowledgeable and careful in applying it.

Guilford has expressed the matter aptly. He says that psychologists have rarely hesitated to apply the statistics that assume interval-scale measurement to ordinal-scale data. He even says that there is little awareness of the interval-scale assumption. Then, comfortingly, he adds:

> . . . experimental data often approach the condition of equal units sufficiently well that there is tolerable error in applying the various statistics that call for them. This is one of those occasions for making use of approximations, even gross ones, in order that one may extract the most information from his data. This is often justified on the basis of evidence of the internal consistency of the findings and the validity of the outcomes. This does not excuse the investigator, however, from being on the alert for intolerable approximations and for results and conclusions that are essentially a function of his faulty application of statistics.[9]

(*Note:* Study suggestions for the three chapters of Part 8 appear at the end of Chapter 27.)

[9]Guilford, *op. cit.*, pp. 15–16. See, also, C. Boneau, "A Note on Measurement Scales and Statistical Tests," *American Psychologist*, XVI (1961), 260–261; N. Anderson, "Scales and Statistics: Parametric and Nonparametric," *Psychological Bulletin*, LVIII (1961), 305–316; F. Lord, "Further Comments on 'Football Numbers,'" *American Psychologist*, IX (1954), 264–265. An excellent analysis of the problem of measurement scales in actual research is: Nunnally, *op. cit.*, pp. 20–30.

CHAPTER 26

Reliability

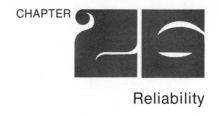

After assigning numerals to objects or events according to rules, an investigator must face the two major problems of reliability and validity. He has devised his measurement game and has administered the measuring instrument to a group of subjects. He has a set of numbers, the end product of the measurement game. He must now ask and answer the questions: What is the reliability of the measuring instrument? What is its validity?

If one does not know the reliability and validity of one's data little faith can be put in the results obtained and the conclusions drawn from the results. The data of the social sciences and education, derived from human behavior and human products, are, as we saw in the last chapter, several steps removed from the properties of scientific interest. Thus they may constitute a major threat to validity. Concern for reliability comes from the necessity for dependability in measurement. The data of all psychological and educational measurement instruments contain errors of measurement. To the extent that they do so, to that extent the data they yield will not be dependable.

Definitions of Reliability

Synonyms for reliability are: dependability, stability, consistency, predictability, accuracy. A reliable man, for instance, is a man whose behavior is consistent, dependable, and predictable—what he will do tomorrow and next week will be consistent with what he does today and what he has done last week. We say he is stable. An unreliable man, on the other hand, is one whose behavior is much more variable. More important, he is unpredictably variable. Sometimes he does this, sometimes that. He lacks stability. We say he is inconsistent.

So it is with psychological and educational measurements: they are more or less variable from occasion to occasion. They are stable and relatively predictable or they are unstable and relatively unpredictable; they are consistent or not consistent. If they are reliable, we can depend upon them. If they are unreliable, we cannot depend upon them.

It is possible to approach the definition of reliability in three ways. One approach is epitomized by the question: If we measure the same set of objects again and again with the same or comparable measuring instrument, will we get the same or similar results? This question implies a definition of reliability in *stability, dependability, predictability* terms. It is the definition most often given in elementary discussions of the subject.

A second approach is epitomized by the question: Are the measures obtained from a measuring instrument the "true" measures of the property measured? This is an *accuracy* definition. Compared to the first definition, it is further removed from common sense and intuition, but it is also more fundamental. These two approaches or definitions can be summarized in the words *stability* and *accuracy*. As we will see later, however, the accuracy definition implies the stability definition.

There is a third approach to the definition of reliability, an approach that not only helps us better define and solve both theoretical and practical problems but also implies other approaches and definitions. We can inquire how much *error of measurement* there is in a measuring instrument. Recall that there are two general types of variance: systematic and random. *Systematic variance* leans in one direction: scores tend to be all positive or all negative or all high or all low. Error in this case is constant or biased. *Random* or *error variance* is self-compensating: scores tend now to lean this way, now that way. Errors of measurement are random errors. They are the sum or product of a number of causes: the ordinary random or chance elements present in all measures due to unknown causes, temporary or momentary fatigue, fortuitous conditions at a particular time that temporarily affect the object measured or the measuring instrument, fluctuations of memory or mood, and other factors that are temporary and shifting. To the extent that errors of measurement are present in a measuring instrument, to this extent the instrument is unreliable. In other words, reliability can be defined as the relative absence of errors of measurement in a measuring instrument.

Reliability is the *accuracy* or *precision* of a measuring instrument. A homely example can easily show what is meant. Suppose a sportsman wishes to compare the accuracy of two guns. One is an old piece made a century ago but still in good condition. The other is a modern weapon made by an expert gunsmith. Both pieces are solidly fixed in granite bases and aimed and zeroed in by a sharpshooter. Equal numbers of rounds are fired with each gun. In Fig. 26.1, the hypothetical pattern of shots on a target for each gun is shown. The target on the left represents the pattern of shots produced by the older gun. Observe that the shots are considerably scattered. Now observe that the pattern of shots on the target on the right is more closely packed. The shots are closely clustered around the bull's-eye.

Let us assume that numbers have been assigned to the circles of the targets: 3 to the bull's-eye, 2 to the next circle, 1 to the outside circle, and 0 to any shot

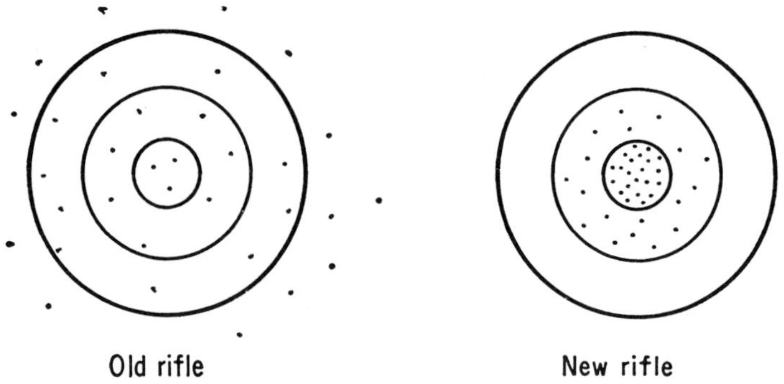

FIG. 26.1

outside the target. It is obvious that if we calculated measures of variability, say a standard deviation, from the two shot patterns, the old rifle would have a much larger measure of variability than the newer rifle. These measures can be considered reliability indices. The smaller variability measure of the new rifle indicates much less error, and thus much greater accuracy. The new rifle is reliable; the old rifle is unreliable.

Similarly, psychological and educational measurements have greater and lesser reliabilities. A measuring instrument, say an arithmetic achievement test, is given to a group of children—usually only once. Our goal, of course, is a multiple one: we seek to hit the "true" score of each child. To the extent that we miss the "true" scores, to this extent our measuring instrument, our test, is unreliable. The "true," the "real," arithmetic scores of five children, say, are 35, 31, 29, 22, 14. Another researcher does not know these "true" scores. His results are: 37, 30, 26, 24, 15. While he has not in a single case hit the "true" score, he has achieved the same rank order. His reliability and accuracy are surprisingly high.

Suppose that his five scores had been: 24, 37, 26, 15, 30. These are the same five scores, but they have a very different rank order. In this case, the test would be unreliable, because of its inaccuracy. To show all this more compactly, the three sets of scores, with their rank orders, have been set beside each other in Table 26.1. The rank orders of the first and second columns covary exactly. The

TABLE **26.1** "TRUE," RELIABLE, AND UNRELIABLE OBTAINED TEST SCORES AND RANK ORDERS OF FIVE CHILDREN

1 "True" Scores	(Rank)	2 Scores from Reliable Test	(Rank)	3 Scores from Unreliable Test	(Rank)
35	(1)	37	(1)	24	(4)
31	(2)	30	(2)	37	(1)
29	(3)	26	(3)	26	(3)
22	(4)	24	(4)	15	(5)
14	(5)	15	(5)	30	(2)

rank-order coefficient of correlation is 1.00. Even though the test scores of the second column are not the exact scores, they *are* in the same rank order. On this basis, using a rank-order coefficient of correlation, the test is reliable. The rank-order coefficient of correlation between the ranks of the first and third columns, however, is zero, so that the latter test is completely unreliable.

Theory of Reliability

The example given in Table 26.1 epitomizes what we need to know about reliability.[1] It is necessary, now, to formalize the intuitive notions and to outline a theory of reliability. This theory is not only conceptually elegant; it is also practically powerful. It helps to unify measurement ideas and supplies a foundation for understanding various analytic techniques. The theory also ties in nicely with the variance approach emphasized in earlier discussions.

Any set of measures has a total variance, that is, after administering an instrument to a set of objects and obtaining a set of numbers (scores), we can calculate a mean, a standard deviation, and a variance. Let us be concerned here only with the variance. The variance, as seen earlier, is a *total obtained variance*, since it includes variances due to several causes. In general, any total obtained variance (or sum of squares) includes systematic and error variances.

Each person has an obtained score, X_t. (The "t" stands for "total.") This score has two components: a "true" component and an error component. We assume that each person has a "true" score, X_∞. (The "∞" is the infinity sign, and is used to signify "true.") This score would be known only to an omniscient being.[2] In addition to this "true" score, each person has an error score, X_e. The error score is some increment or decrement resulting from several of the factors responsible for errors of measurement.

This reasoning leads to a simple equation basic to the theory:

$$X_t = X_\infty + X_e \qquad (26.1)$$

which says, succinctly, that any obtained score is made of two components, a "true" component and an error component. The only part of this definition that gives any real trouble is X_∞, which can be conceived to be the score an individual would obtain if all internal and external conditions were "perfect" and the measuring instrument were "perfect." A bit more realistically, it can be considered to be

[1]The treatment of reliability in this chapter is based on traditional error theory. See J. Guilford, *Psychometric Methods*, 2d ed. New York: McGraw-Hill, 1954, chaps. 13 and 14. While this theory has been shown to have unnecessary assumptions, it is admirably suited to conveying to the beginning student the basic nature of reliability. For a penetrating criticism of the theory, see R. Tryon, "Reliability and Behavior Domain Validity: Reformulation and Historical Critique," *Psychological Bulletin*, LIV (1957), 229–249. In practice, the two approaches arrive at much the same formulas. The most recent development of reliability theory and practice, called generalizability theory, emphasizes multivariate (or multifacet) thinking, components of variance analysis, and decision making. An extended discussion of the theory is given in: L. Cronbach et al., *The Dependability of Behavioral Measurements: Theory of Generalizability for Scores and Profiles*. New York: Wiley, 1972.

[2]This does not mean that X_∞ may not include properties other than the property being measured. All *systematic* variance is included in X_∞. The problem of measuring *the* property is a validity problem.

the mean of a large number of administrations of the test to the same person. Symbolically, $X_\infty = (X_1 + X_2 + \cdots + X_n)/n$.

With a little simple algebra, Eq. 26.1 can be extended to yield a more useful equation in variance terms:

$$V_t = V_\infty + V_e \tag{26.2}$$

Eq. 26.2 shows that the total obtained variance of a test is made up of two variance components, a "true" component and an "error" component. If, for example, it were possible to administer the same instrument to the same group 4,367,929 times, and then to calculate the means of each person's 4,367,929 scores, we would have a set of "nearly true" measures of the group. In other words, these means are the X_∞'s of the group. We could then calculate the variance of the X_∞'s yielding V_∞. This value must always be less than V_t, the variance calculated from the obtained set of original scores, the X_t's, because the original scores contain error, whereas the "true," or "nearly true," scores have no error, the error having been washed out by the averaging process. Put differently, if there were no errors of measurement in the X_t's, then $V_t = V_\infty$. But, there are always errors of measurement, and we assume that if we knew the error scores and subtracted them from the obtained scores we would obtain the "true" scores.

We never know the "true" scores nor do we really ever know the error scores. Nevertheless, it is possible to estimate the error variance. By so doing, we can, in effect, substitute in Eq. 26.2 and solve the equation. This is the essence of the idea, even though certain assumptions and steps have been omitted from the discussion. A diagram or two may show the ideas more clearly. Let the total variances of two tests be represented by two bars. One test is highly reliable; the other test only moderately so, as shown in Fig. 26.2. Tests A and B have the same total variance, but 90 percent of Test A is "true" variance and 10 percent is error variance. Only 60 percent of Test B is "true" variance and 40 percent is error variance. Test A is thus much more reliable than Test B.

Reliability is defined, so to speak, through error: the more error, the greater the unreliability; the less error, the greater the reliability. Practically speaking, this means that if we can estimate the error variance of a measure we can also estimate the measure's reliability. This brings us to two equivalent definitions of reliability:

1. Reliability is the proportion of the "true" variance to the total obtained variance of the data yielded by a measuring instrument.
2. Reliability is the proportion of error variance to the total obtained variance yielded by a measuring instrument subtracted from 1.00, the index 1.00 indicating perfect reliability.

It is easier to write these definitions in equation form:

$$r_{tt} = \frac{V_\infty}{V_t} \tag{26.3}$$

$$r_{tt} = 1 - \frac{V_e}{V_t} \tag{26.4}$$

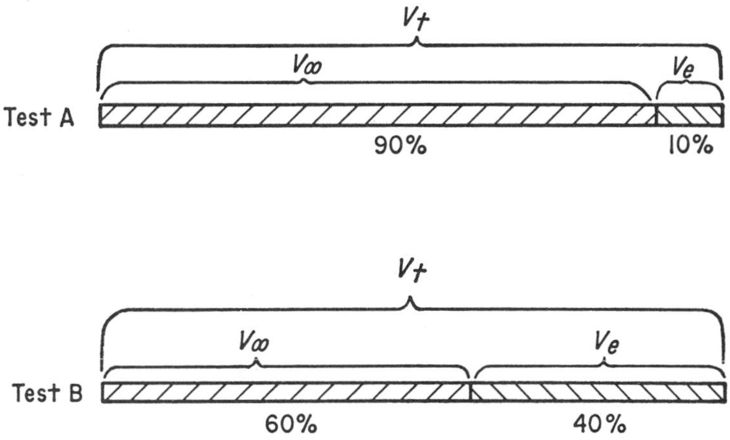

FIG. 26.2

where r_{tt} is the reliability coefficient and the other symbols are as defined before. Eq. 26.3 is theoretical and cannot be used for calculation. Eq. 26.4 is both theoretical and practical. It can be used both to conceptualize the idea of reliability and to estimate the reliability of an instrument. An alternate equation to (26.4) is:

$$r_{tt} = \frac{V_t - V_e}{V_t} \tag{26.5}$$

This alternative definition of reliability will be useful in helping us to understand what reliability is.

Two Computational Examples

To show the nature of reliability, two examples are given in Table 26.2. One of them, labeled I in the table, is an example of high reliability; the other, labeled II, is an example of low reliability. Note carefully that exactly the same numbers are used in both cases. The only difference is that they are arranged differently. The situation in both cases is this: five individuals have been administered a test of four items. (This is unrealistic, of course, but it will do to illustrate several points.) The data of the five individuals are given in the rows; the sums of the individuals are given to the right of the rows (Σ_t). The sums of the items are given at the bottom of each table (Σ_{it}). In addition, the sums of the individuals on the odd items (Σ_o) and the sums of the individuals on the even items (Σ_e) are given on the extreme right of each subtable. The calculations necessary for two-way analyses of variance are given below the data tables.

To make the examples more realistic, imagine that the data are scores on a six-point scale, say attitudes toward school. A high score means a high favorable attitude, a low score a low favorable (or unfavorable) attitude. (It makes no difference, however, what the scores are. They can even be 1's and 0's resulting from marking items of an achievement test: right = 1, and wrong = 0.) In I, Individual 1 has a high favorable attitude toward school, whereas Individual 5 has a low

TABLE **26.2** DEMONSTRATION OF RELIABILITY AND COMPUTATION OF RELIABILITY COEFFICIENTS. HYPOTHETICAL EXAMPLES

I: $r_{tt} = .92$

Individuals	Items a	b	c	d	Σ_t	Σ_o	Σ_e
1	6	6	5	4	21	11	10
2	4	6	5	3	18	9	9
3	4	4	4	2	14	8	6
4	3	1	4	2	10	7	3
5	1	2	1	1	5	2	3
Σ_{it}	18	19	19	12	$\Sigma X_t = 68$ $(\Sigma X_t)^2 = 4624$ $\Sigma X_t^2 = 288$		

$$C = \frac{(68)^2}{20} = 231.20$$

$$\text{Total} = 288 - 231.20 = \mathit{56.80}$$

$$\text{Between Items} = \frac{1190}{5} - 231.20 = \mathit{6.80}$$

$$\text{Between Individuals} = \frac{1086}{4} - 231.20 = \mathit{40.30}$$

II: $r_{tt} = .45$

Individuals	Items a	b	c	d	Σ_t	Σ_o	Σ_e
1	6	4	5	1	16	11	5
2	4	1	5	4	14	9	5
3	4	6	4	2	16	8	8
4	3	6	4	3	16	7	9
5	1	2	1	2	6	2	4
Σ_{it}	18	19	19	12	$\Sigma X_t = 68$ $(\Sigma X_t)^2 = 4624$ $\Sigma X_t^2 = 288$		

$$C = 231.20$$

$$\text{Total} = \mathit{56.80}$$

$$\text{Between Items} = \mathit{6.80}$$

$$\text{Between Individuals} = \frac{1000}{4} - 231.20 = \mathit{18.80}$$

Source	*df*	*s.s.*	*m.s.*	*F*
Items	3	6.80	2.27	2.80 (*n.s.*)
Individuals	4	40.30	(10.08)	12.44 (.001)
Residual	12	9.70	(.81)	
Total	19	56.80		

Source	*df*	*s.s.*	*m.s.*	*F*
Items	3	6.80	2.27	1 (*n.s.*)
Individuals	4	18.80	(4.70)	1.81 (*n.s.*)
Residual	12	31.20	(2.60)	
Total	19	56.80		

By Eq. 26.4:

$$r_{tt} = 1 - \frac{V_e}{V_{\text{ind}}} = 1 - \frac{.81}{10.08} = .92$$

$$r_{tt} = 1 - \frac{2.60}{4.70} = .45$$

By Eq. 26.5:

$$r_{u} = \frac{V_{\text{ind}} - V_e}{V_{\text{ind}}} = \frac{10.08 - .81}{10.08} = .92$$

$$r_{tt} = \frac{4.70 - 2.60}{4.70} = .45$$

Odd-Even:

$$r_{oe} = .91$$

$$r_{oe} = .32$$

favorable attitude toward school. These are readily indicated by the sums of the individuals (or the means): 21 and 5. These sums (Σ_t) are the usual scores yielded by tests. For instance, if we wanted to know the mean of the group, we would calculate it as $(21+18+14+10+5)/5 = 13.60$.

The variance of these sums provides one of the terms of Eqs. 26.4 and 26.5, but not the other: V_t, but not V_e. By using the analysis of variance it is possible to calculate both V_t and V_e. The analyses of variance of I and II show how this is done. These calculations need not detain us long, since they are subsidiary to the main issue.

The analysis of variance yields the variances: Between items, Between individuals, and Residual or Error. The F ratios for Items are not significant in I or II. (Note that both mean squares are 2.27. Obviously they must be equal, since they are calculated from the same sums at the bottoms of the two subtables.) Actually, we are not interested in these variances—we only want to remove the variance due to items from the total variance. Our interest lies in the Individual variances and in the Error variances, which are circled in the subtables. The total variance of Eqs. 26.3, 26.4, and 26.5 is interesting because it is an index of differences between individuals. It is a measure of individual differences. Instead of writing V_t, then, let us write V_{ind}, meaning the variance resulting from individual differences. By using either (26.4) or (26.5), we obtain reliability coefficients of .92 for the data of I and .45 for the data of II. The hypothetical data of I are reliable; those of II are not reliable.

Perhaps the best way to understand this is to go back to Eq. 26.3. Now we write $r_{tt} = V_\infty / V_{\text{ind}}$. If we had a direct way to calculate V_∞, we could quickly calculate r_{tt}, but as we saw before, we do not have a direct way. There *is* a way to estimate it, however. If we can find a way to estimate V_e, the error variance, the problem is solved because V_e can be subtracted from V_{ind} to yield an estimate of V_∞. Obviously we can ignore V_∞ and subtract the proportion V_e/V_{ind} from 1 and get r_{tt}. This is a perfectly acceptable way to calculate r_{tt} and to conceptualize reliability. Reasoning from $V_{\text{ind}} - V_e$ is perhaps more fruitful and ties in nicely with our earlier discussion of components of variance.

It was said in Chapter 13 that each statistical problem has a total amount of variance and each variance source contributes to this total variance. We translate the reasoning of Chapter 13 to the present problem. In random samples of the same population, V_b and V_w should be statistically equal. But, if V_b, the between-groups variance, is significantly greater than V_w, the within-groups (error) variance, then there is something in V_b over and above chance. That is, V_b includes the variance of V_w and, in addition, some systematic variance.

Similarly, we can say that if V_{ind} is significantly greater than V_e, then there is something in V_{ind} over and above error variance. This excess of variance would seem to be due to individual differences in whatever is being measured. Measurement aims at the "true" scores of individuals. The only way that we can know that this aim is accomplished is by learning the "true" *differences* between individuals. When we say that reliability is the accuracy of a measuring instrument, we mean that a reliable instrument more or less measures the "true" scores of individuals, the "more or less" depending on the reliability of the instrument. That "true" scores are measured can be inferred only from the "true" *differences* between individuals, although neither of these can be directly measured, of course. What we do is to infer the "true" differences from the fallible, empirical, measured differences, which are always to some extent corrupted by errors of measurement.

Now, if there is some way to remove from V_{ind} the effect of errors of measurement, some way to free V_{ind} of error, we can solve the problem easily. We simply subtract V_e from V_{ind} to get an estimate of V_∞. Then the proportion of the "pure" variance to all the variance, "pure" and "impure," is the estimate of the reliability of the measuring instrument. To summarize symbolically:

$$r_{tt} = \frac{V_\infty}{V_{\text{ind}}} = \frac{V_{\text{ind}} - V_e}{V_{\text{ind}}} = 1 - \frac{V_e}{V_{\text{ind}}}$$

The actual calculations are given at the bottom of Table 26.2.

Returning to the data of Table 26.2, let us see if we can "see" the reliability of I and the unreliability of II. Look first at the columns where the totals of the individuals are recorded (Σ_t). Notice that the sums of I have a greater range than those of II: $21-5=16$ and $16-6=10$. Given the same individuals, the more reliable a measure the greater the range of the sums of the individuals. Think of the extreme: a completely unreliable instrument would yield sums that are like the sums yielded by random numbers, and, of course, the reliability of random numbers is approximately zero. (The nonsignificant F ratio for Individuals, 1.81, in II indicates that $r_{tt} = .45$ is not significant.)

Now examine the rank orders of the values under the items, *a*, *b*, *c*, and *d*. In I, all four rank orders are about the same. Each item of the attitude scale, apparently, is measuring the same thing. To the extent that the individual items yield the same rank orders of individuals, to this extent the test is reliable. The items hang together, so to speak. They are internally consistent. Also, notice that the rank orders of the items of I are about the same as the rank order of the sums.

The rank order of the values under the items in II is a different case. The rank orders of *a* and *c* agree very well; they are the same as those of I. The rank orders of *a* and *b*, *a* and *d*, *b* and *d*, and *c* and *d*, however, do not agree very well. Either the items are measuring different things, or they are not measuring very consistently. This lack of congruence of rank orders is reflected in the totals of the individuals. Although the rank order of these totals is similar to the rank order of the totals of I, the range or variance is considerably less, and there is lack of spread between the sums (for example, the three 16's).

We conclude our consideration of these two examples by considering certain figures in Table 26.2 not considered before. On the right-hand side of both I and II the sums of the odd items (Σ_o) and the sums of the even items (Σ_e) are given. Simply add the values of odd items across the rows: $a+c: 6+5=11$, $4+5=9$, $4+4=8$, and so forth, in I. Then add the values of the even items: $b+d: 6+4=10$, $6+3=9$, and so forth, in I also. If there were more items, for example, *a*, *b*, *c*, *d*, *e*, *f*, *g*, then we would add: $a+c+e+g$ for the odd sums, and $b+d+f$ for the even sums. To calculate the reliability coefficient, calculate the product-moment correlation between the odd sums and the even sums, and then correct the resulting coefficient with the Spearman-Brown formula.[3] The odd-even r_{tt}'s for I and II are .91 and .32, respectively, fairly close to the analysis of variance results of .92 and .45. (With more subjects and more items, the estimates will ordinarily be close.)

This simple operation may seem mystifying. To see that this is a variation of the same variance and rank-order theme, let us note, first, the rank order of the sums of the two examples. The rank orders of Σ_o and Σ_e are almost the same in I, but quite different in II. The reasoning is the same as before. Evidently the items are measuring the same thing in I, but in II the two sets of items are not consistent. To reconstruct the variance argument, simply remember that by adding the sum of the odd items to the sum of the even items for each person the total sum, or $\Sigma_o + \Sigma_e = \Sigma_t$, can be obtained.

The Interpretation of the Reliability Coefficient

If r, the coefficient of correlation, is squared, it becomes a coefficient of determination, that is, it gives us the proportion or percentage of the variance shared by two variables. If $r = .90$, then the two variables share $(.90)^2 = 81$ percent of the total variance of the two variables in common. The reliability coefficient is also a coefficient of determination. Theoretically, it tells how much variance of the total variance of a measured variable is "true" variance. If we had the "true" scores and could correlate them with the scores of the measured variable and square the resulting coefficient of correlation, we would obtain the reliability coefficient.

Symbolic representation may make this clear. Let $r_{t\infty}$ be the coefficient of correlation between the obtained scores and the "true" scores, X_∞. The reliability coefficient is defined:

$$r_{tt} = r_{t\infty}^2 \tag{26.6}$$

Although it is not possible to calculate $r_{t\infty}$ directly, it is helpful to understand the rationale of the reliability coefficient in these theoretical terms.

Another theoretical interpretation is to conceive that each X_∞ can be the mean of a large number of X_t's derived from administering the test to an individual a large number of times, other things being equal.[4] The idea behind this notion has been explained before. The first administration of the test yields, say, a certain rank order of individuals. If the second, third, and further measurings all tend to yield approximately the same rank order, then the test is reliable. This is a stability or *test-retest* interpretation of reliability.

Another interpretation is that reliability is the *internal consistency* of a test: the test items are homogeneous. This interpretation in effect boils down to the

[3]See any measurement text, for example, Guilford, *op. cit.*, p. 354. The sums of the odd and the sums of the even items are, of course, the sums of only half the items in a test. They are therefore less reliable than the sums of all the items. The Spearman-Brown formula corrects the odd-even coefficient (and other part coefficients) for the lesser number of items used in calculating the coefficient.

[4]*Ibid.*, p. 349.

same idea as other interpretations: accuracy. Take any random sample of items from the test, and any other random and different sample of items from the test. Treat each sample as a separate subtest. Each individual will then have two scores: one X_t for one subsample and another X_t for the other subsample. Correlate the two sets, continuing the process indefinitely. The average intercorrelation of the subsamples (corrected by the Spearman-Brown formula) shows the test's internal consistency.[5] But this means, really, that each subsample, if the test is reliable, succeeds in producing approximately the same rank order of individuals. If it does not, the test is not reliable.

The Standard Error of the Mean and the Standard Error of Measurement

Two important aspects of reliability are the reliability of means and the reliability of individual measures. These are tied to the standard error of the mean and the standard error of measurement. In research studies, ordinarily, the standard error of the mean—and related statistics like the standard error of the differences between means and the standard error of a correlation coefficient—is the more important of these. Since the standard error of the mean was discussed in considerable detail in an earlier chapter, it is only necessary to say here that the reliability of specific statistics is another aspect of the general problem of reliability. The standard error of measurement, or its square, the standard variance of measurement, needs to be defined and identified, if only briefly. This will be done through use of a simple example.

An investigator measures the attitudes of five individuals and obtains the scores given under the column labeled X_t in Table 26.3. Assume, further, that the "true" attitude scores of the five individuals are those given under the column labeled X_∞. (Remember, however, that we can never know these scores.) It can be seen that the instrument is reliable. While only one of the five obtained scores is exactly the same as its companion "true" score, the differences between those obtained scores that are not the same and the "true" scores are all small. These differences are shown under the column labeled "X_e"; they are "error scores." The instrument is evidently fairly accurate. The calculation of r_{tt} confirms this impression: .71.

A rather direct measure of the reliability of the instrument can be obtained by calculating the variance or the standard deviation of the error scores (X_e). The variance of the error scores and the variances of the X_t and X_∞ scores have been calculated and entered in Table 26.3. The variance of the error scores we now label, justifiably, *the standard variance of measurement*, which might more accur-

[5]See L. Cronbach, "Coefficient Alpha and the Internal Structure of Tests," *Psychometrika*, XVI (1951), 297–334; Tryon, *op. cit.* The formulas given by Cronbach and Tryon look different from Eqs. 26.3 and 26.4. They yield the same results, however. The originator of the use of the analysis of variance to estimate reliability seems to have been Hoyt. See C. Hoyt, "Test Reliability Obtained by Analysis of Variance," *Psychometrika*, VI (1941), 153–160. Ebel extended the use of analysis of variance to ratings and stressed the use of the intraclass coefficient of correlation: R. Ebel, "Estimation of the Reliability of Ratings," *Psychometrika*, XVI (1951), 407–424.

TABLE **26.3** HYPOTHETICAL RELIABILITY AND STANDARD ERROR OF MEASUREMENT EXAMPLE

	X_t	X_∞	X_e
	2	1	1
	1	2	−1
	3	3	0
	3	4	−1
	6	5	1
Σ:	15	15	0
M:	3	3	0
V:	2.80	2.00	.80

$$r_{tt} = 1 - \frac{V_e}{V_t} = 1 - \frac{.80}{2.80} = .71 \qquad r_{t\infty} = .845$$

$$r_{tt} = \frac{V_\infty}{V_t} = \frac{2.00}{2.80} = .71 \qquad r_{tt} = r^2_{t\infty} = (.845)^2 = .71$$

$$SV_{\text{meas}} = V_t(1 - r_{tt}) = 2.80(1 - .71) = .81$$

$$SE_{\text{meas}} = SD_t\sqrt{1 - r_{tt}} = \sqrt{SV_{\text{meas}}} = \sqrt{.81} = .90$$

ately be called "the standard variance of errors of measurement." The square root of this statistic is called the *standard error of measurement*. The standard variance of measurement is defined:

$$SV_{\text{meas}} = V_t(1 - r_{tt}) \qquad (26.7)$$

This statistic can only be calculated, obviously, if we know the reliability coefficient. Note that if there is some way to estimate SV_{meas}, then it is possible to calculate the reliability coefficient. This bears further investigation.

We start with the definition of reliability given earlier: $r_{tt} = V_\infty/V_t = 1 - V_e/V_t$. A little algebraic manipulation yields the standard variance of measurement:

$$r_{tt} = 1 - \frac{V_e}{V_t}$$

$$r_{tt}V_t = V_t - V_e$$

$$V_e = V_t - r_{tt}V_t$$

$$V_e = V_t(1 - r_{tt})$$

The right side of the equation is the same as the right side of Eq. 26.7. Therefore $V_e = SV_{\text{meas}}$, or the error variance used earlier in the analysis of variance, *is* the standard variance of measurement. The standard variance of measurement and the standard error of measurement of the example have been calculated in Table

26.3. They are .81 and .90, respectively. As textbooks of measurement show, they can be used to interpret individual test scores. Such interpretation will not be discussed here; these statistics have been included only to show the connection between the original theory and ways of determining reliability.

One more calculation in Table 26.3 needs explanation. If we correlate the X_t and the X_∞ scores, we obtain a coefficient of correlation of .845. Now we obtain this coefficient, $r_{t\infty}$, directly, and square it to obtain the reliability coefficient. (See Eq. 26.6.) The latter, of course, is the same as before: .71.[6]

The Improvement of Reliability

The principle behind the improvement of reliability is the one previously called the *maxmincon principle*—in a slightly different form: "Maximize the variance of the individual differences and minimize the error variance." Equation 26.4 clearly indicates the principle. The general procedure follows.

First, write the items of psychological and educational measuring instruments unambiguously. An ambiguous event can be interpreted in more than one way. An ambiguous item permits error variance to creep in because individuals can interpret the item differently. Such interpretations tend to be random, and hence they increase error variance and decrease reliability.

Second, if an instrument is not reliable enough, add more items of equal kind and quality. This will usually, though not necessarily, increase reliability by a predictable amount. Adding more items increases the probability that any individual's X_t is close to his X_∞. This is a matter of the sampling of the property or the item space. With few items, a chance error, an essentially random response, looms large. With more items, it looms less large. The probability of its being balanced by another random error the other way is greater when there are more items. Summarily, more items increase the probability of accurate measurement. (Remember that each X_t is the sum of the item values for an individual.

Third, clear and standard instructions tend to reduce errors of measurement. Great care must always be taken, in writing the instructions, to state them clearly. Ambiguous instructions increase the error variance. Further, measuring instruments should always be administered under standard, well-controlled, and similar conditions. If the situations of administration differ, error variance can again intrude.

The Value of Reliability

To be interpretable, a test must be reliable. Unless one can depend upon the results of the measurement of one's variables, one cannot, with any confidence,

[6]It would be useful for the student to plot the X_t and X_∞ values of the little example of Table 26.3. On each side of an "average" line (regression line) drawn through the center of the points draw one standard error of measurement. Use the same unit of measurement that is used on the two axes. Note that all the points lie within, or not far outside, these lines. The space enclosed by the two outside lines might be called a "reliability space."

determine the relations between the variables. One goal of science, again, is to discover the relations among variables. Since unreliable measurement is measurement overloaded with error, the discovery of these relations becomes a difficult and tenuous business. Is an obtained coefficient of correlation between two variables low because one or both measures are unreliable? Is an analysis of variance *F* ratio nct significant because the hypothesized relation does not exist or because the measure of the dependent variables is too crude, too unreliable?

Reliability, while not the most important facet of measurement, is still extremely important. In a way, this is like the money problem: the lack of it is the real problem. High reliability is no guarantee of good scientific results, but there can be no good scientific results without reliability. In brief, reliability is a necessary but not sufficient condition of the value of research results and their interpretation.

CHAPTER 27

Validity

The subject of validity is complex, controversial, and peculiarly important in behavioral research. Here perhaps more than anywhere else, the nature of reality is questioned. It is possible to study reliability without inquiring into the meaning of variables. It is not possible to study validity, however, without sooner or later inquiring into the nature and meaning of one's variables.

When measuring certain physical properties and relatively simple attributes of persons, validity is no great problem. There is often rather direct and close congruence between the nature of the object measured and the measuring instrument. The length of an object, for example, can be measured by laying off sticks, containing a standard number system in feet or meters, on the object. Weight is more indirect, but nevertheless not difficult: an object placed in a container displaces the container downward. The downward movement of the container is registered on a calibrated index, which reads "pounds" or "ounces." With some physical attributes, then, there is little doubt of what is being measured.

On the other hand, suppose an educational scientist wishes to study the relation between intelligence and school achievement or the relation between authoritarianism and teaching style. Now there are no rulers to use, no scales with which to weigh the degree of authoritarianism, no clear-cut physical or behavioral attributes that point unmistakably to teaching style. It is necessary in such cases to invent indirect means to measure psychological and educational properties. These means are often so indirect that the validity of the measurement and its products is doubtful.

Types of Validity

The commonest definition of validity is epitomized by the question: Are we measuring what we think we are measuring? The emphasis in this question is on *what* is being measured. For example, a teacher has constructed a test to measure *understanding* of scientific procedures and has included in the test only *factual* items about scientific procedures. The test is not valid, because while it may reliably measure the pupils' *factual knowledge* of scientific procedures, it does not measure their *understanding* of such procedures. In other words, it may measure what it measures quite well, but it does not measure what the teacher intended it to measure.

Although the commonest definition of validity was given above, it must immediately be emphasized that there is no one validity. A test or scale is valid for the scientific or practical purpose of its user. An educator may be interested in the *nature* of high school pupils' achievement in mathematics. He would then be interested in *what* a mathematics achievement or aptitude test measures. He might, for instance, want to know the factors that enter into mathematics test performance and their relative weights in this performance. On the other hand, he may be primarily interested in knowing the pupils who will probably be successful and those who will probably be unsuccessful in high school mathematics. He may have little interest in *what* a mathematics aptitude test measures. He is interested mainly in successful *prediction*. Implied by these two uses of tests are different kinds of validity. We now examine an extremely important development in test theory: the analysis and study of different kinds of validity.

The most important classification of types of validity is that prepared by a joint committee of the American Psychological Association, the American Educational Research Association, and the National Council on Measurements Used in Education.[1] Three types of validity are discussed: *content*, *criterion-related*, and *construct*. Each of these will be examined briefly, though we put the greatest emphasis on construct validity, since it is probably the most important form of validity from the scientific research point of view.

Content Validity and Content Validation

A university psychology professor has given a course to seniors in which he has emphasized the understanding of principles of human development. He prepares an objective-type test. Wanting to know something of its validity, he critically examines each of the test's items for their relevance to understanding principles of human development. He also asks two colleagues to evaluate the content of the test. Naturally, he tells the colleagues what it is he is trying to measure. He is investigating the *content validity* of the test.

[1] *Standards for Educational and Psychological Tests and Manuals*. Washington, D.C.: American Psychological Association, 1966. An important article that explains in detail the system and thinking of the committee in relation to validity is: L. Cronbach and P. Meehl, "Construct Validity of Psychological Tests," *Psychological Bulletin*, LII (1955), 281–302. A detailed and definitive more recent statement is: L. Cronbach, "Test Validation." In R. Thorndike, ed., *Educational Measurement*, 2d ed. Washington, D.C.: American Council on Education, 1971, pp. 443–507.

Content validity is the *representativeness* or *sampling adequacy* of the content—the substance, the matter, the topics—of a measuring instrument.[2] *Content validation* is guided by the question: Is the substance or content of this measure representative of the content or the universe of content of the property being measured? Any psychological or educational property has a theoretical universe of content consisting of all the things that can possibly be said or observed about the property. The members of this universe, U, can be called items. The property might be "arithmetic achievement," to take a relatively easy example. U has an infinite number of members: all possible items using numbers, arithmetic operations, and concepts. A test high in content validity would theoretically be a representative sample of U. If it were possible to draw items from U at random in sufficient numbers, then any such sample of items would presumably form a test high in content validity. If U consists of subsets A, B, and C, which are arithmetic operations, arithmetic concepts, and number manipulation, respectively, then any sufficiently large sample of U would represent A, B, and C approximately equally. The test's content validity would be satisfactory.

Ordinarily, and unfortunately, it is not possible to draw random samples of items from a universe of content. Such universes exist only theoretically. True, it is possible and desirable to assemble large collections of items, especially in the achievement area, and to draw random samples from the collections for testing purposes. But the content validity of such collections, no matter how large and how "good" the items, is always in question.

If it is not possible to satisfy the definition of content validity, how can a reasonable degree of content validity be achieved? Content validation consists essentially in *judgment*. Alone or with others, one judges the representativeness of the items. One may ask: Does this item measure Property M? To express it more fully one might ask: Is this item representative of the universe of content of M? If U has subsets, such as those indicated above, then one has to ask additional questions; for example: Is this item a member of the subset M_1 or the subset M_2?

Some universes of content are more obvious and much easier to judge than others; the content of many achievement tests, for instance, would seem to be obvious. The content validity of these tests, it is said, can be assumed. While this statement seems reasonable, and while the content of most achievement tests is "self-validated" in the sense that the individual writing the test to a degree defines the property being measured (for example, a teacher writing a classroom test of spelling or arithmetic), it is dangerous to assume the adequacy of content validity without systematic efforts to check the assumption. For example, an educational investigator, testing hypotheses about the relations between social studies achievement and other variables, may assume the content validity of his social studies test. The theory from which the investigator derived his hypotheses,

[2] *Standards*, *op. cit.*, pp. 12–13. Two other definitions of content validity can be found in R. Ebel, "Obtaining and Reporting Evidence on Content Validity," *Educational and Psychological Measurement*, XVI (1956), 269–282; R. Lennon, "Assumptions Underlying the Use of Content Validity," *ibid.*, pp. 294–304. The first of these articles stresses the ultimate goals of instruction; the second, like the definition in the text above, is more pertinent to research, because it stresses the representativeness of the sampling of *subjects' responses* to a measurement instrument.

however, may require an *understanding* and *application* of social studies ideas, whereas the test he used may be almost purely factual in content. His test lacks content validity for his purpose. In fact, he is not really testing the hypotheses he thinks he is testing.

Content validation, then, is basically judgmental. The items of a test must be studied, each item being weighed for its presumed representativeness of the universe. This means that each item must be judged for its presumed relevance to the property being measured, which is no easy task. Usually other "competent" judges should judge the content of the items. The universe of content must, if possible, be clearly defined; that is, the judges must be furnished with specific directions for making judgments, as well as with specification of what they are judging. Then, some method for pooling independent judgments can be used.[3]

Criterion-Related Validity and Validation

As the unfortunately clumsy name indicates, *criterion-related validity* is studied by comparing test or scale scores with one or more external variables, or criteria, known or believed to measure the attribute under study.[4] When one predicts success or failure of students from academic aptitude measures, one is concerned with criterion-related validity. How well does the test (or tests) predict to graduation or to grade-point average?[5] One does not care so much *what* the test measures as one cares for its predictive ability. In fact, in criterion-related validation, which is often practical and applied research, the basic interest is usually more in the criterion, some practical outcome, than in the predictors. (In basic research this is not so.) The higher the correlation between a measure or measures of academic aptitude and the criterion, say grade-point average, the better the validity. In short and again, the emphasis is on the criterion and its prediction.[6]

The word *prediction* is usually associated with the future. This is unfortunate because, in science, prediction does not necessarily mean *forecast*. Margenau points out that "pre-" implies "prior to completed knowledge" and does not contrast with "post-."[7] One "predicts" from an independent variable to a dependent variable. One "predicts" the existence or nonexistence of a relation; one even "predicts" something that happened in the past! This broad meaning of prediction

[3]An excellent guide to the content validity of achievement tests is: B. Bloom et al., *Taxonomy of Educational Objectives. Handbook I: Cognitive Domain.* New York: David McKay, 1956. This is a comprehensive attempt to outline and discuss educational goals in relation to measurement. A companion volume that extends the work to affective educational goals—values, attitudes, satisfactions, etc.—is: D. Krathwohl et al., *Taxonomy of Educational Objectives. Handbook II: Affective Domains.* New York: David McKay, 1964.

[4]See *Standards, op. cit.*, p. 13.

[5]Criterion-related validity used to be called *predictive validity.* (It was also called *empirical validity,* because validity is primarily evaluated statistically.) A related term is *concurrent validity,* which differs from predictive validity in the time dimension: the criterion is measured at about the same time as the predictor. In this sense, the test serves to assess the present status of individuals.

[6]For a discussion of desirable qualities of a criterion, see R. Thorndike and E. Hagen, *Measurement and Evaluation in Psychology and Education,* 3d ed. New York: Wiley, 1969, pp. 168–169. They are: relevance, freedom from bias, reliability, and availability. See, also, A. Astin, "Criterion-Related Research," *Educational and Psychological Measurement,* XXIV (1964), 807–822.

[7]H. Margenau, *The Nature of Physical Reality.* New York: McGraw-Hill, 1950, p. 105, footnote.

is the one intended here. In any case, criterion-related validity is characterized by prediction to an *outside* criterion and by checking a measuring instrument, either now or in the future, against some outcome or measure. In a sense, all tests are predictive; they "predict" a certain kind of outcome, some present or future state of affairs. Aptitude tests predict future achievement; achievement tests predict present and future achievement and competence; and intelligence tests predict present and future ability to learn and to solve problems. Even if we measure self-concept, we predict that if the self-concept score is so-and-so, then the individual will be such-and-such now or in the future.

The single greatest difficulty of criterion-related validation is the criterion. Obtaining criteria may even be difficult. What criterion can be used to validate a measure of teacher effectiveness? Who is to judge teacher effectiveness? What criterion can be used to test the predictive validity of a musical aptitude test?

Decision Aspects of Validity

Criterion-related validity, as indicated earlier, is ordinarily associated with practical problems and outcomes. Interest is not so much in what is behind test performance as it is in helping to solve practical problems and to make decisions. Tests are used by the hundreds for the predictive purposes of screening and selecting potentially successful candidates in education, business, and other occupations. Cronbach has particularly stressed the decision aspects of criterion-related validation.[8] Does a test, or a set of tests, materially aid in deciding on the assignment of individuals to jobs, classes, schools, and the like? Any decision is a choice among treatments, assignments, or programs, as Cronbach points out. "To make a decision, one predicts the person's success under each treatment and uses a rule to translate the prediction into an assignment."[9] A test high in criterion-related validity is one that helps investigators make successful decisions in assigning people to treatments, conceiving treatments broadly. An admissions committee or administrator decides to admit or not admit an applicant to college on the basis of a test of academic aptitude. Obviously such use of tests is highly important, and the tests' predictive validity is also highly important. The reader is referred to Cronbach's essay for a good exposition of the decision aspects of tests and validity.

Multiple Predictors and Criteria

Both multiple predictors and multiple criteria can be and are used. In Part 10, when we study multiple regression, we will focus on multiple predictors and how to handle them statistically. Multiple criteria can be handled separately or together, though it is not easy to do the latter. In practical research, a decision must usually be made. If there is more than one criterion, how can we best combine them for decision-making? The relative importance of the criteria, of course, must be considered. Do we want an administrator high in problem-solving ability, high in public relations ability, or both? Which is more important in the particular

[8]Cronbach, *op. cit.*, pp. 484 ff.
[9]*Ibid.*, p. 484.

job?[10] It is highly likely that the use of both multiple predictors and multiple criteria will become common as multivariate methods become better understood and the computer is used routinely in prediction research.

Construct Validity and Construct Validation

Scientifically speaking, construct validity is one of the most significant advances of modern measurement theory and practice. It is a significant advance because it unites psychometric notions with theoretical notions.

The measurement expert, when he inquires into the construct validity of a test, usually wants to know what psychological or other property or properties can "explain" the variance of the test. He wishes to know the "meaning" of the test. If the test is an intelligence test, he may want to know what factors lie behind test performance. He asks: What factors or constructs account for variance in test performance?[11] He may specifically ask: Does this test measure verbal ability and abstract reasoning ability? Does it also "measure" social class membership? He is asking what proportion of the total test variance is accounted for by the constructs: verbal ability, abstract reasoning ability, and social class membership. In short, he seeks to *explain* individual differences in the test scores of a measuring instrument. His interest is usually more in the property being measured than in the test itself.

A researcher generally starts with the constructs or variables entering into the relations. He has discovered, say, a positive correlation between two measures, one a measure of educational traditionalism and the other a measure of the perception of the characteristics associated with the "good" teacher. Individuals high on the traditionalism measure see the "good" teacher as efficient, moral, thorough, industrious, conscientious, and reliable. Individuals low on the traditionalism measure may see the "good" teacher in a different way. The researcher now wants to know *why* this relation exists, what is behind it. To learn why, he must know the meaning of the constructs entering the relation, "perception of the 'good' teacher" and "traditionalism." *How* he can study these meanings is a construct validity problem.[12]

One can see that construct validation and empirical scientific inquiry are closely allied. It is not simply a question of validating a test. One must try to validate the theory behind the test. Cronbach says that there are three parts to construct validation: suggesting what constructs possibly account for test performance, deriving hypotheses from the theory involving the construct, and testing the hypotheses empirically.[13] This formulation is but a précis of the general scientific approach discussed in Part 1.

The significant point about construct validity, that which sets it apart from other types of validity, is its preoccupation with theory, theoretical constructs,

[10] *Ibid.*, pp. 489 ff.

[11] Cronbach and Meehl, *op. cit.*, p. 282.

[12] This example was taken from the following research: F. Kerlinger and E. Pedhazur, "Educational Attitudes and Perceptions of Desirable Traits of Teachers," *American Educational Research Journal*, V (1968), 543–560.

[13] L. Cronbach, *Essentials of Psychological Testing*, 3d ed. New York: Harper & Row, 1970, p. 143.

and scientific empirical inquiry involving the testing of hypothesized relations. Construct validation in measurement contrasts sharply with empirical approaches that define the validity of a measure purely by its success in predicting a criterion. For example, a purely empirical tester might say that a test is valid if it efficiently distinguishes individuals high and low in a trait. *Why* the test succeeds in separating the subsets of a group is of no great concern. It is enough that it does.

Convergence and Discriminability

Note that the testing of alternative hypotheses is particularly important in construct validation because both convergence and discriminability are required. *Convergence* means that evidence from different sources gathered in different ways all indicates the same or similar meaning of the construct. Different methods of measurement should converge on the construct. The evidence yielded by administering the measuring instrument to different groups in different places should yield similar meanings or, if not, should account for differences. A measure of the self-concept of children, for instance, should be capable of similar interpretation in different parts of the country. If it is not capable of such interpretation in some locality, the theory should be able to explain why—indeed, it should predict such a difference.

Discriminability means that one can empirically differentiate the construct from other constructs that may be similar, and that one can point out what is *unrelated* to the construct. We point out, in other words, what other variables are correlated with the construct and how they are so correlated. But we also indicate what variables should be uncorrelated with the construct. We point out, for example, that a scale to measure conservatism should and does correlate substantially with measures of authoritarianism and rigidity—the theory predicts this—but not with measures of social desirability.[14] Let us illustrate these ideas.

A Hypothetical Example of Construct Validation

Let us assume that an investigator is interested in the determinants of creativity and the relation of creativity to school achievement. He notices that the most sociable persons, who exhibit affection for others, also seem to be less creative than those who are less sociable and affectionate. He wants to test the implied relation in a controlled fashion. One of his first tasks is to obtain or construct a measure of the sociable-affectionate characteristic. The investigator, surmising that this combination of traits may be a reflection of a deeper concern or love for others, calls it amorism. He assumes that there are individual differences in amorism, that some people have a great deal of it, others a moderate amount, and still others very little.

He must first construct an instrument to measure amorism. The literature gives him little help, since scientific psychologists have rarely investigated the fundamental nature of love. Sociability, however, has been measured. The inves-

[14]See F. Kerlinger, "A Social Attitude Scale: Evidence on Reliability and Validity," *Psychological Reports*, XXVI (1970), 379–383.

tigator must construct a *new* instrument, basing its content on his intuitive and reasoned notions of what amorism is. The reliability of the test, tried out with large groups, runs between .75 and .85.

The question now is whether or not the test is valid. The investigator correlates the instrument, calling it the *A* scale, with independent measures of sociability. The correlations are moderately substantial, but he needs evidence that the test has construct validity. He deduces certain relations that should and should not exist between amorism and other variables. He reasons that if amorism is a general tendency to love others, then it should correlate with characteristics like cooperativeness and friendliness. Persons high in amorism, he also believes, will approach problems in an ego-oriented manner as contrasted to persons low in amorism, who will approach problems in a task-oriented manner.

Acting on this reasoning, the investigator administers the *A* scale and a scale to measure subjectivity to a number of sixth-grade students. To measure cooperativeness he observes the classroom and playground behavior of the same group of students. The correlations between the three measures are positive and significant.[15]

Knowing the pitfalls of psychological measurement, the investigator is not satisfied. These positive correlations may be due to a factor common to all three tests, but irrelevant to amorism; for example, the tendency to give the "right" answers. (This would probably be ruled out, however, because the observation measure of cooperativeness correlates positively with amorism and subjectivity.) So, taking a new group of subjects, he administers the amorism and subjectivity scales, has the subjects' behavior rated for cooperativeness, and in addition, administers a creativity test that has been found in other research to be reliable.

The investigator states the relation between amorism and creativity in hypothesis form: The relation between the *A* scale and the creativity measure will be negative and significant. The correlations between amorism and cooperativeness and between amorism and subjectivity will be positive and significant. "Check" hypotheses are also formulated: The correlation between cooperativeness and creativity will not be significant; it will be near zero, but the correlation between subjectivity and creativity will be positive and significant. This last relation is predicted on the basis of previous research findings. The six correlation coefficients are given in the correlation matrix of Table 27.1. The four measures are labeled as follows: *A*, amorism; *B*, cooperativeness; *C*, subjectivity; and *D*, creativity.

The evidence for the construct validity of the *A* scale is good. All the *r*'s are as predicted; especially important are the *r*'s between *D* (creativity) and the other variables. Note that there are three different kinds of prediction: positive, negative, and zero. All three kinds are as predicted. This illustrates what might be called *differential prediction* or *differential validity*—or discriminability. It is not enough

[15]Note that we would not expect high correlation between the measures. If the correlations were too high, we would then suspect the validity of the *A* scale. It would be measuring, perhaps, subjectivity or cooperativeness, but not amorism.

TABLE **27.1** INTERCORRELATIONS OF FOUR HYPOTHETICAL MEASURES[a]

	B	*C*	*D*
A	.50	.60	−.30
B		.40	.05
C			.50

[a] *A* = amorism; *B* = cooperativeness; *C* = subjectivity; *D* = creativity. Correlation coefficients .25 or greater are significant at the .01 level. $N = 90$.

to predict, for instance, that the measure presumably reflecting the target property be positively correlated with one theoretically relevant variable. One should, through deduction from the theory, predict more than one such positive relation. In addition, one should predict zero relations between the principal variable and variables "irrelevant" to the theory. In the example above, although cooperativeness was expected to correlate with amorism, there was no theoretical reason to expect it to correlate at all with creativity.

Another example of a different kind is when an investigator deliberately introduces a measure that would, if it correlates with the variable whose validity is under study, invalidate other positive relations. One bugaboo of personality and attitude scales is the social desirability phenomenon, mentioned earlier. The correlation between the target variable and a theoretically related variable may be due to the fact that the instruments measuring both variables may be substantially tapping social desirability rather than the variables they were designed to tap. One can partly check whether this is so by including a measure of social desirability along with the other measures.

Despite all the evidence leading the investigator to believe that the *A* scale has construct validity, he may still be doubtful. He now sets up an experiment (of an ex post facto kind) in which he has pupils high and low in amorism solve problems. He predicts that pupils low in amorism will solve problems more successfully than those high in amorism. If the data support the prediction, this is further evidence of the construct validity of his measure of amorism. It is of course a significant finding in and of itself. Such an experimental procedure, however, is probably more appropriate with achievement and attitude measures. One can manipulate communications, for example, in order to change attitudes. If attitude scores change according to theoretical prediction, this would be evidence of the construct validity of the attitude measure, since the scores would probably not change according to prediction if the measure were not measuring the construct.

The Multitrait-Multimethod Matrix Method

A significant contribution to testing validity is Campbell and Fiske's use of the ideas of convergence and discriminability and correlation matrices to bring evidence to bear on validity.[16] To explain the method, we use some data from a study

[16] D. Campbell and D. Fiske, "Convergent and Discriminant Validation by the Multitrait-Multimethod Matrix," *Psychological Bulletin*, LVI (1959), 81–105.

of attitudes toward education (but not published in the study).[17] It had been found that there were two basic dimensions of attitudes toward education: progressivism, A, and traditionalism, B. Five different kinds of scales were constructed and administered to undergraduates, graduate students of education, and people outside the university. Two of these scales used approximately the same items but utterly different methods of measurement: summated-ratings and forced-choice (see Chapter 29). The correlations between the A and B scales with Method 1 (summated-ratings) and Method 2 (forced-choice) are given in Table 27.2.

TABLE **27.2** CORRELATIONS BETWEEN EDUCATIONAL ATTITUDE DIMENSIONS ACROSS TWO METHODS, MULTITRAIT-MULTIMETHOD APPROACH[a]

		Method 1		*Method 2*	
		A_1	B_1	A_2	B_2
Method 1	A_1	(.70)			
	B_1	−.13	(.70)		
Method 2	A_2	*.59*	−.37	(.70)	
	B_2	−.39	*.62*	−.50	(.70)

[a]Method 1: summated-ratings; Method 2: forced-choice; A: progressivism; B: traditionalism. The diagonal entries in parentheses are approximate internal consistency reliabilities; the italicized diagonal entries are cross-method A-A and B-B correlations.

In a multitrait-multimethod analysis, more than one attribute and more than one method are used in the validation process. The results of correlating variables within and between methods can be presented in a so-called multitrait–multimethod matrix. The matrix (matrices) given in Table 27.2 is the simplest possible form of such an analysis: two variables and two methods. Ordinarily one would want more variables. The most important part of the matrix is the diagonal of the cross-method correlations. In Table 27.2, this is the Method 1-Method 2 matrix in the lower left section of the table. The diagonal values should be substantial, since they reflect the magnitudes of the correlations between the same variables measured differently. The values are .59 and .62—fairly substantial.

In this example, the theory calls for near-zero or low negative correlations between A and B.[18] The correlation between A_1 and B_1 is −.13, in accord with the theory. The cross-correlations, however, are all higher, −.37 and −.39, and the A_2-B_2 correlation is −.50, quite substantial. But the Method 2 A-B correlation was expected to be higher than the Method 1 A-B correlation, because the Method 2 scale was a forced-choice scale. Such scales, because of their response and scoring system, produce spurious negative correlations between the components

[17]F. Kerlinger, "Factor Invariance in the Measurement of Attitudes Toward Education," *Educational and Psychological Measurement*, XXI (1961), 273–285. While this example may not be the strongest one possible because many of the items in the two scales were the same—ideally one would like entirely different items—the totally different methods of measurement and scoring fit the multitrait-multimethod approach.

[18]F. Kerlinger, "Social Attitudes and their Criterial Referents: A Structural Theory," *Psychological Review*, LXXIV (1967), 110–122.

of their items, in this case *A* and *B* items. Therefore, the substantial negative correlations are not unexpected. As far as this evidence goes, then, the construct validity of the educational attitude scales is supported. One will, of course, want considerably more evidence. Further applications of the method with different measures of liberalism and conservatism—the progressivism and traditionalism measures are conceived in the theory to be subsets of the basic underlying liberalism and conservatism dimensions—have given additional support to the theory and the measures of the constructs of the theory.

The model of the multitrait-multimethod procedure is an ideal. If possible, it should be followed. Certainly the investigation and measurement of important constructs, like conservatism, aggressiveness, teacher warmth, need for achievement, honesty, and so on, ultimately require it. In many research situations, however, it is very difficult or impossible to administer two or more measures of two or more variables to relatively large samples. Though efforts to study validity must always be made, research should not be abandoned just because the full method is not feasible.

Research Examples of Construct Validation

In a sense, any type of validation is construct validation.[19] Whenever hypotheses are tested, whenever relations are empirically studied, construct validity is involved. Because of its importance, we now examine three research examples of construct validation. In so doing, we note that aspects of criterion-related validity and content validity are involved and that a variety of methods and approaches are used.

The Environmental Assessment Technique Astin and Holland, in testing the validity of a complex measure of college environment, the Environmental Assessment Technique (EAT), listed the three institutions that had the highest scores on each of the subscales of the EAT: Realistic, Intellectual, Social, Conventional, Enterprising, Artistic.[20] If a test is a valid measure of the intellectual environment of a college, for example, then those colleges that have high average scores should also have environments that are strongly intellectual. Similar reasoning applies to the other measures.

The three schools with the highest EAT Intellectual scores were Union College and University, California Institute of Technology, and Reed College, all three known for their strong emphasis on scholarship and research. Similar findings were obtained for the other variables, evidence for the validity of the EAT. Naturally, Astin and Holland used other methods. One would hardly call a test valid only on the basis of group membership.

A Measure of Anti-Semitism In an unusual attempt to validate their measure of anti-Semitism, Glock and Stark used responses to two incomplete sen-

[19] J. Loevinger, "Objective Tests as Instruments of Psychological Theory," *Psychological Reports*, III (1957), 635–694, Monograph Supplement 9. Loevinger argues that construct validity, from a scientific point of view, is the whole of validity. At the other extreme, Bechtoldt argues that construct validity has no place in psychology. H. Bechtoldt, "Construct Validity: A Critique," *American Psychologist*, XIV (1959), 619–629.

[20] A. Astin and J. Holland, "The Environmental Assessment Technique: A Way to Measure College Environments," *Journal of Educational Psychology*, LII (1961), 308–316.

tences about Jews: "It's a shame that Jews..." and "I can't understand why Jews. . . ."[21] Coders considered what each subject had written and characterized the responses as negative, neutral, or positive images of Jews. Each subject, then, was characterized individually as having one of the three different perceptions of Jews. When the responses to the Index of Anti-Semitic Beliefs, the measure being validated, were divided into None, Medium, Medium High, and High anti-Semitism, the percentages of negative responses to the two open-ended questions were, respectively: 28, 41, 61, 75. This is good evidence of validity, because the individuals categorized None to High anti-Semitism by the measure to be validated, the Index of Anti-Semitic Beliefs, responded to an entirely different measure of anti-Semitism, the two open-ended questions, in a manner congruent with their categorization by the Index.

The Dogmatism Scale Disputing to some extent the validity of the well-known *F* Scale as a measure of authoritarianism, Rokeach, on the basis of rather involved theoretical reasoning, constructed the *D* scale.[22] This instrument consists of a number of items that he believed would tap closed-mindedness, a way of thinking presumably associated with any ideology regardless of content. Central to Rokeach's formulation is the notion that the ideological orientations of individuals are related to their personalities, thought processes, and behaviors. Two examples among many that can be given are his predictions that dogmatism is related to intolerance and to opinionation.

Rokeach undertook an extensive series of investigations aimed at testing his theory and the construct validity of his scales.[23] In one study he used the *known-groups method*, already illustrated in the Astin and Holland study. In this method groups of people with "known" characteristics are administered an instrument and the direction of differences is predicted. For example, if we were validating an attitude scale designed to measure conservatism, we might select groups "known" to be very conservative and groups "known" not to be conservative. Rokeach had college professors and graduate psychology students select graduate students and friends they considered to be open- and closed-minded. The *D* Scale differentiated the two groups.[24]

Perhaps a more cogent demonstration of the validity of the *D* Scale using the known-groups method is Rokeach's testing of different religious groups.[25] He found that Catholic students in Michigan, as predicted, obtained significantly higher *D* scores than Protestant students. These results did not hold up in New York, however, With English subjects, Rokeach found that Communists scored higher on *D* than did liberals, an interesting finding, especially when the same Communists scored lower on the *F* (authoritarianism) Scale.

In more direct tests of the *D* Scale's validity in measuring individuals' total

[21] C. Glock and R. Stark, *Christian Beliefs and Anti-Semitism*. New York: Harper & Row, 1966, pp. 125–127.

[22] M. Rokeach, *The Open and Closed Mind*. New York: Basic Books, 1960.

[23] Rokeach specifically says that he was mainly preoccupied with construct validity. Though he was concerned with predictive and content validities, these were subordinate to construct validity. *Ibid.*, p. 99, footnote.

[24] Chap. 5.

[25] *Ibid.*, chap. 6.

belief systems, Rokeach studied the relation between dogmatism and problem-solving in situations quite different from any encountered in everyday life,[26] between belief-system closedness and perceptual analysis,[27] and even between closedness and acceptance of new and unconventional music.[28] While the results of these studies were not clear-cut, they furnished evidence of the validity of Rokeach's theoretical derivations and the validity of the *D* measure.

Other Methods of Construct Validation

In addition to multitrait-multimethod approach and the methods used in the above studies, there are other methods of construct validation. Any tester is familiar with the technique of correlating items with total scores. In using this technique, the total score is assumed to be valid. To the extent that an item measures the same thing as the total score does, to that extent the item is valid.[29]

Factor analysis is perhaps the most powerful method of construct validation.[30] Factor analysis will be discussed in the last chapter of this book, but its great importance in construct validation requires at least mention here. It is a method for reducing a large number of measures to a smaller number called factors by discovering which ones "go together" (which measures measure the same thing) and the relations between the clusters of measures that go together. For example, we may give a group of individuals twenty tests, each presumed to measure something different. We may find, however, that the twenty tests are really only five measures or factors.

In order to study the construct validity of any measure, it is always helpful to correlate the measure with other measures. The amorism example discussed earlier illustrated the method and the ideas behind it. But, would it not be more valuable to correlate a measure with a large number of other measures? How better to learn about a construct than to know its correlates? Factor analysis is a refined method of doing this. It tells us, in effect, what measures measure the same thing and to what extent they measure what they measure.

Sorenson, Husek, and Yu, in studying the nature and influence of teacher role expectations, constructed a six-subscale measure of such expectations, the six dimensions having been obtained through interviews with teachers, administrators, and others and from reasoning and role theory.[31] The instrument was made up of 30 teaching problem situations and, in effect, 120 items, 20 for each of the six subscales. The 120 items were intercorrelated and factor-analyzed—a good example of analysis that would not have been possible before the computer—and, in a first study, five of the factors agreed with the designations of five of the six sub-

[26]*Ibid.*, chaps. 8, 9, and 12.

[27]*Ibid.*, chap. 14.

[28]*Ibid.*, chap. 15.

[29]For a discussion of item analysis, see J. Guilford, *Psychometric Methods*, 2d ed. New York: McGraw-Hill, 1954, pp. 417 ff., or J. Nunnally, *Psychometric Theory*. New York: McGraw-Hill, 1967, pp. 241 ff.

[30]Cronbach ("Test Validation," *op. cit.*, pp. 469–473) spells out difficulties in using factor analysis for construct validation. I think he understates the positive side of the case.

[31]A. Sorenson, T. Husek, and C. Yu, "Divergent Concepts of Teacher Role: An Approach to the Measurement of Teacher Effectiveness," *Journal of Educational Psychology*, LIV (1963), 287–294.

scales. In a second study and factor analysis, five factors were also found. The five factors seemed to describe the basic dimensions of the teacher's role: disciplinarian, counselor, motivator, referrer, and advice-information giver. In other words, the teacher-role construct and its subordinate constructs were validated by using factor analysis to verify the initial conception of the teacher role.

A Variance Definition of Validity: The Variance Relation of Reliability and Validity[32]

In the last chapter, reliability was defined as

$$r_{tt} = \frac{V_\infty}{V_t} \qquad (27.1)$$

the proportion of "true" variance to total variance. It is theoretically and empirically useful to define validity similarly. Validity, therefore, is defined:

$$\text{Val} = \frac{V_{co}}{V_t} \qquad (27.2)$$

where Val is the validity; V_{co} the common factor variance; and V_t the total variance of a measure. Validity is thus seen as the proportion of the total variance of a measure that is common factor variance.

Unfortunately, we are not in a position yet to present the full meaning of this definition. An understanding of so-called factor theory is required, but factor theory will not be discussed until later in the book. Despite this difficulty, we must attempt an explanation of validity in variance terms if we are to have a well-rounded view of the subject. Besides, expressing validity and reliability mathematically will unify and clarify both subjects. Indeed, reliability and validity will be seen to be parts of one unified whole.

Common factor variance is the variance of a measure that is shared with other measures. In other words, common factor variance is the variance that two or more tests have in common.

In contrast to the common factor variance of a measure is its *specific variance*, V_{sp}, the systematic variance of a measure that is not shared by any other measure. If a test measures skills that other tests measure, we have common factor variance; if it also measures a skill that no other test does, we have specific variance.

Figure 27.1 expresses these ideas and also adds the notion of error variance. The A and B circles represent the variances of Tests A and B. The intersection of A and B, $A \cap B$, is the relation of the two sets. Similarly, $V(A \cap B)$ is the common factor variance. The specific variances and the error variances of both tests are also indicated.

[32]The variance treatment of validity presented here is an extension of the variable treatment of reliability presented in the last chapter. Both treatments follow Guilford, *op. cit.*, pp. 354–357.

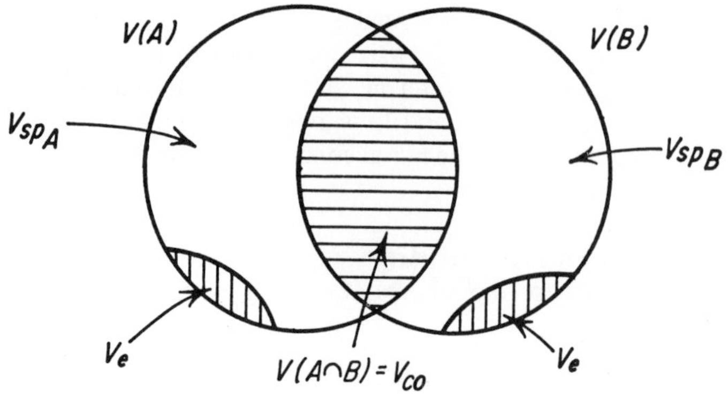

FIG. 27.1

From this viewpoint, then, and following the variance reasoning outlined in the last chapter, any measure's total variance has several components: *common factor variance*, *specific variance*, and *error variance*. This is expressed by the equation:

$$V_t = V_{co} + V_{sp} + V_e \tag{27.3}$$

To be able to talk of proportions of the total variance, we divide the terms of Eq. 27.3 by the total variance:

$$\frac{V_t}{V_t} = \frac{V_{co}}{V_t} + \frac{V_{sp}}{V_t} + \frac{V_a}{V_t} \tag{27.4}$$

How do Eqs. 27.1 and 27.2 fit into this picture? The first term on the right, V_{co}/V_t, is the right-hand member of (27.2). Therefore validity can be viewed as that part of the total variance of a measure that is not specific variance and not error variance. This is easily seen algebraically:

$$\frac{V_{co}}{V_t} = \frac{V_t}{V_t} - \frac{V_{sp}}{V_t} - \frac{V_e}{V_t} \tag{27.5}$$

By a definition of the previous chapter, reliability can be defined as

$$r_{tt} = 1 - \frac{V_e}{V_t} \tag{27.6}$$

This can be written:

$$r_{tt} = \frac{V_t}{V_t} - \frac{V_e}{V_t} \tag{27.7}$$

The right-hand side of the equation, however, is part of the right-hand side of (27.5). If we rewrite (27.5) slightly, we obtain

$$\frac{V_{co}}{V_t} = \frac{V_t}{V_t} - \frac{V_e}{V_t} - \frac{V_{sp}}{V_t} \tag{27.8}$$

This must mean, then, that validity and reliability are close variance relations.

Reliability is equal to the first two right-hand members of (27.8). So, bringing in (27.1):

$$r_{tt} = \frac{V_t}{V_t} - \frac{V_e}{V_t} = \frac{V_\infty}{V_t} \tag{27.9}$$

If we substitute in (27.8), we get

$$\frac{V_{co}}{V_t} = \frac{V_\infty}{V_t} - \frac{V_{sp}}{V_t} \tag{27.10}$$

Thus we see that the proportion of the total variance of a measure is equal to the proportion of the total variance that is "true" variance minus the proportion that is specific variance. Or, the validity of a measure is that portion of the total variance of the measure that shares variance with other measures. Theoretically, valid variance includes no variance due to error, nor does it include variance that is specific to this measure and this measure only.

This can all be summed up in two ways. First, we sum it up in an equation or two. Let us assume that we have a method of determining the common factor variance (or variances) of a test. (Later we shall see that factor analysis is such a method.) For simplicity suppose that there are two sources of common factor variance in a test—and no others. Call these factors A and B. They might be verbal ability and arithmetic ability, or they might be liberal attitudes and conservative attitudes. If we add the variance of A to the variance of B, we obtain the common factor variance of the test, which is expressed by the equations,

$$V_{co} = V_A + V_B \tag{27.11}$$

$$\frac{V_{co}}{V_t} = \frac{V_A}{V_t} + \frac{V_B}{V_t} \tag{27.12}$$

Then, using (27.2) and substituting in (27.12), we obtain

$$\text{Val} = \frac{V_A}{V_t} + \frac{V_B}{V_t} \tag{27.13}$$

The total variance of a test, we said before, includes the common factor variance, the variance specific to the test and to no other test (at least as far as present information goes), and error variance. Equations 27.3 and 27.4 express this. Now, substituting in (27.4) the equality of (27.12), we obtain

$$\frac{V_t}{V_t} = \underbrace{\overbrace{\frac{V_A}{V_t} + \frac{V_B}{V_t}}^{h^2} + \frac{V_{sp}}{V_t}}_{r_{tt}} + \frac{V_e}{V_t} \tag{27.14}$$

The first two terms on the right-hand side of (27.14) are associated with the validity of the measure, and the first three terms on the right are associated with the reliability of the measure. These relations have been indicated. Common factor variance, or the validity component of the measure, is labeled h^2 (*communality*), a symbol customarily used to indicate the common factor variance of a test. Reliability, as usual, is labeled r_{tt}.

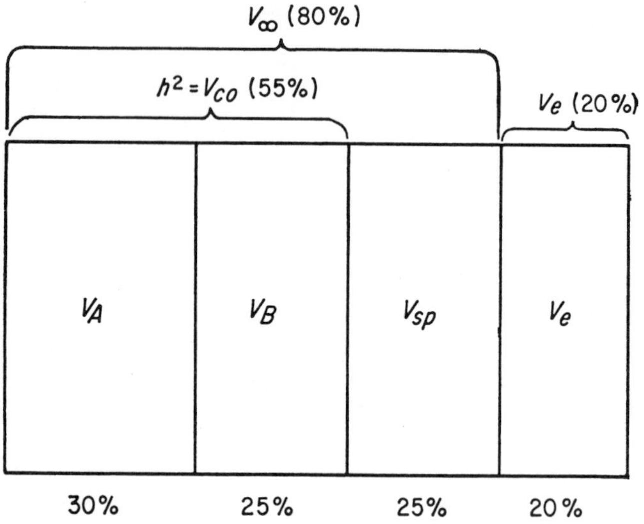

FIG. 27.2

To discuss all the implications of this formulation of validity and reliability would take us too far astray at this time. All that is needed now is to try to clarify the formulation with a diagram and a brief discussion.

Fig. 27.2 is an attempt to express Eq. 27.14 diagrammatically. The figure represents the contributions of the different variances to the total variance (taken to be equal to 100 percent). Four variances, three systematic variances and one error variance, comprise the total variance in this theoretical model.[33] The contribution of each of the sources of variance is indicated. Of the total variance, 80 percent is reliable variance. Of the reliable variance, 30 percent is contributed by Factor *A* and 25 percent by Factor *B*, and 25 percent is specific to this test. The remaining 20 percent of the total variance is error variance.

The test may be interpreted as quite reliable (in most cases), since a sizable proportion of the total variance is reliable or "true" variance. The interpretation of validity is more difficult. If there were only one factor, say *A*, and it contributed 55 percent of the total variance, then we could say that a considerable proportion of the total variance was valid variance. We would know that a good bit of the reliable measurement would be the measurement of the property known as *A*. This would be a construct validity statement. Practically speaking, individuals measured with the test would be rank-ordered on *A* with adequate reliability.

With the above hypothetical example, however, the situation is more complex. The test measures two factors, *A* and *B*. There could be three sets of rank orders, one resulting from *A*, one from *B*, and one from *specific*. While repeat reliability might be high, if we thought we were measuring only *A*, to the extent we

[33]Naturally, practical outcomes never look this neat. It is remarkable, however, how well the model works. The variance thinking, too, is valuable in conceptualizing and discussing measurement outcomes.

thought so to this extent the test would not be valid. We might, however, have a score for each individual on *A* and one on *B*. In this case the test would be valid.[34] Indeed, modern developments in measurement indicate that such multiple scores have become more and more a part of accepted procedure.

The Validity and Reliability of Psychological and Educational Measurement Instruments

Poor measurement can invalidate any scientific investigation. Most of the criticisms of psychological and educational measurement, by professionals and laymen alike, center on validity. This is as it should be. Achieving reliability is to a large extent a technical matter. Validity, however, is much more than technique. It bores into the essence of science itself. It also bores into philosophy. Construct validity, particularly, since it is concerned with the nature of "reality" and the nature of the properties being measured, is heavily philosophical.

Despite the difficulties of achieving reliable and valid psychological, sociological, and educational measurements, great progress has been made in this century. There is growing understanding that *all* measuring instruments must be critically and empirically examined for their reliability and validity. The day of tolerance of inadequate measurement has ended. The demands imposed by professionals, the theoretical and statistical tools available and rapidly being developed, and the increasing sophistication of graduate students of psychology, sociology, and education have set new high standards that should be healthy stimulants both to the imaginations of research workers and to developers of scientific measurement.

Study Suggestions

1. The measurement literature is vast. The following references have been chosen for their particular excellence or their relevance to important measurement topics. Some of the discussions, however, are technical and difficult. The student will find elementary discussions of reliability and validity in most measurement texts.

   Bloom et al. and Krathwohl et al., taxonomies. (See footnote 3.)
   Cronbach and Meehl, construct validity article. (See footnote 1 and Mehrens and Ebel, below.) A most important contribution to modern measurement and behavioral research.
   Cureton, E. "Measurement Theory." In R. Ebel, V. Noll, and R. Bauer, eds., *Encyclopedia of Educational Research*, 4th ed. New York: Macmillan, 1969, pp. 785–804. A broad and firm overview of measurement, with an emphasis on educational measurement.
   Guilford and Nunnally texts. (See footnote 29.) Excellent advanced texts.
   Standards for Educational and Psychological Tests and Manuals. Washing-

[34]Note that even if we thought the test was measuring only *A*, predictions to a criterion might well be successful, especially if the criterion had a lot of both *A* and *B* in it. The test could have predictive validity even though its construct validity was questionable.

ton, D.C.: American Psychological Association, 1966. A definitive statement jointly produced by three large associations concerned with measurement.

Thorndike, R., ed. *Educational Measurement*, 2d ed. Washington, D.C.: American Council on Education, 1971. An outstanding achievement that evidently ranks with its distinguished predecessor: E. Lindquist, ed. *Educational Measurement*. Washington, D.C.: American Council on Education, 1951. Both books have excellent chapters on most aspects of educational measurement, including reliability and validity. The reliability chapters in both editions, by Thorndike (1951) and Stanley (1971), have exceptionally good tables (original table by Thorndike) summarizing the possible sources of variance in measures: Table 8, p. 568, 1951 edition; Table 13.1, p. 364, 1971 edition.

Tryon, R. "Reliability and Behavior Domain Validity: A Reformulation and Historical Critique." *Psychological Bulletin*, LIV (1957), 229–249. This is an excellent and important article on reliability. It contains a good worked example.

The following anthologies of measurement articles are valuable sources of the classics in the field. This is especially true of the Mehrens and Ebel and the Jackson and Messick volumes.

Anastasi, A., ed. *Testing Problems in Perspective*. Washington, D.C.: American Council on Education, 1966.

Chase, C., and Ludlow, G., eds. *Readings in Educational and Psychological Measurement*. Boston: Houghton Mifflin, 1966.

Jackson, D., and Messick, S., eds. *Problems in Human Assessment*. New York: McGraw-Hill, 1967.

Mehrens, W., and Ebel, R., eds. *Principles of Educational and Psychological Measurement*. Skokie, Ill.: Rand McNally, 1967.

2. An important method in validity studies is cross-validation. Advanced students can profit from Mosier's essay in the Chase and Ludlow book mentioned above. A brief summary of Mosier's essay can be found in Guilford, *op. cit.*, p. 406.
3. The more advanced student will also want to know something about response set, a threat to validity, particularly to the validity of personality, attitude, and value items and instruments. *Response sets* are tendencies to respond to items in certain ways—high, low, approve, disapprove, extreme, etc.—regardless of the content of the items. The resulting scores are therefore systematically biased. The literature is extensive and cannot be cited here. An excellent exposition, however, can be found in Nunnally, *op. cit.*, pp. 510–511 and 593–617. Advocates of the effects of response sets on measurement instruments are quite strong in their statements. A considerable dash of salt has been thrown on the response-set tail by L. Rorer: "The Great Response-Style Myth," *Psychological Bulletin*, LXIII (1965), 129–156.

   The position taken in this book is that response sets certainly operate and sometimes have considerable effect but that the strong claims of advocates are exaggerated. Most of the variance in well-constructed measures seems to be due to variables being measured and relatively little to response set. Investigators must be aware of response sets and their possible deleterious effects on measurement instruments, but they should not be afraid to use the instruments. If one were to take too seriously the schools of thought on response set and on what has been called the experimenter effect (in education, the Pygmalion effect), discussed earlier, one would have to abandon behavioral research, except, perhaps, research that can be done with so-called unobtrusive measures.

4. Discuss and criticize the following statements:
   (a) "The reliability of my creativity test is .85. I can therefore be reasonably sure that I am measuring creativity."
   (b) "My creativity test really measures creativity, because I had an expert on creativity carefully screen all the items of the test."
   (c) "Since the reliability of the test of logical thinking is only .40, its validity is negligible."
5. Study the following assertions and decide in each case whether the assertion refers to reliability or validity, or both. Label the type of reliability and validity.
   (a) "The test was given twice to the same group. The coefficient of correlation between the scores of the two administrations was .90."
   (b) "Four teachers studied the items of the test for their relevance to the objectives of the curriculum."
   (c) "The items seem to be a good sample of the item universe."
   (d) "Between a test of academic aptitude and grade-point averages, $r = .55$."
   (e) "The mean difference between Republicans and Democrats on the conservatism instrument was highly significant."
6. An investigator wishes to study the relation between dogmatism and ethnocentrism. He uses a well-established measure of ethnocentrism and constructs an instrument to measure dogmatism. The correlation between dogmatism and ethnocentrism is .60. The investigator does not stop there, however, because it seems to him that the correlation may be due to factors other than those he is trying to measure. He is particularly dubious about the dogmatism measure. What should he do to obtain evidence that his dogmatism measure is really measuring dogmatism? (Pay particular attention to construct validity and construct validation.)
7. Imagine that you have given a test of six items to six persons. The scores of each person on each item are given below. Say that you have also given another test of six items to six persons. These scores are also given below. The scores of the first test, I, are given on the left; the scores of the second test, II, are given on the right.

	I					
	Items					
Persons	*a*	*b*	*c*	*d*	*e*	*f*
1	6	6	7	5	6	5
2	6	4	5	5	4	5
3	5	4	7	6	4	3
4	3	2	5	3	4	4
5	2	3	4	4	3	2
6	2	1	3	1	0	2

	II					
	Items					
Persons	*a*	*b*	*c*	*d*	*e*	*f*
1	6	4	5	6	6	3
2	6	2	7	4	4	4
3	5	6	5	3	4	2
4	3	4	4	5	4	5
5	2	1	7	1	3	5
6	2	3	3	5	0	2

The scores in II are the same as those in I, except that the orders of the scores of Items (*b*), (*c*), (*d*), and (*f*) have been changed.

(a) Do a two-way analysis of variance of each set of scores. Compare the F ratios and interpret them. Pay special attention to the F ratio for Persons (Individuals).

(b) Compute $r_{tt} = (V_{\text{ind}} - V_e)/V_{\text{ind}}$ for I and II. Interpret the two r_{tt}'s. Why are they so different?

(c) Add the odd items across the rows; add the even items. Compare the rank orders and the ranges of the odd totals, the even totals, and the totals of all six items. The coefficients of correlation between odd and even items, corrected, are .98 and .30. Explain why they are so different. What do they mean?

(d) Assume that there were 100 persons and 60 items. Would this have changed the procedures and the reasoning behind them? Would the effect of changing the orders of, say, five to ten items have affected the r_{tt}'s as much as in these examples? If not, why not?

[*Answers:* (a) I: $F_{\text{items}} = 3.79$ (.05); $F_{\text{persons}} = 20.44$ (.001); II: $F_{\text{items}} = 1.03$ (*n.s.*); $F_{\text{persons}} = 1.91$ (*n.s.*). (b) I: $r_{tt} = .95$; II: $r_{tt} = .48$.]

PART

Methods of Observation and Data Collection

Introduction

To implement general plans of research, methods of data collection must be used. There is always a mutual interplay of problem and method. Problems dictate methods to a considerable extent, but methods—their availability, feasibility, and relevance—also influence problems. Some problems cannot be satisfactorily studied, because methods do not at present exist to collect the data implied by the problems; or existing methods and even those that can be invented may not be capable of yielding the precise data needed. In such cases it may be necessary to alter the problems or perhaps even to abandon them temporarily. At any rate, the problem is the more fundamental consideration.

Methods of observation are systematic and standard procedures for obtaining data. They can be considered extensions of measurement theory and methods. The clue is furnished by the definition of measurement: the assignment of numerals to objects according to rules. In the last analysis, almost all methods have the technical purpose of enabling the researcher to so make observations that symbols or numerals can be assigned to the objects or to the sets of objects under study. Put another way, methods of observation help the researcher obtain measures of variables so that he can bring empirical evidence to bear on research questions.

The approach to methods of observation used in this part is dictated by the conviction that such methods can only be learned through experience. It is possible to learn certain principles of schedule construction, but in order to construct an actual schedule, one requires considerable practice in writing and reviewing items and instructions. A book can explain how to interview, but in order to be able to interview, one must interview.

The following chapters, then, have three main purposes. The first is to acquaint the student with the most important observational methods that are available. Graduate students seem to concentrate on two or three methods, perhaps because of a lack of familiarity with available methods. This restriction to two or three methods unduly narrows the range of possible problems and inquiry. Thus one of the prime objectives of these chapters is to broaden the student's knowledge of available methods.

The second purpose is to help the student understand the main characteristics and purposes of the methods. Methods differ considerably in what they can and cannot do. Users of methods must know these possibilities if they are to be able to choose methods suited to their problems. Many a good problem has suffered from an inappropriate and inadequate method.

The third purpose is closely related to the second: to indicate, if incompletely, the strengths and weaknesses of the methods. One method may be well suited to a problem, but it may have grave weaknesses that disqualify it. The mail questionnaire is a case in point. A problem may require a wide geographical sampling of schools, which can be easily accomplished by the mail questionnaire. But its well-known weakness would perhaps disqualify it from consideration, unless it were the only possible way to obtain data.

CHAPTER 28

Interviews and Interview Schedules

The interview is perhaps the most ubiquitous method of obtaining information from people. It has been and is still used in all kinds of practical situations: the lawyer obtains information from a client; the physician learns about a patient; the admissions officer or professor determines the suitability of students for schools, departments, and curricula. Only recently, however, has the interview been used systematically for scientific purposes, both in the laboratory and in the field.

Data collection methods can be categorized by the degree of their directness. If we wish to know something about someone, we can ask him about it directly. He may or may not give us an answer. On the other hand, we may not ask him a direct question. We may give him some ambiguous stimulus, like a blurred picture, a blot of ink, or a vague question; and then ask him for his impressions of the stimulus on the assumption that he will give the needed information without knowing he is giving it. This method would be highly indirect. Most of the data-collection methods used in psychological and sociological research are relatively direct or moderately indirect. Rarely are highly indirect means used.

Interviews and schedules (questionnaires) are ordinarily quite direct. This is both a strength and a weakness. It is a strength because a great deal of the information needed in social scientific research can be gotten from respondents by direct questions. Though the questions may have to be carefully handled, respondents can, and usually will, give much information directly. There is information, however, of a more difficult nature that respondents may be unwilling, reluctant, or unable to give readily and directly, for example, information on income, sexual relations, and attitudes toward religion and minority groups. In such cases, direct questions may yield data that are invalid. Yet, properly handled, even personal or controversial material can be successfully obtained with interviews and schedules.

The interview is probably man's oldest and most often used device for obtaining information. It has important qualities that objective tests and scales and behavioral observations do not possess. When used with a well-conceived schedule, an interview can obtain a great deal of information, is flexible and adaptable to individual situations, and can often be used when no other method is possible or adequate. These qualities make it especially suitable for research with children.[1] An interviewer can know whether the respondent, especially a child, does not understand a question and can, within limits, repeat or rephrase the question. Questions about hopes, aspirations, and anxieties can be asked in such a way as to elicit accurate information. Most important, perhaps, the interview permits probing into the context and reasons for answers to questions.

The major shortcoming of the interview and its accompanying schedule is practical. Interviews take a lot of time. Getting information from one individual may take as long as an hour or even two hours. This large time investment costs effort and money. So, whenever a more economical method answers the research purposes, interviews should not be used.

Interviews and Schedules as Tools of Science

For the most part, interviews and schedules have been used simply for gathering so-called facts. The most important use of interviews should be to study relations and to test hypotheses. The interview, in other words, is a psychological and sociological measuring instrument. Perhaps more accurately, the products of interviews, respondents' answers to carefully contrived questions, can be translated into measures of variables. Interviews and interview schedules are therefore subject to the same criteria of reliability, validity, and objectivity as any other measuring instruments.

An interview can be used for three main purposes. One, it can be an exploratory device to help identify variables and relations, to suggest hypotheses, and to guide other phases of the research. Two, it can be the main instrument of the research. In this case, questions designed to measure the variables of the research will be included in the interview schedule. These questions are then to be considered as items in a measurement instrument, rather than as mere information-gathering devices. Three, the interview can supplement other methods: follow up unexpected results, validate other methods, and go deeper into the motivations of respondents and their reasons for responding as they do.

In using interviews as tools of scientific research, we must ask the questions: Can data on the research problem be obtained in an easier or better way? To achieve reliability, for example, is not a small problem. Interviewers must be trained; questions must be pretested and revised to eliminate ambiguities and inadequate wording. Is it worth the effort? Validity, too, is no small problem. Special pains must be taken to eliminate interviewer bias; questions must be tested for unknown

[1] L. Yarrow, "Interviewing Children," in P. Mussen, ed., *Handbook of Research Methods in Child Development*. New York: Wiley, 1960, chap. 14.

biases. The particular research problem and the nature of the information sought must, in the last analysis, dictate whether or not the interview will be used.[2]

The Interview

The *interview* is a face-to-face interpersonal role situation in which one person, the interviewer, asks a person being interviewed, the respondent, questions designed to obtain answers pertinent to the research problem. There are two broad types of interview: *structured and unstructured* or *standardized and unstandardized.*[3] In the standardized interview, the questions, their sequence, and their wording are fixed. An interviewer may be allowed some liberty in asking questions, but relatively little.[4] This liberty is specified in advance. Standardized interviews use interview schedules that have been carefully prepared to obtain information pertinent to the research problem.

Unstandardized interviews are more flexible and open. Although the research purposes govern the questions asked, their content, their sequence, and their wording are entirely in the hands of the interviewer. Ordinarily no schedule is used. In other words, the unstandardized, nonstructured interview is an open situation in contrast to the standardized, structured interview, which is a closed situation. This does not mean that an unstandardized interview is casual. It should be just as carefully planned as the standardized one. Our concern here is solely with the standardized interview. It is recognized, however, that many research problems may, and often do, require a compromise type of interview in which the interviewer is permitted leeway to use alternate questions that he judges fit particular respondents and particular questions.[5]

The Interview Schedule

Interviewing itself is an art, but the planning and writing of an interview schedule is even more so. It is unusual for a novice to produce a good schedule, at least without considerable prior study and practice. There are several reasons for this, the main ones probably being the multiple meaning and ambiguity of words, the lack of sharp and constant focus on the problems and hypotheses being studied, a lack

[2]The student will find detailed guidance in C. Cannell and R. Kahn, "The Collection of Data by Interviewing." In L. Festinger and D. Katz, eds., *Research Methods in the Behavioral Sciences*. New York: Holt, Rinehart and Winston, 1953, chap. 8. See, also, E. Maccoby and N. Maccoby, "The Interview: A Tool of Social Science," In G. Lindzey, ed., *Handbook of Social Psychology*. Reading, Mass.: Addison-Wesley, 1954, vol. I, pp. 449–487 (pp. 482–484).

[3]*Ibid.*, pp. 451–455.

[4]Cannell and Kahn, *op. cit.*, p. 358; *Interviewer's Manual, Survey Research Center*. Ann Arbor: Institute for Social Research, University of Michigan, 1969, p. 4-2. Although rather close adherence to the interview schedule has been advocated by experts, a somewhat changed view appears to be relaxing this stricture: the interview is seen as an interaction, an active role relation between interviewer and interviewee, in which the interviewer is even a teacher. See C. Cannell and R. Kahn, "Interviewing." In G. Lindzey and E. Aronson, eds., *The Handbook of Social Psychology*, 2d ed. Reading, Mass.: Addison-Wesley, 1968, vol. II, chap. 15. See, also, B. Dohrenwend and S. Richardson, "Directiveness and Non-directiveness in Research Interviewing: A Reformulation of the Problem," *Psychological Bulletin*, LX (1963), 475–485.

[5]The actual procedure of conducting an interview is not discussed in this book. The reader will find guidance in the excellent references given in the study suggestions at the end of the chapter.

of appreciation of the schedule as a measurement instrument, and a lack of necessary background and experience.

Kinds of Schedule Information and Items

Three kinds of information are included in most schedules: face sheet (identification) information, census-type (or sociological) information, and problem information.[6] Except for identification, these types of information were discussed in Chapter 24. The importance of identifying each schedule accurately and completely, however, needs to be mentioned. The careful researcher should learn to identify with letters, numbers, or other symbols, every schedule and every scale. In addition, identifying information for each individual must be systematically recorded.

Two types of schedule items are in common use: *fixed-alternative* (or closed) and *open-end* (or open). A third type of item, having fixed alternatives, is also used: *scale* items.

Fixed-Alternative Items Fixed-alternative items, as the name indicates, offer the respondent a choice among two or more alternatives. These items are also called *closed* or *poll* questions. The commonest kind of fixed-alternative item is dichotomous: it asks for Yes-No, Agree-Disagree, and other two-alternative answers. Often a third alternative, Don't Know or Undecided, is added.

Two examples of fixed-alternative items follow:[7]

> There are always some people whose ideas are considered bad or dangerous by other people, for instance, somebody who is against all churches and religion. If such a person wanted to make a speech in your city (town, community) against churches and religion, should he be allowed to speak, or not?
>
> Yes . . . . ☐
> No. . . . . ☐
> Don't know . . . . ☐
>
> If the school board in your community were to say, some day, that there were no Communists teaching in your schools, would you feel pretty sure it was true, or not?
>
> Would feel it was true. . . . . ☐
> Would not. ☐
> Don't know . . . . ☐

Fixed-alternative questions are probably the commonest form of interview item, and they have many forms. The kind of example just given is used a great deal. There can be several possible responses, however. The following examples are from a survey of over 1600 blacks living in 25 metropolitan areas. Blacks' attitudes toward whites were assessed in a study of the presumed effects of segregated and desegregated schools.[8]

[6]M. Parten, *Surveys, Polls, and Samples*. New York: Harper & Row, 1950, pp. 162–163. For a comprehensive description of information that can be gotten with interviews, see pp. 163–176.

[7]From *Communism, Conformity, and Civil Liberties* by Samuel A. Stouffer. Garden City, N.Y.: Doubleday, 1955, pp. 252 and 256. Copyright © 1955 by Samuel A. Stouffer. Reprinted by permission of Doubleday & Company, Inc.

[8]U.S. Commission on Civil Rights, *Racial Isolation in the Public Schools*. Washington, D.C.: U.S. Government Printing Office, 1967, vol. 2, app. C 5, pp. 211–220.

> Is this neighborhood that you live in all Negro, mostly Negro, half Negro, half white, or mostly white?[9]

Note that four alternatives are given; the respondent chooses one of them. The next question is much more complex: it states a situation and requires tripartite reactions to five statements:

> Most Negroes have some misgivings about being around white people. I want to read a few things that some Negroes have said about how they feel around white people, and you tell me whether you have felt like this frequently when you are around whites, whether you feel like this sometimes, or whether you never feel like this:
> A. When I am around a white person, I am afraid he might say something which will show that he is prejudiced.
> B. When I am around a white person, I am very careful not to make a bad impression.
> C. I am afraid I might tell him what I really think about white people.
> D. I am afraid I might lose my temper at something he says.
> E. I know he is afraid he'll say something he shouldn't and it bothers me.[10]

Although fixed-alternative items have the decided advantages of achieving greater uniformity of measurement and thus greater reliability, of forcing the respondent to answer in a way that fits the response categories previously set up, and of being easily coded, they have certain disadvantages. The major disadvantage is their superficiality: Without probes they do not ordinarily get beneath the response surface. They may also irritate a respondent who finds none of the alternatives suitable. Worse, they can force responses. A respondent may choose an alternative to conceal ignorance. Or he may choose alternatives that do not accurately represent true facts or opinions. These difficulties do not mean that fixed-alternative items are bad and useless. On the contrary, they can be used to good purpose if they are judiciously written, used with probes, and mixed with open items.[11]

Open-End Items Open or open-end items are an extremely important development in the technique of interviewing. *Open-end questions* are those that supply a frame of reference for respondents' answers, but put a minimum of restraint on the answers and their expression. While their content is dictated by the research problem, they impose no other restrictions on the content and manner of respondent answers. Examples will be given later.

Open-end questions have important advantages, but they have disadvantages, too. If properly written and used, however, these disadvantages can be minimized.

[9] *Ibid.*, p. 214.

[10] *Ibid.*

[11] Parten gives good advice on the writing and use of fixed-alternative questions: Parten, *op. cit.*, pp. 184 ff. See, also, Maccoby and Maccoby, *op. cit.*, pp. 457–459.

A *probe* is a device used to find out respondents' information on a subject, their frames of reference, or, more usually, to clarify and ascertain reasons for responses given. Probing increases the "response-getting" power of questions without changing their content. Examples of probes are: "Tell me more about that." "How is that?" Can you please explain that." See Cannell and Kahn, "The Collection of Data by Interviewing," *op. cit.*, p. 359.

Open-end questions are flexible; they have possibilities of depth; they enable the interviewer to clear up misunderstanding (through probing); they enable the interviewer to ascertain a respondent's lack of knowledge, to detect ambiguity, to encourage cooperation and achieve rapport, and to make better estimates of respondents' true intentions, beliefs, and attitudes. Their use also has another advantage: the responses to open-end questions can suggest possibilities of relations and hypotheses. Respondents will sometimes give unexpected answers that may indicate the existence of relations not originally anticipated.

A special type of open-end question is the *funnel*. Actually, this is a set of questions directed toward getting information on a single important topic or a single set of related topics. The funnel starts with a broad question and narrows down progressively to the important specific point or points. Cannell and Kahn say that the funnel has the purposes of preventing early questions in a sequence of questions from affecting those that come later and of determining something of the respondent's frame of reference.[12] Another form of funnel starts with an open general question and uses follow-up, specific closed questions.[13] The best way to get a feeling for good open-end questions and funnels is to study examples.

To obtain information on child-rearing practices, Sears, Maccoby, and Levin used a number of good open-end and funnel questions. One of them, with the authors' comments in brackets, is:

> All babies cry, of course. [*Note that the interviewer puts the parent at ease about her child's crying.*] Some mothers feel that if you pick up a baby every time it cries, you will spoil it. Others think you should never let a baby cry for very long. [*The frame of reference has been clearly given. The mother is also put at ease no matter how she handles her baby's crying.*] How do you feel about this?
> (a) What did you do about this with X?
> (b) How about in the middle of the night?[14]

This funnel question set not only reaches attitudes; it also probes specific practices.

In a study of student attitudes toward the university done at the University of Michigan, one of the relations studied was that between student contact with the faculty and satisfaction with the university.[15] One of the funnel sets used was:

> Do you have any contacts with any members of the faculty outside of classes?
> (a) (If yes) How often is that?
> (b) What is the nature of your contacts (social, counseling, and so on)?
> Are you generally satisfied with the amount of personal contact you have with members of the faculty?
> (If no) What would you like to see done about it?

[12] *Ibid.*, p. 349.

[13] Maccoby and Maccoby, *op. cit.*, p. 459.

[14] R. Sears, E. Maccoby, and H. Levin, *Patterns of Child Rearing.* New York: Harper & Row, 1957, pp. 491–493.

[15] This selection is from an unpublished study done by a class in survey research at the University of Michigan, 1951.

Scale Items A third type of schedule item is the scale item. A *scale* is a set of verbal items to each of which an individual responds by expressing degrees of agreement or disagreement or some other mode of response. Scale items have fixed alternatives and place the responding individual at some point on the scale. (They will be discussed at greater length in Chapter 29.) The use of scale items in interview schedules is a development of great promise, since the benefits of scales are combined with those of interviews. We can include, for example, a scale to measure attitudes toward education in an interview schedule on the same topic. Scale scores can be obtained in this way for each respondent and scale scores can be checked against open-end question data. Or one can measure the *tolerance of nonconformity*, as Stouffer did, by having a scale to measure this variable embedded in the interview schedule.[16]

Criteria of Question-Writing

Criteria or precepts of question-writing have been developed through experience and research. Some of the most important of these are given below in the form of questions. Brief comments are appended to the questions. When confronted with the actual necessity of drafting a schedule, the student should consult more extended treatments, since the ensuing discussion, in keeping with the discussion of the rest of the chapter, is intended only as an introduction to the subject.[17]

1. *Is the question related to the research problem and the research objectives?* Except for factual and sociological information questions, all the items of a schedule should have some research problem function. This means that the purpose of each question is to elicit information that can be used to test the hypotheses of the research.

2. *Is the type of question right and appropriate?* Some information can best be obtained with the open-end question—reasons for behavior, intentions, and attitudes. Certain other information, on the other hand, can be more expeditiously obtained with closed questions. If all that is required of a respondent is his preferred choice of two or more alternatives, and these alternatives can be clearly specified, it would be wasteful to use an open-end question.

3. *Is the item clear and unambiguous?* An ambiguous statement or item is one that permits or invites alternative interpretations and differing responses resulting from the alternative interpretations. So-called double-barreled questions are ambiguous, for example, because they provide two or more frames of reference rather than only one. Cannell and Kahn give a "good" example of a double-barreled and thus ambiguous question: "How do you feel about the development of a rapid transit system between the central city and the suburbs, and the redevelopment of central city residential areas?"[18] Respondents, even if not

[16]Stouffer, *op. cit.*, Appendix C.

[17]Good practical guidance is given in A. Kornhauser and P. Sheatsley, "Questionnaire Construction and Interview Procedure." In C. Selltiz, et al., *Research Methods in Social Relations*, rev. ed. New York: Holt, Rinehart and Winston, 1959. Appendix C; Parten, *op. cit.*, chap. VI; E. Noelle-Neuman, "Wanted: Rules for Wording Structured Questionnaires," *Public Opinion Quarterly*, XXXIV (1970), 191–201.

[18]Cannell and Kahn, "Interviewing," *op. cit.*, p. 559.

baffled by the complexity and alternatives offered by this question, can hardly respond using a common frame of reference and understanding of what is wanted. But ambiguity can arise from much simpler questions: "How are you and your family getting along this year?" Does the questioner mean finances, marital happiness, health, status, or what?

A great deal of work has been done on item writing. Certain precepts, if followed, help the item writer avoid ambiguity. First, questions that contain more than one idea to which a respondent can react should be avoided. An item like "Do you believe that the educational aims of the modern high school and the teaching methods used to attain these aims are educationally sound?" is an ambiguous question, because the respondent is asked about both educational aims and teaching methods in the same question. Second, avoid ambiguous words and expressions. A respondent might be asked the question, "Do you think the teachers of your school get fair treatment?" This is an ambiguous item because "fair treatment" might refer to several different areas of treatment. The word "fair," too, can mean "just," "equitable," "not too good," "impartial," and "objective." The question needs a clear context, an explicit frame of reference. (Sometimes, however, ambiguous questions are deliberately used to elicit different frames of reference.)

4. *Is the question a leading question?* Leading questions suggest answers. As such, they threaten validity. If you ask a person "Have you read about the local school situation?" you may get a disproportionately large number of "yes" responses, because the question may imply that it is bad not to have read about the local school situation.

5. *Does the question demand knowledge and information that the respondent does not have?* To counter the invalidity of response due to lack of information, it is wise to use information filter questions. Before asking a person what he thinks of UNESCO, first find out whether he knows what UNESCO is and means. Another approach is possible. You can explain UNESCO briefly and then ask the respondent what he thinks of it.

6. *Does the question demand personal or delicate material that the respondent may resist?* Special techniques are needed to obtain information of a personal, delicate, or controversial nature. Ask income and other personal matters late in the interview after rapport has been built up. When asking about something that is socially disapproved, show that some people believe one way and others believe another way. Don't make the respondent in effect disapprove himself. Use "soft" rather than "hard" expressions. Don't say "punishment" to a teacher. Softer words might be "correction" and "negative reinforcement." Maccoby and Maccoby's discussion of this subject outlines more precepts that are useful to keep in mind.[19]

7. *Is the question loaded with social desirability?* People tend to give responses that are socially desirable, responses that indicate or imply approval of actions or things that are generally considered to be good. We may ask a person

[19]Maccoby and Maccoby, *op. cit.*, p. 457.

about his feelings toward children. Everybody is supposed to love children. Unless we are very careful, we will get a stereotyped response about children and love. Also, when we ask a person if he votes, we must be careful since everyone is supposed to vote. If we ask respondents their reactions to minority groups, we again run the risk of getting invalid responses. Most educated people, no matter what their "true" attitudes, are aware that prejudice is disapproved. A good question, then, is one in which respondents are not led to express merely socially desirable sentiments. At the same time, one should not question a respondent so that he is faced with the necessity of giving a socially undesirable response.

The Value of Interviews and Interview Schedules

The interview, when coupled with an adequate schedule of pretested worth, is a potent and indispensable research tool, yielding data that no other research tool can yield. It is adaptable, capable of being used with all kinds of respondents in many kinds of research, and uniquely suited to exploration in depth. But do its strengths balance its weaknesses? And what is its value in behavioral research when compared to other methods of data collection?

The most natural tool with which to compare the interview is the so-called questionnaire. As noted earlier, "questionnaire" is a term used for almost any kind of instrument that has questions or items to which individuals respond. Although the term is used interchangeably with "schedule," it seems to be associated more with self-administered instruments that have items of the closed- or fixed-alternative type.

The self-administered instrument has certain advantages. With most or all of its items of the closed type, greater uniformity of stimulus and thus greater reliability can be achieved. In this respect, it has the advantages of objective-type, written tests and scales, if they are adequately constructed and pretested. A second advantage is that, if anonymous, honesty and frankness may be encouraged. This kind of instrument can also be administered to large numbers relatively easily. A somewhat dubious advantage is that it can be mailed to respondents. Further, it is economical. Its cost is ordinarily a fraction of that of interviews.

The disadvantages of the self-administered instrument (when mailed) seem to outweigh its advantages. The principal disadvantage of the self-administered instrument is low percentage of returns. A second disadvantage is that it may not be as uniform as it seems. Experience has shown that the same question frequently has different meanings for different people. As we saw, this can be handled in the interview. But we are powerless to do anything about it when the instrument is self-administered. Third, if only closed items are used, the instrument displays the same weaknesses of closed items discussed earlier. On the other hand, if open items are used, the respondent may object to writing the answers, which reduces the sample of adequate responses. Many people cannot express themselves adequately in writing, and many who can express themselves dislike doing so.

Because of these disadvantages, the interview is probably superior to the self-administered questionnaire. (This statement does not include carefully constructed personality and attitude scales.) The best instrument available for sounding people's behavior, future intentions, feelings, attitudes, and reason for behavior would seem to be the structured interview coupled with an interview schedule that includes open-end, closed, and scale items. Of course, the structured interview must be carefully constructed and pretested and be used only by skilled interviewers. The cost in time, energy, and money, and the very high degree of skill necessary for its construction, are its main drawbacks. Once these disadvantages are surmounted, the structured interview is a powerful tool of behavioral research.

The self-administered questionnaire has been used too much, and the structured interview too little. The success of the interview in sociology and psychology should encourage researchers to master its intricacies and to use it where it is clearly appropriate. At the very least, whenever a questionnaire is contemplated, the question should be asked: Would it be better to use an interview? If the answer is yes, then every effort should be made to do so.

Addendum: Examples of the Interview as a Research Tool

This chapter has emphasized the use of the interview in survey research. Its value as a primary or supplementary method in all kinds of studies must be pointed out. When information is difficult to get with other methods and when it is necessary to probe or go deep, the interview can be invaluable. When a new area is being explored, interviewing may be useful to obtain leads on hypotheses, variables, and items. When research is done with small children, interviewing may be the only way to have them communicate. Rather than labor these points, we give four examples to supplement those given in the chapter.

In their research on the prejudice of former soldiers, Bettelheim and Janowitz used intensive interviews in which the men were encouraged to express their attitudes toward Jews, Negroes, and other minorities.[20] The depth interviews, though costly in time—each took from four to seven hours—unearthed sentiments hardly obtainable by other means.

Jackson, Silberman, and Wolfson ingeniously used 25-minute interviews with third-grade teachers to ascertain their personal involvement with their pupils.[21] First, the teachers were asked to name all their pupils. Then they were asked, "Assume I am a third-grade teacher and this child [the first or last child named by the teacher] is to be transferred to my room. Tell me about him." The descriptions of the teachers were tape-recorded, and typed transcripts were content-analyzed for indicators of teacher involvement, for example, admiration or disdain, judgments of worth, and so on. The results provided measures of involvement. It is hard to imagine obtaining such measures in any other way except, perhaps, through projective devices.

In their study of children's perceptions of social stratification, Simmons and Rosenberg used three-hour interviews as their primary method of determining third- to twelfth-grade children's awareness of stratification and their views of the

[20]B. Bettelheim and M. Janowitz, "Ethnic Tolerance: A Function of Social and Personal Control." In H. Proshansky and B. Seidenberg, eds., *Basic Studies in Social Psychology*. New York: Holt, Rinehart and Winston, 1965, pp. 685–693.

[21]P. Jackson, M. Silberman, and B. Wolfson, "Signs of Personal Involvement in Teachers' Descriptions of Their Students," *Journal of Educational Psychology*, LX (1969), 22–27.

American opportunity structure.[22] One question aimed at the latter was: "Do all kids in America have the same chance to grow up and get the good things in life, or Do some kids *not* have as good a chance as others, or Don't you know."

An example of the exploratory use of interviewing can be taken from the author's research. To obtain educational and social attitude statements and referents, as well as to obtain insights into a new area, a number of adults were interviewed informally by simply mentioning a controversial topic and asking the individuals what their thinking on it was. For example, one question was: "What do you think of the job the public schools are doing today with our children?" The questions were worded in this ambiguous fashion deliberately to elicit a wide range of statements and referents. Pertinent statements and referents were recorded and made parts of item pools.

Study Suggestions

1. There are valuable references on the interview and the interview schedule. A few are given below. Those marked with an asterisk will probably be of most help to the reader whose knowledge of the field is limited.

   Cannell and Kahn chapters. See footnotes 2 and 4.

   **Interviewer's Manual, Survey Research Center.* Ann Arbor: Institute for Social Research, University of Michigan, 1969. An excellent guide to the practical aspects of interviewing.

   Kahn, R., and Cannell, C. *The Dynamics of Interviewing.* New York: Wiley, 1957.

   *Kornhauser, A., and Sheatsley, P. "Questionnaire Construction and Interview Procedure." In C. Selltiz et al. *Research Methods in Social Relations*, rev. ed. New York: Holt, Rinehart and Winston, 1959, app. C.

   *Maccoby and Maccoby chapter. See footnote 2.

   *Parten, M. *Surveys, Polls, and Samples.* New York: Harper & Row, 1950, chaps. VI, X, and XI.

   Richardson, S., Dohrenwend, B., and Klein, D. *Interviewing.* New York: Basic Books, 1965.

2. Good interview schedules are plentiful, though most of them have questions requiring, for the most part, fixed-alternative responses. The reader should carefully study two or three well-constructed schedules. Here are six of them. In addition to illustrating good interview techniques, they have considerable substantive interest. The student should also pay attention to the methodological discussions of these studies (sometimes in appendices).

   Free, L., and Cantril, H. *The Political Beliefs of Americans.* New Brunswick, N.J.: Rutgers University Press, 1967, app. B. Has good questions and probes and fixed-alternative items.

   Glock, C., and Stark, R., *Christian Beliefs and Anti-Semitism.* New York: Harper & Row, 1966. The complete schedule, mostly with fixed-alternative items, is given at the end of the book.

   Miller, G., and Swanson, G. *The Changing American Parent.* New York: Wiley, 1958, app. 3. An involved schedule that required careful planning and work; contains several good funnel questions.

   Sears, R., Maccoby, E., and Levin, H. *Patterns of Child Rearing.* New York: Harper & Row, 1957, app. A. A long and detailed schedule.

   Stouffer, S., *Communism, Conformity, and Civil Liberties.* Garden City, N.Y.: Doubleday, 1955, app. B. This schedule contains many fixed-alterna-

[22] R. Simmons and M. Rosenberg, "Functions of Children's Perceptions of the Stratification System," *American Sociological Review*, XXXVI (1971), 235–249.

tive items and scales especially designed to measure tolerance and perception of Communist threat. See app. C for the scales.

U.S. Commission on Civil Rights, *Racial Isolation in the Public Schools.* Washington, D.C.: U.S. Government Printing Office, 1967, vol. 2, app. C5, pp. 212–214. An abbreviated schedule from a study of the effects of segregated and desegregated schools.

CHAPTER

Objective Tests and Scales

By far the most-used method of observation and data collection in the behavioral sciences is the test or scale. The considerable time researchers spend in constructing or finding measures of variables is well spent, however, because adequate measurement of research variables is at the core of behavioral scientific work. In general, too little attention has been paid to the measurement of the variables of research studies. Consequently, many studies have suffered from inadequate measurement. Of what use is an elegant problem like "Do educational and social values determine educational choices in curriculum, budget, and personnel?" if the researcher measures education and social values inadequately? Recently and fortunately, much more attention has been paid to measurement, and skill, insight, and sophistication are becoming more and more evident.

Objectivity and Objective Methods of Observation

Objective methods of observation are those in which anyone following the prescribed rules will assign the same numerals to objects and sets of objects as anyone else. An objective procedure is one in which agreement among observers is at a maximum. In variance terms, observer variance is at a minimum. This means that judgmental variance, the variance due to differences in judges' assignment of numerals to objects, is zero.

All methods of observation are inferential: inferences about properties of the members of sets are made on the basis of the numerals assigned to the set members with interviews, tests, scales, and direct observations of behavior. The methods differ in their directness or indirectness, in the degree to which inferences are made from the raw observations. The inferences made by using objective methods of observations are usually lengthy, despite their seeming directness. Most such methods permit a high degree of inter-observer agreement because subjects make marks on paper, the marks being restricted to two or more choices among alternatives supplied by the observer. From these marks on paper the observer infers the characteristics of the individuals and sets of individuals making the marks. In one class of objective methods, the marks on paper are made by the observer (or judge) who looks at the object or objects of measurement and chooses between given alternatives. In this case, too, inferences about the properties of the observed object or objects are made from the marks on paper. The main difference lies in who makes the marks.

It should be recognized that all methods of observation have *some* objectivity. There is not a sharp dichotomy, in other words, between so-called objective methods and other methods of observation. There is, rather, a difference in the degree of objectivity. Again, if we think of degrees of objectivity as degrees of extent of agreement among observers, the ambiguity and confusion often associated with the problem disappear.

We will agree, then, that what are here called objective methods of observation and measurement have no monopoly on objectivity or on inference, but that they are more objective and no less inferential than any other methods of observation and measurement. The methods to be discussed in this chapter will by no means exhaust possible methods, since the subject is very large and varied. They are considered only *measures of variables*, to be viewed and assessed the same as all other measures of variables.

Tests and Scales: Definitions

A *test* is a systematic procedure in which the individual tested is presented with a set of constructed stimuli to which he responds, the responses enabling the tester to assign the testee a numeral or set of numerals from which inferences can be made about the testee's possession of whatever the test is supposed to measure. This definition says little more than that a test is a measurement instrument.

A *scale* is a set of symbols or numerals so constructed that the symbols or numerals can be assigned by rule to the individuals (or their behaviors) to whom the scale is applied, the assignment being indicated by the individual's possession of whatever the scale is supposed to measure. Like a test, a scale is a measuring instrument. Indeed, except for the excess meaning associated with *test*, we can see that *test* and *scale* are similarly defined. Strictly speaking, however, *scale* is used in two ways: to indicate a measuring instrument and to indicate the systematized numerals of the measuring instrument. We use it in both senses without worrying too much about fine distinctions. Remember this, however: tests are scales, but scales are not necessarily tests. This can be said because scales do not ordinarily have the meanings of competition and success or failure that tests do. Significantly, we say "achievement testing," not "achievement scaling"; "intelligence testing" and not "intelligence scaling."

Types of Objective Measures

Most of the hundreds, perhaps thousands, of tests and scales can be divided into the following classes: intelligence and aptitude tests, achievement tests, personality measures, attitude and value scales, and miscellaneous objective measures. We discuss each of these types of measure from the research point of view.

Intelligence and Aptitude Tests

While the nature and definition of intelligence are far from being fully determined, there are a number of good individual and group intelligence tests that the research worker can use when he needs a measure of intelligence. To control the intelligence variable, many researchers use short, so-called omnibus measures. (An omnibus measure is one that includes items of different kinds—verbal, numerical, spatial, and others—in one instrument.) These measures are ordinarily highly verbal and correlate substantially with school achievement. Buros' handbook is useful as a guide to such tests.[1]

Aptitude is potential ability for achievement. Although there are good aptitude tests available, they are used mainly for guidance and counseling. Still, general aptitude measures may sometimes be useful to the investigator, particularly as possible control variables. In studies in which school achievement is the dependent variable, pupils' aptitudes—verbal, numerical, and abstract reasoning aptitudes, for example—may need to be identified and controlled.

Achievement Tests

Achievement tests measure the present proficiency, mastery, and understanding of general and specific areas of knowledge. For the most part, they are measures of the effectiveness of instruction and learning. They are, of course, enormously important in education and educational research. Indeed, in research involving instructional methods, achievement, as we have seen, is often the dependent variable.

Achievement tests can be classified in several ways. For our purposes, we break them down into, first, standardized and specially constructed tests. Standardized tests are published group tests that are based on general educational content common to a large number of educational systems. They are the products of a high degree of professional competence and skill in test-writing and, as such, are usually quite reliable and generally valid. They are also provided with elaborate tables of norms (averages) that can be used for comparative purposes. Specially constructed tests are ordinarily teacher-made tests devised by teachers to measure more limited and specific achievements. They may also, of course, be constructed by educational researchers for measuring limited areas of achievement or proficiency.

Standardized achievement tests can also be classified into general and special tests. General tests are typically batteries of tests that measure the most important areas of school achievement: language usage, vocabulary, reading, arithmetic, and

[1]O. Buros, ed., *The Sixth Mental Measurements Yearbook*. Highland Park, N.J.: Gryphon Press, 1965.

social studies. Special achievement tests, as the name indicates, are tests in individual subjects, such as history, science, and English.

Researchers will often have no choice of achievement tests because school systems have already selected them. Given choice, however, they must carefully assess the *kind* of achievement research problems require. Suppose the research variable in a study is achievement in understanding concepts.[2] Many, perhaps most, tests used in schools will not be adequate for measuring this variable. In such cases, the researcher can choose a test specifically designed to measure the understanding of concepts, or he can devise such a test himself. In the former case, he should consult a standard measurement text and actual tests and test manuals. The latter case is more difficult. The construction of any achievement test is a formidable job, the details of which cannot be discussed here. The student is referred to specialized texts, especially those given in Study Suggestion 2, at the end of this chapter.[3]

Personality Measures

The measurement of personality traits is the most complex problem of psychological measurement. The reason is simple: human personality is probably the most complex phenomenon there is. For the purposes of measurement, personality can be viewed as the organization of the traits of the individual. A *trait* is a characteristic of an individual revealed through recurring behaviors in different situations. We say an individual is *compulsive*, or has the trait of *compulsivity*, because he is observed to be overly neat in his dress and speech, to be always punctual, to want everything to be very orderly, and to dislike and avoid irregularities.

The major problem in personality measurement is validity. To measure personality traits validly requires knowledge of what these traits are, how they interact and change, and how they relate to each other—a formidable, even forbidding, requirement. The wonder is *not*, as naive critics love to point out, that personality cannot be measured because it is too elusive, too complex, too existential, or that measurement efforts have not been too successful, but rather that some measure of success in so difficult a task *has* been achieved. Nevertheless, the problem of validity is considerable.

There are two general approaches to the construction and validation of personality measures: the *a priori* method and the *construct or theoretical* method. In the a priori method, items are constructed to reflect the personality dimension to be measured. Since the introvert is frequently a retiring person, we might write items about his preferring to be alone—shunning parties, for instance—in order to measure introversion. Since the anxious person will probably be nervous and

[2]See B. Bloom et al., *Taxonomy of Educational Objectives: The Classification of Educational Goals. Handbook I: Cognitive Domain.* New York: David McKay, 1956, pp. 89 ff.

[3]Unfortunately, little has evidently been written on the construction of tests and scales purely for research purposes. The many texts and other discussions of measurement focus for the most part on the construction and use of instruments for applied purposes. (Exceptions to this statement will be mentioned later and in the Study Suggestions.) Thus, the emphasis of this chapter and certain other chapters is on the research and not the applied connotations of measurement and tests and scales.

disorganized under stress, we might write items suggesting these conditions in order to measure anxiety. In the a priori method, then, the scale writer collects or writes items that ostensibly measure personality traits.

This approach is essentially that of early personality test writers; it is a content validity method that is still used. While there is nothing inherently wrong with the method—indeed, it will have to be used, especially in the early stages of test and scale construction—the results can be misleading. Items do not always measure what we think they measure. Sometimes we even find that an item we thought would measure, say, social responsibility, actually measures a tendency to agree with socially desirable statements. For this reason, the a priori method, used alone, is insufficient.

The method of validation often used with a priori personality scales is the known-group method. To validate a scale of social responsibility, one might find a group of individuals known to be high in social responsibility, and another known to be low in social responsibility. If the scale differentiates the group successfully, it is said to have validity.[4]

A priori personality and other measures will continue to be used in behavioral research. Their blind and naive use, however, should be discouraged. Their construct and criterion-related validities must be checked, especially through factor analysis (see Chapter 37) and other empirical means. Measures of personality, as well as other measures, have been used too often merely because the user *thinks* they measure whatever he is measuring.

The construct or theoretical method of personality-measure construction emphasizes the relations of the variable being measured to other variables, the relations prompted by the theory underlying the research. (See Chapter 27.) While scale construction must always to some extent be a priori, the more personality measures are subjected to the tests of construct validity the more faith we can have in them. It is not enough simply to accept the validity of a personality scale, or even to accept its validity because it has successfully differentiated, say, artists from scientists, teachers from non-teachers, normal persons from neurotic persons. Ultimately, its construct validity, its successful use in a wide variety of theoretically predicted relations, must be established.

Attitude Scales

Attitudes, while treated separately here and in most textbook discussions, are really an integral part of personality. (Intelligence and aptitude, too, are considered parts of personality by modern theorists.) Personality measurement, however, is mostly of traits. A *trait* is a relatively enduring characteristic of the individual to respond in a certain manner in all situations. If one is dominant, one exhibits dominant behavior in most situations. If one is anxious, anxious behavior permeates most of one's activities. An *attitude*, on the other hand, is an organized predisposition to think, feel, perceive, and behave toward a referent or cognitive object. It is an enduring structure of beliefs that predisposes the individual to behave selectively

[4]See, however, Cronbach's analytic admonitions: L. Cronbach, *Essentials of Psychological Testing*, 3d ed. New York: Harper & Row, 1970, p. 543.

toward attitude referents.[5] A *referent* is a category, class, or set of phenomena: physical objects, events, behaviors, even constructs.[6] People have attitudes toward many different things: ethnic groups, institutions, religion, educational issues and practices, the Supreme Court, civil rights, private property, and so on. One has, in other words, an attitude toward something "out there." A trait has subjective reference; an attitude has objective reference. One who has a hostile attitude toward foreigners may be hostile only to foreigners, but one who has the trait *hostility* is hostile toward everyone (at least potentially).

There are three major types of attitude scales: *summated rating scales*, *equal-appearing interval scales*, and *cumulative (or Guttman) scales*. A summated rating scale (one type of which is called Likert-type scale) is a set of attitude items, all of which are considered of approximately equal "attitude value," and to each of which subjects respond with degrees of agreement or disagreement (intensity). The scores of the items of such a scale are summed, or summed and averaged, to yield an individual's attitude score. As in all attitude scales, the purpose of the summated rating scale is to place an individual somewhere on an agreement continuum of the attitude in question.

It is important to note two or three characteristics of summated rating scales, since many scales share these characteristics. First, U, the universe of items, is conceived to be a set of items of equal "attitude value," as indicated in the definition given above. This means that there is no scale of items, as such. One item is the same as any other item in attitude value. The *individuals* responding to items are "scaled"; this "scaling" comes about through the sums (or averages) of the individuals' responses. Any subset of U is theoretically the same as any other subset of U: a set of individuals would be rank-ordered the same using U_2 as U_1.

Second, summated rating scales allow for the *intensity* of attitude expression. Subjects can agree or they can agree strongly. There are advantages to this, as well as disadvantages. The main advantage is that greater variance results. When there are five or seven possible categories of response, it is obvious that the response variance should be greater than with only two or three categories (agree, disagree, no opinion, for example). The variance of summated rating scales, unfortunately, often seems to contain response-set variance. Individuals have differential tendencies to use certain types of responses: extreme responses, neutral responses, agree responses, disagree responses. This response variance confounds the attitude (and personality trait) variance. The individual differences yielded by summated rating attitude scales (and similarly scored trait measures) have been shown to be due in part to response set and other similar extraneous sources of variance.[7]

[5]This definition comes from several sources: D. Krech and R. Crutchfield, *Theory and Problems of Social Psychology*. New York: McGraw-Hill, 1948, p. 152; T. Newcomb, *Social Psychology*. New York: Holt, Rinehart and Winston, 1950, pp. 118–119; F. Kerlinger, "Social Attitudes and Their Criterial Referents: A Structural Theory," *Psychological Review*, LXXIV (1967), 110–122; M. Rokeach, *Beliefs, Attitudes, and Values*. San Francisco: Jossey-Bass, 1968, p. 112.

[6]R. Brown, *Words and Things*. New York: Free Press, 1958, pp. 7–10.

[7]The literature on response set is large and cannot be cited in detail here (see Study Suggestion 4). Good summary discussions can be found in: J. Guilford, *Psychometric Methods*, 2d ed. New York: McGraw-Hill, 1954, pp. 451–456; J. Nunnally, *Psychometric Theory*. New York: McGraw-Hill, 1967,

Here are two summated rating items from a scale designed by the writer to measure attitudes toward the decision of the United States Supreme Court on the New York Regents' Prayer. Respondents are asked to indicate whether they *agree very strongly* (7), *agree strongly* (6), *agree* (5) *disagree* (3), *disagree strongly* (2), *disagree very strongly* (1). The values in parentheses are assigned to the responses indicated. (If there is no response to an item, 4 is given.) Thus, there is a seven-point scale of degree of agreement-disagreement.

> The Supreme Court decision will aid American democracy by strengthening the principle of the separation of church and state.
> The Supreme Court was right; the decision will help to protect religious freedom.

Thurstone *equal-appearing interval scales* are built on different principles. While the ultimate product, a set of attitude items, can be used for the same purpose of assigning individuals attitude scores, equal-appearing interval scales also accomplish the important purpose of scaling the attitude items. *Each item* is assigned a scale value, and the scale value indicates the strength of attitude of an agreement response to the item. The universe of items is considered to be an ordered set; that is, items differ in scale value. The scaling procedure finds these scale values. In addition, the items of the final scale to be used are so selected that the intervals between them are equal, a most important and desirable psychometric feature.

The following equal-appearing interval items, with the scale values of the items are from Thurstone and Chave's scale, Attitude toward the Church:[8]

> I believe the church is the greatest institution in America today. (Scale value: .2)
> I believe in religion, but I seldom go to church. (Scale value: 5.4)
> I think the church is a hindrance to religion for it still depends upon magic, superstition, and myth. (Scale value: 9.6)

In the Thurstone and Chave scale, the lower the scale value, the more positive the attitude toward the church. The first and third items were the lowest and highest in the scale. The second item, of course, had an intermediate value. The total scale contained 45 items with scale values ranging over the whole continuum. Usually, however, equal-appearing interval scales contain considerably fewer items.

The third type of scale, *the cumulative or Guttman scale*, consists of a relatively small set of homogeneous items that are unidimensional (or supposed to be).

---

pp. 593–617. I believe that, while response set is a mild threat to valid measurement, its importance has been overrated and that the available evidence does not justify the strong negative assertions made by response-set enthusiasts. In other words, while one must be conscious of the possibilities and threats, one should certainly not be paralyzed by the somewhat blown-up danger. See *ibid.*, pp. 615–616, and L. Rorer, "The Great Response-Style Myth," *Psychological Bulletin*, LXIII (1965), 129–156.

[8]L. Thurstone and E. Chave, *The Measurement of Attitude*. Chicago: University of Chicago Press, 1929, pp. 61–63, 78.

A *unidimensional* scale measures one variable, and one variable only. The scale gets its name from the cumulative relation between items and the total scores of individuals. For example, we ask four children three arithmetic questions: (a) $28/7 = ?$, (b) $8 \times 4 = ?$, and (c) $12 + 9 = ?$ A child who gets (a) correct is very likely to get the other two correct. The child who misses (a), but gets (b) correct, is likely also to get (c) correct. A child who misses (c), on the other hand, is not likely to get (a) and (b) correct. The situation can be summarized as follows (the table includes the score of the fourth child, who gets none correct):

	(a)	*(b)*	*(c)*	*Total Score*
First Child	1	1	1	3
Second Child	0	1	1	2
Third Child	0	0	1	1
Fourth Child	0	0	0	0

(1 = Correct; 0 = Incorrect)

Note the relation between the *pattern* of item responses and total scores. If we know a child's total score, we can predict his pattern, if the scale is cumulative, just as knowledge of correct responses to the harder items are predictive of the responses to the easier items. Note, too, that both items and persons are scaled.

Similarly, people can be asked various questions about an attitudinal object. If upon analysis the patterns of responses arrange themselves in the manner indicated above (at least fairly closely), then the questions or items are said to be unidimensional. Therefore people can be ranked according to their scale responses. Here are three questions that were designed by Stouffer for his tolerance study:

> Now, I should like to ask you some questions about a man who admits he is a Communist.
> Suppose this admitted Communist wants to make a speech in your community. Should he be allowed to speak or not?
> If some people in your community suggested that a book he wrote favoring government ownership [of all the railroads and big industries] should be taken out of your public library, would you favor removing the book, or not?
> Suppose he is a clerk in a store. Should he be fired, or not?[9]

These items, part of Stouffer's total scale measuring tolerance, were scaled. A person who says "Yes" to the first item will tend to say "Yes" to the other two items. A person who says "Yes" to the second item will tend to say "Yes" to the third. A third person might say "Yes" to the third item and "No" to the first two, and a fourth person might say "No" to all three. The scores and patterns of the four persons are the same as those given for the arithmetic questions: the first person (total score of 3) was the most tolerant; the second person (total score of 2) the next most tolerant; and the fourth person (total score of 0) the least tolerant. Both persons and items are scaled for the degree of tolerance.

[9]From *Communism, Conformity, and Civil Liberties* by Samuel A. Stouffer. Garden City, N.Y.: Doubleday, 1955, pp. 263–265. Copyright © 1955 by Samuel A. Stouffer. Reprinted by permission of Doubleday & Company, Inc.

It is obvious that these three methods of constructing attitude scales are very different. Note that the same or similar methods can be used with other kinds of personality and other scales. The summated rating scale concentrates on the subjects and their places on the scale. The equal-appearing interval scale concentrates on the items and their places on the scale. Interestingly, both types of scales yield about the same results as far as reliability and the placing of individuals in attitudinal rank orders are concerned. Cumulative scales concentrate on the scalability of sets of items and on the scale positions of individuals.

Of the three types of scales, the summated rating scale seems to be the most useful in behavioral research. It is easier to develop, and as indicated above, yields about the same results as the more laboriously constructed, equal-appearing interval scale. Used with care and knowledge of its weaknesses, summated rating scales can be adapted to many needs of behavioral researchers. Cumulative scales would seem to be less useful and less generally applicable. If one clear-cut cognitive object is used, a short well-constructed cumulative scale may yield reliable measures of a number of psychological variables: tolerance, conformity, group identification, acceptance of authority, permissiveness, and so on. It should be noted, too, that the method can be improved and altered in various ways.[10]

Value Scales

Values are culturally weighted preferences for things, ideas, people, institutions, and behaviors.[11] Whereas attitudes are organizations of beliefs about things "out there," predispositions to behave toward the objects or referents of attitudes, values express preferences for modes of conduct and end-states of existence.[12] Words like *equality*, *freedom*, *wisdom*, *peace*, and *happiness* express values.[13] Simply put, values express the "good," the "bad," the "shoulds," the "oughts" of human behavior. Values put ideas, things, and behaviors on approval–disapproval continua. They imply choices among courses of action and thinking.

To give the reader some flavor of values, here are three items.[14] Individuals can be asked to express their approval or disapproval of the first and second items, perhaps in summated-rating form, and to choose from the three alternatives of the third item.

> For his own good and for the good of society, man must be held in restraint by tradition and authority.
> Now more than ever we should strengthen the family, the natural stabilizer of society.
> Which of the following is the most important in living the full life: education, achievement, friendship?

[10]A. Edwards, *Techniques of Attitude Scale Construction.* New York: Appleton, 1957, chaps. 7 and 9. Edwards describes how to construct and evaluate cumulative scales, as well as summated-rating and equal-appearing interval scales.

[11]C. Kluckhohn et al., "Values and Value-Orientations in the Theory of Action." In T. Parsons and E. Shils, eds., *Toward a General Theory of Action.* Cambridge, Mass.: Harvard University Press, 1952, pp. 388–433.

[12]Rokeach, *op. cit.*, p. 159. The relations between attitudes and values and the definitions of both are still not clear in the literature, probably because of the neglect of value theory and research.

[13]Rokeach uses these and other concepts as items in his Value Survey (unpublished).

[14]The first two items were written by the author for a University of Hawaii research project, 1971.

Unfortunately, values have had little scientific study, even though they and attitudes are a large part of man's verbal output and probable influential determiners of behavior. The measurement of values has thus suffered. The only well-known commercially available values scale seems to be the Allport-Vernon-Lindzey *Study of Values*.[15] There can be little doubt, however, that social and educational values will become the focus of much more theoretical and empirical work in the next decade, since social scientists are becoming increasingly aware that values are important influences on individual and group behavior.[16] Rokeach has stated the case for values: "... in shifting ... to a concern with values we would be dealing with a concept that is more central, more dynamic, more economical, ... and that would broaden the range of ... traditional concern to include problems of education and reeducation as well as problems of persuasion."[17]

Miscellaneous Objective Measures

A number of objective inferential measures do not conveniently fall into one of the above categories, although they are closely related to one or more of them. We shall consider several of these measures here to illustrate the variety of work already done and the possible nature of future objective inferential measurement.

Certain scales are important because of their theoretical value and the frequency of their use. The well-known *F* scale is one of these scales.[18] Designed to measure authoritarianism (*F* originally stood for fascism), it has been called both a personality and an attitude measure. Probably closer to being a personality measure, the *F* scale is a summated rating scale in which subjects are asked to respond to a number of general statements, usually 29 or 30. Here are three such items, agreement with which is supposed to indicate authoritarian trends in the respondent.

> Obedience and respect for authority are the most important virtues children should learn.
> What the youth needs most is strict discipline, rugged determination, and the will to work and fight for family and country.
> Science has its place, but there are many important things that can never possibly be understood by the human mind.[19]

The *F* scale seems to tap broad general attitudes or cores of values, as well as personality traits. Many differences have been found between high- and low-scoring persons and groups.[20] More important, however, are the fruitful theoretical reason-

[15] G. Allport, P. Vernon, and G. Lindzey, *Study of Values*, rev. ed. Boston: Houghton Mifflin, 1951.

[16] See W. Dukes, "Psychological Studies of Values," *Psychological Bulletin*, LII (1955), 24–50; B. Friedman, *Foundations of the Measurement of Values*. New York: Teachers College Press, 1946; S. Pittel and G. Mendelsohn, "Measurement of Moral Values," *Psychological Bulletin*, LXVI (1966), 22–35; R. Williams, "Individual and Group Values," *The Annals of the American Academy of Political and Social Science*, CCCLXXI (1967), 20–37.

[17] Rokeach, *op. cit.*, p. 159.

[18] T. Adorno et al., *The Authoritarian Personality*. New York: Harper & Row, 1950.

[19] *Ibid.*, pp. 255–257.

[20] R. Christie, "Authoritarianism Re-examined." In R. Christie and M. Johoda. *Studies in the Scope and Method of "The Authoritarian Personality."* New York: Free Press, 1954, pp. 123–196; J. Kirscht and R. Dillehay, *Dimensions of Authoritarianism: A Review of Research and Theory*. Lexington, Ky.: University of Kentucky Press, 1967; S. Messick and D. Jackson, "The Measurement of Authoritarian Attitudes," *Educational and Psychological Measurement*, XVIII (1958), 241–253; H. Titus and E. Hollander, "The California F Scale in Psychological Research: 1950–1955," *Psychological Bulletin*, LIV (1957), 47–64.

ing behind the scale's construction, the empirical approach to an important social and psychological problem, and the stimulus to research in the measurement of complex variables. The *F* scale has fallen into some disrepute under the critical onslaught of psychologists and sociologists because it allegedly does not hold up under the rigorous application of validity criteria. Recent evidence, however, seems to indicate that, despite its weaknesses, the *F* scale was well conceived theoretically and well fashioned as a measure of authoritarianism.[21]

A number of scales related to the *F* scale have been constructed. One of the Adorno scales is the *E* (Ethnocentrism) scale, which attempts to measure prejudiced attitudes more directly.[22] (The *F* scale measures ethnocentrism indirectly.) Two more related scales that are exceptionally important, but that defy categorization, are Rokeach's Dogmatism (*D*) and Opinionation (*O*) scales.[23] Like the *F* and *E* scales, these are summated rating scales that presumably measure, in the case of the *D* scale, the openness and closedness of individuals' belief systems and general intolerance and authoritarianism, and in the case of the *O* scale, general intolerance. Rokeach built his scales deductively, that is, he studied characteristics of open and closed belief systems and constructed items to tap these characteristics. Here is a sample of Rokeach's *D* scale items:

> Man on his own is a helpless and miserable creature.
> There are two kinds of people in the world: those who are for the truth and those who are against the truth.
> In the long run the best way to live is to pick friends and associates whose tastes and beliefs are the same as one's own.[24]

The first item was designed to measure helplessness, the second intolerance, and the third the avoidance of contact with persons whose beliefs differ from one's own. One outstanding feature of Rokeach's work is his measurement of dogmatism of the right and the left. The *F* scale emphasizes authoritarianism of the right. Rokeach's work is another serious and ambitious attempt to measure important and complex variables—with, it is believed, considerable success.

The measurement of *interests* is relatively easy. The most important measures are the Strong and Kuder tests.[25] In the Strong test, the subject responds to activities presumably related to different vocations: musician, artist, athletic director, physician, and so on. His responses are then compared to the responses of members of the various vocations. Kuder's inventory identifies clusters of occupational interest: scientific, musical, mechanical, and so on. It, too, uses activities presumably related to the different interest areas. An individual's responses identify his

[21]This statement is based mostly on the following research: F. Kerlinger and M. Rokeach, "The Factorial Nature of the F and D Scales," *Journal of Personality and Social Psychology*, IV (1966), 391–399. The data of this study were reanalyzed and the study replicated by other researchers with essentially the same results: P. Warr, R. Lee, and K. Jöreskog, "A Note on the Factorial Nature of the F and D Scales," *British Journal of Psychology*, LX (1969), 119–123.

[22]Adorno et al., *op. cit.*, p. 142.

[23]M. Rokeach, *The Open and Closed Mind*. New York: Basic Books, 1960, pp. 73–84.

[24]*Ibid.*, pp. 75, 78, and 79.

[25]Good discussion of these scales can be found in J. Guilford, *Personality*. New York: McGraw-Hill, 1959, pp. 206–220.

broad interests. The reliabilities of both measures are high and the validities are respectable. For the researcher who wants a quick measure of occupational interests, the Thurstone Interest Schedule takes only ten minutes to administer.[26]

In research studies on group processes, a measure of group cohesiveness, attraction to a group, is sometimes needed. A simple, easily administered and scored cohesiveness measure has been constructed by Libo.[27] Libo developed an interesting picture projective measure of cohesiveness, but he found that the much simpler pencil-and-paper measure yielded better results.

Naturally, there are many other important and useful tests and scales—measures of moral judgment, social responsibility, classroom environment, needs, dominance, and so on. They cannot be discussed here. A few interesting and promising ones, however, are mentioned in Study Suggestion 5 at the end of the chapter.

Types of Objective Scales and Items

Two broad types of items in general use are those in which responses are independent and those in which they are not independent. Independence here means that a person's response to an item is unrelated to his response to another item. True-false, yes-no, agree-disagree, and Likert items belong to the independent type. The subject responds to each item freely with a range of two or more possible responses from which he can choose one. Nonindependent items, on the other hand, force the respondent to choose one item or alternative that precludes the choice of other items or alternatives. These forms of scales and items are called forced-choice scales and items. The subject is faced with two or more items or subitems and is asked to choose one or more of them according to some criterion, or even criteria.

Two simple examples will show the difference between independent and nonindependent items. First, a set of instructions that allows independence of response might be given to the respondent:

> Indicate beside each of the following statements how much you approve them, using a scale from 1 through 5, 1 meaning "Do not approve at all" and 5 meaning "Approve very much."

A contrasting set of instructions, with more limited choices (nonindependent) might be:

> Forty pairs of statements are given below. From each pair, choose the one you *approve more*. Mark it with a check.

[26]L. Thurstone, *Thurstone Interest Schedule*. New York: Psychological Corp., 1947.

[27]L. Libo, *Measuring Group Cohesiveness*. Ann Arbor: Institute for Social Research, University of Michigan, 1953, pp. 24–25. Two excellent reviews of research on cohesiveness are: D. Cartwright, "The Nature of Group Cohesiveness." In D. Cartwright and A. Zander, eds., *Group Dynamics: Research and Theory*, 3d ed. New York: Harper & Row, 1968, pp. 91–109; A Lott and B. Lott, "Group Cohesiveness as Interpersonal Attraction: A Review of Relationships With Antecedent and Consequent Variables," *Psychological Bulletin*, LXIV (1965), 259–309.

Advantages of independent items are economy and the applicability of most statistical analyses to responses to them. Also, when each item is responded to, a maximum of information is obtained, each item contributing to variance. Less time is taken to administer independent scales, too, but they may suffer from response-set bias. An individual can give the same or similar response to each item: he can endorse them all enthusiastically or all indifferently depending on his particular response predilection. Response-set bias, then, can confound the variable property variance with such items. (But see footnote 7.)

The forced-choice type of scale avoids, at least to some extent, response bias. At the same time, though, it suffers from a lack of independence, a lack of economy, and overcomplexity. Forced-choice scales can also strain the subject's endurance and patience, resulting in less cooperation. Still, many experts believe that forced-choice instruments hold great promise for psychological and educational measurement. Other experts are skeptical.

Types of scales and items, then, can be divided into three types: *agreement-disagreement* (or *approve-disapprove*, or *true-false*, and the like), *rank order*, and *forced choice*. We discuss each of these briefly. Lengthier discussion can be found in the literature.[28]

Agreement-Disagreement Items

There are three general forms of *agreement-disagreement* items:

1. Those permitting one of two possible responses
2. Those permitting one of three or more possible responses
3. Those permitting more than one choice of three or more possible responses

The first two of these forms supply alternatives like "agree-disagree"; "yes-no"; "yes-?-no"; "approve-no opinion-disapprove"; "approve strongly-approve-disapprove-disapprove strongly"; "*1, 2, 3, 4, 5.*" The subject chooses one of the supplied responses to report his reaction to each item. In so doing he gives a report of himself or indicates his reaction to the item. Most personality and attitude scales use such items.

The third type of scale in this group presents a number of items; the subject is instructed to indicate those items that describe himself, items with which he agrees, or simply items that he chooses. The adjective check list is a good example. The subject is presented with a list of adjectives, some indicating desirable traits, like *thoughtful*, *generous*, and *considerate*; and others indicating undesirable traits, like *cruel*, *selfish*, and *mean*. He is asked to check those adjectives that characterize himself. (Of course this type of instrument can be used to characterize other persons, too.) A better form, perhaps, would be a list with all positive adjectives of known scale values from which the subject is asked to select a specific number of his own personal characteristics. By using only positive items, response bias can be weakened. The equal-appearing interval scale and its response system of checking those attitude items with which one agrees is, of course, the same idea.

[28]See, especially, Guilford, *Psychometric Methods, op. cit.*

The idea is a useful one, especially with the development of factor scales, scaling methods, and the increasing use of choice methods.

To illustrate the not inconsiderable possibilities, we can examine a scale constructed by the writer to measure perceptions or judgments of desirable characteristics of teachers.[29] The subjects were presented with 18 descriptions of teachers. All elements of the descriptions were balanced in three groups of six items each, except for adjectival descriptions. These adjectival descriptions fell into three groups: *A*, *B*, and *N* (neutral). (*A* and *B* were dimensions derived from empirical studies using the method of factor analysis.) Subjects were asked to play the role of a superintendent of schools and to choose the six teachers he would hire from among the 18 teachers. Here are two of the items, the first a *B* item, the second an *A* item.

1. Davida Lester. Age 27. Single. B.S., University of Buffalo; M.A., City College. Has seven years teaching experience, all of it satisfactory. Her recommendations are good. She has been described by reliable sources as industrious, firm, efficient, moral, dependable, and self-controlled.
2. Ruth Simpson. Age 24. Single. B.S., Potsdam State Teachers College; M.A., New York University. Has five years teaching experience, all of it satisfactory. Her recommendations are good. Reliable evidence indicates that she is insightful, flexible, purposeful, enthusiastic, fair, and sympathetic.

The scoring of agreement-disagreement types of items can be troublesome since not all the items, or the components of the items, receive responses. (With a summated-rating scale or an ordinary rating scale subjects usually respond to all items.) In general, however, simple systems of assigning numerals to the various choices can be used. For instance, "agree-disagree' can be 1 and 0; "yes-?-no" can be 1, 0, −1, or, avoiding minus signs: 2, 1, 0. The responses to the summated-rating items described earlier are simply assigned 1 through 5 or 1 through 7.

The main thing researchers have to keep in mind is that *the scoring system has to yield interpretable data congruent with the scoring system.* If scores of 1, 0, −1 are used, the data must be capable of a scaled interpretation—that is, 1 is "high" or "most," −1 is "low" or "least," and 0 is in between. A system of 1, 0 can mean high and low or simply presence or absence of an attribute. Such a system can be useful and powerful, as we saw earlier when discussing variables like sex, race, social class, and so on. In sum, the data yielded by scoring systems have to have clearly interpretable meanings in some sort of quantitative sense. The student is referred to Ghiselli's discussion of the meaningfulness of scores.[30]

Various systems for weighting items have been devised, but the evidence indicates that weighted and unweighted scores give much the same results. Students seem to find it hard to believe this. (Note that we are talking about the weighting of *responses* to items.) Although the matter is not completely settled, the evidence is strong that, in tests and measures of sufficient numbers of items—say 20 or more

[29]F. Kerlinger and E. Pedhazur, "Educational Attitudes and Perceptions of Desirable Traits of Teachers," *American Educational Research Journal,* V (1968), 543–560. For the rather complex scoring system used, see p. 548.

[30]E. Ghiselli, *Theory of Psychological Measurement.* New York: McGraw-Hill, 1964, pp. 44–49.

—weighting items differentially does not make much difference in final outcomes. Nor does the different weighting of responses make much difference.[31] It also makes no difference at all, in variance terms, if you transform scoring weights linearly. You may have subjects use a system, + 1, 0, − 1, and, of course, these scores can be used in analysis. But you can add a constant of 1 to each score, yielding 2, 1, 0. The transformed scores are easier to work with, since they have no minus signs.

Rank-Order Items and Scales

The second group of scale and item types is *ordinal* or *rank order*, which is a simple and most useful form of scale or item. A whole scale can be rank-ordered—that is, subjects can be asked to rank all the items according to some specified criterion. We might wish to compare the educational values of administrators, teachers, and parents, for instance. A number of items presumed to measure educational values can be presented to the members of each group with instructions to rank-order them according to their preferences.

An excellent example of a rank-order scale is Rokeach's *Value Survey*.[32] Actually, there are two scales in the instrument, one to measure *terminal values* and the other to measure *instrumental values*. In the former, eighteen single-value concepts—A Comfortable Life, A Sense of Accomplishment, Equality, Freedom, Social Recognition, and so on—are presented to the subject to be rank-ordered according to their importance to the subject. Some of the results obtained with this interesting instrument were presented in Chapter 22. Recall that Rokeach found that different groups gave quite different average ranks to *equality* and *freedom* (see Table 22.1).

Rank-order scales have three convenient analytic advantages. One, the scales of individuals can easily be intercorrelated and analyzed. Composite rank orders of groups of individuals can also easily be correlated. Two, scale values of a set of stimuli can be calculated using one of the rank-order methods of scaling.[33] Three, they partially escape response set and the tendency to agree with socially desirable items.

A useful, but relatively untried, method of constructing scales has been suggested by Stephenson in another context.[34] The writer some years ago followed Stephenson's suggestion and constructed sets of four items, each set of which was to be rank-ordered by the respondents. Here is one of the sets of items. (Try responding to it. Assign 1 to the item approved most highly, 2 to the item approved next and 3 to the next, and 4 to the item least approved.)

> It is unrealistic to expect education to be like real life; it is more a preparation for life.
> Pupils should be encouraged to evaluate their teachers, since they must learn to evaluate other people all their lives.

[31]See Guilford, *op. cit.*, pp. 447 ff.; Nunnally, *op. cit.*, pp. 277–279.

[32]J. Robinson and P. Shaver, *Measures of Social Psychological Attitudes*. Ann Arbor: Institute of Social Research, University of Michigan, 1969, pp. 463–467. Some of the research using the instrument has been reported in: Rokeach, *Beliefs, Attitudes, and Values, op. cit.*, pp. 168 ff.

[33]Guilford, *op. cit.*, chap. 8.

[34]W. Stephenson, *The Study of Behavior*. Chicago: University of Chicago Press, 1953, pp. 205–206.

The backbone of the school curriculum is subject matter; activities are useful mainly to facilitate the learning of subject matter.
No subject is more important than the personalities of the pupils.

Items and scales like these are useful with sophisticated individuals. But they have defects, one of which is the lack of independence of the items. Note that, in the set of items above, we have four choices at the start. After choosing the first item three are left. After three items have been chosen and ranked, only one item and one rank remain. This introduces spurious negative correlation between items, correlation that is a result of the measurement procedure. Nevertheless, they can be effective as well as economical.

Forced-Choice Items and Scales

The essence of a forced-choice method is that the subject must choose among alternatives that on the surface appear about equally favorable (or unfavorable). Strictly speaking, the method is not new. Pair comparisons and rank-order scales are forced-choice methods. What is different about the forced-choice method, as such, is that the discrimination and preference values of items are determined, and items approximately equal in both are paired. In this way, response set and "item desirability" are to some extent controlled. ("Item desirability" means that one item may be chosen over another simply because it expresses a commonly recognized desirable idea. If a person is asked if he is careless or efficient, he is likely to say he is efficient, even though he *is* careless.)

The method of *paired comparisons* (or *pair comparisons*) has a long and respectable psychometric past. It has, however, been used mostly for purposes of determining scale values.[35] Here we look at paired comparisons as a method of measurement. The essence of the method is that sets of pairs of stimuli, or items of different values on a single continuum or on two different continua or factors, are presented to the subject with instructions to choose one member of each pair on the basis of some stated criterion. The criterion might be: which one better characterizes the subject, or which does the subject prefer. The items of the pairs can be single words, phrases, sentences, or even paragraphs. For example, Dunkel, in studying the life goals of students, paired items like the following:

Making a place for myself in the world; getting ahead.
Living the pleasure of the moment.[36]

One use of paired comparisons is the pairing of statements in Edwards' Personal Preference Schedule (PPS).[37] One item measuring the need for autonomy, for instance, is paired with another item measuring the need for change. The subject is asked to choose one of these items. It is assumed that he will choose the item that fits his own needs. A unique feature of the scale is that the social desirability values of the paired members were determined empirically and the pairs matched accordingly. The instrument yields profiles of need scores for each individual.

[35]Guilford, *op. cit.*, chap. 7.
[36]H. Dunkel, "An Inventory of Students' General Goals in Life," *Educational and Psychological Measurement*, IV (1944), 87–95.
[37]A. Edwards, *Personal Preference Schedule, Manual.* New York: Psychological Corp., 1953.

In some ways, the two types of paired-comparisons technique, (1) the determining of scale values of stimuli, and (2) the direct measurement of variables, are the most satisfying of psychometric methods. They are simple and economical, because there are only two alternatives. Further, a good deal of information can be obtained with a limited amount of material. If, for example, an investigator has only 10 items, say 5 of Variable A and 5 of Variable B, he can construct a scale of 5×5 or 25 items, since each A item can be systematically paired with each B item. If he has 10 A items and 10 B items, he can construct a scale of 100 items. (The scoring is simple: assign a "1" to A or B in each item, depending on which alternative the subject chooses.) Most important, paired-comparison items force the subjects to choose. Although this may irk some subjects, especially if they believe that neither item represents what they would choose (that is, choosing between *coward* and *weakling* to categorize oneself), it is really a customary human activity. We must make choices every day of our lives. It can even be argued that agreement-disagreement items are artificial and that choice items are "natural."

Forced-choice items of more than two parts can assume a number of forms with three, four, or five parts, the parts being homogeneous or heterogeneous in favorableness or unfavorableness. We discuss and illustrate only one of these types to demonstrate the principles behind such items. By factor analysis, a procedure known as the critical incidents technique, or some other method, items are gathered and selected. It is usually found that some items discriminate between criterion groups and others do not. Both kinds of items—call them *discriminators* and *irrelevants*—are included in each item set. In addition, *preference values* are determined for each item.

A typical forced-choice item is a tetrad. One useful form of tetrad consists of two pairs of items, one pair high in preference value, the other pair low in preference value, one member of each pair being a discriminator (or valid), and the other member being irrelevant (or not valid). A scheme of such a forced-choice item is

(a) high preference—discriminator
(b) high preference—irrelevant
(c) low preference—discriminator
(d) low preference—irrelevant

A subject is directed to choose the item of the tetrad that he most prefers, or that describes him (or someone else) best, and so on. He is also directed to select the item that is least preferrred or least descriptive of himself.

The basic idea behind this rather complex type of item is, as indicated earlier, that response set and social desirability are controlled. The subject cannot tell, theoretically at least, which are the discriminator items and which the irrelevant items; nor can he pick items on the basis of preference values. Thus the tendencies to evaluate oneself (or others) too high or too low is counteracted, and validity is therefore presumably increased.[38]

Here is a forced-choice item of a somewhat different type, constructed by the

[38]For further discussion, see Guilford, *op. cit.*, pp. 274 ff.

author for illustrative purposes using items from actual research:

conscientious
agreeable
responsive
sensitive

One of the items (*sensitive*) is an *A* item, and one (*conscientious*) a *B* item. (*A* and *B* refer to the factors mentioned earlier.) The other two items are presumably irrelevant. Subjects can be asked to choose the one or two items that are most important for a teacher to have.

It is still too soon to evaluate forced-choice methods. They seem to have great promise. Yet there are technical and psychological difficulties, among which the most important seem to be the lack of independence of items, the perhaps too complex nature of some items (see the earlier attitudes-toward-education tetrad), and the resistance of subjects to difficult choices. The reader is referred to Guilford's discussion of the subject: it is authoritative, objective, and brief, and to the reviews by Scott and Zavala.[39]

Ipsative and Normative Measures

A distinction that has become important and that is generally misunderstood in research and measurement is that between normative and ipsative measures. *Normative* measures are the usual kind of measures obtained with tests and scales: they can vary independently—that is, they are relatively unaffected by other measures—and are referred for interpretation to the mean of the measures of a *group*, individuals' sets of measures having different means and standard deviations. *Ipsative* measures, on the other hand, are systematically affected by other measures and are referred for interpretation to the same mean, each *individual*'s set of measures having the same mean and standard deviation. To cut through this rather opaque verbiage, just think of a set of ranks, 1 through 5, 1 indicating the "first," "highest," or "most," and 5 indicating "last," "lowest," and "least," with 2, 3, and 4 indicating positions in-between. No matter who uses these ranks, the sum and mean of the ranks is always the same, 15 and 3, and the standard deviation is also always the same, 1.414. Ranks, then, are ipsative measures.

If the values 1, 2, 3, 4, and 5 were available for use to rate, say, five objects, and four people rated the five objects, we might obtain something like the following:

	1	2	2	3
	2	2	1	2
	3	4	5	3
	4	3	5	3
	5	5	4	2
Sum:	15	16	17	13
Mean:	3.00	3.20	3.40	2.60

[39] *Ibid.*; W. Scott, "Comparative Validities of Forced-Choice and Single-Stimulus Tests," *Psychological Bulletin*, LXX (1968), 231–244; A. Zavala, "Development of the Forced-Choice Rating Scale Technique," *Psychological Bulletin*, LXIII (1965), 117–124.

Note that the sums and means (and standard deviations, too) are different. These are normative measures. Theoretically, with normative measures there are no constraints on the value that individual A can give to object C—except, of course, the numbers 1 through 5.

With ipsative measures, however, the procedure—in this case of ranking—has built-in systematic restraints: each individual must use each of 1, 2, 3, 4, and 5 once and once only, and he must use all of them. This means that when five objects are being ranked and one is given, say, Rank 1, there are only four ranks left to assign. After the next object is assigned 2, there are only three left—and so on until the last object to which 5 *must be* assigned. Similar reasoning applies to other kinds of ipsative procedures and measures: paired comparisons, forced-choice tetrads or pentads, *Q* methodology.

The important limitation on ipsative procedures is that, strictly speaking, the usual statistics are not applicable, since such statistics depend on assumptions that ipsative procedures *systematically* violate. Moreover, the ipsative procedure produces spurious negative correlation between items. In a paired-comparisons instrument, for instance, the selection of one member of a pair automatically excludes the selection of the other member. This means lack of independence and negative correlation among items as a function of the instrumental procedure. Most statistical tests, however, are based on the assumption of independence of the elements entering statistical formulas. And analysis of correlations, as in factor analysis, can be seriously distorted by the negative correlations. Unfortunately, these limitations have not been understood, or they have been overlooked by investigators who, for example, have treated ipsative data normatively.[40]

Choice and Construction of Objective Measures

One of the most difficult tasks of the behavioral researcher faced with the necessity of measuring variables is to find his way through a mass of already existing measures. If a good measure of a particular variable exists, there seems to be little point in constructing a new measure. The question is, however: Does a good measure exist? To answer this question may require much search and study. The student should first know what kind of variable he is trying to measure. Some guidance has been attempted with the structure just provided. One must know clearly whether the variable is an aptitude, achievement, personality, attitude, or some other kind of variable. The second step is to consult one or two texts that discuss psychological tests and measures. Next, consult Buros' justly well-known guides, especially *Tests in Print*.[41] While the Buros books give excellent guidance to published tests, many good measures have not been commercially published. Thus the periodical

[40]L. Hicks, "Some Properties of Ipsative, Normative, and Forced-Choice Normative Measures," *Psychological Bulletin*, LXXIV (1970), 167–184. The reader is encouraged to set up a small matrix of ipsative numbers hypothetically generated by responses to a paired-comparisons scale. Use 1's and 0's and calculate the *r*'s between items over individuals.

[41]O. Buros, *Tests in Print*. Highland Park, N.J.: Gryphon Press, 1961; O. Buros, ed., *The Sixth Mental Measurements Yearbook*. Highland Park, N.J.: Gryphon Press, 1965. (In addition, there are five earlier yearbooks.)

literature may need to be searched. The *F* and *D* scales are examples: they are not commercially available, but anyone can use them for research purposes.

Two valuable sources of information on tests and scales are the journals *Psychological Bulletin* and *Educational and Psychological Measurement*. The former often features reviews of research on and with measurement instruments; the latter features articles on the original development of instruments. The *Journal of Educational Measurement*, as the name indicates, specializes in educational measures. One can track down measures, too, by checking *Psychological Abstracts*, which includes sections on new tests and measures. Another source for educational researchers are pertinent articles in the *Encyclopedia of Educational Research*. A new trend, which is off to a fine start in social psychology, is the publication of anthologies of scales (see Study Suggestion 3). Finally, when one has narrowed the field and found a measure or measures that seem suitable, one can try to find reviews of it in Buros' yearbooks.

An investigator may find that no measure exists for measuring what he wants to measure. Or, if a measure exists, he may deem it unsatisfactory for his purpose. Therefore he must construct his own measure—or abandon the variable. The construction of objective tests and scales is a long and arduous task. There are no shortcuts. A poorly constructed instrument may do more harm than good, because it may lead the investigator to erroneous conclusions. The investigator who must construct a new instrument, then, has to follow certain well-recognized procedures and be governed by accepted psychometric criteria.

Evaluation of Objective Tests and Scales

Tremendous progress has been made in the objective measurement of intelligence, aptitudes, achievement, personality, and attitudes. Opinion is divided, often sharply, on the value of objective measurement, however. The most impressive gain has been made in the objective measurement of intelligence, aptitudes, and achievement. Gains in personality and attitude measurement have not been as impressive. The problem, of course, is validity, especially the validity of personality measures.

Two or three recent developments are most encouraging. One is the increasing realization of the complexity of measuring any personality and attitude variables. A second is the technical advances made in doing so. Another closely allied development is the use of factor analysis to help identify variables and to guide the construction of measures. A third development (discussed in Chapter 27) is the increasing knowledge, understanding, and mastery of the validity problem itself, and especially the realization that validity and psychological theory are intertwined.

Study Suggestions

1. Among the large number of references on objective tests and scales, a few particularly useful ones are listed below. In addition, the student will find information on standardized tests in elementary textbooks.

Buros, O. *Tests in Print*. Highland Park, N.J.: Gryphon Press, 1961.

Buros, O., ed. *The Sixth Mental Measurements Yearbook*. Highland Park, N.J.: Gryphon Press, 1965. Descriptions and reviews of published tests and measures of all kinds. See, also, earlier editions.

Guilford, J. *Personality*. New York: McGraw-Hill, 1959. Good discussions of many personality measures and other measures.

2. Here are five useful references on achievement tests and their construction:

Bloom, B., ed. *Taxonomy of Educational Objectives: The Classification of Educational Goals: Handbook I, Cognitive Domain*. New York: David McKay, 1956. This basic and unusual book attempts to lay a foundation for cognitive measurement by classifying educational objectives and by giving numerous precepts and examples. Pages 201–207, which outline the book, are useful to test constructors and educational researchers.

Gage, N., ed. *Handbook of Research on Teaching*. Skokie, Ill.: Rand McNally, 1963, chaps. 8 and 9 (also 11). These are important chapters for the educational researcher. Chap. 8, by Bloom, reviews achievement and cognitive ability; chap. 9 discusses noncognitive variables and their measurement; chap. 11 reviews studies and measurement of the personality traits of teachers.

Gerberich, J. *Specimen Objective Test Items*. New York: David McKay, 1956. Numerous examples of test items of all kinds.

3. Three excellent anthologies of attitude, value, and other scales have recently appeared. Their excellence inheres not only in the many scales that give in their entirety, but also in perspicacious critiques that focus on reliability, validity, and other characteristics of the scales. The usefulness of these volumes cannot be overemphasized, and the student should be familiar with them.

Robinson, J., Rusk, J., and Head, K. *Measures of Political Attitudes*. Ann Arbor: Institute for Social Research, University of Michigan, 1968.

Robinson, J., and Shaver, P. *Measures of Social Psychological Attitudes*. Ann Arbor: Institute for Social Research, University of Michigan, 1969.

Shaw, M., and Wright, J. *Scales for the Measurement of Attitudes*. New York: McGraw-Hill, 1967.

4. The more advanced student will want to know a good deal about the response-set problem. Here are four basic and important references.

Bass, B. "Development and Evaluation of a Scale for Measuring Social Acquiescence." *Journal of Abnormal and Social Psychology*, LIII (1956), 296–299. One of the principal measures of response set.

Crowne, D., and Marlowe, D. *The Approval Motive*. New York: Wiley, 1964. Has a well-known social desirability scale.

Couch, A., and Keniston, K. "Yeasayers and Naysayers: Agreeing Response Set as a Personality Variable." *Journal of Abnormal and Social Psychology*, LX (1960), 151–174. A fascinating study of agreement response.

Edwards, A. *The Social Desirability Variable in Personality Assessment and Research*. New York: Holt, Rinehart and Winston, 1958. A good monograph by the principal investigator of this troublesome phenomenon.

(*Note:* As an antidote to the above, see the Rorer review cited in footnote 7.)

5. To gain insight into the rationale and construction of psychological measuring instruments, it is helpful to study complete or relatively complete accounts of their development. It is also helpful to study and become familiar with good items in a variety of fields. The references given below describe the development of interesting and important measurement instruments and items.

Allport, G., Vernon, P., and Lindzey, G. *Study of Values*, rev. ed. *Manual of Directions*. Boston: Houghton Mifflin, 1951.

Cattell, R., Saunders, D., and Stice, G. *Handbook for the Sixteen Personality Factor Questionnaire*. Champaign, Ill.: Institute for Personality and Ability Testing, 1957. Based on factor analysis, this is perhaps the most promising of the personality scales.

Edwards, A. *Personal Preference Schedule, Manual*. New York: Psychological Corp., 1953. Measures needs in a forced-choice (pair comparisons) format; used a great deal.

Isaacson, R., McKeachie, W., and Milholland, J. "Correlation of Teacher Personality Variables and Student Ratings." *Journal of Educational Psychology*, LIV (1963), 110–117. A valuable instrument for student evaluation of teacher performance in higher education.

Landis, D., Hayman, J., and Hall, W. "Multidimensional Analysis Procedures for Measuring Self-Concept in Poverty Area Classrooms." *Journal of Educational Psychology*, LXII (1971), 95–103. An intriguing idea: the measurement of the self-concept by using twelve concepts—teachers, policemen, school principals, school counselors, social workers, soldiers, Negroes, white people, Puerto Ricans, my friends, I, school—and determining the distances among them.

Likert, R. "A Technique for the Measurement of Attitudes." *Archives of Psychology*, no. 140, 1932. Likert's original monograph describing his technique, an important landmark in attitude measurement.

Morris, C., and Jones, L. "Value Scales and Dimensions." *Journal of Abnormal and Social Psychology*, LI (1955), 523–535. An unusual measure of values: uses complex items and a rank-order method.

Pace, C. *CUES: College and University Environment Scales, Technical Manual*, 2d ed. Princeton, N.J.: Educational Testing Service, 1969. A well-developed set of five scales to measure aspects of college environment as seen by students. An especially good example of careful and competent scale development.

Sorenson, A., Husek, T., and Yu, C. "Divergent Concepts of Teacher Role: An Approach to the Measurement of Teacher Effectiveness." *Journal of Educational Psychology*, LIV (1963), 287–294. Scale to measure teacher roles—advisor, counselor, disciplinarian, information giver, motivator, referrer—based on role theory.

Thurstone, L., and Chave, E. *The Measurement of Attitude*. Chicago: University of Chicago Press, 1929. This classic describes the construction of the equal-appearing intervals scale to measure attitudes toward the church.

Woodmansee, J., and Cook, S. "Dimensions of Verbal Racial Attitudes: Their Identification and Measurement." *Journal of Personality and Social Psychology*, VII (1967), 240–250. Probably the best measure of attitudes toward the Negro. The inventory is given in the Robinson, Rusk, and Head volume cited in Study Suggestion 3.

6. There is a new development in achievement testing and assessment with which the educational research should be familiar: *criterion-referenced* tests and measures. Actually, the idea appears to be an old one with a new slant. It springs basically from the notion of mastery by the individual of defined instructional goals and task domains and absolute interpretation of test scores. The emphasis is on what is learned by the individual learner, on the criterion of learning set by teacher and pupil, on the goals of instruction. The criterion in the "usual" testing is a group norm: individuals' scores are assessed in relation to group norms, means and standard deviations, for instance. Of course, teachers have for a hundred years or more been giving tests for absolute mastery. The difference seems to be that everyone was expected to attain the

criterion set by the teacher, whereas in this new approach the teacher and the individual pupil set goals, define task domains, and achieve the goals and assess the achievement. The student should read the following chapter:

Glaser, R., and Nitko, A., "Measurement in Learning and Instruction." In R. Thorndike, ed., *Educational Measurement*, 2d ed. Washington, D.C.: American Council on Education, 1971, pp. 625–670, but especially pp. 652 ff.

Criterion-referenced measurement and the educational and measurement ideas behind it will probably have a strong effect on educational research, but it is too soon to assess this effect and its strengths and weaknesses. Even technical problems are affected. The notion of reliability, for instance, has to change or at least be expanded, since present reliability notions are based on the variance among individuals.

CHAPTER 31

Projective Methods, Available Materials, and Content Analysis

Men project some part of themselves into everything they do. Watch a man walk. Examine an artist's paintings. Study a professor's lecture style. Observe a child play with other children or with toys and dolls. In all these ways human beings express their needs, their drives, their styles of life. If we want to know a person, then we can study *what* he does and the *way* he does it.

Men also put part of themselves, their work, their attitudes, and their culture in the materials they create and store. Letters, books, historical records, art objects, artifacts of all kinds express, if often indirectly and remotely, the life, society, and culture of man.

In this chapter, we examine the personal and societal productions of man, the materials deliberately stimulated by scientists, and the materials produced in the course of living and recording, as sources of data. This is the study of projective methods and available materials and their analysis for purposes of scientific research. If we ask children to write stories in order to study their creativity, this is a projective method. On the other hand, if we study stories already written, the stories are available materials. The analysis of both can be essentially the same.

The Idea of Projection

Values, attitudes, needs, and wishes, as well as impulses and motives, are *projected* upon objects and behaviors outside the individual. A hungry individual may invest inedible objects with food properties. An individual with conservative social attitudes may see federal taxes as confiscatory. Each person, then, views the world through his own projective glasses.

It should be possible to study men's motives, emotions, values, attitudes, and needs by somehow getting them to project these internal states onto external objects. This potent idea is behind projective devices of all kinds. A basic principle is that the more unstructured and ambiguous a stimulus, the more a subject can and will project his emotions, needs, motives, attitudes, and values. The *structure* of a stimulus, at least from one important point of view, is the degree of choice available to the subject. A highly structured stimulus leaves very little choice: the subject has unambiguous choice among clear alternatives, as in an objective-type achievement test question. A stimulus of low structure has a wide range of alternative choices. It is ambiguous: the subject can "choose" his own interpretation.

Another important characteristic of projective methods is their relative lack of objectivity, in the sense that it is much easier for different observers to come to different conclusions about the responses of the same persons. Recall that one of the powerful advantages of objective methods was that different observers agree on the scoring of responses. Projectives, on the other hand, are used precisely because they lack this desirable characteristic. Although different observers can score the same data quite differently, a serious weakness from the perspective of objectivity, this is a strength from the projection perspective.

Suppose judges are reading autobiographies written by children in order to rate them on creativity. One judge may rate a passage high in creativity because of its bright, unusual approach; another judge may consider it merely flip and rate it low in creativity. Similarly, two judges observing a child play with dolls may rate the child quite differently in aggressiveness. One may conclude, because the child throws a doll across the room, that this is a manifestation of aggressiveness. Another judge, however, may conclude that throwing the doll was simply a sort of punctuation mark at the end of a play activity. All tests and measures involve inference, as we have seen. Projective tests and measures require large inferential leaps indeed, larger than those of other methods. Thus their reliability and validity are difficult problems.

A significant virtue of projection and projective methods is that almost anything can be used as a stimulus. In addition to the well-known projective tests, like the Rorschach and the TAT—which will not be stressed in this chapter—the principle of projection can be used in many other ways: drawing pictures, writing essays, using finger paints, playing with dolls and toys, role playing, handwriting, telling stories in response to vague stimuli, associating words to other words, interpreting music.

Projective devices are among the most imaginative and significant creations of psychology. There is little doubt of their power, flexibility, and catholicity. But—and the "but" is a large one—can they be used in scientific research? Are their rather shaky reliability and validity inherent obstacles to their profitable use in research?

A Classification of Projective Measures

Lindzey has proposed a five-way classification of projective methods based on types of response: association, construction, completion, choice or ordering, and expression.[1]

[1]G. Lindzey, "On the Classification of Projective Techniques," *Psychological Bulletin*, LVI (1959), 158–168. Discussion of choice or ordering techniques is omitted in this text, since they are not true projective techniques. Essentially, they provide multiple-choice responses to projective stimuli. For

Association Techniques

These techniques require the subject to respond, at the presentation of a stimulus, with the first thing that comes to mind. The most famous and important device of this kind is the Rorschach test. The individual is asked by a highly skilled examiner to respond to ten inkblots of varying shapes and colors. The test is relatively unstructured—inkblots are vague and ambiguous—and allows full play of the subject's reactions and responses. The Rorschach, however, is more useful for clinical work than for research because of the very high skill required of the administrators and scorers of the test and because of its questionable—or at least doubtful—reliability and validity.

Word association methods are more promising. Emotionally tinged words are included with neutral words, and subjects are asked to respond with the first word that comes to mind. Getzels and Jackson, for example, used the technique to measure a presumed aspect of creativity: the ability to shift frames of reference.[2] Among the 25 words used were *arm, bolt, fair, leaf, policy*. Subjects were asked to give as many meanings as possible. The score was the total number of meanings given *and* the number of different categories into which the responses could be put. For instance, a subject might respond to *fair* with beautiful, light, just, equitable, unbiased, legible, average. The score of words produced is 7; the category score might be 4 or 5, depending on the system used.

Construction Techniques

Here the focus is on the *product* of the subject. The subject is required to produce, to construct, something at direction, usually a story or a picture. The stimulus can be simple, like asking children to tell a story about what happened to them yesterday, or complex, like the well-known Thematic Apperception Test (TAT). Generally some sort of standard stimulus is used.

Perhaps the most highly developed use of the construction technique has been the study and measurement of achievement motivation—need achievement, or *n* ach—by McClelland and his colleagues.[3] Subjects were shown four pictures that could be interpreted in a variety of ways. One of these, for example, was a boy sitting before a book, leaning on his left hand, and looking off into space. (Notice the ambiguity and my interpretation: he may be looking at something specific.) They were asked to write, in about a minute, stories about the pictures. The stories were then scored for achievement imagery and motivation.[4] Other variables were then correlated with *n* achievement.

---

example, there is a multiple-choice form of the Rorschach test. Perhaps it would be better to say that the technique is a mechanics of objectifying projective devices. An early general review of projectives is: H. Sargent, "Projective Methods: Their Origins, Theory, and Application in Personality Research," *Psychological Bulletin*, XLII (1945), 257–293.

[2] J. Getzels and P. Jackson, *Creativity and Intelligence*. New York: Wiley, pp. 199–200, 224–225.

[3] D. McClelland et al., *The Achievement Motive*. New York: Appleton, 1953.

[4] This research is exceptionally well documented. In *The Achievement Motive*, sample stories and scoring details are given. Moreover, the work has been carried over into other areas. McClelland has even raised the achievement motive of Indian businessmen by teaching them to score stories for *n* achievement: D. McClelland, "Toward a Theory of Motive Acquisition," *American Psychologist*, XX (1965), 321–333. Kolb has tried to train underachieving boys of high intelligence similarly: D. Kolb, "Achievement Motivation Training for Underachieving High-School Boys," *Journal of Personality*

In a study of religious beliefs, Cline and Richards used TAT-type pictures with religious overtones and had their subjects tell stories about what was happening, what the people were thinking and feeling, and what would be the outcome.[5] The stories were scored for overall religious commitment, religious conflict, and so on. The average correlation between the projective measures of religious commitment and other measures of such commitment obtained from depth interviews and questionnaire items was .66, quite high for such measures.

Veldman and Menaker invented a remarkably simple yet effective projective device of the construction kind.[6] They simply told their subjects, teacher trainees: "Tell four fictional stories about teachers and their experiences." Judges who read the stories of different samples agreed on six general areas of content: Structural Features, Interest Qualities, Emotional Features, Characters and Activity, Role Identity, and Self-Ability and Competence. Within these areas were subareas, like coherence, realism, and general adjustment. A cluster analysis (a method that determines which variables go together, or are correlated with each other) revealed three basic clusters, which corresponded to professional aspects of teaching, problem-solving, and affective aspects of stories. After computer analysis is developed, the method can be almost routinely used with teacher-training candidates and with students in other fields. It is a most interesting example of what can be done with simple means (but rather complex analysis).

Completion Techniques

Schmuck measured the attitudes of school children toward school by having them complete sentences like: "Studying is __________." "This school __________."[7] The completed sentences were rated on a seven-point scale and combined into a single measure (the mean). Schmuck measured attitudes toward self similarly. Getzels and Jackson used a completion technique to measure adjustment.[8] To items such as, "Working with others all the time makes me ____________," subjects might respond: mad, nervous, sick, tired (negative affect), or content, feel good, happy (positive affect).

Completion projective measures, then, supply the subject with a stimulus that is incomplete, the subject being required to complete it as he wishes. Or the stimulus may be loosely structured. It is obvious that responses of completion techniques are simpler than those of association and construction measures, thus simplifying the tasks of scoring and interpretation. The famous sentence-completion method is the best known of such techniques, but other types of completion

---

and Social Psychology, II (1965), 783–792. In addition, McClelland has used available materials to test his ideas cross-culturally: D. McClelland, *The Achieving Society*, New York: Van Nostrand-Reinhold, 1961.

[5]V. Cline and J. Richards, "A Factor-Analytic Study of Religious Behavior and Belief," *Journal of Personality and Social Psychology*, I (1965), 569–578.

[6]D. Veldman and S. Menaker, "Directed Imagination Method for Projective Assessment of Teacher Candidates," *Journal of Educational Psychology*, LX (1960), 178–187. There is also a manual with directions for scoring (see *ibid.*, footnote 5, p. 181).

[7]R. Schmuck, "Some Relationships of Peer Liking Patterns in the Classroom to Pupil Attitudes and Achievement," *School Review*, LXXI (1963), 337–359.

[8]Getzels and Jackson, *op. cit.*, pp. 214–215.

measures, such as story completion, discussion completion, and others, are being developed.

Choice or Ordering Techniques

These methods require simple responses: the subject chooses from among several alternatives, as in a multiple-choice item test, the item or choice that appears most relevant, correct, attractive, and so on. One might wish to measure need for achievement or attitudes toward blacks, for example, and present subjects with sets of pictures or sets of sentences, each item of which expresses different degrees of achievement motivation or attitude toward blacks. Presumably the subject, by choosing pictures or sentences he likes or approves, will project his own need for achievement or attitude toward blacks into the pictures or sentences. Of course, such sets of stimuli can also be ranked by the subject and inferences drawn from the rankings. Later, we will give examples of such methods, though they will appear under other rubrics.

Expressive Techniques

Expressive projective techniques are similar to construction techniques: the subject is required to form some sort of product out of raw material. But the emphasis is on the *manner* in which he does this—the end product is not important. With the construction methods, the content, and perhaps the style, of the story or other product are analyzed. With, say, finger painting or play therapy, it is the process of the activity and not the end product that is important. The subject *expresses* his needs, desires, emotions, and motives through working with, manipulating, and interacting with materials, including other people, in a manner or style that uniquely expresses his personality.

The principal expressive methods are play, drawing, painting, finger painting, and role playing. There are, however, other possibilities: working with clay, handwriting, games, and so on. The discussion that follows is limited to play techniques, finger painting, and role playing.

In the research use of play techniques, a child is brought into the presence of a variety of toys, often dolls of some kind. He may be told that a set of dolls is a family and that he should play with them and tell a story about them. Or he may be given a set of toys representing a miniature life situation. Or he may be put into a planned situation with one or two other children and told to play with them.

Doll play seems well suited to research with young children, probably because it seems so easy and natural for children to project themselves into the dolls.[9] In their study of the effect of the presence of mothers on the aggressiveness of children, Levin and Turgeon used doll play to measure aggression.[10] Aggression was defined as acts that hurt, irritate, injure, punish, frustrate, or destroy the dolls or equipment. Two scores of aggression were used: total number of aggressive units per session and percent aggression (number of aggressive units divided by total number of units).

[9]H. Levin and E. Wardwell, "The Research Uses of Doll Play," *Psychological Bulletin*, LIX (1962), 27–56.

[10]H. Levin and V. Turgeon, "The Influence of the Mother's Presence on Children's Doll Play Aggression," *Journal of Abnormal and Social Psychology*, LV (1957), 304–308.

Finger painting is a particularly rich expressive method. The subject is given pots of a special type of paint and told to draw what he likes with the paints, using his fingers and hands. Variables can be measured by counting numbers of certain kinds of manipulative and approach behavior or by rating subjects on the variables, using predetermined criteria. Alper, Blane, and Adams' study is an excellent and creative example.[11] Sixteen aspects of finger painting were measured: time to begin painting, use of whole hand versus fingertip approach, washing-up behavior, and so on. Significant differences were found between middle-class and working-class children in most of the tasks.

Role playing is the acting-out of an assigned personal or social situation for a brief period by two or more individuals who have been assigned specific roles. It holds considerable promise as an experimental method and as an observation tool of behavioral research, though its research use has been limited.[12] The investigator uses an observation system (see Chapter 31) to measure his variables. Or experimental variables can be manipulated using the technique. Group processes and interpersonal interaction, especially, can be conveniently studied.[13] Hostility, authoritarianism, prejudice, and many other variables can be measured. It has been the experience of role players that they say things they would rarely say under ordinary circumstances. They "come out" with things that surprise even themselves. The method, in other words, tends to bring out motives, needs, and attitudes that are below the social surface.

In studying teacher effectiveness, we might have teacher trainees play various kinds of teacher roles. Or we can ask a teacher or teacher trainee to play the part of a child while another individual plays the part of a teacher. This might be a potent way to measure teacher empathy, or the ability of a teacher to identify with the thoughts and feelings of children. We can ask experienced teachers and teacher trainees to play the role of a teacher discussing a problem of poor work with a student, one of the individuals playing the part of the student.

In using role playing in research, the situation should be structured so that the probability of eliciting behavior pertinent to the variable or variables being measured is high. Suppose one is measuring the attitudes toward authority of small children. The children can be asked to take the roles of teachers and parents. Some specific situation should be assigned so that the subjects can structure their roles and play their parts consistently and spontaneously. To do this, they need instructions that are just the right mixture of generality and specificity. If the instructions are too general, the actors may wander and consequently may not yield behavior relevant to the variables being measured. Rather than say "Play a teacher and a child," it would be better to say something like, "You be a teacher, and you be a child who has misbehaved in class. You (the latter child) have hit other children several times. The teacher has asked you to stay after school to talk to her. You have both just sat down and started to talk. Go ahead." Note that these instructions outline

[11]T. Alper, H. Blane, and B. Adams, "Reactions of Middle and Lower Class Children to Finger Paints as a Function of Class Differences in Child-Training Practices," *Journal of Abnormal and Social Psychology,* LI (1955), 439–448.

[12]J. Mann, "Experimental Evaluations of Role Playing," *Psychological Bulletin,* LIII (1956), 227–234.

[13]See W. Lambert, "Interpersonal Behavior," in P. Mussen, ed., *Handbook of Research Methods in Child Development.* New York: Wiley, 1960, chap. 20.

a general situation that can occur in any class anywhere, but they have a fairly clear structure: the actors know what to talk about. If, on the other hand, the instructions are too specific, the actors may be too bound up in the specificities of the situation. Remember, too, that role playing is projective. A good deal of leeway must be allowed so that the actors can project themselves into the roles they are playing.

Time limits should be carefully planned. Role playing is generally brief, anywhere from 3 to 15 or 20 minutes. Most situations are best ended after about 10 minutes. This is usually sufficient time for the variables to be measured and not so long that the actors lag.

A last point is that the researcher himself or a confederate can always play one of the roles and so be able to control and structure the situation to some extent. Role players sometimes wander off the assigned subjects and roles. Confederates are useful because they can keep the acting of the group concentrated on the assigned situation. More important, maybe, is the possibility of their deliberately saying and doing things to stimulate the actors' behavior relevant to the variable of interest. For example, if attitudes toward authority are measured, the confederate might, in playing the role of a child, say something about hating teachers and other adults.

The possibilities are limited only by the ingenuity and energy of the researcher. Note the ingenuity of Steiner and Field's study of the effects of role taking on attitudes toward the desegregation of schools.[14] Those whose attitudes were for desegregation were put into 34 three-man groups. Two members of each group had similar attitude scores; the third member was an accomplice of the experimenters. The groups were instructed to discuss the desirability of desegregating public schools and to attempt to reach agreement during the 15-minute experimental period. They were urged to take account of the views of a typical Southern segregationist, a typical Northern minister, priest, or rabbi, and a typical member of the National Association for the Advancement of Colored People. Roles were assigned to each group member in half the groups. The experimental subjects in these groups were assigned the Northern clergyman and NAACP roles. The accomplice was always assigned the Southern segregationist role. The treatment for the other 17 groups was the same except that group members were not assigned roles. The results indicated that the role assignment affected group members' perceptions of each other. When specific roles were *not* assigned, for example, subjects yielded more to the segregationist arguments of the accomplice and indicated greater preference for one another (rather than for the accomplice).

Projective Techniques and Behavioral Research: An Assessment

Projective measures are probably the most controversial of psychological measurement instruments. They have been extravagantly praised and extravagantly blamed. In evaluating them, we must not confuse noble sentiments with reliable

[14]I. Steiner and W. Field, "Role Assignment and Interpersonal Influence," *Journal of Abnormal and Social Psychology*, LXI (1960), 239–245.

and valid methods of observation. The position taken in this book is that all methods of observation and measurement must satisfy the same scientific criteria. To argue that a method is valid because it encompasses the whole personality or plunges into the unconscious mind evades the issue. The fact of the projective matter seems to be that the scientific canons of reliability, validity, and objectivity have not been adequately satisfied. What might a balanced view on projective methods be?

First, projective methods must be considered as methods of observation and measurement, just as any other methods are. As such, their purpose is to assign numerals to objects or events according to rules. The questions to be asked, as always, are: Can the numerals be assigned to the objects reliably? How valid are the procedures?

Second, then, projective methods must be subjected to the same type of reliability testing and empirical validation as any other psychometric procedures. This is not too easy to do. Still, it must be done—and done well. Such empirical testing is almost more important with projectives than with other kinds of instruments because of the very long inferential leaps involved.

Third, attempts can and must be made to "objectify the subjective." Projective devices, as we saw earlier, have a large element of subjectivity of interpretation. Objectivity is defined as agreement among observers. This means, to repeat an earlier dictum, that independent and competent judges must agree on the scoring and interpretation of the data yielded by an observation method. How can this be done with projective methods? Suppose an investigator is trying to measure creativity. He shows children a picture and asks them to write a story about it. After the stories are written, he asks judges, whom he has already trained, to read the stories. In addition, he constructs a graphic seven-point rating scale (or a numerical rating scale) of five items. Each item is a criterion of creativity as he defines it. Say that two of them are *originality* and *unusual approach*. He now asks his judges to rate the stories of all the children using the rating scale. To the extent that the ratings correlate highly, to this extent he has achieved objectivity. Other objective procedures can similarly be applied to the products of projective tests.

To sum up, projective methods of observation, when considered as psychometric instruments and subjected to the same canons and criteria of scientific measurement as other instruments, and when used with circumspection and care, can be useful tools of psychological and educational research. A projective instrument should not be used, however, if you have a more objective instrument that adequately measures the same variable. There is no sense in taking the risk if you do not have to. Moreover, it is best to avoid complex projective techniques, like the Rorschach test and the TAT, that require highly specialized training and a great deal of perhaps questionable interpretation.

Available Materials

Uses of Available Materials

A vast store of materials produced by institutions, organizations, and individuals is available for research purposes. Some of the possibilities of these resources are suggested below. We will find that certain available materials are similar to the products of projective methods; thus, the same psychometric criteria apply and similar methods of analysis can be used.

A researcher has to steep himself in his materials. If he is studying boards of education and their functioning, he must not only know a great deal about education and boards of education generally; he must be quite familiar with the particular boards of education he is going to study. To become familiar with a sample of boards of education he can read the documents produced by the boards and their agents and the official and unofficial documents of the boards' policies, activities, and decisions. Thus the first purpose of the use of available materials is to *explore* the nature of the data and the subjects, to get an insight into the total situation.

A second purpose of available materials is to *suggest hypotheses*. While an investigator may have one or two hypotheses which he has deduced, say, from sociological or psychological theory, the study of available materials, like the minutes of board meetings, may suggest further hypotheses. In reading minutes, for example, an investigator may notice that certain boards seem always to reach unanimous decisions, whereas certain other boards rarely reach unanimous decisions. He may also notice that the boards that reach unanimous decisions also seem to have a higher level of education among their members. This suggests an interesting and perhaps theoretically important hypothesis.

A third use of available materials is to *test hypotheses*. For example, Beale, in his great study of freedom—or rather, lack of freedom—in public schools and teachers' colleges, tested implicit hypotheses on the relation between lack of freedom and other variables.[15] Much of Beale's source data came from available materials: newspapers, periodicals, books, public documents, court decisions, and so on.

Although beset with certain methodological difficulties, there is no reason why available materials cannot deliberately be used to test hypotheses. Using the minutes of boards of education, one can test the hypothesis that motivations of board members to become board members is related to the decisions of the boards. Of course, one would have to measure the members' motivations in one of the ways previously discussed. The decisions of the boards and the votes of individual members, of course, are recorded in the minutes. Another hypothesis similarly testable is that the pressure group affiliation of board members is related to decisions. One might predict that boards of education with members who represent pressure groups tend to have split decisions on matters of import to the pressure groups.

Available materials can be used to *check the results of data obtained by one or more other methods*. This is, of course, a validation use. Such validation can take two forms: validation of relations obtained through the use of other methods and validation of measuring instruments. An analysis of newspaper editorials may show that the newspapers enthusiastically support "educational progress" and "better education for all our children." Yet a further analysis of editorials and news

[15] H. Beale, *Are American Teachers Free?* New York: Scribner, 1936.

stories may show that the newspapers take a dim view of new educational policies that require the expenditure of money.[16]

Another use of available materials to check on research findings was mentioned earlier when survey research was discussed: the use of census data to *check sample data*. If one has drawn a random sample of dwellings in a community in order to interview individuals, the accuracy of one's sample should be checked by comparing sociological data of the sample, like income, race, and education, with the same data of the most recent census or with available data in local government offices.

Census and other official data—voting lists, housing registration, license registration, school censuses, and so on—are also used to help *draw samples*. To draw a random sample of a large geographical area is an expensive and difficult job. But it is not too difficult to draw random samples of single, smaller communities. Some school systems, for example, maintain relatively complete and accurate lists of taxpayers or families with school children. The point is that there are a number of available sources that can be used for drawing samples. Though none of these sources is perfect, since records are kept for different purposes, with different degrees of accuracy, by people of different levels of competence, they are much better sources of samples than the informed hunches of investigators.

Important Types of Available Materials

Five or six kinds of available materials seem to be most important for research purposes. *Census* and *registration data* are often invaluable, especially for large field studies and survey research. If census data are needed, perhaps the best source is the United States Government Printing Office, Washington, D.C. Specialized requests for information and help can be sent to the United States Census Bureau. In some cases, the Bureau may even prepare tabulations of data for researchers (at nominal cost).

For information on local registration data, write or visit the nearest county office (the County Clerk). For school data, of course, write or visit the chief administrative officer of the school district or districts in which you are interested. School census and registration data, especially for schools and school districts covering a wide geographic area within a state, can be obtained from state education departments. Interstate school data and information can be obtained from the Office of Education, United States Department of Health, Education, and Welfare, Washington, D.C.

Data on foreign countries can ordinarily be obtained from the consulates and embassies of the countries. (Write the appropriate embassy, Washington, D.C., for information.) A good deal of useful foreign educational and other information can also be obtained from UNESCO. (Write UNESCO, United Nations, New York, N.Y.)

Newspapers and *periodicals*, especially the former, have two principal uses in behavioral research. One, they influence public affairs and policy decisions and often reflect the values and attitudes of many citizens. It would be interesting to

[16]See C. Foster, *Editorial Treatment of Education in the American Press*. Cambridge, Mass.: Harvard University Press, 1938, p. 39.

know, for instance, the relations between editorial policies and social and educational decisions. It is possible that teachers' salaries, bond issues, curriculum policies, and other important educational matters are influenced by newspapers and their reporting and editorial policies.[17]

Two, newspapers maintain files that are useful sources of data. Reporters, editors, and publishers themselves are rich repositories of information about social and educational conditions and issues in their areas. Some newspaper people tend to view things from a larger viewpoint than do other people in a community. Moreover, even when biased, they tend to be more aware of their biases. Thus they can be of considerable assistance to investigators.

A third largely untapped source of materials of possible use to research are the records and the knowledge of the officers and members of *voluntary associations*. Although there has not been too much research on voluntary associations, there is little doubt of their impact on the thinking of millions of Americans. The most important of these associations are probably the fraternal associations (Masons, Oddfellows), church-affiliated associations (Knights of Columbus, Women's Society for Christian Service), and veterans' associations (Veterans of Foreign Wars, American Legion). In addition to being interesting and important objects of study in their own right, these groups and their officers often know a great deal about local communities and their problems.

From an educational research viewpoint, *school records* are the most important available materials. Pupil records and test scores are useful in their own right, since much can be learned about a school system from a simple statistical compilation and analysis of the quantitative data available. It would seem important, for example, to know the average achievement, intelligence, and aptitude levels of the schools in a district in which one is doing research. It would also seem important to know whether the usual relations exist between the various measures of achievement and ability. If one is working in a school that deviates a good deal in one way or another from other schools, one should at least be aware of it.

School records and data have other uses, however. Sampling was mentioned earlier. When drawing samples of schools, classes, and pupils, the first stop should be the school administrative offices. A well-kept school filing system is an invaluable asset to the educational researcher—if he can gain direct or indirect access to it.[18] If a card for each child exists, it is an easy and routine matter to set the

[17]See E. Webb et al. *Unobtrusive Measures: Nonreactive Research in the Social Sciences*. Skokie, Ill.: Rand McNally, 1966, pp. 75 ff.

[18]The whole subject of research-school staff relations is too large to discuss in this book. Besides, there are few set rules. Some advice may be helpful, however. The first person for the investigator to see is the chief administrative officer. If he is understanding and cooperative, half the problem is solved. But many administrators are not cooperative and understanding. In such cases, better abandon the school system—unless you have board of education influence. Next, it is good policy to get board of education approval for the research. The chief administrator can usually get such approval, if he wishes to. Still, it is wise for the investigator to discuss the research directly with the board. Obviously, principals and teachers have to be consulted, too. Planned discussion sessions of representative board members, administrators, and teachers should be arranged if it is possible to do so. In short, the educational investigator, or at least one or more of his colleagues, has to be skilled in social relations. Neglect of this side of research can have unfortunate consequences. On the other hand, successful social relations can yield not only interest and cooperation; they can help the investigator learn a great deal about the school system and the community. See D. Katz, "Field Studies," in L. Festinger and D. Katz, eds., *Research Methods in the Behavioral Sciences*. New York: Holt, Rinehart and Winston, 1953, pp. 85–89.

cards up to draw random samples. Class lists are useful for sampling purposes: one can number each class and draw random samples of classes.

A cautionary word is necessary. The records of many schools and school districts are not well kept. And in most cases no thought has been given to the research use of the records. Scores will be missing or inaccurately recorded. (The tests themselves may have been improperly administered and improperly scored. When using test scores from school records, some discreet attempt should be made to determine the quality of the administration and scoring of the tests.) The researcher who wants to do an analysis of variance or to calculate a coefficient of correlation will most often find that raw scores or standard scores have not been recorded. Grade-point averages and percentiles are common. In such cases, the researcher must make an effort to obtain the raw scores. The day may come when school records are adequately kept. Meanwhile, investigators must be constantly alert to the possibilities of inaccuracies and to the fact that school record scores are often not in adequate form for statistical treatment.

The last important type of available data is the *personal document*. Allport, in his study of personal documents, stresses their use to study the needs, motives, and values of individuals.[19] This is similar to the case study. With the aid of content analysis personal documents can also be used to test hypotheses. Spiegel and Neuringer even tested hypotheses about suicide notes.[20] They are thus considered the same as any other available materials, subject to the same laws and rules. The difficulty with this use of personal documents—or expressive documents, as they have been called—is their relative scarcity, which severely limits sampling possibilities. Adequate samples of expressive materials, however, can be obtained by asking subjects to produce letters, autobiographies, essays, and diaries.

Content Analysis

Content analysis is a method of studying and analyzing communications in a systematic, objective, and quantitative manner to measure variables.[21] Most content analysis has not been done to measure variables, as such. Rather, it has been used to determine the relative emphasis or frequency of various communication phenomena: propaganda, trends, styles, changes in content, readability. In this chapter content analysis is considered a method of observation and measurement.

Content analysis, while certainly a method of analysis, is more than that. It is, as indicated above, a method of observation. Instead of observing people's behavior directly, or asking them to respond to scales, or interviewing them, the investigator takes the communications that people have produced and asks questions of the communications. There is a logic and economy about so viewing con-

[19]G. Allport, *The Use of Personal Documents in Psychological Science*. New York: Social Science Research Council, 1942, p. xii.

[20]D. Spiegel and C. Neuringer, "Role of Dread in Suicidal Behavior," *Journal of Abnormal and Social Psychology*, LXVI (1963), 507–511.

[21]The discussion that follows leans heavily on Berelson's and Holsti's treatments, especially Berelson's: B. Berelson, "Content Analysis." In G. Lindzey, ed., *Handbook of Social Psychology*. Reading, Mass.: Addison-Wesley, 1954, vol. I, chap. 13; O. Holsti, "Content Analysis." In G. Lindzey and E. Aronson, eds., *The Handbook of Social Psychology*, 2d ed. Reading, Mass.: Addison-Wesley, 1968, vol. II, chap. 16.

tent analysis. In effect, we take it out of the purely analytic class and put it into the same class as interviews, scales, and other methods of observation. Thus we realize that we are doing nothing essentially different from previous observational activities: we are observing and measuring variables.

One of the most important characteristics of content analysis is its general applicability, especially now that the use and availability of computers make its application much easier than it used to be. It can be used with the productions of projective methods, with materials deliberately produced for research purposes, and with all kinds of verbal materials. We examine two or three examples from actual research to suggest some of these uses.

Punitiveness and Perceptions of Misconduct

One of the few educational studies to use content analysis is Kounin and Gump's interesting and important study of the effect of punitive and nonpunitive teachers on children's perceptions of misconduct.[22] Three pairs of punitive and nonpunitive teachers were selected from three schools by agreement among raters. Other differences were controlled. Punitiveness-Nonpunitiveness was the independent variable. Individual interviews were held with the 174 first-grade children of these six teachers. The interviews and the content coding were structured around the question, "What is the worst thing a child can do at school?" After a child replied, he was asked, "Why is that so bad?"

The content of the replies to the questions was analyzed with a rather complex code consisting of five major categories with subcategories in all but one of them. Table 30.1 is an abbreviated version of Kounin and Gump's summary table of results.[23] It shows three of the major categories with five of the subcategories. The particular items selected illustrate both the category system and the results. The relations between *punitiveness of teacher* and *perception of misconduct* are clearly demonstrated.

TABLE **30.1** SOME RESULTS OF KOUNIN AND GUMP STUDY[a]

Misconducts and Explanations	Percent *Pu*	Percent *NPu*
I. Content and quality of misconducts		
A. Physical assaults on others	38	17
D. Abstract misconducts	27	52
II. Content and quality of explanations		
C. Serious harm to others	45	18
D. Reality-centered retributions	21	48
V. Concern with school-unique objectives		
A. Learning and achievement losses	20	43

[a] *Pu:* children who have punitive teachers; *NPu:* children who have nonpunitive teachers. $N = 174$. All differences are significant at the .05 level or beyond.

[22] J. Kounin and P. Gump, "The Comparative Influence of Punitive and Nonpunitive Teachers Upon Children's Concepts of School Misconduct," *Journal of Educational Psychology*, LII (1961), 44–49.

[23] *Ibid.*, p. 47.

This study is a good example of the use of content analysis to test research hypotheses. The first of four hypotheses, for example, said that the school misconduct preoccupations of children with punitive teachers would contain more aggression than the misconduct preoccupations of children with nonpunitive teachers. Inspection of Table 30.1 shows that this hypothesis was confirmed. The study is also a good example of choosing methods to fit research purposes. Kounin and Gump reasoned that children would not give the same answers to interview questions that they would to forced-choice questions. And they had to know the misconducts with which the children were preoccupied. The interviews and content analysis naturally followed from this reasoning.

Values and the Madison and Hamilton Papers

Rokeach et al., in a most original study, used results of Rokeach's values research to determine the authorship of twelve of the Federalist papers whose authorship has been disputed.[24] The problem of identifying the twelve papers has been tackled by others using systematic word counts and comparing these counts with known Madison and Hamilton papers. Content analysis and the computer can be extremely useful in such analysis. For example, the two authors probably used words differently. One can determine the frequency "baselines" for words like "and," "in," "the," and so on, of the two authors, and then compare them with the counts in the disputed papers.[25] The procedure is fairly straightforward and can be used with historical and literary documents to test authenticity.

Rokeach and his colleagues had a more interesting idea. They reasoned that the two authors would differ reliably in their use of value words. Using 13 of Rokeach's terminal concepts and 11 of his instrumental concepts, they analyzed 10 Madison, 10 Hamilton, and the 12 disputed essays by recording the values expressed in them (e.g., *a comfortable life*, *freedom*, *equality*, *honor*). Two judges did this; their reliability was .85 or higher. The obtained frequencies of the value concepts for the three groups (Madison, Hamilton, Disputed) were rank-ordered and the ranks correlated. The correlations were all high. The correlations were converted to Fisher z scores and the differences between the mean correlations tested for significance with t tests.

The evidence seemed to indicate that Madison wrote the disputed papers, a result congruent with other research. The evidence also indicated, however, that the values of both men were remarkably similar (making the task of discrimination more difficult).

Some Aspects of Method in Content Analysis

Content analysis, it is clear, can be applied to available materials and to materials especially produced for particular research problems. One can content-analyze

[24]M. Rokeach, R. Homant, and L. Penner, "A Value Analysis of the Disputed Federalist Papers," *Journal of Personality and Social Psychology*, XVI (1970), 245–250.

[25]The advanced student will find an analysis of this kind in: F. Mosteller and J. Tukey, "Data Analysis, Including Statistics." In Lindzey and Aronson, *op. cit.*, pp. 147 ff. This analysis is most ingenious and effective.

letters, diaries, ethnographic materials, newspaper articles and editorials, minutes of meetings, and so on. One can ask children or adults to write autobiographies, stories, essays. As hard as it may be for some people to stomach, essay test questions can be reliably graded using content analysis and the computer. But how is content analysis done? Some ideas were given in the examples above. In addition, a brief introduction to the subject is given below. The student who wants to use content analysis, however, should consult the references given in Study Suggestion 1. Berelson's treatment is particularly helpful.[26]

Definition and Categorization of Universe

The first step, as usual, is to define *U*, the universe of content that is to be analyzed. Kounin and Gump's *U* was all replies to the question on misconduct, or simply breaches of good behavior as perceived by the children. Then *U* was partitioned into five major categories and a number of subcategories. (See Table 30.1.)

Categorization, or the partitioning of *U*, is perhaps the most important part of content analysis, because it is a direct reflection of the theory and the problem of a study. It spells out, in effect, the variables of the hypotheses. One of Kounin and Gump's main hypotheses was that teacher punitiveness is related to children's perceptions of misconduct. The dependent variable, children's perceptions of misconduct, was *U*. To test the basic hypothesis, however, *U* had to be partitioned into *kinds* of misconduct and teacher punitiveness related to it. Study Table 30.1 and note some of the categories of *U* (verbal part of table) and how the categories are juxtaposed against the punitive and nonpunitive categories. A great deal of thought, work, and care must go into this first step.

Units of Analysis

Berelson lists five major units of analysis: words, themes, characters, items, and space-and-time measures.[27] The *word* is the smallest unit. (There can even be smaller units: letters, phonemes, etc.) It is also an easy unit to work with, especially in computer content analysis. An investigator may be studying value words in the writings of high school students. For some reason, he may wish to know the relation between sex or political preference of parents, on the one hand, and the use of value words, on the other hand. The word unit may also be useful in studies of reading. *U* can ordinarily be clearly defined and categorized—for example, value words and nonvalue words; difficult, medium, and easy words. Then the words can simply be counted and assigned to appropriate categories.

The *theme* is a useful though more difficult unit. A *theme* is often a sentence, a proposition about something. Themes are combined into sets of themes. The letters of adolescents or college students may be studied for statements of *self-reference*. This would be the larger theme. The themes making this up might be defined as any sentences that use "I," "me," and other words indicating reference to the writer's self. *Discipline* is an interesting larger theme. *Child training* or *control* is another. Many observers take field notes in a thematic manner. Here

[26]Berelson, *op. cit.*, pp. 507 ff.
[27]*Ibid.*, pp. 508–509.

is an example from the field notes of an observer in a small village in Japan:

> *Food-Training:*... Use cajolery in this family—but it varies. Parents will leave something disliked (if child should be obstreperous about it) out of child's diet.[28]
>
> Informant's first child was fed whenever he cried, and the second child was started out that way; but after one month, informant fed second child on schedule....[29]

It should be emphasized, as Berelson does, that if the themes are complex, content analysis using the theme as the unit of analysis is difficult and perhaps unreliable.[30] Yet it is an important and useful unit because it is ordinarily realistic and close to the original content.

Character and *space-and-time* measures are probably not too useful in behavioral research. The first is simply an individual in a literary production. We might use it in analyzing stories. The second is the actual physical measurement of content: number of inches of space, number of pages, number of paragraphs, number of minutes of discussion, and so on.

Like the theme, the *item* unit is important. It is a whole production: an essay, news story, television, program, class recitation or discussion. Getzels and Jackson used short autobiographies to measure creativity.[31] The unit was the item, the whole autobiography. Each autobiography was judged either "creative" or "noncreative." Children can be asked to write projective stories in response to a picture. The whole story of each child can be the unit of analysis. Judges can be trained to use a rating scale to assess the creativity of the stories. Or judges can be trained to assign each story to a creative or noncreative category.

It is likely that the item as a unit of analysis will be particularly useful in behavioral research. As long as pertinent criteria for categorizing a variable can be defined, and as long as judges can agree substantially in their ratings, rankings, or assignments, then the item unit is profitable to use. But careful checks on reliability and validity must be made. Judges can wander from the criteria, and they can lose themselves in the masses of reading they must do. Yet it is surprising how much agreement can be reached, even for rather complex material. In judging the creativity of student essays, teacher judges in the Hartsdale, New York, public school system achieved agreement coefficients of .70 and .80. Here, again, the whole essays were the units.

Quantification

All materials are potentially quantifiable. We can even rank the sonnets of Shakespeare or the last five piano sonatas of Beethoven in the order of our personal preferences, if nothing else. It is true that some materials are not as amenable to quantification as certain other materials. After all, it is much easier to assign numbers to children corresponding to their knowledge of spelling than it is to assign

[28]Center for Japanese Studies, University of Michigan, Okayama Field Station, *863*, *Niike*, August 25, 1950 (GB). ("*863*" is the Yale field number; "*Niike*" is the Japanese village; "GB" is the observer.)

[29]CFJS, UM, OFS, *853*, *Takashima*, Dec. 18, 1950 (MFN).

[30]Berelson, *op. cit.*, p. 508.

[31]Getzels and Jackson, *op. cit.*, pp. 99–103.

numbers to their original thinking or creativity. This does not mean, however, that no numbers can be legitimately assigned to children's products on the variables originality and creativity. It is not easy, but it can be done.

There are three or more ways to assign numbers to the objects of the content analysis *U*. The first and most common of these corresponds to nominal measurement: count the number of objects in each category after assigning each object to its proper category. Suppose we are reading reports of field observers, and we come to a passage, "... babies are breast fed until two years of age, then gradually weaned to rice and gruel."[32] This theme might be assigned to the category "Permissive" or the category "Late Weaning." Then, in going through the observer's notes, we assign similar passages to these categories. The quantification would simply be the counting of the number of themes in each of the categories.

A second form of quantification is *ranking*, or ordinal measurement. If one is working with not too many objects to be ranked—say not more than 30—judges can be asked to rank them according to a specified criterion. Assume that the relations between religiosity and other variables are being studied, and subjects are asked to write on the subject "What I Believe." Judges might be asked to rank the essays on the degree of religious belief. If a large number of essays are involved, they can still be ranked, but a more manageable system than total ranking can be used, for example, 10 or 11 ranks can be made available, and judges can assign the essays to the ranks.

A third form of quantification is *rating*. Children's compositions, for example, can be rated as wholes for degrees of creativity, originality, inner-direction and other-direction, achievement orientation, interests, values, and other variables.

Certain conditions have to be met before quantification is justified or worthwhile. Berelson has spelled out these conditions.[33] Two of his seven conditions should be noted: (1) to count carefully (or otherwise quantify) when the materials to be analyzed are representative, and (2) to count carefully when the category items appear in the materials in sufficient numbers to justify counting (or otherwise quantifying). The reason for both conditions is obvious: if the materials are not representative or if the category items are relatively infrequent, generalization from statistics calculated from them is unwarranted.

The answer to these two and other conditions, then, is to so select materials or to so have materials produced that quantification is possible and necessary. If materials cannot meet the criteria, they can be used only for heuristic and suggestive purposes and not for relating variables to each other.

The Computer and Content Analysis

The computer has revolutionized content analysis, as it has revolutionized data analysis. Fruitful investigations that could hardly have been conceived a decade ago are now possible. Content analysis is laborious, because it involves the scanning of large quantities of materials, not to mention the preliminary work of setting

[32]CFJS, UM, OFS, *853*, *Niiike*, Aug. 25, 1950.
[33]Berelson, *op. cit.*, pp. 512–514.

up categories, defining units, and so on. Even with the computer, it can be laborious. Nevertheless, the most onerous aspects of the method are no longer onerous. Potentially at least, then, any problems involving verbal materials can be conceptualized and analyzed for research purposes.

It would take far too much space to describe adequately how the computer can be used in content analysis. Besides, this is one field that is rapidly evolving and changing; it certainly has not yet reached the sort of stability necessary for routine instruction. To give some idea of how the computer is used, and to encourage exploration of possibilities, we briefly describe the computer system known as "The General Inquirer."[34] Then we outline Page's system of grading essays with the computer to illustrate a functioning system.

The General Inquirer is a set of computer programs geared to the content and statistical analysis of verbal materials so generalized that it can be applied to a variety of research problems. Its aim is to free the researcher from the details of computer operations and yet to enable him to use the computer flexibly. It locates, counts, tabulates, and analyzes the characteristics of "natural text."

The basis of the system is the "dictionary," which is a large set of words (or short phrases), each word being defined by "tags" or categories. For example, pronouns like *I*, *me*, and *mine* are tagged "self," and *army*, *church*, and *administration* are tagged "large-group."[35] These are called first-order tags; they represent the common or manifest meaning of the dictionary words.[36] Second-order tags represent the connotative meanings of words: status connotations and institutional contexts, for example. Holsti gives the example of a dictionary word "teacher," which is tagged with three meanings: job-role, higher-status, academic. The first is a first-order tag, the second and third second-order tags.[37]

Special-purpose dictionaries for a particular research problem are stored in the computer. For example, one such dictionary to analyze verbal materials for need achievement consists of about 800 entries with 14 tags (categories).[38] The rules for scoring materials for achievement imagery developed by McClelland and his colleagues[39] are behind the dictionary and computer program. Say a child has written a story. The whole story is punched on IBM cards and fed into the computer. The computer scans the words in the story, tags those relevant to need achievement, counts them, and does other analyses. In this case the dictionary consists of words like *wants*, *hopes*, *become*, *gain*, *compete*. The words *wants* and *hopes* are tagged "need"; words like *fame* and *honor* are tagged "success."

The computer needs rules that it can use to identify tag sequences that indicate need for achievement. A simple example is when the tags "need" and "compete" appear in one sentence.[40] The computer prints out the analysis and, on the

[34] P. Stone et al., *The General Inquirer: A Computer Approach to Content Analysis.* Cambridge, Mass., M.I.T. Press, 1966, especially chap. 3. See, too, Holsti, *op. cit.*, pp. 665 ff. The reader would do well at this point to glance at Appendix C.

[35] *Ibid.*, p. 666.

[36] Stone et al., *op. cit.*, p. 174.

[37] Holsti, *op. cit.*, p. 666.

[38] Stone et al., *op. cit.*, pp. 191–206.

[39] McClelland et al., *op. cit.*

[40] Stone et al., p. 201.

basis of rules built into it, arrives at an overall assessment that a passage contains achievement imagery or does not contain it.

An important feature of The General Inquirer is that it has a number of dictionaries that can be used by researchers. The need-for-achievement dictionary just described is one. Another important one is The Harvard Third Psychosociological Dictionary, whose purpose is to provide a computer means of analyzing texts for classifying roles, objects, and dynamic processes. A researcher interested in a particular area can use one or more of these dictionaries to help him build a special dictionary to analyze his own data. For example, if one were interested in values and attitudes, one could provide the first-order words—like *private property*, *equality*, and *civil rights*—and use parts of The General Inquirer (or other system) to suggest tags or categories.

It is not possible to describe computer content analysis adequately. One has to use a system two or three times with actual problems. But to try to fill in a few of the gaps, let's look at Page's highly effective—and highly controversial—computer method of grading essays.[41] In one study, Page analyzed 276 essays written by students in grades 8 through 12. Four judges graded the essays for overall quality. These judgments were the criterion in*trins*ic measures, or "trins," as Page calls them. The computer was programmed to measure 30 ap*prox*imation measures, or "proxes"—again, Page's expression—or various characteristics of the essays: average sentence length, length of essay in words, use of uncommon words, number of commas, and so on. Each of these measures was used in an equation to predict the human ratings of the essays provided by the four judges. What amounts to a coefficient of correlation between a weighted average of the 30 measures and the human judgments was a remarkable .71! Subsequent work confirmed the ability of the computer—rather, the system—to judge and grade essays.

The Use of Content Analysis and Available Materials in Behavioral Research

Projective devices, available materials, and content analysis have been used rather infrequently in behavioral research. To round off the discussion, several uses of these methods are here suggested.

A large number of variables can be measured through content analysis of both available materials and deliberately created materials of a projective kind: needs, values, attitudes, stereotypes, authoritarianism, creativity, and so on. If one were studying ethnocentrism in veterans' associations, for instance, an attitude scale might be resisted. But association members would probably not object to being interviewed. The interview protocols, of course, can be content-analyzed. (Appropriate projective-type questions designed to elicit ethnocentric responses can be included in the interview schedule.)

[41]E. Page, "Grading Essays by Computer: Progress Report." In *Invitational Conference on Testing Problems, 1966*. Princeton, N.J.: Educational Testing Service, 1966, pp. 87–100.

Education has suffered from a lack of analysis of the educational information people absorb from the press and other media of public communication. Educational news articles, editorials, and special features (as mentioned earlier) might well be content-analyzed.

The study of values is difficult because social desirability plays a part in their measurement and, perhaps, because values have been taken for granted. After all, values express socially desirable behaviors, ideals, institutions, and so on. How do we distinguish between responses that are impelled by genuine values and those prompted by their inherent social desirability? But subjects can be asked to produce verbal materials on specified topics, and the materials can be content-analyzed for expressed values.[42] In addition, of course, available materials – newspaper editorials, magazine articles, television interviews, children's essays, and the like – can be content-analyzed for expressed values.

In some educational experiments it may be possible to use content analysis to assess the effects of experimental treatments on dependent variables. For example, is it possible to stimulate the creativity of school children? How much does writing practice help students to write essays? Content analysis can help obtain answers to such questions.

Content analysis can be used to validate other methods of observation and measurement. A scale to measure, say, attitudes toward Jews is hard to validate because there are few external criteria against which to check it. Most people, moreover, know they should not be anti-Semitic. They thus give responses that may not be indices of their true attitudes. But projective-type questions can be asked of subjects, and the responses content-analyzed for their attitudes toward Jews. It is not easy to conceal anti-Semitism if one has to write a short essay on Jews.

Available materials and materials manufactured by request have an extremely valuable use that is often overlooked: as sources of items for objective tests and scales and interview schedules. If one is constructing a scale to measure educational values, for instance, there are vast resources for item construction available: newspaper editorials on education, magazine articles, organizational and institutional propaganda (for example, church and voluntary association literature on education and literature of educational pressure groups), books on education (especially on philosophy of education), speeches of public figures. One of the

[42]For a values content-analysis suggestion, see R. White, *Value-Analysis: The Nature and Use of the Method*, Society for the Psychological Study of Social Issues, 1951. Some features of White's method are excellent; others are not too desirable. While he has touched upon most of the values of man, his system is fundamentally a priori. Furthermore, it is very complicated, though he does suggest that it can be cut down for specific purposes (p. 69). A great deal of research clearly needs to be done on values, their measurement, and their interrelations. As far as the role of content analysis in values research is concerned, the reader can profit from deCharms and Moeller's provocative study of the values and motives expressed in 150 years of children's readers: R. deCharms and G. Moeller, "Values Expressed in American Children's Readers: 1800–1950," *Journal of Abnormal and Social Psychology*, LXIV (1962), 136–142. These authors tested, among other things, the engaging hypothesis that *achievement motivation* is related to *inventiveness* as expressed by the number of patents issued. The coefficients of correlation between these variables was .79 in one sample of readers and .68 in a check sample. The authors also drew two entirely independent and different samples from their materials. The results are a remarkable demonstration of the power of sampling.

main difficulties for the investigator is to cut his way through the morass of pious sentiments to the hard core of the value matter. Though it seems not to have been so used, content analysis can be put to work to analyze such materials.

Other uses suggest themselves, of course. For instance, irrational and illogical thinking on educational matters and matters related to education—financing schools by bond issues at substantial rates of interest, religious manifestations in public schools, transportation for school children, school budgets, teachers, salaries, curriculum changes—can all be content-analyzed. In fact, content analysis would seem to be the only method of analyzing materials on such subjects.

Available materials and content analysis, however, should not be used indiscriminately. Content analysis is not an easy method to use, as we have seen, though it has become much easier with the increased availability and mastery of computers and of programs like The General Inquirer. As usual, it should be used when the nature of a research problem requires it. Although it can be used to measure achievement motivation, it cannot be used to measure achievement (though one can never be too sure). While it can be used to measure attitudes, there are ordinarily better and easier ways to do so. Similarly for available materials. If one can deliberately select, sample, or produce one's own materials, so much the better. Frequently, however, one cannot—so available materials must be used.

Study Suggestions

1. The following references are useful beginnings in the study of the use of available materials and content analysis. There appears to be nothing suitable, in the sense of being specifically oriented to scientific research use, on projective methods (except, perhaps, the Lindzey and Sargent articles mentioned in footnote 1).

   Berelson and Holsti chapters. (See footnote 21.) These chapters are authoritative. Although some of Berelson's discussion is outdated, this chapter is still a good reference on content analysis.

   Stone book, chaps. 1 and 2. (See footnote 34.)

   Angell, R., and Freedman, R. "The Use of Documents, Records, Census Materials, and Indices." In L. Festinger and D. Katz, eds., *Research Methods in the Behavioral Sciences*. New York: Holt, Rinehart and Winston, 1953, chap. 7. One of the only references on available materials.

   Webb et al. book on unobtrusive measures. (See footnote 17.)

2. Read two of the following studies. They show what can be done with knowledge and ingenuity.

   Alper, T., Blane, H., and Adams, B. "Reactions of Middle And Lower Class Children to Finger Paints as a Function of Class Differences in Child-Training Practices." *Journal of Abnormal and Social Psychology*, LI (1955), 439–448. A most ingenious and fruitful use of finger paints; in fact, a lovely study.

   Getzels and Jackson book. (See footnote 2.) See, especially, pp. 99 ff., for creative uses of projective devices to measure creativity.

   Hiller, J., Marcotte, D., and Martin, T. "Opinionation, Vagueness, and Specificity-Distinctions: Essay Traits Measured by Computer." *American Educational Research Journal*, VI (1969), 271–286. An excellent study that used computer analysis of essays; measured three variables or categories of writing style: opinionation-exaggeration, vagueness, specificity-distinctions.

McClelland book. (See footnote 3.) Describes the theoretical and practical development of the famous need-for-achievement measure.

Veroff, D. "Development and Validation of a Projective Measure of Power Motivation." *Journal of Abnormal and Social Psychology*, LIV (1957), 1–8. A provocative study that illustrates a number of points made in this chapter.

Whiting, J., and Child, I. *Child Training and Personality*. New Haven: Yale University Press, 1953. This is a theoretically oriented content-analysis study that fruitfully used the Yale area files as available materials to test psychoanalytic hypotheses.

Winter, D., Alpert, R., and McClelland, D. "The Classic Personal Style." *Journal of Abnormal and Social Psychology*, LXVII (1963), 254–265. Content-analyzed stories to detect basic "themes" of a private secondary school and imaginative processes of its students. Fascinating.

3. A useful class project would be for a class committee to find sources of available data. One huge source, for instance, is the data bank of *Project Talent*, with its more than 500 variables and 400,000 secondary school students.[43] Another more important and, after many years, still relatively unknown source is the so-called Yale area or cross-cultural files. These files are the *ne plus ultra* of available cultural materials. They are outlined in: Murdock, G., et al., *Outlines of Cultural Materials*, 3d ed. New Haven: Human Relations Area Files, 1950. [*Note:* An excellent source for this project is: L. Schoenfeldt, "Data Archives as Resources for Research, Instruction, and Policy Planning," *American Psychologist*, XXV (1970), 609–616. This article gives the names, addresses, and brief descriptions of the major data archives in the United States and certain other countries.]

[43]See J. Flanagan et al., *Project Talent: Five Years After High School*. Palo Alto: American Institutes for Research and University of Pittsburgh, 1971.

CHAPTER 31

Observations of Behavior

A university research institute, collaborating with several public school systems, studied teacher behavior and pupil work outcomes. One hypothesis explored was that flexible and alert teachers would stimulate pupils to more original and independent work. The research group chose Ryans' Classroom Observation Record to measure the behavior of teachers and students.[1]

The Classroom Observation Record is an 18-item objective observation instrument, each item being a bipolar pair of descriptive adjectives, such as partial-fair, harsh-kind, inflexible-adaptable, dull-stimulating. The Record was developed in two ways: by the study of research reports and opinions that named qualities thought to be desirable in teachers and essential to good teaching, and by the use of the critical-incidents technique. The first approach yielded 46 characteristics that seemed relevant. In the *critical-incidents technique*, a large number of experienced teachers were asked what specific behaviors in which specific situations would be used by effective and ineffective teachers.[2] Over 500 critical incidents were obtained, which were reduced to a list of 25 bipolar generalized kinds of behavior.[3] This list was further reduced to a working form of 18 behaviors.

Experienced teachers were used as observers and were carefully trained in the observation technique and use of the Record. In addition, they were retrained at appropriate intervals. Each observer used a glossary containing descriptions or behavioral summaries of the adjective pairs. For example, "inflexible-adaptable"

[1]D. Ryans, *Characteristics of Teachers*. Washington, D.C.: American Council on Education, 1960, p. 86.

[2]See *ibid.*, pp. 79–83. For a long and competent general discussion, see J. Flanagan, "The Critical Incident Technique," *Psychological Bulletin*, LI (1954), 327–358.

[3]Ryans, *op. cit.*, p. 82.

was described as "rigid in conforming to routine" ("inflexible") and "flexible in adapting explanations" ("adaptable"); "impatient with interruptions and digressions" ("inflexible") and "met an unusual classroom situation competently" ("adaptable").[4]

The observers observed a large number of teachers. Each teacher was observed twice by different observers. The unit of observation time was one class period. If there were discrepancies between the two observers in describing a teacher, a third observer was used. Observers made notes during the class hour. Each item of the Record was assessed on a seven-point scale, as in the following pair:

Dull *1* *2* *3* *4* *5* *6* *7* N *Stimulating*

(N means "neutral.") The Record was filled out after each observation period, one class hour.

Averages of two (or three) Record assessments were calculated. Each teacher, then, had scores on the 18 descriptive pairs. The researchers did a number of analyses, using item scores, scores of groups of items, and total scores. These analyses do not concern us here, except to note that the objective observations of the behavior of the teachers yielded measures of the independent variable.

Everyone observes the actions of others. We look at other persons and listen to them talk. We infer what others mean when they say something, and we infer the characteristics, motivations, feelings, and intentions of others on the basis of these observations. We say, "He is a shrewd judge of people," meaning that his observations of behavior are keen and that we think his inferences of what lies behind the behavior are valid.

This day-by-day kind of observation of most people, however, is unsatisfactory for science. The social scientist must also observe human behavior, but he must be dissatisfied with the inadequacy of uncontrolled observations. He seeks reliable and objective observations from which he can draw valid inferences. He treats the observation of behavior as part of a measurement procedure: he assigns numerals to objects, in this case human behavioral acts or sequences of acts, according to rules.

Problems of Observation of Behavior

Basically, there are two modes of observation: we can watch people do and say things and we can ask people about their own actions and the behavior of others. The principal ways of getting information are by either experiencing something directly, or by having someone tell us what happened. In this chapter we are concerned mainly with seeing and hearing events and observing behavior, and solving the scientific problems that spring from such observation.

[4] *Ibid.*, p. 91.

The Observer

The major problem of behavioral observation is the observer himself. One of the difficulties with the interview, recall, was the interviewer, because he was part of the measuring instrument. This problem was almost nonexistent in objective tests and scales. In behavioral observation the observer is both a crucial strength and a crucial weakness. Why? The observer must digest the information derived from his observations and then make inferences about constructs. He observes a certain behavior, say a child striking another child. Somehow he must process this observation and make an inference that the behavior is a manifestation of the construct "aggression" or "aggressive behavior," or even "hostility." The strength and the weakness of the procedure is the observer's powers of inference. If it were not for inference, a machine observer would be better than a man observer. (Sometimes it *may* be.) The strength is that the observer can relate the observed behavior to the constructs or variables of a study: he brings behavior and construct together. One of the recurring difficulties of measurement is to bridge the gap between behavior and construct. Competent observers and well-made observations help bridge this gap.[5]

The basic weakness of the observer is that he can make quite incorrect inferences from observations. Take two extreme cases. Suppose, on the one hand, that an observer who is strongly hostile to parochial school education observes parochial school classes. It is clear that his bias may well invalidate the observation. Referring again to the Ryans Classroom Observation Record, he can easily rate an adaptable teacher as somewhat inflexible because he perceives parochial school teaching as inflexible. Or he may judge the actually stimulating behavior of a parochial school teacher to be dull.

On the other hand, assume that an observer can be completely objective and that he knows nothing whatever about public or parochial education. In a sense any observations he makes will not be biased, but they will be inadequate. Observation of human behavior requires competent knowledge of that behavior, and even of the meaning of the behavior.

The observer-inference problem is the main difficulty. There is, however, another problem: the observer can affect the objects of observation simply by being part of the observational situation. Actually and fortunately, this is not a severe problem.[6] Indeed, it is more of a problem to the uninitiated who seem to believe that people will act differently, even artificially, when observed. The classic educational case of this is the belief that a teacher under observation, especially

[5]In their excellent chapter on observation in classrooms, Medley and Mitzel say that the observer should use the least judgment possible: only a judgment "needed to perceive whether the behavior has occurred or not." This means, of course, the least inference possible. While their argument is well taken, it is perhaps too strong. It would, for example, virtually rule out Ryans' schedule. D. Medley and H. Mitzel, "Measuring Classroom Behavior by Systematic Observation." In N. Gage, ed., *Handbook of Research in Teaching*. Skokie, Ill.: Rand McNally, 1963, chap. 6 (see pp. 252–253). K. Weick, "Systematic Observational Methods." In G. Lindzey and E. Aronson, eds., *The Handbook of Social Psychology*, 2d ed. Reading, Mass.: Addison-Wesley, 1968, vol. II, chap. 13, p. 359, supports Medley and Mitzel's view. At the same time, he argues for a more active role of the observer, as Cannell and Kahn argued for a more active role of the interviewer (see Chapter 28).

[6]*Ibid.*, pp. 306–307.

by superiors, will put her best foot forward. She will act in an exemplary way not necessarily customary with her, it is thought. This may be true. A significant point is missed, however. It is not realized that a teacher cannot do what she cannot do. She cannot act in a way she has not learned to act. She cannot be "adaptable," to use one of Ryans' adjectives, if she has not learned to be adaptable.

Observers seem to have little effect on the situations they observe.[7] Individuals and groups seem to adapt rather quickly to an observer's presence and to act as they would usually act. This does not mean that the observer cannot have an effect. It means that if the observer takes care to be unobtrusive and not to give the people observed the feeling that judgments are being made, then the observer as an influential stimulus is mostly nullified.

Validity and Reliability

On the surface, nothing seems more natural, when observing *harsh-kind* behavior or *partial-fair* behavior, than to believe that we are measuring what we say we are measuring. And when Ryans gives the observer in the glossary of the Record fairly detailed (but not too detailed) definitions of *harsh-kind* or *partial-fair*, then there is good correspondence, presumably, between what is measured and what was intended to be measured. The main point, perhaps, is that, given his definitions, observers can and *do* apply the terms similarly to the same or similar types of behavior. For instance, part of his glossary for *partial-fair* is: "Gave most attention to one or a few pupils" (*partial*) and "Distributed attention to many pupils" (*fair*).[8]

When a greater interpretative burden is put upon the observer, however, validity may suffer (as well as reliability). Fouriezos, Hutt, and Guetzkow's measurement of self-oriented needs in conference behavior is an example.[9] Observers were given a simple ten-point rating scale, ranging from "No expression of self-oriented need" to "All behavior of the self-oriented type," on which they indicate integrated appraisals of group members' self-oriented needs. They were guided by five categories of need expression on which they made notes during conferences. While the system seems to have worked well, there would seem to be a rather large gap between the observed behaviors and the inferred needs. The more the burden of interpretation put upon the observer, then, the greater the validity problem. (This does not mean, however, that no burden of interpretation should be put upon the observer.)

A simple aspect of the validity of observation measures is their predictive power. Do they predict any relevant criteria dependably? The trouble, as usual, is in the criteria. As Heyns and Lippitt point out, independent measures of the same variables are rare.[10] Can we say that an observational measure of teacher

[7]R. Heyns and R. Lippitt, "Systematic Observational Techniques," in G. Lindzey, ed., *Handbook of Social Psychology*. Cambridge, Mass.: Addison-Wesley, 1954, vol. I, p. 399.

[8]Ryans, *op. cit.*, p. 87.

[9]N. Fouriezos, M. Hutt, and H. Guetzkow, "Self-Oriented Needs in Discussion Groups." In D. Cartwright and A. Zander, eds., *Group Dynamics*. New York: Harper & Row, 1953, pp. 354–360.

[10]Heyns and Lippitt, *op. cit.*, p. 398.

behavior is valid because it correlates positively with superiors' ratings? We might have an independent measure of self-oriented needs, but would this measure be an adequate criterion for observations of such needs?[11]

The important clue to the study of the validity of behavioral observation measures would seem to be construct validity. If the variables being measured by the observational procedures are embedded in a theoretical framework, then certain relations should exist. Do they indeed exist? If we are working with a theoretical framework based on needs, for instance, we may deduce from the theory that teachers strong in succorance needs will score high (in Ryans' observation system) on *excitable* and *uncertain*, and low on *understanding*. If these relations hold up, then this is evidence for the construct validity of the observation system.

The reliability of behavioral observation measures is a simpler matter, though by no means an easy one. It is usually defined as the agreement among observers. The reader will recall that this amounts to the definition of objectivity given earlier. While it is satisfactory so to conceive reliability, at least for practical purposes, the broader conception of reliability developed earlier should be applied to observations as it is applied to all other measures.

Practically speaking, then, the reliability of observations can be estimated by correlating the observations of two or more observers. When assessing the reliability of the assignment of behaviors to categories, percentage of agreement between judges is often used. But, as with all kinds of measurement, there are other ways to estimate reliability, for example, repeat reliability and reliability estimated through analysis of variance.[12]

Characteristics of Observations

The first and most important consideration in any observation system is to know clearly what is being observed. This seems so obvious as to be trite. Let us see that it is not so obvious. Suppose we are studying the relation between *independence* and *problem solving*. We hypothesize that the more independent a child the better he will be able to solve problems, other things equal. We wish to observe *independence*, or more accurately, *independent behavior*. Now, what *is* independent behavior? If a child persistently works by himself is this independent behavior? If a child initiates projects and games with other children, is this independent behavior? Take a much more difficult problem: What is democratic behavior in a teacher? If a teacher is nice to children, is this democratic? If she organizes children into groups, is she being democratic? Just what do we mean when we say "democratic behavior"? It should be obvious that clear knowledge of what is being observed is not so obvious.

[11]For an excellent discussion of the criterion problem and validity in relation to teaching behaviors, see Ryans, *op. cit.*, chap. 2.

[12]Medley and Mitzel, *op. cit.*, pp. 309 ff., give a thorough exposition of the reliability of ratings in an analysis of variance framework. But their discussion is a difficult one that requires considerable statistical background. Before tackling the Medley and Mitzel treatment, it would be wise to study Guilford's simpler discussion: J. Guilford, *Psychometric Methods*, 2d ed. New York: McGraw-Hill, 1954, pp. 280 ff.

It is necessary, then, to define fairly precisely and unambiguously what is to be observed. If we are measuring *curiosity*, we must tell the observer what curious behavior is. If *cooperativeness* is being measured, we must somehow tell the observer how cooperative behavior is distinguished from any other kind of behavior. This means that we must provide the observer with some form of operational definition of the variable being measured; we must define the variable behaviorally.

Categories

The fundamental practical job of the observer is to assign behaviors to categories. The categories of the Ryans Record are defined by the adjective pairs. In another comprehensive system for observing classroom behaviors, eight broad behavioral categories or dimensions are used.[13] Two of these, for instance, are *Differentiation* and *Climate-Teacher. Differentiation* includes behaviors aimed at providing or not providing for individual differences of pupils. *Climate-Teacher* includes teacher behaviors that set or influence the emotional and social atmosphere of the class. These broad categories are further broken down into subcategories that indicate where along the dimension measured a particular behavior is to be placed. *Differentiation*, for instance, is broken into 10 subcategories from "identical work —no teacher assistance" to "differentiated work-ability and interest basis—individual-teacher assistance."[14] The observer may note, during an observation period, that the teacher makes no attempt at all to help any individuals and that all pupils are doing the same work. He would assign this set of behavioral acts to the first subcategory.

From earlier work on partitioning, recall that categories must be exhaustive and mutually exclusive. In order to satisfy the exhaustiveness condition, one must first define U, the universe of behaviors to be observed. In some observation systems, this is not hard to do. In others it is very difficult to do. In the Cornell, Lindvall, and Saupe system U was the behavior of all the teachers and pupils in a classroom. But this is much too large and vague. So, these investigators broke U down into subsets: *A: Differentiation; B: Social Organization; C: Pupil Initiative; D: Content; E: Variety; F: Competency; G: Climate-Teacher; H: Climate-Pupil.*[15] Careful study of this partitioning will show that most classroom behaviors can be subsumed under one of these rubrics. Cornell, Lindvall, and Saupe further partitioned the above eight subsets of U into further subsets of the subsets. One of these breakdowns was described earlier.

It might sound as though *all* possible behaviors must be defined and observed. Not so. In many cases, an investigator may be interested only in the variable *social climate* (of a classroom or a group). In such a case the behavior subsumed under *Climate-Teachers* and *Climate-Pupils*, two of Cornell, Lindvall, and Saupe's subsets, would comprise U. (These include items like: "Respected pupil opinion,"

[13]F. Cornell, C. Lindvall, and J. Saupe, *An Exploratory Measurement of Individualities of Schools and Classrooms*. Urbana, Ill.: Bureau of Educational Research, University of Illinois, 1952.

[14]*Ibid.*, p. 53.

[15]*Ibid.*, pp. 53–54.

"Tried to see a pupil point of view," "Corrected or criticized excessively."[16]) In other words, *U* can be large, medium, or small, depending upon the research problem and objectives. One can range from an extremely broad variable like *teacher effectiveness*, including all Ryans' categories to a comparatively narrow variable like *aggressiveness* that may require only two or three subcategories, like *physical and verbal injury to another child* and *takes objects from another child.*

Units of Behavior

What units to use in measuring human behavior is still an unsettled problem. Here one is often faced with a clash between reliability and validity demands. Theoretically, one can attain a high degree of reliability by using small and easily observed and recorded units. One can attempt to define behavior quite operationally by listing a large number of behavioral acts, and can thus ordinarily attain a high degree of precision and reliability. Yet in so doing one may also have so reduced the behavior that it no longer bears much resemblance to the behavior one intended to observe. Thus validity may be lost.

On the other hand, one can use broad "natural" definitions and perhaps achieve a high degree of validity. One might instruct observers to observe *cooperation* and define *cooperative behavior* as "accepting other persons' approaches, suggestions, and ideas; working harmoniously with others toward goals," or some such rather broad definition. If observers have had group experience and understand group processes, then it might be expected that they could validly assess behavior as cooperative and uncooperative by using this definition. Such a broad, even vague, definition enables the observer to capture, if he can, the full flavor of cooperative behavior. But its considerable ambiguity allows differences of interpretation, thus probably lowering reliability.

Some researchers who are strongly operational in their approach insist upon highly specific definitions of the variables observed. They might list a number of specific behaviors for the observer to observe. No others would be observed and recorded. Extreme approaches like this may produce high reliability, but they may also miss part of the essential core of the variables observed. Suppose ten specific types of behavior are listed for *cooperativeness*. Suppose, too, that the universe of possible behaviors consists of 40 or 50 types. Clearly, important aspects of *cooperativeness* will be neglected. While what is measured may be reliably measured, it may be quite trivial or partly irrelevant to the variable *cooperativeness*.

This is the molar-molecular problem of any measurement procedure in the social sciences. The *molar approach* takes larger behavioral wholes as units of observation. Complete interaction units may be specified as observational targets. Verbal behavior may be broken down into complete interchanges between two or more individuals, or into whole paragraphs or sentences. The *molecular approach*, by contrast, takes smaller segments of behavior as units of observation. Each interchange or partial interchange may be recorded. Units of verbal behavior may

[16]*Ibid.*, p. 54.

be words or short phrases. The molar observer will start with a general broadly defined variable, as given earlier, and consider and record a variety of behaviors under the one rubric. He depends on his experience and interpretation of the meaning of the actions he is observing. The molecular observer, on the other hand, seeks to push his own experience and interpretation out of the observational picture. He records what he sees—and no more.

Degree of Observer Inference

Observation systems differ on another important dimension: the *amount of inference* required of the observer. Molecular systems require relatively little inference. The observer simply notes that an individual does or says something. For example, a system may require the observer to note each interaction unit, which may be defined as any verbal interchange between two individuals. If an interchange occurs, it is noted; if it does not occur, it is not noted. Or a category may be "Strikes another child." Every time one child strikes another it is noted. No inferences are made in such systems—if, of course, it is ever possible to escape inferences (for example, "strikes"). Pure behavior is recorded as nearly as possible.

Observer systems with such low degrees of observer inference are rare. Most systems require some degree of inference. An investigator may be doing research on board of education behavior and may decide that a low inference analysis is suited to his problem. He may use observation items like "Suggests a course of action," "Interrupts another board member," "Asks a question," "Gives an order to superintendent," and the like. Since such items are comparatively unambiguous, the reliability of the observation system should be substantial.

Systems with higher degrees of inference required of the observer are more common and probably more useful in most research. The high inference observation system gives the observer labeled categories that require greater or lesser interpretation of the observed behavior. The observation system of Fouriezos, Hutt, and Guetzkow, mentioned earlier, is rather high in observer inference. Though five need areas are supplied and defined, the observer must infer that any particular behavior is self need-oriented. For instance, *dominance* is one of the five needs. It is defined as any individual's attempts to exhibit intellectual superiority over other individuals. The authors say, "Dominance in social situations includes attempts to control and direct in the social situation. . . . The leader here controls with little concern for the needs of the group . . ."[17] Then they say that dominance is shown when an individual refuses to hear arguments against his own ideas and tries to force the group to follow his plans. They stress, however, the necessity for the observer to distinguish between dominance based on ego needs and dominance based on situational demands. It is clear that this system is highly inferential. Lest the reader believe that this necessarily impairs reliability, note that test-retest coefficients of reliability ranged from .67 to .96. To attain such satisfactory reliability, the authors stress the necessity of training observers.

It is not possible to make flat generalizations on the relative virtues of sys-

[17]Fouriezos, Hutt, and Guetzkow, *op. cit.*, p. 684.

tems with different degrees of inference.[18] Probably the best advice to the neophyte is to aim at a medium degree of inference. Too vague categories with too little specification of what to observe put an excessive burden on the observer. Different observers can too easily put different interpretations on the same behavior. Too specific categories, while they cut down ambiguity and uncertainty, may tend to be too rigid and inflexible, even trivial. Better than anything else, the student should study various successful systems, paying special attention to the behavior categories and the definitions (instructions) attached to the categories for the guidance of the observer.

Generality or Applicability

Observation systems differ considerably in their *generality*, or degree of *applicability* to research situations other than those for which they were originally designed. Some systems are quite general: they are designed for use with many different research problems. The well-known Bales group interaction analysis is one such general system.[19] This is a low inference system in which all verbal and nonverbal behavior, presumably in any group, can be categorized into one of twelve categories: "shows solidarity," "agrees," "asks for opinion," and so on. The twelve categories are grouped in three larger sets: social-emotional-positive; social-emotional-negative; task-neutral. The Ryans system was obviously intended for general use in any classroom. The Cornell, Lindvall, and Saupe system, too, is general.

Some systems, however, were constructed for use in particular research situations and may or may not be generally applicable to other situations. Such, evidently, is the Fouriezos, Hutt, and Guetzkow system. Yet it can be applied to situations other than decision-making conferences. Most systems devised for specific research problems, with suitable revision and adaptation, can probably be applied to other research problems.

It should be noted that in much research small observations systems can be used to measure specific variables. One such system was conceived and used by Silberman to measure, through classroom observations of teachers, *contact* (teacher-initiated interaction with pupils), *evaluation* (admiring or approving and criticizing or disapproving behaviors), and *acquiescence* (acquiescent replies to pupil appeals).[20] The observations were aimed only at these behaviors. The measures obtained were correlated with the attachment, concern, indifference, and rejection teachers showed specific pupils.

Sampling of Behavior

The last characteristic of observations, *sampling*, is, strictly speaking, not a characteristic. It is a way of obtaining observations. Before using an observation sys-

[18]Heyns and Lippitt discuss the dimension of inference in observations in each of several rather completely described social psychological observation systems. Heyns and Lippitt, *op. cit.*

[19]R. Bales, *Interaction Process Analysis*. Reading, Mass.: Addison-Wesley, 1951.

[20]M. Silberman, "Behavioral Expression of Teachers' Attitudes Toward Elementary School Students," *Journal of Educational Psychology*, LX (1969), 402–407.

tem in actual research, when and how the system will be applied must be decided. If classroom behaviors of teachers are to be observed, how will the behaviors be sampled? Will all the specific behaviors in one class period be observed? This is what Ryans does. Or will specified samples of specified behaviors be sampled systematically or randomly? In other words, a sampling plan of some kind must be devised and used.

There are two aspects of behavior sampling: *event sampling* and *time sampling*.[21] Event sampling was actually touched upon earlier when units of observation were discussed. An additional meaning attached to the term, however, needs brief explanation. *Event sampling* is the selection for observation of integral behavioral occurrences or events of a given class.[22] Examples of integral events are temper tantrums, fights and quarrels, games, verbal interchanges on specific topics, classroom interactions between teachers and pupils, and so on. The investigator who is pursuing events must either know when the events are going to occur and be present when they occur, as with classroom events, or wait until they occur, as with quarrels.

Event sampling has three virtues: One, the events are natural lifelike situations and thus possess an inherent validity not ordinarily possessed by time samples. Two, an integral event possesses a continuity of behavior that the more piecemeal behavioral acts of time samples do not possess. If one observes a problem-solving situation from beginning to end, one is witnessing a natural and complete unit of individual and group behavior. By so doing, one achieves a whole and realistic larger unit of individual or social behavior. As we saw in an earlier chapter when field experiments and field studies were discussed, naturalistic situations have an impact and a closeness to psychological and social reality that experiments do not usually have.

A third virtue of event sampling inheres in an important characteristic of many behavioral events: they are sometimes infrequent and rare. For example, one may be interested in decisions made in administrative or legislative meetings. Or one may be interested in the ultimate step in problem solving. Teachers' disciplinary methods may be a variable. Such events and many others are relatively infrequent. As such, they can easily be missed by time sampling; they therefore require event sampling.[23]

Time sampling is the selection of behavioral units for observation at different points in time. They can be selected in systematic or random ways to obtain samples of behaviors. A good example is teacher behavior. Suppose the relations between certain variable like *teacher alertness*, *fairness*, and *initiative*, on the one hand, and *pupil initiative* and *cooperativeness*, on the other hand, are studied. We may select random samples of teachers and then take time samples of their

[21]See H. Wright, "Observational Child Study," in P. Mussen, ed., *Handbook of Research Methods in Child Development*. New York: Wiley, 1960, chap. 3. For a review of time sampling, see R. Arrington, "Time Sampling in Studies of Social Behavior: A Critical Review of Techniques and Results with Research Suggestions," *Psychological Bulletin*, XL (1943), 81–124.

[22]Wright, *op. cit.*, p. 104.

[23]If one takes the more active view of observation advocated by Weick (see footnote 5), however, one can arrange situations to ensure more frequent occurrence of rare events.

behavioral acts. These time samples can be systematic: three five-minute observations at specified times during each of, say, five class hours, the class hours being the first, third, and fifth periods one day and the second and fourth periods the next day. Or the time samples can be random: five five-minute observation periods selected at random from a specified universe of five-minute periods. Obviously, there are many ways that time samples can be set up and selected. As usual, the way such samples are chosen, their length, and their number must be influenced by the research problem.[24]

Time samples have the important advantage of increasing the probability of obtaining representative samples of behavior. This is true, however, only of behaviors that occur fairly frequently. Behaviors that occur infrequently have a high probability of escaping the sampling net, unless huge samples are drawn. Creative behavior, sympathetic behavior, and hostile behavior, for example, may be quite infrequent. Still, time sampling is an outstanding contribution to the scientific study of human behavior.

Time samples, as implied earlier, suffer from lack of continuity, lack of adequate context, and perhaps naturalness. This is particularly true when small units of time and behavior are used. Still, there is no reason why event sampling and time sampling cannot sometimes be combined. If one is studying classroom recitations, one can draw a random sample of the class periods of one teacher at different times and observe all recitations during the sampled periods, observing each recitation in its entirety.

Rating Scales[25]

To this point, we have been talking only about the observation of *actual behavior*. The observer looks at and listens to the objects of regard directly. He sits in the classroom and observes teacher-pupil and pupil-pupil interactions. Or he may watch and listen to a group of children solving a problem behind a one-way screen. There is another class of behavioral observation, however, that needs to be mentioned. This type of observation will be called *remembered behavior* or *perceived behavior*. It is conveniently considered under the topic of rating scales.

In measuring remembered or perceived behavior, we ordinarily present the

[24]In a fascinating study of leadership and the power of group influence with small children, Merei points out that time sampling would show only leaders giving orders and the group obeying, whereas prolonged observations would show the inner workings of ordering and obeying. F. Merei, "Group Leadership and Institutionalization," *Human Relations*, II (1949), 23–39.

[25]For an excellent discussion of rating scales, see J. Guilford, *Psychometric Methods*, 2d ed. New York: McGraw-Hill, 1954, chap. 11.

Although rating scales were mentioned earlier in this book, they were not systematically discussed. In reading what follows, the student should bear in mind that rating scales are really objective scales. As such, they might have been included in Chapter 29. Their discussion was reserved for this chapter because the discussion of Chapter 29 focused mainly on measures responded to by the subject being measured. Rating scales, on the other hand, are measures of individuals and their reactions, characteristics, and behaviors by observers. The contrast, then, is between the subject as he sees himself and the subject as others see him. It is important to note, too, that rating scales are used to measure psychological objects, products, and stimuli, such as handwriting, concepts, essays, interview protocols, and projective test materials.

observer with an observation system in the form of a scale of some kind and ask him to assess an object on one or more characteristics, the object not being present. In order to do this, he must make his assessments on the basis of past observations or on the basis of his perceptions of what the observed object is like and how it will behave. A convenient way to measure both actual behavior and perceived or remembered behavior is with rating scales.

A *rating scale* is a measuring instrument that requires the rater or observer to assign the rated object to categories or continua that have numerals assigned to them. Rating scales are perhaps the most ubiquitous of measuring instruments probably because they are seemingly easy to construct and, more important, easy and quick to use. Unfortunately, the apparent ease of construction is deceptive and the ease of use carries a heavy price: lack of validity due to a number of sources of bias that enter into rating measures. Still, with knowledge, skill, and care, ratings can be valuable.

Types of Rating Scales

There are four or five types of rating scales. Two of these types were discussed in Chapter 29: check lists and forced-choice instruments. We consider now only three types and their characteristics. These are the *category rating scale*, the *numerical rating scale*, and the *graphic rating scale*. They are quite similar, differing mainly in details.

The category rating scale presents the observer or judge with several categories from which he picks the one that best characterizes the behavior or characteristic of the object being rated. Suppose a teacher's classroom behavior is being rated. One of the characteristics rated, say, is *alertness*. A category item might be:

How alert is she? (Check one.)
Very alert
Alert
Not alert
Not at all alert

A different form uses condensed descriptions. Such an item might look like this:

Is she resourceful? (Check one.)
Always resourceful; never lacking in ideas
Resources are good
Sometimes flounders for ideas
Unresourceful; rarely has ideas

Numerical rating scales are perhaps the easiest to construct and use. They also yield numbers that can be directly used in statistical analysis. In addition, because the numbers may represent equal intervals in the mind of the observer, they may approach interval measurement.[26] Any of the above category scales can

[26] *Ibid.*, p. 264.

be quickly and easily converted to numerical rating scales simply by affixing numbers before each of the categories. The numbers 3, 2, 1, 0, or 4, 3, 2, 1, can be affixed to the *alertness* item above. A convenient method of numerical rating is to use the same numerical system, say 4, 3, 2, 1, 0, with each item. This is of course the system used in summated-rating attitude scales. In rating scales, it is probably better, however, to give both the verbal description and the numerals.

In graphic rating scales lines or bars are combined with descriptive phrases. The alertness item, just discussed, could look like this in graphic form:

Very alert	Alert	Not alert	Not at all alert

Such scales have many varieties: vertical segmented lines, continuous lines, unmarked lines, lines broken into marked equal intervals (as above), and others. These are probably the best of the usual forms of rating scales. They fix a continuum in the mind of the observer. They suggest equal intervals. They are clear and easy to understand and use. Guilford overpraises them a bit when he says, "The virtues of graphic rating scales are many; their faults are few," but his point is well taken.[27]

Weaknesses of Rating Scales

Ratings have two serious weaknesses, one of them extrinsic, the other intrinsic. The extrinsic defect is that they are seemingly so easy to construct and use that they are used indiscriminately, frequently without knowledge of their intrinsic defects. We will not pause to mention the errors that can creep into the unskillful construction and use of rating scales. Rather, we warn the reader against seizing them for any and all measurement needs. One should first ask the question: Is there a better way to measure my variables? If so, use it. If not, then study the characteristics of good rating scales, work with painstaking care, and subject rating results to empirical test and adequate statistical analysis.[28]

The intrinsic defect of rating scales is their proneness to constant or biased error. This is not new to us, of course. We met this problem when considering response set. With ratings, however, it is particularly threatening to validity. Constant rating error takes several forms, the most pervasive of which is the famous *halo effect*. This is the tendency to rate an object in the constant direction of a general impression of the object. Everyday cases of halo are: believing a person to be intelligent because he agrees with us; believing a man to be virtuous because we like him; giving high praise to Republican presidents and damning Democratic ones.

Halo manifests itself frequently in measurement, especially with ratings. The professor assesses the quality of essay test questions higher than they should be because he likes the testee. Or he may rate the second, third, and fourth questions higher (or lower) than they should be because the first question was well answered

[27]*Ibid.*, p. 268.
[28]Guilford's advice is invaluable: *ibid.*, pp. 264–268 and 293–296.

(or poorly answered). Teacher evaluation of children's achievement that is influenced by the children's docility or lack of docility is another case of halo. In rating individuals on rating scales, there is a tendency for the rating of one characteristic to influence the ratings of other characteristics.

Halo is extremely difficult to avoid. It seems to be particularly strong in traits that are not clearly defined, not easily observable, and that are morally important.[29]

Two important sources of constant error are the error of severity and the error of leniency. The *error of severity* is a general tendency to rate all individuals too low on all characteristics. This is the tough marker: "Nobody gets an *A* in my classes." The *error of leniency* is the opposite general tendency to rate too high. This is the good fellow who loves everybody—and the love is reflected in the ratings.

An exasperating source of invalidity in ratings is the *error of central tendency*, the general tendency to avoid all extreme judgments and rate right down the middle of a rating scale. It manifests itself particularly when raters are unfamiliar with the objects being rated.

There are other less important types of error that will not be considered. More important is how to cope with the types listed above. This is a complex matter that cannot be discussed here. The reader is referred to Guilford's chapter in *Psychometric Methods* where many devices for coping with error are discussed in detail.[30]

Rating scales can and should be used in behavioral research. Their unwarranted, expedient, and unsophisticated use has been rightly condemned. But this should not mean general condemnation. They have virtues that make them valuable tools of scientific research: they require less time than other methods; they are generally interesting and easy for observers to use; they have a very wide range of application; they can be used with a large number of characteristics. It might be added that they can be used as adjuncts to other methods. That is, they can be used as instruments to aid behavioral observations, and they can be used in conjunction with other objective instruments, with interviews, and even with projective measures.

Examples of Observation Systems

Three or four observation systems were mentioned earlier. Other behavioral observation systems are summarized below to help the student get a feeling for

[29]*Ibid.*, p. 279.

[30]Systematic errors can be dealt with to some extent by statistical means. Guilford has worked out an ingenious method using analysis of variance. The basic idea is that variances due to *subjects, judges*, and *characteristics* are extracted from the total variance of ratings. The ratings are then corrected. An easier method when rating individuals on only one characteristic is two-way (correlated-groups) analysis of variance. Reliability can also be easily calculated. The use of analysis of variance to estimate reliability, as we learned earlier, was Hoyt's contribution. Ebel applied analysis of variance to reliability of ratings. See Guilford, *op. cit.*, pp. 280–288, 383, 395–397; R. Ebel, "Estimation on the Reliability of Ratings," *Psychometrika*, XVI (1951), 407–424.

the variety of systems that are possible and the ways in which such systems are constructed and used. In addition, the student may gain further understanding of when behavioral observation is appropriate.

Merrill's Measurement of Mother-Child Interaction[31]

Wishing to measure the variables *Contact between Mothers and Children, Specificity of Control of the Child's Behavior,* and *Facilitation and Inhibition of the Child's Behavior*, Merrill set up an interesting and useful observation system. Mother and child were observed in an experimental room equipped with children's toys and a one-way screen. The mothers were told to imagine that they were at home with their children, unoccupied for half an hour. They had no idea that *they* were being observed, since they had been told that the research was on the child's play behavior.

A mother's behavior was recorded every five seconds, using a fairly complex notational system based on categories derived from the variables mentioned above. For example, *s* means M (Mother) *structurizes*, that is, she uses indirect means to stimulate or influence the child; *t* means M *teaches*, or gives information to increase the child's knowledge; *i* means the mother *interferes* with the child's activity in order to stop it. Each category is accompanied by clear definitions and examples. The category system is comprehensive: it embraces all or most behavior incidents that can occur in a play session. The average reliability for five sessions was .88.

Merrill performed a neat, effective, yet simple experiment using the observation system. Separating the mothers into experimental and control groups, she told the experimental-group mothers, in a second half-hour session, that their children's play potential had not been realized, thus inducing motivation to stimulate the child to do "better." The control-group mothers were told the procedure would be the same as before. If the observation procedure were sensitive enough, it should show the result of the induced motivation. It did.

Medley and Mitzel's Classroom Behavior Observation Record

One of the best-developed observation systems is the Observation Schedule and Record (OScAR) evolved by modifying and combining items from two earlier systems, one of them the Cornell, Lindvall, and Saupe system described earlier.[32] The authors simplified the earlier systems by decreasing the difficulty of the judgments required (see footnote 5, above). Moreover, they required only one judge in each classroom and separated scoring from observing. The schedule was designed to permit the recording of as many significant aspects as possible of what goes on in classrooms.

The individual items were found to group themselves into three relatively

[31]B. Merrill, "A Measurement of Mother-Child Interaction," *Journal of Abnormal and Social Psychology*, XLI (1946), 37–49.

[32]The system, with research data, is described in detail in Medley and Mitzel, *op. cit.*, pp. 278–286. See, also, D. Medley and H. Mitzel, "A Technique for Measuring Classroom Behavior," *Journal of Educational Psychology*, XLIX (1958), 86–92, and "Some Behavioral Correlates of Teacher Effectiveness," *Journal of Educational Psychology*, L (1959), 239–246.

independent and reliable dimensions: *Emotional Climate*, *Verbal Emphasis*, and *Social Organization*. That is, the items belonging to each of these dimensions, or factors, were combined and treated as variables. Two items from each of the first two dimensions, respectively, are: "Teacher demonstrates affection for pupil" (positive), "Pupil ignores teacher's question" (negative); "Pupil reads or studies at his seat," "Pupil (or teacher) uses supplementary reading matter." The third dimension reflects social grouping in classes—for example, a class broken up into two or more groups working independently.[33] It can be seen that this is a low inference system.

Medley and Mitzel say that the three dimensions represent what are probably obvious differences between classes, but that the OScAR fails to tap aspects of classroom behavior related to achievement of cognitive objectives.[34] They are probably too harsh on their own system. The three dimensions of OScAR *are* important. And further work and research on the system may make it possible to get at class behaviors related to pupil cognitive achievement.

The Management of Deviant Classroom Behavior

How should deviant classroom behavior be handled? In one of a series of studies on classroom management, Kounin, Friesen, and Norton used observations of the behavior of both emotionally disturbed and nondisturbed children and the behaviors of teachers handling the deviant behavior of such children.[35] A number of classrooms with both kinds of children were videotaped continuously. The behavior of the children was coded or categorized for work involvement and deviance every 10 seconds and scores were assigned these variables. (Another variable, contagion, was also coded, but we ignore it here.)

The mean scores on the two variables of the disturbed and nondisturbed children were compared and found to be significantly different. The major task of the research, however, was to learn about teaching techniques related to school-appropriate behavior. To do so, the authors studied teacher behavior on the video tapes. Desist, or direct managerial, techniques; overlappingness, or teacher attention to two aspects of a classroom simultaneously; and "with-it-ness," the degree to which a teacher communicates to a class that she knows what is going on, were the teacher behaviors observed and analyzed. Of these, only with-it-ness correlated significantly with child deviance and work involvement. For example, the higher a teacher's with-it-ness, the greater the work involvement of the children and the less their deviance. Moreover, the relations were much the same in both the disturbed and nondisturbed children samples. The authors with some justice advocate that a higher priority be given to group management training in teacher training.

This is significant educational research that could only have been done with observations of behavior. One wonders, indeed, why so little attention has been

[33]*Ibid.*, pp. 282–283.

[34]*Ibid.*, p. 286.

[35]J. Kounin, W. Friesen, and A. Norton, "Managing Emotionally Disturbed Children in Regular Classrooms," *Journal of Educational Psychology*, LVII (1966), 1–13.

paid to the empirical study, especially through direct observation, of classroom management methods and their effects on children's behavior and schoolwork.

Assessment of Parent Behavior

One of the most ambitious attempts to measure parent behavior in natural settings is the research of Baldwin, Kalhorn, and Breese.[36] Observers visit homes and, among other things, rate the behavior of parents on an observation rating scale of 30 items. The items consist of bipolar adjective pairs, such as *disapproving-approving*, *rejecting-devoted*, *nonchalant-anxious*, *dictatorial-democratic*, and so on. Despite the directions, a good bit of inference is required of the observer. The researchers have found that the 30 items group themselves into a smaller number of factors, among which the most important are *warmth*, *democracy*, and *indulgence*. The *warmth* factor, for example, consists of the following items: *child-subordinating–child-centered*, *disapproval-approval*, *rejection-acceptance*, *hostile-affectionate*, *isolation-close rapport*.

Point-Time Sampling of Classroom Activities

Kowatrakul, in studying the relation between student behavior and classroom activities in various subjects, developed a promising method of observation of classroom behavior to be used in conjunction with what he called *point-time sampling*.[37] The observer observes a subject long enough to record one behavior. He then immediately passes on to the next subject. The behavior of the next subject must be independent of that of the first subject. (The author does not say how this is to be achieved, unfortunately.) This procedure is used until one "behavior point" of each subject in the group has been recorded. Then a new round of observation begins. Kowatrakul reports that each round takes between three to five minutes in each class.

The reported reliabilities are high, most of them greater than .90, some as high as .98. (These were odd-even reliabilities.) In a special study of 1689 time samples done by two observers, there was 94 percent agreement. Evidently this is a highly reliable method. The point-time sampling feature of this system deserves further investigation.

Observation and Evaluation of College Teachers

As important as it may seem, there has not been much research on systematic direct or indirect (remembered) observation of college teachers and teaching. In one of the few—and better—studies, Isaacson et al., after considerable preliminary work on items and their dimensions or factors, had college students rate and evaluate their teachers based on their remembered observations and impressions.[38]

[36]A. Baldwin, J. Kalhorn, and F. Breese, "Patterns of Parent Behavior," *Psychological Monographs*, LVIII (1945), No. 3; "The Appraisal of Parent Behavior," *Psychological Monographs*, LXIII (1949), No. 4.

[37]S. Kowatrakul, "Some Behaviors of Elementary School Children Related to Classroom Activities and Subject Areas," *Journal of Educational Psychology*, L (1959), 121–128.

[38]R. Isaacson et al., "Dimensions of Student Evaluations of Teaching," *Journal of Educational Psychology*, LV (1964), 344–351.

They used a 46-item rating scale and instructed the students to respond according to the frequency of the occurrence of certain behavioral acts and not according to whether the behaviors were desirable or undesirable. Their basic interest was in the dimensions or underlying variables behind the items. They found six such dimensions of which the first they thought to be related to general teaching skill.

Although the six factors are important because they seem to show various aspects of teaching—for example, Structure, which is the instructor's organization of the course and its activities, and Rapport, which is the more interactive aspects of teaching and friendliness—we concentrate on the first. Here are three of the items:

He put his material across in an interesting way.
He stimulated the intellectual curiosity of his students.
He explained clearly and his explanations were to the point.

The most effective item, however, was even more general:

How would you rate your instructor in general (all-around) teaching ability?
a. An outstanding and stimulating instructor
b. A very good instructor
c. A good instructor
d. An adequate, but not stimulating instructor
e. A poor and inadequate instructor

While we may question calling this study and others like it observation studies, there is certainly observation, though it is quite different in being remembered and indirect, global and highly inferential, and, finally, much less systematic in actual observation. We ask a student to remember and rate behaviors that he may not have paid particular attention to. Nevertheless, the Isaacson et al. and other studies have shown that this form of observation can be reliably used in instructor and course evaluation.

Behavior Scores System (BSs)

There are a number of important observation systems devised to study group interaction. The best-known is the Bales system mentioned earlier. Flanders has written an interaction analysis system that seems to capture classroom climate and influence and that has an unusual matrix system of analysis.[39] Four of his ten categories are: Accepts Feelings, Asks Questions, Giving Directions, Student Talk-Response. Borgatta has devised a system, called Behavior System Scores (BSs), that is virtually an interaction analysis system.[40] It has the virtues of being brief, fairly simple, and based on factor analysis. Its six categories apparently measure two basic dimensions: *Assertiveness* and *Sociability*. Examples of the

[39]It is described in considerable detail by Medley and Mitzel, "Measuring Classroom Behavior by Systematic Observation," *op. cit.*, pp. 271–274.

[40]E. Borgatta, "A New Systematic Observation System: Behavior Scores System (BSs System)," *Journal of Psychological Studies*, XIV (1963), 24–44. Also described briefly by Weick, *op. cit.*, pp. 400–401.

categories of behavior in each of the factors are: Assertions or dominant acts (draws attention, asserts, initiates conversation, etc.) and Supportive acts (acknowledges, responds, etc.). Such a system may be useful in behavioral research whose focus is group interaction and behavior—decision-making meetings, for example.

Assessment of Behavioral Observation

There is no doubt whatever that objective observation of human behavior has advanced beyond the rudimentary stage. The advances, like other methodological and measurement advances made in the last ten to twenty years, have been striking. The growth of psychometric and statistical mastery and sophistication has been felt in the observation and assessment of actual and remembered behavior. Social scientific research can and should profit from these advances. Many educational research problems, for example, strongly demand behavior observations: children in classrooms interacting with each other and with teachers, administrators and teachers discussing school problems in staff meetings, boards of education working toward policy decisions. Both basic and applied research, especially research involving group processes and group decisions, can profit from direct observation. And it can be used in field studies, field experiments, and laboratory experiments. Here is a methodological approach that is essentially the same in field and laboratory situations.

The difficulty in using full-scale systems, like Ryans' and Medley and Mitzel's, has undoubtedly discouraged the use of observation in behavioral research. But observations must be used when the variables of research studies are interactive and interpersonal in nature and when we wish to study the relations between actual behavior, like class management techniques or group interaction, and other behaviors or attribute variables. Important as is asking about behavior, there is no substitute for seeing, as directly as possible, what people actually do when confronted with different circumstances and different people. Moreover, in much, perhaps most, behavioral research, it is probably not necessary to use the larger observation systems. As shown earlier, smaller systems can be devised for special research purposes. Silberman did this in his study. Kounin, Friesen, and Norton used a limited special-purpose system. Merrill's limited system was highly appropriate for her purpose. In any case, scientific behavioral research requires direct and indirect observations of behavior, and the technical means of making such observations are becoming increasingly adequate and available. The next decade should see considerable understanding and improvement of methods of observation, as well as their increased meaningful use.

Study Suggestions

1. The student should study two or three behavior observation systems in detail. For students of education, the Medley and Mitzel, Ryans, and Cornell, Lindvall, and Saupe systems will yield high returns. Other students will want to expand their study to other systems. The best source for educational systems is Medley and Mitzel's chapter (see footnote 5). It is authoritative and clear

with many examples. The two best general references are the Heyns and Lippitt chapter (footnote 7) and the Weick chapter (footnote 5) in the first and second editions of the *Handbook of Social Psychology*. Recently, an anthology of 79 observation systems was issued in cooperation with Research for Better Schools, Inc., a regional education laboratory: A. Simon and E. Boyer, eds., *Mirrors for Behavior, I and II*. Philadelphia, Pa.: Classroom Interaction Newsletter, 1970.

After getting a general idea of observation systems, the student should study their use in actual research. See, for example, Medley and Mitzel's use of the OScAR (see Footnote 32) and Kounin, Friesen, and Norton's (footnote 35) and Silberman's (footnote 20) use of more limited methods. In addition, here are three studies that have used observations fruitfully:

Borgatta, E. "Analysis of Social Interaction: Actual, Role Playing, and Projective." *Journal of Abnormal and Social Psychology*, LI (1955), 394–405. An outstanding study that compared subjects' responses in three kinds of situations (see title), using the Bales interaction system for observations of role-playing situations.

Brophy, J., and Good, T. "Teachers' Communication of Differential Expectations for Children's Classroom Performance." *Journal of Educational Psychology*, LXI (1970), 365–374. Pairs of subjects, a teacher and a pupil, were observed in actual class situations, in a study of the effect of teachers' achievement expectations on their interaction with pupils. Probably a better test of the well-known expectancy hypothesis because the expectations should affect teacher behavior, but not necessarily pupil achievement.

Klein, S. "Student Influence on Teacher Behavior." *American Educational Research Journal*, VIII (1971), 403–421. An interesting experiment in which the subjects in classes were the teachers and the students the experimenters. Observations were made of both teacher and pupil verbal and nonverbal behavior.

2. There appears to be increasing emphasis, in behavioral and educational research, on observation in "natural" ongoing situations. It is called "naturalistic research." The student will find the following books interesting and stimulating.

   Brandt, R., *Studying Behavior in Natural Settings*. New York: Holt, Rinehart and Winston, 1972.

   Willems, E. and Raush, H., eds. *Naturalistic Viewpoints in Psychological Research*. New York: Holt, Rinehart and Winston, 1969.

CHAPTER 32

Sociometry

Sociometry: A Definition

Sociometry is a broad term indicating a number of methods of gathering and analyzing data on the choice, communication, and interaction patterns of individuals in groups. One might say that sociometry is the study and measurement of social choice. It has also been called a means of studying the attractions and repulsions of members of groups.

A person is asked to choose one or more other persons according to one or more criteria supplied by the researcher: With whom would you like to work? With whom would you like to play? He then makes one, two, three, or more choices among the members of his own group (usually) or of other groups. What could be simpler and more natural? The method works well for kindergartners and for atomic scientists.

Types of Sociometric Choice

Sociometric choice should be rather broadly understood: it not only means "choice of people"; it may mean "choice of lines of communication," "choice of lines of influence," or "choice of minority groups." The choices depend upon the instructions and questions given to individuals. Here is a list of sociometric questions and instructions:

> With whom would you like to work (play, sit next to, and so on)?
> Which two members of this group (age group, class, club, for instance) do you like the most (the least)?
> Who are the three best (worst) pupils in your class?

Whom would you choose to represent you on a committee to improve faculty welfare?
What four individuals have the greatest prestige in your organization (class, company, team)?
What two groups of people are the most acceptable (least acceptable) to you as neighbors (friends, business associates, professional associates)?

Obviously, there are many possibilities.[1] In addition, these can be multiplied simply by asking: Who do you think would choose you to . . .? and Whom do you think the group would choose to . . .? Subjects can also be asked to rank others using sociometric criteria, providing there are not too many to rank. Or rating scales can be used. Members of a group or organization can be asked to rate each other using one or more criteria. For example, we can phrase the sociometric instructions something like this: "Here is a list of the members of your group. Rate each according to whether you would like to work with him on a committee to draft a set of bylaws. Use the numbers 4, 3, 2, 1, 0–4 meaning you would like to work with him very much, 0 you would not want to work with him at all, and the other numbers representing intermediate degrees of liking to work with him." Clearly, any of the methods of measurement, including forced-choice methods, can be used. The main difference is that sociometry always has such ideas as social choice, interaction, communication, and influence behind it.

Methods of Sociometric Analysis

There are three forms of sociometric analysis: *sociometric matrices*, *sociograms*, and *sociometric indices*. Of all methods of sociometric analysis, *sociometric matrices*, to be defined presently, perhaps contain the most important possibilities and implications for the behavioral researcher. *Sociograms* are diagrams or charts of the choices made in groups. We shall discuss sociograms very little, since they are used more frequently for practical than for research purposes.[2] *Sociometric indices* are single numbers calculated from two or more numbers yielded by sociometric data. They indicate sociometric characteristics of individuals and groups.

Sociometric Matrices

We learned earlier that a *matrix* is a rectangular array of numbers or other symbols. In sociometry we are usually concerned only with square, or $n \times n$ matrices, n being equal to the number of persons in a group. Rows of the matrix are labeled i; columns are labeled j; i and j, of course, can stand for any number and any person in the group. If we write a_{ij}, this means the entry in the ith row and jth

[1]For further discussion, see N. Gronlund, *Sociometry in the Classroom*. New York: Harper & Row, 1959, chap. 2. This is an elementary reference. References for the researcher are: G. Lindzey and D. Byrne, "Measurement of Social Choice and Interpersonal Attractiveness." In G. Lindzey and E. Aronson, eds., *The Handbook of Social Psychology*, 2d ed. Reading, Mass.: Addison-Wesley, 1968, vol. II, chap. 14; C. Proctor and C. Loomis, "Analysis of Sociometric Data." In M. Jahoda, M. Deutsch, and S. Cook, *Research Methods in Social Relations*. New York: Holt, Rinehart and Winston, 1951, pt. 2, chap. 17.

[2]See M. Northway, *A Primer of Sociometry*. Toronto: University of Toronto Press, 1952; Gronlund, *op. cit.*, pp. 68–78.

column of the matrix, or, more simply, any entry in the matrix. It is convenient to write *sociometric matrices*. These are matrices of numbers expressing all the choices of group members in any group.

Suppose a group of five members has responded to the sociometric question, "With whom would you like to work on such-and-such a project during the next two months? Choose two individuals." The responses to the sociometric question are, of course, *choices*. If a group member chooses another group member, the choice is represented by 1. If a group member does not choose another, the lack of choice is represented by 0. (If rejection had been called for, −1 could have been used.) The sociometric matrix of choices, C, of this hypothetical group situation is given in Table 32.1.

TABLE **32.1** SOCIOMETRIC CHOICE MATRIX: FIVE-MEMBER GROUP, TWO-CHOICE QUESTION[a]

		j				
		a	b	c	d	e
	a	0	1	0	0	1
	b	1	0	0	0	1
i	c	0	0	0	1	1
	d	0	1	0	0	1
	e	1	1	0	0	0
	Σ:	2	3	0	1	4
				C		

[a] Individual i *chooses* individual j. That is, the table can be read by rows: b chooses a and e. It can also be read by columns: b *is chosen* by a, d, and e. The sums at the bottom indicate the number of choices each individual receives.

It is possible to analyze C in a number of ways. But first let us be sure we know how to read the matrix. It is probably easier to read from left to right, from i to j. Member i chooses (or does not choose) member j. For example, a chooses b and e; c chooses d and e. Sometimes it is convenient to speak passively, "b was chosen by a, d, and e," or "c was chosen by no one."

The analysis of a matrix usually begins by studying it to see who chose whom. With a simple matrix like C this is easy. There are three kinds of choice: *simple* or one-way, *mutual* or two-way, and *no choice*. We look first at simple choices. (This was discussed in the preceding paragraph.) A *simple* one-way choice is where i chooses j, but j does not choose i. In Table 32.1, c chose d, but d did not choose c. We write: $i \rightarrow j$, or $c \rightarrow d$. A *mutual* choice is where i chooses j and j also chooses i. In the table, a chose b and b chose a. We write: $i \leftrightarrow j$, or $a \leftrightarrow b$. We might count mutual choices in Table 32.1: $a \leftrightarrow b, a \leftrightarrow e, b \leftrightarrow e$.

The extent to which any member is chosen is easily seen by adding the columns of the matrix. Obviously, e is "popular": he was chosen by all the other group members; a and b received 2 and 3 choices, respectively. Evidently c is not at all popular: no one chose him; *d* is not popular either: he received only 1 choice. If individuals are allowed unlimited choices, that is, if they are instructed to choose any number of other individuals, then the row sums take on meaning.[3] We might call these sums indices of, say, *gregariousness*.

There are other methods of matrix analysis that are potentially useful to researchers. For example, by relatively simple matrix operations one can determine cliques and chains of influence in small and large groups. These matters, however, are beyond the scope of this book.[4]

Sociograms or Directed Graphs

The simplest analyses are like those just discussed. But with a matrix larger than *C* it is almost impossible to digest the complexities of the choice relations. Here *sociograms* are helpful, provided the group is not too large. We now change the name "sociogram" to "directed graph." This is a more general mathematical term that can be applied to any situation in which *i* and *j* are in some relation *R*. Instead of saying "*i* chooses *j*," it is quite possible to say "*i* influences *j*," or "*i* communicates to *j*," or "*i* is a friend of *j*," or "*i* dominates *j*." In symbolic shorthand, we can write, generally: *iRj*. Specifically, we can write for the examples just given: *iCj* (*i* chooses *j*), *iIj* (*i* influences *j*), *iCj* (*i* communicates to *j*), *iFj* (*i* is a friend of *j*), *iDj* (*i* dominates *j*). Any of these interpretations can be depicted by a matrix such as *C* and by a directed graph. A directed graph of *C* is given in Fig. 32.1.

We see at a glance that *e* is the center of choice. We might call him a leader. Or we might call him either a likable or a competent person. More important, notice that *a*, *b*, and *e* choose each other. This is a clique. We define a *clique* as three or more individuals who mutually choose each other.[5] Looking for more

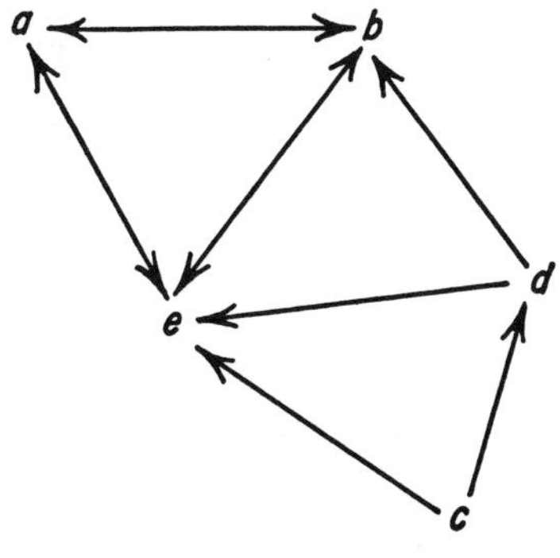

FIG. 32.1

[3]Subjects can be told to choose one, two, three, or more other persons. Three seems to be a common number of choices. The number allowed should be dictated by the research purposes. See Gronlund, *op. cit.*, pp. 48–49; Lindzey and Byrne, *op. cit.*, pp. 455–456.

[4]See *ibid.*, pp. 470–473. A good explanation of elementary matrix operations and sociometric matrices can be found in: J. Kemeny, J. Snell, and G. Thompson, *Introduction to Finite Mathematics*, 2d ed. Englewood Cliffs, N.J.: Prentice-Hall, 1966, pp. 217–250, 384–406.

[5]L. Festinger, S. Schachter, and K. Back, *Social Pressures in Informal Groups*. New York: Harper & Row, 1950, p. 144.

double-headed arrows, we find none. Now we might look for individuals with no arrowheads pointing at them: c is one such individual. We might say that c is not chosen or neglected.

Note that directed graphs and matrices say the same thing. We look at the number of choices a receives by adding the 1's in the a column of the matrix. We get the same information by adding the number of arrowheads pointing at a in the graph. For small and medium-size groups and for descriptive purposes, graphs are excellent means of summarizing group relations. For larger groups (larger than 20 members?) and more analytic purposes, they are not as suitable. They become difficult to construct and difficult to interpret. Moreover, different individuals can draw different graphs with the same data. Matrices are general, and, if handled properly, not too difficult to interpret. Different individuals must, with the same data, write exactly the same matrices.

Sociometric Indices[6]

In sociometry, a large number of indices are possible. Three are given below. The student will find others in the literature.

A simple but useful index is:

$$CS_j = \frac{\Sigma c_j}{n-1} \tag{32.1}$$

where CS_j = the choice status of Person j; Σc_j = the sum of choices in Column j; and n = the number of individuals in the group ($n-1$ is used because one cannot count the individual himself). For C of Table 32.1, $CS_e = 4/4 = 1.00$ and $CS_a = 2/4 = .50$. How well or how poorly chosen an individual is is revealed by CS. It is, in short, his *choice status*. It is of course possible to have a choice rejection index. Simply put the number of 0's in any column in the numerator of Eq. 32.1.

Group sociometric measures are perhaps more interesting. A measure of the cohesiveness of a group is:

$$Co = \frac{\Sigma(i \leftrightarrow j)}{\frac{n(n-1)}{2}} \tag{32.2}$$

Group cohesiveness is represented by Co and $\Sigma(i \leftrightarrow j)$ = sum of mutual choices (or mutual pairs). This useful index is the proportion of mutual choices to the total number of possible pairs. In a five-member group, the total number of possible pairs is 5 things taken 2 at a time:

$$\binom{5}{2} = \frac{5(5-1)}{2} = 10$$

If, in an unlimited choice situation, there were 2 mutual choices, then $Co = 2/10 = .20$, a rather low degree of cohesiveness. In the case of limited choice, the formula is:

$$Co = \frac{\Sigma(i \leftrightarrow j)}{dn/2} \tag{32.3}$$

[6]The discussion that follows is for the most part based on Proctor and Loomis, *op. cit.* Some of the symbols are the author's.

where d = the number of choices each individual is permitted. For C of Table 32.1, $Co = 3/(2 \times 5/2) = 3/5 = .60$, a substantial degree of cohesiveness.

Research Applications of Sociometry

Because the data of sociometry seem so different from other kinds of data, students find it difficult to think of sociometric measurement as measurement. There is no doubt that sociometric data are different. But they are the result of observation, *and they are measures.*[7] They are useful, for example, in classifying individuals and groups. In the Bennington College study, summarized in Chapter 23, Newcomb measured individual prestige by asking students to name five students they would choose as most worthy to represent Bennington College at an important gathering of students from all types of American colleges.[8] He then grouped students by frequency of choice and related this measure of *sociometric prestige* to *political and economic conservatism.* In reading the examples of this section, chosen for their variety of application of the sociometric idea as well as for their importance as research studies, the student should clearly realize that sociometry is a method of observation and data collection that, like any other method of observation, obtains measures of variables.

Prejudice in Schools

In studying the manifestation of prejudice against blacks and Jews in schools, Smith used the simple procedure of asking all the students of entire grades of high schools to name their five best friends.[9] (Smith calls it ". . . a straightforward approach that has been dignified by the label of 'sociometric method' . . . .") He then collated the responses with the responses of the students named to determine ethnic and religious group membership.[10] The students tended to choose their friends from their own racial and religious groups—hardly surprising. More important, Jews and Negroes were not chosen as friends by members of other ethnic and religious groups. White students hardly chose black students at all. While Smith specifically says that he does not want to ascribe his findings to prejudice, it seems clear that "the virtually unpenetrated barrier" between black and white students reflects prejudice. It is evident that a sociometric approach in the study of prejudice can yield important data.

Praise and Sociometric Choice

Most sociometric studies have been ex post facto in nature. Some few have been experimental. One of the latter is Flanders and Havumaki's study of the effects

[7]For a discussion of the basic measurement aspects of sociometric measures, especially their reliability and validity, see Lindzey and Byrne, *op. cit.*, pp. 475–483. See, also, Gronlund, *op. cit.*, chaps. 5 and 6.

[8]T. Newcomb, *Personality and Social Change.* New York: Holt, Rinehart and Winston, 1943, pp. 54–55.

[9]M. Smith, "The Schools and Prejudice: Findings." In C. Glock and E. Siegelman, eds., *Prejudice U.S.A.* New York: Praeger, 1969, chap. 5.

[10]Smith says that this procedure—because students had to name names, shed their own anonymity, and respond to personal questions, and because considerable school time was used—stretched the tolerance of administrator and school boards. In fact, one school system ejected the researchers!

of praise on sociometric choice.[11] The hypothesis was that praise of a student by a prestige figure would increase the student's "choice value." Tenth-grade pupils were divided into 33 groups of 10 subjects each. In 17 of the groups certain individuals were praised for their contributions to discussions about quiz program participation. In the other 16 groups, the subjects were not praised individually; the groups were handled as groups. After the experimental manipulation, the group members were asked to list five members of their groups who would be good quiz program participants. These choices constituted a measure of the dependent variable.

Animal Sociometry

That the sociometric idea is not necessarily limited to human choices is nicely shown in a study of the effects of rearing conditions on the social preferences of rhesus monkeys.[12] Three groups of monkeys were reared from birth to nine months in individual closed cages (A), in a large nursery room in individual bare wire cages (B), and in wire cages in peer groups (C). At 18 months of age, the animals were given social behavior tests in a "selection circus," which was a sociometric choice situation. The "circus" was a circular set of compartments with the test monkey in the center and A, B, and C stimulus monkeys in the compartments in full vision of the test animal. The situation was so arranged that the test animal, after a period of visual orientation, could enter the choice compartments (could select A, B, or C monkeys to be with). As predicted, A animals tended to choose compartments with A animals, B animals compartments with B animals, and C animals compartments with C animals.

Race, Belief, and Sociometric Choice

In a field experiment designed to test Rokeach's controversial hypothesis that differences in beliefs are more influential in determining prejudice than differences in race, Rokeach and Mezei used a realistic employment situation and an ingenious sociometric task.[13] White and black male applicants for various jobs in two mental hospitals were involved individually with four confederates of the experimenters in discussions of rule-oriented and permissive ways of handling patient problems. Two of the confederates were white, two were black; one white and one black confederate espoused the rule-oriented position; the other white and black confederates espoused the permissive position. This arrangement, then, constituted the race and belief conditions. After about 12 minutes of discussion, the experimenter came into the room and asked the five individuals—including the experimental subject, of course—to write down the names of two of the four individuals

[11]N. Flanders and S. Havumaki, "The Effect of Teacher-Pupil Contacts Involving Praise on the Sociometric Choices of Students," *Journal of Educational Psychology*, LI (1960), 65–68.

[12]C. Pratt and G. Sackett, "Selection of Social Partners as a Function of Peer Contact during Rearing," *Science*, CLV (1967), 1133–1135.

[13]M. Rokeach and L. Mezei, "Race and Shared Belief as Factors in Social Choice," *Science*, CLI (1966), 167–172.

with whom he would most prefer to work. This was, of course, a sociometric task whose purpose was to test the prediction that the subjects would express more preference for those individuals whose opinions they shared than for those of the same race. In general, the prediction was supported.

Sociometric Measurement in Social Scientific and Educational Research

Sociometry is a simple, economical, and naturalistic method of observation and data collection. Whenever such human actions as choosing, influencing, dominating, and communicating, especially in group situations, are involved, sociometric methods can usually be used. Sociometry has considerable flexibility. If defined broadly, it can be adapted to a wide variety of research in the laboratory and in the field. Its quantification and analysis possibilities, though not generally realized in the literature, are rewarding. The ability to use the simple assignment of 1's and 0's is particularly fortunate, because powerful mathematical methods can be applied to the data with uniquely interpretable and meaningful results. Matrix methods are the outstanding example. With them, one can discover cliques in groups, communication and influence channels, patterns of cohesiveness, connectedness, hierarchization, and so on.

The student who contemplates using sociometry, however, should study its rationale, its statistical limitations, and, most important for the future, its possibilities of mathematical analysis. (See Study Suggestion 1.) If one considers both matrix algebra and Monte Carlo methods, these possibilities are intriguing and potentially powerful and rewarding to researchers. The student must also be aware that he can use criteria other than those of simple choice based on liking to work with, play with, friendship, and so on. Whenever a conceptual arrow can be drawn between individuals, groups, even objects—the arrow indicating "communicates with," "interacts with," "influences," "dominates," "leads," "accepts," "likes," "is friendly to," "perceives as good," "is like me," and so on—sociometric methods can be used.

Study Suggestions

1. Four useful references on sociometry were cited in the chapter: Gronlund's book, Lindzey and Byrne's chapter, the Proctor and Loomis chapter, and the Northway manual. As the importance and analytic usefulness of sociometric techniques become better known and appreciated, and as computer programs are written to handle the large amounts of data generated, mathematical and Monte Carlo methods of sociometric and related data analysis will probably exert a strong influence on behavioral research. The student is therefore encouraged to explore mathematical treatments of sociometric data. The Kemeny, Snell, and Thompson reference (footnote 4) is a good introduction, though the student needs knowledge of elementary matrix algebra (which,

fortunately, is not difficult). Here are two more references, especially for the advanced student.

Coleman, J. *Introduction to Mathematical Sociology*. New York: Free Press, 1964, pp. 14–16, 444–455. Coleman gives a good example from his own research: pp. 449–454.

Glanzer, M., and Glaser, R. "Techniques for the Study of Group Structure and Behavior: I. Analysis of Structure." *Psychological Bulletin*, LVI (1959), 317–332. This invaluable article reviews a number of matrix operations, sociometric indices, and other methods of studying and analyzing group structure.

2. Let C mean "communicates with." In a four-man group, aCc, bCa, cCa, and dCb.
   (a) Write the matrix expressing these relations.
   (b) Draw a directed graph of the situation. Who would be likely to receive most communications?
   (c) Are there mutual choices? What are they?
   (d) A relation is a set of ordered pairs. Can the present situation be called a relation?
3. An investigator, studying the influence patterns of boards of education, obtained the following matrix from one board of education. (Note that this is like an unlimited choice situation because each individual can influence all or none of the members of the group.) Read the matrix: i influences j.

		j				
		a	b	c	d	e
	a	0	0	1	1	0
	b	0	0	0	0	1
i	c	1	0	0	1	0
	d	1	0	1	0	0
	e	0	1	0	0	0

   (a) What conclusions can you reach from study of this matrix? Is the board divided? Is there likely to be conflict?
   (b) Draw a graph of the influence situation. Interpret the graph.
   (c) Is there a clique on the board? (Define clique as given in the text.) If so, who are its members?
   (d) What members have the least number of influence channels? Are they, then, much less influential than the other members, other things being equal?

   [*Answers:* (c) Yes: a, c, d; (d) b and e.]
4. For the situation in Study Suggestion 3, calculate the cohesiveness of the group using Eq. 32.2.
   [*Answer:* $Co = .40$.]
5. Suppose that you are studying hierarchies in groups and the different influences on group cohesiveness and group decisions of different kinds of hierarchies. One of your research questions is: How do highly centralized group hierarchies influence group cohesiveness in contrast to more diffuse hierarchies? Two of the groups you are studying have sharply differing indices of cohesiveness, say .71 and .32 for groups A and B, respectively. Here are the matrices of *influence* patterns of the two groups, where i

influences j:

A:

i \ j	1	2	3	4	5
1	0	1	0	0	0
2	1	0	0	0	0
3	1	1	0	1	1
4	0	0	0	0	0
5	0	0	0	1	0

B:

i \ j	1	2	3	4	5
1	0	0	0	1	1
2	1	0	0	0	0
3	0	1	0	0	1
4	0	0	1	0	0
5	1	0	0	1	0

(a) Is there a substantial relation between group hierarchy and group cohesiveness?
(b) Which group is highly centralized?
(c) Who probably controls group A? group B?
(d) Draw sociograms for A and B. Do the hierarchical structures become apparent?

(*Note:* Except for the diagonal entries, which are conventionally zero, the entries of B were selected at random.)
[*Answers:* (a) Yes; (b) A; (c) A: no. 3; B: ?]

CHAPTER 33

The Semantic Differential

The semantic differential (*SD*) is a method of observing and measuring the psychological meaning of concepts. Although everyone sees things a bit differently, sometimes very differently, there must be some common core of meaning in all concepts. Indeed the definition of *concept* makes this clear. People must to a great extent share behavioral and verbal definitions of things. We say, "I can't give you a definition of it, but I know what it means." We talk to one another only through shared meanings of words. The public school parent and the parochial school parent share the meaning of the word *school*, even though each has a different perception of the concept. Any concept, then, has a common cultural meaning. It also has other meanings, some of them shared by different groups of people, some of them more or less idiosyncratic.

Osgood invented the semantic differential, henceforth called *SD*, to measure the connotative meanings of concepts as points in what he has called "semantic space."[1] We illustrate the notion of semantic space with two- and three-dimensional examples.

A Spatial Example

Imagine a three-dimensional space—the room you are sitting in, for instance. Assume that there are three sticks at right angles to each other, meeting in the center of the room and touching the walls, the floor, and the ceiling. Label these sticks *X*, *Y*, and *Z*, and call them axes or coordinates. Now imagine there are points

[1]C. Osgood, G. Suci, and P. Tannenbaum, *The Measurement of Meaning*. Urbana, Ill.: University of Illinois Press, 1957.

scattered throughout the three-dimensional space with some of the points clustered near each other and near the X axis, others near the Y axis, and still others near the Z axis. Some points will be situated in the spaces between the axes. Label the points in any order with small letters, $a, b, \ldots, n$. If the axes have been marked off in an equal-interval number system, then any point in the space can be unambiguously identified or "defined" by using the numbers on the three axes. (Let the center of the room, where the three axes meet, be labeled 0 and the numbers on either side of 0 be plus or minus.)

Each point, then, has three numbers attached to it. For example, the point d might be $+6$ units on X, $+3$ units on Y, and -1 unit on Z. This can be written $d = \{6, 3, -1\}$. The point b might be $+4$ units on X, $+3$ units on Y, and 0 units on Z. Thus $b = \{4, 3, 0\}$.

If, through research, we had determined some general "meanings" for the axes X, Y, and Z, then the "meaning" of each point would be some combination of the meanings of X, Y, and Z. If $a = \{4, 0, 0\}$, for example, then a is pure "*X*ness"—4 units of it. If $c = \{1, 1, 6\}$, then c has a little of each of X and Y and a good deal of Z. We might say that a is an X-type and c a Z-type. Notice that if a point, say k, has coordinates $\{0, 0, 0\}$, then k has no meaning. In this circumstance, at least, k is meaningless.

While there is nothing difficult about such a conceptualization, our discussion up to now has been a bit abstract. Therefore let us take a hypothetical, two-dimensional, educational example and try to determine the "meaning" of certain key educational concepts. Suppose we have determined that there are two basic dimensions or factors of meaning. Our research has told us that most educational concepts, like SCHOOL, CURRICULUM, TEACHER, PRINCIPAL, and so on, can be related to two axes, X and Y, which, for good reasons, we have named *Evaluation* and *Potency*. Now, if we have some way to measure things on X, *Evaluation*, and Y, *Potency*, then we can describe these things in the same manner as we did before. Suppose we measured certain concepts in a particular school (by administering an appropriate instrument to teachers, say). SCHOOL may turn out to be $\{6, 1\}$, 6 units on X and 1 unit on Y, or high on *Evaluation* and low on *Potency*. TEACHER may turn out to be $\{5, 2\}$, PUPIL $\{5, -1\}$, PARENT $\{2, 2\}$, PRINCIPAL $\{0, 5\}$, SUPERINTENDENT $\{1, 6\}$, TEACHING $\{6, 2\}$, STUDY $\{5, 1\}$, LEARNING $\{-2, 3\}$, and DISCIPLINE $\{1, 4\}$.

With this information we can "describe" this school (rather, the perception of this school) on the *Evaluation* and *Potency* dimensions. To see what the example just given looks like, we plot the values of the concepts on the X and Y axes. This has been done in Fig. 33.1.

We now have a geometric, spatial, and quantitative description of the school on the two dimensions, X and Y. If X, *Evaluation*, is interpreted as "goodness," and Y, *Potency*, as "strength," and the measurements were obtained from the perceptions of teachers, we might say that the "atmosphere" of the school is such that concepts having to do with teaching—TEACHER, STUDY, SCHOOL, TEACHING, PUPIL—are "good" but not "strong," and that administrative concepts are "strong" but not "good." LEARNING, strange to say, is not "good" but somewhat "strong." PARENT is low on both "goodness" and "strength."

The "meaning" of this school has been specified. Other schools no doubt would have different "meanings." The main point is that concepts have been defined by reference to two known dimensions. If a concept has an ordered pair of numbers assigned to it, this ordered pair of numbers is its "label," which signifies its "meaning." In addition (and very important, as we shall see) the meaning of a concept comes from its relation not only to the two dimensions, X and Y, but also from its relations to other concepts. In Fig. 33.1, TEACHER, STUDY, TEACHING, and SCHOOL are evidently close in meaning. SUPERINTENDENT, PRINCIPAL, and DISCIPLINE, too, are close to each other in meaning, but removed from the first cluster. The meanings of PUPIL and LEARNING are somewhat apart from, though related to, the other meanings.

The Construction and Use of the Semantic Differential

An actual *SD* consists of a number of *scales*, each of which is a bipolar adjective pair, chosen from a large number of such scales for a particular research purpose, together with the *concepts* to be rated with the scales. The scales, or bipolar adjectives, are seven-point (usually) rating scales, the underlying nature of which has been determined empirically. That is, each scale measures one, sometimes two, of

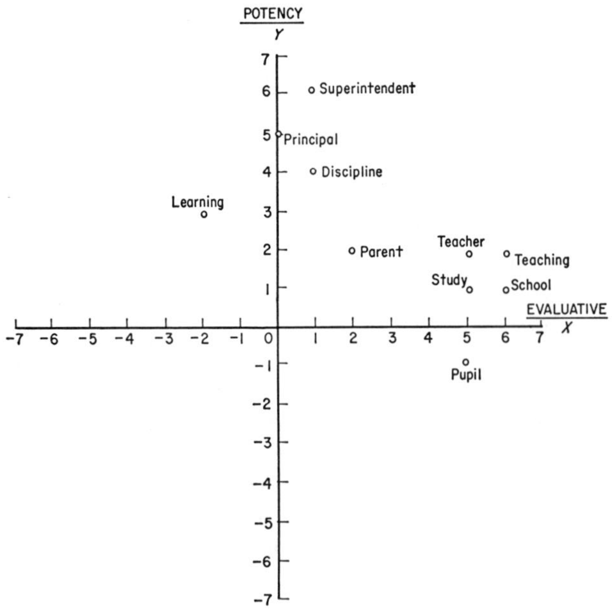

FIG. 33.1

the basic dimensions or factors that Osgood and his colleagues have found to be behind the scales: *Evaluation*, *Potency*, *Activity*. These factors may be called clusters of adjectives.

Through research, Osgood has found that, when analyzed, adjective pairs like *good-bad*, *bitter-sweet*, *large-small*, and *clean-dirty* fall into clusters. The most important cluster seems to consist of adjectives that are *Evaluative*, such as *good-bad* and *pleasant-unpleasant*. A second cluster has adjectives that seem to share strength or *Potency* ideas. *Strong-weak* and *rugged-delicate* are examples. A third important factor is called *Activity* because its adjectives seem to express motion and action. *Fast-slow* and *hot-cold* are examples.

Here are nine of the bipolar adjectives.[2] They are each strongly identified with one of these dimensions or factors. The nature of the dimensions or factors can be ascertained from study of these few scales.

Evaluation	*Potency*	*Activity*
good-bad	large-small	active-passive
beautiful-ugly	heavy-light	sharp-dull
clean-dirty	strong-weak	fast-slow

These are only a few of the bipolar adjective pairs that are available for use and that have been empirically tested. Osgood gives a list of 50 scales with their factor identifications and the strength of the identifications.[3] Investigators can, of course, make up *SD* instruments using these and other adjective pairs.

Concepts

In using the *SD* in research, the first step is to choose the concepts or other stimuli that will be rated with the bipolar adjectives. This is the most important part of the job. The concepts must, of course, be relevant to the research problem. If we were studying educational environments as perceived by teachers, for example, we might use concepts like those in Fig. 33.1: SCHOOL, PUPIL, TEACHING, PRINCIPAL, DISCIPLINE, and so on. Osgood describes a study the main purpose of which was to determine the meaning of political concepts to three groups of subjects.[4] He used names of political leaders as "person" concepts and issues like FEDERAL SPENDING, SOCIALISM, UNITED NATIONS. If one were using the *SD* to measure social attitudes, one would carefully select concepts that are known to tap the attitudes, or are likely to do so, and that would cover substantial parts of the semantic space. These can include the names of public figures of known attitudes, like WALLACE, NIXON, KING, and KENNEDY. One assumes that the meanings associated with such names are related to people's social attitudes. A conservative's meaning space of these four names is probably very different from a liberal's. Perhaps more theoretically fruitful is the rich store of loaded words and expressions that trigger expressions of attitude: CIVIL RIGHTS, UNITED NATIONS, JEWS,

[2] *Ibid.*, p. 37.
[3] *Ibid.*
[4] *Ibid.*, pp. 104–116.

SOCIALIZED MEDICINE, PRIVATE PROPERTY, RELIGION, FREE ENTERPRISE, SCHOOL DISCIPLINE.[5]

There are two general requirements for the selection and use of concepts. One, they must elicit varied responses from different individuals. In other words, they must produce large variance among persons. If they do not, if different people respond to them more or less the same, they are useless for research purposes. Two, they should cover, to some extent, the semantic space. This is not a fixed requirement in all research. In an experimental study in which an investigator is interested only in measuring a single variable, for instance, he might have no interest in covering the semantic space. Studies that pursue meanings of concepts, however, require enough of the semantic space to provide differences in responses to different concepts. These matters will become clearer as we move on.[6]

Scales

The second step in the construction of the instrument, Osgood tells us, is to select appropriate *scales* or *adjective pairs*. Two main criteria determine the selection: factor representativeness and relevance to the concepts used. Perhaps in most cases investigators will want to use scales representative of the three main factors discussed earlier. It is possible, however, that an investigator may wish to use scales of factors other than the three main ones. DiVesta, for instance, in addition to the *E*, *P*, and *A* factors, found other factors: *Warmth, Novelty-Reality, Tautness*.[7] In general, however, the *E*, *P*, and *A* factors have been well-substantiated and should be first considered by researchers.

On the other hand, the investigator may often need only the scales of one factor, most likely the *Evaluation* factor. This would be true in studies of attitudes and values. In some research cases, too, an investigator may decide it is necessary to include scales whose factor identity is not known. After all, Osgood's original 50 scales by no means exhaust adjective possibilities. One might wish to use polarities like *progressive-traditional* and *permissive-restrictive* in a study of educational attitudes. These pairs do not appear in Osgood's original list. Generally, however, the original list will probably be adequate for most purposes.

Osgood and his colleagues use a small sample of factorially related scales to represent each factor, each scale highly "loaded" on one factor and not on the others. For example, nine scales may be used with three *Evaluation*, three

[5]These concepts are attitude objects or referents taken from a scale developed by the author: F. Kerlinger, "The Structure and Content of Social Attitude Referents: A Preliminary Study, "*Educational and Psychological Measurement*, XXXII (1972), 613–630. General sources of concepts are given in Study Suggestion 2.

[6]In some studies, researchers have used only one or two concepts. For instance, to study attitudes toward schools, the single concept SCHOOL may be used with a set of adjective pairs. While this may work, it is not as likely to produce sufficient variance as using three or four related concepts. Moreover, reliability may suffer.

[7]F. DiVesta, "A Developmental Study of the Semantic Structures of Children," *Journal of Verbal Learning and Verbal Behavior*, V (1966), 249–259. Osgood's research indicates that there are certainly other factors or dimensions, in fact no less than seven or eight.

Potency, and three *Activity* scales. The sums or averages of the three scales on each factor are ordinarily used as scores.

The second criterion of scale selection, *relevance* to the concepts used, is much more difficult to satisfy. In many cases, it is quite clear that an adjective pair is related to a concept. If one of the concepts being judged is FATHER, it is obvious that adjective pairs like *good-bad*, *young-old*, *pleasant-unpleasant*, and so on are suitable, since any of these pairs can be used to modify FATHER. But suppose, in a study of prejudice, one were using the concept BIGOT. While most of the cited adjective pairs are suitable, it may very well be necessary to include adjectives not on Osgood's original list. *Flexible-rigid*, *intelligent-stupid*, and, perhaps, *democratic-autocratic* occur to one. If the concept TEACHER were used, one might wish to use adjective pairs presumably appropriate to teaching behavior, for example, *original-stereotyped*, *systematic-disorganized*, and *responsible-irresponsible*.[8] When using such untried scales, however, one should attempt to determine the factorial identity of the scales. It is wise, too, to include scales of known factorial content.[9]

There is a subtle point here that is puzzling. Certain adjective pairs may seem irrelevant to the concepts judged. If one were judging musical compositions, adjective pairs like *loud-soft*, *pleasant-unpleasant*, and *beautiful-ugly* are clearly relevant. Other pairs like *honest-dishonest*, *rich-poor*, and *fair-unfair* would seem not to be relevant. But one cannot always be sure of relevance. Meanings are rich and complex, and an apparently irrelevant adjective pair may turn out to be relevant. If consistent systematic variance can be identified with an adjective pair, then one would have to conclude that the adjective pair is relevant to the concepts. (If an adjective pair is irrelevant to a set of concepts, there should be a large preponderance of midpoint ratings—4 on a seven-point scale—and relatively small variance.) In general, it is probably wise to select adjective pairs that are relevant to the concepts used and to use other adjective pairs sparingly. As Osgood et al. put it, ". . . although there are, we believe, standard *factors* of judgment, the particular scales which may, in any given research problem, best represent these factors, are variable and must be carefully selected by the experimenter to suit his purpose."[10]

Format and Administration of the Semantic Differential

The format of *SD* instruments is simple. Although more complex forms are possible, an effective form is illustrated as follows:

[8]D. Ryans, *Characteristics of Teachers*. Washington, D.C.: American Council on Education, 1960, pp. 86 ff.

[9]Osgood, et al., *op. cit.*, p. 79. The words "factor," "factor structure," and "factorial content" may not be completely grasped at first. For the present think of a factor as a cluster of related things, or as more or less independent subsets of a larger set of things: tests, persons, concepts, and adjective pairs.

[10]*Ibid.*, p. 80.

SCHOOL

(*E*)	1. pleasant	___ : ___ : ___ : ___ : ___ : ___ : ___	unpleasant
(*A*)	2. angular	___ : ___ : ___ : ___ : ___ : ___ : ___	rounded
(*A*)	*3. passive	___ : ___ : ___ : ___ : ___ : ___ : ___	active
(*E*)	*4. ugly	___ : ___ : ___ : ___ : ___ : ___ : ___	beautiful
(*P*)	*5. delicate	___ : ___ : ___ : ___ : ___ : ___ : ___	rugged
(*A*)	6. fast	___ : ___ : ___ : ___ : ___ : ___ : ___	slow
(*E*)	7. good	___ : ___ : ___ : ___ : ___ : ___ : ___	bad
(*P*)	*8. weak	___ : ___ : ___ : ___ : ___ : ___ : ___	strong
(*A*)	*9. dull	___ : ___ : ___ : ___ : ___ : ___ : ___	sharp
(*P*)	10. deep	___ : ___ : ___ : ___ : ___ : ___ : ___	shallow
(*P*)	11. heavy	___ : ___ : ___ : ___ : ___ : ___ : ___	light
(*E*)	*12. dark	___ : ___ : ___ : ___ : ___ : ___ : ___	bright

A concept, SCHOOL, has been inserted to show how a complete page of the instrument might look. The letters before each adjective pair indicate the three factors. The asterisks indicate that the polar adjectives have been reversed, that is, instead of *beautiful-ugly*, *ugly-beautiful* is used. Six of the 12 pairs were reversed at random. Reversals are used to counteract response bias tendencies. A subject cannot go down the list and check all scales at the same point. Notice that the scales are seven-point scales. Although three, five, or even nine-point scales can be used, Osgood has found the seven-point form to be effective. With children, a five-point scale would probably be more suitable.

Each concept appears on a separate sheet with the same set of scales. Subjects are instructed to judge the concepts according to the demands of the research. They might be asked to rate concepts like TEACHER, SCHOOL, ME, and so on, as they see them. This is the usual procedure. But subjects can also be asked to rate concepts "as boys see them," or "by what you think they mean to teachers." For detailed instructions, consult *The Measurement of Meaning*, especially chap. 3.

Analysis of Semantic Differential Data

The *SD* yields a surprising amount of data, and with so many data, a number of analyses are possible. The scores are simply the numbers 1 through 7 assigned as follows:

good 7 : 6 : 5 : 4 : 3 : 2 : 1 bad

That is, if an individual checks the adjective pair *good-bad* between, say, the first and second sets of dots at the left, a 6 is assigned. Other checked points are assigned to the other numerals. It is possible to use the numerical system +3, +2, +1, 0, −1, −2, −3. This has the advantage of having a zero at the neutral point. But this advantage is more than offset by the disadvantage of having to work with negative quantities.[11]

Viewed in variance and set terms, there are three main sources of variance or a three-way cross-partition of the total sample of scores. The sources of variance are: *concepts*, *scales*, and *subjects* (and, of course, *error*). That is, the scores can be analyzed for differences *between concepts*, *between scales*, *between subjects*, or any combination thereof. In most studies, however, there are ways of reducing the data to two categories, usually *concepts* and *scales*, or *concepts* and *factors*. The *SD* data, like *Q* data to be considered later, are unusual in that the data of one individual can be analyzed, as well as the data of groups of individuals.

A small set of hypothetical data may be helpful. Suppose that the matrix of Table 33.1 contains the *SD* raw scores of one individual. This subject judged five

TABLE **33.1** HYPOTHETICAL SEMANTIC DIFFERENTIAL DATA OF ONE SUBJECT: FIVE CONCEPTS, SIX SCALES

	Concepts				
Scales	*A*	*B*	*C*	*D*	*E*
1	6	2	6	5	3
2	5	2	5	5	2
3	6	1	4	6	2
4	7	1	5	6	3
5	5	3	5	7	1
6	6	2	7	7	2
M:	5.83	1.83	5.33	6.00	2.17

concepts: TEACHING, DISCIPLINE, LEARNING, STUDY, CONTROL, against six scales selected from the scales of the *Evaluation* factor: *valuable-worthless*, *pleasant-unpleasant*, *bright-dark*, *good-bad*, *honest-dishonest*, *nice-awful*. (Notice that some of these scales seem relevant to all the concepts, whereas others do not.) We are interested in learning something about the individual's educational "meaning space." How does he "see," how does he evaluate key educational concepts? What relative values does he place on the different concepts? What concepts are close together in his meaning space? Which ones are far apart? We shall try to answer these questions from the data of Table 33.1. At the same time we can learn some of the main analytical possibilities of *SD* data, even though the hypothetical data are limited to only five concepts, judged by one subject using only one *SD* factor (*Evaluation*).

[11]With computer analysis becoming common, however, even this disadvantage disappears. One simply has the positive and negative values punched on IBM cards—of course, the minus signs make the keypunching more difficult and more subject to error—and then writes a short routine in the analysis program to add a constant (in this case 4) to each score, making a 7-point scale of positive values. This can, of course, also be done with all scales that have negative values. The researcher has to decide whether using negative values has advantages that require their use.

Means and Related Statistics

The most obvious analysis of the data of Table 33.1 would be to compare the means of the concepts. There are two distinguishable sets of means: *A*, *C*, *D* and *B*, *E*. The subject puts high values on *A*, *C*, and *D*, and low values on *B* and *E*. That is, TEACHING, LEARNING, and STUDY are highly valued, but DISCIPLINE and CONTROL are not highly valued. With the data of a single individual, there is question of the legitimacy of the use of the usual statistical tests of significance. If the scores in the table were averages of the scores of a group of individuals, it would be possible to use such tests. In this case, we might be interested in the significance of the differences between the five concept means and between the two clusters of means. Such analytic possibilities should be clear to the student. Instead of discussing them, we turn to the type of analysis stressed by Osgood.

Distance-Cluster Analysis

If two concepts are close together in semantic space, they are alike in meaning for the individual or group making the judgments. Conversely, if they are separated in semantic space, they differ in meaning. What is needed is a measure of the distance between any two concepts. The usual product-moment correlation coefficient is not considered suitable as a measure of the relation between two concepts, because it does not take absolute distances into account. Osgood and his colleagues therefore use the so-called *D* statistic, a very simple measure which is defined:

$$D_{ij} = \sqrt{\Sigma d_{ij}^2} \qquad (33.1)$$

where *D* is the linear distance between any two concepts, *i* and *j*, and *d* is the algebraic difference between the coordinates of *i* and *j* on the same factor (*Evaluation*, *Potency*, or *Activity*).[12]

To compute *D* simply subtract the assigned values of one concept from the assigned values of another concept, square each of these differences, and sum the squared differences:

$$\Sigma d_{ij}^2 = \Sigma(X_i - X_j)^2 \qquad (33.2)$$

Then extract the square root of this sum, or

$$D_{ij} = \sqrt{\Sigma(X_i - X_j)^2} \qquad (33.3)$$

Take the values of concepts *A* and *B* of Table 32.1:

$$(6-2)^2 + (5-2)^2 + (6-1)^2 + (7-1)^2 + (5-3)^2 + (6-2)^2 = 106.$$

Then $D_{AB} = \sqrt{106} = 10.30$. The number of *D*'s for any matrix is $n(n-1)/2$, *n* being the number of concepts. For these data: $(5)(4)/2 = 10$. The calculation of the 10 *D*'s yields a symmetric matrix (a matrix that has the same values on both sides of the diagonal). The *D* matrix for the data of Table 33.1 is given in Table 33.2. It is labeled I. (Also given in Table 33.2 is a matrix of *D*'s calculated from the ratings of a subject whose educational semantic space is very similar to that in I. It is labeled II. We consider it presently.)

[12] *Ibid.*, p. 91. Sometimes Σd_{ij}^2 is used instead of D_{ij}.

TABLE **33.2** *D* MATRICES OF TWO SUBJECTS WITH SIMILAR SEMANTIC SPACES

	I						II				
	A	*B*	*C*	*D*	*E*		*A*	*B*	*C*	*D*	*E*
A		10.30	3.00	2.65	9.06	*A*		8.49	3.32	3.32	9.11
B	10.30		8.89	10.44	3.16	*B*	8.49		7.42	7.07	2.45
C	3.00	8.89		3.16	8.19	*C*	3.32	7.42		4.12	8.19
D	2.65	10.44	3.16		9.95	*D*	3.32	7.07	4.12		7.87
E	9.06	3.16	8.19	9.95		*E*	9.11	2.45	8.19	7.87	

One can analyze a *D* matrix in two or three ways. The basis of the different analyses, however, is the same: searching out concepts that cluster together. The *smaller* a *D* between two concepts, the closer the concepts are in meaning. Conversely, the *larger* a *D* the farther apart in meaning the two concepts are. With simple *D* matrices like those in Table 33.2, we can successively pair small *D*'s to define clusters of concepts. Work row by row. For example, look at Row *A* of I. *AC* and *AD* are small: 3.00 and 2.65. Perhaps *A*, *C*, and *D* form a "close cluster." Check the *C* row. Is the *D* between *C* and *D* also small? It is 3.16. *A*, *C*, and *D* form a cluster because the distances between *AC*, *AD*, and *CD* are all small. Now take the next concept (row) that has not been considered, *B*. *BE* is 3.16, a small *D* value. Therefore *B* and *E* are close in meaning. All other *D*'s are large. That is, $AB = 10.30$, $AE = 9.06$, $BC = 8.89$, and so on. There are, then, two clusters: *A*, *C*, *D* and *B*, *E*. Inspection of II will show the same clusters of concepts. We conclude, therefore, that the two subjects (or *groups* if the original scores from which the *D*'s were computed were averages) have similar educational semantic spaces. They perceive the concepts alike.

TABLE **33.3** *D* MATRIX FOR A THIRD SUBJECT

	A	*B*	*C*	*D*	*E*
A		2.00	8.06	9.17	3.46
B	2.00		7.94	9.17	2.83
C	8.06	7.94		2.65	6.86
D	9.17	9.17	2.65		7.75
E	3.46	2.83	6.86	7.75	

Suppose, now, that a third subject's *SD* data yielded the *D* matrix shown in Table 33.3. Analysis of this matrix shows that the concept clusters are *A*, *B*, *E* and *C*, *D*. The first two subjects perceived TEACHING, LEARNING, STUDY as close together but separate from DISCIPLINE, CONTROL, which were perceived as close together. The third subject's data, too, yielded two clusters: (1) TEACHING, DISCIPLINE, CONTROL and (2) LEARNING, STUDY. A little reflection should indicate that these two sets of perceptions are quite different. We might hypothesize that the basic educational value systems of the two sets of perceptions are also quite different. Such a hypothesis, of course, would have to be tested.

The above analysis contains the essence, if not all the substance, of *D* matrix analysis. It is somewhat descriptive and impressionistic. There are more objective methods which can only be briefly described.

If we wish to compare two or more matrices, we can calculate coefficients of correlation between the *D*'s of each pair of matrices. The *D*'s of the same *ij* cells of two matrices form a set of ordered pairs. These pairs of *D*'s are correlated. (Only the values in the upper, or lower, half of the matrices are used.) For instance, take the data of Table 33.2. To find the similarity of the semantic structures of Matrices I and II, take the ordered pairs: (10.30, 8.49), (3.00, 3.32), . . . , (9.95, 7.87), and calculate *r* between the 10 pairs of *D*'s. In this case, $r = .93$, a very high degree of agreement. If we correlate the matrix of I, in Table 33.2, with the matrix of Table 33.3, $r = .06$. This is more objective evidence of the conclusions reached by the more impressionistic method.

Calculating *r*'s between matrices, however, we find out nothing about the clusters within the matrices. A *cluster* is a subset of a set of "objects"—persons, tests, concepts, and so on—the members of which are more similar or closer to each other than they are to members outside the cluster. The key question is how to define and identify clusters and their members. If we are working with correlation coefficients, the answer is easy and direct: we use factor analysis or some simpler form of cluster analysis. But with other statistics, such as *D*, the answer is not so simple. True, the three simple matrices of Tables 33.2 and 33.3 were easily handled. But the method was not objective. Suppose the *D*'s had not been so clearly divided? What if two of the concepts had had values in between 2 to 9? To what cluster do you assign two concepts whose *D* is 4 or 5?

Osgood, Suci, and Tannenbaum discuss this problem and outline methods of clustering concepts. They also outline a factor analytic method.[13] Cluster methods developed by other workers—McQuitty's *elementary linkage analysis*, for example—can be used.[14] Nunnally has outlined a promising method based on the sums of the cross products of the raw scores.[15] Hofman has devised another promising method based on the distances among concepts.[16] Both methods need extensive empirical testing.

The Use of Factor Scores

The term "factor score" in *SD* work means the sum or mean of two or more *SD* adjective pairs on one of the (usually) *E*, *P*, and *A* factors. (In Chapter 37, we will see that "factor score" means something else.) In his significant study of the relations between color names and racial groups, Williams used an *SD* of 12 adjective pairs. Six of the pairs represented the *Evaluation* factor and three each

[13] *Ibid.*, pp. 102–104; 41–42; 332–335.

[14] L. McQuitty, "Elementary Linkage Analysis for Isolating Orthogonal and Oblique Types and Typal Relevancies," *Educational and Psychological Measurement*, XVII (1957), 207–229. The author has tried this method with one or two *D* matrices and found it to work quite well, though not as well as a good factor analytic method.

[15] J. Nunnally, "The Analysis of Profile Data," *Psychological Bulletin*, LIX (1962), 311–319. This is an important article that deserves careful study; its suggestions are applicable to other kinds of data. See, also, J. Nunnally, *Psychometric Methods*. New York: McGraw-Hill, 1967, chap. 11.

[16] J. Hofman, "An Analysis of Concept-Clusters in Semantic Inter-Concept Space," *American Journal of Psychology*, LXXX (1967), 345–354.

represented the *Potency* and *Activity* factors.[17] Williams then used the sums and means of the three factors in his analyses. (His concepts were colors, persons, ethnic groups or names, and five general reference concepts—for example, BLACK, BLACK PERSON, NEGRO, FRIEND.) This is common and good practice: to build *SD* scales on the basis of the three main factors. Researchers often use two or three adjective pairs from each of the factors, as we indicated earlier. Heise, for example, building his *SD* "dictionary," used two adjective pairs from each of four factors, *E*, *P*, *A*, and *Stability* (later dropped).[18] It has been found, too, that only three or four pairs for each factor work very well.[19]

If factor scores for *E*, *P*, and *A* are calculated, then, of course, there will be three sets of scores for each group of subjects. Each of these sets can be analyzed and interpreted in the ways already described. For example, three *D* matrices can be produced and analyzed. Note, however, that it is possible and legitimate to calculate *D*'s over all three factors—that is, from the complete profiles of individual scores or group averages. In any case, *SD* factor scores should probably be used in research. They are psychometrically sound and substantially interpretable. As indicated earlier, *Evaluation* factor scores—sums or means of *E* adjective-pair scales—are the most useful for many behavior research studies.

Some Research Uses of the Semantic Differential

The response to the semantic differential, especially from psychologists, has been enthusiastic. Of course, the simplicity of the *SD* and its ease of use are appealing. But there is more to it. The power and variety of the three studies summarized below may show the reader something of the versatility and usefulness of the method.

Attitude-Conditioning Study

Staats and Staats[20] asked whether attitudes elicited by significant words can be changed by conditioning. Further, can such attitudes be changed without the individuals involved being aware of the change? This is an important problem, because most attitudes are learned, conveyed, and reinforced with words. By attaching positive and negative affects to words, can we change attitudes? Staats and Staats tackled this problem, a problem slightly reminiscent of *Brave New World* and *1984*.

The experimenters used two groups of subjects to whom they presented, in one part of the experiment, six national names: GERMAN, SWEDISH, ITALIAN,

[17]J. Williams, "Connotations of Racial Concepts and Color Names," *Journal of Personality and Social Psychology*, III (1966), 531–540.

[18]D. Heise, "Semantic Differential Profiles for 1,000 Most Frequent English Words," *Psychological Monographs*, no. 601, 1965.

[19]D. Heise, "Some Methodological Issues in Semantic Differential Research," *Psychological Bulletin*, LXXII (1969), 406–422.

[20]A. Staats and C. Staats, "Attitudes Established by Classical Conditioning," *Journal of Abnormal and Social Psychology*, LVII (1958), 37–40.

FRENCH, DUTCH, and GREEK. Each time a name was presented on a screen, subjects heard the experimenter say another word. SWEDISH and DUTCH were always paired with evaluative words. For Group 1 DUTCH was paired with positive words, for example, *happy* and *sacred*; SWEDISH was paired with negative words: *ugly, bitter*. For Group 2 the procedure was reversed. When this conditioning was completed, an *SD* was administered to the subjects. In a second experiment, male names were used instead of national names: HARRY, TOM, and so on. The same conditioning procedure was followed (with different subjects). After this second conditioning procedure, too, the *SD* was administered. The subjects were told that the experimenters had to find out the words they remembered and how they felt about them.

The data of each experiment were analyzed with a 2×2 analysis of variance. The seven-point *SD* scores of the two conditioned words were the dependent variable scores. It was found that the conditioning procedure was effective in attaching positive and negative evaluative effect to the conditioned words—a remarkable finding.

The Generalization of Attitude Change

Suppose we have a source of communication, say a university professor, and suppose a group, say students, has certain attitudes toward the source. Any source is linked to a number of concepts; for example, a professor is linked to certain educational ideas, like teaching machines and learning theories. If the attitudes of a group toward one of the linked concepts is changed, will attitudes toward other related concepts be changed because both are linked to the source? Tannenbaum, in an impressive experiment, showed that attitudes toward linked concepts would be so changed.[21] He first established linkages between a professor (the source) and the ideas Teaching Machines (TM) and Spence Learning Theory (LT). Then (putting it somewhat oversimply) he changed attitudes toward TM by experimental manipulation and showed that predicted attitude changes took place in LT, which was not manipulated.

For our purposes, the study is important because Tannenbaum used a very simple measure, four *SD Evaluation* scales—*good-bad, valuable-worthless, successful-unsuccessful*, and *important-unimportant*—and because he used change or difference scores as the measure of the dependent variable. Recall from an earlier discussion that difference scores are usually much less reliable than the scores from which they are calculated. In this case, however, this was evidently not so. All his predictions were supported by the statistical analyses, which showed appropriate statistical significance. Evidently both the original simple *SD* scores and the change scores were reliable and effective.

A Semantic Differential Study of Emotions

It is striking that emotions, one of the two or three most important aspects of man's life, have not been scientifically studied to any great extent. Some scientists

[21]P. Tannenbaum, "Mediated Generalization of Attitude Change via the Principle of Congruity," *Journal of Personality and Social Psychology*, III (1966), 493–499.

would no doubt say that, since emotional experience is subjective and private, it is not amenable to scientific investigation. Block, in a highly significant and competent study,[22] has shown that it *is* possible to study emotions scientifically. In effect, he asked the questions: What are the factors behind emotions? Do the emotions of men and women differ in meaning? Do the emotions of different national groups differ in meaning?

To answer these questions, Block first had 40 male and 48 female American students judge 15 emotions, such as LOVE, ANGER, PRIDE, FEAR, and GRIEF, on a 20-item *SD*. The sums of all 40 men subjects on each of the 20 items (scales) for each emotion were assigned ranks. The same was done for women separately. That is, the adjective pairs sums for each emotion were rank-ordered. For the emotion FEAR, for example, the adjective pair *tense-relaxed* had a rank of 1, whereas the adjective pair *good-bad* had a rank of 17 (for the female students). This means that FEAR was seen as *tense* and *bad*. The rank-order correlations between men and women were all high, from .84 to .98, except that for GRIEF (.66).

The same procedure was used with 34 Norwegians (after appropriate translation of the instrument from English to Norwegian). Then the similarities and differences in meanings of the emotions to Americans and Norwegians were studied. The results seemed to indicate the appropriateness of the *SD* for cross-cultural study.[23]

The Semantic Differential in Behavioral Research

The semantic differential can be applied to a variety of research problems. It has been shown to be sufficiently reliable and valid for many research purposes.[24] It is also flexible and relatively easy to adapt to varying research demands, quick and economical to administer and to score. And, as Heise points out, "There is probably no social psychological principle that has received such resounding cross-group and cross-cultural verification as the *EPA* structure of *SD* ratings."[25] The main problems, as indicated earlier, are to select appropriate and relevant concepts and appropriate and relevant analyses. In both cases the researcher is faced with a plethora of possibilities. Selection and choice, as usual, are determined by the nature of the problems explored and the hypotheses tested. Here are some suggested uses of the method.

The *SD* should be useful in exploring the meaning structures of children at different ages. Concepts are the foundation stones of the meaning structures of

[22]J. Block, "Studies in the Phenomenology of Emotions," *Journal of Abnormal and Social Psychology*, LIV (1957), 358–363.

[23]There is considerable evidence on the efficacy of the *SD* in cross-cultural research. See the Snider and Osgood book, Part V, cited in Study Suggestion 1. See, also, C. Osgood, "Studies on the Generality of Affective Meaning Systems," *American Psychologist*, XVII (1962), 10–28.

[24]See Osgood et al., *op. cit.*, pp. 140–153, 192–193, *et passim*; Heise, "Some Methodological Issues in Semantic Differential Research," *op. cit.*

[25]*Ibid.*, p. 421.

human beings; they are basic essentials in all human thinking. What concepts has the child of five, six, or nine learned? What are their connotative meanings?[26] What does TEACHER mean to a child of six, a child of nine, a child of twelve? Is the semantic space in which TEACHER is embedded one that will promote learning? Or will it impede learning? Questions such as these can be answered, in part at least, with the aid of the semantic differential.

Concepts are essential parts of the learning of attitudes. The relatively rigid and standardized perceptions of minority group members, called stereotypes, are important parts of prejudiced attitudes. Is it possible to change stereotypes? Attitude learning and change studies might well have a sensitive and helpful companion in the semantic differential. The Staats and Staats and the Tannenbaum studies, summarized earlier, indicate that the *SD* is a fairly sensitive measure of attitude change. Indeed, Osgood believes that the *SD* can be used as a generalized attitude measurement technique.[27]

One of the difficulties in communicating about education is the different interpretations put upon educational ideas. Take "progressive education," the "3 R's," "discipline," and so on. It is likely that different kinds of people have quite different connotative meaning structures of these words. It is likely, for example, that exponents of progressive education have sharply different semantic spaces surrounding these concepts than exponents of more traditional viewpoints. Investigating such structures and their correlates should enrich psychological theory pertinent to education. The *SD* can aid such research.

There has been little cross-cultural scientific educational research. Students of comparative education have done fine work in comparing the educational systems and philosophies of different countries. But little is known of the different meanings put upon educational concepts in different countries. What is the relation between such meanings and educational thinking and practice? Research into such problems is important not only for its own sake; it is also important because it can perhaps yield theoretical information valuable to social psychologists and educators and because it might throw light on American educational problems. The *SD* has already been shown to be a useful adjunct to such cross-cultural research.

It may be possible to study children's values and attitudes by having teachers and other judges rate their compositions on an *Evaluation* form of the *SD*. A related possibility is the study of the attitudes and semantic spaces of teacher trainees. What effect does a teacher training program have on the educational semantic space of teacher trainees? What effect does actual teaching experience have on the semantic space of teachers? And if changes take place, do concomitant changes in educational attitudes take place? Is it possible that there are professional semantic spaces, and that "learning" these spaces is important in the training of professionals?

[26]See F. DiVesta and R. Walls, "Factor Analysis of the Semantic Attributes of 487 Words and Some Relationships to the Conceptual Behavior of Fifth-Grade Children," *Journal of Educational Psychology Monograph*, vol. 61, no. 6, pt. 2, 1970.

[27]Osgood et al., *op. cit.*, p. 195.

These are only a few of the possibilities. We have here a useful and perhaps sensitive tool to help in the exploration of an extremely important area of psychological and educational concern: connotative meaning. We can appropriately end this chapter by saying of the semantic differential what Carroll, in his highly perspicacious review of *The Measurement of Meaning*, said: ". . . it is *good*, it is *active*, it is *potent*."[28]

Study Suggestions

1. Fortunately, there are excellent references on the semantic differential. First, the basic source, *The Measurement of Meaning*, cited so often in this chapter, is not only essential reading (especially the first four chapters); it is a fresh structural approach to a number of research problems. Second, Heise's review of the method (see footnote 19) is very good indeed. Third, Carroll's review (see footnote 28) gives a larger perspective on meaning and its study. Finally, a sourcebook of semantic differential readings is available. It contains many important papers:

   Snider, J., and Osgood, C., eds. *Semantic Differential Technique: A Sourcebook*. Chicago: Aldine, 1969.
2. Valuable atlases or dictionaries of concepts, with adjective pair or *E*, *P*, and *A* values, have been compiled. In addition, there are sources of adjective pairs. The researcher who contemplates using the *SD* will want to have one or more of the concept sources available.

   Heise, D. See footnote 18.

   DiVesta, F., and Walls, R. See footnote 26.

   Jenkins, J., and Russell, W. "An Atlas of Semantic Profiles for 360 Words." *American Journal of Psychology*, LXXI (1958), 688–699.

   Osgood, C., et al. *The Measurement of Meaning*, pp. 37 and 47–66. (*SD* scales.)

   Snider and Osgood (see Study Suggestion 1, above), pp. 625–636.

[28]J. Carroll, Review of *The Measurement of Meaning*. *Language*, XXXV (1959), 58–77 (p. 77).

CHAPTER 34

Q Methodology

Q methodology is a general name used by William Stephenson to characterize a set of philosophical, psychological, statistical, and psychometric ideas oriented to research on the individual.[1] *Q technique* is a set of procedures used to implement *Q* methodology. It centers particularly in sorting decks of cards called *Q sorts* and in the correlations among the responses of different individuals to the *Q* sorts.

Persons Correlations and Clusters

Q technique is mainly a sophisticated way of rank-ordering objects (items, stimuli, etc.) and then assigning numerals to subsets of the objects for statistical purposes. Take a set of six items, each item being a characterization of aspects of university or college courses and teaching. Abbreviations of the items are given in Table 34.1. If we ask individual students to rank-order the items according to the impor-

TABLE **34.1** HYPOTHETICAL RANK ORDERS GIVEN TO SIX TEACHING ITEMS BY FOUR STUDENTS[a]

	PO-1	PO-2	TO-1	TO-2
Contribution to personal growth	1	1	4	3
Stimulates thinking	2	3	1	2
Value of outside work	3	2	6	6
Instructor's ability to explain	4	6	5	5
Course procedure	6	5	3	4
Course organization	5	4	2	1

[a]PO: Person Orientation; TO: Task Orientation

[1]W. Stephenson, *The Study of Behavior*. Chicago: University of Chicago Press, 1953.

tance of the aspects of teaching they express, we would expect different rank orders from different individuals. Four students might give the ranks shown in Table 34.1 (1 being the highest rank and 6 the lowest). Suppose, further, that the first two students are person-oriented and the second two task-oriented.

Inspection shows what might have been expected: the two person-oriented students have similar rank orders, as do the two task-oriented students. The rank orders of the person-oriented and task-oriented students, on the other hand, are unlike. To be more precise, we calculate rank-order coefficients of correlation between all possible pairs of rankers.[2] This yields a 4×4 correlation matrix, as shown in Table 34.2. Note that the clusters (PO-1, PO-2) and (TO-1, TO-2) stand out clearly. The correlations between both pairs are ringed in the table. PO-1 correlates substantially with PO-2 (.77), but virtually zero with TO-1 and TO-2 (−.09 and .03). Similarly, TO-1 and TO-2 correlate highly with each other (.89), but not with PO-1 and PO-2.

TABLE **34.2** CORRELATIONS AMONG PERSON-ORIENTED AND TASK-ORIENTED STUDENTS, TABLE 34.1 DATA

	PO-1	PO-2	TO-1	TO-2
PO-1		.77	−.09	.03
PO-2	.77		−.09	.09
TO-1	−.09	−.09		.89
TO-2	.03	.09	.89	

This oversimplified example illustrates two of the important basic ideas behind *Q*: *correlations between persons* and *persons clusters* or *factors*. The usual correlational procedure, loosely called *R* methodology, uses correlations between tests. The above example might have been four tests given to six persons, the tests measuring two variables. With *Q*, the four persons break down into two clusters.

Q Sorts and *Q* Sorting

The example given above used a straightforward rank-order procedure. *Q* technique uses a rank-order procedure of piles or groups of objects. A set of objects—verbal statements, single words, phrases, pictures, musical compositions—is given to an individual to sort into a set of piles according to some criterion. For example, the cards may have typed on them statements about educational practices. The subject may be asked to sort the cards according to whether he approves or disapproves the statements on them. With a large number of cards—*Q* sorts usually contain between 60 and 120 cards—it would be very difficult to rank order them. For statistical convenience, the sorter is instructed to put varying numbers of cards in several piles, the whole making up a normal or quasi-normal distribution.

[2]The formula is:

$$rho = 1 - \frac{6\Sigma D^2}{n(n^2-1)}$$

where rho = rank-order coefficient of correlation; D = the difference between any pair of ranks; n = the number of ranks.

Here is a *Q*-sort distribution of 90 items:

Most Approve										*Least Approve*
3	4	7	10	13	16	13	10	7	4	3
10	9	8	7	6	5	4	3	2	1	0

This is a rank-order continuum from "Most Approve" to "Least Approve" with varying degrees of approval and disapproval between the extremes. The numbers 3, 4, 7, . . . , 7, 4, 3 are the numbers of cards to be placed in each pile. The numbers below the line are the values assigned to the cards in each pile. That is, the 3 cards at the left, "Most Approve," are each assigned 10, the 4 cards in the next pile are assigned 9, and so on through the distribution to the 3 cards at the extreme right, which are assigned 0. The center pile is a neutral pile. The subject is told to put cards that are left over after he has made other choices, cards that seem ambiguous to him or about which he cannot make a decision, into the neutral pile. In brief, this *Q* distribution has 11 piles with varying numbers of cards in each pile, the cards in the piles being assigned values from 0 through 10. Statistical analyses are based on these latter values.

Sorting instructions and the objects sorted vary with the purposes of the research. Subjects can be asked to sort attitudinal statements on an approval-disapproval continuum. They can be asked to sort personality items on a "like me"-"not like me" continuum. Judges can sort behavioral statements to describe an individual or a group. Aesthetic objects, like pictures or abstract drawings, can be sorted according to strength of preference.

The number of cards in a *Q* distribution is determined by convenience and statistical demands. For statistical stability and reliability, the number should probably be not less than 60 (40 or 50 in some rare cases) nor more than 140, in most cases no more than 100. A good range is from 60 to 90 cards.[3]

In part, *Q* distributions are an arbitrary matter. It is possible to use rectangular distributions. That is, we can have the same number of cards in all the piles. Or we

$n = 80$

2	4	6	9	12	14	12	9	6	4	2
4	6	9	13	16	13	9	6	4		
4	6	10	12	16	12	10	6	4		

$n = 70$

2	3	5	8	11	12	11	8	5	3	2
2	3	4	8	11	14	11	8	4	3	2

$n = 60$

2	3	6	11	16	11	6	3	2		
2	3	4	7	9	10	9	7	4	3	2

[3]The author has gotten good results with as few as 40 items. These 40 items were culled from a larger pool of items, all of which had been tested. It is rarely necessary or desirable to have more than 90 or 100 items.

can even permit subjects to place the cards in a number of piles where they will. The normal or quasi-normal forced distribution had distinct advantages, mainly statistical, that make its use desirable. Some *Q*-sort distributions are shown bottom page 584.

A Miniature Q Sort

A semi-realistic example may help to clarify a number of technical points. Suppose we wish to explore attitudes toward education. We can assemble a large number of statements from which we randomly sample or systematically select a smaller number to put into a *Q* sort. We select 10 statements (naturally many more than 10 would actually be required). Subjects are asked to sort the 10 statements into the following distribution:

Most Approve				*Least Approve*
1	2	4	2	1
4	3	2	1	0

Again, the figures above the line are the numbers of cards in the piles; those below the line are the values assigned to each of the piles.

Suppose four subjects sort the cards as instructed and that the values below the line have been assigned to the cards in the piles. The four sets of values are given in Table 34.3. The numbers in the four columns under *a*, *b*, *c*, and *d* are the values assigned to the cards in the five piles after the four persons, *a*, *b*, *c* and *d*, have sorted the cards. By inspection we suspect that the *Q* sorts of Persons *a* and *b* are very similar. The *Q* sorts of Persons *c* and *d* look similar. (With these two pairs of persons, note that the high values and the low values tend to go together.) We can also see that there seems to be little relation between the *Q* sorts of *a* and *c*, *b* and *c*, and *b* and *d*. To be more precise, we again need to calculate coefficients of correlation.

The calculation of coefficients of correlation with *Q* sorts is quite simple, because the formula for the *r*'s between pairs of subjects has quantities that never

TABLE **34.3** *Q*-SORT VALUES OF FOUR PERSONS: MINIATURE *Q* SORT

	Persons			
Items	*a*	*b*	*c*	*d*
1	2	2	1	1
2	1	1	0	0
3	0	0	3	4
4	2	2	4	2
5	2	1	3	3
6	1	2	2	2
7	3	3	2	2
8	2	2	2	2
9	4	4	2	3
10	3	3	1	1

change. A convenient formula is:

$$r = \frac{\Sigma xy}{\sqrt{\Sigma x^2 \Sigma y^2}} \tag{34.1}$$

(x stands for the deviation scores of one person, and y for the scores of another person.) The denominator of this formula is always the same for a given set of data. The calculation of the denominator requires only the calculation of Σx^2, since $\Sigma x^2 = \Sigma y^2$. On the other hand, Σxy must be calculated for each pair of persons.[4]

The r's between the four sets of values of Table 34.3 are given in the correlation matrix of Table 34.4.

TABLE **34.4** CORRELATION MATRIX FROM THE *Q* SORT VALUES OF TABLE 34.3

	a	*b*	*c*	*d*
a		.92	−.08	−.08
b	.92		−.17	−.17
c	−.08	−.17		.75
d	−.08	−.17	.75	

The interpretation of these correlations presents no difficulties. Obviously Persons *a* and *b* sort the cards very similarly: $r = .92$. Persons *c* and *d*, too, are similar: $r = .75$. All the rest of the r's are near zero. Evidently there are two kinds or "types" of persons, insofar as attitudes toward education are concerned: "*A*-kind" and "*B*-kind."

To get an idea of what *A* and *B* are, we would have to go back to the *Q* sort and examine the items highly approved by *A*'s and those highly approved by *B*'s. Suppose the three highly approved *A* items were:

> Learning is experimental; the child should be taught to test alternatives before accepting any of them.
> No subject is more important than the personalities of the pupils.
> Right from the very first grade, teachers must teach the child at his own level and not at the level of the grade he is in.

Suppose the three highly approved *B* items were:

> Learning is essentially a process of increasing one's store of information about the various fields of knowledge.

[4]The formula is:

$$\Sigma xy = \Sigma XY - \frac{(\Sigma X)(\Sigma Y)}{N}$$

In *Q*, $\Sigma X = \Sigma Y$, and they are always the same; so is N, the number of cards in the *Q* sort. Therefore only ΣXY need be calculated for each pair of persons. This is easily done with such small numbers by mentally multiplying each pair of values and punching the product into a desk calculator.

The curriculum should contain an orderly arrangement of subjects that represent the best of our cultural heritage.
Schools of today are neglecting the three R's.[5]

Obviously, these pairs of people are very different. One, the *A* pair, seems to favor "progressive" educational notions; the other, the *B* pair, seems to favor "traditional" educational notions. Perhaps these individuals are "progressives" and "traditionalists."

The miniature example just discussed contains the essential ingredients of much *Q* analysis. Obviously most *Q* studies have to have more subjects, even though it is theoretically possible to have a *Q* study with one individual.[6] Moreover, the impressionistic kind of analysis used would in most cases not be satisfactory. A more objective method of ascertaining clusters of persons, or persons factors, would have to be used. The highly approved items of clusters of individuals also require a more objective method for their identification. Nevertheless, the example at least outlines the *Q* correlational method.

Theory; Structured and Unstructured Q Sorts; Analysis of Variance

Unstructured Q Sorts

Most published *Q* studies have used unstructured *Q* sorts. An *unstructured Q* sort is a set of items assembled without specific regard to the variables or factors underlying the items. Theoretically, any sample of homogeneous items can be used in an unstructured *Q* sort. The idea is simple. A large number of statements are taken from various statement sources and put together in a *Q* sort. The items of an unstructured *Q* sort are like the items of a personality or attitude scale: they are selected and used because they presumably measure one broad variable, like neuroticism, attitudes toward blacks, or adjustment.

There is a theoretical infinite population of items, and the hope is that the set of items used by the investigator in his *Q* sort is a representative sample of this item population. One important population of items, used by Rogers and others, is focused on the perception of self and others. A large number of statements about the self is assembled or constructed: "I like people," "I am a failure," "I just can't seem to make up my mind on things," and so on.

Individuals are asked to sort the cards to describe themselves as they think they are, as other people see them, and the like. The cards are sorted into a *Q* distribution, the sorts intercorrelated, and the principal analysis focuses on the correlations among persons and on factor or cluster analysis. Inferences about the

[5]Items are from the author's *Q* sort of educational attitudes. See F. Kerlinger, "The Attitude Structure of the Individual: A *Q*-Study of the Educational Attitudes of Professors and Laymen," *Genetic Psychology Monographs*, LIII (1956), 283–329 (see pp. 323–327).

[6]An interesting example of this kind of study is: J. Nunnally, "An Investigation of Some Propositions of Self-Conception: The Case of Miss Sun," *Journal of Abnormal and Social Psychology*, L (1955), 87–92. Nunnally studied, via *Q* sorts, changes in the self-conception of a young woman during two years of therapy. See, also, W. Dukes, "$N = 1$," *Psychological Bulletin*, LXIV (1965), 74–79.

efficacy of therapy or training programs are then drawn from the results of the analysis. For example, trainees—in teacher training, the Peace Corps, doctoral programs—sort the cards before, during, and after the training. Assume that there is an "ideal" or criterion *Q* sort available provided by the trainers. One reasons that if the training has been effective—and one of the important results of training is measured by the *Q* sort—then the correlations between the trainees' sorts and the criterion sort are higher after the training than before it.

Correlation approaches have more or less dominated *Q* studies.[7] One of Stephenson's important contributions, the testing of "theory" and the principle of building "theory" into *Q* sorts by means of structured samples of items, has been neglected.[8]

Structured Q Sorts

In a *structured Q sort*, the variables of a "theory," or of a hypothesis or set of hypotheses, are built into a set of items along Fisherian experimental and analysis of variance design principles. What does this mean? An *unstructured Q sort* is a set of items all of which are in one domain—for example, social-values items, self items, teacher-characteristics items—but which are not otherwise differentiated in the *Q* sort or in the analysis. While the items of a structured *Q* sort, on the other hand, are in one domain, they are partitioned in one or more ways. For instance, a child psychologist may be studying moral growth in children. One aspect of his theory implies that as children get older, control of their behavior becomes more internal. A *Q* sort can be structured as *internal-external*, with half the items reflecting internal control and half external control. This is the simplest possible partition of a structured *Q* sort.

To structure a *Q* sort is virtually to build a "theory" into it. Instead of constructing instruments to measure the characteristics of individuals, we construct them to embody or epitomize "theories." In the use of *Q* as Stephenson sees it, individuals as such are not tested; theoretical propositions are tested. Naturally, individuals must do the *Q* sorting. And *Q* sorts can, of course, be used to measure characteristics of individuals. But the basic rationale of *Q*, as Stephenson sees it, is that we have individuals sort the cards not so much to test the individuals as to test "theories" that have been built into the cards.

One-Way Structured Q Sorts

Building a theory into a measurement instrument, while not frequent, is not new. A well-known example is the Allport-Vernon-Lindzey *Study of Values*, a values instrument based on Spranger's theory of six types of men: Theoretical, Economic, Aesthetic, Social, Political, and Religious.[9] The purpose of the instrument is not to test the theory but to measure the values of individuals. If a person is, say, basically a religious "type," he should select items of the Religious category over items of other categories.

The Stephenson approach to the same problem would be to test the Spranger

[7] J. Wittenborn, "Contributions and Current Status of *Q* Methodology," *Psychological Bulletin*, LVIII (1961), 132–142.

[8] *Ibid.*, pp. 138–139. See Stephenson, *op. cit.*, pp. 66–85.

[9] G. Allport, P. Vernon, and G. Lindzey, *Study of Values*, rev. ed. Boston: Houghton Mifflin, 1951.

theory. (Note that the *Study of Values* can be used to test the Spranger theory.) A *Q* sort would be constructed using the Spranger system as a guide. Items would be selected from various sources and specially written to represent the six Spranger values. There would be 10 to 15 Theoretical items, 10 to 15 Aesthetic items, and so forth, making a total of 60 to 90 items in the entire *Q* sort. Individuals would then be deliberately and systematically selected to "represent" the six values. For example, the investigator might select ministers and priests (Religious), businessmen (Economic), artists and musicians (Aesthetic), scientists and scholars (Theoretical), and so on.[10]

If the theory is "valid," and if the *Q* sort adequately expresses the theory, two rather big "if's," the statistical analyses of the sorts should show the theory's validity. That is, if any individual with "known" values—a minister or priest can be expected to have strong religious values, an artist strong aesthetic values—takes the sort with instructions to place favored or approved statements high and disapproved statements low, we would expect him to place the 10 or 15 statements congruent with his role and its associated values high. Statements associated with other roles and values we would expect him to place lower. If a scientist sorts the cards, we would expect him to place the cards in the Theoretical category high and cards of other categories relatively lower. Naturally, there will be few individuals whose sorts will be so clear-cut. Human beings and their attitudes and values are too complex. But we can expect some such results to occur beyond chance expectation if the theory is valid.

A *Q* sort suggested by the above considerations can be called a "one-way structured sort," because there is one basis of variable classification.[11] This is directly analogous to simple one-way analysis of variance. To make the matter clear, an example from a research study designed in part to test the Spranger theory in *Q* fashion can be given. A 90-item *Q* sort was used. Each item was a single word, each word having been previously categorized by judges in the six Spranger values. There were 15 Theoretical words—*science*, *knowledge*, *reason*, and so on; 15 Religious words—*God*, *church*, *sermon*, and so on; to a total of six categories and 90 words.

The cards were sorted by a number of persons chosen for their presumed possession of the six values. They were asked to sort the cards according to the degree to which they favored or did not favor the words on the cards.

To illustrate the results, here are the mean values in rank order of the sort of one subject, a musician:

a	*s*	*t*	*p*	*e*	*r*
7.13	6.27	6.13	4.73	4.33	1.40

[10]In an interesting *Q* study of religious attitudes, Broen selected 24 clergymen to represent the full spectrum of religious beliefs and attitudes. There were four representatives of each of five major religious groupings. Broen says that the subjects were selected from churches and institutions known to have religious orientations in the directions of his hypothesized religious categories. W. Broen, "A Factor Analytic Study of Religious Attitudes," *Journal of Abnormal and Social Psychology*, LIV (1957), 176–179.

[11]Stephenson does not stress the possibility of *Q* sorts of the one-way type. His *Q* designs are almost all of the factorial two- and three-way type. There seems to be no reason why one-way designs cannot be used.

$F = 26.82$, significant at the .001 level. This means that the musician significantly differentiated the six values. What is the pattern of differentiation? The wider spaces indicate significant gaps.[12] Although it is the highest mean, there is no significant gap between Aesthetic and the next highest mean, Social (6.27). In fact, Aesthetic, Social, and Theoretical form a subset which is separated by a significant gap from all the other means. Political and Economic form another subset. Religious, the lowest mean (1.40), is significantly separated from all the other means. Evidently the musician highly favors Aesthetic, Social, and Theoretical words, and strongly disfavors Religious words. From this analysis we may perhaps draw inferences as to her value system, at least insofar as the measurement system allows. Independent knowledge of the subject confirmed this analysis.

If a set of stimuli can be categorized in this fashion, a one-way structured *Q* sort may be possible to construct and desirable to use. Small theories and hypotheses can be tested in this manner by having subjects of known values, attitudes, personality, roles, and so forth sort the cards. The student should realize that in addition to the analysis of variance structured sort approach, correlation analysis is always applicable. Simply correlate the *Q* sorts of different persons, and disregard the structure built into the sort.

Two-Way (Factorial) Structured Q Sorts

Many theories and hypotheses that can be structured along the lines of analysis of variance paradigms have the potentiality of being tested with *Q* methods. The Spranger example just discussed is a case in point. Other one-way examples might be: introversion-extroversion; oral eroticism-anal eroticism; progressivism-traditionalism; liberalism-conservatism; open mindedness-closed mindedness; and so on. But how about more complex theories and hypotheses? Taking the next logical step, we add another dimension or variable to the *Q* paradigm. This makes a two-variable *Q* sort and a two-variable or factorial analysis of variance design. The *Q* sort is structured in two ways rather than one.

To illustrate two-way structured sorts, the paradigm of an 80-item sort to explore social attitudes and to test a structural "theory" of attitudes is given in Table 34.5.[13] The means of a known conservative individual are also given in the table.

[12]A simple way to do this test is to calculate the standard error of the difference between means. The formula is

$$SE_{M_i - M_j} = \sqrt{V_w\left(\frac{1}{n_i} + \frac{1}{n_j}\right)}$$

where V_w = within-groups variance (from the analysis of variance). Multiply this value by 2:

$$2\sqrt{2.34\left(\frac{1}{15} + \frac{1}{15}\right)} = 2\sqrt{2.34 \times .133} = 2 \times .558 = 1.12$$

Any difference equal to or greater than 1.12 is significant. Perhaps a more legitimate but more conservative test is Scheffé's. See Chapter 13, Study Suggestion 8. Also see A. Edwards, *Statistical Methods*, 2d ed. New York: Holt, Rinehart and Winston, 1967, pp. 265–269.

[13]F. Kerlinger, "A *Q* Validation of the Structure of Social Attitudes," *Educational and Psychological Measurement*, XXXII (1972), 987–995. The theory tested is discussed in: F. Kerlinger, "Social Attitudes and Their Criterial Referents: A Structural Theory," *Psychological Review*, LXXIV (1967), 110–122.

TABLE **34.5** A TWO-WAY STRUCTURED Q SORT WITH THE MEANS OF A KNOWN CONSERVATIVE

		Attitudes		
		Liberal (L)	Conservative (C)	Means
Abstractness	Abstract (A)	3.15	4.70	3.93
	Specific (S)	2.45	5.70	4.07
	Means	2.80	5.20	$M_t = 4.00$

First note the Q-sort structure. The two main variables are *Attitudes* and *Abstractness*. *Attitudes* is partitioned into Conservative (C) and Liberal (L), *Abstractness* into Abstract (A) and Specific (S). Any item of the Q sort must fit into one of the four cells of the cross-partition. Any attitude item must be either Conservative or Liberal and at the same time either Abstract or Specific. The more important variable is *Attitudes*. The second variable, *Abstractness*, was incorporated into the structure because it was conjectured that both liberals and conservatives would react differently to the abstractness-specificity of items. For example, a conservative might strongly endorse *specific* conservative items, while another conservative might endorse *abstract* conservative items—and similarly for liberals. Whether the structure is valid is, of course, an empirical matter. At any rate, here are four items, one for each of the cells of Table 34.5. The labels correspond to those given in the table and above.

social equality (LA)
Supreme Court (LS)
competition (CA)
private property (CS)

The data of this individual's sort can be analyzed with analysis of variance, provided we use care and circumspection in the interpretation of the data. (The questionable nature of using analysis of variance with Q-sort data will be discussed later.) The analysis of variance to use, of course, is the factorial type. The individual whose data (means) are in the table is a "known" conservative who evidently favors conservative referents of the specific kind. The L and C means are 2.80 and 5.20, a difference of 2.40, which is significant at the .01 level. The difference between the A and S means (3.93 and 4.07) is not significant.

Much more interesting, note the Specific row means: 2.45 and 5.70. Contrast this with the Abstract row means: 3.15 and 4.70. The two differences lead to an interaction F ratio of 5.23, significant at .05 level. Although we should treat .05-level differences with caution, these results indicate the subject's preference for conservative and specific referents. Of the four referents given above, he would probably rank *private property* above the others. Since we knew that this individual was conservative before we started, this is some small confirmation of the validity of the reasoning that went into the Q sort.

The use of the *Abstractness* dimension in this sort was not dictated theoretically; it was purely exploratory. A number of individuals (14 out of 33), however, had significant interaction *F* ratios, which indicates that, to some individuals, preferences for conservative referents—and the attitudes they imply—are by no means "pure": for them it makes a difference whether the referents are abstract or specific. This may even mean that we would have to talk about abstract and specific liberalism and conservatism. It may also mean that conservatives tend to favor specific referents, while liberals favor abstract referents. Despite these findings, significant interactions are ordinarily not expected; the principal interest in *Q* is ordinarily in the main effects.[14] Nevertheless, there is no compelling reason why interactions cannot be predicted on the basis of theory or hunch and consciously sought just as in experimental work in learning and teaching.

Before leaving structured sorts, it should be mentioned that *Q* designs are not limited to the simple 2×2 case shown above. Other combinations—3×2, 4×3, 2×4—are possible. Three- and four-variable designs are also possible, if not too practicable. Another possibility, mentioned in an earlier chapter, is the application of the structure idea to objective tests and scales. The items of the referents *Q* sort can be put into summated-rating scale form, for instance, and scored and analyzed accordingly.[15]

Factor Analysis and Factor Arrays in *Q* Methodology

The impossibility of doing justice to *Q* methodology without discussing factor analysis is nowhere more evident than in describing factor arrays, the final technical step of a *Q* study. One of the strong points of *Q* methodology is its analytic possibilities. Of these possibilities, factor arrays are very important. A *factor array* is a *Q* sort constructed from factor analytic results. Conceive factors as similar clusters of objects—in this case persons, or rather, the responses of persons. Those individuals who respond to a *Q* sort similarly will form clusters of persons. Oversimplified, conceive of summing the responses of the individuals of a cluster to any *Q*-sort item. If we do this for every item in a *Q* sort, we will have sums for all items. These sums will, of course, vary a great deal. They can be rank-ordered and then fitted into the original *Q* distribution.[16] This "new" synthetic *Q* sort is literally a description of the factor, which can be directly interpreted. Usually, only the top and bottom two or three piles of the *Q* distribution are used for interpretative purposes. Factor arrays are calculated similarly for each factor.

A Q Study of Perceptions of Teacher Behaviors

In a *Q* study of the relation between attitudes toward education and teachers' perceptions of desirable teaching behaviors, Sontag used an 80-item *Q* sort whose

[14]See Stephenson, *op. cit.*, pp. 103 and 163–164. There are a number of interesting structured *Q* sorts in this volume and in Stephenson's later book: W. Stephenson, *The Play Theory of Mass Communication.* Chicago: University of Chicago Press, 1967.

[15]Some of the possibilities have been described in: F. Kerlinger, "*Q* Methodology in Behavioral Research." In S. Brown and D. Brenner, eds., *Science, Psychology, and Communication: Essays Honoring William Stephenson.* New York: Teachers College Press, 1972, chap. 1.

[16]For details of calculating factor arrays, see Stephenson, *The Study of Behavior*, pp. 176–179.

items were brief descriptions of a large variety of teaching behaviors.[17] Half of 80 elementary and secondary school teachers were instructed to sort the behaviors according to their desirability for elementary teachers and the other half according to their desirability for secondary teachers. The *Q*-sort results for each group were factor analyzed separately and factor arrays calculated. Four factors were obtained in each analysis. These factor arrays are complete 80-item *Q* sorts that describe a weighted average of the relative values the teachers put on the behaviors. Four of the highest values for two of the elementary-teacher behavior factors, with the names of the factors, are:

Concern for Students
Provides individualized material for pupils as required.
Shows sincere concern when confronted with personal problems of pupils.
Teaches students to be sensitive to the needs of others.
Takes advantage of student interest in planning lessons.

Structure and Subject Matter
Presents well-planned lessons.
Is consistent in administering discipline.
In his presentations, shows competent knowledge of subject matter.
Adheres to rules he sets up.

One can readily get a feeling for the underlying themes behind the items, even with these few items. Ordinarily, more positive items are needed to identify and interpret the arrays. In addition, the negative ends of the arrays can and often should be used, since they may be helpful in interpretation. Note, too, that the *Q* sorts of new subjects can be correlated with the arrays, a valuable procedure that has rarely been used. The correlations can be used to identify the factor predispositions of students, teachers in training and in service, administrators, and so on. This kind of use can be particularly valuable in studies of attitude, value, belief, and perception (or judgment) change. The perceptions or judgments of desirable teacher characteristics and behaviors before and after, say, special training can be correlated with "ideal" perceptions of the trainers, as indicated earlier, or with the factor arrays.

Strengths and Weaknesses of Q Methodology

Like factor analysis, which it uses liberally, *Q* methodology is controversial. It has been highly praised and harshly criticized. The truth of the critical matter is probably that the method is not as powerful and all-embracing as Stephenson has claimed it to be, nor is it as poor and defective as some critics have said it is. It is probably safe to say that *Q* is a flexible and useful tool in the armamentarium of the psychological and educational investigator. It also has defects, however, as we shall see.

[17]M. Sontag, "Attitudes Toward Education and Perception of Teacher Behaviors," *American Educational Research Journal*, V (1968), 385–402.

The main strength of *Q* is its close affinity to theory. Structured *Q* sorts, by definition, are theoretically oriented. In order to build a structured sort, one has perforce to enunciate some kind of theory. The theoretical emphasis becomes especially prominent in factorial sorts. In order to build two variables into an instrument, one must relate them to each other in some sensible fashion. While often rudimentary, this is the essence of theory: variables related in logical and empirical fashion.

Many individuals will no doubt believe that the possibilities of *Q* for the objective study of the individual in more than test score fashion are more important than the structured sort idea. With *Q* we have a methodology peculiarly suited to intensive study of the individual. One individual can be given two, three, or more related *Q* sorts. One individual can sort a *Q* sort many times. The data of such sortings can be analyzed objectively without entirely sacrificing the richness of the usual clinical, and much less objective, methods.

In addition, *Q* can be used to test the effects of independent variables on complex dependent variables. One difficulty in studying attitude change under the impact of communication, interaction, and other change agents is that the effects are not simple. Ordinarily the attitude mean of an experimental group is expected to increase or decrease under the impact of the independent variable or variables. With *Q*, we can rather sensitively assess such changes of individuals by using analysis of variance and factor analysis of the data of structured *Q* sorts. Although they have hardly been used, such methods hold great promise for experimental studies.

Two related strengths of *Q* are its heuristic quality and its usefulness in exploratory research. *Q* seems to be helpful in turning up new ideas, new hypotheses. Stephenson's work perhaps best illustrates this quality. One gets the feeling of a curious mind turning up interesting ideas while working with *Q*. *Q*'s exploratory power is shown to some extent by the attitude referents *Q* study outlined above. One can start to get an empirical purchase on slippery problems like the abstractness of attitudes and values.

To illustrate further both the heuristic and exploratory strengths of *Q*, suppose that one has good hunches on some of the content of the variable of a problem. For example, Riesman talks a good deal about inner-direction and other-direction and the presumed characteristics and behaviors of inner- and other-directed individuals. But he has little to say about how his theoretical notions can be tested. An analysis of the things he says about inner-direction and other-direction seems to show certain themes or categories of statements around which one can structure a *Q* sort. Such themes might be *achievement, privacy, abstract principle, conscience, group-interpersonal relations, niceness* or *emphasis on personality*, and *reality*. One might select, say, three or four of these themes and build a two-way structured sort somewhat like this:

	Individual-Group	*Morality*	*Achievement*
Inner-Direction			
Other-Direction			

While this paradigm may or may not be an adequate representation of the Riesman theory, it may at least serve to start its empirical testing. The hard reality of empirical data will hopefully help us refine the theory—or discard it if need be.[18]

Q methodology has other advantages. Analysis of variance and correlational methods can both be used. *Q* sorting is interesting: most persons seem to enjoy sorting *Q* decks, perhaps because the method is both challenging and realistic. Factor arrays are an important contribution to analysis and interpretation, as we saw earlier. One sees, so to speak, the verbal or other expressions of the essence of whatever it is that is common to different groups of individuals. Although seldom used, *Q* can be a strong aid in scale construction. The high items of factor arrays should make good scale items. Other uses and advantages will be discussed in the next section.

As usual, disadvantages accompany advantages. First, take the sampling of persons. One can rarely work with sufficiently large samples in *Q*. It is not a method well-suited to cross-sectional or large sample purposes. One does not draw a random sample of persons for study with *Q*. While Stephenson argues the point vigorously, there is no escaping the inability of the investigator using *Q* to generalize to populations of individuals. *Q* therefore requires cross-sectional supplementation. No matter how promising *Q* results may be, one cannot escape the necessity of testing theory on larger numbers of individuals.[19]

Q has been adversely criticized, mostly on statistical grounds.[20] Remember that most statistical tests assume independence. This means that the response to one item should not be affected by the responses to other items. In *Q* the placement of one card somewhere on the continuum should not affect the placement of other cards. If *Q* placements affect each other, then the independence assumption is violated. *Q* is an ipsative, forced-choice procedure, and it will be recalled that such procedures violate the independence assumption: the placement of one *Q* card affects the placement of other cards. It is, after all, a rank-order method.

The real question is: How serious is the violation of the assumption? Is it serious enough to invalidate the use of correlational and analysis of variance procedures? There is no doubt that in an 80-item sort, there are not really 79 degrees of freedom. Thus, to some extent at least, the analysis of variance procedure is vitiated. It is doubtful, however, that too much is risked in *Q* statistical situations, if there is a fairly large number of items. One can perhaps fall back on Fisher's advice given long ago: raise the requirements for statistical significance. Instead of accepting the .05 level in *Q* sorts, require the .01 level of significance. In most cases of *Q* statistical significance encountered by the author, *F* ratios are so high they leave little doubt as to statistical significance.[21]

[18]See Stephenson, *The Play Theory of Mass Communication*, pp. 83–85, for Stephenson's rather different idea for *Q*-testing the Riesman theory.

[19]Stephenson argues vigorously against this point of view. See *The Study of Behavior*, pp. 193–194, 218.

[20]D. Sundland, "The Construction of *Q* Sorts: A Criticism," *Psychological Review*, LXIX (1962), 62–64; L. Cronbach and G. Gleser, "William Stephenson. *The Study of Behavior: Q-Technique and Its Methodology*. Chicago: University of Chicago Press, 1953," *Psychometrika*, XIX (1954), 327–330 (book review).

[21]It is well, however, to bear the independence stricture in mind. Instructions to subjects should not encourage lack of independence. That is, tell subjects that they can always move any card or cards from one pile to another right to the end of the sorting procedure.

Another criticism of *Q* has focused on the forced-choice feature of *Q* sorting. It has been said that the forced procedure is unnatural, that it requires the subject to conform to an unreasonable requirement. Some subjects, too, complain about the forced-choice constraint of *Q* sorts. Furthermore, important information on elevation and scatter is said to be lost with the forced *Q* procedure. This means, for example, that two individuals can correlate highly because their profiles are alike. Yet these two individuals might be quite unlike: one might be high on a scale and the other low on the scale. (The computation of *r* takes no account of mean differences, or differences in level or elevation.) The *Q* procedure throws away levels differences between individuals.

On the constraint argument, all psychometric procedures are constraints on the individual. Because an individual feels constrained in sorting *Q* sorts, however, is no really good reason for declaring the procedure invalid. Most such inferences are probably made by critics who *think* forced procedures constrain the individual. In the experience of the author and his students, very few individuals complain about the procedure. Most of them, indeed, seem to enjoy it. Livson and Nichols say that the *Q* sorter is his own worst critic and that researchers should not be unduly alarmed by adverse sorter criticisms of the method.[22] They recommend use of the forced procedure after careful study of alternatives.

The evidence on the relative virtues of forced and unforced *Q* sorts is mixed. Block finds forced sorting equal or superior to unforced procedures.[23] Jones, on the other hand, finds the forced procedure wanting.[24] Definitive evidence one way or the other is lacking. So opinion must rule. It is the author's belief that *for its purpose* the forced sorting procedure is a useful device. Whether the distribution of cards is normal, rectangular, or otherwise is not so important, though the normal distribution works well and fits into statistical assumptions nicely. The important thing is to force individuals to make discriminations that they often will not make unless required to do so.

The criticism on the loss of information in *Q* sorting through lack of elevation and scatter is more serious.[25] The argument is too complex to discuss here. The reader should realize, however, that every time a coefficient of correlation is computed, the elevation (mean) and scatter (standard deviation) of the sets of scores are lost. *Q* is not unique here. *Q* is unique, however, in systematically using a procedure that sacrifices level and scatter. All individuals have the same *general* mean and the same *general* standard deviation.

[22]N. Livson and T. Nichols, "Discrimination and Reliability in Q-Sort Personality Descriptions," *Journal of Abnormal and Social Psychology*, LII (1956), 159–165. The author recalls an amusing and instructive incident. Colleagues had been asked to sort a 90-item unstructured *Q* sort the items of which were single words. One colleague, a philosopher, complained about the procedure. When he had finished, he said that the procedure was highly questionable, and that if he had to do it over again the results would certainly be quite different. He did the sort again *eleven months later*. The coefficient of correlation between the first and second sorts was .81!

[23]J. Block, "A Comparison of Forced and Unforced Q-Sorting Procedures," *Educational and Psychological Measurement*, XVI (1956), 481–493.

[24]A. Jones, "Distribution of Traits in Current Q-Sort Methodology," *Journal of Abnormal and Social Psychology*, LIII (1956), 90–95.

[25]See L. Cronbach and G. Gleser, "Assessing Similarity Between Profiles," *Psychological Bulletin*, L (1953), 456–473.

The practical answer is simple to state but not simple to implement: when elevation and scatter are important, do not use ipsative measures. If you are comparing the mean performances of two groups, for example, ipsative scores are of course inappropriate. If, on the other hand, mean differences are not important but the relations among variables *within* individuals or groups are important, then ipsative scores may well be appropriate. In the last analysis, the experience and judgment of the researcher are the final arbiters of whether *Q* sorting should be used.

Q Methodology in Social Scientific and Educational Research

Although it is possible, and sometimes desirable, to use *Q* to assess the effects of experimental manipulations, simpler procedures are usually more appropriate. This stricture applies whenever a hypothesis is tested by comparing the central tendencies, variabilities, or relative frequencies of characteristics of groups of individuals. *Q* can profitably be used for comparing the characteristics of groups of individuals only when comparing the relations *within* the groups. For example, we might test a hypothesis that two specified groups of individuals, categorized on the basis of holding different values or attitudes, will also cluster together similarly on some other measure presumably related to the values or attitudes.

Some research problems lend themselves nicely to *Q*. Complex aesthetic judgments and preferences are examples. Stephenson, in a brilliant *tour de force*, applied the structured *Q*-sort idea to artistic judgments.[26] He used actual squares and rectangles juxtaposed in various ways as items in a *Q* sort. Three variables were built into the sort: *shape dominance* (regular-irregular), *shape concentration* (overlapping-not overlapping), and *color*. He used an artist, himself, and graduate students as subjects, and made statistical predictions based on an aesthetic theory.

Getzels and Csikszentmihalyi followed a related and equally interesting procedure.[27] They had art students, all of whom were highly competent but of differing degrees of artistic talent, produce 31 drawings under controlled conditions. Then they had experts (artists) and nonexperts (graduate students) judge the drawings on *craftsmanship*, *originality*, and *overall aesthetic value* by virtually *Q* sorting the drawings. That is, each judge (total of 20 judges) sorted or rated the drawings three times. Correlations between *Q* sorts enabled the authors to conclude, among other things, that artists differed as much among themselves in judgments as laymen, but that they evidently related originality more to overall value than did the laymen. Both studies are themselves creative and original uses of *Q* to study the complex and highly elusive problem of aesthetic judgment. It is difficult to conceive a better empirical approach to the problem.

As indicated earlier, *Q* can be used to open up new areas, to test preliminary theories, to explore heuristic hunches. Examples were the suggested tentative

[26]Stephenson, *The Study of Behavior*, pp. 128 ff.

[27]J. Getzels and M. Czikszentmihalyi, "Aesthetic Opinion: An Empirical Study," *Public Opinion Quarterly*, XXX (1969), 34–45.

structuring of the Riesman and Spranger theories. The problem of creativity has been tackled up to now almost entirely with large *N* cross-sectional methods. Following the lead of the two aesthetic judgment studies just described, study of the stubborn but fascinating problem of creativity can be tackled. One might take a Guilford theory of convergent-divergent thinking or a Barron originality theory and explore them with *Q*.[28] Complex areas, especially psychological areas where intensive study of the individual is required, do not always yield too readily to large *N* approaches. *Q* methods, adequately used, should be useful in laying some of the research foundations in these areas.

Q is well adapted to studying certain aspects of intensive educational programs. Take attitude change in schools. Most research concentrates on the study of mean changes in attitudes under the impact of educational programs. But attitudes and attitude structures are complex. A group mean may not change much, but there may be pronounced changes in the structure of an attitude. Then, too, a group mean may change significantly, but we may have little or no idea of the nature of the change. Suppose a class is taught for a year with a new approach to social studies, an approach with several facets, say historical, economic, and social. Administration of an attitude scale before and after the program may show a significant change. But this can well leave out of account what aspects changed, the possible interactions of aspects of the general subject, and the changes in attitude factors. Again, *Q* may be a distinct aid in evaluating the program.

Although it cannot replace the methods discussed earlier in this book, *Q* methodology has a valuable contribution to make to behavioral research. In competent and imaginative hands it has an important place, perhaps mainly in opening up new areas of research. It is not well-suited to testing hypotheses over large numbers of individuals, nor can it be used too well with large samples.[29] One can rarely generalize to populations from *Q* persons samples. Indeed, one usually does not wish to do so. Rather, one tests theories on small sets of individuals carefully chosen for their "known" or presumed possession of some significant characteristic or characteristics. One explores unknown and unfamiliar areas and variables for their identity, their interrelations, and their functioning. Used thus, *Q* is an important and unique approach to the study of psychological, sociological, and educational phenomena.[30]

[28]J. Guilford, "Three Faces of Intellect," *American Psychologist,* XIV (1959), 469–479; F. Barron, "Complexity-Simplicity as a Personality Dimension," *Journal of Abnormal and Social Psychology,* XLVIII (1953), 163–172; "The Disposition toward Originality," *Journal of Abnormal and Social Psychology,* LI (1955), 478–485.

[29]At least one adaptation of the *Q* idea, more or less minus its ipsative feature, has been worked out so that some of the advantages of *Q* can be obtained in large-sample surveys. See, for example, E. Cataldo et al., "Card Sorting as a Technique for Survey Interviewing," *Public Opinion Quarterly,* XXXIV (1970), 202–215. In addition, it is possible to construct pencil-and-paper measures that incorporate *Q* ideas. See D. Jackson and C. Bidwell, "A Modification of *Q*-Technique," *Educational and Psychological Measurement,* XXIX (1959), 221–232; H. Webster, "A Forced-Choice Figure Preference Test Based on Factorial Design," *Educational and Psychological Measurement,* XXIX (1959), 45–54. Both methods are ingenious and potentially effective.

[30]For a supplementary discussion in considerable depth of the place of *Q* in behavioral research, see Kerlinger, "*Q* Methodology in Behavioral Research," *op. cit.*

Study Suggestions

1. Unfortunately, there appear to be no widely available elementary references on *Q* methodology. So, to learn the mechanics of *Q*, a good thing to do is work with the examples in Stephenson's book, *Study of Behavior*. Stephenson had the wisdom to include raw *Q* data in the book so that the beginner can grasp what goes on by working with the data. Stephenson also included full *Q* sorts that can be copied and used. Before working with *Q*, some advice is in order, both positive and negative. First, the negative advice: do not try to use *Q* unless you have a pretty fair understanding of analysis of variance and factor analysis. It is hopeless to try to use *Q* mechanically via precept and formula. The positive advice is this: work with as many actual *Q* sorts as you can. Use the data examples in Stephenson's book. Do the analyses of variance. For example, to get a feeling for the intercorrelation of *Q* sorts, type, on 3×5 cards, the Jung *Q* sort that Stephenson gives on pp. 83–85, *The Study of Behavior*. Use the distribution Stephenson gives on p. 72. Ignore the categories. Sort the cards to describe yourself. Have six or seven friends do the same. Pick some introverted friends and some extroverted friends (according to your best judgment). Intercorrelate the sorts.[31] Try a simple cluster analysis by grouping persons with high *r*'s together. After a while, you can acquire a knack for doing this.

   To learn something about the building of structured sorts, study Stephenson's *Q* testing of aesthetic preference in *The Study of Behavior*, pp. 128–141. Then try structuring some problem of interest to yourself. Write or select the items and try out the sort with friends or with other members of your class.
2. Pick 12 prominent political names, six Republicans and six Democrats. Type the names on sheets in random order. Ask some individuals, whom you know to be Republicans and Democrats, to rank order the names according to their preference for the men. Intercorrelate the ranks using the rank-order coefficient of correlation. Enter the *rho*'s in a correlation matrix. Can you identify the individuals who have rank ordered the names by the intercorrelations? Do the political party preferences show in the correlations? Is this like *Q* methodology? (See Table 34.1 and accompanying discussion.)
3. Intercorrelate the data of Table 34.3. Do you get the correlation matrix of Table 34.4? Substitute other persons (and, of course, other variables) and interpret the matrix.
4. Stephenson, in his more recent book (see footnote 14), gives a complex but highly interesting *Q* sort on democratic principles. It would be interesting for a class to have this sort typed, sorted by the class members, and then intercorrelated. If one or more students in the class knows factor analysis, factor-analyze the correlation matrix and calculate the factor arrays of the first two or three factors (see *The Study of Behavior*, pp. 176–179). Interpret the arrays.
5. Here is an easy and perhaps interesting class exercise. Have the following 12 attitude referents typed and reproduced in random order: *civil rights*, *children's interests*, *Supreme Court*, *poverty program*, *Jews*, *socialized medicine*; *private property*, *education as intellectual training*, *subject matter*, *free enterprise*, *school discipline*, *religion*. The first six referents have been found to be

[31]It is useful, in recording an individual's *Q*-sort data, to write the values of the pile placements on the backs of the cards with the individual's initials, being careful to record the initials and numbers of an individual in the same relative position on each card. With structured sorts, record the structure category symbols on the back of each card. Number the faces of the cards with random numbers 1 through *n*, *n* being the number of cards in the deck. There are more elaborate systems for sorting and recording data—for example, racks for sorting and scoring sheets for entering pile placement values—but these are not recommended.

liberal referents and the last six to be conservative referents (see text). Select ten members of the class at random to rank-order the referents according to positive and negative feelings about them. (Rank 1, for instance, can be "strongly positive" and Rank 12 "strongly negative.") Then intercorrelate the rank orders using the rank-order coefficient of correlation (see footnote 2) to produce a 10×10 correlation matrix. See if any of the class members cluster together judged by substantial correlations ($\geqslant .40$). Are there two clusters? If so, go back to the original rank orders of the members of the cluster to identify what is common to the cluster members. (A simple way to do this is to add the values given each item by the members of a cluster. Then rank-order these sums. The nature of the cluster may be deduced from its rank order on this sums set of ranks.)

(*Note:* If the attitudes of the ten individuals are homogeneous, you may obtain only one cluster. It may be necessary to go outside the class for greater heterogeneity of attitudes.)

PART 10

Multiple Regression and Factor Analysis

Introduction

Behavioral research is being revolutionized by multivariate thinking and analysis. *Multivariate analysis* is a general term used to describe a group of mathematical and statistical methods whose purpose is to analyze multiple measures of N individuals: multiple regression analysis, multivariate analysis of variance, canonical correlation, discriminant analysis, and factor analysis. Much behavioral research is multivariate in nature. The phenomena we wish to explain and predict are complex: achievement, learning, aggression, intelligence, creativity, risk-taking, organizational productivity, group cohesiveness, and many others. Many variables influence such phenomena, and multivariate methods are ways of studying multiple influences of several independent variables on one or more dependent variables.

Multivariate methods, then, mirror the actual complexity of behavioral "reality." They make it possible for the behavioral scientist to probe more deeply and realistically into phenomena. The influence is profound: the very nature of the problems that behavioral scientists study is changing radically.

We examine in some depth multiple regression and factor analysis. Other multivariate methods are only briefly characterized. As usual, the three chapters of this section aim at understanding basic ideas rather than mastery of methods. Chapter 35 examines the rationale and working of simple and multiple regression analysis, and Chapter 36 explores the relations between multiple regression analysis and analysis of variance. We will find that multiple regression analysis, properly conceived and used, can accomplish what analysis of variance does—and more. Indeed, we will see that multiple regression analysis is the more general and powerful method, a method that can be used with a wide range and variety of research problems. Part of Chapter 36 briefly defines and illustrates canonical correlation and discriminant analysis.

The book ends, appropriately enough, with a chapter on factor analysis. It can be said, I think, that multiple regression analysis and factor analysis are two of the most powerful, general, and useful modes of analysis available to the behavioral scientist. One of the purposes of Part 10 is to give the student an understanding of the basis for this strong statement.

CHAPTER 35

Multiple Regression Analysis: Foundations

Multiple regression analysis is a method for studying the effects and the magnitudes of the effects of more than one independent variable on one dependent variable using principles of correlation and regression. We turn immediately to research examples and defer explanation until later.

Two Research Examples

Many studies have shown that high school grade-point average (GPA) is a good, perhaps the best, predictor of success in college. Scannell, for example, found correlations of .67 between high school GPA and freshman college GPA and .59 between high school GPA and four-year college GPA.[1] This means that college success can be partially predicted from knowledge of high school achievement as reflected in high school grades. High school GPA, in Scannell's study, accounted for approximately 35 percent of the variance of four-year college grades ($r^2 = .59^2 = .35$).[2]

An important question that should be asked, however, is: Can the prediction of college success be improved by other knowledge? Scannell also had test

[1]D. Scannell, "Prediction of College Success From Elementary and Secondary School Performance," *Journal of Educational Psychology*, LI (1960), 130–134.

[2]Recall that squaring a correlation coefficient yields an estimate of the amount of variance shared by two variables. This notion is used a great deal in regression analysis.

scores of educational achievement for his student subjects. He wanted to improve prediction of the college GPA by adding the predictive power of the achievement measure to that of the high school GPA. The correlation between this measure and four-year GPA was .52. So this test accounted for $.52^2 = 27$ percent of the variance of college GPA. In addition, Scannell knew high school class ranks of his subjects. The correlation between rank in class and college GPA was .39. We have, then, three independent variable measures, high school GPA, high school achievement test scores, and rank in class in high school, and a dependent variable, four-year college GPA. The correlations between the three independent variables and the dependent variable were: .59, .52, and .39. If we combine the predictive powers of the three measures, how much will the prediction improve over what it was when only high school GPA was used? The combination of the three independent variables yielded a correlation coefficient with the dependent variable of .63. This increased predictive power over knowledge of high school GPA alone by about 5 percent ($.63^2 - .59^2 = .40 - .35 = .05$). The addition of achievement-test scores and rank in class increased the accuracy of prediction. The increase, however, was small. Is this always so?

In a study of the prediction of high school GPA, Holtzman and Brown used two independent variable measures: study habits and attitudes (SHA) and scholastic aptitude (SA).[3] The correlations between high school GPA (the dependent variable) and SHA and SA in grade 7 ($N = 1684$) were .55 and .61. The correlation between SHA and SA was .32. How much more variance was accounted for by adding the scholastic-aptitude measure to the study-habits measure? If we combine SHA and SA optimally to predict GPA, we obtain a correlation of .72. The answer to the question, then, is $.72^2 - .55^2 = .52 - .30 = .22$, or 22 percent more of the variance of GPA is accounted for by adding SA to SHA. In contrast to the Scannell example, this is a sharp increase. The reasons for such differences in increases will become apparent later.

These are examples of multiple regression analysis. The basic idea is the same as simple correlation except that k, where k is greater than 1, independent variables are used to predict the dependent variable, the so-called criterion variable. In simple regression analysis, a variable, X, is used to predict another variable, Y. In multiple regression analysis, variables $X_1, X_2, \ldots, X_k$ are used to predict Y. The method and the calculations are done in a manner to give the "best" prediction possible, given the correlations among all the variables. In other words, instead of saying: If X, then Y, we say: If $X_1, X_2, \ldots, X_k$, then Y, and the results of the calculations tell us how "good" the prediction is and approximately how much of the variance of Y is accounted for by the "best" linear combination of the independent variables.

Simple Regression Analysis

We say that we wish to study the regression of Y scores on X scores. We wish to study how the Y scores "go back to," how they "depend upon," the X scores.

[3]W. Holtzman and W. Brown, "Evaluating the Study Habits and Attitudes of High School Students," *Journal of Educational Psychology*, LIX (1968), 404–409.

Galton, who first worked out the notion of correlation, got the idea from the notion of "regression toward mediocrity," a phenomenon observed in studies of inheritance. (The symbol r used for the coefficient of correlation means "regression.") Tall men will tend to have shorter sons, and short men taller sons. The sons' heights, then, tend to "regress to," or "go back to," the mean of the population. Statistically, if we want to predict Y from X and the correlation between X and Y is zero, then our best prediction is to the mean. That is, for any given X, say X_7, we can only predict the mean of Y. The higher the correlation, however, the better the prediction. If $r = 1.00$, then prediction is perfect and we have a functional relation of the form $y = f(x)$. (See the discussion of functions in Chapter 5.) To the extent that the correlation departs from 1.00, to that extent predictions from X to Y are less than perfect. If we plot the X and Y values when $r = 1.00$, they will all lie on a straight line. The higher the correlation, the closer the plotted values will be to the regression line (see Chapter 5).

To illustrate and explain the notion of statistical regression, we use two fictitious examples with simple numbers. The numbers used in the two examples are the same except that they are arranged differently.[4] The examples are given in Table 35.1. In the example on the left, labeled A, the correlation between the X and Y values is .90, while in the example on the right, labeled B, the correlation is 0. Certain calculations necessary for regression analysis are also given in the table: the sums and means, the deviation sums of squares of X and Y ($\Sigma x^2 = \Sigma X^2 - (\Sigma X)^2/n$), the deviation cross products ($\Sigma xy = \Sigma XY - (\Sigma X)(\Sigma Y)/n$), and certain regression values to be explained shortly.

First, note the difference between the A and B sets of scores. They differ only in the order of the scores of the second or X columns. The two different orders produce very different correlations between the X and Y scores. In the A set, $r = .90$, and in the B set, $r = .00$. Second, note the statistics at the bottom of the table. Σx^2 and Σy^2 are the same in both A and B, but Σxy is 9 in A and 0 in B. Let us concentrate on the A set of scores.

The basic equation of simple linear regression is:

$$Y' = a + bX \tag{35.1}$$

where X = the scores of the independent variable, a = intercept constant, b = regression coefficient, and Y' = predicted scores of the dependent variable. A regression equation is a prediction formula: Y values are predicted from X values. The correlation between the observed X and Y values in effect determines how the prediction equation "works." The intercept constant, a, and the regression coefficient, b, will be explained shortly.

The two sets of X and Y values of Table 35.1 are plotted in Fig. 35.1. Lines have been drawn in each plot to "run through" the plotted points. If we had a way of placing these lines so that they would simultaneously be as close to all the points as possible, then the lines should express the regression of Y on X. The line in the top plot, where $r = .90$, runs close to the plotted XY points. In the bottom

[4] These examples are taken from Chapter 15, where, in considering the analysis of variance, we studied the effect on the F test of the correlation between experimental groups.

TABLE **35.1** REGRESSION ANALYSIS OF TWO SETS OF SCORES

	A.	$r = .90$				B.	$r = .00$			
	Y	X	XY	Y'	d	Y	X	XY	Y'	d
	1	2	2	1.2	−.2	1	5	5	3	−2
	2	4	8	3.0	−1.0	2	2	4	3	−1
	3	3	9	2.1	.9	3	4	12	3	0
	4	5	20	3.9	.1	4	6	24	3	1
	5	6	30	4.8	.2	5	3	15	3	2
Σ:	15	20	69		0	15	20	60		0
M:	3	4			$\Sigma d^2 = 1.90$	3	4			$\Sigma d^2 = 10.00$
Σ^2:	55	90				55	90			

A.

$$\Sigma y^2 = 55 - \frac{(15)^2}{5} = 10$$

$$\Sigma x^2 = 90 - \frac{(20)^2}{5} = 10$$

$$\Sigma xy = 69 - \frac{(15)(20)}{5} = 9$$

$$b = \frac{\Sigma xy}{\Sigma x^2} = \frac{9}{10} = .90$$

$$a = \bar{Y} - b\bar{X} = 3 - (.90)(4) = -.60$$

$$Y' = a + bx = -.60 + .90X$$

B.

$$\Sigma y^2 = 55 - \frac{(15)^2}{5} = 10$$

$$\Sigma x^2 = 90 - \frac{(20)^2}{5} = 10$$

$$\Sigma xy = 60 - \frac{(15)(20)}{5} = 0$$

$$b = \frac{0}{10} = 0$$

$$a = 3 - (0)(4) = 3$$

$$Y' = 3 + (0)X$$

plot, however, where $r = .00$, it is not possible to run the line close to all the points. The points, after all, are in effect placed randomly, since $r = .00$.

The correlations between X and Y, $r = .90$ and $r = .00$, determine the slopes of the regression lines (when the standard deviations are equal, as they are in this case). The *slope* indicates the change in Y with a change of one unit of X. In the $r = .90$ example, with a change of 1 in X, we predict a change of .90 in Y. (This is expressed trigonometrically as the length of the line opposite the angle made by the regression line divided by the length of the line adjacent to the angle. In Fig. 35.1, if we drop a perpendicular from the regression line—the point where the X and Y means intersect, for example—to a line drawn horizontally from the point where the regression line intersects the Y axis, or at $Y = -.60$, then $3.6/4.0 = .90$. A change of 1 in X means a change of .90 in Y.[5])

The plot of the X and Y values of Example B, bottom part of Fig. 35.1, is

[5]Raw scores have been used for most of the examples in this chapter because they fit into our purposes better. A thorough treatment of regression, however, requires discussions using deviation scores and standard scores. The emphasis here, as elsewhere in the book, is on research uses of the methods and techniques and not on statistics as such. The student should supplement his study, therefore, with good basic discussions of simple and multiple regression. See the references in the study suggestions at the end of the next chapter.

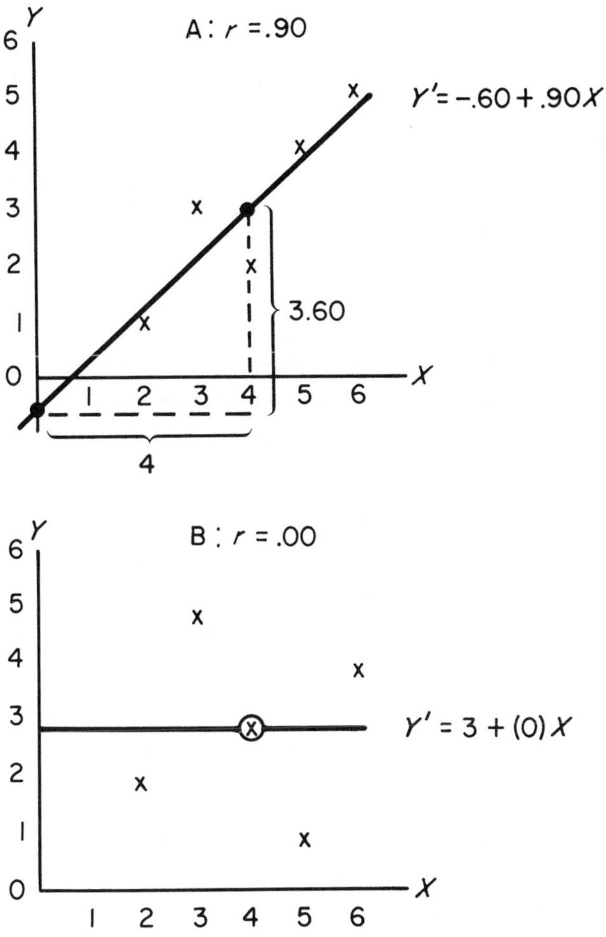

FIG. 35.1

quite different. In Example A, one can rather easily and visually draw a line through the points and achieve a fairly accurate approximation to the regression line. But in Example B this is hardly possible. We can draw the line only by using other guidelines, which we get to shortly. Another important thing to note is the scatter or dispersion of the plotted points around the two regression lines. In Example A, they cling rather closely to the line. If $r = 1.00$, they would all be on the line. When $r = .00$, on the other hand, they scatter widely about the line. The lower the correlation, the more the scatter.

In order to calculate the regression statistics of the two examples, we must calculate the deviation sums of squares and cross products. This has been done at the bottom of Table 35.1. The formula for the *slope*, or *regression coefficient*, b, is:

$$b = \frac{\Sigma xy}{\Sigma x^2} \qquad (35.2)$$

The two b's are .90 and .00. The *intercept constant*, a, is calculated with the formula:

$$a = \bar{Y} - b\bar{X} \tag{35.3}$$

The a's for the two examples are −.60 and 3; e.g., for Example A, $a = 3 - (.90)(4) = -.60$. The intercept constant is the point where the regression line intercepts the Y axis. To draw the regression line, lay a ruler between the intercept constant on the Y axis and the point where the mean of Y and the mean of X meet. (In Fig. 35.1, these points are indicated with small circles.)

The final steps in the process, at least as far as it will be taken here, are to write regression equations and then, using the equations, calculate the predicted values of Y, or Y', given the X values. The two equations are given in the last line of Table 35.1. First look at the regression equation for $r = .00$: $Y' = 3 + (0)X$. This means, of course, that all the predicted Y's are 3, the mean of Y. When $r = 0$, the best prediction is the mean, as indicated earlier. When $r = 1.00$, at the other extreme, the reader can see that one can predict exactly: one simply adds a, the constant, to the X scores. When $r = .90$, prediction is less than perfect and one predicts Y' values calculated with the regression equation. For example, to predict the first Y' score, we calculate:

$$Y'_1 = -.60 + (.90)(2) = \mathit{1.20}$$

The predicted scores of the A and B sets have been given in Table 35.1. (See columns labeled Y'.) Note an important point: If, for Example A, we plot the X and the predicted Y, or Y', values, the plotted points all lie on the regression line. That is, the regression line of the figure represents the set of predicted Y values, given the X values and the correlation between the X and the observed Y values.

We can now calculate the predicted values of Y. The higher the correlation, the more accurate the prediction. The accuracy of the predictions of the two sets of scores can be clearly shown by calculating the differences between the original Y values and the predicted Y values, or $Y - Y' = d$, and then calculating the sums of squares of these differences. Such differences are called *residuals*. In Table 35.1, the two sets of residuals and their sums of squares have been calculated (see columns labeled d). The two values of Σd^2, 1.90 for A and 10.00 for B, are quite different, just as the plots in Fig. 35.1 are quite different: that of the B, or $r = .00$, set is much greater than that of the A, or $r = .90$, set. That is, the higher the correlation, the smaller the deviations from prediction and thus the more accurate the prediction.

Simple Regression and Analysis of Variance

Before beginning discussion of multiple regression, it will be profitable to lay a foundation for understanding the relation between multiple regression analysis and analysis of variance. Recall from earlier discussions how the total variance of a set of dependent variable measures can be broken down into systematic variance and error variance. The simplest form of such a breakdown was: the variance between groups (experimental variance) and the variance within groups (error variance), which, when added, equaled the total variance. Actually, we worked mostly with sums of squares because they are additive. In regression analysis, we do virtually the same thing. The main difference is that the regression approach is more general: It more or less fits and is applicable to most research problems with one dependent variable.

A basic equation of analysis of variance was given earlier:

$$ss_t = ss_b + ss_w$$

where ss_t = total sum of squares; ss_b = between-groups sum of squares; and ss_w = within-groups sum of squares. The transition to regression analysis is easy. We write:

$$ss_t = ss_{\text{reg}} + ss_{\text{res}} \tag{35.4}$$

where ss_t = total sum of squares of Y; ss_{reg} = sum of squares of Y due to regression; and ss_{res} = sum of squares of the residuals, or the deviations from regression.

Before giving the regression formulas for the different sums of squares, let's calculate these sums of squares using the data and statistics of Table 35.1. The total sums of squares, ss_t, are found simply by calculating the sums of squares of the Y columns of Table 35.1:

$$\begin{aligned}\Sigma y_t^2 &= \Sigma Y^2 - (\Sigma Y)^2/N \\ &= (1^2+2^2+3^2+4^2+5^2) - 15^2/5 \\ &= 55 - 45 = 10\end{aligned}$$

for both A and B. The sums of squares for the Y' columns are:

$$(1.2^2+3.0^2+2.1^2+3.9^2+4.8^2) - 15^2/5 = 53.10 - 45 = 8.10$$

for A, and

$$(3^2+3^2+3^2+3^2+3^2) - 15^2/5 = 45 - 45 = 0$$

for B. These are the sums of squares *due to regression*, or due to the regression of Y on X. The sums of squares of the residuals of A and B are calculated similarly:

$$(-.2^2 + -1.0^2 + .9^2 + .1^2 + .2^2) - 0 = 1.90$$

for A, and

$$(-2^2 + -1^2 + 0^2 + 1^2 + 2^2) - 0 = 10$$

for B. We now repeat the symbolic equation and follow it with the numerical values of A and B:

$$ss_t = ss_{\text{reg}} + ss_{\text{res}}$$

$$\text{A:} \quad 10 = 8.10 + 1.90$$

$$\text{B:} \quad 10 = 0 + 10$$

This is the foundation of most further developments. We have the total sum of squares of Y, the dependent variable measures, the sum of squares of Y due to regression, which is analogous to the between groups sum of squares, and the residual sum of squares, which is analogous to the within-groups or error sum of squares. Actually, then, analysis of variance and multiple regression analysis are virtually the same. If this is so, then we should also be able to calculate and interpret F ratios and statistical significance for the regression analysis as we did earlier for the analysis of variance. The formula in one-way analysis of variance was:

$$F = \frac{ss_b/df_1}{ss_w/df_2}$$

where df_1 = degrees of freedom associated with ss_b, and df_2 = degrees of freedom associated with ss_w. Similarly, the formula in regression analysis is:

$$F = \frac{ss_{\text{reg}}/df_1}{ss_{\text{res}}/df_2} \qquad (35.5)$$

The degrees of freedom are: $df_1 = k$, where $k = 1$, and $df_2 = N - k - 1 = 5 - 1 - 1 = 3$. So:

$$F = \frac{8.10/1}{1.90/3} = \frac{8.10}{.633} = 12.80$$

which is significant at the .05 level. Thus we can say that, in Example A, the regression of Y on X is statistically significant.

The test of significance can be done in two or three other ways. One, the correlation of .90 can be checked for significance in a table of r's significant at various levels.[6] In the present case, $r = .90$ is significant at the .05 level. This approach, however, is not helpful when we want to do similar tests with more than one independent variable. A second way is to use the t test: one tests the significance of the regression coefficient, or, in the case of more than one independent variable, regression coefficients.[7] (See footnote 13.)

In using the F test, above, the sums of squares were calculated from the values of Table 35.1. Another way, a more useful one as we will see later, is to calculate the total sum of squares of Y from the observed values of Y and then calculate the regression sum of squares with the following formula:

$$ss_{\text{reg}} = \frac{(\Sigma xy)^2}{\Sigma x^2} \qquad (35.6)$$

The formula requires the cross products of deviation scores, $x = X - \bar{X}$ and $y = Y - \bar{Y}$. The cross products of the X and Y scores are given in Table 35.1. Their

[6]For example, see R. Fisher and F. Yates, *Statistical Tables for Biological, Agricultural, and Medical Research.* New York: Hafner, 1963 (Table VII). Statistics texts ordinarily have such tables.

[7]G. Snedecor and W. Cochran, *Statistical Methods.* Ames, Iowa: Iowa State University Press, 1967, pp. 184–185; 391–393.

sum, for the A data, is 69. Thus,

$$\Sigma xy = \Sigma XY - \frac{(\Sigma X)(\Sigma Y)}{N}$$
$$= 69 - \frac{(15)(20)}{5} = 9$$

Now:

$$ss_{\text{reg}} = \frac{(9)^2}{10} = \frac{81}{10} = \mathit{8.10}$$

The residual sum of squares is obtained by subtraction:

$$ss_{\text{res}} = ss_t - ss_{\text{reg}}$$
$$= 10 - 8.10 = \mathit{1.90}$$

These values, of course, agree with those calculated earlier. Still another method, one that can be conveniently used with multiple regression, will be taken up in the next section.

Multiple Linear Regression

The method of multiple linear regression extends the ideas presented in the preceding section to more than one independent variable. From knowledge of the values of two or more independent variables, $X_1, X_2, \ldots, X_k$, we want to predict to a dependent variable, Y. Earlier in the book we talked about the great need to assess the influence of several variables on a dependent variable. We can, of course, predict from verbal aptitude, say, to reading achievement, or from conservatism to ethnic attitudes. But how much more powerful it would be if we could predict from verbal aptitude together with other variables known or thought to influence reading—for example, achievement motivation and attitude toward school work. Theoretically, there is no limit to the number of variables we can use, but there are practical limits. Although only two independent variables are used in the example that follows, the principles apply to any number of independent variables.

An Example

Take one of the problems just mentioned. Suppose we had reading achievement (RA), verbal aptitude (VA), and achievement motivation (AM) scores on 20 eighth-grade pupils. We want to predict to reading achievement, Y, from verbal aptitude, X_1, and achievement motivation, X_2. Or, we want to calculate the regression of reading achievement on *both* verbal aptitude and achievement motivation. If the scores on verbal aptitude and achievement motivation were standard scores, we might average them, treat the averages as one composite independent variable, and calculate the regression statistics as we did earlier. We might not do too badly either. But there is a better way.

Suppose the X_1, verbal aptitude, X_2, achievement motivation, and Y, reading achievement, scores of the 20 subjects and the sums, means, and raw score sums of squares are those of Table 35.2. (Disregard the Y' and d columns for the moment.) We need to calculate the deviation sums of squares, the deviation cross products, the standard deviations $[\sqrt{\Sigma x^2/(N-1)}]$, and the correlations among the three variables. These are the basic statistics that are calculated for almost any set of data. They are given in Table 35.3.[8] The sums of squares and cross products are given in the diagonal (from upper left to lower right) and above it, and the correlations are given below the diagonal. The r's of prime interest are those of the

TABLE **35.2** FICTITIOUS EXAMPLE: READING ACHIEVEMENT (Y), VERBAL APTITUDE (X_1), AND ACHIEVEMENT MOTIVATION (X_2) SCORES

	Y	X_1	X_2	Y'	$Y-Y'=d$
	2	2	4	3.0305	−1.0305
	1	2	4	3.0305	−2.0305
	1	1	4	2.3534	−1.3534
	1	1	3	1.9600	−.9600
	5	3	6	4.4944	.5056
	4	4	6	5.1715	−1.1715
	7	5	3	4.6684	2.3316
	6	5	4	5.0618	.9382
	7	7	3	6.0226	.9774
	8	6	3	5.3455	2.6545
	3	4	5	4.7781	−1.7781
	3	3	5	4.1010	−1.1010
	6	6	9	7.7059	−1.7059
	6	6	8	7.3125	−1.3125
	10	8	6	7.8799	2.1201
	9	9	7	8.9504	.0496
	6	10	5	8.8407	−2.8407
	6	9	5	8.1636	−2.1636
	9	4	7	5.5649	3.4351
	10	4	7	5.5649	4.4351
Σ:	110	99	104		0
M:	5.50	4.95	5.20		
Σ^2:	770.0	625.0	600.0		81.6091

two independent variables with the dependent variable, r_{y1} and r_{y2}, .6735 and .3946. With these routine calculations out of the way, we can concentrate on the basic notions of multiple regression.

The fundamental prediction equation is:

$$Y' = a + b_1X_1 + \cdots + b_kX_k \tag{35.7}$$

[8]The calculations are not done here because their mechanics were covered in earlier chapters. The student should do them and note that he will probably obtain results slightly different from those reported above. Such differences are due to rounding errors—an ever-present problem in multiple regression analysis. In fact, the results of this problem, obtained on a desk calculator, are slightly different from those obtained by computer.

TABLE **35.3** DEVIATION SUMS OF SQUARES AND CROSS PRODUCTS, CORRELATION COEFFICIENTS, AND STANDARD DEVIATIONS OF DATA OF TABLE 35.2[a]

	y	x_1	x_2
y	165.00	100.50	39.00
x_1	*.6735*	134.95	23.20
x_2	*.3946*	*.2596*	59.20
s	2.9469	2.6651	1.7652

[a]The tabled entries are as follows. The first line gives, successively, Σy^2, the deviation sum of squares of Y, the cross product of the deviations of X_1 and Y, or $\Sigma x_1 y$, and finally $\Sigma x_2 y$. The entries in the second and third lines, on the diagonal or above, are Σx_1^2, $\Sigma x_1 x_2$, and (in the lower right corner) Σx_2^2. The italicized entries *below* the diagonal are the correlation coefficients. The standard deviations are given in the last line.

The symbols have the same meaning as those of the simple regression equation, except that there are k independent variables and k regression coefficients. Somehow, a and the b's must be calculated from knowledge of the X's and Y. These calculations are the most complex of multiple regression analysis. For only two independent variables, algebraic formulas given in statistics books can be used.[9] The calculation of a, once the b's are found, is straightforward. The problem is the calculation of the b's when there are more than two independent variables. Only the general ideas behind the calculations will be explained, since the details would take us too far from our central concern.

What we have, in effect, is a set of linear equations, one equation for each independent variable. The objective of the determination of the b's of Eq. 35.7 is to find those b values that will minimize the sums of squares of the residuals. This is the so-called *principle of least squares.* The calculus provides the method of differentiation for doing this. If used, it yields a set of simultaneous linear equations called *normal* equations (no relation to the normal distribution). These equations contain the coefficients of correlation among all the independent variables and between the independent variables and the dependent variable and a set of weights called beta weights, β_j, which will be explained later (they are like the b weights). The normal equations for the above problem are:

$$\begin{aligned} r_{11}\beta_1 + r_{12}\beta_2 &= r_{y1} \\ r_{21}\beta_1 + r_{22}\beta_2 &= r_{y2} \end{aligned} \qquad (35.8)$$

where β_j = beta weights; r_{ij} = the correlations among the independent variables; and r_{yj} = the correlations between the independent variables and the dependent

[9]See Snedecor and Cochran, *op. cit.*, p. 383.

variable, Y. (Note that $r_{12} = r_{21}$, and that $r_{11} = r_{22} = 1.00$. Note, too, that Eq. 35.8 can be extended to any number of independent variables.)

Probably the best way—certainly the most elegant way—to solve the equations for the β_j is to use matrix algebra. Unfortunately, knowledge of matrix algebra cannot be assumed. So the actual solution of the equations must be omitted. The solution yields the following beta weights: $\beta_1 = .6123$ and $\beta_2 = .2357$. The b weights are then obtained from the following formula:

$$b_j = \beta_j \frac{s_y}{s_j} \tag{35.9}$$

where s_j = standard deviations of variables 1 and 2 (see Table 35.3) and s_y = standard deviation of Y. Substituting in Eq. 35.9, we obtain:

$$b_1 = (.6123)\left(\frac{2.9469}{2.6651}\right) = .6771$$

$$b_2 = (.2357)\left(\frac{2.9469}{1.7652}\right) = .3934$$

To obtain the intercept constant, extend Eq. 35.3 to two independent variables:

$$a = \bar{Y} - b_1\bar{X}_1 - b_2\bar{X}_2$$

$$a = 5.50 - (.6771)(4.95) - (.3934)(5.20) = .1027$$

Finally, we write the complete regression equation:

$$Y' = a + b_1X_1 + b_2X_2$$

$$Y' = .1027 + .6771X_1 + .3934X_2$$

Substituting the observed values of X_1 and X_2 of Table 35.2, the predicted values of Y, or Y', are obtained. For example, calculate the predicted Y's for the fifth and twentieth subjects:

$$Y'_5 = .1027 + (.6771)(3) + (.3934)(6) = 4.4944$$

$$Y'_{20} = .1027 + (.6771)(4) + (.3934)(7) = 5.5649$$

These values and the other eighteen values are given in the fourth column of Table 35.2. The fifth column of the table gives the deviations from regression, or the residuals, $Y_i - Y'_i = d_i$. For example, the residuals for Y_5 and Y_{20} are:

$$d_5 = Y_5 - Y'_5 = 5 - 4.4944 = .5056$$

$$d_{20} = Y_{20} - Y'_{20} = 10 - 5.5649 = 4.4351$$

Note that one deviation is small and the other large: they are the smallest and largest in the set. The residuals are given in the last column of Table 35.2. Most of them are relatively small, and about half are positive and half negative.

The sum of squares due to regression can now be calculated, but the regression of Y on X_1 *and* X_2 must be considered. Square each of the Y' values of the fourth column of Table 35.2 and sum:

$$(3.0305)^2 + \cdots + (5.5649)^2 = 688.3969$$

Now use the usual formula for the deviation sum of squares:

$$\Sigma y'^2 = 688.3969 - \frac{(110)^2}{20} = 83.3969$$

Similarly, calculate the sum of squares of the residuals:

$$\Sigma d^2 = (-1.0305)^2 + \cdots + (4.4351)^2 = 81.6091^{10}$$

As a check, calculate:

$$ss_{\text{reg}} + ss_{\text{res}} = ss_t$$

$$83.3969 + 81.6091 = 165.0060$$

The regression and residual sums of squares are not usually calculated in this way. They were so calculated here to show the student just what these quantities are. Had the formulas that are ordinarily used been used, we might not have clearly seen that the regression sum of squares is the sum of squares of the Y' values calculated by using the regression equation. We also might not have seen clearly that the residual sum of squares is the sum of squares calculated with the d's of the fifth column of Table 35.2. Recall, too, that the a and the b's (or β's) of the regression equation were calculated to satisfy the least-squares principle, that is, to minimize the d's, or errors of prediction—or, rather, to minimize the sum of the squares of the errors of prediction. In sum, the regression sum of squares expresses that portion of the total sum of squares of Y that is due to the regression of Y, the dependent variable, on X_1 and X_2, the independent variables, and the residual sum of squares expresses that portion of the total sum of squares of Y that is *not* due to the regression.

The reader may wonder: Why bother with this complicated procedure of determining the regression weights? Is it necessary to invoke a least-squares procedure? Why not just average the X_1 and X_2 values and call the means of the individual X_1 and X_2 values the predicted Y's? The answer is that it might work quite well. Indeed, in this case it would work very well, almost as well, in fact, as the full regression procedure. But it might *not* work too well. The trouble is that you do not really know when it will work well and when it will not. The regression procedure always "works," other things equal. It always minimizes the squared errors of prediction. Notice that in both cases linear equations are used and that only the coefficients differ:

Regression equation: $Y' = a + b_1X_1 + b_2X_2$

Mean equation: $Y' = \frac{1}{2}X_1 + \frac{1}{2}X_2$

[10]This is a "good" example of the errors that cumulate through rounding. The actual regression sum of squares, calculated by computer, is 83.3909, an error of .006. Note, however, that even though the residuals were calculated from the hand-calculated predicted Y's, the sum of squares of the residuals is exactly that produced by the computer, 81.6091.

Of the innumerable possible ways of weighting X_1 and X_2, which should be chosen if the least-squares principle is not used? It is conceivable, of course, that one has prior knowledge or some reason for weighting X_1 and X_2. X_1 may be the scores on some test that has been found to be highly successful in prediction. X_2 may be a successful predictor, too, but not as successful as X_1. Therefore one may decide to weight X_1 very heavily, say four times as much as X_2. The equation would be: $Y' = 4X_1 + X_2$. And this might work well. The trouble is that seldom do we have prior knowledge, and even when we do, it is rather imprecise. How can the decision to weight X_1 four times as much as X_2 be reached? An educated guess can be made. The regression method is not a guess, however. It is a precise method based on the data and on a powerful mathematical principle. It is in this sense that the calculated regression weights are "best."

The regression and residual sums of squares can be calculated more readily than indicated above. The formulas are:

$$ss_{\text{reg}} = b_1 \Sigma x_1 y + \cdots + b_k \Sigma x_k y \tag{35.10}$$

$$ss_{\text{res}} = ss_t - ss_{\text{reg}} \tag{35.11}$$

In the present case, (35.10) becomes:

$$ss_{\text{reg}} = b_1 \Sigma x_1 y + b_2 \Sigma x_2 y$$

This is easily calculated by substituting the two b values calculated above and the cross products given in Table 35.3:

$$ss_{\text{reg}} = (.6771)(100.50) + (.3934)(39.00) = \mathit{83.3912}$$

$$ss_{\text{res}} = 165.0 - 83.3912 = \mathit{81.6088}$$

Within errors of rounding, these are the values calculated directly from the fourth and fifth columns of Table 35.2. (Note the "most accurate" values given by a computer: $ss_{\text{reg}} = 83.3909$ and $ss_{\text{res}} = 81.6091$, which of course total to $ss_t = \Sigma y^2 = 165.0$.)

The Multiple Correlation Coefficient

If the ordinary product-moment coefficient of correlation between the predicted values, Y', and the observed values of Y are calculated, we obtain an index of the magnitude of the relation between, on the one hand, a least-squares composite of X_1 and X_2, and, on the other hand, Y. This index is called the *multiple correlation coefficient*, R. Although in this chapter it is usually written as R for the sake of brevity, a more satisfactory way to write it is with subscripts: $R_{y.12\ldots k}$, or, in this case, $R_{y.12}$. The theory of multiple regression seems to be especially elegant when we consider the multiple correlation coefficient. It is one of the links that bind together the various aspects of multiple regression and analysis of variance. The formula for R that expresses the first sentence of this paragraph is:

$$R = \frac{\Sigma yy'}{\sqrt{\Sigma y^2 \Sigma y'^2}} \tag{35.12}$$

Its square is calculated:

$$R^2 = \frac{(\Sigma yy')^2}{\Sigma y^2 \Sigma y'^2} \tag{35.13}$$

Using the Y and Y' values of Table 35.2, we obtain: $R^2 = .5054$ and $R = \sqrt{.5054} = .7109$.[11]

R, then, is the highest possible correlation between a least-squares linear composite of the independent variables and the observed dependent variable. R^2, analogous to r^2, indicates that portion of the variance of the dependent variable, Y, due to the independent variables in concert. R, unlike r, varies only from 0 to 1.00; it does not have negative values.

Two other important conclusions can be reached by calculating the correlations of the residuals, d_i, of Table 35.2, with X_1 and X_2, on the one hand, and with Y, on the other hand. The correlations of the residuals with X_1 and X_2 are both zero. This is not surprising when it is realized that, by definition, the residuals are that part of Y not accounted for by X_1 and X_2. That is, when the Y' values are subtracted from the Y values, that portion due to the regression of Y on X_1 and X_2 is taken from them. Whatever is left over, then, is unrelated to either X_1 or X_2. (If the student will take the trouble to calculate the correlation between the d vector—a vector is a single set of measures, either in a column or a row—and either the X_1 or the X_2 vector, he will convince himself of this fact.) An important research implication of this generalization will be discussed later when actual research examples are summarized and discussed.

The correlation of the residuals, d_i, of Table 35.2 with the original Y values also helps to clarify matters. This correlation is: $r_{dy} = .7033$, and its square is: $r_{dy}{}^2 = (.7033)^2 = .4946$. If this latter value is added to the R^2 calculated earlier, the result is interesting: $R^2 + r_{dy}{}^2 = .5054 + .4946 = 1.0000$. And this will always be true. The total variance of Y is represented by 1.0000. The variance of Y due to Y's regression on X_1 and X_2 is .5054. The variance of Y not due to the regression of Y on X_1 and X_2 can be calculated: $1.0000 - .5054 = .4946$, which is, of course, the value of $r_{dy}{}^2$ just calculated directly. The meaning of $r_{dy}{}^2$ can be seen in two ways. The direct calculation of the correlation shows that the residuals constitute that part of the variance of Y not due to the regression of Y on X_1 and X_2. In the present case, 51 percent ($R^2 = .51$) of the variance of the reading

[11]Calculating these values is a good exercise. We already have $\Sigma y^2 = 165$. Then calculate:

$$\Sigma y'^2 = \Sigma Y'^2 - \frac{(\Sigma Y')^2}{N} = 688.3969 - \frac{(110)^2}{20} = 83.3969$$

and

$$\Sigma yy' = \Sigma YY' - \frac{(\Sigma Y)(\Sigma Y')}{N} = 688.3939 - \frac{(110)(110)}{20} = 83.3939$$

It can be shown algebraically that $\Sigma y'^2$ equals $\Sigma yy'$. The difference of .003 is due to rounding errors.

achievement (Y) of the 20 pupils is accounted for by a least-squares linear combination of verbal aptitude (X_1) and achievement motivation (X_2). But 49 percent of the variance is due to other variables and to error. After discussing more usual ways to calculate R and R^2, we will again consider the proportion or percentage interpretation of R^2.

In sum, R^2 is an estimate of the proportion of the variance of the dependent variable, Y, accounted for by the independent variables, X_j. R, the multiple correlation coefficient, is the product-moment correlation between the dependent variable and another variable produced by a least-squares combination of the independent variables. Its square is interpreted analogously to the square of an ordinary correlation coefficient. It differs from the ordinary coefficient, however, in taking values only from 0 to 1. R is not as useful and interpretable as R^2, and henceforth R^2 will be used almost exclusively in subsequent discussion.

The proportion or percentage interpretation of R^2 becomes clearer if a sum of squares formula is used:

$$R^2 = \frac{ss_{\text{reg}}}{ss_t} \tag{35.14}$$

where ss_t is, as usual, the total sum of squares of Y, or Σy_t^2. Substituting the regression sum of squares calculated earlier by formula 35.10, and the total sum of squares from Table 35.3, we obtain:

$$R^2 = \frac{83.3912}{165.0000} = .5054$$

And R^2 is seen to be that part of the Y sum of squares associated with the regression of Y on the independent variables. As with all proportions, multiplying it by 100 converts it to a percentage.

Formula 35.14 provides another link to the analysis of variance. In Chapter 13 on the foundations of analysis of variance, a formula for calculating E, the so-called correlation ratio, was given (Formula 13.4). Square that formula:

$$E^2 = \frac{ss_b}{ss_t}$$

where ss_b = the between-groups sum of squares, and ss_t = total sum of squares. ss_b is the sum of squares due to the independent variable. ss_{reg} is the sum of squares due to regression. Both terms refer to the sum of squares of a dependent variable due to an independent variable or to independent variables.[12]

[12]It should be noted that R and R^2 can be and are often inflated. Therefore, R^2 should be interpreted conservatively. If the sample is large, say over 200, there is little cause for concern. If the sample is small, however, it is wise to reduce the calculated R^2 by a few points. A so-called shrinkage formula can be used:

$$R_c^2 = 1 - (1 - R^2)\left(\frac{N-1}{N-n}\right)$$

where R_c^2 = shrunken or corrected R^2; N = size of sample; n = total number of variables in the analysis. Using this formula, the R^2 in the example reduces to .45.

Tests of Significance

Earlier in this chapter we learned how to test the statistical significance of the regression of Y on X, or, what amounted to the same thing, the statistical significance of r_{xy}^2. (See Eq. 35.5 and the accompanying discussion.) Tests of statistical significance in multiple regression, though more complex computationally, are based on the same relatively simple idea of comparing variances (or mean squares). The same questions asked many times before must be asked again: Can this R^2 have arisen by chance? Or does it depart sufficiently from chance expectation that it can be said to be "significant"? Similar questions can be asked about individual regression coefficients. In this chapter and the next, F tests will be used almost exclusively. They fit in nicely with both regression analysis and analysis of variance, and they are both conceptually and computationally simple.[13]

Take the example of Tables 35.2 and 35.3 again. Is the R^2 of .5054 statistically significant? An F test can be done in two ways. One, Eq. 35.5 used earlier for simple regression is available:

$$F = \frac{ss_{\text{reg}}/df_1}{ss_{\text{res}}/df_2}$$

If df_1 and df_2, the degrees of freedom for the numerator and the denominator of the F ratio, are defined, a formula to test the significance of any multiple regression problem emerges:

$$F = \frac{ss_{\text{reg}}/k}{ss_{\text{res}}/(N-k-1)} \qquad (35.15)$$

where k = the number of independent variables, and N = the sample size. Using the values calculated earlier for the example of Table 35.2, now calculate:

$$F = \frac{83.3912/2}{81.6091/(20-2-1)} = \frac{41.6956}{4.8005} = 8.686$$

Note that the idea expressed by this formula is in the same family of ideas as analysis of variance. The numerator is the mean square due to the regression, analogous to the between-groups mean square, and the denominator is the mean square *not* due to regression, which is used as an error term, analogous to the within-groups mean square, or error variance. The basic principle, again, is always the same: variance due to the regression of Y on $X_1, X_2, \ldots X_k$, or, in analysis of variance, due to the experimental effects, is evaluated against variance presumably due to error or chance. This basic notion, elaborated at length in earlier chapters, can be expressed:

$$\frac{\text{regression variance}}{\text{error variance}} : \frac{\text{experimental variance}}{\text{error variance}}$$

[13]Consideration of t tests of regression coefficients must be omitted because they require matrix algebra calculations beyond our reach. A t test of a regression coefficient, if significant, indicates that the regression weight differs significantly from zero, which means that the variable with which it is associated contributes significantly to the regression, the other independent variables being taken into account.

Another formula for F is:

$$F = \frac{R^2/k}{(1-R^2)/(N-k-1)} \tag{35.16}$$

where k and N are the same as above. For the same example:

$$F = \frac{.5054/2}{(1-.5054)/(20-2-1)} = \frac{.2527}{.0291} = 8.684$$

which is the same as the F value obtained with Eq. 35.15, within errors of rounding. At 2 and 17 degrees of freedom, it is significant at the .01 level. This formula is particularly useful when our research data are only in the form of correlation coefficients. In such a case, the sums of squares required by Eq. 35.15 may not be known. Much regression analysis can be done using only the matrix of correlations among all the variables, independent and dependent. Such analysis is beyond the scope of this book. Nevertheless, the student of research should be aware of the possibility.

Interpretation of Multiple Regression Statistics

The interpretation of multiple regression statistics can be approached in several ways. In order to emphasize and reinforce points already made and to bring out certain new points, we use two or three of these ways.

Plot of Y′ and Y

The predicted Y values, Y', calculated with the regression equation, are a composite of the weighted X values, the weights being chosen to give the best prediction. "Best prediction" means in the least-squares sense: the weights, b, are so calculated that the sum of the squared deviations of $Y - Y'$ is a minimum. To show this graphically the Y' and Y points of Table 35.2 have been plotted in Fig. 35.2. The only difference between this plot and an ordinary plot of a Y against an X is that the present independent variable, Y', is a regression of Y on X_1 and X_2 instead of on a single X.

$R_{y.12} = R_{y'y} = .71$, a fairly substantial correlation. Thus the plotted points of Y' and Y can be expected to lie fairly close to the regression line, which has been drawn through the fixed constant ($a = .1027$) and the point of intersection of the means of Y' and Y (5.50 and 5.50). For the most part they do. $R_{y.12} = .71$ expresses symbolically and quantitatively what the plot expresses graphically. To the extent that the plotted points lie near the regression line, the magnitude of R is high.

Although using and reporting regression plots in this manner is not common practice in education, sociology, and psychology, it probably should be. Not only can the relation be studied in detail; specific features of the data can be singled out for special attention. Deviant cases, for example, may help lead to better explanations and hypotheses. Why is this case deviant? Possible answers can lead to further research, theoretical clarification, and better solutions to research problems.

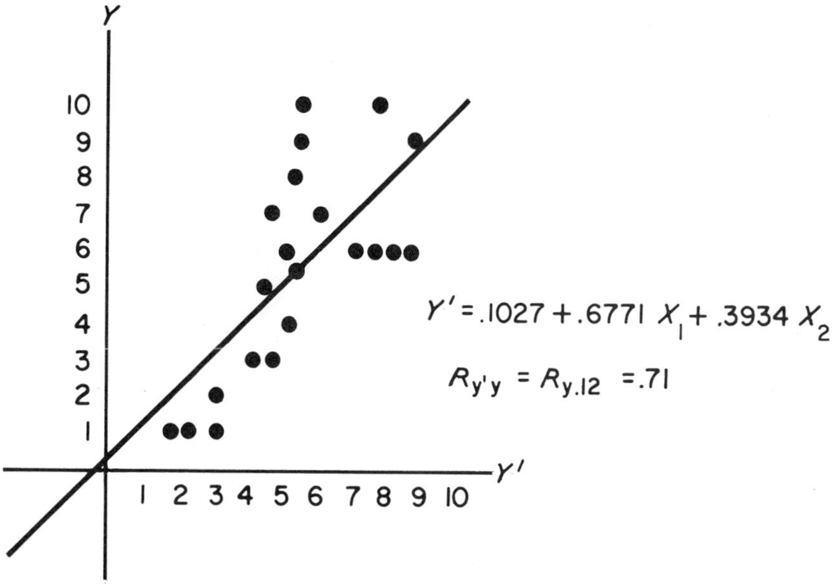

Fig. 35.2

Statistical Significance of the Regression and R^2

The F ratio of 8.684 calculated above tells us that the regression of Y on X_1 and X_2, expressed by $R^2_{y.12}$, is statistically significant. The probability that an F ratio this large will occur by chance is less than .01 (it is actually about .003), which means that the relation between Y and a least-squares combination of X_1 and X_2 could probably not have occurred by chance.

$R = .71$ can be interpreted much like an ordinary coefficient of correlation, except that the values of R range from 0 to 1.00, unlike r, which ranges from -1.00 through 0 to 1.00. $R^2 = .71^2 = .51$ is more meaningful and useful, however. It means that 51 percent of the variance of Y is accounted for, or "determined," by X_1 and X_2 in combination. It is accordingly called a *coefficient of determination.*

Relative Contributions to Y of the X's

Let us ask, somewhat diffidently, a more difficult question: What are the relative contributions of X_1 and X_2, of verbal aptitude and achievement motivation, to Y, reading achievement? The restricted scope of this book does not permit an examination of the answers to this question in the detail it deserves.[14]

[14]The problem of the relative contribution of independent variables to a dependent variable or variables is one of the most complex and difficult of regression analysis. It seems that no really satisfactory solution exists, at least when the independent variables are correlated. Nevertheless, the problem cannot be neglected. The reader should bear in mind, however, that considerable reservation must be attached to the above and later discussions. The technical and substantive problems of interpretation of multiple regression analysis are discussed in two or three of the references given in Study Suggestion 1 at the end of the next chapter.

One would think that the regression weights, b or β, would provide us with a ready means of identifying the relative contributions of independent variables to a dependent variable. And they do, but only roughly and sometimes misleadingly. Earlier it was said that the regression coefficient b is called the *slope*. The slope of the regression line is at the rate of b units of Y for one unit of X. In the little problem A of Table 35.1, for instance, $b = .90$. Thus, as said earlier, with a change of 1 unit in X we predict a change of .90 in Y. In multiple regression, however, straightforward interpretation like this is not so easy because there is more than one b. Nevertheless, we can say, *for present pedagogical purposes*, that if X_1 and X_2 have about the same scale of values—in the example of Table 35.2, the values of X_1 and X_2 are in the approximate range of 1 to 10—the b's are weights that show roughly the relative importance of X_1 and X_2. In the present case, the regression formula is:

$$Y' = .1027 + .6771X_1 + .3934X_2$$

We can say that X_1, verbal aptitude, is weighted more heavily than X_2, achievement motivation. This happens to be true in this case, but it may not always be true, especially with more independent variables.

Regression coefficients, unfortunately for interpretative purposes, are not stable. They change with different samples and with addition or subtraction of independent variables to the analysis.[15] There is no absolute way to interpret them. If the correlations among the independent variables are all zero or near-zero, interpretation is greatly simplified. But many or most variables that are correlated with a dependent variable are also correlated among themselves. The example of Table 35.3 shows this: the correlation between X_1 and X_2 is .26, a modest correlation, to be sure. Such intercorrelations are often higher, however. And the higher they are, the more unstable the interpretation situation.

The ideal predictive situation is when the correlations between the independent variables and the dependent variable are high, and the correlations among the independent variables are low. This principle, commonly cited in statistics and measurement texts, is most important. The more the independent variables are intercorrelated, the more difficult the interpretation. Among other things, one has greater difficulty telling the relative influence on the dependent variable of the independent variables. Examine the two fictitious correlation matrices of Table 35.4 and the accompanying R^2's. In the two matrices, the independent variables, X_1 and X_2, are correlated .87 and .43, respectively, with the dependent variable, Y. But the correlations between the independent variables are different in the two cases. In matrix A, $r_{12} = .50$, a substantial correlation. In matrix B, however, $r_{12} = 0$.

The contrast between the R^2's is dramatic: .76 for A and .94 for B. Since, in B, X_1 and X_2 are not correlated, any correlations they have with Y contribute to the prediction and the R^2.[16] When the independent variables are correlated, as in

[15]See R. Darlington, "Multiple Regression in Psychological Research and Practice," *Psychological Bulletin*, LXIX (1968), 161–182; R. Gordon, "Issues in Multiple Regression," *American Journal of Sociology*, LXXIII (1968), 592–616.

TABLE **35.4** MULTIPLE REGRESSION EXAMPLES WITH AND WITHOUT CORRELATIONS BETWEEN INDEPENDENT VARIABLES

A			*B*		
1	2	*Y*	1	2	*Y*
1.00	.50	.87	1.00	0	.87
.50	1.00	.43	0	1.00	.43
.87	.43	1.00	.87	.43	1.00
$R^2_{y.12} = .76$			$R^2_{y.12} = .94$		

matrix A ($r_{12} = .50$), some of the common variance of Y and X_1 is also shared with X_2. In short, X_1 and X_2 are to some extent redundant in predicting Y. In matrix B there is no such redundancy.

The situation is clarified, perhaps, by Fig. 35.3. Let the circles stand for the total variance of Y, and let this total variance be 1.00. Then the portions of the variance of Y accounted for by X_1 and X_2 can be depicted. In both circles, the horizontal hatching indicates the variance accounted for by X_1, or V_{X_1}, and the vertical hatching X_2, or V_{X_2}. (The variances remaining after V_{X_1} and V_{X_2} are the residual

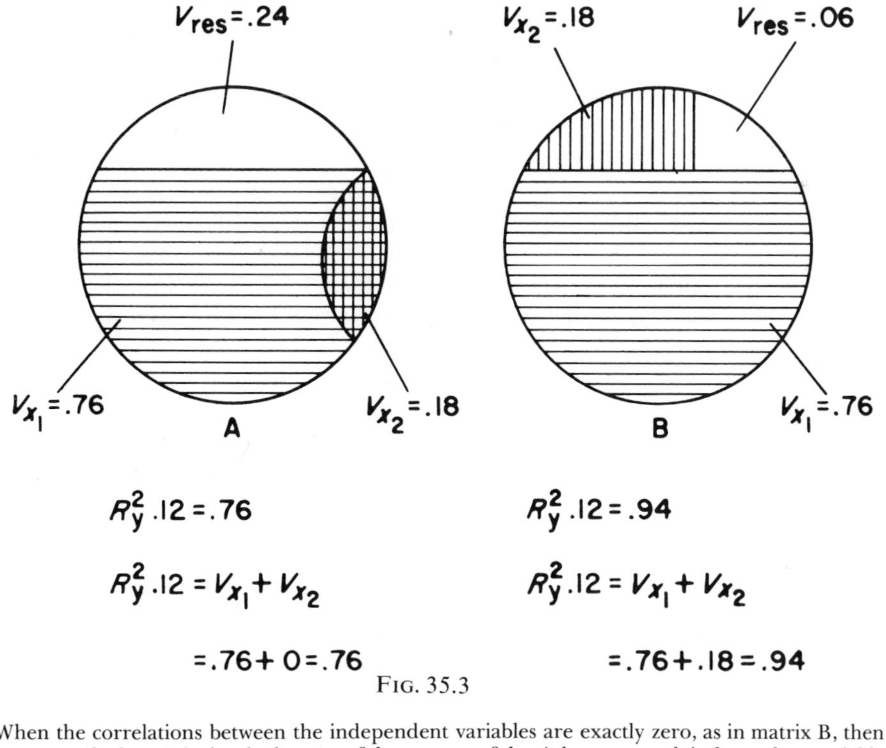

FIG. 35.3

[16]When the correlations between the independent variables are exactly zero, as in matrix B, then R^2 is easy to calculate. It is simply the sum of the squares of the r's between each independent variable and the dependent variable: $(.87)^2 + (.43)^2 = .94$.

variances, labeled V_{res} in the figure.) In B, V_{X_1} and V_{X_2} do not overlap, or in set language, $V_{X_1} \cap V_{X_2} = E$, where E indicates the empty set. In A, however, V_{X_1} and V_{X_2} overlap, or $V_{X_1} \cap V_{X_2} \neq E$. Simply because $r_{12} = 0$ in B and $r_{12} = .50$ in A, the predictive power of the independent variables is much greater in B than in A. This is, of course, reflected by the R^2's: .76 in A and .94 in B.

While this is a contrived and artificial example, it has the virtue of showing the effect of correlation between the independent variables, and thus it illustrates the principle enunciated above. It also reflects the difficulty of interpreting the results of most regression analysis, since in much research the independent variables are correlated. And when more independent variables are added, interpretation becomes still more complex and difficult. A central problem is: How does one sort out the relative effects of the different X's on Y? The answer is also complex. There are ways of doing so, some more satisfying than others, but none completely satisfactory.[17]

Other Analytic and Interpretative Problems

A number of problems in multiple regression analysis cannot in this book be discussed in the detail they deserve. Two or three, however, must be mentioned because of the increasing importance of multiple regression in behavioral research. One, mentioned earlier, is the problem of regression weights. In this chapter and the next, the discussion has been confined to b weights, because in most research uses of regression we predict with raw or deviation scores, and b's are used with such scores. So-called beta, or β, weights, on the other hand, are used with standard scores. They are called *standard partial regression coefficients.* "Standard" means that they would be used if all variables were in standard-score form. "Partial" means that the effects of variables other than the one to which the weight applies are held constant. For example, $\beta_{y1.23}$, or β_1 in a three-variable (independent variable) problem, is the standard partial regression weight, which expresses the change in Y due to change in X_1, with variables 2 and 3 held con-

[17]Perhaps the most satisfactory way, at least in the author's opinion and experience, is to calculate so-called squared semipartial correlations (also called part correlations). These are calculated with the formula:

$$SP^2 = R^2_{y.12\ldots k} - R^2_{y.12\ldots(k-1)}$$

or in the present case, for B:

$$SP^2 = R^2_{y.12} - R^2_{y.1} = .94 - .76 = .18$$

which indicates the contribution to the variance of Y of X_2, after X_1 has been taken into account. The same calculation for A yields: $.76 - .76 = 0$, which indicates that X_2 contributes nothing to the variance of Y, after X_1 has been taken into account. (Actually, there is a slight increase that emerges only with a large number of decimal places.)

The student is referred to the articles by Darlington and Gordon cited earlier for discussions of the problems involved. Kerlinger and Pedhazur also discuss the problem in considerable detail and relate it to research examples: F. Kerlinger and E. Pedhazur, *Multiple Regression in Behavioral Research.* New York: Holt, Rinehart and Winston, 1973 (in press).

stant.[18] The b weights, too, are partial regression coefficients, but they are not in standard form.

Another problem is that in any given regression, R, R^2, and the regression weights will be the same no matter what the order of the variables. If one or more variables are added or subtracted from the regression, however, these values will change. And regression weights can change from sample to sample. In other words, there is no absolute quality about them. One cannot say, for instance, that because verbal and numerical aptitudes have, say, regression weights of .60 and .50 in one set of data, they will have the same values in another set.

Another important point is that there usually is limited usefulness to adding new variables to a regression equation. Because many variables of behavioral research are correlated, the principle illustrated by the data of Table 35.4 and discussed earlier operates so as to decrease the usefulness of additional variables. If one finds three or four independent variables that are substantially correlated with a dependent variable and not highly correlated with each other, one is lucky. But it becomes more and more difficult to find other independent variables that are not in effect redundant with the first three or four. If $R^2_{y.123} = .50$, then it is unlikely that $R^2_{y.1234}$ will be much more than .55, and $R^2_{y.12345}$ will probably not be more than .56 or .57. We have a regression law of diminishing returns, which will be illustrated in the next section when actual research results are discussed.[19]

It was said above that R, R^2, and the regression coefficients remain the same, if the same variables are entered in different orders. This should not be taken to mean, however, that the order in which variables enter the regression equation does not matter. On the contrary, order of entry can be very important. When the independent variables are correlated, the relative amount of variance of the dependent variable that each independent variable accounts for or contributes can change drastically with different orders of entry of the variables. With the A data of Table 35.4, for example, if we reverse the order of X_1 and X_2, their relative contributions change rather markedly. With the original order, X_2 contributed

[18]A second meaning, used in theoretical work, is that β is the population regression weight which b estimates. We omit this meaning. β's can be translated into b's with the formula:

$$b_j = \beta_j \frac{s_y}{s_j}$$

where s_y = standard deviation of Y and s_j = standard deviation of variable j.

[19]When independent variables are added, one notes how much they add to R^2 and tests their statistical significance. The formula for doing so, much like formula 35.16, is:

$$F = \frac{(R^2_{y.12\ldots k_1} - R^2_{y.12\ldots k_2})/(k_1 - k_2)}{(1 - R^2_{y.12\ldots k_1})/(N - k_1 - 1)}$$

where k_1 = number of independent variables of the larger R^2, k_2 = number of independent variables of the smaller R^2, and N = number of cases. This formula will be used later. Although an F calculated like this may be statistically significant, especially with a large sample, the actual increase in R^2 may be quite small. In an example presented later in the chapter (Layton and Swanson's study), the addition of a sixth independent variable yielded a statistically significant F ratio, but the actual increase in R^2 was .0147! The difference between the R^2's in the numerator is the squared semipartial correlation coefficient mentioned in footnote 17.

nothing to R^2, whereas with the order reversed X_2 becomes X_1 and contributes 19 percent $[r^2 = (.43)^2 = .19)]$ to the total R^2, and the original X_1, which becomes X_2, contributes 57 percent $(.19 + .57 = .76)$. The order of variables, while making no difference in the final R^2 and thus in overall prediction, is a major research problem.

Research Examples

The examples used in this section to illustrate multiple regression analysis in research have been chosen to give the student insight into regression thinking, to illustrate certain technical points, and to show the breadth of application of the approach and method.

It has been fairly well known for many years that level of aspiration is related to academic achievement. In a study of this relation, Worell thought that the more realistic an individual's level of aspiration, the more academically successful he will be.[20] Level of aspiration was measured by asking students certain questions about their study habits and grades. Four such measures were used. Two other predictive variables were scholastic aptitude and high school achievement. Of Worell's two dependent variables, only total grade-point average is considered here. An important question to ask is: Does adding the level-of-aspiration measures to scholastic aptitude and high school achievement improve the prediction?

The results were striking. They even seem to contradict the principle stated earlier about the decreasing utility of adding variables to regression equations. Among college sophomores ($N = 99$), the regression of GPA on scholastic aptitude and high school achievement was expressed by $R = .43$. When Worell added his four level-of-aspiration measures to the regression. R leaped to .85! (The student should ask himself why the R increased this much.) The addition of four noncognitive measures to the two more conventional measures resulted in an increase in predictive efficiency of .54 percent $(.85^2 - .43^2 = .72 - .18 = .54)$. This appears to be one of the largest reported increases in R^2 obtained by adding independent variables to other independent variables.

We take the data of a relatively simple study to show in some detail the importance of the order of entry of independent variables. Layton and Swanson used the subtests of the Differential Aptitude Test to predict rank in high school.[21] Using the correlation matrix that Layton and Swanson calculated among the six DAT subtests and high school rank (628 boys in 27 schools), three different orders of entry were used in multiple regression analyses.

To simplify matters, we report only the results with the first four of the six

[20] L. Worell, "Level of Aspiration and Academic Success," *Journal of Educational Psychology*, L (1959), 47–54.

[21] W. Layton and E. Swanson, "Relationship of Ninth Grade Differential Aptitude Test Scores to Eleventh Grade Test Scores and High School Rank," *Journal of Educational Psychology*, XLIX (1958), 153–155. Layton and Swanson also used two other measures which are ignored here. The multiple regression analysis reported above was done by the author.

DAT subtests: Verbal Reasoning (VR), Numerical Aptitude (NA), Abstract Reasoning (AR), and Space Relations (SR). And we report only the R^2's of the first variable entered and the differences between the successive R^2's—that is $R^2_{y.1}$, $R^2_{y.12}-R^2_{y.1}$, $R^2_{y.123}-R^2_{y.12}$, and $R^2_{y.1234}-R^2_{y.123}$. These differences show the contributions, respectively, of X_1 alone, of X_2 after subtracting the effect of X_1, of X_3 after subtracting the effect of X_1 and X_2, and, finally, of X_4 after subtracting the effect of X_1, X_2, and X_3. These indices are squared semipartial (part) correlations (see footnotes 17 and 19). They can be interpreted, with circumspection, as indices of the variance contributions of each of the variables—in that particular order.

The squared semipartial correlations, which are percentages of the total variance (with the particular order of entry of the variables), are given in Table 35.5. The differences are pronounced. VR, for instance, which accounts for 31 percent of the total variance (with all six independent variables) in the first order

TABLE **35.5** SQUARED SEMIPARTIAL CORRELATIONS WITH DIFFERENT ORDERS OF ENTRY OF VARIABLES, DIFFERENTIAL APTITUDE TESTS AND HIGH SCHOOL RANKS, LAYTON AND SWANSON STUDY[a]

Order 1:	VR .31	NA .07	AR .00	SR .00
Order 2:	AR .20	VR .13	NA .05	SR .00
Order 3:	SR .13	AR .09	NA .12	VR .05

[a]VR: Verbal Reasoning; NA: Numerical Ability; AR: Abstract Reasoning; SR: Space Relations. $R^2 = .41$ (for six variables).

of entry, accounts for only 5 percent in the third order. AR, which accounts for almost none of the variance in the first order when it is the third independent variable, jumps to 20 percent in the second order when it is the first independent variable. Obviously, the order of entry of variables in the regression equation is highly important. The reader should note other similar differences—for example, VR.

If the reader feels a bit baffled by the problem of the order of entry of variables, he can hardly be blamed. Indeed, he has company among experts in the field. Actually, there is no "correct" method for determining the order of variables. A researcher may decide that he will let the computer choose the variables in order of the size of their contributions to the variance of Y. For some problems this may be satisfactory; for others, it may not. As always, there is no substitute for depth of knowledge of the research problem and concomitant knowledge and use of the theory behind the problem. In other words, the research problem and the theory behind the problem should determine the order of entry of variables in multiple regression analysis.

In one problem, for instance, intelligence may be a variable that is conceived as acting in concert with other variables, compensatory methods and social class, say, to produce changes in verbal achievement. Intelligence would then probably enter the equation after compensatory methods and before (or after) social class. A researcher doing this would be influenced by the notion of interaction: the compensatory methods differ in their effects at different levels of intelligence. Suppose, however, that the researcher wants only to control intelligence, to eliminate its influence on verbal achievement. The theory underlying his reasoning may say nothing about an interaction between intelligence and other variables. But the researcher *knows* that it will certainly influence verbal achievement and he wants its influence eliminated *before* the effects of compensatory education and social class are assessed. In this case he would treat intelligence as a covariate and enter it into the regression equation first.

Earlier in this book it was said: "Design is data discipline." The design of research and the analysis of data spring from the demands of research problems. Again, the order of entry of independent variables into the regression equation is determined by the research problem and the design of the research, which is itself determined by the research problem.

Although the order of entry of variables and the changes in regression weights that can occur with different samples are difficult problems, one must remember that regression weights do not change with different orders of entry. This is a real compensation, especially useful in prediction. In many research problems, for example, the relative contribution of variables is not a major consideration. In such cases, one wants the total regression equation and its regression weights mainly for prediction and for assessing the general nature of the regression situation.

The next three studies to be cited illustrate special important and useful techniques that can be used with multiple regression analysis. The first of these used residual scores, or $d = Y - Y'$. Recall that a predicted score, Y', is a weighted linear composite of the independent variables, X_j. The predicted Y's, in other words, express whatever sources of variance in Y are due to the X's. Therefore, if they are subtracted from the Y's, the remainders, or residuals, should express sources of variance *other* than those due to the X's. Thistlethwaite and Wheeler, in a highly sophisticated study, developed multiple regression equations to predict the dispositions of college students to seek advanced training.[22] Thus the predicted Y's, or Y_i', were a linear composite of independent variables that best predicted dispositions of students to go into advanced studies after graduation. If so, then the d's $(Y - Y')$, which in effect constitute another variable, should represent *changes* in dispositions to seek advanced study. Thistlethwaite and Wheeler used these residuals as a measure of these changes in disposition. While there can be doubt that the residuals do in fact measure change in disposition, there is little doubt of the ingenuity and depth of these researchers' thinking.

As an illustration of an entirely different kind of research and data and of the effect of high correlations among independent variables—and thus high redundancy of predictors—consider a study of regression of political development (of 77 nations), Y, on communication, X_1, urbanization, X_2, education, X_3, and agriculture, X_4.[23] The lowest r between independent variables was .69 and the highest

[22]D. Thistlethwaite and N. Wheeler, "Effects of Teacher and Peer Subcultures Upon Student Aspirations," *Journal of Educational Psychology*, LVII (1966), 35–47. More advanced students will find careful study of this research profitable.

[23]P. Cutright, "National Political Development: Measurement and Analysis," *American Sociological Review*, XXVII (1963), 229–245. Although Cutright supplied regression statistics, I calculated the R^2's reported above. The student can profit from studying Cutright's solutions to interesting measurement problems.

.88. There is obviously considerable redundancy. This is clearly shown by calculating $R^2_{y.1}$, $R^2_{y.12}$, $R^2_{y.123}$, and $R^2_{y.1234}$. They are: .66, .67, .67, .67! Efficiency of prediction is as good with one independent variable, X_1, as it is with all four independent variables!

We will examine the last example in more depth because it is interesting and instructive and because it comes from what is perhaps the most important single and massive educational study of three decades, *Equality of Educational Opportunity*.[24] One of the basic purposes of the study was to explain school achievement, or rather, inequality in school achievement. Multiple regression analysis was used in a complex manner to help do this. The researchers chose as one of their most important dependent variable measures verbal ability or skill (VA). Some 60 independent variable measures were correlated with VA. From the many correlations reported by the authors, several were selected from those for the total Northern white and Negro samples (in Appendix 9.10), and multiple regression analyses were done.

Five independent variables were chosen to predict to VA because of their presumed importance. They are listed in the footnote of Table 35.6. The R^2's, beta weights, β, and the squared semipartial correlations (SP^2) of the regression analysis of two samples of more than 100,000 each of Northern white and Northern Negro twelfth-grade pupils are given in Table 35.6. In addition to the comparisons between the white and Negro sample results, the variables have been entered into the regression equation in three different orders of entry. The R^2's and the β's for the three orders, of course, are the same, since changing the order does not change R^2 and the β's, as we learned earlier.

Most of the variance of verbal ability appears to be due to Self Concept, a measure constructed from three questions, the answers to which reveal how the pupil perceives himself (e.g., "I sometimes feel that I just can't learn"). Study the SP^2's and see that this is true in all orders of entry for whites (.214, .139, .218). It is less true for Negroes (.111, .063, .120). The only other variable that accounts for a substantial amount of variance ($\geqslant .10$) is Control of Environment, CE, which is another variable involving the concept of self and adding the notion of control over one's fate. Here whites and Negroes are similar, except that CE appears to be somewhat weightier for Negroes.

One of the most interesting comparisons is that between kinds of variables. SC and CE are both "subjective" variables: the pupil projects his own image. The other variables are "objective": they are external to the pupil; they are part of the objective environment, so to speak. This was an important finding of the whole study. Where things like tracking (homogeneous grouping) and school facilities accounted for little of the variance in achievement, the so-called attitude variables, two of which are SC and CE, accounted for more variance for both white and Negro pupils than any other variables in the study.[25]

[24] J. Coleman et al., *Equality of Educational Opportunity*. Washington, D.C.: Dept. of Health, Education, and Welfare, Office of Education (U.S. Govt. Printing Office), 1966.

[25] *Ibid.*, pp. 319–325. The beta weights in Table 35.6 bear careful study. Since they were calculated from very large samples, they are less likely to be unstable. And they accurately reflect the relative importance of the five variables. The contrast between whites and Negroes on self-concept is particularly interesting. See *ibid.*, p. 321, Table 3.26.1.

TABLE **35.6** MULTIPLE REGRESSION ANALYSIS: R^2'S, BETA WEIGHTS, AND SQUARED SEMIPARTIAL CORRELATIONS, SELECTED VARIABLES FROM *EQUALITY OF EDUCATIONAL OPPORTUNITY*

	VAT[a]	PPE	SC	PW	CE	R^2
White:						
β	.033	.074	.396	.069	.198	
SP^2	.001	.007	.214	.006	.034	.262
Negro:						
β	.079	−.019	.265	.161	.277	
SP^2	.016	.000	.111	.020	.070	.217
	CE	PW	SC	PPE	VAT	
White:						
β	.198	.069	.396	.074	.033	
SP^2	.114	.003	.139	.005	.001	.262
Negro:						
β	.277	.161	.265	−.019	.079	
SP^2	.120	.028	.063	.000	.005	.217
	PW	SC	CE	PPE	VAT	
White:						
β	.069	.396	.198	.074	.033	
SP^2	.004	.218	.035	.005	.001	.262
Negro:						
β	.161	.265	.277	−.019	.079	
SP^2	.021	.120	.070	.000	.005	.217

[a]VAT: Verbal Ability, Teacher; PPE: Per Pupil Expenditure; SC: Self Concept; PW: Proportion White; CE: Control of Environment.

Multiple Regression Analysis and Scientific Research[26]

Multiple regression is close to the heart of scientific investigation. It is also fundamental in statistics and inference, and is tightly tied to basic and powerful mathematical methods. From the researcher's point of view, moreover, it is useful and practical: it does its analytic job successfully and efficiently. In explaining these strong and sweeping statements, it may be possible to clarify what we have already learned.

The scientist is concerned, basically, with propositions of the "If p, then q" kind. Such propositions "explain" phenomena. When we say, "If positive incentive, then higher achievement," we are to some extent "explaining" achievement. But this is hardly enough. Even if supported by a good deal of empirical evidence,

[26]Some of the material in this section was published in my essay, "Research in Education," in R. Ebel, V. Noll, and R. Bauer, eds., *Encyclopedia of Educational Research*, 4th ed. New York: Macmillan, 1969, pp. 1127–1144. Note that whenever the expression "If p, then q" appears, it should be taken to mean "If p, then *probably* q.

it does not go very far in explaining achievement. In addition to other if-then statements of a similar kind, the scientist must ask more complex questions. He may ask, for example, under what conditions the statement, "If positive incentive, then higher achievement," is valid. Is it true of black children as well as white children? Is it true of children of both lower and higher intelligence? To test such statements and to advance knowledge, scientists in effect write statements of the kind, If p, then q, under conditions r, s, and t, where p is an independent variable, q a dependent variable, and r, s, and t other independent variables. Other kinds of statements can, of course, be written—e.g., If p and r, then q. In such a case p and r are two independent variables, both of which are required for q.

The point of all this is that multiple regression can successfully handle such cases. In most behavioral research there is usually one dependent variable, though we are theoretically not restricted to only one. Consequently, multiple regression is a general method of analyzing much behavioral research data. Certain other methods of analysis can be considered special cases of multiple regression. The most prominent is analysis of variance, all types of which can be conceptualized and accomplished with multiple regression analysis.

It was said earlier that all control is control of variance. Multiple regression analysis can be conceived as a refined and powerful method of "controlling" variance. It accomplishes this the same way analysis of variance does: by estimating the magnitudes of different sources of influence on Y, different sources of variance of Y, through analysis of the interrelations of all the variables. It tells how much of Y is presumably due to $X_1, X_2, \ldots, X_k$. It gives some idea of the relative amounts of influence of the X's. And it furnishes tests of the statistical significance of combined influences of X's on Y and of the separate influence of each X. In short, multiple regression analysis is an efficient and powerful hypothesis-testing and inference-making technique, since it helps the scientist study, with relative precision, complex interrelations between independent variables and a dependent variable, and thus helps him to "explain" the presumed phenomenon represented by the dependent variable.[27]

[27]Study suggestions for this chapter are given at the end of the next chapter.

CHAPTER 36

Multiple Regression, Analysis of Variance, and Other Multivariate Methods

Close examination shows the conceptual bases underlying different approaches to data analysis to be the same or similar. The symmetry of the fundamental ideas has great aesthetic appeal, and is nowhere more interesting and appealing than in multiple regression and analysis of variance. Earlier, in discussing the foundations of analysis of variance, the similarity of the principles and structures of analysis of variance and so-called correlational methods was brought out. We now link the two approaches to research data.

Our task will be easier if we remember some set theory and put it to work. Relations, which is what science is mostly concerned with, are sets of ordered pairs. In analysis of variance the sets of ordered pairs are those between measures of a dependent variable Y and other "measures" indicating experimental treatments. In regression the sets of ordered pairs are those between the measures of a dependent variable Y and a composite measure derived from one or more independent variables. The independent variable measures can be continuous or categorical (nominal). So can the dependent variable measures. Figure 36.1 may help make these ideas clear. The diagram on the left is meant to indicate the set of pairs of dependent variable (Y) measures with independent variable treatments (A_j). A_1, A_2, and A_3 indicate, say, three methods of teaching reading, and $Y_1, Y_2, \ldots$ are reading achievement scores. The diagram on the right, labeled B, merely indicates the usual set of ordered pairs of independent and dependent variables—the X's are measures of religious attitudes, say, and the Y's measures of educational values. The X's can also be 1's and 0's or some other system of numerals. In multiple regression, the X's are measures that are a composite of several variables, $X_1, X_2, \ldots$.

Ordinarily analysis of variance is used with A and correlation and regression

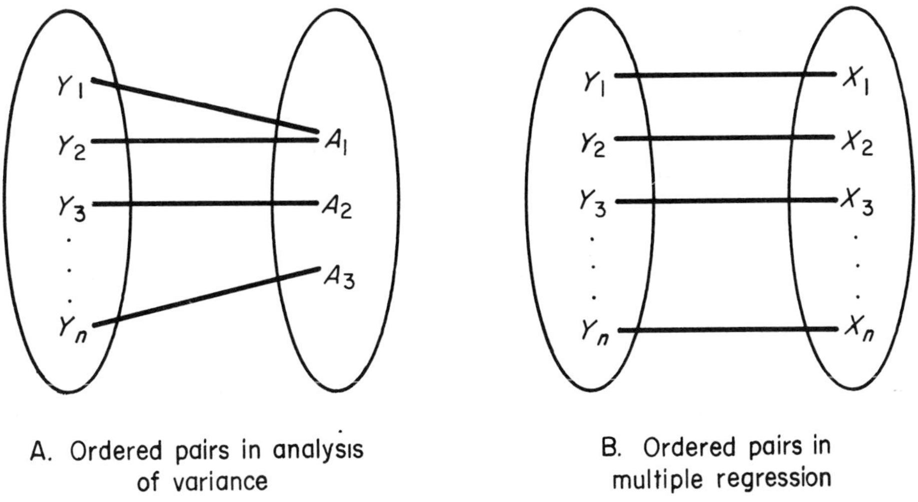

FIG. 36.1

analysis with B. This usage has unfortunately misled us to separate the two conceptually as well as methodologically. *They are in essence the same.* They both express relations. They are both sets of ordered pairs with the independent variable or variables differently defined. That we change both models radically by adding independent variables, for instance, makes no real conceptual difference. A nice practical outcome of this conceptual identity is that the same method of analysis can be used with both models. Multiple regression is a general method that embraces analysis of variance. Any analysis of variance can be done with multiple regression analysis. This does not mean that all data that can be analyzed with multiple regression *should* necessarily be so analyzed. We are merely pointing out the possibility.

One-Way Analysis of Variance and Multiple Regression Analysis

An Example with Two Groups

In Chapter 13 a simple fictitious example was used to illustrate certain analysis of variance calculations. Some of these "data" and the analysis of variance calculations are repeated here for ease of reference. They are given in Table 36.1. Since the calculations and the rationale of analysis of variance of this example were explained in Chapter 13, they will not be repeated. The means of 6 and 3 are significantly different at the .05 level, and, if A_1 and A_2 were two methods of reinforcement, say, and the dependent variable scores were arithmetic skill, we could conclude that Method A_1 produces more arithmetic skill than Method A_2.

Recall, too, that in Chapter 13 the strength or magnitude of relations was discussed and that the coefficient $E = \sqrt{ss_b/ss_t}$, the correlation ratio, was described

TABLE **36.1** DATA AND ANALYSIS OF VARIANCE CALCULATIONS, FICTITIOUS TWO-GROUP EXAMPLE

	A_1	A_2	
	6	3	$N = 10$
	7	1	$n = 5$
	5	5	
	4	2	$k = 2$
	8	4	
ΣX:	30	15	$\Sigma X_t = 45$
M:	6	3	$(\Sigma X_t)^2 = 2025$
			$M_t = 4.5$
			$\Sigma X_t^2 = 245$

$$C = \frac{(\Sigma X_t)^2}{N} = \frac{(45)^2}{10} = 202.50$$

$$\text{Total} = 245 - 202.50 = \mathit{42.50}$$

$$\text{Between} = \left[\frac{(30)^2}{5} + \frac{(15)^2}{5}\right] - 202.50 = \mathit{22.50}$$

Source	*df*	*s.s.*	*m.s.*	*F*
Between Groups	$k-1=1$	22.50	22.50	9.0(.05)
Within Groups	$N-k=8$	20.00	2.50	
Total	$N-1=9$	42.50		

and calculated. Repeating the calculation, we obtain: $E = \sqrt{22.50/42.50} = \sqrt{.5294} = .7276 = .73$. This coefficient, which is statistically significant since the F ratio of Table 36.1 is significant, says that there is a substantial relation between methods of reinforcement and arithmetic skills. Square E to obtain an estimate of the proportion of the variance of the arithmetic skills accounted for by reinforcement: $E^2 = (.73)^2 = .53$.

Now, transpose our thinking from an analysis of variance framework to a regression framework. Can we obtain $E = .73$ "directly"? The independent variable, methods, can be conceived as membership in two groups, A_1 and A_2. This membership can be expressed by 1's and 0's: if a subject is a member of A_1, assign him a 1; if he is a member of A_2, assign him a 0. Or we can assign 1's to A_2 members and 0's to A_1 members. The basic results will be the same.[1]

Treat the ten dependent variable measures as a single set of scores, call this set or vector Y, and treat the ten 1's and 0's as a single set of scores, call this set X, and do a simple regression analysis. The vector of 1's and 0's is called a *dummy*

[1]Indeed, use any two different numbers, for instance, −1 and 10 or 31 and 5, or any two random numbers, and the basic results will be the same. The assignment of 1's and 0's, however, has interpretative advantages that will be mentioned later. See J. Cohen, "Multiple Regression as a General Data-Analytic System," *Psychological Bulletin*, LXX (1968), 426–443.

variable.[2] The new layout of the data is given in Table 36.2. In addition, the sums of squares of X and of Y and the cross products of X and Y are calculated in the table, as is the coefficient of correlation of X and Y.

Note that $r_{xy} = .73$. But this r is the same as the E calculated with analysis of variance. E, then, is the correlation between group membership and arithmetic skills, a point made in an earlier chapter. The statistical significance of $r = .73$ can be tested with formula 35.16 of the preceding chapter, repeated here with a new number:

$$F = \frac{R^2/k}{(1-R^2)/(N-k-1)} \tag{36.1}$$

where R^2 = squared correlation between X and Y or between a linear combination of $X_1, X_2, \ldots$ and Y; k = number of independent variables (in this case 1); N =

TABLE **36.2** FICTITIOUS DATA OF TABLE 36.1 LAID OUT FOR REGRESSION ANALYSIS

	Y	X	XY
	6	1	6
	7	1	7
A_1	5	1	5
	4	1	4
	8	1	8
	3	0	0
	1	0	0
A_2	5	0	0
	2	0	0
	4	0	0
Σ:	45	5	30
Σ^2:	245	5	
M:	4.5	0.5	

$$\Sigma y^2 = 245 - \frac{(45)^2}{10} = 42.50$$

$$\Sigma x^2 = 5 - \frac{(5)^2}{10} = 2.50$$

$$\Sigma xy = 30 - \frac{(45)(5)}{10} = 7.50$$

$$r_{xy} = \frac{7.5}{\sqrt{(2.5)(42.5)}} = \frac{7.5}{10.31} = .73$$

[2]D. Suits, "Use of Dummy Variables in Regression Equations," *Journal of the American Statistical Association*, LII (1957), 548–551; M. Quenouille, *Introductory Statistics*. London: Pergamon, 1950, pp. 148–161.

total sample size. (From this point on we write R and R^2 even though only one X is involved. The reason will become apparent later.) Substituting in the formula, we obtain:

$$F = \frac{(.7276)^2/1}{[1-(.7276)^2]/(10-1-1)} = \frac{.5294}{.4706/8} = 9.00$$

which is the same F value calculated in the analysis of variance manner.

As far as numerical outcomes are concerned, then, the methods are interchangeable. Their interpretations, however, usually differ. In the analysis of variance, the significant F ratio means that the difference between the two means is statistically significant with the usual connotation of departure from chance expectation. The null hypothesis is: H_0: $M_1 = M_2$. In the regression analysis, on the other hand, the significant F ratio means that the R^2 used in formula 36.1 is statistically significant. It expresses the statistical significance of the relation between X and Y, X being group membership, and thus is in a sense more fundamental, since it addresses itself "directly" to the main scientific interest, the relation between X and Y, rather than simply to the difference between the Y means. The null hypothesis in this case is: H_0: $R^2 = 0$. The statistically significant F ratio rejects this hypothesis: R and R^2 differ significantly from zero.

This is not the whole story. What has been shown is that E^2 and R^2 are the same, and that the significance of R^2 can be calculated with the formula earlier used with R^2 when group membership has been coded as a variable and independent and dependent variables subjected to correlation analysis. How about a complete regression analysis? First, calculate the sums of squares due to regression and not due to regression using formulas of the last chapter (but with new numbers):

$$ss_{\text{reg}} = \frac{(\Sigma xy)^2}{\Sigma x^2} \qquad (36.2)$$

Taking the appropriate values from Table 36.2, calculate:

$$ss_{\text{reg}} = \frac{(7.50)^2}{2.50} = \frac{56.25}{2.50} = 22.50$$

Now, the sum of squares of the residuals:

$$\begin{aligned} ss_{\text{res}} &= ss_t - ss_{\text{reg}} \\ &= 42.50 - 22.50 = 20.00 \qquad (36.3) \end{aligned}$$

But $ss_{\text{reg}} = 22.50$ and $ss_{\text{res}} = 20.00$ are the sums of squares obtained in the conventional analysis of variance. The regression sum of squares *is* the between-groups sum of squares, and the residual sum of squares *is* the within-groups sum of squares. R^2 can, of course, be calculated using sums of squares:

$$\begin{aligned} R^2 &= \frac{ss_{\text{reg}}}{ss_t} \qquad (36.4) \\ &= \frac{22.50}{42.50} = .5294 \end{aligned}$$

This is the value of E^2 calculated earlier.

The regression analysis needs only a, the intercept constant, and b, the regression coefficient, for completeness. Repeat formulas from the preceding chapter and substitute values from Table 36.2:

$$Y' = a + bX \tag{36.5}$$

$$b = \frac{\Sigma xy}{\Sigma x^2} \tag{36.6}$$

$$= \frac{7.50}{2.50} = 3$$

$$a = \bar{Y} - b\bar{X} \tag{36.7}$$

$$= 4.5 - (3)(.5) = 3$$

The regression equation, therefore, is:

$$Y' = 3 + 3X$$

If the regression equation is used to calculate the predicted Y values for the ten X scores, the predicted scores for the first five subjects will be 6 and for the second five subjects 3. Calculate Y''s for subjects 4 and 7, for example:

$$Y'_4 = 3 + (3)(1) = 6$$

$$Y'_7 = 3 + (3)(0) = 3$$

And these are the means of A_1 and A_2, illustrating the notion that if one has knowledge only of group membership, then one predicts the mean.

Two reasons for using 1's and 0's for group membership can now be seen: their use will yield an intercept, a, that is equal to the value of the mean of the group that was assigned the 0's, and the regression coefficient, b, will be equal to the difference between the means of the two groups. Numbers other than 1 and 0 will yield the same R^2 and the same F ratio, but a, the intercept, will be a number not corresponding to the mean of either group, and b, the regression coefficient, will not be equal to the difference between the means.

The argument on the relation between multiple regression analysis and analysis of variance can be summarized by listing parallel formulas. This has been done in Table 36.3. The only unfamiliar formula is the first one in the analysis of variance column. It is an adaptation of similar formulas used in theoretical discussions of analysis of variance. It is merely the same kind of formula as the multiple regression prediction formula and has a similar interpretation based on the different contributions of treatments (A, B, etc.) to the scores of individuals. Note the e (for error) in the first equations of each column of the table. Its presence is always recognized. The rest of the table is obvious and needs no explanation.

An Example with Three Groups

To solidify our understanding, we now use the regression method described above with three experimental groups. Suppose an experiment has been done with three

TABLE **36.3** PARALLEL FORMULATIONS OF MULTIPLE REGRESSION ANALYSIS AND ANALYSIS OF VARIANCE[a]

Multiple Regression Analysis	Analysis of Variance
$Y' = a + b_1X_1 + \cdots + b_kX_k + e$	$Y = M_{pop} + A + B + e$
$ss_t = ss_{reg} + ss_{res}$	$ss_t = ss_b + ss_w$
$R^2 = ss_{reg}/ss_t$	$E^2 = ss_b/ss_t$
$F = \dfrac{ss_{reg}/df_1}{ss_{res}/df_2}$	$F = \dfrac{ss_b/df_1}{ss_w/df_2}$

[a] M_{pop} = mean of population; A and B = treatment conditions in analysis of variance; e = error. The remaining symbols are defined in the text.

methods of presenting verbal materials to ninth-grade children. The dependent variable is comprehension measured by an objective test of the materials. Suppose the results were those given in Table 36.4. Obviously an analysis of variance can be and should be done. The analysis of variance results, which the student should calculate himself, are given at the bottom of the table. The F ratio is 18, which, at 2 and 12 degrees of freedom, is significant at the .01 level. The effect of the

TABLE **36.4** FICTITIOUS DATA AND ONE-WAY ANALYSIS OF VARIANCE RESULTS, THREE EXPERIMENTAL GROUPS

	A_1	A_2	A_3	
	4	7	1	
	5	8	2	
	6	9	3	
	7	10	4	
	8	11	5	
Y:	30	45	15	$\Sigma Y_t = 90$
M:	6	9	3	$(\Sigma Y_t)^2 = 8100$
				$M_t = 6$
				$\Sigma Y_t^2 = 660$

$$C = \frac{8100}{15} = 540$$

$$ss_t = 660 - 540 = 120$$

$$ss_b = \frac{30^2}{5} + \frac{45^2}{5} + \frac{15^2}{5} - 540 = 630 - 540 = 90$$

Source	*df*	*s.s.*	*m.s.*	*F*
Between Groups	2	90.0	45.0	18.0 (.01)
Within Groups	12	30.0	2.5	
Total	14	120.0		

experimental treatment is clearly significant. $E^2 = ss_b/ss_t = 90/120 = .75$. The relation between the experimental treatment and comprehension is strong.[3]

Now, turn to multiple regression. The layout of the data for multiple regression analysis is given in Table 36.5. The sums, means, sums of squares, and cross products are also given in the table. (The three columns on the right are included only to show the elements of the regression calculations, in this case the cross products. Conceptually, they are not needed.) The vectors of 1's and 0's are treated as though they were ordinary score vectors. But note an important point when coding experimental treatments: there are only $m-1$ coded vectors, where $m =$ the number of experimental treatments. Expressed differently, there is one vector for each degree of freedom. In this case there are three treatments, A_1, A_2, and A_3, and $m = 3$. Therefore there are $m - 1 = 2$ coded vectors.

TABLE **36.5** REGRESSION LAYOUT AND CALCULATIONS, TABLE 36.4 DATA

	Y	X_1	X_2	X_1Y	X_2Y	X_1X_2
	4	1	0	4	0	0
	5	1	0	5	0	0
A_1	6	1	0	6	0	0
	7	1	0	7	0	0
	8	1	0	8	0	0
	7	0	1	0	7	0
	8	0	1	0	8	0
A_2	9	0	1	0	9	0
	10	0	1	0	10	0
	11	0	1	0	11	0
	1	0	0	0	0	0
	2	0	0	0	0	0
A_3	3	0	0	0	0	0
	4	0	0	0	0	0
	5	0	0	0	0	0
Σ:	90	5	5	30	45	0
M:	6	.3333	.3333			
Σ^2:	660	5	5	30	45	0

As in the last chapter, we take the calculation of the regression weights on faith: $b_1 = 3$ and $b_2 = 6$. The intercept constant, a, is calculated:

$$\begin{aligned} a &= \bar{Y} - b_1\bar{X}_1 - b_2\bar{X}_2 \\ &= 6 - (3)(.3333) - (6)(.3333) = 3 \end{aligned} \tag{36.8}$$

It is necessary to calculate all the deviation sums of squares and cross products. The formulas given in the last chapter are used, treating the 1 and 0 vectors just

[3]The intraclass correlation coefficient or Hays' omega-squared will give better and more conservative estimates than E_2. The intraclass coefficient, however, is .77, and Hays' omega-squared is .69. There is little doubt of the strength of the relation.

TABLE **36.6** SUMS OF SQUARES AND CROSS PRODUCTS OF DATA OF TABLE 36.5[a]

	x_1	x_2	y
x_1	3.3333	−1.6667	0
x_2		3.3333	15.0000
y			120.0000

[a]The values on the diagonal are the deviation sums of squares: Σx_1^2, Σx_2^2, Σy_t^2. The remaining three values above the diagonal are the deviation cross products: $\Sigma x_1 x_2$, $\Sigma x_1 y$, and $\Sigma x_2 y$.

as though they were continuous measures. These quantities are given in Table 36.6.[4]

To calculate the regression and residual sums of squares, use formulas 35.10 and 35.11 of the last chapter (given here with the numbering of this chapter):

$$ss_{\text{reg}} = b_1 \Sigma x_1 y + b_2 \Sigma x_2 y \qquad (36.9)$$

$$= (3)(0) + (6)(15) = \mathit{90}$$

$$ss_{\text{res}} = ss_t - ss_{\text{reg}} \qquad (36.10)$$

$$= 120 - 90 = \mathit{30}$$

Use formula 36.4 to calculate R^2:

$$R^2 = \frac{ss_{\text{reg}}}{ss_t} = \frac{90}{120} = \mathit{.75}$$

and $R = \sqrt{.75} = \mathit{.8660}$. Finally, calculate the F ratio using formula 36.1:

$$F = \frac{R^2/k}{(1-R^2)/(N-k-1)} = \frac{.75/2}{(1-.75)/(15-2-1)} = \frac{.375000}{.020833} = \mathit{18}$$

Another formula for F can also be borrowed from the preceding chapter:

$$F = \frac{ss_{\text{reg}}/df_1}{ss_{\text{res}}/df_2} = \frac{ss_{\text{reg}}/k}{ss_{\text{res}}/(N-k-1)} \qquad (36.11)$$

$$= \frac{90/2}{30/(15-2-1)} = \frac{45.00}{2.50} = \mathit{18}$$

Obviously the values of the sums of squares, the mean squares, and F are the same as those obtained with the analysis of variance. R^2 also equals E^2. In

[4]For example,

$$\Sigma x_1^2 = (1^2 + 1^2 + \cdots + 0^2) - \frac{5^2}{15} = 5 - 1.6667 = 3.3333$$

$$\Sigma x_2 y = (0)(4) + (0)(5) + \cdots + (0)(5) - \frac{(5)(90)}{15} = 45 - 30 = 15$$

$$\Sigma x_1 x_2 = (1)(0) + (1)(0) + \cdots + (0)(0) - \frac{(5)(5)}{15} = 0 - 1.6667 = -1.6667$$

addition, the values of a and the b's tell us something about the data. $a = 3$ is the mean of the group assigned zeroes in both coded vectors. $b_1 = 3$ is the difference between the means of A_1 and A_3, the group assigned zeroes in both vectors: $6-3=3$. b_2 is the difference between the means of A_2 and A_3: $9-3=6$. The means of the three groups are easily found by using the regression equation:

$$Y' = a + b_1X_1 + b_2X_2$$
$$\bar{Y}_{A_1} = 3 + (3)(1) + (6)(0) = 6$$
$$\bar{Y}_{A_2} = 3 + (3)(0) + (6)(1) = 9$$
$$\bar{Y}_{A_3} = 3 + (3)(0) + (6)(0) = 3$$

Note that even though A_3 was not coded—it had no coded vector of its own—its mean is easily recovered by substituting 0's for X_1 and X_2.

While it has been shown that multiple regression analysis accomplishes what one-way analysis of variance does, can it be said that there is any real advantage to using the regression method? Actually the calculations are more involved. Why do it, then? The answer is that with the kinds of data of the example above there is no practical advantage beyond aesthetic nicety and conceptual clarification. But when research problems are more complex—when, for example, interactions, covariates (e.g., intelligence test scores), nominal variables (sex, social class), and nonlinear components (X^2, X^3) are involved—the regression procedure has decided advantages. Indeed, many research analytic problems that analysis of variance cannot handle readily or at all can be fairly readily accomplished with multiple regression analysis.

Coding and Data Analysis

Before enlarging the discussion of multiple regression and analysis of variance, we need to know something about different ways of coding experimental treatments for multiple regression analysis. A *code* is a set of symbols that is assigned to a set of objects for various reasons. In multiple regression analysis, *coding* is the assignment of numbers to the members of a population or sample to indicate group or subset membership according to a rule determined by an independent means. When some characteristic or aspect of the members of a population or sample is objectively defined, it is then possible to create a set of ordered pairs, the first members of which constitute the dependent variable, Y, and the second members numerical indicators of subset or group membership.

In the preceding discussion of the coding of experimental treatments in the multiple regression analogue of one-way analysis of variance, 1's and 0's were used. Vectors of 1's and 0's are correlated. In Table 36.6, for instance, the sum of the cross products, Σx_1x_2, is -1.6667, and $r_{12} = -.50$. Such 1 and 0, or *dummy*, coding works quite well. It is possible to use other forms of coding, however. One of these, *effects* coding, consists of assigning $\{1, 0, -1\}$ or $\{1, -1\}$ to experimental treatments. Although a useful method, it will be discussed only briefly.

To clarify matters, the coding of the data of Table 36.5, a multiple regression analogue of the one-way analysis of variance of the data of Table 36.4, with three experimental groups or treatments, is laid out in Table 36.7. Under the heading "Dummy" is given the dummy coding of Table 36.5, using only two subjects per experimental group. Since there are two degrees of freedom, or $k-1=3-1=2$, there are two column vectors labeled X_1 and X_2. The dummy coding assignment has already been explained: a 1 indicates that a subject is a member of the experimental group against which the 1 is placed, and a 0 that the subject is not a member of the experimental group.

TABLE **36.7** EXAMPLES OF DUMMY, EFFECT, AND ORTHOGONAL CODING OF EXPERIMENTAL TREATMENTS[a]

Groups	*Dummy* X_1	*Dummy* X_2	*Effects* X_1	*Effects* X_2	*Orthogonal* X_1	*Orthogonal* X_2
A_1	1	0	1	0	0	2
	1	0	1	0	0	2
A_2	0	1	0	1	−1	−1
	0	1	0	1	−1	−1
A_3	0	0	−1	−1	1	−1
	0	0	−1	−1	1	−1
	$r_{12}=-.50$		$r_{12}=.50$		$r_{12}=.00$	

[a]In the dummy coding, A_3 is a control group. In the orthogonal coding, A_2 is compared to A_3, and A_1 is compared to A_2 *and* A_3, or $(A_2+A_3)/2$.

Under the "Effects" column, the coding is seen to be $\{1, 0, -1\}$. Effects coding is virtually the same as dummy coding—indeed, it has been called dummy coding—except that one experimental group, usually the last, is always assigned −1's. If the n's of the experimental groups are equal, the sums of the columns of the codes equal zero. The vectors, however, are not systematically uncorrelated. The correlation between the two columns under "Effects" in Table 36.7, for example, is .50. (Contrast this with the correlation between the dummy code columns: $r=-.50$.)

Each of these two systems of coding has its own characteristics. Two of the characteristics of dummy coding were discussed in the previous section. One of the characteristics of effects coding, on the other hand, is that the intercept constant, a, yielded by the multiple regression analysis will equal the grand mean, or M_t, of Y. For the data of Table 36.5, the intercept constant is 6.00, which is the mean of all the Y scores.

The third form of coding is *orthogonal* coding. (It is also called "contrasts" coding, but some contrasts coding can be nonorthogonal.) As its name indicates, the coded vectors are orthogonal or uncorrelated. If an investigator's main interest is in specific contrasts between means rather than the overall F test, orthogonal coding can provide the needed contrasts. In any set of data, a number of contrasts can be made. This is, of course, particularly useful in analysis of variance. The rule is that only contrasts that are orthogonal to each other, or independent, are made. For example, in Table 36.7, the coding of the last set of vectors is orthogonal: each of the vectors totals to zero and the sum of their products is zero, or

$$(0 \times 2) + (0 \times 2) + (-1)(-1) + \cdots + (1)(-1) = 0$$

r_{12} is also equal to zero. (Look at the coded vectors of Table 36.9, too, and note that the three coded vectors are orthogonal.)

Instead of the dummy coding of Table 36.5, suppose we now use orthogonal coding. Suppose we decide to test A_2 against A_3, or $M_{A_2} - M_{A_3}$, and also test A_1 against A_2 and A_3, or $M_{A_1} - (M_{A_2} + M_{A_3})/2$. X_1 is then coded $(0, -1, 1)$ and X_2 is coded $(2, -1, -1)$, as shown by the orthogonal coding of Table 36.7. The interested reader grounded in analysis of variance can follow up such possibilities.[5]

Orthogonal coding becomes particularly important in factorial analysis of variance. A simple example is given below (Table 36.9), where factorial data with two independent variables are coded $(1, -1)$ so that the contrasts between A_1 and A_2, on the one hand, and between B_1 and B_2, on the other hand, are brought out. Note, however, that if the numbers of cases in the different cells are not equal the coding is no longer orthogonal and statistical problems arise. Further discussion of this complex subject is beyond the scope of this book.

No matter what kind of coding is used, R^2, F, the sums of squares, the standard errors of estimate, and the predicted Y's will be the same (the means of the experimental groups). The intercept constant, the regression weights, and the t tests of b weights will be different. Strictly speaking, it is not possible to recommend one method over another; each has its purposes. At first, however, it is probably wise for the student to use the simplest method, dummy coding, or 1's and 0's. He should fairly soon use effects coding, however. Finally, orthogonal coding can be tried and mastered.[6]

The simplest use of coding is to indicate nominal variables, particularly dichotomies. Some variables are "natural" dichotomies: sex, public school-parochial school, conviction-no conviction, vote for-vote against. All these can be scored $(1, 0)$ and the resulting vectors analyzed as though they were continuous score vectors. Most variables are continuous, or potentially so, however, even though they can always be treated as dichotomous. In any case, the use of $(1, 0)$ vectors for dichotomous variables in multiple regression is highly useful.

With nominal variables that are not dichotomies one can still use $(1, 0)$ vectors. One simply creates a $(1, 0)$ vector for each subset but one of a category or partition. Suppose the category A is partitioned into A_1, A_2, A_3, say Protestant, Catholic, Jew. Then a vector is created for Protestants, each of which is assigned a 1; the Catholics and Jews are assigned 0. Another vector is created for Catholics: each Catholic is assigned 1; Protestants and Jews are assigned 0. It would, of

[5]Cohen, *op. cit.* pp. 428–434, especially pp. 432–434. For a detailed discussion, see F. Kerlinger and E. Pedhazur, *Multiple Regression in Behavioral Research*. New York: Holt, Rinehart and Winston, 1973 (in press), chap. 7.

[6]Before using orthogonal coding to any great extent, the student should study the topic of comparisons of means. See W. Hays, *Statistics*. New York: Holt, Rinehart and Winston, 1963, chap. 14.

course, be redundant to create a third vector for Jews. The number of vectors is $k-1$, where $k=$ the number of subsets of the partition or category.

While sometimes convenient or necessary, partitioning a continuous variable into a dichotomy or trichotomy throws information away. If, for example, an investigator dichotomizes intelligence, ethnocentrism, cohesiveness of groups, or any other variable that can be measured with a scale that even approximates equality of interval, he is discarding information. To reduce a set of values with a relatively wide range to a dichotomy is to reduce its variance and thus its possible correlation with other variables. A good rule of research data analysis, therefore, is: *Do not reduce continuous variables to partitioned variables* (dichotomies, trichotomies, etc.) unless compelled to do so by circumstances or the nature of the data (seriously skewed, bimodal, etc.).

Factorial Analysis of Variance, Analysis of Covariance, and Multiple Regression Analysis

Factorial Analysis of Variance

It is with factorial analysis of variance that we begin to appreciate the advantages of multiple regression analysis. First, a fictitious set of factorial data from an earlier chapter will again be used. In Table 14.3 a set of artificial data featuring a significant interaction was given. The same example is given in Table 36.8 with the analysis of variance table. The two independent variables are: methods of teaching, A_1 and A_2, and types of motivation, B_1 and B_2. The dependent variable is achievement. As the analysis of variance indicates, neither of the two main effects is significant, but the interaction between them is.

How can multiple regression analysis be applied to these data? There are two or three ways, differing only in the coding of the independent variables. There are three "effects," each of which must somehow be coded, A, B, and $A \times B$ (the interaction). 1's and 0's can be assigned to members of A_1 and 0's to members of A_2, and similarly with B_1 and B_2. In other words, there is one vector of 1's and 0's for A and another for B. The interaction, $A \times B$, is then simply the product of these two vectors. Recall the principle stated earlier: one independent variable vector for each degree of freedom. All eight dependent variable scores form a fourth or Y vector. This method works quite well: the sums of squares, R^2, and the F ratio will be correct.

We use another method, however: coding that is orthogonal in order to bring out the A, B, and $A \times B$ effects and to obtain independent estimates of the sums of squares associated with these effects. Although it does not matter much with this example, the method has distinct advantages with more complex examples and real data. In any case, no matter what the method of coding, the same R^2 and F ratio will emerge. The method should provide the necessary contrasts between the partitions of the independent variables, i.e., between A_1 and A_2 and between B_1 and B_2. The data of Table 36.8, laid out with the appropriate coding, are given in Table 36.9.

TABLE **36.8** FACTORIAL ANALYSIS OF VARIANCE, FICTITIOUS DATA, FROM CHAPTER 14, SIGNIFICANT INTERACTION

		A_1	A_2	
B_1		8	4	
		6	2	
	ΣX:	14	6	$\Sigma X_{B_1} = 20$
	M:	7	3	$M_{B_1} = 5$
B_2		4	8	
		2	6	
	ΣX:	6	14	$\Sigma X_{B_2} = 20$
	M:	3	7	$M_{B_2} = 5$
	ΣX:	20	20	$\Sigma X_t = 40$
	M:	5	5	$M_{t_2} = 5$
				$\Sigma X_t = 240$

Source	*df*	s.s.	*m.s.*	*F*
Between Methods, A	1	0	0	
Between Types, B	1	0	0	
Interaction: $A \times B$	1	32	32	16.0 (.05)
Within Groups	4	8	2	
Total	7	40		

The multiple regression calculations proceed as usual. First, calculate the deviation sums of squares and cross products. These are given in Table 36.10. (Remember: treat the coded vectors just as though they were continuous variable vectors.) Because this example was deliberately contrived in Chapter 14 to illustrate the presence of an interaction with a complete absence of main effects, the first two values of the last column of the table, $\Sigma x_1 y$ and $\Sigma x_2 y$, which represent the relations between A and B and Y, are zero. In this case, the important value is $\Sigma x_3 y$, which represents the relation between X_3, the interaction, and Y.

The b weights, which must again be taken on faith, are: $b_1 = 0$, $b_2 = 0$, $b_3 = 2$. The remaining regression statistics are calculated as follows:

$$a = \bar{Y} - b_1\bar{X}_1 - b_2\bar{X}_2 - b_3\bar{X}_3 \qquad (36.12)$$
$$= 5 - (0)(0) - (0)(0) - (2)(0) = 5$$

$$ss_{\text{reg}} = b_1 \Sigma x_1 y + b_2 \Sigma x_2 y + b_3 \Sigma x_3 y \qquad (36.13)$$
$$= (0)(0) + (0)(0) + (2)(16) = 32$$

$$ss_{\text{res}} = ss_t - ss_{\text{reg}} = 40 - 32 = 8$$

$$R^2 = \frac{ss_{\text{reg}}}{ss_t} = \frac{32}{40} = .80$$

$$F = \frac{ss_{\text{reg}}/m}{ss_{\text{res}}/(N-k-1)} = \frac{32/1}{8/(8-3-1)} = 16$$

TABLE **36.9** FACTORIAL ANALYSIS OF VARIANCE DATA OF TABLE 36.8 LAID OUT FOR MULTIPLE REGRESSION ANALYSIS[a]

		Y		X_1	X_2	$X_3 = X_1X_2$
A_1		8	B_1	1	1	1
		6		1	1	1
		4	B_2	1	−1	−1
		2		1	−1	−1
A_2		4	B_1	−1	1	−1
		2		−1	1	−1
		8	B_2	−1	−1	1
		6		−1	−1	1
Σ:		40		0	0	0
M:		5		0	0	0
Σ^2:		120		8	8	8

[a]Y = dependent-variable measures; X_1 = Effect A; X_2 = Effect B; $X_3 = X_1X_2$ = interaction of A and B. The A and B main effects are indicated with braces.

TABLE **36.10** DEVIATION SUMS OF SQUARES AND CROSS PRODUCTS, DATA OF TABLE 36.9

	x_1	x_2	x_3	y
x_1	8.0	0	0	0
x_2		8.0	0	0
x_3			8.0	16.0
y				40.0

As usual with factorial analysis of variance, F ratios for each main effect and for the interaction must be calculated. It is obvious that no F ratios can be calculated for the A and B main effects. Only the interaction of A and B generates a sum of squares, 32. The F test is provided by the usual formula except that instead of k, the number of independent variables, we use $m = 1$, the degrees of freedom for the interaction. And, of course, the interaction is statistically significant. R^2 is .80. Thus 80 percent of the dependent variable variance is accounted for by the interaction. The rest of the calculations are familiar and require no explanation.

When the n's in the cells are equal, it is doubtful that there is any particular virtue in using multiple regression analysis. But when the n's are unequal or when one wants to include one or two other variables for control purposes, the multiple regression procedure should be used. This point is most important. In analysis of variance, the addition of other variables—control variables or covariates like intelligence, sex, and social class, or other nominal variables—is difficult and clumsy. With multiple regression, however, the inclusion of such variables is easy and natural.

Analysis of Covariance

In Chapter 21 the analysis of covariance was defined and described but not illustrated. Analysis of covariance *is* a multiple regression procedure, and we now examine it briefly to show how it fits into the kind of analysis under discussion. What analysis of covariance does is to test the significance of the differences among means after taking into account or controlling initial mean differences between the experimental groups on a so-called *covariate*, a variable that is correlated with the dependent variable. (This correlation is also taken into account.)

It has been found in large-scale studies by Prothro and Grigg and by McClosky that people's agreement with social issues is greater the more abstract the issue.[7] Suppose a political scientist believes that authoritarianism has a good deal to do with this relation, that the more authoritarian the person, the more he agrees with abstract social assertions. In order to study the relation between abstractness and agreement, he will have to control authoritarianism. In other words, the political scientist is interested in studying the relation between abstractness of issues and statements, on the one hand, and agreement with such issues and statements, on the other hand. He is not at this point interested in authoritarianism and agreement; he needs, rather to control the influence of authoritarianism on agreement. Authoritarianism is the covariate.

The political scientist devises three experimental treatments, A_1, A_2, and A_3, different levels of abstractness of materials. He obtains responses from 15 subjects who have been assigned randomly to the three experimental groups, five in each group. Before the experiment begins the investigator administers the *F* (authoritarianism) scale to the 15 subjects and uses these measures as a covariate. He wishes to control the possible influence of authoritarianism on agreement. This is a fairly straightforward analysis of covariance problem in which we test the significance of the differences among the three agreement means after correcting the means for the influence of authoritarianism and taking into account the correlation between authoritarianism and agreement. We now do the analysis of covariance using multiple regression analysis.

First, the data are presented in the usual analysis of covariance way in Table 36.11. In analysis of covariance one does separate analyses of variance on the X scores, the Y scores, and the cross products of the X and Y scores, XY. Then, using regression analysis, one calculates sums of squares and mean squares of the errors of estimate of the total and the within groups and, finally, the adjusted between groups. Since the concern here is not with the usual analysis of covariance procedure, we do not do these calculations. Instead, we proceed immediately to a multiple regression approach to the analysis.

The data of Table 36.11, arranged for multiple regression analysis, are given in Table 36.12. As usual, there is one vector for the dependent variable, Y. A second vector, X_1, is the covariate. The remaining two vectors, X_2 and X_3, represent the experimental treatments A_1 and A_2. (It is not necessary to have a vector

[7] H. McClosky, "Consensus and Ideology in American Politics," *American Political Science Review*, LVIII (1964), 361–382; J. Prothro and C. Grigg, "Fundamental Principles of Democracy: Bases of Agreement and Disagreement," *Journal of Politics*, XXII (1960), 276–294.

TABLE **36.11** FICTITIOUS ANALYSIS OF COVARIANCE PROBLEM, THREE EXPERIMENTAL GROUPS AND ONE COVARIATE

Treatments					
A_1		A_2		A_3	
X	Y	X	Y	X	Y
12	12	6	9	12	15
11	12	9	9	10	12
10	11	11	13	4	9
12	10	14	14	4	8
10	12	2	5	8	11

TABLE **36.12** FICTITIOUS ANALYSIS OF COVARIANCE DATA OF TABLE 36.11 ARRANGED FOR MULTIPLE REGRESSION ANALYSIS[a]

	Y	X_1	X_2	X_3
	12	12	1	0
	12	11	1	0
A_1	11	10	1	0
	10	12	1	0
	12	10	1	0
	9	6	0	1
	9	9	0	1
A_2	13	11	0	1
	14	14	0	1
	5	2	0	1
	15	12	0	0
	12	10	0	0
A_3	9	4	0	0
	8	4	0	0
	11	8	0	0

[a] Y = dependent variable; X_1 = covariate; X_2 = treatment A_1; X_3 = treatment A_2.

for A_3, since there is only one vector for each degree of freedom, and there are only two degrees of freedom.)

A regression analysis yields: $R^2_{y.123} = .8612$ and $R^2_{y.1} = .7502$. To test the significance of the differences among the means of A_1, A_2, and A_3, after adjusting for the effect of X_1, the variance in Y due to the covariate is subtracted from the total variance accounted for by the regression of Y on variables X_1, X_2, and X_3:

$R^2_{y.123} - R^2_{y.1}$. This remainder is then tested:

$$F = \frac{(R^2_{y.123} - R^2_{y.1})/(k_1 - k_2)}{(1 - R^2_{y.123})/(N - k_1 - 1)} \qquad (36.14)$$

where k_1 = the number of independent variables associated with $R^2_{y.123}$, the larger R^2, and k_2 = the number of independent variables associated with $R^2_{y.1}$, the smaller R^2, Thus:

$$F = \frac{(.8612 - .7502)/(3-1)}{(1-.8612)/(15-3-1)} = \frac{.0555}{.0126} = 4.405$$

which, at 2 and 11 degrees of freedom, is significant at the .05 level. (Note that an ordinary one-way analysis of variance of the three groups, without taking the covariate into account, yields a nonsignificant F ratio.) $R^2_{y.23}$, or the variance of Y accounted for by the regression on variables 2 and 3 (the experimental treatments), after allowing for the correlation of variable 1 and Y, is .1110. While this is not a strong relation, especially compared with the massive correlation between the covariate, authoritarianism, and Y ($r^2_{1y} = .75$), it is not inconsequential. Evidently abstractness of issues influences agreement responses: the more abstract the issues, the greater the agreement.[8]

The analysis of covariance, then, is seen to be simply a variation on the theme of multiple regression analysis. And in this case it happens to be easier to conceptualize than the rather elaborate analysis of covariance procedure—especially if there is more than one covariate. As Cohen points out, the covariate is nothing but an independent variable. Moreover, a variable considered as a covariate in one study can easily be considered as an independent variable in another study. Cohen neatly says, ". . . one man's main effect is another man's covariate."[9]

The beauty, power, and general applicability of multiple regression emerge rather clearly in this example. And it should be borne in mind that two, even three, covariates can be easily handled with multiple regression. With two covariates and two other independent variables, for instance, we simply write the F ratio:

$$F = \frac{(R^2_{y.1234} - R^2_{y.12})/(k_1 - k_2)}{(1 - R^2_{y.1234})/(N - k_1 - 1)}$$

Carry the reasoning a step further. The use of analysis of covariance with factorial designs is complex. It is simpler with multiple regression analysis. Take a 2×2 factorial design and one covariate. We have, then, the following "variables":

Y	X_1	X_2	X_3	$X_4 = X_2X_3$
Dependent variable	Covariate	Treatment A	Treatment B	Interaction: $A \times B$

[8]Authoritarianism is unlikely to have a correlation with Y of .87. The example was deliberately contrived to show how a strong influence like X_1 can be controlled and the influence of the remaining variables (in this case experimental treatments) evaluated. Note that formula 36.14 can be used in any multiple regression analysis; it is not limited to analysis of covariance or other experimental methods.

[9]Cohen, *op. cit.*, p. 439.

Each of the X's has one degree of freedom, and the analysis proceeds like any multiple regression analysis except at the end when the effect of X_1, the covariate, is subtracted. The remaining "variables," X_2, X_3, and X_4, are then analyzed and the results interpreted.

Canonical and Discriminant Analysis

Canonical correlation and discriminant analysis address themselves to two important research questions. One, what is the relation between two *sets* of data with several independent variables and several dependent variables? Two, how can individuals best be assigned to groups on the basis of several variables? Canonical correlation analysis addresses itself to the first question, and discriminant analysis to the second.

Discriminant Analysis

A discriminant function is a regression equation with a dependent variable that represents group membership. The function maximally discriminates the members of the group; it tells us to which group each member probably belongs. In short, if we have two or more independent variables and the members of, say, two groups, the discriminant function gives the "best" prediction, in the least-squares sense, of the "correct" group membership of each member of the sample. The discriminant function, then, can be used to assign individuals to groups on the basis of their scores on two or more measures. From the scores on the two or more measures, the least-squares "best" composite score is calculated. If this is so, then, the higher the R^2 the better the prediction of group membership. In other words, *when dealing with two groups*, the discriminant function is nothing more than a multiple regression equation with the dependent variable a nominal variable (coded 0, 1) representing group membership. (With three or more groups, however, discriminant analysis goes beyond multiple regression methods.[10])

Although discriminant analysis has not been used much in behavioral research, it has interesting potentialities. It can be used in two main ways: (1) as a classification and diagnosis method, and (2) to study the relations among variables in different populations and samples. The first use will probably be more common than the second. A clinical psychologist, for example, may wish to know whether to classify youths as delinquent or not-delinquent. If he has measures that have in the past successfully predicted delinquency, they can be combined into a discriminant function, and future individuals can be classified with them. Note that this amounts to predicting group membership, represented by 1's and 0's, with a set of measures whose regression weights have been entered into a regression equation.

One can extend such analysis to other dichotomous variables: success or not in college, school dropout or not, sex, vote for-vote against. One can also extend discriminant function analysis to more than two groups. Cooley and Lohnes, for example, describe the discrimination among three career-plans groups: a research

[10]The reader will find excellent guidance in: M. Tatsuoka, *Discriminant Analysis: The Study of Group Differences*. Champaign, Ill.: Institute for Personality and Ability Testing, 1970.

group, those students who enter graduate work to do basic research; an applied-science group, those who continue in science and engineering, but who do not plan a research career; and a nonscience group, those who leave scientific work to enter fields that have direct involvement with people.[11] Science and engineering majors from six eastern colleges were administered the *Study of Values* and other personality measures. The individuals were followed up over a three-year period, and a discriminant function analysis performed, using the *Study of Values* and the three groups indicated above. Cooley and Lohnes were successful in differentiating the members of the groups with the *Study of Values*, and were able to describe some of the differences.

As indicated above, discriminant analysis can be used to study the relations among variables in different populations or samples. Suppose we have ratings of administrators on administrative performance and we also have found, through the In-Basket Test, that three kinds of performance (called factors) are important.[12] We wish to know how successful and unsuccessful administrators, as judged by an independent criterion, perform on the three tests, which are Ability to Work With Others (X_1), Motivation for Administrative Work (X_2), and General Professional Skill (X_3). Suppose the discriminant regression equation were: $Y' = .06X_1 + .45X_2 + .30X_3$. From this equation, we can form the tentative conclusion that Ability to Work With Others seems unimportant compared to Motivation for Administrative Work and General Professional Skill. In other words, the discriminant equation gives us a profile picture of the difference between successful and unsuccessful administrators as measured by the In-Basket Test.

Canonical Correlation

It is not too large a conceptual step from multiple regression analysis with one dependent variable to multiple regression analysis with more than one dependent variable. Computationally, however, it is a considerable step. We will not, therefore, supply the actual calculations. The regression analysis of data with k independent variables and m dependent variables is called *canonical correlation* analysis. The basic idea is that, through least-squares analysis, two linear composites are formed, one for the independent variables, X_j, and one for the dependent variables, Y_j. The correlation between these two composites is the canonical correlation. And, like R, it will be the maximum correlation possible given the particular sets of data. It should be clear that what has been called until now multiple regression analysis is a special case of canonical analysis. In view of practical limitations on canonical analysis, it might be better to say that canonical analysis is a generalization of multiple regression analysis.

In addition to the canonical correlation, sets of regression weights for both the independent and dependent variables are calculated. The weights can be used to determine which of the independent and dependent variables are more closely

[11] W. Cooley and P. Lohnes, *Multivariate Procedures for the Behavioral Sciences*. New York: Wiley, 1962, pp. 119–123.

[12] J. Hemphill, D. Griffiths, and N. Frederiksen, *Administrative Performance and Personality*. New York: Teachers College Press, 1962.

associated. The same strictures mentioned earlier in discussing regression weights apply here, however.

It is not easy to find research studies that have used canonical analysis. In earlier years, of course, the calculations involved were prohibitive. Today, even with computer facilities and programs available, the method is evidently not well known. This is regrettable, because some research problems almost demand canonical analysis. The first of the two studies to be cited is such a problem. Roe and Siegelman, in a study of the sources of interests, tested the notion that early experiences produce later differences in orientations to persons and to things.[13] (They assumed that these orientations influence interests in occupations.) Their basic hypothesis was that extensive and satisfying personal relations early in life produce adults who are primarily person-oriented, while inadequate and unsatisfying personal relations produce adults who are primarily oriented to nonpersonal aspects of the environment.[14] They used a set of independent variables that reflected early home environment and a set of dependent variables that reflected orientation toward people. A canonical analysis yielded a canonical correlation of .47 that was significant, and the greatest contributions to this correlation came from a measure of early social experience, an independent variable, and one of the dependent variables, a composite of questionnaire and inventory items measuring orientation toward people.[15]

The second use of canonical analysis comes from a study by Walberg of the relations between five sets of independent variables consisting of measures of the social environment of learning, student biographical items, and miscellaneous variables (dogmatism, authoritarianism, intelligence, and so on), on the one hand, and a set of dependent variables consisting of cognitive and noncognitive measures of learning.[16] Separate analyses were run between each set of independent variables and the set of dependent variables. Of the five sets of independent variables, three predicted significantly to the learning criteria.

One interesting result was the canonical correlation between the learning environment variables—Intimacy, Friction, Formality, and so on—and the dependent learning variables—Science Understanding, Science Interest, and so on. The canonical R was .61, indicating a fairly substantial relation between the linear composites of the two sets of variables.

In order to understand the significance of what is theoretically perhaps Walberg's most important finding, the reader should know that, as we found out in earlier discussions, there can be more than one source of variation in a set of data. Similarly, there can be more than one source of covariation in the two sets of variables being analyzed by canonical correlation. If there is more than one source, then more than one canonical correlation can be found.

[13]A. Roe and M. Siegelman, *The Origin of Interests.* Washington, D.C.: American Personnel and Guidance Association, 1964.

[14]*Ibid.*, pp. 4, 37–39.

[15]*Ibid.*, pp. 43–44, footnote 9. A more complete description of this analysis and the results is given in Cooley and Lohnes, *op. cit.*, pp. 40–45.

[16]H. Walberg, "Predicting Class Learning: An Approach to the Class as a Social System," *American Educational Research Journal,* VI (1969), 529–542.

Walberg found that 15 of the independent variables each correlated significantly with the set of dependent variables collectively. In a separate canonical analysis of these two sets of variables, two statistically significant canonical correlations were found: .64 and .60.[17] The first canonical variate or component was produced by the independent variables positively correlated with the cognitive learning gains of Physics Achievement, Science Understanding, and Science Processes. The second variate was produced by the gains on noncognitive dependent variables: Science Interest, Physics Interest, and Physics Activities. In short, Walberg was able, through canonical analysis, to present a highly condensed generalization, as he calls it, about the relations between cognitive learning, noncognitive learning, and a variety of environmental and other variables related to learning.

The Computer and Multivariate Analysis

It is pointless to think about anything but computer calculations in any of the techniques of multivariate analysis. The calculations are much too laborious, difficult, time-consuming, and prone to error. While one can still do chi squares, analyses of variance of the usual kind (not multivariate analysis of variance), and a few correlations using a desk calculator, one simply can't, or shouldn't, calculate a multiple regression analysis or a canonical analysis "by hand." (The exception to this statement is the calculation for learning purposes of small model problems such as those in this book.) Fortunately, the availability of electronic computers has increased greatly in the last decade, practical computer know-how has also increased, and behavioral science research data analysis programs are generally available. There is hardly a university that does not have computer facilities and multivariate analysis programs. The serious student of research must know something of the computer and how it operates and, more important, a good deal about computer programs and how to use them.

The best solution of the proper use of the computer is for the student to learn to write programs. More will be said about this in Appendix C at the end of the book. After gaining some knowledge of programming and, hopefully, of matrix algebra—which is really indispensable for adequate grasp and use of multivariate techniques—the student can explore the available programs for multiple regression, canonical correlation, and discriminant analyses, for multivariate analysis of variance, and for factor analysis.

It is not enough to know that a certain program does multiple regression analysis. One has to know *how* the program does it. One has to be able to examine computer output for its validity. Make one or two little mistakes in instructions to the computer and the outcome can be what computer people call garbage. A researcher can reach false conclusions and interpret results quite incorrectly if he does not clearly know, at least in general, how a program does its job. For

[17]The nature of canonical analysis is such that when the second linear component is calculated, it is orthogonal to the first component. Thus the above canonical correlations reflect two independent sources of variance in the data.

example, has the programmer calculated standard deviations with N or $N-1$ in the denominator? If the output is simply labeled "Regression Weights," are the weights b's or β's? These are simple and obvious difficulties. There are more subtle difficulties, especially in highly complex analyses like canonical analysis and factor analysis.

One of the best sets of programs to accomplish multiple regression analysis is the BMD series.[18] The BMD series is not only high art of computer programming; it is also widely available. Some installations have the Cooley and Lohnes routines;[19] some have Veldman's.[20] And there are a number of other good sets of programs, though perhaps not as widely distributed.

Even if the student's institution does not have a special program that will accomplish all he wants, most computer installations will have an ordinary multiple regression program that will at least calculate R and either the b or β weights, or both, in addition to the basic statistics calculated with almost any data. Using the output and intermediate statistics, the student can calculate other desired statistics himself. Soon, general purpose routines will be available for calculating all the necessary operations for multiple regression and other multivariate methods. To use them adequately, however, will require more than superficial understanding of the methods and some knowledge of programming.

Multiple regression programs can be written in several ways. The most popular, evidently, is the so-called *stepwise regression* method. The computer first selects the independent variable, X_a, that has the highest correlation with the dependent variable, Y, and calculates regression statistics. It then selects the variable X_b that, after the first variable, will contribute most to the variance of Y. It then stops to evaluate what it has done. That is, it examines the contribution the first variable would have made had it been entered second. If this contribution turns out not to be statistically significant, the variable is dropped. The process is continued until a statistical test of significance strikes a variable, X_m, that does not contribute significantly to R^2.

The *forward-selection* procedure is much like the stepwise method except that it omits the recapitulatory evaluative step. The *backward-elimination* procedure consists of first calculating the regression of Y with all the independent variables, testing each independent variable for its contribution as though it were the last in the equation, and eliminating that variable which does not meet a certain criterion of significance. There are other methods, of course, but they do not really concern us.[21]

The stepwise method seems to have been accepted as the best by some experts. Draper and Smith, for example, recommend it as the best method. But they also warn against its use by amateur statisticians. Their warning should be under-

[18] W. Dixon, ed., *BMD Biomedical Computer Programs*. Los Angeles: University of California Press, 1970.

[19] W. Cooley and P. Lohnes, *Multivariate Data Analysis*. New York: Wiley, 1971.

[20] D. Veldman, *Fortran Programming for the Behavioral Sciences*. New York: Holt, Rinehart and Winston, 1967.

[21] A good discussion of the different methods with complete computer solutions of the stepwise method is: N. Draper and H. Smith, *Applied Regression Analysis*. New York: Wiley, 1966, chap. 6. See, also, Kerlinger and Pedhazur, *op. cit.*, chap. 11.

lined. The trouble with the stepwise method is that it is too magical: it yields solutions so easily and the method sounds so good that the user can be trapped into believing that a stepwise solution is the best or "correct" solution. Unfortunately, there is no universal best or correct solution. A solution that is correct for one purpose may not be correct for another because it is often legitimate to ask different questions of the same data. Are we interested, for instance, in studying the interaction of social class with, say, methods of teaching science, or are we interested merely in controlling or eliminating the possible effect on the dependent variable of social class? Which question we want answered makes a difference in the order of entry of the independent variables into the regression equation.

The only really dependable guides to the kind of regression solution to use are theory, hypotheses, prior knowledge, and, let's face it, hunch. The researcher has to know what he is doing. Statistical significance is not too happy a criterion. Nor is the amount of variance contributed always suitable. It is possible that an independent variable of little theoretical or practical interest can contribute substantially to the variance of a dependent variable. The important thing is the judgment of theoretical or practical importance and not just the amount of contribution to variance. In short, use the stepwise method but with more circumspection and caution than one would usually use. Like some factor analytic solutions, the results can be misleading if the researcher is not quite alert and aware of the difficulties and complexities of the interpretation of multiple regression analysis data.

Multivariate Analysis and Behavioral Research

Although our study of multivariate methods has been rather superficial, we must still stop to place them into the research scheme of things and to evaluate them. Should we abandon analysis of variance, for example, simply because multiple regression can accomplish all that analysis of variance can—and more? Some such implication has perhaps been picked up by the reader. Isn't multiple regression analysis *really* unsuited to experimental data because it is a so-called "correlational method" (which it is only in part)? Why haven't we described and discussed multivariate analysis of variance? Other important questions can and should be asked and answered, especially at this time in the development of behavioral science research. We are at the point, perhaps, of an important transition. Since Sir Ronald Fisher invented and expounded the analysis of variance in the 1920s and 1930s, the method, or rather, approach, has had great influence on behavioral research, particularly in psychology. Are we now about to leave this stage? Have we entered a "multivariate stage"? If so, it can have an enormously important influence on the kind and quality of research done by psychologists, sociologists, and educators during the next decade. Obviously we can't handle all such questions in a textbook. But we should at least try to open the door to the student.

Should the analysis of variance approach be supplanted by multiple regression analysis? I don't think it should. But is this merely a sentimental clinging to something I have found interesting and satisfying? Perhaps. But there is more to it than that. There is little point to using multiple regression in the ordinary analysis of variance problem situation: random assignment of subjects to experimental treatments; equal or proportional n's in the cells; one, two, or three independent variables. Another argument for analysis of variance is its usefulness in teaching. Multiple regression analysis, while elegant and powerful, lacks the structural heuristic quality of analysis of variance. There is nothing quite so effective in teaching and learning research as drawing paradigms of the designs using analysis of variance analytic partitioning.

The answer is that both methods should be taught and learned. The additional demands on both teacher and student are inevitable, just as the development, growth, and use of inferential statistics earlier in the century made their teaching and learning inevitable. Multiple regression and other multivariate methods, however, will no doubt suffer some of the lack of understanding, even opposition, that inferential statistics has suffered. Even today there are psychologists, sociologists, and educators who know little about inferential statistics or modern analysis, and who even oppose their learning and use. This is part of the social psychology and pathology of the subject, however. While there will no doubt be cultural lag, the ultimate acceptance of these powerful tools of analysis is probably assured.

Multivariate methods, as we have seen, are not easy to use and to interpret. This is due not only to their complexity; it is due even more to the complexity of the phenomena that behavioral scientists work with. One of the drawbacks of educational research, for instance, has been that the enormous complexity of a school or a classroom could not adequately be handled by the too-simple methods used. The scientist, naturally, can never mirror the "real" world with his methods of observation and analysis. He is forever bound to simplifications of the situations and problems he studies. He can never "see things whole," just as no human being can see and understand the whole of anything. But multivariate methods mirror psychological, sociological, and educational reality better than simpler methods, and they enable researchers to handle larger portions of their research problems. In educational research, the days of the simple methods experiment with an experimental group and a control group are almost over. In sociological research, the reduction of much valuable data to frequency and percentage crossbreaks will decrease relative to the whole body of sociological research.

Most important of all, the healthy future of behavioral research depends on the healthy development of psychological, sociological, and other theories to help explain the relations among behavioral phenomena. By definition, theories are interrelated sets of constructs or variables. Obviously, multivariate methods are well adapted to testing fairly complex theoretical formulations, since their very nature is the analysis of several variables at once. Indeed, the development of behavioral theory must go hand-in-hand, even depend upon, the assimilation, mastery, and intelligent use of multivariate methods.[22]

[22]The informed reader may wonder why other multivariate methods, especially multivariate analysis of variance, have not been described. The answer is space and complexity. One simply cannot describe any complex technique effectively, especially in an elementary way, without discussing and illustrating it in some detail. Another limitation is that the explanations had to avoid matrix algebra and matrix notation—without which multivariate analysis of variance can hardly be approached. In any case, multivariate analysis of variance is the generalization of analysis of variance to any number of independent variables and any number of dependent variables. References will be found in Study Suggestion 1.

Study Suggestions

1. Unfortunately, there appear to be no completely satisfactory elementary treatments of multiple regression, especially if one expects concomitant regression treatment of analysis of variance. Perhaps satisfactory elementary treatment of such a complex subject is not possible. The following references may be helpful.

   Kerlinger, F., and Pedhazur, E. *Multiple Regression in Behavioral Research*. New York: Holt, Rinehart and Winston, 1973 (in press). A text that attempts to enhance understanding of multiple regression and its research uses by providing as simple exposition as possible and many examples with simple numbers. Also has a complete multiple regression computer program (Appendix D)

   Snedecor, G., and Cochran, G. *Statistical Methods*, 6th ed. Ames, Iowa: Iowa State University Press, 1967. Chaps. 6 and 13 are pertinent—and very good, indeed.

   Tatsuoka, M. *Multivariate Analysis : Techniques for Educational and Psychological Research*. New York: Wiley, 1971. This clearly written middle-level book has little discussion of multiple regression, but competently attacks many important multivariate problems.

   Two of the following four books contain computer programs for multiple regression with explanations of the theory and the calculations. The third (Dixon) is the manual for the well-known BMD programs.

   Cooley, W., and Lohnes, P. *Multivariate Data Analysis*. New York: Wiley, 1971. Although more difficult than its predecessor, its computer routines can be adapted to different installations. It is also an important textbook.

   Dixon, W., ed. *BMD Biomedical Computer Programs*. Los Angeles: University of California Press, 1970. Describes the rationale of the BMD programs with complete instructions for use. Of six multiple regression programs, BMDO2R and BMDO3R are probably the most useful. Help is usually needed in running BMD programs—or, for that matter, any complex programs.

   Overall, J., and Klett, C. *Applied Multivariate Analysis*. New York: McGraw-Hill, 1972. Has multivariate analysis and factor analysis programs, as well as detailed discussions of methods. Describes techniques for the classification of individuals in depth. Chapter 2 gives a particularly valuable program that calculates the basic statistics used in multivariate analysis.

   Veldman, D. *Fortran Programming for the Behavioral Sciences*. New York: Holt, Rinehart and Winston, 1967. Veldman, like Cooley and Lohnes, offers computer programs that can be adapted to local installations.

   After the student and researcher have mastered the elements of multiple regression analysis and have some experience with actual problems, the following references provide sophisticated guidance in the use of multiple regression analysis and, more important, the interpretation of data.

   Cohen, J. "Multiple Regression as a General Data-Analytic System." *Psychological Bulletin*, LXX (1968), 426–443. Successfully shows the relation between multiple regression and analysis of variance and also suggests general research uses of multiple regression.

   Darlington, R. "Multiple Regression in Psychological Research and Practice." *Psychological Bulletin*, LXIX (1968), 161–182. Excellent, highly sophisticated, and sobering discussion of multiple regression.

   Rulon, P., and Brooks, W. "On Statistical Tests of Group Differences." In D. Whitla, ed., *Handbook of Measurement and Assessment in Behavioral Sciences*. Reading, Mass.: Addison-Wesley, 1968, chap. 2. Lean exposition of the relations among a wide range of tests of statistical significance. Highly recommended for the more advanced student.

2. Suppose that a social psychologist has two correlation matrices:

A

	X_1	X_2	Y
X_1	1.00	0	.70
X_2	0	1.00	.60
Y	.70	.60	1.00

B

	X_1	X_2	Y
X_1	1.00	.40	.70
X_2	.40	1.00	.60
Y	.70	.60	1.00

(a) Which matrix, A or B, will yield the higher R^2? Why?
(b) Calculate the R^2 of matrix A.
[*Answers:* (a) Matrix A; (b) $R^2 = .85$.]

3. Cutright, in a study of the effect of communication, urbanization, education, and agriculture on the political development of 77 nations, found a multiple correlation of .82.[23] The correlations between each of the independent variables and the dependent variable were high: .81, .69, .74, and −.72. But the intercorrelations among the independent variables were also high—mostly in the .70's and .80's. What conclusions can you reach about the relations between the independent and dependent variables? The beta weights were (for the four independent variables): .65, .19, .02, and .00. How much dependence can be put on these weights? What would happen if we reversed the order of entry of the independent variables?

4. Here are three sets of simple fictitious data, laid out for an analysis of variance. Lay out the data for multiple regression analysis, and calculate as much of the regression analysis as possible. Use dummy coding (1, 0), as in Table 36.5. The b coefficients are: $b_1 = 3$; $b_2 = 6$.

A_1	A_2	A_3
7	12	5
6	9	2
5	10	6
9	8	3
8	11	4

Imagine that A_1, A_2, and A_3 are three methods of changing racial attitudes and that the dependent variable is a measure of change with higher scores indicating more change. Interpret the results.
[*Answers:* $a = 4$; $R^2 = .75$; $F = 18$, with $df = 2, 12$; $ss_{\text{reg}} = 90$; $ss_t = 120$. Note that these fictitious data are really the scores of Table 36.4 with 1 added to each score. Compare the various regression and analysis of variance statistics, above, with those calculated with the data of Table 36.4.]

5. Using the data of Table 35.2 in Chapter 35, calculate the sums of each X_1 and X_2 pair. Correlate these sums with the Y scores. Compare the square of this correlation with $R^2_{y.12} = .51$ ($r^2 = .70^2 = .49$). Since the two values are quite close, why shouldn't we simply use the averages of the independent variables and not bother with the complexity of multiple regression analysis?

[23] P. Cutright, "National Political Development: Measurement and Analysis." *American Sociological Review*, XXVII (1963), 229–245.

CHAPTER 37

Factor Analysis

Because of its power and elegance, factor analysis can be called the queen of analytic methods. Even more forbidding in its calculations than other multivariate methods, factor analysis has become accessible with the availability of computers and with increased understanding of its purposes and uses in behavioral research. Until only a few years ago, it was relatively rare to find published factor analytic studies. Not only were the many calculations forbidding; there was too little understanding of the method's purpose and place in research.[1] In any case, factor analysis is an extremely powerful and useful approach to behavioral data, one that can help solve heretofore intractable research problems.

Factor analysis is a method for determining the number and nature of the underlying variables among larger numbers of measures. More succinctly, it is a method for determining k underlying variables (factors) from n sets of measures, k being less than n. It may also be called a method for extracting common factor variances from sets of measures.

Factor analysis serves the cause of scientific parsimony. It reduces the multiplicity of tests and measures to greater simplicity. It tells us, in effect, what tests or measures belong together—which ones virtually measure the same thing, in other words, and how much they do so. It thus reduces the number of variables with which the scientist must cope. It also (hopefully) helps the scientist to locate and identify unities or fundamental properties underlying tests and measures.

A *factor* is a construct, a hypothetical entity, that is assumed to underlie tests, scales, items, and, indeed, measures of almost any kind. A number of factors have been found to underlie intelligence, for example: verbal ability, numerical ability,

[1]The reader can get some idea of the magnitude of the calculations involved in almost any multivariate method from the examples given in the beginning of Appendix C.

abstract reasoning, spatial reasoning, memory, and others. Similarly, aptitude, attitude, and personality factors have been isolated and identified. Even nations and people have been factored!

A Hypothetical Example

Suppose we administer six tests to a large number of seventh-grade pupils. We suspect that the six tests are measuring not six but some smaller number of variables. The tests are: *vocabulary*, *reading*, *synonyms*, *numbers*, *arithmetic* (standardized test), *arithmetic* (teacher-made test). The names of these tests indicate their nature. We label them, respectively, V, R, S, N, AS, AT. (The last two tests, though both arithmetic, have different content. We assume a good reason for including both of them in our little test battery.) After the tests are administered and scored, coefficients of correlation are calculated between each test and every other test. We lay out the r's in a correlation matrix (usually called R matrix). The matrix is given in Table 37.1.

TABLE **37.1** *R* MATRIX: COEFFICIENTS OF CORRELATION AMONG SIX TESTS

		V	*R*	*S*	*N*	*AS*	*AT*
Cluster I	*V*		.72	.63	.09	.09	.00
	R	.72		.57	.15	.16	.09
	S	.63	.57		.14	.15	.09
	N	.09	.15	.14		.57	.63
	AS	.09	.16	.15	.57		.72
	AT	.00	.09	.09	.63	.72	
						Cluster II	

Recall that a matrix is any rectangular array of numbers (or symbols). Correlation matrices are always square and symmetric. This is because the lower half of the matrix below the diagonal (from upper left to lower right) is the same as the upper half of the matrix. That is, the coefficients in the lower half are identical to those in the upper half, except for their arrangement. (Note that the top row is the same as the first column, the second row the same as the second column, and so on.)

The problem before us is expressed in two questions: How many underlying variables, or factors, are there? What are the factors? They are presumed to be underlying unities behind the test performances reflected in the correlation coefficients. If two or more tests are substantially correlated, then the tests share variance. They have common factor variance. They are measuring something in common.

The first question in this case is easy to answer. There are two factors. This is indicated by the two clusters of r's, circled and labeled I and II in Table 37.1. Note that V correlates with R, .72; V with S, .63; and R with S, .57. V, R, and S appear to be measuring something in common. Similarly, N correlates with AS,

.57, and with *AT*, .63; and *AS* correlates with *AT*, .72. *N*, *AS*, and *AT* are measuring something in common. It is important to note, however, that the tests in Cluster I, though themselves intercorrelated, are not to any great extent correlated with the tests in Cluster II. Likewise, *N*, *AS*, and *AT*, though themselves intercorrelated, are not substantially correlated with the tests *V*, *R*, and *S*. What is measured in common by the tests in Cluster I is evidently not the same as what is measured in common by the tests of Cluster II. There appear to be two clusters or factors in the matrix.[2]

By inspecting the *R* matrix, we have determined that there are two factors underlying these tests. The second question (What are the factors?) is almost always more difficult. When we ask what the factors are, we seek to name them. We want *constructs* that explain the underlying unities or common factor variances of the factors. We ask what is common to the tests *V*, *R*, and *S*, on the one hand, and to the tests *N*, *AS*, and *AT*, on the other hand. *V*, *R*, and *S* are vocabulary, reading, and synonym tests. All three involve words, to a large extent. Perhaps the underlying factor is *verbal ability*. We name the factor *Verbal*, or *V*. *N*, *AS*, and *AT* all involve numerical or arithmetic operations. Suppose we named this factor *Arithmetic*. A friend points out to us that test *N* does not really involve arithmetic operations, since it consists mostly of manipulating numbers nonarithmetically. We overlooked this in our eagerness to name the underlying unity. Anyway, we now name the factor *Numerical*, or *Number*, or *N*. There is no inconsistency: all three tests involve numbers and numerical manipulation and operation.

Both questions have been answered: there are two factors, and they are named *Verbal*, *V*, and *Numerical*, *N*. It must be hastily and urgently pointed out, however, that neither question is ever finally answered in actual factor analytic research. This is especially true in early investigations of a field. The number of factors can change in subsequent investigations using the same tests. One of the *V* tests may also have some variance in common with another factor, say *K*. If a test measuring *K* is added to the matrix, a third factor may emerge. Perhaps more important, the name of a factor may be incorrect. Subsequent investigation using these *V* tests and other tests may show that *V* is not now common to all the tests. The investigator must then find another construct, another source of common factor variance. In short, factor names are tentative; they are hypotheses to be tested in further factor analytic and other kinds of research.

Factor Matrices and Factor Loadings

If a test measures one factor only, it is said to be *factorially "pure."* To the extent that a test measures a factor, it is said to be *loaded* on the factor, or saturated with the factor. Factor analysis is not really complete unless we know whether a test is

[2]In this presentation, occasional oversimplifications and somewhat unrealistic examples are used. For example, the *R* matrix of Table 37.1 is unrealistic. All the tests would be positively correlated, though the two factors would probably emerge. In addition, clusters, while similar to factors, are not factors. For simplicity and pedagogy, however, we risk these discrepancies.

factorially "pure" and how saturated it is with a factor. If a measure is not factorially pure, we usually want to know what other factors pervade it. Some measures are so complex that it is difficult to tell just what they measure. A good example is teacher grades, or grade-point averages. If a test contains more than one factor, it is said to be *factorially complex.*

Some tests and measures are factorially quite complex. The Stanford-Binet Intelligence Test, the Otis intelligence tests, and the *F* (authoritarianism) scale are good examples. A desideratum of scientific investigation is to have pure measures of variables. If a measure of numerical ability is not factorially pure, how can we have confidence that a relation between numerical ability and school achievement, say, is really the relation we think it is? If the test measures both numerical ability and verbal reasoning, doubt is thrown upon relations studied with its help.

To solve these and other problems, we need an objective method to determine the number of factors, the tests loaded on the various factors, and the magnitude of the loadings. There are several factor analytic methods to accomplish these purposes. We discuss one of these later.

One of the final outcomes of a factor analysis is called a *factor matrix*, a table of coefficients that expresses the relations between the tests and the underlying factors. The factor matrix yielded by factor analyzing the data of Table 37.1 with the principal factors method, one of the several methods available, is given in Table 37.2.[3] The entries in the table are called *factor loadings*. They can be written a_{ij}, meaning the loading a of test i on factor j. In the second line, .79 is the factor loading of test *R* on factor *A*.[4] In the fourth line, .70 is the factor loading of test *N* on factor *B*. Test *AS* has the following loadings: .10 on factor *A* and .79 on factor *B*.

Factor loadings are not hard to interpret. They range from -1.00 through 0 to $+1.00$, like correlation coefficients. They are interpreted similarly. In short, they express the correlations *between the tests and the factors*. For example, test *V* has the following correlations with factors *A* and *B*, respectively: .83 and .01. Evidently test *V* is highly loaded on *A*, but not at all on *B*.[5] Tests *V*, *R*, and *S* are loaded on *A* but not on *B*. Tests *N*, *AS*, and *AT* are loaded on *B* but not on *A*. All the tests are "pure."

The entries in the last column are called *communalities*, or h^2's. They are the sums of squares of the factor loadings of a test or variable. For example, the com-

[3]Actually, factor analytic methods do not yield final solutions like that in Table 37.2. They yield solutions that require what is called "rotation of axes." Rotation will be discussed later.

[4]Some factor analysts label final solution factors I, II, . . ., or I′, II′, ... In this chapter we label unrotated factors I, II, . . . and rotated (final solution) factors *A*, *B*, ...

[5]Unfortunately, there is no generally accepted standard error of factor loadings. A crude rule is to use the standard error of *r*—or, easier, to find the *r* that is significant for the *N* of the study. For example, with $N = 200$, an *r* of about .18 is significant at the .01 level. Some factor analysts in some studies do not bother with loadings less than .30, or even .40. Others do. The loadings considered "significant" in Table 37.2 are italicized. The use of $1/\sqrt{N}$ as the standard error of factor loadings is recommended in: N. Cliff and C. Hamburger, "The Study of Sampling Errors in Factor Analysis by Means of Artificial Experiments," *Psychological Bulletin*, LXVIII (1967), 430–445. A more conservative formula—that is, it yields larger standard errors—is given in: H. Harman, *Modern Factor Analysis*, 2d ed. Chicago: University of Chicago Press, 1967, pp. 197, 435. Both formulas must be used with circumspection. With large N (> 400), the two estimates are close.

TABLE **37.2** FACTOR MATRIX OF DATA OF TABLE 37.1, ROTATED SOLUTION[a]

Tests	*A*	*B*	h^2
V	*.83*	.01	.70
R	*.79*	.10	.63
S	*.70*	.10	.50
N	.10	*.70*	.50
AS	.10	*.79*	.63
AT	.01	*.83*	.70

[a]See text for identification of the tests. "Significant" loadings are italicized. See footnote to Table 37.5.

munality of test *R* is $(.79)^2+(.10)^2=.63$. The communality of a test or variable is its common factor variance. This will be explained later when we discuss factor theory.

Before going further, we should again note that this example is unrealistic. Factor matrices rarely present such a clear-cut picture. Indeed, the factor matrix of Table 37.2 was "known." The author first wrote the matrix given in Table 37.3. If this matrix is multiplied by itself, the *R* matrix of Table 37.1 (with diagonal values) will be obtained. In this case, all that is necessary to obtain *R* is to multiply each row by every other row. For example, multiply row *V* by row *R*: $(.90)(.80)+(.00)(.10)=.72$; row *V* by row *S*: $(.90)(.70)+(.00)(.10)=.63$; row *S* by row *AS*: $(.70)(.10)+(.10)(.80)=.15$; and so on. The resulting *R* matrix was then factor-analyzed.[6]

It is instructive to compare Tables 37.2 and 37.3. Note the discrepancies. They are small. That is, the fallible factor analytic method cannot perfectly reproduce the "true" factor matrix. It estimates it. In this case the fit is close because of the deliberate simplicity of the problem. Real data are not so obliging. Moreover,

TABLE **37.3** ORIGINAL FACTOR MATRIX FROM WHICH THE *R* MATRIX OF TABLE 37.1 WAS DERIVED

Tests	*A*	*B*	h^2
V	*.90*	.00	.81
R	*.80*	.10	.65
S	*.70*	.10	.50
N	.10	*.70*	.50
AS	.10	*.80*	.65
AT	.00	*.90*	.81

[6]This matrix multiplication operation springs from what is called the basic equation of factor analysis: $R=FF'$, which says succinctly in matrix symbols what was said more laboriously above. A thorough understanding of factor analysis requires a good understanding of matrix algebra. Thurstone has written an excellent exposition: L. Thurstone, *Multiple Factor Analysis*. Chicago: University of Chicago Press, 1947, chap. II. See, too, the Kerlinger and Pedhazur, Tatsuoka, and Veldman references, Study Suggestion 1, Chapter 36.

we never know the "true" factor matrix. If we did, there would be no need for factor analysis. We always estimate the factor matrix from the correlation matrix. The complexity and fallibility of research data frequently make this estimation a difficult business.

Some Factor Theory

In Chapter 27 we wrote an equation that expressed sources of variance in a measure (or test):

$$V_t = V_{co} + V_{sp} + V_e \tag{37.1}$$

where V_t = total variance of a measure; V_{co} = common factor variance, or the variance that two or more measures share in common; V_{sp} = specific variance, or the variance of the measure that is not shared with any other measure, that is, the variance of that measure and no other; V_e = error variance.

The common factor variance V_{co} was broken down into two sources of variance, A and B, two factors (see Eq. 27.11):

$$V_{co} = V_A + V_B \tag{37.2}$$

V_A might be verbal ability variance, and V_B might be numerical ability variance.

This is reasonable if we think of the sums of squares of factor loadings of any test:

$$h_i^2 = a_i^2 + b_i^2 + \cdots + k_i^2 \tag{37.3}$$

where a_i^2, b_i^2, . . . are the squares of the factor loadings of test i, and h_i^2 is the communality of test i. But $h_i^2 = V_{co}$. Therefore $V(A) = a^2$ and $V(B) = b^2$, and Eq. 37.2 is tied to real factor analytic operations.

But there may, of course, be more than two factors. The generalized equation is

$$V_{co} = V_A + V_B + \cdots + V_K \tag{37.4}$$

Substituting in Eq. 37.1, we obtain

$$V_t = V_A + V_B + \cdots + V_K + V_{sp} + V_e \tag{37.5}$$

Dividing through by V_t we find a proportional representation:

$$\frac{V_t}{V_t} = 1.00 = \underbrace{\overbrace{\frac{V_A}{V_t} + \frac{V_B}{V_t} + \cdots + \frac{V_K}{V_t}}^{h^2} + \frac{V_{sp}}{V_t}}_{r_{tt}} + \frac{V_e}{V_t} \tag{37.6}$$

The h^2 and r_{tt} parts of the equation have been labeled as they were in Chapter 27.

This equation has beauty. It ties tightly together measurement theory and factor theory.[7] h^2 is the proportion of the total variance that is common factor

[7]See J. Guilford, *Psychometric Methods*, 2d ed. New York: McGraw-Hill, 1954, pp. 354–357, and Thurstone, *op. cit.*, chap. II.

variance. r_{tt} is the proportion of the total variance that is reliable variance. V_e/V_t is the proportion of the total variance that is error variance. In Chapter 27 an equation like this enabled us to tie reliability and validity together. Now, it shows us the relation between factor theory and measurement theory. We see, in brief, that *the main problem of factor analysis is to determine the variance components of the total common factor variance.*

Take test V in Table 37.2. A glance at Eq. 37.6 shows us, among other things, that the reliability of a measure is always greater than, or equal to, its communality. Test V's reliability, then, is at least .70. Suppose $r_{tt} = .80$. Since $V_t/V_t = 1.00$, we can fill in all the terms:

$$\frac{V_t}{V_t} = 1.00 = \underbrace{\overbrace{(.83)^2 + (.01)^2}^{h^2 = .69} + \overbrace{.11}^{V_{sp}}}_{r_{tt} = .80} + \overbrace{.20}^{V_e}$$

Test V, then, has a high proportion of common factor variance and a low proportion of specific variance.

The proportions can be seen clearly in a circle diagram. Let the area of the circle equal the total variance, or 1.00 (100 percent of the area), in Fig. 37.1. The three variances have been indicated by blocking out areas of the circle. V_{co}, or h^2, for example, is 69 percent, V_{sp} is 11 percent, and V_e is 20 percent of the total variance.

A factor analytic investigation including test V would tell us mainly about V_{co}, the common factor variance. It would tell us the proportion of the test's total variance that is common factor variance and would give us clues to its nature by telling us which other tests share the same common factor variance and which do not.[8]

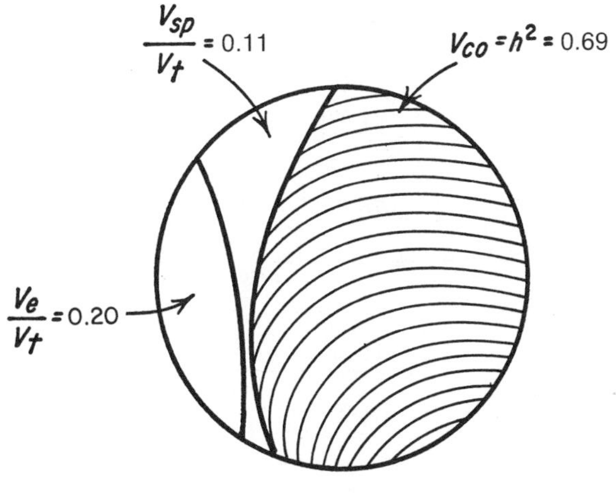

FIG. 37.1

[8]See Fig. 27.1 in Chapter 27 for a diagrammatic two-test illustration of these notions.

Graphical Representation of Factors and Factor Loadings

The student of factor analysis must learn to think spatially and geometrically if he is to grasp the essential nature of the factor approach. There are two or three good ways to do this. A table of correlations can be represented by the use of vectors and the angles between them. We here use a more common method. We treat the row entries of a factor matrix as coordinates and plot them in geometric space. In Fig. 37.2 the factor matrix entries of Table 37.2 have been plotted.

The two factors, A and B, are laid out at right angles to each other. These are called *reference axes*. Appropriate factor loading values are indicated on each of the axes. Then each test's loadings are treated as coordinates and plotted. For example, test R's loadings are (.79, .10). Go out .79 on A and up .10 on B. This point has been indicated in Fig. 37.2 by a circled letter indicating the test. Plot the coordinates of the other five tests similarly.

The factor structure can now be clearly seen. Each test is highly loaded on one factor but not on the other. They are all relatively "pure" measures of their respective factors. A seventh point has been indicated in Fig. 37.2 by a circled cross in order to illustrate a presumed test that measures both factors. Its coordinates are (.60, .50). This means that the test is loaded on both factors, .60 on A and .50 on B. This test is not "pure." Factor structures of this simplicity and clarity, where the factors are orthogonal (the axes at right angles to each other), the test loadings substantial and "pure," almost no tests loaded on two or more factors, and only two factors, are not common.

Most published factor analytic studies report more than two factors. Four, five, even nine, ten, and more factors have been reported. Graphical representa-

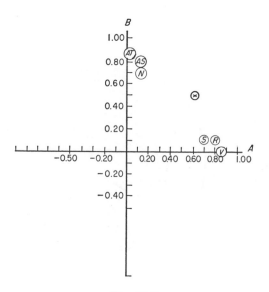

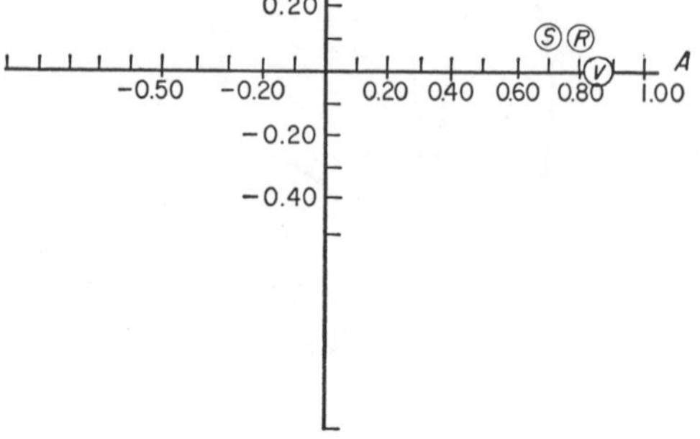

FIG. 37.2

tion of such factor structures in one graph is, of course, not possible. Factor analysts customarily plot factors two at a time, though it is possible to plot three at a time. It must be admitted, however, that it is difficult to visualize or keep in mind complex n-dimensional structures. One therefore visualizes two-dimensional structures and generalizes to n dimensions algebraically.

Methods of Factor Analysis

There are a number of methods of factor analyzing a correlation matrix: principal factors, centroid, diagonal, maximum likelihood, multiple group, minres, image, alpha, and so on.[9] We cannot discuss all these methods. Our purpose is elementary basic understanding. Therefore, we describe the method that is used the most at present and that is widely available at computer installations: the principal factors method.

The reader may ask: Why not use a comparatively simple cluster method like the inspection approach used earlier instead of a complex method like the principal factors method? Cluster methods can be used and have been recommended. They depend upon our identifying clusters and presumed factors by finding interrelated groups of correlation coefficients or other measures of relation (for example, D measures—see Chapter 33). In Table 37.1, the clusters are easy to find. In most R matrices, however, the clusters cannot be so easily identified. More objective and precise methods are needed.

The Principal Factors Method[10]

The principal factors method is mathematically satisfying because it yields a mathematically unique solution of a factor problem. Perhaps its major solution feature is that it extracts a maximum amount of variance as each factor is calculated. In other words, the first factor extracts the most variance, the second the next most variance, and so on.

To show the logic of the principal factors method without considerable mathematics is difficult. One can achieve a certain intuitive understanding of the method, however, by approaching it geometrically. Conceive tests or variables as points in m-dimensional space. Variables that are highly and positively correlated should be near each other and away from variables with which they do not correlate. If this reasoning is correct, there should be swarms of points in space. Each of these points can be located in the space if suitable axes are inserted into the space, one axis for each dimension of the m dimensions. Then any point's location is its multiple identification obtained by reading its coordinates on the m axes. The factor problem is to shoot axes through neighboring swarms of points and to so locate

[9]Harman, *op. cit.*, chap. 6.

[10]See *ibid.*, pp. 99–101 and chap. 8. This is a thorough exposition, with computational and analytic details. A fairly easy-to-follow exposition of the method is given in G. Thomson, *The Factorial Analysis of Human Ability*. Boston: Houghton-Mifflin, 1951, chap. VII. (Thomson really explains the "principal components" method, which differs in the quantities inserted in the diagonal of the R matrix before solution. The term "principal axes" has also been used.)

these axes that they "account for" as much of the variances of the variables as possible.

Take the example we used in the chapter on the semantic differential (Chapter 33): imagine the room you are sitting in to have swarms of points in various parts of its three-dimensional space. Imagine that some of the points cluster together in the upper right center of the room (from your vantage point). Now imagine another cluster of points at another point in the room, say in the lower right center. Part of the problem is to locate axes—three axes in this case, since the room is three-dimensional—so as to identify and appropriately label the swarms and the points in the swarms.

We can demonstrate these ideas with a simple two-dimensional example. Suppose we have five tests. These tests, let us say, are situated in two-dimensional space as indicated in Fig. 37.3. The closer two points are, the more they are re-

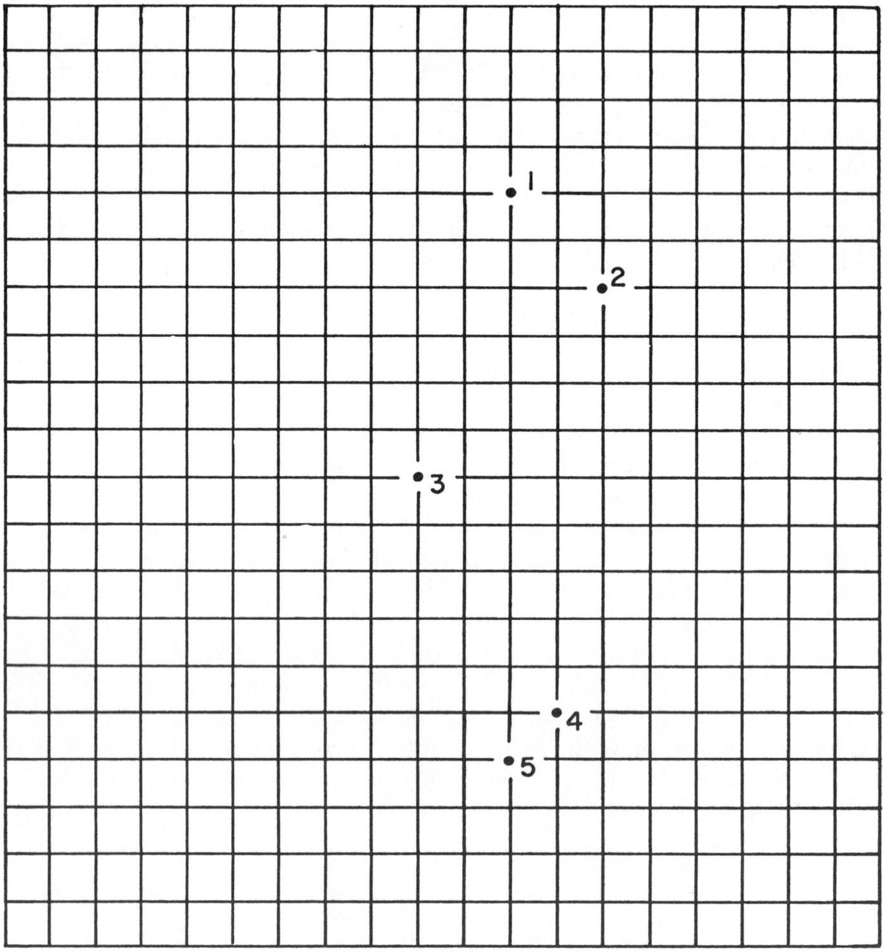

FIG. 37.3

lated. The problem is to determine: (1) how many factors there are; (2) what tests are loaded on what factors; and (3) the magnitudes of the test loadings.

The problem will now be solved in two different ways, each interesting as well as instructive. First, we solve directly from the points themselves. Follow these directions. Draw a vertical line three units to the left of point 3. Draw a horizontal line one unit below point 3. Label these reference axes I and II. Now read off the coordinates of each point, for instance, point 2 is (.70, .50), point 4 is (.60, −.40). Write a "factor matrix" with these five pairs of values.

Rotate the axes orthogonally and clockwise so that axis I goes between points 4 and 5. Axis II, of course, will go between Points 1 and 2. (The use of a protractor is recommended: the rotation should be approximately 40 degrees.) Label these "new" rotated axes *A* and *B*. Cut a strip of four-to-the-inch graph paper. (The points are plotted on this size graph paper.) Count the base of each square as .10 (.10 = 1/4 inch; ten units, of course, equal 1.00). Using the strip as a measure, measure the distances of the points on the new axes. For example, point 2 should be close to (.22, .83), and point 5 should be close to (.71, −.06). (It does not make too much difference if there are small discrepancies.) The original (I and II) and rotated (*A* and *B*) axes and the five points are shown in Fig. 37.4.

Now write both factor matrices, unrotated and rotated. They are given in Table 37.4. The problem is solved: There are two factors. Points (tests) 1 and 2 are high on factor *B*, points 4 and 5 are high on factor *A*, and point 3 has low loadings on both factors. The three questions originally asked have been answered.

TABLE **37.4** UNROTATED AND ROTATED FACTOR MATRICES, POINT-DISTANCE PROBLEM

Points	Unrotated I	II	Points	Rotated *A*	*B*
1	.50	.70	1	−.07	*.86*
2	.70	.50	2	.22	*.83*
3	.30	.10	3	.17	.27
4	.60	−.40	4	*.72*	.08
5	.50	−.50	5	*.71*	−.06

This procedure is analogous to psychological factor problems. Tests are conceived as points in factor *m*-dimensional space. The factor loadings are the coordinates. The problem is to introduce appropriate reference frames or axes and then to "read off" the factor loadings. Unfortunately, in actual problems we do not know the number of factors (the dimensionality of the factor space and thus the number of axes) or the location of the points in space. These must be determined from data.

The above description is figurative. One does not "read off" factor loadings from reference axes; one calculates them using rather complex methods. The principal factors method actually involves the solution of simultaneous linear equations. The roots obtained from the solution are called *eigenvalues*. *Eigenvectors* are also obtained; after suitable transformation, they become the factor loadings. The fictitious *R* matrix of Table 37.1 was solved in this manner, yielding

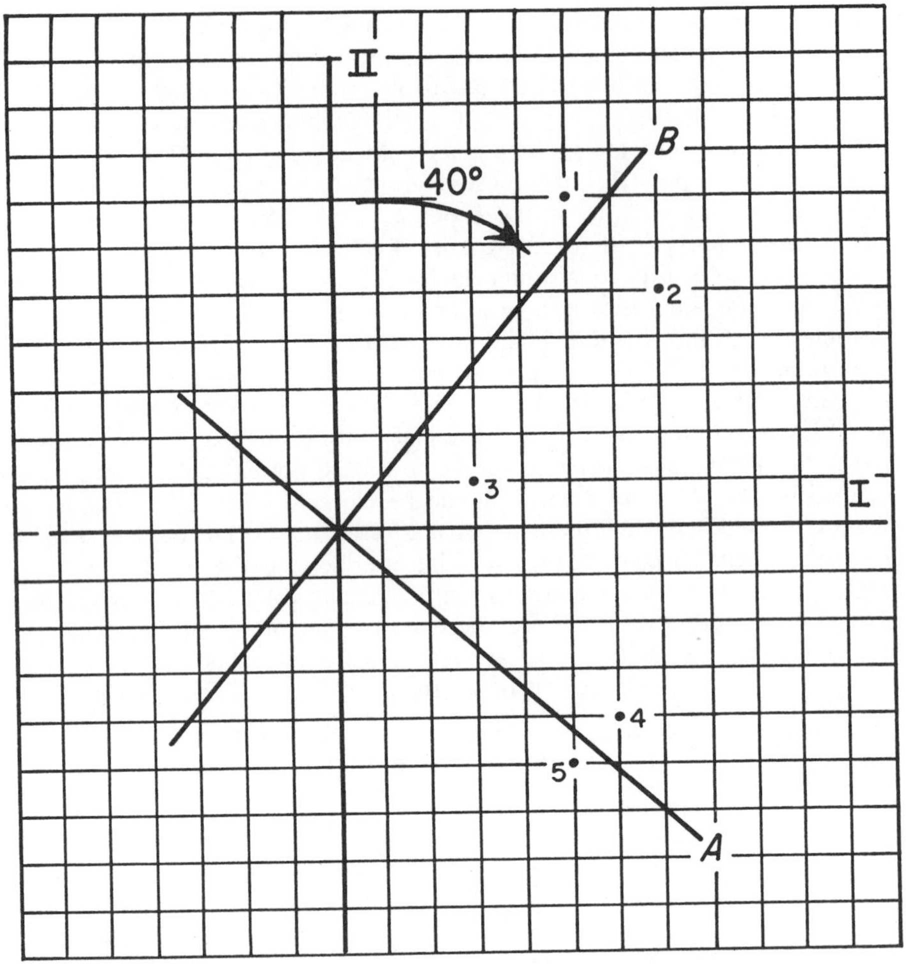

FIG. 37.4

the factor matrix to be given later in Table 37.5. Most computer factor analysis programs use principal factors solutions. And the programs given in published computer program texts use it. The student who expects to use factor analysis to any extent should study the method carefully and at least understand what it does. There is nothing quite so dangerous and self-defeating as using computer programs blindly. This is especially true in factor analysis.[11]

[11]It is possible, perhaps probable, that the principal factors solution will be replaced in the next decade by other methods. Harman (*op. cit.*, pp. 187 ff.) thinks that his minres method, an approach quite different from the principal factors method–and equally if not more complex–will perhaps replace it. Harris also proposes other methods: C. Harris, "Some Recent Developments in Factor Analysis," *Educational and Psychological Measurement*, XXIV (1964), 193–206. These developments cannot be discussed here. The most likely outcome will be that several excellent methods will be readily available, so that researchers can select methods to suit problems.

Rotation and Simple Structure

Most factor analytic methods produce results in a form that is difficult or impossible to interpret. Thurstone argued that it was necessary to rotate factor matrices if one wanted to interpret them adequately.[12] He pointed out that original factor matrices are arbitrary in the sense that an infinite number of reference frames (axes) can be found to reproduce any given *R* matrix.[13] A principal factors matrix and its loadings account for the common factor variance of the test scores, but they do not in general provide scientifically meaningful structures. It is the configurations of tests or variables in factor space that are of fundamental concern. In order to discover these configurations adequately, the arbitrary reference axes must be rotated. In other words, we assume that there are unique and "best" positions for the axes, "best" ways to view the variables in *n*-dimensional space.

There is no intention here of reifying constructs, variables, or factors. Factors are simply structures or patterns produced by covariances of measures. What is meant by "best way to view the variables" is the most parsimonious, the simplest way. A "best" way can be predicted from theory and hypotheses, as Guilford did in his structure of intellect theory and research,[14] or as Cattell did in his theory of crystallized and fluid intelligence,[15] or as Thurstone and Thurstone did in their extensive studies of primary mental abilities (see *Research Examples*, below).[16] Or a "best" way may be discovered from a structure so clear and strong as almost to compel belief in its validity and "reality."

Among Thurstone's important contributions, his invention of the ideas of simple structure and factor axes rotation are perhaps the most important. With them he laid down relatively clear guidelines for achieving psychologically meaningful and interpretable factor analytic solutions. In Table 37.2 we reported a factor matrix obtained from the *R* matrix of Table 37.1. This was the final *rotated* matrix and not the matrix originally produced by the factor analysis. The *unrotated* matrix originally produced by the principal factors method is given on the left side of Table 37.5. The rotated factors are reproduced on the right side of the table. The communalities (h^2) are also given. They are the same for both matrices.

If we try to interpret the unrotated matrix on the left of the table, we run into trouble. It can be said that all the tests are loaded on a general factor, I, and that the second factor, II, is bipolar. (A *bipolar factor* is one that has substantial positive and negative loadings.) This would amount to saying that all the tests measure the same thing (factor I), but that the first three measure the negative aspect of whatever the second three measure (factor II). But aside from the ambiguous nature of such an interpretation, we know that the reference axes, I and II, and conse-

[12]Thurstone, *op. cit.*, pp. 508–509.

[13]*Ibid.*, p. 93. See also R. Cattell, *Factor Analysis*. New York: Harper & Row, 1952, p. 66.

[14]J. Guilford, *The Nature of Human Intelligence*. New York: McGraw-Hill, 1967. [For a distinguished evaluation of this important book, see J. Carroll's review: *American Educational Research Journal*, V (1968), 249–256.]

[15]R. Cattell, "Theory of Fluid and Crystallized Intelligence: A Critical Experiment," *Journal of Educational Psychology*, LIV (1963), 1–22.

[16]L. Thurstone and T. Thurstone, *Factorial Studies of Intelligence*. Chicago: University of Chicago Press, 1941 (reprinted 1968, Psychometric Society).

TABLE **37.5** UNROTATED AND ROTATED FACTOR MATRICES, R MATRIX OF TABLE 37.1[a]

	Unrotated		Rotated		
Tests	I	II	*A*	*B*	h^2
V	.60	−.58	*.83*	.01	.70
R	.63	−.49	*.79*	.10	.63
S	.56	−.43	*.70*	.10	.50
N	.56	.43	.10	*.70*	.50
AS	.63	.49	.10	*.79*	.63
AT	.60	.58	.01	*.83*	.70

[a]Significant loadings (≥ .30) are italicized. Note that the *A* and *B* vectors are reversed in this table. The h^2's calculated from the unrotated and rotated values are slightly different, owing to errors of rounding, e.g., $.60^2 + .58^2 = .70$ and $.83^2 + .01^2 = .69$. The correct computer values have been used in the table (and in Table 37.2).

quently the factor loadings, are arbitrary. Look at the factor plot of Fig. 37.2. There are two clearly defined clusters of tests clinging closely to the axes *A* and *B*. There is no general factor here, nor is there a bipolar factor. The second major problem of factor analysis, therefore, is to discover a unique and compelling solution or position of the reference axes.

Plot the loadings of I and II, and we "see" the original unrotated structure. This has been done in Fig. 37.5. Now swing the axes so that I goes as near as possible to the *V*, *R*, and *S* points and, at the same time, II goes as near as possible to the *N*, *AS*, and *AT* points. A rotation of 45 degrees will do nicely. We then obtain essentially the structure of Fig. 37.2. That is, the new rotated positions of the axes and the positions of the six tests are the same as the positions of the axes and tests of Fig. 37.2. The structure simply leans to the right. Turn the figure so that the *B* of the *B* axis points directly up and this becomes clear. It is now possible to read off the new rotated factor loadings on the rotated axes. (The reader can confirm this by reading off and writing down the loadings of the tests on the rotated axes of Fig. 37.5.) Since the axes are kept at a 90-degree angle, this is called an *orthogonal* rotation.

This example, though unrealistic, may help the reader understand that the factor analyst searches for the unities that presumably underlie test performances. Spatially conceived, he searches out the relations among variables "out there" in multidimensional factor space. Through knowledge of the empirical relations among tests or other measures, he probes in factor space with reference axes until he finds the unities or relations among relations—if they exist.

To guide the factor analyst in his rotations, Thurstone laid down five principles or rules of simple structure.[17] The rules are applicable to both orthogonal and oblique rotations, though Thurstone emphasized the oblique case. (Oblique rotations are those in which the angles between axes are acute or obtuse.) The simple structure principles are as follows:

[17]Thurstone, *op. cit.*, p. 335; Harman, *op. cit.*, pp. 97–99.

1. Each row of the factor matrix should have at least one loading close to zero.
2. For each column of the factor matrix there should be at least as many variables with zero or near-zero loadings as there are factors.
3. For every pair of factors (columns) there should be several variables with loadings in one factor (column) but not in the other.
4. When there are four or more factors, a large proportion of the variables should have negligible (close to zero) loadings on any pair of factors.
5. For every pair of factors (columns) of the factor matrix there should be only a small number of variables with appreciable (nonzero) loadings in both columns.

In effect, these criteria call for as "pure" variables as possible, that is, each variable loaded on as few factors as possible, and *as many zeros as possible in the rotated factor matrix.* In this way the simplest possible interpretation of the factors can be achieved. In other words, rotation to achieve simple structure is a fairly objective way to achieve variable simplicity or to reduce variable complexity.

To understand this, imagine an ideal solution in which simple structure is "perfect." It might look like this, say, in a three-factor solution:

Tests	*A*	*B*	*C*
1	X	0	0
2	X	0	0
3	X	0	0
4	0	X	0
5	0	X	0
6	0	X	0
7	0	0	X
8	0	0	X
9	0	0	X

X's indicate substantial factor loadings, 0's near-zero loadings. Of course, such "perfect" factor structures are rare. It is more likely that some of the tests have loadings on more than one factor. Still, good approximations to simple structure have been achieved, especially in well-planned and executed factor analytic studies. (See the research examples given later.)

Before leaving the subject of factor rotations it must be pointed out that there are a number of rotational methods. The two main types of rotation are called "orthogonal" and "oblique." *Orthogonal* rotations maintain the independence of factors, that is, the angles between the axes are kept at 90 degrees. If we rotate factors I and II orthogonally, for instance, we swing both axes together, maintaining the right angle between them. This means that the correlation between the factors is zero. The rotation just performed in Fig. 37.5 was orthogonal. If we had four factors, we would rotate I and II, I and III, I and IV, II and III, and so on, maintaining right angles between each pair of axes. Some researchers prefer to rotate orthogonally. Others insist that orthogonal rotation is unrealistic, that actual factors are not usually uncorrelated, and that rotations should conform to psychological "reality."[18]

[18]See Thurstone, *op. cit.*, pp. 139–140; Cattell, *op. cit.*, pp. 116–118, 122–123, 210.

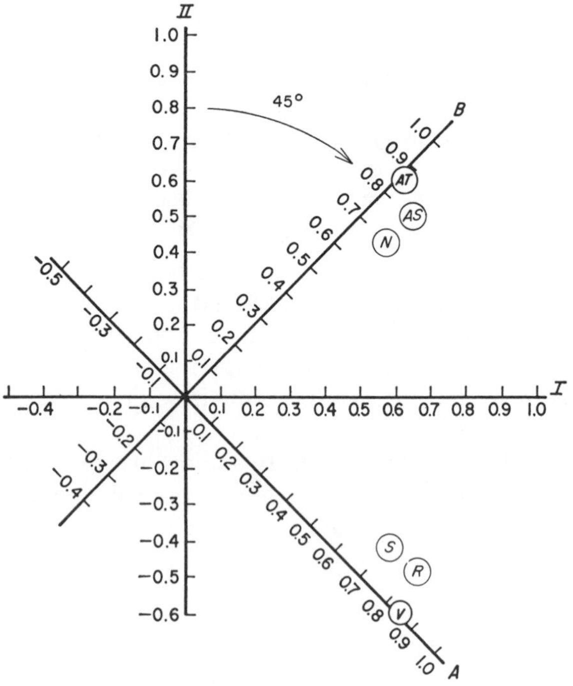

FIG. 37.5

Rotations in which the factor axes are allowed to form acute or obtuse angles are called *oblique*. Obliqueness, of course, means that factors are correlated. There is no doubt that factor structures can be better fitted with oblique axes and the simple structure criteria better satisfied. Some researchers might object to oblique factors because of the possible difficulty of comparing factor structures from one study to another. We leave this controversial subject with two remarks. One, the type of rotation seems to be a matter of taste. Two, the reader should understand both types of rotation to the extent that he can interpret both kinds of factors. He should be particularly careful when confronted with the results of oblique solutions. They contain peculiarities and subtleties not present in orthogonal solutions.

Second-Order Factor Analysis

Second-order factor analysis is a highly important but neglected approach to complex data analysis and hypothesis-testing. When factors are rotated obliquely, there are correlations between factors. In a provocative factor analytic and canonical correlation study of the redundancy present in student test scores, Lohnes and Marshall extracted two factors from 21 ability and achievement tests.[19] The

[19] P. Lohnes and T. Marshall, "Redundancy in Student Records," *American Educational Research Journal*, II (1965), 19–23.

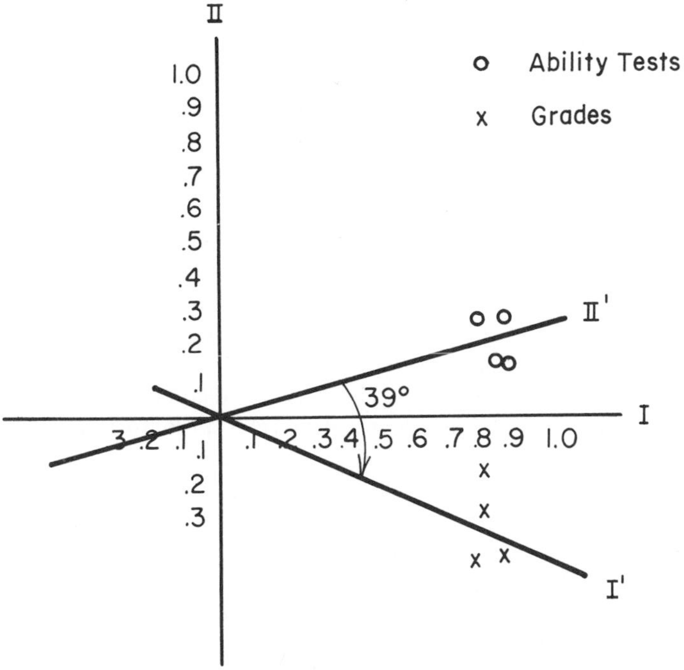

FIG. 37.6

unrotated factor loadings of eight of their measures, four ability tests and four grades (English, arithmetic, social studies, science), have been plotted in Fig. 37.6. The axes have been rotated obliquely so that they will go through the two clusters of loadings. There is an acute angle of about 39 degrees between the rotated axes, now labeled I′ and II′. Any angle other than 90 degrees between axes means correlation between factors. In this case, the correlation is approximately .78, quite high.

Imagine this situation multiplied over six, eight, or ten factors: there would be a set of correlations among the factors. Factor analyze these correlations and we have second-order factor analysis, which is a method of finding the factors behind the factors. The famous "*g*" of intelligence testing is evidently a second-order factor. Whenever large numbers of ability tests are factor-analyzed, the correlations among the tests are usually positive. Factor analyze them and some such pattern, as in Fig. 37.6, though more complex, emerges. Calculate the correlations between the factors and again factor analyze and a single factor, perhaps "*g*," may emerge.

Are there second-order attitude factors? In a large study of social attitudes, which was the *R*-methodological counterpart of a *Q* study outlined in Chapter 34, Kerlinger administered a 50-item summated-rating scale, each item of which was a single word or short phrase (attitude referents or objects)—*private property, religion, civil rights, Social Security*, for example—to several large samples in different parts of the country.[20] The item responses of a combined sample of Texas and North Carolina teachers, $N = 530$, were intercorrelated and factor-analyzed with the principal factors method. Six factors were obtained and rotated obliquely to simple structure. Three of these factors consisted of presumably conservative referents (e.g., *moral standards in education, religion, subject matter*), and the other three factors liberal referents (e.g., *civil rights, children's interests, Supreme Court*).

The correlations among the factors were themselves factor analyzed with the principal factors method. Two factors were obtained and rotated orthogonally to simple structure. The rotated factor matrix is given in Fig. 37.7, together with the identifications of the types of factors, C (Conservatism) and L (Liberalism). The factor loadings are also plotted. The evidence is so clear that it needs little elaboration. There are two clear, relatively orthogonal (uncorrelated) second-order factors, one of which has conservative referent factors, while the other has liberal referent factors.[21]

Factor Scores

While second-order factor analysis is more oriented toward basic and theoretical research, another technique of factor analysis, so-called factor scores or measures, is eminently practical, though not without theoretical significance. *Factor scores* are measures of individuals on factors. Suppose, like Lohnes and Marshall, we found two factors underlying 21 ability and grade measures. Instead of using all 21 scores of groups of children in research, why not use just two scores calculated from the factors? Lohnes and Marshall recommend just this, pointing out the redundancy in the usual scores of pupils. These factor scores are, in effect, weighted averages, weighted according to the factor loadings.

Here is an oversimplified example. Suppose the factor matrix of Table 37.2 were actual data and that we want to calculate the A and B factor scores of an individual. The raw scores of one individual on the six tests, say, are: 7, 5, 5, 3, 4, 2. We multiply these scores by the related factor loadings, first for factor A and then for factor B, as follows:

$$A: \quad F_A = (.83)(7) + (.79)(5) + (.70)(5) + (.10)(3) + (.10)(4) + (.01)(2) = 13.98$$

$$B: \quad F_B = (.01)(7) + (.10)(5) + (.10)(5) + (.70)(3) + (.79)(4) + (.83)(2) = 7.99$$

[20]F. Kerlinger, "The Structure and Content of Social Attitude Referents: A Preliminary Study," *Educational and Psychological Measurement*, XXXII (1972), 613–630.

[21]There are no elementary guides to second-order factor analysis. The best available discussion is the oldest: Thurstone, *Multiple Factor Analysis*, pp. 215, 432–434. A second-order factor analysis computer program can be put together as follows. Use a standard program to factor analyze the R matrix. Use an oblique rotation program to rotate the factors. Have the computer print or punch out the correlations among the factors (see Thurstone formula, *ibid.*, p. 433). Then use the factor analysis program to factor this matrix. You will need a program that accepts R matrices as input, of course. (See Appendix C.)

	A	B	Type
I	*.71*	*.09*	*C*
II	−.22	*.64*	*L*
III	.19	*.61*	*L*
IV	−.13	*.65*	*L*
V	*.78*	.04	*C*
VI	*.68*	−.12	*C*

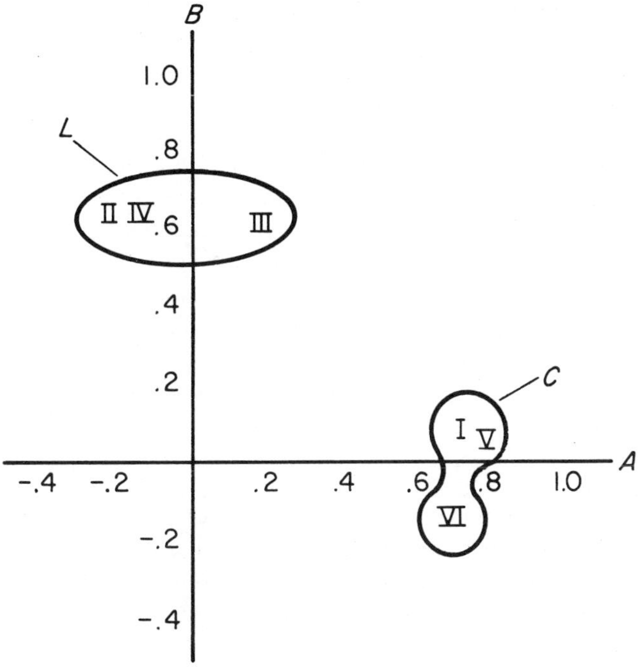

FIG. 37.7

The individual's "factor scores" are $F_A = 13.98$ and $F_B = 7.99$. We can, of course, calculate other individuals' "factor scores" similarly.

This is not the best way to calculate factor scores.[22] The example was made up to convey the idea of such scores as weighted sums or averages, the weights being the factor loadings. In any case, the method, though not extensively used in the past, has great potential for complex behavioral research. Instead of using many separate test scores, fewer factor scores can be used. An excellent real example is described by Mayeske, who participated in the reanalysis of the data of the Coleman report, *Equality of Educational Opportunity*.[23]

First, the scores of fifth-grade students on five achievement tests were weighted with principal component weights (loadings) and added to obtain an

[22]For better methods, see Harman, *op. cit.*, chap. 16.
[23]G. Mayeske, "Teacher Attributes and School Achievement." In *Do Teachers Make a Difference?* Washington, D.C.: U.S. Government Printing Office, 1970, pp. 100–119.

overall achievement composite scores (as in the above example). This was the dependent variable in many subsequent analyses. Second, the intercorrelations of sets of student variables and school variables were factor analyzed. Then "factor scores" were calculated to form indices—for example, socioeconomic status, attitude toward life, training of teacher, experience of teacher. These scores were used in multiple regression and other analyses. In short, more than 400 variables were reduced to 31 "factor variables" calculated from the data of over 130,000 students in 923 schools, thus achieving considerable parsimony and increasing the reliability and validity of the measures.

Research Examples

Several factor analytic studies, including two that used second-order analysis, are summarized below. Most factor analytic studies have factored intelligence, aptitude, and personality tests and scales, the tests or scales themselves being intercorrelated and factor analyzed. The Thurstone example, below, is an excellent example; indeed, it is a classic. Persons, or the responses of persons, as we saw in Chapter 34, can also be factored. The variables entered into the correlation and factor matrices, in fact, can be tests, scales, persons, items, concepts, or whatever can be intercorrelated. The studies given below have been selected not to represent factor analytic investigations in general, but rather to familiarize the student with different uses of factor analysis.

Thurstone Factorial Study of Intelligence

Thurstone and Thurstone, in their monumental work on intelligence factors and their measurement, factor analyzed 60 tests plus the three variables chronological age, mental age, and sex.[24] The analysis was based on the test responses of 710 eighth-grade pupils to the 60 tests. It revealed essentially the same set of so-called primary factors that had been found in previous studies.

The Thurstones chose the three best tests for each of seven of the ten primary factors. Six of these tests seemed to have stability at different age levels sufficient for practical school use. They then revised and administered these tests to 437 eighth-grade school children. The main purpose of the study was to check the factor structure of the tests. In other words, they predicted that the same primary factors of intelligence put into the 21 tests would emerge from a new factor analysis on a new sample of children.

The rotated factor matrix (oblique rotation) is given in Table 37.6. This is a remarkable validation of the primary factors. The seven factors and their loadings are almost exactly as predicted. (See, especially, the italicized loadings.)

Q and R Studies of Social Attitude Referents

Factor analysis of tests and scales as discussed in this chapter has been called *R* methodology in contrast to *Q* methodology. In *R* methodology tests, scales, and

[24]Thurstone and Thurstone, *op. cit.* The student interested in factor analysis and the testing of intelligence can profit greatly from study of this fine monograph.

TABLE **37.6** OBLIQUE ROTATED FACTOR MATRIX, THURSTONE AND THURSTONE STUDY[a]

Tests	*P*	*N*	*W*	*V*	*S*	*M*	*R*
Identification Numbers	*42*	*40*	05	−02	−07	−06	−06
Faces	*45*	17	−06	04	*20*	05	02
Mirror Reading	*36*	09	19	−02	05	−01	09
First Names	−02	09	02	00	−05	*53*	10
Figure Recognition	*20*	−10	02	−02	10	*31*	07
Word-Number	02	13	−03	00	01	*58*	−04
Sentences	00	01	−03	*66*	−08	−05	13
Vocabulary	−01	02	05	*66*	−04	02	02
Completion	−01	00	−01	*67*	15	00	−01
First Letters	12	−03	*63*	03	−02	00	−00
4–Letter Words	−02	−05	*61*	−01	08	−01	04
Suffixes	04	03	*45*	18	−03	03	−08
Flags	−04	05	03	−01	*68*	00	01
Figures	02	−06	01	−02	*76*	−02	−02
Cards	07	−03	−03	03	*72*	02	−03
Addition	01	*64*	−02	01	05	01	−02
Multiplication	01	*67*	01	−03	−05	02	02
3–Higher	−05	*38*	−01	06	*20*	−05	16
Letter Series	−03	03	03	02	00	02	*53*
Pedigrees	02	−05	−03	22	−03	05	*44*
Letter Group	06	06	13	−04	01	−06	*42*

[a] Decimal points are omitted. *P* = Perception; *N* = Number; *W* = Word Fluency; *V* = Verbal; *S* = Space; *M* = Memory; *R* = Reasoning.

items are intercorrelated and factored, whereas in *Q* methodology persons (or their responses) are intercorrelated and factored. A potentially potent research strategy is to use both *Q* and *R* approaches to study the same general problem. One question that can be asked, for example, is: Do the factor analyses in the two approaches yield essentially the same factors? We have seen what *Q* factor arrays are. In *R* methodology, factor arrays are simply the tests, scales, or items that have large loadings on a factor—and preferably on that factor only. In the Thurstone and Thurstone study, the factor array of factor *P* is indicated by the italicized loadings in the *P* column: *.42*, *.45*, and *.36*, beside the items of the array: Identification Numbers, Faces, Mirror Reading. In *Q*, however, the factor arrays are complete *Q* sorts as determined by the persons factors, even though only the high (and sometimes the low) items are used in interpretation.

In Chapter 34 a *Q* study of social attitude referents was described, but the focus of the description was on the structure of the *Q* sort. Now we are concerned with the factor analytic results. After describing the study and its results briefly, we will take up an *R* study of the same problem.[25] Recall that the referents *Q* sort,

[25] F. Kerlinger, "A *Q* Validation of the Structure of Social Attitudes," *Educational and Psychological Measurement*, XXXII (1972), 987–995. The *R* study was cited in footnote 20.

called REFQ, had 80 items, 40 being liberal referents (e.g., *racial integration* and *poverty program*) and 40 conservative referents (e.g., *religion* and *real estate*).

The *Q* sorts of 33 individuals of "known" liberal and conservative social attitudes—known by the investigator or by others—were intercorrelated and factor analyzed. It was predicted, on the basis of a structural theory of attitudes, that liberals and conservatives would appear on separate factors (rather than on one or two bipolar factors, or factors with substantial positive and negative loadings), and that liberals would appear together on a factor, and similarly for conservatives. Of the 33 subjects, 32 were loaded on the factors as predicted. Table 37.7 gives the loadings of six of the 33 subjects on three factors. As can be seen, conservatives appeared on two of the factors. The liberals appeared on a single factor (*A*). The expectations were confirmed. The nature of the factor arrays also was in line with expectations.

TABLE **37.7** TRUNCATED *Q* FACTOR MATRIX, SIX SUBJECTS OF "KNOWN" ATTITUDES, REFQ STUDY

Subjects	*A*	*B*	*C*	"Known" Attitude
4	*.68*	.16	−.26	*L*
15	*.81*	−.04	−.13	*L*
2	−.02	*.68*	.02	*C*
14	−.06	*.71*	.08	*C*
17	−.15	.12	*.63*	*C*
25	.06	*.44*	*.57*	*C*

Independently of the *Q*-sort study, a 50-item referent scale, called REF-I and described in the section on second-order analysis, was constructed and administered to large samples in different parts of the country. Half the items were liberal (*L*) and half conservative (*C*) (judged in ways not relevant here). It was predicted, on the basis of the structural theory of attitudes, that the *L* items would be positively loaded on what would be essentially liberal factors, and similarly for the *C* items. Very few substantial ($\geq .35$) negative loadings were expected.

The responses of 530 individuals, mostly teachers, from Texas and North Carolina were factor analyzed and six factors rotated by the varimax method.[26] To give the reader the flavor of the results, three items from each of the factors are presented in Table 37.8. The factor loadings are also given in parentheses. The remaining factors and loadings were similar: *L* items on *L* factors and not on *C* factors, and similarly for *C* items and *C* factors. There was only one item, *racial purity*, with a substantial negative loading.

The theoretical predictions were supported in both the *Q* and *R* studies. And recall that the second-order analysis of the above six factors yielded two clear second-order factors, one an *L* factor and the other a *C* factor. Liberal persons

[26]H. Kaiser, "The Varimax Criterion for Analytic Rotation in Factor Analysis," *Psychometrika*, XXII (1958), 187–200. Varimax is probably the best method of analytic (computer) orthogonal rotation. It is perhaps the most used, too, being widely available in factor analytic computer programs.

TABLE **37.8** SAMPLE ITEMS FROM SIX FACTORS, REF-I SCALE, TEXAS AND NORTH CAROLINA SAMPLE, $N = 530$

	CONSERVATISM FACTORS	
I. *Religiosity*	II. *Educational Traditionalism*	VI. *Economic Conservatism*
religion (.78)	subject matter (.59)	free enterprise (.62)
church (.73)	school discipline (.44)	private property (.43)
teaching of spiritual values (.53)	homogeneous grouping (.30)	capitalism (.37)
	LIBERALISM FACTORS	
II. *Civil Rights*	III. *Child-Centered Education*	IV. *Social Liberalism*
Negroes (.60)	children's interests (.56)	Social Security (.53)
civil rights (.57)	child-centered curriculum (.54)	Supreme Court (.50)
racial integration (.57)	pupil personality (.54)	poverty program (.48)

cluster together, as do conservative persons. And liberal items cluster together apart from conservative items, which also cluster together. These results seem to indicate that liberalism and conservatism are different kinds of entities and not the polar opposites they are usually assumed to be.

Characteristics of Higher Educational Institutions

Astin wished to know the principal ways in which higher educational institutions differ.[27] He measured 33 attributes of 335 four-year colleges and universities: public vs. private status, teacher-training emphasis, tuition, endowment, total enrollment, student aptitude level, faculty-student ratio, intellectual orientation, and so on. The 33 variables were intercorrelated and the correlations factor analyzed with the principal factors method. Six factors were rotated orthogonally with the varimax method. In addition, the total sample of institutions was subdivided into Public, Private, Universities, Liberal Arts Colleges, and Men's Institutions, and the data of each subsample factor analyzed similarly, providing a useful check on the generality of the factors in different groups.[28]

Some of Astin's most significant findings are presented in the abbreviated rotated factor matrix of Table 37.9. Just enough of the 33 variables and their load-

[27]A. Astin, "An Empirical Characterization of Higher Educational Institutions," *Journal of Educational Psychology*, LIII (1962), 224–235.

[28]Two of the greatest necessities of factor analysis are large samples and replication. A general rule is: Use as large samples as possible. Like any statistical procedure, factor analysis is subject to measurement and sampling error, and the reliable identification of factors and factor loadings requires large N's to wash out error variance. This is especially true for item factor analysis, because item intercorrelations are usually lower and less reliable than test intercorrelations. A loose but not bad rule-of-thumb might be: ten subjects for each variable (item, measure, etc.). Replication is too seldom practiced in any research. And it is particularly needed in factor analytic studies. The "reality" of factors is much more compelling if found in two or three different and large samples.

TABLE **37.9** FACTOR LOADINGS OF SELECTED VARIABLES ON TWO FACTORS, ASTIN STUDY

Variable	*Affluence*	*Size*
Liberal Arts Emphasis	.10	.37
Teacher Training Emphasis	−.22	.35
Endowment	.85	−.08
Operating Budget	.79	.13
Research Funds	.52	.25
Percentage of Merit Scholars	.68	.03
Intellectual Orientation	.50	−.22
Conventional Orientation	−.46	.10
Faculty-Student Ratio	.76	.03
Relative Library Size	.77	.09
Total Enrollment	−.26	.78

ings on two of the six factors is presented to highlight the major features of the results.

The more affluent institutions have greater endowment, operating budget, and so on, as one might expect. More important, the more affluent institutions evidently have high intellectual and low conventional orientations (percentage of majors in business, accounting, etc.). Note, too, that affluence, intellectual orientation, faculty-student ratio, and relative library size (number of books divided by total enrollment) are positively related. Astin also calculated factor scores. He suggests using institution profiles of factor scores (i.e., six scores for each institution, one for each factor) in studies of such institutions.

The main point of this example is to show how factor analysis can be used productively with measures other than tests and in research other than psychometric research. Its results are also intriguing, though somewhat dismal.

Fluid and Crystallized Intelligence

One of the most active, important, and controversial problems of behavioral scientific and practical interest is the nature of mental abilities. Different theories with different amounts and kinds of evidence to support them have been propounded by some of the ablest psychologists of the century: Spearman, Thurstone, Burt, Thorndike, Guilford, Cattell, and others. There can be no doubt whatever of the high scientific and practical importance of the problem. We have alluded, if only briefly, to the work and thinking of Thurstone and Guilford. We now describe, also briefly, one among the many factor analytic studies of Raymond Cattell.[29]

The famous general factor of intelligence, g, can be shown to be a second-order factor that runs through most tests of mental ability. Cattell believes, in effect, that there are two g's, or two aspects of g: crystallized and fluid. *Crystallized intelligence* is exhibited by cognitive performances in which "skilled judg-

[29]Cattell, *op. cit.* For a penetrating critique of this study, see L. Humphreys, "Critique of Cattell's 'Theory of Fluid and Crystallized Intelligence: A Critical Experiment,'" *Journal of Educational Psychology*, LVIII (1967), 129–136.

ment habits" have become fixed or crystallized owing to the earlier application of general learning ability to such performances. The well-known verbal and number factors are examples. *Fluid intelligence*, on the other hand, is exhibited by performances characterized more by adaptation to new situations, the "fluid" application of general ability, so to speak. Such ability is more characteristic of creative behavior than is crystallized intelligence. If tests are factor-analyzed and the correlations among the factors found are themselves factored (second-order factor analysis), then both crystallized and fluid intelligence should emerge as second-order factors.

Cattell administered Thurstone's primary abilities tests and a number of his own mental ability and personality tests to 277 eighth-grade children, factor analyzed the 44 variables, and rotated the obtained 22 factors (probably too many) to simple structure. The correlations among these factors were themselves factored, yielding eight second-order factors. (Recall that oblique rotations yield factors that are correlated.) Although Cattell included a number of personality variables, we concentrate only on the first two factors, fluid intelligence and crystallized intelligence. He reasoned that Thurstone's tests, since they measure crystallized cognitive abilities, should load on one general factor, and that his own culture-fair tests, since they measure fluid ability, should load on another factor. They did. The two sets of factor loadings are given in Table 37.10, together with the names of the tests. The two factors also were correlated positively ($r = .47$), as predicted.

TABLE **37.10** PART OF SECOND-ORDER FACTOR MATRIX, CATTELL FLUID AND CRYSTALLIZED INTELLIGENCE STUDY[a]

	F_1 (g_f)	F_2 (g_c)
Thurstone Tests		
Verbal	.15	*.46*
Spatial	*.32*	.14
Reasoning	.08	*.50*
Number	.05	*.59*
Fluency	.07	.09
Cattell Tests		
Series	*.35*	*.43*
Classification	*.63*	−.02
Matrices	*.50*	.10
Topology	*.51*	.09

[a] g_f: general factor, fluid; g_c: general factor, crystallized. Italics supplied by the author (FNK). These are only two of Cattell's eight factors.

This study demonstrates the power of an astute combination of theory, test construction, and factor analysis. Similar to Guilford's equally astute conceptualization and analysis of convergent, divergent, and other factors mentioned earlier, it is a significant contribution to psychological knowledge of an extremely complex and important subject.

Administrative Performance and In-Basket Factors

What are the factors behind administrative work and performance? There is hardly any area of human activity more important than the work of executives who must run large organizations and constantly take action and make decisions. Hemphill, Griffiths, and Frederiksen, in a major study of the administrative behavior of elementary school principals, based on earlier study of a variety of administrators, used a realistic simulated test of administrative performance called the In-Basket Test.[30] This test, in a form especially adapted to an elementary school situation, had 96 items, each a practical and realistic problem that was presented along with other similar problems to testees for appropriate administrative action in a simulated school. For example, one item was a facsimile of a telegram telling the administrator that a teacher would not report for her classes for several days due to illness. The administrator must take one or more actions—for example, use Miss A as a substitute, convey condolences to the teacher, refer to secretary, and the like. Another item was a letter from a college professor requesting permission to use students of the school in an experiment. Still another was a letter from a mother complaining about the slow progress of her child's class. Although other tests and administrative tasks were used, we omit their consideration.

The sample of subjects consisted of 232 principals of varied backgrounds, experience, and characteristics. Their responses to the In-Basket Test were scored for content and style, yielding 68 categories: Discusses with Subordinates, Unusual Courses of Action, Takes Terminal Action, Delegates Completely, and so on. The scores of 40 of the categories were intercorrelated and the 40×40 matrix of correlations factor analyzed with the principal factors method. Eight factors were rotated obliquely to simple structure. These factors are presumably the first-order bases of the administrative performances of the principals. Two of them are: A: *Exchanging Information* and H: *Directing the Work of Others*.

The authors also factor analyzed the correlations among the factors and obtained two second-order factors: X: *Preparation for Decision* and Y: *Amount of Work* (*Expended in Handling the Items*). The first-order rotated (oblique) factor loadings of the two factors A and H, mentioned in the preceding paragraph are given in Table 37.11. The second-order factor loadings are also given. From the items of factor A, one deduces that exchanging information, especially with subordinates, is an important source of individual differences among administrators. (This says nothing, of course, about the value of exchanging information or the success of the individuals who are high on this variable.) Factor H, *Directing the Work of Others*, seems pretty obvious as a source of differences among administrators. Indeed, it was selected from the eight factors for just that reason. Never-

[30] J. Hemphill, D. Griffiths, and N. Frederiksen, *Administrative Performance and Personality*. New York: Teachers College Press, 1962. Two valuable monographs are: N. Frederiksen, D. Saunders, and B. Wand, "The In-Basket Test," *Psychological Monographs*, no. 438, 1957; N. Frederiksen, "Factors in In-Basket Performance," *Psychological Monographs*, no. 541, 1962.

TABLE **37.11** SELECTED FIRST-ORDER FACTORS, *A* AND *H*, AND LOADINGS FROM IN-BASKET CATEGORIES AND THE CATEGORY LOADINGS ON SECOND-ORDER FACTORS *X* AND *Y*[a]

Categories	First-Order Factors *A*	*H*	Second-Order Factors *X*	*Y*
Usual Actions	*.25*	−.07	.38	.66
Subordinate Groups Involved	*.29*	−.12	.29	.44
Asks Subordinates	*.50*	−.05	.56	.42
Requires Information	*.34*	−.10	.63	.28
Informs Subordinates	*.45*	.10	.29	.52
Informs Outsiders	*.31*	.01	−.04	.47
Subordinates Involved	.11	*.28*	.47	.57
Careless	−.09	*.31*	−.23	.04
Plans Only	.08	*−.67*	.16	−.08
Leading Action	.03	*.64*	.41	.53
Directs	.06	*.47*	.37	.57
Communicates by Telephone	.14	*−.30*	.32	.27
Communicates by Writing	.00	*.59*	.07	.55
Courtesy to Subordinates	.01	*.57*	.38	.27
Courtesy to Outsiders	.10	*.40*	.03	.36

[a]See text for descriptions of factors. Italics mean significant loadings; they were not in the original report.

theless, the loadings are interesting. Note the two negative loadings. Why should there be a negative correlation, for instance, between communicating by writing (.59) and by telephone (−.30)?

The second-order factor loadings are, in this case, not easy to understand. Pay particular attention to the large loadings ($\geqslant .50$) when studying *X* and *Y*. One can well ask: Do these factors fit any particular theory of administrative behavior?

This is an outstanding study from theoretical, practical, and technical points of view, a tour de force of the measurement of complex variables and the persistent and intelligent search, through factor analysis, for the underlying components of educational administrative behavior.

Factor Analysis and Scientific Research

Factor analysis has two basic purposes: to explore variable areas in order to identify the factors presumably underlying the variables; and, as in all scientific work, to test hypotheses about the relations among variables. The first purpose is well known and fairly well accepted. The second purpose is not so well known nor so well accepted.

In conceptualizing the first purpose, the exploratory or reductive purpose, one should keep construct validity and constitutive definitions in mind. Factor analysis can be conceived as a construct validity tool. Recall that validity was defined in Chapter 27 as common-factor variance. Since the main preoccupation of factor analysis is common-factor variance, by definition factor analysis is firmly tied to measurement theory. Indeed, this tie was expressed earlier in the section headed "Some Factor Theory," where equations were written to clarify factor analytic theory. (See, especially, Eq. 37.6).

Recall, too, that construct validity seeks the "meaning" of a construct through the relations between the construct and other constructs. In Part I, when types of definitions were discussed, we learned that constructs could be defined in two ways: by operational definitions and by constitutive definitions. Constitutive definitions are definitions that define constructs with other constructs. Essentially this is what factor analysis does. It may be called a constitutive meaning method, since it enables the researcher to study the constitutive meanings of constructs—and thus their construct validity.

The measures of three variables, say, may share something in common. This something itself is a variable, presumably a more basic entity than the variables used to isolate and identify it. We give this new variable a name; in other words, we construct a hypothetical entity. Then, to inquire into the "reality" of the variable we may systematically devise a measure of it and test its "reality" by correlating data obtained with the measure with data from other measures theoretically related to it. Factor analysis helps us check our theoretical expectations.

Part of the basic life-stuff of any science is its constructs. Old constructs continue to be used; new ones are constantly being invented. Note some of the general constructs directly pertinent to behavioral and educational research: achievement, intelligence, learning, aptitude, attitude, problem-solving ability, needs, interests, creativity, conformity. Note some of the more specific variables important in behavioral and educational research: test anxiety, verbal ability, traditionalism, convergent thinking, arithmetic reasoning, attitude toward self, and social class. Clearly, a large portion of scientific behavioral research effort has to be devoted to what might be called construct investigation or construct validation. This requires factor analysis.

Although a good deal of psychological research pertinent to education and aimed at construct validation has been done, it is remarkable how ignorant we are. Take an obvious example, school achievement, or simply achievement. After almost half a century of educational research we know little about achievement *as a construct*. We know something of the relations between achievement and other constructs, for example, intelligence, social class, anxiety, and sex. But we know strikingly little about the nature of achievement itself. Thousands of tests are constructed and administered by teachers every year. But there is too little research into what these tests measure. Beyond simple factual tests of circumscribed areas, it is evident that most teacher-made achievement tests—and most standardized achievement tests—are factorially complex. If this is so, it is equally evident that the construct validity of achievement tests is seriously in question. Almost any social studies, mathematics, science, or English test probably measures various aspects of achievement. The basic assumption behind most achievement testing is that the tests used to measure whatever achievement is being tested are themselves unitary measures of the achievement in question. And the assumption is probably false (though not necessarily damaging to practical measurement).

The assumption, moreover, is probably false for many other psychological-educational variables and measures. To talk about the relation between achievement and anxiety, for example, is easy. But it is not so easy to say that we are measuring unitary variables. Like achievement, anxiety is evidently multidimensional. Even types of tests and types of items may produce factors.

Many research areas, then, can well be preceded by factor analytic explorations of the variables of the area. This does not mean that a number of tests are thrown together and given to any samples that happen to be available. Factor analytic investigations, both exploratory and hypothesis-testing, have to be painstakingly planned. Variables that may be influential have to be controlled—sex, education, social class, intelligence, and so on.[31] Variables are not put into a factor analysis just to put them in. They must have legitimate purpose. If, for instance, one cannot control intelligence by sample selection, one can include a measure of intelligence (verbal, perhaps) in the battery of measures. By identifying intelligence variance, one has in a sense controlled intelligence. One can learn whether one's measures are contaminated by response biases by including response-bias measures in factor analyses.

The second major purpose of factor analysis is to test hypotheses. One aspect of hypothesis-testing has already been hinted: one can put tests or measures into factor analytic batteries deliberately to test the identification and nature of factors. The design of such studies has been well outlined by Thurstone, Cattell, Guilford, and others. First, factors are "discovered." Their nature is inferred from the tests that are loaded on them. This "nature" is set up as a hypothesis. New tests are constructed and given to new samples of subjects. The data are factor analyzed. If the factors emerge *as predicted*, the hypothesis is to this extent confirmed, the factors would seem to have "reality." This will certainly not end the matter. One will have to test, among other things, the factors' relation to other factors. One will have to place the factors, as constructs, in a nomological network of constructs.

A less well-known use of factor analysis as a hypothesis-testing method is in testing experimental hypotheses.[32] One may hypothesize that a certain method of teaching reading changes the ability patterns of pupils, so that verbal intelligence is not as potent an influence as it is with other teaching methods. An experimental study can be planned to test this hypothesis. The effects of the teaching methods can be assessed by factor analyses of a set of tests given before and after the different methods were used. Woodrow tested a similar hypothesis when he gave a a set of tests before and after practice in seven tests: adding, subtracting, anagrams, and so on.[33] He found that factor loading patterns *did* change after practice.

In like manner, it may be possible to assess the effects of important curriculum changes. A school system that has radically changed its curriculum approach

[31]J. Guilford, "Factorial Angles to Psychology," *Psychological Review*, LXVIII (1961), 1–20. This is an important article that any investigator who uses factor analysis should study.

[32]B. Fruchter, "Manipulative and Hypothesis-Testing Factor-Analytic Experimental Designs." In R. Cattell, ed., *Handbook of Multivariate Experimental Psychology*. Skokie, Ill.: Rand McNally, 1966, chap. 10. See, also, Cattell, *Factor Analysis*, chap. 20, which is a creative discussion of the possibilities of combining factor analysis and experimentation. See also: H. Rawson and S. Rettig, "Factor Analysis as a Controlling Technique," *Educational and Psychological Measurement*, XXII (1962), 725–729.

[33]H. Woodrow, "The Relation between Abilities and Improvement with Practice," *Journal of Educational Psychology*, XXIX (1938), 215–230.

from, say, factual learning to a problem-oriented approach can assess the effects of the change in part through factor analysis. Shifts in factor loading structures and magnitudes can be expected under the impact of so radical a change.

In considering the scientific value of factor analysis, the reader must be cautioned against attributing "reality" and uniqueness to factors. The danger of reification is great. It is easy to name a factor and then to believe there is a reality behind the name. But giving a factor a name does not give it reality. Factor names are simply attempts to epitomize the essence of factors. They are always tentative, subject to later confirmation or disconfirmation. Then, too, factors can be produced by many things. Anything that introduces correlation between variables "creates" a factor. Differences in sex, education, social and cultural background, and intelligence can cause factors to appear. Factors also differ—at least to some extent—with different samples. Response sets or test forms may cause factors to appear. Despite these cautions, it must be said that factors do repeatedly emerge with different tests, different samples, and different conditions. When this happens, we have fair assurance that there is an underlying variable that we are successfully measuring.

There are serious criticisms of factor analysis. The major valid ones center around the indeterminacy of how many factors to extract from a correlation matrix and the problem of how to rotate factors. Another difficulty that bothers critics and devotees alike is what can be called the communality problem, or what quantities to put into the diagonal of the R matrix before factoring. In an introductory chapter, these problems cannot be discussed. The reader is referred to the discussions of Cattell, Guilford, Harman, and Thurstone. A criticism of a different order seems to bother educators and sociologists and some psychologists. This takes two or three forms that seem to boil down to distrust, sometimes profound, combined with antipathy toward the method due to its complexity and, strangely enough, its objectivity.

The argument runs something like this. Factor analysts throw a lot of tests together into a statistical machine and get out factors that have little psychological or educational meaning. The factors are simply artifacts of the method. They are averages that correspond to no psychological reality, especially the psychological reality of the individual, other than that in the mind of the factor analyst.[34] Besides, you can't get any more out of a factor analysis than you put into it.

The argument is basically irrelevant. To say that factors have no psychological meaning and that they are averages is both true and untrue. If the argument were valid, no scientific constructs would have any meaning. They are all, in a sense, averages. They are all inventions of the scientist. This is simply the lot of science. The basic criterion of the "reality" of any construct, any factor, is its empirical, scientific "reality." If, after uncovering a factor, we can successfully predict relations from theoretical presuppositions and hypotheses, then the factor has "reality." There is no more reality to a factor than this, just as there is no more reality to an atom than its empirical manifestations.

[34]See G. Allport, *Pattern and Growth in Personality*. New York: Holt, Rinehart and Winston, 1961, pp. 329–330; G. Allport, *Personality*. New York: Holt, Rinehart and Winston, 1937, pp. 242–248.

The argument about only getting out what is put into a factor analysis is meaningless as well as irrelevant. No competent factor analytic investigator would ever claim more than this. But this does not mean that nothing is discovered in factor analysis. Quite the contrary. The answer is, of course, that we get nothing more out of a factor analysis than we put into it, but that we do not know *all* we put into it. Nor do we know what tests or measures share common factor variance. Nor do we know the relations between factors. Only study and analysis can tell us these things. We may write an attitude scale that we believe measures a single attitude. A factor analysis of the attitude items, naturally, cannot produce factors that are not in the items. But it can show us, for example, that there are two or three sources of common variance in a scale that we thought to be unidimensional. Similarly, a scale that we believe measures authoritarianism may be shown by factor analysis to measure intelligence, dogmatism, and other variables.

If we examine empirical evidence rather than opinion, we must conclude that factor analysis is one of the most powerful tools yet devised for the study of complex areas of behavioral scientific concern. Indeed, factor analysis is one of the creative inventions of the century, just as intelligence testing, conditioning, reinforcement theory, the operational definition, the notion of randomness, measurement theory, research design, multivariate analysis, the computer, and theories of learning, personality, development, organizations, and society are.[35]

It is fitting that this chapter—and the book—conclude with some words of a great psychological scientist, teacher, and factor analyst, Louis Leon Thurstone:

> As scientists, we have the faith that the abilities and personalitities of people are not so complex as the total enumeration of attributes that can be listed. We believe that these traits are made up of a smaller number of primary factors or elements that combine in various ways to make a long list of traits. It is our ambition to find some of these elementary abilities and traits . . .
>
> All scientific work has this in common, that we try to comprehend nature in the most parsimonious manner. An explanation of a set of phenomena or of a set of experimental observations gains acceptance only in so far as it gives us intellectual control or comprehension of a relatively wide variety of phenomena in terms of a limited number of concepts. The principle of parsimony is intuitive for anyone who has even slight aptitude for science. The fundamental motivation of science is the craving for the simplest possible comprehension of nature, and it finds satisfaction in the discovery of the simplifying uniformities that we call scientific laws.[36]

Study Suggestions

1. Fortunately, there are good, even excellent, books and articles on factor analysis. Unfortunately, there is as yet no satisfactory and up-to-date book written at an elementary level. So, to learn factor analysis, one has to work hard at it, using more advanced texts. It is suggested that the student who will not take a course in factor analysis use either the Harman (footnote 5) or the Thurstone

[35]K. Deutsch, J. Platt, and D. Senghaas, "Conditions Favoring Major Advances in Social Science," *Science*, CLXXI (1971), 450–459.

[36]L. Thurstone, *The Measurement of Values*. Chicago: University of Chicago Press, 1959, p. 8.

(footnote 6) text or both. Both are definitive but rather difficult. Thomson's (footnote 10) discussion of the principal factors (axes) method is helpful.

2. The more advanced student will find the following selected articles valuable:

Anastasi, A. "On the Formation of Psychological Traits." *American Psychologist*, X (1970), 899–910. Very good review of (mostly) factor analytic studies of traits and their development.

Coan, R. "Facts, Factors, and Artifacts: The Quest for Psychological Meaning." *Psychological Review*, LXXI (1964), 123–140. A good general theoretical article on factor analysis, with discussion of the interpretation of factors.

Guilford, J. "Factorial Angles to Psychology." *Psychological Review*, LXVIII (1961), 1–20. (See footnote 31.)

Overall, J. "Note on the Scientific Status of Factors." *Psychological Bulletin*, LXI (1964), 270–276. Excellent, even brilliant, analysis of basic factor analytic notions.

Peterson, D. "Scope and Generality of Verbally Defined Personality Factors." *Psychological Review*, LXXII (1965), 48–59. Very convincing on the number of factors problem.

Thompson, J. "Meaningful and Unmeaningful Rotation of Factors." *Psychological Bulletin*, LIX (1962), 211–223. Good article on one of the difficult problems of factor analysis; calls for both objective machine rotation *and* judgmental rotation.

3. The individual who wishes a broad overview—with considerable specificity, however—has a few excellent sources available. Among the following general references, the French monograph and the French et al. reference test kit are valuable. In fact, if you can read and study only one of these, pick the latter. Rather well-established cognitive factors are named, described, and illustrated. The kit has no equal in the literature.

Eysenck, H. *The Structure of Human Personality*. New York: Wiley, 1953. A review of many factor analytic studies of physique, interests, attitudes, and traits.

French, J. "The Description of Aptitude and Achievement Tests in Terms of Rotated Factors." *Psychometric Monographs*, no. 5. Chicago: University of Chicago Press, 1951. An exhaustive review, with data, of many factor analytic studies of aptitude and achievement.

French, J., Ekstrom, R., Price, L. *Manual for Kit of Reference Tests for Cognitive Factors*. Princeton, N.J.: Educational Testing Service, 1963.

Wolfle, D. *Factor Analysis to 1940*. Chicago: University of Chicago Press, 1940. A brief and enlightening review of early factor analysis.

4. As usual, there is no substitute for the study of actual research uses of methods. The student should, therefore, read two or three good factor analytic studies. Select from those cited in the chapter or from the following:

Allen, D., and Ager, J. "A Factor Analytic Study of the Ability to Spell." *Educational and Psychological Measurement*, XXV (1965), 153–161.

Davis, J. "Faculty Perceptions of Students. V. A Second-Order Structure for Faculty Characterizations." Research Bulletin RB-65-12. Princeton, N.J.: Educational Testing Service, 1965. First- and second-order factors in an aesthetically satisfying solution.

Isaacson, R., et al. "Dimensions of Student Evaluation of Teaching." *Journal of Educational Psychology*, LV (1964), 344–351. A competent study of the factors behind student evaluations of instructors. The first factor is important.

Kerlinger, F., and Rokeach, M. "The Factorial Nature of the F and D Scales." *Journal of Personality and Social Psychology*, IV (1966), 391–399. An attempt to clarify a difficult area of measurement: authoritarianism and dogmatism.

Longabaugh, R. "The Structure of Interpersonal Behavior." *Sociometry*, XXIX (1966), 441–460. Use of factor analysis in cross-cultural observations of interpersonal behavior.

Prothro, E. "Patterns of Permissiveness among Preliterate Peoples." *Journal of Abnormal and Social Psychology*, LXI (1960), 151–154. Factor analysis of Whiting and Child cross-cultural data; psychoanalytic orientation.

Thurstone, L. "A Factorial Study of Perception." *Psychometric Monographs*, no. 4. Chicago: University of Chicago Press, 1944. Another Thurstone pioneering and classic study.

Veldman, D., and Peck, R. "Student Teacher Characteristics from the Pupils' Viewpoint." *Journal of Educational Psychology*, LIV (1963), 346–355. Factor analysis of student evaluations; uses factor scores effectively; interesting results.

5. Here is a small fictitious correlation matrix, with the tests labeled.

	1	2	3	4	5	6
1. Vocabulary		.70	.22	.20	.15	.25
2. Analogies	.70		.15	.26	.12	.30
3. Addition	.22	.15		.81	.21	.10
4. Multiplication	.20	.26	.81		.31	.29
5. Recall First Names	.15	.12	.21	.31		.72
6. Recognize Figures	.25	.30	.40	.29	.72	

(a) Do an "armchair" factor analysis. That is, by inspection of the matrix determine how many factors there probably are and which tests are on what factors.

(b) Name the factors. How sure are you of your names? What would you do to be more sure of your conclusions?

6. Given below is the obliquely rotated factor matrix of the intercorrelations among 13 variables produced by the superiors of school principals when they rated the principals.[37] (*Note:* All decimal points are omitted.)

Rating Item	*A*	*B*	*C*	*D*	*E*
Interest in Work	06	15	41	−01	02
Sticking to a Job	03	−18	52	02	02
Getting Along with Teachers	69	07	−07	12	01
Getting Along with Parents	62	−02	04	08	04
Getting Along with Superiors	52	02	05	−17	31
Knowledge of Administration	−07	−11	30	02	26
Knowledge of Teaching	01	33	08	−09	31
Rapport with Children	56	32	−04	09	−12
Written Communication	−03	00	−06	07	45
Understanding	08	−04	05	07	39
Oral Communication (Formal)	−08	01	05	49	01
Oral Communication (Informal)	09	01	−05	48	07
Over-all Impression	25	09	15	01	26

[37]Hemphill et al., *op. cit.*, p. 232.

(a) Name the factors, giving reasons for naming them as you do. (Use loadings .25 and higher to help in this naming.)
(b) Check your names with the names reported in the study.
(c) This is an obliquely rotated matrix, which means that the factors are correlated. For example, the correlation between *A* and *C* is .47. What does this mean? How does this affect the interpretation of the data?

7. Interpret the rotated factor matrix given below. The data are taken from a larger table reported by Sears, Maccoby, and Levin.[38] (*Note:* All decimal points omitted.)

Scale	*A*	*B*	*D*
Permissiveness for Going without Clothes Indoors	*66*	−11	09
Masturbation Permissiveness	*70*	−04	05
Standards for Neatness and Orderliness	*−35*	−19	*38*
Extent of Use of Tangible Rewards	−04	−14	*40*
Extent of Use of Deprivation of Privileges	−16	−08	*51*
Parents' Agreement on Child-Rearing Policies	01	*60*	15
Husband's Reaction to Wife's Pregnancy	13	*51*	07
Mother's Child-Rearing Anxiety	−10	*−56*	−17

[38]R. Sears, E. Maccoby, and H. Levin, *Patterns of Child Rearing*. New York: Harper & Row, 1957, pp. 516–518. Only three factors of seven and eight measures of 44 are given. Some of the original signs (plus and minus) have been changed to facilitate interpretation.

Appendixes

Appendix A

The Research Report

This appendix has two purposes: to outline some of the main points of report writing and to cite appropriate references to guide the reader.

The Purpose

The purpose of the research report is to tell readers the problem investigated, the methods used to solve the problem, the results of the investigation, and the conclusions inferred from the results. It is not the function of the investigator to *convince* the reader of the virtue of the research. Rather, it is to *report*, as expeditiously and clearly as possible, what was done, why it was done, the outcome of the doing, and the investigator's conclusions. The report should be so written that the reader himself can reach his own conclusions as to the adequacy of the research and the validity of the reported results and conclusions.

To achieve this purpose is not easy. The writer must strive for the right blend of detail and brevity, for objectivity, and for clarity in presentation. Perhaps the best criterion question is: Can another investigator replicate the research by following the research report? If he cannot, owing to incomplete or inadequate reporting of methodology or to lack of clarity in presentation, then the report is inadequate.

The Structure

The structure of the research report is simple. It is almost the same as the structure of the research itself: the problem, the methodology, the results. Here is a general outline:

I. Problem
   1. Theory, hypotheses, definitions
   2. Previous research; the literature

II. Methodology-Data Collection
   1. Sample and sampling method
   2. How hypotheses were tested (methodology), experimental procedures, instrumentation
   3. Measurement of variables
   4. Methods of analysis, statistics
   5. Pretesting and pilot studies

III. Results, Interpretation, and Conclusions

The Problem

The problem section differs greatly in different reports. In theses and books, it is usually long and detailed. In published research reports, it is kept to a minimum. The basic precept to keep in mind, though seemingly obvious, is not easy to follow: Tell the reader what the research problem is. Tell it to him in question form. For example, what is the effect of instructional set on the concept learning of children?[1] Does past experience with materials have a negative effect on problem-solving involving the materials?[2] How do race of tester, approval, and need for approval influence Negro children's learning?[3] What is the factorial nature of the *F* and *D* Scales? or, Are authoritarianism and dogmatism parts of the same underlying variable or are they separate though related entities?[4] What are the effects of intelligence, achievement motivation, and educational attainment on occupational status?[5]

The statement of the general problem is usually not precise and operational. Rather, it sets the general stage for the reader. The subproblems, however, should be more precise. They should contain implications for testing. For example: Are principles derived by the learner solely from concrete instances more readily used in new situations than principles given to him?[6] Can a person conversing with another person manipulate that person's conversation by agreeing or disagreeing with him, or by paraphrasing what he has said?[7]

Some report writers, rather than state the problems, state the general and specific hypotheses. A good practice would seem to be to state the broader general problem and then to state the hypotheses, both general and specific. The reader is referred to Chapter 2 for examples. Whatever way is used, bear in mind the main purpose of informing the reader of the main area of investigation and the specific propositions that were tested.

An important part of the statement of the problem is the definition of the variables. At some point in the problem discussion the variables should be defined. The subject of research definitions was handled in Chapter 3 and need not be

[1] H. Amster, "Effect of Instructional Set and Variety of Instances on Children's Learning," *Journal of Educational Psychology*, LVII (1966), 74–85.

[2] H. Birch and H. Rabinowitz, "The Negative Effect of Previous Experience on Productive Thinking," *Journal of Experimental Psychology*, XLI (1951), 121–125.

[3] I. Katz, T. Henchy, and H. Allen, "Effects of Race of Tester, Approval-Disapproval, and Need on Negro Children's Learning," *Journal of Personality and Social Psychology*, VIII (1968), 38–42.

[4] F. Kerlinger and M. Rokeach, "The Factorial Nature of the F and D Scales," *Journal of Personality and Social Psychology*, IV (1966), 391–399.

[5] G. Elder, "Achievement Motivation and Intelligence in Occupational Mobility: A Longitudinal Analysis," *Sociometry*, XXXI (1968), 327–354.

[6] G. Haslerud and S. Meyers, "The Transfer Value of Given and Individually Derived Principles," *Journal of Educational Psychology*, XLIX (1958), 293–298.

[7] W. Verplanck, "The Control of the Content of Conversation: Reinforcement of Statements of Opinion," *Journal of Abnormal and Social Psychology*, LI (1955), 668–676.

repeated here, except for the admonition: Inform the reader not only of the variables but also what you mean by them. Define in general and operational terms giving justification for your definitions.

There are two main reasons for discussing the general and research literature related to the research problem. The first of these is the more important: to explain and clarify the theoretical rationale of the problem. Suppose, like Haslerud and Meyers, one were interested in investigating the relative effectiveness for transfer of self-discovery of principles by learners and systematic enunciation of the principles to learners. Since the problem is in part a transfer of training problem, one would have to discuss transfer and some of the literature on transfer, but especially that part of the literature pertinent to this problem. One may well want to discuss to some extent philosophical and pedagogical writings on the theory of formal discipline, for instance. In this manner the investigator provides a general picture of the research topic and fits his problem into the general picture.

A second reason for discussing the literature is to tell the reader what research has and has not been done on the problem. Obviously, the investigator must show that his particular investigation has not been done before. The underlying purpose, of course, is to locate the present research in the existing body of research on the subject and to point out what it contributes to the subject.

Methodology-Data Collection

The function of the methodology-data collection section of the research report, of course, is to tell the reader what was done to solve the problem. Meticulous care must be exercised to so report that the criterion of replicability is satisfied. That is, it should be possible for another investigator to reproduce the research, to reanalyze the data, or to arrive at unambiguous conclusions as to the adequacy of the methods and data collection. In books and theses there can be little question of the applicability of the criterion. In research journal reports, unfortunately, the criterion is difficult, sometimes even impossible, to satisfy. Owing to lack of journal space, investigators are forced to condense reports in such a way that it is sometimes difficult to reconstruct and evaluate what a researcher has done. Yet the criterion remains a good one and should be kept in mind when tackling the methodology section.

The first part of the methodology-data collection section should tell what sample or samples were used, how they were selected, and why they were so selected. If eighth-grade pupils were used, the reason for using them should be stated. If the samples were randomly selected, this should be said. The method of random sampling should also be specified. If pupils were assigned at random to experimental groups, this should be reported. If they were not, this, too, should be reported with reasons for the lack of such assignment.

The method of testing the hypotheses should be reported in detail. If the study has been experimental, the manner in which the independent variable(s) has been manipulated is described. This description includes instruments used—teaching machines, audio-visual aids, and so on—instructions to the subjects, control precautions, and the like. If the study has been ex post facto, the procedures used to gather data are outlined.

The report of any empirical study must include an account of the measurement of the variables of the study. This may be accomplished in a few sentences in some studies. For example, in an experiment with one independent variable and a dependent variable whose measurement is simple, all that may be necessary is a brief description of the measurement of the dependent variable. Such measurement may entail only the counting of responses. In other studies, the description of the measurement of the variables may take up most of the methodology section. A factor analytic study, for instance, may require lengthy descriptions of measurement instruments and how they were used. Such descriptions will, of course, include justification of the instruments used, as well as evidence of their reliability and validity.

An account of the data analysis methods used is sometimes put into the methodology section, sometimes in the analysis-interpretation section. It is probably better to include these methods in the methodology section, though space can sometimes be saved the other way. Whichever practice is followed, the analysis methods must be outlined and justified. Since most of the common methods of analysis are well known, it is ordinarily sufficient to say, for example, that a $2 \times 3 \times 3$ factorial analysis of variance was done, or that χ^2 was used, or that principal-factors factor analysis with orthogonal rotations was used. If an unusual method of analysis is used, or if a common method is used in an unusual way, the investigator should describe what was done in sufficient detail to enable a competent reader to understand it. If space is at a premium, as it usually is, sometimes a reference to a technical source of the analytic method is sufficient.

In many investigations, pilot studies and pretesting are used. (Indeed, they should be used in most studies.) If so, what was done and the outcome of what was done are reported. If the pilot study was solely for trying out the instruments or the variable manipulation method on a small scale, little need be said. If, however, the pilot study or the pretesting supplied actual research data, the reader is entitled to know methodological details.

Results, Interpretation, Conclusions

This part of the report, though logically a unit, is often broken down into two or three sections. We treat it here as one section, since the interpretation of results and the conclusions drawn from the results are so often reported together in journal research reports. In a thesis or book, however, it may be desirable to separate the data from their interpretation and from the conclusions.

The results or data of a research study are the raw materials for the solution of the research problem. The data and their analysis are the hypothesis-testing stuff of research. Methodology and data collection are tools used to obtain the raw material of hypothesis-testing, the data. The main question is this: Do the data support or not support the hypotheses? It cannot be emphasized enough that methodology, data collection, and analysis are selected and used for the purpose of testing the operational hypotheses deduced from the general research questions. Therefore the report writer must be exceptionally careful to report his results as accurately and completely as possible, informing the reader how the results bear on the hypotheses.

Before writing this part of the report, it is helpful to reduce the data and the results of the data analysis to condensed form, particularly tables. The researcher should thoroughly digest the data before writing. The question, Do the data support the hypotheses? must be clearly answered in his mind. Then, after outlining the results section, he should write. While writing, the investigator should guard against wandering from the task at hand, the solution of the research problem. Everything he writes must be geared to letting the data bear on the problem and the hypotheses.

Somewhere in the final section of the research report the limitations and weaknesses of the study should be discussed. This can be overdone, of course. All scientific work has weaknesses, and many pages can be written belaboring a study's weaknesses. Still, the major limitations, which, of course, may have been mentioned earlier when discussing the problem or the methodology, should be pointed out. This is done, not to show humility or one's technical competence, but rather to enable the reader to judge the validity of the conclusions drawn from the data and the general worth of the study.

Limitations of social scientific and educational research generally come from sampling and subject assignment inadequacies, methodological weaknesses, and statistical deficiencies. Lack of random sampling, as we have seen, limits the conconclusions to the particular sample used. Lack of random assignment casts doubt on the adequacy of the control of independent variables and thus on the conclusions. Statistical deficiencies, similarly, can lead to incorrect conclusions. Deficiencies in measurement always affect conclusions, too. If a measurement instrument, perhaps through no fault of the writer, is only moderately reliable, a finding may be ambiguous and inconclusive. More important, the questionable validity of an instrument may seriously change a conclusion.

These matters have been discussed in the text and need no further elaboration here. It may be added, however, that the writing of the conclusions is naturally affected by the recognized and acknowledged limitations and weaknesses. Not only is the reader entitled to know these things; it is the professional responsibility of the writer to inform him of them.

The Writing

It is not easy to write simply and clearly. One has to work at it. One should realize that almost no writer can escape the necessity of constant revision by reorganizing and paring—deleting circumlocutions, redundancies, and other verbal fat. Suggestions for better research report writing follow.

Although research reports should be fairly detailed, there is no need to waste words. State the problem, the methodology, and the results as clearly, simply, and briefly as possible. Avoid hackneyed expressions like "in terms of," "with respect to," "with reference to," "give consideration to," and the like. Delete unnecessary words and expressions when revising. For example, sentences with expressions like "the fact of the matter is," "owing to the fact that," and "as to whether" can always be revised to remove such clumsy inelegancies. For good advice on simplicity and clarity, study Strunk and White's little classic, *The Elements of Style*. Nicholson's book is most helpful.[8]

Writing scholarly papers and research reports requires a certain amount of routine drudgery that few of us like. Bibliographies, footnotes, tables, figures, and other mechanical details, however, cannot be escaped. Yet a little systematic study can help solve most problems. That is, do not wait until you sit down to write and then find out how to handle footnotes and other mechanical details. Get a good reference book or two and study and lay out footnote and bibliographical forms, tables, figures, and headings. Put three or four types of footnote entries on 3-by-5 cards. Similarly, learn two or three methods of laying out tables. Lay out skeleton tables. Then use these samples when writing. In short, put much of the drudgery and doubt behind you by mastering the elements of the methods, instead of impeding your writing by constant interruptions to check on how to do things.

Presentation of statistical results and analyses gives students considerable trouble. Hit the problem head-on. Perhaps the best way to do this is to study statistical presentation in two or three good journals, like the *Journal of Personality and Social Psychology*, the *Journal of Educational Psychology*, the *American Educational Research Journal*, and the *American Sociological Review*. There are fairly standard ways to present tables of means and standard deviations, analysis of variance results, factor analytic results, and the like. In theses the problem of presenting data is not so acute, since space is not a major consideration. In journals,

[8]See the references at the end of this appendix.

however, the space problem is acute. Tables must be condensed, even omitted. An excellent source of good statistical and tabular reporting help is the manual put out by the American Psychological Association. Turabian's manual is also good.

The purpose of statistical, tabular, and other condensed presentation should be kept in mind. A statistical table, for instance, should clearly tell the reader what the data essentially say. This does not mean, of course, that a statistical table can stand by itself. Its purpose is to illuminate and clarify the textual discussion. The text carries the story; the table helps make the text clear and gives the statistical evidence for assertions made in the text. The text may say, for example, "The three experimental groups differed significantly in achievement," and the tables will report the statistical data—means, standard deviations, F ratios, levels of significance—to support the assertion. There is often no need for a table. If a hypothesis has been tested by calculating one, two, or three coefficients of correlation, these can simply be reported in the text without tabular presentation.

A fairly safe generalization to guide one in writing research reports is: first drafts are not adequate. In other words, almost any writing, as said earlier, improves upon revision. It is almost always possible to simplify first-draft language and to delete unnecessary words, phrases, and even sentences and paragraphs. A first rule, then, is to go over any report with a ruthless pencil toward the end of greater simplicity, clarity, and brevity. With experience this not only becomes possible; it becomes easier.

If an adequate outline has been used, there should be little problem with the organization of a research paper. Yet sometimes it is necessary to reorganize a report. One may find, for example, that one has discussed something at the end of the report that was not anticipated in the beginning. Reorganization is required. In any case, the possibility of improvement in communication through reorganization should always be kept in mind.

Anyone's research writing can be improved in two ways: by letting something one has written sit for a few weeks, and by having someone else read and criticize one's work. It is remarkable what a little time will do for one's objectivity and critical capacity. One sees obvious blemishes that somehow one could not see before. Time helps salve the ego, too. Our precious inventions do not seem so precious after a few weeks or months, We can be much more objective about them.

The second problem is harder. It is hard to take criticism, but the researcher must learn to take it. Scientific research is one of the most complex activities of man. Writing research reports is not easy, and no one can be expected to be perfect. It should be accepted and routine procedure, therefore, to have colleagues read our reports. It should be accepted routine, too, to accept our readers' criticisms in the spirit in which we should have asked for them. There is of course no obligation to change a manuscript in line with criticism. But there is an obligation to give each criticism the serious, careful, and objective attention it deserves. Doctoral students have to consider seriously the criticisms of their sponsors—whether or not they like them or agree with them. All scholarly and scientific writers, however, should voluntarily learn the discipline of subjecting their work to their peers. They should learn that the complex business of communicating scholarly and scientific work is difficult and demanding, and that in the long run they can only profit from competent criticism and careful revision.

Some Useful References

A Manual of Style, 12th ed. Chicago: University of Chicago Press, 1969. A basic reference that should be consulted for moot points—hyphenation, capitalization, tables, types, and so forth.

American Psychological Association. *Publication Manual of the American Psychological Association.* 1967 Revision. Washington, D.C.: American Psychological Association, 1967. The basic manual for writers of reports in psychological journals, especially APA journals. Particularly good for mechanical details such as tables, typing, and the like. Note, however, that many journals, especially education journals, do not use the APA referencing system (giving all references at the end of the report).

Campbell, W. *Form and Style in Thesis Writing*, 3d ed. Boston: Houghton Mifflin, 1969. A useful reference for thesis writers.

Nicholson, M. *A Dictionary of American-English Usage.* New York: Oxford University Press, 1957. A valuable American revision of Fowler's classic, *A Dictionary of English Usage.* Anyone who plans to write much should get this book.

Strunk, W., and White, E. *The Elements of Style.* New York: Macmillan, 1959. This little gem, which every writer should own, is dedicated to clarity, brevity, and simplicity.

Turabian, K. *A Manual for Writers of Term Papers, Theses, and Dissertations*, 12th ed. Chicago: University of Chicago Press, 1969. An excellent, invaluable reference. Can well be called the handbook of the doctoral student. It is based on the *Manual of Style.*

Appendix B

Historical and Methodological Research

The limits of this book forbid adequate discussion of two important and very different kinds of research: *historical research* and what will be called *methodological research*. This appendix will acquaint the reader with the nature of historical and methodological research and point out the part they play in social scientific and educational research.

Historical Research

Historical research is the critical investigation of events, developments, and experiences of the past, the careful weighing of evidence of the validity of sources of information on the past, and the interpretation of the weighed evidence. The historical investigator, like other investigators, then, collects data, evaluates the data for validity, and interprets the data. Actually, the historical method, or *historiography*, differs from other scholarly activity only in its rather elusive subject matter, the past, and the peculiarly difficult interpretive task imposed by the elusive nature of its subject matter.

Historical research is important in behavioral research. The roots of behavioral disciplines have to be understood if behavioral scientists are to be able to put their theories and research in appropriate contexts. This is perhaps more so in disciplines like sociology, economics, and political science than it is in psychology. Nevertheless, even the psychologist must know psychology's origins, since theories develop almost always in a context of earlier theories and research. Reinforcement theory, for example, developed from earlier work by Pavlov, Thorndike, and others, and the psychologist of today must use this earlier work as a cognitive stratum, so to speak, from which he does his work.

Education is a particularly good example of the virtue of historical research. The virtue of historical research in the behavioral sciences probably springs mainly from the need to do present work with earlier work as a cognitive context. In education, however, historical research per se has great value, because it is necessary to know and understand educational accomplishments and trends of the past in order to gain perspective on present and future directions. To understand contemporary movements like the ungraded classroom, the so-called British system, and community control, for example, one should understand progressivism and its roots in Froebel, Rousseau, Dewey, and even Freud. That one has to search for historical roots is nicely shown by the current emphasis on "hard-core" learning, which is understood to be a very old point of view. Psychology and education nicely come together here: hard-core learning is in part the old razor-strop theory of the mind revivified and dressed up in modern clothes. The "British system" is seen to be a version of what Dewey and Parker preached and practiced early in the century.

If we look at one or two canons of historiography, we may be able to understand why historiographical discipline is valuable in and of itself and also valuable for the social scientist. One of the basic rules of research in history is: Always use primary sources. A *primary source* is the original repository of an historical datum, like an original record kept of an important occasion, an eyewitness description of an event, a photograph, minutes of organization meetings, and so on. A *secondary source* is an account or record of an historical event or circumstance one or more steps removed from an original repository. Instead of the minutes of an organization meeting, for example, one uses a newspaper account of the meeting. Instead of studying and citing the original report of a research, one studies and cites someone else's account and digest of it.

To use secondary sources when primary sources are available is a major historiographical error. And with good reason. Materials and data, especially those about human beings and their activities, are changed and often distorted in transmission. The reputable historian never completely trusts secondary sources, though he of course studies them and weighs them for their validity. (Often he is forced to use them for lack of primary sources.) The dangers of distortion and consequent erroneous interpretation are too great.

The precept of the primary source is a good one for behavioral investigators. While the sheer mass of published studies is so great that one has to depend upon secondary sources, such as competent digests and abstracts, one should always attempt to study primary sources, especially of important studies in one's own field. This suggestion applies to both the scientist and the practitioner. If the precept of the primary source were taken more seriously, fewer erroneous generalizations would gain currency. Generalizations like "Democratic group atmosphere produces better learning than autocratic or laissez-faire group atmosphere" would be examined more critically.

Two other canons of historiography are expressed by the terms *external criticism* and *internal criticism*. The historian critically examines the sources of data for their genuineness, or more accurately, for their validity. Is the document or source genuine? Did X really write this paper? If X wrote the paper, was he a competent and truthful witness? This is *external criticism*. *Internal criticism* is preoccupied with the *content* of the source or document and its meaning. Are the statements made accurate representations of the historical facts? A document may survive external criticism and still be suspect as evidence. There may be no doubt of the "true" author or recorder of events—and he may be competent. Wittingly or unwittingly, however, he may have distorted the truth. Internal criticism, in brief, seeks the "true" meaning and value of the content of sources of data.

Social scientific and educational investigators obviously use both external and internal criticism, but particularly internal criticism. If an author of a research report comes to an erroneous conclusion because of inadequate statistical analysis or interpretation, for example, it is clearly the task of other scientists to correct the error. There is a well-known study on transfer of training whose authors seemed to have erred in the interpretation of their data. The study was well done. Its conception and execution were imaginative and competent. But the conclusions and the interpretation of the data are questionable, because of inadequate statistical analysis and inadequate interpretation of the statistical analysis that was done. Any investigator can make, and does make, such errors. This is not the point. The point is that the study has been reproduced in anthologies and cited in texts as evidence of the effect of knowledge of principles on the transfer of learning. Perhaps the conclusion *is* correct. But this study did not yield adequate evidence of its correctness. Careful internal criticism of research studies is clearly needed.

The contributions to knowledge of the educational historian have been many and important. The history of education and historical research in education have declined, in part because of the impact of scientific research.[1] Early in the century, historical and related inquiry occupied a large part of educational attention. After the investigations of men like Thorndike, Terman, and others, however, historical inquiry was subordinated to scientific research. Despite a contemporary recrudescence of historical inquiry among historians in schools of education, the history of education never recovered. This is most unfortunate. Without good history and good historians, a discipline can lose perspective, not to mention the serious consequences on the intellectual development of students of education of this neglect, even derogation, in education of the philosophy and history of education. Rigorous historiography is needed, just as good scientific research is needed.

The following excerpt from a report of a committee of historians on historiography summarizes the importance of historiography to the social sciences:

> Historiography has a necessary relevance to all the social sciences, to the humanities, and to the formulation of public and private policies, because (1) all the data used in the social sciences, in the humanities, and in the formulation of public and private policies are drawn from records of, experience in, or writing about the past; because (2) all policies respecting human affairs, public or private, and all generalizations of a nonstatistical character in the social sciences and in the humanities involve interpretations of or assumptions about the past; and because (3) all workers in the social sciences and in the humanities are personalities of given times, places, and experience whose thinking is consequently in some measure conditioned and determined by the historical circumstances of their lives and experiences.[2].

Methodological Research

Methodological research is controlled investigation of the theoretical and applied aspects of measurement, mathematics and statistics, and ways of obtaining and analyzing data. Without methodological research, modern behavioral research would still be in the research dark ages. Like historical research, it is an extremely important part of the body scientific. This strong statement is made to counteract the somewhat negative sentiments that many professionals in psychology, sociology, and education seem to hold about methodological research.

Methodology is called "mere" methodology. The methodologist is called a "mere" methodologist. This is a curious state of affairs. Some of the most compe-

[1]M. Borrowman, "History of Education." In C. Harris, ed., *Encyclopedia of Educational Research*, 3d ed. New York: Macmillan, 1960, pp. 661–668. (See especially pp. 663–664.)

[2]Social Science Research Council, *Theory and Practice in Historical Study: A Report of the Committee on Historiography*. New York: Social Science Research Council, 1946, pp. 134–135.

tent, imaginative, and creative men in modern psychology, sociology, and education have been and are methodologists. Indeed, it is almost impossible to do outstanding research, though one can do acceptable research, without being something of a methodologist. It is needless to pursue the prejudice further. My point is that methodological research is a vital and absolutely indispensable part of behavioral research. Let us look at what the methodological researcher does and see why these statements have been made.

Perhaps the largest and most rigorous area of psychological and educational methodological research is measurement. The methodologist—and it should be emphasized that good behavioral researchers have to be, to some extent, measurement methodologists—is preoccupied with theoretical and practical problems of identifying and measuring psychological variables. These problems have a number of aspects. Reliability and validity, in and of themselves, are large areas of preoccupation and investigation. Then there are the theoretical and practical problems of the construction of measuring instruments: scaling, item writing, item analysis, and so on. One man can easily spend a lifetime on any one of these aspects of measurement.

Statisticians long ago turned their talents to solving the problem of the objective evaluation of research data. Their contributions were considered at length earlier and need not be repeated here. It is significant to add, however, that some of the most outstanding methodological contributions of statistics have come from applied researchers—Fisher and Thurstone, to name only two.

The application of modern mathematics to social scientific research has begun. There is evidence of a lively stimulus to research. Applications of set theory and thinking were discussed earlier. We are also familiar with probability theory and its application to research. Matrix theory has been successfully applied to multivariate analysis, factor analysis, and sociometry. Its applications to other research problems are being developed; for example, power relations in groups are studied mathematically. Game theory is a new development that may have fruitful applications to behavioral research. A branch of mathematics known as linear programming has promise for the solution of certain complex educational problems. The prospects of the applications of modern mathematics and logic are exciting and important.

The third large area of methodological research, investigations of methods of data collection and analysis, has thrived for many years. This area includes interviews and the construction of interview schedules, content analysis, methods of sampling, systematic observational techniques, and other methods. An example or two may help the student appreciate the significance of such work.

Interviews can yield biased data. The study of the causes and prevention of biases in the schedule and in the interview situation, if successful, can help investigators increase the validity of their data. Which is the more reliable of two methods of direct observation of behavior: the observation and recording of small clearly defined acts of individuals or of larger molar units of behavior? What method of analysis of the content of written documents or of interview material yields the most reliable results? Such questions and many others are being successfully answered by methodologists.

Appendix C

The Computer and Behavioral Research[1]

The high-speed electronic digital computer is profoundly influencing behavioral research and behavioral scientists. The days of statistical and mathematical computational drudgery are over: the computer now does in minutes and seconds statistical and other operations that took days, weeks, and even months of clerical and desk calulator work. Research projects that would not have been attempted ten years ago because of the sheer bulk of necessary calculations to analyze the data of the projects are now readily approachable with the computer and computer auxiliary equipment.

The intent of this appendix is to indicate the importance, even indispensability, of computers in behavioral research, and to try to stimulate the student to learn enough of computer technique to enable him to use the computer as a research tool. A subsidiary purpose is to acquaint the student with the basic characteristics of high-speed computers, with statistical computer programs that are generally available, and with a very remarkable achievement: the intermediary language with which the researcher communicates with the machine.

Some Important Computer Characteristics

The computer is an elaborate complex of electronic hardware whose chief characteristics are tremendous speed, easy ability to do thousands of repetitive operations with a high degree of accuracy, flexibility, and what will here be called "ductility." Everyone has heard that computers are fast. Few people know, however,

[1]I am deeply indebted to the Computing Center of the Courant Institute of Mathematical Sciences, New York University, and particularly its associate director, Professor Max Goldstein, for allowing me to use the computer complex and for helping me to solve programming problems. I owe a special debt to the following highly astute, yet kind and indulgent, computer specialists for their help: Edward Friedman, Eleanor Kolchin, Robert Malchie, Neil Smith, and Howard Walowitz. To my colleague, Professor Nathan Jaspen, who long ago needled my professional conscience until I overcame a curious resistance to learning programming, grateful thanks are also due.

how fast they are. They are faster than almost anything else man works with. Their operations approximate the speed of light. Most students are familiar with the calculation of correlation coefficients. With 100 cases of two sets of one-digit numbers, one correlation coefficient might take about 20 to 30 minutes to calculate. In contrast, here is an actual example of computer speed from the author's work. The responses of 296 individuals to 36 semantic differential items were analyzed on the CDC-6600. The means, standard deviations, and intercorrelations of the items (630 correlation coefficients) and a complete principal factors factor analysis with varimax rotation of two, three, four, five, six, seven, and eight factors were calculated. The factor analysis and rotations alone would take weeks on a desk calculator. In fact, few researchers would be hardy enough to attempt such a task. The machine took 23 *seconds* to do the actual calculations and about 43 seconds to read in and print the data!

This example also illustrates the second basic characteristic of computers: easy ability to do thousands of repetitive operations with high accuracy and dependability. Take a 50-variable problem. There are 50 sums, 50 sums of squares, 50 means, 50 standard deviations, 1225 cross-products sums, and thousands, even millions, of other calculations. The machine handles these lengthy and laborious operations repetitively at great speed. Moreover, by using a special computer language we find it fairly simple to direct the computer to do the calculations.

The ease with which such operations can be implemented, however, can be a hazard to the scientist. The computer calculates with a high but finite accuracy. This is because the computer's memory is limited to numbers of finite accuracy within a wide range of magnitude. In calculating sums of squares or cross products of large sets of numbers, for example, if the number of significant digits exceeds the machine's finite accuracy, the resulting sums will not be correct. In other words, computer output *can* be meaningless.[2] It is therefore necessary for machine users to be constantly alert to the possibilities of inaccurate results.

The third characteristic of computers, flexibility, might better be called a characteristic of the use of the machine. What is meant is that there are several ways to make a computer do a particular job. Virtually identical results can be achieved with different sets of instructions to the machine. In other words, the way the machine operates permits flexibility of programming. It is in this sense that the computer is flexible.

Ductility, the last computer characteristic to be discussed, may be loosely translated as stupidity. The electronic computer is utterly stupid: it will do exactly what a programmer tells it to do. If a programmer solves a difficult problem brilliantly, the machine will perform "brilliantly." If the programmer programs incorrectly, the machine will faithfully and obediently make the errors the programmer has told it to make. This is a great strength, because it means that computers are highly reliable; they seldom make mistakes. Their logic is irrefragable. The researcher can therefore depend upon the machine's "logic" and accuracy, within the limitations mentioned previously.

How Computer Programs Work: Programming and Fortran

A computer program is a set of instructions, in some sort of machine language, that tells the machine what operations to perform and how to perform them in order to analyze data and to calculate solutions of problems.

[2]Some computers have double-precision features, that is, computer accuracy is effectively doubled by means of a special increased storage feature. On the IBM-7094, for example, the usual accuracy is eight significant digits. With double-precision arithmetic, the accuracy is increased to 16 significant digits.

To understand to some extent how computers and computer programs work, let us look at some basic machine or program operations. Before anything else, however, we must be aware that an important problem for the researcher is to be able to communicate with the machine. He must be able to tell it what to do. One common and highly ingenious and useful communication medium is called Fortran (*For*mula *Tran*slation).[3] Fortran and similar languages constitute a major breakthrough in the research use of the computer. Fortran is an intermediary language that enables the researcher, as well as the machine expert, to communicate with the machine. Prior to its invention, the researcher had to communicate with the machine in highly detailed machine language or through a professional programmer. Since direct machine language is very complex, and since professional programmers are scarce and often do not understand research problems, the researcher was severly handicapped. The invention of Fortran and similar languages effectively solved this problem. The researcher writes his program in Fortran, and a computer program called a compiler translates the Fortran into an equvalent machine language program. If Fortran errors are made (that is, actual language and not logical errors), the compiler terminates the translation and prints out a so-called diagnostic, which informs the programmer of his errors and where they are in the Fortran program.[4]

Fortran, among other things, uses several basic statements like DO, GO TO, READ, WRITE, PUNCH, CALL, CONTINUE, and IF. These instructions mean what they say: they tell the machine to do this, do that, go to this instruction, read that instruction, and write the outcome. The power and flexibility of this seemingly simple language cannot be exaggerated. There is almost no numerical or logical operation that cannot be accomplished with it.

The reader who intends doing research is strongly urged to explore the possibilities of learning Fortran (or other intermediary language). To use the computer intelligently demands at least rudimentary knowledge and skill in programming. Many researchers believe that they can depend entirely upon professional programmers and so-called package programs. Such dependence has pitfalls. Many professional programmers are not familiar enough with the purposes and details of the analytical tools of the scientist, particularly those of the social scientist, to be able to help solve many analytic problems adequately. And package programs frequently lack desirable and necessary analyses. For example, an analysis of variance package program may not have relational indices as part of its output. Moreover, while professional programmers are usually highly competent people, many of them would not know the reasons for such special requirements, nor would it be economical for them to adapt package programs or to write new programs for such special use.

One of the most difficult problems associated with computer work, then, is communication between researcher and programmer. It is perhaps unrealistic to expect researchers to be highly expert in programming. But it is even more unrealistic to expect professional programmers to understand the substance and methodology of behavioral science analysis. The best solution of the problem of communication between scientist and programmer is clear: the scientist must learn at least enough about programming to enable him to talk knowledgeably and intelligently to the programmer. The researcher can learn to do this in a matter of months, whereas it would take the programmer years to learn enough about

[3]Although Fortran is here used as an example, it must be remembered that there are other machine intermediary languages. It is quite possible, in fact, that Fortran may in the future be supplanted by other languages. The version now used in most installations is Fortran IV.

[4]This description may make programming sound easy. It is not easy, even though it is a great deal simpler than it used to be. To master Fortran and to program effectively takes considerable application, effort, concentrated thought, and actual machine work. But it is also fun.

behavioral science and behavioral science analysis to communicate with the researcher at the researcher's level.

Available Programs

A fine example of the fruits of intelligent cooperation and open-minded dedication to science is the ready and open availability of many computer programs for scientific use.[5] Most of the following list of programs is available at many computing centers, especially those in universities. To authorized users of machines—and some universities now grant free computer time to unsupported faculty members and students—programs, facilities, and professional help are often available. The programs described below usually come, as indicated above, in ready-made packages. The user needs only familiarity with how to process the programs and the data through the machine complex and, most important, how to interpret the machine output.

Correlation Correlation programs calculate and output means, standard deviations, and correlation matrices. They are probably the most ubiquitous of programs. With the larger machines, the program capacity is large, sometimes well over a 100×100 matrix.

Analysis of Variance Most analyses of variance can probably be done just as well on a desk calculator as on a computer. Certain analytic problems, however, are very laborious and call for computer help. For example, two-way analysis of variance (also called matched-groups or randomized blocks) with large numbers of blocks or subjects is time-consuming, laborious, and subject to error. Simple one-way analysis of variance with large numbers of measures and groups and with post hoc comparisons of means (via the Scheffé test, for instance), too, is often better done on a computer. Standard programs are widely available. The user should be careful, however, to be sure that the form of analysis of variance in a program is the form he needs to analyze his data. One does not need a complex factorial analysis of variance or covariance to do a simple one-way or two-way analysis of variance. And standard programs may not do post hoc comparisons of means or calculate relational indices.

Item Analysis Item-total correlations, reliability, difficulty indices, and intercorrelations among items are best done on a computer because of the large number of calculations involved. Excellent programs have been written. The person in charge of the computing center one plans to use should be consulted.

Multivariate Analysis and Factor Analysis Almost any university computing center will have programs to do multiple regression and factor analysis. Many centers will have canonical correlation, discriminant analysis, and multivariate analysis of variance programs. The virtues of the computer are here particularly evident. In earlier years, many complex problems eluded analysis because of the large amount of calculations involved. This has changed radically. Multivariate methods are now within reach, and factor analysis has actually become commonplace.

But the use of multivariate analysis and factor analysis programs can be

[5]Computer personnel share their programs with each other. It is common to write another installation requesting a program that it has developed. Note, too, that requests for program information to computer manufacturers are attentively answered. Like certain large university centers, the manufacturers maintain libraries and indexes of programs and their sources. They also supply programs. The most important sources of programs for social scientific use, however, are undoubtedly university computing centers. It is suggested that the potential user of the computer consult the individual in charge of the nearest computing center for information on university centers and the programs they have available.

dangerous. Take factor analysis. The uncritical use of package factor analysis programs can lead to misleading results. In order to interpret factor analytic results properly, one needs considerable understanding of, and experience with, factor theory, methodology, and practice. One must know the characteristics of different types of rotations; one must understand the principles of simple structure; one must be able to reach intelligent decisions as to the number of factors to be extracted and rotated. No one can supply this knowledge and understanding but the researcher himself. Factor analysis programs, however, can be rather fixed and rigid. The communality estimates, the type of rotation, and the number of factors extracted may not be suited to the problem being investigated. In other words, while factor analysis programs are readily available and a great boon to the researcher, great care must be exercised in their use. Similar strictures apply to multivariate analysis programs.

Other Programs Many other programs have been written to accomplish a variety of analytic purposes. These include variable plots, factor matching, data transformation, matrix inversion, factor scores, and others. See the references listed at the end of this appendix.

The Computer and Behavioral Research

The computer is revolutionizing behavioral and educational research. This was made clear, I hope, in earlier chapters. One or two aspects of the computer's impact other than numerical analysis, however, need to be mentioned if the reader is to comprehend how far-reaching and deep this impact is. Perhaps the most important development is the computer's versatility and applicability to research problems that go beyond statistical analysis. One of these is the analysis of verbal materials, usually associated with content analysis (see Chapter 30). Texts of all kinds can be effectively analyzed: children's stories, editorials, projective materials, interview protocols, essays, speeches, and so on. The study of attitudes and values, for instance, can be considerably enriched with such analysis. Attitude referents and value objects and themes can be put into a "dictionary" and actual texts fed into the computer for various forms of study and analysis and measures of variables extracted from the texts. This is not a far-off dream; it is present actual reality.

The historian, the English specialist, and the political scientist, as well as the psychologist, can now analyze historical materials, literary productions, and political records in a variety of ways. The possibilities are seemingly endless and fascinating. But it goes further than this. Scholars in virtually all disciplines have no choice: they must use and master the computer. Indeed, it can be said that the scholar of 1975 will be obsolescent, even obsolete, if he does not understand and use the computer in his work.

Some will say that this is an extreme point of view. I don't think it is. Much of the avoidance by scholars of the computer is due to lack of understanding and a a curious fear that the computer will "take over" and somehow hurt scholarly work. This is nonsense. The computer is a completely stupid, if enormously efficient and powerful, piece of hardware. It can only get out of hand through ignorance, avoidance, and misuse. That is, *we* are the masters. *We* use the computer. And we must master and use it not because it is fashionable to do so but because modern research demands that we do.

Concluding Remarks

There is no doubt whatever of the importance and far-reaching implications and consequences of high-speed computers. Like everything else, of course, computers can be used wisely and not so wisely. One of the worst things one can do is to use a computer program without understanding the statistical and analytical principles behind the program. In addition to the danger of uncritically accepting incorrect results—something that occasionally happens, especially with new programs—one can err badly when using programs for complex operations. In the preceding section, the example of factor analysis was used to point up the danger of the uncritical use of computer programs and the necessity for understanding and experience to interpret factor analytic solutions. We can add here that careful judgment always has to be used. In a factor analysis, how many factors should be rotated. Are the machine rotations adequate? With multiple regression, what kind of regression coefficients are calculated and printed? What order of entry of the independent variables should be used? In general, do the results "make sense"? Are they "valid"? Computer results, as noted earlier, can be meaningless because of a machine's finite capacity, because a program is inappropriate for a particular analysis, because the user has made a trivial mistake in his instructions to the computer, and so on. In short, computer output can be what is called "garbage" in one or more ways. The undiscriminating user of computer programs can thus blunder seriously and obtain utterly false or misleading results.

Computers, then, are extremely useful, obedient, and reliable servants, though one must always remember that they are utterly stupid and that their facile output can never substitute for competent and imaginative theoretical, research-design, and statistical thinking. Despite the danger, the reader is urged to explore and learn about this enormously fascinating and powerful analytic tool. One thing is certain: the researcher who learns a little Fortran and who puts one or two programs through a machine complex successfully will never be the same again. He has participated in one of the most exciting adventures he will ever experience. The main problem will then be to maintain the balance and the discretion to keep the machine where it belongs: in the background and not in the foreground of research activity.

References

Behavioral Science and *Educational and Psychological Measurement* These journals regularly feature descriptions and availability of computer programs for social scientific and educational use.

Bernstein, J., "The Analytical Engine," *New Yorker*, XXXIX (Oct. 19, 1963), 58–93; XXXIX (Oct. 26, 1963), 54–108. The author has outlined, in his long and interesting article, the history and characteristics of computers.

Borko, H., ed., *Computer Applications in the Behavioral Sciences*. Englewood Cliffs, N.J.: Prentice-Hall, 1962. This diverse and informative book describes, among other things, machines, programs, and techniques useful to psychologists, sociologists, and educators.

Cooley, W., and Lohnes, P. *Multivariate Data Analysis*. New York: Wiley, 1971. Gives complete Fortran listings (programs) of many important statistical routines.

Dixon, W., ed. *BMD: Biomedical Computer Programs*. Berkeley, Calif.: University of California Press, 1970. The manual for the well-known BMD computer programs. Complete and highly sophisticated, but sometimes not easy to use.

Horst, P. *Factor Analysis of Data Matrices*. New York: Holt, Rinehart and Winston, 1965. Contains listings of many useful multivariate programs.

Lohnes, P., and Cooley, W. *Introduction to Statistical Procedures: With Computer Exercises*. New York: Wiley, 1968. Statistics and analysis courses of the future will probably be taught along the lines of this highly successful effort to integrate elementary statistics with computer thinking and programming. A particularly attractive feature of the book is its use and clear explanations, with examples, of Monte Carlo methods.

McCracken, D. *A Guide to Fortran IV Programming*. New York: Wiley, 1965. A general manual on Fortran IV that effectively and clearly guides the student through programming problems.

Mullish, H. *Modern Programming: Fortran IV*. Waltham, Mass.: Blaisdell, 1968. An excellent guide to Fortran IV; has many useful routines, some of them unusual.

Sterling, T., and Pollack, S. *Introduction to Statistical Data Processing*. Englewood Cliffs, N.J.: Prentice-Hall, 1968. This book is unique, informative, and valuable because it integrates statistics, analysis, and computer thinking. More advanced than Lohnes and Cooley's book (see above), but equally forward-looking.

Veldman, D. *Fortran Programming for the Behavioral Sciences*. New York: Holt, Rinehart and Winston, 1967. A valuable set of computer programs, with excellent discussions of important related topics.

(*Note:* Technical and descriptive materials and manuals are available from computer manufacturers.)

Appendix D

Random Numbers and Statistics[1]

This appendix contains 4000 random numbers organized in 40 sets of 100 each. The numbers are whole numbers evenly distributed in the range 0 through 100. The appendix has three purposes: to supply random numbers and statistics for the text and for the study suggestions of earlier chapters (e.g., Chapters 6, 8, and 12); to give readers at least some more-or-less direct experience with random numbers; and to demonstrate randomness with simple statistics. To achieve the third purpose, basic statistics calculated from the 40 sets of numbers, treating the sets as variables, are also given below: means, variances, standard deviations, and the intercorrelations of the 40 "variables."

Random numbers, or rather pseudorandom numbers,[2] can be generated in a number of ways. One can take the square roots of numbers to several decimal places and extract the middle numbers from each number. Or one can copy the numbers produced by the spins of a roulette wheel. Probably the best way is to use the computer and an addition or multiplication process to produce large numbers and then take parts of these numbers as random numbers. The 4000 numbers given below were produced by such a method. Green and Lohnes and Cooley discuss the method, which is called the *power residue method*.[3]

RANCAL, the random number computer program used, generates k sets of N random numbers each. k and N are read into the computer. In this case $k = 40$ and

[1]I am grateful to Mr. Edward Friedman, Associate Research Scientist, Computing Center, Courant Institute of Mathematical Sciences, New York University, for his help with the program that generated the random numbers given in this appendix. The actual random number computer program used as a subroutine was RANFNYU, a CIMS Computing Center routine.

[2]Oddly enougy, numbers generated by a computer are generated with a completely determined calculation. They are thus called *pseudorandom numbers*.

[3]B. Green, *Digital Computers in Research*. New York: McGraw-Hill, 1963, chap. 9; P. Lohnes and W. Cooley, *Introduction to Statistical Procedures: With Computer Exercises*. New York: Wiley, 1968, chap. 5. Green's discussion is clear and informative—and surprising (about how hard it is to generate random numbers that are really random); Lohnes and Cooley display all the arithmetic to take the mystery out of the procedure.

$N = 100$. The program also calculates the means and standard deviations of each of the 40 sets as well as the mean and standard deviation of all 4000 numbers. The statistics are given below. Since the random properties of the numbers were discussed in Chapter 12, they need not be discussed here. It is, of course, possible to test the randomness of the numbers in a number of ways.[4] One can count the frequencies of odd and even numbers, or the frequencies of any arbitrarily defined groups of numbers, such as 0–9, 10–19, etc., and then do chi-square analysis to test the significance of departures from chance expectations. We now describe a more interesting test.

RANCAL calculates the intercorrelations of the k (= 40) sets of random numbers. Since the numbers are presumably random, the correlations among the 40 sets should hover around zero with occasional r's in the .10's and .20's, but rarely in the .30's (plus and minus). With $N = 100$, an r of .197 is significant at the .05 level and an r of .256 at the .01 level.[5] The number of r's equal to or greater than .197 and the number of r's equal to or greater than .256 were counted. Since 5 percent of the total number of r's $[k(k-1)/2 = (40)(39)/2 = 780]$ is 39 $(780 \times .05)$, we can expect to find about 39 r's equal to or greater than .197. Similarly, 1 percent of the 780 r's, or about 8, can be expected to be equal to or greater than .256.

To provide a better test, three different additional samples of 4000 numbers each were generated with RANCAL, and the r's counted as above. The results of counting the r's in the four samples are given in Table D.1. The departures from chance expectations are not significant (by chi-square test). Most of the r's hover around zero. The highest r of the $4 \times 780 = 3120$ r's is $-.35$. The numbers appear to be random by this test. It would be profitable for the student to make up other tests and use them on the data given below. The importance of understanding and gaining experience with random processes, random numbers, and Monte Carlo methods cannot be overemphasized.[6]

TABLE **D.1** FREQUENCIES OF CORRELATION COEFFICIENTS CALCULATED BETWEEN 40 SETS OF PSEUDORANDOM NUMBERS IN FOUR SAMPLES OF 4000 NUMBERS EACH

	Samples				
	1	2	3	4	Expected
.05 level ($\geq .197$)	46	45	29	48	39
.01 level ($\geq .256$)	12	8	11	13	8
Highest r's	−.33	.31	−.35	−.31	

[4]See Rand Corporation, *A Million Random Digits with 100,000 Normal Deviates*. New York: Free Press, 1955, pp. xi ff., for a good discussion of a number of actual tests. This is an excellent set of random numbers. In addition, behavioral scientists should read this perhaps classic account of the pains taken to produce random numbers and the difficulties encountered in doing so.

[5]A. Edwards, *Statistical Methods*, 2d ed. New York: Holt, Rinehart and Winston, 1967, Table VI, p. 426.

[6]The reader who wishes to generate his own pseudorandom numbers should consult the computer specialists at his computer installation. Random number routines are widely available. The reader will have to write the basic program in which to insert the random number program. This is not hard to do, nor is the writing of the Fortran to calculate the usual statistics. The reader who has not learned to program can have a computer specialist do the job, though this sacrifices a good bit of the fun.

RANDOM NUMBERS

1	53	95	67	80	79	93	28	69	25	78	13	24	100	62	62	21	11	4	5
2	62	12	27	41	5	4	19	34	84	78	71	45	73	79	33	57	29	58	7
3	90	16	47	72	20	60	70	71	2	67	21	65	7	39	58	81	64	11	7
4	10	59	4	76	80	6	82	20	60	92	33	61	76	83	73	12	84	43	9
5	32	17	36	64	8	30	80	95	61	33	65	5	39	88	36	44	42	43	
6	54	71	27	89	41	53	60	10	2	91	76	95	98	91	64	65	23	57	1
7	10	60	18	77	34	59	28	99	15	11	70	34	27	78	67	19	97	30	2
8	42	20	24	36	78	58	82	81	49	91	35	53	30	92	57	19	97	40	5
9	73	55	87	48	49	97	60	92	27	78	2	55	29	76	99	21	45	72	5
10	21	56	41	23	58	57	49	49	70	33	6	79	95	3	70	38	26	26	
11	9	60	37	99	6	41	69	97	18	44	100	18	46	3	90	57	22	82	1
12	63	26	41	8	21	38	15	63	38	100	68	89	24	39	19	29	93	97	4
13	98	72	9	45	69	50	7	86	5	80	0	8	28	96	45	0	0	13	9
14	87	89	65	22	98	55	86	9	66	43	64	55	80	30	15	99	26	25	7
15	5	91	68	44	67	2	71	96	15	73	78	3	12	87	53	9	11	12	2
16	75	93	62	49	95	82	30	81	24	4	11	36	71	96	49	47	65	48	2
17	76	15	55	38	29	0	8	20	71	42	81	51	44	76	93	42	87	89	3
18	26	76	93	84	8	40	96	69	84	82	89	5	16	43	34	37	64	39	1
19	8	35	6	83	76	8	87	81	13	33	14	86	38	23	33	22	58	47	6
20	59	73	37	6	26	44	0	24	89	24	78	80	20	8	19	31	32	53	4
21	87	94	75	45	72	15	39	100	46	99	59	12	22	95	76	18	27	73	8
22	5	74	8	91	37	5	13	55	13	7	19	24	76	4	25	93	78	9	5
23	49	82	39	40	51	15	71	53	68	86	50	93	31	22	64	77	46	17	2
24	2	25	92	97	41	39	98	100	99	67	44	0	99	93	31	69	26	72	5
25	59	41	49	100	13	0	15	33	82	61	28	59	83	8	17	76	24	58	9
26	40	13	20	51	81	15	12	45	16	57	47	54	92	60	70	55	98	12	9
27	80	25	91	36	83	59	19	9	47	61	84	89	98	18	11	56	99	3	2
28	48	33	7	70	61	95	51	32	89	87	72	6	40	88	52	44	19	96	9
29	89	5	7	93	48	60	69	97	61	21	87	68	20	4	61	63	75	8	7
30	97	64	36	36	99	98	23	18	66	28	58	48	34	18	64	71	48	90	6
31	59	73	71	62	66	34	17	41	32	65	50	73	82	7	20	85	1	65	7
32	88	75	43	66	66	38	56	31	25	36	26	91	36	100	88	42	74	27	3
33	34	16	43	38	50	28	34	14	41	2	6	97	56	73	75	17	56	31	10
34	14	61	81	2	69	73	3	89	79	64	67	80	75	5	66	77	97	30	8
35	15	39	5	99	29	36	25	40	46	28	34	63	75	18	21	23	13	85	1
36	68	49	1	55	11	6	63	23	50	33	80	34	82	20	66	48	27	16	8
37	1	72	18	84	84	86	61	41	22	61	45	36	37	16	20	28	98	36	7
38	58	73	55	11	9	96	81	84	21	34	50	92	65	91	69	33	23	4	7
39	91	63	65	63	70	90	57	20	9	13	28	77	72	0	12	30	48	6	2
40	39	45	31	74	91	85	29	45	98	15	11	50	26	16	36	76	1	40	7
41	94	12	62	59	14	42	32	75	41	41	0	58	5	78	89	48	35	1	7
42	3	33	41	22	45	37	65	3	96	27	62	77	16	97	81	78	26	48	9
43	58	2	83	10	100	50	98	57	32	65	31	87	84	45	0	90	42	78	
44	29	73	79	48	66	72	32	1	100	3	2	61	35	0	88	100	45	42	1
45	55	9	63	66	31	5	8	72	4	85	5	44	4	98	2	79	40	44	9
46	52	13	44	91	39	85	22	33	4	29	52	6	82	77	25	0	46	100	4
47	31	52	65	63	88	78	21	35	28	22	91	84	4	30	14	0	97	92	6
48	44	38	76	99	38	67	60	95	67	68	17	18	46	76	83	5	8	20	8
49	84	47	44	4	67	22	89	78	44	84	66	15	56	0	90	21	25	88	9
50	71	50	78	48	65	74	21	24	2	23	65	94	51	82	67	16	35	91	10
51	42	47	97	81	10	99	40	15	63	77	89	10	32	92	86	32	9	33	7
52	3	70	75	49	90	92	62	0	47	90	78	63	44	60	13	55	38	64	6
53	31	6	46	39	27	93	81	79	100	94	43	39	79	2	18	82	40	30	5

44	59	90	78	83	4	97	61	52	75	91	76	98	40	41	2	56	78	62	79	16
20	79	78	68	31	25	30	97	31	82	51	72	23	58	27	17	69	94	75	68	79
4	79	44	47	7	74	34	55	28	90	19	35	15	27	66	20	26	81	37	61	63
71	82	28	21	61	31	92	100	75	22	31	11	5	74	38	84	78	69	70	24	77
88	81	13	63	15	47	92	20	62	5	60	44	83	22	50	59	60	29	12	71	11
0	90	52	26	90	49	31	68	29	58	10	13	8	54	63	58	7	29	25	38	80
60	0	22	11	12	54	50	93	25	69	54	2	60	4	53	16	80	45	30	72	51
13	39	42	25	3	97	64	100	55	24	7	30	58	96	5	30	55	23	39	53	27
24	16	33	50	84	12	65	4	30	48	56	97	74	33	90	0	5	99	3	60	53
89	49	0	68	57	53	91	66	81	53	83	15	81	17	65	0	47	8	65	77	61
38	73	97	74	9	35	82	66	34	84	14	28	36	24	87	76	96	89	34	9	29
91	70	41	95	83	33	25	33	94	44	39	43	23	53	15	54	81	74	31	17	94
24	92	51	11	11	37	91	21	87	89	89	9	68	26	79	43	16	19	89	66	82
87	22	39	97	26	50	12	86	22	65	70	94	86	38	11	60	57	16	41	46	20
32	57	72	16	35	27	51	91	43	58	61	6	62	50	24	11	19	73	14	42	48
8	91	58	40	55	32	7	86	84	95	59	53	70	54	25	96	38	43	5	2	4
51	88	65	83	80	66	91	9	68	30	63	28	75	64	90	11	80	94	99	35	54
77	95	100	52	99	36	81	65	85	21	9	68	57	34	30	29	61	33	49	0	11
36	97	89	20	59	52	9	76	75	52	82	45	65	89	88	39	93	71	55	29	67
32	32	23	57	74	49	17	97	49	71	0	73	11	78	58	58	34	20	30	43	40
41	31	99	37	31	24	89	35	14	14	73	26	59	10	35	75	4	34	38	0	63
85	98	71	37	53	67	75	9	56	95	71	58	15	70	36	19	49	45	18	36	2
25	2	17	69	68	56	44	100	55	80	26	87	85	52	76	40	61	50	68	72	7
25	71	42	28	22	96	76	19	63	97	5	98	44	82	35	0	33	26	68	75	7
25	3	2	76	87	10	18	23	69	93	27	35	39	8	70	79	48	30	65	65	63
27	95	66	23	91	78	86	27	98	16	30	79	82	7	23	41	81	8	32	8	8
67	21	24	80	60	44	42	48	77	84	63	0	30	98	86	100	14	55	86	71	13
62	12	100	82	5	17	62	65	100	63	9	88	88	48	70	64	81	29	71	62	67
92	37	35	40	70	25	86	34	54	53	95	45	62	32	83	60	48	0	44	94	22
57	15	14	24	26	65	29	38	85	99	17	63	8	87	100	28	82	67	65	10	81
85	23	19	45	61	48	98	84	51	63	70	33	6	49	38	55	78	94	26	4	29
40	33	92	18	9	54	51	40	24	82	6	79	51	52	9	38	18	13	16	86	42
84	32	25	33	52	26	78	83	44	0	81	63	29	23	97	64	6	63	74	29	77
82	52	87	25	63	11	67	93	99	61	39	94	16	38	87	3	25	25	49	22	68
43	88	70	92	44	23	73	62	47	60	45	32	6	90	100	29	26	31	39	32	93
78	74	89	9	23	66	62	83	28	34	87	92	99	60	23	79	82	6	62	2	75
39	67	100	71	8	19	29	0	24	95	26	46	1	2	68	40	8	3	99	19	6
93	3	37	95	14	84	27	67	46	61	88	65	55	20	58	89	100	74	77	28	30
89	94	6	58	72	73	16	86	19	95	49	37	58	49	5	51	55	90	22	3	37
1	88	15	60	27	55	0	83	96	36	53	80	47	63	53	58	95	55	25	67	58
70	20	98	38	93	67	35	35	40	38	44	2	48	66	86	47	74	48	87	71	21
59	77	82	54	1	63	24	64	31	31	14	49	71	92	36	55	72	74	13	99	31
17	21	92	92	47	5	29	6	27	62	72	35	48	56	92	76	75	45	23	91	15
18	48	67	36	37	57	12	97	12	95	8	77	61	32	6	66	47	66	0	24	26
75	91	59	66	15	41	19	100	33	23	64	50	83	57	78	38	55	48	97	5	62
35	46	93	11	9	56	82	97	53	18	86	83	94	8	40	14	39	93	51	42	80
87	46	73	55	82	18	76	67	43	76	22	82	1	78	19	94	56	38	8	37	28
87	2	42	65	27	16	22	60	18	78	33	73	74	13	2	42	64	89	86	72	9
100	32	86	30	50	92	48	55	70	35	20	54	43	20	13	39	76	59	7	51	19
35	61	31	75	8	81	58	67	50	28	17	77	32	56	82	56	60	98	80	21	49
69	50	7	61	78	15	60	79	47	73	51	99	27	39	7	32	7	85	14	22	76
63	92	17	100	2	40	93	83	89	88	20	1	14	43	75	65	65	63	53	81	57
31	81	84	62	41	59	4	46	56	100	58	26	51	32	8	24	99	30	36	32	59

54	69	27	97	71	52	38	45	35	14	74	40	96	40	88	38	67	44	81	5
55	2	76	36	72	7	28	55	13	31	78	67	98	50	25	94	39	71	28	0
56	3	4	20	8	63	33	69	31	69	32	35	18	23	84	69	64	13	43	86
57	79	55	89	1	25	68	100	58	44	92	73	29	70	47	3	51	37	24	24
58	99	6	65	35	66	98	66	47	47	22	1	54	94	13	0	31	40	55	69
59	46	98	1	46	43	86	42	91	63	1	93	84	51	8	79	47	54	85	90
60	6	14	71	51	7	10	79	41	58	3	27	33	74	67	18	94	4	57	99
61	92	31	31	40	12	19	74	73	20	94	33	41	40	74	79	42	23	41	29
62	87	8	68	74	61	66	94	27	71	81	37	82	83	7	8	46	65	63	37
63	50	48	52	100	68	75	38	65	59	57	78	24	29	52	24	98	78	48	77
64	67	96	52	88	76	79	16	12	42	33	35	50	54	69	21	57	62	21	84
65	54	42	22	99	28	90	74	46	26	13	48	45	99	3	38	94	86	53	41
66	99	51	72	2	75	81	92	71	85	26	77	73	23	14	2	46	7	13	2
67	35	63	58	46	91	44	56	26	59	56	21	91	19	83	6	61	47	53	10
68	81	98	63	17	77	45	47	96	25	38	23	26	80	20	47	40	39	14	71
69	90	47	44	40	40	9	60	62	13	79	39	0	99	57	37	39	2	8	42
70	29	30	16	54	83	76	50	0	61	100	51	74	78	15	9	16	17	22	44
71	47	94	70	80	51	26	11	78	34	29	10	55	90	42	4	6	83	72	95
72	69	14	17	73	79	25	71	14	52	98	77	82	15	25	8	34	38	80	82
73	54	58	47	9	0	6	36	94	27	3	18	5	36	98	74	36	30	8	87
74	24	63	57	91	8	58	38	29	72	5	56	71	81	50	67	59	41	9	17
75	14	24	69	85	97	51	68	80	16	92	59	72	97	23	89	44	16	71	19
76	86	21	31	59	72	17	77	45	43	29	34	97	67	45	23	88	91	68	12
77	5	28	80	31	99	77	39	23	69	0	15	49	100	2	22	64	73	92	53
78	29	71	48	4	87	32	17	90	89	9	99	34	58	8	61	73	98	48	89
79	90	94	19	80	70	36	2	17	48	63	82	39	85	26	65	27	81	69	83
80	62	66	48	74	86	6	66	41	15	65	6	41	85	57	84	64	70	39	64
81	67	54	3	54	23	40	25	95	93	55	59	46	77	55	49	82	26	8	87
82	75	27	62	15	81	36	22	26	69	42	44	91	55	0	84	48	68	65	5
83	70	19	7	100	94	53	81	76	73	40	22	58	49	42	96	18	66	89	8
84	75	7	9	20	58	92	41	42	79	26	91	44	63	87	45	21	23	15	6
85	55	70	10	23	25	73	91	72	29	47	93	58	21	75	80	52	9	12	36
86	83	42	62	53	55	12	11	54	19	2	45	43	67	13	5	74	30	93	11
87	94	20	76	23	65	72	55	27	44	19	10	72	50	67	83	18	67	22	49
88	51	10	72	9	59	47	66	32	17	6	75	8	54	22	37	3	46	83	95
89	99	50	22	2	92	9	98	9	40	23	34	8	63	58	49	31	70	39	83
90	9	12	3	23	2	0	82	75	36	63	71	19	78	26	66	63	16	75	7
91	20	40	50	29	51	82	81	47	73	69	74	100	80	37	14	67	1	90	92
92	90	92	54	52	74	0	88	71	45	49	38	54	80	2	85	42	75	47	20
93	25	6	92	30	19	31	22	41	0	22	79	87	84	61	6	19	67	97	60
94	13	12	94	76	29	61	50	67	29	76	27	70	97	16	83	88	100	22	48
95	91	77	51	3	92	85	46	22	0	58	84	64	87	93	94	94	13	98	41
96	29	12	39	35	32	47	30	81	40	32	37	8	48	81	50	77	18	39	7
97	43	96	86	14	91	24	22	85	16	51	42	37	41	100	94	76	45	50	67
98	57	44	72	45	87	21	7	29	26	82	69	99	10	39	76	29	11	17	85
99	63	10	10	76	7	75	19	91	2	31	45	94	54	72	10	48	52	7	12
100	34	28	11	95	4	82	51	7	69	53	93	36	81	66	93	88	15	73	54

12	13	98	21	39	36	74	39	83	77	79	37	89	4	20	21	91	98	90	37	49
39	31	69	14	22	50	40	54	12	71	98	25	26	20	61	52	93	90	76	46	19
53	10	28	46	41	29	74	46	64	39	4	47	55	98	22	69	9	15	34	94	16
29	95	79	80	35	0	9	65	42	99	69	90	22	16	34	81	44	3	24	96	70
20	59	12	35	63	52	35	2	56	40	85	2	85	2	58	26	94	48	0	85	70
2	19	26	78	95	1	4	72	81	80	60	49	67	32	10	28	90	72	25	28	53
37	40	96	68	6	95	55	82	16	36	58	68	68	69	7	11	31	17	39	82	85
1	0	13	31	19	63	90	75	17	33	49	13	54	32	26	66	38	1	7	35	16
63	88	20	20	75	16	70	26	75	22	48	6	1	89	99	21	48	6	9	67	85
64	93	100	50	95	76	94	84	25	67	98	94	23	75	40	33	86	87	76	24	98
95	13	66	49	11	48	20	54	51	65	63	33	98	80	13	84	70	85	93	74	22
18	35	10	64	79	70	5	55	92	41	92	14	63	52	94	56	5	40	55	50	17
40	62	28	72	82	81	51	7	45	9	26	47	34	47	47	95	45	38	82	85	20
33	7	97	68	76	44	73	73	0	80	55	84	77	74	27	5	17	57	75	63	2
15	60	83	28	56	78	9	27	52	79	68	90	48	12	51	55	77	48	10	55	21
58	1	28	1	64	50	28	8	69	70	96	26	100	6	31	89	0	31	91	5	23
71	94	59	17	43	50	34	12	14	45	30	79	63	76	72	18	67	87	47	90	93
73	24	19	13	98	0	64	44	90	20	13	66	81	97	81	11	38	7	37	93	64
97	82	87	98	29	97	69	24	62	100	12	28	84	86	10	69	25	66	93	21	57
2	23	76	42	76	87	64	99	5	7	13	33	19	18	37	96	73	95	91	24	24
17	85	42	29	80	53	92	6	44	100	18	24	31	5	6	37	63	93	42	5	97
83	42	53	54	93	63	19	59	30	80	75	8	91	48	79	2	40	6	56	57	60
30	3	41	73	63	76	18	82	8	13	30	78	45	43	77	77	99	98	40	14	82
64	7	19	80	64	4	34	30	65	63	11	72	20	15	22	30	82	77	51	87	61
90	24	25	98	38	79	45	84	30	49	64	98	48	25	14	0	12	63	67	12	77
20	40	25	87	45	88	52	19	33	17	63	60	62	46	12	59	99	5	88	74	89
87	62	78	25	71	57	6	98	59	79	34	20	77	87	83	12	74	29	12	16	99
54	10	53	29	37	82	5	77	54	4	69	7	40	18	32	85	37	73	42	49	49
45	35	11	73	30	16	3	75	56	58	98	46	93	58	96	29	73	6	71	8	46
69	17	54	7	86	29	18	86	98	5	56	78	0	78	24	34	73	95	11	44	36
72	60	78	88	27	45	80	66	25	37	73	7	67	29	27	12	90	60	97	15	94
93	9	58	84	88	90	73	47	49	53	95	62	28	11	61	0	91	49	32	82	28
74	75	27	81	28	48	4	65	87	69	32	14	46	52	52	36	21	13	70	24	76
36	42	53	92	96	19	52	38	2	22	47	26	94	34	57	81	28	49	74	68	50
93	76	77	19	31	74	40	5	0	23	61	15	11	82	35	77	9	28	11	32	30
54	75	23	75	34	69	93	93	20	29	78	24	71	92	75	70	60	80	88	21	11
72	99	15	97	27	48	50	88	2	89	57	18	25	7	100	80	84	97	84	18	53
99	6	34	98	33	77	44	86	95	0	30	34	91	25	98	77	14	95	100	84	19
94	13	95	44	22	63	18	88	37	89	95	98	80	72	72	71	66	13	33	24	12
48	56	64	63	75	27	69	63	29	51	59	22	83	2	33	32	91	78	53	45	63
7	66	52	91	70	34	54	25	71	91	12	41	39	35	37	66	52	80	1	33	94
77	83	71	83	68	55	85	11	69	32	10	30	54	73	21	43	68	65	83	26	90
95	28	92	53	63	46	36	45	62	24	39	65	100	85	12	69	3	72	55	43	5
54	59	91	34	52	75	87	95	30	97	33	57	69	37	7	62	65	36	9	57	73
76	13	93	41	42	27	80	85	61	11	42	44	51	38	59	85	91	51	79	14	26
59	84	46	41	29	7	44	63	27	29	41	39	76	88	46	46	65	72	62	92	67
15	91	53	78	85	78	77	80	36	89	88	84	60	42	55	48	99	44	66	77	27

	MEAN	VARIANCE	ST. DEV.
1	51.8400	895.8144	29.9302
2	46.2000	809.3200	28.4486
3	47.6900	740.6539	27.2150
4	51.8300	872.7611	29.5425
5	53.2100	877.5659	29.6237
6	48.8700	903.9131	30.0651
7	49.6400	778.8704	27.9082
8	51.3700	889.7331	29.8284
9	45.0700	771.7251	27.7799
10	49.2800	872.3016	29.5348
11	48.8700	777.5731	27.8850
12	53.0800	860.2136	29.3294
13	56.5100	773.0099	27.8031
14	47.9900	1110.2299	33.3201
15	49.3700	913.6531	30.2267
16	49.0200	714.0396	26.7215
17	45.6800	842.0776	29.0186
18	47.0400	853.3384	29.2120
19	53.5100	977.2499	31.2610
20	52.7400	853.4924	29.2146
21	50.0600	1001.1564	31.6411
22	53.9500	907.7475	30.1288
23	53.6100	737.3779	27.1547
24	49.3100	807.4139	28.4150
25	49.1600	673.9544	25.9606
26	50.2200	855.3316	29.2461
27	58.3600	877.1904	29.6174
28	49.5700	709.7051	26.6403
29	55.4400	868.3664	29.4681
30	49.4300	791.3851	28.1316
31	48.5200	847.9296	29.1192
32	52.9400	802.3564	28.3259
33	46.7900	784.6259	28.0112
34	48.3300	881.4611	29.6894
35	47.2900	759.3059	27.5555
36	55.5100	854.5499	29.2327
37	52.3900	907.8379	30.1303
38	49.9500	851.3275	29.1775
39	46.0000	817.7800	28.5969
40	47.6500	815.1475	28.5508

Author Index

Subject Index